LANCE PARKIN
and LARS PEARSON

AHISTORY

AN UNAUTHORIZED HISTORY OF THE DOCTOR WHO UNIVERSE

4TH EDITION

mad
norwegian
press

Des Moines, IA

TABLE OF CONTENTS

The following *only* catalogs main story entries for each adventure; some stories occur in multiple time zones, and hence have more than one page number listed. For a complete listing of *all* story references, consult the Index.

Some stories proved undateable and lack main entries; for a list of these, consult the None of the Above section (pages 1353-1356).

For easier reference across what's become a quite sprawling guidebook series, the pages of *Ahistory* Fourth Edition are numbered 1000 and up for Volume 1, 2000 and up for Volume 2, and 3000 and up for Volume 3.

All titles listed are *Doctor Who* stories (or were supplemental comics made for *Doctor Who Magazine*) unless otherwise noted. BBV and Reeltimes Pictures stories include a notation of the particular monster or *Doctor Who* character they feature. For more on the designations used in the Table of Contents, see the Key in the Introduction.

Big Finish box sets, for the most part, are listed under the box set title, then the individual stories therein. (The format is a bit inconsistent – whenever possible, we've gone with whatever's on the cover.)

To save space, Titan's comics are listed under *The Tenth Doctor Year One*, *The Eleventh Doctor Year One*, etc. We've anticipated a collection of *The Ninth Doctor Year One*.

TABLE OF CONTENTS

TABLE OF CONTENTS

TABLE OF CONTENTS

TABLE OF CONTENTS

TABLE OF CONTENTS

TABLE OF CONTENTS

TABLE OF CONTENTS

TABLE OF CONTENTS

TABLE OF CONTENTS

TABLE OF CONTENTS

TABLE OF CONTENTS

TABLE OF CONTENTS

TABLE OF CONTENTS

Footnote Features

Pre-History

History

Present Day

UNIT

Present Day (cont.)

TABLE OF CONTENTS

A very special thank you to our supporters on Patreon: Darren Buckley, David H Adler, Janet Reimer, Maggie Howe, Matt Bracher, Mitchell S Easter, Pat Harrigan, Rick Taylor, Steve Grace, Steven Ashby, Steven Sautter, Steven Mollmann and Tyson Woolman. You guys are awesome!

Volume 1 ISBN: 9781935234227
Volume 2 ISBN: 9781935234234
Volume 3 ISBN: 9781935234241

Word count, Vol. 1 (sans TOC, Introduction and Index): 284,251

Printed in the United States of America.
First Printing (Vol. 1): August 2018.

mad norwegian press | des moines

This book seeks to place every event referred to in *Doctor Who* into a consistent timeline. Yet this is "a" history of the *Doctor Who* universe, not the "definitive" or "official" version.

Doctor Who has had hundreds of creators, all pulling in slightly different directions, all with their own vision of what *Doctor Who* was about. Without that diversity, the *Doctor Who* universe would no doubt be more internally consistent, but it would also be a much smaller and less interesting place. Nowadays, fans are part of the creative process. Ultimately, we control the heritage of the show that we love. The authors of *Ahistory* hope people will enjoy this book, and we know that they will challenge it.

# # # # #

A total adherence to continuity has always been rather less important to the successive *Doctor Who* production teams than the main order of business: writing exciting stories, telling good jokes and scaring small children with big monsters. This, as most people will tell you, is just how it should be.

Doctor Who has always been created using a method known as "making it up as they went along". The series glories in its invention and throwaway lines. When the TV series was first in production, no-one was keeping the sort of detailed notes that would prevent canonical "mistakes", and even the same writer could contradict their earlier work. It's doubtful the writer of *The Mysterious Planet* (broadcast in 1986) had a single passing thought about how the story fit in with *The Sun Makers* (1977)... even though they were both authored by Robert Holmes.

Now, with all the legions of new books, audios, comic strips, short stories and a new TV series, not to mention spin-offs, it is almost certainly impossible to keep track of every new *Doctor Who* story, let alone put them all in a coherent – never mind consistent – framework. References can contradict other references in the same story, let alone ones in stories written forty years later for a different medium by someone who wasn't even born the year the original writer died.

It is, in any case, impossible to come up with a consistent view of history according to *Doctor Who*. Strictly speaking, the Brigadier retires three years before the first UNIT story is set. The Daleks and Atlantis are both utterly destroyed, once and for all, several times that we know about. Characters "remember" scenes, or sometimes entire stories, that they weren't present to witness, and show remarkable lack of knowledge of real world events or events in *Doctor Who* that happened after the story first came out.

"Continuity" has always been flexible, even on the fundamentals of the show's mythology – *The Dalek Invasion of Earth* (1964), *The War Games* (1969), *Genesis of the Daleks*

(1975) and *The Deadly Assassin* (1976) all shamelessly threw out the show's history in the name of a good story. Their versions of events (the Daleks are galactic conquerors; the Doctor is a Time Lord who stole his TARDIS and fled his home planet; the Daleks were created by the Kaled scientist, Davros; Gallifreyan society is far from perfect and Time Lords are limited to twelve regenerations) are now taken to be the "truth". The previous versions (the Daleks are confined to one city; the Doctor invented the "ship" and his granddaughter named it before their exile; the Daleks are descendants of the squat humanoid Dals, mutated by radiation; the Time Lords are godlike and immortal barring accidents) have quietly been forgotten.

# # # # #

However, it would be unfortunate to write a book so vague that it becomes useless. Firm decisions have to be made about where stories are placed, so this book contains abundant footnotes that lay out the evidence pertaining to each story, and to explain each story's placement in this chronology.

In some cases, this is simply a matter of reporting an exact date spoken by one of the characters in the story (*Black Orchid*, for example). In others, no firm date is given. In those cases, we attempt to look at internal evidence given on screen, then evidence from the production team at the time (from the script, say, or from contemporary publicity material), then branch out to cross-referencing it with other stories, noting where other people who've come up with *Doctor Who* chronologies have placed it. What we're attempting to do is accurately list all the evidence given for dating the stories and other references in as an objective way as possible, then weigh it to reach a conclusion.

For a good example of this process at its most complicated, look for *The Seeds of Death* or *The Wheel in Space*. You may not agree with the years we've set, it might make your blood boil, but you'll see how we've reached our answer.

# # # # #

This book is one attempt, then, to retroactively create a consistent framework for the history of the *Doctor Who* universe. It is essentially a game, not a scientific endeavour to discover "the right answer".

All games have to follow a consistent set of rules, and as we attempt to fit all the pieces of information we are given, we have to lay some groundwork and prioritise. If a line of dialogue from a story broadcast in 1983 flatly contradicts what was said in one from 1968, which is "right"? Some people would suggest that the newer story "got it wrong", that the later production team didn't pay enough attention to what came before. Others might argue that the new information "corrects" what came before. In practice, most fans are inconsistent, choosing the facts that best support their arguments or preferences. *The Discontinuity Guide* (1995) has some very healthy advice regarding continuity: "Take what you want and ignore what you don't. Future continuity cops will just have to adapt to your version".

BASIC PRINCIPLES

For the purposes of this book, we have worked from the following assumptions:

• Every *Doctor Who* story takes place in the same universe, unless explicitly stated otherwise. The same individual fought the Daleks with Jo on Spiridon (on TV), Beep the Meep with Sharon (in the comics), the Ice Warriors with Benny in London (the novels), became Zagreus in the Antiverse (the audios), blew up Gallifrey to prevent Faction Paradox taking over the universe (the novels again), saved Rose Tyler from the Autons and married River Song.

For legal, marketing or artistic reasons, it should be noted that some of the people making *Doctor Who* have occasionally stated that they don't feel this to be the case. However there are innumerable cross references (say, Romana being president of Gallifrey in both the books and the audios) and in-jokes that suggest very strongly that, for example, the eighth Doctor of the books is the same individual as the eighth Doctor of the Big Finish audios – or at the very least, they've both got almost-identical histories.

• The universe has one, true "established history". Nothing (short of a being with godlike powers) can significantly change the course of history with any degree of permanency within that universe. The Mars attacked by the Fendahl is the Mars of the Ice Warriors.

• We have noted where each date we have assigned comes from. Usually it is from dialogue (in which case, it's quoted), but often it comes from behind-the-scenes sources such as scripts, publicity material and the like. It is up to the individual reader whether a date from a BBC Press release or draft script is as "valid" as one given on screen.

• In many cases, no date was ever given for a story. In such instances, we pick a year and explain our reasons. Often, we will assign a date that is consistent with information given in other stories. (So, it's suggested that the Cyber War mentioned in *Revenge of the Cybermen* must take place after *The Tomb of the Cybermen*, and probably after *Earthshock* because of what is said in those other stories.) These dates are marked as arbitrary and the reasoning behind them is explained in the footnotes.

• Where a date isn't established on screen, we have also included the dates suggested by others who have compiled timelines or listed dates given in the series. Several similar works to this have been attempted, and we have listed the most relevant in the Bibliography.

• It's been assumed that historical events take place at the same time and for the same reasons as they did in "real history", unless specifically contradicted by the television series. Unless given reason to think otherwise, we assume that the Doctor is telling the truth about meeting historical figures, and that his historical analysis is correct. (It has, however, been established that the Doctor is fallible and/or an incorrigible name-dropper.) When there's a reference in our footnotes to "science", "scientists", "history" or "historians", unless stated otherwise it means scholars and academics from the real world, not the *Doctor Who* universe (they are usually invoked when *Doctor Who*'s version of science or events strays a distance from ours).

• Information given is usually taken literally and at face value, unless there's strong reason to think that the person giving it is lying or mistaken. Clearly, if an expert like the Doctor is talking about something he knows a great deal about, we can probably trust the information more than some bystander's vague remark. (In recent years, it's become trendy to go the other way and invoke River Song's "The Doctor Lies" credo to explain any given point of ambiguity, but – as with not claiming that every discrepancy is the fault of the Last Great Time War – we've resisted that urge as much as possible.)

• *Ahistory*'s version of Earth's future history is generally one of steady progress, and as such stories featuring similar themes and concepts tend to be lumped together – say, intergalactic travel, isolated colonies, humanoid robots and so on. If the technology, transportation or weaponry seen in story A is more advanced than in story B, then we might suggest that story A is set in the future of story B. We also assume that throughout future centuries, humans age at the same rate (unless told otherwise), so their life spans don't alter too dramatically, etc. A "lifetime" in the year 4000 is still about one hundred years.

• All dates, again unless specifically stated otherwise, work from our Gregorian calendar, and all are "AD". It is assumed that the system of leap years will remain the same in the future. For convenience, all documents use our system of dating, even those of alien civilisations. The "present" of the narrative is now, so if an event happened "two hundred years ago", it happened in the early nineteenth century. Often we are told that a specific date takes place on the wrong day: in *The War Machines*, 16th July, 1966, is a Monday, but it really occurred on a Saturday.

• We assume that a "year" is an Earth year of 365 days, even when an alien is speaking, unless this is specifically contradicted. This also applies to terms such as "Space Year" (*Genesis of the Daleks*), "light year" (which is used as a unit of time in *The Savages* and possibly *Terror of the Autons*) and "cycle" (e.g. *Zamper*).

• If an event is said to take place "fifty years ago", we frequently take it to mean exactly fifty years ago, unless a more precise date is given elsewhere or it refers to a known historical event. If an event occurs in the distant past or the far future, we tend to round up: *Image of the Fendahl* is set in about 1977, the Fifth Planet was destroyed "twelve million years" before. So, we say this happened in "12,000,000 BC", not "11,998,023 BC". When an event takes place an undefined number of "centuries", "millennia" or "millions of years" before or after a story, we arbitrarily set a date.

• On occasion we've followed a convention from the TV series: that future-based stories sometimes occur on a rounded number from the year of their broadcast. This is why – to pick a prominent example – *Colony in Space*, broadcast in 1972, takes place in 2472. Likewise with *The Enemy of the World* (1967-1968) quietly taking place fifty years on, in 2018. When and where we've followed this pattern, it's because a story's dating placement is otherwise a bit vague, and – frankly – our gut impulse says it's acceptable to do so. Also, to be honest, one of us grew up a huge fan of *Legion of Super-Heroes*, which magically took place a thousand years after publication. It's been a hard habit to shake.

• A "generation" is assumed to be twenty-five years, as per the Doctor's definition in *Four to Doomsday*. A "couple" of years is always two years, a "few" is less than "several" which is less than "many", with "some" taken to be an arbitrary or unknown number. A "billion" is generally the American and modern British unit (a thousand million) rather than the old British definition (a million million).

• Characters are in their native time zone unless explicitly stated otherwise. Usually, when a *Doctor Who* monster or villain has a time machine, it's central to the plot. On television, the Cybermen only explicitly have time travel in *Attack of the Cybermen*, for example, and they've stolen the time machine in question. It clearly can't be "taken for granted" that they can go back in history. The Sontarans have a (primitive) time machine in *The Time Warrior*, and are clearly operating on a scale that means they can defy the Time Lords in *The Invasion of Time* and *The Two Doctors*, but there's no evidence they routinely travel in time. The only one of the Doctor's (non-Time Lord) foes with a mastery of time travel are the Daleks – they develop time travel in *The Chase*, and definitely use it in *The Daleks'*

Master Plan, *The Evil of the Daleks*, *Day of the Daleks*, *Resurrection of the Daleks*, *Remembrance of the Daleks*, *Dalek*, *Army of Ghosts/Doomsday*, *Daleks in Manhattan*, *Evolution of the Daleks*, *The Stolen Earth/Journey's End*, *Victory of the Daleks*, *Asylum of the Daleks*, *The Day of the Doctor*, *The Time of the Doctor* and *The Magician's Apprentice/The Witch's Familiar*. Even so, in the remaining stories, we've resisted assuming that the Daleks are time travellers.

• Sometimes, stories occur with the sort of impact that means it seems odd that they weren't mentioned in an earlier story. For instance, no-one from *The Power of the Daleks* and *The Moonbase* (both shown in 1966) recalls the Daleks and Cybermen fighting in *Doomsday* (shown in 2006). For that matter, when the Doctor and his companions refer to their past adventures on TV, they rarely mention the events of the Missing Adventures, Past Doctor novels, comic strips or Big Finish audios. (There are exceptions, however, usually when a writer picks up a throwaway line in a TV episode.) In *Doctor Who* itself, this may point to some deep truth about the nature of time – that events don't become part of the "Web of Time" until we see the Doctor as part of them... or it may be simply that it was impossible for the people making *Doctor Who* in the sixties to know about stories authored by their successors – many of whom hadn't even been born then.

• And, in a related note, few people making *The Tenth Planet* (in 1966, depicting the distant space year 1986) would have imagined anyone in the early twenty-first century worrying how to reconcile the quasi-futuristic world they imagined with the historical reality. Whenever the UNIT stories are set, it was "the twentieth century", and that's history now. Some of the early New Adventures novels took place in a "near future" setting. We've therefore accepted the dates given, rather than said that – for example – as we still haven't put a man on Mars, *The Ambassadors of Death* is still set in our future. There's clearly a sensible reason why the "present day" stories made now look like our present day, not *The Tenth Planet: The Next Generation*. The in-story explanation/fudge would seem to be that most *Doctor Who* stories take place in isolated locations, and that there are agencies like UNIT, C19 and Torchwood tasked with keeping alien incursions covered up. This paradigm has broken down over time, however, given the sheer number of public events involving aliens in the new series, *The Sarah Jane Adventures* and (to a lesser degree) *Torchwood*.

• There are still errors of omission, as when a later story fails to acknowledge an earlier one (often in other media) that seems relevant. No-one in *The Christmas Invasion*, for example, notes that it's odd Britain is making a big deal about sending an unmanned probe to Mars, when there were manned UK missions there in the seventies (in *The Ambassadors of Death*) and the nineties (*The Dying Days*). As with Sarah in *School Reunion* remembering *The Hand of Fear* but not *The Five Doctors*, there's got to be an appeal to clarity in storytelling. With so many *Doctor Who* stories in existence, it's almost impossible to tell a new one that doesn't explicitly contradict an earlier story, let alone implicitly. The reason no-one, say, remarks that the second Doctor looks like Salamander except in *The Enemy of the World* is the same reason that no-one ever says Rose looks like the girl who married Chris Evans – it gets in the way of the story, and doesn't help it along.

THE STORIES

This book restricts itself to events described in the BBC television series *Doctor Who*, and its original full-length fiction, audio plays and comics; the spin-off series *The Sarah Jane Adventures, Torchwood, K9, Class* and their related full-length fiction, audio plays and comics; and any spin-off books, audios, comics and direct-to-video/DVD films involving characters that originated in the above, and were used with permission by their rights holders (see Section No. 4 below). To be included in this Fourth Edition of *Ahistory*, a story had to be released before 31st December, 2017. (At our discretion, and as deadlines allowed, we included stray stories from 2018 if they finished an ongoing storyline or had some special significance.)

This is not an attempt to enter the debate about which stories are "canon" (although we have been compelled to make such determinations at times), it is simply an attempt to limit the length and scale of this book. There are two types of information in this book – evidence given in TV stories, and anything provided in another format – and these are distinguished by different typefaces.

1. The Television Series. Included are the episodes and on-screen credits of...
   • *Doctor Who*, from *An Unearthly Child* (1963) to the end of the twelfth Doctor era, *Twice Upon a Time* (2017)
   • The pilot episode *K9 and Company* (1981)
   • *Torchwood* (2006-2011), stars the alien-tech-harvesting group first seen in *Doctor Who* Series 2
   • *The Sarah Jane Adventures* (2007-2011), features the long-running companion Sarah Jane Smith and her teenage friends
   • The *K9* TV series (2009-2010), set in the future, with a new version of K9
   • *Class* (2016), short-lived spin-off set at Coal Hill Academy, following on from *Doctor Who* Series 9.

We have also taken into consideration extended or unbroadcast versions that have since been commercially released or broadcast anywhere in the world – there are few cases of "extended" material contradicting the original story.

Priority is given to sources closest to the finished product or the production team of the time the story was made. In descending order of authority are the following: the programme as broadcast; the official series websites; official guidebooks made in support of the series (*Doctor Who: The Encyclopedia*, etc.), the *Radio Times* and other contemporary BBC publicity material (which was often written by the producer or script editor); the camera script; the novelisation of a story by the original author or an author working closely from the camera script; contemporary interviews with members of the production team; televised trailers; rehearsal and draft scripts; novelisations by people other than the original author; storylines and writers' guides (which often contradict on-screen information); interviews with members of the production team after the story was broadcast; and finally any other material, such as fan speculation.

Scenes cut from broadcast were considered if they were incorporated back into a story at a later time (as with those in *The Curse of Fenric* VHS and DVD). Not included is information from unreleased material that exists, is in release but was kept separate from the story (for instance, the extra scenes on the *Ghost Light* DVD) or that no longer exists (such as with *Terror of the Autons*, *Terror of the Zygons* and *The Hand of Fear*). Neither does the first version of *An Unearthly Child* to be filmed (the so-called "pilot episode") count, nor "In character" appearances by the Doctor interacting with the real world on other programmes (e.g.: on *Animal Magic*, *Children in Need*, *Blue Peter* etc.).

2. The *Doctor Who*, *The Sarah Jane Adventures*, *Torchwood* and *Class* books, audios and webcasts. This present volume also encompasses the *Doctor Who* New Adventures (continued the adventures of the seventh Doctor and Ace after the end of the original TV series) and Missing Adventures (retro Doctor stories) published by Virgin (1991-1997); the BBC's Eighth Doctor Adventures (1997-2005); the BBC's Past Doctor Adventures (1997-2005); the BBC's New Series Adventures (up through *Plague City*, 2017); the *Torchwood* novels (up through *TW: Exodus Code*, 2012); all of the Telos novellas (2001-2004); the three *Class* novels; the four *K9* children's books (1980); and a number of one-off novels: *Harry Sullivan's War, Turlough and the Earthlink Dilemma* and *Who Killed Kennedy*.

The audios covered include *The Pescatons, Slipback, The Paradise of Death* and *The Ghosts of N-Space*; the BBC fourth Doctor mini-series (*Hornets' Nest, Demon Quest* and *Serpent Crest*); and the extensive Big Finish *Doctor Who* audio range... its monthly series (up to *Static*, #233), the

Companion Chronicles (up to Series 11), the Fourth Doctor Adventures (starring Tom Baker, up to Series 6), the Early Adventures (first and second Doctor stories, up to Series 4), the eighth Doctor audios initially broadcast on BBC7 (up to *To the Death*, #4.10), various promotional audios (up to *Trial of the Valeyard*), special releases (up to *The Sixth Doctor – The Last Adventure*), the eighth Doctor box sets *Dark Eyes* and *Doom Coalition*, *Philip Hinchcliffe Presents* (to *The Helm of Awe*), the Lost Stories (unmade TV scripts adapted for audio) and many more. The BBC webcasts *Real Time*, *Shada* and *Death Comes to Time* (the last one somewhat controversially) are included, as well as the *Torchwood* webcast *Web of Lies*.

A handful of stories were available in another form – *Shakedown* and *Downtime* were originally direct-to-video spin-offs, some Big Finish stories like *Minuet in Hell* and *The Mutant Phase* are (often radically different) adaptations of stories made by Audio Visuals. *Ahistory* deals with the "official" versions, as opposed to the fan-produced ones.

This volume covers two stories that appear in different versions, because they were told in two media that fall within the scope of the book and were adapted for different Doctors: *Shada* and *Human Nature*. Those have been dealt with on a case-by-case basis. *Doctor Who* fans have long had different versions of the same story in different media – the first Dalek story, for example, was televised, extensively altered for the novelisation, changed again for the movie version and adapted into a comic strip.

We haven't included in-character appearances in nonfiction books (e.g: the *Doctor Who Discovers...* and *Doctor Who Quiz Book of* series), and *Make Your Own Adventure/Find Your Fate*-style books where it's impossible to determine the actual story. It was tempting, though.

3) The *Doctor Who* comics, including the strip that has been running in *Doctor Who Weekly/Monthly/Magazine* since 1979 (up through "Matildus", *DWM* #518), along with all original backup strips from that publication, and the ones from the various Specials and Yearbooks. With a book like this, drawing a line between what should and shouldn't be included is never as simple as it might appear. Including every comic strip would include ones from the Annuals, for example. This book doesn't include the text stories that *Doctor Who Magazine* has included at various points during its run.

There's a relatively straightforward distinction between the *DWM* comic strip and other *Doctor Who* comic strips: while it's the work of many writers, artists and editors, it also has a strong internal continuity and sense of identity. This book, in all previous editions, has confined itself to "long form" *Doctor Who* and there's a case to be made that the *DWM* strip represents one "ongoing story" that's run for over a quarter of a century. The *Doctor Who Magazine* strip has now run for longer than the original TV series,

and most fans must have encountered it at some point.

That said, this book excludes *DWM* strips that are clearly parodies that aren't meant to be considered within the continuity of the strip. The same logic applies to spoofs like *Dimensions in Time* and *The Curse of Fatal Death*. For the record, the affected strips are "Follow that TARDIS!", "The Last Word" and "TV Action".

DWM has reprinted a number of strips from other publications over the years. We have tended to include these. The main beneficiary of this is *The Daleks* strip from the sixties comic *TV Century 21* (and *DWM*'s sequel to it from issues #249-254).

It's certainly arguable that the *DWM* strip exists in a separate continuity, with its own companions, internal continuity, vision of Gallifrey and even an ethos that made it feel quite unlike the TV eras of its Doctors. This certainly seemed to be the case early on. However, this distinction has broken down over the years – the comic strip companion Frobisher appeared in a book (*Mission: Impractical*) and two audios (*The Holy Terror*, *The Maltese Penguin*); the village of Stockbridge (from the fifth Doctor *DWM* comics) has featured in various audios starting with *Circular Time*; the audio *The Company of Friends* incorporated characters from different book and comic ranges; and for a number of years the strip and the New Adventures novels were quite elaborately linked. In the new TV series, we've met someone serving kronkburgers (in *The Long Game*, first mentioned in "The Iron Legion") the Doctor quoted Abslom Daak in *Bad Wolf*, and Daak's mug shot appeared in *Time Heist*.

The strip tends to "track" the ongoing story (the television series in the seventies and eighties, the New Adventures in the early nineties) – so the Doctor regenerates, without explanation within the strip and on occasion during a story arc. Companions from the television series and books come and go. Costume changes and similar details (like the design of the console room) do the same. It's broadly possible to work out when the strip is set in the Doctor's own life. So, the first *Doctor Who* Weekly strips with the fourth Doctor mention he's dropped off Romana, and he changes from his Season 17 to Season 18 costume – so it slots in neatly between the two seasons. There are places where this process throws up some anomalies, which have been noted.

Also included are the *Doctor Who* comics produced by IDW for the American market; the *Radio Times* comics featuring the eighth Doctor; the comics that first appeared in *Torchwood: The Official Magazine*; and the *Torchwood* and *The Sarah Jane Adventures* webcomics.

We also include the ongoing *Doctor Who* and *Torchwood* comics published by Titan, although – owing to the cut-off point of this guidebook being at the end of 2017 – we've included all of *The Tenth Doctor Year Three* and *The Eleventh Doctor Year Three*, but had to stop partway through *The*

Twelfth Doctor Year Three (#3.9, "The Great Shopping Bill"). All of the Titan comics before that are present, however, as are crossover events up through "The Lost Dimension".

4) Spin-off series featuring characters that originally appeared in *Doctor Who* (whatever the format), and were used elsewhere with permission by their respective rights holders.

This needs some explaining... *Doctor Who* is a very unusual property in that, generally speaking, the BBC retained ownership of anything created by salaried employees, but freelance scriptwriters working on the TV show in the 60s, 70s and 80s (and the novelists working on the books in the 90s) typically wound up owning the rights to any characters they created. Infamously, this has meant that writer Terry Nation (and his estate) kept ownership of the name "Dalek" and the conceptual property therein, but the BBC retained the rights to the likeness of the Daleks, which were created by staff designer Raymond Cusick.

This is very counter-intuitive to how other series work – a world where *Star Trek* is so divided (say, with one person owning the Klingons, another owning the Horta and another owning Spock, while Paramount continues to retain ownership of Captain Kirk and the *Enterprise*) would be unthinkable. Nonetheless, over the years, the rights holders to iconic *Doctor Who* characters and monsters have licensed them for use elsewhere, and – unless given reason to think otherwise – their use in a non-*Doctor Who* story seems as valid as any BBC-sanctioned story.

The spin-offs included in this volume are:

• The Bernice Summerfield novels, audios and novella collections (1997-present), featuring the Doctor's companion who was first seen in the New Adventure *Love and War* (1992). Benny was the lead of the Doctor-less New Adventures novels published from 1997 to 1999; Big Finish took over the license afterward, and has produced Benny audios, novels, short story anthologies, novella collections and one animated story. Later, Benny was folded (after a fashion) back into the main *Doctor Who* range with *The New Adventures of Bernice Summerfield* box sets.

The first five Benny audios were excluded, as they were adaptations of New Adventures novels.

• BBV audios and films (1994-2015?) featuring licensed characters such as the Sontarans, the Rutans and the Zygons, as well as *P.R.O.B.E.* (1994-1996, 2015): a spin-off series featuring Liz Shaw, a third Doctor companion.

• Big Finish audio spin-off series...
  –*Charlotte Pollard* (2014-present), featuring the eighth (and later sixth) Doctor companion who debuted in *Storm Warning* (2001).
  –*The Churchill Years* (2016-present), with Ian McNeice reprising his role as Winston Churchill, first seen in *Victory of the Daleks* (2010).
  –*The Confessions of Dorian Gray* (2012-2016), mature-themed, supernatural stories centered on the "real life" immortal Dorian Gray, a friend of Oscar Wilde. This version of Dorian also appears in the Bernice Summerfield range and *The Worlds of Big Finish*. (For the timeline of the Dorian Gray stories, see the appendix.)
  –*Counter-Measures* (2012-2015), relaunched as *The New Counter-Measures* (2016-present) with the team of the same name that debuted in *Remembrance of the Daleks* (1988).
  –*Cyberman* (2005-2009), original cast of characters fights against the Cybermen in Earth's future.
  –*Dalek Empire* (2001-2008), the same, but against the Daleks.
  –*The Diary of River Song* (2015-present), further escapades of River Song, prior her first appearance in *Silence in the Library* (2008).
  –*Gallifrey* (2004-present), a political drama featuring Romana as president of Gallifrey, as aided by Leela and the two K9s.
  –*Graceless* (2010-present?), mature-themed stories with the two Key to Time Tracers (and sisters), Abby (formerly "Amy") and Zara, who first appeared in *The Judgement of Isskar* (2009).
  –*I, Davros* (2006), covers the early history of the Daleks' creator.
  –*Jago & Litefoot* (2010-2018), Victorian investigations into the strange and the supernatural, starring Henry Gordon Jago and Professor Litefoot from *The Talons of Weng-Chiang* (1977). We've included up through *J&L* Series 13; absent is the coda story *Jago & Litefoot Forever* (2018).
  –*The Lives of Captain Jack* (2017), box set with stories from various points in Jack's history.
  –*Sarah Jane Smith* (2002-2006), features the long-standing third and fourth Doctor companion, in stories set prior to *The Sarah Jane Adventures*.
  –The *Unbound* series (2003-2008), an exercise in having different actors play the Doctor. Considered apocrypha for years, this became part of the main timeline owing to *The New Adventures of Bernice Summerfield* Volume 3 (2016).
  –*UNIT* (2004-present): a mini-series with original characters, then a box set starring the seventh Doctor, and then box sets starring Kate Stewart and Osgood from the new series.
  –*Vienna* (2013-present), with the bounty hunter first seen in *The Shadow Heart* (2012).
  –*The War Doctor* (2015-2017), with John Hurt reprising his role as the War Doctor from *The Day of the Doctor* (2013), in conflicts during the Last Great Time War.
  –*The War Master* (2017), with Derek Jacobi reprising his role as the Master seen in *Utopia* (2007), in conflicts during the Last Great Time War.
  –*The Worlds of Big Finish* (2015) crossover event featur-

ing the Graceless, the Big Finish version of Sherlock Holmes (played by Nicholas Briggs), Dorian Gray, Iris Wildthyme, Vienna and Bernice Summerfield.

• *City of the Saved* anthologies (2012-present), stories set in the end-of-the-universe metropolis first seen in the Faction Paradox guidebook *The Book of the War* (2002). The term "spin-off of a spin-off" is frequently misused, but here it applies.

• *Erimem* books (2005-present), featuring the fifth Doctor audio companion first seen in *The Eye of the Scorpion* (2001), after her departure from the TARDIS in *The Bride of Peladon*.

• *Faction Paradox* books (2002-present), audios and a comic; featuring characters and concepts first seen in the EDA *Alien Bodies* (1997).

• Iris Wildthyme audios and two novels, a novella and many anthologies (2005-present); a character seen in the original fiction of Paul Magrs, and who first appeared in *Doctor Who* in the *Short Trips* story "Old Flames" and the EDA *The Scarlet Empress*.

• *Kaldor City* audios (2001-2011), spun off from *The Robots of Death* and the PDA *Corpse Marker* (1999).

• *Lethbridge-Stewart* novels (2015-present), featuring Colonel (later Brigadier) Alistair Gordon Lethbridge-Stewart in adventures set between *The Web of Fear* and *The Invasion*.

• *Minister of Chance* (2011-2013), undatable audios featuring the lead from the webcast *Death Comes to Time* (2001-2002).

• *Miranda* comic (2003), from the character seen in the EDA *Father Time* (2001).

• Reeltime Pictures direct-to-VHS/DVD films (1988-present), featuring the Sontarans, the Draconians, the Daemons, etc.

• *Time Hunter* novellas (2003-2007), featuring characters from the Telos novella *The Cabinet of Light* (2003), and also involving the Fendahl and the Daemons.

# # # # #

Unhistory, a digital-only supplement to the book you're holding, covers many works that – even with the best of will and a heady desire to be all-inclusive – we viewed as apocrypha (see *Unhistory* for our reasoning on this), so couldn't justify placing in the main timeline. *Unhistory* is a

cornucopia of nearly five hundred such stories, the highlights of which include:

• Comic strips released prior to the advent of the *Doctor Who Magazine* strip, including the *TV Comic* and *Countdown* strips. There are some profound canonicity concerns with these strips, plus it would have taken *Ahistory* to an even more staggering length.

• *The Dalek Book* (1964), *The Dalek World* (1965) and *The Dalek Outer Space Book* (1966), as well as the four *Terry Nation's Dalek Annuals* (1976-1979). Very interesting early texts about the Daleks, often credited to Dalek co-creator Terry Nation and *Doctor Who* script editor David Whitaker.

• Two Big Finish stageplay adaptations *The Curse of the Daleks* and *The Seven Keys to Doomsday*. A third stageplay adaptation, *The Ultimate Adventure,* and its sequel audio, *Beyond the Ultimate Adventure*, were included in *Ahistory* as they are more compatible with the established timeline.

• The 2003 *Scream of the Shalka* webcast, which debuted Richard E. Grant as the ninth Doctor and was then superseded with the advent of the new series. This story was previously included in *Ahistory*, but has been excluded because the sheer preponderance of material establishing the Eccleston version as the ninth Doctor means that almost nobody at time of writing (not even the *Scream of the Shalka*'s creators) accepts the Grant Doctor as canon.

• Short stories from the World Distributors *Doctor Who Annuals* (1966-1986).

• Stories that were explicitly marketed as being apocryphal, mockumentaries and many instances of *Doctor Who* actors portraying their characters in real-life events or commercials (such as the Prime Computers adverts).

# # # # #

However, despite the efforts of *Ahistory* and *Unhistory* combined, there remain some significant omissions:

• Short stories, whether they first appeared in *Doctor Who Magazine*, the *Decalog* and *Short Trips* anthologies, the *Doctor Who Annuals* (1992-present), or any of the innumerable other places they have cropped up.

There are a few exceptions to this... anthologies were included if they were a rare exception in a full-length story range (say, the *Story of Martha* anthology published with the New Series Adventures novels). Or, if they informed upon the New Series so much (as with *The Legends of Ashildr* and *The Legends of River Song* anthologies), it seemed too glaring an oversight to leave them out.

Also, information from the Bernice Summerfield,

Faction Paradox and Iris Wildthyme short story anthologies were included if they were so interwoven into continuity elsewhere that omitting them would have been confusing (prime examples of this are the Benny anthologies *Life During Wartime* and *Present Danger*). Similarly, information from *Faction Paradox: The Book of the War* (itself a guidebook) was included if it directly pertained to characters or events prominently featured in other *Faction Paradox* stories (for instance, the background of Cousin Octavia, the lead character in *FP: Warring States*).

• Unlicensed "cover series" with actors playing thinly veiled counterparts of their *Doctor Who* characters, such as Sylvester McCoy starring as "the Professor" in the BBV audios.

• Proposed stories that were never made, including *Campaign* (a Past Doctor novel commissioned but never released by the BBC; it was later privately published).

• Unauthorised charity anthologies.

• Big Finish's *Sherlock Holmes* audios (see the Sherlock Holmes sidebar), although the detective as played by Nicholas Briggs also appears in *The Worlds of Big Finish* and the audio adaptation of *All-Consuming Fire*.

# # # # #

On the whole, the television series takes priority over what is said in the other media, and where a detail or reference in one of the books, audios or comics appears to contradict what was established on television, it's been noted as much and an attempt made to rationalise the "mistake" away.

The New Adventures and Missing Adventures built up a broadly consistent "future history" of the universe. This was, in part, based on the "History of Mankind" in Jean-Marc Lofficier's *The Terrestrial Index* (1991), which mixes information from the series with facts from the novelisations and the author's own speculation. Many authors, though, have contradicted or ignored Lofficier's version of events. For the purposes of this book, *The Terrestrial Index* itself is non-canonical, and it's been noted, but ultimately ignored, whenever a New Adventure recounts information solely using Lofficier as reference.

Writers' guides, discussion documents and the authors' original submissions and storylines provide useful information; we have, when possible, referenced these.

KEY
The following abbreviations are used in the text:

B – box set (specifically, a Big Finish format)
BENNY – A Bernice Summerfield book or audio
BF – The Big Finish audio adventures
CC – Big Finish's *Companion Chronicles* audios, which switched to a box set format with Series 9
CITY – The *City of the Saved* anthologies
CLASS – *Class*
CD,NM – Big Finish's *Classic Doctors, New Monsters* box sets
CM – *Counter-Measures*
CHARLEY – *Charlotte Pollard* audios
DC – Big Finish's *Doom Coalition* audios, four box sets starring the eighth Doctor. These were released after...
DEyes – Big Finish's *Dark Eyes* audios, four box sets also starring the eighth Doctor
DG – Big Finish's *The Confessions of Dorian Gray* audios, starring the Oscar Wilde creation
DL – *The Darksmith Legacy* novellas
DotD – *Destiny of the Doctor*, an audio mini-series
DWM – *Doctor Who Magazine* (also known for a time as *Doctor Who Monthly*)
DWW – *Doctor Who Weekly* (as the magazine was initially called until issue #44)
1stA – Big Finish's *The First Doctor Adventures* audios, starring David Bradley as the first Doctor
1stD – Big Finish's *The First Doctor* box sets, a continuation of the *Companion Chronicles*
FP – *Faction Paradox*
EA – Big Finish's *Early Adventures* audios, adventures concerning the first and second Doctors
EDA – Eighth Doctor Adventures (the ongoing novels published by the BBC)
ERIMEM – The *Erimem* novels
5thB – Big Finish's *The Fifth Doctor Box Set* audios
IRIS – The Iris Wildthyme books and audios
KC – *Kaldor City*
K9 – The *K9* TV show
JACK – *The Lives of Captain Jack* audio box set
J&L – *Jago & Litefoot* audios
LETH-ST – The *Lethbridge-Stewart* novels
LS – Big Finish's *Lost Stories*, audio adaptations of unmade stories proposed for the TV series
MA – Missing Adventures (the past Doctor novels published by Virgin)
NA – New Adventures (the ongoing novels published by Virgin, chiefly featuring the seventh Doctor)
NAoBENNY – *The New Adventures of Bernice Summerfield*
New CM – *The New Counter-Measures*, a continuation of the *Counter-Measures* audios.
9thC – Big Finish's *The Ninth Doctor Chronicles* audios

NSA – New Series Adventures (featuring the ninth Doctor et al)

PDA – Past Doctor Adventure (the past Doctor novels published by the BBC)

PHP – *Philip Hinchcliffe Presents*, fourth Doctor audios as conceptualised by the TV producer of the same name

RIVER – *The Diary of River Song* audios

S – Season or Series

2ndD – Big Finish's *The Second Doctor* box sets, a continuation of the *Companion Chronicles*

6thLA – *The Sixth Doctor – The Last Adventure*, an audio box set

SJA – *The Sarah Jane Adventures*

SJS – Big Finish's *Sarah Jane Smith* audio series

ST – *Short Trips*, short story anthologies released in print by Virgin, BBC Books and Big Finish, and also on audio by the latter.

TEL – Telos novellas

3rdA – Big Finish's *The Third Doctor Adventures* audios

TimeH – *Time Hunter*

TV – The TV series

TW – *Torchwood*

TWM – *Torchwood: The Official Magazine*

V – Volume

WD – *The War Doctor*

WM – *The War Master*

WORLDS BF – Big Finish's *The Worlds of Big Finish* crossover box set (featuring BF's spin-off characters)

WORLDS DW – Big Finish's *The Worlds of Doctor Who* crossover box set (mostly features TV characters such as Jago and Litefoot)

In the text of the book, the following marker appears to indicate when the action of specific stories take place:

c 2005 – THE REPETITION OF THE CLICHE ->

The title is exactly as it appeared on screen or on the cover. For the Hartnell stories without an overall title given on screen, we have used the titles that appear on the BBC's product (*An Unearthly Child*, *The Daleks*, *The Edge of Destruction*, etc.).

The letter before the date, the "code", indicates how accurately we know the date. If there is no code, then that date is precisely established in the story itself (e.g. *The Daleks' Master Plan* is set in the year 4000 exactly).

• "c" means that the story is set circa that year (e.g. *The Dalek Invasion of Earth* is set "c.2167")

• "?" indicates a guess, and the reasons for it are given in the footnotes (e.g. we don't know what year *Destiny of the Daleks* is set in, but it must be "centuries" after *The Daleks' Master Plan*, so it's here set it in "? 4600").

• "&" means that the story is dated relative another story that we lack a date for (e.g.: we know that *Resurrection of the Daleks* is set "ninety years" after *Destiny of the Daleks,* so *Resurrection of the Daleks* is set in "& 4690"). If one story moves, the linked one also has to.

• "u" means that the story featured UNIT. There is, to put it mildly, some discussion about exactly when the UNIT stories are set. For the purposes of this guidebook, see the introduction to the UNIT Section.

• "=" indicates action that takes place in a parallel universe or a divergent timestream (such as *Inferno* or *Battlefield*). Often, the Doctor succeeds in restoring the correct timeline or erasing an aberrant deviation of history – those cases are indicated by brackets – "(=)". As this information technically isn't part of history, it's set apart by boxes with dashed lines.

• "@" is a story set during the eighth Doctor's period living on Earth from 1888 (starting with *The Ancestor Cell*) to 2001 (*Escape Velocity*). During this period, he was without a working TARDIS or his memories.

• "lgtw" refers to an event pertaining to the Last Great Time War that serves as the background to *Doctor Who* Series 1, and dramatically comes into play in *The Day of the Doctor.*

• "wih" refers to an event that took place during the future War timeline (a.k.a. the War in Heaven, not to be confused with the Last Great Time War featured in New *Who*) in the eighth Doctor books, and which continued in the *Faction Paradox* series. Events in *The Ancestor Cell* annulled this timeline, but remnants of it "still happened" in the real *Doctor Who* timeline, just as *Day of the Daleks* "still happened" even though the future it depicted was averted.

We've attempted to weed out references that just aren't very telling, relevant or interesting. Clearly, there's a balance to be had, as half the fun of a book like this is in listing trivia and strange juxtapositions, but a timeline could easily go to *even more* absurd extremes than presently exist. If a novel set in 1980 said that a minor character was 65, lived in a turn-of-the-century terraced house and bought the Beatles album *Rubber Soul* when it first came out, then it could generate entries for c.1900, 1915 and 1965. We would only list these if they were relevant to the story or made for particularly interesting reading.

We haven't listed birthdates of characters, except the Doctor's companions or other major recurring figures, again unless it represents an important story point.

Before Time

Before our universe, others existed with different physical laws. The universe immediately prior to our own had its own Time Lords, and as their universe reached the point of collapse, they shunted themselves into a parallel universe and discovered that they now possessed almost infinite power.[1]

Rassilon speculated that the beings Raag, Nah and Rok had created and destroyed many universes.[2] **Before the creation of the universe, the Disciples of the Light rose up against the Beast and chained him in the Pit. It was theorised that the Beast would go on to inspire archetypes of evil on many planets, including Earth, Draconia, Skaro (where it was rendered as the Kaled god of war), Damos, Veltino and Vel Consadine.[3]** Abaddon, a grey-skinned creature that apparently hailed from the same race as the Beast, and its opposite number, the blue-skinned Pwccm, were respectively champions of the Light and the Dark – capricious beings of pure halogen that warred against one another, and in time would use the Cardiff Rift to traverse dimensions.[4]

The third Doctor once almost accidentally sent the TARDIS into the void before the universe started.[5]

The Entropy Sirens were born and "danced" before the first hydrogen atoms combined. Their ability to live in our reality was greatly diminished as nucleo-synthesis silenced the universe's scream of creation.[6]

The second Doctor tricked the Vist into travelling back to the start of the universe... where they fell off the edge of it, tumbled into the universe that existed beforehand, and became trapped in a formless, timeless dimension.[7]

The Dawn of Time: Event One[8]

One ship managed to travel to the dawn of creation, albeit by accident. Terminus was a vast spaceship built by an infinitely advanced, ancient race capable of time travel. The ship developed a fault, and the pilot was forced to eject some of its unstable fuel into the void before making a time jump. The explosion that resulted was the Big Bang. Terminus was thrown billions of years into the future, where it came to settle in the exact centre of the universe.[9] The universe was created when the time-travelling starship *Vipod Mor* arrived at this point and exploded.[10]

The Urbankan Monarch believed that if his ship could travel faster than light, it would move backwards in time to the Big Bang and beyond. Monarch believed that he was God and that he would meet himself at the creation of the universe.[11]

The universe was created in a huge explosion known as the Big Bang. As this was the very first thing to happen, scientists sometimes refer to it as "Event One".

---

1 *All-Consuming Fire, Millennial Rites, The Taking of Planet 5.*

2 *Divided Loyalties.* These are the Gods of Ragnarok seen in *The Greatest Show in the Galaxy.*

3 *The Satan Pit*

4 *TW: The Twilight Streets.* "The Light" presumably bears some affiliation with the Disciples of the Light who imprisoned the Beast (*The Impossible Planet*), although *The Twilight Streets* references the Light-Dark conflict as only having run for "millennia". Abaddon appears in *TW: End of Days*; Bilis in the same story almost seems to imply that Abaddon is the "son" of the Beast. The point is unclear, however, especially as "Abaddon" is also given as an alias of the Beast itself in *The Impossible Planet.*

THE CARDIFF RIFT: The ninth Doctor, Rose and Jack's discussion in *Boom Town* about the Cardiff Rift (a central feature of *Torchwood*) seems to indicate that it predates events surrounding it in *The Unquiet Dead* – the Gelth "used" rather than "created" the Rift, and it was only "healed" afterwards. References to the "darkness" might mean that Abaddon is trapped in the void seen in *Army of Ghosts* and *Doomsday*, with the Rift merely providing access. Going just by what's on screen, Abaddon's presence might be what weakens space-time in the Cardiff area, facilitating the creation of the Rift in the first place. *The Twilight Streets*, though, specifies that Abaddon wasn't imprisoned there until 1876.

The Rift is temporarily sealed in 2010 in *TW: The House of the Dead*, which helps to explain why Jack can so readily leave Earth in *TW: Children of Earth*, and the reconstituted Torchwood in *TW: Miracle Day* doesn't have to spend any time worrying about it. The Rift slowly becomes more active, however, and it's returned to being an ongoing concern in *TW: Aliens Among Us.*

5 *Island of Death*

6 *The Demons of Red Lodge and Other Stories*: "The Entropy Composition"

7 *The Forbidden Time*

8 EVENT ONE: The term "Event One" is first used in *Castrovalva* to mean the creation of "the Galaxy", but in *Terminus* the Doctor talks of "the biggest explosion in history: Event One", which he confirms is "the Big Bang" which "created the universe". There are a number of stories where the writers definitely confuse the term "galaxy" and "universe", and a number of others where they seem to. Rather than rule which is which, this book will list what was said in the stories, noting the more egregious examples, rather than ignoring them or trying to rationalise them away.

"Among the adherents of Scientific Mythology [q.v.] the element (Hydrogen) is widely believed to be the basic constituent out of which the Galaxy was first formed [see EVENT ONE] and evidence in support of this hypothesis includes its supposed appearance in spectroscopic analysis of massive star bodies." [12]

(=) The ripple effect caused by the Pyramid Eternia in 2015 caused the Big Bang to fizzle until the Ancients of the Universe put the situation to rights. [13]

TIMELESS [14] -> The eighth Doctor piloted the TARDIS back to slightly after the Big Bang, hoping to avoid a myriad of parallel realities by entering the correct history from the very start. Chloe, a small girl from a devastated planet, arrived on hand. Jamais, her time travelling dog, aided the overstrained TARDIS in reaching London, 2003. The Doctor's party re-visited this era when Sabbath and Kalicum, an agent of the Council of Eight, attempted to seed an intelligence gestated within a heap of diamonds into the start of history. The Doctor failed, and the intelligence became part of the fabric of the universe.

The diamonds allowed the Council of Eight to map out events throughout the whole of history. [15]

CASTROVALVA [16] -> The Tremas Master attempted to kill the newly-regenerated fifth Doctor, Tegan and Nyssa by sending them backwards in time to a hydrogen inrush early in the universe's history.

The Time Lords of Gallifrey monitored the Big Bang, and precisely determined the date of Event One. [17] An eye of the storm resulting from the Big Bang, the Point of Stillness, existed in the difference between 000.000 and 00.0000 (sic). Time Lords were forbidden from visiting the Point of Stillness, as the barriers between reality and imagination were thin there, and defiling it with time anomalies risked destroying the universe. [18]

Insect-like "forces of chaos" fed on the debris of the Big Bang, just as they would feed on the collapse of the universe. [19] The Vess used energy from the Big Bang to power their weapons factory, which was located in a pocket dimension. The sixth Doctor and Peri followed the energy flow to the Vess facility. [20] Amethyst Virus No. 7001B, designated Alpha non-variant 001, fell back to "beyond the beginnings of life in the universe", and endowed all life to come with the ability to evolve and change. [21] As aided by the twelfth Doctor and Clara, the Phaeron succeeded in forever trapping the Glamour, and themselves, in Deep Time: a temporal lockbox reached by drilling a wormhole through time itself. [22]

The Doctor claimed to have been an eye-witness at the origins of the universe. [23]

---

9 *Terminus*

10 *Slipback.* This is a clear continuity clash with *Terminus*, and a discrepancy made all the more obvious as *Slipback* was broadcast within two years of *Terminus* and was written by its script editor, Eric Saward. If we wanted to reconcile the two accounts, we could speculate that the *Vipod Mor* explosion was the spark that ignited the fuel jettisoned in *Terminus*.

11 *Four to Doomsday.* Monarch never achieves this goal.

12 This appears on the console screen in *Castrovalva*.

13 *Big Bang Generation* (ch12).

14 Dating *Timeless* (EDA #65) - The Doctor strategises to enter the universe from its very start, although technically he intends for the TARDIS to "go back in time to just after the Big Bang in our universe and *hold* that point while we slip through the dimensions" (ch4).

15 *Sometime Never*

16 Dating *Castrovalva* (19.1) - The Master's trap entails sending the TARDIS on a one-way (he hopes) journey back to Event One: "the creation" (Nyssa says) "of the galaxy out of a huge in-rush of hydrogen"...

17 *Transit.*

THE AGE OF THE UNIVERSE: The date of the creation of the universe is not clearly established on screen, although we are told it took place "billions of years" before *Terminus*. Modern scientific consensus is that the universe is about 15 billion years old, and books that address the issue, like *Timewyrm: Apocalypse* and *Falls the Shadow*, concur with this date. In *Transit*, the seventh Doctor drunkenly celebrates the universe's 13,500,020,012th birthday (meaning the Big Bang took place in 13,500,017,903 BC). *SJA: Secrets of the Stars* claims the universe is "13 billion" years old. *The Infinity Doctors* establishes that the Time Lords refer to the end of the universe as Event Two.

Hell Bent occurs near the end of the universe, "billions of years" (according to the Doctor and Ashildr) or more specifically "several billion years" (the Doctor says) after Clara's death in the modern day. The same story, however, entails the Doctor having spent "4.5 billion years" trapped in his confession dial (*Heaven Sent*), and the General claiming that Clara has been dead for "half the lifetime of the universe". Treating the two as one and the same would go against scientific consensus, which holds that the universe is *already* more than nine billion years old – it's possible that the General is simplifying to convey the gravity of what's at stake if the Doctor doesn't return Clara to the moment of her death.

18 *The Abandoned*

19 "Hunger from the Ends of Time"

20 *The Light at the End*

21 *Charley S2: The Viyran Solution.* If true, this means the entire universe is a giant paradox.

Fenric and the Elder Gods[24]

"The dawn of time. The beginning of all beginnings. Two forces only: Good and Evil. Then chaos. Time is born: matter, space. The universe cries out like a newborn. The forces *shatter* as the universe explodes outwards. Only echoes remain, and yet somehow, *somehow* the evil force survives. An intelligence. Pure *evil*."

The evil force retained its sentience and spread its influence throughout time and space. It became the entity that the Vikings would call Fenric.[25]

GODS AND MONSTERS[26] **->** The elder gods were powerful beings who played games against one another, and didn't directly interfere in the mortal realm because it wasn't good sport. Some elder gods feared that one of their number, Fenric, would come to destroy them, so had another in their ranks – Weyland – forge the device known as Weyland's Shield as a trap. Fenric believed the Shield would manifest his true form, allowing him to devastate multiple dimensions with "an infinity of limbs", but it actually had the ability to banish him.

The gods created a stable locale – a gameboard – at the dawn of time. A restored Fenric appeared there after the seventh Doctor defeated him in World War II, and openly contested Weyland. Fenric's Vikings warred against Weyland's Saxons. The former king of Persia, Shapur I, served as Fenric's new Ancient One and murdered his son – Prince Hurmzid – when he arrived via a timestorm. Shapur was subsequently slain in battle.

Fenric captured the Doctor during the time of Beowulf,

---

22 *Deep Time*, in which the Phaeron are on "a suicide mission to the dawn of time" (ch19). The term "deep time" actually refers to Earth's age as conceptualized by geological layers, but it here effectively means a temporal prison *so* far in the past that the Glamour stands no chance of transcending the layers of time required for it to threaten sentient life again. *Gods and Monsters* works along similar lines – it's so far back in time, the Doctor must sacrifice the TARDIS' offspring to reach it.

The Glamour, or technology derived from it, also appears in the NSAs *Ghosts of India*, *The Glamour Chase*, *Royal Blood* and *Big Bang Generation*.

23 The Doctor reads the book *The Origins of the Universe* in *Destiny of the Daleks*, and remarks that the author "got it wrong on the first line. Why didn't he ask someone who saw it happen?". The tenth Doctor also claims to have seen the creation of the universe in *Planet of the Dead*.

24 The novels also cite Fenric as a member of the Great Old Ones (see The Great Old Ones sidebar). It's entirely possible that "he" and the "Elder Gods" he's affiliated with (such as Weyland) are a sub-category of that larger group.

25 *The Curse of Fenric*

26 Dating *Gods and Monsters* (BF #164) - It is the very beginning of time – so far back at the start of the universe, the black TARDIS had to perish (at the end of *Black and White*) so the Doctor's Ship could reach it. Fenric says: "To me, Doctor, your universe is less than a millionth of a second old."

27 *Afterlife*

28 *Signs and Wonders*

29 In *An Unearthly Child*, Susan defines the fifth dimension as "space".

30 *The Death of Art*

31 *Autumn Mist*

32 *The Quantum Archangel*

33 *The Shadow of the Scourge*

34 *Blink*

35 *The End of Time*

36 *Time and the Rani*

37 *The Armageddon Factor*. It's possible this is just hyperbole on the Shadow's part.

38 *The Curse of Fenric*

39 *Benny B5: Missing Persons: In Living Memory*

40 THE GREAT OLD ONES: Novels such as *All-Consuming Fire*, *Millennial Rites*, *Business Unusual*, *Divided Loyalties* and *The Quantum Archangel* state that many of the godlike beings seen in *Doctor Who* have a common origin. These Great Old Ones are also referred to in *The Infinite Quest*, and also seem to feature – although they're called "Elder Gods" – in the audio trilogy *Protect and Survive*, *Black and White* and *Gods and Monsters*.

The Great Old Ones were a pantheon of ancient, incomprehensible forces created by horror writer H.P. Lovecraft, and adopted by the novels for this purpose. Perhaps the most well-known of Lovecraft's creations, Cthulhu, had already made an appearance in *White Darkness*. *The Taking of Planet 5* uses Lovecraft's characters, but has them as fictional characters brought to life by Time Lord technology.

Other *Doctor Who* entities explicitly referred to in the books as Great Old Ones include – but aren't limited to – the Great Intelligence (see especially *The Snowmen*, *The Abominable Snowmen*, *The Web of Fear*, *Leth-St: The Forgotten Son*, *Leth-St: Times Squared*, *Leth-St: Night of the Intelligence*, *Millennial Rites*, *Downtime*, *The Bells of Saint John* and *The Name of the Doctor*), the Animus (*The Web Planet*, *Twilight of the Gods*, etc.), the Nestene Consciousness (*Spearhead from Space*, *Terror of the Autons*, *Business Unusual*, the Auton videos, *Synthespians™*, *Rose*, *The Pandorica Opens*), Fenric (*The Curse of Fenric*, *Gods and Monsters*) and the Gods of Ragnarok (primarily *The Greatest Show in the Galaxy*, *Divided Loyalties*). Gog and Magog (or beings with the same name) appeared in "The Iron Legion" comic strip.

and translocated him back to the gameboard. The Doctor's companions – Ace, Hex, Captain Lysandra Aristedes and Private Sally Morgan – arrived in the TARDIS and believed they were part of the Doctor's game against Fenric. In truth, they and the Doctor himself were Weyland's black game pieces, his Volands. The Doctor's companions had obtained Weyland's Shield, which was invisible to Fenric and his game pieces. The elder gods in the forms of Albert and Peggy Marsden sided with Weyland on behalf of their benefactor Moloch, but Fenric slew them both.

Weyland attempted a game-ending move, but Hex used Weyland's Shield to banish him "into the darkness, into null space". Fenric disappeared as the gods began dismantling the game-locale. Fenric took refuge inside Hex's body, but Hex's faith in his mother immobilised him. Lysandra complied with Hex's order to open the TARDIS doors, which swept Hex-Fenric into the chaos outside the Ship.

The TARDIS returned to the future as Fenric and Weyland, situated in null space, agreed to a new game with even higher stakes. Hex had them deal him in.

AFTERLIFE -> Hex won enough against Fenric and Weyland to purchase through Koloon – a fire elemental working for the elder gods – one year of life among mortals. He was physically returned to his native time, with Koloon neglecting to mention that his memories would be walled off, and that Koloon was authorized to "collect" him at the end of that year.[27]

To'Koth, one of the most benevolent of the Elder Gods, and a parent-figure to the likes of Ragnarok, Fenric and Weyland, was already old and sickly when the universe was born. It opted to slumber in the dimensions around what became the northwest of England, but returned to the gods' domain as various parties tried to claim its power. With its dying breath, To'Koth brokered a cessation of hostilities between the Elder Gods and the seventh Doctor.[28]

Eleven physical dimensions existed at first, quickly collapsing down to the five dimensions familiar to us. The other dimensions came to exist only at the subatomic level.[29] Beings named the Quoth evolved inside atoms and were the size of quarks.[30] The Sidhe came to exist in all 11 dimensions.[31] The remaining six dimensions became the Six-Fold Realm, and each of the six Guardians represented one such dimension.[32]

As the universe was formed, an eight-dimensional "radiating blackness" infused space and time. Eventually, the Unity of the Scourge evolved in this darkness.[33] **The Weeping Angels, also sometimes called the Lonely Assassins, were as old as the universe or very nearly. They were quite nice where they hailed from, but developed into quantum-locked hunters who turned to stone if seen.**[34] The "weeping angels of old" were known to Rassilon.[35]

The first few chaotic microseconds of the universe saw extreme temperatures and the forging of bizarre elements that would be unable to exist later. This was the Leptonic Era, and one of the bizarre elements created was Helium 2.[36]

Time and Space as we understand them began as these bizarre elements reacted with each other and cooled.

The Shadow, an agent of the Black Guardian, claimed to have been waiting since eternity began in the hopes of obtaining the Key to Time.[37]

Matter coalesced, elements formed.[38]

The Epoch, survivors from the previous universe, "walked" at the start of our reality. They devoted themselves to viewing, recording and – according to the designs of their master plan, the Scheme – re-mapping creation as it lie before them. The essence of two versions of Bernice Summerfield created by the Epoch in future were scattered from the beginning of time to the end, causing the earlier Epoch to paradoxically identify Benny as a source of timeline disruption. They increasingly meddled in her affairs, determined to eliminate her as a threat to their work.[39]

"The Dark Time, the Time of Chaos": the Great Old Ones[40]

The Time Lords from the pre-universe entered our universe, and discovered that they had undreamt-of powers. They became known as the Great Old Ones: Hastur the Unspeakable became Fenric; Yog-Sothoth, also known as the Intelligence, began billennia of conquests; the Lloigor, or Animus, dominated Vortis; Shub-Niggurath conquered Polymos and colonised it with her offspring, the Nestene Consciousness; Dagon was worshipped by the Sea Devils.

The Doctor claims in *Ghost Light* that Light is "an evil older than time itself". From the context, this appears to mean that Light arrived on Earth before human history started, not that he existed before the universe's creation, but he might also be a Great Old One.

The Great Old Ones in the audio story *The Roof of the World*, and the "Old Ones" mentioned in *Tomb of Valdemar* and *Beyond the Ultimate Adventure* don't seem to be connected to this grouping.

The Tenth Doctor Year Two: "Cindy, Cleo and the Magic Sketchbook" and "Old Girl" depicts a clutch of demi-gods – including the Destroyer (*Battlefield*), the Beast (*The Impossible Planet*), the Vampires (*State of Decay*), the Early Ones and the Death Lords – as having originated from "outside time, outside this universe", somewhat deviating from the idea of there being Old Ones who existed before the universe began.

Other Great Old Ones included Cthulhu, Nyarlathotep, the Gods of Ragnarok, Gog, Magog, Malefescent and Tor-Gasukk. Across the universe, the earliest civilisations worshipped the Great Old Ones.[41] Not even the Time Lords knew much about them.[42]

The Celestial Toymaker was from the old times, "a spirit of mischief from the infancy of the universe". He was a hyper-dimensional being with a whole fragment of reality to himself, but had to obey the rules laid down during the "childhood" of the universe.[43] The Toymaker survived a catastrophe that destroyed his home universe. He carried a part of that universe within him, and so was exempt from the natural laws of our universe. As the Toymaker's universe receded from our own, it pushed back his personal time and extended his life. The Toymaker would live for millions of years – at first he helped life to prosper for hundreds if not of millennia, and created ships, cities, continents and entire planets. He then grew bored, destroyed what he had created... and found destruction as tedious as creation. To distract himself from the endlessness of existence, he amused himself with the chance and uncertainty found in games.[44]

The beings known as the Ancient Lights had existed before the Big Bang, and controlled many of the other beings in the earlier universe in accordance with the laws of astrology. They discovered they had great powers in the new universe, and influenced the development of astrology on many worlds. The Zodiac on Earth would have twelve signs; on Ventiplex, thirteen; on Draconia, seven.[45]

Six almost-omnipotent beings, **the Guardians, existed from the beginning of time. They were the White Guardian of Order and the Black Guardian of Chaos**; the Red Guardian of Justice; the Crystal Guardian of Thought and Dreams; the twins, the Azure Guardians of Mortality and Imagination; and the Gold Guardian of Life. They formed the upper pantheon of the Great Old Ones.[46] Each segment of the Key to Time, which was forged near the end of the universe, represented a particular Guardian.[47]

The universe was able to constantly regenerate itself when the Cosmic Balance between Law and Chaos was maintained. Miggea was the Queen of Seirot – in the great fight between Law and Chaos, when the Archangels of Law fought the Archangels of Chaos, she represented Law. The Doctor remarked that the battle was "a bit Miltonian... only without all that religion". This was the Battle for the Balance, but Miggea's pursuit of Law was ruthless to the point of being evil.[48]

Shug-Niggurath died giving birth, causing the whole planet Polymos to absorb its offspring, the Nestene Consciousness. The Nestene Consciousness went on to colonise many planets, including Cramador, Plovak 6 and the Reverent Pentiarchs of Loorn.[49]

The Chronovores existed outside the space-time continuum, consuming flaws in its structure. They weren't constrained by the laws of physics.[50]

---

41 *All-Consuming Fire, Millennial Rites, Business Unusual, The Quantum Archangel, Divided Loyalties.*

42 *White Darkness*

43 *The Magic Mousetrap*

44 *The Nightmare Fair.* The Doctor says the Toymaker has lived for "millions" of years, but it's somewhat presented as his speculation about the Toymaker's origins. *The Quantum Archangel* and *Divided Loyalties* establish that the Toymaker is both one of the Great Old Ones and one of the Guardians, meaning he's actually much older than that.

45 *SJA: Secrets of the Stars*

46 The White and Black Guardians are first referred to in *The Ribos Operation. Divided Loyalties* says there are six Guardians, adding Justice, Crystal and unnamed twins to the two from the television series. The same book establishes that they are members of the Great Old Ones, and also states that the Guardian of Dreams is the Celestial Toymaker. *The Quantum Archangel* assigns them their colours and adds the Gold Guardian (counting the twin Azure Guardians as one entity).

Whoniverse (BBC, p10) airs suspicions that the Guardians and Eternals (*Enlightenment*) pre-date the universe. Noticeably, a double splash page image (pgs 12-13) show at least six veiled, silhouetted Guardians observing the universe being created.

47 *Divided Loyalties, The Chaos Pool.*

48 *The Coming of the Terraphiles*

49 *Synthespians*™

50 Chronovores first appear in *The Time Monster*; *The Quantum Archangel* and *No Future* clarifies their role.

51 *The Masque of the Mandragora, Enlightenment, Falls the Shadow.*

52 "The Mark of Mandragora"

53 *Beautiful Chaos* (p210). The Doctor also cites the Helix as being from "the Dawn of Time".

54 *TW: Exodus Code* (ch57).

55 The Time Lords' gods were mentioned or seen in a number of New Adventures such as *No Future, Set Piece* and *Human Nature.* The seventh Doctor was often referred to as "Time's Champion". Mortimus (a.k.a. the Monk) is "Death's Champion" in *No Future*, and the decaying Master is hinted as the same in the audio *Master. Vampire Science* has the eighth Doctor as "Life's Champion", and in *The Dying Days* he declares himself to be "the Champion of Life and Time". *Happy Endings* establishes Life's parentage (see that story). In *Seeing I*, Life appears as a cat.

56 *The Gemini Contagion*

57 *Beyond the Ultimate Adventure*

58 The prologue to *Timewyrm: Apocalypse* is a brief history of the formation of the universe, and it follows

The first of our universe's native entities – such as the **Mandragora Helix, the Eternals** and the grey man's race – **sprang into being.**[51] The Mandragora Helix was old even when this universe was born.[52] It claimed to have escaped the Dark Times, and to have created a new home in a nebula, in the heart of "beautiful chaos".[53] The Helix Intelligences were neutral, sentient astral forces that existed before other life. Captain Jack Harkness suspected they had influenced the development of the earliest life forms.[54]

The Time Lords would come to worship some of the more powerful Eternals, such as Death, Pain, Vain Beauty, Life and Time. Certain Time Lords entered a mysterious arrangement to serve as the "champion" of one or more of these Eternals.[55]

Sentient micro-organisms named Meme-Spawn were said to have originated at the dawn of time. They drifted through galaxies for millennia on end, absorbing every spoken language they encountered.[56] Before the beginnings of recorded time, the Old Ones – the old gods – feared the powers of the Eidolon and trapped it in another dimension: the realm known as Ultima Thule.[57]

Over the first few billion years, the first stars were born. Planets and galaxies formed.[58]

The oldest question in the universe, hidden in plain sight, was "doctor who?"[59]

? - THE PANDORICA OPENS[60] -> Planet One, the oldest planet in the universe, had a cliff of pure diamond with fifty-foot letters from the dawn of time – the very first words to be recorded. The words read "Hello Sweetie", and had been placed there, along with a set of space-time co-ordinates, by River Song. The eleventh Doctor and Amy found the message and, as instructed, travel to Stonehenge in 102 AD.

Xaos was the oldest planet in the known galaxy.[61] The Archons were from the "Time before Time", and thought themselves the last survivors of their universe. The few remaining Archons came to live in the Nameless City in the Great Desolation, and "danced" to the Music of the Spheres. The *Necronomicon*, a.k.a. the Book of Dead names, was older than Gallifrey and most star systems, and was the sum total of Archon knowledge.[62]

? - "The Life Bringer"[63] -> The fourth Doctor freed Prometheus, a member of a hyper-advanced race resembling the Greek gods. From their vast city, they co-ordinated the re-engineering of the lifeless galaxy, moving black holes and stars. Prometheus had been imprisoned for releasing the "life spores" before Zeus was satisfied that they would grow into "perfect peaceful loving creatures". The Doctor helped Prometheus escape with a sample of imperfect life spores, and Prometheus went to another planet to spread them once more. The Doctor was unsure whether he was watching the distant past or the distant future.

THE DARK PLANET[64] -> Divergent evolution on the planet Lumia resulted in polar-opposite species: one that transitioned its minds through crystals to become high-energy beings, and a group mind, Krogor, that manifested as shadow and fog. Generations of conflict resulted, even as the Lumia sun – a white dwarf, unusual at this point in time – grew dimmer, threatening both species. The light-elders built a rocket, hoping to re-ignite the sun with their very essences and eradicate the shadow with an "eternal dawn"; instead, this would have triggered a devastating supernova. Simultaneously, Krogor developed a shadow weapon to destroy the light city.

The first Doctor, Ian, Barbara and Vicki convinced the light-elders and Krogor to combine efforts to save their world, but the rebellious children of the light boarded the rocket and launched it. The Doctor's party left as Lumia was destroyed.

---

the modern scientific consensus.

59 *The Wedding of River Song, The Time of the Doctor.*

60 Dating *The Pandorica Opens* (X5.12) - No date given. The Doctor and Amy's reading of the message could happen at any point after the words are carved. This may be the same Planet One that Sebastiane lived on in *The Doctor Trap.*

61 "Warrior's Story". It's unclear if this means it's home to the first known civilisation or physically the oldest planet. As Planet One (seen in *The Pandorica Opens*) is the oldest planet in the *universe*, not just the galaxy, it's older than Xaos.

62 *The Nameless City* (pgs. 41, 58-59).

63 Dating "The Life Bringer" (*DWM* #49-50) - The Doctor puts it best: "As I still don't know whereabout in time we are, I suppose I'll never be able to puzzle it out... if that was Earth I found him on... or if that's Earth he's heading toward." The story is set either in the distant past before life as we know it began, or the distant future after it died out. A character called Prometheus appeared in *The Quantum Archangel* – he was a Chronovore, a race first seen in *The Time Monster*, so it would seem to be a different individual.

64 Dating *The Dark Planet* (BF LS #4.1) - The blurb says it's "somewhere far back in the early days of the universe". The Doctor variously says it's "in the infancy of the universe," "far too early in the history of the universe for a white dwarf" and "We are back at the earliest segments of time. The universe is young." So young, in fact, that Lumia is absent from the TARDIS' star charts. Vicki, echoing the Doctor's words – and possibly revising them to be more accurate – later says it's "the first segment of time".

In future, Lumia's remains and the light's scattered life-essences coalesced into the Singing Nebula: a phenomenon that emanated a sort of singing on certain frequencies. Eventually, the remnants of light and shadow combined into a single mass, and left to explore the universe.

On many worlds, sugars, proteins and amino acids combined to become primordial soup, "the most precious substance in the universe, from which all life springs".[65] Hundreds of millions of years later, the first civilisations began to rise and fall.

Jelloids from the binary quasars of Bendalos were the longest-lived race in the universe, and many think they were the first living creatures.[66]

Thirty thousand million light years from our solar system, the first civilisation came into being. The beings were humanoid, and developed for ten thousand years before wiping themselves out in a bacteriological war. The grey man and his race saw all this, and he constructed the Cathedral, a machine "designed to alter the structure of reality". The grey man's race had been extremely dualistic, but Cathedral formed ambiguities and chaotic forces that ran throughout the universe, breaking down certainty. Its interface with physical reality was the Metahedron, a device that moved from world to world every eighty thousand years, remaining hidden.[67]

The slug-like Teuthoidians originated from near the beginning of time, and were among the universe's first space-faring races. Owing to a fold in hyperspace, some of their number interacted with the universe's final moments on the planet Chaos.[68]

? - "Voyage to the Edge of the Universe"[69] **->** Commander Azal launched a mission from Damos that reached the edge of the universe. There he merged with a version of himself from another universe, gaining infinite power... but couldn't decide which universe was his to return to. Nearby, beings faced the same dilemma... one had waited for ten thousand years, another for twenty-five thousand years, another seventy-three thousand years.

Legend held that Valdemar was the Dark God captured and destroyed by the advanced and philanthropic Old Ones, after centuries of the biggest war in mythology. Following this, the Old Ones vanished. The Time Lords ranked this as the sixth greatest mystery in the universe. The fourth Doctor and the first Romana later learned that the Old Ones had punched a hole into the higher dimensions in an attempt to study them, and unleashed a hole that grew and grew, warping reality. Valdemar was the last

---

65 Primordial soup appears in *City of Death* and *Ghost Light*; the quotation comes from the latter story.
66 *The One Doctor*
67 *Falls the Shadow*
68 *The Chaos Pool*
69 Dating "Voyage to the Edge of the Universe" (*DWM* #49) - The story occurs before the Daemons become extinct, seemingly at the height of their empire. The rocket is nuclear-powered, which doesn't sound terribly advanced, although it does get them to the end of the universe. This can't be the same Commander Azal as in *The Daemons*, for obvious reasons.
70 *Tomb of Valdemar*. The Doctor repeatedly asserts this was "a million years" ago, but others call it "aeons".
71 *The Daemons*. Light appears in *Ghost Light*.
72 *Spearhead from Space*
73 Dating *Deep Time* (NSA #60) - It's "a few billion years" (chs. 19, 20) before the time of the Phaeron. The Doctor claims the Phaeron have been trapped in this null space "for a billion years", but also adds that "they exist beyond time and space" (ch16).
74 It's the universe's early days, variously said to be "millennia"/"millions of years"/"several billion millennia"/"billennia" before *River S1: The Rulers of the Universe*. The Kamishi claim the mantle of "First Race", but that could just be posturing.
75 *The Infinite Quest*
76 *The Forbidden Time*
77 *The Eleventh Doctor Year Three*:"The Memory Feast"

78 "WHEN THE UNIVERSE WAS HALF ITS PRESENT SIZE": The phrase, uttered by a Time Lord in *Genesis of the Daleks*, has no clear scientific meaning and should probably be considered a figure of speech, the Time Lord equivalent of "as old as the hills". Then again, the universe at various points is referred to as having edges, a centre and corners, which suggests a discernible "size".
79 "Agent Provocateur"
80 *Lucifer Rising*
81 *Zagreus*
82 *The Beast Below*
83 *The Quantum Archangel*
84 Dating *Deep Time* (NSA #60) - The blurb says the Phaeron disappeared "over a million years ago" – but that's chump change compared to the idea that the Phaeron established a universal paradise before all other races save the Time Lords existed, "long before the Milky Way was fully formed" (ch3). Professor Vent says the Phaerons existed "millions of years" ago (ch2); the Doctor "billions of years" (ch3).
85 The robot is seen in *The Five Doctors*, *World Game* and *Beyond the Ultimate Adventure*, and cited in *Time in Office*. *The Eight Doctors* says that it comes from a time when "the Time Lords were young". *Alien Bodies* mentions a Raston cybernetic lap-dancer, and Qixotl claims that the ancient legend is just the manufacturer's marketing ploy.
86 *The Ring of Steel*, which describes the Caskelliaks' creators as "an ancient race".

of the Old Ones, and had entombed himself as a way of containing this reality-warping.[70]

What remains of the ancient races suggests awesome power – many had great psychic ability and matter-transmutation powers that were almost indistinguishable from magic. All considered it their right to intervene in the development of whole planets, and to destroy such worlds if they failed to match up to their expectations. Comparatively primitive races worshipped immortal beings such as Light and the Daemons of Damos as gods. The legends and race memories of many planets contain traces of these ancient civilisations. Horns have been a symbol of power on Earth since humans began, and beings of light have been worshipped.

Nothing lasts forever, though, and these great races gradually disappeared from the universe.[71]

New societies sprang up to replace them, and soon the universe was teeming with life. In the late twentieth century, the Institute of Space Studies at Baltimore estimated that there were over five hundred planets capable of supporting life in Earth's section of the galaxy alone.[72]

DEEP TIME[73] **->** A spaceship from the future, the *Carthage*, travelled down the Phaeron's final wormhole and struck a Phaeron vessel as it travelled back to Deep Time. The *Carthage* crew died, and both ships became trapped on a world linked to the wormhole. This freed the Glamour to cause mischief in ages to come, but the twelfth Doctor and Clara assisted the Phaeron in restarting their last journey, which pulled the Glamour back to its fate. Before their end, the Phaeron reunited the Doctor with his TARDIS, and his party returned to the future...

lgtw - The Kamishi, a.k.a. the First Race, existed when the universe "had barely cut its first tooth". A caste within the Kamishi, the Sanakuma, dispatched SporeShips to hasten evolution on many worlds. The Last Great Time War enabled the Sanakuma to interact with the future, where they attempted to destroy the whole of creation, but the eighth Doctor sent them back to their native era with a chrono-mine.[74]

The Dark Times
and the First of the Time Lords

"There was a time when the universe was so much smaller than it is now. Darker, older time of chaos. Creatures like the Racnoss, the Nestenes and the Great Vampires rampaged through the void."

The *Infinite*, a spaceship that could grant your heart's desire, came from this time. It was later lost to legend, and used to be inhabited by one of the Great Old Ones.[75]

Many races evolved before the Time Lords.[76] The Xerxes originated from an era before the Time Lords. Before their deaths in a great plague, they dispatched memory arks so something of them would remain.[77]

The first humanoid civilisation in the universe evolved on the planet Gallifrey, and mastered the principles of transmat technology while the universe was half its present size. They became the first race to master Time. Some legends said the Time Lords existed far in the past; there was some evidence that they lived in the present, and some say they come from the future.[78] Gallifrey was born before the Dark Times.[79]

See the section on Gallifreyan History for more detail.

As the Gallifreyans were the first sentient race to evolve, they established a morphic field for humanoids, making it more probable that races evolving later would also be bipedal and binocular. Non-humanoid races only evolved in environments that would be hostile to humanoids.[80] Rassilon ensured that only humanoid lifeforms survived on many planets, primarily to prevent the Divergents from existing. He used biogenic molecules to restructure the dominant species of sixty-nine thousand worlds.[81]

Time Lords were around before humanity evolved.[82] Evolution on Gallifrey, as on many other worlds, had been accelerated by the mysterious Constructors of Destiny.[83]

DEEP TIME[84] **->** The Phaeron existed "before anyone else" and fashioned a paradise encompassing "all the stars and planets and moons". They constructed the Phaeron Roads, a wormhole-network that stretched everywhere in creation.

The Time Lords warned the Phaeron about an Imperfection: a rogue Phaeron that become what others desired and manipulate their minds, thereby perverting free will. In future times, the rogue became known as the Glamour. Acknowledging their responsibility for destroying this evil, the Phaeron worked to trap the Glamour in a prison within Deep Time – a point before even the Phaeron had existed, as accessed by a special wormhole. The Phaeron accompanied the Glamour on its final journey, and a less perfect universe came about in their absence. The Phaeron Roads gradually closed down.

A civilisation devoted entirely to war developed the Raston Warrior Robot, then vanished without trace.[85] The Caskelliak were created as weapons of war, and were tasked with polluting and destroying entire worlds. Their creators perished in a war that they had initiated.[86]

The Time Lords explored space and time, making

contact with many worlds and becoming legends on many others. Rassilon's experiments created holes in the fabric of space and time, which unleashed monsters from another universe, including the Yssgaroth.[87]

The Time Lords unwittingly loosed the vampires on the universe. Until the Time Lords hunted them, vampires fed off mindless animals to service their needs. They later resorted to feeding off other beings.[88] **Seventeen known worlds, including Earth, have stories of vampires.**[89]

The vampires enslaved whole worlds until the Time Lords defeated them.[90] **The vampires were immune to energy weapons, but Rassilon constructed fleets of bowships that fired mighty bolts of steel and staked the beings through the heart. The Vampire Army was defeated, and only its leader, the Great Vampire, survived by escaping through a CVE into the pocket universe of E-Space. Almost every inhabited planet came to have vampire legends.**[91]

The origins of the Time Lords are obscure, but in the distant past they fought the Eternal War against the Great Old Ones and other invaders from outside our universe, beating them back and imposing Order. Science and Order supplanted Magic and Chaos as the Time Lords mapped, and so defined, the universe.[92] The Time Lords were the first to map "the web of time".[93]

The Carrionites lived at the "dawn of the universe", and discovered a means of manipulating reality – using words as science – that resembled magic. The Eternals found the right word to banish the Carrionites "into deep darkness", and nobody thereafter knew if they were real or imagined.[94] The Hervoken, a race with the ability to shape matter and time, fought a war with the Carrionites millions of years ago. They were eventually banished from the universe by the Eternals.[95]

The vast biomechanical complex known as the Event Synthesizer began operating.

> "Since the dawn of time, the synthesizer has produced the ordered vibrations of the cosmos... creating events in a logical, harmonious sequence to flow into the main time-stream."

87 *The Pit*, further explored in *FP: The Book of the War*.
88 According to a highly suspect account from the vampire Tepesh, part of a historical simulation in *Zagreus*.
89 *State of Decay*. Vampires appear in that story, *Blood Harvest*, "Blood Invocation", *Death Comes to Time*, *The Eight Doctors*, *Goth Opera*, *Jago & Litefoot Series 2*, *Managra*, *Project: Lazarus*, *Project: Twilight*, "Tooth and Claw" (*DWM*), *UNIT: Snake Head*, *Vampire Science*, *World Game*, *Benny: The Vampire Curse* and *Gallifrey IV: Annihilation*.
  Florence Finnegan, a Plasmavore, appeared in *Smith and Jones* is effectively a vampire who uses a straw. Haemovores, who pretty much amount to the same thing as vampires, appeared in *The Curse of Fenric*, *Goth Opera* and *Gods and Monsters*. A type of science-based vampire, Necrobiologicals, featured in *Zaltys*. The vampire-like Corvids are taken for vampires in "The Highgate Horror". *The Vampires of Venice* had "vampires" that were disguised fish people. Vampires also appear as a part of the holographic record in *Zagreus*.
90 *Project: Twilight*
91 *State of Decay*
92 *Cat's Cradle: Time's Crucible*
93 *Gallifrey I: Weapon of Choice*
94 *The Shakespeare Code*. Eternals were seen in *Enlightenment*.
95 *Forever Autumn*
96 "The Tides of Time"
97 *So Vile a Sin*
  THE ETERNAL WAR: On screen, we learn that the Time Lords fought campaigns against the Great Vampires (*State of Decay*), that they time-looped the homeworld of the Fendahl (*Image of Fendahl*), that they protected other races from invaders (*The Hand of Fear*), that they maintained a prison planet that contained alien species (*Shada*) and that they destroyed huon particles and the Racnoss (*The Runaway Bride*). In the New Adventures, particularly *Cat's Cradle: Time's Crucible*, *The Pit* and *Christmas on a Rational Planet*, this was the Eternal War in which the forces of rationality and science defeated the forces of superstition and magic.
98 *The Pit*
99 *Sky Pirates!*, *The Infinity Doctors*.
  THE THREE TIME WARS: This is not the Last Great Time War between the Time Lords and the Daleks that's the backdrop to the 2005 television series. In the *Doctor Who Annual 2006*, Russell T Davies states, "There had been two Time Wars before this – the skirmish between the Halldons and the Eternals, and then the brutal slaughter of the Omnicraven Uprising, and on both occasions, the Doctor's people had stepped in to settle the matter." Although they don't mention those specific incidents, the books concur that there were indeed two previous Time Wars – one in the ancient past (which, to avoid confusion, we might term the Ancient Time War, although it's not a term used in the stories themselves) and the War against the Enemy in the eighth Doctor's future (which has become known in *Faction Paradox* circles as the "War in Heaven").
100 *Sky Pirates!*
101 *Heart of TARDIS*
102 *Sky Pirates!*, *The Infinity Doctors*, *Heart of TARDIS*.
103 *The Gallifrey Chronicles*
104 *The Crystal Bucephalus*
105 Back in "the mists of time", and "countless millennia" ("You can't even comprehend how long ago", the

It was built by the people of Althrace, who were known to Rassilon, to simulate the effects of a white hole.[96] The last form of magic to survive was psionics.[97]

During this war, the great Gallifreyan general Kopyion Liall a Mahajetsu was believed to have died. He actually survived, and vigilantly watched in secret for signs of the Yssgaroth's return. He would deal with the threat of such an incursion in 2400.[98]

This war may or may not be the same conflict as the Time War, in which Time Lords from a generation after Rassilon fought against other races developing time travel. The conflict lasted thirty thousand years. The Time Lords wiped out many races during this time.[99]

One such race was the Charon, who were capable of warping space, and whom the Time Lords destroyed before they ever existed. One Charon survived this and created its own clockwork mini-universe. Another unnamed race used Reality Bombs to disrupt the control systems of time machines. A few of these weapons survived hidden for billions of years.[100]

The Doctor witnessed the horrors of the Time War. At one point, the Time Lords were attacked by an unnamed race in retaliation for something they hadn't yet done.[101]

The Time War ended with all threats to Gallifrey contained, or so completely destroyed that no evidence remained to suggest they even existed. Time Lords were encoded with genetic memories of their ancient enemies and were compelled to destroy any survivors. The Time Lords were ashamed of the Time War, to the point that they deny it ever happened.[102]

Mr Saldaamir, who would become a friend of the Doctor's father, was the last survivor of the Time War.[103] There was a Celestial War in which the Ooolatrii captured at least one primitive TARDIS.[104]

The Bayuun-Hofri-Anat – a race that looked like a cross between hermit crabs and jackals – rampaged in the universe's Dark Times. Such was their devastation, the civilised worlds appealed for help from the Dark Ones in their Twilight Dimension. The Lord of the Dark Ones gave the president of the civilised worlds a pocket realm that outwardly looked like a tin of baked beans, and the Bayuun-Hofri-Anat were sealed within. The pocket realm became the Ringpull: an aperture connecting the universe with the Obverse.[105]

An unidentified party created the Viyrans to clean up a galactic war that happened "far back in universal ancient history". The Viyrans' progenitors fashioned a failsafe device, the Lamentation Cipher, to wipe out their creations if needed. A semi-sentient Amethyst virus escaped back in time to avoid its destruction. The resultant space-time tear created the Ever-and-Ever Prolixity: a phenomena that would prove inexplicable "to all races for the whole of recorded history". The Viyrans' creators learned of the heartless, overreaching creatures the Viyrans would become, and sent a contemporary Viyran through the Prolixity to infect future Viryans with a virus, thereby restoring them to factory settings.[106]

Two galaxies collided in deep space, triggering a stellar collapse that created the Silver Devastation: a vast sector with nothing but dead suns and dark matter, and looked like a huge silver sea in space. Myths about the Silver Devastation suggested that it was populated by the mutant survivors of the two galaxies, or refugees from the Old Time, or monsters from another universe, or that it was just a bottomless chasm in time and space.[107]

The storm raging at the edge of the Proxima System was hundreds of light years across, and was "older than worlds, older than stars". It was the largest storm in the universe.[108]

Several million years ago, a race of carnivores ate rotting meat in the swamps of Malmatine 5, and evolved into Space-Boars capable of space travel. A herd of them travelled around the universe for twenty thousand years before excreting the mass that became the Cassetia asteroids.[109]

Ruta III was an ice world, and the Rutans evolved with no resistance to heat. The Rutans weren't natural chameleons, but instead were "shameleons" who adopted the ability to shapeshift.[110]

The First Sontarans

The Kaveech were native to the planet Sontar, and lived at peace with the other worlds in their star system for eons. It was a time of enlightenment... until the Rutans attacked, instigating a war that went on for years, and killed millions. The Kaveech were heading to total defeat until the head of their Defence Scientific Directorate, Meredid Roath, generated new shock troops with a clone-breeding programme. The first Sontaran clones were hatched on

Doctor claims) before *Ringpullworld*.

106 *Charley* S1: *The Viyran Solution*

107 In *DL: The Game of Death*, the TARDIS data bank says that the galaxies collided "over a hundred billion years ago" – that number was presumably derived from the year in which *Utopia* takes place, but if so, the Devastation must be somewhat younger than that. (If the two numbers were equal, it would mean that the galaxies collided at the universe's very start, before

galaxies had formed.) The Face of Boe is said to hail from the Silver Devastation, and the War Master/ Professor Yana was found there as a small child (*Utopia*). Why dead suns and dark matter look silver is not explained.

108 "Mortal Beloved"

109 *The Forgotten Army*

110 *Castle of Fear*

Elmenus, a high-gravity moon of Sontar, to toughen their physique. Three million Sontarans were produced in a week, devastating the Rutan forces.

The Kaveech celebrated until the clones deemed their creators a weaker species, and a liability because they knew so much about Sontaran physiology. The Sontarans almost entirely killed off the Kaveech, but four hundred survivors reached their city's time-travel facility – which could facilitate limited trips to the future, not the past. The survivors fled to various points in the Milky Way, circa 1862. Roath and his wife lost their children to the Sontaran rampage, but escaped and booby-trapped the time corridor so the Sontarans couldn't follow. The Sontarans erased all knowledge of the Kaveech.

Sontar was a blue-green world while the Kaveech lived there; under Sontaran rule, it became grey, ugly and desolate, with entire continents armoured over.[111]

Around the time the war started, the Sontarans became a clone race. Their greatest warrior, Sontar, had defeated the Isari. He was the model for all future Sontarans. To increase efficiency, the Sontaran body was simplified. All non-clones soon died. The leader of the Sontarans, always called General Sontar, had the memories of all previous General Sontars.[112] The "pureblood" Sontarans were originally less squat, with long hair and five fingers.[113]

The Sontaran-Rutan War

The Sontarans and Rutans became involved in "eternal war".[114] The origins of the conflict between them was lost in the mists of time and was the subject of much propaganda. Much later, the Rutans blamed the war on the Sontarans for attacking the Constellation of Zyt, which the Sontarans claimed was retaliation for a Rutan attack on Holfactur, which the Rutans said had been the base for attacks on the Purple Areas of Rutan Space, which in turn

---

111 *The First Sontarans.* The Kaveech's rudimentary time technology seems to give rise to the osmic projector that Linx uses in *The Time Warrior.*

112 *The Infinity Doctors.* The war has lasted as long as the Time Lord civilisation.

113 "Pureblood". The Doctor's assertion that the Sontaran-Rutan war started "ten centuries" before can't be right, as it would mean it started in the 1500s – in other words, after *The Time Warrior.* Other stories place the start of the war far back in Earth's prehistory.

114 *The Time Warrior, Horror of Fang Rock.*

115 THE PROGRESS OF THE SONTARAN-RUTAN WAR: The length of time we're told the Sontarans and Rutans have been fighting is wildly inconsistent. It's "ten centuries" before "Pureblood" [c.2550]; been raging since before the Time Lords had a civilisation in *The Infinity Doctors;* "six million years" according to *FP: The Eleven-Day Empire,* "13 million years" according to *FP: The Shadow Play;* "fifty thousand years" according to *The Poison Sky, The Taking of Chelsea 426* and *Terror of the Sontarans;* only "thousands of years" in "Prisoners of Time".

We hear a number of status reports from the battlefront of the Sontaran-Rutan War over the course of the TV series. Both sides have periods of success and failure, but implicitly, the Sontarans visit Earth far earlier and far more often than the Rutans. Earth is some way from the front lines (but close enough to strike the enemy using their most powerful emplaced weapons), with the Sontarans between us and the Rutans. According to "Pureblood", when Earth becomes a spacefaring power, its territory borders the Sontaran Empire, but it's in neither human nor Sontaran interests to pick a fight with each other.

It's also worth noting that in *The Time Warrior,* Linx states "there is not a galaxy in the universe which our space fleets have not subjugated", and Styre talks about invading "Earth's galaxy" in *The Sontaran Experiment.* Sontarans and Rutans are both prone to boasting but, even so, a war fought across one galaxy is already incomprehensibly vast, and one suspects the writers – as happens on occasion elsewhere in the TV series – are confusing "solar system" with "galaxy".

We never hear about either the Sontarans and Rutans coming into conflict with other space powers. From this, we might infer that Skaro, Draconia, Telos and Ice Warrior territory are all located on one side of Earth, the Sontarans and (a little further away) the Rutans lie in the other.

In Ancient Egypt ("The Gods Walk Among Us"), Earth is a suitable place for the Sontarans to "outflank" the Rutans (given both sides' use of rhetoric, this might suggest that the Rutans are making a major advance).

In the Middle Ages (*The Time Warrior*), Earth is of no strategic importance, but the Sontarans send a reconnaissance mission there. A pair of Rutans conduct cloning experiments on Earth in 1199 (*Castle of Fear*). The Sontarans and Rutans both have fighter squadrons. Then in the seventeenth century ("Dragon's Claw"), the war is being fought close enough to Earth for a Sontaran ship to crash there.

By the early twentieth century, the Rutans are losing the war. They had dominated the Mutter's Spiral (our galaxy), but now were beaten back to the fringes (curiously, mention of their withdrawal from Mutter's Spiral happens as early as *Castle of Fear*). Earth is of strategic importance. In the late twentieth century (*The Two Doctors*), Earth is "conveniently situated" for the Sontarans' attack on the Rutan-held Madillon Cluster.

As humans spread into space, they encounter the Sontarans and find themselves caught in the crossfire ("Conflict of Interests", *Lords of the Storm*). Humanity and the Sontarans sign a non-aggression pact in 2420.

In Benny's time, the Rutans made great advances,

was revenge for an attack on Mancastovon. The war escalated, and it would rage, ebb and flow across the entire galaxy for many millions of years.[115] The Sontarans would acquire six million years of experience with warfare.[116]

The Time Lords colonised planets such as Dronid and Trion. Sharing their secrets with lesser races, though, led to disaster. Evolution on Klist was reversed, and the civilisation on Plastrodus 14 went insane.[117] **Eventually, the Time Lords recognised the dangers of intervention when their attempts to help the Minyans resulted in the destruction of Minyos.**[118]

The Time Lords interfered on Micen Island, resulting in chemical and biological warfare and the destruction of the entire civilisation. The Time Lords built the Temple of the Fourth on the ruins, and codified the Oath of the Faction. They scattered in repentance for what they had done.[119]

The Time Lords remained content to observe, but monitored the universe and tried to prevent other, less principled races from discovering the secrets of time travel.[120] **They occasionally sent out ambassadors and official observers.**[121] **They also attempted to enforce bans on dangerous technology.**[122]

For more information on the history of the Doctor's people, see the Gallifrey section.

The Ancient Past

Before life evolved on other planets, the Exxilon civilisation was already old.[123] Other races such as the Raab of Odonoto Ceti, a race on Benelisa and the Cthalctose of 16 Alpha Leonis One evolved.[124] The Vondrax were among the universe's oldest sentient races.[125]

The Healers, an ancient race, existed to endow their essences into discarded or derelict objects of a peaceful heritage. Over time, the Healers' efforts would preserve historical artifacts, to the benefit of archaeologists.[126] The Cradle of the Gods, an edifice capable of restructuring entire worlds, was built on the planet Getrhia.[127]

The Proto-Viryans

CHARLEY S2: THE DESTRUCTIVE QUALITY OF LIFE[128] -> Before humanity – or any civilisation of Charley Pollard's acquaintance – had evolved, proto-Viryans determined that life would destroy itself through over-population. To prevent this, the proto-Viryans forced humanoid(ish) beings to collect an orange coral substance on the planet Galracia. The material facilitated Machines that altered a race's behaviour, to cull their ranks some.

Two proto-Viryans, a.k.a. the Identical Men, abducted Charley Pollard and Robert Buchan from the twenty-first

and even manage to devastate the Sontaran homeworld. Following the Doctor's intervention, the Sontarans survive to serve as a buffer between humanity and the Rutans ("Pureblood"). In 2602 (*Benny S4: The Bellotron Incident*), the Sontaran-Rutan war dangerously approaches Earth's trade routes.

There is a demilitarised zone between the later Earth Empire and the Sontarans. The Rutans directly attack the Sontaran homeworld (again) circa 3915 (*Sontarans: Conduct Unbecoming*). The Sontarans menace the outer worlds in Steven Taylor's time (see the Steven Taylor sidebar), and force millions to evacuate the human colonies in Lambda Arietede (*The Sontarans*). Later on, they lose a war to the Federation in the sixty-third century, and their Empire soon lies in ruins.

Then in the far future (*The Sontaran Experiment*), a Sontaran invasion fleet is poised to invade Earth (the story says "Earth's galaxy", but see above), which is of tactical importance. The Doctor says there's a "buffer zone" between human and Sontaran territory. At some point after that (*Heroes of Sontar*), the Sontarans achieve a victory on the planet Samur, but then suffer defeats owing to a flaw in their cloning process, and consolidate their forces within the Madillon Cluster.

The war ended three hundred thousand years before the end of humanity, resulting in the greatest demobilisation in universal history (*The Infinity Doctors*).

Far, far in the future, the two races apparently merge (*Father Time*). Owing to an errant time-scoop, however, Sgt Major Stom survives as the last Sontaran after his race and Sontar are no more (*The Eternal Battle*).

To the Sontarans' immense frustration, they're not allowed to participate in the Last Great Time War (*The Sontaran Stratagem, The Sontaran Ordeal*). There's no record, so far, of how the Rutans viewed that conflict.

116 *FP: The Eleven-Day Empire*
117 *The Quantum Archangel*
118 *Underworld*
119 *Death Comes to Time*
120 *The War Games*
121 *The Two Doctors, The Empire of Glass.*
122 *Carnival of Monsters, The Empire of Glass.*
123 *Death to the Daleks*
124 *Frontier Worlds, The Taint, Eternity Weeps.*
125 *TW: Trace Memory*
126 *Benny B4: New Frontiers: HMS Surprise*
127 *The Dalek Generation.* Hieroglyphics were engraved on the Cradle's walls "many centuries ago", but the Cradle itself is said to be "more ancient than ancient" (ch9).
128 Dating *Charley S2: The Destructive Quality of Life* (*Charley* #2.4) - It's a "long way back in the past", before humankind and most races have evolved. The story ends on a cliffhanger.

century. For "something like" ten years, Charley and Robert laboured with the proto-Viyrans' slaves, and became increasingly intimate. The Rogue Viyran, "Bernard", came back from the future and took up the proto-Viyrans' mission. Fulfilling history, Bernard had Charley send a copy of her journal to the twenty-first century – a lure to summon "him" here.

Bernard moved to kill Charley and Robert, but the Ever-and-Ever Prolixity suddenly became active. Charley recovered, and did not know where she was...

Earth's First Dominant Race

(=) **THE NOWHERE PLACE**[129] -> More than fifty billion years ago, a dominant life-form evolved on Earth and would develop space travel in future. However, a mishap occurred during the race's first attempt to journey out of the solar system. A mis-setting of the spaceship's coordinates – when paradoxically combined with the energy of a nuclear missile strike in 2197 – resulted in the engines getting caught in their own time warp. The hyper-spatial equivalent of a Möbius Strip was created, and ripped the entire race out of space and time. They were consigned to the realm known as Time's End: a point at which all cosmic laws were invalidated.

Other dominant species would evolve on Earth, but the original race – consumed with madness and jealousy, and using the insane logic of Time's End to its advantage – subverted each race's bid for space travel. Each new race was erased from history, made to suffer continuously in the matter-crushing forces of Time's End. Billions of Earth-born species were snared in this fashion.

The original race tried to capture humanity, but the sixth Doctor ventured into Time's End and reprogrammed the original race's spaceship coordinates into a linear fashion. The nuclear strike from 2197 destroyed the vessel rather than creating the Möbius Strip, which obliterated the original species. Time's End was either nullified or moved. The dominance of humanity and its time-stream was assured.

= The Tharils acquired slaves "from the beginning of time", using an innate ability to navigate the timewinds to launch incursions from their stronghold, the Gateway in E-Space. Their vast empire fell when their slaves created the Gundan: powerful robots immune to the timewinds, and which invaded the Gateway. The Tharils themselves were enslaved, and would become highly sought after as navigational tools for spaceships.[130]

The planet Tivoli was home to one of the oldest civilisations in the Milky Way. Its mole-like inhabitants endured because they capitulated to all invaders, and became the most invaded planet in the galaxy. Their anthem was *Glory to [Insert Name Here]*.[131]

---

129 Dating *The Nowhere Place* (BF #84) - The Doctor dates a tool of the original species – a mysterious door in 2197 – as being "more than fifty billion years old". This is a scientific absurdity, given that the universe is no more than fifteen billion years old.

130 *Warriors' Gate*, although the Gundan's mention of "the beginning of time" might not be so literal, but simply mean the start of the Tharils' history.

131 *The God Complex*

132 Dating *A Death in the Family* (BF #140) - The Doctor tells Hex that they've arrived, "billions of years before your time, billions of years before your sun's time... the universe is a baby". Scientific consensus is that Earth's sun formed about 4.6 billion years ago, so this is some time prior to that.

133 *A Death in the Family*. Hex arrives on Pelican in "local year 1871 AC", and the older Doctor takes the Handivale away in "local year 2192 AC". Although it isn't said, "AC" presumably means "After Crash" (of the timeship *Pelican*).

134 9thC: *The Bleeding Heart*

135 *Benny: Adorable Illusion* (ch9).

136 Dating *WD S2: Legion of the Lost* (BF WD #2.1) - The War Doctor says they're "awfully far back"; Co-ordinator Jarad: it's "the earliest days of the galaxy".

137 Dating *Eternity Weeps* (NA #58) - It is "six billion years ago" (p3).

138 Dating *Hide* (X7.10) - The Doctor tells Clara that they've gone back, "About six billion years ago. It's a Tuesday, I think."

139 Dating *The Tenth Doctor Year Two* (Titan 10th Doc #2.13-2.17, "Old Girl") - A caption says it's "Six billion years ago". The Doctor says they're going to Amenthes in the "Deep past, the primordial universe, when [echoing *Genesis of the Daleks*] it was less than half its current size". There's little evidence that Osiran culture stretches back this far, but it's possible it existed for a long time before they became demigods. This aspect of Sekhmet is far more benevolent than the one in *The Bride of Peladon*, but six billion years is plenty of time for an individual to change.

140 Dating "Time Witch" (DWW #35-38) - Brimo was imprisoned "at a time before the Earth was formed" according to the opening caption. She says she was imprisoned for "millions of years", but even that might be an underestimate – the Doctor's encounter with her could well take place at any time in this timeline. Her situation inside the black hole is very like Omega's in

Evelyn Smythe Passes Away

c 7,000,000,000 BC - A DEATH IN THE FAMILY[132] ->

Billions of years before Earth's sun was active, a planet existed with Earth-like conditions. It became the home to English-speaking humans aboard the timeship UNS *Pelican*, who named the planet after their vessel. In the two millennia to follow, their descendants established the Handivale: a living, never-ending tale that was recited by a succession of Storytellers. Remembrances of people who had died were included in the Handivale, and were thereby said to survive in the afterlife.

Evelyn Rossiter (née Smythe) was transported through time to Pelican and lived with the people there. Two years later, she found the wreckage of the original timeship. Five years after that, she had a seat on the ruling Counsel.

An older version of the seventh Doctor left Hex in Evelyn's care as part of his struggle with the Word Lord: a linguistic being from a reality governed by language instead of physics, and who travelled in a Conveyance of Repeating Dialogue in Space-Time (CORDIS). Hex became Evelyn's ward, and read a fictional account of Ace into the Handivale, creating a linguistic version of her in 2028.

At least six months after Hex's arrival, Evelyn suffered a mortal heart attack while lecturing at Pelican University. The seventh Doctor and Ace arrived with the comatose Captain Stillwell of UNIT, who had within him the future version of the Handivale. Convinced that the Word Lord posed a threat to all living matter in the universe, Evelyn consented to have the Handivale transferred into her from Stillwell. She became the last Storyteller, and as she died, the Handivale died, and the Word Lord trapped within the Handivale died also.

About three hundred and twenty Pelican years after Evelyn's passing, the older seventh Doctor was given the contemporary Handivale so he could "combat great evil" with it. He became the Handivale's Storyspeaker, trapped a younger version of the Word Lord within the living story, and then sealed himself inside a Gallifreyan sarcophagus that would came to reside in the archives of the Forge.[133]

A tear in interstitial space, the Compassionate, was "already old when the universe was young".[134] The earliest interstellar civilizations knew of the energy rift later known as the Rapture, but the phenomena's energy releases made it hard to examine.[135]

lgtw - (=) WD S2: LEGION OF THE LOST[136] ->

When the universe was "very, very young", the Horned Ones escaped their native dimension into our own. The physics governing our reality proved so different, the Horned Ones slept while a techno-mage cult arose to resurrect them. During the Last Great Time War, the Time Lords brokered an allegiance with the techno-mages of the planet Aldrus. The mages tapped the dormant Horned Ones' power to bring fallen Gallifreyan soldiers back to life, but while doing so embedded each restored Time Lord with the splinter-essence of a Horned One. In time, the Horned Ones' essence would have gained a critical mass, restoring them. The War Doctor used the techno-mages' Crypt of Non-Time – a means of accessing worlds that no longer existed – to reclaim a timeline-erasing Annihilator. With that device, the Doctor erased the techno-mages and the Horned Ones from history.

c 6,000,000,000 BC - ETERNITY WEEPS[137] ->

Jason Kane used a time ring to reach 16 Alpha Leonis One, the home of the Cthalctose. He met the Astronomer Royal, who had detected a black hole in their solar system and provided force field technology. Jason was placed in a stasis field and watched the Cthalctose civilisation develop for five hundred years. The Cthalctose attempted to contain the black hole, but eventually could no longer power the force fields. Unable to save themselves, they built a device, "the Museum", that could convert another world to resemble their own. This entailed using a terraforming virus that would generate sulphuric acid, which was present in the seas on their homeworld. The Cthalctose launched the Museum out of their solar system, and the forces of the black hole destroyed 16 Alpha Leonis One. Jason Kane's stasis field failed and he returned to 2003.

6,000,000,000 BC (a Tuesday) - HIDE[138] -> The eleventh Doctor and Clara photographed the future site of Caliburn House during Earth's pre-historic days. They then jumped forward at intervals of a few million years to take more photos, on through Earth's life cycle to its death.

c 6,000,000,000 BC - THE TENTH DOCTOR YEAR TWO[139] ->

Aeons before Sutekh was born, the tenth Doctor and Cindy raided equipment from an Osiran energy facility: Amenthes, a moon of Phaester Osiris and part of the Osiran Reefworlds Colony. As the Doctor had previously helped to defeat the Racnoss Imperium and the Cyclopean Alliance, the colony worlds of Phaester Osiris were in his debt, and so Sekhmet smoothed over the theft with Atum and the Guild of Aged Souls.

? - "Time Witch"[140] ->

Before the Earth was formed, Brimo was imprisoned in an eternity capsule for attempting to dominate the planet Nefrin. She watched civilisations rise and fall, and when Nefrin's sun went nova, the capsule fell into the resulting black hole. Once there, she entered a realm where her thoughts became reality.

Later, the TARDIS was torn apart and the fourth Doctor

and Sharon were pulled into a dimensional rift to Brimo's domain. The presence of the TARDIS started draining Brimo's abilities, and the Doctor fought a battle of wits with her, finally trapping her by getting her to imagine the eternity capsule. Restoring the TARDIS aged the Doctor and – more noticeably – Sharon by four years.

A bloated star, born in a stellar nursery, obliterated the sun of the planet Home in a super-nova. Before the end, the people of Home constructed the super-computer ArkHive to facilitate their being remembered. The super-nova that destroyed the Home System created the cosmic detritus from which many new systems, including Sol, eventually formed. The ArkHive was damaged when Home was destroyed, fell through space for a million years, and eventually became part of an ice moon accreting above Saturn. ArkHive's hull seeped into the ice, creating substantial bernalium deposits.[141] The Doctor helped ArkHive to send its creators a message, which avoided a paradox by arriving after the ArkHive was dispatched through space.[142]

The Doctor visited the Kystra, a race of traders, during their Era of Embodiment. A Kystra museum contained some technology from Home, as well as displays of worlds menaced by the Great Vampires. The age gave way to an Era of Disembodiment.[143]

? – THE EDGE OF DESTRUCTION[144] **->** The first Doctor tried to take Ian and Barbara back home to 1963 from Skaro, so used the Fast Return Switch on the TARDIS console. When the Switch stuck, the Ship steadily kept travelling into the past – but refused to

destroy itself in the birth of a new solar system. The Ship's efforts to convey its impending doom caused all manner of strange happenings, prompting the Doctor to accuse Ian and Barbara of sabotague. He apologised, and reflected upon his behaviour, after discovering the true culprit and repairing the Switch.

The Formation of the Sol System

As Earth's solar system formed from dust, the Tractite named Kitig arrived through time via a time tree. As Kitig intended, this destroyed the time tree at the cost of his own life.[145] **The Veil, reptilians who could take command of other beings' bodies, were conquering worlds "when Earth was little more than a ball of superheated gas".**[146]

Earth formed billions of years ago.[147] **The Time Lords "got rid" of huon particles, which were capable of unravelling atomic structure.**[148]

An unknown race came under threat from an enemy – perhaps the Racnoss, the Null or the Movellans – and so designed the Clades, ruthless intelligent projectile weapons that bonded with their users. The Clades prevailed and went dormant for some centuries, their mere existence warding off potential threats. Eventually, the Clades found they lacked purpose without war, and destroyed their creators, leaving their star cluster burning. They became mercenaries, and would encounter the Doctor on Sierra Secundus, Tannhauser and New Mitama.[149]

The Three Doctors (and *The Infinity Doctors*), although there's no indication she's trapped there.
141 "Five billion years" before *The Wheel of Ice* (p215, 262).
142 *The Wheel of Ice.* As the message would have arrived after the ArkHive's creators were dead, this seems little more than an exercise in keeping ArkHive pacified.
143 Also "five or six billion years" before *The Wheel of Ice* (p162).
144 Dating *The Edge of Destruction* (1.3) - The Doctor muses that they've arrived "at the very beginning, the new start of a solar system... a new birth of a sun and its planets". The unnamed newborn solar system is quite possibly (but not necessarily) that of Earth or Skaro. Without further details, most commentators have shrugged their shoulders as to when exactly *Edge* occurs. *About Time* didn't attempt to figure it out, *The Terrestrial Index* punted (perhaps by virtue of its time-line starting with Earth's creation) and *The Universal Databank* off-handedly suggested (in the Fast Return Switch entry) that the item "nearly sent the TARDIS and

its crew back to the very beginning of time".
Jon Preddle's *Timelink* makes the most detailed run at the problem, and arrives at "5,000,000,000 BC" by reasoning that the TARDIS must have gone *quite* far into the past because it takes most of *The Edge of Destruction* to get there, comparable with the extend-ed trip in *Castrovalva* to Event One and the (relatively) shorter trips some "millions" of years into the future or past in *Image of the Fendahl*, *City of Death* and *Frontios*. It's hard to escape the sense that – whatever its loca-tion – *The Edge of Destruction* entails a trip billions rather than millions of years into the past, so we've gone with Preddle's number (even if the same author tosses out the Doctor's claim in *Edge* that "Skaro was in the future" and instead dates *The Daleks* to 900 AD). See also the dating notes on *The Daleks* and the Fast Return Switch sidebar.
145 *Genocide* (p279).
146 *SJA: Prisoner of the Judoon*
147 *Inferno*
148 "Billions of years" before *The Runaway Bride*.
149 *Peacemaker*. The Racnoss were an ancient race,

The Gallifrey-Racnoss Conflict and the Formation of Earth

CD,NM V1: EMPIRE OF THE RACNOSS[150] **->** At the dawn of time, with the cosmos still forming, Gallifrey pressed home its attack on the Racnoss forces. The Racnoss Empress betrayed her husband, the Emperor, by using a huon pulse to birth one of their hatcheries early. The ravenous offspring grievously wounded the Emperor, who nonetheless raised the children to become his shock troops. The Racnoss plunged into civil war.

A distress signal ripped the TARDIS out of the Vortex, and the fifth Doctor found himself in Gallifrey's past. The Empress killed the Emperor, but the Doctor and a Gallifreyan, Alayna, relocated a remaining Racnoss hatchery to a safe world. They then watched the birth of some of the universe's nebulae.

4,600,000,000 BC - THE RUNAWAY BRIDE[151] **->** The Time Lords and the "fledgling empires" all but eradicated the Racnoss: spider-like monsters who were born starving, and devoured entire planets. Four point six billion years ago, as the tenth Doctor and Donna witnessed, Earth formed around one of the last of the Racnoss ships. Without the huon particles needed to revive the Racnoss within, the creatures would sleep until the twenty-first century. The Empress of the Racnoss also survived, and retreated to the edge of the universe to hibernate.

c 4,500,000,000 BC – EXPLORATION EARTH[152] **->** A force rapidly dragged the TARDIS back four thousand, five hundred million years, into Retrograde Time. The fourth Doctor and Sarah boarded a two-person TARDIS pod, and watched a early stage of Earth's development. Sarah's homeworld was currently an enormous billowing mass of space gasses, with a core of rock in the centre.

They returned to the TARDIS and went forward some

millions of years. The fiery mass that would become Earth was much smaller and starting to solidify, as the sun eroded away all the hot gas. Suddenly, they encountered a demon-like creature: Lord Megron, High Lord of Chaos, Chief of the Carrions and Lords of Chaos. Megron claimed Earth as part of his kingdom of chaos, while the Doctor argued that it was moving toward order. Megron's lightning forced the Doctor and Sarah back to the TARDIS, and they went forward more millions of years...

Volcanoes and earthquakes now wracked the surface of the Earth. Megron declared that order would never come, but the Doctor insisted that the planet was generating just a bit of oxygen. As a granite crust formed, chaos receded. The Doctor and Sarah went forward in the TARDIS, and would meet Megron once more...

When the Earth was formed, the Blessing – a space set between two rock edges, and possibly alive – was established as a secondary "magnetic" pole that ran West to East, exiting at the future locations of Singapore and Buenos Aires. Humanity would develop a symbiotic relationship with the Blessing, which transmitted a morphic field that encompassed every person. Anyone living in a two-mile radius of one of the Blessing's access points had a life expectancy equal to the average life expectancy of humanity.[153]

A Helix Intelligence became trapped within the Earth during its formation, and might have influenced development of life on its surface.[154] Seneschal, a being whose "heart was forged in the fiery magma of the once-was", claimed to have seeded the Milky Way with life. He patiently watched the results of his labours unfold on Earth.[155]

While the Earth was still forming, the Time Lords were in negotiations with the Tranmetgurans, trying to organise a planetary government and end the war that was ravaging the planet. The Hoothi – a fungoid group-mind that lived off dead matter and farmed entire sentient species – attacked Tranmetgura, introducing their dead soldiers into

around before the Earth formed. Even if the Movellans were not the historic foes of the Clades' creators, the Doctor seems comfortable implying that the Movellans existed many billions of years ago. *A Device of Death* and *War of the Daleks* have different (and also mutually incompatible) accounts of the origins of the Movellans.

150 Dating *CD, NM V2: Empire of the Racnoss* (*CD,NM #2.2*) - The fifth Doctor, ripped out of Gallifrey's normal timestream, unwillingly finds himself in the Racnoss War described in *The Runaway Bride*. Alayna opts to not return to Gallifrey, but it's left unsaid if she and the Doctor keep travelling together.

151 Dating *The Runaway Bride* (X3.0) - The Doctor and Donna witness the Earth's formation.

152 Dating *Exploration Earth*, a.k.a. *Exploration Earth:*

The Time Machine (BBC Schools radio series) - The first phase of the story takes place during Earth's early days, "four thousand, five hundred million years" ago – so, a bit after the tenth Doctor and Donna witness the formation of Earth in 4.6 Billion BC in *The Runaway Bride*. The Doctor and Sarah make two jumps equal to some "millions of years" each, but Earth is just forming a crust on their second stop.

153 *TW: Miracle Day.* Jack says, "The world's been turning for over four billion years", in rough approximation with the age of Earth as given in *The Runaway Bride*.

154 *TW: Exodus Code*

155 "4.5 billion years" before "The Sentinel!", supposedly concurrent with the start of life on Earth. The degree to which Seneschal influences humankind's

the battle. War broke out, and two thirds of the population were killed. The Hoothi harvested the dead, taking them aboard their silent gas dirigibles. When the Time Lords sent an ambassador to the Hoothi worlds, the Hoothi used him as a host and attempted to conquer Gallifrey. The Time Lords counter-attacked, and the Hoothi fled into hyperspace. The Hoothi vanished from the universe.[156]

The father of the Osirians, Geb, said that he was around "when the world burned the skin to touch it". He claimed to have torn open the Earth with his hands, and pulled his offspring – including Osiris, Sutekh and Nephthys – from it.[157] The elder god To'Koth saw the Earth being born, and – before the creation of humanity and its languages – came to rest near the area that would become Liverpool.[158]

A plague wiped out the Curcurbites: machines that were fuelled by the blood of their enemies. The last of them fell into the magma of primeval Earth.[159] When the Sol System and its sun were new, and before life formed on Earth, a young space explorer passed nearby and activated his remote viewer. The device connected with a dimension that had no time, life or death – it was an empty darkness that hungered. The explorer died, and his ship eventually drifted into the Cardiff Rift.[160]

The universe passed the point when it would naturally collapse. The people of Logopolis sustained it by opening CVEs into other universes.[161] When Earth's moon was in its infancy, a black, spherical rock from another galaxy crashed onto its surface. The alien bacteria on the rock would remain dormant for 3.9 billion years.[162]

Three billion years ago, carvings were made of the Great Old Ones on the planet Veltroch.[163]

Venus

c 3,000,000,000 BC - VENUSIAN LULLABY[164] **->** The Venusians were an advanced race, surprisingly so since all metals were poisonous to them with the exception of gold, platinum and titanium. Their cities were crude, with the buildings in cities such as Cracdhalltar and Bikugih resembling soap-bubbles made from mud and crude stone, but the civilisation lasted for three million years.

By measuring the day, which got steadily longer, the Venusians calculated that their planet was dying. For tens of millennia, most of the Venusians were resigned to their fate. Most of the Venusian animal species had become extinct: the shanghorn, the klak-kluk and the pattifangs. To conserve resources, Death Inspectors killed Venusians who had outlived their useful lives. Anti-Acceptancer factions such as the Rocketeers, the Below the Sun Believers, the Magnetologists, the Water-breathers, the Volcano

development is debatable, as he bemoans how the results don't at all match his designs.

156 *Love and War*

157 *FP: The Judgment of Sutekh*

158 *Signs and Wonders*

159 "Tooth and Claw" (*DWM*). The Curcurbites know of the Time Lords.

160 *TW: Long Time Dead*

161 *Logopolis*. It's unclear when this happened, but there have been "aeons of constraint", and an aeon is a billion years.

162 "3.9 billion years" (pgs. 120, 146) before *Heart of Stone*. The rock must have impacted the moon long before it started orbiting the Earth (*The Silurians*).

163 *White Darkness*

164 Dating *Venusian Lullaby* (MA #3) - The Doctor tells Ian and Barbara that they have travelled back "oh, about three billion years I should think". *&L: Voyage to Venus* suggests the second Doctor visited Venus in the far future.

165 The background to *J&L: Voyage to Venus*.

166 *The Harvest of Time*

167 *Interference*

168 "Billions of years" before *The Day of the Troll*.

169 "A thousand million years" before *Spearhead from Space*. This date is confirmed in "Plastic Millennium".

170 *Auton 2: Sentinel*

171 "A billion years" before *The Caves of Androzani*.

172 *The Impossible Planet*

173 *The Harvest of Time* (p129). For the phrase "a billion or so years ago" to make any sense in the history laid out in this book, it must refer to the main universe's timeline, not that of Gallifrey.

174 *In the Forest of the Night*. The Doctor refers to the modern-day threat as a "once in a billion years solar event" (not strictly true in *Doctor Who* terms; see The Solar Flares sidebar).

175 "The Stockbridge Horror"

176 Dating *Power Play* (BF LS #3.5) - The Doctor specifies that it's the "Cambrian Period of the Paleozoic Era of the Phanerozoic Eon", which happened 541 to 485.4 million years ago.

177 Dating *The Beginning* (BF CC #8.5) - It's during Earth's pre-history, at least "four hundred and fifty million years" before the first human colony on the moon. The title isn't to be confused with the DVD set of the same name, which includes *An Unearthly Child*, *The Daleks* and *The Edge of Destruction*.

178 Dating *Exploration Earth: The Time Machine* (BBC Schools radio series) - The fossil record suggests that the first land plants appeared in the Ordovician Period, around 450 million years ago.

179 "4x10(2d8) yrs" ago, according to *The Gallifrey Chronicles*.

180 "A few hundred million years" before "Ghost Stories".

181 Dating *City of Death* (17.2) - Scaroth and the Doctor both state that the Jagaroth ship came to Earth

People and the Cave-Makers believed that they could escape their fate, but the majority saw them as cranks.

The first Doctor, Ian and Barbara visited Venus at this time, just as the Sou(ou)shi arrived to offer the Venusians a place within their spacecraft. The Sou(ou)shi were vampires, and wanted to consume the entire Venusian race as they did the Aveletians and the Signortiyu. The Venusians discovered this with the Doctor's help and destroyed the Sou(ou)shi craft. The debris from the ship entered the Venusian atmosphere, blocking some of the sun's rays and lowering the planet's temperature. This prolonged the Venusians' existence for another one hundred generations. The consciousness of the Sou(ou)shi survived and travelled to primeval Earth.

Species native to Venus included the rhino-like, herbivore shanghorns and the sapient Cytherians – the latter of whom created a greenhouse effect on their world through use of fossil fuels. The Cytherians entered suspended animation, along with caches of Venus' plant and animal life, to reclaim their world in future.[165] The Doctor could hum a rendition of one of the greatest tragic operas in the history of the Venusian arts.[166]

wih - Time Lords from the future launched an unmanned warship to destroy Earth, the original homeworld of the Enemy. The ship travelled at sublight speeds, and three billion years would elapse before it arrived there in 1996.[167]

A plant-creature, Sphereosis, fell to Earth and grew beneath the soil.[168] **The Nestene, a race of pure energy, began their conquests a billion years ago.**[169] Nestene gestation chambers were established on many worlds – including Earth – long before intelligent life evolved on them.[170] **Around this time, the last seas dried up on Androzani Minor in the Sirius System.**[171] **The Scarlet System became home to the Pallushi – a mighty civilisation that would last a billion years until it fell into a black hole.**[172]

A billion years ago, the seahorse-like Sild evolved the ability to animate dead bodies and use their knowledge. The Sild overwhelmed whole planets through infiltration and sheer force of numbers, causing the deaths of billions. The Time Lords judged the Sild a threat to creation, and imprisoned them all aboard the *Consolidator*.[173]

The Here, the spirit of the trees on Earth, came to the great North Forest, and then the vast Southern Forest. When needed, the trees could rapidly expand in size to protect Earth against potential ecological disaster. Humanity forgot about the trees' benevolence, and worked a fear of forests into its fairy tales.[174]

The TARDIS was possessed by an elemental alien around 1983 and travelled back five hundred million years. Here the alien revelled in the forces of primeval Earth. The TARDIS returned, but the alien was free.[175]

The Cambrian Period (c 500,000,000 BC) - POWER PLAY (BF)[176] **->** The planet-assassin Dominicus furthered a scheme that entailed dumping vast amounts of nuclear waste into Earth's past, where it could harmlessly decay. The sixth Doctor directed missiles targeted to destroy twenty-first century Earth down Dominicus' time corridor, causing a series of contained detonations. Victoria Waterfield's associate David died to prevent Dominicus from escaping the resultant explosion.

The Doctor and Susan's First Adventure Away from Gallifrey

c 450,000,000 BC - THE BEGINNING[177] **->** Immediately after leaving their homeworld, the first Doctor and Susan – accidentally accompanied by the Gallifreyan technician Quadrigger Stoyn – arrived on Earth's moon, where the TARDIS' exterior transformed into a large boulder. The Doctor thwarted Stoyn's efforts to signal their people, and explored outside the Ship. They encountered the Archaeons – propagators who thought themselves tasked with creating order on primitive planets, and were using a cannon to seed life onto Earth with red lightning.

The Archaeons tinkered with a temporal stasis capacitor from the TARDIS, inadvertently creating a time field around everyone present. The Doctor, Susan, Stoyn and the Archaeons would remain frozen until the construction of Earth's first moon colony.

c 450,000,000 BC - EXPLORATION EARTH[178] **->** The fourth Doctor and Sarah saw Earth when it had trees, flowers, and abundant oxygen. The Doctor engaged Lord Megron in a telepathic duel, and banished him.

The Great Provider began its intergalactic conquests four hundred million years ago.[179] The Vigilant Eremites of Andurax became caretakers of the Gate of Tersimmon, a.k.a. Bertha. Four gemstones, including the Ghost, were forged to let the Gate syphon away a potentially lethal build-up of dark energy in the universe, which occurred naturally every million years.[180]

Life on Earth

c 400,000,000 BC - CITY OF DEATH[181] **->** An advanced race, the callous Jagaroth, wiped themselves out in a huge war. The last of the Jagaroth limped to primeval Earth in an advanced spaceship. The ship's pilot, Scaroth, attempted to take his vessel to power three – warp thrust – too close to the Earth's surface and the spacecraft detonated over what would later become the Atlantic Ocean.

Scaroth was splintered into 12 fragments and materialised at various points in human history. He would influence humanity's development for tens of thousands of years. This culminated in the building of a time machine in 1979, which he used to return to the past in an attempt to prevent his ship exploding. The fourth Doctor, the second Romana and their ally Duggan prevented Scaroth from changing history.

Earth was a barren volcanic world, but it had already produced primordial soup, and the anti-matter explosion acted as a catalyst. Life on Earth began.

The explosion of the Jagaroth ship left a radiation trace that the Euterpians detected many millions of years later.[182]

Life evolved much as palaeontologists and geologists think that it did.

Earth was home to a species of malignant wraiths that resided in the "lost lands". It was said that they hailed from the dawn of time, but these creatures, who resembled evil fairies, had their origins in humanity's children. They came to reside backwards and forwards in time, became invisible to detection and took to murdering people in their sleep. They had control of the elements, and were especially protective of their own: children named the "chosen ones".[183] These fairies, *homo fata vulgaris*, were ultra-terrestrials who lived in the

Invisible: a realm in a "groove" of existence adjacent to our own. The fairies' influence and that of their kin, including the elves and Boggarts, waned as Earth civilisation developed straight lines and buildings rather than natural spaces.[184]

Werewolves were among the oldest races on Earth. The werewolf Stubbe claimed to have been around at the Earth's creation.[185]

Around two hundred and sixty million years ago, the Permians – skeletal, lizard-hipped carnivores, bound together by a bioelectric field – were top of the food chain on Earth. They had a degree of intelligence, and the ability to mentally guide other creatures. They consumed electrical energy from living things, and were so efficient as predators that they wiped out 96% of life on Earth. With food becoming scarce, the Permians fed off each other. The last few of them went dormant and became fossils.[186]

wih - Two hundred and twelve million years ago, the Great Attractor, a.k.a. Grandfather's Maw, came into existence and became a hazard to timeship navigation. Robert Scarratt suspected that House Lineacrux had created the Attractor. Its sheer magnitude provoked interest from the other Great Houses and the Enemy.[187]

A time-jumping Death's Head left footprints in the

"four hundred million years ago". Contemporary science has a number of estimates of when life on Earth started, but all are far, far earlier than that. *The Terrestrial Index* takes that as a cue to set this story three and a half billion years ago.

SCAROTH OF THE JAGAROTH: In *City of Death*, we actually *see* Scarlioni, Tancredi and four other Scaroth splinters: an Egyptian, a Neanderthal (the one some fans think looks like Jesus – the DVD commentary notes that Julian Glover thought the same), a Roman and a Celt (although most reference books, including the earlier versions of this one, describe him as a Crusader), in that order, in the flashback at the start of episode three.

Further examination of this story can account for all 12 Scaroth splinters, assuming that none of them live for more than a century, and that they acquire Scarlioni's antiques while they are new. One Scaroth version (presumably the Neanderthal that we see) demonstrates "the true use of fire"; a second gives humankind the wheel; a third "caused the pyramids to be built" (we see this one both as a "human" Egyptian Pharaoh and as a Jagaroth on an ancient Egyptian scroll); a fourth caused "the heavens to be mapped"; the fifth is an ancient Greek; the sixth is the Roman that we see (a Senator, or possibly even an Emperor); the seventh is the Celt that we see; the eighth gives humankind the printing press (presumably, this accounts for why Scarlioni has more than one Gutenberg Bible); the ninth is Captain Tancredi; the tenth is an Elizabethan nobleman (who

obtains the first draft of *Hamlet*); the eleventh lives at the time of Louis XV (and is presumably the splinter who purchases the Gainsborough that's just been sold at the start of the story – he's named as Cardinal Scarlath in *Christmas on a Rational Planet*); and the twelfth is Carlos Scarlioni.

182 *Invasion of the Cat People*

183 *TW: Small Worlds.* Jack says the fairies are "from the dawn of time" – it's possible that he's speaking metaphorically, although in truth the fairies reside "backwards in time" and might pre-date humanity, even though they hail from it. Mention of the "lost lands" might suggest that they held more of a foothold on Earth until Scaroth's spaceship sparked humanity's birth. It might be far simpler, however, to assume that their development coincides with that of humankind.

184 *The Shining Man* (ch14).

185 *Loups-Garoux*

186 *The Land of the Dead*

187 *FP: The Brakespeare Code* (ch5, 7).

188 "Time Bomb!". The Triassic Period happened 251 to 199 million years ago.

189 *Doctor Who and the Silurians*

CONTINENTAL DRIFT: According to scientists, continental drift is a continuing process. In *Doctor Who*, there's evidence that it was a single event. The Doctor talks of "the great continental drift, two hundred million years ago" in *Doctor Who and the Silurians*. In the broadcast version of *Earthshock*, the Earth of sixty-five million years ago looks like it does today. Continental

Triassic Period, to the befuddlement of future geologists.[188] In the 1970s, Dr Quinn discovered a colony of reptile people living below Wenley Moor in Derbyshire. They were the remnants of an advanced lost civilisation, and had spent many million years in hibernation. Quinn mistakenly believed that they came from the Silurian Period, and had a globe showing the Earth as it was before the great continental drift, two hundred million years ago.[189]

c 200,000,000 BC - "Time Bomb"[190] -> The Time Cannon of the Hedrons sent the sixth Doctor, Frobisher and TARDIS from the year 2850 far into the past of Earth. This was the destination for all the genetic impurities of that world – including many dead bodies that went on to influence genetic development on Earth.

The seventh Doctor watched the first Lungfish walk on a Devonian beach.[191] Humanity crawled out of the sea, contrary to the Doctor's advice.[192]

The Age of Dinosaurs

One hundred and sixty-five million years ago, dinosaurs started to emerge on Earth.[193] In a different galaxy from Earth, which had become known as Home Galaxy, a number of advanced races made contact and reengineered themselves so that they could interbreed. They developed advanced artificial intelligence technology. The People and Also People constructed the Worldsphere: a Dyson sphere that completely enclosed the star Whynot, with a surface area six hundred million times larger than that of Earth. The regulating intelligence of the Worldsphere became known as God.[194]

An unnamed race created the Omnethoth, a sentient weapon that could alter its physical state, to conquer the universe. The Omnethoth killed its creators, seeded the universe with colonisation clouds and went dormant.[195] The Erogem – an "old, old" civilisation – conquered half a galaxy with an occult-like technology, but eventually fell from power. A Coalition restricted their activities.[196]

The Millennium War

While dinosaurs walked the Earth, the Millennium War was fought across the galaxy. The Constructors of Destiny had created the Mind of Bophemeral – the ultimate computer and the most massive object ever built – from black holes, blue dwarfs and strange matter. Bophemeral, though, went insane within instants and destroyed the Constructors. A thousand races, including the Time Lords, Daemons, Euterpians, Exxilons, Faction Paradox, Greld, Grey Hegemony, Kastrians, Maskmakers of the Pageant, Ministers of Grace, Nimon, Omnethoth, Osirians, People of the Worldsphere, Uxariens, Rutans and Sontarans fought the Mind of Bophemeral and its drones. The planets Kastria and Xeraphas were devastated in the war, but Bophemeral was defeated. The Time Lords and the People time-looped Bophemeral and the Guardians intervened, using the Key to Time to erase all knowledge of this War.[197]

c 150,000,000 BC - THE HAND OF FEAR[198] -> On Kastria, the scientist Eldrad built spacial barriers to keep out the solar winds that ravaged the planet. He also devised a crystalline silicon form for his race, and built machines to replenish the earth and the atmosphere. Once this was done, he threatened to usurp King Rokon.

The Kastrians did not share Eldrad's dreams of galactic conquest, and so Eldrad destroyed the barriers. The Kastrians sentenced Eldrad to death. As killing a silicon lifeform was almost impossible, they constructed an Obliteration Module and sent it out into space, beyond all solar systems. The Module was detonated early at nineteen spans, while there was still a one-in-three-million chance that Eldrad might survive. The Kastrians elected to destroy themselves and their race banks rather than lead a subterranean exist-

drift was a reality according to *Invasion of the Cat-People*. In *The Ark*, the Earth of ten million years hence also looks exactly like contemporary Earth, although we saw the continents devastated in *The Parting of the Ways*, and *The End of the World* acknowledges that technology was used to arrest continental drift.
190 Dating "Time Bomb" (*DWM* #114-116) - "Earthdate 200 Million Years BC", according to the caption.
191 *Transit*. This may be a dream sequence or an allegory.
192 Or so he claims in *The Silurian Candidate*.
193 In *Earthshock*, the Doctor states that the dinosaurs existed for "a hundred million years or so" and died out "sixty-five million years ago", which is in tune with scien-

tific consensus.
194 *The Also People*. No date is given, but the People fight in the Millennium War in *The Quantum Archangel*.
195 "Millions of years" before *The Fall of Yquatine*. The Omnethoth also fight in the Millennium War according to *The Quantum Archangel*.
196 *The Blood Furnace*. The Erogem have waged war "since dinosaurs ruled [Earth]", the seventh Doctor says.
197 *The Quantum Archangel*. The Millenium Wars (consistently misspelled with one "n") were a feature of the early *Doctor Who Weekly/Monthly* comic strips, but this would appear to be a different conflict.
198 Dating *The Hand of Fear* (14.2) - The Doctor identifies the rock in which Eldrad's hand was discovered,

ence. **Eldrad's hand eventually reached Earth in the Jurassic Period, where it became buried in a stratum of Blackstone Dolomite.**

King Rokon feared that Eldrad would survive his premature obliteration, and so dispatched Mulkris the Executioner to search thousands of worlds for his remains. She would slay a hundred Eldrads that regenerated on a hundred different worlds.[199]

(=) 150,000,000 BC - "Time Bomb"[200] **->** The sixth Doctor and Frobisher returned to the distant past from 2850 to discover that the Hedrons were disposing of bodies in this era, too. History might never be restored.

A time-expedition from the sixty-third century collected samples of flora and fauna from the Jurassic period. A member of the group, Baskerville, desired one of his col-

leagues, Laura Lyons, and sabotaged their time engine. All save Baskerville and Lyons died as the expedition ran aground in London, 1894.[201] The Vardon-Kosnax War was meant to run fifty years, but time-disruption made it last three hundred.[202]

During the final days of the fifty-first star fall campaign, the Sontarans suffered great losses at the tentacles of the Rutan Horde. The Sontarans built a world engine, the Warsong, as a final offensive against the Rutans, but were unable to deploy it. The Sontaran Surnat Gaq died after hiding the Warsong on Earth in the dinosaur age.[203]

The twelfth Doctor and Clara spiralled back in time following his regeneration. A tyrannosaur caught the TARDIS in its maw, and was transported along with the Ship to Victorian times.[204]

THE TWELFTH DOCTOR YEAR TWO[205] **->** To show comic book-creators Sonny Robinson and Val Kent *actual* adventures in time and space, the twelfth Doctor took

and twice tells Eldrad that he has been away from Kastria for "a hundred and fifty million years".
199 *Eldrad Must Die!*
200 Dating "Time Bomb" (*DWM* #114-116) - The caption reads "Earthdate 150 Million BC".
201 *J&L S7: The Monstrous Menagerie.* Baskerville says his beasts haven't had a meal in "150 million years".
202 *Neverland.* The war is referred to as over by *Time-Flight.* The Vardons are probably not the Vardans seen in *The Invasion of Time.* A Kosnax appears in *Cold Fusion.*
203 "Instruments of War"
204 *Deep Breath*
205 Dating *The Twelfth Doctor Year Two* (Titan 12th Doc #2.14-2.15, "Invasion of the Mindmorphs") - It's the "late Jurassic era".
206 Dating *Time-Flight* (19.7) - The Doctor informs the flight crew of the second Concorde that they have landed at Heathrow "a hundred and forty million years ago". He states, correctly, that this is the "Jurassic" era, but then suggests that they "can't be far off from the Pleistocene era", which actually took place a mere 1,800,000 to 10,000 years ago. *The Seeds of Doom* gives a more accurate date for the Pleistocene.
207 *Carnival of Monsters.* The Doctor states that the Pleisosaurus "has been extinct for a hundred and thirty million years". The MiniScope presumably captures its specimens in a Timescoop like those seen in *Invasion of the Dinosaurs* and *The Five Doctors.*
208 *Doctor Who and the Silurians, The Happiness Patrol.*
209 *Invasion of the Dinosaurs.* Whitaker tries to take Earth back to a "Golden Age," but there's no indication that this is the age of the dinosaurs, which would hardly be an Earthly paradise for humans. He uses dinosaurs to scare people out of London.
210 *The Mark of the Rani, Time and the Rani.*
211 "Matildus". Pretending for the moment that colos-

sosaurus rex even existed, it probably walked the earth in the Cretaceous Period, when most of the large carnivores were around. Perhaps the Doctor lost his book on an alien world with such beasts.
212 *6thLA: The End of the Line*
213 "The Eye of Torment". These Umbra are of no relation to the Umbra creature from *Shadowmind.*
214 Enough "generations" before *The Eleventh Doctor Year One*: "The Eternal Dogfight"/"The Infinite Astronaut" that even the Time Lords must speculate about the conflict's origins.
215 "Cuckoo"
216 The Doctor says this happened "millions of years" before *The Twelfth Doctor Year Three*: "Beneath the Waves", but also that the ship was built "before humanity was even a twinkle in the universe's eye".
217 *Made of Steel.* The two dinosaurs seen are apatosaurus and tyrannosaurus, from the Upper Cretaceous.
218 *Mission to Magnus.* The Doctor says that Anzor's TARDIS has been dispatched back to "the beginning of time", but his subsequent comments about the things Anzor might encounter there suggest he didn't mean the term literally. The Mesozoic era started 250 million years ago, and ended about 65 million years ago.
219 *Antidote to Oblivion*
220 *The Twelfth Doctor Year Two*: "Clara Oswald and the School of Death"
221 *I, Davros*: "Corruption". This is a cheeky explanation for why the male Thals so outnumber the females in all three of their TV stories. The Planistavian Age was "a hundred million years" ago according to Davros.
222 "One hundred million years" before *The Wheel of Ice* (p259).
223 *Terrible Lizards*
224 Dating "A Glitch in Time" (*DWM* #179) - It's "the Cretaceous", so between 145 and 65 million years ago.

them to the late Jurassic era... where they ran like mad from a T-Rex, who told the Doctor, "A pleasure to meet you too, Old Chap. And even more of a pleasure to eat you."

140,000,000 BC - TIME-FLIGHT[206] **-> The planet Xeraphas was the home of the Xeraphin, a legendary race with immense mental powers. It was rendered uninhabitable when it was caught in the Vardon-Kosnax War. The surviving Xeraphin came to Earth, hoping to colonise the planet, but they suffered from radiation sickness. They abandoned their physical forms, and became a psychic gestalt of bioplasmic energy until they were able to regenerate. The Tremas Master became trapped on Earth five hundred years after this and attempted to harness the power of the Xeraphin Consciousness.**

Building a Time Contour Generator, the Master kidnapped a Concorde from the 1980s, and used the passengers as slaves in an attempt to penetrate the Xeraphin citadel. He was defeated when the fifth Doctor, Tegan and Nyssa followed him back through time and broke the slaves' conditioning.

About one hundred thirty million years ago, the Plesiosaurus became extinct. Before this, the owner of a MiniScope kidnapped one of the species.[207]

The Doctor visited Earth at the time of the dinosaurs. He reckoned the Cretaceous Era was "a very good time for dinosaurs".[208] Professor Whitaker kidnapped various dinosaurs using his Timescoop.[209] The Rani visited this period and collected tyrannosaur embryos, one of which almost killed her later. She also expressed an interest in reviving the era with a Time Manipulator.[210] A book the Doctor had checked out from Cornucopia, on the anatomy of the colossosaurus rex, was eaten by a colossosaurus rex.[211]

Millions of years ago, the Parallel Sect emerged as a race of dimensional pioneers that traversed reality by linking dimensional nexus points. Whatever became of the Parallel Sect, their organic creations – "the Normans" – labored to maintain the stability of the dimensional web they instigated.[212] An alien race created the Umbra: a psychic fabric that removed guilt and regret, giving rise to a golden age. The Umbra consumed its creators, prompting a dying scientist to send the Umbra into a young star, Earth's sun, via a trans-warp tunnel. They were trapped within for millions of years.[213]

The Armstrons of the Great Wheel and the Ja'arrodic Federation sponsored a joint venture, in the starship *Infinite*, to see what lay beyond a mysterious wormhole: the Gate of Creation. When the *Infinite* and subsequent missions failed to return, the Armstrons and Ja'arrodic disagreed over the nature of the reality and fell into open warfare. The resultant struggle, the Eternal Dogfight,

destroyed the homeworlds of both races, and their mobile space armadas periodically lashed out at one another.[214]

Millions of years ago, a Surcoth explorer was lost on Earth. His body eventually fossilised and was discovered in 1855.[215] An alien fell to Earth while in hypersleep, and became buried in sediment in Devon.[216] The tenth Doctor and Martha visited the Cretaceous, and a tyrannosaurus chased them.[217]

Due to the Doctor's sabotage of his TARDIS on the planet Magnus, the Time Lord Anzor was sent on a slow ride back to an earlier era of time. The Doctor thought that Anzor could spend his time trying to bully molluscs and pterodactyls, and studying Mesozoic slime molds.[218] Anzor's TARDIS was recalled from antediluvian times to the twenty-fourth century.[219] Clara Oswald went for a picnic in prehistoric times, and nearly caused an evolutionary disaster when a pterodactyl flew off with her tuna sandwich.[220]

Davros believed that any similarity between the Kaleds and Thals on Skaro was entirely superficial, and that their last common ancestors, if they ever had them, existed in the Planistavian Age, not long after life evolved on the planet. Thals were descended from urvacryls, a type of water snake; Kaleds from clam-like creatures. His evidence for this was that the two species' internal organs were completely different and that while there was a 50:50 ratio of male and female Kaleds, seven male Thals were born for every female.[221]

The amulet that the ArkHive sent back in time fifty million years – a distress beacon of sorts – arrived on Earth. In time, it became part of a dinosaur fossil.[222] A time fracture temporarily relocated a variety of dinosaurs to the Florida everglades in 1881.[223]

(=) c 100,000,000 BC - "A Glitch in Time"[224] **->** The seventh Doctor and Ace arrived at a nexus point in Earth's history, the Cretaceous, and immediately met a team of time-travelling dinosaur hunters. Despite the Doctor's objections, they were convinced they were part of history and couldn't change it. They shot an early mammal... and a team of reptilian time-travelling hunters materialised to hunt apes. The two parties fighting inside the nexus cancelled each other out, and both returned to their respective futures.

(=) The paleontologist George Williamson tested his time travel prowess by watching dinosaurs. Williamson's presence encouraged some saurian lizards to walk upright and gain an evolutionary advantage, creating a parallel timeline. A dimensional doorway opened in Siberia, 1894, and some saurians went through it. The timeline was erased due to the Doctor and Williamson's actions in 1894.[225]

(=) 80,000,000 BC - BENNY: THE SWORD OF FOREVER[226] -> A botched use of the Sword of Forever flung Bernice eighty million years back in time, where she was eaten by an intelligent velociraptor. The Sword destroyed Earth, but Benny's use of the item in 2595 re-created Earth's timeline.

The homeworld of a race of snake-like beings disintegrated, scattering chunks of itself across the Sol System. A few survivors would hide away on Earth's moon.[227]

The Dinosaur Extinction Event

Adric is Lost to His Friends

c 65,000,000 BC - EARTHSHOCK[228] -> Sixty-five million years ago, the dinosaurs became extinct when the anti-matter engines of a space freighter that had spiralled back through time from 2526 exploded in Earth's atmosphere. The fifth Doctor's companion, Adric, seemingly died trying to prevent the disaster.

c 65,000,000 BC - BENNY: THE ADOLESCENCE OF TIME[230] -> The freighter impact caused a giant dust cloud to settle on the Earth's surface, and released all manner of psychic forces. A race of reptile-people continued to reside on land and in the sea, even as their winged sister race farmed fish on a chain of islands floating above the devastation. The psychic forces slowly altered the reptiles' brains. A worm-monstrosity sought the blood of a time traveller, and – after reconstituting Benny's time ring – brought Peter Summerfield back through time. Peter misguidedly triggered warfare between the flying reptiles and the worm's misshapen minions, the worm-callers. The flying reptiles' farm belt was destroyed, and they started looking for food on the surface with their kin. Peter realised his mistake and asked the worm to return him to the future; the reptiles subsequently built a statue that regarded him as an abomination and a destroyer.

Bernice Summerfield didn't know what had killed off the dinosaurs.[229]

---

225 "Several million years" before *Time Zero*.
226 Dating *Benny: The Sword of Forever* (Benny NA #14) - The timeframe is given.
227 *Horror of the Space Snakes*. The Doctor estimates this as "seventy million years ago," and further speculates that the moon was perhaps part of the disintegrated planet – or just that the snakes hitched a lift as the moon roamed through space.
228 Dating *Earthshock* (19.6) - The Doctor dates the extinction of the dinosaurs, and confirms that the freighter has travelled to that era, back "sixty-five million years". In the original TV version, the pattern of prehistoric Earth's continents are those of modern-day Earth. A correction was attempted for the DVD release, where an effects option allows the viewer to see an updated special effect. However, the correction itself is historically awry, as it features the super-continent Pangea, when the proper configuration should be somewhere between Pangea and the present day.
229 Dating *Benny S9: The Adolescence of Time* (Benny audio #9.2) - The blurb says that the story occurs "many years" after the freighter collided with Earth (*Earthshock*) and enough time has passed that only one of the characters involved is old enough to have remembered the impact. The story helps to bridge the freighter impact with the rise of the Silurians; it's implied that the "psychic forces" released by the collision helped to develop the Silurians' third eyes, and the relocation of the flying reptiles to the ground presumably unifies the reptile-people into a single society. See the When Did the Silurians Rule the Earth? sidebar.
230 *Benny B1: Epoch: Judgement Day*
231 Dating *The Boy That Time Forgot* (BF #110) - Adric claims to be "more than five hundred years old", so that long (give or take) has passed since *Earthshock*.
232 Dating "The Sentinel!" (*The Incredible Hulk Presents* #7) - The Doctor estimates that he's arrived on Earth in the Cenozoic Period – the current geological period, stretching from the death of the dinosaurs (*Earthshock*) to today. The humans seen are primitive, so it's presumably early in the era.
233 *SJA: The Lost Boy*
234 "Millions of years" before *Deep Breath*, with the Doctor alternatively mentioning the droids as "rubbish robots from the Dawn of Time", but also that the ship's been buried "for centuries".
235 *Worlds BF: The Feast of Magog*
236 Dating *The Company of Friends*: "Benny's Story" (BF #123a) - It's "fifty million years" into the past.
237 *All Consuming Fire*
238 *Doctor Who and the Silurians, The Sea Devils, Benny S9: The Adolescence of Time*. See the When Did the Silurians Rule the Earth? sidebar.
239 According to the Doctor in *The Hungry Earth*. This line accounts for the physical differences between the Silurians in that story and their previous appearances, and presumably also accounts for the differences between the Silurians in *Doctor Who and the Silurians* and those in *Warriors of the Deep* (and, by extension, the winged race in *Benny S9: The Adolescence of Time*).
240 *UNIT S4: Assembled*
241 *The Scales of Injustice*
242 *The Silurian Candidate*
243 *Doctor Who and the Silurians*
244 *Blood Heat*
245 *UNIT S4: Assembled*

(=) & 64,999,500 BC - THE BOY THAT TIME FORGOT[231] **->** The fifth Doctor's application of Block Transfer Computation in Victorian England made real his subconscious desire that Adric should live, and enabled Adric to enter new course computations into the freighter's computer before impact. The vessel still grounded itself on Earth, but Adric survived.

Adric found that the Cybermen's alien computer – which he named Star – could act as a psychic booster and make his ideas manifest. He created giant spiders that, using the crashed freighter as a foundation, built a City of Excellence. He also manifested millions of giant scorpions, who chanted Block Transfer Computations in "counting houses". This "song of the scorpions" sustained Adric beyond his normal lifespan – he lived for five hundred years as the scorpions' king.

The Doctor, Nyssa, novelist Beatrice Mapp and faux adventurer Rupert Von Thal arrived from Victorian England in search of the hijacked TARDIS. The scorpions' bloodthirsty progenitors spurred a rebellion against Adric. Rupert was killed, but Adric used Star to relocate himself and the Doctor's remaining party back to Victorian England.

In Adric's absence, this timeline was sealed off into its own bubble of existence.

c 64,600,000 BC - "The Sentinel!"[232] **->** The enigmatic being Seneschal was bitterly disappointed that humankind had spent the last four hundred thousand years as stupid knuckle-draggers, and – sensing the seventh Doctor might have the solution to the problem – pulled his TARDIS to Earth with a temporal rubicon. The Doctor objected to Seneschal's meddling in humanity's development, enraged the elder being and fled – but not before Seneschal procured his genetic material, and from it pledged to create a race of Time Lords.

Sixty million years ago, a meteorite containing some Xylok – crystalline lifeforms – crashed to Earth and was buried.[233] **The time-travelling *SS Marie Antoinette* crash-landed on Earth in prehistoric times. The clockwork droids on board set about harvesting organs from lifeforms (including, eventually, humans), and maintained their systems for millions of years.**[234] The demonic force summoned by Alexander Korvo in 1927 claimed to have watched over the Earth since humanity's distant ancestors first climbed down from the trees.[235]

c 50,000,000 BC - THE COMPANY OF FRIENDS: "Benny's Story"[236] **->** A time fissure briefly relocated the eighth Doctor and Benny to the distant past on Epsilon Minima. During a lion attack, the Doctor lost some but-

tons and the TARDIS key – in future, both would get buried in a coal seam. He also located the fissure, enabling him and Benny to return to her era.

A hundred thousand years before the Silurians, the Earth had been ruled by "gargantuan entities".[237]

The Age of the Reptile People

On Earth, some reptiles had evolved into intelligent bipeds. There were three **distinct species: the land-based Silurians, who built a great civilisation in areas of extreme heat; their amphibious cousins, the Sea Devils; and a winged race.**[238] **There were different races of Silurians, "cousins" to one another.**[239] Silurian society reflected a wide range of politics and beliefs.[240]

Silurian civilisation started as scattered clans, which were eventually united by Panun E'Ni of the Southern Clan, whose deeds were recorded in the Hall of Heroes. Panun E'Ni was deposed by Tun W'lzz, who freed the enslaved tribes to create a united Silurian civilisation.[241] The Silurians' Parliament, capital city and highest ruling Silurian triad – Spenodus, Avvox and Chordok – were located in what would become Motuo, China.[242]

Silurians had advanced psychic powers, which seemed to be concentrated through their third "eye". They had telekinetic and hypnotic abilities, could project lethal blasts of energy and establish invisible force fields. Much of their equipment was operated by mental commands, although the Silurians were also known to use an almost-musical summoning device. Much of Silurian technology appears to have been organic. The Silurians domesticated dinosaurs, using a tyrannosaur species as watchdogs. They constructed the Disperser, a device capable of dispersing the Van Allen Belts.[243]

They used brontosaurs to lift heavy loads, and dilophosaurs as mounts. They communicated using a sophisticated language that was a combination of telepathy, speech and gesture. They had Gravitron technology which allowed a sophisticated degree of weather control. They travelled in vast airships.[244]

Silurian scientists hybridized aquatic, airbourne and land-dwelling dinosaurs, creating creatures they could control psionically. Out of compassion, the Silurian Kralix disobeyed orders to destroy his weaponized hybrids, and kept them in hibernation.[245]

The Silurians had technology far in advance of humanity in 2020, including methods of energy generation and water supply.[246] **Their science was more advanced than human technology of the late twenty-first century, with particle suppressors and advanced genetic engineering. They also created creatures such as the Myrka, a ferocious armoured sea monster. Silurian law forbid all but defensive wars, but the Sea**

Devils had elite army units and hand-held weaponry, and the Silurians built submarine battlecruisers.[247] **Silurian bioengineering technology was usually only seen on jungle planets.**[248]

The Silurians lived in vast crystalline cities with imposing architecture.[249] One estimate is that their technology was three or four hundred years more advanced than Earth in the twentieth century. A provision of Silurian law was to execute members of different castes who mated. Strict laws also prevented experiments into genetic engineering and nuclear fission.[250]

Turtles existed at the time of the Sea Devils, much as they do in our time. Sea Devils didn't eat meat.[251] The Silurians worshipped the Great Old Ones, with the Sea Devils venerating Dagon in particular.[252] They also worshipped a lizard "devil god", Urmungstandra.[253]

The Prime Serpent was a Silurian deity.[254] The Old Ones visited Earth when humans were just apes.[255]

= The Silurian scientist Mortakk performed illegal genetic experiments. He was tried and executed before the great hibernation.[256]

The Silurians saw apes as pests who raided their crops, and developed a virus to cull them.[257] Silurians also ate the apes, using Myrkas to hunt them.[258] Apes were caged and tortured.[259] **The Silurian warrior Restac and others of her group hunted apes for sport.**[260] Some Silurians lost the ability to generate fear in humankind, and technologically replicated the talent. An anti-toxin protected Silurians vulnerable to their fellows' venom.[261]

As a little Silurian, Madame Vastra saw a tyrannosaur.[262] The Silurians "did not rule Earth alone". **Madame Vastra witnessed the suffering caused by her people's deadliest nemesis, a breed of red leech that poisoned the Silurians' drinking water.**[263]

(=) ? - "Supremacy of the Cybermen" -> The eleventh Doctor and Alice Obiefune visited prehistoric Earth, to collect some nanjura fruit – Madame Vastra's favourite, and long-extinct – as an anniversary present from Jenny Flint. Cyber-technology from the end of time overcame some Silurians, and the Doctor failed in his efforts to usurp their network. The twelfth Doctor would go on to avert these events.

The ArkHive's damaged programming made it seek a means of travelling back to reunite with its doomed creators. Its failed attempt to create a time machine detonated one of Saturn's ice moons, spreading frozen detritus that would become Saturn's rings. The ArkHive subsequently sent an amulet back in time, hoping it would compel Earth's dominant species to develop space travel and visit Saturn with technological support. The Silurians, distracted by a rogue planet's approach, failed to heed this...[264]

The Arrival of Earth's Moon; the Silurians Enter Hibernation

Silurian scientists detected a rogue planetoid, and calculated that as it passed by Earth, it would draw away Earth's atmosphere and destroy all life on the surface. The Silurians built hibernation shelters deep underground to survive the catastrophe.[265]

The Silurians' preparations took twelve years. Silurian hybrids were sent to Shelter 429.[266] **A Silurian spaceship the size of Canada left Earth before the predicted planetary disaster; it was an Ark with some thousands of Silurians and at least fifty dinosaur species aboard.**[267] A Silurian base at the South Pole facilitated scientific research, but also housed a small army of Myrka. Prior to entering hibernation, the Silurians there stockpiled Fire

---

246 According to Eldane in *Cold Blood*.

247 *Warriors of the Deep*

248 *The Hungry Earth*. The implication is that Silurians lived in jungle areas, although the next episode, *Cold Blood*, suggests they lived in deserts.

249 *Blood Heat, The Scales of Injustice, Bloodtide.*

250 *The Scales of Injustice*

251 "The Devil of the Deep"

252 *All-Consuming Fire*

253 *The Crystal Bucephalus*, named in *The Taking of Planet 5*. The name was spelled Urgmundasatra in *Benny: Twilight of the Gods.*

254 "Final Genesis"

255 *Tomb of Valdemar*

256 "Final Genesis". This is set in a parallel universe, and it's unclear if Mortakk also lived in ours.

257 *Doctor Who and the Silurians*

258 *Bloodtide*

259 *The Scales of Injustice*

260 *Cold Blood*

261 *UNIT S4: Assembled*, highlighting discrepancies between the new-series Silurians and those in *Doctor Who and the Silurians*.

262 *Deep Breath*

263 "Sixty five million years", Vastra claims, before *The Crimson Horror*. The Doctor concurs that the leech originates from "the time of the dinosaurs".

264 "Fifty million years" before *The Wheel of Ice* (p257, 260), and prior to the Silurians going into hibernation. The American Geophysical Society, using data harvested from NASA's Cassini spacecraft, determined in 2013 that Saturn's rings likely date back to the formation of the planet itself, some 4.4 billion years ago.

265 *Doctor Who and the Silurians*

266 *The Scales of Injustice*

267 *Dinosaurs on a Spaceship*. It's never stated why this

WHEN DID THE SILURIANS RULE THE EARTH?: There are a number of contradictory accounts in the TV episodes and the tie-in series of when the Silurian civilisation existed, and it's impossible to reconcile them with each other, let alone against scientific fact.

A lot of the dating references are vague: *Doctor Who and the Silurians* says the Silurians "ruled the planet millions of years ago". *The Scales of Injustice* states the Silurians existed "millions of years" and "a few million years" ago, but also uses the term "millennia". *Bloodtide* says it was "many hundreds of thousands of years ago" and "over a million years ago". *Eternity Weeps* shows the arrival of the moon in Earth orbit. However, it's inconsistent with its dating, stating that this happened both "twenty million" (p127) and "200 million" (p117) years ago.

In *The Silurian Candidate*, a space programme worker (so not necessarily a historical expert) reiterates that the Silurians should be called Eocenes, and ruled the Earth some "fifty million years" ago. In the same story, the seventh Doctor ballparks it as "several million years" ago. "The Lost Dimension" names the Myrka (*Warriors of the Deep*) as a genetically engineered species that's "been extinct for 65 million years".

In *Kill the Moon*, the twelfth Doctor says that the moon has been "tagging along beside" Earth for "a hundred million years" and, later, "a hundred million years or so". In *The Hungry Earth*, the eleventh Doctor says that a Silurian is "300 million years out of [her] comfort zone". The approach of the rogue planet that prompts the Silurians to enter hibernation distracts them from acknowledging the ArkHive's message "fifty million years" before *The Wheel of Ice* [c 2060].

Ironically, the one thing we can safely rule out is that the Silurians are from the actual Silurian Era, around 438 to 408 million years ago. Life on Earth's surface was limited to the first plants, and the dominant species were coral reefs. The first jawed fishes evolved during this era. If nothing else, in terms of *Doctor Who* continuity (according to *City of Death*), this is before life on Earth starts. It's Dr Quinn who coins the name "Silurian" in *Doctor Who and the Silurians*. Despite the name being scientifically inaccurate, everyone at Wenley Moor – including the Doctor – uses it. We don't learn what the reptile people call themselves, but the Doctor calls them "Silurians" to their face and they don't correct him. The on-screen credits also use the term.

In *The Sea Devils*, when Jo calls the reptile people "Silurians", the Doctor replies, "That's a complete misnomer. The chap that discovered them must have got the period wrong. Properly speaking, they should have been called the Eocenes". Yet the Doctor never uses the "correct" term. The novelisation of *Doctor Who and the Silurians* (called *The Cave Monsters*) called them "reptile people", and the word "Silurian" only appears as a UNIT password. The description "sea devil" is coined by Clark, the terrified sea fort worker in *The Sea Devils*, and the term appears in the on-screen credits for all six epi-

sodes. Captain Hart refers to them as "Sea Devils" as though that's their name. For the rest of the story, the humans tend to call them "creatures" while the Doctor and Master refer to them as "the people".

By *Warriors of the Deep* and *Blood Heat*, however, the reptiles have adopted the inaccurate human terms for their people. *Bloodtide* starts with a flashback where Silurians refer to themselves by that name in their own era. In *Love and War*, we learn that the Silurians of the future "liked to be called Earth Reptiles now", and that term is also used in a number of other novels. The designation "homo reptilia" that crops up in a number of places is scientifically illiterate. In *Blood Heat*, the Doctor uses the term "psionsauropodomorpha".

In *Doctor Who and the Silurians*, Quinn has a globe of the Earth showing the continents forming one huge land mass, the implication being that it's the world the Silurians would have known. *The Scales of Injustice* follows this cue. Scientists call this supercontinent Pangaea, and date it to 250 to 200 million years ago. Again, this seems too early, as it predates the time of the dinosaurs.

That said, while most fans have assumed, and the tie-in media stories have often stated, that the Silurians come from the same time as the dinosaurs (around 165 to 65 million years ago, according to science, *Benny: The Adolescence of Time* and the Doctor in *Earthshock*), only recently has the new series acknowledged – particularly through the Silurian ark-ship with fifty dinosaur species aboard (*Dinosaurs on a Spaceship*) – that the Silurians were contemporaries of any known dinosaurs. *UNIT: Assembled* states that the Silurians experimented upon dinosaurs from the Cretaceous Period (which follows the end of the Jurassic, and lasted 145 million BC to about 66 million BC).

In *Doctor Who and the Silurians*, the Silurians have a "guard dog" that's a mutant, five-fingered species of tyrannosaur that the Doctor can't identify, and in *Warriors of the Deep*, we see the lumbering Myrka. While it might seem obvious to cite the extinction of the dinosaurs and the fall of Silurian civilisation as owing to the same events, it's a connection only made (loosely) on screen when Madame Vastra says she witnessed the horrors inflicted on her people by the red leech "sixty five million years" ago (*The Crimson Horror*), and later mentions in *Deep Breath* that she last saw a tyrannosaur when she was a little girl. However, we know from *Earthshock* that the dinosaurs were wiped out in completely different circumstances than the catastrophe that made the Silurians enter hibernation.

The key plot point with the Silurians' story is not whether or not they existed at the time of the dinosaurs, it's that as their civilisation thrived, the apes who were humanity's ancestors were mere pests. The Sea Devil leader in *The Sea Devils* says "my people ruled the Earth when man was only an ape". *Bloodtide* says the

continued on page 1037...

Ice: a crystalline energy storage method.[268]

Madame Vastra was among those to enter hibernation, and would awaken in the nineteenth century.[269]

? - "Twilight of the Silurians"[270] **->** Apes in the wild were beginning to organise into packs and attack vulnerable Silurians. One ape, Kin, had emerged as a leader and was captured. Many Silurians viewed the threat of the approaching moon as a scare story, but new calculations revealled they were merely five days from disaster. Led by Kin, the apes escaped by rebelling against their captors.

? - BLOODTIDE[271] **->** The surface of the Earth became a freezing wasteland. The Silurian scientist Tulok genetically augmented some of the apes to improve their flavour, and as a side-effect they also become sentient. As the Silurian Triad entered hibernation, Tulok was banished to the sur-

face for the crime of illicit experimentation. He was rescued by his friend Sh'vak. They went to the hibernation chambers, and sabotaged the controls so that most of the species would not revive when planned.

> = The Valeyard and Ellie deposited an alarm clock that would wake up the Silurian scientist Tulok and the clans with him. In future, the Silurians would accept humanity into their culture.[272]

The entire Silurian civilisation went into hibernation; they planned to sleep for thousands of years.[273] The Silurians entered hibernation over a prolongued period.[274]

The Silurians retired to their vast subterranean hibernation chambers, but the catastrophe they had predicted didn't happen – instead, the rogue planetoid

group of Silurians overslept the chosen time that *homo reptilia* was supposed to awaken, unless their ship was slaved by remote to systems on Earth, so was subject to the sabotage perpetrated in *Bloodtide*.

268 *The Silurian Gift*

269 *A Good Man Goes to War*

270 Dating "Twilight of the Silurians" (*DWW* #21-22) - It's "millions of years before history began". There's a note to the effect that the Silurians are also known as Eocenes.

271 Dating *Bloodtide* (BF #22) - It's set at the time the Silurians are going into hibernation, "over a million years ago", and "ten years" after Earth's surface has become uninhabitable. In *Doctor Who and the Silurians* and *The Scales of Injustice*, it's stated that the Silurians don't revive because Earth's climate stabilises below the levels the Silurians set. In *Bloodtide*, Tulok claims he prevented the reactivation, and the Doctor finds evidence of his sabotage.

272 *Unbound: He Jests at Scars*, playing off *Bloodtide*.

273 *Cold Blood*

274 *UNIT S4: Assembled*, at odds with *Bloodtide*.

275 *Doctor Who and the Silurians*

276 *Cold Blood*. It's unclear if Malokeh's family remained awake the whole time, or periodically woke up to check progress, just as it's not explained why they didn't bother waking the other Silurians at any point after they realised the Earth was habitable once more.

277 "Twenty million years, give or take" before *Eternity Weeps*, according to Benny.

278 See The Creation of the Cybermen sidebar.

279 *The Doctor Falls*, referencing Cybermen first seen in, respectively, *The Tenth Planet*; *The Tomb of the Cybermen* (or possibly earlier in *The Moonbase*); *Rise of the Cybermen/The Age of Steel* (or, arguably, *Dark Water/ Death in Heaven*); *The Invasion* and "The World Shapers" (or, pedantically, *The Keys of Marinus*); *World Enough and Time/The Doctor Falls*. (This creates a curious contradic-

tion, in that "The World Shapers" established that Marinus and Planet 14 were in fact the same planet, but here they're named separately.)

The fan consensus has long been that all Cybermen had a common origin, although there were alternate theories. (Earlier versions of this book suggested that it might be more of a common process than something that originated in one place – see the "Cybermen... Fashion Victims?" sidebar, which has been updated for this edition.) While the first draft script of *The Moonbase* and the Target novelisations of sixties Cybermen stories insisted that the Cybermen originated on Telos, and *Rise of the Cybermen/The Age of Steel* had shown the Cybus Industries models as developing on Earth in a parallel universe, most *Doctor Who* reference works took it as read that the Cybermen originated on Mondas, and all Cybermen to follow (from our universe, at least) were in some sense "descended" from them. *The Doctor Falls* makes it clear this is not the case. According to that story, Cybermen flourish wherever humanity exists.

280 The first Doctor attributes this as happening "millions of years" before *The Tenth Planet* [1986]. *Whoniverse* (BBC, p158), however, thinks Mondas was thrown from orbit "billions of years ago".

281 *The Tenth Planet*, and elaborated in *Spare Parts*.

282 According to the sixth Doctor in *Attack of the Cybermen*. The implication seems to be that Mondas left the solar system deliberately and under its own power. However, *Spare Parts* shows the propulsion unit first being used at the far end of Mondas' journey.

283 *The Quantum Archangel*

284 Dating "The Cybermen" (*DWM* #215-238) - "The Cybermen" strip covered the early history of Mondas. It places the creation of the Cybermen in the Age of the Reptile People, which may or may not support the date for the creation of the Cybermen less than five million years ago given in "The World Shapers" (see the When

settled into orbit around Earth and become its moon. Because the Silurians' hibernation mechanism was defective, they failed to revive as planned. In the Silurians' absence, the apes began to evolve a greater degree of intelligence. Before long, the only trace remaining of the reptile people were the race memories of these first hominids, the ancestors of humankind.[275] Through the millennia, the family of the Silurian scientist Malohkeh monitored the evolution of the apes as they became human.[276]

The planetoid was the moon containing the Museum of the Cthalctose. The gravitational forces wrecked havoc on Earth, destroying many Silurian shelters. Race memories of this event survived in human mythology as a great flood.[277]

The Birth of the Cybermen

There have been a number of accounts of the origins of the Cybermen.[278]

Owing to parallel evolution, the Cybermen were born in multiple locations through a progression of people plus technology minus the humanity. Wherever people existed, the Cybermen came to exist. The Cybermen would establish themselves on worlds including Mondas, Telos, Earth, Planet 14 and Marinus, and aboard a Mondasian colony ship.[279]

Millions of years ago, a twin planet to Earth – Mondas – was home to a race identical to humanity (indeed, Mondas was an old name for Earth). Mondas started to drift out to the edge of space.[280]

It soon became clear that the Mondasian race was becoming more sickly. Their life spans were shortening dramatically and they could only survive by replacing diseased organs and wasted limbs with metal and plastic substitutes. A new race was born.[281]

> "Mondas had a propulsion unit, a tribute to Cyber-engineering – though why they should want to push a planet through space, I have no idea." [282]

Mondas had been created by the Constructors of Destiny to research collective intelligence.[283]

? - "The Cybermen"[284] **->** On Earth's twin planet of Mondas, the Silurians created monsters: the all-devouring Titan R'lyeh and the giant Golgoth, the distillation of the greatest reptilian bloodstock. The Silurians eventually imprisoned them.

Mondas spun away from the sun, but was still habitable. The Silurians became tyrants, the unquestioned rulers of the world and augmented the apes to make cybernetic servants. Eventually, the reptiles were driven into hiberna-

continued from page 1035...

Silurians ruled "while humanity was still in its infancy", and goes on to specify that the apes at the time were Australopith-ecus. The earliest evidence for that genus is around four million years ago – which ties in with the date for the earliest humans in *Image of the Fendahl*. Although *Doctor Who* continuity has established that humanity dates back millions of years more than scientists would accept, it doesn't seem to stretch anything like as far as the Eocene, 55 to 38 million years ago.

We don't know how long Silurian civilisation stood. One solution to the dating problem might be to say that it lasted for tens or even hundreds of millions of years, from before the dinosaurs (and surviving their extinction) through to the time of the apemen. But, all accounts have the reptile people as a technologically-advanced, innovative, stable and centrally-controlled civilisation. When they entered hibernation, they were merely "centuries" ahead of the twentieth century humans. This would seem to point to a civilisation lasting thousands of years rather than millions.

tion by worsening conditions.

After a thousand years, and the Millennium Winter, the Cybermen had evolved from the augmented apes. They destroyed their former masters and set out to conquer the planet, but soon discovered – when they accidentally released R'lyeh – that they were not the only surviving creations of the lizard kings. A lost Cyber-mission returned as phantoms, then the Cybermen fought necromantic Sea Devils and their deity, Golgoth. He created a son, then destroyed himself and the Cybermen in a battle lasting 40 days and nights. The Cyber-civilisation fell.

Marinus, the Voord and the Cybermen

Mondas and Marinus were the same planet.[285]

The Voord sought to bring the "gift" of their leadership to all people, believing that peace wasn't possible while opposing cultures existed. The original Voord – their "blood tree" – included Tarlak, Nebrin and Yartek, who were fitted with Voord masks at an early age. The Voord "harvested" other races, bestowing their masks – equipped with neuro-analyzers that could assess loyalty – onto those who submitted to Voord rule. Subjects deemed worthy became Voord, and were amalgamated into the Voord telepathic network, whereas the masks killed those who felt doubt. The new Voord were genetically augmented, and could live for a thousand years. Voord custom prohibited forcing masks upon the unwilling.

Yartek led an expedition of Voord to the planet Marinus...[286]

? – THE KEYS OF MARINUS[287] **->** The people of the planet Marinus built the Conscience: a machine that originally served as an impartial judge, but eventually became capable of radiating a force that eliminated crime, fear and violence for seven centuries. Yartek, the Voord leader, learned how to resist the Conscience, and thus his followers robbed and cheated without any resistance. The scientist Arbitan deactivated the Conscience, hiding the five micro-keys needed to operate it around the planet; this prevented the Voord from using the device to control the population.

The first Doctor, Susan, Ian and Barbara arrived on Arbitan's island. They recovered all the keys on Arbitan's behalf, but returned to find that Yartek had killed Arbitan and taken control of the Conscience. Ian tricked Yartek by giving him a facsimile of one of the keys, but once it was inserted into the Conscience, the duplicate broke under the strain. The Conscience exploded, killing Yartek.

DOMAIN OF THE VOORD[288] **->** The Voord's water-based technology helped them dominate the ocean planet Hydra, which had only one land mass: the continent of Predora. A year after, the first Doctor, Ian, Barbara and Susan aided the Predoran resistance in ruining the Voord telepathic network. The Predorans reclaimed their world as Overseer Tarlak and other natural-born Voord were deprived of footsoldiers.

(=) "Four Doctors" (Titan) -> Owing to paradoxes and timeline alterations in the Last Great Time War, the Voord became a formidable power. The tenth, eleventh and twelfth Doctors combined efforts to regress the Voord along their own timeline, returning them to their original state. The eleventh Doctor proposed arranging for the Voord to become members of the wider community of species.

? - "The Cybermen"[289] **->** Three thousand years after the fall of their civilisation, the Cybermen were legends to the humans that ruled Mondas. Once again, the planet's orbit decayed. All life on the planet was extinguished, except for the reborn Cybermen.

Did the Silurians Rule the Earth? sidebar).
285 "The World Shapers"
286 The background to *The Keys of Marinus*, as given in *Domain of the Voord*. The latter story establishes that Voord can live for a thousand years, which patches a continuity hole in *The Keys of Marinus* (in which errant statements add up to Yartek being at least seven hundred years old). Also, as Tarlak and Yartek are of the same generation (meaning Tarlak must be at least eight hundred when *Domain of the Voord* rolls around), the Voord must come into being no more than a couple of centuries before *Marinus*.

Domain of the Voord indicates that Marinus isn't the Voord's original homeworld, which is reportedly destroyed in the UNIT Era (*DC 2: Beachhead*). The eighth Doctor's insistence in that story that the Voord homeworld "didn't [historically] die at any point anywhere near this timezone" also mitigates against it being Mondas, which perished in 1986 (*The Tenth Planet*).
287 Dating *The Keys of Marinus* (1.5) - There is no way of dating this story in relation to Earth's history, but taking the comic strips into account, it has to happen before "The World Shapers". As it's set on Mondas, the only place it can fit is after the first fall of the Cyberman civilisation seen in "The Cybermen".

There's confusion within the chronology of the story – Arbitan seems to state that Yartek is at least 1300 years old (as the Conscience was built two thousand years ago, and Yartek broke its conditioning after seven centuries). Arbitan has been working to upgrade the Conscience to defeat the Voord, and he and his followers have hidden the micro-keys around the planet, but there's no indication of how long Arbitan's been at work. Arbitan is mortal and feeling the effects of old age, and there's nothing to suggest anyone on Marinus has anything other than a normal human lifespan. *Domain of the Voord* reconciles some of the aforementioned discrepancies, claiming that the Voord are genetically enhanced beings who can, in fact, live for a thousand years.
288 Dating *Domain of the Voord* (BF EA #1.1) - It's "over a hundred years"/"a century" since Yartek died (*The Keys of Marinus*). At least two months pass within the story.
289 Dating "The Cybermen" (*DWM* #215-238) - It's "three thousand years" after the previous strip.

THE CREATION OF THE CYBERMEN: The origin of the Cybermen (in our universe, at least) has never been depicted on television, but the broad facts were established in *The Tenth Planet*, with additional information in *Attack of the Cybermen*. *World Enough and Time/The Doctor Falls*, it seems, occurs in the same time zone, but pertains to a different group.

DWM has offered two distinct origins of the Cybermen on Mondas itself, Big Finish a third. (The creator of the Cybermen, Gerry Davies, pitched his own origin story for television in the eighties, and this was reprinted in Virgin's *Cybermen* book.)

The three origin stories that were made might seem to contradict each other, but none of them contradict what we learn on TV. They can, with a little imaginative licence, all be reconciled with each other.

"The World Shapers" appears to diverge the furthest from the television account, roping in the planet Marinus and making the Cybermen the descendants of the Voord from *The Keys of Marinus*, but the story doesn't contradict anything like as much as it seems. The Voord are human underneath their wetsuits, and they become Cybermen to survive global environmental collapse. It would mean Marinus is Earth's twin planet – which is a stretch, but not an enormous one. (We know from *The Keys of Marinus* that it's a planet where humans, wolves, chickens, grapes and pomegranates can all be found.) The issue of Marinus/Mondas leaving the solar system isn't addressed, but neither is it ruled out.

"The Cybermen" strip in *DWM* takes fan speculation that links the Cybermen and Silurians, and is more consciously mythological in tone.

Spare Parts has, perhaps, the most orthodox interpretation of what we're told in *The Tenth Planet* – the civilisation on Mondas is roughly the equivalent of the mid-twentieth century, with a sickly population surviving in subterranean cities. Mondas travels into interstellar space, and as it does so, the population need to take existing medical technology to extremes to survive. Note that for a third time, an established *Doctor Who* race is part of the Cyberman recipe, as here the fifth Doctor's physiology provides the template for the future Cybermen.

These stories can be placed in order. The *DWM* *Cybermen* strip comes first – it's the only one that depicts Mondas leaving its original orbit. Not only that, it establishes that there's a period of three thousand years when Mondas settled into a new orbit where the Cyber-civilisation has collapsed and an advanced, fragmented human civilisation dominates. This is an ideal place to fit *The Keys of Marinus* and "The World Shapers" – all it needs is for (some of) the humans on Mondas now to think of their planet as "Marinus".

Again, this seems like a stretch – and, of course, it isn't what any of the writers intended or planned. But there *are* elements of Marinus technology in *The Keys of Marinus* that look remarkably like remnants or precursors of Cyber-technology: the Conscience itself is based around the idea of negative emotions being eliminated to create an ordered society and is built with "micro circuits"; the Troughton era Cybermen had hypnotic and sleep-inducing technology much like that of the city of Morphoton; in episode three, Darrius' experiments, like those of the Voord in "The World Shapers", have increased the "tempo" of nature; there's a group of soldiers frozen in ice; the Voord and Cybermen are the only two monsters the Doctor's ever met who were human once, have handles on their heads and wear wetsuits.

So... Mondas settled into its new orbit and became known as Marinus. Within a thousand years, the Conscience of Marinus was built and soon came to control the population. For seven hundred years, the planet knew total peace. Then Yartek learned how to resist the Conscience's influence – it's hard not to picture the second Doctor breaking Cyber-hypnosis in *The Wheel in Space* and *The Invasion*. The Voord's physical appearance might mean they've found some remnants of the legendary Cyber civilisation. They haven't abandoned emotions in favour of logic and the good of society, though – ironically, it's rather the opposite. If Yartek is part-Cyberman, it might explain why he apparently lives at least thirteen hundred years. Neither is it a paradox that Yartek manages to resist the Conscience – yes, the Conscience should have quelled his urge to break the conditioning if his intent was purely malicious, but it could have been an accident or motivated by... well, the fairly uncontroversial belief that having free will is a good thing. (The Doctor says as much at the end of *The Keys of Marinus* itself, and in many other stories.)

"The World Shapers" sees the Voord consciously evolving into Cybermen to survive sudden environmental collapse. We have to speculate to join the dots, but it's not a wild thing to do. The surface of Mondas is, once again, uninhabitable for humans. The *DWM* "Cybermen" strip explicitly states it also leaves its new orbit. The Voord understand the problem and are ready for it – they now achieve their aim, and take control of the planet (presumably there are at least some other survivors), and build subterranean cities (or merely extend them – their base is already underground in "The World Shapers"). Perhaps the most highly-evolved Voord – the ones who had become the Cybermen at the end of "The World Shapers" – became the Committee from *Spare Parts*. It fits together surprisingly well, save for the Doctor in *The Doctor Falls* suggesting that Mondas and Marinus are in fact different planets.

Spare Parts itself is set later – how much later isn't specified – when the people of Mondas are used to their sickly, subterranean life. Without the Worldshaper, while they know their destiny, the early Cybermen have had to learn the science of cybernetics gradually – until the fifth Doctor comes along, at any rate.

The Death of Jamie McCrimmon

? - "The World Shapers"[290] **->** The sixth Doctor, Peri and Frobisher landed on a deserted area of the ocean on Marinus. They discovered a TARDIS and its dying pilot, who whispered "Planet 14" before dying, his regenerations exhausted. His TARDIS was an ostentatious new model that told the Doctor they had been sent by the High Council to investigate temporal disturbances.

Time had sped up on Marinus. The new TARDIS returned to Gallifrey, the Doctor and his companions to their Ship. The Doctor remembered hearing about Planet 14 in his second incarnation, but not the context. The travellers headed to the eighteenth century to meet up with Jamie McCrimmon – his companion at the time – to see if he remembered. As they left, a Worldshaper ship arrived at Marinus – Worldshapers reformed uninhabited planets, but were banned years after the Yxia System collapsed.

The Doctor's TARDIS returned a week later than it left... but the planet was a now rocky desert. The Voord captured the Worldshaper and used it to rapid-evolve themselves and sculpt time. They were becoming the Cybermen. The Doctor and Jamie sneaked into the Voord base and met the future CyberController. Jamie sacrificed himself, aging to death to destroy the Worldshaper. Time accelerated so that geological processes occurred in front of the Doctor's eyes. The effect died down, and the Doctor emerged from the TARDIS to find a group of Time Lords present.

Marinus had become Mondas. The Doctor lobbied for the Cybermen to be prevented from coming into being, but the Time Lords told him things were in hand.

A sect from Mondas, the Faction, believed in total conversion into cyborgs. They were at odds with the mainstream, who viewed the technology as a last resort. The Faction left Mondas for Planet 14.[291]

---

290 Dating "The World Shapers" (*DWM* #127-129) - The story is set no more than five million years in the past, as the Time Lords calculate that the Cybermen will become a force for peace in that time, and they haven't even by our far future.

The Doctor mentions the Fishmen of Kandalinga, from the first *Doctor Who Annual*, and the TARDIS initially lands on a platform very like the one seen in the illustrations from that story. However, as the name suggests, that story was set on Kandalinga, not Marinus. WHEN WERE THE MONDASIAN CYBERMEN CREATED?: It's unclear when Mondas leaves the solar system. In *The Tenth Planet*, the Doctor says it was "millions of years" ago. The Cyberman Krang says it was "aeons", and an aeon is a billion years. But the Mondasians were "exactly like" humans when Mondas started to drift away. As the land masses of the "twin" planets of Earth and Mondas are identical, it seems logical that life evolved in the same way and at the same rate on both worlds (we have to gloss over the fact that aliens such as the Daemons and Scaroth accelerated human development on Earth, but presumably not on Mondas).

"The World Shapers" sets the origins of the Cybermen within five million years of the present day – the Time Lords, at least, believe the Cybermen will be a force for good five million years after their creation. David Banks, in both his *Cybermen* book and his novel *Iceberg*, dated Mondas' departure to 10,000 BC. *The Terrestrial Index* concurred. Banks suggested that the "edge of space" was the Oort Cloud surrounding the solar system. The audio *Spare Parts* contradicts that, saying that Mondas reaches the Cherrybowl Nebula, and states that Mondas left orbit because of the moon's arrival. *Real Time* says Mondas left "millennia" ago. In a story outline for a proposed sixth Doctor story, *Genesis of the*

Cybermen, Gerry Davis set the date of the Cybermen's creation at "several hundred years BC". *Timelink* notes that as the Fendahl planet was the "fifth" 12 million years ago, Mondas must have already left its orbit by that point.

Over the years, a number of fans – including the first two versions of *Ahistory* – have speculated that the Mondasians and the Silurians were contemporaries, linking the disaster that put the Silurians into hibernation with the one that threw Mondas out of its orbit. There's little to either support or contradict this in the stories themselves. The Cyberman design seems to echo the Silurian third eye at the top of the head, but the Cybermen clearly aren't cyborg Silurians. Not only are we told in *The Tenth Planet* that the Cybermen "were exactly like you [humans] once", the same story shows them with human hands, not reptilian ones. "The Cybermen" strip in *DWM*, though, ingeniously solves that problem by depicting the Cybermen as descendents of apes augmented by the Silurians.

The Virgin edition of *Ahistory* suggested that Mondas was subject to time dilation, explaining why the Cybermen weren't more advanced. *Timelink* and *The Death of Art* reached the same conclusion. However, the continents on Mondas are exactly like those on Earth, so this theory doesn't account for the identical continental drift, assuming such a thing affected the ancient Earth in the *Doctor Who* universe.

291 "Ten thousand years" before the novel *Iceberg*, which uses the same dating system as David Banks' book *Cybermen*. This schism is the given explanation for the difference in appearance – and apparent lack of contact – between the Cybermen from *The Tenth Planet* and *The Invasion*.

292 Dating *World Enough and Time/The Doctor Falls* (X10.11-12) - While Missy initially assumes that the col-

The Last Days of Humanity on Mondas, Bill and Nardole Leave the TARDIS, Missy and Harold Saxon Kill One Another

WORLD ENOUGH AND TIME / THE DOCTOR FALLS[292] -> En route to pick up its charges, a 400-mile colony ship of Mondasian manufacture fell under the pull of a black hole. The ship's skeleton crew reversed engines – while the ship slowly pulled away, the black hole's gravity slowed time on the ship's upper floors. Mere minutes passed on Floor 000 as centuries went by on the lower decks. The progeny of the crewmembers there soon numbered in the thousands. Some resided in a solar farm on Floor 507.

The Harold Saxon Master burnt out his TARDIS' dematerialization circuit while trying to escape the black hole's gravity well. He ruled the lower decks for a time, but the people rebelled, and he hid among them as "Mr Razor". As the environment decayed, Razor and various physicians developed Cyber-technology, to upgrade the populace into Mondasian Cybermen.

The twelfth Doctor, Bill, Nardole and Missy – Harold's future self – answered a distress call from the ship's bridge. Bill was fatally wounded, and so proto-Cybermen figures took her to the lower decks for repair. By the time the Doctor's trio could follow, Bill had spent ten years in Razor's company... and been upgraded into a Cyberman. The Doctor turned the Cybermen against Harold, and his band withdrew to Floor 507.

---

ony ship is from Earth, she later confirms this ship is "from Mondas". Missy's computer scan registers Mondas as an upside-down Earth (as in *The Tenth Planet*), and the readout identifies it as the fourth world in a solar system with ten planets (presumably Sol). The story's background, at least, has to be set before the Mondasians become Cybermen – in other words, the ship was launched (and this story is set) the "aeons ago" spoken of in *The Tenth Planet*, before *Spare Parts*.

It's easy to imagine a link between the construction of the colony ship and the disaster that befalls Mondas – that the ship has been built by the Mondasians to evacuate at least some of the population. If that was the plan, then it would seem viable. While the exact sizes of the human space arks in *The Ark*, *The Ark in Space*, *Frontios* and *The Beast Below* are never specified, judging by the model shots, they seem almost tiny by comparison. This 400-mile long colony ship would serve very well as a space ark, and Mondasian civilisation would be preserved.

There are problems with this interpretation. No one in the story ever suggests that Mondas is in imminent danger (the "Project Exodus" referred to is deliberately misleading, but proves to be the plan the Cybermen have to leave their deck and conquer the rest of the colony ship). The ship is never referred to as an ark, or in any similar terms. Nardole calls it a "colony ship" and the janitor Jorj doesn't contradict him, adding "it's brand new. The colonists haven't arrived yet. We were on our way to pick them up". It's possible Missy is looking at an old archive of Mondas before the disaster that saw it break orbit, but the very strong inference is that her information is current, and the disaster hasn't happened yet.

While it's not entirely clear, it seems Missy's wrong, and the ship isn't "from Mondas", it's been built somewhere *other* than Mondas, and is being delivered there, where the plan is to pick up colonists and take them to another (unspecified) planet. Whatever the case, there's a black hole on the route of its maiden voyage, so it's travelling outside the Solar System. Jorj is blue-skinned, and apparently a member of the same unnamed species which has popped up a lot in the revived series (see the Blue in the Face sidebar). Even if this is the only colony ship the Mondasians ever had, and even if alien shipbuilders constructed it for them, in this story the Mondasians are a spacefaring culture, in contact with at least one other spacefaring culture.

The picture of Mondas we get from *World Enough and Time* looks very different from the desperate, desolate, impoverished world of *The Tenth Planet* and *Spare Parts*. These Mondasians would find preserving their civilisation almost trivially easy. If they are contemporaries of the Silurians, that might rule out the conquest of Earth, as the Silurians seem more advanced – it's worth noting that the Silurian ark in *Dinosaurs on a Spaceship* is "approximately ten million square kilometres" and "a ship the size of Canada". If they are contemporaries of the Ice Warriors, the natives of Mars might have been able to fight off a Mondasian invasion. The colony ship, though, is able to sustain its population for centuries and can apparently travel interstellar distances. The galaxy would seem to be its oyster... right up to the point it gets snagged by a black hole.

Harold Saxon names the events of this story as "the genesis of the Cybermen", and Missy says we're "watching the Cybermen get started". They clearly think that the Cybermen here will return to Mondas, convert the population there, and then begin their galactic conquests. The Doctor quickly proves them wrong – the colony ship Cybermen evolve independently. The first models are "Mondasian Cybermen", but they develop into the Cyberiad (*Nightmare in Silver*) and Cybus (*Rise of the Cybermen*) models without any contact with the outside universe. Perhaps after *The Doctor Falls*, the colony ship will break free, return to Mondas and Cyber-convert the people there – but that's not something we see on screen, and the Doctor makes it clear that even if they don't, the people of Mondas will become Cybermen. All civilisations discover the technology. *The Tenth Planet* and *Spare Parts* state that the people of Mondas convert out of necessity (so, not

The Doctor readied to fight a hopeless battle on behalf of the Floor 507 settlers. Missy decided to aid the Doctor, and fatally stabbed her former self. In turn, Harold vowed that he would never stand with the Doctor, and killed Missy with his laser screwdriver – an energy burst powerful enough to cancel out regeneration. Harold returned to his TARDIS with Missy's spare dematerialisation circuit, fated to regenerate into Missy and not remember these events.

Nardole evacuated the settlers to another solar farm on Floor 502. The Doctor endured many fatal Cyberblasts, but largely wiped out the Cybermen by detonating Floor 507. As Bill mourned for her fallen friend, her tears summoned the Pilot – who made Bill into a space-oil being like herself. They laid the Doctor to rest in his TARDIS, then left for new adventures.

The Ship took the dying Doctor to meet his first self, in 1986. Nardole looked over the settlers on 502, and vowed to deal with the Cybermen in the lower decks.

The Birth of the Cybermen on Mondas

? - SPARE PARTS[293] **->** The fifth Doctor and Nyssa arrived on Mondas when it was at the furthest point in its journey away from the Sun, on the edge of the Cherrybowl Nebula, "a crucible of unstable energy". Civilisation survived under the surface of the planet. Mondas was rife with diseases like TB, and "heartboxes" were common for cardiovascular problems. Mondas was ruled by a bionic group mind, the Committee, who were building Cybermen capable of working on the desolate surface of Mondas. The Cybermen were engineering a propulsion system to deflect Mondas away from the Nebula.

A scan of a tertiary lobe in the Doctor's brain solved various organ rejection problems that had plagued the planet's Cyber-program; the Cyber-templates were augmented with this new design. The Doctor realised he could do little to prevent history from unfurling as planned.

During the Miocene Era, around twenty-five million

because droves of colony ship cybermen suddenly descended from the skies and forced the change upon them), as a last resort, but this doesn't contradict the Doctor – while all civilisations develop the technology and see a proportion of their population become Cybermen, clearly in the normal course of events, others in those civilisations resist conversion (see *The Age of Steel* and *The Doctor Falls*). On Mondas, those who didn't convert perished, because of the harsh conditions.

Where does this leave the dating of this story? It's set at a time when Mondas is still in its original orbit, populated by an advanced human civilisation with the ability to travel interstellar distances, in contact with at least the blue-skinned alien race. This story is not set around the time Mondas is blasted out of its orbit, it's set comfortably before, during some prior – the term is a little ironic when referring to Cybermen – golden age.

BLUE IN THE FACE: The revived TV series has featured a number of appearances by bald, blue-skinned humanoids, presumably because blue facepaint is a relatively easy way to make a television extra look alien for a show on a budget. There have been more substantial roles – the Steward and the plumber Raffalo in *The End of the World*, Dorium Maldovar (*The Pandorica Opens*, *A Good Man Goes to War*, *The Wedding of River Song*), the mining station worker Dahh-Ren in *Oxygen* and the janitor Jorj in *World Enough and Time*. (Here we're not including blue-skinned beings with significant non-human attributes, such as the Moxx of Balhoon in *The End of the World*, or the insectoid steward Flemming in *The Husbands of River Song*, who is jubilant because his offspring have recently eaten their mother.)

Raffalo says she is from Crespallion, which she clarifies isn't a planet, adding "Crespallion's part of the

Jaggit Brocade, affiliated to the Scarlet Junction, in Complex 56". *The Doctor Who Encyclopedia* duly names the species "Crespallions". Crespallions have yellow eyes with quasi-reptilian pupils. They may not be the same species as the other blue people we see, who have eyes like human beings. Then again, as humanity itself has evolved into a vast array of posthuman species by that time, this might represent what the Blue People become in the far future. *Gridlock*, set in the same historical era, doesn't feature blue people, but does feature red and white people.

It's notable, and surely no coincidence, that Dahh-Ren and Jorj have names that are homonyms of common modern British names.

Just as there are many planets in the *Doctor Who* universe with species who look remarkably like human beings, there may be many planets with people who look remarkably like human beings except they have blue skin. In the 1960s *Doctor Who* comic strips, there was something of a trend for blue-skinned aliens, most notably the "original Daleks", the Dals of Skaro.

No official source has confirmed whether these are all meant to be members of the same race. If they are, then the blue people have quietly become one of the most oft-recurring *Doctor Who* alien races, who were a spacefaring culture in the extremely ancient past (*World Enough and Time*) and the eyewateringly distant future (*The End of the World*).

293 Dating *Spare Parts* (BF #34) - There is no dating evidence in the story itself. It takes place when Mondas is at its farthest point from Earth and the implication is that the return journey will be much faster than the outward one, as it will be powered. *Spare Parts* could, then, take place a matter of decades before *The Tenth Planet* (and further evidence for this might be the Mondasian society of *Spare Parts* resembles Earth's in

years ago, the rocks on which Atlantis would later be built were formed.[294] Certain minerals that caused blue grass to grow would not be present in Wales for twenty million years.[295] Twenty million years ago on Earth, Creodonts – a cross between a hyena and a bear, and the largest mammalian predators ever to walk the planet – went extinct.[296]

The Origins of Man

It's unclear when humanity evolved, and it depends on one's definition of humanity. Some estimates have men walking the Earth six million years ago. The scientific consensus in the 1970s was about four million.[297] The Osirians helped a race of giant insects to build a civilisation on Mars, but became bored with them. The insects died out as other forces emerged on Mars.[298]

The Time Lords Time-Loop Planet Five

Twelve million years ago, on a nameless planet in our solar system that no longer exists, evolution went up a blind alley. Natural selection turned back on itself, and a creature – the Fendahl – evolved which prospered by absorbing the energy wavelengths of life itself. It consumed all life, including that of its own kind.

The Time Lords decided to destroy the entire planet, and hid the fact from posterity. But when the Time Lords acted it was too late, as the Fendahl had already reached Earth, probably taking in Mars on its way through. The Fendahl was buried, not killed. The energy amassed by the Fendahl was stored in a fossilised skull, and dissipated slowly as a biological transmutation field. Any appropriate life form that came within the field was altered so it ultimately evolved into something suitable for the Fendahl to use. The skull did not create man, but it may have affected his evolution. This would explain the dark side of man's nature.[299]

---

the mid-twentieth century).

That said, while it's never quite stated, Mondas seems to have left the solar system within the lifetimes of the older characters, not the "millions of years" the Doctor spoke of in *The Tenth Planet*. There's no indication that Mondas immediately set course for a return to the solar system. We know that the Cybermen didn't attend the Armageddon Convention (*Revenge of the Cybermen*) and that the Convention was signed in 1609 (*The Empire of Glass*), so that they were a force to be reckoned with by the seventeenth century.

It therefore seems fair to speculate that the Cybermen piloted Mondas around the galaxy for a long time (certainly millennia) before finally returning to their native solar system.

294 *The Underwater Menace*

295 The presence of blue grass in *The Hungry Earth* tips the Doctor off to the presence of Silurians.

296 *Forty-Five:* "False Gods". The terminology is a bit off here; creodonts were an entire order of mammals whose members included the Megistotherium, said to be the largest mammalian predator.

297 When asked in *Autumn Mist* when humanity evolved, the Doctor says "the accepted figure's about half a million years, though its really nearer six". It's only one suggestion that human origins in the *Doctor Who* universe stretch further than conventional scientific wisdom would have you think. According to *Image of the Fendahl*, the Fendahl skull arrived on Earth 12 million years ago, just as the first humanoid bipeds evolved – this is eight million years before Dr. Fendelman had believed.

298 "Millions of years" before *FP: Ozymandias*. Presumably, these are the Martians wiped out by the

Fendahl. It may also be a *Quatermass* in-joke, as *Quatermass and the Pit* depicted insectoid Martians who had become extinct millions of years before.

299 *Image of the Fendahl*

LIFE ON MARS: The Fendahl couldn't have wiped out all life on Mars, as the Ice Warriors come from Mars and lived there at least from the time of the Ice Age on Earth (*The Ice Warriors*) until the twenty-first century (*The Seeds of Death*) and apparently far further into the future (*The Curse of Peladon*). It should be noted that in *Image of the Fendahl*, the Doctor only speculates that the Fendahl attacked Mars.

As it happens, *Image of the Fendahl* is not the only occasion that the show seemingly ignores the existence of the Ice Warrior civilisation on the Red Planet. *The Ambassadors of Death* has manned missions to Mars that don't encounter the Ice Warriors (yet they *do* meet another alien race there – one that's not from Mars itself). *Pyramids of Mars*, as the name suggests, has the Doctor and Sarah visiting a pyramid on Mars and never mentioning the Ice Warriors. We never see UNIT encounter the Ice Warriors, although *Castrovalva* has the fifth Doctor mimic his previous selves, and seems (unless, in his post-regeneration confusion, he's just marrying together two unrelated elements) to refer to an adventure with the Brigadier and the Ice Warriors. In *The Christmas Invasion*, UNIT knows that there are Martians, and that they don't look like the Sycorax.

Humanity hasn't got as far as Mars by *The Seeds of Death*, explaining why they don't know about the Martians. It's harder to explain why Zoe, who is from a time when the solar system has been explored, is unaware of them.

Some fans (as well as sources like the FASA roleplay-

The Singing Towers of Darillium were built.[300] The Jovians evolved as sentient collections of dust, gas and vapour in Jupiter's atmosphere. They crafted a society that existed within their shared minds – a civilisation with ideas serving as its architecture – and kept their existence secret. There was no historical record of their impact on Earth's solar system after the emergence of humanity.[301]

c 12,000,000 BC - THE TAKING OF PLANET 5[302] ->

A Celestis outcast became concerned that the Celestis base of Mictlan might attract the Swimmers – beings large enough to crush the universe. The outcast hoped to destroy Mictlan before this occurred.

Using a Fictional Generator, the outcast brought the Elder Things from HP Lovecraft's work to life in Antarctica. This attracted Time Lord shock troops from the future, who slaughtered the Elder Things and subsequently readied a fleet of War-TARDISes. They intended to break the time-loop around Planet Five, hoping to use the Fendahl trapped within against the Time Lords' future Enemy.

A wounded TARDIS created a time fissure that would later be exploited by Professor Fendelman. The time-loop was breached, but this actually released the hyper-evolved Fendahl Predator: a Memeovore, capable of consuming conceptual thought. The Memeovore consumed Mictlan, and thus destroyed the Celestis, before the eighth Doctor banished it to the outer voids.

By now, the planets Delphon and Tersurus had developed their unique forms of communication.

The first true human became aware of herself and immediately developed a sense of self-doubt. The Scourge had established themselves in our universe.[303] It was believed that the 001 variant of Amethyst icosahedral plasmic virus No. 9007/41 came to reside in humanity during humankind's earliest evolution. Each human possessed one dormant particle of the virus, and passed it to their offspring.[304] The owl evolved on Earth around this time.[305]

Ten million years ago, a derelict primitive TARDIS from the war against the Vampires began orbiting the planet Clytemnestra. Human colonists from the Earth Empire of the thirtieth century would mistake it for a moon, and name it Cassandra.[306]

The Vo'lach feared that as the expanding universe would one day exhaust its matter. They constructed the Spire – a tower that would syphon matter from the future into the past – to prolong the universe's lifespan. From the moment of its activation, the Spire was a temporal paradox: if too successful, it would rob the Vo'lach of the motivation to build it in the first place. Two Planetcracker missiles came back from the twenty-sixth century and resolved the paradox by damaging the Spire, reducing its efficiency. As the missiles were of Vo'lach design, the Vo'lach became alarmed that their descendents were conquerors. To prevent this, the Vo'lach committed mass suicide.[307]

The Carnash Coi, monstrous entities from a distant galaxy, conquered Earth six million years ago. Their violent empire self-destructed, and one of their citadels submerged itself off the coast of what would become Alaska.

---

ing game) concluded that the Ice Warrior civilisation was subterranean – a view that for decades was practically taken for granted in the books and audios, even though evidence for it on screen only arrived with 2017's *Empress of Mars*. The books and audios have made further attempts to explain why the Ice Warriors are not well-known to future humanity. In particular, *Transit* featured a genocidal war fought in the late twenty-first century between Earth and Mars. Its vision of most Martians leaving the planet – with a few left behind as an underclass to the human colonists – is depicted in later stories such as *GodEngine* and *Fear Itself* (PDA).

Benny Summerfield is an expert on Martian history, but most accounts have her believing that the Martian civilisation is a dead one (or at the very least, that there are no Ice Warriors on Mars itself).

The Dying Days attempted to reconcile some of the UNIT-era accounts by depicting a Martian culture influenced by the Osirians, who are disturbed by a British space mission (and there's a fleeting reference to the aliens from *The Ambassadors of Death*). As it's set in 1997, it would explain why UNIT know what Martians look like in *The Christmas Invasion*, and some fans have interpreted the line in the TV episode as a reference to

the book.

300 "Millions of years" before *The Husbands of River Song*.

301 *The Jupiter Conjunction*

302 Dating *The Taking of Planet 5* (EDA #28) - It is "about twelve million years ago" (p71). The Elder Things aren't the same as the Great Old Ones seen in Lovecraft's work, so there's no direct clash with this story and the Great Old Ones seen elsewhere in the *Doctor Who* novels.

Delphon was mentioned in *Spearhead from Space*, Tersurus got a mention in *The Deadly Assassin* but didn't appear until the Comic Relief sketch *The Curse of Fatal Death*. According to *Alien Bodies*, the Raston robots (*The Five Doctors*) are built on Tersurus.

303 *The Shadow of the Scourge*

304 *Blue Forgotten Planet*

305 *Just War*

306 *So Vile a Sin*

307 9.25 million years before *Benny: Ghost Devices*.

308 *Lurkers at Sunlight's Edge*

309 *Frontios*. Date unknown, but it's long enough before the twentieth century that Turlough has the race memory, but doesn't otherwise seem to know the Tractators by name.

The Carnash Coi within slept, dreaming of future conquests.[308] **The people of Trion were so horrified by an infestation of Tractators, it became embedded in their race memory.**[309]

Five million years ago on Earth, the climate of Antarctica was tropical.[310] Millions of years ago, an advanced civilisation on Betrushia built an organic catalyzer to test species for survival traits. The catalyzer exceeded its design and threatened all life it encountered, causing the inhabitants to build an artificial ring system that constrained the creature to Betrushia.[311] The people of Kirbili wiped themselves out millions of years ago.[312] The Kaloczul were engineered as silicon-based lifeforms, more machine than organic, by a species that went extinct. They began terraforming worlds to make them agreeable to silicon-based life.[313]

Millions of years ago, the neighbouring worlds of Janus Prime and Menda – respectively inhabited by giant spiders and a race of humanoids – ended a war. They agreed to build a doomsday device as a deterrent against further hostilities, and constructed a device that, if needed, would move a moon of Janus Prime and a moon of Menda into parallel orbit around the Janus System's sun. A hyperspace link between the two moons would then turn the sun into a black hole. The spiders wiped out the Menda humanoids anyway, but not before the Mendans seeded Janus Prime with isotope decay bombs. This made the spiders devolve into savagery, leaving the doomsday device untouched until 2211.[314]

By the time of the Pliocene on Earth, the Martian civilisation equivalent of the Industrial Revolution had already taken place.[315]

c 3,639,878 BC - GENOCIDE[316] **->** A group of Tractites arrived from the future using a time tree. They established a colony on Earth, which threatened to wipe out humanity and give rise to a future where the Tractites controlled the planet. The eighth Doctor, aided by Jo Grant and Samantha Jones, tried to prevent this. Jo obliterated the Tractites and their colony with a laser cannon, preventing the aberrant future. The Doctor's Tractite ally, Kitig, stayed in this period to carve messages in rock for Jo and Sam to find 1.07 million years hence. At the end of his life, Kitig travelled back in time to destroy the time tree.

Three million years ago, civilisation had started on Veltroch.[317] When the People of the Worldsphere were young, their metaphors were powerful enough to restructure reality. In this manner, the concept of the "inner world" was seeded throughout the universe, and came to hollow out and reshape interior of the planet later known as Tyler's Folly. This facilitated the creation of Mankind Expects Pain, However Much It Seems To Outsiders (MEPHISTO), a conceptual entity who represented the need to feel pain even in a utopia.[318]

2,579,868 BC - GENOCIDE[319] **->** Captain Jacob Hynes, a genocidal UNIT member, arrived through time with a virus intended eliminate all mammalian life on Earth. Jo Grant and Sam Jones prevented him from releasing a deadly prion, and some primitive humans killed Hynes. A message from the eighth Doctor's Tractite ally, Kitig, enabled Jo and Sam to find the buried TARDIS and locate the Doctor 1.07 million years in the past.

The Seventh Doctor is Frozen for Millions of Years

? 2,500,000 BC - FROZEN TIME[320] **->** The Martians gave one of their number, Arakssor, a life sentence because he wanted to lead his people to war. Arakssor and about 20 of his followers were frozen in Antarctica, with a group of Martians watching over them. The guards were betrayed and Arakssor's warriors broke free. A firefight led to everyone involved being covered in ice – the seventh Doctor was present, fell into freezing water and went comatose. Sediment congealed around him in the centuries to follow, and he would remain frozen until 2012.

wih - Godfather Morlock of Faction Paradox studied a South American missing link that was two million years old.[321] A humanoid race sent probes out into the galaxy to build transference pylons capable of teleporting people between solar systems at the speed of light. Ninety-nine

---

310 *The Seeds of Doom*
311 *St. Anthony's Fire*
312 *The Quantum Archangel*
313 "Millions of years" before *TW: Fallout*.
314 *The Janus Conjunction*
315 *The Dying Days*
316 Dating *Genocide* (EDA #4) - It's 1.07 million years before 2,569,868 BC.
317 *The Dark Path*
318 Millions of years before *Benny: Down*.

319 Dating *Genocide* (EDA #4) - The precise date is given (p260).
320 Dating *Frozen Time* (BF #98) - The Doctor, upon his revival, says he was frozen "millions of years" ago. There is no evidence that Arakssor's imprisonment bears any relation to Varga's mission (*The Ice Warriors*), and it could substantially pre-date it.
321 *FP: The Eleven-Day Empire*

percent of the probes failed, but the remaining 1% allowed the Slow Empire to be established.[322]

The Ulanti developed "bioharmonics", wherein they transformed their entire planet into a musical instrument and produced a natural melody using the biological rhythms of their ecosystem. The Ulanti homeworld was an unspoilt wilderness, and its music was incredibly sublime. Nonetheless, the Ulanti died out two million years ago. Some of their music would survive in the archives on Nocturne.[323]

After crashing in what would become Chihuahua, Mexico, a cyborg-squid slathered itself in time-suspending vortex ice.[324] A million years ago, the Mastons of Centimminus Virgo became extinct.[325] Rocinate's TARDIS, with its Qwerm eggs inside, went dormant.[326] The Hoothi made the first moves in their plan to conquer Gallifrey. They enslaved the Heavenites, keeping them as a slave race and turning their planet into a beautiful garden world.[327]

The Tralsam-mavarians died out.[328] The planet Wrouth was an enormous diamond with a monetary value in excess of the number of molecules in the universe. For a million years, the planet had been defended by war asteroids. In that time, it attracted a number of attackers, including the Daleks (driven away by the Doctor and Captain Nekro) and the Gantacs.[329] An entity said to be "the spirit of the trees, the life force of nature" came to slumber in what would become Wells Wood in Stockbridge. A pagan cult came to worship this Green Man, a.k.a. Viridios.[330]

The Ice Warriors of Mars had space travel a million years ago.[331] Around the same time, diamonds were formed in the remnants of a Jovian planet in the Caledonian Reef.[332] **The earliest splinter of Scaroth gave humankind the secret of fire in his efforts to accelerate human development.**[333]

The Thal civilisation had begun half a million years ago on Skaro, and writings survive from this time.[334] A quarter of a million years ago, the Monks of Felsecar began collecting objects and information.[335] **Two hundred thousand years ago, *homo sapiens* – "the most vicious species of all" – began killing one another.**[336] As humans evolved, the alien entity that the TARDIS dropped off on primeval Earth was summoned. It took human form and existed "on the edge of fear", always seeking the TARDIS.[337] The Lobri were created in the collective unconscious of primitive humankind. They were xenophobia incarnate, living symbols of our fear of the alien.[338]

The planet Hitchemus was 7/8ths covered by ocean, and the shifting climate there threw the genetics of the indigenous species of tigers into flux. A generation of tigers

---

322 "Millions of years" before *The Slow Empire*. The Empire lasts "two million years" once it has been set up.
323 *Nocturne*
324 A cave expert hastily estimates this as "a million years" before *Vortex Ice*.
325 *Slipback*
326 "A million years" before *The Legends of River Song*: "River of Time".
327 *Love and War*
328 *A Device of Death*
329 "A million years" before "Invaders from Gantac".
330 Viridios claims to have slept for "a million years" before *The Eternal Summer*. In real life, Viridios is a Celtic deity whose name means "Green Man" in the Celtic languages and Latin. Altar stones to Viridios have been recovered from Roman Britain; in *Doctor Who* terms, though, there's no evidence that Viridios-worship went any further than the Stockbridge area, with the Doctor describing it as "highly localized".
331 *The Dying Days*. They would send an expedition to Earth, as seen in *The Ice Warriors*. Its loss presumably convinced them to use their scarce resources another way, and put them off conquering our planet.
332 *Synthespians™*
333 *City of Death*. The earliest known use of fire was around 700,000 BC. Supporting this, the "second splinter" of Scaroth seen on screen is presented (somewhat confusingly) as a Neanderthal.
334 Measured from *The Daleks*, in which the Doctor says that the Thal records "must go back nearly a half a million years".
335 *Love and War*
336 *The War Games*
337 "The Stockbridge Horror"
338 "Ground Zero"
339 "Hundreds of thousands of years" before *The Year of Intelligent Tigers*.
340 *DotD: Trouble in Paradise*
341 *The Ice Warriors*. Arden states that the Ice Warrior Varga comes from ice dating from "prehistoric times, before the first Ice Age". Arden's team have discovered the remains of mastodons and fossils in the ice before this time. In *Legacy*, the Doctor states that Varga "crashed on Earth millions of years ago". *Timelink* favoured that Varga's ship fell to Earth in "10,000 BC"; *About Time*, acknowledging the vagueness of the evidence, said it was some undetermined point between "1,000,000 BC" and "8,000 BC".
342 According to Benny in *The Dying Days*.
343 *An Unearthly Child, Ghost Light*.
THE FIRST ICE AGE: According to *Doctor Who*, the Ice Age was a single event around one hundred thousand years ago. In reality, there were waves of ice ages that lasted for hundreds of thousands of years as the ice advanced and retreated. We may now be living in an interglacial period. *An Unearthly Child* seems to take place at the end of the Ice Age: the caveman Za speaks of "the great cold" – although this might simply mean a

was born hyper-intelligent and built a weather control system. However, the tigers' progeny lacked the increased intelligence of their parents – presumably as a survival mechanism to prevent the tigers from over-developing their limited resources. Before passing on, the intelligent tigers built a hidden storehouse to preserve something of their developments. A generation of intelligent tigers would sporadically be born from time to time, with multiple generations of instinctive tigers in-between.[339]

The buffalo became the dominant race on Earth during a time of ice and snow, and was revered by humanity – who painted their likenesses on cave walls. Their reign ended on the Day of Disaster, when the linchpin of their mental gestalt – Bovin the Herd-Leader – was entombed in ice. The buffalo became ordinary livestock without Bovin's guiding influence, assuring humanity's ascendancy.[340]

The First Ice Age and Cavemen

A Martian ship crashed on Earth, and became encased at the foot of an ice mountain.[341] Ice Warrior spaceship designs changed little after this time.[342]

One hundred thousand years ago on Earth, the First Ice Age began. By this time, two rival groups of intelligent primates had developed: Neanderthals and *homo sapiens*.[343] Another group, the Titanthropes, became an evolutionary dead end. They possessed more intelligence than Neanderthals, but were more hostile and killed themselves off before the emergence of *homo sapiens*.[344]

The being named Light surveyed life on Earth for several centuries during the Ice Age. Ichthyosaurs were included in Light's catalogue, as were the Neanderthals. The Doctor visited a Neanderthal tribe and acquired the fang of a cave bear.[345]

The Daemon Azal wiped out the Neanderthals. Race memories of beings with horns and their science survived in human rituals. Light had preserved a single specimen – Nimrod – and a few individual examples of the race survived for tens of thousands of years.[346]

The Dalek Project was initiated as a long-term analysis of how humans warred against one another, working to develop anti-human tactics. Three time-active Dalek survey ships observed some cavemen, then jumped forward to different periods of Earth history, erasing all evidence of their presence in each era.[347]

A sentient spaceship, a Psycholops, fell to Earth during the ice age and went dormant. Edinburgh would be built atop it.[348]

The Cave of Skulls

c 100,000 BC - AN UNEARTHLY CHILD / THE EIGHT DOCTORS[349] -> The first Doctor, Ian, Barbara and Susan met a prehistoric tribe struggling to survive "the great cold", and was in the throes of a leadership struggle between Kal and Za. Ian made fire, and the leader-

---

particularly harsh winter. Similarly, the butler Nimrod talks of "ice floods" and "mammoths" in *Ghost Light*, and he's one of the last generation of Neanderthals. In *The Daemons*, the Doctor says that Azal arrived on Earth "to help *homo sapiens* take out Neanderthal man", and Miss Hawthorne immediately states that this was "one hundred thousand years" ago.

344 *Last of the Titans*

345 *Ghost Light*

346 *The Daemons, Ghost Light*. Science tells us that the Ichthyosaurs actually died out at the time of the dinosaurs. In *Timewyrm: Genesys*, Enkidu is one of the last Neanderthals. In reality, Neanderthals only evolved about one hundred thousand years ago and survived for about sixty thousand years, until the Cro-Magnon Period.

347 *The Dalek Project*

348 *Plague City* (chs. 13, 15). The Doctor deduces that the Psycholops crashed during the "last ice age" (which ended about 11,500 years ago), and has slept for "what, ten thousand years? Fifty thousand?" The blurb mentions that "something which has lain dormant for two hundred million years is due to destroy the entire city..." – possibly meaning the Psycholops' grief-leeches, but more likely the dormant volcano near the town.

349 Dating *An Unearthly Child* (1.1) and *The Eight Doctors* (EDA #1) - Ian confirms in *The Sensorites* that the story is set "in prehistoric times". (*An Unearthly Child* itself never explicitly states that it's set on Earth, rather than another primitive planet.) Now that we know that the production team called the first televised story *100,000 BC* at the time it was made (the title appears on a press release dated 1st November, 1963), dating the story has become a lot less problematical. Anthony Coburn's original synopsis of the story also gives the date as "100,000 BC".

The first edition of *The Making of Doctor Who* placed the story in "33,000 BC" (which is more historically accurate), but the second edition corrected this to "100,000 BC". *The Programme Guide* said "500,000 BC", *The Terrestrial Index* settled on "c.100,000 BC". *The Doctor Who File* suggested "200,000 BC". *The TARDIS Special* claimed a date of "50,000 BC", *The Discontinuity Guide* "500,000 BC – 30,000 BC". *Timelink* says 100,000 BC. *About Time* leaned toward a date of "not much earlier than 40,000 BC".

A History of the Universe in 100 Objects (p31) dates the entry for The Doctor's Pipe to "100,000 BC". In "Hunters of the Burning Stone", the Prometheans say that events in *An Unearthly Child* took place on Earth "one hundred millennia ago".

ship dispute was settled in Za's favour when Kal was exposed as a murderer.

The eighth Doctor observed his earlier self.

The Prometheans regarded themselves as "gift-bearers, teachers and shapers" who "since the birth of conscious thought" had a duty to help lesser species develop. They meddled in the affairs of many worlds, but overlooked *homo sapiens* until they detected the time-field distortion caused by the TARDIS' visit to Earth. The Doctor's party had caused the Tribe of Gum to consider the benefits of fire, unity and subterfuge, and the Prometheans sought to further advance them with an offering of psychic metal.

The Tribesmen – including Hur of the dancing flame, Horg of the crying trees and Za the leader – transformed the metal into spears, gaining such abilities as flight, strength and the power to channel energy bolts. They became masters of their land and took many slaves, but left for space to obtain more psychic metal. The Tribesmen patterned their garb after their worship of Orb, as well as the flaming bones they'd witnessed in the Cave of Skulls. They experienced time dilation during their journey, and aged only a handful of years before arriving in 2013.

The Prometheans seeded psychic metal at key locations in history, including London, Athens and Prague. They also made sure that every human society – Celtic, Aztec, Greek, Sumerian and more – worshipped the sun, causing sun iconography to embed itself in humanity's collective consciousness.[350]

(=) 100,000 BC - TW: THE MEN WHO SOLD THE WORLD[351] -> CIA agent Rex Matheson was thrown back in time from 2010 by a Ytraxorian Reality Gun. A caveman, Bent Low, confronted him.

The super-assassin Mr Wynter altered events so that the rogue CIA operative Cotter Gleason was displaced to 100,000 BC instead. Bent Low killed Gleason, and used the man's meat to feed his family.

The Doctor's First Encounter with the Master Away from Gallifrey

? 100,000 BC - 1stA: THE DESTINATION WARS[352] ->The first Master's TARDIS – in disrepair when he stole it – fell apart, stranding him billions of light years away from the Milky Way. To restore his ruined Ship, he spurred an arms race between the humanoid colonists on the planet Destination and the indigenous population, the Delmari. The Master adjusted each society as "a benefactor", the Inventor, then slowed time inside his lab to "jump ahead" at 12-year intervals, to gauge his progress. In time, he hoped to achieve nuclear power and restart his Ship's dimensional engines.

The first Doctor, Susan, Ian and Barbara stopped the Master's meddling, and trapped him within his own laboratory. The Doctor spent two years rebuilding the societies on Destination, with temporal trickery enabling Susan, Ian and Barbara to catch up with him afterward.

The Cold, a form of intelligence, evolved in the Siberian ice. It became dormant as the planet warmed, but would emerge in the savage winter of 1963.[353] The Gappa were a race of telepathic hermaphrodites from Hydropellica Hydroxi, on the far side of the Milky Way. They became so adept at hunting, they consumed each another until only one remained. Some Modrakanians transported the last Gappa to a snowy portion of Earth, but their spaceship disintegrated. Fire-wielding humans drove the Gappa

---

350 "Hunters of the Burning Stone"
351 Dating *TW: The Men Who Sold the World* (*TW* novel #18) - The year is given.
352 Dating *1stA: The Destination Wars* (BF *The First Doctor Adventures* #1.1) - The action occurs "billions of light years" away from Earth, and the participants aren't human.

The Master says it's "the earliest segments of time". That brings to mind the dating convention in *The Ark* – there, the First Segment of Time incorporated "Nero, the Trojan Wars, the Daleks" (the last being, quite possibly, a reference to *The Dalek Invasion of Earth*). Destination's calendar isn't of any help, since the date of "March the 3rd, 2003" (the Master presumably having seeded the Gregorian calendar into this society) just reflects when the colonists left their homeworld. Matt Fitton, the writer of this story, told us: "It's just supposed to be totally disconnected from Earth once the reveal happens, so just 'a long time ago in a galaxy far far

away' really..."

As played by James Dreyfus, the first Master outwardly looks noticeably younger than the first Doctor. It's not a product of the slow-time effect in the Master's laboratory; Fitton remarked: "It could be more to do with the Master staying longer on Gallifrey after the Doctor departs, given we've seen Romana, Leela, etc., age much more slowly. And, as we know from River Song, it is possible for a Time Lord to focus and change how their appearance ages."
353 *Time and Relative*
354 "A hundred thousand years" before *Snowglobe 7*.
355 "The Vanity Box". Events on the asteroid take place in *The Wishing Beast*.
356 *Dreamtime*
357 More than a hundred thousand years before *The Sandman*.
358 "A hundred thousand years of conflict" before *Heroes of Sontar*.

underground, where an icefall buried it. The tenth Doctor and Martha, having defeated the Gappa in 2099, recovered the bodies of the Modrakanians for burial.[354]

The box entity that the sixth Doctor flung into a space-time tear in 1965 fell into "the distant past", and arrived on a desolate asteroid. In the ages to follow, a spaceship crashed on the asteroid and the box entity merged with a young boy to become The Wishing Beast. It subsisted off hapless travellers for three centuries until the sixth Doctor and Mel defeated it.[355]

The Galyari evolved as an intelligent lizard race that was descended from avians. They sought to overrun the home-world of the Cuscaru, but the Doctor obtained the Galyari's Srushkubr, the "memory egg" deposited on every colony world. He destroyed it when General Voshkar of the Galyari refused to withdraw. This released a dose of neural energy that would taint the descendants of the Galyari present for generations. The Galyari later became nomads aboard a fleet of spaceships named the Clutch.[356]

The Doctor's role in this affair made the Galyari regard him as "the Sandman", a legendary killer of Galyari children. The threat of the Sandman's return helped to keep the Galyari's aggression in check.[357] The Witch Guards, an amorphous gestalt that absorbed their opponents' attributes, began operating as mercenaries.[358]

Scaroth, the Fendahl and the Daemons all continued to influence human development until the late twentieth century.[359] At some point humankind will become embroiled in a conflict with the Leannain Sidhe, an energy-based race dimensionally out of phase with humanity, existing in all eleven dimensions rather than the "visible" four but sharing the same planet. A truce between the two races will eventually be reached.[360]

The Gubbage Cones were the dominant empire in the galaxy.[361] The Master had a Vortex Cloak stolen from the ruins of the Gubbage Cone Throneworld on the edge of the Great Attractor.[362]

The ozone layer of Urbanka collapsed around 55,500 BC. The Monarch of the planet stored the memories of his population, some three billion, on computer chips which could be housed in android bodies. Monarch built a vast spacecraft and set out for Earth. The ship doubled its speed on each round trip, and the Urbankans landed and kidnapped human specimens.[363]

It was thought that humankind made the Great Leap Forward from animal to human around 50,000 BC. Humans started burying their dead, and created art and money.[364]

The P'Shiem created millions of mechanical beings – the Omicron – to explore different worlds via the Cardiff Rift, and then pool any information they gleaned into a tesseract fold. The Rift proved so hazardous that only one Omicron survived to the twenty-first century; the P'Shem themselves died when a monstrous creature came through the Rift and ate their world.[365]

The Flurrgh and the Wfflmibibiki initiated a long-lasting war with each other.[366]

Cavemen Days

Cave paintings on one Mediterranean island date from the Cro-Magnon period, forty thousand years ago, demonstrating that a primitive human culture had

---

359 *City of Death, Image of the Fendahl, The Daemons.*
360 *Autumn Mist*
361 "Seventy thousand years" before *The Crystal Bucephalus* (p34). The fungoids on Mechanus in *The Chase* were named "Gubbage Cones" in the script but not on screen.
362 *The Quantum Archangel*
363 *Four to Doomsday*
    MONARCH'S JOURNEY: There is a great deal of confusion about the dates of Monarch's visits to Earth, as recorded in *Four to Doomsday*. The story is set in 1981. The Greek named Bigon says he was abducted "one hundred generations ago [c.500 BC], and this is confirmed by Monarch's aide Enlightenment – she goes on to say that the visit to ancient Greece was the last time the Urbankans had visited Earth. Bigon says that the ship last left Urbanka "1250 years ago", that the initial journey to Earth took "twenty thousand years" and that "Monarch has doubled the speed of the ship on every subsequent visit."
    This is complicated, but the maths do work. The speed only doubles every time the ship arrives at *Earth*,

perhaps because of some kind of slingshot effect. Monarch's ship left Urbanka for the first time in 55,519 BC, it arrived at Earth 20,000 years later (35,519 BC), the speed doubled so the ship arrived back at Urbanka ten thousand years later (25,519 BC), it returned to Earth (15,519 BC), the speed doubled and the ship travelled back to Urbanka (arriving 10,519 BC). Monarch returned to Earth (in 5519 BC), the speed doubled once again and the ship arrived back at Urbanka (in 3019 BC). The ship made its final visit to Earth around 519 BC, and now the trip back to Urbanka only took 1250 years. The ship left Urbanka (731 AD) and reached Earth in 1981.
    However, this solution leaves a number of historical problems – see the individual entries.
364 *TW: Miracle Day*. The advent of money occurred a lot later than this, though.
365 "Fifty thousand years" before the 2008 portion of *TW:* "Rift War".
366 Fifty thousand years before *Benny: The Infernal Nexus.*

developed by this time.[367] Three demigods, the Ancients of the Universe, sometimes went out into reality to party and enjoy themselves. The trio skydived in Australia around 36,000 BC, "give or take a century or ten", and slammed through a portion of the Blue Mountains, creating the rock formation known as the Three Sisters.

(=) One of the Ancients dropped the trigger device to the Pyramid Eternia. It would be known by many names, including the Glamour, Locke, the Stone of Destiny, and the Rock of Ages, and remain buried in New South Wales until 1934.[368]

Around 35,500 BC, the Urbankans kidnapped the Australian Aborigine Kurkurtji and other members of his race.[369] An Onihr captain took charge of a vast Onihr ship thirty thousand years ago. The same captain would seek to acquire time-travel technology on Earth, the twenty-first century.[370]

c 35,000 BC - "The Doctor and the Nurse"[371] -> The eleventh Doctor and Rory spotted a mammoth at the La Brea Tar pits, and incapacitated a saber-tooth tiger with tranquilized meat when it got into the TARDIS. They resumed their haphazard attempts to steer the TARDIS back to 1814.

c 30,000 BC (Spring) - THE TENTH DOCTOR YEAR TWO[372] -> Mr Ebonite employed alien slavers – the Monaxi – to harvest Neanderthals to fight in his Arena of Fear, so he could collect the life energies of the fallen. The tenth Doctor and Gabby curtailed the Monaxi's operation, but were swept down a time corridor to Ebonite's Arena...

29,185 BC (24th May) - ONLY HUMAN[373] -> The ninth Doctor and Rose arrived from the twenty-first century, on the trail of a "dirty rip" time engine. They quickly discovered a group of researchers from the far future who were monitoring the local Neanderthal tribe. Rose accidentally married the prince of the caveman tribe, Tillun, while the Doctor discovered that Chantal – one of the time travellers – had engineered fearsome Hy-Bractor creatures. She planned to release them, changing history to wipe out the inferior *homo sapiens*. The Doctor defeated her.

A rock sculpture, the Venus of Galgenberg, would withstood the test of time aboard *The World*.[374]

The Neanderthals died out around twenty-eight thousand years ago.[375] A "framily" (friends who become like family) took up residence inside a space-faring Ghaleen.[376]

The T'Zun began space conquests around 23,000 BC. They defeated the fungoid Darkings of Yuggoth, but their genetic structure became corrupted and they mutated into three subspecies.[377] The energy fields of the dormant Permians influenced the early Inuit legends.[378]

Two Krynoid pods landed in Antarctica in the Late Pleistocene Period, twenty to thirty thousand years ago. They remained dormant in the Antarctic permafrost until the twentieth century.[379] The older religions on the planet Vortis claimed that "the light" made the universe and the sky, but a being named Pwodarauk made time and the ground so that things might wither but also grow. The first Menoptera, Hruskin, went to Pwodarauk and described the world she envisioned for her offspring. They agreed that slaves would build the temples for the light and raise harvests while the Menoptera enjoyed themselves, and so Pwodarauk made the Zarbi.[380]

Humans hunted centaurs (an "extremely unpleasant

---

367 Peri has just turned down an opportunity to visit the caves with her mother at the beginning of *Planet of Fire*. Although filmed on Lanzarote and named as such in the story, in real life Lanzarote was nowhere near any ancient Greek trading routes.

368 *Big Bang Generation* (chs. 5, 13).

369 *Four to Doomsday*. Bigon states that Kurkurtji was taken "thirty thousand years" ago. Examples of Australian Aboriginal art that are at least twenty-five thousand years old survive.

370 *Trading Futures*

371 Dating "The Doctor and the Nurse" (IDW Vol. 4 #3-4) - A caption reads: "35,000 years ago, give or take."

372 Dating *The Tenth Doctor Year Two* (Titan 10th Doc #2.4-2.5, "Medicine Man") - The blurb says it's the "deep, deep past", and also "the dawn of humankind". "True" Neanderthals lived starting around 200,000 and 250,000 years ago, and finally died out in southern Spain about twenty-eight thousand years ago. In issues #2.6-2.7 ("Arena of Fear"), there's some suggestion that

Ebonite's operations contributed to the Neanderthals' eventual extinction, but didn't wipe them out entirely. The snows have started melting; "it's a new season".

373 Dating *Only Human* (NSA #5) - The Doctor and Jack calculate the precise date.

374 *The Wreck of the World*. The Venus of Galgenberg dates back about 30,000 years. It wasn't discovered until 1988 – making it a bit of an anachronism, as this story moulds itself into shape as an "unused" Season 6 adventure.

375 According to the Doctor in *Only Human*, which doesn't take into account the two survivors he met in *Ghost Light* and *Timewyrm: Genesys*.

376 Thirty thousand years before *The Song of the Megaptera*.

377 "Twenty-five thousand years" before *First Frontier*. Yuggoth is another reference to H.P. Lovecraft (it's his name for the planet Pluto).

378 "Twenty-five thousand years" before *The Land of the Dead*.

lot") to extinction.[381] Around 16,000 BC, a Tregannon scout, Sancreda, was marooned on Neolithic Earth.[382]

Circa 15,000 BC, Mars began to flourish as a world of builders, craftsmen and farmers.[383] **Around 15,000 BC, the Urbankans returned to Earth. They kidnapped the princess Villagra.**[384] Circa 13,000 BC, the Canavitchi of the Pleiades begin conquering neighbouring star systems, building an empire that would eventually stretch over seven galaxies.[385]

The being named Martin was born on Frantige Two, a dull planet and home to a species with an extraordinarily long lifespan. He would live fourteen thousand years into the twenty-first century.[386] Circa 9000 BC, Traken outgrew its dependency on robots.[387] Around 8000 BC, the Euterpian civilisation died out.[388] Around the same time, the Jex from Cassiopeia started their conquests. They eventually dominated several galaxies, including a planet in the Rifta System where the Doctor encountered them.[389]

Homogenite was a mono-crystal forged in supernovae. One such crystal collided with Earth – the immense heat of its arrival changed the local geography, and gave rise to Calcutta's precious gems industry.[390] The homogenite crystal became a prized emerald – "the Emerald Tiger" – and could facilitate biological restoration and re-combination. Three siblings – the brothers Shardan (a.k.a. Shardul Khan) and Ayyappa, and their sister Dawon – found the Emerald Tiger while playing as children, and were gifted with extended life and transmogrification abilities. They jointly ruled over a hidden valley in India and kept the crystal within the Temple of the Emerald Tiger, giving rise to a Hindu story about the island fortress of Lanka.[391]

The wolf-like Valethske had worshipped the insectile Khorlthochloi as gods, but the Khorlthochloi believed the Valethske were becoming too dominant. They destroyed the Valethske warfleets, and released a plague that devas-tated the race. The Khorlthochloi later abandoned their physical bodies for a higher plane of existence. A threat to their new forms made the Khorlthochloi try to reunite with their bodies, but this proved impossible, as the bodies had become too independent. The threat killed the Khorlthochloi's minds, but their bodies lived on as sedate herds of giant beetles.[392]

About ten thousand years ago, the inhabitants of a dying planet encoded everything about their world – including its genetic information – onto a crystal. This was dispatched via a slow-travelling spaceship to another solar system, where the crystal would rebuild their civilisation. Half the races in the universe coveted the crystal, and its transport was obliterated. The Doctor acquired the crystal, but its magnetic fields prevented it from undergoing time travel. He deposited it for safekeeping in Earth's past; various royalty would guard it for millennia.[393]

Azrael emerged as the first necrotist: an artist who regarded murder as the only worthy form of creativity. His people attained immortality, but he found a means of killing them anyway. Later, he killed a race of giants, the Kasareen, and fused their corpses into his greatest work – the fabled Wasting Wall – as a tribute to genocide. The slaughter that Azrael perpetrated lasted for three centuries, but he was eventually caught and executed. Some of Azrael's memories remained in his mask, which was carved from the skull of the last Magellan Emperor.[394]

Around ten thousand years ago, humanity developed the wheel – with a helping hand from Scaroth.[395] **The leaders of the Silence claimed to have ruled the Earth "since the wheel and fire".**[396]

The seventh Doctor, mesmerized by Renk Van Magnastein's drugged lemonade, engineered life on a prehistoric planet using a mutagenic field, a genetically-tailored dragon skeleton and fast-growing embryos that

---

379 *The Seeds of Doom*
380 *Return to the Web Planet.* "Pwodoruk" is the name the Optera give to the Animus, evidently taking after this legend.
381 "Thirty thousand years" before "A Fairytale Life".
382 "Eighteen thousand years" before *The Spectre of Lanyon Moor*.
383 "Twelve thousand years" before Martian civilisation's downfall in *The Judgement of Isskar* [c.3000 BC].
384 *Four to Doomsday.* Bigon claims that Villagra is a "Mayan". Although the Doctor boasts of his historical knowledge, he then suggests that the Mayans flourished "eight thousand years ago", but the civilisation really dated from c.300 AD to c.900 AD. The Urbankans, though, don't visit Earth after 500 BC. It would appear that Villagra must come from an ancient, unknown pre-Mayan civilisation.
385 "A dozen millennia" before *The King of Terror*.

386 *The Tomorrow Windows* (p256).
387 "Eleven thousand years" before Nyssa's time, according to *Cold Fusion*.
388 "Ten thousand years" before *Invasion of the Cat-People*.
389 "Ten thousand years" before *King of Terror*.
390 *The Emerald Tiger.* This happens some "thousands of years" prior to the crystal empowering Shardul Khan and his siblings.
391 "Ten thousand years" before *The Emerald Tiger*.
392 "Many thousands of years" before *Superior Beings*.
393 *The Veiled Leopard*
394 "Ten thousand years" before "The Blood of Azrael".
395 *City of Death.* Scaroth says that he "turned the first wheel". Archaeologists think that humankind discovered the wheel around 8000 BC.
396 *Day of the Moon*

started out as frogs and developed into serpentine humanoids. Van Magnastein fitted the planet with "custom plates" with a name derived from his own: Arvien 2.[397]

Flowers last grew on Mars around ten thousand years ago.[398]

In the Prion System, the Zolfa-Thurans developed a powerful weapon. When the Dodecahedron, a power-source, was aligned with the giant Screens of Zolfa-Thura, an energy beam – "a power many magnitudes greater than any intelligence has ever controlled" – was formed. The beam was capable of obliterating any point in the galaxy.

Zolfa-Thura fell into bloody civil war, and everything on the planet's surface except the Screens was devastated. The Dodecahedron was taken to Zolfa-Thura's sister-planet, Tigella, where the Deons worshipped it.[399] A crystal sculpture was made of Arincias, one of the lost gods of Atlantis.[400]

Two factions of evolved spiders lived on the planet Jaiwan: the Alpha spiders were a federation of cultures, but the Omega spiders – calling themselves the Laughing People, a.k.a. The Way of Life that Works – sought to eradicate the Alphas. The Omega spiders diverted an asteroid toward Jaiwan, then went into hibernation, intending to ride out the devastation and awaken to claim the planet. Some Alphans, however, survived in cryo-sleep.[401]

Jack Harkness suggested that Norwegians, the Scottish, the Irish, the Danish and the Icelandic all had a bit of alien inheritance, owing to a spaceship that crashed in Iceland. The ship had been looking for volcanoes, and originated from somewhere near Pyrovillia.[402]

Around 6000 BC, the humanoid Thains, arch-enemies of the Kleptons, died out.[403] Circa 5900 BC, the inhabitants of Proxima 2 created the Centraliser, which linked

them telepathically.[404] **Around 5500 BC, the Urbankans visited Earth for the third time. The Urbankans kidnapped the mandarin Lin Futu, along with a number of dancers.**[405] A new "framily" formed inside a space-faring Ghaleen that the sixth Doctor and Peri would encounter.[406] The Mogor, a warlike race, lived on Mekrom.[407]

The "hammies", inhabitants of Tollip's World, developed a symbiotic relationship with a type of indigenous flora: the Trees of Life. The Trees engineered a virus to wipe out some ape-like predators, but this killed all animal life on the planet. The hammies merged their bodies with Trees, waiting for the virus to burn itself out, but the slow-thinking Trees forgot to revive their charges.[408]

---

397 "Exactly ten thousand years" before *NAofBenny* V1: *The Revolution*.

398 *The Waters of Mars*

399 "Ten thousand years" before *Meglos*.

400 This is suspected to have occurred "twelve thousand years" before *Benny* S10: *Secret Origins*.

401 At least ten thousand years before *Benny: Genius Loci*.

402 *TW: The Sin Eaters*. Date unknown, but this is presumably early on in each race's history. Proto-Indo Europeans settled Norway toward the end of the third millennium BC; Ireland has been inhabited for about nine thousand years. Pryovillia is the home of the Pyroviles from *The Fires of Pompeii*.

403 *Placebo Effect* (ch6) commits something of a math error here, claiming this happened "ten thousand years" prior to 3999, but in reference to aliens that appeared in the *TV Comic* story "The Klepton Pirates" – which takes place in either the twenty-ninth or thirtieth centuries. So, the Thains at best would have died

out about a thousand years beforehand.

404 "Eight thousand years" before *The Face-Eater*.

405 *Four to Doomsday*. There is no "Futu dynasty" in recorded Chinese history. The Doctor has heard of it, however, and claims it flourished "four thousand years ago". The date does not tie in with the details of Monarch's journey as described in the rest of the story. Archaeologists have discovered a piece of tortoiseshell with a character from the Chinese alphabet on it that is seven thousand years old, so it seems that an early Chinese civilisation was established by that time, and the timescale does tie in with the dates established by Bigon.

406 Ten thousand years before *The Song of the Megaptera*.

407 "Six thousand years" before "Echoes of the Mogor".

408 "Eight thousand years" before *Benny: The Tree of Life*.

Charley and the Viyrans Arrive in the Past

Some Viyrans and Charley Pollard had been thrown back in time by the temporal explosion at Amethyst Station. Over the millennia to come, the Viyrans occasionally woke up Charley – who otherwise remained in stasis – to assist them on missions. They would next encounter the Doctor in the twenty-first century.[1]

The planet Trion founded colonies on other worlds, forming an empire. Science and technology drove the ruling Clans, who developed a vacuum transport system that revolutionised on-planet travel. Non-Clansmen incorporated cold fusion into their spaceships.[2] The Time Lord passing as "Jane Templeton" – unwilling to face her punishment on Gallifrey for meddling with human history – piloted her dying TARDIS into Earth's sun, inadvertently causing a small shift in the Earth's axial rotation.[3]

Ancient Egypt

Seven thousand years ago in the Nile delta, Egyptian civilisation was flourishing. A variety of extra-terrestrials visited Egypt around this time, and were seen as gods. The Egyptian god Khnum was either one of the Daemons or a race memory of them, and Scaroth of the Jagaroth posed as an Egyptian god and Pharaoh, building the earliest Pyramids.[4]

"Assimilation 2"[5] -> In ancient Egypt, the eleventh Doctor, Amy and Rory exposed an escaped alien convict masquerading as one of Pharaoh's viziers, and banished him back to a Visendi detention area.

The Osirians

By 5000 BC, the highly-advanced Osirian race had influenced the cultures of many planets, including Earth, Mars, Youkali (the scene of a devastating battle between the Osirians and Sutekh), Exxilon and Adorandus Calimorfus.[6] A final generation of the giant insects aided by the Osirians hatched in 5000 BC.[7]

Some Osirians were as powerful as decent-sized planets. Many of them bore different animal heads to keep up appearances, and to reflect their biodiversity. Osiris founded the Osirian Court, which existed in its own timeframe – its past and future could interact in varying ways with different eras of different planets, including the Homeworld of the Great Houses.[8]

Sutekh married his sister Nephthys on the same day that Osiris cut the court off from history.[9] The Osirians had a slave force of more than two billion – nearly one billion of those in the inner court alone – and had influence on six hundred and sixty worlds.[10]

The Osirians constructed the Ship of a Billion Years – a formidable vessel that would pass through the noospheres of different planets, and facilitated a "thousand year cruise" of the gods. The Ship was powered by Ra: a miniature sun that the Osirians, even mighty as they were, revered. Four Osirians (Osiris, Sutekh, Upuat and Kepri) were designated "the divine shields of Ra" – they could tap Ra's energies to defend the Ship. Ra's voice spoke through the Lady Nut, and it was said that no man could reach the throne of Osiris without earning passage on the Ship. Whichever Osirian sat on the throne could receive the loyalty of the Ship, but had no jurisdiction over it.[11] The Ship was forged inside a star, and had a hull of solid gold.[12] Booji juice was an Osiran delicacy.[13]

Osirian technology depended on magnetic monopoles, and the Osirians built a power relay system on Earth. The Sphinx was carved from living rock, and made to serve as a dispersal point. The Osirians then left instructions on how to build pyramids to serve as receptacles for their power. They either constructed similar pyramids and a Sphinx on Mars, or found a religiously fanatical group to do it for them.

The face of the Sphinx originally had perfect alignment

---

1 Variously said, by Charley, to happen "several"/"a few" millennia before *Blue Forgotten Planet*.
2 "Nine thousand years" before *Turlough and the Earthlink Dilemma*. *Kiss of Death* also mentions Trion's colonies.
3 *Forty-Five*: "False Gods". In *Doctor Who* terms, this accounts for why ancient calendars denote a difference in the rising and setting of the sun. As this event is recorded on the box of hieroglyphs in Userhat's tomb, "Jane" must chronologically kill herself before Userhat acquires her TARDIS.
4 *The Daemons, City of Death*.
5 Dating "Assimilation 2" (IDW *Star Trek: The Next Generation/Doctor Who* mini-series) - The locale is simply named as "Earth, ancient Egypt". The Pharaoh seen here has never encountered the Doctor before. Bananas are on display in the marketplace, but were unknown in the classical world.
6 *Pyramids of Mars. Return of the Living Dad, GodEngine, The Quantum Archangel* and *The Tenth Doctor Year Three*: "The Good Companion" contain the further references.
7 *FP: Ozymandias*
8 *FP: Coming to Dust, FP: The Ship of a Billion Years*.
9 *FP: Words from Nine Divinities*
10 *FP: Coming to Dust, FP: The Ship of a Billion Years, FP: Body Politic, FP: Words of Nine Divinities*.
11 *FP: The Ship of a Billion Years*
12 *FP: The Judgment of Sutekh, FP: Body Politic*.
13 *The Tenth Doctor Year Two*: "Old Girl"

with the path of the sun, but this became imperfect as the angle of the Earth altered over time. Also, sand would periodically cover the Sphinx and fog the reception. The Sphinx was equipped with a mental pulse that would influence individuals to dig it out.[14] The original face of the Sphinx on Earth was that of Horus.[15]

Sutekh once visited a carnival on the world of Cairos, and was moved to make a snake-performer actually swallow all of his serpents, one by one.[16] The Osirians reshaped entire galaxies using quantum harvesters, a.k.a. their Great Keys, which imposed desired parallel universes on our reality. Sutekh the Destroyer used one such quantum harvester, the Hand of Sutekh, to extinguish life on millions of worlds.[17]

The Osirians fought a war in our solar system. Sutekh, a.k.a. the Typhonian Beast, destroyed his homeworld of Phaester Osiris and left a trail of destruction across half the galaxy. Sutekh became known by many names, including Set, Sadok and Satan.[18]

Sutekh the World-Destroyer is Bound

Sutekh was instrumental in the downfall of his brother Osiris. There were at least two accounts pertaining to Osiris' overthrow and Sutekh's eventual defeat.[19]

In the first account, Sutekh and his sister Nephthys captured Osiris and sent him into space in a capsule without life support. Sutekh and Nephthys tracked the body of Osiris to Egypt and totally destroyed it. Osiris' sister-wife Isis looked for her lost husband, and the remains of his mind endowed themselves in the mind of her spacecraft pilot. This psi-child became Osiris' son Horus.[20]

Along with seven hundred and forty of his fellow Osirians, Horus located Sutekh on Earth, trapping and sealing him in a pyramid. Nephthys was imprisoned in a human body and mummified. Her mind was fragmented, the evil side placed in a canopic jar.[21]

---

14 All according to the Doctor in *The Sands of Time* (pgs 233-235); he says the Sphinx was built "between eight and ten thousand years ago" (p234).
15 *The Sands of Time* (p235).
16 *NAofBenny V2: The Pyramid of Sutekh*
17 *The Tenth Doctor Year One*: "Spiral Staircase"
18 *Pyramids of Mars*
THE DEVIL'S IN THE DETAIL: Both *Pyramids of Mars* and *The Satan Pit* feature a god-like being – Sutekh and the Beast, respectively – who is said to be the inspiration for the Biblical Satan. The two of them even sound the same (because Gabriel Woolf portrayed Sutekh and voiced the Beast; in a knowing bit of casting, he also played a manifestation of Lucifer in *DG: All Through the House*). *The Daemons* also features a devil-like being, but no-one in the story quite says that he's Satan – it's just that the Daemons have inspired myths of powerful horned beings. Finally, *TW: End of Days* has another creature named Abaddon that's apparently of the same race as the Beast in *The Satan Pit*.

The Beast and Sutekh do not appear to be the same being – not if the Beast truly was imprisoned before the universe began, and only released in Earth's future – but the two beings' stories do contain parallels. Much of human mythology in the *Doctor Who* universe seems to be a mish-mash of dimly-remembered ancient encounters with alien races. It therefore seems possible – and forgivable – that people have elided legends of the Beast and Sutekh, although the extent of this isn't clear.
19 Respectively given in *The Sands of Time* and Series 2 of the *Faction Paradox* audios.
20 *The Sands of Time*. Egyptian mythology can't decide on Horus' exact relationship to Set; *The Sands of Time* (pgs. 142, 158) solves this by making Horus a "psi-child"

of Osiris, which simultaneously makes him Sutekh's brother and nephew. The Cult of Sutekh also appears in the New Adventure *Set Piece*. In the scripts for *Pyramids of Mars*, the name Osirians is also sometimes spelt (and is always pronounced) "Osirans".
21 *Pyramids of Mars*, *The Sands of Time*.
22 Dating *FP: Ozymandias*, *FP: The Judgment of Sutekh* (*FP* audios #2.5-2.6) - The story ends in accordance with Sutekh's status in *Pyramids of Mars*.
23 *Pyramids of Mars*, *The Sands of Time*.
24 *NAofBenny V2: The Pyramid of Sutekh*
25 *The Tenth Doctor Year One*: "Sins of the Father"
26 "Five thousand years"/"a hundred generations" (only 2500 years by this guidebook's counting) before *The Tenth Doctor Year One*: "Spiral Staircase".
27 According to *The Legends of Ashildr*: "The Arabian Knightmare", which has an unreliable narrator.
28 *The Big Bang*. This could happen at any time, but it has an Osirian ring to it.
29 This happened "generations" before *K9: The Curse of Anubis*, with the Huducts ruling the Anubians for millennia. K9 did this at some unknown point before *K9: Regeneration* (possibly while working for the Time Lords). We see pictures of the races the Anubians conquered, not their names. The Anubians resemble the Egyptian god Anubis, and their technology, design, written language and imagery all looks Ancient Egyptian. There's no suggestion they've been to Egypt or even Earth before, though, and so they could well be a race influenced by the Osirians.
30 Variously said to occur "thousands of years" and "countless millennia" before *The Bride of Peladon*. In Egyptian mythology, Sekhmet was Ra's daughter and a warrior goddess of Upper Egypt, but was sometimes regarded as a more vengeful aspect of Hathor. Her cult

Cousin Eliza of Faction Paradox Dies

wih - c 5000 BC - FP: OZYMANDIAS / THE JUDGMENT OF SUTEKH[22] **->** The second account of Sutekh's defeat pertained to the War in Heaven. An assembly of more than seven hundred Osirians gathered on Mars, which was still under Osirian jurisdiction, to render a final judgement concerning Sutekh's claim to the throne of Osiris – whom Sutekh had secretly killed and buried near Mount Vesuvius in the eighteenth century. Sutekh now challenged his rival to the throne – Cousin Eliza of Faction Paradox, who was endowed with Osiris' biomass and calling herself Horus – to a fight to the death.

Cousin Justine of Faction Paradox brokered a deal with the Osirians. The more than seven hundred Osirians that historically defeated Sutekh were instead dispatched to the Homeworld of the Great Houses, and "dealt with" the living timeship Lolita. Justine and Eliza separately laid a trap for Sutekh that, at the cost of Eliza's life, severed Sutekh's neural connections and psionic centres, leaving him paralysed. It was believed that Sutekh had lost his challenge, and he was imprisoned beneath a pyramid. As before, history recorded that the Osirians had bested Sutekh.

Corwyn Marne and Abelard Finton had travelled back from 1764 to aid the Cousins. Finton returned to the eighteenth century, but Marne remained trapped on Mars.

The Pyramid of Mars was built to house the Eye of Horus, and the Osirians set up a beacon there to broadcast a warning message. The Egyptians worshipped Horus and the other Osirians. Even Sutekh was worshipped by many on Earth, and the Cult of Sutekh survived for many thousands of years. The influence of the Osirians unified the Egyptian kingdoms, and the local humans were genetically enhanced, becoming taller and with increased mental capacity.[23]

Some of the Osirians who defeated Sutekh were laid to rest – simultaneously dead and merely sleeping in the Pyramid of Osiris. The Osirian named Isis survived, and had her followers build a vault for her on Earth.[24] At Horus' request, Anubis – the son of Sutekh – built the Circle of Transcendence, which enabled the Osirians to leave our reality for a higher, four-dimensional plane.

Anubis himself remained behind to guard the Circle, and to eradicate all remaining traces of Osirian technology.[25] The Cult of the Black Pyramid pledged to further the Osirians' interests.[26]

As the time of the Egyptian gods drew to a close, the goddess Zekahmet remained in her City of Brass. One of her followers, the Wizard of Marabaia, failed in his duties and enabled Zekahmet's enemies to locate the City. Zekahmet banished the Wizard prior to the City's downfall and her death. The Wizard lost an amethyst that granted access to the City and, cursed with immortality, wandered the earth looking for it.[27]

The Doctor was at the prayer meeting when an Egyptian goddess was sealed in the Seventh Obelisk.[28] The Anubians resembled creatures from Egyptian myth. K9 freed them from the mind control of the Huducts, and earned their almost godlike reverence. After K9 left, the Anubians used the mind-control technology of their former oppressors and to conquer races that apparently included the Sea Devils, Alpha Centaurians, Mandrels, Aeolians and Jixen.[29]

An Egyptian legend held that Ra the sun god chose to live amongst the people as a human. Ra transformed his "divine eye" into Sekhmet the Powerful One, the Avenger. She killed Ra's enemies, but continued the slaughter until Ra ordered his high priest at Heliopolis to dye seven thousand jars of beer with pomegranate juice, then to pour it onto the ground. Sekhmet drank from what she thought was a lake of blood, and became stupefied. She was imprisoned in trisilicate, the hardest form of salt in the galaxy, as its negatively charged atoms weakened her. She was bound under four blood locks; three sealed her in space, the fourth in time. Sekhmet was blasted into space and was finally entombed on the planet Peladon. The Doctor suspected that Ra eventually died.[30]

Dilvpod Tentacle wrote a story that was later adapted to become *Peter Pan*.[31]

The Doctor restored the rotting "soul" of the homeworld of the Weave: creatures who existed as flexible protein ribbons, and had numbers for names. He took a young Weave, 6011, to see a star system being born before returning her home. After the Doctor left, the xenophobic Tahnn conducted a war against the Weave. One Weave

---

was particularly dominant in the twelfth dynasty (1991 BC to 1802 BC), only a few centuries before Erimem's time. The "dying beer with pomegranate juice" story comes from a myth focused around an annual Sekhmet festival, although this has Ra dying the entire Nile (which turns red every year when it fills with silt).

The Curse of Peladon says that trisilicate can be found on Mars, where Sutekh was imprisoned, so it makes sense that the Osirians would use it to bind Sekhmet. It's not entirely clear, though, if Sekhmet was deliber-

ately entombed on Peladon or if she was blasted into space at random and happened – very coincidentally – to wind up on a planet loaded with trisilicate, the best means of restraining her. Sekhmet's claim that she "created" the desert and set Sutekh to rule over it can probably be excused as propaganda, as with talk that she's the "Queen of the Osirians" (if she is, it's probably only by virtue of the rest being dead).

31 "Several millennia" before Barrie wrote *Peter Pan*, according to *The Tomorrow Windows*.

ship, the WSS *Exalted*, crashed to Earth with the reality-warping Glamour aboard. The local tribe buried it, and the Glamour extended the lifespan of one of them – Owain – to watch over the Weave.[32]

The troll-like Vykoids stood only seven centimetres tall, and were frustrated because the universe didn't take them seriously. They developed tools of conquest: assault vehicles and a Time Freeze that immobilised the larger races, enabling the Vykoids to transport them to slave planets. The Vykoid machines of war caused chaos across the galaxies.

The Ninety-Ninth Vykoid Expeditionary Force came to Earth, expecting to capture Triceratops and Diplodocuses for use as beasts of labour. Instead, the Force entered cryosleep in Svalbard, the Arctic, within one of their conveyances: a mechanical mammoth.[33]

The exploration ship *Vesuvius* arrived after traveling back nearly five thousand years through a wormhole. The cosmonauts Mortan Hardak and Sheira Rynn killed the third member of their party, Rickard Karne, to protect their secrets. The killers used DNA-rewriting medical spores to transform Rynn into a double of Karne, then entered cryostasis, intending to awake in five millennia and misidentify Karne's skeleton as belonging to Rynn.[34]

Around 3600 BC, a Sontaran ship landed in Ancient Egypt. Its pilot was worshipped as the Toad-God Sontar and set the natives to work building an ion cannon emplacement. The Sontaran planned to outflank the Rutans with it, knowing that the Rutan counter-strike would destroy the planet. A priest learned of these plans, and had Sontar entombed.[35]

The TARDIS became represented in some Egyptian hieroglyphs[36], as did Irving Braxiatel's name.[37]

Around 3500 BC, the Trakenite living god Kwundaar re-engineered Traken's sun to become a vast computer – the Source – which regulated the climate, provided energy, stored information and destroyed all who were evil. With the Source performing such duties, the people of Traken had no further need for a god and exiled Kwundaar from their star system.[38] Brierly, a parliament of personas, came into being.[39] An empire ruled by a family of Primearchs collapsed when their final leader – Ceatul XVI – fought to the death with another race.[40]

c 3400 BC - GODS AND MONSTERS[41] -> The elder god disguised as Peggy Marsden briefly bought Lysandra Aristedes and Sally Morgan from the dawn of time to see Weyland's Smithy: a Neolithic burial site in Oxfordshire constructed as a game piece by Weyland, as part of his chess game against Fenric. The Smithy, in conjunction with the Doctor's TARDIS, served as Weyland's rooks. A chalk horse crafted near the Smithy served as Fenric's white knight, keeping watch over the locale.

A group of Pyroviles – stone creatures animated by internal magma – crashed into Vesuvius and were obliterated on impact. Their particles mixed with the volcano's inner core.[42]

On a three-sunned planet in the fourth galaxy, the males of an unnamed race used their group mind to subjugate their females. One female formed a mental circuit with the enslaved women and attacked the men's gestalt – the males killed the revolutionary's body, but her consciousness survived in other women. The females prevailed, but feared the power their leader had amassed. Her mind was isolated, and her severed head was deposited on Earth.[43]

Alien Centuripedes bred in oak forests on Earth for thousands of years.[44] The Vam existed as a universal force that could wrap itself around a sun, eradicate entire planets or destroy an entire warfleet. It killed billions, excreting

---

32 "Six thousand years" (pgs. 149, 178) before *The Glamour Chase*.

33 "Several thousand years" before *The Forgotten Army*. The Vykoids must be working from wretched intelligence, if they came to Earth expecting to find T-Rexes, Triceratops and Diplodocuses some tens of millions of years after they died out.

34 Karne enters stasis "4,979 years, two months, twelve days, eight hours and twelve minutes" before *Benny B3: Legion: Vesuvius Falling*. His killers corrupt the ship's logs "4,978 years, three months, four days, seventeen hours, forty-three minutes" before the same story.

35 "The Gods Walk Among Us". The archaeologists estimate that the tomb is "five thousand five hundred" years old in 1926, so it was built around 3574 BC.

36 The TARDIS is plainly seen in some hieroglyphs in *Love & Monsters*, even though the Ship would not be represented as a phone box icon under such a language system. Egyptian hieroglyphs were in use from

3200 BC to 400 AD.

37 *Benny B5: Missing Persons: The Brimstone Kid*

38 "2523 years" before *Primeval*.

39 "She" is "six thousand years old" (ch4) in *FP: Spinning Jenny*.

40 "Millennia" before *Benny: A Life in Pieces*.

41 Dating *Gods and Monsters* (BF #164) - Real-life excavations conducted in 1962-1963 concluded that one barrow of Weyland's Smithy was built around 3700 BC, a second about 3400 BC. It's anyone's guess as to when, exactly, Peggy's trio view it.

42 "Thousands of years" before *The Fires of Pompeii*.

43 "Thousands of years", if not more, before *The Suffering*. The "fourth galaxy" could be a reference to the home of the Drahvins in *Galaxy 4*, and for all we're told, the exiled woman might hail from their race. Interestingly, both the Drahvins and the race in *The Suffering* have culled the males of their population.

44 *K9: The Last Oak Tree*

its waste as oil.[45] The Kamishi, having technology that merged the physical with the spiritual through mental discipline, began conquering galaxies.[46]

Tribal Scots discovered a gateway to the dimension of the Eaters of Light, and contained it with a cairn. The structure briefly vented energy every year, necessitating that a Keeper go into the gate and hold the Eaters at bay. Because of time dilation, the sacrifice of one Keeper per generation was required.[47]

> (=) The eleventh Doctor, Amy and Rory took photographic evidence demonstrating how the temporal anomalies in Swallow Woods were making people avoid that area as early as the Bronze Age.[48]

The Rise and Fall of Martian Civilisation

The indigenous population of Mars, later known as the Ice Warriors, founded a vast empire five thousand years ago. Mars emerged as the crowning jewel of the Sol System.[49] The pre-Ice Warrior Martians were excellent engineers.[50]

> (=) Martians were superstitious about Pandas, owing to a legend from the dawn of their history, which said that a Panda deity visited them in a scarlet chariot from the stars.[51]

Damage to the Ecology of Mars

c 3000 BC - THE JUDGEMENT OF ISSKAR[52] **->** Mars had prospered as a world of builders, craftsmen and farmers for twelve thousand years. The whole of the planet was criss-crossed with waterways, and while the Martians had learned to hunt, they didn't fight one another and had yet to experience warfare. The Martians thought themselves protected by their gods, and had a gift economy in which water and other goods were offered for free; a strict code of honour demanded that something be given in return. Alien visitors were rare, but not unknown. A town on the Martian equator was home to a pyramid that had taken nineteen thousand masons, six hundred carpenters and forty-six overseers to complete.

The fifth Doctor and the living Key-tracer Amy visited Mars during the second quest for the Key to Time. The segment was undergoing decay and formed a gravity well through the middle of Mars, generating earthquakes and boiling away the canals. The Doctor and Amy left with the segment, preventing it from forming a black hole. The warped gravity eventually corrected itself, but the Martian environment was left permanently altered. Millions died as earthquakes and hurricanes persisted for thirty years. Some Martians left their world during this time.

The Birth of the Ice Warriors

LORDS OF THE RED PLANET[53] **->** The ecology on Mars became so poisoned that even the Martians' underground communities succumbed. Only the subterranean complex of Gandor remained, as it was near mines from which a vitamin-rich food source – the Life Drink – could be processed. The thousand Martians living in Gandor had temples, markets and more. Martian sensors detected spacecraft journeying between worlds, but such travellers rarely stopped at Mars' inhospitable climate.

One race of indigenous herbivores, Saurians – outwardly a cross between an armadillo and a tortoise – with-

---

45 "Millennia" before the 2009 portion of *TW: Risk Assessment*.

46 "Millennia" before *UNIT S2: Shutdown*.

47 An unknown number of generations before *The Eaters of Light*. Scottish cairns date back to a portion of the Neolithic Period (4000-2500 BC).

48 *The Way Through the Woods*. In Europe, the Bronze Age lasted 3200-600 BC.

49 The background to *Cold War*.

50 *Empress of Mars*

51 This appears to be true, if nowhere else, in an alternate dimension in *Iris: Enter Wildthyme*.

52 Dating *The Judgement of Isskar* (BF #117) - This is the backstory to the downfall of the Martians, and (for some of them) their forced relocation from Mars. Exactly when the Martian ecology goes into decline is open to debate – on screen, the only real clue is the Doctor's claim (*The Waters of Mars*) that flowers last grew on the Red Planet "ten thousand years" ago; such flora would seem unlikely once the toxic Red Dawn

(the Big Finish audios *Red Dawn*, *The Judgement of Isskar* and *Thin Ice*) becomes a factor. Another approach would be to consider if Varga's ship (*The Ice Warriors*) crashed to Earth before or after Mars was devastated, but so little is said of Mars itself in that story, it's hard to make that determination.

Cold War is fairly insistent that the Ice Warriors built their Empire "five thousand years" ago, meaning that the root of its ecological decline – as seen in *The Judgement of Isskar* – likely takes place c.3000 BC, as opposed to *Ahistory* Third Edition's dating of c.8000 BC. Doubling down on that, the Ice Warriors we meet in another story by Mark Gatiss, *Empress of Mars* [1881], have been asleep for "five thousand years".

53 Dating *Lords of the Red Planet* (BF LS #4.3) - The story features the first development of the Ice Warriors, an event that *Cold War* loosely ascribes to "five thousand years ago" [3000 BC]. The second Doctor here tells Jamie: "We're back in the past. The early days of your solar system..." Quandril seems vague as to the cause of

stood the surface's colder temperatures and fed off the remaining vegetation there. Quandril, a Martian genetics expert, sought to create a toughened breed of Martian that could thrive on the surface, and so induced forced evolution upon the Saurians to find their ultimate form. He initially created two "daughters" – the elegant Princess Veltreena and her smarter "younger sister" Zaadur – then produced an armoured race of manual labourers: the Evolutionaries. The first of these, Risor, was under-developed and became Quendril and Veltreena's servant.

Zaadur viewed the Gandorans as beneath her evolved form – she wiped out Gandor's leaders in a coup, then made plans to blow up Gandor after escaping in a rocket with crates of her eggs and squadrons of Evolutionaries. In time, she hoped to make her offspring the dominant force in the galaxy. Zaadur compelled Quandril to create a smarter Evolutionary – Aslor, the first Evolutionary "Lord" – to lead her troops in battle.

The second Doctor, Jamie and Zoe recognised the Evolutionaries as the first generation of Ice Warriors. Zaadur killed Veltreena, launched her rocket into space and succeeded in exploding Gandor. Hundreds of Gandorians fell through chasms to their deaths. Aslor developed fealty to Zoe, and sacrificed himself to kill a

cadre of Ice Warriors assigned to eliminate any survivors. Risor avenged Veltreena by triggering the self-destruct aboard Zaadur's rocket, killing them both.

The Doctor synthesized a substitute for the Life Drink, and told Quandril that his people would go on. He privately knew, however, that new Ice Warriors would either emerge from Quandril's stockpiles or evolve naturally from the Saurians, then wipe out the Gandorans and become the dominant form of Martian.

The Martians adopted bio-mechanoid armour as temperatures dropped across their homeworld, becoming the Ice Warriors. According to the Doctor, "The Ice Warriors... could build a city under the sand, yet drench the snows of Mars with innocent blood. They could slaughter whole civilisations, yet weep at the crushing of a flower."

Grand Marshal Skaldak was renowned as the greatest hero the Martians had ever produced; he was known as the Sovereign of the Tharseesian Caste, the Vanquisher of the Phobos Heresy and Commander of the Nix-Thassis Fleet. Rumours claimed that even Skaldak's enemies held him in such regard, they carved his name onto their bodies before perishing.

Mars' ecological decline, commenting only: "We Martians poisoned the surface so very long ago. Nobody could live up there." The Doctor says he's heard "all manner of disturbing rumours" concerning this (possibly a reference to his future self being involved in it; see *The Judgement of Isskar* and, by extension, *Red Dawn*). Temperatures on Mars have fallen, but cultivating food seems the biggest issue; the Doctor clarifies to Zoe that "the atmosphere doesn't get ruined for quite some years to come". The Saurians eat a type of remaining vegetation that, presumably, can't sustain the Gandorians.

Aslor is the original "Ice Lord", a type of Ice Warrior first seen in *The Seeds of Death*.

54 The background to *Cold War*. The Doctor's quote is from *Empress of Mars*.

55 *Empress of Mars*

56 *Cold War*, even though, to judge by Skaldak's performance aboard a Soviet submarine, an Ice Warrior sans armour is actually more dangerous than while inside it. **57** *The Waters of Mars*

58 *The Silent Stars Go By*, *Thin Ice* (BF), respectively.

59 *The Waters of Mars*. A deleted scene said that the Martians left Mars because they could not beat the monsters from that story, the Flood. Nonetheless, because the scene *was* omitted, it's unclear within the fiction if the Flood was frozen after the Martian ecology went into decline (*The Judgement of Isskar*), or in one of Mars' polar regions beforehand.

60 *The Judgement of Isskar*, based upon the history of

Izdal given in *Red Dawn*.

61 "Five thousand years" before *Empress of Mars*.

62 *The Creed of the Kromon*, which we might retroactively think is referring to *Lords of the Red Planet* and *The Judgement of Isskar*.

63 *Deimos*/*The Resurrection of Mars*.

64 *Demon Quest: A Shard of Ice*. This may be a reference to *Pyramids of Mars*.

65 *Wishing Well*. We're assuming that the Doctor and Martha visited when the castles were at their height, rather than in ruins.

66 Dating *Gallifrey VII: Intervention Earth* (*Gallifrey* #7.0) - The year is given, but *Gallifrey* Series 8 annuls these events.

67 "Five thousand years" before *Mummy on the Orient Express*.

68 "Thousands of years" before *Mummy on the Orient Express*.

69 Dating *Timewyrm: Genesys* (NA #1) - The Doctor says the TARDIS is heading for "Mesopotamia, 2700 BC".

70 A total of three thousand years before *Leth-St*: "The Black Eggs of Khufu". The Pyramid of Khufu (a.k.a. the Great Pyramid of Giza) was built c.2580-2560 BC, Menkure was c.2510 BC.

71 "City of Devils"

72 Dating "The Forgotten" (IDW *DW* mini-series #2) - It is "most likely around the twenty-sixth century BC". Menkaure ruled in the late twenty-sixth century BC, although historians can't be sure of the exact dates. In the Doctor's personal timeline, this is after *Marco Polo*

Skaldak sang to his daughter of the Old Times, the Songs of the Red Snow. Later on, he became trapped in ice at Earth's North Pole, and slept until 1983.[54]

The Ice Warriors built hibernation hives, sometimes with sarcophagi containing their monarchs. The Doctor served as an honorary guardian of the Tythonian Hive.[55] An attack on one Ice Warrior constituted an attack on all. It was considered the greatest dishounor for an Ice Warrior to leave its armour.[56]

The Ice Warrior language had the dialect Ancient North Martian.[57] Some Ice Warriors were herbivorous, others ate glacier fish from the polar regions.[58]

Legends spoke of how the Ice Warriors built an empire on Mars out of snow. The Doctor suspected that they found a malevolent entity that lived in water and *created* water, and used their might and wisdom to freeze it beneath Gusev Crater on Mars.[59]

The Red Dawn, the Ice Warrior Hibernation and the Migration from Mars

The Martians remaining on Mars wanted to rebuild their world, but Lord Izdal concluded that the cause was lost, and that the Martian atmosphere could no longer filter out deadly radiation. To prove this, Izdal gave himself to the Red Dawn: the time of day when the atmosphere was the most toxic. Izdal's sacrifice, as witnessed by the magistrate Isskar, convinced the Martians to abandon their homeworld. Isskar entered cryo-freeze, hoping to exact revenge upon the Doctor for his role in Mars' decline.[60]

The Ice Warrior later known as Friday went into space during Mars' downfall, and hoped to return for the sleeping Empress of Mars: Iraxxa.[61] As Mars' ecology went into decline, some Ice Warriors entered hibernation in caverns on the Martian moon of Deimos. Another group went to sleep in the asteroid belt.[62]

The Doctor visited Mars before it became a dead world.[63] The Doctor visited the tombs on Mars.[64] The tenth Doctor and Martha visited the Frozen Castles of the Ice Warriors.[65]

- -
(=) 2986 BC - GALLIFREY VII: INTERVENTION EARTH[66] **->** The Time Lord Rexx, secretly an Adherent of Ohm, manipulated Ace into transporting the Hand of Omega in her TARDIS back to Greater Henge, a network of stone circles on Earth. Rexx hypnotised Ace, then used her Ship and the Hand to generate a black hole through which Omega could return to our universe. Narvin arrived from Gallifrey and fatally shot Rexx, causing him to regenerate and stand revealled as Adjutant Coordinator Tauras. Using Ace's TARDIS, he took Ace and Narvin through to Omega's universe of anti-matter...
- -

The myth of the Foretold spoke of a mummy that appeared to doomed individuals. Anyone who bore the Foretold's stare had sixty-six seconds to live, although some versions spoke of a riddle or secret that would make it stop. In actuality, the Foretold was a soldier from a forgotten war, who leeched energy from its victims after taking sixty-six seconds to move them out of phase.[67]

The Doctor visited Thedion Four – a world constantly bathed in acid rain, and where he had a lovely picnic in a gas mask. The Magellan black hole came to devastate that world, the perpetually dark planet Obsidian, a planet of shrubs, and many others.[68]

Ancient Mesopotamia

Creation of the Timewyrm

c 2700 BC - TIMEWYRM: GENESYS[69] **->** The human race had developed from hunters into city-dwellers, and had irrigation. In the Middle East, walled cities were built and a warrior aristocracy developed. The earliest human literature was written at this time, and commerce had begun between cities. The deeds of one warrior-king – and his contact with extra-terrestrials – soon became legend.

Gilgamesh refused the advances of the alien Ishtar, who had crashed near Uruk. Ishtar went on to the temple of Kish, taking the form of a metal snake woman, and had a vast temple built. The seventh Doctor, Ace and Gilgamesh travelled to the mountains of Mashu and led Utnapishtim, a member of Ishtar's race, to his prey. Ishtar infiltrated the TARDIS computer, and the Doctor ejected her into the Vortex... inadvertently turning her into the Timewyrm, a creature foretold to herald the end of the universe. The Timewyrm became capable of independent travel through space-time. The Doctor and Ace pursued her.

The Great Pyramids

Aliens interconnected the pyramids of Khufu, Menkaure and Queens as an energy source.[70] Around 2650 BC, Zoser was one of the first Egyptian Kings.[71]

c 2610 BC - "The Forgotten"[72] **->** The TARDIS materialised in Menkaure's Pyramid, the smallest of the three being constructed at Giza. The first Doctor, Ian, Barbara and Susan were immediately arrested by Egyptian soldiers, but accidentally foiled an assassination attempt on Pharaoh Menkaure's life. In the confusion, they made their escape.

Sutekh and Osiris were depicted in paintings in Menkaure's Pyramid.

c 2566 BC - THE DALEKS' MASTER PLAN[73] **->** The first Doctor, Steven and Sara Kingdom were pursued to the time of the construction of the Great Pyramids by both the Daleks in their time machine, and the Monk in his TARDIS. The travellers escaped during a pitched battle between the Daleks and Egyptian soldiers, but the Daleks and Mavic Chen recovered the Taranium Core the Doctor had stolen and returned to the future.

c 2560 BC - BENNY S5: THE GREL ESCAPE[74] **->** Bernice Summerfield, Jason Kane and Benny's son Peter, in fleeing from a pack of time-travelling Grel, briefly visited the Great Pyramid of Khufu in ancient Egypt. Anubis, the Egyptian god of the dead, had full knowledge of Peter's life to come – and told Benny that her son was unworthy to enter the kingdom of Heaven.

A race of crocodilians ruled the planet Sobek, an old imperial world founded on centuries of slavery. The aristocrat Snabb deemed the ruling prince of Sobek as too corrupt and led an uprising; the ensuing war devastated the planet. A few royals escaped with "the great Skull" – a molecular data encryption system containing all of Sobek's memories and history. In time, it was concealed in a sanctuary on Indigo 3.[75]

Some Sumerian stone tablets displayed Irving Braxiatel's name.[76] The dominant life on the planet Bubastis developed as cat creatures, the Nobal, who had twenty-two long, slender fingers and a tradition of burning their dead. The Nobal ate a new type of insanity-causing bug, and in their madness stuffed themselves inside five enormous, but hollow, stone cats. The insectoid Bal evolved on Bubastis in the millennia to come, and wrote the Bal Rule Book (forbidding the eating of insects) for benefit of space travellers to their world. To archaeologists, Bubastis became known as "that world with the giant stone cats", with differing theories existing to the cats' origins.[77]

Around 2350 BC, the inhabitants of Uxarieus had used genetic engineering to become a psychic super-race powerful enough to come to the attention of the Time Lords. They built a Doomsday Weapon, a device capable of making stars go supernova. The Crab Nebula was formed as a result of testing the device. Soon, though, radiation began leaking from the weapon's power source. It poisoned the soil and the race began to degenerate into primitives.[78] The space explorer Moriah conquered Krontep and built a civilisation there. He left the planet shortly after his wife Petruska killed herself. Their descendants, including King Yrcanos, would rule the planet for millennia.[79]

---

but before *The Aztecs*. He already knows of the Osirians.

73 Dating *The Daleks' Master Plan* (3.4) - The three time machines land at the base of a "Great Pyramid" that has nearly been completed. This might well be the Great Pyramid of King Khufu (Cheops in Greek), one of the Seven Wonders of the World. John Peel's novelisation of the story names it as such, and also says "Khufu lay in his final illness" (p72). Khufu died in 2566 BC; the Great Pyramid was built over a twenty year period, ending around 2560 BC.

The Terrestrial Index pins the date at "2620 BC"; *The Discontinuity Guide* offers a wider range of "2613 BC – 2494 BC". *Timelink* says 2635 BC. According to *The Dalek Handbook* (p136), the Daleks battle Egyptian soldiers – in *The Daleks' Master Plan* episodes nine and ten – "circa 2560". The Pyramid entry in *A History of the Universe in 100 Objects* (p34) ends at "2650 BC", presumably denoting the same. *Whoniverse* (BBC, p253) has the pyramid kerfuffle with the Daleks happen "about 2500 BC".

Dalek: The Astounding Untold History of the Greatest Enemies of the Universe (p88) claims this all happened during the "height of the Ancient Egyptian Middle Kingdom (approximately 2200 BC)".

74 Dating *Benny S5: The Grel Escape* (Benny audio #5.1) - The story takes place in ancient Egypt, and it's entirely possible that the Anubis seen here was an Osirian.

75 *Benny B5: Missing Persons: The Brimstone Kid*

76 *The Skull of Sobek*; see the dating notes on this story. It's not entirely clear if Sobek's downfall triggered a

migration of its culture to other planets, or if the crocodilians had dealings with other species beforehand. If the former is true, the crocodilians must have immense lifespans, as the prince and Snabb are still around ten thousand years later. The fact that Snabb spends a full century scouring one sector of space for the Skull somewhat supports this notion, as does the fact that he only eats once a year (which suggests a slow, life-extending metabolism).

77 "Thousands of years" (pgs. 77, 78, 111) before *Benny: The Slender-Fingered Cats of Bubastis* (Nobal detail, pgs 198-200). *The Nobal: My Part in the Discovery of a Lost Civilisation* by Chilton Christopher determines that Nobal-made bowls go back "more than five thousand years" (p39).

78 *Colony in Space*. The date isn't given, but this is when the Crab Nebula was formed. It was first visible on Earth from 1054.

79 Unspecified "thousands of years" before *Bad Therapy*.

80 *City of Death*. Scaroth says that he caused "the heavens to be mapped", and humankind's first star maps were made in China around 2300 BC.

81 "Over four thousand years" before *The Burning*. The entity is drawn to Earth as the result of events in Siberia, 1894, in *Time Zero*.

82 According to the Doctor in *Four to Doomsday*.

83 *Deadly Reunion*. It's suggested the "gods" were the product of the Daemons' experiments.

84 *The Woman Who Lived*. This is evidently a separate

Around four thousand three hundred years ago, the Chinese were making the first astronomical measurements with Scaroth's help.[80] Over four thousand years ago, various cultures on Earth worshipped an elemental "burning" entity. It was known as Agni the fire god in India, and Huallallo to the Peruvians.[81] **Four thousand years ago, the Futu dynasty was flourishing in China.**[82]

The Time of Greek Myth

On Earth, the classical Greek gods were long-lived beings with psionic abilities. They had forgotten their origins. Some of them believed they were aliens, although Hermes came to suspect they were an early mutation of humanity. Zeus, Poseidon and Hades were the oldest of the gods, although they were not yet five thousand years old.[83]

The twelfth Doctor suspected that the mythology of the Greek Underworld originated with aliens from Delta Leonis.[84] A psychic parasite from space was mistaken for the goddess Artemis, and fed off the people's greed. The priests serving the parasite rose up and bound it in a circle of iron within its temple. The creature's presence gradually made some of the women in the area psionic.[85] A group of physicists in the 1960s postulated that the Helix intelligences inspired the Greek myths of the Titans.[86]

The Chronovore Prometheus and the Eternal named Elektra broke an ancient covenant to sire the Chronovore Kronos. The Guardians spared the half-breed's life, but sealed him in a trident-shaped crystal prison and threw it into the Time Vortex. The crystal came to simultaneously exist on many worlds.[87]

Five hundred and thirty-seven years before the fall of Atlantis, the priests of that land captured the god Kronos. At this time, a young man called Dalios was king. Kronos transformed a man, one of the king's friends, into a fearsome man-beast: the Minotaur. After this, the King forbid the use of the Crystal of Kronos, for fear of destroying the city.[88]

c 2000 BC - FALLEN GODS[89] -> The Titans had evolved at the bottom of the sea. Most left to live in the Vortex, but some remained on Earth as humanity amused them. Humans bound these Titans using special crystals. The Titans could manipulate time, and were compelled to grant the people on the island of Thera four harvests a year. They ended a war between Athens and Thera by stealing life energy from the Athenians – which was taken to be a plague – and using it to extend the lifespan of the elite on Thera.

Fiery demon bulls attacked Thera, and King Rhadamanthys believed that Athens was seeking revenge. However, the Titans themselves were causing the attacks, hoping the king would free them to repel the "invaders". Rhadamanthys was killed, and his son Deucalion succeeded him. Deucalion felt the Titans' abilities had been used unwisely, and ordered their crystals scattered far and wide, curtailing their power.

The blessings the Titans had bestowed on Thera were stolen from the future. In the times to come, the island would experience barrenness and a volcanic eruption.

Around 2000 BC, Pharaoh forbade his daughter, Hentopet, from seeing her suitor, Temhut. The giant cat-like creature Bubastion, an agent of the Shadow Proclamation sent to oversee the forward development of Earth, manifested in response to Hentopet praying to the goddess Bast. Hentopet deceived Bubastion into attacking Pharaoh's associates, giving Hentopet the opportunity to kill her father. Pharaoh's death meant Bubastion had failed in his mission, and so he cursed Hentopet and her servant Sheeq to immortality.[90]

In the fourth year of the twelfth dynasty, around 2000 BC, Kephri the beetle god was one of the seven hundred forty gods that captured Sutekh. It was given an area of Egypt as a reward, but wanted the whole of Africa. Horus had it sealed in a casket, where it would wait, plotting revenge for four thousand years. The Doctor witnessed at least some of these events.[91]

The true meaning of the burial mound containing the WSS *Exalted* had now been forgotten. Rumours and myths about it would circulate for four thousand years.[92]

---

incident than Leandro's excursion, as there's no sign that he's been lurking about on Earth for centuries.

85 "Thousands of years" before *The Hounds of Artemis*.

86 *TW: Exodus Code* (ch55).

87 *The Quantum Archangel*

88 *The Time Monster*

89 Dating *Fallen Gods* (TEL #10) - It's "the Bronze Age" (p91). This is a retelling of the creation of the Atlantis as related in *The Time Monster*.

90 "Nearly four thousand years" before the 1974 component of "Agent Provocateur".

91 "The Curse of the Scarab". The casket is "four thousand" years old. The fourth year of the twelfth dynasty would be around 1988 BC. *Pyramids of Mars* placed the imprisonment of Sutekh "seven thousand" years ago, but this dating does coincide with the dating given for events of *The Sands of Time*, perhaps suggesting that the Osirians maintained some sort of presence in ancient Egypt for millennia.

92 "Four thousand years" (p21) before *The Glamour Chase*.

c 2000 BC - "The Power of Thoueris"[93] -> The eighth Doctor easily defeated the "third rate" Osirian – the hippo-like Thoueris – while on holiday in ancient Egypt. Thoueris was devoured by crocodiles.

c 2000 BC - THE SANDS OF TIME[94] -> Tomb robbers entered the pyramid of Nephthys, breaking the canopic jar that contained her evil intellect. The Egyptian priests sought a pure vessel to contain it and chose the fifth Doctor's companion Nyssa, sealing her in a sarcophagus until the 1920s.

At around the same time, Cessair of Diplos, a criminal accused of murder and stealing the Great Seal of Diplos, arrived on Earth. She would pose as a succession of powerful women over the millennia, while her ship remained in hyperspace above Boscombe Moor in Damnonium, England. A stone circle named the Nine Travellers was set up, and subsequent attempts to survey the circle proved hazardous.[95] Unknown parties, perhaps aliens, installed a stone circle on Earth to resurrect their fallen members. The circle included a quarantine zone to contain bodiless intruders: the Static.[96]

The warrior Ravage captured the throne of the planet Amital, but was defeated by republican forces. He was turned into stone and imprisoned on Earth; twelve sentries transformed themselves into rock to monitor him.[97]

The Arcasian Lights were visible from Earth four thousand years ago.[98] A group of ten Therrin – a race of alien explorers surveying worlds for their resources – established a series of recumbent stone circles in the British Isles to act as data collectors. Primitive men killed six Therrin, but the survivors would hibernate in buried healing capsules. They remained dormant for more than four millennia.[99] In 1936 BC, the Emperor Rovan Cartovall of the planet Centros became bored with his imperial life. He disappeared without a trace, and took the immense palace treasury with him. His younger brother Athren suc-

93 Dating "The Power of Thoueris" (DWM #333) - No date is given, and this is clearly not the height of Osirian power, so it's been placed at the same time as events of the backstory for "The Curse of the Scarab".

94 Dating The Sands of Time (MA #22) - The date is given (p57).

95 The Stones of Blood. The Terrestrial Index dated Cessair's arrival on Earth at "3000 BC", but this contradicts the Doctor and the Megara, both of whom claim that only "four thousand" years have elapsed since Cessair came to Earth.

96 Static. The Doctor muses that the resurrection circle has been "buried in the Earth since before the dawn of mankind".

97 SJA: The Thirteenth Stone. There's no evidence that the practice here of turning alien convicts into rock has any relation to The Stones of Blood.

98 SJA: The Lost Boy

99 DotD: Vengeance of the Stones

100 "Five thousand years" before The Ultimate Treasure.

101 "Thousands of years" (p236) before Fear Itself.

102 Dating Worlds BF (1.4, Kronos Vad's History of Earth (Vol. 36,379)) - The year is given.

103 Carbon-dating confirms the bodies are "considerably older" than decorative lids dated to 4,500 years before Benny: Filthy Lucre.

104 Deadly Reunion (p115). The first part of the book takes place in 1944, and Persephone says she is three thousand, seven hundred and two years old.

105 "Several millennia" before "Invaders from Gantac". The Daleks do not appear to have been created until after this point, so the ones referred to here must be time travellers.

106 Dating The Slitheen Excursion (NSA #32) - The year is given as "1500 BC" on the back cover and page 25. Real-life renderings of the founder of Athens (Cecrops

I) do, in fact, depict him as a human with a giant fish tail for legs. Events here are unrelated to the fall of Atlantis.

107 THE FALL/S OF ATLANTIS: We hear of/witness the destruction of Atlantis in three stories: The Underwater Menace, The Daemons and The Time Monster. In The Underwater Menace, the island in question is in the Atlantic, and in The Time Monster, "Atlantis" is another name for the Minoan civilisation in the Mediterranean. In The Daemons, Azal warns the UNIT Master that "My race destroys its failures. Remember Atlantis!". The Terrestrial Index attempts to explain this by suggesting that the Daemons supplied the Minoan civilisation with the Kronos Crystal. This might be true, but there is no hint of it on screen.

The Magician's Apprentice codifies the discrepancies by having UNIT analysts determine that the Doctor has visited "three possible versions of Atlantis", which also suggests the TARDIS at some point landed in the one the Daemons destroyed.

108 Dating The Time Monster (9.5) - The traditional date for the fall of Atlantis is around 1500 BC. The Doctor says that the crystal was used to capture Kronos "four thousand years ago", but states on returning to the twentieth century that the downfall of Atlantis he and Jo just witnessed was "three thousand five hundred years ago". The Terrestrial Index, The Discontinuity Guide and About Time all suggested the traditional date of 1500 BC, the FASA Role-playing game claimed 10,000 BC. The TARDIS Logs included the presumed misprint of 1520 AD. Timelink goes for 1529 BC.

109 The Underwater Menace

110 The Underwater Menace, The Daemons.

111 The background to Benny S11: Year Zero, given in Benny B1: Epoch: Judgement Day.

112 Benny S11: Year Zero, Benny S11: Dead Man's Switch

ceeded him to the throne. The mystery of Rovan and his missing treasure became legendary.[100]

An alien race – possibly as an experiment, possibly as part of a battle – released two viruses, Fear and Loathing, into Jupiter's atmosphere. They remained there for millennia, grappling with each other for supremacy.[101]

1911 BC - WORLDS BF: KRONOS VAD'S HISTORY OF EARTH (VOL. 36,379)[102] -> Iris Wildthyme got her wires crossed while trying to reach London, 1911, and her bus briefly set down during the Egyptian-Nubian war of 1911 BC...

Time worshippers on Turgara murdered twelve adolescents and buried their bodies in a Clock of Children formation.[103] In 1758 BC, the "goddess" Demeter gave birth to Persephone, the future beloved of Hades. The Greek gods passed into legend, and some attempted to live quiet existences among humankind.[104] The seventh Doctor helped the people of Wrouth defeat the Daleks "in '38".[105]

1500 BC - THE SLITHEEN EXCURSION[106] -> The tenth Doctor, having promised to show ancient Greece to June, a twenty-first century university student, diverted to look into a temporal anomaly in 1500 BC. King Actaeus told the Doctor and June that a group of Slitheen, who originated from circa 34,600 and were running time-travel package tours for other aliens, had ruled the region since before his father had been born. The Slitheen had provided food via molecular repurposing that kept the people from starving, and in return demanded a small number of humans compete in games for the tourists' amusement. The Doctor had the sinking feeling that the Slitheen's intervention was part of established history, and that the visiting aliens were the basis for the creatures of Greek myth.

The Slitheen were scheming to accuse one of their clients, a fish-tailed humanoid named Cecrops, of corporate espionage, but Actaeus sacrificed himself to destroy the Slitheen's temporal drives. The resultant explosion destroyed the island of Thera, the modern island of Santorini. The Doctor taught the Greeks some farming techniques, and then took everyone home – except Cecrops, who was thought dead in his native era, but instead became the legendary founder of Athens. Three of the Slitheen were made dormant inside some stalagmites, and wouldn't revive until the twenty-first century.

The Fall of Atlantis[107]

The Master Fails to Contain Kronos

c 1500 BC - THE TIME MONSTER[108] -> The UNIT Master arrived in Atlantis, claiming to be the emissary of the gods. King Dalios didn't believe the stranger,

who seduced his wife, Queen Galleia. The Master and the Queen plotted to steal the Crystal of Kronos. King Dalios died of a broken heart, and the Master seized power, proclaiming himself King. Queen Galleia, filled with remorse, ordered his arrest. The third Doctor and Jo were present as the Master released Kronos the Chronovore, and Atlantis was destroyed.

Some Atlanteans survived beneath the ocean, off the Azores.[109] The Daemons would later claim to have destroyed Atlantis.[110]

Bernice Summerfield in the Epoch's alt-reality

(=) ? 1500 BC (fourth month) - BENNY S11: YEAR ZERO / DEAD MAN'S SWITCH -> The Epoch created alternate timelines to observe and alter the progression of life itself, largely to eliminate potential threats to themselves. Earth's solar system, and particularly Bernice Summerfield's ability to "see the truth" of reality, posed a danger to the Epoch. They decided to evaluate her – then either eliminate her from all potential timelines, or choose which version of Bernice would confront them.[111]

Following her defeat of the Deindum in 2610, Benny found herself on Raster – one of twenty inhabited worlds in a timeline restarted by the Epoch. It was currently the fourth month (springtime) of Year 54. All knowledge of anything before Year 1 had been eradicated. The Great Leader, a computer, further obscured the past by regularly assigning new names to the people and places of the twenty worlds. Studying history or archaeology warranted a death sentence. Bernice thought that only about three dozen stars existed in this reality. She sought answers at the capital of the twenty worlds: the planet Zordin...[112]

The demon-looking Kadept excelled as solicitors, accountants, insurance brokers, mortgage brokers and bankers, and survived largely by being meek and cowardly. Jack, a future friend of Bernice, had been raised by his father Jacques and aunt Jacquelette after his mother died. His best friend, Lara, died playing a crooked card game when Jack was late and she stepped in for him. Another of Benny's associates, Ruth, had been an unscrupulous member of the Morris Prime royal family who had killed her parents during an insurrection and gone into hiding. In future, Dorian Gray would claim to have known Ruth when she was both "revered and reviled".

Bernice first met Ruth and Jack on the shuttle to Zordin. Jack had tried and failed to collect an unpaid bill on Raster for his father's law firm: Jack, Jackson and Jack's Sons. Avril Fenman traversed time via the crystals of Hera, and implanted Jack and Ruth with mind-controlling crystals.

The Epoch's revisions to reality meant that Benny, Ruth and Jack all forgot meeting one another. Jack operated as Avril's agent in this time zone. The Epoch's remapping endowed Ruth with an entirely new persona and history, making her a priestess of Poseidon who secretly aided the historian Leonidas. Bernice arrived on Zordin after spending three years in stasis aboard the spaceship...[113]

(=) & 1497 BC - BENNY B1: EPOCH / BENNY: MANY HAPPY RETURNS[114] -> Benny awoke in Year 57 to find that Zordin looked like Earth... and that just three months beforehand, the Great Leader had just renamed the planet "Atlantis". The world was an amalgamation of elements from Greek mythology – Minotaurs were "commonplace", and winged horses, Pegasii, could fly to great heights. Benny spent a few weeks assisting Acanthus the Tale-Smith. Two secret historians – Leonidas and Ruth – recruited Benny to conduct an examination of the Underground,

potentially the remains of a previous civilisation. They confronted and destroyed the Great Leader, hoping to end its clandestine manipulation of the twenty worlds.

More alterations occurred to Atlantis per the Epoch's design. Many citizens were revised into law-enforcers named Hierophants, and the temple of Ando offered a two-for-one sale on blessings. Leonidas and Benny became lovers; the next day, Leonidas and his fellow Historians were changed en masse into Hierophants. An erasure wave wiped out Atlantis...

... but Benny and Ruth awoke in a pocket reality from which the Epoch observed the timelines they'd created. The Epoch gave Bernice a final test: she was shown a Jurassic era-timeline and a Victorian era-timeline, with a Benny and Ruth in each of them. The Epoch-Prime reality Benny was to deduce which timeline was genuine, and delete the other two. Benny deleted the Jurassic timeline, and threw the Epoch off balance by deleting the Epoch-Prime reality. Before its eradication, Ruth forced Benny into a stasis capsule, which held Benny in a timeless state until she returned to her native era, the year 2616.

---

113 *Benny* B3: *New Frontiers: The Curse of Fenman, Benny: Many Happy Returns, Benny* S11: *Dead Man's Switch, Benny: Adorable Illusion* (ch19). Dorian Gray's claim to have known Ruth "when the very mention of your name could make whole empires flee" (in *Benny* B3: *Legion: Shades of Grey*) doesn't really match Ruth's origin story in *The Curse of Fenman*, and presumes that Gray must have traveled through time at least once in the centuries between *The Confessions of Dorian Gray* series and *Shades of Grey*.
114 Dating *Benny* S11: *Year Zero* (*Benny* audio #11.3), *Benny* S11: *Dead Man's Switch* (*Benny* audio #11.4) and *Benny: Epoch* (box set #1, contains *The Kraken's Lament*, 1.1; *The Temple of Questions*, 1.2; *Private Enemy No. 1*, 1.3; *Judgement Day*, 1.4) and *Benny: Many Happy Returns* (Benny 20th anniversary special) - These seven stories occur in a central alternate reality (and two subsidiary realities) as crafted by the Epoch. Three years elapse between *Dead Man's Switch* and the *Benny: Epoch* stories, with Benny in stasis. In *Judgement Day*, she returns to her native era in a timeless state while the universe ages around her, which very much suggests that the Epoch's timeline/s are located in the past; Benny suspects as much as early as *Year Zero*. Big Finish producer Gary Russell (who took over the Benny audios from John Ainsworth after *Dead Man's Switch*) confirmed that the dating was left vague, and that, "the Atlantis Benny knows [in *Benny: Epoch*] could be any time from real Atlantis to Victorian times, or indeed the twenty-fifth century". In *Judgement Day*, Benny tells a robot

attendant in 2616 to not recite everything that's happened in the "last however-many-millennia..." while she was in stasis. An interlude in *Many Happy Returns* has Benny enjoying Leonidas and Ruth's company, prior to *Private Enemy No. 1*.

The *Benny* stories to follow consistently assume that Atlantis was some thousands of years in the past, with *Benny* B2: *Road Trip: Brand Management* being predicated on the idea that a corporation capitalizes on the cult that arises around Benny while she's in stasis. Back at home in the twenty-seventh century, Benny claims to have spent "many millennia" in stasis and that Ruth "should have died a couple of thousand years ago" (*Brand Management*). In *Benny* B5: *Missing Persons: In Living Memory*, Benny says that Atlantis was "a few millennia back and slightly to the left". *Benny: The Weather on Versimmon* states that Benny "slept for centuries" (p26), and Benny glibly says, "You've have thought exercise would be good for you after being in bed for five hundred years" (p56).

With all of that in mind, the path of least resistance is to place the *Epoch* stories roughly concurrent to the Atlantis seen in *The Time Monster*.
115 *Benny* B1: *Epoch: Judgement Day*, and the *Benny* B5: *Missing Persons* stories *The Winning Side* and *In Living Memory*.
116 *Benny* B4: *New Frontiers: The Curse of Fenman*
117 *SLEEPY* (p102).
118 As theorised by the Doctor in *The Sands of Time* (p234); the fifth Doctor and Peri visit a chamber *under*

Aftermath of the Epoch's alt-reality

A dinosaur ate the Jurassic version of Bernice Summerfield. The version of Benny from Victorian times was thought dead, but escaped and had adventures in other times and places, including a city ruled by King Theon.[115] The Epoch's final remapping of this era translocated a shuttle that Jack was aboard to the year 2613. Avril Fenman saved Ruth and transported her to the same era, where she was reunited with Benny circa 2616.[116]

The Ikkaban Period of Yemayan history was in progress around 1500 BC.[117] The Great Sphinx was now buried up to its neck by sand. It mentally influenced the young Thutmose, who was on a hunting trip, to dig it out.[118]

Two Time Lord students visited Earth as part of Academy History Module 101, hoping to study Osirian cosmic influence. A freak surge in the Vortex damaged their TARDIS, stranding them. They were worshipped as the gods Amun and Thoth, but "Amun" died in an uprising. Thoth escaped, but their TARDIS was disguised as a shabti figure – a representation of servants who wait upon royals in the afterlife – and was stolen by Userhat, one of Amun's servants. Thoth spent several lifetimes searching for his tomb.[119]

The resurrected Sutekh landed on Earth, having escaped the Pyramid of Horus in the twenty-seventh century. Limited in power, he walked the land as an old man. The seventh Doctor found himself in ancient Egypt following contact with the secondary Eye of Horus in 1941, and – to cloak himself from the world-destroyer – compressed his mind and stored it within the brain of the Pharaoh Hatshepsut. As "Senenmut", the Pharaoh's beloved and one of her advisers, the Doctor set about building a network of obelisks.[120]

1458 BC - NAofBENNY V2: THE EYE OF HORUS[121]

-> After nearly twenty years of walking the Earth, the resurrected Sutekh's body was nearing its end. Because gods could not enter Pharaoh's palace without an invitation, Sutekh goaded Thutmose III to dethrone his stepmother, Hatshepsut, and become Pharaoh. Bernice Summerfield emerged from a wormhole from the twenty-first century, and was mistaken for an aspect of Hathor: "the goddess of hope and beer". To fulfill causality, she left a message in hieroglyphs for her younger self to find.

Sutekh usurped the obelisk network the Doctor (as Senenmut) had built, and placed the Eye of Sutekh at its focal point. Instead of concentrating humanity's goodwill to repel Sutekh, it threatened to harvest humankind's evilness as fuel for the world-eater. Owing to the Doctor's machinations, Sutekh was drawn to a devastated Earth in the future. The Doctor retrieved his mind from Hatshepsut, and she departed as Tut moved to wipe her name from history. Ace arrived in the TARDIS, and took the Doctor and Benny to a final confrontation with Sutekh.

An unnamed entity became embodied in the Pharaoh of Egypt, the future grandfather of Erimemushimteperem. As such, the Pharaoh fought the otherworldly Ash-Ama-Teseth, and through his own blood banished the fiend from our universe. The effort weakened Pharaoh, who died many years before Erimem was born, and diluted the potency his bloodline. The new Pharaoh had many wives and concubines, but would father only four children...[122]

Erimem

Erimemushimteperem, "Daughter of Light" – a companion of the fifth Doctor, and later a time-space adventurer in her own right – was born to Pharaoh Amenhotep II and one of his sixty concubines, Rubak.[123] She had three half brothers: the eldest, Thutmose; Teti; and the youngest, Mentu.[124] When Erimem was a child, her father trapped the Great Old Ones in a pyramid in the Himalayas.[125]

Erimem's father, Amenhotep II, defeated a rival king and came to possess the alien crystal that the Doctor had deposited on Earth many millennia ago. Amenhotep II also

---

the Sphinx in *The Eye of the Scorpion*, so if Thutmose did dig out the Sphinx, he'd finished his work prior to that. **119** *Forty-Five:* "False Gods". Howard Carter says that Userhat's tomb was sealed "three thousand years" prior to 1902. In real life, Amun was a patron deity of Thebes, and rose to prominence in the eighteenth dynasty (1550-1292 BC). The cult of Thoth gained notoriety somewhat before this, when its base of operations – Khnum – became the capital of the Hermopolite nome (a "nome" being an administrative district in ancient Egypt).
120 "Nearly twenty years" before *NAofBenny* V2: *The Eye of Horus.*
121 Dating *NAofBenny* V2: *The Eye of Horus* (*NAofBenny*

#2.3) - Historically, Hatshepsut and Thutmose III jointly ruled Egypt starting in 1478 BC (he had ascended to the throne a year earlier, at age five) until Hatshepsut's death in 1458 BC. As this story claims, Tut did try to scrub her name from history.
122 The background to *Erimem: The Last Pharaoh*. Although unnamed, Erimem's grandfather is presumably Menkheperre Thutmose III, who ruled 1458 BC until his death in 1425 BC.
123 *The Eye of the Scorpion*; Erimem's father is named in *The Roof of the World* and *Erimem: The Coming of the Queen*.
124 *Erimem: The Coming of the Queen*
125 *The Roof of the World*

claimed one thousand slaves and the rival king's sister as a wife, but he prized the crystal most of all. It was regarded as a diamond, but became known as the Veiled Leopard because it almost seemed to glow, and possessed odd spots that looked like leopard markings.[126]

Erimem's brother Mentu fathered a child with one of Erimem's handmaidens, a Mitannite named Miral, who fled from Thebes when false charges of treason were brought against her family. The offspring's lineage would produce one of Erimem's close associates, the Egyptian curator Ibrahim Hadmani.[127]

c 1401 BC - ERIMEM: THE COMING OF THE QUEEN

[128] -> Amenhotep II had recently won a war against King Gadamere of Mitanni, and even after the final battle ordered the small fingers cut from the hands of five hundred Mitanni captives, and another five hundred of them taken as slaves. Pharaoh desired an alliance with his former rival, and arranged that his son Mentu should marry Gadamere's daughter Miral. The Mitanni sought revenge, and although a plot to install a puppet ruler as Pharaoh failed, Miral killed Erimem's brothers. For this treachery, Pharaoh killed Gadamere, and Erimem, age 16, slit Miral's throat and stabbed her through the heart. Some months later, Hyksos mercenaries attacked the Pharaoh's chariot escort, and Amenhotep – standing his ground to prove his divinity – was killed. Erimem became ruler of Egypt.

When her father died, Erimem ordered priests to place the Veiled Leopard inside Amenhotep's bandages as he was prepared for burial. The diamond was later separated from his body, possibly owing to graverobbing, and would become one of the world's most famous jewels.[129]

Erimem Joins the TARDIS

c 1400 BC - THE EYE OF THE SCORPION[130] -> A starship containing prisoners crashed near Thebes, and a stasis box holding a dangerous gestalt energy being broke open. It began possessing local mercenaries. The fifth Doctor and Peri joined forces with Erimem to defeat it. Following this, Erimem – now age 17 – joined the Doctor on his travels; Fayum, a junior council member, became Pharaoh in her absence. The face of the Sphinx was damaged, and Peri whimsically issued orders that it be reconstructed with Elvis' features, confident that Napoleon's troops would damage it in the late eighteenth century.

1366 BC - SET PIECE[131] -> Ace arrived via a space-time rift in Egypt during the rule of Pharaoh Akhenaten. She served as a bodyguard to Lord Sedjet, and eluded the robotic Ants pursuing her. After burying the TARDIS for Benny to find some centuries on, she escaped through a rift to nineteenth-century France.

The shapeshifting Vondrax subsisted on the tachyon energy generated when probabilities compressed into parallel timelines. They fashioned and dispersed spheres, the Vondraxian Orbs, to harvest such energy. The Vondrax spent centuries collecting their energy-laden Orbs, and

---

126 *The Veiled Leopard*

127 *Erimem: The Last Pharaoh* (ch13).

128 Dating *Erimem: The Coming of the Queen* (BF New Worlds novel #2) - Erimem is 16 according to the blurb and pages 6-7; she was the same age "last year" in *The Eye of the Scorpion* [c.1400 BC]. Hypothetically, then, she was born in 1417 or 1418 BC, depending on when her birthday falls.

In the real world, Thutmose (here named as Erimem's half-brother) ruled Egypt as Menkheperura Thutmose IV from about 1400-1390 BC, and historically – as in the *Doctor Who* universe – he was the son of Amenhtep II. His death as reported in *Erimem: The Coming of the Queen* is a fairly significant deviation from history; writer Iain McLaughlin had privately decided that Erimem's successor to the throne, Fayum, would get renamed and become the historical Thutmose. While this seems like a fairly convoluted way of going about things, nothing rules it out either.

129 *The Veiled Leopard*

130 Dating *The Eye of Scorpion* (BF #24) - The Doctor estimates the date as "about 1400 BC" from environmental conditions and hieroglyphics; in the real world, it's unclear as to whether the reign of Amenhotep II

ended in 1401 BC or 1397 BC. Peri's claim that Napoleon's troops damaged the Sphinx's face (historically, they arrived in Egypt in 1798) owes to an urban legend that they used it for target practice. The Doctor doesn't correct Peri, but there's otherwise no evidence that Napoleon's troops perpetrate the crime in the *Doctor Who* universe. In the real world, at least, erosion is the far more likely culprit.

The blurb to *Erimem: The Last Pharaoh* says Erimem is "from 1400 BC", and she's cited in Chapter Nine as being from "around 1400 BC". The same book (ch5) claims that Erimem was "in her eighteenth year" when she left Egypt (*The Eye of the Scorpion*, however, says she was 17), and names her father as Amenhotep II (ch3).

Erimem's friend Andy Hansen claims (*Erimem: Buccaneer*) that Erimem was Pharaoh "about 1450BC" – but she's not the best informed about this, having only known Erimem after she's lost many of her memories.

131 Dating *Set Piece* (NA #35) - The date is given as "1366 BCE".

132 *TW: Trace Memory*

133 *The Time Meddler.* The earliest parts of Stonehenge were built around 2800 BC, although the surrounding

almost inevitably caused a slaughter at each retrieval zone. One such massacre occurred in Egypt, 1352 BC.[132]

The Monk helped build Stonehenge using anti-gravity lifts.[133] A Glassa took over the body of Eowin, a warrior guarding Stonehenge. "He" would walk the Earth for millennia.[134] The Ragman had been born at the other end of the universe as a psionic force. It had travelled on Earth in a stone, drawn to the power inherent in Earth's ley lines. The rock containing the Ragman was incorporated into the stone circle at Cirbury, and the creature was dormant.[135]

1334 BC - DINOSAURS ON A SPACESHIP[136] -> The eleventh Doctor saved Queen Nefertiti's people from a giant alien locust attack. A grateful Nefertiti accompanied the Doctor to address a crisis in 2367.

A bust of Nefertiti wound up in the Monk's TARDIS, another aboard the *Erewhon*.[137] King Tutankhamun died. His coffin would wind up in Madame Karabraxos' private collection.[138]

Classical History

The Doctor claimed to have met Theseus.[139] The eleventh Doctor took Amy to the Trojan Gardens.[140] The Rani was present at the Trojan War, extracting a chemical from human brains.[141]

The Trojan War:
Vicki Leaves the TARDIS, Katarina Joins

c 1184 BC - THE MYTH MAKERS[142] -> Captured by the Greeks outside Troy, the first Doctor was given two days to come up with a scheme to end the ten-year siege. He rejected the idea of using catapults to propel the Greeks over the walls of Troy – if only after

Agamemnon insisted that the Doctor would be the first to try such a contrivance – and came up with the idea of using a wooden horse containing Greek troops. Vicki left the Doctor and Steven's company to marry young Troilus; she re-named herself "Cressida". Katarina, one of Cassandra's handmaidens, joined the Doctor on his travels.

Vicki and Troilus married, but the Trojans came to believe that she was cursed or possessed. While Prince Aeneas and the main party travelled onward, Vicki and Troilus settled in Carthage. They had two children – "two young heroes", as Vicki called them.[143]

The Doctor procured a first edition of Homer's *The Iliad*, and later gave it to the Reneath Archive on Cornucopia.[144]

1164 BC - FROSTFIRE[145] -> Vicki wept alone one day, and discovered the Cinder – all that remained of the phoenix she had encountered in 1814 AD – amongst her tears. She contained it in an oil lamp, and kept it beneath the Temple of Astarte. It amused her to call the Cinder "Frosty", and to visit it and share memories of the Doctor.

Knowing that the phoenix would devour Earth if it hatched again, Vicki cared for the Cinder – and thereby set up a loop that would end its cycle of rebirth. The Cinder would remain in Carthage until the nearby city of Tunis arose. It then became part of Captain McClavity's Collection of Curiosities in the nineteenth century – and then travelled back with Vicki again to ancient Troy.

Troilus was supervising the building of a new quinquereme.[146]

Interstellar authorities captured a Medusa – a predatory species that quantum-locked others into stone – and began the journey home. The Medusa took mental command of the Scryclops (cyclopes who could see back-

---

earth bank goes back to 3100 BC. The final building activity occurred between 1600-1400 BC.

134 Eowin is "4,725" years old in *Leth-St: The Life of Evans* (ch1), set by its internal logic in 1970, which would date Eowin to 2755 BC.

135 *Rags* (p160).

136 Dating *Dinosaurs on a Spaceship* (X7.2) - A caption provides the year. Competing theories exist as to Nefertiti's fate in real life, but she died c.1330 BC.

137 Busts of Nefertiti are seen in episode four of *The Time Meddler* (squint, and you can just see it between Vicki and Steven) and *Smile*. The sculptor Thutmos crafted the infamous Nefertiti Bust in 1345 BC, but it's been copied many times. Knowing the Monk, he probably has the original.

138 *Time Heist*. Tutankhamun died c.1323 BC.

139 *The Horns of Nimon*

140 *Vincent and the Doctor*. This presumably means the gardens of ancient Troy.

141 *The Mark of the Rani*

142 Dating *The Myth Makers* (3.3) - The traditional date for the fall of Troy is 1184 BC, although this date is not given on screen.

143 *Frostfire*

144 "Matildus"

145 Dating *Frostfire* (BF CC #1.1) - The audio booklet concurs on a dating of 1184 BC for *The Myth Makers*, and the back cover dates *Frostfire* to 1164 BC, something that is reiterated within the story itself.

146 *Frostfire*. A quinquereme is an oar-powered warship, and was developed from the earlier trireme. It was in use from fourth century BC to the first century AD.

wards and forwards in time) crewing her jailor's ship, and it crashed to Earth. A limitation field kept the Medusa contained.[147]

The Master hid his TARDIS in a burial chamber in the Valley of Kings in Egypt, prior to the Daleks putting him on trial on Skaro.[148] A Vondraxian Orb wound up buried in the Arctic on Earth.[149] The Sorshans let the hostile Lom past their planetary defence shield, then reactivated it and released a biological toxin – deliberately killing themselves and their planet to prevent the Lom from spreading.[150] The Doctor was given a copy of the *I Ching* by Wen Wang.[151]

Thousands of years ago, the Exxilons were "the supreme beings of the universe... Exxilon had grown old before life began on other planets". Bernice Summerfield once wrote, "There are half a dozen worlds where the native languages develop up to a point, and then are suddenly replaced by one of the Exxilon ones."

Worlds visited by the Exxilons include Yemaya and Earth, where they helped to build temples in Peru. The Doctor visited one of these temples, and examined the carvings there. On their home planet, the Exxilons created one of the Seven Hundred Wonders of the Universe: their City, a vast complex designed to last for all eternity. It was given a brain to protect, repair and maintain itself, and thus it no longer needed the Exxilons, who were driven from the City and degenerated into primitives.

The City needed power, and began to absorb electrical energy directly from the planet's atmosphere. The City also set an intelligence test that granted access to those who might have some knowledge to offer it. Over the centuries, a few Exxilons attempted the test, but none returned.[152]

c 1000 BC - THE EXXILONS[153] -> The Exxilons visited many worlds, and negotiated with local populations to construct advanced beacons. These opened portals back to Exxilon, and siphoned away the indigenous populations' mental energy to feed the living City there. The fourth Doctor, Leela and K9 stopped a party of Exxilons on the *Locoyun* from draining Planet E9874, the home of the Tarl.

Mawdryn and seven of his companions stole a metamorphic symbiosis generator from the Time Lords,

---

147 "Gaze of the Medusa", during the Homeric Era. The spaceship's hologram avatar looks like Zeus, and the Doctor speculates that it inspired Greek mythology – but there's no evidence of that, and it's just as likely the reverse.

148 *Mastermind*, explaining what became of the Master's Ship prior to *Doctor Who – The Movie*. Tombs were constructed in the Valley of Kings from the sixteenth to eleventh centuries BC.

149 "Three thousand years" before the 1953 component of *TW: Trace Memory*.

150 "Three thousand years" before "The Grief".

151 *Timewyrm Revelation* (p14). Wang was the last king of the Shang dynasty.

152 *Death to the Daleks*. The Peruvian temples influenced by the Exxilons are around three thousand years old, so the collapse of Exxilon civilisation must be after that. In *SLEEPY*, Benny detects Exxilon influence in the Yemayan pyramid, dating from around "1500 BCE".

153 Dating *The Exxilons* (4th Doc #4.1) - The story occurs during the Exxilons' exploration phase (as referenced in *Death to the Daleks*).

154 *Mawdryn Undead*. The ship has been in orbit for "three thousand years" according to the Doctor.

155 "Millennia" before *Phantoms of the Deep*.

156 Litefoot estimates this happened "thousands of years" before *J&L S11: The Woman in White*, but it's also said that the *Demeter* lay undisturbed "for centuries".

157 "Three thousand years" before *River S1: The Boundless Sea*.

158 *DotD: Vengeance of the Stones*

159 Dating *Primeval* (BF #26) - It is "three thousand years" before Nyssa's time.

160 "Thousands of years" before *Scapegoat*.

161 "Millennia" before *Forever Autumn*.

162 "Millennia" before *SJA: The Shadow People*.

163 "Three thousand years" before *SJA: Eye of the Gorgon*.

164 "Thousands of years" before *The Sorcerer's Apprentice*.

165 *Other Lives*. The Queen was a contemporary of King Solomon, who lived circa 970-928 BC.

166 "Three thousand years" before *SJA: Enemy of the Bane*.

167 *The Daemons*

168 *ST: "All Hands on Deck"* – implying she met Leir, a semi-legendary King of the Britons who lived around the time of the founding of Rome.

169 *The Song of the Megaptera*. The Biblical book *Jonah* is set during the reign of Jeroboam II (786-746 BC).

170 *K9: Dream-Eaters*. No date is specified, and the information that the obelisk dates to "Celtic" times doesn't pin one down.

171 *The Eleventh Doctor Year One: "The Rise and Fall"*. King Midas of Phrygia, a possible inspiration of the Midas myth, lived in the late eighth century BC.

172 *Seasons of Fear*

173 "A few thousand years" before *The High Price of Parking*.

174 Dating *Benny: Walking to Babylon* (Benny NA #10) - The year is given.

175 *Option Lock*. Pythagoras lived 580-500 BC.

176 "Gaze of the Medusa"

hoping to become immortal. Instead they became horrific undying mutations, and the elders of their planet exiled them. Their ship entered a warp ellipse. It reached an inhabited planet every seventy years, allowing one of the crew to transmat down to seek help.[154] Moisture-harvesting microbots fell to Earth, and became trapped in a tomb in Mesopotamia.[155]

The planet Therris, the fourth world of the Valerian System, was destroyed in an inter-planetary conflict more than three millennia ago.[156] Prior to its extinction, a goblin-like race programmed a vessel to travel to another world, upgrade the intelligence of the most advanced species there, and psionically imprint their dead minds into them. The ship became trapped in the Mariana Trench and stayed there, awaiting a species susceptible to telepathic influence.[157]

The *Demeter*, a Galactic Zoological survey vessel, crashed to Earth. In future, the Prince Albert Theatre would be built over it.[158]

c 1000 BC - PRIMEVAL[159] **->** Kwundaar launched a bid to reconquer Traken. He engineered an illness for Nyssa, knowing the fifth Doctor would seek out Shayla, the greatest physician in Trakenite history. Kwundaar then implanted a psychic command in the Doctor's mind, getting the Doctor to deactivate Traken's defences. Kwundaar's forces consequently invaded the planet, but the Doctor tricked Kwundaar and harnessed the Source's power for himself. The Doctor thus became the first Keeper of Traken. He reactivated the defences, which destroyed Kwundaar, then abdicated. Shayla became the second Keeper.

The Baroks were humanoids with heads like those of goats. They were an advanced species who, each hunting season, would turn into wild, ferocious cannibals. They finally developed a ritual to siphon away their bloodlust – each tribe of Baroks would nominate a "scapegoat" into whom they could project their violent tendencies. The scapegoat would be driven into the wilderness, enabling the tribe to refrain from tearing itself apart. When a "cosmic" catastrophe befell the Barok homeworld, the surviving tribes dispersed throughout the galaxy.[160]

A spaceship containing some Hervoken crashed to Earth in what would become New England in America. In the millennia to come, the ship psychically influenced people to build the town of Blackwood Falls over it.[161]

The Shaydargen were a race of space pioneers. One of their spaceships crashed in Snowdonia, Wales, where the ten surviving crewmembers lived out their natural lives. Their craft remained buried in a mountain as the crew died off, and an empathic artificial entity created to meet their needs went dormant.[162]

Three parasitic Gorgons arrived on Earth through a portal, and inspired the legends of Medusa and her sisters in Greek mythology. They took human hosts – one of them was killed, and a sisterhood devoted to Demeter protected the remaining two. The Gorgons lost the talisman that would re-open the portal.[163]

On the planet Avalon, a technologically advanced race created a system that focused solar energy to deflect the large number of asteroids in their system away from their world. They also built thought-operated nanobots that allowed them to affect matter and energy. This discovery prolonged the race's existence but made their lives futile. They drained the machines of energy, but it was too late. Their civilisation fell, and the natives regressed to being reptilian cephlies, lacking all ingenuity.[164]

The Doctor met the Queen of Sheba.[165] **The cybernetic organism Horath ruled the Dark Empire, a period of tyrannical galactic rule. Horath crushed many civilisations, but was finally banished to another dimension. A portal leading to Horath was sealed below the standing stones in the village of Whitebarrow.**[166]

Evidence found by Professor Horner in the twentieth century suggested that pagan rituals took place at Devil's Hump at around 800 BC.[167] Susan told one of her Coal Hill teachers, Ms Ireland, that King Lear was "nothing like what really happened".[168] The Doctor met the Jonah of legend – a confirmed vegan with white and wrinkled skin.[169] **The Bodach attempted to send humanity permanently to sleep and feast on its dreams, but the plan failed. The crystals the Bodach needed – the Eyes of Oblivion – were set on an obelisk that ended up buried outside London.**[170]

King Midas of Phrygia backed the Doctor in his efforts to stage a hostile takeover of SERVEYOUinc.[171] Around 600 BC, a Nimon scout arrived on Earth and was killed by his own sword by Mithras, who was later worshipped throughout the known world as a result of his deed.[172]

The artificial planetoid Parking was built, to handle traffic to and from the tourist world Dashrah.[173]

570 BC - BENNY: WALKING TO BABYLON[174] **->** Benny pursued two Worldsphere rogues (!Ci!ci-tel and WiRgo!xu) and their drone (I!qu-!qu-tala) down a time corridor to ancient Babylon, and met a linguist, John Lafayette, who had fallen down the corridor from 1901. I!qu-!qu-tala curtailed the rogues' goal of triggering war between the People and the Time Lords, and terminated the corridor after sending Benny home. !Ci!ci-tel was killed, but WiRgo!xu and I!qu-!qu-tala travelled across the world with the Babylonian priestess Ninan. The Time Lords returned John to his native time.

The Doctor was present when Pythagoras discovered the connection between mathematics and the physical world.[175] The Doctor said that Pythagoras was a "Lovely fellow. Very good at billiards. All those tricky angle shots."[176] Daedalus tried to confound the Doctor, as did Pythagorus – a "brilliant man" who "thought his beans were evil".[177] King Croesus' funding helped the eleventh Doctor purchase shares of SERVEYOUinc.[178]

The Doctor regarded the Gautama Buddha – whose golden tooth would survive aboard *The World* – as a "lovely chap".[179]

c 516 BC - CASUALTIES OF TIME[180] **->** The TARDIS' Randomiser didn't fool the Black Guardian in the slightest, and so the Guardian backtracked along the Doctor's timeline and laid a trap for his foe. The Guardian created a causal loop that involved his construct, Cuthbert, travelling back in time to enable creation of his own company: the Conglomerate, a corporation heavily interwoven into Earth history. Cuthbert first brought about the Conglomerate by shooting down a spaceship over a village in Scotland, but the fourth Doctor – as the Guardian intended – moved to stop him, an act that would negate the Conglomerate's existence and rip the whole of time asunder. The Doctor did thwart Cuthbert, having deduced that the spaceship was low on power and would crash nearby, preserving history. Having stymied the Guardian, the Doctor took Cuthbert back to the future.

c 500 BC - "Gaze of the Medusa"[181] **->** The Lamp of Chronos, as derived from Time Lord technology, enabled the Medusa imprisoned on Earth to make contact with 1887. The fourth Doctor, Sarah, Professor Odysseus James and his daughter Athena travelled back and confronted the fiend. The Medusa turned James and Sarah into stone – James was shattered, but Sarah remained in that state until the Victorian era. The Doctor and Athena escaped back to the future, and caused the Medusa to die when its spaceship self-destructed.

Around 500 BC, the Doctor met Sun Tzu at least twice and discussed the *Art of War*.[182] The Doctor replaced Sun

---

177 *The Labyrinth of Buda Castle.* Pythagorus lived c.570 to c.495 BC. It's sometimes claimed that Pythagorus didn't like consuming beans, possibly in deference to the doctrine of metempsychosis (i.e. the transmigration of spirit). Daedalus sired the doomed Icarus; his being a real person in *Doctor Who* would be in keeping with *The Myth Makers*, which depicts the Trojan War.

178 *The Eleventh Doctor Year One:* "The Rise and Fall". King Croesus of Lydia lived 595 BC to circa 547 BC, and was known for his wealth.

179 *The Wreck of the World.* According to legend, the Gautama Buddha died in 543 BC. His tooth currently resides at the Temple of the Sacred Tooth Relic in Kandy, Sri Lanka.

180 Dating *Casualties of Time* (BF 4th Doc #5.8) - Reading off the TARDIS instruments, the Doctor says it's "Scotland, sixth century BC", "the Iron Age". The Black Guardian is remarkably stupid here – laying a trap that, if the Doctor falls for it, will cause the Guardian to lose.

181 Dating "Gaze of the Medusa" (Titan 4th Doc Vol. 1 #1-5) - The Doctor estimates that it's "500 BC?... give or take half a century either way". Professor James finds a Corinthian helmet from the same period.

182 The fourth Doctor name-drops Sun Tzu in *The Shadow of Weng-Chiang*, and the seventh Doctor and Ace refer to meeting him in *The Shadow of the Scourge*.

183 *Set Piece*, during the "Fourth Century BCE".

184 Three thousand years before *Benny: Tempest*.

185 *Benny S7: The Empire State.* The legend of the Stone claims it's "about three thousand years old", and Benny (speaking from 2607) says it has existed for "the whole of recorded human history". Braxiatel concurs, but also says he was inert as the Stone "for a couple of millennia". In *Benny S8: The Judas Gift*, Bev Tarrant says Braxiatel spent "three thousand years asleep".

186 *The Daemons, City of Death.*

187 "One hundred generations" before *Four to Doomsday.*

188 *The Vampires of Venice.* Records suggest that the Olympic Games were first held in 776 BC.

189 *Pond Life*

190 *The Spectre of Lanyon Moor.* This would be around 440 BC.

191 *Enlightenment.* Pericles died, age 70, in 429 BC.

192 *Robot.* Alexander lived 356-323 BC.

193 *The Keys of Marinus.* Pyrrho lived c.360-270 BC.

194 *The Slitheen Excursion*

195 *Omega.* This would have been around 350 BC.

196 *Horror of Fang Rock, Logopolis.*

197 "Voyager"

198 *City at World's End, The Two Doctors.* Archimedes lived c.287-212 BC.

199 *Island of Death*

200 *Eye of Heaven* (p181). Eratosthenes lived c.276-194 BC.

201 *Cat's Cradle: Witch Mark*

202 "The Crimson Hand". Depictions of Zephyrus and Hyacinth (a target of Zaphyrus' love, and killed by him when Hyacinth favoured Apollo) date back to the fifth century BC.

203 *DEyes 4: A Life in the Day.* The Marbles were sculpted circa 447-438 BC.

204 Dating *Benny S6: The Oracle of Delphi* (Benny audio #6.5) - The year is given. Historically, the plague that struck Athens in 430 BC returned in 429 and 427 BC.

205 *Iris S5: Oracle of the Supermarket*

206 *3rdA: Storm of the Horofax*

207 *Mask of Tragedy.* Historically, Cleon died in 422 BC.

208 Dating *Mask of Tragedy* (BF #190) - The year is given. *Peace* was first performed in 421 BC. As the story also claims, *The Wasps* debuted "last year", in 422 BC.

Tzu as the Chinese emperor's military advisor but wasn't terribly effective, as he kept holding conflict resolution seminars rather than fighting.[183] The Way of Drell, a religion devoted to universal harmony, was founded in the Mother Temple on Karnor.[184]

After Irving Braxiatel left the Braxiatel Collection in 2606, he wanted some "me" time and facilitated his transformation into a rock: the Stone of Barter. It became a legendary item that was passed between nomadic tribes, and enabled a literal exchange of qualities such as intelligence, knowledge and paranormal abilities.[185]

Ancient Greece

The Daemons and Scaroth both influenced ancient Greek civilisation.[186] The Athenian philosopher Bigon lived in Greece around two thousand five hundred years ago. In Bigon's fifty-sixth year, the Urbankans kidnapped him. For the first time in their visits to Earth, the Urbankans encountered resistance.[187]

The eleventh Doctor thought that Amy and Rory might like to visit the first Olympic Games as a wedding present.[188] The eleventh Doctor crashed into ancient Greece while leaving a phone message for Amy and Rory.[189] The Doctor visited Athens and saw the Parthenon being built.[190] **The Eternals kidnapped a trireme of Athenian sailors from the time of Pericles.[191] The Doctor met Alexander the Great[192] and Pyrrho[193], possibly on the same visit.**

The tenth Doctor planned to take June to Greece in 480 BC, but they ended up in 1500 BC instead.[194] The Doctor met Praxiteles, who sculpted the Venus de Milo.[195] **The Doctor visited one of the Seven Wonders of the Ancient World: the Pharos lighthouse.[196]**

The first lighthouse was built at Alexandria; Astrolabus provided the fire of its lamp. Within a year, starships began to land. "The city had become a crossroads in time. Past and future had conjoined – sorcery and science now walked hand in hand." The aliens stole Astrolabus' charts. Alexandria fell, destroyed by a sea monster.

"It was then that Voyager came... from the realms of old time, from the dawn of myth... the very spirit of legend."

Astrolabus attempted to navigate the timelines, but the disturbances were too great.[197]

The first Doctor and Susan met Archimedes, and **the Doctor acquired his business card.[198]** The third Doctor visited Athens and spent time with Archimedes.[199] The Doctor taught the playwright Eratosthenes at least some of his craft.[200] The Doctor wrote many of the Greek Classics.[201] He judged that Zephyrus, the Greek god of the west wind, was "a lovely bloke, bit of a swinger. Should have seen what he did to poor old Hyacinth".[202] The Doctor modelled for one of the Elgin Marbles.[203]

430 BC - BENNY S7: THE ORACLE OF DELPHI[204] ->
Benny and Jason travelled back in time to ancient Greece, hoping to consult with the Oracle of Delphi pertaining to future events concerning the Braxiatel Collection. The Oracle, a.k.a. Lady Megaira, had gained the gift of prophecy from the Stone of Barter. She unleashed a plague upon Athens as vengeance against the patriarchy for their treatment of women, but herself fell victim to the illness. Benny and Jason distributed a plague-vaccine, and returned home. During these events, Benny met Socrates and Plato.

Iris Wildthyme saw the auguries of Rome, where birds were an ancient symbol of prophecy. The priests of Greece summoned an inter-dimensional being from the shadowlands to serve as their Oracle, and trapped it. The Oracle was passed on, and by the twentieth century was endowed in a fairground relic.[205] Some oracles of ancient Earth were time-sensitives, akin to the Horofax Provosts.[206]

The Athenian general Cleon fell in battle, but Tyrgius – an alien xenosurgeon taking his holiday in ancient Greece – impulsively healed him. Cleon led Athens through the period of plague and war to follow.[207]

421 BC - MASK OF TRAGEDY[208] ->
Ancient Athens held such notoriety in the history of time, some of its key citizens knew that time travellers and extraterrestrials discretely visited them. Aristophanes found that his serious works never sold, but the seventh Doctor – who visited the playwright, accompanied by Ace and Hector Thomas – had been commissioning a comedy from him on a yearly basis.

The time-tourist Tyrgius used a thought-intensifying mask to endow plague victims with his natural healing ability, but this created increasing numbers of the walking dead. The power-mad leader of Athens, Cleon, attempted to contain and incinerate both the plague-carriers and his political opponents – a situation that Hector curtailed by donning Tyrgius' mask and declaring himself the fun-loving god Dionysus. Cleon stole the mask and exerted his will over the Athenians, further destabilising matters. Tyrgius destroyed the mask, Ace allied herself with female Spartans who doused a blaze threatening to consume Athens, and Aristophanes used the Doctor's Metebelis crystals to temporarily calm the populace, making them think they were choruses from his various works. The Athenians drove Cleon into exile.

The first performance of Aristophanes' play *Peace* concluded with Tyrgius revealing his true form, a giant beetle, and flying "up to Heaven". *Peace* won a theatrical contest, prompting the history books' claim that the Athenians had "voted for peace" with Sparta. The Spartans' aid to Athens led to an accord against the Persians and Macedonians. The Doctor pledged to nip forward and edit out the anomalous developments from Wikipedia (and other historical resources).

Hector denounced the Doctor and Ace's cavalier attitude toward a potentially disastrous situation, and insisted they take him home to the twenty-first century...

410 BC - "The Chains of Olympus"[209] -> Aristophanes' *The Clouds* had caused such character assassination and widespread mockery of Socrates, all of the great philosopher's students save Plato abandoned him. Socrates became such a drunken waste of a man, not even his wife abandoning him lifted his spirits.

The statue of Athena containing psychic metal had, for decades, been serving as a belief engine – i.e. absorbing the faiths of the people of Athens – but now manifested that faith as constructs of the Greek gods. Athens came under threat from Zeus and various creatures of myth: a harpy, a cyclops, a griffin and more. The eleventh Doctor, Amy and Rory contained the situation and secured the psychic metal, even as Socrates posed enough philosophical conundrums to the faux Zeus that his entire pantheon was uncreated.

The seventh Doctor was fairly certain that he'd discussed Athenian jurisprudence with Socrates.[210] Benny thought that Plato was a "miserable old git who talked a lot of rubbish".[211]

The Doctor met the real Sybil, "a hell of a woman" who could dance the Tarantella and had "nice teeth". She had a bit of a thing for the Doctor, but when he told her it could "never last", she replied, "I know."[212]

A spaceship fell onto the planet Kasagrad. Rablev, the chief engineer of King Hieronimes, tried to harness its power and capture the throne, but the ship's atomic stacks overloaded, killing thousands if not millions. The people believed Rablev's arrogance had offended the gods, and

---

209 Dating "The Chains of Olympus" (*DWM* #442-445) - The year is given. Socrates lived 470/469 to 399 BC. Socrates' wife – presumably Xanthippe, the mother of his three sons – has left him, but almost nothing factual is known about her life.
210 *Mask of Tragedy*
211 *Benny B1: Epoch: The Kraken's Lament*
212 *The Fires of Pompeii*. Presumably this refers to the original Sybil, at Delphi.
213 "Three thousand years, give or take" (p51) years before *Benny: The Doomsday Manuscript*.
214 *TW: The Sin Eaters*. The year isn't given, but the historical record suggests that eruptions occurred at Etna in 396 BC, 122 BC, 1030, 1160 (or possibly 1224), 1669, 1928, 1949, 1971, 1981, 1983 and 1991 to 1993.
215 *The Drosten's Curse*. Hippocrates lived circa 460 to circa 370 BC. Historians believe that he, or one of his students, wrote the Oath sometime between the fifth and third century BC.
216 "Decades" before "The Chains of Olympus". Calidora is here a young girl, an older woman when the story takes place.
217 *Survival of the Fittest*. Aristotle lived 384 to 322 BC.
218 *The Nu-Humans*
219 *Mask of Tragedy*. Euclid's birth and death years are unknown, but he worked during the reign of Ptolemy I (323-283 BC).
220 Dating *Farewell, Great Macedon* (BF LS #2.1a) - The year is given at least three times. The Doctor's group spends some "long weeks" with Alexander before leaving on the day of his death, which is cited as "June 13th". (A solid claim, although his passing is alternatively ascribed to the 10th or the 11th.)

Many of the events in *Farewell, Great Macedon* are drawn from historical accounts, but extreme liberties have been taken with the timeframe, and entirely disparate events have been rolled into a single narrative. Cleitus is thought to have died about five years before Alexander (in autumn 328 BC), Calanus about a year and a half beforehand (in late 325 BC), and Hephaestion some months beforehand (in autumn 324 BC) – here, they all perish in a matter of weeks. Calanus and Cleitus died in circumstances similar to those described here, but Hephaestion likely died from typhoid fever, and here succumbs to a snake bite. Antipater is rumoured to have orchestrated Alexander's death, while the historian Plutarch rejects this idea, and it's equally likely that Alexander died from natural causes. Either way, Antipater isn't implicated as having anything to do with Cleitus, Calanus and Hephaestion's deaths. Nor did Antipater die at Selecus' hand – he was, in fact, named regent of Alexander's empire and given control of Greece before dying from an illness, after returning to Macedon in 320 BC.
221 *The Movellan Grave*
222 *FP: The Brakespeare Voyage* (ch9, 12).
223 Dating *Erimem: Three Faces of Helena* (Erimem novel #8) - The year is given.
224 "A thousand years" before *Genesis of the Daleks*.
225 *Marco Polo*
226 Or so the artificial version of Huang claims in "The Immortal Emperor". Huang was born in 246 BC.
227 *Enlightenment*
228 *The Nightmare Fair*. Imperial China started in 221 BC; the Toymaker's involvement could have happened at any point until its end, in 1912 AD.
229 An unseen adventure, referenced in *The Tenth Doctor Year Three*: "Sharper than a Serpent's Tooth".
230 Dating *The Angels Take Manhattan* (X7.5) - The year is given. The Qin dynasty lasted 221 to 206 BC.

sealed him in the ship. His lost tomb became legendary.[213]

Jack Harkness fled a lava flow emanating from Mount Etna on a goat cart.[214] The Doctor helped Hippocrates write the Hippocratic Oath.[215]

The Prometheans deposited an egg of psychic metal near Athens. A young girl named Calidora found it, and incorporated some of its substance into a gold statue of Athena forged by her father.[216] The Doctor met Aristotle, who whittered on about bees.[217] The Doctor claimed to have written speeches for Aristotle, characterizing him as a "lovely chap with a dreadful beard".[218] Melanie Bush corrected some of Euclid's geometry.[219]

323 BC (May to 13th June) - FAREWELL, GREAT MACEDON[220] -> The first Doctor, Ian, Barbara and Susan met Alexander the Great during his final days. One of Alexander's generals, Antipater, tired of Alexander's refusal to return home to Macedon and led a conspiracy to replace the king with another general, Selecus. The conspirators' actions led to the deaths of those in line to succeed Alexander: Cleitus, Calanus and Hephaestion. The Doctor's party was implicated in the deaths, but Alexander judged them innocent – especially after the Doctor and Ian respectively proved their worthiness by walking barefoot on hot coals and winning a wrestling match.

Alexander fell ill (or was poisoned) and refused treatment upon learning from the Doctor's group that his dream of uniting the entire world was destined to fail. Antipater's plot was exposed, and Selecus killed Antipater to keep his own treachery secret. Within minutes of Alexander's death, his remaining generals started squabbling over his throne. Ptolemy aided the Doctor and his friends in making their getaway, and pledged to improve upon the city of Alexandria – and to build an immense library there in Alexander's honour.

A Movellan ship buried itself near the Pilgrims' Way in the fourth century BC, and stayed dormant until 1980.[221]

wih - Robert Scarratt of the Great Houses worked against the Celtic alliance that sacked Delphi in 279 BC. Thanks to his efforts, the Celtic leader Brennus died and was thought to have killed himself – which caused a backlash against his co-commander, Acichorus, and lent aid to the Houses' Eighth Earth Front. As part of Scarratt's payment for captaining *The Brakespeare*, House Lineacrux agreed to snatch the Celtic tribes an instant before their deaths, and transport them to a safe world far away in space-time.[222]

Erimem's Friend Helena Becomes Immortal

276 BC and 272 BC - ERIMEM: THREE FACES OF HELENA[223] -> Helena, a close friend of Erimem, was born and worked as a slave to Asha, an honourary Princess in Alexandria. Egypt's old families resented the Greek influence upon the throne following Alexander's rule – Asha, as one of their number, heard stories of a traveller guarding a powerful device in Africa's depths, and led an expedition there.

Four years after leaving Alexandria, Princess Asha's expedition found a crashed spaceship up a mountain in Africa. The traveller inside possessed nanites that repaired all wounds, granting immortality. Asha mortally wounded her slave, Helena, for her infidelity with Asha's beloved, Ikrates. Helena's future self, Erimem, Andy Hansen and Ibrahim Hadmani healed Helena with the traveller's medical casket, then facilitated her escape. She would live into the twenty-first century.

Asha also gained immortality, and came to rule the isolated city of Kurr.

The Thousand Year War on Skaro

On the planet Skaro, the Thals and the Kaleds went to war. During the first century of the conflict, chemical weapons were used, and monstrous mutations developed in the Thal and Kaled gene pool. To keep their races pure, all Mutos were cast out into the wastelands that now covered the planet. As the war continued, resources became more scarce for the foot soldiers – plastic and rifles gave way to animal skins and clubs, but both sides developed ever-more potent missiles. The war would last for a thousand years until there were only two cities left, protected by thick domes.[224]

Ancient China

The Great Wall of China was built around 300 BC.[225] As a young boy, Qin Shi Huang found a spaceship bearing an alien: Meng Tian. Huang used Meng Tian's knowledge to unite China's warring states and become its first emperor.[226] At the time the Ch'in dynasty ruled in China, the Eternals kidnapped a crew of Chinese sailors.[227]

At some point, the Celestial Toymaker's games became interwoven into the fabric of Imperial China.[228] The Doctor lived in ancient China for a time, and – deprived of the TARDIS' telepathic circuits – learned some local dialects.[229]

221 BC - THE ANGELS TAKE MANHATTAN[230] -> The eleventh Doctor and Amy changed the markings on a vase in the early Qin dynasty. River Song would read the word "Yowzah!" on the vase in 1938, and send the appropriate homing signal.

The First Emperor of China

In 210 BC, an alien intelligence copied the minds of Qin Shi Huang and two of his generals into a stone engram. They would remain dormant until 1865 AD.[231] The Doctor witnessed a shadow puppet theatre performed during the Han Dynasty.[232]

c 210 BC - THE EMPEROR OF ETERNITY[233] -> The TARDIS materialised in space, and deflected a meteor toward China. Li Si, a chancellor to the Emperor Qin Shi Huang, regarded the meteor landing as a bad omen and had the people of Dongjun put to death lest they speak of it. The second Doctor, Jamie and Victoria arrived in the village ten days later. Li Si captured the travellers and the TARDIS, but Qin – who had been masquerading as a monk – was saddened to learn the atrocities committed in his name and gave the Doctor's party permission to leave.

c 210 BC - "The Immortal Emperor"[234] -> The tenth Doctor and Donna saw the Great Wall of China, and found that Emperor Qin Shi Huang's first general – Meng Tian – was an alien who had built an army of terracotta robots. Following an assassination attempt, Meng Tian had given the Emperor an artificial body. The Emperor learned of Meng Tian's plans to conquer Earth and slew him – but in doing so became inert and destroyed his palace.

c 200 BC - LUNA ROMANA[235] -> Ancient Rome was a sub-Level 1 civilisation.

An accident on the moon threw Quadrigger Stoyn back in time – and also splintered him into six copies of himself. On arrival in Rome, Stoyn traded gold on his person for the local currency, and commissioned the playwright Titus Maccius Plautus to write *Luna Romana* (as inspired by the moon goddess Luna and Stoyn's encounter with Romana), which concerned General Pyrgotrogus returning after three months abroad to find debauchery in his household.

---

231 "Two thousand years" before *The Eleventh Tiger*.
232 *The Darkness of Glass*. The Han Dynasty lasted 206 BC to 220 AD.
233 Dating *The Emperor of Eternity* (BF CC #4.8) - The evidence is confusing when weighed against the historical accounts. The Doctor specifies that it's "210 BC", within a few days of the Emperor's death (on September 10th of that year), but the meteor incident that prompted the slaughter of Dongjun is historically dated to 211 BC. It's possible that the meteor event happened a year later in the *Doctor Who* universe, but it's equally likely that the Doctor has just gotten the year wrong.

THE FIRST EMPEROR OF CHINA: Qin Shi Huang (who ruled under the name "First Emperor" from 221-210 BC) is featured in three *Doctor Who* stories, in three different formats: the novel *The Eleventh Tiger*, the *DWM* comic "The Immortal Emperor" and the audio *The Emperor of Eternity*. All are reasonably reconcilable if one is flexible as to the final fate of the original Emperor. For all that we're told, the real Huang might, as history claims, have simply died after ingesting a series of "immortality pills" that gave him mercury poisoning – but that his mind was copied (by both Meng Tian and the Mandragora Helix, for entirely different purposes) beforehand. In *The Eleventh Tiger* (p267), the first Doctor concurs with this, saying that the "Emperor" he meets is a duplicate of the original's memories "in a personality matrix", and isn't the genuine article. (That, certainly, would explain why the Emperor is portrayed a lot more ruthlessly in *The Eleventh Tiger*, and seems very intent on obtaining the immortality that he forsakes in *The Emperor of Eternity*.) Similarly, it's possible that the "Emperor" in "The Immortal Emperor" is nothing more than a robotic construct crafted by Meng Tian, who wants to remain the power behind the throne once the original Huang has died/otherwise become unavaila-

ble. The robot might even *think* he's the genuine article, although it's admittedly an oversight on Meng Tian's part to leave out a failsafe that would prevent his faux Qin Shi Huang from becoming outraged and killing him. The only remaining stumbling block is that the tenth Doctor claims ("The Immortal Emperor") that Huang just disappeared one night and that "no-one knows how he died" – something that isn't true in real life, as the first Doctor knows (*The Eleventh Tiger*, p267 again).

Whatever the case with Huang, it's possible that Meng Tian built the terracotta army (found in real life in 1974) as robots that collect dust after Meng Tian's death until the Mandragora Helix makes use of them in 1884 (in *The Eleventh Tiger*), once the stars align as it requires.

234 Dating "The Immortal Emperor" (*The Doctor Who Storybook 2009*) - It's "a couple of centuries BC", at the end of the First Emperor's reign.
235 Dating *Luna Romana* (BF CC #8.7) - It's the height/middle of the Roman Republic, typically dated as 509 to 27 BC. A coin in the street – a quadrigatus – suggests that it's "around the second century BC". The second Romana judges a local wine as "Minus 200. Quite a good year", and later reiterates that it's "200 BC". It's "more than five centuries" after Rome's founding in 753 BC. The script specified that it's "more than two thousand years" since the Doctor and the first Romana's previous visit to Earth (in *The Stones of Blood*, presumably), but actress Juliet Landau mis-delivers the line as "two hundred". The Doctor licks a finger, puts it up in the air and decides that it's "August".

Titus Maccius Plautus lived circa 254-184 BC, and shows no confusion when the Doctor compliments his play about the twins (*The Menaechmii*, year of authorship unknown), even though the Doctor later claims

Stoyn's mask-wearing duplicates publicly performed the play, an act of repetition that enabled Stoyn's prime version to better concentrate his mind in his own body.

The six Stoyns accessed the TARDIS when the fourth Doctor and the first Romana randomly arrived in Rome a year later, and returned to Stoyn's moonbase in the future. The second Romana sent the TARDIS back to Rome, allowing the Doctor and her previous self to leave and continue seeking the Key to Time.

An older fourth Doctor and the second Romana returned to Rome after falling down a time portal from circa 8000, and battled the robotic Legionnaries that followed them on stage. The Legionnaries ran out of power, and were broken up for the gold they contained. Stoyn retrieved the Doctor and Romana in the TARDIS, and took them to the future for a final confrontation.

The T'Keyn, a time-active race, "audited" worlds to determine their worthiness to survive. One of the T'Keyn, Sondrah, audited Earth and approved its continued existence.[236] The Doctor met the original Vandals.[237]

c 104 BC - THE WATER THIEF[238] -> A seed pod of the Water Thief – a reed designed to thrive in arid regions – was somehow transported through time to ancient Egypt. The eleventh Doctor and Amy, having come back in time from 1896, stopped it from overrunning the city of Oxyrhynchus by creating a flood using the TARDIS force field. Bits of the Water Thief remained dormant in papyrus that would be recovered in the late nineteenth century. The Doctor and Amy returned there, after the Doctor left behind a helpful note saying, "Dear Doctor... here are the coordinates you need", for himself to find in future.

The Jex brutally subjugated the Canavitchi, killing two-thirds of them. The Canavitchi successfully revolted, and swore to eradicate their former masters.[239] Two thousand years ago, Varan Tak from the Anthropology Unit on Oskerion was marooned in the asteroid belt when his spacecraft was damaged. He began collecting specimens from Earth.[240] The Star Abacus of Beta Phoenii 9 was destroyed by the Paragon Virus in 87 BC.[241]

Ancient Rome

101 BC (January) - 100: "100 BC"[242] -> The sixth Doctor and Evelyn, mistakenly thinking they'd gone forward to 100 BC instead of backwards to 101 BC, arrived as the parents of Julius Caesar hailed the birth of a girl, Julia. The travellers wrongly concluded their "previous visit" had altered Julius' conception, causing him to be born with two X chromosomes. They attempted to "go back" in time, hoping to put history back on course.

101 BC (October) - 100: "100 BC"[243] -> The sixth Doctor and Evelyn happened to meet Senator Gaius Julius Caesar the elder and his wife Aurelia – the parents of Julius Caesar – and left upon realising that love was in the air.

They returned after an erroneous trip back in time, convinced that their presence had delayed Julius' conception, causing him to be born a girl. They eventually realised that they'd witnessed the birth of Caesar's sister, and that Julius hadn't been born yet. Aurelia, suitably in the mood, lured her husband into bed.

A Dalek fell to Earth, and presented itself to a young British girl as "the Bronze God". With the Dalek's backing, the girl grew up to become Queen Tristanha of the Britons, and oversaw the construction of windmills and turbines needed to repower the Dalek's spaceship.[244]

---

the man has yet to write it.

236 Sondrah audits Earth an unknown number of times (but, it appears to have happened more than once), in thousand-year intervals prior to "Dead Man's Hand".

237 *Breaking Bubbles and Other Stories*: "The Curious Incident of the Doctor in the Night-Time"

238 Dating *The Water Thief* (BBC children's 2-in-1 #6) - It's "about 2000 years" (ch3) before the circa 1900 component of the story, although the back cover blurb dials this down to being only "hundreds of years" beforehand. Oxyrhynchus (part of the modern-day village of Behneseh) historically went into decline throughout the Roman and Byzantine times, and was finally abandoned after the Arab invasion of Egypt circa 641.

239 "Two thousand years" before *The King of Terror*.

240 "The Collector"

241 *The Quantum Archangel*

242 Dating *100*: "100 BC" (BF #100a) - The Doctor attempts to go forward nine months in time from October 101 BC, but appears to instead go backward by the same amount. Julius Caesar's older sister Julia was indeed born in 101 BC. Nothing is here said about Julius' *other* older sister, who was also named Julia, and is only mentioned in the accounts of the biographer/historian/gossip monger Suetonius.

243 Dating *100*: "100 BC" (BF #100a) - The month and year are given, and are extrapolated from Caesar's birth on 13th July, 100 BC. The story title was doubtless intended to tie into Big Finish's 100th audio release, but is deliberately misleading in that – as the Doctor and Evelyn figure out – they were never in 100 BC.

244 *Phantoms of the Deep*. In Shakespeare's *Julius Caesar*, Cassius relates how he saved Julius from drowning in the Tiber during a swimming competition gone awry. Caesar lived 100 BC to 44 BC.

The Doctor met Julius Caesar.[245] The Doctor pulled Julius Caesar out of the Tiber.[246]

c 54 BC (early Autumn) - CHURCHILL: LIVING MEMORY[247] **->** The eleventh Doctor, Winston Churchill and a young Kazran Sardick arrived to chat with Julius Caesar during the first invasion of Britain, but engine leakage from the Bronze God's spaceship put the TARDIS – with the Doctor inside – a nano-second out of phase, isolating it. Churchill was conscripted to serve as one of Caesar's strategists as the Bronze God's technology gave Queen Tristahna's soldiers a formidable advantage against the Romans. Tristanha realized that the Bronze God – actually a Dalek – intended to lift off and eradicate her people with dystronic missiles, so threw in with Caesar and Churchill. A combined British-Roman front destroyed the Bronze God's technology, even as Churchill and Kazran recalibrated the engines of the Dalek's spaceship, eradicating it and the Dalek. The Doctor restored the TARDIS to normal, even as Caesar withdrew from Britain.

The eighth Doctor, Fitz and Trix defeated Thorgan of the Sulumians. He had been planning to prevent the signing of the Treaty of Brundusium.[248] **At the height of the Roman Empire, the War Lords lifted a Roman battlefield.**[249] The Dalek Project examined some Roman soldiers.[250] The Celestial Toymaker abducted a Roman legionary.[251]

The second Doctor, Jamie and Victoria attended a gladiator fight in ancient Rome, and Victoria was appalled by the violence.[252] **One of the splinters of Scaroth was a man of influence in Ancient Rome.**[253]

Cleopatra

The Doctor visited Rome, met Hannibal and Cleopatra, and was very impressed by the swordsmanship of Cleopatra's bodyguard.[254] The captain of Cleopatra's guard was a "friend of a friend" to Ace, and taught her the

---

245 "Two decades" before *Churchill: Living Memory*.

246 *Empire of Death*, and evidently a separate occasion from *100*: "100".

247 Dating *Churchill: Living Memory* (*The Churchill Years* #1.3) - Churchill names the year as "55 BC", in accordance with Julius Caesar's first withdrawal from Britain (he returned in 54 BC), and estimates – from the local trees – that it's "early Autumn. September, I'd guess". Two details, however, support this actually *being* the 54 BC invasion: Caesar here displays little appetite for making another attempt to invade Britain and – more noticeably – he mentions the "recent" death of his daughter, who passed in 54 BC, not 55. Caesar was already mourning her when he wrote to Cicero on 1st September, 54 BC, during the second invasion.

Sardick appeared in *A Christmas Carol*. Tristahna is fictional.

248 *The Gallifrey Chronicles*

249 *The War Games*

250 *The Dalek Project*

251 "The Greatest Gamble"

252 *The Colony of Lies*

253 *City of Death*. He's listed as "Roman Emperor" in the script, but it's possible he's a senator or other Roman of rank.

254 The Doctor has already visited Rome on his travels before *The Romans*. He mentions Hannibal (247-182 BC, he crossed the Alps in 219 BC) in *Robot*, and Cleopatra (68-30 BC) in *The Masque of Mandragora*.

255 *The Settling*

256 *The Girl in the Fireplace*

257 *Ghosts of India*

258 Or so River seems to imply in *The Husbands of River Song*, with the Doctor – a little weirdly, depending upon one's interpretation – counter-claiming that it's akin to her marrying actor Stephen Fry.

259 "Supremacy of the Cybermen"

260 *The Wedding of River Song*

261 *Loups-Garoux*

262 *Iris: Enter Wildthyme* (p83).

263 *FP: The Brakespeare Voyage* (ch11). Cleopatra lived late 69 BC to 30 BC.

264 Dating *Erimem: The Last Pharaoh* (*Erimem* novel #1) - Erimem's crew first arrives in the days, or possibly some weeks, before the Battle of Actium, which happened 2nd September, 31 BC. Erimem time-jumps to the day that Cleopatra died, which happened on 12th August, 30 BC.

265 "At least two thousand years", if not more, before *Leth-St: Mind of Stone* (chs 4, 5, 14).

266 *The Alchemists*. Augustus ruled 27 BC to 14 AD.

267 "Two thousand years" before *Trail of the White Worm*.

268 An undetermined number of millennia before *Night of the Stormcrow*.

269 Dating *State of Change* (MA #5) - The Doctor thinks that it is "the year 10 BC, approximately" (p41). The Cleopatra of this world died around 15 BC (p45). Terra Nova is part of the universe's timeline by the end of the story, yet despite its prosperity and technological advantage over the proper Earth, it's never heard of again.

270 Dating *The Tenth Doctor Year Three* (Titan 10th Doc #3.3-3.5, "Sharper than a Serpent's Tooth") – No date given, but it's ancient China. Some of the locales are drawn from Chinese mythology, the idea presumably being that they're lost to history after the Para-Nestene's defeat. In "Vortex Butterflies" (*TDY3* #3.6-3.8, 3.10), Cindy – a high schooler circa 2015 – says that "Sharper Than a Serpent's Tooth" happened "two thousand years" before she was born.

271 *Voyage of the Damned*

art of sword fighting.[255] **The tenth Doctor mentioned meeting Cleopatra,**[256] and was familiar with the size of Cleopatra's bedchamber.[257]

The Doctor married Cleopatra.[258] The eleventh Doctor spent his wedding anniversary on the loo, having warned Cleopatra that he didn't like prunes.[259] According to the Doctor, Cleopatra was a pushover.[260] with "the grace of a carpet flea".[261] Iris Wildthyme's companion Panda said Cleopatra was an "incorrigible woman".[262] wih - Robert Scarratt met Cleopatra.[263]

31 BC, 30 BC (12th August) - ERIMEM: THE LAST PHARAOH[264] **->** Erimem, curator Ibrahim Hadmani and university students Andrea Hansen, Tom Niven and Anna Whitaker were transported through time to the days before the Battle of Actium. Members of the cult of Ash-Ama-Teseth pursued them there. Erimem was agonized to hear that Rome's defeat of Egypt was a matter of recorded history, and she failed to convince Mark Antony and Cleopatra to move against Gaius Octavius' forces before this could happen. The cultists were killed, but their leader forcibly took Erimem back to 2015. Whitaker died, but Hadmani, Hansen and Niven used the cultists' time-devices to return home.

Erimem later returned to witness the victory of Octavius' fleet, and Antony and Cleopatra fleeing back to Egypt. Later still, Erimem went to see Cleopatra following Mark Antony's death, and discussed the public shame and slow execution that Cleopatra would experience if Octavius took her alive. Cleopatra concurred that the Pharaoh of Egypt could not be seen to suffer such humiliation, and – after giving Erimem with a ring-bracelet shaped like a golden scorpion – ended her own life with a goblet of poisoned wine. Erimem kicked over a basket with a snake as she left: a final surprise for the first Roman to find Cleopatra's body.

A stone containing the mind of Rakis of the planet Glastra was expelled from his native reality, and fell to ancient Egypt. It caused madness in those who touched it, and – given sufficient energy – turned people into stone. Following Antony and Cleopatra's deaths, Octavian's troops looted the stone from Egypt's treasures.[265]

The first Doctor and Susan came into possession of Roman aurei from the time of Augustus.[266]

An immense worm created through quasi-organic engineering, and capable of boring wormholes "millions of centuries and billions of light years apart", was bisected in space and fell to Earth. It took refuge in Dark Peak, Derbyshire.[267] The void of space gave birth to a species of vulture – what the people of Ganaldos Beta called No Things – that fed on dying worlds. One such creature took to circling the Earth, drawing near every thousand years to see if its end was approaching.[268]

10 BC - STATE OF CHANGE[269] **->** After watching Cleopatra's barge on the Nile in 41 BC, the sixth Doctor and Peri had decided to travel a little way into the future to follow the history of Rome. The Rani compelled a Vortex entity, Iam, to copy the Doctor's TARDIS console, but this also duplicated a section of the Earth around 32 BC, creating a flat disc-shaped world. The TARDIS console was duplicated and came to rest on the copied Earth, where it was regarded as an Oracle.

With information from this Oracle, the Roman Empire made great advancements. The battle of Actium went against Octavian and Agrippa because they faced opponents with steamships. Electric lighting, airships and explosives were developed. The culmination of this technology was Ultimus, the Roman Empire's atomic bomb programme. Capable of kiloton yields, Ultimus could destroy any known city. Cleopatra's three children – Cleopatra Selene, Alexander and Ptolemy – ruled as a triumvirate.

The Doctor defeated the Rani's plans, and convinced Iam to relocate Terra Nova into the real universe. It settled into an unoccupied sector of space.

Cindy Wu Begats Herself

c 2 BC - THE TENTH DOCTOR YEAR THREE[270] **->** A chase through time between the Doctor's TARDIS and the Para-Nestene in the form of a red, tentacled police box ended when the latter ran aground in ancient China. The Para-Nestene manifested as the Red Jade General, built a power base near Mount Buzhou, and infused five hundred locals with the biodata of its captive, Cindy Wu – thus producing five hundred Cindy-clones to serve as its army and engineer corps. As the Para-Nestene tried to leech energy from the TARDIS, the tenth Doctor – accompanied by Gabby and Noobis – briefly relocated the Ship, which pulled the Para-Nestene through a pinhole entrance to the Time Vortex, destroying it through ectoplasmic inversion.

The five hundred Cindys lived their own lives, and furthered their bloodline. It was believed that in this way, the original Cindy had become her own ancestor.

The Time Sentinel rescued the Red TARDIS, and press-ganged it into service.

Anno Domini

The Doctor claimed he was at the original Christmas, and "got the last room" at the inn.[271] The Doctor took Leonardo da Vinci back to the very first Christmas in Bethlehem, so Leo could study the local light and colour for his adoration painting. Leonardo was fearful of visiting Christ's manager, so he and the Doctor had a slap-up dinner before returning to the fifteenth century.[272]

> = The Valeyard thought it possible that, owing to his meddling in history, human-Silurian culture would have daily flights to Mars by the time of Jesus' birth. The Roman Empire, he believed, would go on to conquer space and aid in his designs.[273]

Captain Jack is Buried for Two Millennia

27 AD - TW: EXIT WOUNDS[274] -> Jack Harkness' brother, Gray, forced Captain John Hart to bury the immortal Jack beneath the future site of Cardiff. He would remain trapped until 1901.

The Doctor remembered the original Easter.[275] Joseph Liebermann, who would encounter the seventh Doctor in 1888, claimed to be the Wandering Jew of legend.[276] wih - Robert Scarratt was present for a relatively minor campaign, near the Sea of Galilee.[277]

The Doctor visited the court of Caligula.[278] Caligula tried to have the Doctor thrown to the lions, as he didn't like the cut of his trousers.[279] The Monk and his companion Lucie Miller met Caligula.[280]

c 39 AD - IRIS S2: THE TWO IRISES[281] -> Iris Hilary Wildthyme – a projection of Iris' bus – and Panda visited Caligula's Rome for a toga party and some tai chi.

In the spring of 43, the Romans invaded Britain. They were led by Emperor Claudius, who was in Britain for a total of sixteen days.[282] **The Doctor had much experience with Roman Britain... he lived there, governed, farmed, juggled and was a Vestal virgin, second class.**[283]

46 AD (winter) - DEMON QUEST: THE RELICS OF TIME[284] -> The fourth Doctor and Mrs Wibbsey arrived on the trail of the TARDIS' spatial geometer. A group of Celts considered Mrs Wibbsey a soothsayer, and she went

---

272 *Relative Dimensions.* The Doctor mentions that this was "right about Zero BC/AD", although estimates of Christ's birth year by historians generally range from 6 BC to 6 AD.

273 *Unbound: He Jests at Scars...*

274 Dating *TW: Exit Wounds* (*TW* 2.13) - The year is given.

275 *Planet of the Dead*

276 *FP: The Brakespeare Voyage* (ch12). This happens during "the year three thousand, seven hundred and ninety" in the Hebrew calendar, which is 30 AD in the Gregorian one.

277 *Matrix.* The Wandering Jew was a shoemaker or tradesman who mocked Jesus on his way to the Crucifixion, and was reportedly condemned to walk the Earth until the Second Coming of Christ. There is little Biblical evidence for this, but records of the legend go back to the thirteenth century.

278 *The Slow Empire*

279 *The Labyrinth of Buda Castle*

280 *The Resurrection of Mars.* Caligula ruled 16th March, 37 AD, to 24th January, 41 AD, presuming this meet-up happened during his reign as emperor.

281 Dating *Iris S2: The Two Irises* (BF *Iris* #2.3) - It's during Caligula's time as Emperor (37-41 AD).

282 *Demon Quest: The Relics of Time*

283 *The Eaters of Light*

284 Dating *Demon Quest: The Relics of Time* (BBC fourth Doctor audio #2.1) - The Doctor says it's "nearly two thousand years earlier" than the present day. A Celt says Julius Caesar invaded "almost a century ago", and it's referred to a couple of times as "the first century". Although "Claudius" is actually a shapechanging demon, it would seem to be later in the year that the Doctor knows the real Claudius came to Britain: 43 AD. However, Mrs Wibbsey dates this story to 46 AD in *Demon Quest: Starfall.*

285 *Demon Quest: Sepulchre*

286 *Human Nature* (NA)

287 *TW: Small Worlds*

288 *Trail of the White Worm.* This is during the Roman occupation of Britain, which lasted 43 AD to 383.

289 Dating *The Wrath of the Iceni* (BF 4th Doc #1.3) - The Doctor says that it's "approximately seventeen years after the Roman invasion [of Britain]", which happened in 43 AD. Historians can't agree if Boudica's uprising (and her death because of it) occurred in 60 or 61 AD, but these events concern the sacking of the Roman base at Camulodunum (modern-day Colchester), the start of her doomed insurrection. There are different ways to spell "Boudica" (including "Boudicca" and "Boadicea"); this write-up reflects Big Finish's preference.

290 *Unbound: A Storm of Angels*

291 *The Blue Angel.* Salome lived in the first century AD.

292 "Seventeen years" before *The Fires of Pompeii.*

293 Said to be "over two thousand years" before *The Stolen Earth,* although in truth it's slightly less than that.

294 *Paradise 5.* Pliny the Elder (23-79 AD), author of *Naturalis Historica* (*Natural History*) wrote about smelling salts.

295 *The Nightmare Fair*

296 Dating *The Rescue* (2.3) and *Byzantium!* (PDA #44) - The TARDIS topples over right at the end of *The Rescue,* as a literal cliffhanger. The date is established in *The Romans,* but *Byzantium!* establishes that the TARDIS crew have another adventure first.

297 Dating *The Romans* (2.4) - The story culminates in the Great Fire of Rome. The TARDIS crew have spent "a month" at the villa.

298 Archaeologists date the site to "about 70 AD" in *I am a Dalek* (p24).

into a trance, displaying knowledge she couldn't possibly possess. This convinced them to attack a rival tribe, which had a "wizard" and "monster". The next morning, the Doctor and Wibbsey went to the village and discovered that the monster was an elephant and the wizard was a disguised Emperor Claudius, who had run away from his army for a quiet life. Except... "Claudius" was not the genuine article, but the shapechanging Demon luring the Doctor and Wibbsey through time.[285] As the two British tribes made their peace, "Claudius" entered a dematerialisation chamber in his dwelling and vanished. The Doctor rescued the elephant from the hungry Celts, and the TARDIS headed for its next destination: the Moulin Rouge.

The Iceni, a Celtic tribe led by Boudicca, razed many Roman-occupied British towns to the ground.[286] **Roundstone Wood in England always "stayed wild"; in ancient times, it was considered bad luck to collect wood there. The Romans in Britain stayed clear of it.**[287] A group of Romans in Britain came to worship the space worm hiding in Derbyshire, and one of Caesar's legions made a mascot of it.[288]

c 60 AD - THE WRATH OF THE ICENI[289] **->** The TARDIS set down in ancient Norfolk, at the height of the Roman occupation of Britain. Leela saved Boudica, the Queen of the Iceni, from two soldiers and thought her impending uprising seemed just – the Romans had reneged on a deal with Boudica's late husband and seized her kingdom, publicly flogged the Queen and had her daughters raped in front of her.

Boudica thought the fourth Doctor was a seer, and threatened the life of one of her own people, Bragnar, until the Doctor revealed the future. He advised that Boudica's attack on the Roman settlement at Camulodunum was a trap, and that the Roman army led by Gaius Suetonius Paulinus would strike at her force's rear flank. Boudica positioned soldiers to guard against Paulinus' advance, and sacked Camulodunum.

Leela realised that Boudica had no honour – the Queen was willing to murder her way through the infirm, the aged and even her own people to gain revenge. Leela bested Boudica in single combat and freed the Doctor – who revealed that he had lied about the Roman ambush. Events would proceed as history dictated, with Boudica's people suffering a catastrophic defeat in a muddy field. The Romans would rule Britain for another three centuries.

= The Auld Mortality Doctor congratulated Susan for having successfully impersonated Boudicca.[290]

Iris Wildthyme claimed that Salome did the fan dance with the Doctor's scarf.[291] **A great earthquake in Vesuvius**

in 62 AD released some of the Pyroviles from their ancient slumber. The eruption of Vesuvius in 79 AD caused a rift in time that retroactively gave some of the young girls of Pompeii the gift of prophecy. Some of their number formed the Sybiline Cult. The TARDIS' arrival was foretold in the Thirteenth Book of the Sybiline Oracles.[292] **The Pyroviles were unable to return to their homeworld, Pyrovillia, because it had been stolen by the Daleks for their reality bomb.**[293]

Pliny the Elder gave the Doctor some smelling salts.[294] The Celestial Toymaker took some inspiration for his games from the Roman Coliseum.[295]

64 AD - THE RESCUE / BYZANTIUM![296] **->** The **TARDIS landed, only to topple from the side of a hill...**

The TARDIS had materialised just outside Byzantium. The Romans mistook Ian for a contemporary Briton and granted him some respect as a citizen of the Empire. Ian helped the Roman General Gaius Calaphilus and his political opponent, city praefectus Thalius Maximus, to settle their differences. Calaphilus and Maximus united efforts to purge corruption from the city, instigating a period of reform.

The first Doctor met the scribes Reuben, Rayhab and Amos, and helped them to translate the Gospel of Mark into Greek, producing a version that complemented the writings of Matthew the tax-gatherer.

Returning to the TARDIS, the travellers discovered that the Roman Germanicus Vinicius has found the TARDIS and taken it to his villa near Rome. They followed it there...

The Burning of Rome

64 AD (June to July) - THE ROMANS[297] **->** The first **Doctor, Ian, Barbara and Vicki spent nearly a month at a deserted villa just outside Rome. Becoming bored by the lack of adventure, the Doctor and Vicki travelled to the capital. Captured by slave traders, Ian and Barbara were sold at auction. Ian escaped, but ended up as a gladiator in Rome. Barbara became the servant of the Emperor Nero's wife, Poppea, and the object of the Emperor's attentions. The Doctor, meanwhile, was posing as the musician Maximus Pettulian (despite a complete lack of musical ability). When the Doctor accidentally set fire to Nero's plans to rebuild Rome, the Emperor was inspired. As Rome began to burn, the four time travellers returned to the TARDIS.**

A Dalek arrived in Roman Britain from the Time War, with orders to imprint the population with the Dalek Factor. Its capsule malfunctioned, and it was only able to release a tiny amount of the Factor before being buried.[298]

Volcano Day

79 AD - THE FIRES OF VULCAN[299] **->** The seventh Doctor and Mel arrived in Pompeii, just as Mount Vesuvius became active. The TARDIS was trapped in the rubble of a collapsed building, preventing their escape. The Doctor managed to antagonise the gladiator Murranus by beating him in a dice game. The Doctor and Mel escaped to the TARDIS just as the volcano erupted, destroying Pompeii and the surrounding area.

> (=) Temporal distortion resulted in an alternate history where Vesuvius took much longer to erupt, and the city's populace evacuated in their boats.[300]

The tenth Doctor and Martha had some "unlucky business" at Mount Vesuvius.[301]

79 AD (22nd-23rd August) - THE FIRES OF POMPEII[302] **->** The tenth Doctor and Donna arrived in what they thought was Rome, but which turned out to be Pompeii, the day before the great eruption. The Doctor told Donna that Vesuvius erupting was a fixed point in time, and so they couldn't save the doomed people. They learned that the Pyroviles intended to convert all of humanity into stone creatures, and so used the Pyroviles' own technology to engineer the historic eruption of Vesuvius, destroying them.

Twenty thousand people died in Pompeii, but Donna persuaded the Doctor to save the family of Lobus Caecilius, a marble trader.

> (=) Had the Doctor and Donna not intervened, the Pyroviles would have created a Pompeii-based empire that would have overthrown Rome and encompassed the whole world.[303]

---

299 Dating *The Fires of Vulcan* (BF #12) - The story ends with the eruption of Vesuvius.
300 *The Algebra of Ice* (p15).
301 *Made of Steel.* It's not specified that this was during the famous historical eruption.
302 Dating *The Fires of Pompeii* (X4.2) - The date is a matter of historical record. The Doctor claims he's been to Rome "ages ago" before during the great fire, a reference to *The Romans* - but as we've seen, he's made a couple of other trips to the city.
303 *The Fires of Pompeii*, according to a vision the High Priestess of the Sybilines has of the "Pyrovile alternative" timeline.
304 *The Girl Who Died.* While this explains why Caecilius (*The Fires of Pompeii*) looks exactly like the twelfth Doctor (as Peter Capaldi played both parts), it introduces all sorts of corollary questions - such as what "message" if any lies behind the sixth Doctor and Maxil (*Arc of Infinity*) having the same features, as both were played by Colin Baker.
Speaking to the *Radio Times* (15th November, 2015), Steven Moffat revealed Russell T Davies' theory that the civil servant John Frobisher (also played by Capaldi in *TW: Children of Earth*) was descended from Caecilius - the idea being that the Doctor had defied time in saving Caecilius, but that time had reasserted itself by ending the bloodline with Frobisher and his family. The Doctor's choice of both Caecilius and Frobisher's identical faces, then, is yet another defiance of time, and part of his ongoing battle with destiny. Caecilius and Frobisher looking exactly the same, Moffat claims, owes to "a [remarkable] level of genetic throwback", i.e. not temporal trickery, as is the case with the multiple Clara Oswalds.
305 *The Fires of Pompeii*
306 "Hunters of the Burning Stone"
307 *Shroud of Sorrow*, p147, and possibly an in-refer-ence to David Tennant touring Pompeii for *Doctor Who Confidential.*
308 *The Tenth Doctor Year One:* "The Weeping Angels of Mons"
309 Dating *The Pandorica Opens/The Big Bang* (X5.12-5.13) - The Doctor says it's "102... not am, not pm, AD". The real Cleopatra, as is mentioned, has already died (in 30 BC).
The Cybermen seen here warn that "all the universes are deleted", which is in keeping with their having the Cybus logo (meaning they're from Pete's World). However, they now have Cyberships, teleportation and their heads sprout tentacles and can operate independently - all of which seems more advanced than the Cybus models first seen in *Rise of the Cybermen/The Age of Steel.* Those Cybermen discarded the whole body apart from the brain, but the faceplates of these newer models open up to reveal bone skulls, and hunt for "organic components". The conclusion is either that these Cybermen are the first from *our* universe seen in the new series (having melded the Cybus tech with their own), or that they're from the future of Pete's World.
310 *The Big Bang*
311 "Two thousand years" before *The Art of Destruction.*
312 *TW: Trace Memory*
313 *Benny: Many Happy Returns.* Hadrian lived 76-138 AD.
314 Dating *The Stone Rose* (NSA #7) - The date is given.
315 Dating *The Eaters of Light* (X10.10) - Bill says it's the "second century AD".
In real life, the Ninth Legion was stationed in Britain after the Roman invasion (43 AD), but disappeared from the official records in 120 AD. Some sources claim the legion went missing as early as 117 AD. Tellingly, the Ninth isn't listed amongst the legions active during the reign of Marcus Aurelius (161-180), so it was presuma-

In future, the Doctor chose Caecilius' face for one of his incarnations... a reminder that he should save people.[304] Six months after the eruption, Caecilius and his family had set themselves up in Rome, and had an altar dedicated to the Doctor, Donna and their temple: the TARDIS.[305]

The icon of a police box was implanted in humanity's collective consciousness as the TARDIS' exterior was rendered in cave walls, tapestries, parchments and more throughout history.[306] The Doctor visited Pompeii some years after Vesuvius erupted, and learned the state of the bodies covered in ash.[307]

A World War I soldier found himself in the Colosseum, Rome, 97 AD, after a Weeping Angel sent him there.[308]

The Lone Centurion Begins His Watch, Amy Pond Enters Stasis for ~Two Millennia

102 - THE PANDORICA OPENS / THE BIG BANG[309] **->** Projections made by a number of alien races indicated that the Doctor's TARDIS would explode in such a way that would destroy history. All universes were threatened. A coalition of alien races, brought together using the Cracks in Time for travel, sought to prevent this and laid a trap that the Doctor couldn't resist. Psychic blueprints were taken from Amy Pond's house in 2010, and used to construct a vault under Stonehenge – Underhenge – in 102 AD. Within the vault was placed the Pandorica: a fabled prison rumoured to contain "a nameless, terrible thing, soaked in the blood of a billion galaxies", but which was actually patterned from one of Amy's childhood storybooks, *The Legend of Pandora's Box*.

The alliance against the Doctor included the Daleks, Cybermen, Sontarans, Terileptils, Nestenes and their Autons, Drahvins, Chelonians, Slitheen, Sycorax and their roboforms, Haemo-goths, Zygons, Atraxi, Draconians, Hoix, Judoon, Uvodni, Blowfish, Weevils and Silurians. Autons posed as Roman soldiers, as patterned from *The Story of Roman Britain*. The conspirators also used Amy's psychic residue to bring Rory Williams back to life as an Auton – he was unaware that he wasn't human.

The Underhenge broadcast a signal: "The Pandorica is opening." Per instructions that Vincent van Gogh left on the painting *The Pandorica Opens*, River Song arrived at Stonehenge and posed as Cleopatra. She summoned the eleventh Doctor and Amy, and they all examined Underhenge and the Pandorica.

A vast fleet of diverse starships appeared above the Earth – a Dalek fleet (a minimum of twelve thousand Dalek battleships), Cybership and four Sontaran battlefleets. River attempted to relocate the TARDIS to aid the Doctor, but was taken to the year 2010 instead.

Rory's Auton programming activated, and he mortally wounded Amy. The Doctor insisted that he wasn't responsible for the destruction of the TARDIS, but the leaders of the alliance sealed him in the Pandorica. The TARDIS exploded in 2010 anyway.

The eleventh Doctor's future self travelled back from 1996, and had Rory free his past self from the Pandorica. They put Amy's body in his place, knowing that the Pandorica would keep her in stasis, healing her when it obtained a sample of her future DNA. Rory remained behind to guard the Pandorica – he would do so for nearly two thousand years, spurring the legend of the Lone Centurion.

In 118, the Pandorica was taken back to Rome under armed guard.[310] Valnaxi refugees hid themselves and some of their works of art in a warren on Earth, to prevent destruction by their enemy, the Wurms.[311] The Vondrax killed many in Syria, the second century AD, while retrieving one of their Orbs.[312] Iris Wildthyme was intimately acquainted with the Emperor Hadrian.[313]

120 - THE STONE ROSE[314] **->** The tenth Doctor and Rose arrived in Rome, hoping to explain how a statue of Rose from the second century ended up in the British Museum in the twenty-first. They discovered a GENIE from the year 2375 and captured it, preventing the damage its reality-altering powers could cause.

The Lost Legion

120 - THE EATERS OF LIGHT[315] **->** Crows on Earth stopped talking when humans ceased having decent conversations with them.

For generations, the Keeper of the Gate near Aberdeen had sacrificed him/herself to fight back the Eaters of Light: inter-dimensional locusts seeking to consume the stars themselves. In the wake of the Roman invasion, one Keeper – Kar – let an Eater through, and it slaughtered the five thousand strong of the Ninth Legion in an hour. The twelfth Doctor, Bill and Nardole rallied a few surviving legionnaires and Kar's Picts to drive the Eater back home. Kar and the legionnaires entered the gateway – the slowed time dilation within meant they would hold back the Eaters for millennia. The cairn collapsed behind them. Music played by Kar's band endured for ages to come.

Kar's brother told the crows her name, and they repeated it to honour her.

The planet Quagreeg developed in the Sirius System as a marsh world that was home to a race of unpleasant reptilians. One reptilian – later named the Sepulchre, after St Sepulchre's Church – developed within its mental landscape overlapping recreations of London in various time periods. The Sepulchre used dimensionally transcendental beams to transport various humans into the London-recreations within its mind, and did so with a Roman legion.[316]

    (=) The eleventh Doctor, Amy and Rory photographed a Roman-built road in England that had been diverted around Swallow Woods.[317]

Jack Harkness attempted to sell tickets to horse racing in second century Rome to the Cephalids, but they didn't understand the concept.[318] On a visit to Condercum, the Doctor debated military ethics with a group of Romans fighting the Caledonians.[319] A group of third-century Romans was kidnapped by Varan Tak.[320] The Romans drove the Celts from their lands. Gallifreyan intervention allowed King Constantine to pass into the parallel world of Avalon. Even while sleeping, Constantine ruled Avalon for two thousand years.[321]

A time warp briefly sent a Roman soldier to the late twentieth century.[322] **A Roman legionary fell through the Rift to arrive in twenty-first century Cardiff.**[323] Ptolemy was immune to the Doctor's psychic paper, meaning he was a genius.[324] **The Doctor put together a band that included Emperor Marcus Aurelius, "a superlative bass guitarist".**[325]

    = On one parallel Earth, later designated Roma I, the Roman Empire enjoyed a golden age as successive Emperors Nerva, Trajan, Hadrian, Antonius Pius, Marcus Aurelius, Avidius Cassius, Septimus Severus, Publius Septimus, Claudius Gothicus, Domitius Aurelianus and Diocletian ruled wisely. The Rhine and Danube were crossed, and the Germanic peoples fled East; they spent centuries fighting the Huns, Vandals and Ostrogoths. Rome was free to concentrate elsewhere. Constantine conquered Asia.[326]
-----

bly "lost" prior to that. Films inspired by this historical oddity include *The Last Legion* (2007) starring Colin Firth, and *Centurion* (2010) starring Dominic West, with Noel Clarke in the cast.

316 *Dead London*, providing an alternate explanation for the Ninth Legion's fate (see Unfixed Points in Time).

317 *The Way Through the Woods*. The Roman invasion of England began in 43 AD, and formally ended in 410.

318 *Only Human*

319 *Ghost Ship*

320 "The Collector"

321 *The Shadows of Avalon*

322 "The Tides of Time"

323 *TW: End of Days*

324 "Ripper's Curse". Ptolemy lived 90 to 168 AD.

325 *Deep Breath*. Aurelius was Roman Emperor from 161 to 180.

326 *FP: Warlords of Utopia*. In our history, Commodus succeeded Marcus Aurelius in 192, and was the first in a long line of weak and/or short-lived Emperors. Roma I's Emperors were all historical figures, and potential Emperors. Claudius Gothicus did rule and scored notable military victories, but died of plague. In Roma I, he survived to rout the Germanic tribes. Diocletian also ruled in our history.

327 The Ninexie lands on Teymah "three thousand years" before *Absolute Power*, finishes off the population there "two thousand years" beforehand.

328 *The Stone Rose*

329 "The Tides of Time"

330 "Seventeen centuries" before *The Curse of Fenric*. The novelisation likens this contest to an ancient Arabian tale that takes place in "the White City".

331 *Gods and Monsters*. The Battle of Edessa happened in 260, and ended with Valerian becoming the only Roman Emperor ever taken as a prisoner of war. The "magic genie" is presumably Fenric (*The Curse of Fenric*), and plague is, in fact, historically blamed for weakening Valerian's forces.

332 *Gods and Monsters*. Historically, Shapur I died of an illness in May 270.

333 *Gods and Monsters*, in which Hurmzid is presented as a prince, although he briefly succeeded his father as king, from May 270 to June 271. The name is rendered as "Hurmzid" in the CD booklet, although it's usually Anglicised as "Hormizd".

334 Dating "The Futurists" (*DWM* #372-374) - It is "the late third century".

335 "A thousand years" before *Marco Polo*.

336 *The Masque of Mandragora*

337 *The Time of the Daleks*

338 Dating *Seasons of Fear* (BF #30) - The date is given.

339 Dating *The Eleventh Doctor Year One* (Titan 11th Doc #1.12-1.14, "Conversion"/"The Comfort of the Good") - A caption gives the year. The Battle of Milvian Bridge happened on 28th October, 312. Maxentius drowned while retreating from Constantine's forces on the same day.

340 Dating *The Council of Nicaea* (BF #71) - The year is given. The Doctor says the TARDIS has landed "a few days before the council is set to begin", but Athanasius more accurately says it is "the night before the council starts". Historically, the Council opened on 20th May.

341 "The Tides of Time". The date is given – this is the opening battle of the Millenium (sic) wars. See the main entry (c.1983) for more.

342 *Memory Lane*

343 *The Vampires of Venice*

344 *CD,NM* V1: *Judoon in Chains*. Ambrose lived circa 340 to 397.

The Ninexie, a race of electroparasites, all-but died out in a nine-hundred year war against Wrechon Four. The last Ninexie crashed onto the planet Teymah, and burnt out the entire populace before going dormant.[327] Circa 200, the Doctor defeated a silicon-based life form, the Ogre of Hyfor Three; its foot ended up in the British Museum.[328]

The Demon Melanicus was a native of Althrace, a member of the race of Kalichura. He sought to conquer the advanced culture, generating legends of gods and demons. His armies were defeated and Melanicus fled to third century Earth, where he came in a dream to the tyrant king Catavolcus. Melanicus bestowed great power on him and the secrets of time travel.[329]

The Doctor challenged Fenric to solve a chess puzzle. Fenric failed, and the Doctor imprisoned him in a flask, banishing him to the Shadow Dimensions.[330]

The Persian king Shapur I forged a pact with a "magic genie" after winning a game of dice against it on the road to Byzantium. The genie riddled an opposing Roman army with anthrax, facilitating its defeat at the Battle of Edessa. The Roman Emperor, Valerian, was captured. The Doctor refrained from objecting as Shapur used Valerian as a footstool from which to mount his horse, lest he invent the Geneva Convention some two thousand years early.[331]

Following his defeat in World War II, Fenric translocated Shapur I back to the dawn of time to become his new Ancient One.[332] The seventh Doctor warned King Shapur's son, Hurmzid, that he shouldn't tangle with demons. Hurmzid ignored his friend's advice, and used an enchanted hammer to create a timestorm, then travel to the dawn of time in search of his father.[333]

c 275 - "The Futurists"[334] -> Valente and Secundus, two Roman soldiers fighting in Wales, saw a green fire in the sky. The energy enveloped Valente. Shortly afterwards, the tenth Doctor and Rose arrived from 1925 and defeated the alien Hajor, who were attempting to master Time.

By the third century's end, the Old Silk Road to and from Cathay had been opened.[335] **The Cult of Demnos had apparently died out by the fourth century.**[336]

> (=) In a potential timeline, the Daleks used time machines to invade Roman Britain in 305.[337]

(=) 305 - SEASONS OF FEAR[338] -> The Roman Decurion Gralae worshipped Mithras, and had made contact with the Nimon, who posed as his god. They granted Gralae eternal life in return for his making sacrifices to them.

The eighth Doctor met Gralae at this time. Between now and his next meeting with the Doctor, seven hundred and fifty years later, Gralae would become known as "Grayle" and spend eighty years repenting with monks. He married twelve times, all his wives dying of old age while he stayed young.

The eighth Doctor sent some Nimon from 1806 to here, and rallied the Roman troops to wipe them out. He then rewrote history by buying out Gralae's commission before he met the Nimon.

312 (28th October) - THE ELEVENTH DOCTOR YEAR ONE[339] -> The eleventh Doctor and John Jones reunited with Alice, ARC and the TARDIS after driving a motorbike though a wormhole in 1976. The Entity they sought fell to Earth, appearing as a comet in Northern Rome. At the Battle of Milvian Bridge, Constantine I looked upon the comet after a young Christian died while saving him, and considered it a good omen.

The traumatized Entity sought to protect itself with an army, and overcame a Cyber-Ship. The Entity's telepathic effect caused Constantine's forces and those of his rival, Maxientus, to perceive the Cybermen as what they desired most – including a variety of gods and goddesses. Maxientus drowned when some Cybermen pulled him into the Tiber.

ARC re-merged with the Entity, making it whole once more, and freeing the Cybermen to withdraw. The TARDIS found the Doctor's actions so questionable, it lost faith in him and acted on pre-programming to seek out the nearest Time Lord. The time-active Entity took the Doctor's group to 2015 to retrieve his Ship...

325 (May) - THE COUNCIL OF NICAEA[340] -> The Roman Emperor Constantine held a conference in Nicaea so bishops could settle issues of dispute within the Christian Church. Among other concerns, the assembled council sought to decide the matter of Christ's divinity. The deacon Athanasius believed Christ was divine, but the presbyter Arius held that Christ was subordinate to God. Erimem found Arius to be honourable and aided his cause, threatening to derail history. Tensions mounted, but the fifth Doctor encouraged Constantine to defuse the situation with his oratory skills. In accordance with history, the Council adopted Athanaisus' views.

In 375, Mongol hordes swept into central Europe... and were wiped out by Nazi tanks.[341] The Doctor suggested that the joke "What's the most ruthless thing in the bakery... Attila the Bun!" was much funnier if you had known the man.[342] **Venice was founded by refugees from Attila the Hun.**[343] The Doctor was friends with St Ambrose.[344]

The Library of Alexandria

c 410 (Autumn) - THE LIBRARY OF ALEXANDRIA[345]

-> Following the TARDIS landing in Alexandria, Ian took a job in the customs office to pay for rooms while the first Doctor, Barbara and Susan enjoyed the city and watched lost plays by Sophocles. Before long, Ian befriended the schoolteacher Hypatia.

A Mim scouting expedition to the Sol System lost their assessment book: *The Pathway to the Stars*, which fell into the library's possession. Fearful that the book could accelerate human knowledge, the shapechanging Mim attacked the library as giant squid monsters. A fire ravaged much of the facility, but the Doctor convinced the Mim to take their book and withdraw. Barbara and Susan saved much of the library's holdings and – unable to return the scrolls for history's sake – stored them within the TARDIS. Works in the library included writings by the philosopher Plotinus.

The Doctor impishly put to some of Hypatia's students the question of how much effort was required to move a

---

345 Dating *The Library of Alexandria* (BF CC #7.10) - The blurb and the script say it's the "5th Century AD"; Ian specifies that it's the "early fifth century AD". The story features Hypatia, who was purportedly killed by a mob in 415. The season is "Autumn".

The time of the library's real-life destruction (which might owe to more than a single disaster) is unknown, with scholars tending to favour four possibilities: A) Julius Caesar's troops besieging Alexandria in 48 BC, B) the Emperor Aurelian (who ruled 270-275) putting down a revolution by Queen Zenobia of Palmyra, C) the Coptic Pope Theophilus ordering its destruction in 391, or D) the army of 'Amr ibn al-'Aas purging non-Muslim works after capturing Alexandria in 642. In *The Library of Alexandria*, Susan acknowledges that multiple accounts of the library's end exist, and scoffs at one mentioning "sea monsters"... which, of course, proves to be correct.

346 *Eye of Heaven* (p181).

347 *Iris: Enter Wildthyme*

348 *Timewyrm: Apocalypse*

349 *CD,NM V2: The Carrionite Curse*

350 *Time and the Rani*. Hypatia of Alexandria, a neo-Platonic philosopher and mathematician, lived circa 370-415 AD. There's no mention of her Rani-kidnapping in *The Library of Alexandria*, so it presumably happens afterward.

THE RANI'S TIME BRAINS: The Rani kidnaps eleven geniuses before we see her plans nearing fruition in *Time and The Rani*. In the televised version, only three of these are named: Hypatia, Pasteur and Einstein. The rehearsal script and the novelisation both mention three more: Darwin, Za Panato and Ari Centos. The novelisation also states that the Danish physicist Niels Bohr is kidnapped.

351 *The Big Bang*

352 *Day of the Moon*

353 "Millennia" before *Point of Entry*.

354 The Darksmiths' origins go back "countless generations" before *DL: The Colour of Darkness* (p49), and are here arbitrarily estimated as fifteen hundred years, in accordance with at least a millennia passing after the Darksmiths were commissioned by the Krashoks (presuming said "millennia" has happened concurrently from the Darksmith's point of view). There's no mention of the colonists of Karagula being human.

355 "Millennia" before *The Pyralis Effect*. Gallifrey is in Kasterborous, and it's not impossible that the unnamed race that defeated the Pyralis was the Time Lords.

356 Dating *Black and White* (BF #163) - The story is clearly intended as the inspiration behind the epic poem *Beowulf*. The general consensus among historians is that King Hrothgar and the Scyldings were based on real-life people, and that events in the poem seem to take place around the turn of the sixth century, although it's possible that the poem itself was first composed in the seventh century. Certainly, it's after the migration to England that created the Anglo-Saxons in the fifth century.

Lysandra Aristedes, without any classics training that we're made aware of, says that the Doctor's copy of *Beowulf* is "a twenty-second century edition of a nineteenth century translation of an eleventh century Anglo-Saxon manuscript based on a story that originates in the fifth or sixth century". She also off-handedly counts off as the TARDIS travels back through the "ninth, eighth, seventh century...", but might not bother to finish her statement, meaning the Ship could arrive earlier than that.

Beowulf's claim that he met Ace "50 years ago" is called out as a tall tale, as he doesn't even look 50 now.

357 *Toy Soldiers* (p208). The novel takes place in 1919, and the war on Q'ell has been going on for "fourteen hundred and five years" by that point.

358 "Twelve years" after the earlier portion of *Black and White*.

359 Dating *Black and White* (BF #163) - "Sixteen years, three months" have passed since the story's earlier part, according to the TARDIS read-outs.

360 *Starlight Robbery*

361 *Benny B3: Legion: Shades of Gray*, referencing the Quechua dramatic play *Ollantay*. Differing theories exist as to the play's origin; it possibly survived in oral tradition, and the earliest known manuscript belonged to the priest Antonia Valdes (1744-1816). *Shades of Gray* has a bit of a misnomer in calling the item "Quena Ollantay's flute", as Quena is the type of flute in question, not the main character's name or title.

362 *Iris S3: Iris Rides Out*. Saint Benedict of Nursia lived circa 480 to 543 or 547, and was the inspiration behind

monolith in the Alexandria gardens – which depicted a newly crowned king in three languages – to the port town of Khito. The monolith would be relocated there in future, and become renowned as the Rosetta Stone.

The Doctor was ejected from the staff at the Library of Alexandria after he misshelved the Dead Sea Scrolls.[346] Iris Wildthyme paid a visit to the library at Alexandria.[347] The Doctor saved two Aristophanes plays from the destruction of the Great Library of Alexandria.[348] The sixth Doctor's TARDIS held scrolls from Alexandria.[349] **The Rani kidnapped Hypatia to become part of her Time Brain.**[350]

In 420, the Pandorica was taken from Rome during a raid by the Franks.[351] **The Roman Empire fell; both the Doctor and Rory Williams witnessed it.**[352]

The world of the Omnim was lost when the resonances they created shattered it. Remnants of the Omnim's mental energies existed in a few fragments, one of which became rogue asteroid D35XQ2.[353] The original colonists of the planet Karagula found the heat of its twin suns unbearable – some went underground and became the Darksmith Collective, practitioners of the dark arts. They learned to break and reassemble reality, moulding time and space much like a child would play with wet sand. For centuries, the Darksmiths accepted commissions to make "impossible, wonderful frightening things".[354]

Energy beings, the Pyralis, swarmed throughout the constellation of Kasterborous and were defeated after a century-long war. They were imprisoned within a temporal void for millennia, even as their obelisk-shaped dimensional gateways remained dormant on some worlds.[355]

c 505 - BLACK AND WHITE[356] **->** The Xybrox, a race of cybernetic insect hybrids, created technology that was exceedingly rare and lucrative. Garundel – an Urodelian black marketer with four mothers, who was contesting with his eighty two siblings to see who could gain the most credits with the fewest kills – attempted to bring down a Xybrox ship with his own spacecraft, but the encounter caused both vessels to crash to Earth.

Weohstan, an attendant to the warrior Beowulf, pulled Garundel from his burning wreckage and struck a deal with him. In exchange for the gold plating needed to repair his ship, Garundel would use the Xybrox robot he'd captured to terrorize King Hrothgar, enabling Beowulf to charge to the rescue. Weohstan hoped that Beowulf's reputation would become so grand, he would net Hrothgar's blessing and become king in his homeland.

The seventh Doctor, accompanied by Captain Lysandra Aristedes and Private Sally Morgan in the black TARDIS, arrived in search of Weyland's Shield: a prized artifact in the Doctor's third contest with Fenric. The Doctor was left behind as a recall signal from Hex and Ace summoned the TARDIS to the future with Lysandra and Sally aboard, and

was gravely wounded by the Xybrox robot. Beowulf "thwarted" the robot – completely unaware that it was a ruse – and took both its arm and the Doctor's sonic screwdriver as trophies.

The Doctor recovered in Garundel's biopod, but Fenric possessed Weohstan via his bloodline, and spirited the Doctor away to the dawn of time. Weohstan/Fenric also decapitated Garundel, whose alien biology enabled his head to survive in a chest beneath Beowulf's throne.

Ace and Lysandra subsequently arrived in this time zone in the black TARDIS, were mistaken for Valkyries, and jumped forward 16 years to reunite with Hex and Sally.

In 514 AD, warfare broke out on the planet Q'ell. The Recruiter, a device created to destroy the Ceracai race, extended the war as part of its programming. The conflict would last until the twentieth century, and cause at least 2,846,014,032 casualties.[357]

Weohstan was believed to have died in his bed in 517 AD, but was instead taken back to the dawn of time to become Fenric's new Ancient One.[358]

& 521 - BLACK AND WHITE[359] **->** Beowulf was now king of his homeland. Hex and Sally Morgan arrived in the white TARDIS as the Xybrox robot that had formerly terrorised Hrothgar's castle now destroyed Beowulf's hall. The king died from injuries incurred by dispatching the metal beast off a cliff. Ace and Lysandra arrived in the black TARDIS to retrieve their friends, and reunited Garundel's severed head with his body – only to have it parted again by Wilaf, Weohstan's son. The four companions bundled Gardundel's body parts into his biopod, expecting that his mothership would collect him.

The seventh Doctor's associates found the prized Weyland's Shield, which – when placed on the TARDIS console – activated a pre-programmed journey. The black and white TARDISes initiated a symbiotic propulsion "back through the birth pangs of this universe, sideways through the Vortex, diagonally through several relative dimensions..." The black TARDIS perished, but its additional shielding enabled the white TARDIS – which returned to its normal hue of blue – to reach the dawn of time, where the companions hoped to rescue the Doctor from Fenric...

Garundel eventually recovered, but sixty of his siblings exiled him. He would later found Garundel Galactic as a trafficker of advanced weaponry.[360]

Ollantay's flute was among the items later found in Jennifer Alford's collection of supernatural items.[361] The supernatural investigator Thomas Carnacki claimed to own chalk blended from the ground bones of St Benedict, the patron saint of exorcists.[362]

(=) 540 - THE SECRET HISTORY[363] **->** The Monk saved the time-sensitive Sophia, a Nikopolis resident, and incorporated her abilities into a master plan to undo the Doctor's history. After two failed attempts, the Monk swapped the fifth and first Doctors as the latter, Steven and Vicki witnessed the Emperor Justinian postponing the restoration of the Roman Empire in Italy.

The Monk and Sophia awakened the Ostardi: exiled aliens who manifested as giant stone heads of Medusa, and possessed Justinian and the Empress Theodora. The fifth Doctor hesitated while rectifying the situation... and thereby contradicted his earlier self's actions, injecting a paradox into his history. The Time Lords contained the temporal damage and erased the Doctor from time. Sophia's abilities let the Monk move into the resultant temporal breach, and he *became* the Doctor...

Sophia pulled the fifth Doctor back into reality from a space-time tear. Acknowledging the Monk's duplicity, she aided him... Six days later, the Doctor (formerly the Monk) landed in Constantinople with Steven and Vicki, and entertained thoughts of mucking about with history to create a lasting Roman Empire. The fifth Doctor turned the Ostardi against the Doctor-Monk, who was forced to restore the Doctor's timeline. The Ostardi left Earth, taking the Monk with them for punishment. The fifth Doctor and his younger self again swapped places...

In Constantinople, the first Doctor, Steven and Vicki dealt with both the Ostardi and the virulent Antoim pursuing the TARDIS. Procopius, the future author of *The Walls of Justinian* and *The Secret History*, declined to include these events in his chronicles.

= On Roma I, Roman Emperor Justinian was crowned Emperor of India. By the time of his death, he was also Emperor of America. The Romans had discovered the continent and the Native Americans, like so many previous civilisations, were keen to be togafied.[364]

The eleventh Doctor claimed that in his earlier years, he spent a few nights out with some Icelandic friends in the sixth century. After a generous amount of honey mead, the Doctor convinced a blind man to shoot Edda the bard with mistletoe – a cheap trick that not-at-all-amused Edda worked into his tales of the gods, and gave rise to the legend of Loki.[365] In the seventh century, Lord Roche's

---

the Saint Benedict Medal. Laypeople aren't allowed to perform exorcisms in the Catholic faith, but can use the Medal to ward off evil.

363 Dating *The Secret History* (BF #200) - The year is given.

364 *FP: Warlords of Utopia*

365 *Dark Horizons* (p196, 306). The Doctor's story is rather dubious, as "Edda the bard" never existed. The *Poetic Edda* (a crucial source of Norse mythology, along with the *Prose Edda*) is a compilation of works by different poets, but while different theories exist for why it's named as such, none of them entail a person actually named Edda. The leading thought is that the word stems from a derivation of the Latin "edo", as used in a treatise on poetry by Snorri Sturlson (1179-1241).

366 *The Suns of Caresh*

367 Dating *TW: "Rift War"* (*TWM* #4-13) - Jack "reckons" from the carbon buildup in some grass that he chews that it's "around 600 AD, slap bang in the middle of the Dark Ages".

368 "Two thousand years"/"over four score generations ago" before *Benny B2: Road Trip: Bad Habits.*

369 "Two thousand years" before *Benny B4: New Frontiers: A Handful of Dust.*

370 "Three millennia" before *Worlds BF: The Archive* [c.3630].

371 *The Talons of Weng-Chiang, The Flames of Cadiz.* Bede lived c.673-735, although he never went to London, only leaving Jarrow once to visit Canterbury.

372 *Companion Piece.* This is a neat trick on Bede's part, as he died in 735 and the building of Westminster Abbey didn't start until 1050.

373 *The Banquo Legacy.* It was attributed to the Silurians in *White Darkness* (p89).

374 *Four to Doomsday*

375 *The Mark of the Rani*

376 *The Tomorrow Windows*

377 "Twelve hundred and twenty-four Terran years" before *First Frontier.*

378 *Battlefield.* The archaeologist Warmsley thinks that Excalibur's scabbard dates "from the eighth century".

379 *Wolfsbane*

380 *Royal Blood* (ch2).

381 *Silhouette*

382 *I, Davros:* "Purity". In *The Daleks*, the Dals are cited as being forebears of the Daleks.

Dalek: The Astounding Untold History of the Greatest Enemies of the Universe suggests that the Thal history simply amalgamated the Dals and the Kaleds into a single enemy. The same book (p50) claims that Skaro has three satellites: the naturally occurring Flidor and Omega Mysterium, and the construct Falkus – a fallback position in case of overwhelming attack. Flidor was first mentioned in "Genesis of Evil" (it's also the name of the gold that forms the Dalek Emperor's casing). Falkus and Omega Mysterium originate from "The Forbidden Planet" feature published in the *Doctor Who and the Daleks Omnibus* collection (1976). *Dalek...*

TARDIS crashed in England and died on impact. One of the Furies trapped within starved to death, but the other survived until the Ship was discovered in 1999.[366]

c 600 - TW: "Rift War"[367] -> The Cardiff Rift briefly transported Jack Harkness and Gwen Cooper back in time. Their duplicitous ally Vox went through the Rift and guided them back home.

A humanoid species charted much of the Milky Way "when other [races] were just out of short trousers". One of their number, an astronaut named Celestion, arrived on the planet Agora and was later regarded as the prophet St Celestion. Talishanti Monastery was founded over terrain thought to contain St Celestion's tomb.[368]

The indigenous people of the planet Nemeqit practiced Gaia worship, as their world was indeed a single entity. As part of its life cycle, Nemeqit sterilized its surface and constructed a dome to shield its two children, Bel and Lud, during their development. The souls of the dead were thought to walk Nemeqit, and it became known as the most haunted planet in Legion's part of the galaxy.[369]

The original keepers of the Department of Eschatology within the Archive erected new platforms.[370]

The first **Doctor** and Susan **caught a huge salmon in Fleet and shared it with the Venerable Bede (who "adored fish").**[371] Bede made the Doctor the Dean of Westminster Abbey.[372] The *Necronomicon* was written by Abdul Al-Hazred, a mad poet of Sanaa, in Damascus around 730.[373] **Around this period, Monarch left Urbanka for the last time.**[374] **The Rani visited Earth during the so-called "Dark Ages".**[375]

The Galactic Heritage Foundation emerged as an organisation to halt alien property development on planets with indigenous populations. In the eighth century, the third princess Tabetha of Cerrenis Minor spent a weekend in Lewisham. Despite her finding it all a bit gauche, Earth was accorded a low-level ranking of Grade 4, which put it under the Foundation's protection.

With planets under such development bans selling for cheap, the Frantige Two native named Martin purchased a hundred or so worlds for next to nothing. Among his acquisitions, he bought the planet Earth for a few thousand Arcturan ultra-pods from a Navarino time-share salesman going through a messy divorce. The Navarino threw in the rest of Earth's solar system for free.[376]

The Doctor defeated the Tzun at Mimosa II in 733.[377]

= "Sideways in time" on an Earth where the truth about King Arthur was closer to the myths of our world, a future incarnation of the Doctor was known as Merlin. During the eighth century, Arthur and Morgaine fought against one another, despite their childhood together at Selladon. The

---

Doctor cast down Morgaine at Badon with his mighty arts.

Eventually, though, Morgaine was victorious and Arthur was killed. The Doctor placed Arthur's body and Excalibur in a semi-organic spaceship, and transferred it to the bottom of Lake Vortigern in our dimension. Morgaine imprisoned the Doctor forever in the Ice Caves, and went on to become Empress of the solar system.[378]

Godric, a swordsman in the age when Arthur ruled, found the Holy Grail in a freshwater spring. A wood dryad seduced Godric into her tree, where he slept until 1936. The Doctor claimed to have taught Lancelot how to use a sword at King Arthur's court.[379] The twelfth Doctor insisted that King Arthur was an actual warlord/Duke, but that Sir Lancelot, the Lady of the Lake and the Holy Grail were all the stuff of myth.[380]

When King Arthur was very young, he ran along shouting that he needed a sword, prompting a confused Doctor to pull Excalibur from the stone. The Doctor spent a day as the King of England before abdicating in Arthur's favour.[381]

The Birth of the Daleks

The planet Skaro was the birthplace of the Kaleds and the Thals, and had formerly been home to such wiped-out races as the Tharons and the Dals. Skaro had two moons: Falkus and Omega Mysterium.[382] Varga plants were native to Skaro.[383] Skaro's history included a rural economy phase.[384]

Young Davros

& 677 - THE MAGICIAN'S APPRENTICE / THE WITCH'S FAMILIAR[385] -> The Kaled-Thal war was now being fought with a mixture of technology including bows and arrows and laser-equipped biplanes, and lethal weaponry such as clam drones. A young boy fled across a battlefield and found himself surrounded by deadly hand-mines. The twelfth Doctor arrived nearby, having lost his way while looking for a bookshop, and encouraged the boy to seize upon the one chance in a thousand that he had to survive... until he realised that the young boy was Davros, the future creator of the Daleks. Mortified, the Doctor fled in the TARDIS.

The Doctor returned, eliminated the hand-mines with a Dalek gun, and escorted Davros home. In doing so, the Doctor taught the young boy the importance of mercy – a quality that Davros would be unable to eliminate entirely from the Daleks' worldview.

& 683 - I, DAVROS: INNOCENCE[386] -> The Kaleds and Thals had warred with each other for centuries, and neither side remembered what started their conflict. Davros was born to an influential Kaled family – his mother was Lady Calcula, a personal assistant to Councillor Quested, and his father was acknowledged as Nasgard, a senior military officer. Quested was actually Davros' biological father. Davros' half-sister, Yarvell, was in the Military Youth. A House of Congress governed the Kaleds.

When Davros was 16, Calcula murdered her husband and his sister, Tashek, to keep secret the truth about Davros' parentage. Brogan, a major, was framed for the crime and executed. Davros' interest in science grew, and

he brutally subjected his tutor, Magrantine, to radiation to understand its effect on living tissue. He also killed Quested in a domestic dispute.

& 696 - I, DAVROS: PURITY[387] -> The Kaled-Thal war experienced a hiatus that some called the Unsigned Truce. The increasing chemical pollutants and radioactivity on Skaro mutated the Varga plants: flesh-eating vegetation that was formerly rooted in the ground, but now gained the ability to walk and hunt its prey. The name "Varga", as deciphered from old cave paintings, came from the old Dal word for "devourer".

Davros had enlisted in the military because his family's

Astounding Untold History (p50) also names Skaro as the twelfth planet from its sun, and the only habitable world in the seven surrounding galaxies.

383 *WD* S2: *The Neverwhen*

384 *WD* S2: *Legion of the Lost*

385 Dating *The Magician's Apprentice/The Witch's Familiar* (X9.1-9.2) - It's during Davros' childhood. This placement extrapolates from him being 16 in *I, Davros: Innocence.*

386 Dating *I, Davros: Innocence* (*I, Davros* #1.1) - Davros is currently 16, so it's thirteen years before *I, Davros: Purity.* Yarvell's name is doubtless a play on "Yarvelling", the creator of the Daleks according to *The Dalek Book* (1964) and the *TV Century 21* comic.

387 Dating *I, Davros: Purity* (*I, Davros* #1.2) - Davros was 16 in *I, Davros: Innocence,* and he's now 29; we know this partly because the product blurb says he's "approaching thirty", and because his sister (two years his elder, according to *Innocence*) is cited as being 31.

388 *Genesis of the Daleks*

389 Dating *Davros* (BF #48) and *I, Davros: Corruption* (*I, Davros* #1.3) - Events pertaining to Davros having Shan killed are told in flashback in *Davros* and expanded upon in *Corruption.* Davros claims in *Genesis of the Daleks,* "Many times in the last fifty years, factions of the government have tried to interfere with my research here" – "here" indicating the Kaled bunker and the work of the Scientific Elite. It seems reasonable to assume that said fifty years pass between Davros schisming the Elite off from the Kaled government (as happens in *Corruption*) and *Genesis.* That matches with Davros being thirty when he's crippled in *Corruption,* but his being "an old man" – owing to his life-support systems, which make him the first Kaled to enjoy a natural (if one can call it that) lifespan in ten generations – in *I, Davros: Guilt.*

390 *Davros* and *I, Davros: Corruption,* drawing on sources such as the novelisations of *Genesis of the Daleks* and *Remembrance of the Daleks.* The circumstances of how Davros came to be in his life support system are never given on screen – it's described as "an accident", which doesn't directly support the idea that it was a Thal attack.

391 *Genesis of the Daleks.* There's no indication how old Davros was when he was crippled, or how much time passed between the accident and *Genesis of the Daleks.*

392 *NAofBenny* V1: *The Lights of Skaro.* The Kaleds' "metal into gold" discovery pairs with the carrot the Daleks dangle Professor Maxtible in *The Evil of the Daleks.* The existence of "Kaled artists" reconciles why – in a city otherwise without culture – the first Doctor's party conveniently finds a statue to drop down a lift shaft in *The Daleks.*

393 Dating *I, Davros: Guilt* (*I, Davros* #1.4) - The story ends with the Mark I Dalek coming to life. The Daleks seen in *Genesis of the Daleks* are Mark III, so some time must pass – probably just weeks or months, but possibly some years – between the audio mini-series and the TV story.

394 *Gallifrey VI: Ascension*

395 Dating *Genesis of the Daleks* (12.4) - The date of the Daleks' creation is never stated on television. *The Dalek Invasion of Earth, The Daleks' Master Plan* and *Genesis of the Daleks* all have the Doctor talk of "millions of years" of Dalek evolution and history. *Destiny of the Daleks,* however, suggests a much shorter timeframe of "thousands of years", and Davros has only been "dead for centuries". The Daleks seem to have interstellar travel at least two hundred years before *The Power of the Daleks* (so by 1820), although *War of the Daleks* suggests those were time-travelling Daleks from the far future.

The dating of *Genesis of the Daleks* in this chronology is derived from the *TV Century 21* comic strip (for full details, see the dating notes on "Genesis of Evil" [1763]). *Timelink* puts *Genesis* at around "300", keying off its preferred dating of *The Daleks* to "900". *About Time* suggests "all we can say for sure is that it's well before the twenty-second century" before proposing a date of the eighteenth century "for mostly spurious reasons".

Both the Mark I Travel Machine entry in *A History of the Universe in 100 Objects* (p50) and the Dalek Timeline in *The Dalek Handbook* (p18) cite the creation of the Daleks as "circa 1450". *The Dalek Handbook* also proclaims – in bold letters even – that the Doctor's intervention in Skaro's past creates a new timeline, then backtracks and gets ambiguous concerning what if any

long tradition of service demanded it, but he longed to join the Scientific Corps. To win reassignment, he complied with the wishes of the Supremo, a high-ranking Kaled official, that he investigate an advanced Thal weapons facility. Davros' team destroyed the facility, but Davros alone survived the mission. Calcula discovered that Yarvell, now a peace supporter, feared Davros' potential for destruction and had warned her allies about his mission. Seeing her daughter as a threat to Davros' advancement, Calcula drowned her. A Thal infiltrator was blamed for Yarvell's death, and Davros joined the Scientific Corps.

& 709 - I, DAVROS: CORRUPTION -> Skaro's environment took a turn for the worse. There hadn't been a summer for three years, nearly all animal life was extinct, and what little wildlife survived was in the Lake of Mutations, formerly known as Drammakin Lake. Now established within the Scientific Elite, Davros developed a blast ray with a range of three miles – its use consumed enough energy to power the Kaled city for seventy-three years, but a shot from it obliterated a fortified Thal command facility.

The Supremo became wary of Davros' ascent and desire to eradicate the Thals entirely, and sent an underling – Section Leader Fenn – to wreck his equipment and kill Calcula. She stopped Fenn by subjecting them both to fatal doses of radiation. Davros learned of the Supremo's involvement in his mother's death, and blackmailed him Henceforth, the Kaled Science Division would have autonomy, and the Elite could requisition any and all resources. Councillor Valron was framed for Calcula's murder.

Fifty years before the end of the war between the Thals and the Kaleds on Skaro, the Kaleds set up an Elite group, based in a secret bunker below the Wasteland. It was run by chief scientist Davros, the greatest mind Skaro had ever seen.[388]

Davros is Gravely Injured

& 709 - DAVROS / I, DAVROS: CORRUPTION[389] -> Although he continued to develop weapons – one of which sunk the entire Thal Navy in a day – Davros had come to realise the war was futile. Prolonging the war with the Thals and using increasingly deadly weapons would mean that soon Skaro would become a dead planet. He believed that no other world could support life, and it was impossible to end the fighting, as both races would inevitably compete to exploit the same ecological niche. Logically, the Kaled race could not possibly survive.

One of his research students, Shan, came up with what she called The Dalek Solution, a plan to reengineer the Kaled race to survive the pollution on Skaro. Fearing that Shan would become a more brilliant scientist than him, Davros framed her for treason and had her hanged.

Davros was greatly injured, and the only survivor, when the Thals shelled his laboratory. He was given a poison injector to kill himself, as none of the Kaleds could bring themselves to put Davros out of his misery. At that moment, Davros realised how weak the Kaleds were and how true power was being able to grant life and death.[390]

Davros was crippled, but survived by designing a life support system for himself. He created energy weapons, artificial hearts and a new material that reinforced the Kaled Dome.[391]

The Kaleds developed the ability to turn metal into gold. Poets and artists were unwelcome in the Kaled dome in the final days of the Kaled-Thal war. The Kaled Klinus, having crafted the statue *Eternal War*, was used as raw material to create the very first Daleks.[392]

& 759 - I, DAVROS: GUILT[393] -> Lieutenant Nyder successfully rescued Davros when the Thals briefly captured him, and thereby became his trusted aide.

Davros demanded that the ruling Council of Twelve make all Kaled children the property of the state, so his biological experiments had access to the widest available stock. The Councillors unanimously voted against Davros, and so he killed them, attributing their deaths a faulty heat exchanger. Davros took charge until a new legislative body could be elected, and instigated a mandatory "child protection program" to oversee any Kaled younger than five.

Davros successfully developed a Mark I travel machine, based upon his own life-support chair, that would house the form he believed the Kaleds would eventually mutate into. He and Nyder looked on as the first "Dalek" – a Dal word meaning "gods" – switched on and came to life.

End of the Thousand Year War

The First Engagement Between the Daleks and the Time Lords

Narvin, the head of the Gallifreyan CIA, initiated the first strike on the Daleks' origins in a bid to save President Romana. He dispatched a disguised Chancellor Valyes back to brief the fourth Doctor, Harry and Sarah on their mission to interfere with the Daleks' development...[394]

The First Daleks are Entombed, Force Davros Into Stasis

? 760 - GENESIS OF THE DALEKS[395] -> Davros selectively bred an intelligent creature that could survive in the radiation-soaked, environmentally desolate world of Skaro. Using the Mark III Travel Machines, the Daleks could live in virtually any environment.

The Time Lords foresaw a time when the Daleks had become the supreme power in the universe, and sent the fourth Doctor, Sarah and Harry back to the Daleks' creation. They gave the Doctor three options: avert the Daleks' creation; affect their genetic development so they might evolve in a less aggressive fashion; find an inherent weakness that could be used against them.

Facing opposition to his work, Davros turned against his own people, leading to the obliteration of the Kaled dome. He intended that only the Daleks and his Scientific Elite would survive, but the Daleks threw off Davros' control and exterminated him.

The Doctor destroyed the Daleks' incubator room and entombed them in their bunker; he reckoned he had set Dalek development back a thousand years. He believed the existence of the Daleks would serve to unite races against them.

Davros' back-up systems suspended his life-functions while healing him. He would remain inert until the Dalek-Movellan War.[396] Davros had compelled the fourth Doctor to yield information about future Dalek defeats, but while the recording of this interrogation was destroyed, Davros programmed the details he could remember into his Daleks' memory banks. The Davros clone Falkus would scrub the information, believing the Daleks needed to learn from their mistakes.[397]

The Doctor's interference on Skaro spared thousands of worlds from enduring the Dalek wars. The Time Lords calmed the resulting time disruption.[398] At some point, at least a thousand years later, the Daleks developed space travel and began their galactic conquests.[399]

= The Valeyard gave the Thals a formula that destroyed the Daleks in their infancy, preventing them from ever having left their bunker.[400]

= On the Skaro of an alternate reality, the Thals served as the dominant military culture while the Kaleds were scholars. The Quatch Empire, ethereal beings from another dimension, sought to tap the powerful energy source at Skaro's core: a collapsed dimensional pathway. A space war resulted, with the Thals conscripting the Kaleds to fight against the Quatch. Though the Thals and Kaleds prevailed, Davros was heavily injured in the fighting.

Many of Davros' Daleks retained the capacity for pity, so did not turn on him, but seemed weak to his eyes. Davros left Skaro and, failing to realize the Quatchs' culpability with his injuries, joined them as their Chief Technician. A number of Daleks went into space to find their creator.[401]

A group of Gantha, intergalactic mercenaries, crashed on the Arabian Peninsula, Earth, and died on impact. The Shalaki they were transporting – a creature capable of assuming the shape of other beings – survived. It assumed a sultan's form, and imprisoned the genuine article. The Shalki adapted the Gantha's technology to extend his life, living on for a century.[402] The Hornet Swarm, a hivemind of tiny insects ruled by a powerfully telepathic Queen, drifted through space. In the early ninth century, the Swarm accidentally ended up on Earth. They would

---

meaningful changes have actually occurred. "Perhaps the Doctor was correct – he'd set the Daleks back a thousand years, and Earth was not now invaded until 3157, for example. Or, possibly, their history was played out more or less the same" (pgs. 70-71).

The Dalek Handbook (p16) bridges *Genesis of the Daleks* and *The Daleks* by naming the futuristic city in the latter as Kalaann (as it's called in the Series 5 adventure game *City of the Daleks*), and claiming that it was built "amidst the ruins of the destroyed Kaled city and the underground Bunker, with corridors, doors, elevators and walkways designed specifically for Dalek use. There were, however, still significant numbers of Thal forces. They regrouped and, possibly recruiting Mutos, resumed hostilities against the Daleks. From secure levels beneath their city, the Daleks exploded a neutron bomb, finally ending the war."

Dalek: The Astounding Untold History of the Greatest Enemies of the Universe (pgs. 30-31) claims "over five hundred years" pass with the Daleks trapped within the confines of their city prior to *The Daleks*. The Thals in that story achieve victory after – including Skaro's thousand year war – "a millennium and a half", meaning Kalaann is built not long after *Genesis of the Daleks*.

Entertainingly, *The Dalek Handbook* points out (p65) that while Davros' interrogation equipment was calibrated to detect lies, it couldn't compensate for the Doctor's erratic memory concerning future events.

Dalek: The Astounding Untold History of the Greatest Enemies of the Universe (p84) suggests that in future, Davros and the Daleks will have a more-than-casual focus on Earth because Sarah and Harry's presence at their origins drew their attention to it. Given that Davros and the Daleks open *Genesis of the Daleks* convinced that life on alien planets doesn't exist, the idea that they'd fixate on the first aliens they meet (other than the Doctor) sounds worryingly plausible.

396 Davros returns to life in *Destiny of the Daleks*.

397 *Genesis of the Daleks*, *Daleks Among Us*.

398 *A Device of Death*

399 *The Dalek Invasion of Earth*, and most subsequent Dalek stories. Again, taking what the Doctor says at face value, the Daleks are set back a thousand years by the Doctor in *Genesis of the Daleks*.

400 *Unbound: He Jests at Scars...*

401 An alternative version of how Davros was injured prior to *Genesis of the Daleks*, at a point variously said to be "centuries", "hundreds" and "thousands" of years

ARE THERE TWO DALEK HISTORIES?: There are a number of discrepancies between the accounts of the Daleks' origins in *The Daleks* and *Genesis of the Daleks*. In the first story, the original Daleks (or Dals) were humanoid, and it is implied they only mutated after the Neutronic War. This version was also depicted in the *TV Century 21* comic strip, where the Dalek casings are built by a scientist called Yarvelling and a mutated Dalek crawls into a casing to survive. Whereas in *Genesis of the Daleks*, we see Davros deliberately accelerate the mutations that have begun to affect the Kaled race (a process the Doctor calls "genetic engineering" in *Dalek*).

Fans have attempted to reconcile these accounts in a number of ways. Perhaps the most common nowadays is to completely dismiss the version in *The Daleks*, and declare the Thal version of events to be a garbled version of the true history seen in *Genesis of the Daleks*. This would mean that the Doctor's comment that the Thal records are accurate is wrong – which isn't too difficult to justify. The idea that Skaro's civilisation lost knowledge following a nuclear war and that the two races would have subjective, propaganda-driven history is tempting... but it *doesn't* explain why both the Thals and the Daleks in *The Daleks* believe in exactly the same version of events, especially as they've had no contact with each other for some time. It's also suggesting that Skaro's historians are so incompetent that they can't tell the difference between a war that lasted a thousand years with one that lasted a day.

Another possible explanation is that the Doctor changes history in *Genesis of the Daleks* – before then, history was the version in *The Daleks*, afterwards it's the *Genesis* version. This is tempting, because altering history *was* the Doctor's mission, after all, and he says at the end that he's set the Daleks back "a thousand years". *The Discontinuity Guide* suggested that in their appearances after *Genesis of the Daleks*, the Daleks are nowhere near as unified a force as they had been before. Morever, Davros – who previously wasn't even mentioned – plays a major part in Dalek politics. *The Discontinuity Guide* credits all of this to the Doctor changing history – looking closely at the evidence, though, the Doctor hasn't actually made much of a difference. The Daleks are an extremely feared, powerful and unified force in the first of the post-*Genesis* stories (*Destiny of the Daleks*), and it's their defeat to the Movellans after that story which weakens them. In other words, no alteration of the timeline need be invoked to explain the change in the status quo. Perhaps the clincher is that *The Dalek Invasion of Earth* still happens in the post-*Genesis* stories – Susan remembers it in *The Five Doctors* (indeed, she's been snatched from its aftermath), and *Remembrance of the Daleks* contains references both to the Daleks invading Earth in "the twenty-second century" and to events on Spiridon (*Planet of the Daleks*). That's before factoring in the dozens of references to pre-*Genesis of the Daleks*

stories in the novels, audios and comic strips featuring later Doctors.

All told, it looks like the Doctor setting the Daleks back a thousand years in *Genesis of the Daleks* is part of the timeline we know, not a divergence from it – again, they still invade Earth in 2157, not 3157. With that in mind, it's interesting to note that the 60s strip has the Daleks developing space travel very soon after they take to their mechanical casings, but that this happens a thousand years after the end of the Thousand Years War (which we would later see ending in *Genesis of the Daleks*). If the Doctor hadn't been there, the Daleks would have developed space travel very soon after *Genesis of the Daleks*, and so the Doctor – as part of the original timeline – *has* set them back a thousand years.

There's a second problem: We have to reconcile the fact that *The Daleks* shows a group of Daleks confined to their city on Skaro and wiped out at the end, while all the other stories have them as galactic conquerors. Nothing in any *Doctor Who* story, in any medium, accounts for this.

The FASA roleplaying game and *About Time* both explain the discrepancy by theorising that soon after *Genesis of the Daleks*, there's a schism between Daleks who want to stay on Skaro to exterminate the Thals and those who want to conquer other planets. The FASA game names them the "exterminator" and "expansionist" factions, and states that the exterminator Daleks never leave Skaro, eventually wither on the vine and end up confined to their city – finally dying out in *The Daleks*. (In this scenario, spacefaring Daleks later recolonise their home planet.)

In *About Time*'s version, the "exterminator" Daleks do venture beyond Skaro, but only on limited sorties – like the invasion of Earth – and they're not galactic conquerors. There's nothing on screen to suggest an early divergence in Dalek history, and only a line in *Alien Bodies* (p138) supports it. *If* this was the case, it seems the spacefaring "expansionist" Daleks completely broke contact with the Daleks on Skaro. Adding speculation to speculation, we might infer this schism was because the Daleks on Skaro continued to mutate – indeed, perhaps they become the humanoid Dals mentioned in *The Daleks*, a different race altogether. Given what we know of Dalek history, it seems unlikely that this was an amicable arrangement, so there could have been a Dalek civil war of some kind.

While we're speculating, we might wonder if the Thals joined the Dals in their efforts to rid the planet of Daleks. Following this, the Dals and Thals lived together in (relative) peace on Skaro for a long time – until the Neutronic War, placed in this guidebook in 1763. The spacefaring Daleks eventually return to Skaro somewhere between *The Daleks* (?2263) and *Planet of the Daleks* (2540).

It might be straightforward, then: the "expansionist"

continued on page 1093...

develop plans to conquer it.[403]

Radiation started to increase to dangerous levels on the planet Oseidon.[404] **The Saxons mentioned the Caliburn Ghast – actually an echo of the time traveller Hila Tacorien – in their poetry. The Ghast alternatively became regarded as the Wraith of the Lady, the Maiden in the Dark and the Witch of the Well.**[405] As the Romans in Britain had done before them, some Saxons provided sacrifices to the space worm in Derbyshire. The worm gave rise to a tale of brave Sir Edgar, who went looking for a terrible wyrm (i.e. dragon) that lived in the fires of the gap of Dark Peak.[406]

The Viking Age

The Vikings were active from roughly the late eighth century to the mid-eleventh century.

Two rival warships crashed on the isle of Hoy in Orkney, Scotland, where the crews' bodies became embedded in a bog. The disembodied minds of the dead sought out those with psychic potential, hoping to reintegrate their psyches. In time, their presence spurred legends about mud-creatures: the Marsh Wains. Viking sagas would speak of two armies resurrected by magic, forced to fight on Hoy until Ragnarok. It was additionally possible that the TARDIS' double arrival on Hoy in the 1950s rippled back through time and gave rise to the Viking legend of the Wissfornjarl – a protective spirit whose name meant "wise old chieftain". The Wissfornjarl was said to live under a barrow, where the first Doctor would stash away the TARDIS.[407]

c 800 - "Doctor Conkerer!"[408] **->** The seventh Doctor invented the game of conkers.

The Book of Kells – a collection of manuscripts including the four Gospels, and which would become regarded as Ireland's greatest national treasure – was created in an abbey founded by St Columbia on the island of Iona. Vikings raided the abbey, and the monks fled to Ireland and Scotland, taking the Book with them.[409] The Vikings regarded the alien Vostok – who came to sleep beneath the polar icecap – as "the gods of the ice age".[410]

The first Doctor was present when a fire ravaged Charlemagne's library.[411]

> = On Roma I, the Roman Emperor Carolus Magnus, that Earth's Charlemagne, defeated the Vikings.[412]

The tenth Doctor rescued Charlemagne from the clutches of an insane computer.[413] The Catholic Church founded the Library of St John the Beheaded in the St Giles Rookery, a notorious area of Holborn, London. The library contained unique, suppressed and pagan texts, including information on "alternative zoology and phantasmagorical anthropology".[414]

The imprisoned Fenric still had influence over the Earth and the ability to manipulate the timelines. He summoned the Ancient One – a powerful Haemovore – from half a million years in the future. Over the centuries, the Ancient One followed the flask containing Fenric. It was stolen from Constantinople; Viking pirates took it to Northumbria. Slowly, the Ancient One followed it to Maiden's Bay.

By the tenth century, a nine-letter Viking alphabet

before *Unbound: Masters of War*.

402 *1001 Nights:* "1001 Nights".

403 "Twelve hundred years'" before *Hornets' Nest: Hive of Horror*. The *Hornets' Nest* series sees the Doctor travelling through time to meet the Hornets, so that he encounters them in reverse historical order.

404 *The Oseidon Adventure*, marking the start of the decline of the Kraals (*The Android Invasion*).

405 *Hide*

406 *Trail of the White Worm*. The "story" of Sir Edgar – invented for this audio – seems to be a Middle Ages story akin to the fable of the Lambton Worm.

407 "Hundreds of years" before *The Revenants*. Viking and Norse settlers first gained a hold on Scotland in the eighth century, with Scottish influence increasing from the thirteenth century onward.

408 Dating "Doctor Conkerer!" (*DWM* #162) - No date is given, but it's set at the time of the Vikings.

409 *The Book of Kells*. This is historical, and dates to the ninth century.

410 *TW:* "The Return of the Vostok"

411 *The Drowned World*. Charlemagne ruled 768 to 814. The library fire isn't historical, and is writer Simon Guerrier's way of establishing a "missing" *Doctor Who* story concerning the great works that went absent from Charlemagne's archive, as specifically inspired by Umberto Eco's *The Name of the Rose*. In Eco's book, a monastery library is said to own works by Aristotle, etc., that were formerly housed in Charlemagne's court library. Real-life scholars aren't quite sure, though, what works Charlemagne's library may have contained.

412 *FP: Warlords of Utopia*

413 *The Unicorn and the Wasp*

414 The Library of St John the Beheaded was mentioned in *Theatre of War*, and made its first appearance in the following New Adventure, *All-Consuming Fire*. In that book, we learn much about the library, including the fact that it has been established for a "thousand years" (p15). The library still exists at the time of *Millennial Rites*. In *The Empire of Glass*, Irving Braxiatel

continued from page 1091...

Daleks are the ones with slats in their mid-section, the "exterminators" are the ones with bands (as seen in the first two TV stories, *The Space Museum* and the *TV Century 21* strip). However, the Daleks in *The Chase* are based on Skaro and are out to avenge the defeat in *The Dalek Invasion of Earth*, so that would also seem to be the "exterminator" faction (unless the first order of business when the "expansionists" return to Skaro is to go after the man who twice inflicted crushing defeats – and so wiped out – the "exterminators").

Alternatively, it could be that the Doctor changes history in *The Daleks* – his first encounter with them might affect Dalek development. We know from *The Evil of the Daleks* and *Dalek* that the Daleks can be altered by contact with aliens, particularly time-travelling ones. Their first contact with the Doctor in *The Daleks* might have been the catalyst that set any Daleks that survived on course to conquer the universe and challenge the Time Lords' supremacy. Again, though, there's no evidence from the series that this is the case – and every Dalek on Skaro appears dead at the end of *The Daleks*.

Ironically, the *one* thing fans seem to agree on is that the Doctor is simply wrong in *The Dalek Invasion of Earth* when he said *The Daleks* was set "a million years" in the future. At the time, it was the television series' own attempt (and in only the second Dalek story!) to explain the discrepancies in Dalek history, but virtually nobody credits the Doctor's statement now.

So... reconciling the account given in *The Daleks* and *TV Century 21* with *Genesis of the Daleks* may not be as difficult as it appears, but merely needs a little *speculation* to smooth things over. The Thousand Years War ends in *Genesis of the Daleks* with the Kaleds wiped out and the first Daleks buried underground. These Daleks either leave Skaro to become galactic conquerors or they simply die out. For the purposes of this chronology, it's been assumed the Doctor set the Daleks back a thousand years, so no Daleks leave Skaro at this time. Six hundred years later (according to *The Dalek Outer Space Book*), the Daleks evolved... meaning the blue-skinned humanoid Daleks (or "Dals"). We could speculate that the Dals are mutated Kaled survivors, or perhaps Dalek mutants who've escaped from the buried bunker.

A thousand years after *Genesis of the Daleks*, Yarvelling builds a "metal casing" that looks like Davros' Mark III travel machine – even though it's not exactly the same design (the mid section and colour scheme is different, matching the ones from *The Daleks* and *The Dalek Invasion of Earth*), it's too similar to be a coincidence. Perhaps Yarvelling has based it on a design from history that he knows will scare the Thals, although it seems more likely he's got access to ancient records of Davros' work, or maybe he's even managed to excavate an old Dalek casing from the Kaled bunker. The Dals

also develop the Neutron bomb, which goes off (deliberately according to *The Daleks*, accidentally according to the *TV Century 21* strip) and all but wipes out life on Skaro. A mutated Dal – the creature predicted by Davros' experiments, perhaps even a thousand-year-old survivor of those experiments – crawls into one of the casings, and becomes the sort of Dalek we're familiar with.

Very quickly, these Daleks develop a thirst for galactic conquest, the early days of which are recounted in the *TV Century 21* strip. At some point, apparently soon after *The Dalek Invasion of Earth*, there's a split – one group of Daleks completely abandons Skaro to become fearsome conquerors elsewhere in the universe, another group becomes confined to their city and dies off in *The Daleks*. Eventually spacefaring Daleks return to Skaro and reoccupy their planet, sharing it with the Thals, at least for a while (as seems to be the case in *Planet of the Daleks* – although, ominously, there are no Thals seen on Skaro in later TV stories).

was in use, although the later Vikings used a 16-letter version. Carvings in the earlier alphabet claimed that the Vikings were cursed, and they buried the flask in a burial site under St Jude's church.[415]

c 817 - THE TWELFTH DOCTOR YEAR THREE[416]->
Haathi, an Ice Warrior infected by the Flood, fled to Earth. The twelfth Doctor and Bill bested Fenric's efforts to poison Earth with the Flood, leaving Fenric trapped in his bottle. As history dictated, the surviving Vikings continued on to Northumbria. The Ancient One followed.

Merlin banished the Demon Melanicus from our universe. Melanicus waited a thousand years for an opportunity to escape the black, formless void.[417] Viking legends referred to the Timewyrm as Hel.[418] The seventh Doctor, Ace and Bernice were at an Angle settlement when the Vikings attacked it.[419] The Doctor met the Anglo-Saxon king Alfred the Great and his cook Ethelburg, "a dab hand at bear rissoles".[420] The Doctor became known as Shango the thunder god of the Yoruba tribe when he demonstrated static electricity.[421]

During the second quest to find the Key to Time, the White and Black Guardians found that their powers were greatly diminished. The Black Guardian transported the fifth Doctor and Amy the Key-tracer to the location of the next Key segment – ninth-century Sudan – then crashed there himself, four decades prior to their arrival, in a spaceship. The Black Guardian became Lord Cassim Ali Baba, and sired a son named Prince Omar. He partnered with a stranded Djinn – a race of collectors who went from world to world in search of profit – to repair the spaceship and leave Earth. Meanwhile, the weakened White Guardian lived as the Legate of the Caliphate of Baghdad.[422]

The master vampire Gabriel Saunders embarked upon a breeding programme that developed the Ruthven family into formidable monsters protected by bone spikes, but could pass as human. Saunders hoped to create a prey worthy of being hunted by him, possibly even one that offered the chance of ending his undead existence.[423]

c 820 - THE MEMORY BANK AND OTHER STORIES: "The Last Fairy Tale"[424] ->
Grayling Frimlish had become the oldest living being in Europe – the last of a race of Storytellers who had fallen into our dimension. In the medieval village of Vadhoc, some uncomely people took hostages to protest how the Storytellers always portrayed hags, dwarves and anyone who wasn't conventionally beautiful as evil. The fifth Doctor and Turlough watched as Frimlish assuaged those present by telling the story of a cranky old witch, an axe-wielding dwarf and a smart hell hound who were all good friends and very nice, and had marvellous travels together.

---

acquires manuscripts for the library (p245).

415 *The Curse of Fenric.* The Ancient Haemovore arrived in "ninth-century Constantinople" according to the Doctor. Ace says the inscriptions are "a thousand years old".

416 Dating *The Twelfth Doctor Year Three* (Titan 12th Doc #3.5-3.7; "The Wolves of Winter") - Captions name the century. This is a prequel to *The Curse of Fenric.*

417 Melanicus has waited for "a thousand years" before "The Tides of Time". It's tempting to link the void he was in with "Hell", the gap between the worlds in *Doomsday*. Merlin here is the Merlin from our universe, a recurring character in the *DWM* strip, not the future Doctor who will pose as Merlin in a parallel universe (*Battlefield*).

418 *Timewyrm: Revelation*

419 *Sky Pirates!*

420 *The Ghosts of N-Space*

421 *Transit* (p204).

422 "Forty years" before *The Destroyer of Delights.*

423 "Over a thousand years" before *J&L S2: The Ruthven Inheritance.*

424 Dating *The Memory Bank and Other Stories*: "The Last Fairy Tale" (BF #217b) - The blurb claims that it's Old Europe (6500-2800 BC), but within the story it's "Medieval Europe" (fifth to fifteenth centuries).

425 Dating *The Girl Who Died* (X9.5) - It's during the Viking Age. Electric eels are native to South America; the Vikings must have found those seen here during their travels and brought them back to Scandinavia. The official BBC synopsis for *The Woman Who Lived* says that Ashildr and the Doctor first meet in the "ninth century". In the same story, set in 1651, Ashildr claims to have had "eight hundred years of experience" in adventuring.

426 Dating *The Destroyer of Delights* (BF #118) - The back cover says it's the "ninth century", which is reiterated within the story. It's cited as the time of Caliph al-Mutawakkil, who ruled 847-861 AD. These events presumably serve as the inspiration for "Ali Baba and the Forty Thieves" and other stories contained within *One Thousand and One Nights* (vaguely dated by scholars to the ninth century) – but curiously, neither the Doctor nor either of the Guardians comments upon this.

427 *The Chaos Pool*

428 *DotD: Babblesphere.* Alfred the Great lived 849 to 899, and was King of Wessex from 871 to 899. His most famous culinary exploit was burning some cakes he was meant to be attending to, and this is almost certainly a sly reference to that.

429 Dating *1001 Nights*: "1001 Nights" (BF #168a) - The framing sequence takes place in an unspecified city on

Ashildr Gains Immortality

c 850 - THE GIRL WHO DIED[425] **->** Vikings took the twelfth Doctor and Clara captive as a leader of the Mire – one of the most lethal races in the galaxy – appeared as Odin in the skies over their village. "Odin" asked the warriors present to accompany him to "Valhalla" – i.e. his spaceship, where the warriors became fodder for an adrenaline-testosterone serum that nourished the Mire. Ashildr, daughter of Einarr, unwisely challenged the Mire rather than letting them just leave, prompting a Mire assault.

The Doctor hardwired Ashildr into the Mire's sensor network, enabling her to trick them into retreating before the image of a giant serpent. The Mire left for space, fearing the damage to their reputation if the Doctor distributed evidence of their cowardice on the Galactic Hub. Ashildr died from the effort, but the Doctor revived her with a Mire medical patch. It would continue to heal her body, making her immortal but not indestructible.

c 855 - THE DESTROYER OF DELIGHTS[426] **->** The Black Guardian, a.k.a. Cassim Ali Baba, had spent two years amassing enough gold to hyper-compress into a warp manifold – the last component needed to restore his grounded spaceship. Upon its creation, the compressed gold shard became incarnated as the fifth segment of the Key to Time. Prince Omar killed the Djinn, and – along with forty others – plundered the treasures in the Djinn's spaceship. The ship self-destructed upon the Djinn's death, and the fifth Doctor and the Key-tracer Amy acquired the segment.

The second Romana met the Black Guardian while trying to answer the Doctor's distress call, and transported him in her TARDIS to the planet Chaos in the far future.[427]

The Doctor did the catering for Alfred the Great.[428]

c 875 - 1001 NIGHTS: "1001 Nights"[429] **->** The fifth Doctor and Nyssa tracked a distress signal from a downed Gantha ship in the Arabian Penninsula. The shapeshifting Shalaki posing as a sultan locked up the Doctor, and commanded Nyssa to tell him tales of the Doctor's adventures in time and space. Her recounting aided the Shalaki in feeding off the Doctor's psyche, enabling him to *become* the Doctor. The creature's psionic abilities clouded Nyssa's perceptions, and she mistook it for a new incarnation of her friend. They left in the TARDIS, stranding the real Doctor for three years...

? 875 - THE LEGENDS OF ASHILDR: "The Arabian Knightmare"[430] **->** *Third-hand accounts suggested that the bored King of Samarkand offered his hand in marriage to the woman who could keep him amused – and executed those who failed in this duty. The Lady Sherade, possibly Ashildr, told him the story of the servant Ash El Dir, who accompanied the sailor Sinbad in search of treasure. They found a prized amethyst, which Ash El Dir gave to her beloved, Prince Karim, the King's grandfather. Eventually, Ash El Dir and Karim confronted the Wizard of Marabaia in the City of Brass, where Karim abandoned Ash El Dir for the sake of treasure.*

Upon finishing her tale, Sherade – as she believed that queens were preferable to kings – strangled her husband to death, and so fulfilled the role of the Destroyer of Delights.

c 878 - 1001 NIGHTS: "1001 Nights"[431] **->** The fifth Doctor had lived on the streets of an Arabian city for three years. The TARDIS returned to him when the Shalaki-Doctor became unable to contain the Doctor's memories, and suffered a mental breakdown. The Doctor and Nyssa reunited, and arranged for the Shalaki to receive treatment in an off-world medical facility.

---

the Arabian Peninsula, "many centuries" prior to one of the related stories (*1001 Nights*: "The Interplanetarian") set in 1892. The faux Sultan knows of Scheherazade – the storyteller in *One Thousand and One Nights*, which is loosely dated to the ninth century.

430 Dating *The Legends of Ashildr*: "The Arabian Knightmare" (NSA #61a) - The introduction makes clear that the story, as obviously inspired by *One Thousand and One Nights*, stems from an unreliable third-hand source. The chief reason to discount much of what we're told is that Ash El Dir and Prince Karim go adventuring when Karim's father Caliph Harun al-Rashid, is still alive – he died 24th March, 809, i.e. almost certainly before Ashildr meets the twelfth Doctor and Clara in *The Girl Who Died*, making it physically impossible that Ashildr could have been involved in those events.

Similarly, Lady Sherade seems remarkably talented, adept and worldly compared to the young Ashildr we meet on TV – a bit of a problem even if one generously makes an exception to *Ahistory*'s normal rule that a generation constitutes twenty-five years, and presumes that more than fifty years have elapsed between the King of Samarkand and Karim, his grandfather. One way of pounding this square peg into a round hole is to assume that Ash El Dir and Sherade are the older Ashildr/Lady Me who takes up traveling with Clara in *Hell Bent*, except that *The Legends of Ashildr* stories were touted as filling in the gaps of the younger Ashildr's history.

431 Dating *1001 Nights*: "1001 Nights" (BF #168a) - It's "three years" after the story's main events.

At the Peace of Wedmore, the Doctor suggested to King Alfred and the Viking Guthrum that Watling Street was a natural boundary.[432] The auditor Sondrah re-authorised Earth's continued survival.[433]

c 885 - "They Think It's All Over"[434] -> The eleventh Doctor, Amy and Rory attempted to see England play Germany in the 1966 World Cup Final, but instead landed in Wemba's Lea, a Saxon area marauded by the Vikings. Henghist, the son of King Ragnar, killed his father as a means of spurring the Vikings against the Saxon. The Doctor and Rory forced the Vikings to retreat after besting Henghist in a penalty shootout.

918 (June-July) - THE LADY OF MERCIA[435] -> A time machine created by Professor Bleak's wife catapulted Tegan back to the Dark Ages, and also pulled Aelfwynn, the daughter of Queen Aethelfrid of Mercia, to 1983. The Queen had achieved a victory against the Danes at Derby, but was beset by her brother – the Earl of Wessex – from the south. She was required to travel to York to receive a blessing at the Minster there, and assure the people of the strength of her bloodline... by showing them her daughter. Tegan posed as Aelfwynn in exchange for her life.

At York, the Queen surprised those assembled – and Tegan – by announcing her abdication, and that her "daughter" would succeed her. The fifth Doctor and the older Nyssa returned Aelfwynn to her native time in the TARDIS as a party of Danes led by Arthur Kettleson instigated a massacre. Kettleson insisted that "Aethelfrid" should marry him, which would make him king, but he died after being accidentally impaled on a sword that Tegan held. Wessex killed the Queen, then escaped with Tegan, thinking she was the princess.

The Doctor, Nyssa and Aelfwynn jumped forward in the TARDIS to Aelfwynn's last recorded appearance – the nunnery where she spent the remainder of her life – and recovered Tegan. Aelfwynn accepted her fate, and the Doctor's trio returned to 1983 to collect Turlough. As history recorded, Wessex became king and helped to unite the north and the south, facilitating the creation of England.

Weyland summoned men from Mercia to the dawn of time, to fight against the forces of Fenric.[436] **The Cup of Aethelstan was made in 924 as a gift from the first King of England to Hywel, king of the Welsh. The Doctor visited Aethelstan's court around this time.**[437] A

432 *The Mega*. The Peace of Wedmore happened in 878, when the King of Wessex, Alfred the Great (849-899), formally adopted the defeated Viking leader Guthrum. Watling Street, the name given to an ancient trail in England and Wales, today is part of the A2 and A5 roads.
433 "Dead Man's Hand"
434 Dating "They Think It's All Over" (IDW *DW* Vol. 2, #5) - The Doctor initially says they are "a thousand years" too early for 1966, so it's 966. Then he says it's the "ninth century", so it's the 800s. It's then established that Alfred the Great is king – he ruled from 871 to 899, and it's after the Doctor met him in such a capacity.
435 Dating *The Lady of Mercia* (BF #173) - The Doctor says, "Here we are, 918 AD", and that Aethelred has ruled "all these seven years" – both statements concur with her historically being on the throne from 911 to 918. Nyssa comments, "This is it? July 918 AD?", when the TARDIS hops forward to fetch Tegan, whose run-of-the-mill bad temper suggests that she's been at the nunnery for a few weeks rather than anything longer.
   Many of the events rendered here (particularly the Danes triggering a slaughter during Aethelfrid's appearance at York) aren't part of the historical record, with Professor Bleak noting that the Dark Ages are called just that for a reason. In real life, it's believed that the Queen was supposed to appear at York so the people could pledge loyalty, but that she died on 12th June, 918, some two weeks before they could do so. Aelfwynn actually succeeded her mother as monarch for about six months before her uncle dethroned her;

no record exists of what happened to her afterward.
436 *Gods and Monsters*. Mercia existed from 527 to 918.
437 *Planet of the Dead*
438 "Centuries" before *The Jade Pyramid*.
439 "Ten hundred years" before *Thin Ice* (BF), during the "Third Martian Polar Epoch".
440 *3rdA: Prisoners of the Lake*. Nobody can agree if these events happened "centuries" or "thousands of years" ago. The spaceship's logs indicate the former, and the Doctor hedges his bets by telling the Dastrons they've been asleep for "centuries, perhaps millennia".
441 "A millennium" before *The Helm of Awe* [1977], during the Viking Age.
442 *The Keeper of Traken*
443 *Kiss of Death*. The palace that Turlough's family owns is "almost a thousand years" old.
444 *The Cloisters of Terror*
445 Dating *Graceless III: The Battle* (*Graceless* #3.2) - Abby and Zara arrive two miles from Maldon on "9th of August, 991 AD". The battle commences the next day.
446 *FP: The Brakespeare Voyage* (ch5).
447 *Pond Life*. The helmic regulators were first mentioned when Harry Sullivan gave them a hard twist in *The Ark in Space*. With the TARDIS' exterior impervious to almost any harm, one presumes the arrow sped through the open door and struck the console.
448 *Ghosts of India*

group of benevolent space travellers landed in Japan and were killed by the scared natives. The ogre-like, animated mannequins – the Otoroshi – built to aid the travellers were incorporated into a holy shrine.[438]

Marshall Sezhyr founded the Ice Army, and united the nations of Mars, when the planet was in peril. He successfully defended the City of Chebisk against the rebel Dust Riders, and also fought the Kings of the Blood Gullies. Sezhyr's banners flew in a hundred Martian cities and on the planet's moons, but such was his tyranny that thousands of dissenters were killed. His mind survived his physical demise, encoded into his body armour.[439]

The Dastrons, a callous lupine race, overran many worlds and killed millions. The Federal Jurasdictorate levelled sanctions that wrecked the Dastron economy, and the Dastron military leaders were dispatched, in stasis, aboard a Jurasdictorate vessel to face trial. A rescue attempt caused the ship to crash in what would become Dunstanton Lake in Britain.[440] The Barbezzas, amoral galactic pirates famed as the ugliest creatures in the universe, established a bolthole on the Shetland isle of Bothness.[441]

A thousand years ago, a new Keeper of Traken was inaugurated. The Union of Traken in Mettula Orionsis had enjoyed many thousands of years of peace before this time.[442] The family of Vislor Turlough owned a planet in a system where wealthy Trions established stellar retreats. A millennia later, these were abandoned at start of the Trion civil war.[443]

In late Spring 985, a spaceship fell to Earth near Oxford. It was preprogrammed to return home if any of its three operators died, but its damaged warp-ignition field would have destroyed Earth in the process. A local named Matilda became the ship's first replacement operator, keeping the ship dormant. The three operators used the ship's telepathic circuits to influence the townsfolk to build St Matilda's convent over the vessel. For centuries, the nunnery served as a source of replacement operators.[444]

991 (9th-10th August) - GRACELESS III: THE BATTLE[445] -> The living Key tracers Abby and Zara travelled to Essex, 991, believing that their lost lover Marek was present as the Vikings sacked the town of Maldon. The sisters feared the slaughter to come, and – with the Vikings mistaking them for Valkyries – attempted to negotiate a peace between the Earl of Northumbria, Byrhtnoth, and the Viking chief Olaf Tryggvason. An ill-fated arrow triggered the battle; as history dictated, Byrhtnoth was killed, and the Vikings lay waste to the town's men, women and children. King Aethelred would later buy off the Vikings with a tribute, and Tryggvason became King of Norway.

(=) Unsatisfied with this outcome, Abby and Zara teleported back to before the battle. They arranged for Byrhtnoth to have a better shield, and for his men to better guard him in battle. The Vikings still prevailed, but suffered greater losses. Tryggvason consequently demanded more gold from Aethelred, leading to a war in which thousands died. He never became King of Norway, averting the Viking invasion of England.

(=) Abby and Zara went back and again intervened, making it rain and bogging down the Vikings in mud. Maldon still fell, but the battle lasted longer.

(=) On another attempt, the sisters moved the clouds so the sun shone in the Vikings' faces. Byrhtnoth's men prevailed, but the Vikings extracted revenge a few months later, burning every village down the coast.

(=) Abby and Zara meddled in the battle again, hoping for a better result...

(=) ... and again...

(=) ... and again...

The repeated historical revisions caused so much temporal damage, it created a black hole that represented time itself coming undone. Abby and Zara went into the future and returned with the historian Chi Shin-Kylie, whose expertise helped them put history back on its proper course. The Vikings won, but the arrival of Persephone Kreekpolt's spaceship – as part of her researching Abby and Zara's history – scattered the Vikings before they could massacre the village's women and children.

Abby, Zara and Chi amended a commemorative tapestry made for Byrhtnoth's widow, removing Persephone's spaceship and adding Marek into the background – the clue that would bring them to Maldon in search of him. The tapestry would be lost, but not before it inspired a poem about the battle, which mis-identified "the messenger of the Vikings" as male.

wih - The Enemy of the Great Houses launched a massive assault on the history of the eleventh century.[446]

The eleventh Doctor rode a horse through eleventh-century Coventry. An arrow struck the TARDIS at Hastings Hill, deactivating the Ship's helmic regulators and making it difficult for the Doctor to return to Amy and Rory.[447] Some space-faring races plundered more primitive species to create Gelem warriors – fierce cannon fodder soldiers, each created from an amalgamation of five living bodies. Gelems were used in the first battles of the War of Five Hundred Worlds, but were banned by the Pact of Chib in the eleventh century.[448]

c 1001 - EXCELIS DAWNS[449] -> Numerous civilisations had come and gone on the planet Artaris. The populace was mostly relegated to communities living on mountainsides for defensive purposes. A nunnery emerged on Excelis, the highest mountain on the planet.

The fifth Doctor landed on Artaris and met the warlord Grayvorn, who was on a quest for "the Relic", a powerful artifact and purported gateway to the afterlife. The Doctor also met Iris Wildthyme, who couldn't remember how she ended up there. Grayvorn found the Relic, which was shaped like Iris' handbag, but he went missing. The Relic's energies inadvertently made Grayvorn immortal.

1006 - THE BOOK OF KELLS[450] -> The TARDIS fell down a temporal wormhole to Ireland, diverting the eighth Doctor and Tamsin from their journey to Charisima Maxima – a pleasure world with billion-year-old forests. A new incarnation of the Monk, with Lucie Miller as his companion, tried and failed to repair his faulty directional unit. As the Monk's TARDIS dematerialised, it backfired and scorched *The Book of Kells* – ruining its cover, and charring its pages. The Doctor hid the *Book* under some sod, knowing it would be recovered eighty days later.

The Doctor saved Aethelred the Unready from what would have been a fatal fever.[451] An amoral Time Lord used a twenty-fourth century flood controller to turn back the tide for Canute, giving him great influence. The Doctor set history back on course.[452] The Doctor talked philosophy with the ruler of Ghana, King Tenkamenin.[453]

The Hyperions, a race of sentient suns, went forth from their homeworld of Hyperios to advance the lesser races. Tragically, the Hyperions turned malevolent as they mutated during the final stage of their development, and prolonged their lives by draining their home sun and many other stars. Rassilon led an alliance of powerful races against the Hyperions and mostly wiped them out, although a few survived in stasis.[454] After the Hyperion War, Rassilon's alliance purged other malevolent species including the Kaliratha: four-dimensional beings who styled themselves as deities. One Kaliratha made plans for her resurrection, even after her body was destroyed.[455]

Around one thousand years ago, Martin instigated a get-rich-quick scheme that entailed the washed-up actor Prubert Gatridge posing as a god on planets that Martin owned. This seeded "selfish memes" – philosophical concepts that led each world's populace to destroy themselves. Each genocide lifted the Galactic Heritage Foundation's development ban, allowing Martin to sell the worlds at fantastic profit.[456] A being that fed off life energy came to reside by the River Mersey, and inspired the legend of the river hag Jenny Greenteeth.[457]

The Doctor offered Lady Godiva a stick of celery with which to cover her modesty.[458]

During the building of the Cathedral of St Sophia, a casket fell from the sky. It was believed to contain an angel and was placed in the catacombs.[459] In 1033, Clancy's Comet was mistaken for the Star of the West, sent to com-

449 Dating *Excelis Dawns* (BF *Excelis* mini-series #1) - It's a thousand years before *Excelis Rising*.

450 Dating *The Book of Kells* (BF BBC7 #4.4) - The year is given. The loss and recovery of "the great Gospel of Clumnkille" – thought to be The Book of Kells – is recorded in the Annals of Ulster, although some historians date the Book's disappearance to 1007, not 1006.

The Doctor only acknowledges his encounters with the Monk in *The Time Meddler* and *The Daleks' Master Plan*, and seems to overlook their meetings in the tie-in media. Along those lines, he claims to have regenerated "several times" since they last met, and the Monk's directional unit – stolen by the Doctor in *Master Plan* – is still faulty. Then again, the Doctor describes the Monk as "someone I thought was dead", which doesn't describe how matters are left in *Master Plan*, but is a reasonable interpretation of the Monk's encounter with the seventh Doctor in *No Future*.

451 *Seasons of Fear.* The meeting is also mentioned in *The Tomorrow Windows.* Aethelred was king of England, and lived from circa 978 to 23rd April, 1016.

452 *The Twelfth Doctor Year One.* There's conflicting information in "Terrorformer" about when this occurred – a recap blurb says that the Hyperion Rann-Korr wakes up after "millions of years" of dormancy, but the Doctor

claims, "The fires of Hyperios were extinguished a thousand years ago". In "The Hyperion Empire", the Doctor claims the Hyperions were benevolent "millennia ago". "Gangland" shows Rassilon with the listed races.

453 *The Twelfth Doctor Year One*: "The Swords of Kali"

454 *Invaders from Mars*

455 *Transit*

456 *The Tomorrow Windows*

457 "A millennium or two" before *Signs and Wonders.*

458 *DC 3: The Eighth Piece.* Historical records indicate that Godiva, who infamously rode naked as a protest against excessive taxation, was active 1010-1067.

459 *Bunker Soldiers*

460 *The Ghosts of N-Space*

461 *Terror of the Zygons*

462 *Extremis.* This is admittedly part of a computer simulation, but one which is otherwise uncannily accurate to reality, so we can assume these details are true there as well. Benedict IX (c.1012-c.1056) served as Pope three times: from October 1032 to September 1044, then April to May 1045, and then November 1047 to July 1048. There are stories alleging there has been a Pope who was secretly female – the most prominent concerning Pope Joan, said to have reigned for a few

memorate the millennium of the crucifixion.[460] A monastery was established on the site of Forgill Castle in the eleventh century.[461]

Pope Benedict IX, a "lovely girl", radiated trouble, but was beguiling with her castanets. She founded a library of heretical texts, the Haereticum, within the Vatican's depths. Benedict judged her friend, the Doctor, as the man most needing confession – but he declined, as it would have taken too long.[462]

1039 (Midwinter) - HORNETS' NEST: A STING IN THE TALE[463] -> The fourth Doctor visited Tilling Abbey in Northumbria to investigate what he suspected was the earliest activity of the Hornet Swarm on Earth. He discovered that the nuns had been besieged by fierce dogs for three months, and that their Mother Superior was a pig that had been possessed by the Queen of the Swarm. The Doctor realised the Queen was trapped because the nuns freely sampled the products of their distillery, and the Hornets couldn't possess a person if they were drunk. The Doctor left, but only after being bitten by a dog – the new host of the Queen – that had also got inside the TARDIS. The Doctor put the TARDIS into the Vortex, taking the Hornets away from Earth. They would materialise in 1768.

> (=) During his time in the Godwins' court, Grayle was once bishop of all Cornwall. The Doctor defeated Grayle's plan to stockpile plutonium for the Nimon, and rewrote history to prevent Gralae from making contact with the Nimon in 305 AD.[464]

Edward the Confessor's reign was one of the Doctor's favourite times and places.[464] **The Aeolians were wiped out in the Centaurian Catastrophe.**[465]

The Battle of Hastings

1066 (late summer) - THE TIME MEDDLER[466] -> Landing on a beach in Northumbria, the first Doctor, Steven and Vicki learnt that the Monk – a renegade from the Doctor's own people – was planning to destroy a Viking invasion with futuristic weapons. Harold's army would be fresh for the Battle of Hastings, and after defeating the Norman invasion, Harold would usher in a new period of peace for Europe. The Doctor foiled the Monk's plans, and removed the dimensional control from the Monk's TARDIS, stranding him.

It "took a bit of time" to fix, but the Monk resumed his travels.[467] The Weeping Angels threw a future incarnation of the Monk back centuries, perhaps even millennia, from 1970s New York.[468]

> (=) The knock-on effect of the alternate history created at Maldon, 991, meant that the Vikings thought better of invading England, and the Battle of Hastings never occurred.[469]

> = The Chapel of Night originated from a reality where the Norman conquest didn't happen, and the Anglo-Saxons established an empire.[470]

The eighth Doctor and Mary Shelley met King Harold at the Battle of Hastings.[471] **The Shopkeeper implied that he possessed the arrow pulled from the eye of King Harold after the Battle of Hastings, although some said the king wasn't shot in the eye at all.**[472] In 1066, debris from Haley's Comet damaged a spaceship from the planet Persopolis, causing it to crash to Earth. The components of a powerful Persopolis construction device were separated, and the ship's occupant, Janxia, went into stasis.[473] Joanna Harris, a future geneticist and vampire, was born.[474]

c 1085 - BENNY: MANY HAPPY RETURNS[475] -> Irving Braxiatel popped back in time to nick a copy of the *Domesday Book* while one of the six monks writing it

---

years during the Middle Ages.
463 Dating *Hornets' Nest: A Sting in the Tale* (BBC fourth Doctor audio #1.4) - The Doctor says it is 1039. It is midwinter.
464 *Seasons of Fear.* The date is given, and it is exactly seven hundred and fifty years after the Doctor and Charley met Decurion Gralae.
465 A thousand years before *K9: Aeolian.*
466 Dating *The Time Meddler* (2.9) - The story takes place shortly before the Battle of Hastings (14th October, 1066), the Doctor judging it to be "late summer". The Doctor discovers a horned Viking helmet, although the Vikings never wore such helmets.
467 *The Daleks' Master Plan*

468 *DC 4: The Side of the Angels.* It's indeterminate if this tosses the Monk further back than *The Time Meddler.*
469 *Graceless III: The Battle*
470 *J&L S13: Chapel of Night*
471 *The Company of Friends:* "Mary's Story"
472 *SJA: Lost in Time*
473 *SJA: The Time Capsule*
474 *Vampire Science.* Joanna says she was born before the end of the first millennium, but also on the day William the Conqueror died, which was in 1087.
475 Dating *Benny: Many Happy Returns* (Benny 20th anniversary special) - The *Domesday Book* is a survey of England and Wales finished in 1086 on behalf of William the Conqueror. Braxiatel comments that it's

answered the call of nature. He offered the *Book* to Bernice as proof of what they could professionally accomplish together. Benny insisted that Braxiatel return the item, but agreed to help his efforts to create an archive of the universe's extant and extinct civilisations, giving rise to the Braxiatel Collection...

(=) Sir Walter Raleigh, having traveled back from 1592 in the TARDIS, encountered the Semestran Interlude – a.k.a. the Mirror Unto Nature, spectral beings from Galaxy 4 who changed to resemble the races they formed a bond with – at the future site of Roanoke. Raleigh convinced the Interlude to spare him in exchange for laying claim to the Roanoke colonists. Thanks to the Interlude's prowess, he survived for five centuries until the deal came to fruition.

The sixth Doctor arranged for the TARDIS to land at Roanoke without Raleigh, preventing the Interlude from meeting him. The Ship stayed buried until 1590.[476]

First of the Draconian Emperors

The White Emperor, the first of the Deathless Emperors, came to rule on Draconia. He tyrannically conquered fifty-two worlds and formed an empire that would last a millennia; scribes said that owing to his actions, the suns ran purple with blood. Each successive emperor was designated by a colour, which came to include gold, green, pearl grey, blood purple and dusk blue. As each emperor neared the end of his reign, the Draconian priesthood slowed his metabolic functions and placed him in Imperial Heaven – a tomb orbiting Draconia. The priesthood could

about "eight hundred years" too early for Hollandaise sauce; there's debate as to the origin of that, but a recipe for it appears in a Dutch cookbook (1593) by Carel Baten.

476 *J&L: Voyage to the New World,* "four hundred and ninety-eight years" before 1590, or exactly "five hundred years" before 1592.

477 "A thousand years" before *Paper Cuts.*

478 *Benny S8: The Judas Gift*

479 Dating *TimeH: Deus Le Volt (TimeH #8)* - The year is given. Historically, the siege was broken on 2nd June; Honoré and Emily seem to arrive two days beforehand. "Reynald" appears to be loosely based on Raymond IV, the Count of Toulouse (circa 1041/1042-1105). He was an associate of the soldier/mystic Peter Bartholomew, who claimed to find the Spear of Longinus during a church excavation that occurred in mid-June. Faked or not, the "discovery" is credited with motivating the crusaders against their foes.

480 "One thousand years, at least" before *The Shield of the Jotuun.*

481 *The Return of Doctor Mysterio*

482 Dating *Dark Horizons* (NSA #51) - The Doctor says that it's the "twelfth century" (p11), but his claims and math get increasingly suspect as the story goes along. He states that it's "three hundred years" prior to *The Tempest* (probably written in 1610-1611, so actually four if not five centuries after this story, p139), and that humanity won't enjoy the benefits of electricity for "a thousand years" (p151) when it's more like six hundred. He follows *Star Wars'* lead in expressing a parsec as a unit of time, not distance (p192), and airs a fairly nonsensical tale about the wholly fictional Edda the Bard (p196, 306). Cumulatively, *Dark Horizons* is another story where it's hard to believe a word that he says (see also *The Forgotten Army*).

Complicating matters, the book contains a number of historical falsehoods. The twelfth century is a bit late for Vikings to be active (historians generally mark the

Viking Age as ending with the Battle of Hastings in 1066; see *The Time Meddler*). Some raids continued into the 1100s, but the people of Lewis would have been less likely to fear the Vikings (as is the case here), since the isle at the time was considered part of Norway.

A more glaring anomaly is the fictional King Gissar Polvaderson, as an assembly (the Albingi) governed Iceland in this era, and the country didn't have any monarchy, at all, until it entered into a treaty with Norway in 1262. Also, the Doctor facilitates the creation of the aurora borealis – while the Old Norse records don't mention the Northern Lights until the Norwegian chronicle *Konungs Skuggsja* (1230), other cultures acknowledge them long before that, with the earliest written document originating from c.2600 BC.

A twelfth-century dating *does* work in one important regard: the commemorative chess pieces carved for Freydis' marriage are clearly the Lewis Chessmen, a twelfth-century whale ivory chess set found on the isle in 1831. (Even here, though, the Doctor exaggerates in telling Freydis, p306, that she will be remembered as a Queen forever – if the set was intended for a specific event or person/s, it's been lost to history.) However, while some historians concur with *Dark Horizons* in thinking that Trondheim craftsmen made the Chessmen, they differ in believing that the set was lost en route to a relatively affluent Norse town on the east coast of Ireland. If the set was truly bound for Iceland, as *Dark Horizons* claims, there'd be no need for Freydis' party to sail near Scotland at all.

Mention is made of Siegried and Brynhild of the *Volsunga* saga (p45), Vinland (the Viking name for North America, p55), and *The Wisdom of Odin* – all of which originate no later than circa 1000 AD. The Viking named Erik seen here bears no relation to Eric Thorvaldsson, a.k.a. Erik the Red (950 to c.1003). The Doctor directs Freydis' party to relocate to the modern-day site of Martha's Vineyard (p304) - presumably at Staumsey, a settlement that founded by Thorfinn

then call upon the emperors' wisdom as needed.[477]

Early in his reign, the First Emperor used The Judas Gift – a gauntlet that detected treachery in those who wore it – to determine that one of his nobles, Lord Salak, was a traitor. Salak was executed. As he had duelled left-handed, fighting with one's left-hand became a mark of shame on Draconia. Only royals were deemed "trustworthy" enough to exercise such a privilege.[478]

1098 (31st May to 2nd June) - TIMEH: DEUS LE VOLT[479] -> The time-travelling Honoré Lechasseur and Emily Blandish investigated mysterious events at siege of Antioch, 1098. Honoré's actions inadvertently enabled the crusaders to open the city gates, triggering a massacre. Reynald – the former Earl of Marseille, whom the crusaders had branded a traitor – had become the core of the Fendahl, but Honoré and Emily helped to prevent the creature from manifesting. A "warrior preacher" named Peter suspected Reynald's lance of being the Spear of Longinus – the weapon used to pierce Christ's side as he was crucified – and used it to rally the crusaders against the Muslims.

The Talessh, a techno-psionic race, lived in a Dyson sphere until its star, Ororah, began to collapse. Nine thousand Talessh fled in a transmat beam, and their shield-like transmat receptacle arrived on Earth. One of the Talessh manifested from the shield and was taken for a "frost giant" from Jotunheim. Herger, the last of the high chieftains of the North, and his men turned the murdering Talessh into stone with calcium, then broke the creature apart with hammers. Chief Herger and his men took the shield and travelled further than any Northmen before – to Arizona, where they believed the icy Jotuun could not reform. The Vikings entombed themselves there, and the shield absorbed their minds into its buffer.[480]

Nardole took a side trip in the TARDIS to twelfth-century Constantinople, where he claimed to have ruled "firmly, but wisely".[481]

c 1105 (September) - DARK HORIZONS[482] -> The Arill was a race of pure thought, requiring energy networks to survive. One group of Arill lost their way and

arrived near the Isle of Lewis, Scotland, as a Viking ship bore Freydis, the daughter of the Duke of Trondheim, to her intended marriage to King Gissar Polvaderson of Iceland. The Arill's failed attempt to form a network from the electrical impulses of human minds caused many incinerations, and burnt down the Viking ship.

The eleventh Doctor dispersed the Arill with a group of chained swords, and channeled their impulses into Earth's upper atmosphere to form the *aurora borealis*. He also aided Freydis in avoiding her forced marriage by directing her party to the Norse settlement at the modern-day Martha's Vineyard. A commemorative chess set carved for Freydis' marriage was recovered in future.

The militaristic Argians destroyed all knowledge on many planets, including Venedel, Zerinzar and Athrazar. The Argians were undone by their own arrogance, and, over the course of a millennium, their empire fell apart.[483] Humanoids bearing the Jax – a sentient virus – settled on the planet Saturnia Regna. They built a cathedral, but were killed by indigenous wolves. The virus adopted the wolves as its new hosts and retreated into the cathedral, awaiting the arrival of more humanoids.[484]

In 1120, the Pandorica was the prize possession of the Knights Templar.[485] The Treaty of the Marshes was signed at Cadogan Castle in 1123.[486]

Two bright green children were seen in Wulpit in Suffolk, and viewed with suspicion by an angry mob. These were actually alien Lampreys.[487] "Smart implants" – devices that could turn those fitted with them into dust – were outlawed under the Hexen-Brock Treaty. The Doctor prevented the assassination of Janakin Brock by a Tamaranian death-squad, who used the implants in a war against the Pashkul.[488]

The order of the Knights Templar was founded in 1128.[489] The Canavitchi claimed responsibility for founding the Knights Templar.[490] The Doctor rode with the templars in Palestine. Elsewhere, the Templars recovered the Imagineum, a mirror-like device built by an ancient race of extra-terrestrial alchemists. It could create a dark duplicate of anyone who looked into it.[491]

The Doctor saw the completion of Durham Cathedral in 1133. Sir Brian de Fillis built Marsham Castle in Yorkshire

---

Karlsefni (the *Saga of the Icelanders* claims) after 1010. The time of year is given as "September" (p101) and "autumn" (p117).

483 *Benny: The Gods of the Underworld.* Venedel has crawled back to having a feudal society circa 2100, so the Argians' millennium of decline presumably concludes before that point.

484 "A thousand years" before *Kursaal*. Given the time-frame involved, the humanoids weren't of Earth descent.

485 *The Big Bang*

486 *Rat Trap.* The castle and the Treaty are fictional. The Doctor seems awfully keen to enjoy the celebration of the Treaty, considering the conditions of this period make it a less-than-ideal holiday stop.

487 *Spiral Scratch.* This was in "the twelfth century".

488 "Eight centuries" before *Freakshow*.

489 *Sanctuary*

490 *The King of Terror*

491 "End Game" (*DWM*)

in the twelfth century. The knight went mad, believing his wife was haunting him.[492] The Doctor warned King Henry I about a surfeit of lampreys.[493]

1138 - THE DOCTOR'S MEDITATION / THE MAGICIAN'S APPRENTICE[494] -> The twelfth Doctor went to Essex, 1138, to meditate before confronting Davros. A warrior named Bors assisted him... even as the Doctor procrastinated by digging a well for water, and overseeing construction of a visitors' centre and a throne room extension. On Day 21 of the Doctor's "meditation", Bors insisted that if the Doctor had only one night left, he should spend it celebrating...

Clara and Missy journeyed to this era using vortex manipulators, and found the Doctor wielding a guitar atop a tank, as he was engaged in an "axe fight" against Bors. The Doctor had won the last bout using a daffodil, given many of those present maths tuition, and introduced the word "dude" several centuries early. Colony Sarff arrived to take the Doctor to Davros, and Clara and Missy insisted on going with him. The Daleks transported the TARDIS to Skaro.

1139 - THE KRILLITANE STORM[495] -> The tenth Doctor found that people in medieval Worcester feared the legendary Devil's Huntsman, who had made a number of people disappear recently. He quickly identified the culprits as the Krillitane. The Doctor met an Ertrari bounty

---

492 *Nightshade*

493 *The Helm of Awe*. Henry I of England died in 1135, apparently from food poisoning. A chronicler, Henry of Huntingdon, claimed he ate lampreys against his physician's advice.

494 Dating *The Magician's Apprentice* (X9.1) - A caption names the year.

495 Dating *The Krillitane Storm* (NSA #36) - The year is given.

496 *The Stones of Blood*

497 *The Church and the Crown*

498 *Tragedy Day*. Genghis Khan was born circa 1162, and died in 1227. The seventh Doctor must have delivered Genghis, as he claims in *Thin Ice* (BF) that he's never delivered a child before – but does so in that story, here, and in *The Settling*.

499 *An Earthly Child*. It's possible that she met Khan at the same time her grandfather delivered him.

500 *The Daemons*

501 *Doctor Who – The Movie*

502 *Rose*

503 *Borrowed Time*. Either Khan or Al Capone told the Doctor this.

504 *The Left-Handed Hummingbird*

505 *Timelash*

506 *The Taking of Planet 5*

507 *The Eleventh Doctor Year Three*: "Fooled"; the arrow-shooting attacker isn't named.

508 Two accounts of Stefan's game are given, in *The Nightmare Fair* and *Divided Loyalties*. Both versions have Stefan serving with Barbarossa, but the former story has him losing a game of dice to the Toymaker after wagering a Greek family. *Divided Loyalties*, however, says that Barbarossa drowned after Stefan bet the Toymaker that Barbarossa could successfully swim the Bosporus.

The account is slightly at odds with established history. Frederick Barbarossa was made Holy Roman Emperor in 1155, and died in 1190 after being thrown from his horse into the Saleph River in Cilicia (part of modern-day Turkey), whereupon his heavy armour made him drown in hip-deep water. As if that weren't enough, one chronicler claimed the shock additionally made Barbarossa have a heart attack.

509 *The Dalek Project*

510 Dating *Robot of Sherwood* (X8.3) - The Doctor at first says it's "Earth, England, Sherwood Forest, 1190AD-ish", but later tells Clara more directly: "It's 1190." Robin gives the season: "Dame Autumn has draped her mellow skirts about the forest, Doctor. The time of mists and harvest approaches." The spaceship contains record banks of various depictions of Robin Hood throughout the centuries, including a photo of Patrick Troughton – who in 1953 became the first actor to play Robin Hood for the BBC.

511 Dating *The Crusade* (2.6) - A document written for Donald Tosh and John Wiles in April/May 1965 (apparently by Dennis Spooner), "The History of Doctor Who", stated that the story is set between the Second and Third crusades, with the Third Crusade (1189-1192) starting when Richard's plan fails. David Whitaker's novelisation of his own story has the Doctor tell Ian: "We are on Earth at the time of the Third Crusade... some time between A.D. 1190 and 1192."

Richard is already in Palestine at the start of the story, and the events depicted within *The Crusade* happened in either October or November 1191 – Leicester mentions the desire for "a new victory like Arsuf" (that battle happened 7th September of that year), Queen Joan (or Joanna, as she's called here) joined the King in the Holy Land in October (seen in episode two), and de Preaux's capture – which opens episode one, so occurs out of sequence – happened in November. Ian claims in *The Space Museum* that *The Crusade* took place in the "thirteenth century", seemingly an error on his part.

The *Radio Times* and *The Making of Doctor Who* both set the story in the "twelfth century". *The Programme Guide* gives a date of "1190", *The Terrestrial Index* picks "1192". *Timelink* admirably sifted through the aforementioned evidence and narrowed it down to "20-21 October, 1191". *About Time* more-or-less agreed, favouring it being circa November 1191.

hunter, Emily Parr, who was seeking to capture Lozla Nataniel Henk: the man who had killed her father a month ago. Henk and his associates had captured a giant Krillitane, the Krillitane Storm, and were milking it for its oil. A Krillitane ship arrived, and although the Doctor drove the combating factions away, the Krillitane Storm died. Parr turned Henk in for the bounty, and decided to go to university.

During the twelfth century, the Convent of the Little Sisters of St Gudula was founded with Vivien Fay posing as the Mother Superior.[496] In the same century, the Doctor saw the King of France, Phillippe Auguste, lay the first stone of the Louvre.[497]

Genghis Khan

The Doctor delivered Genghis Khan.[498] Susan was familiar with Genghis Khan.[499] **The Doctor claimed to have heard Genghis Khan speak.**[500] **The Deathworm Master implied that the Doctor** *was* **Genghis Khan.**[501] **Genghis Khan's hordes couldn't break down the TARDIS doors.**[502] The Doctor suspected that Genghis Khan told him that villains liked to keep record of their villainy.[503]

Around 1168, the Aztecs left their original home of Aztlan and became nomads. They took a holy relic, the Xiuhcoatl, with them.[504] **The other end of the time corridor formed by the Timelash was in 1179 AD.**[505] The Borad was disgorged from the Timelash and quickly killed by operatives of the Celestis, the investigators One and Two.[506] The eleventh Doctor, Alice and the Sapling tried to go shopping in 1189, but wound up dodging arrows fired by one of the Doctor's "old friends".[507] In 1190, Stefan, a Crusader, lost a game to the Celestial Toymaker and became his agent.[508] A researcher for the Dalek Project fought a Crusader.[509]

1190 (Autumn) - ROBOT OF SHERWOOD[510] **-> A time-vessel crashed in England and disguised itself as a twelfth-century castle. The robots therein presented themselves to the Sheriff of Nottingham as robotic knights, and offered him dominion of Earth in exchange**

for the gold needed to repair their engine circuitry.

The twelfth Doctor granted Clara's wish of meeting Robin Hood, and she found herself in the company of Robin, Will Scarlet, Friar Tuck, Alan-a-dale and Little John. She also, inadvertently, coined the phrase "Robin Hood and his Merry Men". After much bickering, the Doctor and Robin aided Clara and the Merry Men in defeating the Sheriff, who fell into a vat of molten gold while duelling Robin. The robots attempted to launch their ship into space, but lacked the critical mass of gold required. The Doctor, Robin and Clara fired off a golden arrow that enabled the ship to reach orbit, where it harmlessly exploded. Afterward, the Doctor helped to reunite Robin with his beloved Marion. The history records would believe that Robin and his associates were only a fable.

c 1191 (Autumn) - THE CRUSADE[511] **-> The first Doctor, Ian, Barbara and Vicki saved Richard the Lionheart from an ambush, and became embroiled in court politics. Richard planned to marry his sister Joanna to the brother of Saladin, the Saracen ruler, but Joanna refused. The Doctor was mistaken for a sorcerer and the TARDIS crew narrowly escaped.**

Richard the Lionheart instructed the Doctor on the art of swordsmanship and in use of the broadsword.[512] The immortal Helena served King Richard in the Holy Land, and later claimed that his sister was named Joanna, not Joan.[513]

c 1191 - KRYNOIDS: THE GREEN MAN[514] **->** The Earl of Godfrey and his supporters dispatched two Krynoids that hatched in the English woods.

The Middle Ages was the native time of Justin, a knight who would help the fifth Doctor fight Melanicus – and would later be canonised.[515] Hubert, the earl of Mummerset, died in Palestine while serving with King Richard. A hapless herbalist's apothecary took his place, and spent seven years in a Saracen prison before escaping.[516] **K9 met the real Robin Hood.**[517] The time-traveller Arianda visited the Middle Ages.[518]

---

512 *Robot of Sherwood, Leviathan,* evidently on a different meeting (or two) with the King than *The Crusade.* Richard lived 1157-1199.

513 *Erimem: Three Faces of Helena,* impishly canonising Joanna as seen in *The Crusades* (in real life, the king's sister was Joan of England, Queen of Sicily).

514 Dating *Krynoids: The Green Man* (BBV audio #33) - King Richard is on the throne. Mention is made of stories pertaining to the Saracen; a sign, but not a guarantee, that it's during the Third Crusade (1189-1192).

515 "The Tides of Time" doesn't specify at what point of the Middle Ages Justin comes from. However, a mercenary in *Castle of Fear,* set in 1199, has met Justin and gives a correct description of him.

516 "Seven years" before *Castle of Fear*

517 *K9: The Last Oak Tree.* This possibly, but not necessarily, happened when K9 was travelling with the Doctor.

518 *3rdA: Storm of the Horofax*

The village of Stockbridge was named after a bridge over the river Stock, which dated back to medieval times.[519] The Lokhus, a creature from the universe after ours, fell to Stockbridge and went into a chrysalis stage.[520]

1199 - CASTLE OF FEAR[521] -> The Rutan Empire was withdrawing from Mutter's Spiral. Two Rutans took up residence in Stockbridge Castle in Mummersetshire, and began cloning experiments, hoping to clone Rutans in human form for use as cannon fodder. The fifth Doctor and Nyssa defeated the Rutans, a.k.a. "the demons of Stockbridge Castle", nine months later. One Rutan clone, Osbert, survived; his offspring in Stockbridge had some Rutan inheritance, but this became more diluted with each generation.

These events influenced the names of local establishments such as the Green Dragon Inn and the Turk's Head, and originated the legend of St George – in reality the apothecary masquerading as the earl of Mummerset – besting a dragon. Future residents of Stockbridge remembered the Rutans' defeat – and the Doctor's role in it – as both a hereditary memory and a mummery performance.

The alien Berserkers were active on Earth in the thirteenth century.[522] **Whitaker's Timescoop accidentally kidnapped a peasant from the Middle Ages.**[523] **Scaroth possibly posed as a Crusader.**[524] **Around 1205, a man was boiled in oil for the entertainment of King John.**[525]

1207 - THE BELLS OF SAINT JOHN[526] **-> The eleventh Doctor retired to a monastery in Cumbria, 1207, to ponder the strange case of Clara Oswald. Clara was connected to the Doctor via the TARDIS' exterior phone when she tried to call Internet support, prompting him to visit her in the twenty-first century...**

In the early thirteenth century, a Yogloth Slayer ship attacked a Khameirian spaceship rounding Rigellis III. The Khameirian vessel crashed to Earth and destroyed the chapel at Abbots Siolfor, home of a secret society led by Matthew Siolfor. The Khameirians put their life essences into what would later be called the Philosopher's Stone. They enthralled six of the brotherhood to work toward restoring them. The society's descendants would spread throughout the world, influenced by the Khameirians.[527]

The sunburst icon became known as a sigil of extraterrestrial power from the thirteenth century.[528]

1212 (late summer) - BENNY: THE VAMPIRE CURSE: "Possum Kingdom"[529] **->** Benny and a Yesterways, Ltd., time travel tour group visited Marseilles during the Children's Crusade. Nepesht arrived from the twenty-sixth century, and sacrificed his liberty to again imprison the last of the Utlunta, Lilu, in a pocket universe.

Kamelion Joins the TARDIS

1215 (4th-5th March) - THE KING'S DEMONS[530] **->** The Tremas Master attempted to pervert the course of

---

519 *The Eternal Summer*
520 "The Stockbridge Child". The accompanying illustration suggests this was during medieval times.
521 Dating *Castle of Fear* (BF #127) - The back cover and – within the story – the Doctor agree that it's 1199. *Plague of the Daleks* reiterates that *Castle of Fear* occurs in the "twelfth century". What's perplexing is that the Doctor determines the year to which he and Nyssa must go based upon a statement that one of the Stockbridge residents makes in 1899 – "It's the year when the ant by the lion was slain." It's a reversal of the real-life phrase "when the lion by the ant was slain", denoting how King Richard was fatally shot by a boy wielding a crossbow, who was angered because Richard had killed his father and brothers. (Richard was shot on 25th March, 1199, and died on 6th April.) Even more strangely (unless this is a deliberate choice as part of the story's comedy), the Doctor here says that the "ant" refers to Saladin – in real life it does no such thing, as Saladin died in 1193.

This adventure originates the tale of St George and the dragon, the earliest text of which dates to the eleventh century, although George himself dates back to at least the seventh century. The Green Dragon Inn is mentioned in "The Tides of Time".

For benefit of non-UK readers, "Mummerset" is a deliberately awful depiction in plays and films of a West Country accent. Twelfth-century Stockbridge is said to reside in Mummerset; "The Tides of Time" says that the modern-day Stockbridge is in Gloucestershire.
522 *SJA: The Mark of the Berserker*
523 *Invasion of the Dinosaurs*
524 *City of Death*. Most fans have interpreted the last of the four Scaroths we see as a Crusader, although the DVD says it's a "Celt". Although Julian Glover plays both Richard the Lionheart in *The Crusade* and Scaroth in *City of Death*, it doesn't seem likely that Scaroth posed as King Richard.
525 "Ten years" before *The King's Demons*.
526 Dating *The Bells of Saint John* (X7.7) - A caption names the year.
527 *Option Lock*
528 "End Game" (*DWM*)
529 Dating *Benny: The Vampire Curse*: "Possum Kingdom" (Benny collection #12b) - The year and season are given.
530 Dating *The King's Demons* (20.6) - The TARDIS readings say it is "March the fourth, twelve hundred and fifteen".

constitutional progress on Earth by preventing the signing of Magna Carta. On 3rd March, 1215, an android controlled by the Master – Kamelion – arrived at Fitzwilliam Castle posing as the King. The Master accompanied him, disguised as the French swordsman Sir Giles Estram. The Fitzwilliams had served the King for many years before this, giving him their entire fortune to help the war against the abhorrent Saracens, but the King now demanded even more of them. "King John" began to challenge the loyalty of even the King's most devoted subjects, but the fifth Doctor, Tegan and Turlough exposed the Master's plan. They took Kamelion with them in the TARDIS.

The eleventh Doctor owned a copy of the Magna Carta.[531] Around 1225, the Doctor defeated Thorgan of the Sulumians, who was attempting to kill the mathematician Fibonacci before he wrote the *Liber quadratorum* (*The Book of Squares*), a text on Diophantine equations.[532] **In 1231, the Pandorica was donated to the Vatican.**[533]

1240 - BUNKER SOLDIERS[534] **->** The first Doctor, Steven and Dodo landed in Kiev. The Doctor was asked to help fend off the Mongols, but knew that history recorded the sacking of the city and refused – so the governor of the city, Dmitri, imprisoned him. Dmitri sought supernatural aid, uncovering a casket under the Church of St Sophia. This held an alien soldier, who started a killing spree. He infected Dmitri with a virus that drove him mad, leading to Dmitri refusing the Mongols' offer of sparing the city in return for an honourable surrender. The Mongols ransacked Kiev, but the Doctor deactivated the soldier.

> = Upon leaving Kiev, the first Doctor, Steven and Dodo found themselves on Logopolis. The Valeyard derailed that trip by venturing back to Kiev and killing Dodo with one of Jack the Ripper's knives.[535]

1242 - SANCTUARY[536] **->** The seventh Doctor and Benny made an emergency landing in the Pyrenees. The Doctor discovered a plot to recover the skull of Jesus Christ from the heretical Cathare sect, even as Benny fell for the knight Guy de Carnac. The Church forced an attack on the Roc of the Cathares sanctuary and set it afire, but the Doctor found the skull was a fake. The Doctor and Benny escaped the destruction – it's possible that Guy de Carnac did also...

c 1245 - GUY DE CARNAC: THE QUALITY OF MERCY[537] **->** Guy de Carnac protected a space traveller from an Inquisition, and helped him return to his people.

> = On Roma I, only Seres (China) stood against the might of the Roman Empire thanks to their Great Walls. They had little contact with Rome. By the mid-thirteenth century of our calendar, Roman roads and bridges linked every part of the world. The Seric Navy under Zheng He launched attacks on Roman ports, and war raged for twenty-eight years as the Serics made great territorial gains.
>
> Then Emperor Yung Lo met the Roman Emperor Cosimo. They agreed that rather than destroy the world with a devastating war, they should settle the matter on the toss of a coin. Rome won, and Yung Lo knelt at the feet of his new Emperor. The merging of Roman and Seric philosophies led to a new golden age. A perfect world was built.[538]

The Doctor let Henry III's polar bear out for a swim in the Thames.[539] **River Song and the eleventh Doctor visited Easter Island; the inhabitants made many statues of him.**[540] **Marco Polo was born in Venice.**[541] The sixth Doctor's TARDIS contained papers from the House of Wisdom.[542]

---

531 As seen in *The Doctor, the Widow and the Wardrobe.*
532 *The Gallifrey Chronicles*
533 *The Big Bang*
534 Dating *Bunker Soldiers* (PDA #39) - The Doctor says "we are in Kiev in 1240" (p16).
535 *Unbound: He Jests at Scars...*, adding onto *Bunker Soldiers.* The Doctor had, we're told in *Logopolis*, previously visited Logopolis at some point in his lives.
536 Dating *Sanctuary* (NA #37) - Benny "persuaded someone to tell her that the year was 1242".
537 Dating *Guy de Carnac: The Quality of Mercy* (BBV audio #35) - The audio features Guy de Carnac from *Sanctuary*, but it's not expressly said whether this is a prequel or a sequel to that book (presuming for the moment that Guy survived the Roc of the Cathares – his body is never found, after all). That said, a conversation concerning Guy and an "unrequited love" could

well be a reference to Bernice. Seven years passed in the real world between the release of the two stories; the placement here somewhat arbitrarily splits the difference.
538 *FP: Warlords of Utopia*
539 *The Twelfth Doctor Year Three*: "The Wolves of Winter". The King of Norway gave Henry III a pale bear (presumably a polar bear) in 1252.
540 *The Impossible Astronaut*, possibly contradicting the origin of the statues given in *Eye of Heaven*. The first moai on Easter Island were carved in the thirteenth century.
541 *Marco Polo.* Barbara states that Marco Polo was born in "1252", although actually it was two years later.
542 *CD, NM* V2: *The Carrionite Curse.* The Mongols destroyed the House of Wisdom, a major library in Baghdad, in 1258.

Destruction of the Zygon Homeworld

According to the Doctor, the Zygons hailed from "the deepest, murkiest fathoms of space".[543] A sub-set of Zygons – called Zynogs (sic) – were exiled from Zygor, the Zygon homeworld, as punishment for breaking the oldest of Zygon laws: using the body-print of another Zygon. The Zynogs' original forms were destroyed, and they were trapped within stunted forms incompatible with Zygon body-print technology. Some Zynogs found a technological means of transferring their essences into brain-dead individuals.[544]

The arachnid Xaranti destroyed Zygor.[545] The Zygons retaliated and destroyed the Xaranti homeworld in Tau Ceti. The Xaranti consequently became nomadic.[546] **A Zygon spacecraft crashed in Loch Ness. While awaiting a rescue party, they fed on the milk of the Skarasen, an armoured cyborg creature that was often mistaken for the locals as a "monster".**[547] Another Zygon craft, led by the warlord Hagoth, crashed elsewhere on Earth. The crew entered hibernation, but would later revive and promote industry throughout the twentieth century.[548]

The fourth Doctor didn't fret about the possibility of being stuck in Italy, 1265, as he could always pick a bow with Thomas Aquinas – or "Big Tom", as they called him.[549] **In the Middle Ages, Stangmoor was a fortress.**[550] **A medieval knight was kidnapped by the UNIT Master using TOM-TIT.**[551] **When Marco Polo was 12, English crusaders occupied the African port of Accra.**[552]

The Doctor was based for a time around 1268 at Ercildoune in Scotland. He cured a crippled stable hand called Tommy. Two years later, the Queen of the Charrl contacted Tommy from the far future, promising him immortality in return for his stealing the Doctor's TARDIS. Tommy came to be known as the wizard Jared Khan.[553]

In 1270, a mysterious doctor who tended King Alexander sent his stable boy Tom away. The legends of Kebiria claimed that the Caliph at Giltat was visited by mysterious demons, the Al Harwaz, who promised him anything he wanted – gold, spices, slave women – if his people learnt a dance, "dancing the code". The arrangement continued for a time, until the Caliph broke the agreement and flying monsters destroyed his city.[554] In the 1270s, Marco Polo witnessed oil seeping out of the ground in the vicinity of the Aural Sea.[555]

---

543 *The Zygon Who Fell to Earth*
544 *Death in Blackpool*
545 *The Bodysnatchers*; Zygor is also named in *The Zygon Who Fell to Earth*.
546 "Several centuries" before *Deep Blue*.
547 *Terror of the Zygons*. The Zygon leader Broton tells Harry Sullivan that they crashed "centuries ago by your timescale". While disguised as the Duke, Broton later tells the Doctor that there have been sightings of the Loch Ness Monster "since the Middle Ages", the implication being that the Zygons and Skarasen have been on Earth since then.

In *Timelash*, we're made to believe that the Borad has been similarly swimming around Loch Ness from 1179 onwards, but the Borad's death in *The Taking of Planet 5* suggests he doesn't contribute to the Loch Ness sightings. *The Programme Guide* claimed that the Zygon ship crashed in "50,000 BC", *The Terrestrial Index* preferred "c.1676". *Timelink* linked the Zygon ship's arrival to the first "sighting" of Nessie in 565 (or a bit beforehand, depending on how fast Skarasen embryos develop).
548 The eighth Doctor believes that the Zygon craft in *The Zygon Who Fell to Earth* crashed concurrent to the one that landed in Scotland in *Terror of the Zygons*.
549 *The Haunting of Malkin Place*. Aquinas asserted that as inanimate objects were not aware, but moved as though they had purpose, God must be directing them. He used the analogy of an inanimate arrow being directed to its target by an archer.
550 *The Mind of Evil*
551 *The Time Monster*
552 *Marco Polo*

553 *Birthright*
554 "Seven hundred years" before *Dancing the Code*.
555 *Brave New Town*
556 *Pond Life*. Conflicting theories exist as to when pasta was invented, although (and this is real) the International Pasta Organisation cites the idea that Marco Polo introduced pasta to Italy after returning home from China in 1271 – which would concur with the Doctor here feeding pasta to an unnamed Mongol.
557 *Marco Polo*
558 Dating *The Time Warrior* (11.1) - The story seems to be set either during the Crusades, as Sir Edward of Wessex talks of "interminable wars" abroad, or quite soon after the Conquest as Irongron refers to "Normans". The Doctor tells Professor Rubeish they are in the "early years of the Middle Ages". However, in *The Sontaran Experiment*, Sarah says that Linx died "in the thirteenth century". According to *The Paradise of Death*, this was "eight hundred years back" (p12), and it's "three centuries" before "Dragon's Claw".

The Programme Guide set a date of "c.800", but *The Terrestrial Index* offered "c.1190". *The TARDIS Logs* said "1191 AD", *Timelink* said "1272" and *About Time* "1190-1220". *A History of the Universe in 100 Objects* (p47) classifies Lynx's Sontaran Scout Ship as being from the "13th century", and further stipulates that "The clone race from Sontar have been fighting a war with the Rutan Host for over 70,000 years" (p48).

In what's almost certainly an in-joke about potatoes anachronistically appearing in *The Time Warrior* (the novelisation, at least; some heroic efforts to identity the root vegetables in the TV story have proved inconclu-

The eleventh Doctor accidentally invented pasta.[556] In 1271, Marco Polo left Venice to explore China.[557]

c 1273 - THE TIME WARRIOR[558] -> The third Doctor arrived from the twentieth century on the trail of the Sontaran Linx, who had kidnapped scientists and pulled them back in time. For his own amusement, Linx was supplying a local warlord, Irongron, with advanced weapons. The third Doctor and Sarah Jane – who had stowed away in the TARDIS – thwarted both Linx and Irongron, and the destruction of the Sontaran's ship also destroyed Irongron's castle.

Marco Polo arrived in Cathay in 1274, the same year the beautiful maiden Ping-Cho was born. Three years later, Polo entered the service of Kublai Khan.[559]

1278 (29th August) ASYLUM[560] -> An alien dispatched from 1346, now hosted in Brother Thomas of the Franciscan Order, tried to further philosopher Roger Bacon's research into the Elixir of Life – a possible cure to the impending Black Death seventy years hence. The fourth Doctor and Nyssa prevented the alien from disrupting history, and Nyssa dislodged the alien presence from Thomas' mind. Bacon burned his unsuccessful Elixir Manuscript, but the Franciscan Order imprisoned him for twelve years for committing "heretical" research into alchemy. Bacon would become renowned to future generations as a great philosopher, not a scientist.

In 1283, a meteorite from the Jeggorabax Cluster – a dark nebula said to contain entities created by emotions – fell to Earth in the Weserbergland Mountains in Lower Saxony. The next year, the people of Hamelin's collective fear of rats caused the energy within the meteorite to manifest as the Pied Piper – a being who needed fear to survive, and stole Hamelin's children to create it. In the centuries to come, aspects of the Piper would steal children for similar effect.[561] The Doctor spent time as a ratcatcher in Hamelin.[562]

On Earth, the country of Goritania brokered a pact with alien Mefistoles. In exchange for a single soul, the Mefistoles' perception filter kept Goritania shrouded from the world. The country would enjoy five hundred years without war, famine or plague.[563]

Hughes de Chalons, a Knights Templar, took refuge in a hidden chamber beneath the Sphinx in 1287. A woman bearing the seal of the Knights gave him a box of scrolls, and said he was the new Guardian of Forever.[564]

1289 - MARCO POLO[565] -> Kublai Khan refused permission for Marco Polo to return to Venice. In 1289, Polo led a caravan across the Roof of the World to the court of the Khan. He took with him Tegana, the emissary of the Mongol warlord Noghai, and Ping-Cho, who was destined to marry a 75-year-old nobleman. They discovered the first Doctor, Ian, Barbara and Susan – along with their blue cabinet, which Polo decided to present to the Khan. They traversed Cathay and the Gobi Desert, arriving at Shang-Tu. Tegana's plan to murder the Khan was exposed, and he killed himself. In gratitude to the travellers, the Khan returned their cabinet.

Astrolabus claimed to have an appointment with Marco Polo.[566] Jared Khan narrowly missed acquiring the TARDIS at this time.[567] The immortal Ashildr had many guises across the centuries. At one point, she became a medieval queen – a post that entailed a lot of paperwork and backgammon. She faked her death, and escaped being eviscerated.[568]

The Forgill family served the nation from the late thirteenth century.[569] The Doctor met Dante and acquired his business card.[570] The Doctor met William

---

sive), the Monk chronicles (*The Doctor: His Lives and Times*, p18) how he fixed his TARDIS using spare parts from a toaster and a crystal set, and adds that he mischievously left behind some potatoes in the 11th century before he left following *The Time Meddler*. "Maybe the Doctor will land in the Middle Ages and wonder why he's being served chips. Ha!"

559 *Marco Polo*

560 Dating *Asylum* (PDA #42) - The blurb says it's "1278"; 1266 was "twelve years previously" (p116).

561 *SJA: The Day of the Clown*. The first Doctor met the Pied Piper in the *TV Comic* story "Challenge of the Piper" (outside the bounds of this chronology), and this may well have been the same entity. The Pied Piper also menaced Sarah Jane and company in *SJA: The Day of the Clown*.

562 *Antidote to Oblivion*

563 "Five hundred years" before *Death and the Queen*.

564 *Benny: The Sword of Forever*

565 Dating *Marco Polo* (1.4) - Marco gives the year as "1289". *The Programme Guide* gave the date as "1300".

566 "Voyager"

567 *The Woman Who Lived*. It's not specified which medieval queen Ashildr posed as, but one candidate is Eleanor of Castile (1241-1290), as it wasn't unusual for embalming in the thirteenth century to involve evisceration.

568 *Birthright*

569 *Terror of the Zygons*

570 *The Two Doctors*. Dante lived from 1265-1321.

Tell.[571] The Doctor met Robert the Bruce in the early fourteenth century.[572] He also visited the citadel that became the Kremlin.[573]

wih - The fourteenth century came under fire from the Enemy.[574] The Doctor slayed a dragon in Krakow.[575] The fourteenth century saw the rebirth of the organic statues of Es-Ko-Thoth Park in the city-state of Tor-Ka-Nom.[576] The fifth Doctor's pockets contained fourteenth-century gold florins, which he spent in 1864.[577]

Seth was a grand schemer in fourteenth-century Rome known to the Doctor. He would go on to be known as Vance Galley, Van Giefried, Virgil Gaustino, Vincent Grant and the twenty-fourth century entrepreneur Varley Gabriel.[578] **The Cardiff Rift transported a fourteenth-century plague victim to the twenty-first century.**[579] King Philip IV of France moved against the Knights Templar in 1307. Hughes de Chalons was captured while enjoying the pleasures of a whore's bed.[580]

In March 1314, the last key members of the Knights Templar (Grand Master Jacques de Molay; Geoffrey de Charnay, the Order's Preceptor of Normandy; and Hughes de Chalons) were burnt at the stake. de Molay's nephew, Guillaume de Beaujeu, procured a relic sacred to the Order – the finger of John the Baptist – and secured it in his castle in Arginy.[581] The Kindred of Fel, fabled telepaths from the Dushanka Forests, were believed extinct. A few of their number survived in captivity.[582]

In the 1300s, a "demon" fell from the sky near a convent near London. A "sainted physician" (i.e. the Doctor) "smote" the demon and it disappeared. This created The Legend of the Blue Box, which was commemorated in stained glass at the church later built on that site.[583]

The Doctor almost gave William of Ockham a nervous breakdown trying to get him to work out the history of the planet Skaro.[584] **The Monk calculated that if his plan to prevent the Norman Conquest had worked, then humankind would have developed aircraft by 1320.**[585]

1320 - RENAISSANCE OF THE DALEKS[586] **->** The fifth Doctor dropped off Nyssa to look into an anomalous time track in Rhodes, 1320, then ventured off to investigate a second anomaly. Nyssa made the acquaintance of a Mulberry, a member of the Knights of Templar, but they both fell down a wormhole to Petersburg at the time of the American Civil War.

---

571 *The Face of Evil.* William Tell lived in the early fourteenth century.

572 *Lords of the Storm.* Robert the Bruce was one of Scotland's greatest kings, and ruled from 1306-1329.

573 "Centuries" before *Thin Ice* (BF). The site of the Kremlin has been occupied since the second century BC, but the first stone structures were built there in the fourteenth century.

574 *FP: The Brakespeare Voyage* (ch5).

575 "Thirteen hundred years" before Rose's time, according to *Only Human.*

576 "By Hook or by Crook"

577 *The Contingency Club*

578 "Profits of Doom". The Doctor doesn't recognise him face-to-face, so they probably don't meet at this time.

579 *TW: End of Days*

580 *Benny: The Sword of Forever.* Historically, Philip did move against the Knights in 1307; Pope Clement V declared the Order disbanded in 1312.

581 *Benny: The Sword of Forever.* De Molay and de Charnay are historical, and were burned to death in March. In real life, Guillaume was the twenty-first Grand Master of the Knights (de Molay was the twenty third) and died during the siege of Acre in 1291. The character in *The Sword of Forever,* however, wasn't born until 1292 (perhaps the one is the son of the other, born after the father's death?).

582 "Seven centuries" before "The Blood of Azrael".

583 *The End of Time*

584 *The Gallifrey Chronicles.* Ockham was a philosopher and friar during the Middle Ages. He was responsible for the principle of Occam's Razor (also spelled "Ockham's Razor") and lived c.1287 to c.1349.

585 *The Time Meddler*

586 Dating *Renaissance of the Daleks* (BF #93) - The date is given.

587 "Twenty years" before *The Legends of Ashildr:* "The Triple Knife".

588 *The Awakening,* "centuries" before the village was destroyed in the English Civil War.

589 In the travellers' personal timelines, this occurs between *Boom Town* and *Bad Wolf.*

590 *The Legends of Ashildr:* "The Triple Knife", based upon Essie being eight years old in 1348.

591 *Asylum*

592 *Rat Trap*

593 *SJA: The Time Capsule.* This story might actually be true, even allowing for the diamond's extra-terrestrial origins.

594 Dating *The Legends of Ashildr:* "The Triple Knife" (NSA #61c) - The story expands upon a flashback scene of Ashildr grieving for her children in "1348" in *The Woman Who Lived.* The datelines of Ashildr's journal specify the days.

595 "Change of Mind". This was in 1349.

596 Dating *TimeH: Kitsune* (TimeH #4) - It's medieval Japan, complete with samurais, but the dating is otherwise left unsaid.

597 *The Twelfth Doctor Year One:* "The Swords of Kali". The Thugee were founded prior to 1356.

598 *Benny: The Sword of Forever*

599 "Centuries"/"many centuries"/a vague "endless, numberless ages" before *J&L S9: Island of Death.*

Ashildr fell for a handsome fisherman named Tomas circa 1328.[587] **The Malus, a psychic probe from Hakol, arrived in Little Hodcombe.**[588] **The ninth Doctor, Rose and Jack "only just escaped" Kyoto in 1336.**[589] The first of Ashildr and Tomas' children, Essie, was born in 1340, and later followed by two sons, Johann and Rue.[590]

Aliens emerged from a null dimension and into London in 1346. They took control of human bodies, which were vulnerable to a plague that the aliens knew would arrive in two years. They discovered that philosopher Roger Bacon wrote of a possible cure for the plague, and sent one alien back several decades to ensure Bacon's research succeeded. The alien's host in that era, Brother Thomas, survived and felt drawn to the aliens in 1346, but they failed to heed his warnings about the futility of their efforts.[591]

Cardogan Castle suffered a large outbreak of the Black Death shortly before the plague's end.[592] The black diamond of Ernfield, a cursed gem, was said to have been stolen from a mid-fourteenth-century temple.[593]

1348 (9th-27th August) - THE LEGENDS OF ASHILDR: "The Triple Knife"[594] **->** Ashildr left Marseilles for London with her children – Essie, Johann and Rue – to avoid her husband's questions about why twenty years and three births had not aged her. As the plague worked its way through London, and infected Ashildr's children, Ashildr briefly encountered a trio of aliens – mask-wearing Scientists examining disease to develop cures for their own kind – but declined an offer to leave with them, as she was unwilling to abandon her offspring. **Ashildr was briefly ill as her medical patch learned to cope with the Black Death. The plague claimed her children; she vowed not to have any more.**

The Doctor was at the university of Prague when it opened.[595]

c 1350 - TIMEH: KITSUNE[596] **->** While investigating the history of mischievous fox-spirits – the kitsune – Emily Blandish briefly visited medieval Japan.

Guillaume de Beaujeu, age 62, went off to war in 1354 and didn't return. The finger of John the Baptist remained at the Castle of Arginy.[597] In India, one of the Kaliratha appeared as a manifestation of Kali and inspired the Thugee gang of assassins.[598] The alien Kibu fell to Earth in a meteorite, and landed on an island near Sumatra. The natives coaxed Kibu to sleep, and constructed a temple over its slumbering form.[599]

Iris and Panda faked insanity to infiltrate Bedlam, 1357, to stop a psychic vampire feeding off the inmates.[600] The eleventh Doctor claimed to have spent a gap year in Bedlam: "A nice place, once you got used to all the wailing and gnashing of teeth."[601]

On the planet Skaro, a small, squat blue-skinned warlike race had evolved... the Daleks.[602]

c 1360 (November) - DL: THE ART OF WAR[603] **->** A Krashok warship materialised several miles from London, having fled into the past using a Dalek temporal shift device. The tenth Doctor and his companion, Gisella, pursued the Krashoks to prevent their activating the fake Eternity Crystal in their possession – an act that could have triggered an explosion large enough to destroy Earth. The Doctor incapacitated the Krashoks with sonic waves, and medieval knights slew many of them. The surviving Krashoks returned to the future with both the real Crystal and Gisella, and the Doctor followed them.

wih - 1375 - FP: AGAINST NATURE[604] **->** Ordnance-Tetrarch Goralschai of House Xianthellipse harvested bio-data from a Mexica, Acamapichtli, to further his goals pertaining to the New Fire Ceremony in 1506.

Trakenites colonised the planet Serenity. The being named Malador created an energy-supplying labyrinth there that later helped to power the super-computer Prophecy. Malador's ambitions were such that he had his conscience removed from his mind, "liberating" his thought processes, and his reign became increasingly despotic. He developed the statuesque Melkur – the name of which meant "like a fly caught in honey" – and scattered them among the stars as a sleeping army, awaiting his

600 *Iris S3: The Iris Wildthyme Appreciation Society.* Panda says this happened "the year the original Bedlam opened", which is a bit misleading. Initially known by names such as St Mary Bethlehem and Bethlem Hospital, Bedlam first opened as a hospital in 1330, but didn't admit the mentally ill until some decades later. 1357 and 1377 are often cited as when this happened, but in truth the date is lost to history.
601 *Shroud of Sorrow* (p109).
602 "Genesis of Evil". This was in the year 1600 of the New Skaro Calendar.

603 Dating *DL: The Art of War* (*DL* #9) - The story occurs in "November" (p34) in "medieval London" (p27). The TARDIS databank makes mention (p28-29) of the Black Death ravaging London in 1348, and that the population had been halved by 1350, so the story is here – a little arbitrarily – placed after that. For the Doctor and Gisella, the story concludes in *DL: The End of Time.*
604 Dating *FP: Against Nature* (*FP* novel #7) - The year is given. "Mexica" is the more accurate term for the Westernized word "Aztecs".

activation signal. The people of Serenity tricked Malador into locking himself in a timeless state in his own labyrinth, and afterward formed the Benign Union.[605]

The Canavitchi faked the Turin Shroud in an attempt to slow man's progress.[606] The Phiadoran Clan Matriarchy came to power in the Phiadoran Directorate. They ruthlessly weeded out their political opponents.[607] Cartophilius lived in Italy under the name John Buttadaeus.[608]

The Doctor met Chaucer in 1388 and was given a copy of *The Doctour of Science's Tale*.[609] The Doctor drank ale with Chaucer in Southwark.[610]

Around this time, the Doctor acquired his ticket to the Library of St John the Beheaded.[611]

1399 (December) to 1400 (January to February) - THE DOCTOR'S TALE[612] -> Henry of Bolingbroke had deposed Richard II and been crowned Henry IV. The first Doctor, Ian, Barbara and Vicki passed themselves off as pilgrims at the Sonning Bishop's Palace, and the Doctor became a tutor to Isabella, the former Queen. The travellers later attended an epiphany feast to celebrate the New Year, with the Doctor serving as the Lord of Misrule. Afterward, the Doctor and Barbara left on a pilgrimage to Canterbury to satisfy Barbara's interest concerning Geoffrey Chaucer.

Thomas Arundel, as the Archbishop of Canterbury, moved against those opposed to the king's rule. Sir Robert de Wensley, as Arundel's agent, inveigled himself into Ian's confidence and used Ian's credentials as a Knight of Jaffa to infiltrate a group of conspirators including the Earl of Huntingdon, the Earl of Gloucester and Chaucer himself. Arundel burned down Chaucer's house, destroying many of his writings. Chaucer gave his original copy of *The Canterbury Tales* to Barbara, who fled to Suffolk. An uprising to reinstate Richard II failed, and he starved to death in Pomfret Castle.

---

605 Malador goes into stasis "a thousand years" before *The Guardians of Prophecy*; the Benign Union has been at peace that same duration of time. It's not explicitly stated that Malador was a Trakenite, although his psionic might does seem reminiscent of Kwundaar's abilities (*Primeval*). The cadaverous Master disguises his TARDIS as a Melkur in *The Keeper of Traken*.

606 *The King of Terror*. The Shroud is first recorded in the fourteenth century.

607 *Imperial Moon*. This takes place at "611,072.26 Galactic Time Index".

608 *Matrix*

609 *Cat's Cradle: Time's Crucible*, and a separate meeting from *The Doctor's Tale*.

610 *Synthespians*™

611 *All-Consuming Fire*

612 Dating *The Doctor's Tale* (BF EDA #1.2) - The blurb says it's "England 1400", and Barbara estimates the year as "around 1400". The narration suggests the story opens slightly before that, in the "cold and frosty season of December". Vicki's narration soon mentions, "With the New Year just begun...", and the Doctor and company are captured at the New Year's revels at the Sonning Bishop's Palace.

It's twice said that Henry IV became king "three months" ago, after deposing Richard II (on 30th September, 1399). Events play out into February, with Isabella seeing her husband's body – historically, he died around 14th February, he was laid in rest in St Paul's Cathedral on 17th February, and was buried later, on 6th March. The Earl of Gloucester and the Earl of Huntingdon are here killed for conspiring against Henry IV; they respectively died on 16th January and 13th January, 1400.

Chaucer increasingly vanishes from the historical record following the downfall of Richard II, his patron. The cause of Chaucer's death isn't known, and the "official" date of his passing (25th October, 1400) appears on a tomb engraving made more than a century later.

613 *The Daemons*

614 *TimeH: The Child of Time* (p64).

615 *Terrible Lizards*

616 "A hundred years" before *The Masque of Mandragora*.

617 *Shadowmind*

618 At least "five hundred years" before *Iris S3: Iris Rides Out*, if the age of the Grange's floorboards is anything to go by.

619 *The Talons of Weng-Chiang*, *Shada*, *The King of Terror*. Agincourt was fought on 25th October, 1415.

620 *The Woman Who Lived*

621 Dating *DC 3: The Eighth Piece* (BF DC #3.2) - The Doctor says it's "early fifteenth-century Prague. The very height of enlightened science on Earth in this period." It's "six centuries" (possibly an approximation, possibly not) before the story's modern-day component [2016].

622 *DC 3: The Doomsday Chronometer*

623 *The Memory of Winter*. Joan was born 6th January, circa 1412.

624 Dating *The Memory of Winter* (BBC audiobook #25) - The year is given. Joan of Arc at present "couldn't have been more than seventeen years old"; she lived 6th January circa 1412 to 30th May, 1431. Gallifreyan memory lanterns were mentioned in *Engines of War*, also by George Mann.

THE WINTER FAMILY: The four-part *Tales of Winter* audios (*The Gods of Winter*, *The House of Winter*, *The Sins of Winter* and *The Memory of Winter*) entail variously benevolent or malevolent generations of the Winter family owning a psychic-paper card that can recall the TARDIS to help with a crisis/use the Doctor and Clara as dupes in a diabolical scheme. In *The Memory of Winter*, we learn that the whole situation derives from yet-another ontological paradox (see also *Destiny of the*

The Doctor, Ian, Vicki and Chaucer reunited with Barbara, who had beguiled patrons at the Tabard Inn with a recitation of *The Canterbury Tales*. Arundel tried to capture Chaucer, but the barfolk aided the travellers in making it appear that Arundel's victims had returned from the dead to haunt him. Sir Robert, besotted with Barbara, slipped and drowned while trying to betray her party. Ian neglected to tell Barbara of Sir Robert's death, claiming simply that "he ran away," as the travellers returned to the TARDIS and Chaucer left to live in Wales.

The Renaissance

The Daemons inspired the Renaissance.[613] A cult, Sodality, achieved limited time travel through a book linked to the Daemons, and used conventional and psionic science to alter human development. Select individuals were born as time-channellers (humans with the innate ability to travel through time) or time-sensitives (empathic humans who served as the channellers' navigators during time-jumps). Through such individuals, Sodality hoped to gain command of time and space travel.[614]

The eleventh Doctor, Amy and Rory were en route to the Renaissance when the TARDIS collided with a makeshift time machine built by the Calibas: a gaunt race near the Soronax Nebula, which scavenged from such races as the Utraxan and the Saturnynians. The Calibas' time drive was sent into the past, even as their vessel and the TARDIS were catapulted forward to the nineteenth century.[615] **By the end of the fourteenth century, wire-drawing machinery had been developed.**[616] Constantinople was renamed Istanbul.[617] Mocata Grange was built.[618]

The Doctor was present at the Battle of Agincourt.[619] **Ashildr's first stint as a man happened at the Battle of Agincourt, where she helped to end the Hundred Years' War. She also cured a village of scarlet fever, and for**

her troubles was nearly drowned as a witch. On another occasion, the Doctor observed Ashildr founding a leper colony, but left her there.[620]

c 1416 - DC 3: THE EIGHTH PIECE[621] **->** The Eleven's TARDIS briefly touched down in fifteenth-century Prague, and left behind molten residue from the destroyed planet Syra. A Time Lord artisan, the Clocksmith, forged the residue into the Doomsday Chronometer: a device that would bring about the Apocalypse. A disguised River Song, the eighth Doctor, Liv Chenka and the Solvers thwarted the Clocksmith's efforts. The Chronometer was broken into eight pieces; the Solvers scattered seven of these through history. River nicked a ninth piece as leverage, then gave Liv a lift to 2016. The Doctor and the Solvers' Queen followed in the TARDIS.

The Eight – an earlier, more benevolent incarnation of the Eleven – tried and failed to intervene in his own past, so remained on Earth for another century.

Forewarned of his defeat, the Clocksmith founded the Revelation Sect in the mid-fourteenth century. For the next six centuries, the group searched for the Chronometer pieces.[622] The Time Lord Hiroth's memory lantern fell to Earth. A parasitic Thrake boosted Joan of Arc's latent psionic talent – at age 13, in father's garden, she started hearing voices – so that one day, it could use her as a medium to feast upon Hiroth's memories.[623]

The Winter Family Gains a TARDIS Card

1429 - THE MEMORY OF WINTER[624] **->** Julius Winter, an amateur historian from the twenty-fifth century, time-jumped to 1429 to look into his family's history. He found a party travelling to the French Court – a group that included a seventeen-year-old Joan of Arc and Julius'

Doctor, *Vanderdeken's Children*, etc.) as the card has no starting and ending point... the Doctor winds up taking the card from its last owner, Julius Winter, and giving it to the first, Marianne de Winter. To avoid further paradoxes, the card is coded to always summon the twelfth Doctor and Clara, but there's a small glitch in that *Gods* describes the card as yellowing and creased from having experienced "several" owners by that point. *House*, by contrast, says it's made from "indestructible magnalinium".

Not every generation of Winters uses the card, and the Doctor and Clara keep mentioning off-screen adventures with some of the ones who do. We the audience meet four Winters who invoke the card: Diana Winter (twice, in *Gods*), Harrison Winter (*House*), Shadrak Winter (*Sins*) and Julius Winter (*Memory*). (These Winters, incidentally, have no known relation to Emily

Winter, a tenth Doctor companion in the IDW comics.) Marianne de Winter also uses the card, but only to get the Doctor and Clara out of a tight spot. For the Doctor and Clara, Diana Winter represents the first time they're made to answer the card's call.

We know that the card-paradox starts in 1429, and we know when it ends, since Julius Winter hails from the "twenty-fifth century". *The House of Winter* takes place in the same century. *The Sins of Winter* definitely takes place later than *The Gods of Winter* – the Doctor and Clara piss off Baldrassian Corp in the latter, and its legal department tries to seek revenge in the former. There's nothing to otherwise demand that *Sins* actually takes after *House*, but it's not unreasonable to think that, after Diana, the card calls the Doctor and Clara in the chronological order of the Winters who deploy it.

That only leaves the dating for *The Gods of Winter*

ancestor: a handmaiden, Marianne de Winter. Joan's psionic talents let her more directly commune with the Time Lord Hiroth's memory lantern.

The memory-eating Thrake stalking Joan increasingly gained corporeal form and killed four people, scaring Julius into using the mysterious TARDIS-summoning psychic-paper card that had been in his family for generations. The twelfth Doctor and Clara confiscated Julius' card, but were later imprisoned, and coded the card to Marianne's genetic make-up so she could summon the TARDIS to free them.

Julius intervened as the Thrake attacked Joan, and lost his recent memories. The Doctor discharged Hiroth's memory lantern, destroying the Thrake with an overload of raw memories. Clara and the Doctor returned Julius to his native time, then realised that they had left Julius' psychic-paper card with Marianne. With it, the Winter dynasty would summon them many more times.

The Doctor had already met Joan of Arc – an event to come in her lifetime.

The Doctor enjoyed a crepe during confidence-building lunch with Joan of Arc – a meeting which went a bit too well.[625] The Doctor assisted the great-great-great grandfather of the Duke of Medici in some bother with the Borgias.[626] The Doctor survived dinner with the Borgias.[627] The Viyrans' creators constructed many temples across the cosmos, including a hidden one in the forests of Scotland.[628]

A renegade Time Lady, also a friend of the Doctor, founded a restaurant on Earth during the time of the Hapsburgs.[629] Legends about a "beast" which terrorized the German town of Orlok circulated in the Middle Ages.[630] The planets of the Radzera System fell into a pattern of constant war.[631]

The Doctor was acquainted with the specifications of the Duke of Exeter's Daughter, a fifteenth-century torture rack in the Tower of London.[632] The Doctor was stretched out on a rack in the Tower of London.[633] At some point, River Song escaped from the Tower of London.[634]

---

somewhat uncertain, and even that can be narrowed down to a human colony world prior to the twenty-fifth century. See the individual entries for more.

625 "Four Doctors" (Titan). Joan was martyred on 30th May, 1431.

626 *The Doomsday Quatrain*. The Doctor refers to the man who was Duke in 1560, i.e. Cosimo de Medici. His paternal grandfather was Givoanni di Bicci de' Medici (circa 1360 to 1429). The Borgia family (mentioned in *City of Death*) became prominent in politics and the church in the fifteenth and sixteenth centuries.

627 "Sticks and Stones"

628 "Centuries" before *Charley S1: The Shadow at the Edge of the World*.

629 "Urban Myths". The country where the restaurant is located isn't specified, but it's evidently where goulash was invented – originally, that would be Hungary. The Hapsburgs ruled there from 1437 to 1918, and it's possible that the Doctor's comment "since the time of the Hapsburgs" refers to the start of their reign.

630 Four hundred years before *The Beast of Orlok*.

631 "Centuries" before *The Beast of Orlok*.

632 *Trial of the White Worm*. This doesn't mean that the Doctor was actually strapped to the rack.

633 *The Middle*. This, however, says he was actually strapped to *a* rack.

634 *DC 2: The Sonomancer*

635 *The Kingmaker*. Richard III was born October 1452.

636 *The Many Hands*

637 By the Doctor's best guess, this happened "more than two thousand years" before *Cobwebs*.

638 *Leth-St: Travers & Wells: Other Wars, Other Worlds*. It's unclear as to how, exactly, these kontron crystals came to Earth. The logical guess is that they originate with the Borad, but he doesn't conspicuously keep any

about his person in *Timelash*.

639 *FP: Coming to Dust*. *FP: The Book of the War* says that the Mal'akh are monstrosities tainted by the blood of the Yssgaroth (*The Pit*).

640 *A Death in the Family*. The year is unknown, but the Great Vowel Shift – a sea change in how the English language is pronounced – occurred at some point between 1450 and 1750.

641 *City of Death*. Movable type was developed in China during the ninth century, but as Scaroth possessed a number of Gutenberg Bibles (printed 1453-1455), we can infer he was responsible for *Europe's* development of printing.

642 *Son of the Dragon*. Vlad II was killed in 1447.

643 *Son of the Dragon*. Vlad very briefly ruled in 1448 before being cast into exile; this event must occur after he grained the throne in 1456.

644 *Matrix*

645 *The Labyrinth of Buda Castle*

646 "Two centuries" before *The Witch from the Well*.

647 Dating *Son of the Dragon* (BF #99) - The story begins on 17th June, 1462, the night of an infamous attack by Dracula's forces on the Turks. Act Three opens on July 2nd, and events unfold relatively soon thereafter. The name of Dracula's first wife is lost to history, although there's a problem with this woman being Erimem – Dracula's first wife bore him a son, Mihnea cel Rau, who ruled Wallachia 1508-1510. As the Doctor here says, Dracula did briefly regain his throne after this... for all of two months in 1476, before he was killed in battle.

648 *The Kingmaker*. Edward and Richard were respectively born in 1470 and 1473.

649 Dating *Unbound: He Jests at Scars...* (BF *Unbound* #4) - The year is given, although the Valeyard displays a

Richard III

From the time he was knee high, Richard III was a subject of huge interest to alien time tourists and academics. Random time travellers would repeatedly show up to question Richard about the future murder of his nephews – one of history's greatest mysteries – and had strong views about whether he should kill the boys or not. This puzzled Richard, who at around age 12 had no intention of doing anything of the sort. By accident, Richard discovered that most of the travellers were afraid of someone called "the Doctor", and he continually dropped the Doctor's name as a means of making the visitors leave.[635]

Many of those who died in the Nor' Loch, Edinburgh, from the fifteenth century onwards were likely to be resurrected by the Onk Ndell Kith in 1759.[636] An unknown race established itself on the planet Helhine, then fell to ruin.[637] In the fifteenth century, an ancestor of Edward Travers found a kontron crystal on the shores of Loch Ness. H.G. Wells would come to own another such crystal, from the same source.[638]

wih - Sutekh sent hordes of Mal'akh to fifteenth century Earth, where they became involved in the conflict between the European Christians and the Ottoman Turks. He withdrew his forces after the Great Houses, to protect their involvement in this crucible of history, signed a treaty with the Osirian Court. Ellainya of the Great Houses, a.k.a. Merytra, was bound by blood into Sutekh's service.[639]

The Doctor tripped the Word Lord's CORDIS on the lost twenty-seventh letter of the English alphabet, which made him crash into the entire alphabet, and caused the Great Vowel Shift.[640]

In the mid-fifteenth century, Scaroth gave humankind the printing press, although he kept a number of Gutenberg Bibles for himself. It was possibly this splinter of Scaroth that acquired a Ming vase.[641]

Vlad III: Dracula

Upon the murder of his father, Vlad III took the name "Dracula" – which means "son of the dragon".[642] During the first Easter of his reign, Vlad III invited two hundred boyars to his banqueting hall – and afterwards had them slaughtered for the roles they played in the deaths of his father and brother.[643] The Wandering Jew once shared a bottle of Tokay with Vlad Tepes, who was unable to end the man's immortal life.[644]

Alien material gave Zoltan Frid vampire-like attributes, as well as the ability to syphon information from his victims' minds. Frid served as one of Vlad the Impaler's interrogators until – out of fear that he knew too much – he was buried alive in the labyrinth beneath Buda Castle.[645]

The Varaxil Hegemony developed a science based upon Odic power, an energy associated with the supernatural. They became such despised outcasts on so many worlds, they renounced their technology and began hunting down any beings who could innately channel Odic energy, imprisoning them on Varix Beta.[646]

1462 (17th June to July) - SON OF THE DRAGON[647]**->** Turkish forces led by Sultan Mehmed II invaded Wallachia, part of what would later become Romania. Prince Vlad III (a.k.a. Vlad the Impaler, a.k.a. Dracula) ruled Wallachia and ravaged his people's own crops, livestock and water supplies to stop his enemies making use of them.

The fifth Doctor, Peri and Erimem arrived during this conflict, and Erimem wound up saving Dracula's life. Dracula welcomed her as a guest at his palace, Poienari Castle. Events led to the Doctor being captured and Peri earning a death sentence, whereupon Erimem bargained with Dracula – in exchange for letting her friends go, she'd become his wife. The Turks surrounded Poienari, and the King of Hungary withdrew his support from Dracula. Erimem was released from her promise, and Dracula fled to Transylvania. Radu, Dracula's brother, became the head of Wallachia.

A legend concerning these events claimed that an archer (actually the Doctor) had warned Dracula of the impending siege of Poienari. It was further said that Dracula's first wife threw herself to her death (a misinterpretation of Dracula briefly dangling Peri off the Poienari battlements), and the portion of the Arges River marking this point became known as Raul Doamenei, "the princess' river". The Doctor stole Radu's journal to keep the name of Dracula's "first wife" – even though he and Erimem hadn't formally married – a secret.

The "sons" of King Edward IV – who were historically fated to die in the Tower of London – were actually born as girls. Edward feared this would throw the line of royal succession into doubt, and spark decades of fighting amongst the power-crazed nobility. He therefore announced that the girls were in fact boys: the future Edward V and Richard of Shrewsbury.[648]

= 1471 - UNBOUND: HE JESTS AT SCARS...[649]
-> Accompanied by Ellie, the Valeyard located the Doomsday Weapon on Uxarius and used it to destroy Gallifrey. He later trained the weapon on Logopolis, hoping to deprive the fourth Doctor of the incentive to go there, which would undo the Valeyard accidentally killing his past self. However, the Web of Time grew increasingly resistant to the Valeyard's changes to history, and subtly influenced him into targeting Logopolis in 1471 – the year that the first Doctor was

present there. Having still committed retroactive suicide, the Valeyard went back to Kiev in the thirteenth
century to fix the problem...

In 1478, George, the Duke of Clarence, was convicted
of treason against his brother, King Edward IV. He was
slated for execution, but their other brother, Richard of
Gloucester, quietly rescued him. George was believed dead
and lived in disguise as Clarrie, the barkeep of The
Kingmaker tavern.[650]

**In 1479, a wall was built around the parish of St
James – which would one day be known as Cardiff – to
keep out plague victims. A little girl named Faith died,
but a priest brought her back to life with a resurrection
gauntlet. Her revival enabled an aspect of Death to
manifest in St James – its hold on Earth would have
solidified had it killed thirteen people, but it had only
murdered twelve when Faith stopped it. The gauntlet
was hidden within St Mary's Church.[651]**

= The alt-first Doctor, along with his granddaughter Susan, visited 1480 and took Leonardo da Vinci
on a few trips in the TARDIS. He witnessed the spaceships constructed by the One, and gained other
insights into future technology.[652]

A "Northern chap with big ears" left a pair of messages
for Peri and Erimem at The Kingmaker tavern on Fleet
Street in London. They would receive the notes in 1483.[653]

**The year 1482 was full of temporal glitches, making
it difficult for the TARDIS to land there.[654]**

1483 (April to October) - THE KINGMAKER[655] ->
The wayward TARDIS deposited Peri and Erimem in Stony
Stratford, 1483. William Shakespeare, having stowed
aboard from 1597, snuck out of the Ship. Shakespeare
presented himself to Richard III as "Mr Seyton", someone
from the future who advocated that Richard should murder his nephews.

King Edward IV died, so Richard escorted the new monarch – his nephew, King Edward V – back to London.
Along the way, Richard discovered that his nephews were
female. He rounded up anyone who might know this
secret, and executed Hastings, a friend of the old king.
Three days after Richard's discovery, Peri and Erimem
arrived at The Kingmaker tavern and – based upon the
Doctor's messages – realised they were doomed to stay in
1483 for a time. They worked as waitresses there for about
six months.

Commemorative mugs, plates and tea towels were made
in anticipation of Edward V's coronation on 24th June, but

poor grasp of mathematics in telling Ellie that it's "ten
thousand years" before the TV story featuring the
Doomsday Weapon, *Colony in Space* [2972].
650 *The Kingmaker.* History says George was executed
on 18th February, 1478.
651 *TW: Dead Man Walking.* It's never said what became
of Faith after Death was banished, and for all anyone
knows, she's the ageless, fortune-telling little girl whom
Jack consults in *Dead Man Walking* and *TW: Fragments*.
652 *Unbound: A Storm of Angels*
653 "Two years" before Peri and Erimem's arrival in *The
Kingmaker.* The "big-eared" chap is almost certainly a
veiled reference to the ninth Doctor, who apparently
passes through the fifteenth century and completes
this task, fulfilling the line of communication between
his previous self and his companions.
654 Or so he claims in *The Impossible Astronaut.* It's
entertaining to think this could be related to all the
conflicting stories about the fate of the nephews of
King Richard III, per *Sometime Never* and *The Kingmaker*,
especially given the temporal shenanigans in the latter.
655 Dating *The Kingmaker* (BF #81) - Edward IV died
on 9th April, 1483, and Edward V's short-lived reign
began on 18th April (he's one of three British monarchs
to have never been crowned). Peri and Erimem arrive at
least three days beforehand, and work at The Kingmaker
for about six months. A minor anomaly is that Henry
Stafford later claims Peri and Erimem turned up "about
eighteen months" before what's clearly August 1485,

meaning it's more accurately two years plus change.
656 Dating *The Kingmaker* (BF #81) - One of the
Doctor's notes to Peri and Erimem dates their arrival to
1st August, 1485. Bosworth Field was fought on 22nd
August, and it's a little puzzling to wonder how the run-
up to the conflict unfolded, given that Richard III time-
jumps with the Doctor to 1597 and is apparently
absent some days beforehand. Henry Stafford was historically executed on 2nd November, 1483, so in the
Doctor Who universe, he languishes in prison for twenty-one months beyond that point.
657 *The King of Terror*
658 *Blood Harvest*
659 *Project: Twilight*
660 According to Harrison Chase in *The Seeds of Doom*.
The Wars of the Roses lasted from 1455-1485.
661 Dating *The Legends of Ashildr:* "The Fortunate Isles"
(NSA #61b) - The year is given.
662 Dating *Sometime Never* (EDA #67) - The date is
given.
663 Dating *The Left-Handed Hummingbird* (NA #21) -
The date is first given on p39.
664 The Doctor has Christopher Columbus' business
card in *The Two Doctors.* Columbus lived 1451-1506 and
discovered the New World in 1492.
665 *Eye of Heaven*
666 *Cobwebs*
667 Dating *DotD: Trouble in Paradise* (*Destiny of the
Doctor* #6) - Columbus' journal repeatedly gives the

the event didn't occur. Parliament declared Edward and his "brother" Richard illegitimate; their uncle had Mr Seyton conduct a press conference on this development with the finest gossips in England, including the *Lincolnshire Tattletale* and the *Wessex Busybody*. Richard was subsequently crowned as Richard III.

The now-illegitimate Princes were relocated to the Tower of London – the king invited Peri and Erimem to serve as their handmaidens. Henry Stafford, the Second Duke of Buckingham, sought to bring the Woodville family into conflict with the king as a means of claiming the throne for himself. He hoped to trigger this by convincing Peri and Erimem to poison the "boys", but the king discovered the plot and threw Stafford in prison.

Richard III had Peri and Erimem double as the Princes while the genuine article went to work as waitresses with their uncle Clarrie at The Kingmaker. Peri and Erimem routinely appeared in public as the Princes, seen from afar playing tennis or exercising. The king got fed up with Shakespeare/Seyton and had him tortured, learning much about the web of time. Peri and Erimem spent the next two years masquerading as the Princes, but the public didn't take much notice of the "lads". History would record that the Princes were last seen in 1484.

Pointy beards were all the rage in France, and considered a fashion statement for the 1480s (as distinguished from the large, open-necked beards of the 70s).

Bosworth Field:
The Death of Shakespeare

1485 (August) - THE KINGMAKER[656] **->** The fifth Doctor, Peri and Erimem arrived from 1597, wanting to investigate the death of Richard III's nephews. But while the Doctor departed to patronize The Kingmaker tavern, the TARDIS – telepathically resonating with the Doctor's recent boozing – hiccupped and slipped back to 1483 with Peri and Erimem aboard.

Henry Stafford was tortured to death by Sir James Tyrell, the king's Royal High Concussor. The barkeep Clarrie – formerly George, the Duke of Clarence – was identified and died in a chase, drowning in the Thames. In future, the play *Richard III* would spread the belief that he had drowned in a vat of Malmsey wine.

William Shakespeare, a.k.a. Mr Seyton, escaped imprisonment and demanded that the Doctor take Richard III to stand trial in Queen Elizabeth's era. Much calamity ensued, and after a brief visit to 1597, the TARDIS arrived at the Battle of Bosworth Field. Shakespeare was forcibly hauled out of the TARDIS by a sixty-fourth century publishing robot that eventually exploded. Erimem had broken Shakespeare's arm, and a laser pistol wound had singed his foot and given him a limp, so Shakespeare was mistaken for the king. He was killed, blubbing like a child, after

scrambling up a tree.

The Doctor relocated Richard III's nieces, Susan and Judith, to join their uncle in 1597.

The Canavitchi helped guide the Spanish Inquisition.[657] Agonal, an immortal who gained strength from suffering, fed on its fear and death.[658] The Doctor was present during the Spanish Inquisition.[659] **The earliest parts of Chase Mansion were built during the Wars of the Roses.**[660]

1485 - THE LEGENDS OF ASHILDR:"The Fortunate Isles"[661] **->** The *Makaron*, the largest of the Bet-Zone's timeships, journeyed from era to era and posed as a subtropical isle: a locale where a planet's inhabitants would be lured to compete in deadly games. Ashildr, now working as a thief, fled Seville by stowing aboard the carrack *El Galgo*, and happened upon a map to the alleged "Fortunate Isles". The *El Galgo* set sail for the Fortunate Isles, a land seemingly covered in massive diamond and gold deposits. Ashildr emerged as the winner of the games – as aided by the fact that she couldn't remain drowned for long – and escaped back to the *El Galgo*. The *Makaron* departed, leaving a featureless sea behind.

1485 - SOMETIME NEVER[662] **->** An Agent of the Council of Eight kidnapped the two nephews of Richard III to prevent their having an impact on history. The eighth Doctor and Trix later rescued the boys, and took them to the early twenty-first century.

1487 - THE LEFT-HANDED HUMMINGBIRD[663] **->** In the Aztec city of Tenochtitlan, the god Huitzilopochtli's taste for blood grew every year. By 1487, his priests demanded twenty thousand sacrifices. These fed the psychic Huitzilin – a human mutated by the Xiuhcoatl, an Exxilon device that leaked radiation. Huitzilin used his powers to remain alive, and used the Xiuhcoatl to make his people worship him. For centuries, he would visit the most violent places in human history, feeding off the carnage of such events. He would become known as the Blue.

Christopher Columbus

The Doctor met Christopher Columbus.[664] He travelled on the *Santa Maria*, but Columbus refused his suggestion of plotting courses with an orange and a biro.[665] The Doctor told Columbus that there was more to travelling than going from A to B.[666]

1492 (12th October) - DotD: TROUBLE IN PARADISE[667] **->** The number of buffalo sharply dropped as the Native Americans killed them for food and clothing. In a bid to save his race, a time-travelling Bovin the Herd-Leader used a tractor beam to steer Christopher Columbus' ships to America, hoping to change history so the buffalo could thrive after the Europeans curtailed the Native Americans. Columbus, a dreadful navigator, would never have found North America on his own.

The eleventh Doctor directed the sixth Doctor and Peri to this era, and instructed them to secure the energy of an omniparadox – a rare and potentially universe-shattering event caused by a massive collision of time – in the TARDIS for his future use. Columbus realised that the Doctor was a much greater explorer than himself, and petulantly resolved to kill him.

A second version of Bovin travelled back to tell his younger self that the Europeans, owing to his intervention, had similarly whittled down the buffalo's numbers. The Doctor nicked the central time element from the younger Bovin's ship to prevent further mischief, and was holding the device behind his back as Columbus tried to run him through with a sword. Peri screamed a warning, enabling the Doctor to dodge and causing Columbus to skewer the

time element instead. Its destruction retroactively prevented the older Bovin from warning his younger self about his failed plan, guaranteeing the European settlement of North America.

The United States continued to exist only due to massive historical revision, as well as the omniparadox stemming from Peri, an American, contributing to the destruction of the time element that helped to create her home country. The Doctor and Peri secured the omniparadox in the TARDIS, and the Doctor predicted that the stranded younger Bovin would be hunted down and killed as a devil figure in Japan.

The omniparadox later powered the TARDIS as it escaped the Creevix's universe back to Oxford, 2013.[668]

In the late fifteenth century, the Doctor visited China.[669] He believed the best Chinese takeaway came from the Ming dynasty.[670] The Doctor encountered Torquemada in Toledo, where an *auto-da-fé* didn't go as

---

date as 12th October, 1492.

668 *DotD: The Time Machine*

669 *The Talons of Weng-Chiang*. The Doctor notes, "I haven't been in China for four hundred years" – presumably four hundred years ago in history, as opposed to when the Doctor was four hundred years younger.

670 *Dreamland* (DW)

671 *Managra*. This happened "seven years" before Torquemada's death in 1498.

672 Dating *The Masque of Mandragora* (14.1) - It's said that the Helix will return to Earth in five hundred years at the "end of the twentieth century", so the story is set at the end of the fifteenth century.

The second edition of *The Making of Doctor Who* said that the story is set in "the fifteenth century". The novelisation by producer Philip Hinchcliffe specified the date as "1492", *The Terrestrial Index* and *The TARDIS Logs* both set the story "about 1478". *The Discontinuity Guide* said it must be set "c.1470-1482 when Da Vinci was in Florence". *Timelink*, among other things factoring in Hieronymous' remarks about the summer solstice, decided it was "April 1492". *About Time* commented: "The novelisation specifies 1492, which fits."

In *SJA: Death of the Doctor*, Sarah Jane would seem to remove any ambiguity about this when she says that she visited "Italy, San Martino, 1492".

The entity that encroaches on Earth in *The Eleventh Tiger* (set in 1865) also seems to be the Mandragora Helix, even though the Doctor says in *Masque* that it's been banished for five hundred years. There's either another conjunction taking place that he doesn't know about, or he's discounting events of 1865 because he knows he already won the day then.

The novel *Beautiful Chaos* not only agrees that *Masque of Mandragora* occurs in 1492 (pgs. 41, 167), it takes the added step of saying that the Doctor and

Sarah fought the Helix "five hundred and seventeen years, one month, four days" (p43) prior to 15th May, 2009. According to *A History of the Universe in 100 Objects* (p56), and in a fairly obvious nod to this story, "the fourth Doctor was keen to meet Leonardo in 1492 San Martino".

673 *Beautiful Chaos*

674 *SJS: Buried Secrets*, *SJS: Fatal Consequences* and *SJS: Dreamland*. Sarah's research-minded friend Natallie says that Giuliano wrote his journal in the "sixteenth century", suggesting that Giuliano didn't record events from *The Masque of Mandragora* until some years afterwards. Alternatively, it's possible that Natallie is just guessing based upon the sketchy records at her disposal, and Giuliano wrote his journal before the turn of the century. A continuity glitch exists in that the Doctor doesn't tell Sarah until the very end of *The Masque of Mandragora* that the Mandragora Helix will return to Earth in five hundred years, so there's no opportunity for Giuliano to learn of this and later record it in his journal. It's possible, though, that Giuliano – even from a distance – overhears the Doctor and Sarah's final conversation, which would explain why he seems a bit disconcerted even before witnessing the TARDIS dematerialise. If so, however, it's strange that Sarah so repeatedly flogs herself in *Sarah Jane Smith* Series 2 because her "loose lips" told Giuliano of the future, when if anything it's the Doctor's fault.

675 *Spiral Scratch*

676 *Managra*. Torquemada died 16th September, 1498.

677 *So Vile a Sin*. Vasco da Gama, a Portuguese explorer, was the first European to journey by sea to India.

678 *Instruments of Darkness*

679 *Absolution*. *The Garden of Earthly Delights* is Bosch's best-known work, painted somewhere between 1490 to 1510. The idea that the Doctor posed for this

planned, and "mini-Beelzebubs" hauled Torquemada from his bed.[671]

The Mandragora Helix on Earth

1492 - THE MASQUE OF MANDRAGORA[672] **-> The fourth Doctor and Sarah Jane accidentally brought the Mandragora Helix to Renaissance Italy, where it made contact with the Brotherhood of Demnos cult. The Doctor drained and dissipated the Helix's energy before it could plunge Earth into an age of superstition and fear.**

What remained of the Helix seeped into the ground and water around San Martino. The people there became endowed with traces of Helix energy – by 2009, the Helix would be able to control their descendants. In the centuries to come, San Martino would become uninhabited and lost to history.[673]

Following the Mandragora incident, Duke Giuliano formed the Orphans of the Future: a secret society dedicated to helping humankind. In the centuries to come, Giuliano's written account of the Mandragora affair became known as *The Book of Tomorrows*, and was regarded as a work of prophecy. The Orphans eventually split into two camps – the White Chapter and the Crimson Chapter – based upon their interpretation of *The Book*, particularly its prediction that an "alien intelligence" would return to Earth in half a millennium. The White Chapter believed that the returning aliens would take humanity away to a better life; the Crimson Chapter thought the aliens wanted to eradicate humanity.[674]

> = The sixth Doctor visited the planet Yestobahl in 1494.[675]

The Doctor was present when Torquemada died in Avila – an event that involved the arrival of the personification of Death, complete with scythe.[676] The Doctor was with Vasco da Gama when he sailed into the harbour of Zanzibar in 1499.[677]

The Cylox were immensely powerful psionics and a very long-lived species, being the equivalent of adolescents after surviving for millennia. Two of the Cylox, Lai-Ma and his brother Tko-Ma, had spent several millennia annihilating planets in another dimension. Around the late fifteenth century, an intergalactic court exiled them to a pocket realm located on Earth. The brothers later loosed their shackles and agreed to see who could destroy Earth the fastest. The Ini-Ma, the brothers' jailor of sorts, endowed its essence into female members of the bloodline that would produce Loretta van Cheaden.[678]

The painter Hieronymus Bosch was a friend of the Doctor, who posed for one of Bosch's triptychs: *The Garden of Earthly Delights*. The Doctor spent hours lying against a table, and Bosch went mad if he so much as twitched.[679] **Gueiseppe di Cattivo, a contemporary of Leonardo da Vinci, was known in fifteenth-century Florence as the Artist of Nightmares.**[680]

The Sixteenth Century

During the sixteenth century, the Ancient Order of St Peter existed to fight vampires.[681] Stattenheim and Waldorf created working plans for a TARDIS during the sixteenth century.[682] Jack Harkness visited a dying galaxy and found a sole survivor. He relocated it to Earth, where it came to inspire myths about the shapeshifting Selkie.[683] Veec-Elic-Savareen-Jal-9 became a fugitive after speaking out against the warmongering Hive Council on Jal Paloor. Darac-Poul-Caparrel-Jal-7 was dispatched to capture him.[684] The Doctor visited Venice in the sixteenth century.[685]

Legends spoke of Hetocumtek as a vicious warrior god who descended from the heavens, and tried to conquer the peoples of the Great Plains. The most powerful medicine men of the Mojave tribe trapped Hetocumtek in a totem pole that was buried in the Mojave Desert. It was said that if ever the totem fell back into the hand of men, Hetocumtek would be freed.[686]

The second Doctor and Jamie met Copernicus.[687] A young Prince Henry found a quill made from a temporal phoenix feather. It could rewrite time – so Henry had his Scrivener use the quill to kill his brother, Arthur the Prince

---

becomes even more fanciful once you realise that the depicted figures are nude.
680 *SJA: Mona Lisa's Revenge.* The artist's name is spelled "Giuseppe" in the closed captioning, but "Gueiseppe" in the art book Rani consults on screen.
681 *Minuet in Hell*
682 *The Quantum Archangel,* doubtless extrapolating from use of a Stattenheim remote control in *The Two Doctors,* with a dash of *Muppets* influence.
683 *TW: "The Selkie".* Some women on Seal Island have been aiding the Selkie for some "centuries".

684 "Four hundred years" before *Ghosts of India.*
685 *The Stones of Venice*
686 *SJA: The Curse of Clyde Langer.* Date unknown, but at a rough guess, it's probably some centuries prior to the Mojave surrendering to United States forces in 1859. Mojave culture stretches back that far, but very little is known about it.
687 An unseen adventure inferred from *The Wreck of the World.* Alternatively, the Doctor is just quizzing Jamie about his historical knowledge. Copernicus lived 1473-1543.

of Wales. This paved the way for him to become King Henry VIII.[688]

The Time Agency's paradox crew worked to eliminate a causal loop igniting in the sixteenth century, preferably without losing Sir Francis Drake in the process.[689]

c 1500 - THE GHOSTS OF N-SPACE[690] **->** Around the turn of the sixteenth century, the third Doctor and Sarah were briefly seen as ghosts.

Leonardo da Vinci

Both the Monk and Scaroth claimed credit for inspiring Leonardo to consider building a flying machine.[691] The Doctor told da Vinci that coleopters were more trouble than they were worth.[692] The Doctor personally instructed Leonardo da Vinci in the art of draughtsmanship.[693] **Leonardo had a cold when he drew a sketch of a young woman's face.**[694] The Doctor took Leonardo to attend the wedding of Bernice Summerfield and Jason Kane; Leonardo designed their wedding cake.[695]

The Doctor believed that Leonardo initially painted a lot of eels before Christ in *The Last Supper*; River Song attested

that, actually, Leonardo didn't eat meat or fish, just a lot of garlic.[696] Leonardo convinced the Doctor to take him back to the time of Christ, and following this journey produced a "marvellous adoration painting"... that he didn't finish. The Doctor ended up owning some of Leo's designs, and gifted them to his great-grandson Alex, to further the boy's interest in architecture.[697]

Although nobody took notice of Leonardo da Vinci's sketches of helicopters or tanks at the time, his drawings would "seed" the idea for such inventions, and help to facilitate their creation in future.[698]

> = Leonardo da Vinci founded the DaVinci Corporation in 1500.[699]

The Mona Lisa

The Doctor visited Leonardo while he was painting the Mona Lisa, "a dreadful woman with no eyebrows who wouldn't sit still".[700] The model who sat for the Mona Lisa was "a dreary Italian housewife who laughed like a camel and farted like a donkey". Leonardo painted the Mona Lisa using oils he blagged from his neigh-

---

688 *Recorded Time and Other Stories:* "Recorded Time". Prince Arthur died on 2nd April, 1502.
689 *Jack: Month 25*
690 Dating *The Ghosts of N-Space* (MA #7) - The Doctor says it is "somewhere near the turn of the century".
691 *The Time Meddler, City of Death.*
692 *Kingdom of Silver*
693 *The Harvest of Time* (p360).
694 *Doctor Who – The Movie*
695 *Happy Endings*
696 *River S3: A Requiem for the Doctor*
697 *Relative Dimensions*
698 *The Nowhere Place*
699 *Unbound: A Storm of Angels*
700 *City of Death.* The Doctor's note to Leonardo ends "see you earlier". In *The Two Doctors,* the Doctor has Leonardo's business card. According to *The Doctor: His Lives and Times* (p88), Leonardo at some point drew a sketch of the fourth Doctor, scarf and all.
701 *SJA: Mona Lisa's Revenge.* It seems reasonable to presume that all seven Mona Lisas were created using paint made from the alien rock, as the original painting is destroyed in 1979 (*City of Death*). In both *City of Death* and *Mona Lisa's Revenge,* various characters attribute Leonardo as having painted the Mona Lisa between 1503 and 1519, in accordance with the painting's real-world history. *City of Death,* however, specifies that the original Mona Lisa, at least, was completed by 1505.
702 Dating *The Twelfth Doctor Year One* (Titan 12th Doc #1.3, "The Swords of Kali") - A caption gives the year. Clara posing for the Mosa Lisa contracts events in *SJA: Mona Lisa's Revenge.*

703 Dating *City of Death* (17.2) - Tancredi asks what the Doctor is doing in "1505".
704 Dating *FP: Against Nature* (FP novel #7) - The year is given. The history books claim that the last New Fire Ceremony occurred in 1507, with the Spanish conquest of Mexico curtailing the practice.
705 Dating *The Aztecs* (1.6) - The obvious point is that it's before Cortes ended the Aztec Empire by capturing its territory for Spain. Related to that, but perhaps proving that we shouldn't put too much stock in any one person's remarks, Susan (normally a brainiac), asks, "Cortes landed in 1520, didn't he?", and Barbara affirmatively replies, "Mrm-hrm". Which is curious, since he actually landed in 1519. John Lucarotti corrects the error in his novelisation of his own script (published twenty years after the TV story was made), and has the same exchange go (p4) Susan: "The Spanish landed in the early 1500s, didn't they?", Barbara: "1519, to be exact".

The core dating assessment in the TV version comes from Barbara, a history teacher who specialised in Aztec culture. Straight out of the TARDIS, she judges that Yetaxa "must have died around 1430, I should think", as the items in his tomb – she believes – hail from the Aztecs' early period (their empire peaked 1440-1519). Her estimate isn't supported, or directly contradicted (see below), by the story itself. However, the warrior Ixta (played by Ian Cullen, age 29) is the son of the man who built Yetaxa's tomb, which presumably means that *The Aztecs* happens within living memory of Yetaxa's death. In the novelisation, Lucarotti repeats Barbara's "1430" estimate of Yetaxa's passing, but also writes: "The Doctor pressed the digital time-orientation

bour, Guieseppe di Cattivo, and had been made from minerals found in a rock that fell from space.[701]

1505 - THE TWELFTH DOCTOR YEAR ONE[702] ->
While the twelfth Doctor watched on, Leonardo da Vinci used Clara as the model for the Mona Lisa. The travellers left as the Doctor's friend Tiger Maratha phoned to warn about an impending threat in India, 2134.

1505 - CITY OF DEATH[703] -> Captain Tancredi, one of
the splinters of Scaroth the Jagaroth, kept Leonardo a virtual prisoner and ordered him to begin making six additional copies of the Mona Lisa. Scaroth hoped to sell them at great profit to fund his time experiments in 1979. The fourth Doctor arrived, and wrote "This is a Fake" in felt-tip on many of Leonardo's blank canvasses. Leonardo painted the copies over them.

The New Fire Ceremony

1506 - FP: AGAINST NATURE[704] -> Every fifty-two
years, the Mexica held a version of the New Fire Ceremony: a means of restarting the Nahua calendar via a young man representing Xiuhtecuhtli – the God of Fire and the Passage of Time – so that the universe could continue. Ordnance-Tetrarch Goralschai, a first-wave veteran of the Great Houses, adapted the ceremony for his own purposes. As part of this, Rhodenet of House Meddhoran had been reincarnated as Momancani – an orphan with no discernable beginning or ending, and a vessel in which Xiuhtecuhtli could manifest. Primo Acamapichtli Isleno de la Vega, one of Goralschai's totems, was transported to this era as part of the impending ritual.

Goralschai succeeded in using the ceremony to gain godlike abilities – possibly in the pursuit of ending his life, possibly to destroy the entire universe (an aspiration from which he relented), or possibly another aim still. The ceremony participants acknowledged a benign outcome, even if their memories of the proceedings were muddled. Primo remained in this time, and Momancani left on a pilgrimage to find Aztlan (the mythic island home of the Aztecs), knowing that the arrival of foreigners would soon change the land.

The history books wrongly recorded that no new Fire Ceremony was held in 1506, and that Motechuhzoma postponed it until 1507 for political reasons.

1507 - THE AZTECS[705] -> When the first Doctor, Ian,
Barbara and Susan emerged from a sealed tomb, Barbara was taken for the reincarnation of the Aztec priest Yetaxa, who was buried there. She attempted to use her "divine" power to end the Aztec practice of human sacrifice, knowing it would horrify the European conquerors in future, and hoped this would

button [in the TARDIS] and the year 1507 lit up" (p6). It's possible Lucarotti intended this as the year from the start, or, given two decades to think the matter over, he concluded that 1507 worked better.

In *The Left-Handed Hummingbird* (ch5), Benny fails to "come across a single reference to the Doctor's original visit to [Aztec] civilization", but, from his own description, she's fairly certain that he "turned up during the drought of 1454, when the Aztecs had been busy sacrificing humans to Tlaloc". There's a bit of leeway with that one, if Benny is chiefly going off the Doctor's relating of events, since he isn't always the most reliable. (Besides, he evidently doesn't remember the year, or he'd have told her.) Also, Benny can't be entirely right, because while 1454 saw one of the Aztecs' most widely reported calamities – the drought-caused famine of One Rabbit (their calendar used animal icons) – the drought itself seems to have started earlier, in 1452. There's no mention of famine in *The Aztecs*, save for Barbara forecasting it. The Doctor chats with Cameca about their prioritizing water for the flowers in the garden rather than food, but if anything that suggests things aren't *so* dire that they're on the verge of starvation. In fact, Autloc says the Rain God has looked away from his people "For many days", not years, so it's even less likely to be 1454.

More recent decades have witnessed some rethinking of Aztec culture, and a new theory holds (see in particular Ross Hassig's *Time, History, and Belief in Aztec and Colonial Mexico*) that Motechuzoma II revised the Mexica model of the universe from nine heavens to thirteen in 1502. Ergo, in episode two, when Tlotoxl asks Barbara "How many heavens are there?" and she correctly answers, "thirteen", it's likely during Motechuzoma II's reign (1502-1520), or Tlotoxl would have cause to arrest her on the spot. Knowing that, it seems more likely than ever that Lucarotti's naming of "1507" in the novelisation is right after all, although he probably had less cause to know that at the time.

The Programme Guide dated the story "c.1200 AD". *The Terrestrial Index* suggested "1480", claiming that fifty years elapsed between Yetaxa being buried and the TARDIS landing inside the tomb. *About Time* leaned toward "a date around 1460-80", while conceding that Lucarotti's date in the novelisation was feasible if Barbara's estimate was a bit off. Both editions of *The Making of Doctor Who* placed the story in "1430".

The Cup of Cocoa entry in *A History of the Universe in 100 Objects* dates *The Aztecs* to "circa 1507". *Whoniverse* (BBC Books) seems to have skipped mention of *The Aztecs*, possibly because it lacks an SF element beyond the TARDIS. *Timelink* favoured Barbara's estimate and dated the story to "1450", but also noted that while a prominent eclipse features in episode four, the only recorded instances in that period happened on 7th June, 1415 and 16th March, 1485.

save the Aztec civilisation from the Spanish. Her efforts failed.

Owing to a misunderstanding with some cocoa, the first Doctor was briefly engaged to an honourable Aztec lady, Cameca.

(=) The first Doctor came under threat from the Great Intelligence while visiting Aztec times.[706]

= The Aztecs mistook the alt- first Doctor for their reincarnated high priestess, as he was the first out of the tomb, and thereafter had to dress the part. The Doctor's loose lips forewarned the Aztecs about Cortez's arrival, enabling the Mayan Alliance to rout the invasion of the Americas.[707]

The Doctor visited his friend Cameca now and again.[708] The tenth Doctor and Martha had a drink of chocolate in

Aztec times.[709] They also visited the Italian Renaissance.[710]

= Owing to the advances of the DaVinci Corporation, humanity achieved space travel. In 1508, Vasco da Gama stepped foot on Mars.[711]

Guieseppe di Cattivo painted a self-portrait in 1509. He also painted his masterpiece, *The Abomination*, but discovered that nobody could look upon it without losing their sanity. He locked *The Abomination* in a special case made from hangman's gallows, and the next morning was found in his Florence apartments, completely insane.[712] The Doctor found Gioffre Borgia so intimidating that when the man asked, "What do you think of our Leaning Tower of Pisa?", the Doctor leaned to the side and said, "It looks okay to me."[713]

The Doctor watched Michelangelo paint the Sistine Chapel, and told him that if heights frightened him, he shouldn't have accepted the commission.[714] Michelangelo

---

706 Or so it appears from a clip of *The Aztecs* shown in *The Name of the Doctor*.
707 *Unbound: A Storm of Angels*, providing an alternate take on *The Aztecs*.
708 *The Tenth Doctor Year One*: "Revolutions of Terror"
709 "Agent Provocateur". They presumably, unlike the first Doctor in *The Aztecs*, don't wind up engaged because of this.
710 *Wishing Well*
711 *Unbound: A Storm of Angels*
712 *SJA: Mona Lisa's Revenge*. The number of years that elapse between Guieseppe painting *The Abomination* and his death in 1518 isn't specified.
713 *Time Heist*. Gioffre Borgia was born 1481 or 1482, and died in 1516 or 1517. The Leaning Tower was finished in 1372.
714 *Vincent and the Doctor*. The Sistine Chapel was painted 1508-1512.
715 "Changes". Peri is surprised to find the picture in a store room, so she wasn't with the Doctor at the time.
716 *The Stone Rose*
717 *The Resurrection of Mars*
718 "Centuries" before *The Rising Night*. As the Baobhan Sith are enemies of the Time Lords of old, it's odd that they were, historically speaking, allowed to create an Empire. Then again, the fall of their Empire here might well owe to Gallifrey's intervention.
719 "Eight years" before "Dragon's Claw".
720 Dating *The Ravelli Conspiracy* (BF EA #3.3) - The year is given. Some writings published after Leo X's death indicated he was gay, but later historians couldn't decide if this was the case.
721 Dating *DC 3: The Doomsday Chronometer* (BF DC #3.3) - Exact time unknown, but it's set in Leo's studio.
722 *SJA: Mona Lisa's Revenge*
723 *Hornets' Nest: The Stuff of Nightmares*. The expres-

sion is first cited in a 1520 poem by Conrad Goclenius.
724 Susan says in *The Aztecs* that this happened in 1520; as the novelisation of that story and *The Left-Handed Hummingbird* correctly identifies, it was actually 1519.
725 *Point of Entry*. The Spanish invasion of the Aztecs happened 1519-1521.
726 *Point of Entry*. Agrippa lived 1486-1535.
727 Dating "Dragon's Claw" (DWW #39-43, DWM #44-45) - "It is 1522...the summer of death!" according to the opening captions.
728 *Benny S6: The Lost Museum*
729 *The Sensorites*. Henry VIII reigned from 1509-1547. In *Tragedy Day*, the seventh Doctor says he has "never met" Henry VIII (p74); but the sixth Doctor says he has in *The Marian Conspiracy*, and is seen doing so in *Recorded Time and Other Stories*: "Recorded Time".
730 "The Gift"
731 *Iris S2: The Panda Invasion*
732 *Iris: Enter Wildthyme*. This happens "four hundred years" before the destination they flee to, a Shirley Bassey concert (so, likely the twentieth century, but possibly the twenty first).
733 *Terror Firma*. It's unclear if this refers to the same occasion mentioned in *The Sensorites*.
734 *The Stones of Blood*. The dissolution of the monasteries took place in the fifteen-thirties.
735 *Black Orchid*
736 *A Town Called Mercy*
737 Dating *The Power of Three* (X7.4) - This is separate from the time Rory's phone charger was left in the King's en suite (*A Town Called Mercy*).
738 *Unbound: A Storm of Angels*. Date unknown, but Henry VIII lived 1509-1547.

drew the sixth Doctor.[715] The tenth Doctor learned how to sculpt from Michelangelo.[716] The Monk owned a cupid that Michelangelo had sculpted.[717]

The Baobhan Sith, and their empire, were all but exterminated in a galactic war. A few Baobhan females crashed in Yorkshire, and feasted upon the locals until a Sisterhood killed them. One Baobhan survived, trapped within a pile of rocks that became known as Lucifer's Tombstone. The village of Thornton Rising grew up around it.[718]

In 1514, a Sontaran ship crashed near Mount Omei in China. A monk, Yueh Kuang, investigated the starfall. The Sontarans taught him martial arts for three months. He then returned to share his new knowledge with his fellow monks, deposed Abbot Hsiang and took over as Abbot.[719]

1514 - THE RAVELLI CONSPIRACY[720] -> Pope Leo X increasingly was made to understand that the Ravelli family sought to assassinate him, in revenge for the Pope's brother – Guiliano de Medici, the ruler of Florence – having executed their eldest son last winter. The statesman Niccolo Machiavelli was under house arrest, deemed an enemy of the Medicis, but drew the first Doctor, Vicki and Steven into a complicated and devious plan to regain his power. The Pope became fond of Vicki – as it was expected that he should enjoy female company, he asked her to become his consort, a cover story for his true orientation.

The Doctor deduced that Guiliano and Machiavelli had invented the Ravellis: an "enemy" by which Guiliano could justify a crackdown on his enemies, and Machiavelli could regain the Pope's favour. The Pope punished Machiavelli by publishing his grand opus on how government should function, ruining his reputation for years to come. The travellers timed the TARDIS' dematerialisation so that Guiliano became convinced of his brother's divine power, whereupon the Pope made Guiliano a Cardinal.

c 1516 - DC 3: THE DOOMSDAY CHRONOMETER[721] -> The Revelation Sect seeded clues as to their operations into Leonardo da Vinci's artwork. While River Song distracted Leonardo with a game of tiddlywinks, Helen Sinclair grabbed paintings of his – including *The Climbing Maiden with Foal* and *Church of Brindisi* – that would be lost to history. Leonardo proved a bad loser, so the two ladies made their escape into time...

The Eight, now posing as Brother Octavian, stowed himself aboard the Clocksmith's TARDIS and went to Rome, 2016.

Guieseppe di Cattivo died in 1518 in a lunatic asylum.[722] The Doctor thought that he invented the expression "mind like a sieve".[723] **Cortez landed in South America.**[724] A fragment from the Omnim planet fell to Earth and was carved into an Aztec stone knife of sacrifice. The knife was included in the plundered treasure aboard the Spanish ship *Santa Isabella*, but the crew surrendered the knife to English raiders. The hilt was taken to Madrid.[725] The Doctor met the magician Heinrich Cornelius Agrippa von Netteshiem, and thought him an example of how dark powers destroyed great talent.[726]

1522 (summer) - "Dragon's Claw"[727] -> For years, Japanese pirates attacked ports along the coast of the East China Sea. The Shaolin monks of Mount Omei repelled one such group. Abbot Yueh Kuang, their leader, had an advanced energy weapon. The fourth Doctor, Sharon and K9 arrived and found people killed by the gun. They were captured by the monks and taken four hundred miles to their monastery, where the Doctor discovered they'd been taught martial arts by the mysterious "eighteen bronze men". The Doctor snuck into the Hall of the Eighteen Bronze Men and survived a series of death traps to discover a group of Sontarans. The aliens were planting hypnotic commands in the monks, creating a deadly fighting force. The Doctor discovered their crashed ship, and learned its transmitter was damaged. The Sontarans needed a rock crystal to repair it, and only the Emperor had one large enough. The Doctor returned to the monastery, and one of the monks, Chang, slew the Sontarans in a hypnotic killing frenzy.

The Trib Museum was established in 1528. Its treasures would include fifteenth-century longbows from Earth.[728]

Henry VIII

On one of their earliest visits to Earth, the first Doctor and Susan met Henry VIII, who sent them to the Tower after the Doctor threw a parson's nose back at the King. The TARDIS had landed in the Tower, and this enabled the Doctor and Susan to make good their escape.[729] The Doctor had six wedding invitations from Henry VIII.[730] An early incarnation of Iris Wildthyme met Henry VIII and two of his wives – and a good time was had by all.[731] Iris and Panda hobnobbed at Hampton Court, then left for the future to avoid being beheaded.[732]

King Henry VIII mistook the Doctor for a jester.[733] Henry VIII dissolved The Convent of Little Sisters of St Gudula.[734] Priests from around the country hid at Cranleigh Hall.[735] Rory Williams left his phone charger in Henry VIII's en suite.[736]

THE POWER OF THREE[737] -> Amy Pond accidentally married Henry VIII on a trip through time intended to celebrate her wedding anniversary to Rory Williams.

= Spain surrendered when Henry VIII, a.k.a. Henry Glorianus, sent his English Armada there.[738]

By the 1530s, the Spanish knew of an Incan myth about a fire god. It was based on the "burning" sentience.[739]

1533 (19th July) - SJA: LOST IN TIME[740] **->** Rani Chandra was transported back in time to find a piece of chronosteel, and met the doomed Queen Lady Jane Grey on the last day of her nine-day reign. The chronosteel had adopted the form of a dagger and threatened to derail history, but Rani prevented a Protestant from using the blade to martyr the Queen. Rani returned with the item to 2010.

Superstitious townsfolk in London burned a World War I soldier at the stake, after a Weeping Angel caused him to suddenly manifest in 1535.[741]

1536 (4th May) - RECORDED TIME AND OTHER STORIES: "Recorded Time"[742] **->** Anne Boleyn learned that King Henry VIII wanted his time-rewriting Scrivener to make him the immortal King of Time. She used the Scrivener's phoenix pen to summon the sixth Doctor and Peri, who became one of the Queen's ladies in waiting. Henry proposed marriage to Peri. He also exacted venge-

ance on the Queen, making the Scrivener write that she was an adulterer, a sorceress and had a sixth finger on one hand. The Scrivener expired after defying the King's wish that the Queen be burned alive, writing instead that she would receive a clean sword-strike to the head. The Doctor destroyed the phoenix pen.

The Doctor witnessed the execution of Anne Boleyn.[743]

1538 (18th May) - DC 3: THE EIGHTH PIECE / THE DOOMSDAY CHRONOMETER[744] **->** The eighth Doctor searched for a Doomsday Chronometer piece in England, but for his trouble wound up on Thomas Cromwell's rack as a suspected Papal spy. Risolva, the Queen of the Solvers, purchased the Doctor's freedom so he could save her people. After they had left for 2016, Cromwell covered up the Doctor's unearthly visitation by drafting a document confirming his execution.

In 1540, under the reign of King James V, a shooting star landed near the Torchwood Estate in Scotland. Only a single cell of an alien – a werewolf – survived. In the generations to come, the cell would take host

739 *The Burning*
740 Dating *SJA: Lost in Time* (*SJA* 4.5) - The date is given.
741 *The Tenth Doctor Year One*: "The Weeping Angels of Mons"
742 Dating *Recorded Time and Other Stories*: "Recorded Time" (BF #150a) - King Henry VIII states the exact day. Anne Boleyn was killed about two weeks later, on 19th May. That Anne is still at liberty – and arguing with Henry in the court about his affairs – is a bit ahistorical; in real life, she was arrested on 2nd May and imprisoned in the Tower of London.
743 *Deadly Reunion*, unrelated to the sixth Doctor meeting Boleyn in *Recorded Time and Other Stories*: "Recorded Time". Boleyn was executed on 19th May, 1536.
744 Dating *DC 3: The Eighth Piece* and *DC 3: The Doomsday Chronometer* (BF DC #3.2-3.3) - A parchment lists the exact date of the Doctor's "execution". As if to demonstrate that people sometimes speak in approximations, the Doctor tells Cromwell: "So you're inviting me in for tea... oh no, 1500. You don't have any yet."
745 *Tooth and Claw* (TV)
746 *Benny: The Vampire Curse*: "Possum Kingdom". The Tigra, a.k.a. the Tiwa, are first mentioned in 1541 by the conquistador Francisco Coronado, although Nepesht's sojourn with them could predate that.
747 Dating *The Jade Pyramid* (BBC *DW* audiobook #10) - The Doctor and the blurb vaguely identify the period as "medieval Japan". A much earlier version of this story was set in Korea and dated between 1592 and 1598. Foreigners from across the seas are mentioned, possi-

bly denoting the Portuguese, who arrived in 1543. Firearms are cited in such a way that they don't appear to be common. Ultimately, while author Martin Day didn't have a year in mind for the final version of *The Jade Pyramid*, he was inclined to think that it was during the early years of Ashikaga Yoshiteru's shogunate, which lasted 1546-1564. But even Day concedes that this was more of a generalisation on his part than a hard and fast rule.
748 Dating *Sleepers in the Dust* (BBC *DW* audiobook #20) - It's "three hundred years" back from the Doctor and Rory's visit to Nadurniss in the nineteenth century.
749 "Ten years" before *The Room with No Doors*.
750 *Hexagora*
751 *The King of Terror*
752 *The Ark in Space*. Nostradamus lived from 1503-1566, and published his prophecies in 1556.
753 Dating *The Marian Conspiracy* (BF #6) - It is one month after the Wyatt Uprising, at the end of 1554.
754 *The Curse of Peladon*, although the Doctor admits he might be confusing it with the Coronation of Queen Victoria. Elizabeth was Queen from 1558, but the Coronation wasn't until the following year.
755 *Cat's Cradle: Witch Mark*. There wasn't an Earl of Essex at the time of Elizabeth's Coronation.
756 *Terror Firma*. Elizabeth ruled 1558-1603.
757 *Only Human*
758 Dating *The Room with No Doors* (NA #59) - It is "probably March 1560", and "early spring".
759 Dating *The Day of the Doctor* (X7.15) - The year is given in a caption.

after host and grow stronger. **The local monks in the Glen of St Catherine tended to the creature, and made plans to facilitate the Empire of the Wolf.**[745]

The Utlunta were slavers who purportedly drained the blood of other races to power their organic spaceships. The leader of a benevolent race trapped the Utlunta, and himself, in a pocket universe. He went mad, forgot his purpose and fled back to the proper universe – which also freed Lilu, the last Utlunta. While Lilu and her spaceship were pitched forward to the fifty-first century, the leader wound up with the Tigua Indians of pre-Columbian America. He became the source of a Comanche legend of the demon Nepesht and his vampiric offspring.[746]

c 1550 - THE JADE PYRAMID[747] **->** The ruler of Japan sent his samurai to collect the prized jade pyramid in the town of Kokan, and to bring it to Kyoto. The eleventh Doctor and Amy prevented bloodshed and made off with the pyramid. They also disabled a spaceship and the Otoroshi that it animated.

c 1550 - SLEEPERS IN THE DUST[748] **->** The rat-like, six-eyed Nadurni founded an empire on the strength of their scientific achievements. The eleventh Doctor and Rory traveled back in time to the Nadurni homeworld, Nadurniss, and went to the High Directorate of Science to find a cure for the bacteria killing Amy in the thirty-ninth century. Mordax – the Nadurni Science Dictator and Head of Biological Weapons – captured them and extracted the Doctor's DNA for use in his new creations: the Prokarians, enormous colonies of sentient bacteria that could turn a target population into incubators for Prokarian spawn.

The Doctor's regenerative abilities greatly enhanced the Prokarian biomass; in time, they brought Nadurniss to ruin, averting an expanded Nadurni conquest. Mordax's own creations smothered him. The Doctor added a biological trigger to the Prokarian genome, making it vulnerable to Rory's DNA, then returned with Rory to the thirty-ninth century.

Around 1550, a jiki-ketsu-gaki, or vampire, attacked the Doctor in Japan. He was buried in a snowdrift and spent three months recovering in a monastery. He confronted the vampire, let her drain his blood until she was sated and fell asleep – and then burnt down her castle.[749]

Hexagoran scouts reconnoitered sixteenth-century London, but judged Earth as unsuitable for colonisation.[750] The Canavitchi supplied Nostradamus with many of his prophecies.[751] **The fourth Doctor's long scarf was made by Madame Nostradamus, "a witty little knitter".**[752]

1555 (January) - THE MARIAN CONSPIRACY[753] **->** The sixth Doctor helped Evelyn Smythe explore her ancestry. While the Doctor visited the court of Queen Mary,

Evelyn stumbled on a Protestant plot to poison the Queen and replace her with Elizabeth. The time travellers were both imprisoned in the Tower of London. They met Reverend Thomas Smith, Evelyn's ancestor, before escaping and preventing the assassination.

The Elizabethan Age

The Doctor attended the Coronation of Queen Elizabeth I.[754] The Doctor was appalled by the Earl of Essex's behaviour at the Coronation.[755] The eighth Doctor, Samson and Gemma also visited the Court of Queen Elizabeth.[756] Jack Harkness had fun with a lady at Elizabeth's court.[757]

1560 (spring) - THE ROOM WITH NO DOORS[758] **->** A Kapteynian slave escaped from a Caxtarid slaver ship, and its capsule crashed in the Han region of Japan. Within days, the Victorian time traveller Penelope Gate also visited Japan. A month later, the seventh Doctor and Chris Cwej arrived and became embroiled in a dispute between rival warlords Guffuu Kocho and Umemi, both wanting possession of the capsule. The Doctor managed to prevent either of them from taking control of it.

The Tenth Doctor Marries Elizabeth I

lgtw - 1562 - THE DAY OF THE DOCTOR[759] **->** During a pleasant outdoor excursion and picnic, the tenth Doctor proposed marriage to Queen Elizabeth I... as a ruse, as he wrongly believed she was a Zygon in disguise. The Doctor's white horse transformed into the Zygon in question, then into Elizabeth's double.

The Moment sought to give the War Doctor perspective into the momentous decision he was facing by creating time portals – these enabled the eleventh Doctor to come through from the twenty-first century, and the War Doctor from the final day of the Last Great Time War. Clara Oswald also arrived from the twenty-first century via a vortex manipulator.

The Zygons who had infiltrated Elizabeth's court judged Earth in this era as too primitive, and went into stasis within multi-dimensional Gallifreyan paintings so they could invade Earth some centuries on. The Queen killed her doppelganger, but insisted that the tenth Doctor fulfill his proposal. They were married. Afterwards, the tenth Doctor, the eleventh Doctor, the War Doctor and Clara returned to the future by placing themselves in stasis within the painting *No More*, a.k.a. *Gallifrey Falls*...

The Queen later named the Doctor as curator of the Under Gallery, a clandestine cache of art considered a danger to the realm. Its holdings included a painting of the Queen with the tenth Doctor.

The tenth Doctor married and deflowered Elizabeth I.[760] **The Queen waited in a glade to elope with the Doctor.**[761] Elizabeth I knighted the Doctor for "more intimate reasons" than Victoria would in future.[762]

Iris saved the fourth Doctor and Sarah Jane in Scotland, in an escapade involving Mary Queen of Scots – who crocheted Iris a nice seat cushion.[763] The Doctor advised Mary Queen of Scots to change her muckspreader.[764] The Doctor taught Tycho Brahe everything he knew about astronomy.[765]

"The Beast" were flying creatures that would move from planet to planet by way of dimensional interfaces, and invisibly feed off other beings. This was normally harmless, but on the planet Benelisa, the Beast wiped out the native populace as their numbers were few. The Beast moved on, but at least one Benelisan construct – Azoth – endured and pledged to eradicate the Beast.[766]

In 1564, an Agent of the Council of Eight prevented an Italian blacksmith from gaining the insight needed to invent the steam engine.[767] The Fulgurites – aliens who looked like mushroom-headed men – secretly established themselves on Earth and traded various commodities with other planets.[768] The Doctor said that the stories didn't lie: Ivan the Terrible really was *that* terrible.[769]

lgtw - c 1566 - 1STD V2: THE PLAGUE OF DREAMS[770]

-> During their final assault on Gallifrey in the Last Great Time War, the Daleks worked to undermine the Doctor's timeline. As the first Doctor, Polly and Ben found themselves in Wyld Heath, the Daleks released a psychoactive virus that converted dreams into reality. Infected persons generated menaces such as dragons; the Doctor and Ben also succumbed and projected steam-powered robots and pirates. The Player, a Time Lord touring through the six-

---

760 *The End of Time, The Beast Below, Amy's Choice.*

761 *The Wedding of River Song*

762 *"A Fairytale Life"*

763 *Verdigris.* Mary Queen of Scots ruled 1542-1567.

764 *Tragedy Day*

765 *Revenge of the Swarm.* Brahe lived 1546-1601.

766 *The Taint.* The Beast arrive on Earth in 1944, according to *Autumn Mist.*

767 *Sometime Never*

768 "Centuries" before *The Perpetual Bond.*

769 *Thin Ice* (BF). Ivan ruled 1533 to 1584.

770 Dating *The Plague of Dreams* (BF CC #11.4) - The Time Lords monitoring the situation say it's the sixteenth century; the Doctor judges the same, from the appearance of the houses. The Doctor and the Player can't decide if *A Midsummer Night's Dream* has been written yet; that happened 1595-1596.

771 *Leth-St: The Daughters of Earth* (ch2).

772 "Well over four hundred years" before *Leth-St: The Forgotten Son* (ch11).

773 "Centuries" before *The First Sontarans.*

774 "Three centuries" before *A Town Called Mercy.*

775 Dating *The Massacre* (3.5) - The first three episodes take place over a single day each, the last picks up nearly twenty-four hours after the end of the third late on the evening of the 23rd and runs into the 24th. The Admiral Gaspar de Coligny was shot on the 22nd. This story is sometimes referred to as *The Massacre of St Bartholomew's Eve*, based on some production documents, but this is historically erroneous. The event is more accurately named "the massacre of St Bartholomew's *Day*". Nonetheless, in *Masquerade*, the Doctor refers to the events of this story as "The Massacre of St Bartholomew's Eve".

776 *The Time of the Daleks,* which implies that Shakespeare used some of the names of individuals he met in the future in plays such as *Hamlet, King Lear, Twelfth Night, Titus Andronicus* and *The Tempest.*

777 "Four hundred years" before *Hide.*

778 *The Cloisters of Terror.* The Wakefield Mystery Plays were thirty-two Bible-based plays that were most likely enacted in Wakefield, England, prior to 1576.

779 "The Broken Man". Rudolf II reigned as Emperor from 1576 to 1612. In real life, Rabbi Judah Loew Ben Bezalel (1525-1609), a.k.a. the Maharal of Prague, is a central figure in a nineteenth-century legend about the Golem.

780 Dating *The Vampires of Venice* (X5.6) - The opening caption says "Venice 1580". This is another story affected by the Cracks in Time, so it's possible – given that the Saturnynians would never have come to Venice but for benefit of one – that this story was removed from history when the cracks were sealed (see the Cracks in Time sidebar, however, for why this probably isn't the case). The Doctor references this story's "sexy fish vampires" in *A Good Man Goes to War*, giving no indication that they're now the stuff of alternate history.

The aliens are called "Saturnynians" on the BBC website, "Saturnynes" in *Doctor Who: The Encyclopedia.* The story ends with the canals of Venice still containing ten thousand Saturnynian males, and it's the subject of fan-conjecture that, somehow, they become the progenitors of the fish-people seen in *The Stones of Venice.*

781 *Timewyrm: Revelation*

782 *The Stones of Blood*

783 *Unbound: A Storm of Angels.* In real life, Henry VIII initiated construction of Nonsuch Palace in Surrey, and it stood until 1682-83, when the Countess of Castlemaine had it pulled down to pay off her debts.

784 Dating *TimeH: Child of Time* (TimeH #11) - The year is given (p68). It's possible that these events occur in an alternate timeline; see the 2586 entry of this story.

785 Dating *The Flames of Cadiz* (BF CC #7.7) - The year is given. Ian comments that it's "Scorching, even for April." Historically, Drake's fleet entered the Bay of Cadiz on 19th April, 1587. *Don Quixote* was published in two

teenth century, infected himself and Polly so they could stage these events in a shared dreamscape, to spread a cure. Afterward, the Player convinced the Doctor to right his timeline by going to the South Pole, 1986.

The Lethbridge-Stewart Bloodline Begins

William Stewart, the first Lethbridge-Stewart on record, was born in 1567. He was related to the Stuart Kings, and friends with James VI when he ascended to the English throne in 1603. Stewart married Mary Lethbridge, the daughter of the influential Lethbridge family in England, on condition that their surnames were cojoined. Stewart's family mostly stayed in Scotland, while Mary's relations remained English.[771]

The Lethbridge-Stewarts had a history of military service that went back to when the Stewarts of Lanark and the Lethbridges of Devon intermarried.[772]

The Rutans conquered the Killiban Confederacy, which had one of the largest standing armies in Earth's sector of space.[773] **Abaraxas Security software began incinerating intruders.**[774]

1572 (21st-24th August) - THE MASSACRE[775] **-> The first Doctor and Steven arrived in Paris in August 1572. The Protestants of the city, the Huguenots, were massing to celebrate the wedding of Henry of Navarre to Princess Marguerite. Yet they lived in fear of the Catholic majority, particularly the Queen Mother – Catherine de Medici – and the ruthless Abbot of Amboise. One hundred Huguenots had been killed at Wassy ten years ago, and a full-scale massacre was now instigated. The Doctor and Steven fled and left Anne Chaplet, a serving girl befriended by Steven, behind to her fate. Immediately thereafter, they arrived in the 1960s and met Dodo Chaplet, whom they believed to be Anne's descendant.**

Rebels from the mid-twenty-first century kidnapped the young Shakespeare to prevent time-travelling Daleks assassinating him. This removed Shakespeare from time, but history was restored upon his safe return.

> (=) In a version of history without Shakespeare, the Daleks had a compound in Warwick in 1572.[776]

Caliburn House was built.[777] The Doctor saw one of the Wakefield Mystery Plays.[778]

Sixteenth-century Prague served as a tolerant, diversified trading centre until the Mavora – two-dimensional energy panes that fed on fear and distrust – spread the lie that Jews were slaughtering Christian children in dark ritu-

als. In the violence to follow, Gerhard Frankel, a scholar in Emperor Rudolf II's court, found a sphere of psychic metal. Rabbi Judah Loew Ben Bezalel worked the material into a Golem, and Frankel endowed the creature with his mind. The Frankel-Golem contained the Mavora within a book, *The Sorrows of Prague*. It was stored in the archives of Bezalel's synagogue until 1989.[779]

1580 - THE VAMPIRES OF VENICE[780] **-> The planet Saturnyne was "lost" to the Silence, but a small group of fish-like Saturnynians escaped through a Crack in Time and arrived at Venice. Their leader used a perception filter to pose as Signora Rosanna Calvierri, a powerful figure who convinced the Venetians that the surrounding countryside was afflicted with plague. Calvierri also established an exclusive school – a means of genetically altering the girls there into Sisters of the Water, mates for the males. The human survival instinct would override the Sisters' perception filters in time of danger, making them look like vampires.**

The eleventh Doctor, Amy and Rory stopped Calvierri from sinking Venice with an earthquake device, thus turning the city into the Saturnynians' new domain. Calvierri killed herself, taunting the Doctor that he had wiped out another species.

In 1582, the Doctor visited Rome while trying to track the Timewyrm.[781] **Boscombe Hall was built on the site of the Convent of the Little Sisters of St Gudula in the late sixteenth century.**[782]

> = A space station, Nonsuch Palace, was constructed in Earth orbit. In 1585, Sir Francis Drake set sail in his spaceship, the *Golden Hind*, to begin charting the great asteroid reef.[783]

1586 - TIMEH: CHILD OF TIME[784] **->** The cult Sodality sought further power and summoned the Daemon Mastho during a masked ball at the Palazzo Bembo, Venice. Mastho decried Sodality, and ordered that the group destroy the time-sensitives and channellers it had created, lest their existence interfere with the Daemons' experiments on humanity. Sodality was given exactly one millennium to complete this task; Mastho threatened to return at that time, and to destroy the world if Sodality failed.

1587 (April) - THE FLAMES OF CADIZ[785] **->** The execution of Mary, Queen of Scots had moved England and Spain closer to war. The first Doctor, Ian, Barbara and Susan witnessed religious strife in Saville, and Ian was arrested for trying to stop agents of the Church from burning the house of a paper-merchant family. Barbara and Susan rescued their friends after the Doctor unsuccessfully impersonated a Cardinal, and was arrested while trying to persuade King Phillip II to release Ian.

The Doctor's quartet befriended Don Miguel, a supplier of the Armada intending to invade England. Ian set off with a fellow ex-prisoner, Esteban Aribi – Sir Francis Drake's contact – to tell Drake to attack the Spanish fleet at Cadiz as history dictated. The Doctor wrongly believed that Ian was trying to change history, leading to an escapade with the Doctor fruitlessly racing along on a burro in front of a burning windmill. Drake heeded Ian and Esteban's information, and directed his fleet to attack the supply ships at Cadiz – an event called "the Singeing of the King of Spain's Beard". The Spanish Armada was delayed from moving against England for a year.

In future, Don Miguel – the author Cervantes, fully convinced the Doctor was some sort of madman – incorporated these events into *Don Quixote*.

The Doctor met Cervantes.[786] **The West Wing of Chase Mansion was completed in 1587.**[787] The Doctor may have been at the execution of Mary, Queen of Scots.[788]

Governor John White left the Roanoke colony to bring back needed supplies from England. He would return in 1590 to find the colony abandoned.[789] In 1587, the Greld wiped out the Roanoke colony in the New World. They implanted the colonists with components for a meta-cobalt bomb, hoping to sabotage the Armageddon Convention. Christopher Marlowe, an agent of the crown, investigated the tragedy but escaped.[791] A member of the timeship *Makaron* claimed responsibility for the disappearance of the Roanoke colonists.[792]

The Spanish Armada

The Doctor met Francis Drake just before he faced the Spanish Armada.[793] He played bowls with Drake and met William Cecil at Elizabeth's court.[794] The Doctor let Drake win at bowls so Drake could leave early to face the Spanish Armada on time.[795] The first Doctor and Dodo spent some time aboard the *Golden Hind*.[796]

An Agent of the Council of Eight released a single butterfly in Africa. The slight disturbance it caused in the atmosphere triggered a storm that helped to destroy the Armada. The Council of Eight's leader, Octan, arrived in 1588 to try and stop this. The Agent, unable to recognise Octan, pushed him into the Time Vortex.[797]

1588 (19th July) - THE LOST MAGIC[798] **->** John Dee learned many secrets by communing through an obsidian mirror – a gift from Sir Francis Drake – with his "angel", Merdinia. Drake subsequently plundered Dee's journals (many of which were expressed in Enochian, a.k.a. Old High Gallifreyan), branded himself with Gallifreyan tattoos and summoned the time-warping Tenebrous Glist to destroy the Spanish Armada. The twelfth Doctor, travelling with the siblings Alex and Brandon Yow, feared Drake's power-mad efforts would destroy the world.

halves, in 1605 and 1615. In real life, Cervantes was indeed a purveyor for the Spanish Armada.

786 *Endgame* (EDA), which can be retroactively taken to mean *The Flames of Cadiz*.

787 *The Seeds of Doom*

788 *EarthWorld.* This was in 1587.

789 Said to happen "three years" before *J&L: Voyage to the New World* (so, 1587), although White's diary also says he left the colony in 1586. Historically, he sailed for England in late 1587.

790 *The Empire of Glass,* which consistently renders "Roanoke" as "Roanoake".

791 *The Legends of Ashildr:* "The Fortunate Isles"

792 *Four to Doomsday*

793 *The Marian Conspiracy*

794 *Birthright*

795 *Maker of Demons.* The *Golden Hind,* Sir Francis Drake's ship, was originally named the *Pelican,* but renamed in 1578.

796 "Dead Man's Hand"

797 *Sometime Never*

798 Dating *The Lost Magic* (BBC *DW* audiobook #28) - The exact day, when the Spanish Armada was historically sighted, is given.

799 Dating *PHP: The Devil's Armada* (BF *PHP* #1.2) - The year is given. The story begins some days in advance of the Spanish Armada setting sail, and ends not long after the Doctor and Leela witness its defeat in August of that year.

800 Dating *Unbound: A Storm of Angels* (BF *Unbound* #7) - The year is given. It's "twenty days" before "St Barnabas' Eve", a creation of this alternate timeline.

801 Dating "The Doctor and the Nurse" (IDW Vol. 4 #3-4) - A caption says: "1588 A.D."

802 "Dead Man's Hand"

803 *The Empire of Glass*

804 *Loups-Garoux*

805 "Seven centuries" before *Zaltys* [c.2290].

806 Dating *Voyage to the New World* (*J&L* #4.6/BF *DW* Special Release #2) - The blurb says that it's "Roanoke Island, 1590", the Doctor broad-brushes it as "the 1590s", and John White's journal names the days of 17th, 18th and 19th August. Historically, White returned to Roanoke on 18th August, 1590.

The Empire of Glass provides an alternate explanation as to what became of the Roanoke colonists. The enduring enigma of the Roanoke colony (to this day, no firm evidence exists as to the colonists' fate) might mean that it's an Unfixed Point in Time.

The Glist de-regenerated the Doctor back to being a young boy age seven or eight, but Alex completed a circuit that banished the creature. Drake awoke sans tattoos or memory of these events, and the young Doctor advised him on how to defeat the Armada. Merdinia sent through the mirror an elixir that restored the Doctor to normal. Sensing the Sisterhood of Karn's involvement, the Doctor, Alex and Brandon left to confront Ohila...

1588 (August) - PHP: THE DEVIL'S ARMADA[799] ->

The fourth Doctor and Leela intervened as William Redcliffe hunted Catholic priests on behalf of Queen Elizabeth I, and rescued Father D'Arcy from his torture rack. On behalf of Sir Robert Harney, one of the Queen's fleet commanders, the Doctor made a rousing speech to the Privy Council that they should trust their men of the sea – such as John Hawkins, Lord Howard and the pirate Francis Drake – to protect England from the oncoming Spanish invasion.

The Doctor and Leela witnessed the Spanish Armada's defeat, and realised that some Vituperon – devil-like imps from another dimension – were feeding on the hysteria of these events, a prelude to their overrunning Earth. Redcliffe sacrificed himself to hold the First of the Vituperon at bay as the Doctor modified the TARDIS' dimensional field to seal off the Vituperon realm, forever denying it access to Earth's reality.

= 1588 - UNBOUND: A STORM OF ANGELS[800] -> Jewel-like beings with a collective mind had developed in the Sol System's asteroid belt, and yearned for a less isolated existence. They mentally appeared to John Dee as angels, and through him guided the *Golden Hind* to their location. Sir Francis Drake's men dug up three hundred caskets of the jewels, and set sail to give them to the publicly elected Empress of half of Earth: Gloriana, Queen Elizabeth I.

The alt-first Doctor, accompanied by the Susan fashioned by his Probability Generator, temporarily eluded Agent Zero by grounding the TARDIS in this time. The Ship disguised itself as a barrel, and landed on the *Hind* as Mayan priests sensed that Drake's ship contained a "jeweled demon". The jewel-creatures manifested as a storm of angels and destroyed the oncoming Mayan galleons, then swept the *Hind* from Mars to Earth in fifteen minutes.

At Nonsuch Palace in Earth orbit, the jewel-creatures physically invaded and took control of many in Elizabeth's court, and transformed Agent Zero into their envoy. The real Susan arrived from Gallifrey, and the Doctor tricked the jewel-people, including Zero, into dancing, which shook their physical forms apart. The conflict against the jewel-creatures caused Nonsuch Palace to fall to Earth as Elizabeth and her

allies escaped aboard the *Hind*. The Queen let the people elect a new Gloriana while she and Drake set sail to dispose of the jewel-creatures' motherstone.

Susan regretted not leaving Gallifrey with her grandfather, and agreed with him that they couldn't let people suffer because it was historically necessary. The Doctor's Probability Generator was failing, and so the Susan copy returned to Gallifrey to confuse the High Council while the genuine article posed as her restored doppelganger. The Doctor privately knew the two had switched places, but welcomed new travels with his granddaughter.

1588 - "The Doctor and the Nurse"[801] -> Rory popped his head outside the TARDIS, saw a horse in London, 1588, and confirmed that he and the Doctor had not reached 1814 as intended.

The mind-parasite Es'Cartrss, thrown back in time by the TARDIS' explosion in 2010, hosted itself in the alien auditor Sondrah.[802] Around 1589, Irving Braxiatel began a diplomatic effort that culminated in the signing of the Armageddon Convention.[803] On 28th October of the same year, the ancient werewolf Pieter Stubbe escaped after being sentenced to death for sorcery in Cologne.[804]

The third Doctor and Jo curtailed an outbreak of Necrobiologicals, a.k.a. vampires, on the planet Sekhmet. Nonetheless, some hundreds escaped aboard the spaceship *Exemplar*, and hid on the planet Occhinos for seven centuries.[805]

(=) 1590 (August) - J&L: VOYAGE TO THE NEW WORLD[806] -> The sixth Doctor, Professor Litefoot and Henry Gordon Jago found that the Semetran Interlude – owing to the pact made with Sir Walter Raleigh in 1092 – had lured the colonists of Roanoke, Virginia, away to the island of Croatoan. The Interlude manifested as children, then "bonded" with the colonists, reducing them to a ghostly state. The Doctor's trio found the TARDIS, which had been buried for nearly five hundred years, and forged a communications link with its past self in 1592. The Doctor convinced an Algonquin named Wanchese to avert this timeline...

The Roanoke colonists remained on Croatoan island and went native. Virginia Dare, John White's granddaughter, was the first child born in the Americas to English parents. The sixth Doctor attempted to take Jago and Litefoot back home, but accidentally deposited them in 1968 instead...

c 1592 (summer) - POINT OF ENTRY[807] **->** The Omnim, largely existing as mental energy in rogue asteroid D359XQ2, locked onto the TARDIS' flight trail as a means of drawing close to Earth. A Spaniard, Don Lorentho Velez, found the Omnim-tainted stone hilt in Madrid, and so fell under the Omnim's power. He was made to find the Omnim stone knife the English had taken from the Aztecs, and recruited help from the dramatist Christopher Marlowe – an agent of the crown, who was busy writing *The Tragical History of the Life and Death of Doctor Faustus* – by allowing him to experience astral projection. The sixth Doctor and Peri destroyed the Omnim as they attempted to manifest during a lunar eclipse. Marlowe wrote a line in *Doctor Faustus* ("Where the philosopher ceases, the Doctor begins") in the Doctor's honour.

(=) In 1592, the sixth Doctor's TARDIS, having been seized at Roanoke by John White, came into the Sir Walter Raleigh's possession. Raleigh activated the Ship's Fast Return Switch, but his tinkering with the console sent the Ship back to the correct location, albeit five hundred centuries too early. The Doctor communed with the TARDIS from 1590, and directed Wanchese to render Raleigh unconscious and send the Ship back to 1092 without him.[808]

Christopher Marlowe continued serving as a secret agent of the British government. He conspired with Walsingham, the Secretary of State, to fake his death.[809]

Towards the end of the sixteenth century, the Xaranti attacked a Zygon fleet. A Zygon ship survived the fighting

---

807 Dating *Point of Entry* (BF LS #1.6) - The Doctor judges that they've arrived "1590 local time, or thereabouts. The Elizabethan Age." A slightly later dating, however, is indicated in the Doctor telling Peri that while "Shakespeare's hardly started yet", they can potentially see *Henry VI, Part 1, Part 2* and *Part 3*. The real-life evidence suggests that at the very earliest, those three plays were written in 1591, and first performed no later than September 1592. Whatever the case, it's after Marlowe's *Tamburlaine* - the first part of which was first performed in late 1587 - has been performed for Queen Elizabeth I.

Certainly, *Point of Entry* happens before Marlowe's real-life death on 30th May, 1593 – although *The Empire of Glass* details how he faked his demise. That story and *Point of Entry* are reasonably compatible as far as Marlowe's life is concerned, although the sixth Doctor curiously tells Peri that Marlowe – as history claims, and as the Doctor should know better from *The Empire of Glass* – will die young in a bar fight.

It's twice said to be summer.

808 *J&L: Voyage to the New World*

809 *The Empire of Glass*. History tells us Marlowe died on 30th May, 1593.

810 "Three centuries" before *The Bodysnatchers*. This is a different ship from the one seen in *Terror of the Zygons*.

811 "Hundreds of years" before *Jago & Litefoot & Strax*.

812 SHAKESPEARE: Going on just the information in the television series, the Doctor has met Shakespeare at least three times. Taking all the other media into account, we can infer that the Doctor has met Shakespeare a bare minimum of eight separate occasions, in at least six incarnations.

We actually see five of these meetings. In chronological order of Shakespeare's life, these are *The Time of the Daleks* (when Shakespeare is a child), "A Groatsworth of Wit" (set in 1592), *The Kingmaker* (set in 1597, and in which Shakespeare is replaced by Richard III), *The Shakespeare Code* (set in 1599) and *The Empire of Glass* (set in 1609, but with an epilogue that shows Shakespeare's death in 1616). Additionally, *The Chase* has the first Doctor, Ian, Barbara and Vicki using the Time-Space Visualizer to observe Shakespeare in the court of Elizabeth I, presumably at some point between *The Shakespeare Code* (as *Hamlet* has still not been written) and *Hamlet*'s real-life registry in 1602 (years before *The Empire of Glass*, then).

In one regard, this is all far less contradictory than it might seem. None of the stories (save for *The Chase* and *The Shakespeare Code*, in which Shakespeare twice receives inspiration to write *Hamlet*) bear different accounts of the same event. Indeed, none of the adventures even occur in the same year – the closest pairing (*The Kingmaker* and *The Shakespeare Code*) are set two years apart. Taking the general events in the five stories that directly involve Shakespeare, then, at face value is not very difficult.

Two impediments remain, however. One is that Shakespeare does not remotely look or act the same in some of his appearances. All things being equal, it's hard to believe that Shakespeare as voiced by Michael Fenton-Stevens in *The Kingmaker*, as played by Dean Lennox Kelly in *The Shakespeare Code*, and as played by Hugh Walters in *The Chase* are all the same person. (Note that this problem isn't limited to the different *Doctor Who* media, but occurs even in Shakespeare's two appearances on television.) Shakespeare's personality varies wildly between stories, even allowing that we're witnessing different points of his life.

The other problem is that Shakespeare in his later appearances never acknowledges having met a stranger named "the Doctor" before. He is admittedly never seen to meet the same incarnation twice, but it's implausible to think that he never makes a connection between the various men who keep appearing during turbulent and strange events, all of them named "Doctor". *The Kingmaker* actually helps a little in this regard – the Doctor and Shakespeare are on very chummy terms, but Shakespeare dies on Bosworth Field, eliminating the need for Richard III to acknowledge having met the Doctor in *The Time of the Daleks* and crashed on Earth.[810] An ion storm damaged an alien survey ship, which limped into Earth orbit and passively recharged from the mental energy below.[811]

Shakespeare[812]

The Doctor encouraged Shakespeare, a "taciturn" young man, to take up writing.[813] Shakespeare and John Fletcher wrote *Cardenio – A Spanish Comedie*.[814] Iris suspected that Shakespeare's genius owed to his interacting with the universe on an advanced quantum level.[815]

1592 (September) - "A Groatsworth of Wit"[816] **->** The alien Shadeys took Robert Greene, a staunch critic of Shakespeare, from his deathbed and transported him over four hundred years into the future. The ninth Doctor and Rose arrived, hot on Greene's trail. The Doctor quoted from *Richard III* and was mistaken for an actor, while Shakespeare tried to seduce Rose. Greene attacked Shakespeare, but the Doctor suggested that if Greene destroyed the great playwright *now*, Greene himself would lose what little future fame he currently enjoyed. Greene banished the Shadeys and returned to his deathbed.

Caravaggio painted *Narcissus*; the billionaire Neil Redmond would eventually own it.[817]

Richard III Adopts Shakespeare's Identity

1597 - THE KINGMAKER[818] **->** Peri and Erimem watched an exceedingly bad preview of *Richard III*, while the fifth Doctor went boozing at The White Rabbit tavern with his friend William Shakespeare. A loyalist to the Queen, Shakespeare became greatly disturbed by the Doctor's suggestion that in future, suspicion for the murder of Richard III's nephews would fall on Henry Tudor. Shortly afterwards, the Doctor and his companions left for 1485, and Shakespeare – determined to convince Richard to kill his nephews and thereby preserve the Queen's family name – stowed aboard.

Events in 1485 caused the TARDIS to materialise back in 1597 during a subsequent performance of *Richard III*. The genuine King Richard III had stowed away and remained behind as Shakespeare re-entered the TARDIS and met Richard's historical fate on Bosworth Field.

To preserve history, Richard III lived out Shakespeare's life and wrote his remaining plays, historicals, tragedies and comedies. He was moved to write his late brother George into *Henry IV, Part 1*, but kept misspelling Shakespeare's name. The Doctor suggested that Richard look up Francis Bacon to help with his writing.

Shakespeare's only child, Hamnet, had died, so the Doctor relocated Richard's nieces to live with him as "Shakespeare's daughters", Susanna and Judith.

---

and "A Groatsworth of Wit". Obviously, this doesn't explain why Richard himself doesn't acknowledge the Doctor in the next story in the line – *The Shakespeare Code* – or thereafter.

The Kingmaker is a particular sticking point, as it has Richard III living out Shakespeare's life from 1597 onward. This would mean that the "Shakespeare" that the tenth Doctor and Martha meet in *The Shakespeare Code* is actually a disguised Richard III installed by the fifth Doctor... but who is somehow driven to great depression by the death of the original Shakespeare's son, who has acquired two perfectly functional arms and who doesn't limp. It might be best to assume events in *The Kingmaker* happened, then the Time War or some other intervention (allowing for Shakespeare's importance to history) reversed them. This would carry the double benefit of not having to rationalise the conflicting fates of Richard III's nephews/nieces in *The Kingmaker* and *Sometime Never*.

The Shakespeare Notebooks deliberately go overboard in chronicling many, many more meetings between Shakespeare and multiple versions of the Doctor, but it's a toss-up as to how much we're to take it all seriously (see The Shakespeare Notebooks sidebar, in the Appendix).

813 *City of Death.* This unseen encounter would have to be before 1590, when we know Shakespeare was writing, and must have involved one of the Doctor's first four incarnations.

814 *TW: Trace Memory.* Shakespeare and Fletcher are credited as writing the lost play *Cardenio* in a 1653 Stationers' Register that otherwise makes false use of Shakespeare's name. In the *Doctor Who* universe, it appears he and Fletcher did author the work.

815 *Iris* S4: *Iris at the Oche,* which would certainly explain the Carrionites' interest in him in *The Shakespeare Code.*

816 Dating "A Groatsworth of Wit" (*DWM* #363-364) - Greene's death on 3rd September, 1592 is historical record. Greene is famous for dismissing Shakespeare both for plagiarism and because he was mainly – at that time – an actor, not a writer. When Rose asks if the Doctor knows Shakespeare, he says he's "known him for ages. Just not yet". This would suggest that the meeting mentioned in *Planet of Evil* didn't involve too much familiarity.

817 *TW: Uncanny Valley. Narcissus* was painted c.1597-1599; the story doesn't specify that Redmond has the original, but it seems likely. In real life, the Galleria Nazionale d'Arte Antica in Rome owns it.

818 Dating *The Kingmaker* (BF #81) - The date is given. It's believed that *Richard III* was written in 1592-93, and

The grief Shakespeare suffered after Hamnet's death allowed three Carrionites entrance back into history, and they manipulated him in a bid to free their sisters. They also influenced Peter Streete – the architect of the Globe Theatre – to design the stage area with fourteen sides, in accordance with the fourteen stars of the Rexel planetary configuration. Streete lost his mind as a result, and was consigned to Bedlam.[819]

1599 - THE SHAKESPEARE CODE[820] **->** The tenth Doctor and Martha were surprised when a performance of *Love's Labour's Lost* in London ended with an announcement by Shakespeare that the sequel, *Love's Labour's Won*, would debut the following night. Three witch-like Carrionites were manipulating Shakespeare

– *Love's Labour's Won* was embedded with coordinates that would open a spatial rift, and allow the rest of their race freedom. Shakespeare used his command of language to seal the portal and banish the Carrionites; all copies of *Love's Labour's Won* were destroyed.

Shakespeare took note of the Doctor's use of the word "Sycorax"[821], and a few choice phrases. The Doctor and Martha escaped when a wrathful Elizabeth I called for his head – owing to events that hadn't yet happened in the Doctor's personal timeline.

The first Doctor used the Time-Space Visualiser to watch Shakespeare at the court of Elizabeth I. The Queen was interested in Falstaff, but Francis Bacon gave Shakespeare the idea to write *Hamlet*.[822]

---

it was entered into the Register of the Stationers Company on 20th October, 1597 by bookseller Andrew Wise. The Doctor and Shakespeare go drinking at The White Rabbit – a London establishment mentioned in Big Finish projects such as *The Reaping*.

819 *The Shakespeare Code*. Hamnet Shakespeare was buried on 11th August, 1596.

820 Dating *The Shakespeare Code* (X3.2) - The date is given in a caption at the start, and confirmed by the Doctor. In real life, it's thought that *Love's Labour's Lost* was performed in 1597; *Love's Labour's Won* is on a list of Shakespeare's plays dating from 1598. Historically, the Globe Theatre opened in the autumn.

The tenth Doctor claims that he "hasn't met" Queen Elizabeth I yet (he later does so in *The Day of the Doctor*). It's possible he means his current incarnation (which she recognises on sight), as *Birthright* establishes that she's been familiar with the seventh Doctor since at least 1588.

821 The implication is that (among other things) the Doctor inspires Shakespeare to use the name Sycorax – not just the aliens from *The Christmas Invasion*, but also the name of Caliban's mother in Shakespeare's final play, *The Tempest*. (A moon of Uranus is named after the same character.)

822 *The Chase*. Literary scholars disagree when *Hamlet* was written, but we know it was entered in the Stationers' Register in 1602. It was almost certainly written and performed around 1600.

823 *Endgame* (EDA), *The Gallifrey Chronicles*.

824 *The Ultimate Treasure*. *The Merry Wives of Windsor* was written around 1597, but could have been a little later, so this is just possibly the same visit as the one where the Doctor helped with *Hamlet*.

825 *City of Death*. Historically, Shakespeare was known as an actor by 1592, and tradition has it that he continued to act even when he was better known as a writer. This reference seems to contradict the one in *Planet of Evil*, and clearly represents a different, subsequent visit (or visits). We can therefore infer that it's the fourth Doctor who helped with *Hamlet*, after *Planet of Evil*. The

encounter is mentioned again in *Asylum*. One problem is that it's also mentioned by the first Doctor in *Byzantium!* – if that needs explaining away, it's possible the first Doctor has seen the manuscript, recognised his handwriting (we know from *The Trial of a Time Lord* that the Valeyard and sixth Doctor have the same handwriting, so presumably all the Doctors do) and so inferred a future meeting.

826 *City of Death*

827 *The Time Meddler,* although there's no evidence of any contact between the Monk and Shakespeare.

828 *The Cabinet of Light*. *King Lear* appeared in the Stationers' Register for November 1607, so this is another meeting. *Island of Death* implies it has to involve one of the Doctor's first three incarnations.

829 "Changes". This play, unlike the ones Braxiatel acquires in *The Empire of Glass*, is completely unknown to Shakespearean scholarship.

830 *Hide*

831 *DC 3: The Doomsday Chronometer*

832 *The Suns of Caresh*

833 *Pier Pressure*

834 *Dead London*

835 *Grand Theft Cosmos*

836 *Iris S5: Dark Side*

837 *Time in Office*. Azal appeared in *The Daemons*.

838 *3rdA: Storm of the Horofax*

839 *The Banquo Legacy*. In the real world, the *Necronomicon* was a fictional book of magic invented by H.P. Lovecraft.

840 *Spare Parts*

841 *The Mind of Evil*. Raleigh lived 1552-1618, and was imprisoned 1603-1616.

842 "Centuries" before *The Way Through the Woods*.

843 *Scavenger*. In real life, Salim was born 30th August, 1569; crowned on 15th October, 1605; and died 7th November, 1627.

844 Dating "The Devil of the Deep" (*DWM* #61) - It's "the early seventeenth century" when Diego is rescued according to a caption. The Sea Devil revived "ten years" before rescuing Diego, who is rescued "twenty years"

The Doctor helped Shakespeare write his plays, and saw Burbage take the title role in the first performance of *Hamlet*.[823] The Doctor suggested that *The Merry Wives of Windsor* needed to be redrafted, but the Queen wanted it performed as soon as possible.[824]

The fourth Doctor said Shakespeare was a "charming fellow", but a "dreadful actor".[825] The Doctor transcribed a copy of *Hamlet* for Shakespeare, who had sprained his wrist writing sonnets. Scaroth later acquired the manuscript.[826]

If the Monk's plan in 1066 had worked, *Hamlet* would have been written for television.[827] The Doctor wrote Poor Tom's dialogue in *King Lear*[828]. The Doctor had a copy of *Mischief Night*, or *As You Please*, an unknown Shakespeare play, in a TARDIS storeroom.[829]

The Seventeenth Century

A local clergyman saw the Caliburn Ghast in the seventeenth century.[830] River Song and Helen visited the south of France, the seventeenth century, while tracking down the Doomsday Chronometer.[831]

The planet Caresh was in a binary star system containing the larger, warmer sun Beacon and the smaller, colder Ember. Caresh randomly orbited one of the two stars each solar cycle, causing unpredictable warm and cold years. In the seventeenth century, a protracted cold period killed off a large amount of the population. As the warm years returned, scientists on Dassar Island built a scanner capable of seeing into the future, giving them advance warning of cold years. The Time Lords ruled the scanner a violation of their monopoly on time travel, and dispatched agents Solenti and Lord Roche to shut down the device.[832]

Centuries ago, invaders dominated the planet Indo. The surviving microscopic natives travelled to Earth on a meteorite. They fed off the latent emotions of humans in the Brighton area, and would gain in strength by 1936.[833]

The Sepulchre transported a resident of the seventeenth century – "Springheeled Sophie", a funambulist and thief – into the London-recreation that existed in its mental landscape. Following the Sepulchre's defeat by the eighth Doctor and Lucie, Sophie remained in the Sepulchre's recreation of her native time.[834]

In the seventeenth century, an inhabitant of the planet Parrimor was exiled to Earth. He became Claudio Tardelli – an artist whose paintings and sculptures warped reality, and had a "malign influence" on anyone who looked at them. In Rome, the Doctor stopped Tardelli from using his artworks to influence the Pope. Tardelli was discredited, and the Doctor worked to keep him obscure, destroying many of Tardelli's works. Tardelli fled to Florence and sequestered himself inside a black diamond he'd created – one that contained a compressed universe about three light years across. The King of Sweden later acquired the diamond in 1898.[835]

One of Iris Wildthyme's selves had a terrible gambling habit, and commissioned the construction of a home, Pink Gables, on Earth's Moon. The house served as a spirit trap for a disembodied intelligence that Iris caught slinking around Earth, and so became a self-cleaning haunted house that also made soup. Various ghosts came to reside in Pink Gables over the centuries – including Edward, a seventeenth-century native whose earlobes were cut off because he practiced the dark arts.[836]

Inec, an Arimeci, longed for a grudge match against the Daemon Azal. The fourth Doctor and Leela found Inec in seventeenth-century Japan, trying to power his portal home with thousands of souls, and pitched him into a pocket dimension. In trying to escape, Inec collapsed the pocket realm and died.[837] Arianda, a time traveller, realised that humankind lacked the ability to destroy itself in the seventeenth century, and jumped ahead some centuries.[838]

Around 1600, the *Necronomicon* was translated into Spanish.[839] In the early seventeenth century, Emperor Tokugawa Ieyasu of Japan gave the Doctor tea.[840] **The Doctor shared a cell with Walter Raleigh, who "kept going on about this new vegetable he'd discovered".[841]**

Neighbouring empires fought The Long War, a conflict that went on for generations. During this, a space explorer, Reyn the were-fox, crashed on Earth near the village of Foxton. Reyn's spaceship *learned* from its travels, attaining some sentience through a process called The Shift.

(=) Reyn's ship needed to absorb living minds every half-century, and so extruded a number of temporal and spatial anomalies through Swallow Woods from the Bronze Age to the present day. People subconsciously avoided the Woods, save for when the ship mentally lured in people to drain their minds. It would claim three hundred and nine victims.

The eleventh Doctor, Amy and Rory undid the temporal anomalies. The Long War ended very badly for Reyn's homeworld, but the Doctor and Rory retroactively established a legend that "the Traveller" would one day return with knowledge of lost technology.[842]

In 1600, Crown Prince Salim returned to his palace after spending fourteen years in India's military. An extraterrestrial space probe – later dubbed Scavenger – scanned Earth for salvageable materials, and abducted Salim's beloved, the slave girl Arriani. Scavenger absorbed Arriani's mind and went dormant, sleeping until Earth developed technology more worth harvesting. As a side effect of Scavenger's beam, Salim lived for five centuries.[843]

c 1600 - "The Devil of the Deep"[844] -> The ship of Diego da Columba of Cordoba vanished off the coast of South America. It had been attacked by pirates led by

Korvo. Diego was rescued after walking the plank by a Sea Devil who had revived ten years previously. The pirates discovered the Sea Devil's island and he was captured by Korvo. One of the pirates accidentally activated a Caller, a device that summoned a giant marine reptile that sank the pirate ship. Diego was left alone for twenty years until he was rescued and could tell his tale – his proof was that he still had the Caller.

c 1600 (5th May) - "The Road to Hell"[845] **->** The eighth Doctor and Izzy arrived in Japan and were brought before aliens known as Gaijin, who sought to understand the concept of honour. They had a nano-sculptor that turned thoughts into reality, and could make people immortal – they did so with Katsura Sato. The Doctor was angry at the interference, but the Gaijin didn't understand the objections. One of the Japanese, Asami, saw a vision of Japan's future in Izzy's mind, including the atomic bombs of World War II. He decided to launch a preemptive attack on the West. The Gaijin now understood that honour was linked to responsibility and deactivated the nano-sculptor even though it killed them.

c 1601 - THE LEGENDS OF ASHILDR: "The Ghosts of Branscombe Wood"[846] **->** The AI governing a crashed spaceship in Branscombe Wood was scanning memories of intruders to ward them away, but had thereby driven one young woman insane. Ashildr left London and wandered until she reached Branscombe, and ended the ship's threat by destroying it.

Katsura Sato, unable to commit seppuku, wandered the Earth, became a pirate and ended up incarcerated in Saragossa for fifty years. The Master wrote the *Odostra*, a fake holy book, and gave it to Katsura in his cell. Katsura was filled with crusading zeal and set out to conquer the world. History changed because of this.[847]

Jared Khan had adopted the guise of John Dee, and had served as Queen Elizabeth's counsellor for twenty years. In 1603, the Queen diverted Dee's attention so he would not discover that the seventh Doctor was at her court.[848]

The ley lines in Greenwich, London, were a source of energy akin to the Cardiff Rift; in future, Greenwich would become the primary meridian of all Earth time, and the naval college would be full of ghosts. A group of alien conquerors, the Enochians, were drawn to Greenwich's ley

after being marooned.

845 Dating "The Road to Hell" (*DWM* #278-282) - The Doctor asserts "I'm fairly sure I've set us down in the tenth century", but quickly corrects this to "the early seventeenth century".

846 Dating *The Legends of Ashildr*: "The Ghosts of Branscombe Wood" (NSA #61d) - Ashildr's journal reports, "And now, all too soon, 1600 has come and gone".

847 "The Glorious Dead"

848 *Birthright*. It's entirely possible that after this point, Jared Khan passes off the identity of "John Dee" to a successor who later starves to death while containing the Enochians ("Don't Step on the Grass").

849 "Don't Step on the Grass". The head Enochian says its spaceship arrived on Earth "over five hundred years" prior to 2009 (so, concurrent with Dee's lifetime), and the date is given as "sixteenth century Greenwich" in "Final Sacrifice". Seemingly without any evidence, the Doctor also claims that the spaceship has been on Earth for "thousands of years". Enochian is an occult/angelic language found in Dee's journals in real life.

850 "Final Sacrifice"

851 *The Dying Days*

852 Dating *The Plotters* (MA #28) - The year is given (p23).

853 Before *Revenge of the Cybermen*. The signing of the Convention is the central event of *The Empire of Glass*.

854 "Don't Step on the Grass". In real life, it's unknown if Dee died in 1608 or 1609, as both the parish registers and his gravestone are missing.

855 Dating *The Empire of Glass* (MA #16) - The Doctor

states that it "must be the year of our lord, 1609" (p30).

856 "Matildus"

857 *DC: The Galileo Trap*. Virginia Galilei was born in 1600.

858 *Managra*. Bathory lived 1560-1614; her trial commenced on 7th January, 1611, with her in absentia.

859 *The Carrionite Curse*

860 "A thousand years" before *Benny B2: Road Trip: Bad Habits*.

861 *The Empire of Glass*

862 *FP: Weapons Grade Snake Oil* (ch34). Jonson's *Christmas, His Masque* (1616) gave renown to the traditional conceptualisation of Father Christmas.

863 Three hundred years before *Year of the Pig*.

864 *The Settling*. The person who bestows the forceps upon the Doctor is merely referred to as "Chamberlen". Peter Chamberlen is regarded as the inventor of forceps, although the name actually refers to two brothers (respectively 1560-1631 and 1572-1626). The elder Peter is apparently the creator of the device, which was a family secret for generations.

865 *DL: The End of Time*, p40. There were actually two "Defenestrations of Prague", in 1419 and 1618, although the term more often refers to the latter. Some real-life texts do claim that those thrown out the third window of the Bohemian Chancellory lived owing to a large heap of manure.

866 *Silver Nemesis*

867 *Sometime Never*

868 "Ten generations" before *Imperial Moon*.

lines, but their colony ship encountered a systems failure. They sought help from John Dee by speaking through his associate, the medium Edward Kelley. Dee parted ways with Kelley in 1589 and returned to England, then moved his private library and the Enochian spaceship to Duke Humphrey's house. He hoped to help the aliens, whom he regarded as "angels", and created the Enochian language to better communicate with them.[849] The Enochians had unknowingly been diverted to Greenwich by the Tef'Aree, as a means of enabling its own creation.[850]

General William Lethbridge-Stewart was among King James' retinue on his initial arrival in London in 1603.[851]

1605 - THE PLOTTERS[852] -> The first Doctor and Vicki decided to investigate the Gunpowder Plot while Ian and Barbara set off for the Globe Theatre. The Doctor and Vicki – who was disguised as a boy named Victor – met King James I, and learned that the statesman Sir Robert Cecil was encouraging the Plot to draw out the conspirators and discredit the Catholics. Some Catholics captured Barbara, leading to Guy Fawkes befriending her. Robert Catesby, a member of the Plot, argued with Fawkes and killed him... which isn't how the history books reported events.

The King's courtier, Robert Hay, was a secret member of a grand order devoted to mysticism. Hay sought to create anarchy, but the Doctor manoeuvred Hay to the cellar under Parliament, where Cecil arrested him. Hay was tortured and executed in Fawkes' place, preserving history.

The Armageddon Convention was signed, and banned the use of cobalt bombs.[853] John Dee learned that the Enochian "angels" were actually conquerors and destroyed their physical forms, but their essences were absorbed into the Earth. One Enochian remained aboard their spacecraft in a clockwork body, and so Dee sealed the ship within the cellars of Duke Humphrey's house. He finally starved to death aboard the spacecraft.[854]

The Armageddon Convention

1609 - THE EMPIRE OF GLASS[855] -> Irving Braxiatel and the first Doctor – accompanied by Steven and Vicki – hosted a meeting, the Armageddon Convention, that saw doomsday weapons such as temporal disrupters and cobalt bombs banned. Although the Daleks and Cybermen refused to attend, many other races did sign. The Convention was nearly sabotaged by the Greld, a race of arms dealers who stood to lose money from it; and the Jamarians, who craved an empire for themselves.

The first performance of *Macbeth* had the last minute substitutions of Shakespeare in the role of Lady Macbeth, and the Doctor and Vicki in the roles of the doctor and his servant. The spy Christopher Marlowe died in a duel.

Thanks to the Doctor, an original manuscript of *Macbeth* wound up in the Reneath Archive on Cornucopia.[856] Galileo Galilei's daughter Virginia, age ten, gave the Doctor some recorder lessons.[857]

The Doctor dropped Sarah Jane off at Skye for a few days, and stopped a monstrous undertaking by the serial killer Elizabeth Bathory, a.k.a. the Blood Countess. He was present at her trial in 1611. The Mimic, a creature banished from Gallifrey, copied a demonic creature that Bathory had summoned. On 29th June, 1613, the talentless playwright Francis Pearson – a follower of Countess Bathory – burnt down Shakespeare's Globe Theatre during a production of *Henry VIII*. He later vanished, transported by the ancient Mimic to the thirty-first century.[858] Stones from the original Globe Theatre were removed for future benefit of the Carrionites.[859]

The infamous thousand-year dig at the Semprini Colonnade on the planet Persinnia began.[860]

The Death of (the Other) Shakespeare

In April 1616, a dying William Shakespeare handed over three unpublished plays – *Love's Labours Won*, *The Birth of Merlin* and *Sir John Oldcastle* – to Irving Braxiatel in return for memories of events in Venice, 1609.[861]

The public's conception of Father Christmas was shaped when the poet Ben Jonson had a dig at Father Christèmas of Faction Paradox, and the idea went viral.[862] On one occasion, the Doctor saw a beached whale lie on the shore for four days until its bowels exploded – some of the eyewitnesses died from disease after being splattered by rotten whale meat.[863]

Chamberlen, the inventor of modern obstetrical forceps, bequeathed a pair of his creations upon the Doctor. He would use this item in 1649 to deliver a child during the sacking of Wexford.[864]

The Doctor was present at the Defenestration of Prague, and saved the lives of the intended victims with a pile of manure. The TARDIS stank for a week.[865]

In 1621, the infamous Lady Peinforte poisoned her neighbour Dorothea Remington.[866] In 1624, the Doctor met an Agent of the Council of Eight in Devon.[867]

The Phiadoran Directorate Systems were dominated by the Phiadoran Clan Matriarchy, who influenced males with genetically augmented pheromones. The Matriarchy instigated ten generations of tyranny that lasted Galactic Time Index 611,072.26 to 611,548.91. The Sarmon Revolution brought down the Matriarchy, and exiled its members to die in a safari park built on Earth's moon. Thirty-two years later, the carnivorous Vrall killed the Matriarchy, and disguised themselves as the Phiadorans by wearing their skins. Lacking space-travel, the Vrall launched RNA spores encoded with technical information to Earth.[868]

The immortal Padmasambhava, a.k.a. the Guru Rinpoche, returned to the mortal plane in 1625, and took to living at the Det-Sen Monsatery in Tibet.[869]

wih - Nathaniel Silver, a Roundhead soldier involved in the War in Heaven, was born in 1625.[870]

1626 - THE CHURCH AND THE CROWN[871] ->

At the court of King Louis, the Musketeers and Cardinal Richelieu were in constant dispute. The fifth Doctor, Peri and Erimem arrived, and it transpired that Peri was the double of Queen Anne. The Duke of Buckingham kidnapped Peri – he was planning a British invasion of France by dividing the French court. Erimem rallied the troops, and averted a major diplomatic incident.

The Doctor apparently visited the Det-Sen monastery in Tibet on a number of occasions, and in 1630 helped the monks there to survive bandit attacks. He was entrusted with the holy Ghanta when he left.[872] **It was possibly on this visit that the Doctor learned the Tibetan language and meditation techniques.**[873]

The Doctor witnessed philosopher Francis Bacon conduct an experiment on the preservation of meat by stuffing snow into a chicken. Bacon later contracted pneumonia from the incident and died.[874] **The War Lords lifted a battlefield from the Thirty Years War.**[875]

1636 - BORROWED TIME[876] ->

Jane Blythe, now a fugitive from the Time Market following her economic ruin in 2007, fled into the past and established a low-level time commodities scheme. Her avatars, Mr Hoogeveen and Mr Verspronck, loaned out time to certain residents of the Netherlands – before long, this created an economic bubble pertaining to the value of tulips.

Bishop Mazain arrived in Paris in 1636, and became

---

869 *Leth-St: Night of the Intelligence* (ch15) says Padmasambhava came to Earth in "1625", the Haisman Timeline says it was "1630" – both play off the Doctor visiting Det-Sen three hundred years before *The Abominable Snowmen*. The earliest sources referencing Padmasambhava as an actual person date back to the ninth century.

870 *FP: Newtons Sleep* (p14). Silver says he was born "the year the last king came to the throne" – meaning Charles I, in 1625.

871 Dating *The Church and the Crown* (BF #38) - The date is given.

872 *The Abominable Snowmen*. This was "1630" according to the Doctor. *The Programme Guide* suggested "1400 AD". *Leth-St: Night of the Intelligence* (ch13) says the Doctor was "a different man" both times he visited Det-Sen, meaning Padmasambhava met the first Doctor in 1630.

873 The Doctor speaks Tibetan in *Planet of the Spiders* (but can't in *The Creature from the Pit*), and uses Tibetan meditation in *Terror of the Zygons*.

874 *Heart of TARDIS*. Bacon died in April 1626.

875 *The War Games*. The Thirty Years War ran from 1618-1648.

876 Dating *Borrowed Time* (NSA #49) - The year is given (p253). The peak of "tulip mania" was February 1637.

877 *The Twelfth Doctor Year Two*: "Terror of the Cabinet Noir"

878 *The Church and the Crown*

879 "Two years" before *DC: The Galileo Trap*.

880 Dating *Silver Nemesis* (25.3) - The Doctor gives the date of the launch, but there is no indication of exactly how long afterwards Lady Peinforte leaves for the twentieth century. Quite how "Roundheads" can be involved in this business when the term wasn't used until the Civil War is unclear. As a letter to *Radio Times* after *Silver Nemesis* aired noted, the adoption of the Gregorian calendar in 1752 means that eleven days were "lost" in Britain, so had the Nemesis *really* landed exactly three hundred and fifty years after 23rd November, 1638, it would have landed on 3rd December, 1988.

The statue passes over the Earth every twenty-five years (in 1663, 1688, 1713, 1738, 1763, 1788, 1813, 1838, 1863, 1888, 1913, 1938, 1963 and finally 1988). *The Terrestrial Index* offers suggestions as to the effects of the statue on human history, but the only on-screen information concerns the twentieth century. *The Curse of Fenric* establishes Fenric's involvement.

881 Dating *DC: The Galileo Trap/The Satanic Mill* (*Doom Coalition* #1.3-1.4) - The year is given. No time-displacement occurs when the Doctor and company relocate from Earth to Phyton.

882 *The Drosten's Curse*, which implies the incident had something to do with Cardinal Richelieu (1585-1642).

883 "Instruments of War"

884 *Robot of Sherwood*. Bergerac lived 1619-1655.

885 Dating *FP: Newtons Sleep* (FP novel #6) - The date is given on the back cover, in accord with the English Civil War starting in 1642. The publisher of *Newtons Sleep*, Random Static, has stated that the lack of an apostrophe in the title was deliberate; it's a quote from William Blake.

886 *The Twelfth Doctor Year Two*: "Terror of the Cabinet Noir". In real life, Richelieu died 4th December, 1642.

887 Dating *Plague City* (NSA #63) - The year is given. The Doctor here seems responsible for the advent of the Edinburgh Hogmanay Festival, "Hogmanay" being the last day of the year.

888 *The War Games*. The English Civil Wars ran from 1642-1649.

889 *The Time Monster*

890 *The Awakening*

curator of the Black Library: a repository of forbidden texts confiscated by Cardinal Richelieu's intelligence network.[877] The Doctor met Louis XIII in 1637.[878] Galileo saw a new planet, Phyton, through his telescope, but lost his sight in doing so.[879]

The Journey of the Nemesis Begins

1638 (November) - SILVER NEMESIS[880] **->** On 23rd November, 1638, the seventh Doctor was present as some Roundheads fought Lady Peinforte's soldiers, and as the Nemesis asteroid was launched into space from a meadow in Windsor. Following this, the Doctor set his watch alarm to go off on 23rd November, 1988, the day that the Nemesis would return to Earth.

The Nemesis passed over the Earth every twenty-five years, influencing human affairs. Lady Peinforte employed a mathematician to work out the asteroid's trajectory, and then used his blood in a magical ceremony – one that also involved the Validium arrow in Peinforte's possession – to transport Peinforte and her servant Richard Maynarde to its ultimate destination. The imprisoned Fenric aided her time travel.

1639 - DC: THE GALILEO TRAP / THE SATANIC MILL[881] **->** Two leech-like alien mercenaries, Fortuna and Cleaver, accepted a commission from the Eleven to capture the Doctor. The pair donned full body masks and inveigled themselves into the household of the Doctor's old friend Galileo, with Fortuna posing as Galileo's daughter Virginia – who had died five years earlier. Cleaver drained so many souls from the people nearby, rendering them mindless, that officials believed a new plague was at work.

The eighth Doctor, Liv and Helen showed up in response to a message Galileo had been made to etch into a stone tablet, having overlooked Galileo's hints that they were walking into a trap. Cleaver was incinerated while trying to feast on the Doctor. The cyborg Cavalli, of the Cosmos Security Squad, Sol Division, arrested Fortuna on charges of gross moral turpitude and wrongful infiltration of an alien culture. The Doctor and his companions went to confront the Eleven...

The Eleven had transformed Omega's prototype stellar manipulator into Phyton: a satellite located between Mercury and the Sun. The workings there generated disposable humanoids, the Orbs, who tread on mills to create power. The Eleven intended to bring down all the Doctor held dear by scorching him in the sun, and using the resultant regenerative energy to trigger the manipulator into collapsing Earth's star into a black hole. The Age of Reason, as well as the Doctor's friends and humanity's luminaries, would never exist.

The Doctor, Liv and Helen ended the Eleven's plans, and the Eleven was lost in a radiation surge as the TARDIS – navigating by instructions from the Sonic – rescued the Doctor and his friends. Afterward, the Doctor relocated the surviving Orbs to a stable planet, and suggested that he, Liv and Helen go on a holiday together.

The Doctor experienced a dew-laden Earth dawn in seventeenth-century France.[882] The twelfth Doctor and Clara enjoyed a frost fair in 1641.[883] **Cyrano de Bergerac taught the Doctor how to handle a sword.**[884]

wih - 1642 - FP: NEWTONS SLEEP[885] **->** Nathaniel Silver, a Roundhead soldier, was shot dead at Edgehill. Representatives from humanity's posthuman era, seeking to guarantee the stability of their timeline, meddled with Silver's biodata and resurrected him. Silver didn't age from this point onward. The posthumans also gave him possession of a mysterious egg that aided his efforts to learn the secrets of natural philosophy.

As his death approached, Cardinal Richelieu used alchemists' spellbooks to summon sentient dark matter – The Darkness – which extended his lifespan for decades.[886]

1645 (? 31st December) - PLAGUE CITY[887] **->** An outbreak of bubonic plague in Edinburgh awoke the living spaceship, an empathic Psycholops, buried beneath a group of hills: Arthur's Seat. Grief-consuming leeches on the Psycholops also revived, and feasted off the city's misery. To contain the leeches, the twelfth Doctor – accompanied by Bill and Nardole – deployed his guitar, and staged a concert in which he played selections including *The Very Best of the Smiths*, Radiohead's "Creep" and The Proclaimers' "My Old Friend the Blues". The temporary abatement of suffering drove the leeches underground, enabling the travellers to destroy them with a contained volcanic blast.

The Doctor dosed Catherine Abney, age 19, with a touch-transferable bacteriophage – this would cause a steep and historical drop in plague cases. The Doctor's concert gave rise to the annual Edinburgh Hogmanay Festival, which generated some happiness to counter-balance the overall level of Scottishness.

The English Civil War

The War Lords kidnapped a Civil War battlefield.[888] A division of Roundheads was also kidnapped by the UNIT Master using TOM-TIT.[889]

On 13th July, 1643, the Royalists and Roundheads met in Little Hodcombe, wiping out themselves and the entire village. The Malus fed from the psychic energy released by the deaths and briefly emerged from its dormancy. The fifth Doctor returned the time-flung Will Chandler to this, his native era, shortly afterwards.[890] Returning Will Chandler was not a straightforward business.[891]

A group of Roundheads was torn apart on Lanyon Moor, apparently by wild beasts.[892] In 1644, "strange fire" consumed the castle of Crook Marsham.[893] **Witches hid from Matthew Hopkins in Devil's End.**[894] The Doctor met King Charles II.[895]

The cyber-assassin Death's Head momentarily appeared in a garden in Thetford, 1646, prompting the execution of Mistress Thorogood as a suspected witch.[896]

c 1647 - "Witch Hunt"[897] -> As part of her game against the twelfth Doctor, the time-travelling jester Miss Chief brought Clara back to the seventeenth century – where she was nearly drowned by the Witchfinder General, Matthew Hopkins. The Doctor and Clara successfully painted Hopkins as an agent of Satan, causing some townsfolk to throw him in a lake. The Doctor also gave Miss Chief's time-travel device, Mini-Mischief, a good soaking, knowing it would hamper her shenanigans.

Iris Wildthyme was at the Siege of Colchester.[898]

1648 - THE ROUNDHEADS[899] -> Ben Jackson and Polly were mistaken for Parliamentarians. Polly was kidnapped by Royalists, while Ben was press-ganged. Meanwhile, Oliver Cromwell's men arrested the second Doctor and Jamie. Cromwell's belief that Jamie was a fortune teller aided the TARDIS crew in escaping, but they were accompanied by King Charles... who according to history should have stayed in prison. Polly was forced to betray Christopher Whyte, a new friend and a Royalist, to protect history. Charles was duly recaptured and executed.

The Doctor met Inigo Jones in 1649, and either helped him find his cat or defeat an army of cats – he couldn't remember which.[900]

1649 (12th September to 11th October) - THE SETTLING[901] -> The seventh Doctor, Ace and Hex arrived in Ireland as Oliver Cromwell's forces successfully besieged

---

891 *The Hollow Men*
892 *The Spectre of Lanyon Moor*
893 *Nightshade*
894 *The Daemons.* The witchhunter Matthew Hopkins died in 1647.
895 *Players*
896 "Time Bomb!"
897 Dating "Witch Hunt" (*DWM* #497-499) - Hopkins hunted witches from March 1644 to 1647. The story explains the "passing legend" that Hopkins himself was drowned as a witch – probably wishful thinking, as historical records indicate otherwise.
898 *The Elixir of Doom.* The siege occurred 12th June to 28th August, 1648.
899 Dating *The Roundheads* (PDA #6) - The Doctor says it's "1648, December I should say" (p39).
900 "Don't Step on the Grass"
901 Dating *The Settling* (BF #82) - Cromwell's ultimatum to Wexford is issued on 12th September, 1649, and the story begins shortly beforehand. The sacking of Wexford lasted from 2nd to 11th October. The "Dr Goddard" in this story apparently refers to Dr Jonathan Goddard (1617-1675), a distinguished Society member and a favourite of Cromwell.
902 Dating *FP: Newtons Sleep* (*FP* novel #6) - Newton was born on 4th January, 1643, and is currently "a child of nine summers with shite on his brow" (p1). René Descartes is "freshly-dead" (p2) - he died on 11th February 1650. Newton is constantly referred to in *Newtons Sleep* by his pseudonym, "Jeova Unus Sanctus" (more commonly rendered as "Jeova Sanctus Unus") - the letters of which can be rearranged (allowing that J's in Latin are rendered as I's, as demonstrated in that great and seminal documentary of archaeology, *Indiana Jones and the Last Crusade*) to spell *Isaacus*

Neutonuus, an invented rendering of his name in Latin.
903 Dating *FP: Newtons Sleep* (*FP* novel #6) - Behn, a real-life historical figure, was born on 10th July 1640, and is age 10 when she meets Larissa.
904 Dating *The Woman Who Lived* (X9.6) - The Doctor names the year. According to an interview with writer Catherine Tregenna in *DWM* #492, the story occurs in Hounslow.
905 "The seventeenth century", says *Rags* (p39).
906 *The Shining Man*
907 *The Androids of Tara.* Izaak Walton lived 1593-1683, and published *The Compleat Angler* in 1653.
908 *Ghost Ship.* Hobbes lived 1588-1679.
909 According to the monument in *Silver Nemesis*.
910 *The Stones of Blood.* The English writer John Aubrey (best known for his collection of biographies, *Brief Lives*) lived 1626-1697.
911 *Ghost Light.* The Royal Geographical Society was formed in 1645 during the Civil War.
912 The Doctor says that these should have been outlawed "centuries" before *The Many Deaths of Jo Grant*.
913 Dating *The Waters of Amsterdam* (BF #208) - The year is given. Rembrandt lived 1606-1669. Rembrandt's prime concerns are more in line with the events of one, even two decades previous: he's still mourning his wife (1642), angered at his lover Geertje Dircx besmirching his good name (1649), and upset that so many of his clients squandered their fortunes on investments such as tulips (1637). Mention is made of his son, but not his daughter Cornelia, born in 1654.
914 *River S3: A Requiem for the Doctor*
915 Dating *The Witch from the Well* (BF #154) - It's the "seventeenth century", and "three and a half centuries"/"350 years" from the present day. The Varaxils landed in spring, and it's now six months later.

Drogheda. Weeks later, Cromwell's army threatened Wexford, and he demanded that the town recognise the authority of Parliament. Conflict ensued until Cromwell received a surrender notice and ordered the fighting to cease. Hex, having witnessed the horror at Drogheda, roused the townsfolk to resist. The fighting resumed, and hundreds of fleeing women and children drowned on crowded boats. Cromwell's troops prevailed.

The seventh Doctor met Dr Goddard, who helped to found the Royal Society.

wih - 1650 - FP: NEWTONS SLEEP[802] **->** When Isaac Newton, a.k.a. Jeova Unus Sanctus, was a young boy, the wounded babel that had escaped from Thessalia of the Order of the Weal hid within his timeline. Newton carried on with his life, unaware of this.

wih - 1651 - FP: NEWTONS SLEEP[903] **->** The mortally wounded Thessalia, a member of the Great Houses, arrived from 1678 and regenerated. A young girl named Aphra Behn – later a dramatist and spy for King Charles II – mistook the reborn Thessalia, later named Larissa, for a beautiful nymph and pledged allegiance to her.

1651 - THE WOMAN WHO LIVED[904] **-> The immortal Ashildr became a highwayman, the Knightmare, for the sport of it. "He" was renowned as being faster than Sam Swift the Quick, and more lethal than Deadly Dupont. One day, Ashildr found the lion-like Leandro – an alien from Delta Leonis – on her estate. He claimed to be stranded, having lost his portal-making talisman, the Eye of Hades, upon crashing to Earth. The twelfth Doctor again met Ashildr while tracking the Eye's exoplanetary energies, and aided her in recovering it.**

Ashildr wanted to experience adventures in space, **and triggered the Eye with the life-energy of Sam Swift. Leandro rejoiced as a portal formed... the start of his people's invasion of Earth. Ashildr acknowledged Leandro's betrayal and healed Swift with her remaining Mire medical patch, closing the portal. Leandro's people executed him for his failure. The Doctor speculated the patch had made Swift healthy, but not immortal.**

Afterward, in the pub Ye Swan With Two Necks, the **Doctor and Ashildr parted as uneasy friends. Ashildr agreed to become the patron saint of the people the Doctor left behind.**

An act of murder within the standing stones in Cirbury awakened the Ragman. Emily, the mayor's daughter, was raped by a corpse that the Ragman animated. The Ragman triggered acts of class warfare, but was driven back into the stones. The townsfolk relocated the stones to Dartmoor. Emily was left pregnant and later died in poverty, but her

bloodline led to the journalist Charmange Peters and the lout Kane Sawyer in the twentieth century.[905]

In 1654, a Fairy Finder captured a Boggart near Manchester, and imprisoned it beneath a rowan tree.[906] **The Doctor fished with Izaak Walton.**[907] He also met Thomas Hobbes.[908] **Lady Peinforte's servant Richard Maynarde died on 2nd November, 1657, and was entombed at Windsor.**[909]

According to the Doctor, Aubrey invented Druidism "as a joke".[910] **The Doctor was a founder member of the Royal Geographical Society.**[911] Mindscape generators, devices capable of crafting fake scenarios in a subject's mind, were invented.[912]

1658 - THE WATERS OF AMSTERDAM[913] **->** The Countess Mach-Teldak destroyed her homeworld, Corus-Valletine, and fled the judgment of a water-based race, the Nix, to Earth. She commissioned Rembrandt van Rijn to paint schematics of spaceships, then tasked the Mayor of Amsterdam – also the President of the East India Company – with realising the designs. Meanwhile, Teldak's android servant, Kylex-Twelve, spent three centuries trying to find a time traveller to aid his mistress, then returned to this time with the fifth Doctor, Nyssa and Tegan.

The Nix drowned Teldak, averting the creation of a Dutch Galactic Company fleet of spaceships in 1983. Kylex left to find his own way. The Doctor convinced Rembrandt to burn his spaceship paintings, and eased the man's financial struggles with a bag of Teldak's diamonds.

Prior to her execution in 1659, the poisoner Giulia Tofana passed along the psychic substance Aqua Tofana, AKA Aqua Galatea, to Frau Bruner. It extended Bruner's lifespan.[914]

c 1660 (autumn) - THE WITCH FROM THE WELL[915] **->** Two shapeshifting Varaxils arrived in the village of Tranchard's Fell while hunting beings who could channel Odic power. They killed Finicia and Lucern, the children of Squire Portillon, and assumed their forms. The eighth Doctor and Mary Shelley arrived six months later, but the older versions of "Finicia and Lucern" with them used the TARDIS' Fast Return Switch to return to the twenty-first century with Mary, stranding the Doctor.

A botched attempt by the Varaxils to leech Odic energy from the midwife Agnes Bates, who had the "second sight", resulted in her becoming a monstrosity that attacked the village. The Doctor drained her Odic energy, and tricked everyone involved into thinking that the monster-Agnes was imprisoned down a well. In actuality, only an energy echo of monster-Agnes was trapped. The Doctor aided Agnes, who had been found guilty of witchcraft, in moving to another village.

Finicia and Lucern pledged to spend their lengthy lifespans searching for their Odic scanner – a.k.a. the Witch Star – which Squire Claude Portillon had hidden. Mary returned in the TARDIS, and the Doctor left with her.

In 1661, the astronomer Clancy discovered a comet that returned to Earth every one hundred and fifty-seven years.[916] **The mathematician Pierre de Fermat died in a duel, his last theorem unproven, because the Doctor slept in.**[917] Earth was now a Level 2 civilisation. Moan'na, a political dissident from the Hakuai homeworld, restructured his DNA to hide among humans, but died in 1665 from the bubonic plague.[918]

In 1665, an alien stranded on Earth adopted the guise of Erasmus Darkening, an alchemist. James, the Third Earl of Marchwood, hired Darkening to find the secret of turning common metal into gold – but Darkening instead built trans-dimensional equipment in the hopes of getting home, and powered it with the life force of Marchwood's children. Marchwood stabbed at Darkening, damaging Darkening's device – which reduced them both to a ghost-like state. In the centu-

ries to follow, Darkening's ghost turned at least thirteen people into shades, using their life-energies to fuel his immortality.[919]

wih - 1665 - FP: NEWTONS SLEEP[920] **->** A commoner, Thomas Piper, died from the plague. A Faction Paradox delegation that included Cousin Hateman, Mother Sphinx, the androgynous Father-Mother Olympia and their cat, Faction Cat, recruited his widow to join the Faction as Little Sister Greenaway.

1665 - THE DEMONS OF RED LODGE AND OTHER STORIES: "The Demons of Red Lodge"[921] **->** The fifth Doctor and Nyssa visited the village of Red Lodge. The alien Spira were busy replicating the townsfolk as a precursor to a takeover of Earth, but died from imperfections upon incorporating the non-human Doctor into their genetic matrix.

---

916 *The Ghosts of N-Space*

917 *The Eleventh Hour*. This was in 1665.

918 "The Pestilent Heart"

919 *SJA: The Eternity Trap*

920 Dating *FP: Newtons Sleep* (FP novel #6) - The year is given in the blurb.

921 Dating *The Demons of Red Lodge and Other Stories*: "The Demons of Red Lodge" (BF #142a) - The Doctor twice comments that it's 1665, and it's "twenty years" after the time of Matthew Hopkins, who operated as a witchhunter from 1645 to 1647.

922 *TW: Hidden*. In real life, Vaughan was a member of the Society of Unknown Philosophers, established his reputation by writing the pseudo-mystical work *Anthroposophia Theomagica*, and lived 1621 to 1666.

923 *K9: Fear Itself*

924 Dating *The Visitation* (19.4) - The Doctor, trying to get Tegan home to 1981, suggests "we're about three hundred years early". The action culminates with the start of the Great Fire of London, which took place on the night of 2nd to 3rd September, 1666, so the story would seem to start on 1st September. According to the novelisation, the Terileptils crashed on "August 5th". On screen, Richard Mace says this was "several weeks ago".

925 The Doctor says he was blamed for the Great Fire in *Pyramids of Mars*. He refers to Mr and Mrs Pepys in *Robot*, and to Mrs Pepys' coffee-making prowess in *Planet of the Spiders*. Pepys lived 1633-1703 and began his diary in 1660. His wife Elizabeth died in 1669. Mention of the Doctor's reluctance to talk about the Great Fire is from *Doctor Who and the Pirates*.

926 *Doctor Who and the Invasion from Space*

927 "Hundreds of years" before *The Scorchies*.

928 Dating "Black Death White Life" (IDW *DW* one-shot #6) - "It's the year of our Lord sixteen hundred and sixty-nine" according to a villager.

929 Dating *The Impossible Astronaut* (X6.1) - No date is given. The affronted man is not named in the story, and is only referred to as "Charles" in the end credits. However, the story implies that he is king, and the man's attire, moustache and impressive hair all match that of Charles II (who reigned 1660-1685) as painted by John Michael Wright. *Doctor Who: The Encyclopedia* cites the man as a "seventeenth-century nobleman", and also says that Matilda is the man's daughter. None of Charles' real-life children have that name, although he did have an awful lot of illegitimate issue.

930 Dating *FP: Newtons Sleep* (FP novel #6) - The back cover names the year.

931 *The Twelfth Doctor Year Two*: "Terror of the Cabinet Noir"

932 *Unbound: A Storm of Angels*

933 *Sometime Never*

934 *The Forgotten Army*. New Amsterdam reverted to the name "New York" in November 1674, but the Bronx wasn't incorporated into New York until 1874. Either this discrepancy owes to some aspect of time travel on the Doctor's part, or – as with a lot of the Doctor's spurious and inaccurate claims in this novel – one does have to wonder if he's just making it all up.

935 "Don't Step on the Grass"

936 *The Happiness Patrol*. Wallis lived 1616-1703, and is credited with furthering the development of modern calculus.

937 Dating *FP: Newtons Sleep* (FP novel #6) - Events follow the death of the courtier Edward Coleman (p143), who was hanged on 17th May, 1678. Rochester

The Welsh philosopher Thomas Vaughn studied alchemy, and found a means of living for centuries.[922] **In 1665, a plague spread across London, killing thousands.**[923]

The Great Fire of London

1666 (early September) - THE VISITATION[924] **-> A group of escaped Terileptil prisoners made planetfall on Earth. They planned to wipe out the human population with rats infected with the bubonic plague virus, but were thwarted by the fifth Doctor, Tegan, Nyssa and Adric. A final confrontation resulted in the Doctor dropping a torch that caused the Terileptils' equipment to explode – which killed the Terileptils and caused the Great Fire of London.**

Prior to this in his lifetime, the Doctor had already been blamed for the Great Fire. The Doctor perhaps met Mr and Mrs Pepys on the same visit. Mrs Pepys "makes an excellent cup of coffee". The Doctor doesn't like to talk about the Great Fire of London.[925]

The Mortimer family – George, Helen and their children Ida and Alan – stumbled into the TARDIS when the first Doctor landed during the Great Fire. Much to the Doctor's irritation, they thought he was a warlock. Together, they travelled to the Andromeda Galaxy in the far future.[926]

Dawn of the Scorchies

The people of an unnamed planet watched so much television, they were powerless when invaders overran their world. A native scientist transmitted some of his people into space as television signals, but miscalculated the compression algorithm needed to convert their physical forms. The survivors lost their moral centre, vowed revenge on anyone with a planet or physical form, and infiltrated worlds as a children's show called *The Scorchies*.[927]

1669 - "Black Death White Life"[928] **->** The tenth Doctor and Martha found an English village in the grip of a plague. A "fallen angel" in the local church was healing people, and the Doctor identified it as an Immunoglobulin from Mimosa 3 in the Crux Constellation. The Immunoglobulins and the Macroviruses had been locked in an ongoing war, but recently the Macroviruses had gained an advantage – and were now on Earth. The Doctor coaxed the Immunoglobulin to reproduce and destroy the Macroviruses on Earth, then returned it to Mimosa 3.

c 1670 - THE IMPOSSIBLE ASTRONAUT[929] **->** Charles II found the eleventh Doctor nude and hiding under the skirts of Matilda, a woman who had just painted him in that state. The Doctor was imprisoned in the Tower, but flew out of his cell two days later.

wih - 1671 - FP: NEWTONS SLEEP[930] **->** On behalf of Sir Samuel Morland, Aphra Behn infiltrated a gathering of alchemists and ritualists in Cambridge, as hosted by a man named Salomon. Those present – including Isaac Newton (a.k.a. Jeova Unus Sanctus); representatives of Faction Paradox; and Valentine, a member of the French secret society *le Pouvoir* – had gathered to watch an advanced science demonstration by "the Magus", Nathaniel Silver. Salomon was actually Dr Alexander Bendo, the head of the Secret Service – he had arranged the gathering to round up the attendees with his soldiers, but largely failed. Little Sister Greenaway's performance during these events earned her a promotion to Cousin.

The singer-swordswoman Julie D'Aubigny, seemingly a companion of the twelfth Doctor, was born in 1673.[931]

> = The alt-first Doctor rescued the Princes in the Tower.[932]

The Doctor placed skeletons in the Tower of London, which were found in 1674 and identified as the lost Princes.[933] The eleventh Doctor claimed to know the bar where the Governor of New Amsterdam lost the city in a bet. The Doctor wasn't present, as he was busy with the "Bronx peace talks", which he said were more akin to a "barn dance".[934]

Operating on instructions from John Dee, the Society of Horticultural Historians, a.k.a. the Knights of the Arboretum, worked to prevent the last of the imprisoned Enochians from escaping. Christopher Wren, Inigo Jones and William Boreman were members of the group. In 1675, Wren convinced John Flamsteed, the royal astronomer, to move the location for the proposed Greenwich Observatory to thirteen degrees off magnetic north. The Observatory was built over the foundations of Duke Humphrey's house, further sealing off the Enochian vessel. The Doctor would receive notes that Wren left for him concerning these events in 2009.[935]

In 1677, the mathematician John Wallis gave a paper on sympathetic vibration to the Royal Society.[936]

wih - 1678 - FP: NEWTONS SLEEP[937] **->** Dr Alexander Bendo sought to learn more about Faction Paradox and dispatched the spy Aphra Behn to a brothel called the Inferno, where a mysterious woman had appeared out of thin air. This was Thessalia of the Great Houses, who had arrived following the Violent Unknown Event on the planet Zo La Domini. Determining that Thessalia had less value than he had hoped, Bendo shot her. Thessalia's biosuit automatically "jumped" her to safety along Behn's timeline, depositing her in 1651. An enraged Behn stabbed Bendo with a biodata needle engineered to erase people from history – henceforth, he would only be remembered as a disguise of John Wilmot, the second Earl of Rochester.

> = Around 1679, on an alternate Earth where Rome never fell, a race of genetically engineered soldiers – the Bestarius – were created but proved uncontrollably violent. Robots were deemed to be far more useful, and around this time the first robot, Vesuvius, was built. Centuries later, by 1979, Rome's iron legions had conquered the entire galaxy.[938]

A legendary soul-eater, the Bah-Sokhar, reincarnated as an egg. The now-benevolent creature became fond of a young girl, Julia Fetch, and extended her lifespan.[939] The Chalnoth – horned, militaristic beings – expanded their territory and would come into conflict with the Sontarans, the Rutans, the Varlic Horde and the Delphons.[940]

The fourth Doctor and Leela left the racehorse Shergar in pasturelands that would become the New Forest in southern England, where he could graze to his heart's content.[941] **In the late seventeenth century, Professor Chronotis retired to St Cedd's College, Cambridge.**[942] **The Eternals kidnapped a seventeenth-century pirate**

crew.[943] Nikolas Valentine, actually an extra-terrestrial stranded on Earth, received a knighthood in the 1680s.[944] The tenth Doctor and Martha visited Mauritius in 1681.[945]

1682 - THE NINTH DOCTOR YEAR ONE[946] **->** As a Time Agent, Jack Harkness conducted surveillance in this era as "Father Julian Horta". The ninth Doctor, Rose, Jack and Tara Mishra visited a Tupi Village in Brazil to learn more about Jack's missing two years, and freed some mer-creatures there from cruel alien slavers: the Sereia. Rose learned that Jack had assassinated the scientist Zloy Volk, and a shamed Jack left using his vortex manipulator. They would reunite in the fifty-fourth century.

wih - 1683 - FP: NEWTONS SLEEP[947] **->** Nathaniel Silver, having worked for *le Pouvoir* since the botched Cambridge raid in 1671, stretched the mysterious egg in his possession to create a series of mirrors that displayed possible futures. Cousin Greenaway, in a fit of anger against the babel within Isaac Newton, stabbed Newton with a biodata needle designed to wipe people from history. Silver removed the needle and saved Newton, but enough of a temporal anomaly appeared within Newton's

---

in real life went underground as "Dr Bendo" following a brawl with the night watch, in which one of his companions was killed. "The Inferno" is presumably a precursor to the nightclub seen in *The War Machines*. (Writer Daniel O'Mahony also mentions the Inferno – the nightclub, that is, not the brothel – in *The Cabinet of Light*, so the name of the brothel here is looking less and less like coincidence.)

938 "Centuries" before "The Iron Legion". Vesuvius is the oldest robot, and a guard says he "should have been dealt with centuries ago". Likewise, the Bestarius have lain in their suspended animation "for centuries".

939 "Something like three hundred years" before *The Drosten's Curse*.

940 "A thousand years" before *3rdA: The Havoc of Empires*.

941 "A few centuries" before *The Oseidon Adventure*.

942 "Three centuries" before *Shada*.

943 *Enlightenment*

944 *Phantasmagoria*

945 *The Last Dodo*

946 Dating *The Ninth Doctor Year One* (Titan 9th Doc #1.9-1.10, "Slaver's Song") - The year is given.

947 Dating *FP: Newtons Sleep* (FP novel #6) - The back cover cites the year.

948 *Upstairs*. Construction of 10 Downing Street was completed in 1684.

949 "Two hundred years old, at least" before *Kiss of Death*. Mention of the Arar-Jecks suggests this is the time of the Twenty Aeon War cited in *Frontios*.

950 *Ghost Ship*. Purcell lived from 1659-1695.

951 *Battlefield*. This is the date on the capstone above

the hotel's fireplace.

952 *The Hollow Men*

953 *The Pirate Planet*. Newton lived 1642-1727, and published his theories of gravitation in 1685. This meeting clearly predates the fifth Doctor encountering Newton in *Circular Time*.

954 *Circular Time*: "Summer"

955 *Psi-ence Fiction*

956 Dating *The Glorious Revolution* (BF CC #4.2) - It's 1688, the year of the Glorious Revolution. The specific day isn't mentioned, but historically, the king fled on 10th of December and was captured the next day.

957 Dating *FP: Newtons Sleep* (FP novel #6) - Behn died 16th April, 1689. The real-life cause of her death isn't known, but she was buried in Westminster Abbey.

958 Dating *Erimem: Buccaneer* (Erimem novel #6) - Andy and company have gone back "a bit over three hundred years" to the "late seventeenth century". Governor Parson writes an account of these events on "July 1689".

959 *Erimem: Three Faces of Helena*

960 The background to *Iris S5: An Extraterrestrial Werewolf in Belgium*. The legend of Oude Rode Ogen ("Old Red Eyes") began in the late seventeenth century.

961 "A few hundred years" before *The Ultimate Adventure*.

962 *Winner Takes All*. This would be around 1690.

963 "Final Sacrifice"

964 *TW: Trace Memory*

965 *Cat's Cradle: Witch Mark*. The Ceffyl have lived at peace with the humans on Tír na n-Óg for "three centuries" (p169).

timeline to net the attention of parties in humanity's post-human era. The babel was trapped in Silver's egg, and killed when the egg compressed into a dark pebble. Greenaway and her fellow Cousins performed rituals to stabilise Newton's history. On Aphra Behn's recommendation, Larissa of the Great Houses forged a personal alliance with the Faction.

A time-active fungus established itself in the attic of 10 Downing Street, and set about spreading its mycelia into various eras. The servants at No. 10 formed a conspiracy that directed the fungus to feed off prized members of the elite. The cabal believed that, in time, the fungus would absorb the best attributes of its victims, and develop into a Prime Minister to lead the British Empire to glory. The first Doctor suspected that the ruckus he, Steven and Vicki made in the Downing Street attic in July 1900 rippled through time and caused the rumour that Sir George Downing – the property speculator who built Downing Street in the 1680s – continued to haunt the locale.[948]

Vislor Turlough's great-great-great grandfather was a member of the royal court on Trion, and an ambassador to alien worlds. By the time the Arar-Jecks had fought their way to Trion's borders, Turlough's ancestor had negotiated with neutral powers for use of a dimensional vault – a final hiding place for the Trion Queen and her entourage. In future, rumours spoke of the Queen's "lost treasure horde", which remained in the vault for safekeeping.[949]

The Doctor met the Baroque composer Henry Purcell.[950]

The Gore Crow Hotel was built in 1684.[951]

In 1685, the Hakolian battle vehicle Jerak arrived on Earth, but failed to find its partner, the Malus, as planned. The scheduled invasion didn't happen, and the battle vehicle went dormant. Its radiating malevolence ensured that local legends sprang up of an evil spirit named "the Jack i' the Green".[952]

The fourth Doctor claimed to have met Isaac Newton. At first he dropped apples on his head, but then he explained gravity to him over dinner.[953] Newton was furious about the Doctor dropping an apple on his head, as his nose bled for three days.[954] Newton showed the Doctor around Cambridge University.[955]

1688 (10th-11th December) - THE GLORIOUS REVOLUTION[956] -> The second Doctor, Jamie and Zoe arrived just prior to the Glorious Revolution – the relatively bloodless transfer of power from King James VII to William of Orange – and aided Queen Mary and her son, James Stewart, in fleeing to France as history recorded. They soon met King James VII. Jamie, having fought for James Stewart's right to the throne in future, persuaded the king to stay and fight rather than fleeing London – the act that would doom his kingship...

(=) A paradoxical timeline was created in which the king became mad with power and vowed to burn those who didn't convert to Catholicism. The historical alterations cast doubt upon whether Jamie had ever met the Doctor, and so a Celestial Intervention Agency operative circa 1786 intervened...

... enabling Jamie to realise his terrible mistake. Jamie and his friends abducted the king, then ratted him out to the locals. It was believed that the king had abdicated. The Doctor's party also met the infamous "hanging judge", George Jeffries, who was captured while trying to escape.

wih - 1689 (16th April) - FP: NEWTONS SLEEP[957] -> Aphra Behn was dying, having been poisoned by remedies prescribed by a quack. Nathaniel Silver visited Behn and comforted her on the last day of her life.

c 1689 - ERIMEM: BUCCANEER[958] -> Erimem's friend Andrea Hansen decided to enjoy some Me Time in the past as a heroic highwaywoman. Governor William Arthur Parson oversaw England's interests in islands off the Americas, and Andy rescued his niece, Olivia Parson, from the clutches of a lustful mine owner. Erimem, Ibrahim and Helena visited this era to find Andy, and passed themselves off as foreign nobility. At one of the Governor's dinner parties, Helena sang "In My Life" three hundred years before it was written.

Andy and Olivia became lovers, but were captured by Olivia's ex-fiance: Captain Winston, thought dead at sea, but now a pirate. Winston directed his ship, the *Behemoth*, to attack Port Thorpe, but Erimem defeated Winston in single combat, and Olivia killed the man when he tried to shoot Erimem after yielding. Olivia thereby became the mistress of the *Behemoth*, renamed it *Future's Hope* and embarked on a career of sailing cargo. Andy and her friends returned to 2016, but Andy and Olivia remained in a long-distance relationship.

As part of her visits with Andy, Olivia attended the wedding of Ibrahim Hadmani and Helena.[959]

An extraterrestrial werewolf visited Belgium, becoming less-than-whole when local residents skinned it. The werewolf survived for centuries as a human, its story inspiring the legend of "Old Red Eyes", a.k.a. the Beast of Flanders.[960] The Doctor visited Altair III, and fought off a Dalek invasion with the help of the insectoid natives there.[961] The Doctor visited Hampton Court maze soon after it was planted.[962] The Doctor took Newton to Practas Seven, and it made the man sit in a corner and whimper.[963] The Vondrax assumed the forms of samurai, and killed many in Japan, 1691.[964] Goibhnie, a member of the Troifran race, took samples from Earth and created the mystical world of Tír na n-Óg.[965]

1692 - THE WITCH HUNTERS[966] -> The TARDIS landed in Salem, and the first Doctor, Ian, Barbara and Susan quickly retreated to avoid becoming implicated in the witch trials. Susan, however, wanted to help those who were accused and took the TARDIS back there. She and Ian were soon accused of witchcraft. The Doctor saved his friends, but to preserve history, he persuaded the governor not to pardon the alleged witch Rebecca Nurse, age 71.

Later, the Doctor returned and took Rebecca to 1954. He convinced her that her death would encourage future tolerance, and she agreed to return to her native time and face her historical demise.

Julie D'Aubigny became adept at fencing, and fancied herself a swashbuckling hero. She fell in love with a woman named Brigitte – when their relationship was discovered, Brigitte was sent to a convent in Avignon, and Julie was married off to Monsieur Maupin, a diplomat. She tied him up on their wedding night, and made off with Brigitte after setting her nunnery on fire – but Brigitte ended their relationship to devote herself to God.

Julie became a travelling singer and thief working with Seranne, a swordsman from Marseille, but killed him when he tried to steal their earnings. King Louis XIV pardoned Julie of duelling, arson and kidnapping, on the condition that she sang in the Paris Opera. She did so as Mademoiselle Maupin.[967]

1695 (9th-11th June) - THE TWELFTH DOCTOR YEAR TWO[968] -> The twelfth Doctor attended the Paris Opera, and thought it very strange that Cardinal Richelieu was still alive, since he officially had died in 1642. The singer-swordswoman Julie D'Aubigny aided the Doctor as the Darkness within Richelieu capitalised on an eclipse, and opened a portal to let more Darkness loose on Earth. The Doctor used the TARDIS to open a time tunnel to the Saberhagen Quasar – its intense light eradicated the Darkness and ended Richelieu's extended lifespan. Julie suggested she and the Doctor duel with swords, to see if she could join him on his travels...

An extra-terrestrial was "lost in darkness" for many centuries, but fell to Earth and adopted human form. In 1695, she fell in love with a man named Tobias Williams – who decried her as a witch and had her burned at the stake. The shapeshifter survived, and vowed vengeance upon Williams and his descendants. Whenever sons were born to the family, the creature rendered its grandparents immobile with a potion. They were believed dead... and then buried, but remained aware for a hundred years.[969]

c 1696 - THE SMUGGLERS[970] -> A group of pirates led by Captain Samuel Pike of the *Black Albatross* attempted to locate Captain Avery's treasure in Cornwall, with only a rhyme as a clue to its whereabouts. Avery had

---

966 Dating *The Witch Hunters* (PDA #9) - Each section states the date. Nurse was executed on 19th July, 1692.
967 The King pardons Julie the year before *The Twelfth Doctor Year Two*: "Terror of the Cabinet Noir" [1695].
968 Dating *The Twelfth Doctor Year Two* (Titan 12th Doc #2.11-2.13, "Terror of the Cabinet Noir") - The year is given. An eclipse occurred on 11th June, 1695; the story happens at least "two days" beforehand.

Julie is something of a Schrodinger's Companion... the Previously On blurbs keep naming her as the newest companion, but it's a bit open-ended as to whether she joins the TARDIS at story's end. The Previously On for the *next* story, "Invasion of the Mindmorphs", claims that the Doctor's let Julie go off to her own adventures. There's no other sign that they actually travel together, or what those adventures entailed.
969 *100*: "Bedtime Story"
970 Dating *The Smugglers* (4.1) - The Doctor notes that the design of the church he sees on leaving the TARDIS means that they could have landed "at any time after the sixteenth century". Later, he says that the customers in the inn are dressed in clothes from the "seventeenth century". *The Terrestrial Index* and *The TARDIS File* set the story in "1650", *The TARDIS Logs* in "1646". *Timelink* went for "1672", *About Time* said it's "likely to be after 1685".

The Discontinuity Guide states that as a character says "God save the King" (and, perhaps more to the point,

Josiah Blake is the "King's Revenue Officer"), it must be when England had a King (between 1603-1642, 1660-1688 or 1694 onwards). However, William III ruled as King from 1688-1702, and even though this was alongside Mary at first, legally and in the minds of the public he was King. The *Guide* further speculates that the costumes suggest this story is set in the latter part of the century.

A "SMUGGLERS" PREQUEL?: It's become fashionable in fandom to say that *The Curse of the Black Spot* (X6.3), set in April 1699, is either a sequel or a prequel to *The Smugglers*. The problem being: on balance, it isn't. It's possible that the captain's name in *The Curse of the Black Spot*, "Avery", was intended as an homage to a referenced character in *The Smugglers*, but the ties between the two stories run no deeper than that. *The Smugglers* claims that Avery died a drunken pauper, while *The Curse of the Black Spot* has him leave Earth in a spaceship. Even one assumes that rumours of Avery's death were greatly exaggerated, the ships seen in the two stories have different names – in *The Smugglers*, it's the *Black Albatross*; in *The Curse of the Black Spot*, it's *The Fancy*, in accordance with the ship of the real-life, seventeenth-century pirate Henry Every. Most glaringly, Avery's gold in *Black Spot* is dumped into the ocean, making it exceedingly unlikely that it could be the same gold buried amongst some tombstones in

died a drunk pauper, and his treasure was said to be cursed. The first Doctor, Ben and Polly became embroiled in efforts to find the treasure. It was found in the local church, and the names in the rhyme appeared on tombs in the crypt. The King's militia arrived, killing Pike and many of his crew.

Toby Avery's mother died, two years after he last saw his father.[971]

1699 (April) - THE CURSE OF THE BLACK SPOT[972] -> The pilot of a Skerth spaceship had died when exposed to human bacteria. The ship's holographic medical system continued on automatic, and took to teleporting injured sailors and pirates into its medical bay. The system manifested as a glowing Siren and appeared through reflected surfaces – shining treasure was an excellent medium for this, and the Siren inspired folklore about gold-laden ships being cursed.

The eleventh Doctor, Amy and Rory landed aboard a becalmed pirate ship, the *Fancy*, on which the Siren had apparently disintegrated anyone with even a slight scratch. The Doctor freed the Siren's patients. Captain Avery and his son Toby took command of the Skerth ship, and left with the crew of the *Fancy* to explore the stars, starting with Sirius.

Calling in a debt, the eleventh Doctor summoned Avery and Toby to help him storm Demons Run and rescue Amy.[973] The Hussar and Anne Bonny raided sailing vessels with their timeship, the Kraken, and obtained a vast proportion of the *Gank-I-Sawai's* fabled plunder, as well as Long Ben Avery's treasure. One of their attacks resulted in *The Black Diana* and its captain, James "Porkbelly" Corker, being forgotten from history.[974]

The Eighteenth Century

Select members of the Hawthorne family began their watch over Devil's End. The mother of Dulcin Hawthorne was the first to own the family's prized grimoire.[975]

Biochemical warfare wiped out the population of Anima Persis. The ghosts of the dead haunted this geopsychic planet. The Time Lords used the world as a training ground.[976] The Talichre once attacked Anima Persis.[977] The alien scientist Raldonn travelled the universe peacefully for hundreds of years. He would crash on Earth in the nineteen sixties.[978]

An alien force arrived in Earth's dimension, and was separated into a ghostly ectoplasmic form and a disembodied bundle of psychic energy. Henry Deadstone encountered the creature's psychic aspect and buried it in a pit, but was mentally compelled to feed it children and animals. Gypsies hanged Deadstone for "feeding children to the Devil". The creature remained in the pit and artificially extended Deadstone's life.[979]

A Vurosis – a proto-molecular parasite from the Actron Pleiades System – fell to Earth as a seed, and germinated beneath a well in the English village of Creighton Mere. It spawned an eighteenth-century legend that a highwayman had lost his gold treasure down the well, and drowned in it while hiding from the Duke of York.[980]

By the late twentieth century, no documents from before 1700 existed at Boscombe Hall. This was the year before Dr Thomas Borlase was born.[981] Weed creatures were seen in the North Sea during the eighteenth century.[982] The Doctor "ran Taunton for two weeks in the eighteenth century and I've never been so bored".[983]

An inter-clan marriage between the Blathereen and the Slitheen resulted in some tan-skinned hybrids.[984] During the eighteenth century, the Ragman inhabited the

---

Cornwall in *The Smugglers*.

Whoniverse (BBC, pgs 58-60) puts the accounts of *The Curse of the Black Spot* and *The Smugglers* side by side without trying to reconcile them.

971 "The previous winter" and "three years" before *The Curse of the Black Spot*.

972 Dating *The Curse of the Black Spot* (X6.3) - The Doctor says it's the "seventeenth century". The BBC website preview for the episode has Avery give the date as "April 1st, 1699", and says the ship has been becalmed for eight days. The Skerth are named in *Doctor Who: The Encyclopedia*, but not on screen.

973 *A Good Man Goes to War*

974 *FP: Weapons Grade Snake Oil*. Avery captured the *Gank-I-Sawai*, a Mughal trading ship, on 7th December, 1695.

975 "Centuries" before *Daemons: White Witch of Devil's End* (story #4, "The Poppet"). Dulcin's mother wouldn't

naturally be so far removed from Olive Hawthorne (*The Daemons*), but the Hawthorne women chosen as guardians of Devil's End don't appear to age naturally – save, oddly enough, for Olive herself.

976 "Hundreds of years" before *Death Comes to Time*. Anima Persis is also mentioned in *Relative Dementias* and *The Tomorrow Windows*.

977 *Relative Dementias*

978 "Operation Proteus"

979 Unspecified "centuries" before *The Deadstone Memorial*.

980 *Wishing Well*

981 *The Stones of Blood*

982 *Fury from the Deep*

983 *The Highest Science*

984 "Many generations" before *SJA: The Gift*.

body of an executed highwayman.[985] The Doctor visited Rio de Janero in 1700.[986] **The Uvodni-Malakh War began in the eighteenth century.**[987]

On the planet Artaris, civilisation divided itself into fortified city-states. The planet began to industrialize, and "Reeves" emerged as a type of government overseer in the city-state of Excelis. Within a hundred years, a Reeve had commissioned volunteers among the citizens to become law-enforcement officers named Wardens. The immortal Grayvorn worked as one of the earliest Wardens and rose through the ranks.[988]

The Doctor learned to cook in eighteenth-century Paris.[989] He told the philosopher David Hume that you couldn't have an effect without a cause.[990] **A Cyber-ship crashed in Colchester and went dormant.**[991]

Two humanoid life forms – the carbon-based Fleshkind and the boron-based Metalkind – lived in a binary system at the eye of the Tornado Nebula. The Fleshkind mined the Metalkind's world for ores, which were actually the Metalkind's children, and so the two races warred with each other for centuries.[992]

The homeworld of the Veritas – a race of beings with no concept of lying – was obliterated when an unscrupulous merchant released an energy virus there. Three Veritas survived, and pledged to pass sentence on any being they found to be practicing deceit.[993]

- -
(=) Katsura Sato had conquered the Europe of his alternate timeline. Africa and Asia soon followed.[994]
- -

Will Butley, a clerk in Shanghai, fell in love with a Taoist philosopher who taught him the secrets of the *chi*: the life force itself. Butley murdered his lover, and spent the next three centuries draining the life essences from young men as a means of prolonging his own.[995]

The Doctor met the Scottish outlaw Rob Roy.[996] The Doctor studied with the Miccosukee for a time.[997]

---

985 *Rags*

986 *Loups-Garoux*

987 *SJA: Warriors of Kudlak*

988 "Three hundred years" before *Excelis Rising*.

989 *The Lodger* (TV)

990 "The Child of Time" (*DWM*). Hume lived 1711-1776.

991 Unspecified "centuries" before *Closing Time*.

992 "Centuries" before *SJA: Sky*.

993 "Centuries" before *SJA: Judgement Day*.

994 "Within a century" of his crusade beginning, according to "The Glorious Dead".

995 "Three hundred years" before *SJS: The Tao Connection*.

996 *Masters of Earth*. "Rob Roy", full name Robert Roy MacGregor, lived 1671-1734.

997 *The Drosten's Curse*. The Miccosukee inhabited the American South, and migrated to northern Florida in the eighteenth and nineteenth centuries.

998 Dating *Phantasmagoria* (BF #2) - The exact date is given.

999 Dating *River S2: The Eye of the Storm* (BF *The Diary of River Song* #2.4) - The story centres around the Great Storm of 1703, which struck Britain on 26th November (going by the Julian calendar) or 7th December (the Gregorian one). Defoe, the author of *Robinson Crusoe* and *Moll Flanders*, was indeed released from prison a week before the Great Storm, and wrote a pioneering work of journalism (*The Storm*, 1704) based upon accounts of it. River inspiring Moll Flanders is a deliberate wink at the actress who portrays River Song, Alex Kingston, having played Moll in a 1996 ITV adaptation.

1000 Dating *Doctor Who and the Pirates* (BF #43) - The date isn't specified beyond it being "the eighteenth century".

1001 *Leth-St: Times Squared*

1002 Dating "Ravens" (*DWM* #188-190) - It's "four hun-

dred years" before the main event of this story.

1003 Dating *Circular Time*: "Summer" (BF #91) - The year isn't specified, but the month is given as July. The story occurs while Newton is warden of the Royal Mint – he was appointed to the post in 1696, and served until his death in 1727. This date is otherwise arbitrary, based upon actor David Warner's age of 65 when he voiced Newton (who was born in January 1643 by the Gregorian calendar) for this audio.

Historically, counterfeiting in this period was treated as high treason, and those found guilty were put to death. Convictions proved difficult to achieve, but Newton – often venturing out in disguise, as occurs here – personally collected evidence against such criminals. His most notable prosecution was against the counterfeiter William Chaloner – who was hanged, drawn and quartered on 23rd March, 1699.

1004 Dating *The Rising Night* (BBC DW audiobook #4) - The Doctor guesses that it's the seventeenth or early eighteenth century; the back cover says that it's the eighteenth. The Baobhan is freed in October, and the Doctor arrives three weeks later.

1005 *Only Human*. Montagu, an aristocrat chiefly known for her letters from Turkey (when she was the wife of the British ambassador) lived 1689-1762.

1006 *The Android Invasion*. The Doctor presumably means the first Duke, who lived 1650-1722 and was made a Duke in 1702.

1007 *The Wages of Sin*. This would have to be between 1712-1725.

1008 "Three hundred years" before *UNIT S5: Encounters: Invocation*.

1009 *The English Way of Death* (p46).

1010 *FP: Weapons Grade Snake Oil*. Not much is known of Bonny outside of Capt Charles Johnson's *A General History of the Pyrates* (1724), but it seems she was

1702 (8th-10th March) - PHANTASMAGORIA[998] -> The fifth Doctor and Turlough witnessed phantoms abducting a gambler, Edmund Carteret, who died from a heart attack. This was the latest of many such disappearances. The Doctor discovered that a stranded alien, Karthok of Daeodalus, was operating on Earth as Sir Nikolas Valentine, a card-playing member of the Diabola Club. Valentine had been absorbing human minds into his ship's computer, then using the amassed calculating power to help the ship heal itself. The phantoms were the collected consciousness of the minds absorbed, directed by Valentine to snatch more victims. The Doctor tricked Valentine into seeding his own bioprint into the ship's computer, whereupon the phantoms tore Valentine to pieces. Valentine's ship was programmed to self-destruct.

1703 (Summer to November) - RIVER S2: THE EYE OF THE STORM[999] -> A Sperovore Queen laid its eggs in the home of Sir Robert Hardy, the Speaker of the House of Commons, so they could feed off the potential futures of the seamstress Sarah Dean and the tilemaker Isaac George, as well as all their offspring. The seventh Doctor and River Song arrived from four centuries on, but the Doctor – not quite trusting River – had her detained in Newgate. While jailed, she met the author Daniel Defoe, who had been imprisoned when Queen Anne took a dim view of his satire.

Six months later, the sixth Doctor arrived and mistook River for a Time Lord operative. Defoe was released, and arranged River's liberty. The Great Storm of 1703 signalled the start of events that would culminate in Earth existing in a Schrodinger's state four hundred years on. River explained the stakes to Sarah and Isaac, and convinced them to sacrifice their lives by walking into the storm. Their deaths deprived the Sperovore Queen of their futures, killing her eggs.

As River told Defoe her name was "Moll", he based *Moll Flanders* on her. She once more smooched the sixth Doctor with her memory-robbing lipstick. When the seventh Doctor didn't fall for any of her ploys, she shot him unconscious and had the TARDIS edit out his memories of her.

c 1705 - DOCTOR WHO AND THE PIRATES[1000] -> The TARDIS landed on board a ship as the pirate Red Jasper attacked it. The sixth Doctor and Evelyn were taken on board Jasper's vessel. Jasper was looking for treasure in the Ruby Islands, and was unimpressed by the Doctor's reluctance to kill. The Doctor incited mutiny on Jasper's ship, leaving Jasper stranded.

A 19 year old living in the Nyainquentanglha mountain range, Jemba-wa, fell under the influence of the Great Intelligence, in 1706. He would assist Padmasambhava with constructing the Intelligence's Yeti.[1001]

c 1707 - "Ravens"[1002] -> The seventh Doctor saw patterns in history and convinced a warrior in seventeenth-century Japan, the Raven, that although his wife and children were dead, he could still save others. The Doctor took Raven to the future to confront a street gang: the Ravens.

c 1708 (July) - CIRCULAR TIME: "Summer"[1003] -> The fifth Doctor was distracted by an alchemy demonstration in London, and handed Nyssa some coins from other eras. Sir Isaac Newton, disguised as an Algerian juggler with a false chin, witnessed this and – under his authority as director of the Royal Mint – had them incarcerated for counterfeiting. Newton's formidable brain pieced together many details about the coins, and made several correct guesses about the future and the Doctor and Nyssa's origins. The knowledge triggered one of Newton's seizures, and the Doctor prevented him from swallowing his own tongue and choking to death. Newton ordered the travellers' release, hoping they would never meet again. The Doctor thought that Newton would have a headache for some days, then become bored with the memory of the time travellers and move on to something new.

c 1709 (November) - THE RISING NIGHT[1004] -> In Thornton Rising, Yorkshire, the last of the Baobhan Sith was freed from its cairn. Its spaceship projected a force field that trapped the locals within, and kept the sun at bay. Three weeks later, the tenth Doctor confronted the Baobhan as it infected other women with its taint and started slaughtering the men of the town. The Doctor deactivated the force field, slaying those with Baobhan DNA via exposure to ultraviolet. A tainted young woman named Charity survived, and the Doctor – possibly after a few side-adventures with her – relocated Charity to a planet where the sun never rose.

Events in Thornton Rising were attributed to the Devil's work. The village was removed from all the maps of the kingdom, as if it had never existed.

The Doctor knows that marrying for love is a mistake, due to his experience with Lady Mary Wortley Montagu.[1005] **The Doctor once met the Duke of Marlborough.**[1006] He also met Peter the Great in Russia, and saw the Peter and Paul Cathedral being built.[1007] Sir John Ealdon built Ealdon House, but in doing so accidentally created a madness-inducing infrasound, and threw himself to his death.[1008]

In 1720, the Doctor saw the Earth's fury at Okushiri.[1009] A Great House member, the Hussar, rescued the pirate Anne Bonny from her cell in Jamaica. She became his lover, and disappeared from the historical record.[1010] The Tristian Cluster was a series of asteroids that had been a planet, and settled in orbit around the planet's moon. They became much colder, but retained enough sunlight that the planet's albino-skinned natives could live there. A family of criminals from the Cluster came to reside on Earth in a West Sussex village, Wolfenden – so named for the white wolf that was carved into the rocks there. Most of the family remained in cryo-sleep, awaiting the day that their sentence had passed.[1011]

Through the millennia, the Silurian Malohkeh's family had monitored humankind's evolution. From around 1720, only Malohkeh remained to perform this task.[1012]

Casanova was born in 1725.[1013] A Cyber-ship fell onto the village of Klimtenburg, shattered the local church tower and buried itself in the graveyard behind it. The dozens of Cybermen inside remained in hibernation.[1014] *Gulliver's Travels* was published in 1726.[1015]

The Tenth Doctor and Reinette

1727 - THE GIRL IN THE FIREPLACE[1016] **->** The tenth Doctor passed through a time window from the fifty-first century and met Reinette for the first time.

c 1728 - THE GIRL IN THE FIREPLACE[1017] **->** Weeks or months later, he met her again and saved her from a clockwork man.

An alien creature, the Onk Ndell Kith, was damaged when it fell into the water near Edinburgh. Its consciousness was split into multiple units programmed to self-replicate. A brewster found one of these, and sold it to a man named Alexander Monro. The unit sampled Monro's DNA, and transformed itself into a mechanical hand. He experimented on the hand using electricity, and it split into two – one of which turned into a younger copy of Monro. Without the critical mass needed to restore it to life, the Onk Ndell Kith remained disembodied until 1759.[1018]

wih - c 1730 (spring) - FP: NEWTONS SLEEP[1019] **->** Nathaniel Silver's extended lifespan came undone, and he died at the Inferno brothel, in the bed of a French prostitute named Madame Machine.

Padmasambhava encountered the Great Intelligence – and was the first to name it as such – on the astral plane. The fiend took over Padmasambhava's body; with Jemba-wa, he spent the next two centuries constructing the Intelligence's robot yeti.[1020] **The Aliens Act was passed in 1730.**[1021] **In the same year, a Mr Chicken resided at 10 Downing Street.**[1022]

A Nixi colonisation vessel landed in Britain, near Briarwood House. Madeline, the great-great-great-great-

---

imprisoned in Jamaica in October 1720.

1011 "Hundreds of years" before *SJA: The White Wolf*.

1012 Malohkeh has been watching humankind "for the last three hundred years" according to *Cold Blood*.

1013 "One hundred forty-five years" after *The Vampires of Venice* (which is in accordance with Casanova's real-life birth year).

1014 Vaguely said to happen "ages back" (p122) and "all those years ago" (p159) before *Plague of the Cybermen*, but certainly long enough that the event has become the stuff of legend.

1015 *The Mind Robber*

1016 Dating *The Girl in the Fireplace* (X2.4) - Reinette says it's 1727. The Doctor tells her that August of that year is "a bit rubbish", but he's no way of knowing if August has already passed or not. We might expect Reinette to correct him if it has, but he's gabbling and doesn't really give her a chance.

1017 Dating *The Girl in the Fireplace* (X2.4) - It is "weeks, months" after the Doctor and Reinette's first meeting. It's snowing outside, so it's winter. The older Reinette later says she has "known the Doctor since she was seven" – as she was born 29th December, 1721, she would have been that age almost exclusively in 1728. If the initial meeting takes place in 1727 and the second is "months" later in 1728, then Reinette's comment about her age makes some sense – although it means (not unreasonably) that she's more referring to the Doctor saving her from the clockwork man than their initial, very brief conversation through the fireplace.

This probably isn't what was intended on screen, but it fits the available evidence fairly well. The alternative is that the Doctor and Reinette first meet in the last three days of 1727 – which would again push their second meeting into 1728.

1018 "Thirty years" before *The Many Hands*.

1019 Dating *FP: Newtons Sleep* (FP novel #6) - It's "nearly sixty years" (p135) after the raid at Salomon's house in 1671. It's also spring (p134).

1020 "Over two hundred years" before *The Abominable Snowmen* according to the Abbot Songsten, and reiterated in *Leth-St: Night of the Intelligence* and the Haisman Timeline.

1021 *The Highlanders*

1022 *World War Three* strongly implies that the Doctor met this man. Mr Chicken is historical, and was the last private resident of the building before King George II put it at the disposal of Sir Robert Walpole, the first British Prime Minister.

1023 "Two hundred years" before "A Matter of Life and Death" (issue #4).

1024 *PHP: The Ghosts of Gralstead*

1025 "Pay the Piper." Turpin died 7th April, 1739.

1026 Dating *The Doomwood Curse* (BF #111) - The back cover says it's "England, 1738". The story is a little more vague – the Doctor estimates that it's about "twenty years" after 1720, the date he spies on a tombstone. In real life, as in the *Doctor Who* universe, Turpin was a petty criminal and murderer whose exploits were over-romanticized in the likes of *The Genuine History of the*

grandmother of Bertie Bingham, found a system key that forced the Nixi king back into slumber for two hundred years.[1023] Sir Joseph Scrivener built Gralstead Hall in 1733.[1024] The eleventh Doctor owned a signed photo of Dick Turpin.[1025]

1738 - THE DOOMWOOD CURSE[1026] **->** The sixth Doctor and Charley arrived in 1738, having just encountered some Grel at the Archive of Alexandria IV. The literal-minded Grel – only able to acknowledge verifiable fact – had developed the Factualizer, a device that contained particles that made fictional tales manifest in the real world. The time travellers unknowingly released some of these particles, and people started acting in accordance with the novel *Rookwood* (1834). The Doctor eventually contained the particles after they concentrated for a time in Dick Turpin – a heroic highwayman as depicted in *Rookwood*, but a violent criminal and petty thief in real life. Turpin departed, historically fated to be tried and executed the following year.

c 1738 - THE GIRL IN THE FIREPLACE[1027] **->** The tenth Doctor met Reinette when she was a young woman, and snogged her.

In 1740, the man who would become known as Sabbath – a rival of the eighth Doctor – was born.[1028] On 8th September, 1742, the first Doctor and his companions spent some time in New England after their adventure in Salem, 1692.[1029]

Alexander Monro's father, John Monro, died in 1740. Alexander loved his father so much, he sought to use the Onk Ndell Kith's replication abilities to bring John back to life as an infant.[1030] Lady Clara, an orphaned rhinoceros,

began to tour and entertain the crowned heads of Europe.[1031] Smugglers killed Mrs Mountford on the moor in 1742. Her spirit would inhabit Malkin Place.[1032] Time travellers Penelope Gate and Joel Mintz briefly visited the year 1743.[1033]

1744 - THE GIRL IN THE FIREPLACE[1034] **->** The King's mistress, Madame de Chateauroux, was ill and near death. The tenth Doctor spied on Reinette as she walked through the grounds of a stately home, plotting to take Chateauroux's place.

1745 (February) - THE GIRL IN THE FIREPLACE[1035] **->** Shortly afterwards, the Doctor used another time window to visit Reinette the night she became the royal mistress.

A battlefield from the Jacobite Uprising was kidnapped by the War Lords.[1036]

Jamie McCrimmon Joins the TARDIS, Returns Home

1746 (April) - THE HIGHLANDERS / THE WAR GAMES[1037] **->** The second Doctor, Ben and Polly prevented the crooked solicitor Grey from selling Scottish prisoners into slavery. The highlanders had signed six-year plantation work contracts, but the Doctor sent the boat to the safety of France. Jamie McCrimmon, a Scots piper, joined the Doctor on his travels. The Time Lords later returned Jamie to his native time, but walled off his memories of all of his adventures with the Doctor save the very first.

Life of Richard Turpin (1739), *Black Bess and the Knight of the Road* (1867-68), *Rookwood* and other stories. Historically, as here, Turpin was executed in April 1739.
1027 Dating *The Girl in the Fireplace* (X2.4) - Reinette's age as a young woman isn't given, although she's "23" the next time they meet.
1028 *The Adventuress of Henrietta Street*, and specified on the back cover of *FP: Sabbath Dei*.
1029 *The Witch Hunters*
1030 *The Many Hands*
1031 "Fifteen years" before *The Behemoth*.
1032 *The Haunting of Malkin Place*
1033 *The Room with No Doors*
1034 Dating *The Girl in the Fireplace* (X2.4) - It is said that Madame de Chateauroux, the King's mistress prior to Reinette, is "ill and close to death". She died on 8th December, 1744. The scene probably occurs a few months beforehand, as Reinette is seen walking across a sunny patch of grass.
1035 Dating *The Girl in the Fireplace* (X2.4) - It is the

night that Reinette meets the King – historically this occurred in February 1745, after Chateauroux's death. The Doctor says Reinette is "23", which she historically would have been at the time. Incidentally, *The Girl in the Fireplace* fails to mention that the real-life Reinette was married at age 19 and later had two children, neither of whom lived beyond age ten.
1036 *The War Games*
1037 Dating *The Highlanders* and *The War Games* (4.4, 6.7) - The provisional title of *The Highlanders* was *Culloden*, and it is set shortly after that battle. Despite references in *The Highlanders*, *The War Games* and other stories, Culloden took place in April 1746, not 1745. This is first explicitly stated in *The Underwater Menace*, (although the draft script again said "1745"). The *Radio Times* specified that *The Highlanders* is set in April. The 1745 date has been perpetuated by the first edition of *The Making of Doctor Who*, and surfaces in a number of books, such as *The Roundheads*. *Birthright* has Jared Khan narrowly miss the TARDIS' departure after *The*

Once again, Jared Khan – this time known as Thomas – narrowly missed acquiring the TARDIS. After this time, he posed as "Alessandro di Cagliostro".[1038] The Kith-spawned version of Alexander Monro married a woman named Katherine.[1039] In 1750, a ship was wrecked off Haiti. Washed ashore was Nkome, a six-year-old African slave kept alive by voodoo, who began plotting his revenge against the white landowners – the blancs.[1040] The Doctor knew the landscape architect Lancelot Brown, a.k.a. Capability Brown.[1041]

Around 1750, a "Mr Sun" arrived in England from China. He inherited business space in Covent Garden, and opened a toy store there. A successive number of "Mr Suns" would operate the shop for two hundred years.[1042]

The Daemons inspired the Industrial Revolution.[1043] **The Doctor lost a bet to Casanova, and wound up owing the man a chicken.**[1044]

The Eleven-Day Empire Begins

Britain decided to adopt the Gregorian calendar, meaning that eleven days (from 2nd to 14th September) would be removed from the current calendar. Faction Paradox approached King George II and offered to purchase and occupy those missing days, intending that they would become their centre of operations, the Eleven-Day Empire.

The future George III was present in January 1752, when a Faction representative performed a six-armed "shadow dance" for the King at St James' Palace. The compact governing the sale of the eleven days was later signed in the upstairs room of a public house.[1045]

The father of Corwyn Marne, a founding member of the Society of Sigismondo di Rimini, attended the compact signing. At this time, Faction Paradox placed race banks and biodata codices at secret locations on Earth – a precaution if they required more troops and agents in this era. Sutekh ruined one such cache at Mount Vesuvius, and hid the body of Osiris there. In the decade to come, Osiris' biomass, co-mingled with Faction Paradox genetic material, seeped into the soil and was distributed amongst different lifeforms, including cows and flowers with black petals – "the buds of the hours".[1046]

On 14th September, 1752, as the calendar moved forward eleven days, one soul in a thousand – including a young Sabbath – saw, just for a moment, London bathed in shadow as the intervening days passed into Faction Paradox's care.[1047]

& 1754 - THE GIRL IN THE FIREPLACE[1048] **-> Rose appeared and warned Reinette that the clockwork men would come for her in five years. Reinette briefly travelled to the fifty-first century, then returned home.**

Highlanders, in a scene dated to 1746. Jamie returns to his native time in *The War Games*.

1038 *Birthright.* Cagliostro, an occultist in real life, lived from 1743-1795.

1039 "Eleven years" before the *The Many Hands*.

1040 *White Darkness*

1041 *The Doomwood Curse*. Brown lived 1716 to 1783.

1042 *The Cabinet of Light* (p85).

1043 *The Daemons*

1044 *The Vampires of Venice*

1045 *Interference, FP: Sabbath Dei, FP: In the Year of the Cat, FP: "Political Animals", FP: "Betes Noires and Dark Horses".*

1046 *FP: Coming to Dust*

1047 *Interference, FP: "Betes Noires and Dark Horses".*

1048 Dating *The Girl in the Fireplace* (X2.4) - It is "five years" before Reinette is 37. Owing to her 29th December birthday, she would have been that age almost the entirety of 1759, so it's now 1754.

1049 *Smith and Jones*. History says this happened 15th June, 1752. This is definitely a separate occasion from the tenth Doctor and Martha later (in their timelines) helping Franklin with kite-flying in *The Many Hands* [1759], but might reference the first Doctor's business with Franklin in *1stD* V1: *The Founding Fathers* [1762].

1050 *The Stones of Blood*

1051 *The Also People*

1052 "Nearly ten" Krillitane generations before *School Reunion*.

1053 *Hornets' Nest: The Circus of Doom*

1054 Dating *The Behemoth* (BF #231) – The year is given. This story is a pure historical.

1055 "A century" before "The Screams of Death".

1056 *The Wrong Doctors*

1057 Dating *The Girl in the Fireplace* (X2.4) - Rose says the clockwork men will come for Reinette "some time after your thirty-seventh birthday", which was on 29th December, 1758, so it must now be 1759.

1058 Dating *The Many Hands* (NSA #24) - The back cover and a caption before the first part of the book confirm the year.

1059 *...ish, Synthespians™, The Gallifrey Chronicles*

1060 *The Underwater Menace*

1061 *Benny B3: Legion: Shades of Gray*

1062 "The Collector"

1063 *The Silent Stars Go By*. Chingachgook appeared in the writings of James Fenimore Cooper, in stories set from 1740 to 1793.

1064 *CD,NM* V1: *Fallen Angels*. The advent of the sandwich is credited to Lord Sandwich (referenced in *FP: Sabbath Dei*), but the exact details of its invention are unknown.

1065 Dating *FP: Sabbath Dei/FP: In the Year of the Cat* (*FP* audios #1.3-1.4) - The narrator says, "In the calendar of the West, this is the winter in the year seventeen hundred and sixty-two".

1066 Dating *1stD* V1: *The Founding Fathers* (BF CC #9.3) - The year is given; Steven says it's "mid-summer","hot".

The Doctor received mild injuries when he helped Benjamin Franklin fly his kite.[1049] **Dr Borlase was killed surveying the Nine Travellers in 1754.**[1050] In the same year, the seventh Doctor discovered Kadiatu Lethbridge-Stewart half-dead in a slaver off Sierra Leone. He took her to the Civilisation of the People.[1051]

The Krillitanes, a race who are a genetic amalgam of all the species they've conquered, invaded the planet Bethsan and made a million widows in a day. They also absorbed the natives' wings into their own physiology.[1052] Antonio, a hideous dwarf, was born around 1755.[1053]

1756 - THE BEHEMOTH[1054] **->** The sixth Doctor, Constance and Flip tried to enjoy the springs in Bath, but wound up liberating the slaves at the Bristol Brassworks. The freed workers became handlers to Lady Clara, a touring rhinoceros.

The Doctor saw a performance of *Eurydice*.[1055] Stapleton Petherbridge, the first in a daisy chain of Pease Pottage residents linking a Time Demon to Melanie Bush through their very lives, was born in 1758.[1056]

& 1759 - THE GIRL IN THE FIREPLACE[1057] **->** The tenth Doctor saved Reinette from the clockwork men, but was apparently trapped in the past. However, Reinette had arranged to move her fireplace to her new residence, and it was still capable of working as a time window. The Doctor returned to the future, promising he would return for her.

1759 - THE MANY HANDS[1058] **->** The tenth Doctor and Martha landed in Edinburgh and briefly encountered Benjamin Franklin – who was there to pick up an honorary degree from St Andrews University – as the self-replicating biological material of the Onk Ndell Kith approached a critical mass. This caused the dead to rise from the city's Nor' Loch, and much of the Onk Ndell Kith's substance was animated as hundreds of hands. Many of the Onk Ndell Kith's parts merged into a larger creature, but it required the genetic information of eighty thousand people to fully repair itself. The Doctor tried to avert chaos, but the Onk Ndell Kith learned of the TARDIS and coveted it. Inspired by Franklin, the Doctor used a kite, the TARDIS key and a bolt of lightning to destroy the creature.

The last hand of the Onk Ndell Kith remained in Franklin's possession. The elder Alexander Monro died during this conflict – his younger self took over "father's" position as Chair of Anatomy at St Andrews.

The Doctor met Doctor Johnson.[1059] **Scottish poet Robert Burns was born in 1759, so Jamie McCrimmon had never heard of him.**[1060] Lord Elliot Marwick commissioned a tapestry to celebrate the wedding of his first-born

son in 1759. Successive generations of Marwicks were thought to add images of themselves to the work, but, in truth, the tapestry claimed the Marwicks' souls – and trapped them screaming – upon their deaths.[1061]

A salon full of people from the eighteenth century was kidnapped by Varan Tak.[1062] The Mohican named Chingachgook refined the Doctor's tracking abilities.[1063] The Doctor claimed to have invented the sandwich.[1064]

wih - 1762 - FP: SABBATH DEI / FP: IN THE YEAR OF THE CAT[1065] **->** Cousins Justine and Eliza, having fled the ruined Eleven-Day Empire, took refuge with the Order of St Francis. The arrival of their timeship caused such a commotion at Portsmouth Docks, they used lethal force against bystanders in fighting their way out. With Lord Dashwood absent, the Earl of Sandwich served as their host. The Cousins routed Special Forces assassins dispatched against them by the Service (over Sabbath's recommendation against such a move).

The living timeship Lolita sought to strengthen her hold on this era by giving King George III an army of three hundred clockwork automata, the commanders of which originated from circa the year 5000. Lolita overlaid her personality onto Queen Charlotte; it was possible that Prince George IV was actually of Lolita's blood.

The rival timeship Compassion, as channelled through the famous prostitute/witch Mary Culver, aided the Cousins against Lolita. Sabbath discretely helped Eliza, Lord Sandwich and the Sieur d'Eon – a French spy, transvestite and special envoy to King Louis IV – in destroying the automata army sequestered at Queen's House. A speech that the King had made to both houses of Parliament about bringing in "troops from outside the country" was dismissed as a symptom of his growing madness. Eliza informed Sandwich that history would forget his role in helping to save the world, and that he would chiefly be remembered for "those snacks you always have brought to your desk while you're working – where you stick the beef between the two slices of bread".

The Great Houses captured Justine, put her on trial and sentenced her to perpetual imprisonment in their prison asteroid.

1762 (Summer) - 1STD V1: THE FOUNDING FATHERS[1066] **->** The first Doctor stepped out into London on a hot summer day, and absent-mindedly threw his coat back into the console room... only to realize that the TARDIS key was still in his pocket, meaning he, Steven and Vicki were now locked outside the Ship. The trio tracked down Benjamin Franklin at the Pennsylvania Coffee Shop, and aided with his experiments to deduce the nature of lightning. Using a kite, the Doctor conducted lightning down a bit of twine into the TARDIS lock, which succeeded in opening the Ship – but Franklin followed the

Doctor inside. Franklin touched the controls, but received a shock that rendered him unconscious. The Doctor carried Franklin outside the Ship, and the latter – being a rational man who didn't believe in miracles – believed that he'd imagined the incident after being jolted by lightning.

wih - 1763 - FP: A LABYRINTH OF HISTORIES[1067] **->** Compassion spent six months using her influence to liberate Justine, who was reunited with her friends in 1763.

wih - 1763 - FP: COMING TO DUST / THE SHIP OF A BILLION YEARS[1068] **->** Three members of the Society of Sigismondo di Rimini – Corwyn Marne, John Pennerton

and Abelard Finton – summoned Cousins Justine and Eliza to Naples to consult on reports of renewed activity from the Mal'akh. Justine vowed to kill Sutekh upon discovering that he had destroyed what was probably the last cache of Faction biomass on Earth. Merytra's cadre of Mal'akh self-immolated themselves – a sacrifice to open an interdimensional tunnel for benefit of their master. Justine used this tunnel to travel to the Osirian Court.

wih - Cousin Eliza joined Justine at the Court, and spent weeks tracking down what remained of Osiris' biodata, which was now spread across thousands of miles.[1069]

1067 Dating *FP: The Labyrinth of Histories* (FP audio #1.6) - Compassion tells Justine, "I'll explain once you're back here with us in 1763", indicating that the New Year has come and gone.

1068 Dating *FP: Coming to Dust/FP: The Ship of a Billion Years* (FP audio #2.1-2.2) - The year is given. Corwyn expects his ailing daughter will die "by this summer", so it's earlier than that in the year.

1069 *FP: Body Politic*

1070 Dating *FP: Ozymandias* (FP audio #2.5) - Marne says that it's been "more than six months", since they last saw Justine, but Finton later comments that it was "a year ago". Either way, it's most likely 1764 now.

1071 Dating *The Girl in the Fireplace* (X2.4) - The final sequence takes place shortly after Reinette's death. This historically happened on 15th April, 1764 – the same year as is listed on the painting at the end of the story. The King says Reinette was "43" when she died, but historically she was only 42. (Writer Steven Moffat has conceded this as a mistake.)

1072 Dating *FP: The Judgment of Sutekh* (FP audio #2.6) - The dates are given in Pennerton's letters.

1073 *P.R.O.B.E.: The Devil of Winterborne*

1074 "Five hundred years" before *The Daleks*.

THE NEUTRONIC WAR ON SKARO: The Neutronic War referred to in *The Daleks* is clearly a different conflict from the Thal-Kaled War seen in *Genesis of the Daleks*, given that the Neutronic War in *The Daleks* lasted just "one day", whereas the Thal-Kaled War lasted "nearly a thousand years". In the first story, a Dalek tells the Doctor that "We, the Daleks and the Thals" fought the Neutronic War, implying that this was after the Daleks were created (a version of events supported by the *TV Century 21* comic strip). The Thal named Alydon speaks of this as the "final war", maybe suggesting that there was more than one.

It's interesting to note that after the Neutronic War, both the Thals and Dals mutated until they resembled the state they'd been in at *Genesis of the Daleks* – the Thals becoming blond humanoids, the Dals becoming green Dalek blobs.

1075 This is the opening caption of the first "The Daleks" *TV Century 21* strip.

1076 Dating "The Daleks: Genesis of Evil" (*TV21* #1-3, *DWW* #33) - This is the first story in "The Daleks" comic strip printed in *TV Century 21*. As the story starts with the birth of the Daleks, but ends at a time when Earth has spaceships (shortly before *The Dalek Invasion of Earth*, it seems), and "Legacy of Yesteryear" is explicitly "centuries" after "Genesis of Evil", the strips have been broken into two blocks, with events of each block happening over a relatively short time, but with hundreds of years between the two.

The year this story – and so the rest of its block – is set isn't given in the strip, but Drenz was killed in 2003 according to both *The Dalek Book* and *The Dalek Pocketbook and Space-Travellers Guide*, both of which are otherwise consistent with the strip. However, this isn't 2003 AD: *The Dalek Outer Space Book* mentions the "New Skaro Calendar", with Year Zero being the year the "Thousand Years War" started. It also says the Daleks emerged in the year 1600 and "The Year of the Dalek" lasted until the year 1,000,000 (the original date given in scripts for *The Daleks' Master Plan*, which may or may not be a coincidence). This would account for a line in "The Dalek World" stating it's not unusual to find Daleks that are a million years old. See the Are There Two Dalek Histories? sidebar for how this can be reconciled with *Genesis of the Daleks*.

So... the blue-skinned original Daleks appear in 1600, "Genesis of Evil" is set in 2003, and *The Daleks* takes place five hundred years after "Genesis of Evil" (so around 2503). We also know that *Genesis of the Daleks* is set at the end of the Thousand Years War, so in 1000. Making the assumption that a "year" is the same length as a year on Earth (as this chronology does, unless stated otherwise), and using other dates from this chronology, we can work back. *The Daleks* is set in 2263 AD and 2503 according to the New Skaro Calendar, so to calculate an Earth date, you subtract two hundred and forty from the Skaro date. Therefore, "Genesis of Evil" starts in 1763 and *Genesis of the Daleks* is set in 760 AD.

1077 "Legacy of Yesteryear"

1078 Dating *ST:* "Old Flames" (BBC *Short Trips* #1b) - The "eighteenth century" is repeatedly named, and Sarah

wih - 1764 - FP: OZYMANDIAS[1070] -> Justine and Eliza sent a telepathic message to Corwyn Marne and Abelard Finton, who comprehended it through their dreams and poetry writing. The two men felt compelled to journey via an interdimensional tunnel to Mars, circa 5,000 BC, where they assisted the Cousins in defeating Sutekh.

1764 (15th April) - THE GIRL IN THE FIREPLACE[1071] -> The tenth Doctor once again travelled to France to meet Reinette, but arrived to find that she had died. He took a letter she had written to him back to the future.

wih - 1764 (16th October to 8th November) - FP: THE JUDGMENT OF SUTEKH[1072] -> Sutekh mentally compelled John Pennerton to write letters urging that the Society of Sigismondo di Rimini destroy Faction Paradox wherever it found them. Sutekh released Pennerton from his servitude about three weeks later, and also returned Abelard Finton home. Finton's encounter with Sutekh proved so horrifying, he soon died.

Winterborne was built in Surrey, 1764, by Sir Isaac Greatorex for use as a charity house, but was later sold off and became a public boys' school. Greatorex himself was charged with being the leader of a dark cult, and was tried in secret and hanged.[1073]

Neutronic War on Skaro - and the Dalek Conquests Begin

& 1763 – There were two races on Skaro: the original Daleks (or Dals) and the Thals. The Daleks were teachers and philosophers, the Thals were a famous warrior race. Skaro was a world full of ideas, art and invention.

However, there were old rivalries between the two races, and this led to a final war. Skaro was destroyed in a single day when the Daleks detonated a huge neutronic bomb. The radiation from the weapon killed nearly all life on the planet, and petrified the vegetation. The only animals that survived were bizarre mutations: the metallic Magnadons, their bodies held together by a magnetic field, and the monsters swarming in the Lake of Mutations.

After the Neutronic War, the Daleks retired into a huge metal city built as a shelter, where they were protected from the radiation. They became dependent on their machines, radiation and static electricity. Most of the Thals perished during the final war, but a handful survived on a plateau a great distance from the Dalek City, where they managed to cultivate small plots of land. The Thals mutated, evolving full circle in the space of five centuries, becoming physically perfect blond supermen.[1074]

"Deep in Hyperspace is Planet Skaro. This world is the most feared globe in all the universe. Many thousands of years ago, it was already the scene of a vicious conflict. On the continent of Davius, the Thals, a tall, handsome, peaceful race went in constant dread of attack from the short, ugly Daleks who inhabited Dalazar across the Ocean of Ooze."[1075]

& 1763 - "The Daleks: Genesis of Evil"[1076] -> The Daleks discovered cobalt in a mountain range, and developed a neutron bomb. In the year 2003 of the New Skaro Calendar, Minister Zolfian, Warlord of the Daleks, killed the peaceful leader Drenz. The scientist Yarvelling developed war machines ("metal slaves") to kill Thal survivors. As the Dalek factories prepared for war, a meteorite storm struck, starting fires which spread to where the neutron bombs were stored. There was a vast atomic explosion which wiped out the entire continent of Dalazar and reached as far as the Thals' homeland, Davius. Radiation spread across the planet.

The explosion shifted the north pole of the planet, freezing three scientists who had recently discovered a planet nine galaxies away: Earth.[1077]

Captain Turner Joins Iris' Bus

1764 - ST: "Old Flames"[1078] -> Iris Wildthyme sought to own a house in every century on Earth, and conspired to marry off Captain Turner, her travelling companion, to Bella, the granddaughter of Lady Huntington. If successful, Iris would inherit Huntington's estate via her friend. The fourth Doctor and Sarah attended Lady Huntington's annual ball, and discovered that Huntington and Bella were the last of a race of were-tigers. Huntington tried to travel back in the TARDIS to prevent her race's extinction, but the Doctor trapped her within a Time Lord message pod, in which she'd have ample room to roam around. Turner awoke one morning to find that Iris, the Doctor and Sarah had all left without him.

Turner married Bella, but as an alien were-tiger, she wasn't the sort to mate for life. Iris returned for Turner, and he resumed his travels with her.[1079]

& 1765 - "The Daleks: Genesis of Evil"[1080] -> Two years later, Yarvelling and Zolfian emerged from a shelter. Exploring their continent, they failed to locate any other survivors, and began to succumb to radiation poisoning. They were ambushed by one of the war machines, learning that a mutated survivor had crawled inside. This was the first of a new race of Daleks, with brains a thousand times superior to the original. Zolfian and Yarvelling rebuilt the war factory, creating a Dalek production line. The first

Dalek declared himself Emperor and had a special casing constructed – it was finished as Zolfian and Yarvelling died. The Emperor realised the Daleks needed slaves to continue their work.

The Black Dalek was built – it had even more firepower than a standard Dalek, and was the Emperor's deputy.[1081]

& 1765 - "The Daleks: Power Play"[1082] -> Within two months, the Daleks had built a vast new city and begun to develop new inventions and weapons. A Krattorian slave ship arrived to collect valuable radioactive sand. The Daleks encouraged a slave revolution, then took the spaceship and the slaves for themselves. Two of the slaves managed to recapture the ship and escape with the slaves... but not before the Daleks learned the spaceship's secrets.

& 1765 - "The Daleks: Duel of the Daleks"[1083] -> All the Daleks lacked was the ability to make a material strong enough to withstand the heat stress of space travel. Dalek Zeg was bathed in chemicals and found that he had become stronger (and that his casing had become red and gold). Zeg announced that he had discovered metalert, a

substance strong enough to build spaceships from, and would only share it if he was declared Emperor. Zeg attracted followers, and the Emperor consulted the Dalek Brain Machine, which ordered the two fight a duel. Realising that Zeg was resistant to heat, not cold, the Emperor froze Zeg – thus destroying him.

& 1765 - "The Daleks: The Amaryll Challenge"[1084] -> The first three prototype spacecraft failed, but the fourth succeeded... until it tried to break the light barrier, when it was destroyed. Proto 9 broke the light barrier, but metalert proved too weak to resist the heat barrier. The saucer-shaped Proto 13 passed every trial, and soon a space armada left Skaro. The Emperor led the fleet, from the golden flagship Proto-Leader.

Dalek saucers landed on Alvega, the nearest planet to Skaro. It was the home of the Amarylls: plant creatures who resisted the Dalek scouts. They wiped out the Amarylls, and destroyed the world-root – and with it, the entire planet. The Emperor declared a new law: what the Daleks could not conquer, they would destroy.

---

and Captain Turner agree that it's "1764" (p21). Iris' bus is here regarded as a TARDIS (not the case once it's revealed that she hails from the Clockworks; see *Wildthyme Beyond!*, etc.).

1079 *Iris S5: An Extraterrestrial Werewolf in Belgium*
1080 Dating "The Daleks: Genesis of Evil" (*TV21* #1-3, *DWW* #33) - It is two years later.
1081 "Duel of the Daleks"
1082 Dating "The Daleks: Power Play" (*TV21* #4-10, *DWW* #33-34) - "Two months" after "Genesis of Evil".
1083 Dating "The Daleks: Duel of the Daleks" (*TV21* #11-17, *DWW* #35-36) - It's set soon after "Power Play".
1084 Dating "The Daleks: The Amaryll Challenge" (*TV21* #18-24, *DWW* #36-37) - It's not stated how long the Daleks experiment with spacecraft, but they design and build thirteen different prototypes, test them and then build a fleet of the winning design in the first installment. This allows one of only two gaps in the narrative (the other is between "Impasse" and "The Terrorkon Harvest"), which have to add up to the "centuries" between "Genesis of Evil" and "Legacy of Yesteryear". That said, there's no indication it takes the Daleks very long to develop space travel.
1085 Dating "The Daleks: The Penta Ray Factor" (*TV21* #25-32, *DWW* #37-39) - The story follows straight on from "The Amaryll Challenge".
1086 Dating "The Daleks: Plague of Death" (*TV21* #33-39, *DWW* #39-40) - The Emperor is summoned back at the end of "The Penta Ray Factor", so this story starts while that story is running.
1087 Dating "The Daleks: Menace of the Monstrons" (*TV21* #40-46, *DWW* #40-42) - The Monstron ship arrives

while the Daleks are rebuilding after "Plague of Death".
1088 Dating "The Daleks: Eve of the War" (*TV21* #47-51, *DWM* #53-54) - It's "a few months" after "The Menace of the Monstrons", and the Daleks have spent the time rebuilding their city. The Mechanoids in the *TV Century 21* strip physically resemble the ones seen in *The Chase*, but see the dating notes on that story for more.
1089 Dating "The Daleks: The Archive of Phryne" (*TV21* #52-58, *DWM* #54-55) - The story is set shortly after "Eve of the War", with the Daleks gearing up to fight the Mechanoids.
1090 Dating "The Daleks: Rogue Planet" (*TV21* #47-51, *DWM* #53-54) - The Daleks are still preparing to fight the Mechanoids, so this is shortly after "The Archive of Phryne". The rogue planet is accidentally called Skardel in a couple of the later instalments.
1091 Dating "The Daleks: Impasse" (*TV21* #63-69, *DWM* #62-66, 68) - The story ends the immediate threat of war between the Mechanoids and Daleks.
1092 *TW: Trace Memory*. Sheridan was an Irish actor, educator and proponent of elocution movement.
1093 *Minuet in Hell*
1094 *Upstairs*. Townshend died 4th September, 1767.
1095 Dating *Hornets' Nest: The Circus of Doom* and *Hornets' Nest: A Sting in the Tale* (BBC fourth Doctor audios #1.3-1.4) - The date is given.
1096 "Two centuries" before *Revolution Man*.
1097 *The Adventuress of Henrietta Street*. Sabbath is working with the service prior to this in the *Faction Paradox* audios; this must represent his initiation into its higher echelons.

& 1765 - "The Daleks: The Penta Ray Factor"[1085] -> The fleet went onward to Solturis, home of a humanoid race that had been at peace for a hundred years. The Daleks were welcomed, and pretended to be friendly while they discovered the extent of the planet's defences. The penta ray (which combined alpha, infra, omega, ultra and beta rays) was a threat. The Daleks swapped the real weapon for a fake, but needed the key to operate it. The main fleet left while Daleks from two saucers attacked the city of Bulos, but were destroyed by the ray. Instead of avenging this, the Emperor received a message from Skaro that demanded his immediate return.

& 1765 - "The Daleks: Plague of Death"[1086] -> Skaro had become a huge war factory that was overseen by the Black Dalek, but a dalatomic rust cloud escaped from one research base and began eating through every Dalek it came into contact with. Dalek hoverbouts were sent to investigate the cloud, and it was contained with magnets, but mutated into a plague. The Daleks began destroying each other, rather than risk infection. The Emperor returned and deduced that the Black Dalek carried the plague. The Black Dalek's casing was recast, and the planet was rebuilt.

& 1765 - "The Daleks: The Menace of the Monstrons"[1087] -> The Monstrons landed in a dead volcano on Skaro, and set their Engibrain robots to building a bridgehead. A Dalek was captured, and the city bombarded with missiles. The Daleks seemed defeated, but the captured Dalek broke free and set off the volcano, destroying the Monstrons.

& 1765 - "The Daleks: Eve of War"[1088] -> A few months later, a new Dalek City had been built, with improved defences. The Daleks constantly monitored against surprise attack. The Daleks built a space station as a staging post to the planet Oric, with construction supervised by the Red Dalek. Workers there were attacked by the Mechanoids' "suspicion ray", and began fighting amongst themselves. The Daleks detected the Mechanoid ship and destroyed it. Two Mechanoid ships quickly retaliated, destroying the Dalek saucer and warning the Daleks to avoid their territory.

& 1765 - "The Daleks: The Archive of Phryne"[1089] -> The Emperor ordered the Daleks to prepare new weapons to fight a galactic war, and began searching nearby planets for new inventions. A force led by the Black Dalek discovered the planet Phryne behind an invisibility screen, and landed to seize "the genius of a hundred planets". But the Phrynians kept the information in their own memories, and fled the Dalek invasion.

& 1765 - "The Daleks: Rogue Planet"[1090] -> The Astrodalek observed a newborn rogue planet in the Eighty-Fourth Galaxy, which they named Skardal. It collided with the planet Omega Three, altering its course so that it was heading for Skaro. Upgraded Dalek saucers fitted with Magray Ultimate deflected Skardal until it was aimed at the home planet of the Mechanoids, Mechanus.

& 1765 - "The Daleks: Impasse"[1091] -> The leaders of the planet Zeros were alarmed at the prospect of galactic war between the Daleks and Mechanoids, and sent a robot agent, 2K, to prevent either side from winning. 2K arrived on Skaro and discovered the existence of Skardal. 2K launched himself towards the rogue planet in a Dalek missile. 2K was captured by the Mechanoids, but diverted the Dalek missile to destroy Skardal. He tricked the Mechanoids into thinking the Daleks had saved them, and the threat of war receded.

As a time agent, Jack Harkness stole a rare manuscript of Shakespeare and Fletcher's *Cardenio – A Spanish Comedie* from Thomas Sheridan, an Irish stage actor, in 1765.[1092] Sir Francis Dashwood, an ancestor of Brigham Elisha Dashwood III and Chancellor of the Exchequer to King George III, founded the Hellfire Club as a social organisation. The group peaked in the 1760s, becoming a debauched haven for the aristocracy. The generations to follow exaggerated the group's dabblings with the black arts.[1093] Official reports said that Charles Townshend, the Chancellor of the Exchequer, died from a fever; in actuality, he fell victim to the time fungus in 10 Downing Street.[1094]

1768 - HORNETS' NEST: THE CIRCUS OF DOOM / A STING IN THE TALE[1095] -> The Hornets mentally compelled the fourth Doctor to bring them to this time, and they took control of the hideous dwarf Antonio was he was 13. He met the Hornets in the lagoons outside Venice, and they granted him vast psychic powers – that he used to burn out the minds of those who had taunted him. Freed of the Hornets' influence once they possessed Antonio, the Doctor and a dog the Hornets had previously possessed – which he named Captain – tried to find the dwarf for four days, but to no avail.

Rubasdpofiaew, a drug from Tau Ceti Minor, found its way to Earth and started growing in Tibet as a "miracle flower" named Om-Tsor. Those who consumed Om-Tsor could turn thought into reality. Starving Tibetan lamas ate the Om-Tsor flowers, and used their newfound abilities to found the peaceful "Om-Tsor" valley.[1096]

Sabbath was initiated into the British intelligence service in 1762, adopting the name by which we know him.[1097] He was not supposed to survive the initiation, but the

Council of Eight saved him. The Council claimed to be humans from the future who wanted to become the Lords of Time. They recruited Sabbath as a counterpart to the Doctor, but he did not hear from them for another twenty years.[1098]

1770 (April to June) - TRANSIT OF VENUS[1099] -> The TARDIS arrived on the sailing ship *Endeavour*, which was commanded by Captain James Cook. His expedition had recently left Tahiti after observing a transit of Venus – a rare event when Venus moves across the disc of the sun. The transit would aid astronomers in creating a map of the skies, and the *Endeavour* was now headed toward Cook's historical discovery of Australia.

Superstitious sailors pitched the TARDIS – with Barbara and Susan inside – into the water. The first Doctor and Ian

were mistaken as hailing from Venus, and enjoyed Cook's hospitality while worrying about their lost friends. Susan had tied the TARDIS to the *Endeavour* with some rope, and the time machine had been pulled behind Cook's vessel. Barbara passed some time relating details of the period to Susan, whose latent empathy had unknowingly influenced Cook's chief scientist, Joseph Banks, to write and talk about historical events, tunes and poems from the future.

In June, the Doctor's party were reunited when the *Endeavour* reached Australia; Cook's nephew, Isaac Smith, was the first to step ashore. Banks promised to remain silent about these events – and the extra-terrestrial travellers he'd purportedly met.

Banks named a plant "Barberer" after "barber", meaning Latin for beard, possibly because his telepathic link with Susan brought the word "Barbara" to mind.

1098 *Timeless*
1099 Dating *Transit of Venus* (BF CC #3.7) - The adventure occurs over a period of "less than two months" in 1770, and concludes "days" after the *Endeavour* gets stuck on the Great Barrier Reef on June 11. Susan's empathic link with Banks is deemed an offshoot of the telepathy she used in *The Sensorites*. Ian claims to have seen "the metal seas of Venus", but it's not stated that he actually met any Venusians; the Doctor, Ian and Barbara do so in *Venusian Lullaby*.

Transits of Venus are extraordinarily rare – pairs of transits will occur at eight-year intervals, then not be seen again for two hundred and forty-three years. A transit of Venus occurred in 1761; Cook's party witnessed its "pairing" in 1769.
1100 *The Many Hands*
1101 "Two hundred years" before *The Many Deaths of Jo Grant*.
1102 Dating *FP*: "Political Animals" and *FP*: "Betes Noires and Dark Horses" (*FP* comic #1-2) - The year and month are given. The story was interrupted by the cancellation of the *Faction Paradox* comic after two issues.
1103 *The Adventuress of Henrietta Street*
1104 *The Unquiet Dead*
1105 *The Mark of the Rani*. The American War of Independence ran from 1775-1783.
1106 *The King of Terror*
1107 *The Impossible Astronaut*
1108 *Survival of the Fittest*. Jefferson lived 1743 to 1826.
1109 *Seasons of Fear*. No date is given, but Franklin died in 1790. The modern-day American government didn't start until 1789, so unless Franklin was President in the *Doctor Who* universe under its predecessor, the Articles of Confederation, then he must have served during the term normally attributed to George Washington.

The mistake wasn't deliberate – writer Paul Cornell genuinely believed that Franklin had been President. In *Neverland*, a line that the "wrong man became

President" was meant to denote the Bush-Gore election in 2000, but fans have cited it to cover this mistake.
1110 *FP: Warlords of Utopia*
1111 "Two hundred years" before *The Daemons*.
1112 *City of Death*
1113 We see the portrait of Ace hanging in Windsor Castle in the extended version of *Silver Nemesis*. In Ace's personal timeline, she had not yet sat for the painting. Gainsborough lived from 1727-1788, painting society portraits 1760-1774 before turning to landscapes.
1114 *Timeless* (p93). Kalicum says that D'Amantine, who's alive in 1830, is the third generation affected by his alterations.
1115 *The Nightmare Fair*
1116 *The Devil Goblins from Neptune*. He ruled 1780-1790.
1117 *The Stones of Blood*. Allan Ramsay, a Scottish portrait painter, lived 1713-1784.
1118 Three months before *Catch-1782*.
1119 Dating *Catch-1782* (BF #68) - The dates of Mel's arrival and departure from this era are given.
1120 Dating *The Adventuress of Henrietta Street* (EDA #51) - It is "March 1782" on p2, more specifically "March 20, 1782" on p15. The Siege of Henrietta Street happens on "February 8", 1783 (p259). Scarlette's funeral is dated 9th February on p269 and the back cover, with the Doctor departing Henrietta Street on February 13 (p273), and his final conversation with Scarlette occurs on the same day. An epilogue with Sabbath and Juliette happens on "August 18 1783" (p278).

The book is told in a style reminiscent of a history book, and some of the key facts are open to dispute. With that in mind, novels after this one state that Anji has been travelling with the Doctor only for "months", suggesting the timeframe of *Henrietta Street* might be more condensed than the book itself suggests.

Scarlette is the young girl Isobel from the *Faction Paradox* comic series, which covers some of her early history and takes place in 1774.

In 1771, Alexander Monro reclaimed the last Hand of Onk Ndell Kith from Benjamin Franklin, who was staying at the home of the philosopher David Hume. Two years later, Alexander used the hand to "rebirth" his father as a baby, and presented it to his wife Katherine as an abandoned infant that they should raise as their own.[1100] The Xoanthrax Empire subjugated the Hargarans.[1101]

wih - 1774 (December) - FP: "Political Animals" / "Betes Noires and Dark Horses"[1102] -> Empress Catherine of Russia gifted the court of King George III with a mammoth – a relic of history from a different time. Mother Francesca of Faction Paradox arrived, along with her unnamed second, as various parties gathered at the court for a ritualistic hunt. The event drew the attention of Sabbath. The American delegation intended on using a Mayakai warrior, Mayakatula, as their hunting dog, but she freed herself and made the acquaintance of a young servant named Isobel...

Sabbath first met the Mayakai warrior Tula Lui in 1776, when she was ten. She would eventually become his apprentice. In 1780, Sabbath failed to seduce Scarlette, a brothel owner and ritualist. The same year, he was present during the Gordon Riots. He left the Service, and dealt with the agents of the Service – the "Ratcatchers" – sent to assassinate him. Tula Lui, as Sabbath's only real company from 1780 to 1782, eliminated some high-ranking Service officials as a message for them to leave Sabbath alone.[1103]

The American War of Independence

The Doctor was at the Boston Tea Party in 1773.[1104] The Rani was present during the American War of Independence.[1105] The Canavitchi were involved in the same conflict.[1106] **The Doctor met American founding fathers Thomas Jefferson, John Adams and Alexander Hamilton – two of them fancied him.[1107]** The Doctor was once stuck at a tea party with Thomas Jefferson, who wouldn't shut up about bees.[1108]

Benjamin Franklin became President of the United States.[1109]

> = On Roma I, Americanus crushed a republican insurrection in America. As a reward, the Emperor granted his family stewardship of the continent.[1110]

Devil's End became notorious when the Third Lord of Aldbourne's black magic rituals were exposed.[1111] In the late eighteenth century, Scaroth lived in France at the time of Louis XV. He acquired a Gainsborough.[1112] **Gainsborough also painted a portrait of Ace that ended up in Windsor Castle.[1113]**

Kalicum, an agent of the Council of Eight, made genetic alterations to the grandfather of the Frenchman D'Amantine. The alterations would work their way through thirteen successive generations.[1114] Shardlow lost a game of backgammon at the Hellfire Club in July 1778, and became the Celestial Toymaker's thrall.[1115]

The Doctor met Emperor Joseph II of Austria-Hungary.[1116] **Cessair of Diplos posed as Lady Montcalm and was painted by Ramsay.[1117]** In September 1781, Jane Hallam – the wife of Henry Hallam, one of Mel's ancestors – died from a horse-riding accident.[1118]

1781 (12th December) to 1782 (June) - CATCH-1782[1119] -> Melanie Bush arrived through time from 2003, and the transition left her extremely confused and disorientated. Henry Hallam cared for her and, failing to recognise Mel as one of his descendants, became intent on making her his second wife. The sixth Doctor and Mel's uncle, John Hallam, arrived and intervened. The travellers returned with Mel to the twenty-first century, and Henry eventually married his housekeeper, Mrs McGregor. Henry's journal and other documents from the period would note the existence of "Eleanor Hallam" – actually Mel, who was erroneously believed to have been born about 1760 and died in 1811.

The Eighth Doctor Marries Scarlette

1782 (20th March) to 1783 (13th February) - THE ADVENTURESS OF HENRIETTA STREET[1120] -> At the limit of human consciousness was the "horizon", and beyond that was the Kingdom of the Beasts and the babewyns, bestial ape creatures. The destruction of Gallifrey destabilised time, allowing the babewyns to escape to Earth as humans were beginning to conceive of time as a dimension.

The eighth Doctor arrived in this era, suffering physical symptoms as a result of his being linked to his homeworld, which no longer existed. He allied himself with a brothel owner and ritualist, Scarlette. Together, they agreed that the Doctor should marry Juliette, a young woman working in the brothel, as this would link him to Earth and allow him to serve as its protector.

The Doctor came to the attention of Sabbath, who thought the Doctor had brought the babewyns to Earth. Sabbath was building a time machine, the *Jonah*. The Doctor and Sabbath teamed up upon realising they both wished to repel the monsters. Juliette abandoned the Doctor for Sabbath, so the Doctor instead married Scarlette in the Caribbean. The Doctor's illness got worse, and the babewyns transported his party to their domain (possibly the ruins of Gallifrey). Sabbath saved the Doctor by removing one of his hearts.

The babewyns assaulted Scarlette's brothel, and Scarlette was believed killed in the fighting. The Doctor defeated the babewyns, and beheaded the King of Beasts with the sonic screwdriver. A funeral was held for Scarlette on 9th February, 1783, but she had survived and parted company with the Doctor on 13th February.

After implanting the Doctor's heart in his chest, Sabbath gained the ability to travel through time. The Doctor wrote the novel *The Ruminations of a Foreign Traveller in his Element* during this time.

1783 (4th-10th December) - DEAD OF WINTER[1121]
-> Dr Bloom, the head of a clinic in St Christophe, Italy, preformed miracle cures in conjunction with a water-dwelling hive-creature that had visited Earth at various times. The creature could heal disease, and also generated Familiars: ghost-like recreations of lost loved ones. A Familiar had raised Prince Boris, a Russian aristocrat, and cured him of his wasting disease. The eleventh Doctor, Amy and Rory were present as Boris tried to use the creature's psionic abilities to conquer the world. A distraught

Bloom fatally shot the Doctor after learning that his wife Perdita was also a Familiar. The hive-creature exploded after healing the Doctor, unable to process the weight of his life's memories. Many of Bloom's patients, including Boris, regained their ailments. Two last Familiars remained: an 11-year-old girl named Maria and her mother, both of whom were unaware of their true nature.

Sir Percival Flint excavated a fogou in Cornwall in 1783 and heard ghastly screams.[1122] Sythorr, the warlike progenitor of the plant-like Haluu, became stranded on Titan after his people banished him.[1123] The TARDIS wine cellar contained a bottle of 1784 Madeira, which was the property of Benjamin Franklin.[1124]

The Pathfinders – androids who prided themselves on "always getting their man", i.e. obliterating their opposition – participated in what would become one of the most pointless interplanetary wars in modern history.[1125] The insectoid Hexagora colonised Zagara IX and came into

1121 Dating *Dead of Winter* (NSA #46) - The six days that pass within the story – starting with "4th December 1783" (p10) and ending with "10th December 1783" (p251) – are listed in various journal entries and letters.
1122 *The Spectre of Lanyon Moor*
1123 "Centuries" before "The Soul Garden".
1124 *The Haunting of Thomas Brewster*. Franklin died in 1790.
1125 A bit more than two hundred years before *The Nightmare Fair*.
1126 *Hexagora*. Date unknown, but this is within the lifetime of Queen Zafira, who as a Hexagoran has a lifespan of five hundred years.
1127 Dating *Helicon Prime* (BF CC #2.2) - The next Companion Chronicles audio starring Frazer Hines, *The Glorious Revolution*, suggests that the same amount of time has passed for Jamie as has passed in the real world since the broadcast of *The War Games* in 1969. If that's the case, the framing sequence of *Helicon Prime* (released in 2007) probably takes place c.1784.
1128 Dating *The Glorious Revolution* (BF CC #4.2) - The Time Lord says that it's been "forty years" since *The Highlanders*, which is set in 1746, evidently mirroring the real-life time that's passed for Frazer Hines since he left *Doctor Who* in 1969. Additionally, it's said that 1688 was "a hundred years ago", and that King James VII died "eighty years ago" (he lived 1633-1701). Jamie's wife, named as "Kirsty", is presumably Hannah Gordon's character of the same name from *The Highlanders*.
1129 Dating *Death and the Queen* (BF 10th Doc #1.3) - The Doctor says it's the "1780s", and makes some fanciful claims about General Hortense and her all-female army mopping the floor with Napoleon. Shorthand has not been invented yet; it was created in 1837. Start to finish, the story runs "a few weeks".
1130 *The Death of Art*

1131 *Silver Nemesis*
1132 *9thC: Retail Therapy*. The earliest documented case of pasta with a meat-based sauce hails from Imola, near Bologna, in the late eighteenth century.
1133 Dating *The Ultimate Adventure* (BF stageplay adaptation #1) - The Doctor states the year, which is confirmed in *Beyond the Ultimate Adventure*. Bizarrely, the Doctor in that same story claims that the Nazis "were from about 150 years *before*" Jason's time.
1134 *Leth-St: Beast of Fang Rock* (ch3).
1135 "A little over one hundred years" before *Jago & Litefoot & Strax: The Haunting*.
1136 *The Taint*. Fitz is named after Freddie's brother.
1137 *Erimem: Three Faces of Helena*
1138 Dating "The World Shapers" (*DWM* #127-129) - It's "the eighteenth century" according to a caption, and the Doctor thinks he's miscalculated by "about forty years". The previous edition of *Ahistory* dated this story to circa 1785, but the inclusion of *The Glorious Revolution* at circa 1786 makes it advisable to bump "The World Shapers" ahead in time a bit, under the assumption that personal matters go downhill for Jamie afterwards. Peri remembers *The Two Doctors* as being "a couple of years ago". The reference to Planet 14 first appeared in *The Invasion*, and later in *The Doctor Falls*.
1139 Dating *The Sword of the Chevalier* (BF 10th Doc #2.2) – The blurb names the year. The Chevalier lived 1728-1810, and also appears in *FP: Sabbath Dei/In the Year of the Cat*. Herschel's forty-foot telescope made its first observation in 1787, was decommissioned in 1840.
1140 *Doctor Who and the Pirates*. The Spinning Jenny was invented in 1797.
1141 *The Space Museum*. James Watt lived 1736-1819.
1142 *Day of the Daleks*, Alex Macintosh, the television commentator in that story, states that the house is "Georgian".

conflict with the Agelli – hostile ape-like creatures native to the Acteon Galaxy, but had ventured into the Milky Way. The Hexagora obliterated the Agelli warfleet – one hundred thousand starships were destroyed, and the cause of the Agelli defeat would remain a mystery.[1126]

c 1784 - HELICON PRIME[1127] **->** Mindy 'Voir believed the second Doctor had made off with the prized memory bank of the Fennus colony, and travelled back to eighteenth century Scotland to see if Jamie knew its location. The data bank was a pendant around Jamie's neck – and when Mindy attacked Jamie, it absorbed her, trapping her mind with the memories of the Fennus colonists.

c 1786 - THE GLORIOUS REVOLUTION[1128] **->** Jamie McCrimmon had married a young woman named Kirsty, and they'd had "more bairns than there are days in the week". Their children had grown up, and made them grandparents.

A representative of the Celestial Intervention Agency visited Jamie about forty years after he'd encountered the Doctor, having detected a fluctuation in Earth's timeline.

> (=) Jamie's encounter with King James VIII in 1688 had created a paradoxical timeline in which the king never left England and stayed on the throne, causing the ascension of King Charles III. The CIA operative stabilized the temporal integrity of Jamie's past self in 1688, enabling him to put history right...

Jamie decided that he'd had a full life and was better off not knowing about his adventures with the Doctor. At his request, the CIA agent re-instated Jamie's memory block.

c 1786 - DEATH AND THE QUEEN[1129] **->** While relaxing at a French Riviera casino, Donna Noble became quite taken with Crown Prince Rudolph of Goritania – who whisked her away to his homeland to become his queen. As the intended monarch, Donna introduced her maids to shorthand some decades too early, as well as the writings of Jackie Collins.

The five-hundred-year pact that had kept Goritania protected from the outside world was coming due, and the alien Mefistoles required another soul, that of the country's queen, to continue it. A Mefistole avatar of Death appeared to claim Donna's soul at her wedding, but was exorcised because her maids had sewn the Goritanian Royal Standard – which contained the inviolable text of their contract with the Mefistoles – into her undergarments. The perception filter concealing Goritania continued, and Donna rebuked her fiance for trying to sacrifice her. Afterward, she resumed travelling with the tenth Doctor.

Six months later, Goritania came under the control of General Hortense and her all-female army.

In the late 1780s, Montague and Tackleton, a firm making dolls' houses, scandalously made a house that resembled the haunted Ilbridge House.[1130] **In 1788, the Nemesis Bow was stolen from Windsor Castle.**[1131] Of all the races in the universe, humans invented spaghetti bolognese.[1132]

1789 - THE ULTIMATE ADVENTURE[1133] **->** Jason, a French nobleman during the French Revolution, met the Doctor and joined him on his travels. The Doctor accidentally returned Jason to this time while fighting the Daleks and Cybermen, but saved him from the guillotine and escaped.

John Smeaton designed the Fang Rock lighthouse in 1789, based on his work on the Eddystone lighthouse. Fang Rock's lighthouse was first lit on 18th March, 1790.[1134] An alien survey ship created a genetically engineered entity. The creature inspired rumours that Brutan Street was haunted, and spent years developing its form to become "Mrs Multravers" of Cobbletown.[1135] Fitz Kreiner's great-great-grandfather and his twin, Freddie Tarr and Neville Fitzwilliam Tarr, were born in 1790.[1136]

In the 1790s, the immortal Helena – passing as Ms Helena de Planchet, a survivor of the Reign of Terror – had a marriage of convenience with Lord Percival Marjoribanks. They adopted a French child, Adele, who died three years later.[1137]

c 1791 - "The World Shapers"[1138] **->** The sixth Doctor, Peri and Frobisher arrived in the Scottish Highlands, looking for Jamie and clues about the mysterious Planet 14. The Time Lords had failed to erase Jamie's memory after all, and he was now known as "Mad Jamie" because he had told people about his adventures with the Doctor. Jamie remembered the reference to Planet 14 – the Cybermen referred to it when they invaded Earth. The Doctor let Jamie go back to Marinus with him, dematerialising the TARDIS in front of the other villagers to prove that Jamie wasn't mad.

1791 - THE SWORD OF THE CHEVALIER[1139] **->** The tenth Doctor took Rose to Slough, eagerly hoping to see William Herschel's forty-foot telescope, but soon ran afoul of an association of criminal factions: the Consortium of the Obsidian Asp. As aided by the Chevalier d'Eon, a French exile and spy, the travellers ended the Consortium's human slavery operation.

The Doctor claimed to be the first person to spin a jenny.[1140] **The first Doctor met James Watt, an engineer who influenced the Industrial Revolution.**[1141] **Auderly House was built in Georgian times.**[1142]

In the late eighteenth century, a cabin boy named Varney served aboard a treasure galleon. A storm left him shipwrecked, and he wasn't seen for five years. During that time, the last of the Curcurbites entered "communion" with Varney, altered his blood and gifted him with a knowledge of biochemistry. He rejoined civilisation as a vampire pirate, made his fortune and settled on an island in the Atlantic. Like Varney, his descendents worked toward the Curcurbite's restitution.[1143]

Mozart

Mozart hated cats.[1144] Mozart's talent stemmed from his gaining low-level quantum abilities, or so Iris Wildthyme believed.[1145] The immortal Helena separately met Goya and Robert Burns. A time-travelling Andy Hansen met Mozart.[1146]

(=) 1791 (5th December) - 100: "My Own Private Wolfgang"[1147] **->** A Mozart clone from the far future travelled back in time, intending to damage the reputation of his original self. He appeared, masked, at the dying Mozart's bedside and offered him immortality in exchange for his producing a new symphony every year. Mozart agreed, and the clone pumped him full of self-regenerating fluid, curing his tuberculosis. As the clone intended, Mozart lived for centuries – and proved the rule that while the good die young, the mediocre stick around forever.

The sixth Doctor and Evelyn convinced Mozart to not sign the life-extending deal. To hobble Mozart's reputation just a little, the Doctor – with Mozart's consent – tore out the last twelve pages of his finished *Requiem*.

1143 "One and a half centuries" before "Tooth and Claw" (*DWM*).
1144 "The Golden Ones"
1145 *Iris* S4: *Iris at the Oche*
1146 *Erimem: Three Faces of Helena*. Goya lived 1746-1828, Burns 1759-1796, Mozart 1756-1791.
1147 Dating *100: "My Own Private Wolfgang"* (BF #100b) - It's the day of Mozart's death. His last composition, *Requiem in Mass D minor*, is regarded as one of his most popular works – but it's unfinished, and was completed by Franz Xaver Sussmayr or other parties after Mozart's death. In *Time and Relative*, Susan relates that her grandfather regards Mozart as a "bad-mannered show-off with a silly hairstyle" – but as Susan herself hasn't met Mozart, this is likely just the first Doctor's opinion without benefit of having met the man.
1148 Dating *River* S3: *A Requiem for the Doctor* (BF *The Diary of River Song* #3.2) - Mozart died 5th December, 1791, and bits of *Requiem in Mass D minor* were performed at his memorial on 10th December. *100: "My Own Private Wolfgang"* provides an entirely different explanation for why *Requiem* went unfinished. Perhaps he finished two copies.
1149 According to Susan in *The Reign of Terror*.
1150 In *An Unearthly Child*, Susan borrows a book about the French Revolution, but already knows a great deal about the subject.
1151 *The Scapegoat*. The Bastille was in operation as a fortress prison from 1370 until its storming on 14th July, 1789.
1152 *Christmas on a Rational Planet*
1153 *Just War*
1154 The lockpick is mentioned in *Pyramids of Mars*, and again in *Vampire of the Mind*. The Doctor also mentions Marie Antoinette in *The Robots of Death*.
1155 *The Adventuress of Henrietta Street*

1156 *The Beautiful People*
1157 *The Resurrection of Mars*. Antoinette was Queen of France from 1774 to 1792.
1158 *The Crystal Bucephalus*
1159 *The Daemons*
1160 *The Burning*
1161 *The Banquo Legacy*
1162 "The Pestilent Heart". This must have entailed some time travel shenanigans, as Boucher – one of the most celebrated eighteenth-century painters – died in 1770, but the Louvre wasn't established until 1793. Madame de Pompadour (*The Girl in the Fireplace*) was Boucher's patroness.
1163 Dating *1stD* V2: *Fields of Terror* (BF CC #11.1) - It's been lightly snowing, and it's said of the murderous, monk-clad survivor: "This is no winter ghost". According to the Doctor, Robespierre will be overthrown "in a few months' time" (in late July 1794; see *The Reign of Terror*). It's after the statesman Pierre Victurnien Vergniaud was guillotined (that happened 31st October, 1793). The National Convention authorised the Infernal Columns on 1st August and 1st October 1793, but their worst atrocities happened 21st January to May 1974.
1164 Dating *The Reign of Terror* (1.8) - The date is given on screen. *The Programme Guide* offered the date "1792", but *The Terrestrial Index* corrected this. The story shows the arrest of Robespierre, which occurred on 27th July.
1165 The background to *Gallery of Ghouls*.
1166 *The Man in the Velvet Mask*
1167 Dating *World Game* (PDA #74) - Serena gives the date of the Doctor's arrival as 9th August, 1794. The Duke of Wellington was a leading military and political figure. He was a Field Marshall during the Napoleonic Wars, and oversaw Napoleon's defeat at Waterloo.

1791 (10th December) - RIVER S3: A REQUIEM FOR THE DOCTOR[1148] **->** The fifth Doctor, Brooke and River Song looked into the presence of alien material in this time zone: Frau Bruner's poison of choice, the psychic substance Aqua Galatia. It had tainted the final portion of Mozart's *Requiem*, the debut of which threatened to kill everyone in the concert hall. One of Bruner's descendants was present and at risk, and so she sacrificed her life to nullify the substance's negative impulses. The Doctor's group made sure the end of *Requiem* was lost to history.

The French Revolution

This was the first Doctor's favourite period of Earth history.[1149] Susan visited France at this time with the first Doctor.[1150] A rack used at the Bastille would later, in German-occupied Paris, be occupied by Lucie Miller.[1151]

In 1791, the first Doctor and Susan were imprisoned in Paris, but escaped by using an artillery shell. Transcripts of the Doctor's interrogation would end up with the Shadow Directory.[1152] It was the Doctor and Susan's first-ever visit to Earth. It demonstrated to the Doctor that the old order could be toppled, and that people wanted freedom and a hope for the future.[1153]

The Doctor met Marie Antoinette and obtained a lockpick from her.[1154] The Doctor claimed to have been invited into Marie Antoinette's boudoir.[1155] He judged that Marie Antoinette had a lovely cook, and decided that eating cake was a good way of passing the time.[1156] The Monk said he had cakes from the kitchen of Marie Antoinette.[1157]

In 1791, the fifth Doctor, Tegan and Turlough were dining at the Cafe de Saint Joseph in Aix-en-Provence when they were accidentally scooped up by the Crystal Bucephalus and whisked thousands of years into the future.[1158] In 1793, the attempted opening of Devil's Hump by Sir Percival Flint resulted in disaster.[1159] The Daniells brothers unearthed a statuette of a dancer in Pakistan in 1793.[1160] In 1793, the actor Robert Dodds built Banquo Manor using money he inherited. The rumour was that Dodds had murdered his aunt for her money.[1161]

Somehow, the Doctor snuck a drunk Francois Boucher back into the Louvre.[1162]

lgtw - 1794 (first quarter) - 1STD V2: FIELDS OF TERROR[1163] **->** Infernal Columns rained hell upon royalist supporters in the Vendee region, western France. Captain Lagrange's column destroyed a hospital run by an order of monks, the Blue Penitents, and a traumatised survivor adopted their hooded robes. The first Doctor, Steven and Vicki bore witness as the survivor vengefully killed Lagrange, and likely died from his own wounds.

The Daleks in the Last Great Time War here targeted the first Doctor's history, but two Time Lords repaired the damage.

1794 (late July) - THE REIGN OF TERROR[1164] **->** The first Doctor and his companions landed in France during the Reign of Terror. Ian met the British spy James Stirling, but Barbara and Susan were arrested as aristocrats and sentenced to the guillotine. Posing as a Citizen, the Doctor rescued his companions. Ian and Barbara helped Stirling to identify Napoleon as the next ruler of France, but were unable to prevent his predecessor, Robespierre, from being arrested.

The Slough, the fourth planet from the left, was home to an intelligent amoeboid species that couldn't experience pain or pleasure. One of their number came to Earth with an android to witness and record the experience of death, but wound up on the block during the Reign of Terror. The android rescued its master and took the guise of Marie Antoinette, as such a body had looked quite nice on the Queen. The amoeboid took the name Mr Goole, and the two of them fled to Brighton.[1165]

> (=) A group of curious aliens performed experiments on reality control and used a "world-machine" device to slip the entire Earth out of N-Space. The planet was remade according to the philosophies of a single human: the Marquis de Sade. However, the world-machine's operator threw off the aliens' control and became Minski, a dwarf. Minski created an automaton of the Marquis, who began ruling France the day Robespierre was arrested, and the real Marquis was imprisoned. The fake Marquis ruled France, with Minski as his deputy, for ten years.[1166]

1794 (August) - WORLD GAME[1167] **->** The immortal Players interfered in Earth history for their amusement. After an attempt to kill the future Duke of Wellington failed, the opposing Player countermoved by having Napoleon arrested.

The second Doctor and Serena – an ambitious Time Lady sent to keep him in check – arrived in Antibes to monitor the time disturbances caused by the Players' actions. The Doctor saved Napoleon from execution and came into contact with the Countess, one of the Players, who was working to see Napoleon defeat the British. The Doctor worked out that she hoped to kill Nelson and Wellington, and that the two only met once, in 1805. The Doctor and Serena departed for that meeting.

The theatrical illusionist Thomas Houghton Bloodchild, a household name at the peak of his success, hoped to obtain immortality by translating a Welsh-written volume of forbidden arts from the Dark Ages. A dozen copies of the resultant grimoire, *The Bloodchild Codex*, were made, but all save one perished in a 1794 housefire thought to have killed Bloodchild. In actuality, the remaining

Bloodchild Codex became endowed with Bloodchild's essence. He remained dormant in its pages until 1968.[1168]

In 1795, the Directory was running France after Robespierre's arrest. They learned of many unusual visitations and encounters on Earth, and set up the Shadow Directory to capture or destroy such things. At some point, the Shadow Directory autopsied a Time Lord and knew of them as *les betes aux deux coeurs,* or "the devils with two hearts". One of the Shadow Directory's agents, the psychic aristocrat Marielle Duquesne, investigated the Beautiful Shining Daughters of Hysteria in Munchen.[1169] A barometer, of late-eighteenth-century German vintage, would endure in the archives of *The World*.[1170]

Samuel Taylor Coleridge and the Visitor from Porlock

Samuel Taylor Coleridge was the "last man" to read every book in circulation; he was the last true "universal expert". But as a result, he kept falling asleep and forgetting his poems.[1171] The sixth Doctor planned to visit Coleridge.[1172]

While Samuel Taylor Coleridge's body slept in 1797, his mind aided the twelfth Doctor, Bill Potts and Rudy Zoom about two centuries later, on Titan, against the plant-like Haluu. Upon his return, Coleridge vaguely depicted the event in his poem "Kubla Khan".[1173] Coleridge's musings about Xanadu were interrupted by the sudden arrival of Panda, Iris Wildthyme (who was dolled up like Olivia Newton-John) and some men dressed as the Electric Light Orchestra, all of them on roller skates.[1174]

The Doctor met the artist Turner.[1175] The Quoth gave psychic abilities to the toymaker Montague in 1797.[1176] In 1798, Napoleon undertook an expedition to colonise Egypt. He entered the Great Pyramid, and was mentally influenced to dig out the sand-covered Sphinx.[1177] Maleficums from Napoleonic times would wind up in the collection of Jennifer Alford.[1178] A bronze bust of Napoleon would endure aboard *The World*.[1179]

1798 - SET PIECE[1180] **->** Benny fled the robot Ants, and ended up with archaeologist Vivant Denon as he began to

---

1168 *J&L* S5: *The Bloodchild Codex*

1169 *Christmas on a Rational Planet*

1170 *The Wreck of the World*

1171 *The Scarlet Empress* (p90). Coleridge lived 1772-1834.

1172 *CD,NM* V1: *Judoon in Chains*. The notorious "person from Porlock" is said to have interrupted Coleridge while he was writing the poem "Kubla Khan" in 1797, which is why it went unfinished.

1173 "The Soul Garden"

1174 *Wildthyme Beyond!* (p202), with Iris and company taking their cue from the movie *Xanadu* (1980).

1175 *The Hollow Men, Blood Heat*.

1176 *The Death of Art*

1177 *The Sands of Time*. Napoleon began his expedition in March 1798, and the year is given (p203).

1178 *Benny* B3: *Legion: Shades of Gray*. The word "maleficium" more typically refers to an act of black magic rather than a magical item.

1179 *The Wreck of the World*

1180 Dating *Set Piece* (NA #35) - It is "1798 CE" (p57).

1181 *The Zygon Who Fell to Earth*. William Wordsworth lived 1770-1850, and his magnum opus is generally regarded as *The Prelude* – a work he started working on when he was 28, but was published posthumously.

1182 *The Banquo Legacy*

1183 *Interference* (p59, p147).

1184 Dating *Christmas on a Rational Planet* (NA #52) - It's "1799. At Christmas" (p24).

1185 "The early nineteenth century" according to *The Eight Doctors*.

1186 *Instruments of Darkness*. In our history, the dodo was extinct by 1700.

1187 *A Thousand Tiny Wings*. This presumably occurred when the Arapaho lived on the plains – they were relocated, in the mid-nineteenth century, to reservations in Wyoming and Oklahoma.

1188 *Moonflesh*. Crazy Horse lived c.1840 to 1877.

1189 *FP: The Brakespeare Voyage* (ch3).

1190 *The Demons of Red Lodge and Other Stories*: "Special Features"

1191 *Upstairs*. Pitt died, age 46, on 23rd January, 1806, from ill health exacerbated by his heavy drinking. The claim that five Prime Ministers "died in office" in a 22-year span isn't 100% accurate, as Robert Banks Jenkinson died in 1828 after resigning the year before.

1192 *The Lazarus Experiment, Under the Lake*

1193 *Unbound: A Storm of Angels*. Beethoven lived 1770-1827, and started going deaf in his late 20s.

1194 "The Glorious Dead"

1195 "Millennia" before *Earth Aid*.

1196 In *Iris* S5: *Comeback of the Scorchies*, Iris claims that Turner is from "18thinga-mabobs", and he's the sort of person who references Horatio Walpole (1717-1797). It's perhaps best to assume that he's from earlier in the nineteenth century than later, because *ST*: "Old Flames" claims that his uniform came into service about 1776. Also, Turner says in *Iris* S5: *An Extraterrestrial Werewolf in London* that rugby came about "after [his] time" – it started at Rugby School in the 1830s, and was popularized in the 1850s and 60s.

1197 Dating *Foreign Devils* (TEL #5) - It's "December 1800" (p22).

1198 Dating *The Man in the Velvet Mask* (MA #19) - The Doctor and Dodo see a poster that gives a date of "Messidor, Year XII", and the Doctor calculates that they

uncover ancient Egyptian treasures for Napoleon. She located the TARDIS, thanks to a message Ace left in 1366 BC, and programmed it to find the Doctor. It did so in Paris, 1871.

The Doctor had a close friendship with Wordsworth, and was present when the writer did a first draft of his most famous poem.[1181] Robert Dodds was murdered at Banquo Manor in 1798. A Time Lord agent was dispatched to wait for the Doctor, who eventually showed up a century later.[1182] In 1799, Mother Mathara of Faction Paradox and two thousand refugees from Ordifica arrived from 2596. They began building the city of Anathema. With the help of the remembrance tanks that Mathara left, this society would become the Remote.[1183]

1799 (9th November to 25th December) - CHRISTMAS ON A RATIONAL PLANET[1184] ->

Napoleon returned to France from Egypt, shutting down the Directory and replacing it with the Consulate. The Shadow Directory secretly survived. The mysterious Cardinal Scarlath gave the Vatican's Collection of Necessary Secrets certain documents that described the creation of ancient Egyptian civilisation by a one-eyed monster.

Roz Forrester accidentally ended up in Woodwicke, New York state, after investigating a temporal anomaly in 2012. She set herself up as a fortune-teller and met Samuel Lincoln, whom she mistook for an ancestor of Abraham Lincoln. Roz planned to assassinate Samuel, thus changing history and enabling the seventh Doctor to locate her.

The Doctor arrived and stopped Roz, but a vast psychic disturbance started in the town. This was caused by the Carnival Queen, also known as Cacophony, who sought to create an irrational universe. The Queen was releasing irrational gynoid monsters into the area, and sought to create further disruption through the latently telepathic Chris Cwej. He chose Reason over the Carnival Queen's irrationality, and the defeated Queen departed into eternity, where she hoped to inspire more ideas.

The Doctor learned afterwards that the TARDIS had planted a memory in Chris' mind that swayed his decision, as the TARDIS feared becoming denationalised under the Queen's rule. Jake McCrimmon, agent of the American Special Congress, investigated the aftermath.

The Nineteenth Century

Lord Aldbourne formed a branch of the Hellfire Club and played at devil worship.[1185] The Doctor brought the ornithologist James Bond to the 1800s to see a live Dodo.[1186] The Doctor learned tracking skills from the Arapaho tribe: experts in pursuing buffalo across the American plains.[1187] Crazy Horse taught the Doctor how to use a bow and arrow. The Doctor had one or two encounters with the

Sioux, who he thought could do marvellous things with chokecherries, wild turnips and buffalo liver.[1188]

wih - In an early campaign of the War in Heaven, Robert Scarratt served on a nineteenth-century whaling vessel.[1189] Mind parasites, the Racht, germinated throughout space via "seed discs". One such disc infected a town in Norfolk in the 1800s; the fifth Doctor and Nyssa cleansed the populace, but the seed disc went missing.[1190]

The time fungus in 10 Downing Street fed upon and killed a number of UK Prime Ministers in the early nineteenth century, including William Pitt the Younger.[1191]

The Doctor met Beethoven, and thought him "a nice chap, bit intense, loved an arm-wrestle".[1192]

> = The alt-first Doctor who defeated Auld Mortality fashioned a hearing aid for Beethoven.[1193]

> (=) By this time, Katsura Sato had conquered the Earth. He renamed the world Dhakan.[1194]

A sentient planet birthed grub-creatures that ravaged her resources and returned nothing. The planet then birthed a warrior race, the Metatraxi, to eliminate the grubs. The Metatraxi developed a highly refined sense of honour and left their homeworld, returning only to supply their Great Mother planet with minerals. Some grubs survived, off world.[1195]

Captain Edwin Turner, a companion of Iris Wildthyme, hailed from the nineteenth century. He couldn't actually remember the first time he met her.[1196]

1800 (December) - FOREIGN DEVILS[1197] ->

The Emperor became sickened by the foreign-sponsored opium trade afflicting China, and ordered the removal of all "foreign devils". The Chief Astrologer to the Emperor placed a curse on one such opium trader, Roderick Upcott. The curse was designed to first endow the Upcott family with prosperity, making their inevitable downfall all the more crushing.

The TARDIS arrived in China, and while the second Doctor was caught up with local politics, Jamie and Zoe disappeared through a "spirit gate" – a stone ring traditionally designed to keep demons at bay. The Doctor realised the gate was a teleporter and used the TARDIS to follow his companions to 1900.

> **(=) 1804 - THE MAN IN THE VELVET MASK[1198] ->** The first Doctor and Dodo arrived on Earth, which had been remade ten years ago by a world-machine. The dwarf Minski, in control of the remade France, attempted to start a war between France, Britain and America that would spread a virus. Anyone infected would have fallen under Minski's control. Minski's

plan fell to ruin and he was killed. Dodo acquired Minski's virus while sleeping with an actor named Dalville, but the virus was harmless without its creator. The Doctor and the real Marquis de Sade sabotaged the world-machine, and the machine's creators returned Earth to N-Space, erasing this history.

River Song made her escape from the Marquis de Sade's private boudoir.[1199] The vampire Lilyana murdered the family of a man named Victor, and turned him.[1200]

1805 - TIMEH: THE CLOCKWORK WOMAN[1201] **->** The time travellers Honoré Lechasseur and Emily Blandish helped a clockwork woman named Dove – the creation of Sir Edward Fanshawe, a genius builder – to become self-actualised. Dove was influenced by the writings of Mary Wollstonecraft, and pledged to become a writer who advocated gender equality.

The Battle of Trafalgar

Vice Admiral Horatio Nelson **"was a personal friend"** of the Doctor.[1202] The Doctor breakfasted with Nelson in 1805, the day before Nelson's final battle with Napoleon at Trafalgar.[1203] The Doctor was "instrumental" at Trafalgar.[1204]

His sextant calculated the position of Napoleon's fleet.[1205]

1805 (12th September) - WORLD GAME[1206] **->** The second Doctor and Serena narrowly saved Wellington and Nelson when Valmont, one of the immortal Players, attempted to kill them with a bomb.

The Doctor and Serena travelled to Paris to discover more about the Players' plans. They saved Napoleon from assassination, and learned that another Player, the Countess, was also in Paris. The Doctor learned that Napoleon had a secret weapon – a submarine – and in part survived a vampire assassin because of all the garlic he'd been eating since arriving in France. The Countess had designed the submarine's omega drive propulsion system, and had tasked a Raston Warrior Robot to serve as a guard. When this vanished, the Doctor deduced that someone on Gallifrey had sent the Robot and the vampire. The Doctor and Serena sabotaged the submarine, but with no more leads to the Players' grand plan, they departed for 1815.

c 1805 - STARBORN[1207] **->** The first Doctor, Ian, Barbara and Vicki found a planet where the people lived in symbiosis with the star-network supporting their world. As individual stars died, one of the populace transformed to take its place. A race of plunderers, the Waneshi, sent one

---

are in "June or July 1804".
1199 *DC 2: The Sonomancer*
1200 "A century and a half" before *Daemons: White Witch of Devil's End*: "Half Light".
1201 Dating *TimeH: The Clockwork Woman* (*TimeH #3*) - The year is given.
1202 *The Sea Devils*. Nelson lived 1758-1805.
1203 *Eye of Heaven*. The Battle of Trafalgar occurred on 21st October, 1805.
1204 *The Scarlet Empress*
1205 "Fire and Brimstone"
1206 Dating *World Game* (PDA #74) - The date is given, and is indeed the only day Nelson and Wellington met historically.
1207 Dating *Starborn* (BF CC #8.9) - It's "a century or so"/"a hundred years" before the early-twentieth-century portion of the story. The first Doctor wore a particular ring – in *The Daleks' Master Plan*, he uses its mysterious properties to open the TARDIS door. The second Doctor discards the ring in *The Power of the Daleks*, as it no longer fits his finger.
1208 Dating *Seasons of Fear* (BF #30) - The date is given.
1209 *Benny: The Medusa Effect*. This presumably denotes *The Battle of Trafalgar* by J.M.W. Turner (1775-1851), painted in 1806, and currently owned by the Tate Gallery in London.
1210 "Forty years" before *Demon Quest: A Shard of Ice*.
1211 "Many years" (p52) before *Plague of the Cybermen*, in which Victor is still a young boy.

1212 Twenty years before *The Beast of Orlok*.
1213 *The Darkness of Glass*
1214 "About two hundred years" before *The Raincloud Man*.
1215 "Two hundred years" before *Planet of the Dead*. There is no International Gallery in real life, but we see it again in *SJA: Mona Lisa's Revenge*.
1216 "Two hundred years" before *SJA: Eye of the Gorgon*.
1217 According to a gravestone in *The Curse of Fenric*.
1218 *The Wrong Doctors*. This happens "three years" before Petherbridge dies in the War of 1812.
1219 *Upstairs*. Cavendish-Bentinck died 30th October, 1809.
1220 "The Forgotten"
1221 *The Pit*
1222 *The Eye of the Tyger*, which sounds like a different visit to the one seen in *The Pit*.
1223 *Hornets' Nest: The Stuff of Nightmares*
1224 *Night of the Humans* (p16). Pond lived 1767-1836, and served as Astronomer Royal 1811-1835.
1225 *The Devil Goblins from Neptune*. Other references to meeting the Duke of Wellington around this time appear in *The Tomorrow Windows*, *Synthespians™* and *The Book of the Still*.
1226 *TW: Greeks Bearing Gifts*. Mary is evidently from the same race as the peaceful "star poet" seen in *SJA: Invasion of the Bane*, which suggests that – as Mary speculates in the *Torchwood* episode – her planet has undergone a regime change.

of their number – Stella – to gather information from Annet, the newest of the Starborn, prior to the Waneshi siphoning away the planet's energy. The Waneshi's efforts interrupted Annet's ascension, and the Doctor sacrificed his ring to plug a potentially catastrophic leak in the star-network – a temporary measure until the Waneshi forced Stella to ascend. The Waneshi left, defeated, and the victimized Stella sent her consciousness forward a hundred years to try and avert her fate.

> **(=) 1806 - SEASONS OF FEAR**[1208] **->** The eighth Doctor and Charley confronted the long-lived Grayle once again. This time, Grayle built a transmat and brought his masters, the Nimon, to Earth. The Doctor engineered a time corridor that returned the Nimon to Britain in 305 BC.

An original painting by Turner would come to adorn Irving Braxiatel's study.[1209] Albert Tiermann was the son of a successful writer, but had no imagination of his own. As part of his plan to trap the Doctor, the Demon working for the Hornets granted Tiermann an imagination in return for implanting a shard of ice in his heart. The Demon also created a hotel in the Murgin Pass.[1210]

A clockmaker in Klimtenburg found a damaged Cyber-unit from the dormant spaceship there, and thought it an Oracle. The unit guided the clockmaker to fashion a power-converter that could revive the sleeping Cybermen. When Lady Marie Ernhardt died birthing her son Victor, the clockmaker fashioned a robot double that had Marie's memories.[1211]

Golems were unthinking killing machines crafted from virtually indestructible aluminosilicate; many civilised worlds and Article 12 of the Galactic Code outlawed them. Experiments were undertaken to create intelligent Golems that could integrate themselves into a society. A humanoid-looking boy and girl Golem were birthed, but one of their creators had a crisis of conscience and sent them away in a spaceship.

In the quiet German town of Orlok, Baron Teufel had systematically dismembered fourteen people as part of experiments on the reanimation of human tissue using electricity – the savage deaths were attributed to the fabled "Beast of Orlok". The spaceship with the young Golems arrived in the Black Forest near Orlok, just as the Baron attempted to make a local, Frau Tod, his fifteenth victim. She permanently blinded the Baron and claimed the Golems as her own children, naming them Hans and Greta. The Baron left town.[1212]

Mannering Caversham became one of the greatest lanternists of his age, and staged performances in his castle on Michael's Island. On 15th November, 1807, Caversham's innovation with light weakened a dimensional barrier, and allowed a demon-creature entry to our reality. Caversham

trapped the demon in a stained-glass window and – as it was mentally linked to the darker aspects of his mind – shot himself to keep it imprisoned.[1213]

The Tabbalac were an orange-skinned, aggressive species who could innately sense lies by reading body language, and were skilled at matter transmission. One Tabbalac – a technical genius who feared that his government would use his talents for killing – adopted the name "Brooks" and escaped his homeworld by building a casino boat, The High Straights, that teleported from planet to planet. The casino served an elite clientele, and another of Brooks' inventions, the reality-warping High Stakes table, enabled patrons to bet such abstract commodities as their youth, skills, emotions and their very history.[1214]

The Cup of Aethelstan was put on display in the International Gallery in London.[1215] **One of the surviving Gorgons possessed an Abbess.**[1216] **Joseph Sundvik, an ancestor of Captain Sorin, was born on 8th April, 1809.**[1217]

> (=) In 1809, a Vortex-dwelling Time Demon – having identified Melanie Bush as a means of creating temporal chaos – usurped the lifetime of Stapleton Petherbridge, a toll-bridge worker in Pease Pottage. Upon the Time Demon's defeat, Petherbridge's life resumed its normal course.[1218]

William Cavendish-Bentinck, the Third Duke of Portland and UK Prime Minister, died owing to the time fungus.[1219] A squad of Parisian soldiers were lost in the Catacombs in 1810. They found themselves in 2000.[1220]

In 1811, the poet William Blake vanished from his home and met the Doctor.[1221] The Doctor also met William Blake at home once.[1222] William Blake was a personal friend of the fourth Doctor.[1223] The Doctor said that John Pond, the Astronomer Royal, was a "lovely chap" who once told him a filthy joke.[1224] The Doctor was with a British rifle brigade when he met Sir Arthur Wellesley. He was a prisoner of the French at Salamanca in 1812.[1225]

In 1812, the alien criminal "Mary" arrived on Earth. She would later claim to hail from a savage, repressive world that punished dissent with death. The beings there communicated with pendants that granted telepathy. Mary killed the guard escorting her, and hosted herself within a passing young woman.[1226]

Stapleton Petherbridge was drafted into the Royal Navy in 1810, and died on the seas in the War of 1812.

> (=) The Time Demon within him became linked to Jebediah Thurwell, who was born the same year.[1227]

1812 - EMOTIONAL CHEMISTRY[1228] **->** The Magellans were essentially living stars. One such creature broke a rule among its kind by giving birth; its child was named

Aphrodite. The Doctor acted as defence council when the Magellan was put on trial. The Magellan's people ruled to spilt the creature in half and place each part in separate time zones on Earth. The emotional side of the Magellan became the female Dusha, and by the early nineteenth century had been adopted by Count Yuri Vishenkov. The Magellan's intellectual half became Lord General Razum Kinzhal, a strategist around the year 5000. Aphrodite was contained and given the extra-dimensional locale of Paraiso as her home.

Living as a Russian noblewoman, Dusha Vishenkov had the ability to alter probability and affected her "sister" Natasha Vishenkov. Natasha's descendants would look virtually identical for millennia to come, and be predisposed to good luck. Dusha's influence also turned the Vishenkov family's possessions into empathic capacitors that amplified the emotions of those nearby. One such item, a painting, would be on display in the Kremlin Museum in 2024 and start a fire there.

The eighth Doctor helped Dusha reunite with her lover, Kinzhal, in the year 5000.

Napoleon's Russian Campaign

In 1812, a battlefield from Napoleon's Russian campaign was kidnapped by the War Lords.[1229] The Doctor met Napoleon and told him that an army marches on its stomach.[1230] The Doctor kept a bottle that Napoleon threw at him. He later drank it in 2011 with Amy, Rory and River Song on the shore of Lake Silencio.[1231]

While on the Russian front, Napoleon had coffee with Iris Wildthyme.[1232] The Celestial Toymaker beat Napoleon at Risk.[1233] Illeana (later Illeana de Santos) fled with her wealthy merchant father from Smolensk, but bandits killed her father. The werewolf Stubbe turned her into a werewolf and bound her to him for a century or two.[1234]

(=) **1812 - "The Time of My Life"**[1235] -> The tenth Doctor and Donna found that time had been interfered with, and that Napoleon's troops were attacking Cossacks with impulse weapons.

1812 (summer to 18th October) - MOTHER RUSSIA[1236] -> The first Doctor, Steven and Dodo spent some time at the home of Count Gregori Nikitin, where the Doctor tutored Nikitin's son. A spaceship carrying an infiltration unit – one designed to adopt the form of an enemy's leaders to assassinate them – crashed to Earth and impersonated the Doctor just prior to Napoleon's invasion of Russia. The disguised unit served as an advisor to Napoleon once he'd captured Moscow. The public set fire to the city rather than surrender it – Napoleon withdrew, and a Russian mob killed the infiltration unit.

c 1813 - THE MARK OF THE RANI[1237] -> The Rani was present during the Industrial Revolution, extracting a chemical from human brains. Her project was interrupted by the arrival, and rivalry, of the Tremas Master

1227 *The Wrong Doctors*

1228 Dating *Emotional Chemistry* (EDA #66) - The date is given in the blurb.

1229 *The War Games*

1230 *Day of the Daleks*. The Doctor does not meet Napoleon in *The Reign of Terror* (although Ian and Barbara do). The third Doctor is still exiled in the twentieth century timezone, so he must have met Napoleon in an earlier incarnation (see *Mother Russia* and *World Game*). Napoleon lived 1769-1821. The meeting is also mentioned in *Escape Velocity* and *Warmonger*.

1231 *The Impossible Astronaut*. Napoleon lived 1769-1821.

1232 *Iris S2: The Panda Invasion*

1233 "End Game" (*DWM*)

1234 *Loups-Garoux*

1235 Dating "The Time of My Life" (*DWM* #399) - Jonathan Morris' behind-the-scenes notes in *The Widow's Curse* graphic novel specifies that this scene originated from a pitch of his where "Napoleon attacks Moscow with nuclear bombs". The resolution to this dilemma is never told, but said temporal interference is presumably (but not necessarily) erased from history.

1236 Dating *Mother Russia* (BF CC #2.1) - As the back cover says, "it's 1812". The Doctor's party lodges with Nikitin for some "weeks" before Napoleon marches on Moscow and the battle of Borodino, which occurred on 7th September. Steven claims that it's "spring" when the TARDIS arrives, but that would mean that the TARDIS crew spends entire months with Nikitin, so he's probably just estimating and it's actually summer.

Troublingly, the historical 1812 fire of Moscow and the withdrawal of Napoleon's troops from the city (concurrent with the arrival of winter, which is why it starts snowing in the final scene) are here conflated into the same day. In real life, the fire occurred 14th-18th September, but Napoleon's troops didn't withdraw until a month later, on 18th-19th October. It's possible that Napoleon have left sooner in the *Doctor Who* universe than in real-life – but mid-September still seems a bit early for snow, even for Moscow.

The fifth Doctor recalls witnessing Napoleon's invasion of Russia in *Loups-Garoux*, and that the occasion had stormy weather – retroactively, this could be taken as a reference to *Mother Russia*.

1237 Dating *The Mark of the Rani* (22.3) - The date is never stated on screen or in the script, but *DWM* reported that the production team felt that the story was set in "1830". *The Terrestrial Index* set the story "c1825", the novelisation simply said "the beginning of

and the sixth Doctor. The Master attempted to disrupt human history as the greatest scientific minds of the era converged on Killingworth. The Doctor trapped the two renegades in the Rani's TARDIS and banished them from Earth.

The Last Frostfair

The Doctor helped River Song celebrate her birthday on a frozen Thames in 1814, at the last of the great frost fairs. Entertainment was provided by Stevie Wonder, who didn't realise the Doctor had brought him back in time.[1238]

1814 (February) - FROSTFIRE[1239] **->** The first Doctor, Steven and Vicki arrived at the last-ever frost fair – literally a fair situated upon ice – on the River Thames. Captain McClavity owned a Collection of Curiosities there, as well as a phoenix egg that he had acquired from the Medina in Tunis. The travellers encountered Jane Austen, much to the Doctor's delight, as he had read all of her novels and thought them very witty. Soon afterwards, McClavity was murdered and the phoenix egg stolen.

The phoenix inside the egg had been responsible for the destruction of a thousand worlds, and now sought to be reborn on Earth. Its essence possessed Georgina Mallard, whose husband – Sir Joseph Mallard – worked for the Royal Mint. The phoenix hoped to use the Mint's metal-melting furnace as a hatchery for itself, but Austen assisted the Doctor's group in turning down the heat. The newly hatched phoenix chick died, but a cinder from the fire –

endowed with a small piece of the phoenix's being – remained in Vicki. She only learned of its presence after she left the Doctor's company and became Lady Cressida.

1814 (4th February) - THIN ICE (TV)[1240] **->** The TARDIS insisted upon taking the twelfth Doctor and Bill to the last great frostfair in 1814. The Doctor had visited the occasion "a few times".

For generations, Lord Sutcliffe's family profited from the energy-rich excretions of an enormous sea-creature kept shackled in the Thames. The creature's energy-exchange periodically froze the Thames over, and now – to maximize his take – Lord Sutcliffe heavily advertised the frostfair to boost attendance. The Doctor and Bill prevented Sutcliffe from detonating the ice and feeding those present to the creature – instead, it ate Sutcliffe and left to avoid humanity, possibly in Greenland. The frostfairs ended without the creature's freezing effect. The Doctor's forged documents enabled some street urchins to inherit Sutcliffe's riches.

Jane Austen, in Clara Oswald's opinion, was a phenomenal kisser. Clara expressed her love for Jane – the two of them repeatedly pranked one other.[1241] The Doctor danced a *cotillion* with Jane Austen, and deemed her "a very nifty mover".[1242] Iris and Jane Austen visited the Moulin Rouge – not the one in Paris, but a space station near Betelgeuse.[1243] The immortal Helena met Jane Austen, and bought a first edition of *Pride and Prejudice*.[1244]

the nineteenth century". Tony Scupham-Bilton concluded in *Celestial Toyroom* that, judging by the historical evidence and the month the story was filmed, the story was "set in either October 1821 or October 1822". As that article states, the story must at the very least be set before the Stockton-Darlington line was opened in September 1825, and after Thomas Liddell was made Baron Ravensworth on 17th July, 1821. However, co-writer Jane Baker later told *DWM* that her research was confused by the Victorian convention of biographies referring to Lords by their titles even before they were given them. Given that, Jim Smith in *Who's Next* suggested that the date given in *DWM* was a mishearing of "1813", which fits all the evidence apart from the existence of Lord Ravensworth.

Timelink opted for it being "October 1813" based upon Stevenson constructing his first engine, the Blucher, in that year, and October being the month the story was filmed (so it fitting with the seasonal conditions on screen). *About Time* laid out the evidence but didn't especially come to a conclusion, noting that Stevenson's creation of Blucher suggested 1813, but that wartime travel restrictions would make the pro-

posed meet-up of Davy, Farraday and Telford more feasible after the end of the Peninsula War or Waterloo.
1238 *A Good Man Goes to War*
1239 Dating *Frostfire* (BF CC #1.1) - The year is given. Historically, the last River Thames frost fair started on 1st February, 1814, and only lasted four days. The issue of whether the first Doctor only had one heart or not is complicated by the phoenix's comment about the cold "in the Doctor's hearts". As Austen claims, she had only published two novels by 1814: *Sense and Sensibility* (1811) and *Pride and Prejudice* (1813). *Mansfield Park*, her third book, saw print in July 1814.
1240 Dating *Thin Ice* (X10.3) - The Doctor gives the exact day. The first Doctor visited the last frostfair in *Frostfire*, and the eleventh Doctor and River Song skated there (*A Good Man Goes to War*).
1241 *The Magician's Apprentice, Face the Raven*. Austen lived 1775 to 18th July, 1817.
1242 *The Behemoth*
1243 *Iris* S2: *The Panda Invasion*
1244 *Erimem: Three Faces of Helena*. *Pride and Prejudice* was first released on 28th January, 1813.

1814 (17th October) - "The Doctor and the Nurse"[1245] **->** Amy lost patience with the arguing eleventh Doctor and Rory, and ordered them to bond over a Boys' Night Out. The TARDIS arrived at a tavern in London, 1814, following the Doctor asking the Ship to find "lots of beer". Amy left to sightsee, but the Doctor and Rory found the idea of spending time together so horrifying, they tried to skip ahead a few hours in the TARDIS... only to discover that delayed damage from an attack in 7213 had harmed the Ship's chronolabe. They spent weeks bouncing between various points in space-time.

In their absence, an agent of the Silence – seeking to fulfill upon a fixed point in time – placed a bomb that triggered the London Beer Flood: a crushing wave of 323,000 gallons of beer from the Horse Shoe Brewery. Amy deduced that the flood itself was a fixed point, but its victims weren't, and used her TARDIS phone's foreknowledge to save many lives. When the Doctor and Rory finally returned, she castigated them for enjoying themselves while she was saving lives and covered in beer, and cancelled future Boys' Nights.

In 1815, the aged Toussaint ritually summoned a Loa to liberate him from slavery. The Loa possessed his granddaughter Zara, and "fulfilled" its promise by creating a slow-time duplicate of Keynsham village. The zone, known as the Keysham Triangle, would snare victims throughout the decades.[1246]

The Battle of Waterloo

1815 (June) - WORLD GAME[1247] **->** Using psychic paper, the second Doctor gatecrashed a ball being held by Wellington, and warned him of the Players' plans. Serena died saving Wellington from an assassination attempt. The Doctor impersonated Napoleon in order to infiltrate the French lines at Waterloo and divert reinforcements arranged by the Players. History was returned to its normal course and the Players – worried about further intervention from the Time Lords – suspended their games.

The Doctor told his good friend Wellington at Waterloo: "Hope for luck, but put trust in your strategy."[1248] Major General Fergus Lethbridge-Stewart served alongside the Duke of Wellington, and was at his side at Waterloo.[1249] Oliver Blazington, later a big game hunter, was a rifleman who fought alongside Wellington at Waterloo.[1250] The Doctor met Wellington after the conflict.[1251]

1245 Dating "The Doctor and the Nurse" (IDW Vol. 4 #3-4) - A caption says it's "October 17, 1814", the same day as the historical London beer flood. It remains one of history's stranger catastrophes, on par with the Boston Molasses Disaster, which killed twenty-one people on January 15, 1919.
1246 The background to *Leth-St: The Dreamer's Lament*.
1247 Dating *World Game* (PDA #74) - The Doctor arrives on the eve of the Battle of Waterloo, so therefore it's 17th June, 1815.
1248 *3rdA: Storm of the Horofax*
1249 *The Dying Days, Leth-St: The Daughters of Earth* (ch2), *Leth-St: The Dreamer's Lament*. *The Scales of Injustice* provided Fergus' first name and rank.
1250 *The Eye of the Jungle*
1251 *The Eight Doctors*
1252 Dating *The Curse of Davros* (BF #166) - The story picks up in "the early hours of the morning of the 18th of June, 1815", the day of the Battle of Waterloo, with everything up to Flip and Jared's arrival being told through exposition or in flashback. The Duke of Wellington here meets Flip and Jared, but - as with *Other Lives* – doesn't actually meet the Doctor.
1253 *J&L S9: The Flying Frenchmen*
1254 Dating *World Game* (PDA #74) - The date is given.
1255 *Players*, almost certainly the same meeting mentioned in *The Eight Doctors*. The bank account is also mentioned in *World Game*.
1256 *The Land of the Dead*
1257 Dating *The Company of Friends*:"Mary's Story" (BF #123d) - "It was 1816," says Mary, later adding that it

was "one dreary night in June". Interestingly, Mary *was* calling herself "Mary Shelley" (as opposed to "Mary Godwin", her maiden name) by this point, even though she and Percy weren't actually married. They wouldn't wed until late 1816, after his first wife killed herself. The Doctor having familiarity with Byron, Mary Shelley and/or the night that *Frankenstein* was created was also mentioned in *Storm Warning, Neverland, Zagreus* and *Terror Firma*. *Managra* mentions a separate incident involving the Doctor, Byron and Percy Shelley.
1258 *The Silver Turk*
1259 *The Company of Friends*: "Mary's Story"
1260 The epilogue to *Army of Death* has Mary deciding to ask the Doctor to take her home. That story also implies, however, that they've only experienced events in *The Silver Turk, The Witch from the Well, Army of Death* and a side trip to the planet Mayhem. Given that she and the Doctor travel together for "years" (*The Company of Friends*:"Mary's Story"), perhaps she reconsiders for a time, or she goes home for a bit and travels with him again.
1261 *Antidote to Oblivion. Frankenstein (or, The Modern Prometheus)* was first published in 1818.
1262 *Managra*. This happened to one of the first three Doctors.
1263 *9thC: The Window on the Moor*. The Bronte sisters and their brother, Branwell, were born 1816-1820.
1264 "A couple of centuries" before *The Lost Angel*.
1265 Dating *The Ghosts of N-Space* (MA #7) - It is "eighteen eighteen" (p63), one hundred and fifty-seven years before the present-day setting (p200).

Flip Jackson Joins the TARDIS

1815 (18th June) - THE CURSE OF DAVROS[1252] -> Davros and his Daleks arrived from the future to field-test a mind-transfer device that he had engineered. Napoleon's military genius impressed Davros, who theorised that if Napoleon's history were revised, the resultant French Empire would inspire significant technological advancement on Earth, turning humanity from an opponent into an ally. Davros cured Napoleon's ill health with some pills, then took Napoleon through time to meet his older self – who explained the details of his defeat and exile.

Napoleon and Davros returned to 1815, even as the sixth Doctor detected the Dalek mothership operating in this time period. To stymie Davros' efforts, the Doctor used the mind-swapper to switch their bodies. Davros, in the Doctor's body, subsequently escaped in a Dalek pursuit ship to the twentieth century...

The Daleks retrieved Davros, who was accompanied by Philippa "Flip" Jackson and her boyfriend Jared. Napoleon had used his foreknowledge to head off the Prussian Army at the town of Wavre, preventing the Prussians from aiding the British. The Doctor and Davros returned to their proper bodies, and the Doctor informed Napoleon that the Daleks intended to swap the French Emperor's mind with that of a Dalek – turning it into a super-computer that would harness his genius to subjugate Earth and a thousand other worlds. Napoleon resigned himself to his historical fate, allowing the British victory to happen. Jared supplied twenty Dalek gun-sticks to a small team of British soldiers, enabling them to frighten off General Gracey's troops at Wavre. The soldiers were sworn to secrecy about the weaponry, and the Prussians captured Prince Nous, preserving history.

The Doctor erased the Daleks' minds with the mind-switcher, and stranded them – along with Davros – aboard their mothership in the Vortex. He programmed a Dalek pursuit ship to take Flip and Jared home... but Flip exited at the last second, preferring to travel with the Doctor.

(=) Mallory Riverstock's portal machine created a short-lived, errant timeline in which the French won the Battle of Waterloo, and all of Europe eventually fell to Emperor Napoleon V.[1253]

(=) 1815 (18th November) - WORLD GAME[1254] -> The second Doctor and Serena arrived in a Paris that was celebrating a great victory over the British and Wellington's mysterious death. The Doctor and Serena first travelled fifty years into the future – to see the end result of the Countess' Grand Design – then went into the past to prevent it happening.

In 1816, the Doctor visited the Duke of Wellington, and made a lot of money at a gambling den. He set up an account at Chumley's Bank that he occasionally dipped into while on Earth.[1255] The Doctor was present when Peter the Great sent an expedition to Alaska.[1256]

Mary Shelley Joins the TARDIS, Returns

1816 (June) - THE COMPANY OF FRIENDS: "Mary's Story"[1257] -> A temporal storm infected the TARDIS and the eighth Doctor with corrosive "vitreous time". He arrived, charred and misshapen, at the Villa Diodati at Lake Geneva, 1816, just as Lord Byron challenged his friends – Mary and Percy Shelley, Mary's step-sister Claire and John William Polidori – to each write a ghost story. The Doctor muttered, "Dr Frankenstein", lay injured for a week and appeared to have died. Percy suggested they test whether an electro-static spark could make his body twitch, as had been reported with frog's legs. The experiment revived the Doctor, and he wandered off.

Mary found the Doctor in his ransacked TARDIS. An earlier version of the eighth Doctor answered his later self's distress call after dropping Samson and Gemma off in Vienna. The younger Doctor activated the TARDIS' self-repair systems, which healed his older self via their symbiotic link. The older Doctor left, and Mary accepted the younger one's offer to become his travelling companion.

The Doctor tried to relocate the TARDIS in space, not time, to reunite with Samson and Gemma in Vienna... but he and Mary instead found themselves in that city in 1873.[1258] The Doctor and Mary travelled together for years, encountering foes such as Cybermen and Axons.[1259] Mary eventually ended her travels with the Doctor, and returned home to be with her soul mate, Percy Shelley.[1260]

The Doctor spent time in Geneva with Frankenstein.[1261] The Doctor met Byron at the Parthenon, and had an episode with him that involved five oranges, a purple handkerchief and a misplaced nostrum. He also met Percy Shelley.[1262]

In their childhood, the Bronte siblings caught stray "visions" of alien travellers on the moor, and amused themselves with tales of fantastical lands. Anne indulged Emily in her belief, but Charlotte told Anne to set aside such childish things. In future, Emily helped the travellers to route to other worlds.[1263] A quartet of Weeping Angels became trapped in a buried street in Rickman, New York.[1264]

1818 - THE GHOSTS OF N-SPACE[1265] -> Travelling back in time, the third Doctor and Sarah witnessed the early life of the wizard Maximillian.

c 1818 - PLAGUE OF THE CYBERMEN[1266] -> The eleventh Doctor cured an outbreak of Hapthoid Radiation Sickness in Klimtenburg, as caused by pieces of shattered reactor housing from the crashed Cyber-ship there. The residents formed a mob as some dozen Cybermen revived from stasis, and the robotic Marie Ernhardt fell to her death while struggling with one of them. The Doctor destroyed the Cybermen by overloading their energy intake, but Marie's son Victor died in the process.

1819 (14th-16th August) - THE PETERLOO MASSACRE[1267] -> Travelling backwards through decades of carbon emissions caused the TARDIS to malfunction and ground itself in Manchester. The Ship's glitching instruments reported the year as 1816, but it was actually 16th August 1819: a fixed point in time, as tens of thousands of people converged in the city to demand parliamentary reform. The gentry instigated a slaughter to keep the lower classes in their place, killing at least fifteen and wounding more than six hundred. The fifth Doctor, Tegan and Nyssa had to let history unfold. The event was later called the Peterloo Massacre, reflective of the Battle of Waterloo in 1815.

In the early nineteenth century, the Doctor met Beau Brummel, who told him he looked better in a cloak.[1268] The sixth Doctor owned a fob watch gifted to him by Beau Brummel.[1269] The Doctor told Walter Scott that all that sentimental stuff about the tartan and the heather would lead to no good.[1270]

A Dalek scoutship crashed on the planet Vulcan. By this time, the Daleks had already encountered the second Doctor.[1271] The Dalek ship was from the far future.[1272] The New Church of Wonderment split from what became the Old Church of Wonderment.[1273]

The Reverend Thomas Bright surveyed the Nine Travellers. At some point between now and the late twentieth century, Cessair of Diplos posed as Mrs Trefusis for sixty years, then Senora Camara.[1274]

Davros took Napoleon to meet his older self on the isle of St Helena. The older Napoleon demonstrated with toy soldiers how he had lost the battle of Waterloo, and that defeat would result in his exile. The younger Napoleon left with Davros to try and avert this outcome.[1275]

On 3rd July, 1820, Florence Sundvik – later the wife of Joseph Sundvik – was born.[1276] Napoleon died in 1821, still traumatised by what he had witnessed in the Great Pyramid in 1798.[1277]

1266 Dating *Plague of the Cybermen* (NSA #52) - The blurb says it's the "19th-century village of Klimtenburg". The story has no blatant ties to *Frankenstein* (first published in 1818), but thematically resembles bits of it (mobs with pitchforks, lightning storms, Marie's son being named Victor, etc). It's not said, but to judge by the cover, the Cybermen involved are the former Cybus-Industries models, so must be time travellers (as with *The Next Doctor*).
1267 Dating *The Peterloo Massacre* (BF #210) - The exact day of the massacre is given, and the Doctor's party arrives two days beforehand.
1268 The Doctor mentions Beau Brummel in *The Sensorites*, *The Twin Dilemma* and *The Two Doctors*. Brummel lived 1778-1840. He was an arbiter of fashion in Regency England, and helped further the style known as "dandyism".
1269 *The Red House*
1270 *The Wheel of Ice* (p307). The English like to suspect that novelist Walter Scott made up all the business about the tartan and the bagpipes about 1820; this is a dig at the Scottish, basically.
1271 The Dalek ship crashed "two hundred years" before *The Power of the Daleks*. This is an early Dalek expedition of our solar system assuming, of course, that Vulcan is (or was) in our solar system. *War of the Daleks* states that this capsule is from the far future (after *Remembrance of the Daleks*), and this fits some of the circumstantial evidence – a Dalek from this mission recognises the Doctor, despite his regeneration (and despite no recorded adventures with any Doctor –

except for *Genesis of the Daleks* – up to this point). In *Day of the Daleks*, the Daleks must use the Mind Analysis Machine to establish the Doctor's identity. On the other hand, the Daleks are silver and blue, and dependent on external power supplies – quite unlike the Davros Era Daleks.
1272 *War of the Daleks*
1273 Some "eight centuries" before *Vienna* S1: *Bad Faith*. As such, neither church is likely to have originated with humanity.
1274 *The Stones of Blood*
1275 *The Curse of Davros*. Napoleon spent the last six years of his life on St Helena, and died on 5th May, 1821. His older self, aware of Davros' duplicity and the historical importance of his younger self capitulating at Waterloo, must advocate the opposite to fulfill upon his personal history.
1276 *The Curse of Fenric*
1277 *The Sands of Time* (p220). The year is given, and Napoleon died 5th May, 1821.
1278 "Bloodsport", "Doorway to Hell". *The Hay Wain* was finished in 1821.
1279 *The Rings of Ikiria*. Champollion published the first translation of the Rosetta Stone in 1822.
1280 The background to *Leth-St: Beast of Fang Rock*. *Horror of Fang Rock* mentions the Beast being seen "eighty years" beforehand.
1281 Dating *Leth-St: Beast of Fang Rock* (*Leth-St* novel #3) - The year is repeatedly named, and the day is also given (ch11).

The painter John Constable added the twelfth Doctor and his TARDIS into *The Hay Wain*.[1278] Shortly before deciphering the Rosetta Stone, the Doctor told Jean-Francois Champollion: "There is a profound difference between translation and interpretation."[1279]

The First Incursion of Fang Rock

Jacob Travers inherited a strand of morphic DNA that had infected his father Lawrence in India. The mutant gene remained dormant until Jacob and his associate, Archibald Goff, took shelter near the Fang Rock lighthouse. A Rutan scout arrived through time from the late 1960s, and its mutagenic field briefly transformed Jacob into a werewolf. He killed one of the lighthouse keepers, Davy Williams, and was then institutionalised at Bethlem Hospital. The scout killed another lighthouse keeper, Alfred Scott, before taking his form. **The sighting of the Beast of Fang Rock became part of the local folklore.**[1280]

1823 (26th September) - BEAST OF FANG ROCK[1281] **->** Archibald Goff and Jacob Travers – both ancestors of Professor Edward Travers and his daughter Anne – returned to Fang Rock to better ascertain the cause of Jacob's insanity. The "Alfred Scott" Rutan, isolated from the Rutan Host, had developed a conscience and an appreciation for humanity. Jacob again became a werewolf and died in combat with a hostile Rutan. The benevolent scout took on Jacob's form and returned to the man's family. The real Jacob already had a son, guaranteeing the Travers line.

1825 - THE TWELFTH DOCTOR YEAR ONE[1282] **->** The Scindia family became devotees of the last of the Kaliratha, and constructed a life-harvesting necro-cloud to facilitate the Kaliratha's resurrection. Khair-un-Nissa Kapoor, the daughter of a spice merchant, was among the necro-cloud's victims. Kapoor's lover Rani Jhulka, the former captain of an Amazon guard, met the twelfth Doctor as he came down a time portal to investigate the Scindia's operations. Priyanka Maratha sweet-talked the TARDIS into going to

this time zone, and the three of them retreated to 2314.

In 1826, the *Camara* was lost in the Irish Sea after snaring a stone "demon" in its nets.[1283] James Fenimore Cooper struck a deal to include Chingachgook, an actual Mohican, as a fictional character in his writings.[1284] Mary Shelley's *The Last Man* was published in 1826.[1285] Prime Minister George Canning died, after just a few months in office, because of the time fungus in 10 Downing Street.[1286]

Golden control-coins belonging to alien pirates, the Flight, wound up in the booty of a smuggler, Isaac Gulliver. Captain Witherley and his men died trying to reclaim Gulliver's hidden treasure in Wiltshire, July 1826.[1287]

1827 - THE BEAST OF ORLOK[1288] **->** General Zoff, the commander-in-chief of the Radzera Planetary League, now possessed Golems that were halfway between mindless brutes and the "civilised" versions represented by Hans Tod and his "sister" Greta. Hoping to create an army of the enhanced versions, Zoff tracked Hans and Greta across sixty thousand light years to Earth.

Baron Teufel returned to Orlok, and a Golem under Zoff's command killed him, which enabled Zoff to adopted Teufel's form using a "metamorphiser". The eighth Doctor and Lucie visited Orlok by mistake after the TARDIS entirely failed to materialise in Alton Towers. The Doctor destroyed Zoff's Golem and Orlok Castle in the process. Zoff's people made him suffer a humiliating loss of rank, and Hans and Greta remained on Earth.

1827 - THE EYE OF THE JUNGLE[1289] **->** The eleventh Doctor, Amy and Rory found themselves in the Amazon rain forest, and confronted the Nadurni: aliens who were harvesting animals to transform into biological weapons for a war effort. The big game hunter Oliver Blazington, who was aiding an expedition to collect animals for the opening of the London zoo, was hideously transformed by the Nadurni's experiments. He attacked his tormentors, and died as their space station was destroyed.

1282 Dating *The Twelfth Doctor Year One* (Titan 12th Doc #1.3, "The Swords of Kali") - The year is given.
1283 "Seaside Rendezvous"
1284 *The Silent Stars Go By*. Chingachgook (misspelled here as "Chingachook") appeared in Fenimore Cooper's *Leatherstocking Tales*, published from 1826 to 1841.
1285 The liner notes to *Army of Death* hint that this book was inspired by Mary's trip to the planet Draxine, and her encountering an army of skeletons there.
1286 *Upstairs*. Canning died 8th August, 1827. His tenure of 119 days is the shortest of any UK Prime Minister.
1287 "Two hundred years" before *Leth-St: The Flaming Soldier* (ch11).

1288 Dating *The Beast of Orlok* (BF BBC7 #3.3) - The year is given. Greta says that she and Hans can't leave Earth because Frau Tod will kill them if they "weren't home for Christmas", and she makes an "early gift" to the Doctor by returning his sonic screwdriver – but the statements are offhanded enough that the story doesn't necessarily take place in winter.
1289 Dating *The Eye of the Jungle* (BBC *DW* audiobook #13) - The year is given in the blurb, and when the Doctor whispers to his companions, "Ahhhh... this is 1827, the year before London Zoo opens".

(=) c 1827-1828 - MEDICINAL PURPOSES[1290] ->

A human researcher from the future acquired a Type 70 TARDIS from a Nekkistani dealer of Gryben, and a dying alien race employed him to research a virus that was killing them. The aliens' immune systems resembled those of humans, so the researcher set up shop in Edinburgh, 1827. He took the guise of "Dr Robert Knox", the anatomist who employed the graverobbers William Burke and William Hare to provide cadavers for study. Not content with unearthing corpses, Burke and Hare started murdering people to fulfill Knox's demands.

Knox infected some Edinburgh residents with the alien virus, but anyone who consumed alcohol proved immune. Failing to make progress, Knox used his illicit technology to roll back time in Edinburgh and start with "new" bodies. He grew ambivalent toward his employers' survival, and turned the enterprise into an elite tourist attraction; patrons paid to witness the "Hale and Burke Experience". The memories of the locals grew cloudy as time repeatedly looped. The sixth Doctor and Evelyn arrived inside of Knox's time loop, and discovered his operations.

The Doctor found it hard to perform hands three and four of *Fantasia in F minor*, as Franz "the hands" Schubert kept tickling him.[1291] The Doctor was at the opening of the London Zoo.[1292] The Second Earl of Liverpool passed on, as a result of the time fungus feeding off him.[1293]

On 28th January, 1829, the Doctor and Evelyn observed Burke's hanging. The Doctor tricked Knox into leaving his time loop and infected him with the alien virus. Knox fled in his TARDIS, and history was restored to its proper path. The Doctor and Evelyn took the mentally disabled "Daft Jamie", who was fated to become one of Burke and Hare's victims, back to meet his appointed demise.

Knox was dying from a flu virus that he'd contracted in Edinburgh. He found an emotion-eating Indo in a crater of congealed iron magma on Mercury – in exchange for the Indo extending Knox's lifespan, Knox agreed to facilitate the creature feasting upon the emotions of John Wilkes Booth, one of history's most famous assassins, in 1865.[1294]

Francesca Farrow ran away with the Circus of Delights in 1829 and became its bearded lady.[1295] Octopoid psychovores, the Saiph, inhabited a planet of the same name in the constellation of Orion. In 1829, some of their number relocated to Earth after a cosmic storm struck their satel-

---

1290 Dating *Medicinal Purposes* (BF #60) - The back cover says 1827. Burke and Hare met the real Knox in November 1827, but the majority of their murders occurred throughout 1828, until they were caught in November of that year. The audio concurs with the historical date for Burke's execution. Hare was granted immunity because he turned King's Evidence against Burke. The real Knox was never prosecuted.

1291 *Dinosaurs on a Spaceship*. Schubert wrote *Fantasia in F minor* from January to March 1828; it was first performed in May of that year.

1292 *The Eye of the Jungle*. The zoo opened on 27th April, 1828, at first as a collection for benefit of scientists. It opened to the public in 1847.

1293 *Upstairs*. The Earl died 4th December, 1828, having left office as Prime Minister on 9th April, 1827.

1294 *Assassin in the Limelight*

1295 "Three years" before *Hornets' Nest: The Circus of Doom*. Novelist William Makepeace Thackeray lived 1811-1863, poet Charles Baudelaire lived 1821-1867, artist Eugene Delacroix lived 1798-1863, and painter Edouard Manet lived 1832-1883.

1296 *The Stealers from Saiph*

1297 *DC: The Red Lady*. Peel, later Prime Minister, established the Metropolitan Police Force in 1829, while he was Home Secretary.

1298 *Leth-St: Beast of Fang Rock*

1299 "Bloodsport". Turner lived 1775-1851, and would spit upon paintings to bind the pigments together.

1300 *The Wreck of the World*. The Great Wave off

Kanagawa was published some time between 1829-1833.

1301 *Timeless*

1302 Dating "Prisoners of Time" (IDW *DW* mini-series) - The year is given.

1303 *Reckless Engineering*

1304 The architect Isambard Kingdom Brunel lived 1806-1859, and also features in *Reckless Engineering*. The sixth Doctor has Brunel's business card in *The Two Doctors*.

1305 *Shroud of Sorrow* (p25).

1306 *The Haunting of Thomas Brewster*

1307 Dating *Hornets' Nest: The Circus of Doom* (BBC fourth Doctor audio #1.3) - The Hornets told the Doctor they met "over a hundred years ago" in *Hornets' Nest: The Dead Shoes*. It's "June" and "1832" according to the Doctor here. The CD sleeve includes a *Radio Times* entry saying it's "1832", and a letter from Sally's father – dated "15th June 1832" – warning against the circus.

1308 "One hundred seventy-six years" before *Voyage of the Damned*.

1309 "The Parliament of Fear"

1310 Dating *Gallery of Ghouls* (BF 4th Doc #5.5) - The Doctor: "1833! You see, Romana, 1833!" Romana: "Early evening, certainly."

1311 "Twenty years" before the 1854 part of *FP: Spinning Jenny*.

1312 Dating *Bloodtide* (BF #22) - The date is given.

1313 "These past ten years" before *Demon Quest: A Shard of Ice*.

lite. The Saiph reverted to protoplasm, and were nourished by the minerals in a cave near Antibes, France.[1296]

The Doctor gave Sir Robert Peel the idea for a metropolitan police force, and served as one of the "peelers".[1297] The Rutan disguised as Jacob Travers went for a walk in the snow in 1829, and never returned. Vina Travers blamed Archibald Goff for the loss of her husband, the start of a feud between their families. "Jacob" shifted form again to become Rupert Slant, and established Morecombe & Slant solicitors in 1830.[1298]

The Doctor thought that painter J.M.W. Turner's spitting was a bit much, but conceded that "talent is undiscerning".[1299] Eventually, the archives of *The World* would contain the woodblock print *The Great Wave off Kanagawa* by Katsushika Hokusai.[1300]

In early May 1830, the time traveller Chloe and her dog Jamais happened upon Sabbath in St Raphael, France. She sensed part of his history but fell unconscious. When she awoke, Sabbath had left her a diamond and a book purporting to speak of the future. Her belief in the book allowed Sabbath to manipulate her activities.[1301]

1830 - "Prisoners of Time"[1302] -> Two Aeroliths – alien "creatures of light and wind" – adopted human form and took up residence in Scotland as Gibson and Ruth Campbell. The Tremas Master captured the Campbells, and used a gulwort beast to siphon away their life energy for benefit of his unseen partner in crime (Adam Mitchell). The seventh Doctor and Ace blew up the gulwort, and the Campbells pursued the Master in their natural forms, intending to torment him. Adam spirited Ace away to his base of operations. The Aeroliths tortured the Master for decades before he escaped from them.

> (=) In 1831, energy beings from the Eternium, a doomed pocket universe, manipulated the aspiring poet Jared Malahyde to work on the Utopian Engine: a device intended to temporally age Earth to extinction. The Eternines wanted to harvest the life force energy released by Earth's demise. Malahyde partnered with architect Isambard Kingdom Brunel, and they pioneered the Malahyde Process, a means of developing superior steel. Malahyde spent the next twelve years working on the Utopian Engine.[1303]

The Doctor met Brunel.[1304] The eleventh Doctor claimed that Isambard Kingdom Brunel was mad, and built so many bridges because he feared that at ground level, pixies would bite his ankles.[1305] The TARDIS arrived in 1831 on the fifth Doctor's preset instructions, having travelled from an alternate version of 2008. The Ship buried itself in the muck of the Thames, and remained inert for thirty-four years.[1306]

1832 (June) - HORNETS' NEST: THE CIRCUS OF DOOM[1307] -> The fourth Doctor arrived in Blandford and learned from a shop assistant, Sally, that the strange Circus of Delights had come to town. Almost the whole population watched the show until two in the morning, amazed by the lion act and the Clown Funeral. An Italian dwarf, Antonio, served as ringmaster. The Doctor met Dr Adam Farrow, who was looking for his sister Francesca.

On the second night, all the villagers returned to watch the show again, and the Doctor discovered that the Hornets had both possessed Antonio and infiltrated the entire circus. Various villagers were compelled to join the circus and perform incredible acts.

The Doctor realised that the withered feet he'd seen in the ballet shoes in the future belonged to Francesca. He hypnotised Antonio to learn of the dwarf's history – and was shocked to find that the Hornets had somehow used the TARDIS to take control of him, an event that had not happened yet in the Doctor's timeline. The Hornets swarmed out of Antonio. Francesca was killed, but the Doctor left with Antonio's body, now in stasis.

Farrow took his sister's body and had it embalmed. Eventually, only her feet survived, still in their ballet shoes.

Max Capricorn started running Max Capricorn Cruiseliners in 1832.[1308] The child of a Seminole medicine woman, Mother Totika, died on the Trail of Tears in Winter 1832.[1309]

1833 - GALLERY OF GHOULS[1310] -> The Randomiser took the fourth Doctor and the second Romana to Brighton, 1833, and they wondered how they might fill the intervening eighteen years until the Brighton Pavilion opened. The duo became embroiled in an escalating contest between rival waxwork exhibitions: Goole's Gallery of Ghouls, and that of Madame Marvel Tissot.

Mr Goole, an amoeboid alien desperate to experience pain and pleasure, attempted to steal the Doctor's memories, but the Doctor reduced the temperature inside the TARDIS and froze Goole solid. Tissot and Goole's android, looking like Marie Antoinette, decided on a new waxworks venture that included a frosty Goole. The Doctor and Romana realised that the android only had enough power to stay active for one more season – but *what* a season!

A Loa, Spinning Jenny, was pulled back to the start of the Industrial Revolution from 1931. It would live its life in reverse, and be killed by one of its fellows, Baron Samedi. Elizabeth Howkins was dragged into this era by Spinning Jenny's time-wake, and would spend two decades learning to harness power through ritualism.[1311]

1835 - BLOODTIDE[1312] -> The sixth Doctor took Evelyn to meet Charles Darwin, her personal hero, in the

Galapagos Islands. They learned of "devil creatures" on the island, identifying them as Silurians. The Doctor confronted their leader, the renegade scientist Tulok, who planned to wipe out all human life with a virus. The Doctor tricked the Silurians' Myrka into destroying a Silurian submersible, which killed Tulok before he could launch his bacterial warheads. The Doctor suggested that Darwin not mention the Silurians in his writing.

Albert Tiermann began entertaining the blind King with stories.[1313] The Doctor took tackling lessons from Webb Ellis.[1314] In May 1837, in the Pyrenees, the archaeologist Louis Vosgues stood on the verge of formulating the theory of evolution years before Darwin. An Agent of the Council of Eight ensured that Vosgues fell off a cliff to his death.[1315] The killer Springheeled Jack was first reported in London in 1837.[1316] Engineer Alan Stevenson drew heavy inspiration from Fang Rock when he designed the Skerryvore lighthouse in 1837.[1317]

The Victorian Era

The Doctor attended the coronation of Queen Victoria.[1318] Archibald Goff died, only three years after the birth of his grandson, John Goff. As Archibald had failed to write a letter to Anne Travers as history dictated, Rupert Slant wrote her one instead on 23rd September, 1839.[1319]

In the 1840s, a tenant farmer who tried to flatten the tumulus on Lanyon Moor died of a heart attack. The crops nearby failed for the next seven years.[1320] A crashed alien asked for help in Lewes, the 1840s – but as it was Bonfire Night, the riotous people threw it onto a fire. The alien crawled back to its ship and plotted its revenge.[1321]

Professor Litefoot's Chinese fowling piece was last fired around this time.[1322] **The Doctor gave Hans Christian Andersen the idea for "The Emperor's New Clothes".**[1323] **The International Gallery took possession of Guieseppe di Cattivo's works in Victorian times.**[1324] Benny, Jason and Peter, in fleeing from a party of time-travelling Grel, stopped off in Victorian times. The Grel took the opportunity to test their Great Grel Gun, and atomized a group of schoolgirls.[1325]

The eleventh Doctor and Clara stopped in Victorian

1314 *Cuddlesome.* William Webb Ellis is the alleged inventor of rugby, and lived 1806-1872.
1315 *Sometime Never*
1316 "Three years" before "The Curious Tale of Spring-Heeled Jack".
1317 *Leth-St: Beast of Fang Rock* (ch3).
1318 *The Curse of Peladon.* Victoria was crowned 1838.
1319 *Leth-St: Beast of Fang Rock* (ch1).
1320 *The Spectre of Lanyon Moor*
1321 *1stD V2: The Bonfires of the Vanities*
1322 According to Professor Litefoot in *The Talons of Weng-Chiang*, the gun "hasn't been fired for fifty years".
1323 *The Romans*
1324 *SJA: Mona Lisa's Revenge*
1325 *Benny S5: The Grel Escape*
1326 *Hide*
1327 *Benny B1: Epoch: Judgement Day*, and the *Benny B5: Missing Persons* stories *The Winning Side* and *In Living Memory.* Bernice wonders if it's the "eighteenth or nineteenth century", the blurb says it's "Victorian London". It's not clear, however, if *this* Victorian London coincides with the genuine article, or is in another era per the Epoch's machinations.
1328 Dating "The Curious Case of Spring-Heeled Jack" (*DWM* #334-336) - The date "1840" is given.
1329 *Eye of Heaven.* The date of Stockwood's first expedition is given (p1).
1330 "A hundred and fifty years" (p222) before *Cat's Cradle: Witch Mark.*
1331 *Unbound: Sympathy for the Devil.* In the real world, Britain took over Hong Kong in 1841.

1332 Dating *The Snowmen* (X7.6) - The year is given.
1333 *All-Consuming Fire*
1334 *1001 Nights:* "The Interplanetarian".
1335 Dating *Reckless Engineering* (EDA #63) - The date is given as "19 July 1843" (p5).
1336 Dating *Worlds BF: The Archive* (*Worlds BF* #1.1) - The year is given.
1337 *Beyond the Ultimate Adventure*
1338 *The Church and the Crown*
1339 *In the Blood* (ch12). *The Snow Queen*, written by Hans Christian Andersen, was published in 1844.
1340 According to *The Tomorrow Windows. The Unquiet Dead*, on the other hand, certainly presents itself as the first meeting between them.
1341 *The Death of Art*
1342 Dating *The Twelfth Doctor Year One:* (Titan 12th Doc #1.11, "Unearthly Things") - The year is given.
1343 Dating *9thC: The Window on the Moor* (BF *The Ninth Doctor Chronicles* #1.2) - Emily names the exact days. *Wuthering Heights* was written between October 1845 and June 1846, and published in December 1847. Emily is "a little older than Rose" – born 30th July, 1818, she'd now be 27.
1344 *The Helm of Awe.* Effectively, the last of the Bronte sisters' novels were: Emily with *Wuthering Heights* (her only novel) in 1847, Anne with *The Tenant of Wildfell Hall* in 1848 and Charlotte with *Shirley* in 1849. Charlotte's *The Professor* was published posthumously in 1857. The reason they stopped publishing, however, is that Emily and Anne died of tuberculosis in 1848 and 1849. Charlotte died a little later, in 1855.

times during their time-tour, to photograph the site of Caliban House.[1326]

> (=) The version of Benny from a Victorian London created by the Epoch escaped and had adventures in other times and places.[1327]

1840 - "The Curious Tale of Spring-Heeled Jack"[1328] ->

The eighth Doctor investigated the case of Springheeled Jack, who had apparently been assaulting young women in London. He discovered that Jack was innocent, and the killings had been performed by the alien Morjanus, a bitter rival of Jack's race. Morjanus released the fire-beings named the Pyrodines, and the Doctor destroyed them. Jack remained in London to fight crime.

An alien race, on the verge of losing a war, had long ago seeded its DNA into space in millions of head-shaped *moai*. The aliens' rivals killed them, but the *moai* distributed the DNA like a virus, creating hybrids of the aliens on multiple worlds. On Earth, such *moai* had settled on Rapa Nui (also known as Easter Island) and turned some Polynesians into alien hybrids. But in October 1842, Horace Stockwood's expedition to the island carried a disease that would kill off the hybrids.[1329] The Welsh town of Dinorben mysteriously emptied overnight. Goibhnie had taken the people to populate a town on the world of Tír na n-Óg.[1330]

> = The Doctor saw people in Hong Kong crying as a British flag was run up a flagpole, marking that the territory had come under British administration.[1331]

1842 - THE SNOWMEN[1332] ->

When Walter Simeon was a young boy, he craved isolation. The Great Intelligence, as manifested in a snowman, reflected Simeon's thoughts and fears back at him. Simeon became devoted to the Intelligence's goals, and came to found the Great Intelligence Institute.

In 1843, the first Doctor and Susan met Sherlock Holmes' father, Siger Holmes, in India and learnt that the natives believed in a gateway to another world.[1333] In the same year, the Doctor saved the life of Elizabeth Spinnaker's father during the Second Great Crookback Incursion in Mesopotamia.[1334]

> (=) 1843 - RECKLESS ENGINEERING[1335] -> The Eternine gambit reached fruition in 1843, when Malahyde activated the Utopian Engine. The eighth Doctor's intervention meant that instead of aging Earth to death, the device advanced time on the planet's surface forty years. This created an alternate timeline in which an estimated 95% of mature

humans and animals either aged to death or died from shock. Humanity's children, suddenly aged to adulthood, became savage creatures of instinct named the Wildren. The remaining pockets of civilisation struggled to survive in disparate settlements. In some parts, cannibalism became acceptable.

The Graceless Plant Kronos Vad's *A History of Earth* (Vol. 36,379) on Earth

1843 - WORLDS BF: THE ARCHIVE[1336] ->

The living tracers Abby and Zara went to 1843 and left a copy of Kronos Vad's *A History of Earth* (Volume 36,379) in a newly established bookshop. They departed, hoping the book would warn humanity about the future threat of Gomagog.

The Eidolon, trapped in Ultima Thula, contacted Edgar Allen Poe in dreams. The mental contact influenced the writing of Poe's *Dream-Land* (1844).[1337] In 1844, the Doctor helped Alexandre Dumas with *The Three Musketeers*.[1338] The tenth Doctor claimed *The Snow Queen* was a historical document.[1339] The Doctor met Charles Dickens.[1340] Dickens' work became far darker in tone after he encountered Montague's killer dolls in 1845.[1341]

1845 - THE TWELFTH DOCTOR YEAR ONE[1342] ->

Charlotte Bronte and her friend Ellen lodged at North Lees Hall, the home of Lord Marlborough in Derbyshire, and happened upon the twelfth Doctor and Clara. A stranded, spider-like Aranox attempted to refuel its ship with psychic energy drained from Marlborough's party guests, but the Doctor broke the Aranox's mental control, and the guests set the creature on fire. These events inspired Bronte to write *Jane Eyre*, which entailed a schoolmistress, a begrudging hero and dark secrets.

1845 (3rd-4th December) - 9thC: THE WINDOW ON THE MOOR[1343] ->

For some years, Emily Bronte had met humanoid alien exiles who appeared on the moor through a trans-dimensional window, and guided them to their departure point. Civil war erupted on the aliens' homeworld when Prince Julius seized power from his nephew, Duke Alexandro. Due to trans-dimensional echoing, Emily was the spitting image of Alexandro's beloved, the Duchess Aida. The ninth Doctor, Rose Tyler and Emily helped Aida isolate Julius and his army on another world, but Alexandro was lost also. The Doctor believed these events inspired Emily's only novel, *Wuthering Heights*.

The Doctor took the Bronte sisters to Hollywood, where exposure to close-harmony singing caused them to never write another book.[1344]

Thomas Brewster, a companion of the fifth and sixth Doctors, was born in or around 1846.[1345] River Song escaped a lecherous baker in Venice, 1846, by overturning a bucket of pig entails on his head.[1346] Mycroft Holmes, the elder brother of Sherlock, was born in 1846 or 1847.[1347]

The Boyhood Lives of Henry Gordon Jago and Professor George Litefoot

Around this time, **the stage impresario Henry Gordon Jago and the pathologist Professor George Litefoot** – a pair of Victorian investigators, and associates of more than one Doctor – **were born.**[1348]

Henry Gordon Jago grew up in a set of rooms over butcher's shop. His father abandoned the family, leaving behind only an African greyparrot.[1349] As a fan of Charles Dickens, Jago was beside himself when he read that Little Nell had died.[1350] As a boy, Litefoot saw cojoined twins on exhibition. Jago was friends at school with Toby Brooksmith.[1351] Jago's mother warned that drinking led to death. He placed last in races at school.[1352] Jago's Aunt Maude took him swimming in Highgate.[1353]

1847 (winter) - DEMON QUEST: A SHARD OF ICE[1354] **->** Writer Albert Tiermann was being rushed through the Murgin Pass for an audience with the King at his Winter Palace in San Clemence when the TARDIS materialised in front of his carriage. The fourth Doctor and Mike Yates showed Tiermann a book of his fairy tales – a book which had yet to be written. Tiermann had run out of stories to tell the King, and was desperate to lay hands on the book. The lodge was menaced by a monster, which killed Hans the footman. The Doctor and Tiermann tracked the monster – the shapeshifter Demon that the Doctor encountered in Roman Britain and Paris – to its lair. The Doctor revealled that on this occasion, the Demon had assumed the guise of Albert's Queen. She had engineered the Doctor's arrival and wanted to take him to her

---

1345 *The Haunting of Thomas Brewster* suggests that Brewster is about four or five in 1851. Even Brewster is unclear about this, however, as "it's hard to judge [your age] when you have no birthdays."
1346 *The Legends of River Song:* "Death in New Venice"
1347 He's "64" as of *Worlds BF: The Adventure of the Bloomsbury Bomber* [June 1911].
1348 Jago and Litefoot first appear in *The Talons of Weng-Chiang*, then in thirteen seasons of the *Jago and Litefoot* audios from Big Finish. Their birth years are never nailed down. The placement here derives from Trevor Baxter (who played Litefoot) and Christopher Benjamin (Jago) respectively being age 44 and 42 while recording *Talons* – which is set in this guidebook to c.1889. Going off that, Litefoot was born around 1845, Jago around 1847.
The *Mahogany Murderers* claims that Jago attended the Great Exhibition in Crystal Palace in 1951, but never specifies his age, so he may indeed have been taken there at age four. *Talons* has Jago claim to have logged "thirty years" in the theatre halls, but we might imagine that the figure owes to his well-known talent for exaggeration, or that he started there very young in *some* capacity but not necessarily acting (*J&L* S10: *The Year of the Bat* has him sweeping the stalls in 1867).
1349 *J&L* S6: *Return of the Repressed*
1350 *J&L* S4: *Beautiful Things*. Little Nell featured in Dickens' *The Old Curiosity Shop*. If Jago was born circa 1847, he probably read the 1841 collected book version of *The Old Curiosity Shop* years after the fact, not the original version (an 88-part serial in *Master Humphrey's Clock*, released from April 1840 to November 1841) as it was coming out.
1351 *J&L* S13: *Chapel of Night*
1352 *J&L* S8: *The Backwards Man*
1353 *J&L* S8: *Jago & Litefoot & Patsy*
1354 Dating *Demon Quest: A Shard of Ice* (BBC fourth Doctor audio #2.3) - Tiermann says "the year was 1847".
1355 *Face the Raven*. The camp has been there "since Waterloo Station" (Britain's busiest passenger railway station). A railway station for the site opened on 11th July, 1848; the present structure was inaugurated in 1922.
1356 No year given, but Eleanor is a child when this happens, and seems middle-aged (actress Joanna Monro was 54 when she played the adult Eleanor) in *J&L* S3: *The Man at the End of the Garden*.
1357 *The Wrong Doctors*
1358 *FP: Weapons Grade Snake Oil*. Beddoes lived 1803-1849.
1359 Dating *Nevermore* (BF BBC7 #4.3) - The Doctor says his meeting with Poe occurred "three days" prior to the man's death, although technically, Poe was found delirious on the Baltimore streets on 3rd October, 1849, and died on October 7th.
1360 *The Algebra of Ice* (p8-11).
1361 *Heaven Sent*. Jacob Grimm lived 1785-1863, his brother Wilhelm lived 1786-1859.
1362 *FP: The Book of the War*. From the original Cwej's perspective, this happens some time after *Benny: Twilight of the Gods*.
1363 "One hundred forty-seven years" before *Unbound: Sympathy for the Devil*. The mind-parasites would seem to be the same species as the one seen in *The Mind of Evil*.
1364 Dating *Sleepers in the Dust* (BBC *DW* audiobook #20) - The Doctor and Rory have gone "two thousand years in the past" from their starting point in the thirty-ninth century.
1365 "A year" before "Hypothetical Gentleman".
1366 *1963: The Assassination Games*
1367 Fifteen years prior to *Other Lives*.
1368 "Nine years" before *A Town Called Fortune*
1369 *The Next Doctor*, "Hypothetical Gentleman".

home, called Sepulchre. The Doctor and Yates escaped her clutches, and the Doctor took Tiermann to safety, before heading back to Nest Cottage.

Tiermann related this story to his King.

Ashildr became the mistress of a Quantum Shade, and established a trap street in London to serve as an alien refugee camp – even for belligerent species such as the Cybermen and Sontarans. As Mayor Me, she enforced the peace there.[1355]

A fairy-like man gave little Eleanor Maycombe a pocketbook that could make real anything she wrote within its pages. The deal required Eleanor to wake the little man up after a year and a day – but she didn't, and he slept as she grew to adulthood. The family housekeeper, Mrs Hitch, confiscated the pocketbook and in future used it to keep herself and Eleanor off parish relief.[1356]

Jebediah Thurwell was sent to Victoria, Australia, as a convict in 1849. He eventually worked for his freedom, married a woman named Patsy, and had four children and fifteen grandchildren.[1357] Thomas Lovell Beddoes, an English poet, joined Faction Paradox as Cousin Rupert.[1358]

1849 (3rd October) - NEVERMORE[1359] -> The eighth Doctor attended to some business in Baltimore, Maryland, and happened upon an ailing Edgar Allan Poe. He begged the Doctor to look after his "final message to the world", which he'd written on some sheets of paper he kept in a bottle. After hospital orderlies took Poe away, the Doctor found that Poe hadn't emptied the bottle before putting the paper inside – meaning the ink had run, and Poe's text now read, "[obscured] [obscured] verdigris [obscured] [obscured] manifold [obscured] a shadow over the [obscured] [obscured] principia of the human [obscured]..." With a sigh, the Doctor poured Poe's final writings into the gutter. Poe died soon after.

> (=) Time distortion threw Edgar Allen Poe's death into flux. In alternate histories, he either died in a gutter four days before history recorded or happily survived and stayed on a drinking binge. The distortion abated, and he expired on 7th October, 1849.[1360]

The Doctor thought the Brothers Grimm were "lovely fellas", and had them on his darts team.[1361]

wih - The Great Houses' military wing established a training facility at the future site of the Japanese city of Kobe, circa 1850. Chris Cwej, already their agent, served as the template for the Army of One project and underwent mass replication. Cwej's duplicates, collectively called the Cwejen, fell into three types: the original blonde version ("Cwej-Prime"), a shorter, dark-haired version ("Cwej-Plus") and an extremely rare armoured version ("Cwej Magnus"). The original Cwej increasingly became a loner,

wanting less and less to do with himself.[1362]

> = A spaceship containing mind-parasites crashed in China. The creatures within were taken to various temples and monasteries, where monks chanted round the clock to contain their evil.[1363]

c 1850 - SLEEPERS IN THE DUST[1364] -> The eleventh Doctor and Rory, in researching a cure to a bacteria that was killing Amy, arrived on Nadurniss on the day the Prokarian staged a sky-assault in their "death clusters", reducing the whole planet to ruin. The time travellers discovered that a Nadurni named Mordax had created the Prokarian, and went back three centuries to learn more. Once Nadurniss was sterilised, Prokarian bacteria went dormant in the planet's dust. The Nadurni became a displaced race, and the location of Nadurniss was lost for three millennia.

The Hypothetical Gentleman trapped within the Doctor's TARDIS reached out through the Ship's telepathic circuits, and sent blueprints for a quantum resonator – through which it hoped to manifest on Earth – to the psionic Emily Fairfax. She interpreted the communication as a message from angels, constructed the resonator with her husband Charles, and depleted their savings while doing so. They failed to make the device work, and, starved for cash, sold it to the Great Exhibition.[1365]

The Light, whispered about as the secret rulers of the universe, were widely regarded as the invention of conspiracy mongers – but had infiltrated a thousand worlds by engendering their essences into the native populations there. On Earth, the Light founded a nursery to birth their members inside human children, with the intent of controlling the British Empire.[1366]

The traveller Edward Marlow married his beloved Georgina at Camden Chapel. They lived in his uncle's house in Camden Town, and had two sons: Edward and Henry. The elder Edward explored the world and wrote about his discoveries, but went missing in 1850.[1367] In Dry Creek, a town in America, Sheriff Samuel P Hayes secretly killed the prospector William Donovan over the love of a woman. The town's mayor and owner, Thaddeus Sullivan, blackmailed Hayes into keeping quiet as he stole the rights to Donovan's gold mine, and in the process renamed the town "Fortune".[1368]

The tenth Doctor considered 1851 to be a bit dull, but the eleventh Doctor said that it was "A very good year. One of my favorites!" As such, the Hypothetical Gentleman knew the Doctor would visit there eventually.[1369]

The wormhole conveying a spaceship with the cyborg child Alex, his guardian Boolin and a Skishtari gene egg overshot its intended destination and deposited them in the village of Hexford, 1851. Boolin lost his memory, and became known as "Mr Bewley". He tutored Alex, who was taken in by a rector, and made to wear a paper bag on his head to disguise his cyborg nature.[1370]

The Great Exhibition

1851 (30th April) - "Hypothetical Gentleman"[1371]

-> The eleventh Doctor, Amy and Rory reached the Crystal Palace the day before the opening of the Great Exhibition, having first been diverted to the Palace's destruction in 1936. Emily and Charles Fairfax's quantum resonator syphoned away the TARDIS' artron energy, enabling the Hypothetical Gentleman to partly manifest and steal time from people. Amy smashed the resonator, consigning the Gentleman – unknown to those involved – back to his imprisonment within the TARDIS. The Exhibition's displays included an Osirian robot mummy and force-field generator, and a statue of a Myrka.

1851 - OTHER LIVES[1372]

-> At the Great Exhibition of the Works of Industry of All Nations, civil unrest was threatened when two French visitors – Monsieur de Roche and his wife Madeleine – went missing. Charley and C'rizz aided the Duke of Wellington in a deception to cover up their disappearance, but the visitors had simply time-jumped ahead in the TARDIS and returned without incident. The eighth Doctor was mistaken for the absent traveller Edward Marlow, and assisted the man's wife in retaining her household. C'rizz was briefly imprisoned in a freak show and crippled its owner, Jacob Crackles.

1851 (12th September) - "Claws of the Klathi!"[1373]

-> The seventh Doctor landed in London at the time of the Great Exhibition, and met Nathaniel Derridge of the New Lunar Society, a scientific club. The Doctor learned that some curious murders had taken place in Docklands, and was attacked by a robot at the scene of the crime. He evaded the robot to discover a crashed spacecraft.

1370 "Ten years" before *Serpent Crest: The Broken Crown.*

1371 Dating "Hypothetical Gentleman" (IDW Vol. 4 #1-2) - The caption reads "London, 1851". The Doctor confirms the year, and it's the day before the Great Exhibition's grand opening, which happened 1st May, 1851. The story picks up from the Doctor, Amy and Rory witnessing the Crystal Palace's destruction in "The Eagle and the Reich"."Sky Jacks" gives the origin of the Hypothetical Gentleman. Osirian mummies appeared in *Pyramids of Mars*, the Myrka in *Warriors of the Deep*. The Doctor acknowledges the need to avoid running into himself at the Exhibition, possibly in reference to *Other Lives*.

1372 Dating *Other Lives* (BF #77) - The year is 1851, and the Great Exhibition was held from 1st May to 15th October. The Doctor's comment that the Exhibition did a lot of business in its "first six months" is therefore an approximation, as it was only open five and a half months total. As the Duke of Wellington claims, he would have been 82 in this story, and he died the following year.

1373 Dating "Claws of the Klathi!" (*DWM* #136-138) - Derridge says it's "the twelfth of September, year of Our Lord Eighteen Hundred and Fifty-One".

1374 *The Mahogany Murderers*

1375 Dating *The Haunting of Thomas Brewster* (BF #107) - The year is given.

1376 *Enlightenment*

1377 *In the Blood* (ch6).

1378 "Three weeks" before *The Next Doctor.*

1379 *J&L S4: Beautiful Things*

1380 "Nine years" before *PHP: The Ghosts of Gralstead.*

1381 Dating *The Next Doctor* (X4.14) - An urchin tells the Doctor it's "Christmas Eve" and "the year of our Lord 1851", with the action continuing through the night to Christmas Day.

A glaring oddity is that the CyberKing here rampages across London, and destroys patches of it with heavy weaponry. Lake comments that the "events of today will be history, spoken of for centuries to come", and even though said events are wildly nonhistorical, the Doctor only comments "Funny, that". The eleventh Doctor later implies in *Flesh and Stone* that the Cracks in Time ate away at the CyberKing, explaining why it's not recorded in the history books. (He speculates this, however, before knowing that he's going to restore everything the Cracks destroyed upon rebooting the universe in *The Big Bang*; see the Cracks in Time sidebar.) It could equally be the case, however, that the CyberKing event isn't well remembered because it happened at night (severely limiting the number of people who could have actually *seen* the CyberKing) in an era without suitable photography to record the proceedings (even had they occurred in the daytime), meaning the resultant damage was attributed to other causes or left as a mystery.

1382 *The One Doctor.* Peter Roget was a physician and lexicographer who lived 1779-1869. He compiled *Roget's Thesaurus.*

1383 *J&L: Voyage to Venus*

1384 *Cryptobiosis.* "Livingstone" is presumably David Livingstone (1813-73), the famed Scottish medical missionary and explorer of Africa (from 1852-56).

1385 *State of Decay.* Grimm lived 1785-1863.

1386 *Tooth and Claw* (TV). Prince Albert and Sir Robert's father seem to have begun collaborating as early as Robert's childhood, but the exact dating is unclear. The Koh-i-Noor was presented to Queen Victoria in 1850, and Albert died 14th December, 1861. The recounting of the diamond in *Tooth and Claw* deviates a little from history – the story implies that Albert

Nearby, the Wyndham's Freakshow included some live aliens. The Doctor met one, Caval of the Joebb, whose race was lifted out of squalor by the Klathi – ruthless aliens who were also in London. The Klathi need a large crystal to power their ship, but activating the reflective lattice would kill people over a vast area. The Doctor confronted the Klathi at Crystal Palace, but they didn't care about the human casualties. Joebb rebelled, and the aliens were killed when their spacecraft exploded.

Henry Gordon Jago attended the Great Exhibition in Crystal Palace, 1851, and saw Michael Faraday demonstrate the benefits of electricity.[1374]

1851 - THE HAUNTING OF THOMAS BREWSTER[1375]

-> When Thomas Brewster was four or five, his mother killed herself by jumping off the Southwark Bridge. Brewster never knew his father, and his first memory was that of his mother's funeral. Brewster's aunts and uncles blamed him for his mother's suicide, and it was decided that he should be sent to a workhouse, to be raised by the parish.

The fifth Doctor and Nyssa were briefly at the funeral, as they were trying to determine when young Brewster came under psychic influence from beings from an alternate 2008. From his mother's graveside, Brewster glimpsed the departing TARDIS.

The *America* crossed the Atlantic in seventeen days in 1851.[1376] The tenth Doctor left the TARDIS right in the middle of Old Kent Road for a fortnight, when he and Donna attended the Great Exhibition.[1377]

Jackson Lake, a mathematics teacher from Sussex, arrived in London with his family to take a post at university. They encountered a group of Cybermen that had fallen through time from the Void. Lake's wife Caroline was killed, his son Frederic was abducted and Lake himself was riddled with energy from an infostamp – a device containing the Cybermen's database on the Doctor's activities. Lake believed he *was* the Doctor, and as such saved a young woman, Rosita, from the Cybermen at Osterman's Wharf.[1378]

Warren Gadd, a foe of Professor Litefoot and Henry Gordon Jago, was born in Liverpool, 1851. As Gadd grew up, his mind created an inter-dimensional library that contained every possible book, every possible painting. The library became so vast, it drained energy from living minds to maintain itself and consumed Gadd's parents. He periodically moved to avoid suspicion as the library found more victims. An avatar of Gadd within the library absorbed his sins and corruption, which slowed his aging process.[1379]

Mordrega, the Captain General of the Hosts of Alcyon in the Gravora Sector, lost a challenge against her people's ruler. She was cast into the shade-worlds while her people's icon, the life-restorative Corona of Alcyon, was taken to Earth. The Corona's arrival in England instigated the "Scrivener family curse": from that night, Sir Cedric Scrivener's daughter Clementine failed to age. Cedric hid the Corona in his late wife's grave in Africa.[1380]

1851 (Christmas Eve to Christmas Day) - THE NEXT DOCTOR[1381]

-> The tenth Doctor was surprised to encounter "the Doctor" – actually Jackson Lake – and his "companion" Rosita as they fought the Cybermen and the Cybershades, their beast-like servants. Mercy Hartigan, the matron of St Joseph's Workhouse, aided the Cybermen operating in this time zone as they built a CyberKing: a Dreadnought-class mechanoid that would be the front line of an invasion, and housed a Cyberfactory capable of converting millions. To this end, they rounded up children from workhouses to serve as a workforce.

The Cybermen Cyber-converted Miss Hartigan into the last component of the CyberKing, but her mind proved strong enough to resist total conversion, and she took control of the Cybermen. The Doctor and his allies freed the children, including Lake's son Frederic. The CyberKing emerged as a vast robot that began to stomp across London, but the Doctor confronted the CyberKing in Lake's hot air balloon, the Tethered Aerial Release Developed In Style (TARDIS). The Doctor offered to send Hartigan and her Cybermen to an uninhabited world, and when she refused, he destroyed them all. He also sent the CyberKing's remains into the Vortex, where it would disintegrate.

The Doctor stayed on to have Christmas Dinner with Jackson Lake, Frederic and Rosita.

Roget was a very good friend of the Doctor.[1382] The Doctor claimed to have met Livingstone, and said the man couldn't read a map to save himself.[1383] The Doctor claimed that he once told Livingstone: "That's all very well… but the elephant in the gorilla suit has to go."[1384]

Around this time, Jacob Grimm discovered the Law of Consonantal Shift.[1385]

Albert, the Prince Consort, frequently lodged at Torchwood Estate with the father of Sir Robert MacLeish. The two of them dared to imagine that local stories about a werewolf and the brethren that protected it were true, and fashioned a trap for the beast. A light chamber was constructed, and Albert had the Koh-i-Noor, the diamond given to Victoria as spoils of war, recut to serve as the chamber's focusing device.[1386]

Iris Wildthyme bought an account of Fanny Hill at the Vandermeer bookshop in 1852, and continued to patron-

ize the shop for centuries.[1387]

Victoria Waterfield, a companion of the second Doctor, was born.[1388] The Doctor met Thackeray, Baudelaire, Delacroix and Manet.[1389] In 1853, Saul, a living church in Cheldon Bonniface, was baptised in his own font.[1390]

c 1853 - FP: HEAD OF STATE[1391] **->** The Star Chamber tasked one of its agents, the explorer Richard Burton, with investigating reports that the Mal'akh had possession of a book that could devastate the British government's interests in Arabia. During Burton's travels, his older self recruited him into Faction Paradox.

The timeship Lolita approached Burton as "the Lady of the Last Night", and gave Burton a copy of *The Thousand and Second Night*: an alternate chronicle of the fate of Shahrazad. In the years to come, Burton would translate *One Thousand and One Nights* to familiarize himself with the language in both books.

1853 (October) - FP: SPINNING JENNY[1392] **->** An older Elizabeth Howkins had backtracked along her own timeline. Baron Samedi, the Loa locked in combat with the Loa Spinning Jenny, provided Elizabeth with a knife that would liberate her husband Bill from Spinning Jenny's flesh. Making use of James Braddock's enhanced biodata, Howkins opened a portal to 1931...

1854 (January) - FP: SPINNING JENNY[1393] **->** A time-hopping Elizabeth Howkins came into conflict with Cousin Isabella of Faction Paradox. The shadow weapon Isabella had stolen from Howkins felt such conflicted loyalties, it literally split into two and warred against itself. Isabella's future self killed her younger self, per the Faction tradition of ritually converting one's own timeline into a paradox.

1854 (June) - FP: SPINNING JENNY[1394] **->** The auguries provided Elizabeth Howkins, now a few weeks shy of age 64, with the time and locale – the Goyt Valley – where she could confront Spinning Jenny. Howkins' efforts resulted in her jumping through time via various means. Howkins' porter, James Braddock, became embroiled in these events; his biodata became ritually linked to a bubble reality, and facilitated space-time travel.

---

whittled down the stone through constant recuttings, when most of the lost mass was shed in a single cutting in 1852.

1387 *Worlds BF: Kronos Vad's History of Earth (Vol. 36,379)*

1388 *Downtime* provides conflicting clues with regards Victoria's birth year... she's "11" (p14) when her mother dies in November 1863, meaning – depending on when Victoria's birthday falls – she was born in 1851 or 1852. However, she also claims, at age 28 (p14), to have been "ten years" younger when she visited the Det-Sen monastery (*The Abominable Snowmen*). The statement carries the smallest of wiggle room, but she was presumably that same age when she met the Doctor (in *The Evil of the Daleks*, in 1866), so would have been born in or around 1848. Tilting the scales in favour of a circa 1852 birth, perhaps, Victoria tells Sarah Jane in *Downtime* that she was born "over a hundred and forty years" before 1995 (p105). Actress Deborah Watling, born 2nd January, 1948, was 19 when she first played Victoria.

1389 *Ghost Ship*. Novelist William Thackeray (*Vanity Fair*) lived 1811-1863; poet Charles Baudelaire 1821-1867; painter Eugéne Delacroix 1798-1863; painter Édouard Manet 1832-1883. While there's no indication these meetings were on the same trip, it's possible.

1390 *Timewyrm: Revelation* (p4).

1391 Dating *FP: Head of State* (FP novel #9) - Year unknown. The Burton entry in *FP: The Book of the War* suggests that he was recruited into the Faction after (or perhaps during) 1843 and prior to (or perhaps during) 1845. That would concur with the younger Burton esti-

mating his elder self's face as "some forty years older", presumably in accordance with Burton relocating to the Eleven Day Empire in 1890. However, Burton went to Meccah and Medina as a pilgrim – as happens here – in 1853 and 1854. It's after Sir Richard Owen coined the term *dinosauria* (in 1842).

1392 Dating *FP: Spinning Jenny* (FP novel #11) – The month and year are given (ch12).

1393 Dating *FP: Spinning Jenny* (FP novel #11) – The month and year are given (ch16).

1394 Dating *FP: Spinning Jenny* (FP novel #11) – The month and year are given (ch15).

1395 Dating *The Four Doctors* (BF subscription promo #9; also numbered as #142b) - The year is given.

1396 *The Angel of Scutari*

1397 *White Ghosts*

1398 Dating *The Angel of Scutari* (BF #122) - The Doctor provides all of the specified dates, which historically match the siege of Sevastopol and the Charge of the Light Brigade. The attempted rescue of Hex happens "10:14 on 19th of November". The only small deviation from history is that Nightingale seems to have arrived in Scutari in early November, not mid-month.

1399 *Gods and Monsters*

1400 "Maybe forty years" before *J&L S12: The Flickermen*.

1401 *J&L S6: Return of the Repressed*, when Litefoot is "about ten".

1402 Dating "Perceptions" and "Coda" (*Radio Times* #3805-3816) - It's broadly said to be "Victorian London".

1403 Dating "Cuckoo" (*DWM* #208-210) - The date is given at the beginning of the story.

1404 *The Evil of the Daleks*

1854 - THE FOUR DOCTORS (BF)[1395] **->** The seventh Doctor visited Professor Michael Faraday, and dealt with a Dalek time corridor that ended at Faraday's laboratory at the Royal Institution of Great Britain.

On 20th September, 1854, during the Crimean War, the British readied to besiege the port city of Sevastopol. A British officer, Brigadier-General Bartholomew Kitchen, tried to avert bloodshed by inventing a story that the Russians were preparing to surrender, causing the British fleet to hold back and according the Russians time to fortify themselves. Kitchen had expected that the British would withdraw entirely once they learned of the Russians' preparations, but the attack proceeded anyway, causing massive casualties...[1396] The fourth Doctor owned a lantern that had belonged to Florence Nightengale.[1397]

1854 (25th September to 19th November) - THE ANGEL OF SCUTARI[1398] **->** The seventh Doctor and Ace arrived during the siege of Sevastopol on 25th September, 1854, to investigate accounts that the Doctor was a traitor to the crown. A cannonball hit the TARDIS and triggered the Ship's Hostile Action Displacement System (HADS), causing it to retreat into the Vortex to heal.

The Russians incarcerated the Doctor and Ace, and accused him of trying to signal the British fleet; Tsar Nicholas I was indifferent as to the Doctor's guilt or innocence. Ace befriended the future author Leo Tolstoy, who was currently a Russian soldier. He had lost his family home – and three hundred fifty peasants – while playing cards, and to date had only published two stories in *The Contemporary*.

On October 7th, the Doctor learned that the Tsar had authorised his execution; Ace escaped at roughly the same time. Brigadier-General Kitchen pinned his traitorous actions at Sevastopol on the Doctor, and reported to his superiors that the Russians were mistakenly executing one of their own double agents. The Doctor fulfilled causality by making sure that correspondence from Sir Hamilton Seymour – the British ambassador in St Petersburg – to the Minister of War backed up Kitchen's claims, then escaped with Seymour's help. Ten days later, the Doctor and Ace were reunited in Kursk and summoned the TARDIS, intending to retrieve Hex from mid-November of the same year. Kitchen became unhinged upon witnessing the Ship's departure, and reported that he'd killed the Doctor.

On 17th October, the Doctor, Ace and Hex made their initial landing in this era, at the British army barracks at Scutari. William Russell, a *London Times* war correspondent, accused the Doctor of being a traitor, prompting the Doctor and Ace to go back four weeks to investigate his claims and Seymour's reports. Hex remained to care for the wounded and meet his idol, Florence Nightingale, who was scheduled to arrive in about a month. The Charge of

the Light Brigade occurred on 25th October.

Ten days after the Doctor and Ace departed Kursk, Kitchen was taken off active service and accompanied Nightingale to the hospital at Scutari. They arrived mid-November, and Hex met Nightingale. On 19th November, Kitchen hotly confronted Hex concerning his affiliation with the Doctor and Ace. Hex's friends arrived through time to collect him – just as Kitchen shot him. The Doctor and Ace bundled their wounded friend into the TARDIS, and set course for St Gart's Hospital in the twenty-first century. Nightingale was left to pray, with a distraught Kitchen, for Hex's recovery.

The elder god Weyland extended his power and stopped Hex's injuries from becoming mortal – but in the process, Hex became one of Weyland's pawns in his game against Fenric.[1399] Construction operations near the Thames caused inter-dimensional beings, the Flickermen, to become trapped in a disued tunnel.[1400]

When George Litefoot was about ten, his father took his two sons every Sunday to play on the grounds of the district commissioner – who had made an unrequited advance on Litefoot's mother. Litefoot felt traumatised upon being made to feed an aged baboon on the property with rats, and was doubly scarred when his father, a weak man, made him beat the baboon with a stick to prove his manhood.[1401]

c 1855 - "Perceptions" / "Coda"[1402] **->** The eighth Doctor, Stacy and Ssard helped P'fer'd and M'rek'd, two purple and yellow-spotted Equinoids stranded on Earth, to get home.

1855 (13th December) - "Cuckoo"[1403] **->** The seventh Doctor, Benny and Ace landed in the seaside village of Lifton, where it was rumoured the devil had shown himself. This was the location of one of the richest fossil beds in Southern England. Mary Anne Wesley was pioneering the field of paleontology at this time, despite the fact the locals disapproved. The Doctor was here to stop her, as Wesley was about to unearth the fossil of an alien – and set science back by decades as it pursued a false trail. While the Doctor and Benny met Wesley, Ace found a body on the beach. The Doctor realised that one of the Wesleys' other guests was a lizard-like shapeshifter, a Surcoth, looking to repatriate the fossilised remains of an ancient explorer. The Doctor let him leave.

The Crimean War

The Crimean War was fought 1853-1856. On 25th October, 1854, the Doctor was present at the "magnificent folly" of the Charge of the Light Brigade.[1404] **The Doctor claimed he had been wounded in the Crimea.**[1405]

The War Lords lifted a Crimean War battlefield.[1406]

In 1854, J. Clark Maxwell experimented with electromagnetism.[1407] The Ogron homeworld was discovered in 1855. From this point, the ape-like race would be used as slaves and hired muscle by more than a dozen races.[1408]

Two residents of the Euphorian Empire, the artisan brothers Jude and Gabriel, travelled to Earth in 1855 via a dimensional portal. On the island of Es Vedra, the monk Francisco Belao mistook them for angels.[1409]

(=) 1856 (27th January) - 100: "My Own Private Wolfgang"[1410] -> The Mozart who bargained for immortality was all-too horrifyingly aware that he'd become a hack. Along with scores of time-travelling Mozart clones, the sixth Doctor and Evelyn attended a ball to celebrate Mozart's 100th birthday – and bore witness as a despondent Mozart tried and failed to kill himself on stage. Evelyn was accidentally transported to the future, while the Doctor – learning how Mozart had been manipulated and mistreated – travelled in the TARDIS back to Mozart's deathbed.

In Scotland, 1856, a young boy named James Lees encountered a different dimensional portal while swimming in the River Clyde near the Corra Linn falls. Lees remained on the other side of the portal, but the aliens who lived there sent a doppelganger of him back through as an ambassador. The ersatz James could tap people's memories to "speak with the voices of the dead" and was committed to an asylum. Within a few years, he'd become renowned as a spiritualist.[1411]

1856 (winter) - THE HAUNTING OF THOMAS BREWSTER[1412] -> Thomas Brewster had spent five years at the workhouse, taking lessons and enduring regular beatings from Mr Shanks, the master there. Brewster experienced recurring dreams of his dead mother – the result of a psychic "test signal" sent to him from the future. The fifth Doctor and Nyssa arrived and quickly departed, deciding they were still too early in Brewster's timeline.

wih - Gillian Rose Petra came into information suggesting that Sherlock Holmes had been born in late February, 1857 (and not January 1854, as was more commonly

---

1405 *The Sea Devils*
1406 *The War Games*
1407 *The Evil of the Daleks*
1408 *Interference* (p191).
1409 *The Rapture.* The brothers' portal isn't related to the portal that abducts James Lees in the same era.
1410 Dating *100: "100 My Own Private Wolfgang"* (BF #100b) - Mozart was born 27th January, 1756, and it's now his 100th birthday.
1411 *Empire of Death.* James is replaced in 1856, as dated on the back cover and p5.
1412 Dating *The Haunting of Thomas Brewster* (BF #107) - Brewster has been at Shanks' workhouse for five years, and the season of the year is stated.
1413 FP: *Erasing Sherlock* (p27). The traditional date for Holmes' birth, January 1854, is extrapolated from clues in the Conan Doyle story "His Last Bow". With *Erasing Sherlock*, the differing birthdate accommodates Holmes being 25 when the story opens in 1882.
1414 Dating *Downtime* (MA #18) - It's "Oxford, 1857, a golden afternoon" (p1). Carroll would have been 25 at the time; *Alice's Adventures in Wonderland* was published later, in 1865.
1415 *Downtime* (p259).
1416 "Ten years" before *The First Sontarans.*
1417 *The Nightmare Fair.* It's not said which shelling during the Opium Wars (the first of which lasted 1839-1842, the second 1856-1860) this is meant to denote.
1418 *Worlds DW: Second Sight*, extrapolating from actor Jamie Glover being 45 when he played Rees in *Worlds DW: Mind Games* [1894].
1419 Dating "The Screams of Death" (*DWM* #430-431) - The year is given.

1420 "The Child of Time" (*DWM*)
1421 *J&L* S6: *The Skeleton Quay*
1422 Dating *A Town Called Fortune* (BF CC #5.5) - The story is oddly circumspect about when it's set, given that it's a historical. Fortune is an American town, but we're not told the state in which it resides, let alone the year. The only tangible clue is that it's nine years after Donovan was engaged in the gold prospecting business – such activity generally dates to the mid-nineteenth century, and the most famous example of this, the California Gold Rush, lasted 1848-1855.
1423 Dating *The Pursuit of History* (BF 4th Doc #5.7) - The exact date is given.
1424 *The Shadows of Avalon*
1425 "Cuckoo"
1426 *Island of Death.* The third Doctor remembers the meeting, so it's a different occasion than when the sixth Doctor met him in *Bloodtide.*
1427 *The Forgotten Army.* The Doctor says this was in "1829" (p156) - probably either a typo or the result of him misremembering, as the Plug Uglies and Dead Rabbits operated in the 1850s, not the 1820s.
1428 *The Eleventh Tiger*
1429 Dating *Benny: The Vampire Curse*: "Possum Kingdom" (Benny collection #12b) - The tour group members dress up for the Victorian era (1837-1901), but nothing more specific is given.
1430 *The Talons of Weng-Chiang.* Jago claims to have had "thirty years in the halls".
1431 Dating *PHP: The Ghosts of Gralstead* (BF PHP #1.1) - The blurb gives the year; the story says it's "October". The Doctor tells Leela that it's "nearly forty years" before they met Jago and Litefoot, which seems an exaggera-

believed) and that his first name was Edmund (not William).[1413]

1857 - DOWNTIME[1414] **->** A friend of the Waterfield family – Charles Dodgson, later known as Lewis Carroll – photographed a young Victoria Waterfield on a stone bench holding a doll. He told her to "imagine a frozen teatime, when the tea never gets cold" – something of a difficulty, as Victoria didn't like tea. The photo was later found among Dodgson's effects.

The Doctor met Lewis Carroll on some other occasion, and regarded him as a brilliant mathematician who served rather good lemonade and muffins.[1415] The surviving four hundred Kaveech arrived via a time corridor from the distant past. They acclimatised to the populations of various worlds, avoiding detection from the Sontarans of this era. One of the Kaveech, Meredid Roath, took to living on Earth with his wife, and set about developing anti-Sontaran weaponry.[1416]

During the Opium Wars, the Doctor recreated a tapestry from a grubby Han-Sen original as the British fleet shelled a city. The Celestial Toymaker was not present, but would later acquire the copy.[1417] A young boy named Rees came to own the Art, an ancient device in the form of a music box, when his late mother bequeathed it to him. The Art focused Rees' budding psychic talents, which first manifested when he compelled his abusive father to jump down a well to his death.[1418]

(=) 1858 - "The Screams of Death"[1419] **->** The time-child Chiyoko transported a criminal from the future, Monsieur Valdemar, into the past. He used a DNA sequencer to transform young women to his agents, and excellent opera singers to boot. The eleventh Doctor and Amy enjoyed the best performance of *Eurydice* that the Doctor had seen in a century, and stopped Valdemar from eliminating the ancestors of the four men who had betrayed him. Valdemar's slaves turned on him, and threw him to his death.

The TARDIS absorbed a young woman, Cosette, into itself, but she was restored to life when Chiyoko cancelled out her own existence.[1420] A member of Parliament ignored the pleas of experts, and had the stone that protected the village of Shingle Cove from the ocean removed to construct docks. He became rich in the process. In 1859, an alien machine aboard a spacecraft bore witness as the villagers all died in a landslide while fleeing a fierce storm. The shingle's removal remained a dark family secret – in time, the MP's daughter, Camilla Tevelyan, inherited her father's business.[1421]

c 1859 - A TOWN CALLED FORTUNE[1422] **->** The sixth Doctor and Evelyn visited the town of Fortune, and helped to bring Mayor Sullivan to justice for crimes. Sheriff Hayes turned himself in for the murder of William Donovan.

1859 (15th November) - THE PURSUIT OF HISTORY[1423] **->** Urbain Le Verrier, a French mathematician, discovered the planet Vulcan in 1859. According to the Bi-Al Foundation's geological database, Earth's population on 15th November, 1859 was 1,000,300,558 humans.

The time-jumping Cuthbert hired men in Ampleforth Junction, Yorkshire, to help him mine and irradiate tritonium from a crashed spaceship in ancient Scotland. The substance furthered Cuthbert's plans some two centuries on, so the fourth Doctor and K9 followed him there.

The Doctor talked to Lewis Carroll about the sleeping King Constantine, which influenced Carroll's writing.[1424] Darwin published *The Origin of the Species* in 1859.[1425] The Doctor met Darwin.[1426] The Doctor dropped by New York as the Plug Uglies and Dead Rabbit gangs were tearing into each other. He helped to resolve the conflict, either by sorting it out with them over a pack of Jammy Dodgers, or just sending them back to Sligo, Ireland.[1427] In 1860, Ian Chesterton's great-grandfather, Major William Chesterton, was a member of a Hussar company at Jaipur, India.[1428]

c 1860 - BENNY: THE VAMPIRE CURSE: "Possum Kingdom"[1429] **->** Benny and the Yesterways Ltd. tour group visited Transylvania during Victorian times.

In 1860, Litefoot's father was a Brigadier-General on the punitive expedition to China. Afterward, he stayed on as a palace attache. Around this time, Henry Gordon Jago began working in the entertainment business.[1430]

1860 (October) - PHP: THE GHOSTS OF GRALSTEAD[1431] **->** Mordrega travelled to Earth to find the Corona of Alcyon, and arrived in such a diminished state, she required brain matter to sustain her form. The fourth Doctor and Leela, accompanied by Sir Cedric Scrivener, went in the TARDIS to find the Corona, and arrived in Africa some months ahead...

1861 - THE HAUNTING OF THOMAS BREWSTER[1432] **->** Mr Shanks sold Thomas Brewster to a man named Creek, who offered the lad an apprenticeship in his shop on Jacob's Island – a notorious rookery on the south bank of the Thames. The boys in Creek's employ scavenged the river for all manner of valuables, including items thrown overboard to avoid the revenue man. Brewster endured Creek's regular beatings.

1861 (April) - PHP: THE GHOSTS OF GRALSTEAD[1433]
-> The fourth Doctor, Leela and Sir Cedric Scrivener recovered the Corona of Alcyon in Africa. The Corona resurrected the warriors slain by King Obingo, and facilitated his downfall. The TARDIS returned to England – Mordrega had turned Gralstead Hall into a larder to sustain her hunger, and also used a Corona-splinter to perform "miracle cures", attracting attention from such notable persons as the Prince of Wales.

Mordrega manifested in her true armoured form and fought with a rival from her homeland, Pelito. The Doctor opened a portal that sent the Corona and a diminished Mordrega back to her native domain.

1861 (June) - THE GOOD, THE BAD AND THE ALIEN[1434] -> A Jerinthioan, a psionic vampire, became trapped on Earth. It mentally enticed two space smugglers – members of the Cemar race, who looked like humanoid meerkats – to come to Mason City, Nevada, so it could escape. The eleventh Doctor, Amy and Rory ran afoul of the Jerinthioan, the Cemars and some bank robbers: the Black Hand Gang. The Jerinthioan over-fed on the Doctor's psionic energy and died, and the Doctor took the Cemars back to their homeworld to face trial for smuggling.

Earth was now classified as a Level Three[1435] planet.

1861 - SERPENT CREST: THE BROKEN CROWN / ALADDIN TIME[1436] -> The cyborg Alex was now a teenager, and had become attuned to the Skishtari egg in his possession. It created within itself fictional worlds based upon the books he read. The fourth Doctor and Mrs Wibbsey arrived down a wormhole from the far future as the egg made Alex increasingly capricious. The Doctor and Wibbsey were briefly trapped inside the egg's dimensions, and experienced a realm based upon *Arabian Nights*. The Doctor's scarf manifested as a genie and granted Alex some wishes – which he used to close down the egg's fictional constructs. The Doctor buried the egg and gave instruc-

tion wherever one places *The Talons of Weng-Chiang*.

1432 Dating *The Haunting of Thomas Brewster* (BF #107) - Brewster is sold after having lived at Shanks' workhouse for ten years.

1433 Dating *PHP: The Ghosts of Gralstead* (BF *PHP* #1.1) - There's some discussion that the Doctor can return the TARDIS to when it left in October 1860, but this doesn't appear to happen, and ultimately the Ship seems to jump "months" ahead. Clementine Scrivener confirms that "months and months, and all through winter and Christmas" have passed. Cedric Scrivener, an accomplished explorer of Africa, notes that the grass is dry, like he'd expect to find in "May".

1434 Dating *The Good, the Bad and the Alien* (BBC children's 2-in-1 #3) - The story takes place "three months" (p109) after "18 April 1861" (p7).

1435 See the A Level Five World sidebar.

1436 Dating *Serpent Crest: The Broken Crown* and *Serpent Crest: Aladdin Time* (BBC fourth Doctor audios #3.2-3.3) - The Doctor tells Mrs Wibbsey, "You saw that newspaper in the village shop, this is 1861. We have to get acclimatised."

1437 He's 38 in *TW: The Victorian Age* [1899].

1438 *Just War*

1439 "The Forgotten"

1440 *A Good Man Goes to War*. The Underground first opened in 1863; it's not specified if the Doctor met Vastra as part of the initial construction or as it continued. *Doctor Who: The Encyclopedia* says that the Underground tunnelling accidentally obliterated the shelter in which Vastra's people lived. Vastra is already acquainted with the ninth Doctor in "The Lost Dimension" [1886], and has been friends with him "for years", possibly suggesting that this incarnation first met her.

1441 *The Name of the Doctor*

1442 *Tooth and Claw* (TV)

1443 *The Eleventh Tiger*

1444 "The Tides of Time"

1445 "Half a century" before *Year of the Pig*, provided the age of Chardalot's journals is anything to go by.

1446 *An Earthly Child*, *Wooden Heart*. "Blondin" is Charles Blondin (a.k.a. Jean François Gravelet-Blondin), a French tight-rope walker and acrobat who lived 1824–1897. He first performed the Niagara Falls feat in 1859, but repeated it a number of times after that.

1447 *The Three Companions*. The Metropolitan line opened 10th of January, 1863.

1448 Dating *Empire of Death* (PDA #65) - The story's starting and ending dates are given on p37 and p235.

1449 *Logopolis*. Thomas Huxley lived 1825-1895.

1450 *The Evil of the Daleks*, with further details in *Downtime*.

1451 *The War Games*

1452 *The Chase*. The TARDIS crew supposedly watch this on the Time-Space Visualiser, although it's possible that they're just watching Lincoln rehearse the speech beforehand. The actual event had Lincoln surrounded by a huge crowd in close quarters; the Visualiser shows him very much isolated.

1453 *Iris S2: The Panda Invasion*

1454 *An Earthly Child*. This happened in 1864.

1455 Dating *The Runaway Train* (BBC *DW* audiobook #9) - The year is given, and it's after the battle of Galveston (there were actually two of these, fought on 4th October, 1862, and then on 1st January, 1863).

1456 Dating *The Contingency Club* (BF #222) - The year is given.

1457 Dating *Renaissance of the Daleks* (BF #93) - The date is given toward the end of episode two. As stated, the detonation killed three hundred Confederates, but the Union army miscalculated in the explosion's aftermath, and lost fifty-three thousand troops. The crater

tions that Nest Cottage, which he would come to own, be built over it. Alex used his last wish to transport himself, Boolin, the Doctor and Wibbsey to Nest Cottage in 2010.

Archie, a long-standing Torchwood archivist, was born.[1437] The Doctor met Victor Hugo in Guernsey.[1438] The Doctor showed Victor Hugo the catacombs of Paris. Hugo was so spooked by this that he changed the plot of *Les Miserables*, which he had planned to make a comedy.[1439]

Madame Vastra in the Underground

The Doctor encountered the Silurian warrior Madame Vastra, who was trying to avenge the deaths of her sisters on innocent workers in the London Underground. He warned her that "anger is always the shortest distance to a mistake". The two of them formed an enduring friendship.[1440] The Doctor saved the life of Jenny Flint, Madame Vastra's associate and future wife, when she and Vastra first met.[1441]

A child born ten miles from the Torchwood Estate was stolen from a cultivation, and became the newest host to the essence of an alien werewolf.[1442] In 1863, the stone-imprinted minds of Qin Shi Huang and his two generals were transferred into Abbot Wu and two warrior monks.[1443] A time warp in the USA sent a Cheyenne War Party to the twentieth century, where they attacked a trucker.[1444]

A time traveller of unknown origin arrived in the nineteenth century, and – as far as could be determined – conducted experiments to improve the cognitive and intellectual abilities of pigs. Two "children" were born in the laboratory: the human-looking Charlie and his brother Toby, a walking, talking pig who passed in polite society as a swine of culture. Charlie and Toby were both endowed with false memories of their childhood.

The traveller died, taking his secrets to the grave. Charlie adopted the name "Alphonse Chardalot". In the years to follow, he sought to continue the work of his "father", often mistakenly believing himself to be the deceased time traveller. Meanwhile, Toby became a stage performer who shared his "life story" (such as he knew it) with audiences, and would perhaps sing an aria or two.[1445]

The Doctor took tightrope-walking lessons from Blondin and accompanied him on one of his tightrope walks across Niagara Falls.[1446] Thomas Brewster and his mates visited the new Metropolitan line, and had a contest to see who could ride it the furthest without paying.[1447]

1863 (14th-21st February) - EMPIRE OF DEATH[1448] **->** The duplicate James Lees was now performing séances for the heads of Europe, and Queen Victoria commissioned him to hold one for her late husband, Prince Albert.

Earth's physical laws were affecting the other side, and the beings who lived there became increasingly desperate to seal off the dimensional rift. The fifth Doctor and Nyssa used the TARDIS to close the rift, and the Queen vowed to never speak of the matter again. The false James expired, and the real one was returned, having barely aged since he entered the rift in 1856.

The Doctor lost track of whether he had met Queen Victoria before now.

Around this time, the Doctor befriended biologist Thomas Huxley.[1449] Victoria Waterfield's mother, Edith Rose, **died** on 23rd November, 1863.[1450]

The American Civil War

The American Civil War was fought 12th April, 1861 to 9th May, 1865.

A battlefield from the American Civil War was lifted by the War Lords.[1451] The Gettysburg address was made on 19th November, 1863.[1452] Iris had breakfast with Abraham Lincoln on the White House lawn after seeing off Martian invaders for the third time.[1453] The Doctor was present at the opening of the Clifton Suspension Bridge in Bristol.[1454]

1864 - THE RUNAWAY TRAIN[1455] **->** The Cei were on the losing side of an inter-planetary war, and their last warship attempted to use a terraformer to transform Earth into a Cei-compatible planet. The eleventh Doctor and Amy destroyed the terraformer, and the Doctor assisted the warship in returning to its homeworld.

1864 - THE CONTINGENCY CLUB[1456] **->** The Contingency – both a family and race of game-players – gambled for entire worlds. One of their number bet his sister, the Red Queen, that she could not take control of Earth with only contemporary technology. Her spaceship constructed The Contingency: a gentleman's club from which she worked to blow up notable London landmarks and replace Queen Victoria. The fifth Doctor, accompanied by Adric, Tegan and Nyssa, planted Tegan's CD player on the Red Queen, which violated the game rules. Her spaceship automatically jumped into hyperspace with her aboard, and The Contingency club collapsed.

1864 (30th July) - RENAISSANCE OF THE DALEKS[1457] **->** Nyssa and the knight Mulberry arrived in Petersburg, Virginia, via a wormhole from 1320. The Siege of Petersburg was underway, and Union troops set explosives in a mine tunnel running under Confederate lines. The bombs detonated early in the morning on 30th July, killing about three hundred Confederate soldiers.

> (=) The fifth Doctor arrived too late to rescue them, and Nyssa and Mulberry were present at 3:15 am when the bombs exploded.

The Doctor overrode the TARDIS' time-track crossing protocol, and rescued Nyssa and Mulberry at 3:14 am.

Auguste Denayrouze gave his friend, the Doctor, an item he'd co-invented with Benoit Rouquayrol: a diving suit.[1458]

Phoenixes entered our universe every few eons to deposit eggs – which would hatch, and return to their native dimension – in heart of dying stars. One such egg was discharged during a supernova, and came to rest in the pneumatic railway that designer Thomas Webster Rammell had connected to the Crystal Palace. Rammell buried the egg after it weakened his lifeforce, and discontinued the railway after only a few months of service. The egg remained hidden until 1936.[1459]

The brilliant Victorian scientist Harriet Dodd created a feasibility generator, and used it to make Wonderland – a subterranean locale designed to contain creatures that broke through from other dimensions. Dodd allied herself with the earliest form of the Ministry for Incursions and other Alien Ontological Wonders (MIAOW), but the group deemed her work as too subversive and weird, and sealed up Wonderland with Dodd inside. She and the whole of Wonderland slept for more than a century.[1460]

Jeremiah Castle, a man with a hook for a hand, became the king of Jacob's Island – a rookery east of St Xavier's Docks in London. Montague Finish gambled there, and lost his companion, Patsy, in a dice game. For ten years, she was one of Castle's "queens". Jacob's Island eventually turned against Castle, and the police hung him and slung his body into the Thames. Patsy became homeless.[1461]

Ellie Higson, a friend and ally of Professor Litefoot and Henry Gordon Jago, was born circa 1865.[1462]

The Assassination of Abraham Lincoln

1865 (February to April) - BLOOD AND HOPE[1463] -> The fifth Doctor, Peri and Erimem attempted to visit the Wild West but arrived in the waning days of America's Civil War instead. The Doctor assisted the Union army as the medic "Doctor John Smith", and was present on 26th March, 1865, when Billingsville Prison was captured. On 5th April, the Doctor saved President Lincoln from an assassination attempt in Richmond, Virginia. On the same day, Peri shot dead the Confederacy's Colonel Jubal Eustace when he attempted to murder her friends as Union collaborators. Lincoln was killed days later.

caused by the mine explosion is still visible to this day.
1458 *Dark Horizons* (p143). Denayrouze, a co-inventor of the diving suit along with Benoit Rouquayrol, lived 1837-1883 and filed their patent for the suit in 1864.
1459 "The Eagle of the Reich". The Crystal Palace railway closed in 1864, shortly after its opening. Rammell evidently survived his encounter with the phoenix's egg; in real life, he died in 1879 from diabetes.
1460 "Over one hundred years" before *Iris S2: The Land of Wonder*. The implication is that Lewis Carroll's work was based upon Dodd's Wonderland, but it's not explained how this is the case. Perhaps the malleable Wonderland creatures patterned themselves after the characters in Carroll's books. Either way, *Alice in Wonderland* saw print in 1865; Dodd's Wonderland was presumably created around the same time.
1461 *J&L S8: Jago & Litefoot & Patsy*, as related by Patsy. Her timeline is a bit off, in that she opens her story with "thirty years ago", claims that she spent ten years in Castle's company, then says he was hung "thirty years ago".
1462 Or so Summer, Thomas Bloodchild's descendant, estimates after researching Ellie's past in *J&L S5: The Bloodchild Codex*.
1463 Dating *Blood and Hope* (TEL #14) - Judging by a letter on p29, the TARDIS crew arrive in America on 21st February, 1865. The Doctor's saving Lincoln is dated on p49; Eustace's death is dated on p69.
1464 *Minuet in Hell*
1465 "Fifteen years" before *Evolution* (p107).

1466 *Downtime* (p23).
1467 Dating *Assassin in the Limelight* (BF #108) - The story takes place on the day Lincoln was shot (14th April, 1865; he died the following day). The Civil War had concluded a mere five days beforehand on 9th April, when General Lee surrendered the Army of Northern Virginia.

Knox here passes himself off as Oscar Wilde – who is only age ten when this story takes place – but the few people to see him as "Wilde" either die or (in Henry Rathbone's case) go insane and become institutionalized before the real Wilde became famous, suggesting none of them would have noticed the discrepancy in future. An exception is the theatre manager, Henry Clay Ford, who would have lived to hear of Wilde's fame – but who also, having deduced that the Doctor and Evelyn were time travellers, would perhaps be inclined to keep quiet about it all.

It's fancifully implied that Knox, his mind in Pops' dead body, assumes the life meant for Arthur Conan Doyle (1859-1930) from this point on. Conan Doyle is actually seen in three *Doctor Who*-related stories: *Evolution* [set in 1880], *J&L S7: The Monstrous Menagerie* [1894] and *Revenge of the Judoon* [1902]. In all of these, Conan Doyle is presented as the genuine article, not a lively corpse-person with Knox's mind.

The more one considers Knox's plan to swap himself for Conan Doyle, the more unlikely it seems that he succeeded. Such a scheme begs the question of a) what exactly Knox did to the real Conan Doyle, b) how,

The Doctor warned Lincoln not to go to the theatre.[1464] Lord Kelvin laid transatlantic telegraph cables in 1865.[1465] In July 1865, Edward Waterfield had his solicitor, Mr Byle, draw up a will that left his estate to his daughter Victoria Maud.[1466]

1865 (14th April) - ASSASSIN IN THE LIMELIGHT[1467]

-> Dr Robert Knox had exchanged his Type 70 TARDIS for a newer model, and he imprisoned the Indo accompanying him within the Ship. The Indo summoned one of its own kind, who hoped to alter the events surrounding Lincoln's assassination so that the American Civil War would resume, enabling both Indo to feast upon the resulting emotional trauma.

Knox died from his disease. The Doctor trapped the second Indo inside Knox's TARDIS, then deactivated the Ship's temporal shields and sent it hurtling through the Vortex – aging both creatures to death. Knox had absorbed some of the Indo's power, and used it to put his consciousness in the dead body of Pops, a stagehand at Ford's Theatre. In such a form, Knox adopted the identity of Arthur Conan Doyle and booked passage to England.

An earlier version of Knox was in the audience when Booth, as history dictated, killed Lincoln.

1865 - THE HAUNTING OF THOMAS BREWSTER[1468]

-> Creek tried to interrogate Thomas Brewster after the fifth Doctor and Nyssa inquired about him, but lost his footing and drowned in the Thames. Brewster escaped with a fellow scavenger named Pickens.

The Doctor and Nyssa returned with Brewster's older self, having identified this as the point when the "test signal" from the future formed a psychic link with Brewster's mind. The older Brewster persuaded his younger self that the dreams he'd experienced of his mother were an illusion, and the younger Brewster's conviction about this caused the alternate 2008 timeline to cease to exist.

Creek's scavengers recovered the TARDIS from the Thames, where it had been buried since 1831. It would remain in Creek's abandoned shop for two more years.

1865 - THE ELEVENTH TIGER[1469] -> Earth prepared to

enter a unique stellar conjunction for the first time in two thousand years. Qin Shi Huang, controlled by the intelligence that revived him, assembled an army and started securing "sacred sites" that would serve as conduits to the intelligence's power, enabling it to seize control of China. The first Doctor, Ian, Barbara, Vicki and their allies flooded a tomb seeped with the intelligence's power. Qin took control of his host long enough to step into the water, shorting out the intelligence's energy. Qin's mind dissipated, and the possessed Abbot Wu recovered.

Major William Chesterton served in China at this time, and suffered a concussion while fighting bandits in Qiang-Ling. The Doctor and his friends encountered the Ten Tigers of Canton, the top ten kung fu masters in Guangdong.

> **(=) 1865 - WORLD GAME**[1470] -> The Countess created an alternate time line in which Napoleon won the Battle of Waterloo. As she had foreseen, he died of pneumonia during his victory parade in Moscow, whereupon his empire collapsed. The Players took advantage of the empire's disintegration and created numerous small territories, which they pitted against each other in endless "games" of war. The Countess described this as her "Grand Design", but the second Doctor restored the correct timeline by travelling back and preventing Napoleon's victory.

Following the Players' defeat, they abandoned the Grand Design. All Games were suspended indefinitely due to the amount of disruption the Countess had caused, which drew the attention of the Time Lords.

---

exactly, everyone who knew Conan Doyle could have possibly mistake Knox-Pops for him, and c) how, exactly, Knox is meant to have married three times and sired five children when his animated Pops-body reeks of decay and death. Some of these issues are solved if Knox transfers his consciousness into Conan Doyle's body after arriving in England, but this isn't actually said, and it's very odd that Knox is already telling people that he's Conan Doyle before he's even left America. Conan Doyle in real life was a doctor of medicine, so Knox would be able to fake that expertise, at least.

The Doctor and Evelyn are mistaken for Pinkertons – the Agency got its start in 1850, after Allan Pinkerton thwarted an attempt to kill president-elect Lincoln.

1468 Dating *The Haunting of Thomas Brewster* (BF #107) - It's "two years" before the 1867 component of the story, and it's said that the TARDIS is recovered "thirty-four years" after 1831.

1469 Dating *The Eleventh Tiger* (PDA #66) - The date is given. Although not referred to by name, the alien intelligence bears the characteristics of the Mandragora Helix (*The Masque of Mandragora*), and it's intimated (p274) that the Doctor defeated its attempt to dominate Earth "four hundred years" previous.

1470 Dating *World Game* (PDA #74) - The TARDIS travels "fifty years" beyond 1815.

1866 (2nd-3rd June) - THE EVIL OF THE DALEKS[1471]
-> The second Doctor and Jamie were brought to the Waterfield household from 1966 by the Daleks, who ran tests on them in the hopes of discovering the Human Factor. That done, the Doctor, Jamie, Victoria Waterfield and her father Edward were taken to Skaro.

Edward Waterfield was thought to have died when an explosion obliterated his home near Canterbury. His daughter Victoria was supposedly in Paris, as part of a cover story that Professor Maxtible had propagated.[1472]

c 1866 - THE MORTON LEGACY[1473] -> Josiah Morton inherited a museum of curiosities from his uncle, but a relative, Prof Matthew Tenderton, mounted a legal challenge. The second Doctor, Polly, Ben and Jamie found that Morton's butler, Blazzard, had taken it upon himself to eliminate Tenderton and his lawyer with a poison blowd-art — and that their deaths did not, as the Doctor speculated, owe to an alien necklace that focussed mental energy (rather, it was just a necklace). Blazzard died saving Morton from criminals robbing the museum.

1866 (6th October) - "A Matter of Life and Death"[1474] **->** The Silversmith, the master of a mirror realm that existed opposite Edinburgh, escaped into our reality and became a stage magician at the Theatre Royal. He assembled an army from the dark reflections of audience members who passed through his mirrors. The eighth Doctor and Josie restored the Silversmith's victims, rescued his original self and sealed the doppelganger within the mirror reality.

A massive time breach in the TARDIS caused the fifth Doctor to become separated from Nyssa, and he performed an emergency materialisation that caused him to arrive in London, on or about November 1866. While awaiting Nyssa's arrival, he resided at 107 Baker Street as an English gentleman. As "Doctor Walters", he became a Royal Society member so he could collect the materials he needed to repair the damaged TARDIS. For appearance's sake, he took on Robert McIntosh — a medical student at Edinburgh — as his assistant-cum-protégé.[1475]

K9 was programmed with all grandmaster chess games from 1866 onwards.[1476] The Doctor implied he was present when Brighton's West Pier opened in 1866.[1477]

Clara Oswin Oswald, a Victorian iteration of Clara Oswald, was born 23rd November, 1866.[1478] Sherlock Holmes' younger sister, Genevieve, was left mentally handicapped owing to the birth trauma that killed her mother.[1479] **The War Lords lifted a battlefield from the Mexican Uprising of 1867.**[1480]

The Early Adult Lives of Jago and Litefoot

George Litefoot left China in 1866, to make his name as a surgeon.[1481] The New Palace Theatre was formerly the site of a Kibble dog food factory.[1482]

For a time, young George Litefoot took up with Jean Basemore, and enjoyed a memorable New Year's Eve with her by the fountain in the Great Quadrangle of Christchurch. At some point, he refused to return to Peking for the summer, and had a secret rendezvous with her in Buckinghamshire at a filthy but charming tavern, the Mausoleum.[1483]

A young Henry Gordon Jago wished for good luck while playing cards, and unknowingly became indebted to fifth-dimensional beings: the Gentlemen of the Dice.[1484]

1867 - J&L S10: THE YEAR OF THE BAT[1485] **->** As a young man, George Litefoot studied medicine at St Thomas' Hospital. Henry Gordon Jago lacked the talent to be an actor, and was employed sweeping theatre stalls. An unknown party — possibly the Doctor — strategically

---

1471 Dating *The Evil of the Daleks* (4.9) - An early storyline gave the date of the Victorian sequence as "1880" (and the date of the caveman sequence which was later deleted as "20,000 BC"). The camera scripts gave the date of "1867", as did some promotional material, but this was altered at the last minute to dovetail *The Faceless Ones* and *The Evil of the Daleks*. *Downtime* states that Edward Waterfield was presumed dead in 1866.
1472 *Downtime* (p23).
1473 Dating *The Morton Legacy* (BF EA #4.3) – The broad idea, as the blurb notes, is that Ben and Polly (having originated in 1966) have arrived home "a hundred years too early". To that end, Polly says the locale is "Less 1960s, more 1860s".
1474 Dating "A Matter of Life and Death" (Titan 8th Doc #1-5) - The day was given in issue #1.

1475 "Twelve months" before the November 1867 component of *The Haunting of Thomas Brewster*.
1476 *The Androids of Tara*
1477 *Pier Pressure*
1478 According to her tombstone in *The Snowmen*.
1479 *FP: Erasing Sherlock*. Genevieve is "ten years" younger than Sherlock, who is said to have been born in 1857.
1480 *The War Games*
1481 "The year before" *J&L S10: The Year of the Bat*. It's possible that Litefoot spent some years prior to his father's death living in both England and China, since he says in *The Talons of Weng-Chiang*: "We came home in [18]73".
1482 *J&L S7: The Night of 1000 Stars*
1483 *J&L S11: Jago & Son*

deployed a Yesterday Box so that both men could receive letters from their older selves, who identified themselves only as "J" and "L", from thirty years in the future. "J" wrote that Jago had a bright future as the manager of the Palace Theatre, encouraging the young man along a new path.

Jago and Litefoot instructed their younger selves to independently – so as to avoid their meeting prior to the Weng-Chiang affair – investigate why street urchins had gone missing. Aided by Sgt Quick Sr, Jago and Litefoot discovered that vampire nannies were stealing children to feed to their Queen, who was nested in Wyld's Great Globe: a disused tourist attraction in Leicester Square. The Queen was vulnerable to water, so Quick's men rolled the Globe into the river, killing her.

On Quick Sr's recommendation, Jago made the Red Tavern his establishment of choice, and pale ale his preferred drink. The Master of Ceremonies at the Regency Theatre received a sprained ankle from the runaway Globe, and Jago was asked to take his place. The older Litefoot instructed his younger self to hide the Yesterday Box for thirty years, and also to keep a water-based fire pump at his home in future.

As a medical student, an eager-to-please George Litefoot had a patient, Elizabeth, die on his operating table during a routine procedure. Litefoot felt she died from his error,

and delivered the news to one of his colleagues, Elizabeth's fiancé. The blow this dealt to Litefoot's confidence made him switch from treating the living to examining the dead.[1486] At some point, and for one week only, Jago took the place of the Honourable Arthur Lloyd at the Round Room at the Rotunda.[1487]

1867 (14th November) - THE HAUNTING OF THOMAS BREWSTER[1488] -> Nyssa, who had been expelled by the TARDIS, arrived in Seven Dials on the day the Doctor was addressing the Royal Society. He unreservedly lauded a paper by the physicist Leon Foucault, which calculated the speed of light as 298 km per second. The Doctor was now friends with physicist James Maxwell.

Under the direction of his mother's shade, Thomas Brewster had spent the last two years stealing various bits of scientific paraphernalia – and thereby lashed together a machine capable of creating a time breach. Smoke-beings from an alternate 2008 travelled down this corridor to help guarantee that their timeline became the dominant one; they murdered Brewster's friend Pickens and the Doctor's protégé, Robert McIntosh. Their deaths, and others caused by the smoke beings, were attributed to yet-another lethal London smog.

The Doctor severed the time corridor, but the smoke-beings tricked Brewster into stealing the Doctor's TARDIS

1484 *ST: The Jago & Litefoot Revival*, probably when Jago is "well and twenty".
1485 Dating *J&L S10: The Year of the Bat (J&L #10.2)* - The year is given. Wyld's Giant Globe opened in 1851, closed in 1862.
1486 *J&L S7: The Night of 1000 Stars*
1487 *J&L S11: Jago & Son*
1488 Dating *The Haunting of Thomas Brewster (BF #107)* - The day and year are given. James Clerk Maxwell lived 1831-1879. The Doctor here tries to seem older by growing a beard - a rare occurrence, but something he also does in *The Adventuress of Henrietta Street* and *The Wedding of River Song*.

THE HOUSE AT 107 BAKER STREET: To listen to the earliest two stories involving it, the Doctor's ownership of a house at 107 Baker Street (just down the road, then, from the infamous 221B Baker Street) is fairly straight-forward. The fifth Doctor lives there from circa November 1866 to mid-November 1867 (*The Haunting of Thomas Brewster*), while he's stitching the TARDIS back together and waiting for Nyssa to arrive through time. Not long after, from his point of view, he signs the property over to Thomas Brewster in 2008 ("A Perfect World"), intending that proceeds from its sale will fund Brewster's new lease on life. We're not told that the fifth Doctor personally bought the property, but that seems implicit in his remark that the house is of "no [continued] use" to him (once he's got the TARDIS back), and that it's just "standing empty", so Brewster might as well

see some benefit from it.

Later Big Finish stories, however, reveal that various Doctors, companions and associates cycle through the Baker Street house more frequently in the Victorian era and the twentieth century. For nearly all of 1894, a fugitive Jago and Litefoot use the house - with the sixth Doctor's permission - as an invaluable safe harbour while they work to clear their names (*Jago & Litefoot* Series 7). The next year, Jago and Litefoot leave a message at the house for the same Doctor, who dutifully shows up to help them against the cadaverous Master (*Jago & Litefoot* Series 11). Things get a little confusing from 1917-1922, when the fourth Doctor splits some of his five-year sojourn on Earth between the Baker Street house and Paris, necessitating that he surreptitiously evade himself at the former (*The Haunting of Malkin Place*). The ease with which the fourth Doctor stays at 107 Baker Street suggests the property pre-dates the fifth Doctor; that, or - as with Jago and Litefoot - the Doctors have been passing notes to one another offering the house as a sort of timeshare. Meanwhile, Molly O'Sullivan, an eighth Doctor companion at loose ends as World War I draws to a close, squats in the house for an unknown length of time until November 1918 (*DEyes 2: The White Room*).

For more than half a century, however, 107 Baker Street is home to David Walker - a former patient of Molly, who takes it upon herself, in 1918, to insist that he live there even though it's not actually her property

and travelling to their native time. The Doctor and Nyssa retrieved an older version of the TARDIS that had been sitting in Creek's shop since 1965, and followed Brewster into the future.

The travellers defeated the smoke beings, then returned to the Doctor's house. Brewster, fearing a return to a life of scavenging and near-starvation, hijacked the TARDIS a second time.[1489]

In 1868, the Doctor opened a bank account at Coutts Bank in London under the name R.J. Smith Esq.; Susan Foreman, Victoria Waterfield, Sarah Jane Smith, Melanie Bush and Bernice Summerfield were named as signatories on the account.[1490] In the same year, Wychborn House burnt down.[1491] In 1868, the Phiadoran spores enabled Professor Bryce-Dennison to create a solar-powered impeller drive.[1492] Shotgun manufacturer Purdeys received the Royal Warrant in 1868.[1493]

A Sontaran fleet menaced the Mephistra Enclave, but the Doctor captured an advance party before they could penetrate the Enclave's defence shield. The Sontarans deemed the operation a failure, and purged the senior officers responsible. Mingus Jaka, a mere ensign, was spared and eventually promoted to Fleet Marshal.[1494]

A group of American frontiersmen encountered Daleks working on the Dalek Project.[1495]

1868 - "Prisoners of Time"[1496] **->** The first Doctor, Ian, Barbara and Vicki visited the Doctor's friend, the biologist Thomas Huxley, and learned that some of Huxley's students had gone missing while searching for specimens. A tendril of the Animus had arrived on Earth via a portal, and generated a new Carsenome in the London Underground. The Animus brought a small army of Zarbi drones to Earth, but Ian pulverised the Animus with a speeding underground train. The Zarbi were sent back to Vortis, and the Doctor convinced Huxley to keep quiet about what he'd witnessed.

Before the travellers could leave, Adam Mitchell kidnapped Ian, Barbara and Susan.

1868 - "The Heralds of Destruction"[1497] **->** Having moved his Electronicon Ltd. complex through time, Ramon Salamander tried to woo Prime Minister Benjamin Disraeli and Parliament with "magic" technology which could speed up the United Kingdom's advancements. The third Doctor, Jo Grant, the Brigadier and the UNIT Master tracked Salamander, and entered Parliament via a secret passage the Master kept in the statue of the Earl of Derby. The Master hypnotised the politicians into forgetting about Salamander, then escaped after failing to seize control of Salamander's micro-machines. The Doctor and UNIT arrested Salamander and returned to their native time...

c 1868 - THE MAKING OF A GUNSLINGER[1498] **->** A nine-year war devastated the homeworld of the Kahler, one of the most technologically innovative races in the galaxy, until the scientist Kahler-Jex and his colleagues routed the enemy with a cyborg army.

(The White Room). Walker and his family occupy the house until the UNIT Era (DEyes 2: Eyes of the Master), and, one presumes, until whatever year Walker passes away. Following directly on from that same story, Liv and Molly spend "months" at the house while the Doctor's off colluding with some Daleks against the Eminence (ST: "Damascus" and ST: "The World Beyond the Trees"); a little weirdly, Liv makes no mention of Walker also being around. Doubly strange, the eighth Doctor and Liv later (to them) stop by the house in 1963 (DC: The Red Lady), and it's unoccupied. Perhaps the Walkers are conveniently off on holiday.

The Baker Street abode doesn't seem germane to The Crimes of Thomas Brewster (set in c.2011), meaning Brewster probably did cash it out to fund his operations, or squirrel away for a rainy day. Either way, it wouldn't be surprising if more lodgers at the house – there with the Doctor's blessing or not – came to light.

1489 Brewster has possession of the TARDIS for five months (from his perspective), and has such adventures as The Three Companions during that time. The Doctor and Nyssa catch up with him in The Boy That Time Forgot.

1490 Birthright

1491 Strange England (p157).

1492 Imperial Moon

1493 Revenge of the Judoon

1494 Jaka is an ensign when this happens, a Fleet Marshal by The First Sontarans. While it's a guess as to how long such a career rise would take, A Good Man Goes to War suggests that Sontarans have shorter lifespans, and it's reasonable to think the incessant warring against the Rutans encourages a relatively rapid promotion.

1495 The Dalek Project

1496 Dating "Prisoners of Time" (IDW DW mini-series) - The year is given. It's suggested that the first Doctor steered the TARDIS to see his old friend Thomas Huxley (the Doctor: "I recently wrote [Huxley] a letter, and he invited us to pay him a visit."), in defiance of his being unable to control the Ship in the TV stories (Seasons 1 and 2, in particular, are predicated on it).

1497 Dating "The Heralds of Destruction" (Titan 3rd Doc #1-5) - The year is given. Disraeli's first term as prime minister was 27th February to 1st December, 1868.

1498 Dating The Making of a Gunslinger (Series 7 webcast) - The background to A Town Called Mercy. The

The victorious Kahler cyborgs were decommissioned, but one of them – Kahler-Tek, seeking revenge for the wrongs perpetrated on his fellow soldiers – began murdering his creators. Kahler-Jex fled to Earth, became a physician in the Western US town of Mercy and cured a cholera outbreak there.[1499]

The Death of Adric

c 1868 - THE BOY THAT TIME FORGOT[1500] -> The fifth Doctor gathered twelve of the finest minds in the Empire – including Professor Quandry, the novelist Beatrice Mapp and the fraudulent explorer Rupert Von Thal – in Mapp's sitting room in Bloomsbury to conduct an experiment. Those present read off ones and zeroes; by this use of Block Transfer Computation (BTC), the Doctor and Nyssa could locate the hijacked TARDIS. The Doctor's subconscious guilt over Adric's death usurped the BTC, creating a prehistoric timeline where Adric had survived. The Doctor, Nyssa, Beatrice and Rupert were transported there.

The Doctor, Nyssa and Beatrice – along with an aged Adric – returned six weeks after they'd left. Adric's health was failing, and he died while using the last of his strength to recall the TARDIS. Adric was buried in the same cemetery as Thomas Brewster's mother.

The Doctor said that other Time Lords, "Iris especially", had travelled in this period.

The Doctor told Jules Verne to leave the Silurians out of *20,000 Leagues Under the Sea*.[1501] Bilis Manger served as the manager of the Amser Hotel in Roath, which never recovered from "eerie pink flames" gutting it in 1869. The incident linked Bilis to a Rift entity – he both had to do its bidding and set about engineering its destruction.[1502]

The Doctor visited the New York Natural History Museum quite a lot when it first opened, as he hadn't properly cleaned up after himself, and some of the items recovered from the Gobi were "far too unstable" to be put on display.[1503]

The Doctor saw Monet and Renoir painting outside a cafe on the Seine.[1504] The Doctor got Leo Tolstoy to autograph his first edition of *War and Peace* in 1869.[1505]

Charles Dickens and the Gelth

1869 (24th December) - THE UNQUIET DEAD[1506] -> **The ninth Doctor and Rose landed in Cardiff. A dramatic recital by Charles Dickens was interrupted by what seemed to be a ghost. These were gas creatures, the Gelth, who had travelled to Earth by a time rift, a.k.a. the Cardiff Rift. The Gelth posed as refugees, but sought to invade Earth. The Doctor and his allies sent the Gelth back through the Rift and closed it behind them. Dickens hoped to write the adventure as *The Mystery of Edwin Drood and the Blue Elementals*, with the killer being an extra-terrestrial instead of the boy's uncle as originally planned, but died the following year before completing it.**

The "healed" Rift left a residual dimensional scar; this was harmless to humans, yet useful as a means of refuelling time vessels. The Rift would continue to attract all manner of alien beings and technology to the Cardiff area.[1507] The existence of the Rift created a "field of despair" over Cardiff that normally just made the people there a bit miserable, but intensified in times of approaching crisis and increased the suicide/homicide rate.[1508]

Gwen Cooper, a future Torchwood operative, had an old Cardiff family dating back to the 1800s. Gwyneth Cooper, a maid the Doctor and Rose met and who died fighting the Gelth, was linked to her through "spatial genetic multiplicity".[1509]

Making of a Gunslinger occurs at least two years beforehand, as Kahler-Tek has been on Earth that long.

1499 At least "two years" before *A Town Called Mercy*.

1500 Dating *The Boy That Time Forgot* (BF #110) - It's unclear how much time has passed since Brewster stole the TARDIS in mid-November 1867, and so it's possible that it's either late 1867 or some time in 1868. For the Doctor, Nyssa and Brewster, this story continues in the undatable *Time Reef*.

1501 *Peacemaker*. *20,000 Leagues Under the Sea* was published in 1869.

1502 *TW*: "Broken". The incident seems unrelated to events in *The Unquiet Dead*, even though they occur in the same year. The Rift entity isn't Abaddon, whom Bilis is seen serving in *Torchwood* Series 1.

1503 *The Forgotten Army* (p163). The American Museum of Natural History – presumably the same building that this novel keeps calling the "New York Natural History Museum", and identified down to its street address (p26) – opened in 1869.

1504 "The Pestilent Heart". Monet and Renoir did so (the painting bit, not the meeting the Doctor bit) in Summer 1869.

1505 "Gaze of the Medusa"

1506 Dating *The Unquiet Dead* (X1.3) - The Doctor gives the year (having originally aimed for 1860). The date is given a number of times, first on a poster in Dickens' dressing room. The Doctor, Rose and Jack's discussion about the Rift in *Boom Town* seems to indicate that it predates events in *The Unquiet Dead*.

1507 The Doctor uses the Rift to refuel the TARDIS in *Boom Town* and *Utopia*. Evidence of the Rift attracting alien beings and technology to Cardiff is witnessed throughout *Torchwood*.

1508 *TW: Ghost Train*

1509 *Journey's End*, providing an explanation as to why

Jack Harkness Begins His Century of Waiting for the Doctor

Captain Jack Harkness used his vortex manipulator to travel back from the year 200,100 to find the Doctor. He arrived in 1869, would discover in 1892 that he was now immortal, and live on Earth until the early twenty-first century.[1510]

The Doctor knew Mary Ann Evans, a.k.a. George Eliot, the author of *Middlemarch*.[1511] The eleventh Doctor, Amy, Rory and Kevin the Tyrannosaur met Sitting Bull.[1512]

Just before his 400th birthday, the Doctor saw Buffalo Bill outside Wichita.[1513] Admiral Hamish Ravenscaur, a hero of the British Empire, founded Ravenscaur School in 1870 as a haven for the poor and orphans. His descendants would refashion it for the elite.[1514] On 10th Nov, 1870, the Flickermen abducted an eight-year-old boy named Sammy.[1515]

1870 - A TOWN CALLED MERCY[1516] -> Toast crumbs on the TARDIS console prevented the eleventh Doctor, Amy and Rory from reaching Mexico for a Day of the Dead festival, and they instead found themselves in the town of Mercy in the American West. They prevented the cyborg-soldier Kahler-Tek from executing the fugitive Kahler-Jex – a standoff that resolved with Kahler-Jex committing suicide to atone for his crimes. Kahler-Tek found a new purpose as the secret sheriff of Mercy.

Thomas Brewster Leaves the TARDIS

c 1870 - INDUSTRIAL EVOLUTION[1517] -> The sixth Doctor and Evelyn returned Thomas Brewster to the town of Ackleton in his native era. Rival bits of alien technology – a "catalyser" that dissected machines and improved upon their designs, and a living mechanical "inhibitor" designed to create malfunctions and make a planet's inhabitants frightened of technological developments – competed with one another. Brewster saved the Industrial Revolution by destroying the inhibitor, but earned the Doctor's disgust because he had slain a living being. The Doctor and Evelyn left without Brewster, who struck up a partnership with "Samuel Belfrage" – a Karlean working the interplanetary black market. Their first haul was half a ton of Earth's rock salt, which was considered a delicacy on other planets.

Gwen and Gwyneth look identical (both were played by Eve Myles). From her conversation with Rose about boys, Gwyneth is very clearly not a mother in *The Unquiet Dead*, and so Gwen is not her descendant, and the physical resemblance seems more like a result of (to coin a phrase) "time echoing" than genetics.

1510 *Utopia*. It may or may not be coincidence that 1869 is the year the TARDIS landed at the Rift in *The Unquiet Dead*. Jack's immortality is first revealed in *TW: Everything Changes*.

1511 *The Criminal Code*. Evans lived 1819 to 1880.

1512 "Your Destiny Awaits". This happens when Sitting Bull is a Sioux leader, which started no later than 1864, and ended with his surrender in 1881.

1513 "Gaze of the Medusa". The Doctor thinks this happened in "1869", then decides it was "probably 1870".

1514 *The Twelfth Doctor Year Two*: "Clara Oswald and the School of Death"

1515 *J&L* S12: *The Flickermen*

1516 Dating *A Town Called Mercy* (X7.3) - Isaac says, "The War only ended five years back", presumably meaning the American Civil War (1861-1865), so it's now 1870. The Doctor's claim that it's about "ten years too early" for electric street lamps concurs with that, as Wabash, Indiana, became the first US city to test such lights on March 31, 1880.

1517 Dating *Industrial Evolution* (BF #145) - The period is generalised as "nineteenth century Lancashire", but the Doctor would hardly want to deposit Brewster in his personal past, and there's no sign on this occasion of the TARDIS missing its mark. It's probably relevant that when the Doctor offers to take Brewster home in *The Feast of Axos*, he suggests a destination of "about 1870", to which Brewster replies, "That'll do."

1518 According to Angus in *Terror of the Zygons*.

1519 *Horror of Fang Rock*

1520 *The War Games*

1521 *Companion Piece*

1522 *The Devil Goblins from Neptune*

1523 Dating *Set Piece* (NA #35) - It is "1871 CE" (p62). The Commune fell on 28th May, 1871. Ace's departure in *Set Piece* deliberately echoes the epilogue to *The Curse of Fenric* novelisation, in which the Doctor visits an older Ace in nineteenth-century Paris, some time after she's departed his company. Reconciling the epilogue with the New Adventures is difficult, as the epilogue takes place in 1887 (p186 and 188) when Ace is still a "young lady". Given her aging in the New Adventures, this makes it unlikely that she lives in Paris for all of the sixteen years between 1871 and 1887. Fortunately, the New Adventures have Ace taking up time travel after *Set Piece*, and using a time-jump to facilitate her meeting with the Doctor in 1887 would explain a great deal.

1524 *The Talons of Weng-Chiang*. Greel arrived in 1872, according to *The Shadow of Weng-Chiang*.

1525 *The Curse of Fenric*

1526 *FP: The Book of the War*. She's in her "eleventh year" in 1883 according to *FP: Warring States* (p52).

1527 *The Girl Who Never Was*

1528 *TW: The Twilight Streets*

1529 *TW: Risk Assessment*. Havisham says that the zom-

In 1870, the Jameson boys were out cutting peat when they encountered the Zygons on Tulloch Moor. The elder brother Robert was driven mad by the experience and never spoke again; his younger brother Donald simply disappeared.[1518] Around that time, Reuben joined the lighthouse service. He spent twenty of the next thirty years in a gas-powered lighthouse.[1519] In 1871, a battlefield from the Franco-Prussian War was lifted by the War Lords[1520] and the Doctor was given a Gladstone bag by Gladstone.[1521]

The Doctor met Tsar Nicholas at the Drei Kaiser Bund of 1871.[1522]

Ace Leaves the TARDIS

1871 - SET PIECE[1523] **->** The time-lost seventh Doctor, Benny and Ace were reunited in Paris. After they defeated the robotic Ants, Ace chose to leave the TARDIS and joined the ruling Paris Commune. She was the last soldier to leave the barricades when the Commune fell from power. She had possession of a time-hopper built by Kadiatu Lethbridge-Stewart, a means of travelling through time.

During this time, Magnus Greel arrived in the Time Cabinet from the year 5000. The Chinese peasant Li H'sen Chang sheltered Greel, thinking he was the god Weng-Chiang. The Emperor acquired Greel's Cabinet.[1524]

Joseph Sundvik died on 3rd February, 1872.[1525] Cousin Octavia of Faction Paradox was born in Scotland, 1872.[1526] The Doctor had a permanent suite on Floor Six of the Singapore Hilton from 1872 until at least 2008.[1527] A mine owner, Gideon ap Tarri, established the Tretarri in Cardiff as a housing district for his employees in 1872.[1528] Agnes Havisham found herself shooting at zombies – a clue that perhaps the Cardiff Rift was becoming more active.[1529]

Edward Waterfield, Victoria's father, was officially reported as missing in 1872. It was thought that he'd gone off to Africa. Victoria sold his estate, but let the Doctor use the house on Dean Street as a base in London. Edward's sister, Margaret, looked after the place. Victoria visited her a few times – sometimes with the Doctor, and once when she was studying graphology.[1530]

1872 - THE FIRST SONTARANS[1531] **->** The Sontarans had an empire. The First Sontaran Battlefleet contained one of the largest clone hatcheries outside of Sontar; it was equipped with six hundred thousand incubator vats, ready for rapid deployment of fresh troops into battle. Sontar itself had tens, even hundreds of millions of incubators. Sontaran fleet marshals pledged to protect the Sontaran unborn, and could be charged under the Sontaran Military Code for offenses such as ordering deaths for no sound military reason.

The sixth Doctor and Peri landed in the Sea of Nectar on Earth's moon, and found a communications device that Meredid Roath – the creator of the Sontarans – was using to summon his fellow Kaveech to Earth. Based in Sussex, Roath had developed bio-specific guns that caused total cellular collapse in Sontarans while leaving all other organic matter unaffected. Roath's estranged wife, Liandra, had brokered a deal with the Killibans for a larger deployment of the same artillery, unaware that the Rutans had enslaved the Killibans and coveted Roath's technology.

The surviving Kaveech gathered in Sussex, but the Sontarans – eager to remove their progenitors as a liability – wiped them out save for Roath and Liandra. The Doctor, Peri, Roath and Liandra were taken aboard a Sontaran vessel bound for Sontar, to stand trial before the Grand Marshal and the Table of Seven. Rutan fighters engaged the First Sontaran Battlefleet between Neptune and Pluto, and Fleet Marshal Mignus Jaka self-destructed his own warships to prevent the Rutans laying claim to Roath and his weaponry. The resultant explosion obliterated both fleets as the Doctor's party escaped in the TARDIS.

Believed dead, a reconciled Roath and Liandra pledged to hide away from Sontaran space and start a new family, continuing the Kaveech line.

1872 (August to December) - EYE OF HEAVEN[1532] **->** Horace Stockwood organized a second expedition to Easter Island, and the fourth Doctor and Leela joined his group aboard the sailing ship *Tweed*. On the island, Stockwood's party discovered a giant stone head containing a teleport device. This transported some of the group to the homeworld of the aliens who built Easter Island's *moai*. They searched an alien library, but their presence triggered a booby trap that turned the alien sun black. The

---

bie incident occurred "a few years" after a space-time disturbance "shifted" the Rift – presumably a reference to *The Unquiet Dead*.
1530 *Birthright*
1531 Dating *The First Sontarans* (BF LS #3.6) - The year is given. Jaka's full name of "Mingus Jaka" is in keeping with Commander Linx's full name being revealed as "Jingo Linx" in *The Time Warrior* novelisation. A grievously wounded Liandra is rapidly cured when the

Doctor places her in the TARDIS' Zero Room – a different application of what's seen of it in *Castrovalva*. Perhaps it's an upgrade from the Zero Room destroyed in that story, but this begs the question of why the Doctor doesn't keep such an astonishingly useful and life-saving facility about the TARDIS all the time (see *The Angel of Scutari* and others).
1532 Dating *Eye of Heaven* (PDA #8) - The date is given (p17).

party returned to Earth, hoping the sun would return to normal in their absence. From Leela's blood, the Doctor created an antidote to the sickness that had killed the Polynesian/alien hybrids thirty years ago. Stockwood remained on the island to help protect the Polynesians until the alien DNA the *moai* carried could re-infect them.

The *Mary Celeste*

1872 (25th November) - THE CHASE[1533] **->** The first Doctor, Ian, Barbara and Vicki arrived on the *Mary Celeste*, and left moments before the Daleks pursuing them. The crew were so terrified by the Daleks, they abandoned ship.

As the Enzomodons communicated by digesting one another, the Enzomodan ambassador worked his way through the whole crew of the *Mary Celeste*, then choked on a lifeboat.[1534] The eleventh Doctor's TARDIS had lifebelts labeled *SS Mary Celeste*.[1535]

c 1872 - 100: "The 100 Days of the Doctor"[1536] **->** The sixth Doctor learned that an assassin working for the Tharsis Acumen — a technocracy of scientists who were

enraged because he freed their political prisoners — had tainted him with an intelligent virus that would eventually kill him. The Doctor and Evelyn backtracked his various destinations to find the point of infection, and in so doing observed two versions of the eighth Doctor — respectively accompanied by Lucie; Charley and C'rizz — playing cards in a Western saloon in the 1870s.

George Litefoot's father died in China; per custom, fireworks were used at his funeral. When the Litefoot family returned to England in 1873, the Emperor gifted Litefoot's mother with the Cabinet of Weng-Chiang.[1537] The Emperor also bequeathed Litefoot's mother with a little jade frog — a good luck charm — which she passed along to her son. It slipped from Litefoot's fingers, but he recovered it, on the boat trip back to London.[1538]

Ace witnessed some of the rebuilding of Paris in 1873, then used her time-hopper to meet up with the Doctor and his friends in 2001.[1539] The homeworld of the yellow-skinned Lurons became uninhabitable, and so the survivors miniaturised their sun in a pocket warp, and used it as a power-source for their space exploration vessel. They sought to deploy the ship's genetic stocks — which could have generated a million new Lurons — on a new planet,

1533 According to Nardole in *The Eaters of Light*.
1534 *The Water Thief* (ch15).
1535 Dating *The Chase* (2.8) - The emptied *Mary Celeste* was discovered in November 1872.
1536 Dating *100*: "The 100 Days of the Doctor" (BF #100d) - It's the "1870s". The Tharsis Acumen is said to lack time travel, and to have existed for "only a few centuries", so the Doctor could theoretically have freed their slaves at just about any point from (say) the 1500s to the twenty-second century.
1537 *The Talons of Weng-Chiang*
1538 *J&L* S13: *How the Other Half Lives*
1539 *Head Games*
1540 *The Valley of Death*. Perkins' journal records that it's "The first of May, 1873, Day 36 of our quest into the Amazon rain forest". Godrin later claims that the Luron homeworld was obliterated "hundreds of years ago", as part of a false narrative he gives about his origins.
1541 *Pyramids of Mars*
1542 *Doctor Who and the Pirates*. The Doctor says he "paced" Webb, which indicates he was swimming ahead of Webb to increase the man's pace rather than trying to defeat him.
1543 Dating *The Silver Turk* (BF #153) - A newspaper has the dateline "11th September, 1873". The Doctor mentions the real-life Turk — an automation exhibited starting in 1770, was exposed as a fraud in the 1820s and incinerated in a fire in 1854.
1544 Dating *Strange England* (NA #29) - The Doctor says that the "temporal location" is "1873" (p229).

1545 Churchill features in *Victory of the Daleks, Players, The Shadow in the Glass* and *The Churchill Years* audios. He was born 30th November, 1874.
1546 *The Stones of Blood*
1547 *Asylum of the Daleks*. This is tricky to place, as we don't know the exact recording being referenced. *Carmen* was first performed on 3rd March, 1875.
1548 "Twenty years" before *J&L* S10: *The Year of the Bat*.
1549 Dating "Bad Blood" (*DWM* #338-342) - The date is given in a caption.
1550 *The Pirate Planet*. Bandraginus V disappeared "over a century" ago according to the Doctor, when the Zanak native Balaton was young. As Zanak is not capable of time travel, it must have been operating at least that long. The planets attacked by Zanak are named in production documents, and plaques were made up with the names on... but only those for Bandraginus V, Granados, Lowiteliom and Calufrax are clearly visible on screen. *First Frontier* gives a little more detail about Bandraginus V (p129).
1551 "About twenty years" before *J&L* S11: *Jago & Son*.
1552 Dating *Jack: Month 25* (BF *The Lives of Captain Jack* #1.4) - The year is given.
1553 *TW: The Twilight Streets*; this is how Abaddon came to be imprisoned beneath Cardiff (*TW: End of Days*).
1554 *The Android Invasion*. Bell lived 1847-1922.
1555 *Father's Day*. Bell's famous phone call occurred on 10th March, 1876.
1556 *Players* (p62), *Festival of Death*. Custer was killed 25th June, 1876.

but the sun's radiation drove the ship's crew mad, causing them to purge their ranks until only twenty-two increasingly amoral Luron remained.

In 1873, the Luron named Godrin reconnoitered Earth, but meteorites caused his scoutship to crash in the Amazon. At the time, Professor Cornelius Perkins was leading an expedition into the so-called Valley of Death to discover the lost city of the Maygor tribe. Awaiting the day that humanity would develop communications technology powerful enough to contact the Luron mothership, Godrin used his scoutship to generate a slow-time field within the Valley – while a month passed for those within, more than a century elapsed in the outside world. The Luron mothership stayed in orbit around Jupiter, encased in a similar time field.[1540]

Old Priory, a Victorian folly, was built for the Scarman family. After this time, Marcus and Laurence Scarman played in the priest-hole there as children.[1541] The Doctor swam with Captain Webb in the Channel.[1542]

1873 (11th September) - THE SILVER TURK[1543] **->** Mondas was now within two hundred light years of Earth. A scoutship with two Cybermen, Graham and Brem, reconnoitred the space around Mondas and crashed on Earth. Dr Johan Drossel and Alfred Stahlbaum acquired Brem, who was badly damaged, and turned him into a touring curiosity that could play checkers and the piano. The eighth Doctor and Mary Shelley stopped Graham – who cannibalised Brem for needed parts – from contacting Cyber-Control on Mondas. Graham's systems failed, and the Doctor and Mary burned a number of advanced marionettes that he had constructed. Stahlbaum toured with one such marionette – a wooden Doctor-duplicate, "the Silver Doctor", which challenged people to play games.

1873 - STRANGE ENGLAND[1544] **->** The TARDIS landed on an asteroid shaped by Gallifreyan Protyon units to resemble an idyllic Victorian country house based on Wychborn House. It was sculpted by a friend of the Doctor, the Time Lady Galah, who had reached the end of her regenerative cycle. With the seventh Doctor's help, Galah lived on as one of her human creations, Charlotte. She returned to Earth and married Richard Aickland, who became a renowned Gothic novelist (of such books as *Cold Eyes* and *The Wine Press*) in the early twentieth century.

Winston Churchill, Prime Minister of the United Kingdom and a close friend of the Doctor's, was born.[1545] **The Nine Travellers were surveyed in 1874.**[1546] **The Doctor played the triangle during a recording of *Carmen*.**[1547] The temporary site of St Thomas' Hospital became the Surrey Gardens Music Hall.[1548]

Destrii Joins the TARDIS

1875 - "Bad Blood"[1549] **->** In the Dakota Hills, the eighth Doctor found that Chief Sitting Bull had been told he would arrive in a vision. Miners had awoken an ancient evil, and Indians and General Custer's forces were both attacked by wolf-like creatures: the Windigo. The Doctor was reunited with Destrii when she arrived with her uncle, Count Jodafra, but the two aliens started to arm Custer's men with laser weapons.

Jodafra had made a deal with the Windigo, as it could navigate the timestream. Destrii sided with the Doctor, and helped destroy the Windigo. Jodafra savagely attacked Destrii, leaving her for dead, but the Doctor brought her back aboard the TARDIS.

The *Vantarialis* crashed on Zanak, where its injured captain was remade as a cyborg. With the assistance of old Queen Xanxia, the Captain converted the entire planet into a hollow world capable of teleporting between star systems and sucking the life out of planets by materialising around them. After this time, and with increasing frequency, Zanak attacked and destroyed Bandraginus V, Aterica, Temesis, Tridentio III, Lowiteliom, Bibicorpus and Granados.[1550]

Henry Gordon Jago enjoyed his drink a bit too much, and cavorted with a stage performer, Ruby Valentine. She secretly bore his son, Henry Jr., then fled to Europe to escape a cult intent upon resurrecting their dark lord in her child. Henry Jr. grew up in various cities, including as a stable boy in Versailles, with Valentine claiming that his father had died saving dozens of people from a rampaging elephant at the London Zoological Gardens.[1551]

1876 - JACK: MONTH 25[1552] **->** Magrin Shank and Kim Pollensa – respectively the superior and best friend of the young Time Agent Javic Piotr Thane, a.k.a. Captain Jack – found him cavorting in 1876. They hauled his sorry arse back to the Time Agency.

Gideon ap Tarri bore witness in 1876 as an earthquake wracked Cardiff, because Abaddon was fighting Pwccm for control of the Rift. The combatants each had a second: the twins, Bilis and Cafard Manger. The contest left Abaddon trapped under Cardiff, and Pwccm stuck the Rift. Cafard merged with Bilis. On Bilis' advice, ap Tarri relocated his workers to newer accommodations in the Windsor and Bute Esplanades. The Tertarri would remain uninhabited for a century, and become a place of hauntings.[1553]

The Doctor met Alexander Graham Bell.[1554] **Bell initiated the first phone message while asking for his assistant Watson. The message would later dominate phone lines during a time paradox in 1987.**[1555] The Doctor warned General Custer against taking his Seventh Calvary over the ridge, but Custer ignored him.[1556] **The Doctor met Gilbert and Sullivan.**[1557] The Doctor claimed to have inspired the *Mikado*, a comic operetta.[1558]

1887 - "Gaze of the Medusa"[1559] -> Lady Emily Carstairs obtained the time-active Lamp of Chronos and allied herself with the Medusa in Homeric Greece, hoping to learn how to travel back and save her two deceased children. The Lamp variously transported the fourth Doctor, Sarah, Carstairs, the chrononautologist Odysseus James and his daughter Athena back to ancient Greece. Carstairs, James and the Medusa all died, but the Doctor and Athena returned and restored Sarah, who had been a Medusa-made statue in the intervening centuries.

Afterward, the Doctor and Sarah attended the wedding of Athena and Lt Albert Sullivan, a ship's surgeon in the Royal Navy. They were the great-grandparents of Harry Sullivan.

On Earth, the first phonograph recording (of Thomas Edison reciting, "Mary had a little lamb...") trapped a disembodied extraterrestrial, later called the Second Voice.[1560] The Doctor's acapella group included Thomas Edison.[1561]

In 1878, the Vondrax collected an Orb from Canada.[1562] The Doctor knew Billy the Kid, who wasn't like Emilo Estevez's portrayal in *Young Guns II*.[1563] Oscar Wilde's heart was broken when his childhood sweetheart, Florence Balcombe, married the theatre manager Bram Stoker.[1564]

1878 (September) - IMPERIAL MOON[1565] -> Using Bryce-Dennison's impeller drive, the British government had crafted three spaceships: the *Cygnus*, *Draco* and *Lynx*. The fifth Doctor and Turlough arrived as the ships explored Earth's moon, and mistook the deadly Vrall for the exiled Phiadorans. While returning to Earth, the Vrall were exposed aboard the *Draco* and a deadly struggle took place. The crewless *Draco* sped into space.

The *Cygnus* and *Lynx* arrived on Earth, where Queen Victoria greeted the "Phiadorans" as emissaries from another world. The Vrall self-replicated and instigated a slaughter. The Doctor and Turlough used advanced weapons from the lunar safari park to wipe out the Vrall on Earth. At the Doctor's command, Kamelion disguised himself as the late Prince Albert and appeared to the Queen "in a vision". Kamelion convinced the Queen to dismantle the remaining spaceships and never mention the

---

1557 *The Edge of Destruction.* Gilbert and Sullivan collaborated between 1875-1896.
1558 *Doctor Who and the Pirates*
1559 Dating "Gaze of the Medusa" (Titan 4th Doc Vol. 1 #1) - The year is given. The fourth Doctor says he's not sure if the Weeping Angels of legend (*Blink* et al) exist. The fifth Doctor already knows of them in *CD,NM* V1: *Fallen Angels*.
1560 *Ghost in the Machine.* Edison demonstrated the first phonograph on 29th November, 1877.
1561 "The Parliament of Fear"
1562 *TW: Trace Memory*
1563 "When Worlds Collide". Billy the Kid lived 1859-1881.
1564 Four years before "Dead Man's Hand". Historically, Balcome married Stoker in 1878.
1565 Dating *Imperial Moon* (PDA #34) - It's "the year of our Lord 1878" (p7).
1566 Dating *Tooth and Claw* (X2.2) - The Doctor gives the date as "1879". The book *Creatures and Demons* (a nonfiction book about various *Doctor Who* monsters) suggests that the parallel universe first seen in *Rise of the Cybermen* diverged from our history because Queen Victoria was killed in their (Doctorless) version of these events. The series itself was going to state this, but Russell T Davies decided against it. While it might explain why the Britain of that universe is a Republic, it doesn't explain why the Queen's successor would create Torchwood – an organisation founded in response to the Doctor and Rose irritating Victoria. Perhaps the Queen's death at the hands of a werewolf triggered an urge to defend Britain against such foes.

A letter to the Lord Provost dated "October 23, 1879" absolves him of the Doctor's deceptions to the Crown in *The Doctor's His Lives and Times* (p189).
1567 *TW: Children of Earth*
1568 *Army of Ghosts,* with the date of the Charter's establishment stated in *The Torchwood Archives* (BBC) and on Home Office files in *TW: Children of Earth.*
1569 *TW: Risk Assessment. The Torchwood Archives* (BBC) establishes that Victoria gave orders for the founding of Torchwood Cardiff in 1879. *TW: Slow Decay* provides confirmation that it was operating no later than 1885.
1570 *TW: Golden Age*
1571 *TW:* "World Without End"
1572 *TW: Corpse Day*
1573 *TW:* "Rift War"
1574 Dating *The Tenth Doctor Year One* (Titan 10th Doc #7, "The Weeping Angels of Mons") - A dateline on the *Dundee Herald* states the day, which is when the real-life Tay Bridge disaster occurred.
1575 "Wormwood"
1576 *Storm Warning.* Roarke's Drift occurred on 22nd to 23rd January, 1879.
1577 *Death Match.* Freud, born in 1856, began smoking when he was 24.
1578 *DC 2: The Sonomancer*
1579 Dating "The Parliament of Fear" (*DWM* #515-517) – A caption gives the year and season.
1580 Dating *Evolution* (MA #2) - It is the "year of grace eighteen hundred and eighty" (p6, p108). Events here seem to influence Conan Doyle regarding *The Hound of the Baskervilles*, which was written in 1902. Kipling lived

incident. The moon safari park self-destructed, leaving only a large crater.

The Founding of Torchwood

1879 - TOOTH AND CLAW (TV)[1566] **->** The tenth Doctor and Rose met Queen Victoria in Scotland. She was en route to the royal jewellers, but was diverted by the brethren who served a werewolf-like alien to Torchwood Estate. The alien intended to bite Victoria and through her foster the Empire of the Wolf, but the Doctor deduced Prince Albert's plan to defeat the creature and killed it.

Queen Victoria knighted the Doctor for saving her life, and named Rose as "Dame Rose of the Powell Estate". However, the Queen was not amused – she was fearful that the Doctor and Rose had strayed from all that was good, and therefore posed a danger. She banished them from her empire, and secretly ordered the formation of the Torchwood Institute to protect the realm from such alien threats.

It was possible that the werewolf scratched the Queen before it died. The Doctor theorised that the Queen might similarly nip her children, and that the "royal disease" (unknown in Victoria's bloodline before her, and thought to be haemophilia) might actually be the alien werewolf taint.

Torchwood was established by royal decree, and was funded directly by the Crown. Victoria stated:

> "Torchwood is also to administer to the Government thereof in our name, and generally to act in our name and on our behalf, subject to such orders and regulations as Torchwood shall, from time to time, receive from us through one of our Principal Secretaries of state." [1567]

The Doctor was named as an enemy of the Crown in the Torchwood Foundation Charter, which was established on 31st December, 1879.[1568]

Torchwood Cardiff – per Victoria's decree and on the advisement of Agnes Havisham, a Torchwood associate – was established as a means of monitoring Rift activity.[1569] Torchwood India was founded to recover alien artifacts in the Raj.[1570]

The Torchwood House observatory would remain unused until the twenty-first century.[1571] Queen Victoria decided that from time to time, Torchwood should assist the local constabulary on unsolved cases – thus giving rise to the tradition of Corpse Day.[1572] Torchwood took to studying a stone circle near Cardiff, which was a focus for Rift energy.[1573]

1879 (28th December) - THE TENTH DOCTOR YEAR ONE[1574] **->** Jamie Colquhoun's friend Henry, thrown back in time by a Weeping Angel, found himself aboard a Dundee train moments before the Tay Bridge collapsed – and all aboard were killed.

Creation of the Threshold

In 1879, an Arkansas Bible salesman named Abraham White touched a shooting star and was exposed to images from a thousand worlds, including visions of Time Lords. The "star" was actually the consciousness of Pariah – a predecessor to Shayde, and now an enemy of Gallifrey. White hosted her essence within him. Armed with Pariah's knowledge, White sought to boost humanity's technology development. He nudged a generation of geniuses and inventors – including Thomas Edison, Nicola Tesla, Rudolf Diesel, Henry Ford and Albert Einstein – along.

Pariah grew herself a new body within White's form, and learned to replicate her basic sphere influence. White infused select agents with the spheres and turned into living gateways. In this fashion, he founded the Threshold: an organisation that traded its services (moving clients through spatial doorways) in exchange for alien technology. The Threshold mastered space as the Time Lords had mastered time, and avoided Gallifrey's detection by refraining from time travel technology.

Threshold began developing an energy wave, but this would take over three thousand years to perfect. The group came into conflict with the seventh and eighth Doctors; events between them climaxed on the moon in the fifty-third century.[1575]

The Doctor met Afrikaaners during the Boer War and was at the battle of Roarke's Drift.[1576] The Master found Sigmund Freud to be "a joy", and gave the man his first box of cigars.[1577] River Song was an honorary member of the Royal Society. She also went to "outrageous" parties in the 1880s.[1578]

1880 (Spring) - "The Parliament of Fear"[1579] **->** In the Indian Territory (later Oklahoma), Mother Totika – a Seminole medicine woman hungry for vengeance against the white settlers – became the psychic linchpin by which Dreamscape-denizens, the Stikini, could possess human bodies and manifest as were-owls. Although the Stinkini war-queen, Cocheta, temporarily inhabited Bill Potts, the twelfth Doctor banished all of the Stikini back to the Dreamscape... where an unknown force incinerated them. The Doctor found a sigil carved into the TARDIS's exterior wood, and put their trip to the Ragnarok Club at New Asgard on the back-burner to learn more...

1880 - EVOLUTION[1580] **->** Percival Ross witnessed a Rutan scoutship crashing in Limehouse, and recovered a flask of Rutan healing salve from the wreckage. The alien gel had a miraculous healing effect on humans, but it also could merge human and animal genetic material, as Ross discovered when a boy he was treating became a ferocious dog-like creature. Ross interested the industrialist Breckingridge, the owner of a vast cable factory in the town of Bodhan, in the creation of a race of hybrid dolphin-men. Ross kidnapped fifteen children, and conducted experiments that turned them into mer-children.

Breckingridge died when one of his mutated guard dogs turned on him; Ross drowned. The fourth Doctor relocated the mer-children to a water planet in the Andromeda Galaxy. A young Arthur Conan Doyle witnessed the happenings on Dartmoor, and his chance encounter with the Doctor inspired two of his most famous characters: Sherlock Holmes and Professor Challenger. An even younger Rudyard Kipling, future author of *The Jungle Book*,

also witnessed the events surrounding the closure of Breckingridge's factory.

The Doctor "borrowed" Conan Doyle's stethoscope and kept meaning to return it.[1581] The Doctor was friends with Rudyard Kipling.[1582] In 1880, the HMS *Courage* ran aground on the island containing the slumbering Kibu, and all hands perished.[1583]

The Doctor claimed to have studied medicine under Bell in Edinburgh.[1584] The Doctor met Geronimo.[1585] He also met Mark Twain.[1586] The Doctor edited the first manuscript of *Huckleberry Finn*, as Mark Twain was such a terrible speller. By way of thanks, Twain gifted the Doctor with an original Paul E. Wirt pen.[1587]

Panda swore Iris to secrecy after a visit to Montmartre, France, the 1880s, entailed his wearing lipstick and rouge, and cavorting with some dancing girls and a bottle of Absinthe.[1588]

1865-1936, so he is "15" here (p45).

1581 *Storm Warning*. No date given, but the Doctor did meet him in *Evolution*. Conan Doyle lived 1859-1930.

1582 *Cold Vengeance*. The Doctor here quotes from Kipling's "If—" (1910).

1583 *J&L S9: Island of Death*. Captain Pettigrew's journal reports mysterious happenings from 21st-22nd March, 1880, with the last entry dating to May.

1584 *Tooth and Claw* (TV). Bell lived 1837-1911, and Conan Doyle studied under him. Note that in *The Moonbase*, the Doctor remembers studying in Glasgow under Lister in 1888. Either he studied under both, or has altered the details slightly here.

1585 *Storm Warning*, "The Golden Ones". Despite the eleventh Doctor using "Geronimo" as a catch-phrase, only these two stories claim that he actually met the man. Geronimo lived 16th June, 1829, to 17th February, 1909. He instigated revenge attacks after soldiers killed his family in 1858, and surrendered in 1886.

1586 *The Crooked World*

1587 *Shroud of Sorrow*. Twain wrote *Adventures of Huckleberry Finn* (1885), the sequel to *The Adventures of Tom Sawyer* (1876), from 1876 to 1883.

1588 *Iris S3: The Midwinter Murders*

1589 Dating "The Greatest Gamble" (*DWM* #56) - The date is given.

1590 *TW: The Twilight Streets*

1591 *TW: To the Last Man*

1592 Dating *Terrible Lizards* (BBC children's 2-in-1 #5) - Captain Bartholomew tells the travellers that it's "the year of Our Lord Eighteen Hundred and Eighty-One, of course" (ch4). Though the gaunt "Calibas" brings to mind Caliban from *The Tempest*, there's no evident connection.

1593 Dating *Empress of Mars* (X10.9) - The year is given. Godsacre participated in the Battle of Isandlwana (22nd January, 1879). This initial contact between Alpha Centauri and the Ice Warriors, no doubt, eventu-

ally facilitates the formal relations between them (*The Curse of Peladon*). The Doctor's claim that this marks the genesis of the Martian Golden Age, while perhaps true overall, somewhat glosses over their attempts to destroy humanity along the way – the most glaring examples being *The Seeds of Death* [c.2040] and the Thousand-Day War in the New Adventures.

1594 Dating *The Gunfighters* (3.8) - The story ends with the Gunfight at the OK Corral. The depiction of events owes more to the popular myths and Hollywood treatment of the story than historical accuracy.

1595 Dating "Dead Man's Hand" (IDW Vol. 4 #13-16) - The caption says, "Deadwood, Dakota Territory. March 1882", and the Doctor confirms the month and year.

Wilde has been in America for "three months now"; historically, he arrived in New York aboard the SS *Arizona* on 3rd January, 1882. It's "four years" since Florence Balcombe married Bram Stoker in 1878, and "two years" after Edison created the "electric lamp" (or, more specifically, the first commercial incandescent light; the first successful test of this actually happened on 22nd October, 1879, but Edison didn't patent it until 27th January, 1880). The Doctor says it's "six years" prior to Wilde considering at the Langham Hotel that he should write *The Picture of Dorian Gray* – actually more than seven years, if he means the dinner between Wilde, Arthur Conan Doyle and *Lippincott's Monthly* editor J.M. Stoddart on 30th August, 1889, which also resulted in Conan Doyle being commissioned to write *The Sign of Four*. Hickock died on 2nd August, 1876, so should probably have decomposed more than is depicted here.

The unnatural nature of these events presumably resulted in a cover-up that scrubbed the historical record. Wilde did spend 1882 touring America, but, as the Doctor and Clara discuss, there's no evidence of his visiting the Dakota Territories. Similarly, the US Seventh Cavalry – here massacred – had no major battle in 1882; the group is best known for the Battle of Little

c 1880 - "The Greatest Gamble"[1589] -> Gaylord Lefevre, a gambler on a Mississippi riverboat, played the Celestial Toymaker and lost, like so many before him.

On the instructions of Bilis Manger, Gideon ap Tarri recorded the Abaddon-Pwccm battle that he'd witnessed into his diary on 12th June, 1880. On 18th September, 1881, an operative from Torchwood London approached ap Tarri about the document. Ap Tarri fled to prevent it falling into Torchwood's hands, but he died in the same year, and Torchwood exhumed his grave to obtain the item.[1590] **Torchwood Cardiff was equipped with cryogenics in the Victorian era.**[1591]

1881 - TERRIBLE LIZARDS[1592] -> The Calibas crew of a damaged time vessel adapted the wrecked sailing ship *Venture* to suit their needs, and set off to Florida to find their time vessel's missing drive. The malfunctioning item had given rise to the myth of the Fountain of Youth, but now created a time fissure that brought liopleurodon, stegosaurs, tyrannosaurus rex and other dinosaurs through from pre-historic times. The eleventh Doctor, Amy and Rory sent the dinosaurs back, sealed off the fissure, and aided the Calibas in returning home.

1881 - EMPRESS OF MARS[1593] -> **A British officer, Colonel Godsacre, found a dormant Ice Warrior vessel on the South African veldt. The Warrior within, Friday, took Her Majesty's soldiers to Mars, ostensibly to help them mine precious gems. Secretly, he worked to find and revive the dormant Empress of Mars, Iraxxa. The twelfth Doctor, Bill and Nardole turned up as Iraxxa's warriors and Godsacre's men tumbled into conflict. Godsacre quelled the fighting by offering his life and service to Iraxxa, who accepted his tribute.**

On the Martians' behalf, the Doctor broadcast a messaged to the nearby space-faring civilisations. Alpha Centauri, a future ambassador to the Federation, answered the call and welcomed the Ice Warriors into universal society. Centauri dispatched ships to assist Iraxxa's hive – the Doctor, Bill and Godsacre guided them down by spelling out "God Save the Queen" in stones. An ice cap later covered up the message.

The Doctor speculated that the Martian Golden Age was about to begin.

1881 (25th-26th October) - THE GUNFIGHTERS[1594] -> **The first Doctor, Steven and Dodo landed at Tombstone shortly before the Gunfight at the OK Corral. As the Doctor searched for a dentist, the gunman Johnny Ringo found one – Doc Holliday – who he'd been tracking for two years. Marshall Wyatt Earp and his allies killed Ringo and some members of the renegade Clanton family.**

1882 (March) - "Dead Man's Hand"[1595] -> The mindparasite Es'Cartrss, as hosted in the T'Keyn auditor Sondrah, attempted revenge upon the Doctor by bringing about Earth's destruction. Es'Cartrss-Sondrah captured Thomas Edison and put him to work overhauling the technology at Sondrah's disposal. The corpses buried at Mount Moriah cemetery in Deadwood, the Dakota territory, were re-fashioned into undead gunmen wearing red masks, and the eleventh Doctor and Clara arrived as the animated body of Wild Bill Hickock began terrorizing the town. Calamity Jane and Oscar Wilde, the latter on a yearlong American tour to lecture on interior design, aided the travellers.

The T'Keyn approved Es'Cartrss-Sondrah's audit that Earth should be destroyed, and dispatched a cadre of shock troops to fortify Es'Cartrss' undead army. The US Seventh Cavalry, as led by Captain Lacey, took heavy casualties while confronting the invaders. A fragment of Hickock's personality remained, and he died a final time while hampering Es'Cartrss' operations.

The Doctor took Wilde – whose clothes were torn, forcing him to don the eighth Doctor's garb – to the T'Keyn mothership, where the T'Keyn ruled in favour of humanity's survival based upon Wilde's impassioned arguments. They also pledged to separate Es'Cartrss from Sondrah's mind and imprison the parasite.

The Doctor went out on the town with Oscar Wilde.[1596] The Dalek Project studied the prowess of the French Cavalry.[1597] Captain Jack shot at a Malevilus in the Wild West.[1598]

The Eruption of Krakatoa

wih - 1882 (autumn) to 1883 (26th August) - FP: ERASING SHERLOCK[1599] -> The time traveller Gillian Petra became a maid in Sherlock Holmes' household to observe him for her doctoral thesis. She was unaware that

---

Bighorn, with Custer, in June 1876. The point is raised that Thomas Edison should be in New York building the Pearl Street Power Station, but it's not said how his absence was explained.
1596 *The Silurian Gift*
1597 *The Dalek Project*

1598 *The Ninth Doctor Year One*: "Secret Agent Man"; the Malevilus first appeared in "The Iron Legion".
1599 Dating *FP: Erasing Sherlock* (FP novel #5) - The story ends with the eruption of Krakatoa on its historical date of 26th August, 1883; many dating notations mark the progression of the story through the year

her benefactor, Jimmy Moriarty, and his associate Thomas Peerson Corkle were conducting an experiment to see if the history of a "dynamic individual" such as Holmes could be derailed, and his notoriety erased, early on in his career. Petra and Holmes became lovers. Corkle murdered Holmes' father and sent a serial killer, Francis Black, to debase and kill his sister Genevieve. An anguished Holmes shot Corkle dead, and set about rescuing his sister. The energy released by the eruption of Krakatoa powered Petra's return to the future.

The Doctor witnessed the eruption of Krakatoa.[1600] The Krakatoa eruption released a Xylok crystal from under the Earth. It would form the heart of Sarah Jane Smith's computer Mr Smith.[1601] C-19's Vault would come to own some damaged crystals from Krakatoa, 1883.[1602]

The Rani kidnapped microbiologist Louis Pasteur.[1603] Penelope Gate built herself a time machine using a miniature Analytical Engine. She left her husband in 1883 for a life of time travel. She first headed to the year 2000, actually landing in 1996. The seventh Doctor returned Penelope to her native time after meeting her in feudal Japan.[1604] In 1883, the Time Lord Ulysses exiled his fellow Time Lord Marnal to the home of Penelope Gate's parents on Earth. Marnal's memories were locked off, and he wouldn't recover them until his regeneration in the twenty-first century.[1605]

There was a single account of a pocket of dinosaurs surviving on one plateau in Central Africa, but most scientists and reporters, including a young Arthur Conan Doyle, dismissed it as the ravings of a madman:

beforehand. Gillian says that the woman whose identity she adopts, "died in early August, just before I arrived" – but Gillian is already ensconced in Holmes' household when the story opens, and it's said to be "autumn" on p13, "November" on p27 (how much time passes between the two isn't immediately clear). While the adventure is based upon the premise that nefarious parties are trying to change Holmes' timeline, it's also implied that he regains his moral compass enough to become the same detective seen in Conan Doyle's stories (and, by extension, in *Doctor Who*).

1600 *Inferno, Rose*. The ninth Doctor also visited the scene. Krakatoa erupted in 1883.

1601 *SJA: The Lost Boy*

1602 *Leth-St: Beast of Fang Rock* (ch2), presumably referencing *SJA: The Lost Boy*.

1603 *Time and the Rani*. Pasteur lived 1822-1895.

1604 *The Room with No Doors*

1605 *The Gallifrey Chronicles*

1606 *Ghost Light*. It is unclear from the story whether the plateau really existed or was merely a delirious Fenn-Cooper's rationalisation of his adventures in Gabriel Chase.

1607 Dating *Ghost Light* (26.2) - Set "two years" after 1881, when Mackenzie is sent to investigate the disappearance of Sir George Pritchard, and "a century" before Ace burns down Gabriel Chase in 1983. It's a time of year when the sun sets at six pm (so either the spring or autumn). The script suggested that a caption slide "Perivale – 1883" might be used over the establishing shot of Gabriel Chase. Queen Victoria was a Hanover, not a Saxe-Coburg, but late in her reign she did acquire the nickname "Mrs Saxe-Coburg".

1608 *Gods and Monsters*, per mention of the "village blacksmith" in *Ghost Light*.

1609 "The Time Machination"

1610 Justine is "barely 16" in *FP: Movers*, set circa March 1899. If the word "barely" can be taken at all literally, she was born in 1883.

1611 *Assassin in the Limelight*. This is historical, and

remains a secondary tragedy inflicted on those attending Ford's Theatre with Lincoln. After killing his wife, Rathbone lived in an asylum in Hildesheim, Germany, and died himself in 1911. He was buried alongside Clara in Hildesheim until the authorities deemed their graves as unattended, and had the gravesites destroyed in 1952. Rathbone and Clara's eldest son served as a U.S. Congressman from Illinois, Lincoln's home state.

1612 *The Green Death*

1613 *The Harvest of Time* (p128). Khartoum siege, a victory by Muhammad Ahmad's Mahdist forces against the British-held Khartoum, began March 13, 1884.

1614 *The Three Companions*. Stevenson lived 1850-1894.

1615 *The Drosten's Curse*

1616 *The Wrong Doctors*

1617 Dating *SJA: The Ghost House* (*SJA* audiobook #4) - The year is given. Skak's time manipulator relies upon Zygma energy (*The Talons of Weng-Chiang*).

1618 Dating *Erimem: Three Faces of Helena* (*Erimem* novel #8) - The year is given. Quatermain first appeared in *King Solomon's Mines* (1885) by H. Rider Haggard; his narration establishes that his travels "inspired" Haggard's stories rather than being gospel.

1619 Dating *Peacemaker* (NSA #21) - It's the "1880s" according to the back cover. Similarly, the Doctor licks his thumb, holds it up to the air, and determines, "This is 1880-something, I reckon. A Monday. Just after breakfast." *The Time Machine* was published "ten years" after this (in 1895).

1620 Dating *Timelash* (22.5) - The Doctor applies "a time deflection coefficient of 706 years" to the timelash's original destination of 1179, and concludes that Vena will arrive in "1885... AD". *The Terrestrial Index* set this in "c.1891", after *The Time Machine* was written.

1621 *The Ghosts of N-Space*

1622 *Deadly Reunion*

1623 *Christmas on a Rational Planet*. No date given, but Blavatsky lived 1831-1891.

"The pygmies from the Oluti Forest led me blind-fold for three whole days through uncharted jungle. They took me to a swamp full of giant lizards, like giant dinosaurs."[1606]

Gabriel Chase

1883 - GHOST LIGHT[1607] **->** While Light slumbered, the Survey Unit assisting him had established itself in Gabriel Chase north of London as Josiah Samuel Smith, arch-advocate of Darwinist theories. Two years after Inspector Mackenzie vanished while investigating the goings-on at the house, Smith was plotting to use a pass to Buckingham Palace given to his associate – the adventurer Redvers Fenn-Cooper – to assassinate Queen Victoria and bring new order to the "anarchic" British Empire. The seventh Doctor brought Ace to Gabriel Chase to confront her having burned it down in a hundred years' time. Light awoke and sought to destroy Earth in a firestorm, but was goaded by the Doctor into dispersing itself. Josiah and Light's Control Unit swapped places on the evolutionary ladder. Control, Fenn-Cooper, the servant Nimrod and the diminished Josiah left in Light's spaceship, and the house remained abandoned for a century.

The seventh Doctor knew "a nice little restaurant on the Khyber Pass".

Perivale would eventually have a blacksmith, which the elder god Weyland used to monitor Fenric's activities.[1608] The Torchwood Institute learned about events pertaining to the Doctor, Krakatoa and Gabriel Chase.[1609]

Justine McManus, later Cousin Justine of Faction Paradox, was born to Jake McManus.[1610] On 23rd December, 1883, Major Henry Rathbone – his mental health having deteriorated after witnessing Abraham Lincoln's assassination, and after being repeatedly stabbed at the event – murdered his wife Clara.[1611]

In 1884, a book was published detailing many types of Amazonian fungus.[1612] The finest swami in old Calcutta taught the Doctor the rudiments of snake charming, just prior to the siege of Khartoum.[1613]

Robert Lewis Stevenson gifted the Doctor with a tumbler of whiskey.[1614] Robert Louis Stevenson told his friend the Doctor that there was usually an extremely pressing reason for someone to be in Arbroath, so what was it?[1615]

Jebediah Thurwell died on his farm in 1884, age 71.

(=) The Time Demon with a special interest in Melanie Bush became linked to Muriel Wilberforce, who was born that year.[1616]

1884 - SJA: THE GHOST HOUSE[1617] **->** The genocidal war criminals Skak and Efnol fled from the twenty-first century to a Victorian villa built in 1865, and attempted to produce a time bubble that, when shattered, would help them escape but destroy Earth in the process. Sarah Jane, Luke, Clyde and Rani briefly went back to 1884 and thwarted their plan. An alien bounty hunter – whose name translated in Russian to "Death Kill Massacre" – took the criminals away for trial.

1884 - ERIMEM: THREE FACES OF HELENA[1618] **->** The immortal Helena grew bored with life, and – hoping that Princess Asha would end her existence – commissioned the explorer Allan Quatermain to escort her to the lost city of Kurr in Africa. Erimem, Helena's future self, Andy and Ibrahim arrived to intercede at this crucial juncture of Helena's history, but Asha fatally stabbed Ibrahim. The older Helena sacrificed her immortality, via the medical cabinet that had granted her long life, to heal him. Asha's subjects rebelled against her cruelty, and threw her into a geological fissure to be vaporized. While Erimem's party returned to the future, the younger Helena and Quatermain parted ways in Cape Town.

c 1885 - PEACEMAKER[1619] **->** The tenth Doctor and Martha learned that a smallpox outbreak in the Wild West town of Redwater, Colorado, had been contained by a travelling salesman: Alvin Godlove. They were attacked by gunslingers with energy weapons, but escaped and discovered that Godlove was making a fortune from his miracle cures. The Doctor determined the involvement of the Clades, sentient weapons whose only rationale was to destroy; Godlove's miracle cure was part of the Clades' self-repair system. The Doctor destroyed the Clade before they "sterilised" the Earth.

H.G. Wells

1885 - TIMELASH[1620] **->** Vena, the daughter of a Councillor on Karfel, was transported to Earth in the Timelash and met Herbert George Wells, who was conducting an experiment with a ouija board. Wells travelled to Karfel with the sixth Doctor, and the experience inspired him, upon his return home, to write his scientific romances.

The Doctor helped "Bertie Wells" with invisibility experiments.[1621] He discovered that H.G. Wells was a ladies man.[1622]

The Doctor met the mystic Madame Blavatsky.[1623] **Lady Clemency Eddison met and fell in love with a man named Christopher, actually a Vespiform in human guise, in India in 1885. She became pregnant by Eddison – who died when the Jumna river flooded – and returned to England, secretly giving birth the following year. The child would become the Reverend**

Arnold Golightly.[1624] The Doctor coined the phrase "Beware that when fighting monsters, you yourself do not become a monster", and later kicked himself for giving it away rather than collecting royalties.[1625]

1886 - "The Lost Dimension"[1626] -> Madame Vastra set sail – as captain of the good ship *Mary Anning* – with Jenny Flint for Sumatra, to learn if Sir Robert Napton's recent discovery of a Silurian corpse there heralded a reactivated Silurian colony. The ninth Doctor happened upon Vastra while taking Rose to see his wise Silurian friend Horlak, the Master with Three Eyes. A Myrka protecting Horlak's colony destroyed the *Mary Anning*, killing half of Vastra's crew. As Horlak's Silurians were carriers for the deadly Raldoma Syndrome, Vastra couldn't rejoin her people. The ninth Doctor temporarily left Rose in Vastra's care while he answered the fourth Doctor's summons, and left for 2017.

c 1887 - ZYGONS: THE BARNACLED BABY[1627] -> The Zygon named Demeris, the sole survivor of a wrecked expedition that was searching for Zygon colonies, became part of Jethro's Travelling Freak Show as "the Barnacled Baby". Phineas T. Barnum expressed interest in buying the Baby, or at least arranging for him to be on display in New York. Demeris' notoriety gained him an audience with Queen Victoria – he subdued the queen, adopted her form and went forth to rule the British Empire...

For a time, Madame Vastra performed in a freakshow as the Sensational Scaled Siren. Later, she became a member of respectable Victorian society after saving Her Majesty from a Zygon plot.[1628]

The Doctor Meets Sherlock Holmes

1887 - ALL-CONSUMING FIRE[1629] -> Sherlock Holmes and Dr Watson were travelling through Austria on the Orient Express when the train was stopped by Pope Leo XIII. The Pope commissioned Holmes to investigate the theft of occult books from the Library of St John the

---

1624 *The Unicorn and the Wasp*
1625 *The Twelfth Doctor Year One*: "The Swords of Kali". The phrase originates from Nietzsche in *Beyond Good and Evil* (1886).
1626 Dating "The Lost Dimension" (Titan mini-series #2, #8) – The year is given.
1627 Dating *Zygons: The Barnacled Baby* (BBV audio #30) - The story ends with a shapechanging Zygon replacing Queen Victoria, and nothing is said about what happens next. Victoria definitely isn't killed, as Demeris – as with the TV Zygons at this point – can only assume the body print of a living subject, so it's easy enough to imagine that the substitution is discovered and the real Victoria rescued. For that matter, it's easy to retroactively think that the Victoria seen here is a ringer sent by Torchwood to investigate the mysterious and potentially extra-terrestrial "Baby" – would the actual Queen have been allowed to travel to the baby's bedroom without a single escort? Prince Albert (1819-1861) has died, but Barnum (1810-1891) is alive.
1628 "The Lost Dimension". Spuriously, we might connect the dots and suggest that Vastra settled the unresolved threat to the Crown in *Zygons: The Barnacled Baby*.
1629 Dating *All-Consuming Fire* (NA #27) - It is "the year eighteen eighty seven" according to both Watson (p5) and Benny (p153). References to *The Talons of Weng-Chiang* (p42, p64), including the Doctor's claim that he's currently lodging with Professor Litefoot, suggest this book is set after that story, but aren't conclusive.
SHERLOCK HOLMES: Whereas the Dorian Gray seen in *The Confessions of Dorian Gray* audios is very compatible with *Doctor Who*, Sherlock Holmes offers the challenge that it's not immediately clear if he's an actual character in the *Doctor Who* universe or some flight of

fancy on Arthur Conan Doyle's part. On screen, the only real evidence is Dr Simeon implying (*The Snowmen*) that Madame Vastra inspired the print version of Holmes, and stray references in *Deep Breath* indicate that Vastra dealt with two off-screen Holmes adventures mentioned – but not seen – in Conan Doyle's stories. Accepting that the obvious conclusion from all of this is that Holmes is fictional, the evidence itself isn't so rock-solid as to negate other interpretations.

The tie-in works, however, mostly favour Holmes as an actual person... he appears in the New Adventures *All-Consuming Fire* and *Happy Endings*, Benny shares an escapade with Mycroft Holmes while Sherlock is out of town in *Benny S9: The Adventure of the Diogenes Damsel*. In *Evolution*, Conan Doyle takes note of the fourth Doctor's deerstalker attire and later on – it seems – instructs his illustrators to make use of it for Holmes' look, but that doesn't rule out his encountering the actual Holmes.

Additionally, Big Finish's *Sherlock Holmes* audios entail Roger Llewellyn playing an older Sherlock musing on his past adventures in the first two stories, with Nicholas Briggs playing Holmes after that. Just to bring things full circle, Briggs voices Sherlock in both the audio adaptation of *All-Consuming Fire* and *The Worlds of Big Finish* – a crossover story involving the Graceless, Iris, Dorian Gray, Vienna and Benny. Likewise, David Warner, who played Mycroft in *The Adventure of the Diogenes Damsel*, reprises the role in *The Worlds of Big Finish*. To make everything even more incestuous, Holmes and Dorian Gray meet face to face in that series and reference their previous meeting in *DG: Ghosts of Christmas Past*.

The glaring exception in this is the *Jago & Litefoot* audio *The Monstrous Menagerie*, which is predicated on

Beheaded. With help from the seventh Doctor, Ace and Benny, Holmes discovered that his eldest brother Sherringford had allied himself with the Baron Maupertuis. They planned to use incantations in the books to open a gateway to the planet of Ry'leh. Sherringford was under the thrall of the Great Old One named Azathoth, and hoped this would facilitate her escape to Earth. Maupertuis and Sherringford were both killed, and the Doctor transported Azathoth and her followers to 1906, where they also perished. The Doctor and Holmes sealed the portal to Ry'leh forever.

Arthur Conan Doyle would later write the book *All-Consuming Fire*, but it never saw print.

The Doctor told Ace that he met Sherlock Holmes.[1630] After leaving the Doctor's company in 1871, Ace became lovers with Count Nikolai Sorin, the great grandfather of Captain Sorin. They pretended to be married, but Ace's violent nature frightened the Count, and he left her. Ace continued travelling on her time-hopper, and would attend the wedding of Bernice Summerfield in 2010.[1631]

Henry Gordon Jago met the fortune-teller Gentila Cooper, a.k.a. Gypsy Nancy Lee, on "a balmy night in August", but failed to commission her for the Palace Theatre even after she correctly predicted that a vicious snowstorm would sweep across Sussex. Mary Elizabeth Reilly and her beloved, George William Nevil, froze to death when the snowstorm struck Brighton on 14th August, 1887. A mirror belonging to Lee captured Reilly's spirit. Nevil's shade, failing to realise he was dead, spent years searching for her.[1632]

Jago enjoyed a drunken night out in Soho with his stagehand, Casey.[1633] At one point, Casey lost the whole set of costumes for Madame LeGrand's Luscious Ladies, including the ostrich feathers.[1634]

Ms Matilda Vane, renowned as a showgirl and strumpet at the New Palace Theatre, rejected Henry Gordon Jago's offer to make an honest woman of her. A few weeks later, Jago fired Vane – to protect the theatre's reputation, and also his personal hurt – when another man left her in the family way. She was found dead soon after, floating in the Thames.[1635]

The Guild of Clockmakers dismissed one of its most honoured members, Edward Merridew, after the Queen's Little Jubilee Clock exploded from internal stress at its unveiling, and showered the Royal Family with clock-pieces. Merridew died a broken man, but his daughter Edwina used his designs to transform Moorsey Manor into a death trap, and set about killing the Guild heads who had disgraced her father.[1636]

The inventor Sir Joseph Montague obtained a probe from the future, and incorporated it into the metal mind of his Difference Golem: a robot named Adam. Montague established a factory so that Adam's offspring could eliminate the need for human servants, which he viewed as a form of slavery. The events of Bloody Sunday, 1887, made Montague fear that his robots would be misused for injustice or war, and he deactivated them all.[1637]

the idea that Holmes is purely Conan Doyle's creation – so much so that when Conan Doyle decides on the fly to write *The Hound of the Baskervilles* as a clue to allies in the future, the plan works and time travellers arrive to save everyone's bacon. Also, *Jago & Litefoot* Series 7 entails the lead characters staying in the Doctor's house at 107 Baker Street, which is down the street from the 221B house that Conan Doyle maintains in *The Monstrous Menagerie* as a front to collect fan mail and such. Jago and Litefoot also speculate in *J&L S7: Jago in Love* that *they* are the inspirations behind Holmes, but that's assuredly not the case when *The Monstrous Menagerie* rolls around.

So the TV series leans toward Holmes *not* being real, but the tie-in works largely (but not entirely) keep presenting him as an actual person. The gray area this all creates has enabled some works to have some fun with Holmes' status... *Timewyrm: Revelation* and *The Gallifrey Chronicles* suggest that Holmes straddles some sort of line between fiction and reality; *The Secret Lives of Monsters* "reference book" indicates that Madame Vastra's crew *did* meet Holmes and Watson, in an adventure chronicled in *A Study of Green*, but that Vastra's group confiscated all copies of it; and the City of the Saved-related stories claim that when everyone of human inheritance is resurrected at the end of time, multiple versions of Holmes are present.

For now, *Ahistory* omits Big Finish's Sherlock Holmes audios, partly because Holmes' canonicity is more opaque than some, but also because it dodges the issue – in a guidebook already bursting at the seams – of how much to incorporate the broader Conan Doyle mythology.

1630 *Timewyrm: Revelation*. This was before *All-Consuming Fire*. The eighth Doctor also encountered Holmes, according to *The Gallifrey Chronicles*.

1631 *Happy Endings*, elaborating upon details about Ace given in *The Curse of Fenric* novelisation; see the dating notes on *Set Piece*.

1632 *J&L S4: Jago in Love*

1633 *J&L S9: Island of Death*, and prior to Casey's death in *The Talons of Weng-Chiang*.

1634 *J&L S12: Picture This*

1635 *J&L S7: The Night of 1000 Stars*. Matilda Vane has no known relation to Sibyl Vane (*DG: The Picture of Dorian Gray*).

1636 *J&L S7: Murder at Moorsey Manor*

1637 *SJA: Children of Steel*. Bloody Sunday occurred on 13th November, 1887.

Princess Annajanine, the grandniece of Queen Victoria, died of consumption in 1887.[1638]

In 1888, the Doctor gained a medical degree in Glasgow under Lister.[1639] **The Doctor obtained a doctorate from Glasgow University, but accidentally graduated in the wrong century.**[1640] The Doctor learned about "painless anaethesia" from Lister, and folded that knowledge into his Venusian karate.[1641]

Around that time, the Doctor sparred with John L Sullivan, the first modern world heavyweight champion.[1642] The Doctor discovered the truth behind the mysterious Pale Man in nineteenth-century Whitechapel.[1643]

In the Winter Gardens in Berlin, 1888, Miss Alice Bultitude was in the front row of the stalls as Toby the Sapient Pig's European tour opened. Toby performed with such entertainers as Professor Prometheus, the fireproof Secasian, the "incomparable" Hildebrand and the Blondin Donkey. Bultitude would also attend Toby's farewell concert at the Black Castle, Alhambra, and acquire a first edition copy of his memoirs.[1644]

1888 (12th March) - 1stA: THE GREAT WHITE HURRICANE[1645] **->** The first Doctor, Ian, Barbara and Susan became entangled in hostilities between two gangs, the Mad Boars and the Alley Dogs, as the Great White Hurricane – a massive snowstorm – struck the East Coast of America. The travellers aided whom they could, then made their escape as the storm paralyzed the city, killing hundreds.

The Amnesiac Eighth Doctor Begins 113 Years of Living on Earth

@ The eighth Doctor lived on Earth from 1888 to 2001, without benefit of his memories or his companions...[1646]

@ 1888 - THE ANCESTOR CELL[1647] **->** Compassion brought the eighth Doctor to Earth to recuperate following Gallifrey's destruction. He woke up in a carriage with no memory of what had happened, and found he possessed a tiny cube, all that remained of his TARDIS.

1638 *J&L S7: The Wax Princess*
1639 *The Moonbase.* Surgeon Joseph Lister lived 5th April, 1827, to 10th February, 1912. *Apollo 23* says the Doctor was given an honourary degree in rhetoric and oratory by the University of Ursa Beta. In *The God Complex*, he claims to have a degree in cheese-making.
1640 *Death in Heaven*, smoothing out the anomaly created on this topic in *The Moonbase*.
1641 "The Heralds of Destruction"
1642 *Carnival of Monsters*
1643 *Synthespians™*
1644 *Year of the Pig*
1645 Dating *1stA: The Great White Hurricane* (BF *The First Doctor Adventures* #1.2) - Barbara finds a newspaper with the dateline "12th of March, 1888". Historically, the storm formed on 11th March and dissipated on the 14th. The resultant isolation and cold killed four hundred people, half of those in New York City.
1646 As chronicled in *The Ancestor Cell, The Burning, Casualties of War, The Turing Test, Endgame* (EDA), *Father Time* and *Escape Velocity*.
1647 Dating *The Ancestor Cell* (EDA #36) - It's "more than a hundred years" (p282) before 2001, and "one hundred and thirteen years" before *Escape Velocity* (p184), which would make it 1888.
1648 *Vanishing Point*
1649 *The Burning*
1650 Dating *The Pit* (NA #12) - Blake sees a newspaper dated "the thirtieth of September, 1888". There's some indication this takes place in a parallel timeline, so it's not "the" Jack the Ripper murders.
1651 Dating "Ripper's Curse" (IDW *DW* Vol. 2 #2-4) - The opening caption says it's "30 September 1888. 12:30 a.m.", which matches the real-life murder of Elizabeth

Stride, the Ripper's third canonical victim.
1652 Dating "Ripper's Curse" (IDW *DW* Vol. 2 #2-4) - Amy confirms that it's "9th November", the night of the final Ripper murder. *Matrix* and *A Good Man Goes to War* offer alternate explanations for Jack the Ripper (see the Unfixed Points in Time sidebar). "Ripper's Curse", very oddly, seems to ignore some new-series rules pertaining to historical alteration – the Doctor says that the Ripper's victims are all "static" points in time, but tries to alter the final one anyway (see the Fixed Points in Time sidebar). Moreover, time *is* altered in this story – Mary Warner is "meant" to die, but the timeline is left with Mary Kelly (who died in our history) being killed instead.

It's arguably an anachronism that a member of the Metropolitan police is so well acquainted with both Sherlock Holmes and Conan Doyle's methodology in creating the character – the first Holmes story, *A Study in Scarlet*, was published prior to this in 1887, but the character's popularity didn't take off until the first series of short stories emerged in *The Strand*, starting in 1891. However, the Earl of Upper Leadworth is fictional, suggesting that Holmes' history in the *Doctor Who* universe is a deviation from the real world.

UNFIXED POINTS IN TIME: Reconciling the four accounts of Jack the Ripper in *Matrix*, "Ripper's Curse", *J&L S7: The Wax Princess* and on screen in *A Good Man Goes to War* does tend towards absurdity – the Ripper is respectively shown to be the Valeyard, to be a murderous alien, to be a man engaged to a member of the Royal Family, and to be an unnamed party dispatched by Madame Vastra, in seemingly unrelated adventures.

As a unifying theory about this, though, perhaps there's a class of events that are destined to remain

@ The Doctor was found wandering and was placed on a hospital ward for five days.[1648] He travelled in England for a few years, still having no memories.[1649]

Jack the Ripper

There were multiple explanations as to the identity of Jack the Ripper. His five "canonical" victims – the ones officially recognised as having died as his hand – were murdered 31st August to 9th November, 1888.

1888 (30th September) - THE PIT[1650] **->** The seventh Doctor and William Blake were conveyed by a space-time tear to the East End at the time of the Jack the Ripper murders, then departed to the late twentieth century.

1888 (30th September) - "Ripper's Curse"[1651] **->** The eleventh Doctor, Amy and Rory intended to watch Accrington Stanley play football in London, but instead materialised just after Jack the Ripper – actually a ferocious alien reptile, a Re'nar, using a shimmer suit to disguise itself as human – murdered Long Lizzie Stride. The Doctor's psychic paper established Amy and Rory's credentials as Miss Marple and Inspector Clouseau of CSI London, then named Rory as the Earl of Upper Leadworth, Conan Doyle's inspiration for Sherlock Holmes.

Amy remembered that the Ripper would next murder Catherine Eddowes, who died later that very night. She led the police to the scene... to find that Eddowes had already been murdered. The Doctor, found kneeling over her dead body, was arrested on suspicion of being the Ripper. Inspector Abbeline, the detective investigating the Ripper crimes, quickly released him.

Mary Warner was fated to become the Ripper's final victim, and Amy was horrified to learn that the Doctor planned to let Warner die because each of the Ripper's victims was an unalterable static point in space and time. Amy warned Mary anyway, but she didn't listen. The Doctor discovered that an alien Ju'wes was passing as Sir Charles Warren of Scotland Yard, and had pursued the Re'nar from the future. The Re'nar was committing the murders to discredit the Ju'wes, retroactively undermining them in the Re'nar-Ju'wes war to come. The Doctor was convinced by Amy that they should try to save Warner, and jumped forward five weeks in the TARDIS...

(=) 1888 (9th November) - "Ripper's Curse"[1652] **->** Mary Warner was Jack the Ripper's final victim.

Amy's warning to Mary Warner five weeks previous had altered time – she had survived, but the Ripper instead killed Mary Kelly. The Re'nar-Ripper captured Amy, and the Doctor and Rory took the TARDIS to 2011 to examine the historical alteration. They returned forewarned that the Ripper would kill both Amy and Mary Warner. The Ripper took Amy and Mary to a cellar, but they escaped. The Ju'wes posing as Warner pulled the Re'nar into an unstable space-time tunnel, killing them both.

Possible Death of the Valeyard

1888 (November) - MATRIX[1653] **->** The Valeyard now had control of the Dark Matrix – the embodiment of the dark thoughts of the Time Lord minds within the Matrix – and journeyed with it to Whitechapel, 1888. While the Dark Matrix lodged itself in a tomb, the Valeyard renamed

mysteries. After all, the main historical significance of the Jack the Ripper is that it's famous *as a mystery*. Perhaps what happened remains unknown and open to question *even after we've seen an explanation*. (A whimsical example of this from real life: IDW's publicity materials proclaimed that "Ripper's Curse" would be the "first" time that *Doctor Who* had dealt with Jack the Ripper, a statement the company retracted when it was pointed out that actually, it wasn't.)

This doesn't rule out *all* mysteries being unsolved – the Doctor seems to conclusively solve the mystery of Agatha Christie's real-life disappearance in *The Unicorn and the Wasp*, for example. But it might account for why there are historical mysteries with multiple solutions in the *Doctor Who* universe. Candidates might include the beginning of the universe, the extinction of the dinosaurs, the exact origin of man, how and why the Pyramids were built, the purpose of standing stones, the Fall of Atlantis, what became of the Ninth Legion of the Roman army, the fate of the Roanoke colonists, the Great Fire of London, what happened to the *Mary*

Celeste, what happened at Tunguska, the sinking of the *Titanic* as well as a whole host of Fortean mysteries (the Loch Ness Monster, Yeti, Roswell, flying saucers, etc.). Within the fiction of the *Doctor Who* universe, the exact origins of the Daleks, the start of the Sontaran-Rutan war, the beginnings of the Time Lords and the reason the Doctor left Gallifrey might be "unfixed".

Great care should be taken, however, to distinguish between "unfixed" historical mysteries and simply things where there's one explanation that's not been uncovered. It's also probably best not to use this as a handwave for any continuity problems – like, say, why the manned space program of the UNIT years is more advanced than the one seen in the new series, or the final fate of the planet Earth. But where *Doctor Who* has multiple explanations for the same historical mystery, we might usefully think the reason is that it's "unfixed".

1653 Dating *Matrix* (PDA #16) - It's during the time of the Ripper murders (the later part of 1888); the month is given as "November" (p155, 231). The last of the canonical Jack the Ripper murders took place on 9th

himself "the Ripper" and set about killing prostitutes. The Dark Matrix fed off the psychic potential of these murders.

The seventh Doctor and Ace arrived from an alternate timeline in 1963, and the Doctor was mentally assaulted by the Dark Matrix so much, he downloaded his mind into a telepathic circuit. The amnesiac Doctor became a cardshark named Johnny, and was aided by a man named Joseph Liebermann (possibly the Wandering Jew of legend), even as Ace tried to make ends meet as a maid.

The Doctor's memories were restored, and he confronted the Valeyard. The Dark Matrix imploded, and the Valeyard was struck by lightning and killed.

> = The Valeyard acquired a knife from a man in Whitechapel who produced terrible paintings.[1654]

The Jack the Ripper murders continued beyond the canonically recognised five victims. Following the discovery of a headless torso at Pinchin Street, Inspector Frederick Abberline captured the Ripper: a surgeon formerly engaged to Princess Annajanine. Owing to the Ripper's Royal Family connections, the arrest was kept secret. Publicly, Abberline's "failure" to stop the Ripper ruined his career, and he became the Queen's secret advisor on law and order.[1655]

Madame Vastra and Friends Investigate

The Silurian warrior Madame Vastra had become a formidable crimesolver, known to some as the Veiled Detective. She operated from a house on Paternoster Row, and was aided by her human wife, Jenny Flint.[1656]

1888 (November) - A GOOD MAN GOES TO WAR[1657] -> On the very night that Vastra caught and ate Jack the Ripper, the Doctor sought her and Jenny's help in storming Demons Run and saving Amy.

After the Battle of Demons Run, Vastra and Jenny returned to London, 1888, with the Sontaran named Strax. He agreed to serve as their butler and aided them in thwarting criminals and protecting the Empire.[1658] The digital copy of River Song in the Library sometimes advised Madame Vastra's group.[1659]

In 1889, H.G. Wells felt strangely drawn to the kontron crystal in his possession. It transported him to an alternate version of Britain, 1899.[1660] In 1889, Jago had the singular honour of introducing "the shocking sight of that sinister double-headed duo from Siam".[1661]

Sir Robert Napton claimed credit for finding a fairy mound in the mountains of Narakhstan. Although fairies were in fact real, he was chancing his arm.[1662]

November, 1888, so this is presumably after that.

1654 *Unbound: He Jests at Scars...*, and a nod to *Matrix*.

1655 *J&L* S7: *The Wax Princess*, which attributes three of four deaths listed in the Whitechapel murder files – Rose Mylett (20th December, 1888), Alice McKenzie (17th July, 1889) and the Pinchin Street torso (10th September, 1889) – to the Ripper, but evidently not that of Frances Coles (13th February, 1891).

1656 The background to *A Good Man Goes to War* and the Vastra-centric episodes to follow.

1657 Dating *A Good Man Goes to War* (X6.7) - As with *Matrix*, this is presumably after the last of the Ripper killings.

1658 *The Battle of Demons Run: Two Days Later*, helping to explain the status quo in *The Snowmen*.

1659 Vastra's trio becomes acquainted with River's younger self in *A Good Man Goes to War*, and – it seems – has received help from the Library version of her prior to *The Name of the Doctor*.

1660 *Leth-St: Travers & Wells: Other Wars, Other Worlds*. The Haisman Timeline dates this to August. Kontron crystals appeared, as did Wells, in *Timelash*.

1661 *J&L* S13: *Chapel of Night*

1662 "Three years" after the 1886 portion of "The Lost Dimension".

1663 Dating *SJA: Lost in Time* (SJA 4.5) - The year is given.

1664 Dating "The Time Machination" (IDW *DW* one-shot #2) - A caption says it's "London 1889". Wells claims that he met the Doctor in *Timelash* "four or five years back" (even if this version of Wells is hard to reconcile against the version seen on screen). The story ends with the fourth Doctor and Leela arriving at the beginning of *The Talons of Weng-Chiang*. Lewis and Cooper seem attached to the Torchwood branch operating out of the West India Docks, although they are acquainted with Jack Harkness by "Final Sacrifice".

1665 "Final Sacrifice"

1666 Dating *The Talons of Weng-Chiang* (14.6) - No date is given, and the story is trying to encapsulate an era, rather than a precise year. The story is set soon after the Jack the Ripper murders (1888), as Henry Gordon Jago refers to "Jolly Jack". In the draft script, Casey went on to say that the new batch of disappearances can't be the Ripper because he "is in Canada".

Litefoot is seen reading a copy of *Blackwood's Magazine* from February 1892 in episode four... then again, there's also a modern newspaper visible in Litefoot's laundry in episode three, with a headline that references British politician Denis Healey, so both could be considered set dressing rather than definitive dating evidence. The seventh Doctor claims to briefly lodge with Litefoot in *All-Consuming Fire*, set in 1887 – although given that story's unreliable narrative structure, it's perhaps safe to overlook that one.

Big Finish's *Jago & Litefoot* spin-off series claims, for

1889 - SJA: LOST IN TIME[1663] -> Sarah Jane Smith was transported to the wrong time zone on her mission to find a piece of chronosteel, and met the ghost-hunter Emily Morris. The chronosteel had taken the form of a key, and was causing a temporal overlap with a future time in which two children were under threat from a fire. Sarah and Emily used the chronosteel key to open the children's bedroom door, saving their lives. A mishap caused Sarah to return to 2010 without the key. Emily kept it, went on to become a doctor and founded a hospital for children.

1889 - "The Time Machination"[1664] -> "Jonathan Smith", a time traveller from the mid-fifty-first century, became an acquaintance of H.G. Wells as part of a scheme to kill the fourth Doctor and avert Magnus Greel's demise. The tenth Doctor learned of Smith's plot, and collaborated with Wells to thwart it. Robert Lewis and Eliza Cooper of Torchwood were tricked into thinking that Smith was the Doctor, and imprisoned him. They also learned that the Doctor had the ability to change his appearance. Wells said goodbye to the Doctor and vowed to start writing a story called "The Time Machine".

By this time, Torchwood had hubs in Cardiff, Glasgow and the West India Docks.

Torchwood subsequently dissected Mr Smith.[1665]

Prof. Litefoot and Henry Gordon Jago Meet During the Weng-Chiang Affair

c 1889 - THE TALONS OF WENG-CHIANG[1666] -> The fourth Doctor and Leela arrived in London during a search by the stage magician Li H'sen Chang for the time cabinet of Magnus Greel, a war criminal who had escaped the fifty-first century. Greel lurked in the sewers, reliant on draining the life force of young women to continue surviving. He had brought the Peking Homunculus – a.k.a. Mr Sin, who assisted Chang on stage – with him to act as his agent. Chang died after Greel disavowed him.

With the help of an eminent pathologist, Professor George Litefoot, and the manager of the Palace Theatre, Henry Gordon Jago, the Doctor tracked Magnus Greel to his headquarters – the House of the Dragon – and destroyed him and the Homunculus. The Doctor stomped his foot on the crystal key that opened Greel's cabinet, smashing it to pieces, then bought his friends some muffins from a muffin man.

> = Without the Doctor's help, Luke Betterman and Aubrey started their heroic careers by dealing with Greel and Mr Sin.[1667]

Publicly, it was thought that Chang had "gone potty and died in a pot house".[1668] After leaving Litefoot and Jago's company, the fourth Doctor and Leela answered a distress signal originating from Kent, 1985.[1669]

The Zygma beam powering the time cabinet had an affinity with the human brain, and stored Greel's mind inside the crystal key. The Great Godiva – who had assisted Li H'sen Chang on several occasions – spent two days collecting every last shard of the key from the floor of the House of the Dragon. Godiva's son and grandson spent lifetimes trying to reassemble the key, and it – as well as the time cabinet and Mr Sin – ultimately passed on to Godiva's great-granddaughter, Guinevere Godiva.[1670]

---

the most part, to open in 1892, some "years" after events in *Talons*. *J&L* S5: *The Final Test*, set in 1968, says it's been "eighty years" since Jago and Litefoot rode the dumb-waiter in the House of the Dragon in *Talons*, and the Time Agent Cara indicates that Greel arrived in London by boat in "1889" in *J&L* S13: *The Stuff of Nightmares*. Against the grain of that, however, *Destination: Nerva* says that *Talons* occurred "three years" before 1895, and *The Final Act* has Guinevere Godiva claim that Li H'sen Chang's final performance at the Palace Theatre (in *Talons*) was in 1892. Knowing where *The Talons of Weng-Chiang* happens, therefore, becomes an uneasy contest of weighing those two statements against the cumulative evidence given in *J&L* Series 1 and 2 (see the dating notes on that series). *The Ghosts of Gralstead* overshoots all of this a bit, with the fourth Doctor telling Leela that 1860 is "nearly 40 years" too early for them to visit Jago and Litefoot.

In *J&L* S11: *Maurice*, Jago picks up a bottle of wine and says, "1891. Good year, that. It was before [astonish-

ing] things like this kept happening to us", presumably in reference to *The Talons of Weng-Chiang*. Similarly, the Master in *J&L* S11: *Masterpiece* [1895] admits to having "overshot by a few years" while trailing the Doctor to the Victorian Era, and the Doctor concedes that his TARDIS has visited the period lots "after the last few years" – both statements presumably denoting *Talons*.

The first edition of *Timelink* stated that *Talons* took place in 1895; the Telos version of the book goes for February 1892. *About Time* roughly concurred with the latter. *The Terrestrial Index* went for "c1890". *Whoniverse* (BBC, p71) places *Talons* before discussion of Vincent van Gogh, the latter dated to 1890. *A History of the Universe in 100 Objects* (p71) broadly places its Peking Homunculus entry at "circa 1890". According to Sarah Jane in that book, Professor Litefoot was – for a time – suspected of being Jack the Ripper (p88).

1667 *J&L* S13: *How the Other Half Lives*
1668 *J&L* S13: *The Stuff of Nightmares*
1669 *Destination: Nerva*

The Eighteen-Nineties

An expedition led by Captain Fowler hit upon a means of traveling, via a gateway, to another world. The natives there warmly greeted Fowler's crew, but the visitors stole a precious artefact from a temple. A demon tasked with protecting the artefact followed the visitors to Earth and progressively murdered them. Three of the survivors – Fowler, Mallory Riverstock and Aubrey – spent years failing to recreate the portal and return the item.[1671]

The Prime Cluster ruling the Takala Empire – an extra-dimensional race of energy beings – fell victim to one of their number committing murder. The rogue element fled, and was attracted to Earth when the Sioux Indian named Silver Crow performed the Ghost Dance when he was 18. Silver Crow fell into a trance, and awoke to find a large red crystal, later called the Moonflesh, in his hand. The rogue element remained dormant within for more than twenty years.[1672]

Human sacrifice was still taking place in Moreton Harwood in the early 1890s.[1673] The Doctor met the French novelist Emile Zola.[1674] **Jack Harkness had a boyfriend in the 1890s – a Slovenian who took arsenic to improve his skin.**[1675] A female ancestor of Jo Laws discovered the ArkHive amulet in a dinosaur fossil. In 1890, Sir Iain Laws gave the item to his daughter Josephine. Henceforth, each new generation of Laws women received the amulet when they turned 16.[1676]

Vincent van Gogh

Van Gogh painted the Doctor.[1677] The Monk owned two paintings by van Gogh.[1678]

1890 (early June) - VINCENT AND THE DOCTOR[1679] **->** The eleventh Doctor and Amy visited Auvers to investigate the mystery creature painted into Vincent van Gogh's *The Church at Avers*. They found Vincent at a cafe, but were attacked by a creature invisible to everyone but the painter. Vincent painted *The Church at Avers*, which showed the creature behind one of the church windows. The Doctor identified it as a Krafayis, a predatory creature abandoned on Earth. The Krafayis was blind and died, impaled on Vincent's painting stand. The Doctor and Amy briefly took Vincent to a museum in Amy's time; after Vincent returned home, he signed one of his works, *Still Work: Vase with Twelve Sunflowers*, "For Amy, Vincent."

1890 (26th June) - THE POWER OF THREE[1680] **->** The eleventh Doctor arranged for Amy and Rory to celebrate their wedding anniversary at the recently opened Savoy Hotel – an event somewhat spoiled upon the discovery that half the hotel staff were Zygons. The Doctor and his friends dealt with the situation, but were afterward left out in the snow.

1670 *J&L S5: The Final Act*
1671 "Several years" before *J&L S9: Return of the Nightmare.*
1672 "Over twenty summers" before *Moonflesh.*
1673 "Ninety years" before *K9 and Company.*
1674 *Ghost Ship.* Zola lived 1840-1902.
1675 *TW: Miracle Day*
1676 *The Wheel of Ice* (p87). Mention is made (p89) of the "famous Li H'sen Chang" from *The Talons of Weng-Chiang*, but it's not necessarily after that story.
1677 According to the sixth Doctor in "Changes". *Vincent and the Doctor* doesn't rule out that van Gogh and the Doctor (in another body) have met before; in fact, that story has van Gogh claim, "My brother's always sending doctors..."
1678 *The Resurrection of Mars*
1679 Dating *Vincent and the Doctor* (X5.10) - The story entails Vincent painting *The Church at Auvers*, which Dr Black says was completed "somewhere between the 1st and 3rd of June 1890, less than a year before [van Gogh] killed himself". Vincent died on 29th July, so while Black is technically right, it was more accurately about two months beforehand.
　　The story has a few anachronisms... Vincent has both ears, but in real life, he'd cut one off in December 1888. *The Church at Avers* was painted in 1890, but Vincent's

series of sunflower paintings (the creation of which Amy here influences) were done August 1888 to January 1889. The episode opens with Vincent painting *Wheatfield with Crows*, which was actually completed some weeks *after* this story, around 10th July. (Then again, the opening might be more thematic than literal.) It's perhaps excusable that Vincent appears to have signed "For Amy" in English, assuming the TARDIS is translating it; in real life, the work just bears Vincent's signature.
1680 Dating *The Power of Three* (X7.4) - The Doctor gives the exact date. The Savoy opened on 6th August, 1889.
1681 Dating *The Pandorica Opens* (X5.12) - The year appears in a caption. *Doctor Who: The Encyclopedia* says this happened "a few weeks" after *Vincent and the Doctor*, so it's very close to van Gogh's death.
1682 Dating *The Story of Martha*: "The Frozen Wastes" (NSA #28d) - The year and month are given.
1683 *Vincent and the Doctor.* This happened on 29th July, 1890.
1683 *The Vampires of Venice*
1684 *TW:* "Fated to Pretend"
1685 The prologue to *FP: Erasing Sherlock*, as published in *FP: Warring States.*
1687 *The Eleventh Tiger*

1890 (June) - THE PANDORICA OPENS[1681] **->** Vincent van Gogh was sensitive to the signals being broadcast by the Underhenge, and experienced mental anguish. One of his last paintings, *The Pandorica Opens*, depicted the destruction of the TARDIS.

> **(=) 1890 (July) - THE STORY OF MARTHA: "The Frozen Wastes"**[1682] **->** The tenth Doctor and Martha attended a presentation by the explorer Pierre Bruyere to the London Geographical Congress – an event that puzzled the Doctor, as history claimed that Bruyere's expedition had vanished three months previous, in April 1890. The Doctor and Martha accompanied Bruyere on a balloon trip to the North Pole, and were caught in a time loop – an unidentified entity was forcing Bruyere to make his journey again and again, so it could harvest his memories. The creature tried to feed upon the Doctor and Martha, but their memories were so voluminous, it burst...

Pierre Bruyere happily settled into a life of being a baker, as his parents had been before him.

Vincent van Gogh killed himself.[1683]

The eleventh Doctor suggested that the Moulin Rouge in 1890 would be a suitable romantic destination for Rory and Amy.[1684] Jack Harkness met a man named Alec at the Moulin Rouge, 1890, and fought with the painter Toulouse Lautrec over him. An extra-terrestrial con man, Monsieur Jechiel, was on commission to recruit an army of the undead to fight the Togomil Heresy, and transformed Alec into such a soldier. Jechiel subsequently left – partly because Jack told him to get lost, partly because he'd not been paid.[1685]

wih - In October 1890, the pair of boots that Sherlock Holmes lost during his time with Gillian Petra was returned to him.[1686] By 1890, a retired William Chesterton had translated Ho Lin Chung's *Mountains and Sunsets* into English.[1687]

1890 (19th-20th October) - FP: HEAD OF STATE[1688] **->** Sir Richard Burton finished translating *The Thousand*

and Second Night on 19th October, 1890. The next day, he left a dead clone of himself to be found and immigrated to the Eleven-Day Empire, where he was known as Faction Paradox's Father Abdullah. Burton's wife Isabel deemed many of his works sinful and burned them, but Burton secretly recovered his writings with a Faction memecatcher. He refrained from reconstructing *The Thousand and Second Night*, believing it was nothing more than anti-Faction propaganda. *An Account of Some Travels in the Arabian Desert* recorded, for benefit of the Faction archives, some of Burton's history.

c 1890 (December) - THE DEVIL IN THE SMOKE[1689] **->** A menacing smoke-creature fell from space, and established itself in the foundry of the industrialist Able Hecklington. Madame Vastra, Jenny and Strax realised that snow could absorb the smoke monster, and snuffed it out during a confrontation at the Crystal Palace.

1891

Molly O'Sullivan, a companion of the eighth Doctor, was born in Ireland, 1891, to Patrick and Cathy Sullivan. She grew up with four brothers, but had two brothers and three sisters who didn't live past their fifth birthdays.[1690] **The governess of Captain Latimer's children drowned in a pond in the front of Latimer's house. The pond froze over, and her body was found a month later.**[1691]

1892

Ace was on the Red List of the Shadow Directory by 1892.[1692] An advanced society on Duchamp 331 had built the Warp Core, an energy being, to combat the Krill. The Warp Core killed off the Krill and its creators also, reducing Duchamp 331 to a dust planet. The creature wandered through space and time before seeking refuge in the mind of the Norwegian artist Edvard Munch. He painted *The Scream*, which exorcised the Warp Core from his mind into the painting.[1693]

Following his battle with Moriarty at Reichenbach Falls,

1688 Dating *FP: Head of State* (FP novel #9) - The days are given (ch42), and coincide with Burton's real-life death on 20th October, 1890.

1689 Dating *The Devil in the Smoke* (BBC Series 7 ebook #2) - No year given, but it's after Strax joins Vastra and Jenny in 1888 (following *The Battle of Demons Run: Two Days Later*). The month is specified as "December", it's prior to "Christmas" and "November the fifth" was "weeks ago" (ch1). Mention is made of Sherlock Holmes (ch2), so it's after his debut in 1887. It's a bit of a misnomer to call this a "prequel" to *The Snowmen*, as the two share no ties other than Vastra, Jenny and Strax being

involved in a curious and devilish affair at Christmastime. There's not even a mandate that it happen prior to *The Snowmen*, although that was probably the intention, and there's a convenient four-year gap between Strax joining and *The Snowmen* for *The Devil in the Smoke* to take place.

1690 *DEyes: Tangled Web/X and the Daleks*.

1691 "A year" before *The Snowmen*.

1692 *The Death of Art*

1693 *Dust Breeding*. There are actually four different versions (and a lithograph) of *The Scream*, all created by Munch between 1893 and 1910.

Sherlock Holmes went into hiding.[1694] **In 1892, Captain Jack got into a fight on Ellis Island. He was shot through the heart and lived – and thereby came to realise that events in 200,100 had rendered him immortal.**[1695]

1892 - TIMEH: THE SEVERED MAN[1696] **->** The Cabal of the Horned Beast formed as a middling demon-worshipping cult, an excuse to engage in debauchery. The group obtained a book that could control time and summon representatives of the Daemons. Although the book was eventually stolen, the Cabal's surviving members reclaimed it in the twenty-sixth century and used it to retroactively give their forefathers more wealth and influence, leading in future to the creation of Sodality.

1892 - 1001 NIGHTS: "The Interplanetarian"[1697] **->** The Lingua-Technicians of the Melian Cube, located near the Styxheimer Cluster, created a weaponised form of

"mind virus" against an unknown foe. One such virus arrived on Earth, becoming responsible for a ghost story or two. The virus infected Nyssa, and so the fifth Doctor left her with Elizabeth Spinnaker, the daughter of one of his associates, while he went to the Melian Cube for a cure. In gratitude for the Doctor aiding them against the Covetous Shoal of Majestrix Prime, the Melians gave him tea coded with a liquid firewall that destroyed the virus.

Jago & Litefoot Series 1-4[1698]

Professor Litefoot and Henry Gordon Jago continued to team up after the Weng-Chiang affair, investigating infernal incidents and cracking complex conundrums. They resolved a mystery with a trained anteater and an aluminium violin, then didn't see each other for a time. Litefoot had a laboratory in the basement of St Thomas' Hospital, which the trustees made available to the police. Jago was forced to close the Palace Theatre, and became the master

---

1694 *Benny S9: The Adventure of the Diogenes Damsel*, following the continuity established in Conan Doyle's stories. "The Final Problem", where Sherlock seemed to perish, was set in 1891. Series 4 of Big Finish's *Sherlock Holmes* audios examine what Sherlock got up to in his post-Reichenbach years, when he was thought dead.

1695 *Utopia*

1696 Dating *TimeH: The Severed Man* (*TimeH* #5) - The year is repeatedly given. The Cabal's links to Sodality are explained in *TimeH: Child of Time* (p64).

1697 Dating *1001 Nights*: "The Interplanetarian" (BF #168c) - The year is given.

1698 Dating *The Mahogany Murderers* (BF CC #3.11) and *Jago & Litefoot* Series 1, 2, 3 and 4 (*The Bloodless Soldier*, 1.1; *The Bellova Devil*, 1.2; *The Spirit Trap*, 1.3; *The Similarity Engine*, 1.4; *Litefoot and Sanders*, 2.1; *The Necropolis Express*, 2.2; *The Theatre of Dreams*, 2.3; *The Ruthven Inheritance*, 2.4; *Dead Men's Tales*, 3.1; *The Man at the End of the Garden*, 3.2; *Swan Song*, 3.3; *Chronoclasm*, 3.4; *Jago in Love*, 4.1; *Beautiful Things*, 4.2; *The Lonely Clock*, 4.3; *The Hourglass Killers*, 4.4) - The production notes for *Jago & Litefoot* Series 1 say, "The year is 1892. It is a short while after *The Talons of Weng-Chiang*, in which Litefoot reads the February 1892 edition of *Blackwood's Magazine*. But unless we absolutely have to, we won't mention specific dates. The stories exist in the limbo of the classic late Victorian era. Queen Victoria is on the throne, the British Empire seems to control most of the world, and science is the answer to all problems. London is a perpetual murk of... fogs and industrial pollution, and you can always charter a special railway train to get you wherever you need to go."

Despite this intended ambiguity, however, Series 1 both indicates that the year is 1892 (the revolution that occurred in Eastern Rumelia in 1885 happened "seven years ago", *J&L* S1: *The Bellova Devil*) and that a fair

amount of time – years, most likely – has passed since *Talons*. Jago says in *J&L* S1: *The Similarity Engine* that the "demonic deflagration" that closed the Palace Theatre happened "a few years back"; Litefoot calls Jago one of "his oldest friends" in *J&L* S1: *The Spirit Trap*; Litefoot says in *J&L* S2: *Litefoot and Saunders* that the events which brought him and Jago together happened "some time ago"; and even *The Mahogany Murders* has Jago stating that the "adventure in Limehouse", presumably meaning *Talons*, was "a while back". He and Litefoot appear to have working together off and on since then; Litefoot tells Quick in *The Similarity Engine* that his experience of supernatural matters includes "a handful" of cases.

Contrary to all of that, statements made in *Destination: Nerva* and *J&L* S5: *The Final Test* claim that *Talons* itself happened in 1892 (see the dating notes on *Talons* for more), which would mean that Series 1 opens after Litefoot and Jago have known each other for just a few months rather than some years.

Either way, *Jago & Litefoot* Series 4 serves as a lynchpin for dating purposes – Jago and Litefoot leave in the TARDIS at the end of it, and Series 5 (in which they are stranded in 1968) repeatedly and clearly states that they did so in 1893. They return to that very year in Greel's time cabinet, after the resurrected Greel has specifically programmed it to do so (*The Final Test*).

With Series 4 resolutely ending in 1893, it's possible to backtrack and establish a framework for the first four *Jago and Litefoot* series. Series 1 opens in 1892 and progresses over some months, with Series 2 happening in the same year – Jago claims it's "the middle of summer" in *J&L* S1: *The Similarity Engine*, but it's gone to having "frosty air" and Litefoot wishing he were in front of a warm fireplace in *J&L* S2: *The Necropolis Express*. At least "a month" seems to pass during *J&L* S2: *The Theatre of Dreams*, and another goes by in *The Ruthven*

of ceremonies at the Alhambra Theatre in Putney.

Dr Heinrich Tulp, having studied astral projection in Tibet, projected his mind into the future and witnessed technological developments to come. This also, however, brought his mind into contact with a formless entity in the dark recesses of space. It compelled Tulp to undertake many experiments with his future knowledge, searching for a means of making Earth akin to its homeworld, a radioactive wasteland. To finance his experiments, Tulp embarked upon many criminal endeavours.[1699]

Jago and Litefoot were often assisted in their escapades by Sgt Quick and Ellie Higson – a barmaid at their favourite watering hole, the Red Tavern.[1700] Carruthers Summerton secretly became a devotee of Jago and Litefoot, and was determined to chronicle and further their adventures. Dr Tulp gave Summerton one of his first interviews.[1701]

c 1892 (summer) - THE MAHOGANY MURDERERS
-> Jago and Litefoot discovered that Dr Tulp had engineered a device that could transfer a person's spirit into inanimate objects. He had done so with several convicts at Newgate, creating a gang of men made from wood. The leader of this bunch, Jack "the Knife" Yeovil, proposed that they shift their spirits into bodies made from more impervious materials, then rally an army of convicts to take over the Empire, then the world. Litefoot disconnected Tulp's machinery, making the convicts' spirits return to their discarded, buried bodies.

c 1892 (summer) - J&L S1: THE BLOODLESS SOLDIER / THE BELLOVA DEVIL / THE SPIRIT TRAP / THE SIMILARITY ENGINE / J&L S2: LITEFOOT AND SAUNDERS ->
Jago and Litefoot intervened in mysterious happenings that included a British army captain who was infected with lycanthropy. Ellie Higson's brother, Private Jim Higson, also acquired the werewolf taint – when Litefoot balked at euthenising Jim, Jago saved lives by doing so.

Jago and Litefoot also brought down the Far-Out Travellers Club, a con run by Dr Tulp to swindle patrons out of their estates. On yet another case, Jago and Litefoot stopped beings from the forty-ninth century from projecting their minds into people via seances, part of a plan to take control of the British Empire. They finally stopped Dr Tulp from cornering the world's supply of uranium, and

---

Inheritance. If it isn't already autumn when *The Theatre of Dreams* begins, it almost inescapably is when Series 2 finishes. The diary of Dr Ormond Sacker (*J&L S5: The Age of Revolution*) dates his escapades with Jago and Litefoot in Series 2 to 1892, and given that Sacker dies at the end of that series, it's reasonably clean to imagine that the calendar year changes between Series 2 and 3.

The dating clues in Series 3 all point to the year being 1893... Jago states in *J&L S3: The Man at the End of the Garden* that "It's August" – as Series 2 concluded so late in the year, it must now be the *following* August, i.e. August 1893. Also, *J&L S3: Chronoclasm* has Jago referring to the panto performance held at the New Regency in Christmas – he only inherited the theatre in Series 2, so, again, it must now be the following year. (However, mention is made in *J&L S3: Swan Song* that Jago has only been at the New Regency "a few months", when, if it really *is* 1893, it's been more like a year.) Litefoot tells Sgt Quick in the Series 3 finale (*J&L S3: Chronoclasm*) that, "You and I, and Jago and Miss Leela, we've come across some of the most vile and appalling things over the past year or so...", which can only be true if Series 3 begins earlier in 1893 than later. This would mean that Leela literally spends about a year dashing around resolving time breaks with Litefoot and Jago, but there's nothing to especially rule that out. In *Chronoclasm*, Payne is suitably vague when he tells the time-displaced Nikolas Tesla that it's "1890, give or take a few years."

Series 4 – which irrefutably ends in 1893 – begins immediately after Jago and Litefoot meet "Professor Claudius Dark" at the end of Series 3. The decision to holiday in Brighton (*J&L S4: Jago in Love*) commences no more than "three days" afterward, the holiday itself seems to only last a few days (a fever afflicts Litefoot for "two days"), repairs to Litefoot's house (following *Chronoclasm*) are still incomplete upon everyone's return, and the final three installments (*J&L S4: Beautiful Things*, *J&L S4: The Lonely Clock*, and *J&L S4: The Hourglass Killers*) all feed into one another. All told, Series 4 seems to take place over days, weeks at most.

In *Beautiful Things*, Litefoot and company attend Oscar Wilde's "new" play *A Woman of No Importance*, which premiered 19th April, 1893 (although "new" in this instance might be interpreted to mean "some months old", to avoid a conflict with *The Man at the End of the Garden* taking place in August of the same year). *Beautiful Things* also references George Bernard Shaw's play *Widowers' Houses* (which debuted 9th December, 1892), *The Picture of Dorian Gray* (printed in the July 1890 issue of *Lippincott's Monthly Magazine*) and Wilde's acquaintance with Lord Alfred Douglas (the two of them met in mid-1891). A glitch is that Litefoot seems to quote Lord Alfred Douglas'"Two Loves", which wasn't published until 1894.

1699 The background to *Jago & Litefoot* Series 1, largely given in *The Mahogany Murderers* and *J&L S1: The Similarity Engine*.

1700 Sgt Quick appeared, briefly, in *The Talons of Weng-Chiang*. Ellie, played by Lisa Bowerman (Bernice Summerfield), is original to the *Jago & Litefoot* audios.

1701 *J&L S10: The Museum of Curiosities*

embarking upon a scheme to replace prominent government officials and businessmen with his wooden simulacra. The entity influencing Tulp turned him into a tentacled monster, which Jago and Litefoot dispatched.

The day after defeating Tulp, Jago and Litefoot challenged – and badly burned – Gabriel Saunders, a purported vampire expert who was himself a master vampire.

> = In their reality, Betterman and Aubrey sorted out Dr Tulp.[1702]

Ellie Higson Becomes a Vampire

1892 (autumn) - J&L S2: THE NECROPOLIS EXPRESS / THE THEATRE OF DREAMS / THE RUTHVEN INHERITANCE -> Jago inherited the New Regency Theatre. His continuing adventures with Litefoot entailed their defeating Dr Sibelius Crow, a mad scientist who wanted to turn corpses into bestial creatures to serve as soldiers for the Empire; besting the Theatre de Fantasie,

a living story that fed off the dreams and fantasies of mortals; and killing the fiend Gabriel Saunders – but not before Saunders had fed off and killed Ellie Higson. She awoke as a vampire, but Litefoot's treatments calmed the condition, and let her live a relatively normal life.

The Sibelius Crow affair made Litefoot the UK's leading expert on the undead. Carruthers Summerton had helped Gabriel Saunders to learn that Jago and Litefoot were investigating him.[1703]

The Great Intelligence, Walter Simeon and Clara Oswin Oswald

> (=) A future version of the Great Intelligence murdered the Doctor in Victorian London.

Clara Oswin Oswald, a version of Clara Oswald, was present in this period because her personal history had overwritten the Intelligence, saving the Doctor.[1704]

1702 *J&L S13: Too Much Reality*

1703 *J&L S10: The Museum of Curiosities*

1704 *The Name of the Doctor, The Snowmen.*

1705 Dating *The Great Detective /Vastra Investigates: A Christmas Prequel* (Series 7 webcasts) - These two minisodes lead into *The Snowmen*. Jenny says, "Well, it is nearly Christmas" in *Vastra Investigates*, and wishes the Doctor "Merry Christmas" in *The Great Detective*.

1706 Dating *The Snowmen* (X7.6) - A caption states that it's "50 years" after "1842". Clara's tombstone establishes that she died on "December 24, 1892", and the main story begins and ends a day on either side of that (with the epilogue taking place after Clara's funeral).

1707 *The Snowmen*, rationalizing the Intelligence's attacks to come in *The Abominable Snowmen* and *The Web of Fear*.

THE GREAT INTELLIGENCE: *The Snowmen*, while a bit vague on the details, presents itself as something of an origin story of the Great Intelligence – a recurring villain first seen in *The Abominable Snowmen* (5.2) and then *The Web of Fear* (5.5). In *The Abominable Snowmen*, the Intelligence is described as being "formless in space", drawn to Earth when the high lama Padmasambhava's mind goes wandering on the astral plane. In *The Snowmen*, the eleventh Doctor more clinically calls the Intelligence a "multi-nucleate crystalline organism with the ability to mimic and mirror what it finds". He also deduces that its modus operandi is to "turn up on a planet... generate a telepathic field" to assess the local conditions, then adapt/evolve accordingly to perpetrate conquest.

In other words, it's a mere shadow of the cosmic force that's seen in *The Abominable Snowmen* and *The Web of Fear*, with events in *The Snowmen* seemingly goosing the not-so-self-actualised Intelligence to think

that invasion by Yeti and an assault on the London Underground circa 1967 (prominent elements in the *The Abominable Snowmen* and *The Web of Fear*) are a sensible way of going about things. The main snag with this is that (according to both *The Abominable Snowmen* and the Haisman Timeline) the Intelligence has been active on Earth a lot longer than the Victorian era, as Padmasambhava met the Doctor during his first visit to Det-Sen monastery in 1730 and is still alive in 1935, with the Intelligence having extended his lifespan. It's possible that the Intelligence only directs Padmasambhava to start building his robot Yeti after its encounter with the eleventh Doctor in 1892, although the abbot Songsten concludes in *The Abominable Snowmen* that "[Padmasambhava] laboured for nearly two hundred years. With the help of the Intelligence, he built the [Yeti] and the other wonderful machines." Either way, the Intelligence is demonstratively established on Earth some centuries prior to *The Snowmen*.

The novel range, notably *All-Consuming Fire* and *Millennial Rites*, names the Intelligence as belonging to the Great Old Ones: a group of monsters from the universe before our own. The easiest way to reconcile all of this, then, is just to presume that the Intelligence is at a diminished state when it inveigles itself to Padmasambhava circa 1730 and Simeon in 1842, that it's flying by the seat of its pants in *The Snowmen*, that it gradually regains its footing and becomes the cosmic menace seen in *The Abominable Snowmen*, *The Web of Fear*, *Downtime* and *Millennial Rites*, and that it's potent and time-active enough to endanger the Doctor's entire life history by *The Bells of Saint John* and *The Name of the Doctor*.

However, the *Lethbridge-Stewart* novels go a differ-

1892 (December) - THE GREAT DETECTIVE / VASTRA INVESTIGATES: A CHRISTMAS PREQUEL[1705] -> The eleventh Doctor visited his friends Madame Vastra, Jenny and Strax, but had no appetite for adventure given that Amy and Rory were forever lost to him. Vastra's trio could find nothing to spark the Doctor's excitement – not even with the case of Professor Erasmus Pink, who vowed to tear Earth open with a giant drill, but was probably just a singing drunk. Strax advocated declaring war on the moon; with nobody was living there, it was the perfect time for a sneak attack.

As the Doctor rebuffed his friends' suggestions, Vastra's trio assisted Scotland Yard in solving crimes.

1892 (23rd to 25th December) - THE SNOWMEN[1706] -> Madame Vastra, Jenny and Strax looked into the mysterious affairs of the Great Intelligence Institute. Its head, Dr Walter Simeon, believed that Vastra was the inspiration behind Conan Doyle's Sherlock Holmes stories. An ice copy of Captain Latimer's dead governess was gestating within a pond; using this as a template, the Great Intelligence intended to craft an army of ice people and plunge Earth into an eternal winter.

An iteration of Clara Oswald – Clara Oswin Oswald, jointly working as a barmaid at the Rose & Crown and a governess to Latimer's children – met the eleventh Doctor as he looked into the strange case of snow that could mirror human thought and transform into monstrous snowmen. The rampaging Ice Governess broke free of the pond and made Clara fall from a great height, gravely injuring her. The Doctor became convinced, wrongly, that the Intelligence had no true consciousness and erased Simeon's memories with a Memory Worm. This enabled the Intelligence to occupy Simeon's body as an army of fiendish snowmen formed. Clara's tears caused the critical mass of thought-mirroring snow to make it rain, which melted the snowmen. Simeon's body died, and Clara died shortly after.

The Doctor realised that Clara was an exact double of the "Oswin Oswald" he'd met at the Dalek Asylum, and left to investigate her history.

The Intelligence survived and, acting on instinct from the knowledge gained in this encounter, in future thought it a good idea to invade the world with snowmen. Based upon a map on the Doctor's lunchbox, the Intelligence suspected that the London Underground in 1967 was a strategic weakness.[1707]

---

ent route – one that entails the Intelligence looping back on its own lifetime at least twice.

The *Lethbridge-Stewart* books depict the Intelligence as the result of a mind that experiences multiple reincarnations (including the Brigadier's brother Gordon and Owain Vine) before culminating in Jiva Mukta, a.k.a. Mahasmatman, on the planet Sathanasi circa 11,926 (the Haisman Timeline). Mahasmatman's botched attempt at astral travel transforms his mind into the Intelligence, a being (Sunyata) that exists in the void between realities, and whose tendrils extend into different dimensions. Thus, the *Lethbridge-Stewart* short story "Legacies" tries to reconcile any discrepancies in the Intelligence's history by fronting the idea that *Downtime*, *Millennial Rites* and *The Roof of the World* (not actually a Great Intelligence story) occur in different continuities. The idea assumes, however, that the *Doctor Who* TV, books and independent videos ranges exist in separate continuities, which creates far more more problems than it solves.

Nonetheless, the progression of the Intelligence's life-cycle, as detailed in the Haisman Estate's "The Great Intelligence Official Background" document, is...

• **Time Track A (TV/Big Finish continuity):** The Intelligence is "born" on Satahanasi circa 11,926, but loops back in time and meets Padmasambhava – the first to name it "the Great Intelligence" – circa 1730. Its various efforts to fully manifest, or otherwise conquer Earth with robotic yeti, go down in defeat in *The Abominable Snowmen* [1935], *The Web of Fear* [UNIT Era]

and *New CM S2: Time of the Intelligence* [1974]. From there, the Official Background document says the Intelligence "eventually found its freedom, in a story as yet untold", but then, while "the details remain unknown", the Intelligence loops back in time *again*, and...

• **Time Track B (TV/Big Finish continuity):** ... encounters Dr Simeon and brings about *The Snowmen*. Outwardly Simeon, the Intelligence dogs the eleventh Doctor in *The Bells of Saint John* and *The Name of the Doctor*, rips itself to pieces while trying to punch holes in the Doctor's timeline (an assault undone by Clara Oswald), and in defeat tumbles back in time yet a third time...

• **Time Track C (TV/Lethbridge-Stewart books continuity):** ... to interrupt its own history by causing Gordon Lethbridge-Stewart to die some years too early, bringing about the *Lethbridge-Stewart* books timeline. (This means, by the way, that *The Snowmen* didn't happen in the *Lethbridge-Stewart* continuity.) Colonel/Brigadier Alistair Lethbridge-Stewart and his allies deal with the Intelligence in *Leth-St: The Forgotten Son* and *Leth-St: Night of the Intelligence* [both UNIT Era]. Eventually, the Official Background document says, Ally Landlaw – a second cousin of the Brigadier's grandson Conall – was born in 2017 as a reincarnation of the Intelligence freed of its corruptive aspects.

In *all* realities, the Intelligence always winds up at the Det-Sen Monastery in 1935 (*The Abominable Snowmen*). For much, much more on this, see the Haisman Timeline sidebar.

1893

Jago's old school chum Toby Brooksmith had failed as a journalist, so took a modest job at Jago's theatre to get himself off Queer Street.[1708]

1893 - THE CRIMSON HORROR[1709] -> A red leech of the variety that vexed the Silurians survived from prehistoric times, and formed a symbiotic relationship with the prize-winning chemist and engineer Mrs Winifred Gillyflower. She named the leech Mr Sweet, and with it founded the Sweetville community in Yorkshire as a haven from society's moral decay. Gillyflower plotted to launch a rocket that would contaminate Earth's atmosphere with Mr Sweet's toxin, enabling the "worthy" people she'd sealed away within Sweetville to inherit the planet. Experiments on human subjects with Mr Sweet's poison resulted in rejects that were dumped in the river, their red-skinned corpses giving rise to talk in the newspapers of "the Crimson Horror".

Madame Vastra, Jenny and Strax assisted the eleventh Doctor and Clara against Gillyflower, and spirited Sweet's toxin away before take-off, causing the rocket to harmlessly explode in the sky. Gillyflower fell to her death, and her victimized daughter Ada squashed Mr Sweet.

1893 - CLARENCE AND THE WHISPERMEN / THE NAME OF THE DOCTOR[1710] -> Using Dr Simeon's guise as an avatar, the Great Intelligence returned to this era after attaining a level of power that put the whole of time and space at its disposal. The Intelligence sent its Whisper Men to embed the coordinates for the Doctor's gravesite into the mind of Clarence DeMarco, a Polish serial killer convicted of murdering fourteen women. DeMarco's knowledge gained the attention of Vastra, Jenny and Strax, who all entered into a trance to mentally commune across the ages with Clara Oswald and River Song. The Whisper Men incapacitated Vastra's group and took them to the planet Trenzalore in the future...

c 1893 - "The Crystal Throne"[1711] -> Lady Cornelia Basildon-Stone, having discovered a Silurian gene-splicer in a hibernation chamber in South Africa, financed a Brazilian rainforest exhibition at Crystal Palace. The gene-splicer transformed Basildon-Stone into a wasp-hybrid, but Madame Vastra, Jenny and Strax ended her scheme to lay eggs in the rainforest, which would hatch to create a new British Empire. Suddenly deprived of her biological upgrade, Basildon-Stone fell to her death.

Prior to this, Vastra and her friends had dealt with the affair of the Hounslow Dragon.

c 1893 - WORLDS DW: MIND GAMES[1712] -> Rees found that he had developed the ability to control minds,

---

1708 "A handful of years" before *J&L* S13: *Chapel of Night.* "Queer Street" refers to someone in financial difficulty.

1709 Dating *The Crimson Horror* (X7.12) - The story is set after *The Snowmen*, and a caption reads "Yorkshire 1893". The Doctor names the year on arrival.

1710 Dating *Clarence and the Whispermen* (Series 7 DVD minisode) and *The Name of the Doctor* (X7.14) - A caption in *The Name of the Doctor* reads "London 1893". The minisode explains how DeMarco attains the information that nets Vastra's interest.

1711 Dating "The Crystal Throne" (*DWM* #475-476) - The story is a filler piece, published before the start of *DWM*'s twelfth Doctor comics.

1712 Dating *Worlds DW: Mind Games* (*Worlds DW* #1.1) - Mention is made of Jago consulting with Sigmund Freud in *J&L* S6: *Return of the Repressed*, but Jago and Litefoot aren't currently fugitives (*J&L* S6: *Military Intelligence* to the end of *J&L* Series 7). Sgt Quick hasn't yet been promoted to Inspector, so it's before *J&L* S7: *The Wax Princess.* So, *Mind Games* must fall between *Return of the Repressed* and *Military Intelligence.*

1713 *Worlds DW: The Reesinger Process*

1714 Dating *Benny* S9: *The Adventure of the Diogenes Damsel* (Benny audio #9.3) - Benny guesstimates her arrival in this era as being "late spring" based upon the "filthy weather", and she seems to spend some weeks helping Mycroft solve cases. Her diary states that her confrontation with Straxus begins on "7th of May", and events spill over to the next day. It's doubtful that Benny spends much more time in 1893 after getting a working time ring on 8th May, as she seems awfully eager to check on Peter.

The legendary figure of the Cwejen, "Mr Seven", also here called Time's Champion, is almost certainly the seventh Doctor. Mycroft's housekeeper is named as "Mrs Grose", presumably the character seen in *Ghost Light.* Cloisterham is a fictional town from *The Mystery of Edwin Drood*, Charles Dickens' unfinished work. A different incarnation of Straxus appeared in Big Finish's BBC7 range.

1715 Dating *Camera Obscura* (EDA #59) - It's the "nineteenth century" (p6), Maskelyne (presumably the magician John Nevil Maskelyne, 1839-1917) is alive (p7) and it's a "century" before Anji's time (p35). Fitz here meets George Williamson, so this is before *Time Zero.*

1716 *Camera Obscura.* William is the human version of Spike from *Buffy the Vampire Slayer.* However, the dating is awry – in *Buffy*, Spike became a vampire in 1880.

1717 *Army of Death*

and sadistically made people commit murder or suicide. He became a successful stage performer, using his appearances at the New Regency to mesmerise audience-members into later performing grotesque acts of violence. Litefoot, Jago, Sgt Quick and Ellie deduced Rees' *modus operandi*, and a confrontation at Rees' estate led to his falling down a well. Jago threw Rees' mental focal point, a music box, down after him.

Before his death, Rees transferred his mind into the music box.[1713]

1893 (spring to 8th May) - BENNY S9: THE ADVENTURE OF THE DIOGENES DAMSEL[1714] ->

Straxus, a Time Lord who was stranded on Earth, diverted Benny's time ring as she travelled from prehistoric times. Dr Watson and his wife were away on a recuperative cruise, so Benny made the acquaintance of Mycroft Holmes – who worked for Her Majesty's Foreign and Commonwealth Office, and looked nothing like his illustrations in *The Strand*. She aided him in solving a number of crimes, including the Case of the Peculiar Pig. They also stopped the Choirmaster of Cloistersham from selling cipher keys to the Shah of Iran.

Benny and Mycroft stopped Straxus' assistants, two Cwejen, from committing murders that prominently featured the number 7, in an attempt to create a pattern in history that would attract the attention of a "pale god" named Mr Seven. A past version of Straxus locked up his successor, and also gave Benny a working time ring.

Mycroft Holmes currently possessed the only copy of *All-Consuming Fire*.

1893 (July to August) - CAMERA OBSCURA[1715] ->

The eighth Doctor and Sabbath both arrived in Victorian England after detecting disturbances in time. A faulty time machine, based on the principles of temporal interferometry, had splintered the stage magician Octave into eight individuals. Octave attacked the Doctor, who lived because Sabbath had placed the Doctor's second heart in his own chest, which tethered the Doctor to the living world. Sabbath's assassin, the Angel-Maker, killed Octave.

The time machine had also twinned the insane psychologist Nathaniel Chiltern. One of the Nathaniels attempted to further use the machine, which could have punctured the space-time continuum, but the Doctor destroyed the device by flinging himself into it. Nathaniel killed the Angel-Maker, but was then killed by Sabbath. By extension, this killed the other Nathaniel.

At this time, the Doctor, Fitz and Anji attended a séance. Also in attendance was a young man named William.[1716] The Doctor collected some oolong tea in Peking in either 1893 or 1983.[1717]

1893 - J&L S3: DEAD MEN'S TALES ->

Operating from 2011, the temporal engineer Elliot Payne tried to harvest all of Earth's temporal energy – enough raw power to free his wife, who was trapped in an event horizon millennia in the future. Payne's experiments created time breaks, and so Leela was dispatched from Gallifrey to aid Litefoot and Jago in dealing with the situation. One of Payne's experiments translocated the doomed Navy seaman Johnny Skipton from 1958; the resultant time break resolved when the spirits of Skipton's crewmates claimed him, and they all drowned as intended.

1893 (August) - J&L S3: THE MAN AT THE END OF THE GARDEN ->

Eleanor Naismith, née Maycombe, had become a famed author of fantasy stories. Litefoot, Jago and Leela helped to stop the fairy-man whom Eleanor had bargained with as a child from vengefully killing Eleanor's daughter Clara – who had been formed via the fairy-man's magic pocketbook. Clara used the book to make jackdaws carry the fairy-man away to the moon, where one of their number kept him company.

1893 (summer) - J&L S3: SWAN SONG / CHRONOCLASM ->

Prior to this, Professor Litefoot had met Oscar Wilde.

Litefoot, Jago and Leela found that Elliot's experiments had forged a temporal link between the New Regency Theatre and Elliot's laboratory, which stood on the same locale in 2011. Payne's equipment was ruined, but he successfully journeyed down the link and arrived in the 1890s. Because it amused him, Payne kidnapped Nikola Tesla from a future year to serve as his assistant.

(=) Leela and her allies failed to find Payne, who converted Earth's temporal energy. Roads split and the Thames boiled as the whole history of London happened all at once. Jago witnessed the cataclysm and was thrown back in time a few hours...

Leela's temporal register triangulated Payne's location from the future Jago. A cadre of Time Eaters arrived to collect the energy Payne had promised them. Payne realised the Time Eaters had killed his wife, and, on Litefoot's suggestion, temporally connected his lair with 12th October, 1940 – when a bomb was slated to destroy the New Regency. The Time Eaters were obliterated, Payne also seemed to perish and Tesla was returned to his native year. Leela said farewell to her friends, but her time ring failed to return her home – indicating that danger was still present – even as Jago and Litefoot were approached by Professor Claudius Dark...

The Temperon Empire devised vessels that warped time to shorten space journeys, but failed to achieve actual time travel. Elliot Payne's temporal experiments interfered with the workings of a Temperon ship, and it crashed in Bedfordshire. The ship's synthetic "pilots" adopted the names Kempston and Hardwick from the nearby town of Kempston Hardwick, and searched for the Doctor and his TARDIS, hoping to extract from them the secrets of full-fledged time travel. The sixth Doctor went incognito as Professor Claudius Dark to elude Kempston and Hardwick, and worried they would strike at him through his friends Jago and Litefoot.[1718]

1893 (summer) - JAGO & LITEFOOT SERIES 4 -> As "Professor Dark", the sixth Doctor arranged for Jago, Litefoot and Leela to holiday together in Brighton, to keep them away from Kempston and Hardwick. The two villains followed and tried to fracture their opponents by creating a human simulacrum – the singer Abigail Woburn – to seduce Jago. He fell for Abigail's charms and proposed marriage, but rejoined his friends as the spirit of Mary Elizabeth Reilly, who had been trapped in a mirror in Brighton since 1887, possessed Litefoot. Leela smashed the mirror, enabling Reilly's ghost and that of her beloved, George Nevil, to cross to the great beyond. Jago deemed Abigail's affections as lost to him.

Litefoot, Jago and Leela returned to London, where Professor Dark offered tickets to a performance of the new Oscar Wilde play, *A Woman of No Importance*. Litefoot's trio

consequently encountered the psionic Warren Gadd, whose infinite library drained energy from living minds. Gadd failed to trap Litefoot's party and Wilde in his library, and was forever rendered immobile as his mental energy held back a bullet fired at him from within the library.

Leela returned to the Red Tavern as Kempston and Hardwick tried to snare Jago and Litefoot in a temporal trap involving an underground train circling Charing Cross. Litefoot and Jago found the corpse of the housebreaker Winnie O'Connor, who had actually died twice thanks to a time-cracker that Kempston provided, creating a paradox. Jago smashed Winnie's time cracker, ending the temporal dilemma. The sixth Doctor acknowledged that the time for hiding was past, and revealed his true identity to his friends.

The Doctor and his allies backtracked Kempston and Hardwick's origins to a town in Bedfordshire. Jago and Ellie posed as the Doctor and Leela to distract Kempston and Hardwick while the Doctor, Leela and Litefoot found the spaceship that brought Kempston and Hardwick to Earth – the source of their power – and arranged for its destruction. Kempston and Hardwick used their ability to assimilate local materials to create an army of sandmen, but terminated their Abigail Woburn simulacrum. They sought to capture the TARDIS, but the Doctor's party tricked Kempston and Hardwick into bringing a tunnel wall down upon themselves. The incoming Thames for-

---

1718 The background to *Jago & Litefoot* Series 4, as given in *J&L S4: The Hourglass Killers*. The Temperon Empire has no evident relation to the Temperon creatures seen in *The Sirens of Time*.
1719 *Voyage to Venus, J&L S5: The Final Act*
1720 *J&L S6: The Skeleton Quay*
1721 The background to *Jago & Litefoot* Series 6.
1722 *J&L S10: The Museum of Curiosities*
1723 Dating *J&L S6: The Skeleton Quay* and *Return of the Repressed* (*J&L #6.1-6.2*) - *The Skeleton Quay* opens with Jago and Litefoot having returned to 1893 in Greel's time cabinet (at the end of Series 5), having suffering no evident loss of time from when they left. These two installments of Series 6 seem to happen at lightning speed – the Colonel literally approaches Jago and Litefoot just as they've returned from 1968, they dutifully go to Shingle Cove (*The Skeleton Quay*) and soon after deal with the alien intelligence they encountered there (*Return of the Repressed*). It's said to be a "warm summer day" in *J&L S6: Return of the Repressed*, which would suggest that not long has passed since as far back as *J&L S3: The Man at the End of the Garden* in Series 3, when it was "August". That would also concur with it being warm enough for Leela to sleep in Litefoot's flowerbed in *J&L S4: Beautiful Things*.
1724 Dating *DEyes: Tangled Web* (BF *DEyes* #1.3) - The year is given. It's Molly's second birthday, with *DEyes: X*

and the Daleks confirming that she was born in 1891. That same story sees all of Kotris' actions erased from history, although the Doctor and Molly retain the memory of them.
1725 Dating *DEyes: Tangled Web* (BF *DEyes* #1.3) - The Doctor tells Molly that it's "around the late 1800s". The two of them spy on Kotris in Ireland in the same time zone, at virtually the same time or perhaps a few years apart.
1726 *Leth-St: Beast of Fang Rock* (ch1). Baum lived 1856-1919.
1727 The month before *J&L S6: Military Intelligence*.
1728 Dating *Deep Breath* (X8.1) - For Vastra's trio, the Doctor and Clara, events follow on from *The Name of the Doctor* [1893].
Clara, Vastra and the Doctor separately examine a copy of the *Times*, but - even if one freeze-frames the Hi-Def version of the story - the dateline is only discernable as "Friday, January [two-digit date] [unreadable year]." Most of the dated adverts within the paper indicate that it's June... Mr Leonard Borwick's Chamber Concert is scheduled for "Friday evening next, July 1"; a Covent Garden performance of *Gotterdummerung* slated for "Friday the 24th" has been rescheduled to "Monday July 4 to Tuesday July 5"; an issue of *The Humanitarian*, edited by Victoria Woodbe, is to publish in July; and the fictional "Ecce Homo!", touted as

ever swept away Kempston, Hardwick and their sandmen.

Leela bid her friends farewell and returned home using her time ring. The Doctor suggested that Jago and Litefoot take a trip with him in the TARDIS, and they soon found themselves on Venus in the far future...

The Doctor erroneously dropped Jago and Litefoot off at the Red Tavern in 1968, and they had adventures in that year before returning to their own era in Magnus Greel's time cabinet.[1719] The time cabinet seemed broken beyond repair upon the completion of its journey, and Litefoot had it put into storage for safekeeping.[1720]

A man known only as the Colonel was dismissed from governmental service, and privately worked to construct an army of advanced warboats, dirigibles and mechanised soldiers. With such an army, the Colonel hoped to secure the Empire's fortunes across the globe, as well as depose Her Majesty and name himself as Emperor of Europe. Unfinished blueprints from the late Charles Babbage's notebooks aided the Colonel in developing Babbage Engines that governed the actions of his mechanical men, but the robots' efficiency remained limited.[1721]

To further Jago and Litefoot's exploits, Carruthers Summerton arranged for the Colonel to take an interest in them...[1722]

1893 (summer) - J&L S6: THE SKELETON QUAY / RETURN OF THE REPRESSED[1723] -> Prior to this, Jago's mother had died in a women's hospital.

The Colonel became concerned that reports of a ghostly fog along the Suffolk coast would draw attention to an experimental warship he kept in the area. He misrepresented himself as an agent of the Crown to Jago and Litefoot, and tasked them – as experts on the supernatural – with investigating the affair. Jago and Litefoot went to Suffolk, communed with the alien intelligence that had witnessed the destruction of the town of Shingle Cove some thirty years prior, and exposed the culpability of Camilla Tevelyan's father in the villagers' demise. Tevelyan had killed anyone who suspected her family's secret, but became scared by the intelligence and fell to her death.

The alien intelligence's psyche was fractured, and reached out to Litefoot's mind to mend itself. Repressed trauma that Litefoot had experienced as a child in China surfaced, and caused the intelligence to manifest as a duality: a rough recreation of Litefoot's mother and a savage baboon. Jago experienced dreams of an ape and sought professional help from the visiting Dr Sigmund Freud. The two of them deduced the cause of Litefoot's affliction, enabling the intelligence to integrate its various personas into Madame Anna: a talented acrobat and singer. Litefoot, Jago and Freud lost all memory of Madama Anna's origins, and Jago commissioned her to perform at the New Regency.

(=) 1893 - DEyes: TANGLED WEB[1724] -> The rogue Time Lord named Kotris infused young Molly O'Sullivan with retrogenitor particles as part of his scheme to erase the Time Lords from the universe. The eighth Doctor and an older Molly secretly observed as Kotris – his TARDIS disguised as a horse and coach – examined the two-year-old Molly to see how the particles were gestating. Kotris returned young Molly to her parents, claiming she'd temporarily become lost in a storm.

(=) c 1893 - DEyes: TANGLED WEB[1725] -> The eighth Doctor and Molly visited the pre-industrial world Shrangor, during the early days of the Daleks' underground base there. The Time Lord Straxus picked up the Doctor, Molly and the Doctor's TARDIS in a mothballed Type 40 TARDIS, and took them some centuries the future to confront the Daleks.

1894

Margaret Goff, the future wife of Edward Travers and mother of Anne, was born in 1894 to Matthew Goff. Amongst Margaret's possessions was an *Oz* book autographed to her by L. Frank Baum.[1726] An acrobatic fire-eater from Shanghai nearly burned down the New Regency while appearing on stage there.[1727]

c 1894 - DEEP BREATH[1728] -> The clockwork droids stranded on Earth had established Mancini's Family Restaurant in London as a front for their organ-harvesting operation. Madame Vastra was looking into the Conk-Singleton forgery case, and expected to have the Camberwell child poisoner for dinner.

Vastra, Jenny and Strax investigated the curious incident of a tyrannosaur that appeared by the Thames, having been accidentally drawn through time with the TARDIS caught in its throat. Vastra's trio contained the T-Rex with signal-emitters, then took Clara and the newly regenerated twelfth Doctor back to Paternoster Row to recover. The droids, as led by their control node – the Half-Face Man – incinerated the T-Rex to cover up their plundering its optic nerves.

The Doctor and his allies went to Mancini's, where the Half-Face Man activated his long-dormant ship – now revamped as a dirigible made from human skin – in an attempt to reach the Promised Land. The Half-Face Man was either thrown to his death by the Doctor, or accepted the Doctor's argument that his half-existence had no purpose and committed suicide. Whatever the case, Missy greeted the Half-Face Man upon his awakening in the Promised Land. Without the Half-Face Man's guidance, the clockwork droids went dormant. The Doctor took Clara back to her own era...

Missy had placed a newspaper ad that lured the Doctor and Clara to Mancini's, which helped to keep them in each others' company.[1729]

1894 (11th January) - THE BODYSNATCHERS[1730] ->

Henry Gordon Jago had been a bit dyspeptic of late, and on Professor Litefoot's orders had gone to see his sister in Brighton for a few weeks. With Litefoot's help, the eighth Doctor and Sam Jones discovered that a series of grisly murders were part of a Zygon plot to conquer the world. The Doctor confronted Balaak, the Zygon leader, and accidentally killed some of the Zygons by poisoning their milk. The Zygons' pack of Skarasen threatened London until the Doctor lured them into the TARDIS. He relocated them and a Zygon survivor, Tuval, to an uninhabited planet.

c 1894 - J&L S6: MILITARY INTELLIGENCE / THE TRIAL OF GEORGE LITEFOOT[1731] ->

The Colonel again visited Litefoot and Jago, and insisted that they provide him with a full and detailed account of their adventures, as he hoped to perfect his soldiers with their knowledge of the late Dr Tulp's technology. Litefoot and Jago learned of the Colonel's schemes, and, with help from Agatha Worthing – a true agent of the Crown – destroyed one of the Colonel's munitions factories. The corpse of one of the Colonel's henchmen was found at the site, and wrongly identified as Jago's body while the genuine article recovered in secret. The Colonel used his clout to have Litefoot arrested for Jago's death and swiftly put on trial.

Disguised as a barrister, Jago defended Litefoot in court while Worthing trailed the Colonel to his base of operations: the Statchford Observatory. The Colonel had adapted the telescope to fire a high artillery shell onto Buckingham Palace, intending to kill the Queen and her senior ministers. Litefoot was found guilty, and Jago's revelation of his true identity resulted in both of them being arrested on murder charges. They escaped and reunited with Worthing, who died trying to stop the Colonel. Jago reprogrammed the observatory cannon to send the artillery shell straight up and back down again. The shell destroyed the observatory and killed the Colonel.

The authorities erroneously concluded that Jago and Litefoot were behind the plot to kill Her Majesty, and that Worthing and the Colonel had died foiling them. The Queen was devastated to hear of Worthing's death, and a reward was issued for Jago and Litefoot's capture – dead or alive. Without Worthing to clear their names, Jago and Litefoot went on the run...

"Munkeacsy's Sacred masterpiece", is "open till August". The adverts also mention a dinner to celebrate Dominion Day at the Imperial institute on July 1, as well as performances of the invented plays *Crossing the Line or Crowded Rooms* and *The Maid With Her Milking Pail*.

However, none of these dates match the real world – in 1894, June 24th was a Sunday, July 1st a Sunday, July 4th a Wednesday and July 5th a Thursday. In 1893, they were respectively a Saturday, a Saturday, a Tuesday and a Wednesday. It's also germane to say: *Deep Breath* was filmed in January 2014, and on-screen everyone looks as if they're dressing for that time of year, making a June dating even more dubious.

Whoniverse (BBC, p77) seems to presume that each Paternoster Gang adventure happens a year apart, so puts *Deep Breath* in 1894. That works as well as anything – to presume that a year passes for Vastra and company between Series 7 and 8, until the twelfth Doctor and Clara turn up on their doorstep.

Vastra's other cases are off-screen Holmes adventures referenced in Arthur Conan Doyle stories: the Camberwell poisoning (cited by Watson as occurring in 1887) in "The Adventure of the Five Orange Pips", and the forgery incident in "The Adventure of the Six Napoleons".

1729 *Death in Heaven*

1730 Dating *The Bodysnatchers* (EDA #3) - It is "11.01.1894" (p15). It is six years since the Ripper murders (p2), and five years since *The Talons of Weng Chiang*

(p37). Thrillingly for continuity-keepers, *Jago & Litefoot* Series 6 and 7 establish that Jago and Litefoot spend almost all of 1894 (and possibly the tail end of 1893 too) either incarcerated or on the run as fugitives – potentially leaving no room for *The Bodysnatchers* to occur as seen, with Litefoot at home as if everything is normal. It's not totally beyond the pale, however, to squeeze *The Bodysnatchers* into the very start of 1894 before all of that happens (see the dating notes on *J&L S6: Military Intelligence*).

Previous editions of *Ahistory* postulated that the minor character "Mr Stoker" (no first name given) was *Dracula* author Bram Stoker, but a closer examination of Stoker's life voids this idea. Stoker was living in London in 1894, but served as the business manager of the Lyceum Theatre from 1878 to 1905 – it doesn't seem likely that such an established businessman, husband and father would moonlight (as "Stoker" does here) as a thuggish enforcer to a factory-owner. Stoker does, however, appear in *J&L S11: The Woman in White*.

1731 Dating *J&L S6: Military Intelligence* and *The Trial of George Litefoot* (*J&L* #6.3-6.4) - The final two installments of Series 6 happen relatively quickly, concluding on the fifth of the month in "1894" (according to *J&L S7: The Monstrous Menagerie*). Notably, Jago and Litefoot have their second meeting with the Colonel on a Thursday (*Military Intelligence*), with it later being said that Jago "was killed" on that same evening, the night of the 14th (*The Trial of George Litefoot*). In 1893, the

In 1894, Frederick Simonsson purchased two of Claudio Tardelli's reality-warping paintings for the King of Sweden.[1732] **Thomas Reginald Brockless, a soldier in World War I, was born on 7th February, 1894.**[1733]

1894 - TIME ZERO[1734] ->

Keen to be an adventurer in his own right, Fitz accompanied palaeontologist George Williamson on an expedition to Siberia. Tsar Alexander III was present when the expedition left Vladivostok.

Reptiles from another timeline attacked the expedition, killing everyone but Fitz and Williamson. A huge explosion encased the two of them in ice, where they would remain for over a hundred years. The eighth Doctor and Williamson later went back to 1894 and averted the saurians' timeline by arranging Williamson's death. The billionaire Maxwell Curtis, travelling down a time corridor to this era from 2002, died in a minor explosion.

As a result of these events, an energy being from an o-region – a sort of isolated, mini-universe – was drawn to Earth. Bits of it seeped through Williamson's time corridor into the past, where it was worshipped by some cultures. The main portion of the fire elemental that arrived in 1894, however, achieved enough critical mass to work toward its agenda of consuming Earth entirely.

The elemental allied with Roger Nepath, who believed it could restore his dead sister to life.[1735] Marnal's first story, "The Giants", was published in the *Strand* in 1894.[1736]

1894 (19th May) - CD,NM V1: JUDOON IN CHAINS[1737] ->

A fugitive Judoon, Captain Kybo, fled to Victorian England after one-dimensional beings, the Ayishas, stimulated the creative centre of his brain. As part of a carnival exhibit, he enjoyed reading books such as *Great Expectations* and *Moby Dick*, and developed a penchant for poetry. Owing to jurisdictional issues, Kybo's fellow Judoon temporarily relocated an English court to the future so Kybo could stand trial for desertion...

1894 (June) - DEMON QUEST: THE DEMON OF PARIS[1738] ->

The fourth Doctor and Mrs Wibbsey dropped off the elephant they picked up in Roman Britain and proceeded by train to Paris to investigate the Doctor's appearance on one of Henri Toulouse-Lautrec's posters. Lautrec's recent behaviour had been erratic, and a number of girls had been found murdered. Moreover, all of the paintings in the artist's studio had been slashed to pieces. The Doctor and Wibbsey found Lautrec at the Moulin Rouge, and discovered that even Lautrec has begun to doubt his own sanity. The travellers found desiccated corpses in Lautrec's attic, along with the missing component from the TARDIS – but this made the Doctor suspect Lautrec wasn't the murderer. The concierge was a shapeshifter who drained life energy, and the same demonic being who posed as Claudius in the first century. The alien once again escaped in a dematerialisation chamber, and the Doctor and Mrs Wibbsey returned to 2010.

Shortly after this time, Mrs Wibbsey's parents died. Her younger self was sent to live with her aunt.[1739]

= 1894 (a Thursday in June) - IRIS: ENTER WILDTHYME[1740] ->

Iris Wildthyme's favourite month and year to spend in Paris was June 1894, and she worked to avoid running into herself there. She, Kelly, Simon and Panda saw the Martians invade the Paris of an alternate dimension. Between now and the turn of the century, the city would be levelled.

1894 - J&L S7: THE MONSTROUS MENAGERIE / THE NIGHT OF 1000 STARS[1741] ->

A time machine from the sixty-third century heading back from the Jurassic Period became grounded in London, killing the crew save for Baskerville and Laura Lyons. Baskerville covertly let his specimens feed on locals in the East End, their savaged bodies causing rumours concerning "the Beast of Burden Green". Arthur Conan Doyle, having

---

14th was a Thursday in July, September and December. It's fairly simple to believe, then, that *Military Intelligence* happens on 14th December, 1893, that Litefoot is incarcerated for a short time, and that his trial ends on 5th January, 1894. Alternatively, the calendar might have changed before Jago and Litefoot again meet the Colonel, and all of these events happen in 1894.

1732 "Four years" before *Grand Theft Cosmos*.

1733 *TW: To the Last Man*

1734 Dating *Time Zero* (EDA #60) - This was in "1894" (p15).

1735 *The Burning*

1736 *The Gallifrey Chronicles.* This is the same issue of the *Strand* the Doctor is looking for in *The Bodysnatchers*.

1737 Dating *CD,NM V1: Judoon in Chains* (*CD,NM* #1.2)

- The presiding judge names the exact day.

1738 Dating *Demon Quest: The Demon of Paris* (BBC fourth Doctor audio #2.2) - The Doctor dates the poster to "1894" in *Demon Quest: The Relics of Time*. Mrs Wibbsey affirms that year in *Demon Quest: Starfall*, and it's "June 1894" according to the sleeve notes.

1739 *Demon Quest: The Demon of Paris*

1740 Dating *Iris: Enter Wildthyme* (Iris novel #1) - The year and month are given (p80). It's a Thursday (p82).

1741 Dating *J&L S7: The Monstrous Menagerie* and *The Night of 1000 Stars* (*J&L* #7.1-7.2) - *The Monstrous Menagerie* opens two days after the end of Series 6, on the "7th" of the month (likely January; see the dating notes on *J&L S6: The Trial of George Litefoot*). The year is given as "1894", and Baskerville says the time-expedi-

killed off his creation Sherlock Holmes in "The Final Problem", desperately wanted to focus on new projects including *The Stark Munro Letters*. Nonetheless, he often collected – and felt chagrinned by – the fan mail sent to 221B Baker Street, with correspondence from The Sherlock Society A) pointing out all the discrepancies in the Holmes stories, and B) asking for more Holmes adventures.

The Doctor let the fugitive Jago and Litefoot take shelter at his house at 107 Baker Street, and sent Conan Doyle their way when Lyons wrote to "Sherlock Holmes" for help with Baskerville. The villain set his favourite beasts – luminescent hounds – upon the investigators, but Conan Doyle vowed, reluctantly, to summon Lyons' associates from the future by writing a new Holmes adventure with elements of what he'd seen. A Temporal Retrieval Squad arrested Baskerville, secured his animals and rescued Lyons. Conan Doyle also considered basing a new character upon elements of this adventure, giving rise to his Professor Challenger stories.

Afterward, the embodiment of Remourse adopted Leela's form and tried to make Jago, Litefoot and Ellie Higson submit to their past regrets. The trio deduced Remouse's identity, and banished it with a rousing chorus of "Where Did You Get That Hat?"

1894 - 9thC: THE OTHER SIDE[1742] -> The ninth Doctor was ejected from a Birmingham theatre, after the Bigon Horde's temporal tsunami made him materialise on stage. Stranded on Earth, he would reunite with Rose in 1922.

1894 (December) - J&L S7: MURDER AT MOORSEY MANOR / THE WAX PRINCESS[1743] -> Edwina Merridew beheaded nearly all of the clockmaker guild-members responsible for her father's disgrace. As the last one, Professor Potter, was a Sherlock Holmes fan, Merridew hosted a party for Holmes aficionados – a gathering timed to celebrate the "passing" of the Great Detective one year previous. Merridew's murder devices killed most of those assembled, but – in self-defence – Litefoot manipulated Merridew into plunging to her death.

Frederick Abberline recruited Jago and Litefoot's help when Jack the Ripper escaped from custody. The Ripper had a Madame Tussauds sculptor craft a replica of his beloved Princess Annajanine, then harvested organs from his new victims to animate her. He intended to overthrow Queen Victoria, but a confrontation at Windsor Palace led to a small fire consuming both the faux Annajanine and the Ripper. Jago and Litefoot thought they saw the Ripper's body melting alongside Annajanine's before the end.

tion crashed in that same year "three weeks ago". Conan Doyle's father died, and his wife was diagnosed with consumption, "last year" – which happened in 1893. From then until 1897, Conan Doyle and his wife lived in Switzerland; here, he claims to return to 221B Baker Street "every few weeks" to collect the mail.

The Stark Munro Letters were published in 1895. *The Hound of the Baskervilles* was serialized from August 1901 to April 1902. Professor Challenger first appeared in *The Lost World* (1912). (The Doctor met Conan Doyle, and seemed to serve as an inspiration for Challenger, in *Evolution*. Alternatively to both of these possibilities, *someone* named Professor Challenger is name-checked as an actual person in *ST: The Jago & Litefoot Revival*.) One of the late time-expedition members, Professor Presbury, bears the same name as a character from the Holmes story "The Adventure of the Creeping Man" (1923). Jago comments upon "smoke damage in the kitchen" of No. 107, which happened in *The Haunting of Thomas Brewster* [1867].

The story treats Sherlock as nothing more than Conan Doyle's invention (see the Sherlock Holmes sidebar), but also helps to establish that Knox's plan (*Assassin in the Limelight*) to possess Conan Doyle's body and identity didn't come to pass.

1742 Dating *9thC: The Other Side* (BF *The Ninth Doctor Chronicles* #1.3) - It's "twenty-eight years" before 1922. If the ninth Doctor lives out said twenty-eight years on Earth (see The Doctor's Age sidebar for more), it's perhaps odd that he doesn't visit Jago and Litefoot. According to *ST: The Jago & Litefoot Revival*, however,

the investigators never meet the Eccleston version.

1743 Dating *J&L S7: Murder at Moorsey Manor* and *The Wax Princess* (*J&L* #7.3-7.4) - Events at Moorsey Manor open on the first anniversary of Sherlock Holmes' "death" at Reichenbach Falls, presumably indicating the publication of "The Final Problem" in December 1893. (Events in "The Final Problem" itself take place in 1891.) Merridew complains that it's "freezing" outside. *The Wax Princess* immediately follows on from the previous story.

1744 "Three years" before *Grand Theft Cosmos*.

1745 Dating *The Burning* (EDA #37) - It's "a few years" since the Doctor arrived on Earth (p142), dated in *Escape Velocity* to 1888. The most precise indication in *The Burning* itself is that it's "the late nineteenth century". It is "fifty years" before *The Turing Test* (p59), which is set in January 1943.

The fire elemental first manifests on Earth in *Time Zero* and writer Justin Richards has confirmed that whereas bits of the creature seep through Williamson's time corridor (causing a residual presence of it to be worshipped by ancient cultures, etc.), it's only when the main chunk of it arrives in 1894 that the elemental attains enough critical mass to work toward its own insidious agenda. Therefore, *The Burning* – in which the elemental works to its own design, and the Doctor defeats it – manifestly has to occur after *Time Zero*.

The Burning (p238) specifies that it's January, so allowing that some time (a few months at least) probably pass while the elemental and Nepath forge their pact and start to implement it, January 1895 seems the

Jago and Litefoot received a Royal pardon, and were recommended to succeed Abberline as the Queen's secret advisor while he left to helm a European office of the Pinkerton Agency. Sgt Quick was promoted to Inspector.

An exonerated Litefoot and Jago enjoyed a pint as Jago commissioned a new act: entertaining puppets called the Scorchies...

1895

In 1895, Frederick Simonsson acquired one of Claudio Tardelli's sculptures. It was actually a silicate-based life-form tasked with protecting the diamond containing Tardelli's micro-universe.[1744]

@ c 1895 (January) - THE BURNING[1745] **->** The amnesiac eighth Doctor ended up in Middletown, just in time to investigate a mysterious geological fault. He realised that it was the home of a fire elemental that was in league with local developer, Roger Nepath. The Doctor blew up a dam, flooding the fault and extinguishing the elemental. The Doctor callously killed Nepath.

c 1895 (January) - SILHOUETTE[1746] **->** The Shadow Proclamation found Orestes Milton, a.k.a. Milton Orestes, guilty of illicit genetic augmentation and weapons development. Milton fled to Earth and usurped the Carnival of Curiosities in England, then adapted three of its members – the telekinetic Silhouette, the desire-inducing Affinity and the emotion-draining David Rutherford, a.k.a. Empath. The trio eliminated anyone who guessed the Carnival's true purpose.

Milton advanced plans to destroy London with a cloud of anger generated by Empath – a show-room demonstration of his talents for prospective clients – but the twelfth

Doctor, Clara, Madame Vastra, Jenny and Strax liberated Silhouette and Affinity. The Shadow Proclamation dispatched Dekseller-class Smart Torpedoes to eliminate Milton's spaceship as he fled. Silhouette and Affinity left to make their own way, and the latter met a young woman who loved him for himself.

On February 14th, 1895, the Doctor attended the debut performance of *The Importance of Being Earnest*.[1747]

@ In March 1895, the Doctor met George Bernard Shaw at a party hosted by Oscar Wilde. Around that time, Sherlock Holmes solved the McCarthy murders before the Doctor could.[1748] The Doctor claimed to have acquired a walking stick and shroud after an encounter with Oscar Wilde and a theatre of midget assassins.[1749]

The fourth Doctor claimed he was asked to be George VI's godfather.[1750] Nikola Tesla was temporarily transported back in time by Elliot Payne.[1751] The immortal Helena worked as Helena Johnson, a New York schoolteacher, in the late nineteenth century.[1752]

1895 - DESTINATION: NERVA[1753] **->** The fourth Doctor and Leela investigated a distress signal originating from a spaceship in Kent, 1895. Lord Jack Corrigan's men had slaughtered a party of peaceful Dellierian space explorers – ten-foot tall beings with yellow skin – and captured their space-vessel. Lord Corrigan sought glory for the British Empire, and departed in the ship to the Dellerian home-world with about two dozen men, using the technology aboard to extend their lives. The Doctor and Leela tried to follow, but warp distortion threw the TARDIS into the future. They encountered Lord Corrigan's ship upon its return to Earth, at Nerva spacedock...

---

most likely time for *The Burning* to occur. The date was given as 1889 in the original story synopsis.

1746 Dating *Silhouette* (NSA #56) - It's a while but not *too* long after *Deep Breath*. (Clara: "You been busy since we last visited?"; Jenny: "Nothing too exciting. We did have a haunted house to investigate last month.") There's reason to think that the New Year has come and gone, however, in that the the Prologue gives the time of year as "January". Unsurprisingly, a warm fire provides comfort (ch6).

1747 *Assassin in the Limelight*

1748 *The Gallifrey Chronicles*, a reference to Nicholas Meyer's novel *The West End Horror*, which features Holmes and Shaw. Holmes at this point would have resurfaced following his encounter with Moriarty at the Reichenbach Falls, per Conan Doyle's "The Adventure of the Empty House", set in 1894.

1749 "The Forgotten". He actually got the stick from Kublai Khan, and the shroud from the San Francisco

hospital where he regenerated for the seventh time.

1750 *Wolfsbane*. George was born in 1895.

1751 *J&L* S3: *Chronoclasm*. Year unknown, but Tesla lived 1856-1943. Duncan Wisbey, who played Tesla, was 40 when this story was recorded. Tesla might well be the same age when Payne abducts him, but that only puts him a few years ahead of the *Jago & Litefoot* stories, and begs the question of why Payne didn't just look up Tesla's contemporary self.

1752 *Erimem: Three Faces of Helena*

1753 Dating *Destination: Nerva* (BF 4th Doc #1.1) - The year is given. The story picks up (for the Doctor and Leela) directly after *The Talons of Weng-Chiang*; the Doctor claims that the distress signal hails from "three years" after their current position, which seems to indicate that *Weng-Chiang* occurred in 1892. (See the dating notes on that story and Big Finish's own *Jago & Litefoot* series, however, for why it's more likely 1889.)

1895 - DL: THE VAMPIRE OF PARIS[1754] -> Brother Varlos of the Darksmiths buried the Eternity Crystal on Earth's moon and took up residence in Paris. A timeship followed Varlos to Earth, and the time vampire that powered the vessel killed the crew and escaped. The tenth Doctor and Varlos' android daughter, Gisella, tracked down her "father". Together, they reversed the strange temporal effects that the creature was causing, and allowed it to peacefully escape into the Time Vortex, but Varlos died while doing so. The Doctor and Gisella left to find a means of obliterate the Eternity Crystal, but destronic particles jolted the TARDIS, catapulting it to the Silver Desolation in another time zone...

Jago & Litefoot Series 8-12[1755]

1895 - JAGO & LITEFOOT SERIES 8 -> The Scorchies became a top act at the New Regency, even as they fed off the emotions of those present, twice nightly and three times on Saturday. Two of the Scorchies, the Mister and Missus, sought to forever trap an audience as a continual emotional battery, but Ellie Higson arrived and sang about how she was going to save the day. The Scorchies combusted, and the doomed Mister and Missus sang about how they were burning and full of sawdust.

The being named Mr Wednesday had caused the alien Kind to go extinct, and – feeling repentant – travelled to different worlds with his freakshow, Wednesday's World of Weird Wonders, with machinery that physically transformed his audiences into new Kind. Jago and Litefoot intervened when Wednesday's devices found it easiest to reverse the human body rather than transform all of its joints, and a defeated Wednesday burst while trying to to transform himself into a Kind.

The eggs of the alien Darkling Façade crashed into Mulberry Gride's factory in Yorkshire, burning it down. The alien material possessed Gride, who took to gestating Darkling Façade eels in facilities on Jacob's Island. Jago and Litefoot prevented the eels from reaching maturity, but although Gride's operations went up in flames, Darkling

---

1754 Dating *DL: The Vampire of Paris* (*DL #5*) - The year is given (p10). This "time vampire" has different attributes from those described in *The Time Vampire*, and follows Varlos' "time trail" – suggesting that he has, in fact, come back in time (see Dating *The Darksmith Legacy*). For the Doctor and Gisella, the story continues in *DL: The Game of Death*.

1755 Dating *Jago & Litefoot* Series 8-12 (*Encore of the Scorchies*, 8.1; *The Backwards Men*, 8.2; *Jago & Litefoot & Patsy*, 8.3; *Higson & Quick*, 8.4; *The Flying Frenchman*, 9.1; *The Devil's Dicemen*, 9.2; *Island of Death*, 9.3; *Return of the Nightmare*, 9.4; *The Case of the Missing Gasogene*, 10.1; *The Year of the Bat*, 10.2; *The Mourning After*, 10.3; *The Museum of Curiosities*, 10.4; *Jago and Son*, 11.1; *Maurice*, 11.2; *The Woman in White*, 11.3; *Masterpiece*, 11.4; *Picture This*, 12.1; *The Flickermen*, 12.2; *School of Blood*, 12.3; *Warm Blood*, 12.4) - Series 8 opens with the Scorchies ensconced as a hit at the New Regency, and Ellie telling Litefoot "We've not heard a peep from Mr Jago in weeks": the duration of time since he commissioned the Scorchies at the end of *J&L S7: The Wax Princess* [December 1894]. When the Mister and Missus burn up, they mention feeling "warm for the time of year". (Similarly, at the end of Series 8, there's "a definite nip in the air".) With nothing being said of Christmas or holiday-themed acts at the New Regency, it's fair to think that the "weeks" reference means *Encore of the Scorchies* opens in 1895, and the rest of Series 8 unfolds from there.

However, the third episode of *Jago and Litefoot* Series 11, *The Woman in White*, rather unavoidably takes place somewhere in the last half of 1895, as it's after Sir Henry Irving was knighted (16th July, 1895), but while he's starring in J. Comys Carr's *King Arthur* (which happened that same year). Moreover, events in this story

form the inspiration for *Dracula*, which was published in 1897, but was doubtless written by Bram Stoker beforehand. Historians believe that Stoker based Dracula's mannerisms on Irving, but here the man serves as the template for his lackey Renfield. So, we know that Series 8 opens in 1895, and it's not yet 1896 when Series 11 finishes.

Confirming that, in the final episode of Series 12 (*J&L S12: Warm Blood*), Litefoot asks Ellie as to her whereabouts "three Wednesdays ago, the 16th". In 1895, the 16th only fell on a Wednesday in October. That would match (more or less) with Series 12 ending "a few weeks" later in early November, when Jago and Litefoot wrap up warm for their night escapades, as the evening chill is "eating right through" them.

Relatively speaking, none of these five series seem to happen over a long stretch of time, and each follows directly on from a cliffhanger at the end of the previous one. The Darkling Façade goo quietly infects Litefoot's trio in *J&L: Jago & Litefoot & Patsy* (8.3), and it's manifestly taken over their minds by *J&L: Higson and Quick* (8.4). *J&L: Return of the Nightmare* (9.4) establishes that no time dilation occurs in the *Fata Morgana*'s various teleportations in Series 9, and Ellie noticeably thinks Jago and Litefoot are back from their holiday a bit early; Litefoot concedes that their trip was "cut short." *J&L: The Museum of Curiosities* (10.4) opens on the heels of *J&L: The Mourning After* (10.3), with Jago remarking, "This being dead takes it out of you." And in *J&L: Masterpiece*, the final story of Series 11, Inspector Quick establishes that only "weeks" have passed, start to finish, since he first encountered the cadaverous Master at the end of Series 10. "About a week" passes during *Masterpiece* itself, and there's still no mention of Christmas or the holiday season. Series 12 is fairly definitive in taking

Façade matter mentally dominated Jago, Litefoot and a homeless ghoul, Patsy. The trio coordinated efforts to boil the remaining Darkling Façade matter in a steam engine, thereby tainting everyone in London. Ellie and Inspector Quick cleared their friends' minds by sedating them with brandy, and incinerated the remaining Darkling goo.

Fatigued by their recent escapades, Jago and Litefoot decided to take a relaxing cruise that was sure to be absent of strange happenings...

1895 - JAGO & LITEFOOT SERIES 9 -> Still hunted by a demon creature, Captain Fowler, Mallory Riverstock and Aubrey crafted a device that would transport a sailing vessel back to the island from which they had stolen a sacred artefact. As such, the trio booked passage with other passengers – including Jago and Litefoot – aboard the *Fata Morgana* for Casablanca.

The portal machine misfired, creating a fog that deadened the ship's engines for some days. The machine's instability caused dozens of *Fata Morgana*s from alternate histories to appear – Jago and Litefoot met versions of themselves who were French, Prussian, Italian, Dutch, Spanish and more. The variant *Fata Morgana*s eventually vanished as the "true" *Fata Morgana* escaped...

The *Fata Morgana* arrived at Monte Carlo, where Jago became the target of a con involving the Dark Casino. This clandestine operation tricked wealthy patrons into signing away their estates, then frightened them to death by staging Satanic rituals. Jago saw through the theatrical production, and with Litefoot brought the operation to an end.

The fog transported the *Fata Morgana* to an island off Sumatra, where the operations of a French company, Empire Mining, had stimulated the slumbering alien Kibu to produce hundreds of larvae. With help from Lady Isobelle Danvers, Jago used techniques he had learned from a master of stage mesmerism, Harry Hypno, to send Kibu back to sleep.

The demon-creature hunting the stolen artefact murdered Riverstock, and began slaughtering everyone aboard the *Fata Morgana*. Jago and Litefoot repaired Riverstock's portal-device enough to relocate the *Fata Morgana* back to the London coast. The demon killed Fowler, but Aubrey returned the purloined artefact to the creature.

Jago and Litefoot retired to the Red Tavern, where Ellie delivered a letter from an author, Caruthers Summerton, who knew about their escapades with Dr Tulp, the Colonel and more, and wanted to write a book about them....

c 1895 - 6thLA: STAGE FRIGHT[1756] **->** The Valeyard drew strength from the Doctor's darker impulses, and rented out the New Regency Theatre as "Timothy Yardvale": would-be playwright and owner of Yardvale Costumiers.

weeks rather than months, as it's said in the final episode that one of Ellie's victims (killed at the end of Series 11) was murdered "a few weeks" back.

All told, then, we can only conclude that Series 8, 9, 10, 11 *and* 12 of *Jago & Litefoot* all happen in 1895 – which means Jago, Litefoot, Quick and Ellie experience at least twenty escapades in no more than a year, although that's perhaps not out of range for investigators of their calibre.

The assorted dating clues that remain are vague... According to the "infernal" contract that Jago signs, *J&L: The Devil's Dicemen* (9.2) takes place on "the 17th" of an unspecified month. It's probably best to take the repeated claim in *J&L: The Year of the Bat* (10.2) that events in 1867 happened "thirty years ago" as an approximation (the alternative is that two years have passed throughout these *Jago & Litefoot* series without there otherwise being any sign of it). *The Year of the Bat* happens on the night of the "13th", but the month isn't given. At one point in *J&L: The Mourning After*, Jago gets cut off while asking, "What was she doing in the year 189—?"

Stoker tells Irving in *The Woman in White*, "We've been friends for fifteen years!", when it's actually been more like twenty, as they formally met in 1876. It's possible that the events here also moved Stoker to write *Lair of the White Worm*, although that didn't see print until 1911. His noted biography of Irving came out in 1906, sans mention of alien bloodsucking leeches. A reference to Irving having played Malvolio "last year" seems like a simple mistake – he actually appeared in *Twelfth Night* in 1884, not 1894.

It's sometimes assumed that the "Patsy" seen in Series 8 is the woman seen on the riverbank (and credited only as "Ghoul") in *The Talons of Weng-Chiang* episode one, but nothing within the *Jago & Litefoot* stories confirms that. The Big Finish crew seems of two minds as to whether the character voiced on audio by Flaminia Cinque is the same one played on screen by Patsy Smart, or if the latter just inspired the former.

In *Masterpiece*, Ellie says Jago and Litefoot first stepped into the Red Tavern "a few years ago", on the night they discussed the nefarious activities of Dr Tulp (*The Mahogany Murderers*, set in this chronology c.1892). Soon after in *J&L S12: Warm Blood*, Litefoot remarks that there's been no sign of Ellie's vampirism "for years" (by *Ahistory*'s count, given the placement of Series 2 to c.1892, it's been about three years).

1756 Dating *6th LA: Stage Fright* (*The Sixth Doctor – The Last Adventure* #3) - Jago and Litefoot have already met the sixth Doctor (*J&L* Series 4 et al). Jago mentions that the Valeyard's patronage means that he doesn't have to pinch his pennies "from now until Christmas." It's said that Richard Mansfield played Jekyll and Hyde at the Lyceum Theatre "not so long ago", when he chiefly did so in 1887 and 1888 – so, actually, it was quite a while ago.

He commissioned actors and actresses to don clothes similar to the Doctor's companions, and to re-enact the Doctor's previous deaths with the script to *Death of a Prydonian* – then drained their life forces via a psychic extractor, and left their bodies to gain the Doctor's attention.

The sixth Doctor and Flip visited Jago and Litefoot and confronted the Valeyard... who used the psychic extractor to harvest the rage and fear the Doctor had felt prior to his regenerations. The negative emotions made the Valeyard stronger than ever, but Litefoot drove the Valeyard away with a mob of actors angered over their comrades' fates.

c 1895 - JAGO & LITEFOOT SERIES 10 -> Carruthers Summerton, viewing himself as Jago and Litefoot's greatest fan, had built the Museum of Curiosities to showcase their adventures. To better learn their methods, he became their official biographer ...

Accompanied by Summerton, Jago and Litefoot dealt with Sir Hartley Harecourt, who had combined Hetty Kindred's Speciation Serum with Dr Jasper Cornish's Fissipation Formula to create a Potentiation Potion that could hyper-evolve individuals into two components: an ape-like being and a dead husk. No evidence existed to prosecute Harecourt, who lost interest in genetics and thought about investing in shoe umbrellas instead.

Litefoot accepted delivery of the Yesterday Box that his younger self had concealed thirty years previous, and discovered that he and Jago could use it to send letters to their younger selves. On their instructions, the younger Jago and Litefoot stymied some vampire nannies in Leicester Square... but the survivors came to Litefoot's house to capture the Yesterday Box and undo their defeat. As the vampires were vulnerable to water, Litefoot instructed his younger self to place a fire pump in a handy location, enabling Jago to destroy them.

Summerton furthered a ruse in which a drug made Jago appear dead, causing Litefoot, Ellie and Inspector Quick to bury their friend. Summerton's associate Adella revived Jago, and convinced him he'd woken up in the post-apocalyptic world of 2000. Jago related some of his adventures to Adella, who escaped as Litefoot rescued his friend.

Moving toward his end game, Summerton framed Jago and Litefoot's associate – the virologist Dr Luke Betterman – for a series of bizarre murders. Events led Jago and Litefoot to the Museum of Curiosities, where Summerton hoped to drop the duo into a vat of wax, as concocted from Jack the Ripper's formulas, and immortalize them as the masterpiece of his collection. Jago, Litefoot, Ellie, Quick and Betterman dodged animated exhibits of the Scorchies, the Mahogany Murderers, the Necropolis Express and more, and confronted Summerton – who fell into his own vat of wax and died. Afterward, while Jago and Litefoot relaxed at the Red Tavern, the cadaverous Master hypnotised Inspector Quick...

c 1895 - JAGO & LITEFOOT & STRAX: THE HAUNTING[1757] **->** The alien construct known as Mrs Multravers gave humans intelligence tests, then stole the brains of suitable candidates to refuel her spaceship, which ran on mental power. Strax investigated the dinochromic energy emanating from Multravers' ship, but gave such a violence-laden and nonsensical answer to her question pertaining to a kitchen sink that she deemed him very stupid, then erased his short-term memory with a perception weapon and left him in a back alley.

A confused Strax believed that Litefoot and Jago were Madame Vastra and Jenny Flint, but "in disguise" as Victorian gentlemen. Strax accompanied Litefoot and Jago to the Palace Theatre, where he took an offer to "cut the cards" during a magic act rather too literally, and executed the magician's parrot – which he believed to be a Rutan spy with a malfunctioning language device – on stage for all to see. Accompanied by Litefoot, Jago and Ellie, Strax destroyed Multravers' spaceship with a fragmentation grenade. Afterward, he returned to Paternoster Row.

1757 Dating *Jago & Litefoot & Strax: The Haunting* (BF unnumbered one-shot) - The story saw release between *Jago & Litefoot* Series 10 and 11, but can occur at any point after Quick becomes an Inspector (*J&L S7: The Wax Princess*, set in December 1894).
1758 This is the first *Jago & Litefoot* series in a great long while to end without a cliffhanger.
1759 Dating *ST: The Jago & Litefoot Revival* (BF ST #7.3-7.4) - The start of year has come and gone. With 1895 being so full of adventures anyway (see the Dating notes on *Jago & Litefoot* Series 8-12), it seems the perfect time to flip the calendar and decide it's 1896.
Litefoot says he last saw the Doctor "almost a year" ago, when they fought the Master (*J&L Series 11*). If so, whole months have probably elapsed in 1896 with little happening (no wonder he and Jago are bored). This story was released to coincide with the 40th Anniversary of *The Talons of Weng-Chiang* (broadcast 26th February to 2nd April, 1977); the time of year could easily fall in that timeframe. At least two weeks pass - one in transit, one there - during Litefoot's trip to Minos, which is cut short when he returns to the New Regency via the Gentlemen's dimension.
Jago reminisces about his days at the "Glasgow Empire" - strange if he means the Glasgow Empire Theatre, as it didn't open until 1897. For the dying tenth Doctor, it's been "well over a century" since he saw the investigators, suggesting that the ninth Doctor (and possibly the War Doctor too; see The Doctor's Age sidebar) never met them.

1895 - JAGO & LITEFOOT SERIES 11 -> Henry Gordon Jago's great aunt Fanny was now 94, and thought she was the Duke of Cambridge. By now, Professor Litefoot had met a moon man who stole moth balls from the housewives of Brixton.

The cadaverous Master had arrived in London, having missed the Doctor during the Weng-Chiang affair. The Master's condition worsened, and so he drained the life-force of various lowlifes to sustain himself.

Henry Gordon Jago's illegitimate son, Henry Gordon Jr., a.k.a. "Harry", asked for his father's help when a Satanic cult kidnapped and murdered his mother, Ruby Valentine. The cult hoped to resurrect their infernal lord in Harry's body, but instead did so in a man named Hodgson. Harry shot Hodgson dead, then left for parts unknown. Litefoot was briefly reunited with an old flame, the archaeologist Jean Bazemore.

An alien mercenary – a worm capable of imitating other people via physical and mechanical means – accepted a commission to capture the Doctor, and detected the Prydonian pocketwatch he had retroactively gifted to com-poser Maurice Pavel. The worm adopted Pavel's form, but Jago, Litefoot, Ellie and Quick drove the Pavel-worm away after it fashioned itself into a mechanical simulacrum of Litefoot. The worm proposed an alliance with the Master against the Doctor – but the Master instead paralysed the worm with drug-laced asparagus. The affair would later influence Ravel's *Gaspard de la nuit* (1908).

The renovation of the Prince Albert Theatre's founda-tion, as ordered by manager Bram Stoker, caused a builder – Stanley Harker – to discover the Galactic Zoological spaceship buried there. Blood-feasting specimens within the ship, the Draxus worms, possessed Harker and extend-ed their influence into famed actor Sir Henry Irving; he became demented and prone to eating flies, and received the worst reviews of his career in *King Arthur*. The Draxus worms sought access to the elite class through Irving's membership in the Hermetic Society of the Golden Dawn, and hoped to sire an entirely new species. Stoker asked his old friend Jago for help, and the two of them – along with Litefoot – reactivated the spaceship's AI, which appeared as a mysterious woman in white. The AI exterminated the Draxus, killing Harker. Irving survived, but with no memory of his corruption. Jago suggested that Stoker refrain from mentioning giant leeches from space in his biography of Irving, but that he could get away with just about anything in a Gothic melodrama.

Having identified Jago and Litefoot as the Doctor's friends, the Master slowly drained away their life essences with energy dampeners disguised as mirrors. They became so withered that – as the Master intended – they left a note asking for help at the Doctor's Baker Street house. The sixth Doctor received his friends' message in future, and went incognito as assistant to a stage hypnotist, Madame Sosotris. She broke Inspector Quick's conditioning, and he restored Jago and Litefoot by revering the mirror-drain. Stymied, the Master escaped in his TARDIS.

While interrogating Ellie about her friends, the Master used a device to "correct" the metabolic anomaly he had detected within her. Ellie's vampiric nature took hold, and she murdered the assistant curator at the Scarlet Gallery...

1895 (16th October to early November) - JAGO & LITEFOOT SERIES 12 -> Ellie stole *Death on the Platform* – a painting that showed Jago killing her brother Jim while Litefoot looked on – from the Scarlet Gallery, then pledged fealty to the most ancient vampire in London: the Old One. Jago, Litefoot and Quick investigated the murder, and found that the Gallery's curator, Mr Kindred, was extending his life by trapping people in paintings. Quick shot Kindred in self-defence, freeing his captives.

Afterward, Jago and Litefoot enabled the Flickermen – inter-dimensional creatures largely imperceptible to the naked eye – to return to their native realm. They also became embroiled in the schemes of Mr Ravener, one of the Old One's lieutenants, as part of his mission to elimi-nate vampires who strayed from the fold. The detectives saved Lucilla Fredericks, a young vampire at St Cecilia's School for Girls, from Ravener's clutches – but were unaware when Ellie returned later and murdered her.

As the Old One's slumbering vampire army prepared to wake and take over London, Ellie lured Jago and Litefoot to the fiend's lair. Ellie recanted her murder spree upon realising that Jago had mercy-killed her brother, and staked the Old One to death. The Old One's army perished without his influence, and Jago staked Ravener through the heart. The battle wounded Ellie, and a transfusion of Litefoot's blood seemed to again make her vampirism dor-mant.[1758]

1896

1896 - ST: THE JAGO & LITEFOOT REVIVAL[1759] -> For some time after the New Year, Henry Gordon Jago and Professor Litefoot experienced a distinct lack of challenges and adventures, and became melancholic. Litefoot joined Jean Basemore on a dig at Minos, and wound up summon-ing the fifth-dimensional Gentlemen of the Dice (who manifested as cowboys) with a mouth organ. The dying tenth Doctor, on his farewell tour, banished the Gentlemen. Litefoot threw the harmonica into the Aegean.

The eleventh Doctor returned with the harmonica, and helped Jago and Litefoot confront the Gentlemen in their home dimension. Jago and Litefoot told so many stories involving luck and chance, the Gentlemen became engorged on Fortune Energy and burst. Afterward, the Doctor enjoyed a glass of ginger beer with his friends at the Red Tavern.

Not long after, Jago gatecrashed Litefoot's retelling of these events at the thirteenth meeting of the Club for Curious Scientific Men, whose members included Professor Challenger and Mr Griffen. Litefoot entitled the adventure *Some Observations Pertaining to a Succession of Events Which Took Place Both Upon the Island of Minos and Within a Nameless Dimension*, Jago preferred *The Triumph of H.G. Jago, a Melodrama in Two Acts*, and they compromised on *The Jago & Litefoot Revival*.

1896 - JAGO & LITEFOOT SERIES 13[1760] **->** A Time Agent, Cara, pursued Magnus Greel but arrived some time after his death. She eliminated Jago's stage magician, Harry Hypno, as a potential witness. Cara's damaged vortex manipulator leaked chronoplasm, which interacted with her brain-scanning Cortex Manipulator...

= ... and the resultant chrono-cortoplasm transported Jago, Litefoot and eventually Cara to parallel realities that best matched their insecurities. Litefoot found himself on Professor Jago's mortuary slab, and an audience pelted Jago with fruit. In another reality, they were murderous agents of the Old One. In yet another, Commissioner Litefoot and Sgt Jago of the Time Agency prosecuted Cara's court-martial. Cara's vortex manipulator detonated, propelling Jago and Litefoot into still another parallel timeline...

= Mrs Bartholomew, of the enigmatic Chapel of Night, worked to bring across souls from yet-another reality where the Anglo-Saxons ruled. Jago and Litefoot foiled the Chapel's intended invasion of this world, but Bartholomew escaped.

Aspects of the Weng-Chiang affair remained unresolved in this timeline. The alt-Jago was married to the barmaid Xiu Xiu, but hoped to regain his lost standing by killing and exhibiting the Giant Rat of the River Fleet. The alt-Litefoot, a noted Sinophile and pathologist, had purchased Weng-Chiang's artefacts from the Palace Theatre on auction. "Our" Jago and Litefoot aided their counterparts in foiling a robbery at Litefoot's house, even as the infernal investigators Betterman and Aubrey shot the Giant Rat with the Eye of the Dragon...

Mrs Bartholomew, a.k.a. Angelica, began losing her toehold on this reality, and tried to recorporealise herself by technologically syphoning the reality from others. Her attempt to do this to Jago and Litefoot backfired, as they hailed from a different reality, destroying Angelica and the Chapel of Night's spaceship. The alt-Litefoot and alt-Jago teamed up with Betterman and Aubrey against supernatural threats.

1760 Dating *Jago & Litefoot* Series 13 (*The Stuff of Nightmares*, 13.1; *Chapel of Night*, 13.2; *How the Other Half Lives*, 13.3; *Too Much Reality*, 13.4) - The new season opens without preamble or a pick-up from previous stories, and saw release after *ST: The Jago & Litefoot Revival* [1896]. Conspicuously, while explaining Greel's fate to Cara, neither Jago nor Litefoot mention the fiend's resurrection and final death in *J&L* Series 5 (but that happened in 1968, so perhaps it wasn't relevant to say). Nonetheless, it's possible Litefoot means that second meeting when he says he encountered Greel "at least three years ago" (in, relative to Litefoot's lifetime and "modern-day" perspective, 1893).

Cara suggests that Greel arrived by boat in London in "1889", evidently indicating when *The Talons of Weng-Chiang* takes place. Other *Talons* references are a bit varied – Jago says that story happened "a few years ago, you know"; Chang performed at the Palace Theatre "around five years" ago and "several years ago".

1761 *Jago & Litefoot* Series 13 ended on a cliffhanger. The passing in 2017 of actor Trevor Baxter, who portrayed Litefoot, brought the series to an end save for a coda story, *Jago & Litefoot Forever*.

1762 CD, *NM V2: The Carrionite Curse*

1763 Dating *The Water Thief* (BBC children's 2-in-1 #6) - Grenfell and Hunt's excavation of Oxyrhynchus – a rich source of historical artifacts – happened from 1896 to 1906.

1764 Dating *The Sands of Time* (MA #22) - The date is given (p29).

1765 *The Tenth Doctor Year One*: "The Weeping Angels of Mons"

1766 *DotD: Enemy Aliens*

1767 "Six months" before Christmas Day, 1897, according to *TW: The Torchwood Archive* (BF).

1768 *Paper Cuts*. Queen Victoria's reign began on 20th June, 1837, and her Diamond Jubilee was held in 1897.

1769 *DEyes 4: The Monster of Montmartre*. Zidler died 12th November, 1897.

1770 Dating *The Death of Art* (NA #54) - It's "26 November 1897" (p16).

1771 *The Torchwood Archive* (BF). The Tsar is named as "Tsar Alexander", and the timeframe involved suggests that it's Tsar Alexander III (who ruled 1881-1894). Notably, Russia suffered a famine in 1891-1892. The Bad Penny is the locket that makes Alex Hopkins go off the rails and kill his teammates in *TW: Fragments*. Archie's account suggests the Tsar passes the Bad Penny along to Victoria in 1897 (so he obtained it in 1895).

1772 "Just over one hundred years" before *TW: The Conspiracy*.

1773 Dating *The Torchwood Archive* (BF *TW* special release #1) - Archie names the exact day.

1774 *TW: The Dying Room*. Wilhelm II ruled 15th June, 1888 to 9th November, 1918.

> "Our" Litefoot used a stabiliser taken from the Chapel of Night to reopen a portal back home. He and Jago stepped through, to see a hot air balloon in the night sky...

How Jago and Litefoot dealt with this conundrum is unknown, but they continued to have strange and peculiar adventures together.[1761]

Professor Litefoot authored *Reminiscences of the Peculiar*, a summation of some of the foes he'd encountered.[1762]

c 1896 - THE WATER THIEF[1763] **->** The eleventh Doctor, Amy and Rory were present as Bernard Grenfell and Arthur Hunt excavated the village of Behneseh, formerly the Egyptian city of Oxyrhynchus. Some Papyrus books, including a Book of the Dead, recovered from the site had been made from a super-robust reed – the Water Thief – that revived when Rory spilled tea on it, and threatened to overrun Earth. The Doctor and Amy went back to Oxyrhynchus per a note from the Doctor to himself, then returned and moved the reed to a water world.

1896 (10th November) - THE SANDS OF TIME[1764] **->** The fifth Doctor, Tegan and Nyssa arrived in the Egyptian Room of the British Museum. At the invitation of Lord Kenilworth, they attended the unwrapping of an ancient mummy, only to discover that the mummy was the perfectly preserved body of Nyssa herself. The Doctor came to realise that the intelligence of the Osirian Nephthys was in Nyssa's body.

Father Thomas Monaghan, the victim of a Weeping Angel, found himself in Scotland, 1896, just as Jamie Colquhoun was born.[1765] The Doctor had a season ticket to Division Two football's 1896-97 season.[1766] Torchwood hired a man named Archie, who would serve as its archivist for more than a century.[1767] Lord Salisbury lent the Doctor a morning coat for the Queen's Diamond Jubilee.[1768] The Doctor attended the funeral of Charles Zidler, the co-owner of the Moulin Rouge.[1769]

1897 (November) - THE DEATH OF ART[1770] **->** The seventh Doctor, Chris and Roz investigated a psychic disturbance in France. They encountered the Brotherhood, a secret society researching psychic activity. A man called Montague ruled one faction of the Brotherhood, but another, "the Family", were working against him. The outbreak of psychic powers was because the Quoth, multidimensional beings, had taken shelter in human brains. The Doctor sided with the Family against Montague, who was killed. The Doctor retrieved all the Quoth and took them to a new home in a neutron star.

The Committee of Erebus and the Bad Penny[1771]

Tsar Alexander III learned of Queen Victoria's Torchwood, and founded his own alien-fighting organisation: the KVI. Fearing that the sporadic nature of alien threats to Earth might usher in periods of appeasement or disarmament, the Queen and the Tsar collaborated to create a mutual foe that Earth's champions could remain vigilant against. They parlayed with alien leaders who, in exchange for a stipend of Torchwood and the KVI's technology stores, formed "the Committee". The group would periodically test Earth's defences, and operated out of Erebus.

Clandestinely, the Committee expanded its purview and invaded other worlds, to sell them off for massive profit. In time, the Committee members would shed their physical form and adopt bodies, either artificial or physical, on target planets. When the Tsar learned of the Committee's ambitions, they gave him with a locket variously known as the Bad Penny, the Red Key and Object One. It served as a bad-luck charm that scanned all possible futures and moved events toward the worst of them. While the Tsar had the Bad Penny, Russia suffered crop failure, infant mortality, political unrest and a strengthening of Royal blood disease. Two years later, he passed it along to Victoria as "a present", weakening the British Empire. Victoria ordered Captain Jack Harkness to get rid of the Bad Penny, but he instead named it "the Red Key" (owing to the instability it caused in Russia) and stored it in the Torchwood Cardiff archives.

The Bad Penny would be repeatedly discarded or lost, but always return to Torchwood throughout the decades – even to its very end in the far future.

During his time as a rogue Time Agent, Jack Harkness worked as an Enabler for the Committee: a nefarious organisation that exploited Capris V, in the constellation of Fornax, as well as worlds in Cygnus A, Omega Centauri and Andromeda. Jack falsified records to stop the Committee from taking an interest in the Milky Way, but the Committee did so anyway, and began studying Earth.[1772]

1897 (25th December) - TW: THE TORCHWOOD ARCHIVE (BF)[1773] **->** Archie, as head of Torchwood House's library, used a Computational Organic Processing Device – a "knowledge sponge" – to create a new catalogue for alien technology obtained by field agents. Having done so, he logged the Bad Penny into the Archive and designated it Object One.

Kaiser Wilhelm II founded the Institute of Alien Technology as a counterpart to Torchwood.[1774]

1898

Sir Toby Kinsella, the head of Counter-Measures, was born.[1775] **In 1898, humanity's average life expectancy was forty-nine years, nine months and five days.**[1776] The Martian landing at Horsell Common, as depicted in *War of the Worlds*, was indeed fictional.[1777] The Valeyard claimed that the Doctor owned a photograph from the Stockbridge Second Eleven of 1898.[1778] The fifth Doctor was once up against the cricketer Wilfred Rhodes, the best left-arm spinner the Doctor had ever met... save for the Doctor himself.[1779]

wih - (=) ? 1898 - FP: WARRING STATES[1780] **->** The timeship Compassion required an independent power source, and extruded part of her internal dimensions into Chinese history as a White Pyramid. Compassion's machinations brought Cousin Octavia of Faction Paradox and a Chinese girl named Liu Hui Ying into conflict over a casket found within the pyramid in 1900, and they both travelled (Octavia by derailing a Faction Paradox train while doing so) to the pyramid itself. Compassion time-looped the bat-tle between the two women – sometimes Octavia prevailed, sometimes Ying would. Each "winner" became a mummy within the casket, enabling Compassion to power herself from their witchblood.

Compassion sustained herself in this manner for "thousands of years", but Octavia and Ying finally combined efforts to defeat her, and vanished into another reality.

Enigmatic circus people, the Night Travellers, per-formed in the dead of night and left a trail of "damage and sorrow" – as well as claiming children to "live with them forever" – wherever they performed. In 1898, they were responsible for a number of disappearances and coma victims in the town of Wellsfield.[1781]

1898 - THE BANQUO LEGACY[1782] **->** A scientist, Harris, built a machine that could share thoughts. He demonstrated it at Banquo Manor as a Time Lord device trapped the eighth Doctor, Fitz and Compassion. The Doctor discovered that the butler, Simpson, was a Time Lord searching for Compassion. The Doctor unravelled the web of blackmail and murder involving Harris and his

---

1775 Extrapolating from actor Hugh Ross, born 28th April, 1945, being age 66 when he started playing Kinsella in *Counter-Measures* Series 1 (set in 1964).
1776 *TW: Miracle Day*
1777 According to the Doctor in *Heart of Stone* (p79). *War of the Worlds* was published in 1898 and had a contemporary setting.
1778 *Trial of the Valeyard*
1779 *Alien Heart*. Rhodes lived 1877-1973, and began his career in 1898.
1780 Dating *FP: Warring States* (FP novel #4) - The White Pyramid seems to (mostly) be located outside linear time, so the dating here, based upon the year in which Compassion allows the Pyramid to become his-torically noticeable (p187), might be a bit of a cheat. One interpretation of the ending is that Octavia and Ying leave the realm of fiction altogether.
1781 *TW: From Out of the Rain*
1782 Dating *The Banquo Legacy* (EDA #35) - The date is given (p7).
1783 *The Curse of Fenric*
1784 "Ten long summers" before the main portion of *The Emerald Tiger*.
1785 Dating *Grand Theft Cosmos* (BF BBC7 #2.5) - Lucie expresses frustration to the Doctor that as it's 1898, she can't play her MP3 player in public.
1786 According to Alice's diary on Torchwood.org.uk. A morgue inventory on the website suggests that Holroyd's partner was named Philip Lyle. Holroyd and Guppy appear in *TW: Fragments*.
1787 "Thirty, forty years", the Doctor estimates, before

The Angels Take Manhattan.
1788 The Haisman Timeline. *Leth-St: Beast of Fang Rock* [1902] has Ben Travers mention his "three year old" nephew Edward.
1789 *Leth-St: The Schizoid Earth* (ch2).
1790 Dating *FP: Movers* and *FP: The Labyrinth of Histories* (FP audios #1.5-1.6) - It's "one hundred and twenty-five years" after 1764. More specifically, it's "about six months" before the Siege of Mafeking, which commenced in October 1899. Emma comments that Justine's step-mother is always "drunk after a Saturday", so it's probably Sunday.
1791 Dating *TW: Fragments* (TW 2.12) - It's before 1900 per the prediction of The Girl (who everyone calls the tarot-reader according to Torchwood.org.uk). Jack gen-eralises that Earth is "a century away" from official first contact with alien life, also hinting that it's closer to 1900 than not.
   Transcripts of Jack's bar conversations (briefly seen on screen, but better illustrated on the official Torchwood website and in BBC Books' *The Torchwood Archives*) are dated to 12th February, 1987; 16th December, 1897; and 4th April, 1898. However, as Alice Guppy joins Torchwood in mid-September 1898 and seems very adept when she meets Captain Jack, it's probably 1899 when she and Holroyd approach him.
1792 Dating *TW: The Victorian Age* (BF TW #2.1) - Jack's audio log names the exact day. It's "twenty years" since Torchwood's foundation in *Tooth and Claw* [1879].
   The historical details all match with it being 1899... Victoria says she's "79" (she was born 4th February, 1819), and no assassination attempt on her life has

sister, Catherine. Simpson was thought killed, and the Doctor's trio left before Simpson was missed by Gallifrey.

On 12th January, 1898, Florence Sundvik died. Mary Eliza Millington was born on 3rd March, dying four days later. At the end of the nineteenth century, the grandfather of Reverend Wainwright translated the Viking Runes in the crypt of his church.[1783]

The were-tiger Dawon became distant from her brother, Shardul Khan, and attempted – and failed – to destroy the Emerald Tiger crystal that granted them eternal life. She became locked in her tiger form, and was captured as a prized animal. Bereft of both of his siblings, Khan swallowed the Emerald Tiger whole.[1784]

1898 - GRAND THEFT COSMOS[1785] **->** The eighth Doctor and Lucie went to Stockholm by train to see Strindberg's new play, and made the acquaintance of Frederick Simonsson, an art buyer for the King of Sweden. The time-travelling Headhunter summoned Tardelli forth from the black diamond that Simonsson had obtained, as the Emperor Vassilar-G of Ralta wanted to hire him as an official court artist. The Doctor convinced Tardelli to perform a fifth-dimensional dump on the diamond, sending its pocket universe into the gap between universes, where it could exist independently. He also confiscated the Tardelli paintings in Simonsson's possession while the diamond's stone guardian wandered off into the woods around Stockholm. The Headhunter and Karen took Tardelli away to work for the Emperor Vassilar-G, but the Doctor believed that the Emperor had notoriously fickle tastes, and would likely eat Tardelli on a balcony, in front of a crowd, when he got bored with him.

Having failed to sell the diamond as an energy source to the industrialist Yashin, the Headhunter thought it best to avoid Earth between now and his death in 1905, lest he exact retribution.

Emily Holroyd of Torchwood Cardiff burned her partner to death when a mutative infection transformed him into a giant snake. His replacement, Alice Guppy, was hired on Tuesday, 13th September, 1898.[1786]

> **(=) The Weeping Angels at Winter Quay sent Rory Williams back in time. He lived out his days, alone, before dying in bed in 1938.**[1787]

1899

Professor Edward Travers, an associate of the second Doctor and a host of the Great Intelligence, was born in May 1899 – as was his twin, Vincent.[1788] Edward Travers spent a chunk of his youth exploring the snow-capped Himalayas.[1789]

wih - 1899 (a Sunday in March) - FP: MOVERS / A LABYRINTH OF HISTORIES[1790] **->** Godfather Sabbath had just been appointed the head of Faction Paradox's military wing. To insulate his bloodline from temporal interference by the Faction's enemies, he began systematically killing off his family tree. The godfather murdered his mother, then his mother's father – after each slaying, the historical equations governing Godfather Sabbath's existence were rebalanced so he could exist without progenitors. He next tried to kill his maternal grandfather's mother, Fiora Vend, but arrived after she was already pregnant. As killing his grandfather twice would be in very bad form, the godfather instead murdered Fiora's niece, Emma James, hoping it might open up further avenues of attack in his family history.

Godfather Morlock recruited Emma's cousin and best friend, Justine McManus, to join Faction Paradox.

Jack Harkness Begins a Century of Service for Torchwood

1899 - TW: FRAGMENTS[1791] **-> Jack Harkness had taken to wandering from drinking den to drinking den. He had been "killed" fourteen times in the proceeding six months when Emily Holroyd and Alice Guppy of Torchwood investigated statements Jack had made in taverns concerning the Doctor. Holroyd offered Jack employment as an uncontracted field agent, and he accepted after a mysterious young girl who read tarot predicted that "the century would turn twice" before he would see the Doctor again.**

1899 (17th May) - TW: THE VICTORIAN AGE[1792]

> "The nineteenth century is when everything changes, and We are ready."
>
> —Her Majesty Queen Victoria

Torchwood had quietly thwarted ten plots to kill Queen Victoria, and another to replace her with a clockwork waxwork. The group also dealt with a metal plague designed to reverse the Industrial Revolution, a thief who moved through mirrors and killer caterpillars in Kew Gardens. Incidents involving aliens and Torchwood enhanced the legend of Spring-Heeled Jack.

Jack Harkness assisted the Queen as she inspected Torchwood's new base in the London History Museum. The Queen was surprised that Jack would so freely approach her "after last time". A humanoid alien capable of draining people of their youth awoke from a sarcophagus in the HQ, and aged the head of Torchwood London – the thirty-eight-year-old Archie – an additional fifty years. Jack and the Queen hotly pursued the alien through

London, an escapade that ended when Her Majesty inspired the elderly people in a pub to join her on one last adventure. Victoria and the pensioners surrounded the creature, depriving it of a food source and causing it to disintegrate.

Afterward, Jack politely turned down the Queen's offer that he lead Torchwood London, as he was committed to Torchwood Cardiff. He accepted, however, her invitation that they go and enjoy some strawberry ice.

Archie recovered from the alien's attack and discovered it had left him with an extended lifespan. He would work as a Torchwood archivist into the twenty-first century. [1793]

c 1899 - THE JUSTICE OF JALXAR[1794] **->** The Jalxar Peninsula existed in a heavily regulated but undeniably peaceful end of the Milky Way, where mind-scanning justice robots terminated those guilty of serious crimes without benefit of a jury or judge. A humanoid adjudicator partnered with each robot, to guarantee that they respected the laws of different planets and acted with a reasonable morality. A coach driver, Bobby Stamford, found a justice robot when it landed by accident in Victorian London, and adapted its technology to become a crime fighter: the Pugilist.

A month later, the fourth Doctor and the first Romana detected emissions coming from the Jalxar vessel, and consulted with Professor George Litefoot and Henry Gordon Jago. The Jalxar robot had been running amok and slaughtering criminals, and the Pugilist died saving his beloved, the pickpocket Mary Brown, from it. The Doctor's group caused the robot to fall into the Thames, where it sank into the mud and deactivated. Before he and Romana departed, the Doctor was delighted to buy his friends muffins from the same vendor who served them after the Weng-Chiang affair a decade ago.

1899 - TW: CONSEQUENCES: "The Baby Farmers"[1795] **->** Admiral Sir Henry Montague financed an operation aboard the decommissioned HMS *Hades* to breed extra-terrestrials and create an army of superstrong amphibious assassins for the Empire. Torchwood – led by Emily Holroyd, and otherwise composed of Alice Guppy, Charles Gaskell and Jack Harkness – destroyed the operation. Jack allowed members of the race that Montague was farming to kill the man.

Holroyd received a sentient alien book that Jack had sent through the Rift from 2009, and per his instructions filed it away in the University College library. This caused the book to become aware of Torchwood's existence, and it desired stories pertaining to the group.

= 1899 (September) - LETH-ST: TRAVERS & WELLS: OTHER WARS, OTHER WORLDS[1796] **->** Mars became a dying world, the Martians killing one another over its dwindling resources. To survive, the Martians invaded Earth with giant tripods armed with heat rays. The whole of Europe fell, as likely did India, Singapore and South Africa. Queen Victoria fled to Canada, and died of a broken heart.

occurred (because Torchwood has been eliminating the potential threats, Jack says) in "seventeen years"; in real life, the last documented effort to kill her happened in 1882. Victoria ends this story by vowing to lay the foundation stone for the Victoria Museum and then retire from public life – she did so in May 1899, in what was her last public ceremony. There's some intimation that the alien's life-transference powers actually give Victoria an extra jolt of vitality, but it can't be long-lasting – historically, she died about a year and a half after this story, on 22nd January, 1901.

Mention of replacing Victoria with a "clockwork waxwork" brings to mind *J&L* S7: *The Wax Princess*, although it's hard to see how Torchwood was involved in that.
1793 *TW: The Torchwood Archive* (BF). Archie is the enigmatic leader of Torchwood Two in the modern day (*TW: Everything Changes*).
1794 Dating *The Justice of Jalxar* (BF 4th Doc #1.4) - The blurb touts "It is the dawn of a new century". Jago and Litefoot note that they haven't seen the fourth Doctor since "That business with Greel over ten years ago" (*The Talons of Weng-Chiang*), so it's quite some time after their own adventures in the *Jago & Litefoot* series.
1795 Dating *TW: Consequences*: "The Baby Farmers"

(*TW* novel #15a) - Charles Dickens' reading at the Taliesin Lodge (in *The Unquiet Dead*) happened some "thirty Christmases past". Moreover, the future Jack writes a letter to Holroyd (p241) that says, "I'm guessing the year [where you are] is 1899."
1796 Dating *Leth-St: Travers & Wells: Other Wars, Other Worlds* (*Leth-St* novella #3) – The month and year are given (ch1). Travers misspeaks a little in saying that Wells published *The War of the Worlds* in 1898; it was first serialised in *Pearson's Magazine* in 1897.
1797 *The War Games.* The Boer War ran 1899-1902, the Boxer Rising was in 1900.
1798 *TW: Miracle Day.* It's not specified that this was for Torchwood, and it might've been during his time as a Time Agent.
1799 *The Flames of Cadiz.* The Boxer Rebellion lasted Autumn 1899 to September 1901.
1800 *Unbound: Sympathy for the Devil.* The Boxer Rebellion happened August 1899 to September 1901.
1801 "Just over twenty years" before *DotD: Smoke and Mirrors.*
1802 Mentioned in *Planet of the Spiders, Revenge of the Cybermen, The Vampires of Venice*, "Voyager", "Facades", *Cat's Cradle: Time's Crucible, The Pit, Head Games, The*

America marshalled its forces – although Chicago was lost and Menlo Park burned, Nikola Tesla developed effective weaponry against the intruders. Governor Teddy Roosevelt and his Rough Riders crossed to England, and encountered Travers and Wells. The time travellers destroyed the Martians' facility at Dartmoor, and the humanity-ending bacteria inside it. That done, Travers and Wells' kontron crystals bore them away from this reality...

The Boxer Rebellion

Battlefields from the Boxer Rising and the Boer War were lifted by the War Lords.[1797] **Jack Harkness was in China for the Boxer Rebellion.**[1798] The first Doctor and Susan used a smokescreen to make their escape from the Boxer Rebellion.[1799]

= The chanting that kept the mind-parasites in China docile was interrupted, resulting in the Boxer Rebellion.[1800]

Harry Houdini

Harry Houdini aided the first Doctor, Polly and Ben in 1890s New York against the Ovids: stranded beings of pure thought who went from world to world via crystal spheres, and were giving people nightmares while trying to communicate with them. The incident caused Houdini to learn about the existence of things beyond the spiritual, and became part of a lifelong friendship he held with different Doctors. One Ovid sphere survived, and resurfaced at a fairground in the 1920s.[1801]

The Doctor learned a great deal from Houdini.[1802] **Houdini was slightly shorter than five slightly scary girls that the Doctor encountered: the Vampires of**

Venice.[1803] The sixth Doctor elaborated that he didn't study with Houdini, Houdini studied with *him*.[1804] The Doctor showed Houdini how to escape from ropes.[1805] The Doctor taught Houdini everything he knew.[1806] **The Doctor also learned sleight of hand from Maskelyne.**[1807]

The first Master also met Houdini.[1808]

The Panoptican Theatre in Cardiff opened in 1899, and hosted touring dramatic companies.[1809] Nikola Tesla received the fright of his life in 1899, thinking he was hearing Martians, when a radio receiver vocalized Jupiter's radiation pulses.[1810] The Doctor met Nikola Tesla, and together they thwarted a Vardan invasion.[1811]

1899 - PLAYERS[1812] **->** The sixth Doctor and Peri stopped the murder of a 24-year-old Winston Churchill, who was serving as a war correspondent in South Africa. The Doctor helped Churchill escape from a P.O.W. camp, and Churchill returned home a hero.

1899 (26th December) - CASTLE OF FEAR[1813] **->** The fifth Doctor and Nyssa visited Stockbridge, and witnessed a mummery that entailed Father Christmas, St George, a dragon... and a rendition of the fifth Doctor himself and his TARDIS. The travellers went back to 1199 to investigate the source of the play. They returned to 1899 to find that the Rutan spaceship in Stockbridge Castle had regrown in the interim, and was influencing the town residents to dig it out. The Doctor and Nyssa piloted the weakened ship into the stratosphere, but its engines triggered a hyperspatial warp-core explosion that flung them to Stockbridge in the early twenty-first century.

The Doctor and Iris met Oscar Wilde in Venice after his imprisonment. They also fought some "fish people".[1814]

In 1899, twenty years to the day after Torchwood's for-

Sorcerer's Apprentice, The Devil Goblins from Neptune, Project: Twilight, The Church and the Crown, Eye of Heaven, Independence Day, Frontier Worlds, Circular Time: "Summer", *The Mind's Eye,* "Prisoners of Time", *Dreamland* (DW), "Don't Step on the Grass", *1001 Nights, DotD: Smoke and Mirrors, DEyes 3: Masterplan, The High Price of Parking,* "Theatre of the Mind" and *The Twelfth Doctor Year One:* "The Swords of Kali".

There's no date given in any of those stories. Houdini lived 1874-1926. In *Planet of the Ood,* a bound Donna asks the Doctor, "You must have met Houdini", but he's too busy trying to wriggle free to answer.
1803 *The Vampires of Venice*
1804 *The Ultimate Adventure*
1805 *DEyes 3: Masterplan*
1806 *The Twelfth Doctor Year One:* "The Swords of Kali"
1807 *The Ribos Operation.* No date is given, but this is

presumably the magician John Neville Maskelyne (1839-1917, and also mentioned in *Camera Obscura*), although it could be his grandson, the magician Jasper Maskelyne (1902-1973).
1808 *1stA: The Destination Wars*
1809 Torchwood.org.uk, elaborating on *TW: From Out of the Rain.*
1810 *Iris S4: A Lift in Time*
1811 *Maker of Demons*
1812 Dating *Players* (PDA #21) - The year is given (p15). The Doctor says it's "just at the beginning of the [Second] Boer War!", which started 11th October, 1899.
1813 Dating *Castle of Fear* (BF #127) - The exact day is given. The fifth Doctor here says that he hasn't visited Stockbridge prior to 1899.
1814 *The Scarlet Empress.* Although never specified, the "fish people" could be the amphibious gondoliers that

mation, Queen Victoria recorded a confession of how her actions and those of the Tsar had created the Committee. [1815] **Gerald Carter**, age 24, **joined Torchwood** after being trained in military intelligence. One of his earliest missions was the Centurian Incident of New Year's Eve, 1899. [1816]

The Twentieth Century

Joan Redfern had married Oliver, her childhood sweetheart, but he died at the Battle of Spion Kop. [1817] **The first Doctor was present at the Relief of Mafeking.** [1818]

Matthew Lethbridge-Stewart, the paternal uncle of Brigadier Lethbridge-Stewart, was born in 1900. [1819] In 1900, Emily Holroyd drafted a manifesto pertaining to Torchwood's Rules and Regulations, including guidelines concerning the group's succession of leadership. [1820] Professor Angelchrist saw H.G. Wells speak about *The War of the Worlds* at a bookshop on Charing Cross Road. [1821] The Empress Alexandria praised the Doctor's oratory skills. [1822]

Nurse Albertine studied battle surgery and saw some action during the South African War. She would come to work for Toby the Sapient Pig. [1823] **Colonel Hugh served in the Boer War.** [1824]

The first Master dropped in on Earth from time to time. [1825] The painter Millicent Mary Litehorne, born in Cork, produced eleven major works, including *When the Boats Come In* and *The Fisherman's Friend*, before dying of consumption. [1826] The artist John Singer Sargent painted the third Doctor's portrait. [1827] The Doctor met the celebrated cricket-player W.G. Grace, during an incident with the Medusoids. [1828]

> (=) By the beginning of the twentieth century, Dhakan – the alternate Earth ruled by Katsura Sato – had interstellar travel. [1829]

The Doctor told L. Frank Baum that if monkeys had wings, they technically would no longer be monkeys. [1830]

Iris met Arthur Balfour, a British statesman and Prime Minister, in the Reform Club. [1831]

1900 (January) - TALES FROM THE VAULT [1832] **->** Kalicarache, an extra-terrestrial being composed of psionic energy and could possess dead bodies, escaped when the prison transport carrying it crashed in Africa. The first Doctor, Steven and Dodo confronted Kalicarache during the Battle of Spion Kop, after he had possessed the late Lt Thornicroft. Kalicarache's consciousness was left trapped inside the fabric of a coat worn by a killed solider, Tommy Watkins. In the decades to come, Kalicarache could control anyone wearing the item.

> **wih - (=) 1900 (May) - FP: WARRING STATES** [1833] **->** Compassion furthered her gambit with the White Pyramid by placing the Empress Dowager Ci Xi in a garden within her internal dimensions, and then impersonating her. Cousin Octavia, accompanied by her Red Burial and Prester John, arrived in this time zone to lay claim to a casket found within the Pyramid by an archaeological team, as she believed that it held the secret of immortality. Compassion pitted Octavia against Liu Hui Ying, and they both travelled back to the Pyramid.

When Compassion's stratagem finally failed, the archeological team found only an empty tomb.

1900 (July) - UPSTAIRS [1834] **->** The first Doctor, Steven and Vicki discovered the enlarged time fungus in the attic of 10 Downing Street, and released a fast-growing, benign fungus from the TARDIS' Xenovegetative Laboratory to take over its territory. With the locale cleansed, Lord Salisbury was the last Prime Minister to decline to make No. 10 his official residence.

---

appear in Paul Magrs' *The Stones of Venice*. This meeting must have occurred after Wilde's release from prison on 19th May, 1897, but before his death on 30th November, 1900.
1815 *TW: The Torchwood Archive* (BF)
1816 Per Torchwood.co.uk. There's some confusion regarding Gerald's surname – on screen he's credited as just "Gerald", the official Torchwood website gives his last name as "Carter", but *The Torchwood Archives* (BBC) and *Torchwood: The Encyclopedia* both claim that it's "Kneale".
1817 *Human Nature* (TV). The Battle of Spion Kop occurred on 23rd and 24th January, 1900.
1818 *The Daleks' Master Plan, The Invasion of Time, The Unicorn and the Wasp.* This occurred on 17th May, 1900, when British troops ended the Siege of Mafeking dur-

ing the second Boer War.
1819 *Leth-St:* "What's Past is Prologue". Matthew is 17 at Christmas 1917.
1820 *TW: Consequences:* "Kaleidoscope"
1821 *Paradox Lost*
1822 *The Next Life.* Alexandra Feodorovna, the wife of Nicholas II, was empress of Russia from 26th November, 1894 to 17th July, 1918.
1823 *Year of the Pig.* The South African War (also known as the Second Boer War) lasted 1899-1902.
1824 *The Unicorn and the Wasp*
1825 *1stA: The Destination Wars.* Based upon these trips, it amuses him to pattern Destination's society after Earth's.
1826 *The Renaissance Man.* Litehorne appears to be an actual Victorian/Edwardian painter in the *Doctor Who*

& 1900 - THE BEAST OF KRAVENOS[1835] **->** The fourth Doctor, the second Romana and K9 visited Jago and Litefoot when nucleaonic energy readings kept emanating from the New Regency Theatre. To better trace the anomaly, K9 performed on stage as a modern mechanical marvel, and introduced such acts as Mystic Margaret and her Hierarchical Hamsters. Sir Nicholas Asquin had found a spaceship from Kravenos, and – as its teleport was not properly calibrated for humans – increasingly became a shuffling savage monster. The Doctor cured Sir Nicholas of the condition, and safely disposed of the ship.

Thomas Carnacki had Father Ignatious of the Holy Order of Glistening Tattooists tattoo arcane symbols on his chest in blessed ink, which turned his body into a lethal weapon against the supernatural.[1836]

The toadstool-like xXltttxtolxtol discovered their homeworld would extinguish in a few thousand years, and sent a stardrive through the Rift to "invite" to other species to travel to them... a means of identifying a world to conquer. The Queen granted George Herbert Sanderson of Torchwood permission to visit the stardrive's planet of origin, a few solar systems distant, on behalf of the Empire. Sanderson experienced time dilation during the journey, and aged little as a century passed in the outside universe.

Late in her life, Queen Victoria commissioned Agnes Havisham to serve as the Torchwood Assessor. Havisham would enter cryo-sleep at a storage facility in Swindon, and only awaken when automatic systems predicted deadly peril for a Torchwood station. Havisham was to have absolute authority over Torchwood in such cases. Her hibernation chamber was finally ready in late 1901. She would only awaken four times in the next hundred years – for "two invasions, one apocalypse and a Visitation by the Ambassadors of the Roaring Bang".[1837]

Queen Victoria passed away on 22nd January, 1901. Jack Harkness never definitively concluded whether the Queen or her clockwork duplicate had died. Despite the prime minister's advocacy of Torchwood, Victoria's successor, Edward VII, failed to understand its importance. Jack won the group some short-term funding by taking the King to Paris and getting him drunk.[1838]

1900 (December) - FOREIGN DEVILS[1839] **->** The second Doctor followed Jamie and Zoe's passage through the "spirit gate" in 1800, arriving exactly a hundred years later. The Chief Astrologer's curse started murdering the descendants of Roderick Upcott, and the Doctor teamed up with Carnacki, an investigator of the supernatural, to look into events at Upcott House. The curse used the spirit gate's dimensional energy to remove the house from time and space, and transformed Roderick Upcott's corpse into a dragon. The Doctor destroyed the spirit gate, which returned the house and made the dragon crumble to ash.

Capt. Jack Awakens, Goes Back Into Stasis

1901 - TW: EXIT WOUNDS[1840] **->** Alice Guppy and Charles Gaskell of Torchwood unearthed Jack Harkness, who had been buried since 27 AD. At Jack's urging, they placed him into cryo-freeze and timed his revival for the twenty-first century. Jack's younger self continued working for Torchwood.

---

universe but not real life, unlike the fictional "Mont Morensy Pescaville" whom the fourth Doctor invents.
1827 *Time in Office.* Sargent lived 1856-1925.
1828 *3rdA: The Havoc of Empires.* Grace lived 1848-1915.
1829 "The Glorious Dead"
1830 *A Thousand Tiny Wings.* Baum lived 1856-1919; *The Wonderful Wizard of Oz* saw print in 1900, but the described argument could have taken place either before or after publication.
1831 *Iris S2: The Two Irises.* Arthur Balfour, UK Prime Minister from 1902 to 1905, lived 1848-1930.
1832 Dating *Tales from the Vault* (BF CC 6.1) - Steven says that "The year is 1900". The Battle of Spion Kop lasted from 23rd to 24th January.
1833 Dating *FP: Warring States* (FP novel #4) - It's "a May afternoon in Peking, 1900" (p4). Prester John, here a member of Faction Paradox, is a legendary figure said to have ruled over a lost Christian nation.
1834 Dating *Upstairs* (BF CC #8.3) - The time fungus extends into many eras, but the central mass exists at a point a maid says is "July 1900."
1835 Dating *The Beast of Kravenos* (BF 4th Doc #6.1) - Jago and Litefoot met the first Romana in *The Justice of Jalxar* [c.1899]; here, they comment upon the oddity of two of the Doctor's companions having that name (a fun joke, even if they *surely* must know that the Doctor manifests in different bodies by now). With the first Romana featuring in Season 16, and *Kravenos* set in the interim between Seasons 17 and 18 – and sporting the Season 18 theme – it seems fair to keep with that and say that a year has passed since *Jalxar*.
1836 "A few years" before *Iris S3: Iris Rides Out.*
1837 *TW: Risk Assessment.* Victoria died on 22nd January, 1901, and as her conversation with Havisham occurs in December of a year that Victoria fears will see "her last Christmas", it's likely December 1900.
1838 Dating *Foreign Devils* (TEL #5) - It's "December 1900" (p35).
1839 *TW: The Torchwood Archive* (BF)
1840 Dating *TW: Exit Wounds* (TW 2.13) - The year is given.

> = Iris was "instrumental" in the final battles against the Martians in an alternate dimension.[1841]

In 1901, the Night Travellers were responsible for the disappearances of eight people from Church Stretton.[1842] In the same year, an English author began to write boy's stories for *The Ensign*.[1843] The Doctor saw the assassination of President McKinley.[1844] Henri de Toulouse-Lautrec, a painter affiliated with the Moulin Rouge, died in 1901.[1845]

1901 (20th October) - CRYPTOBIOSIS[1846] **->** The sixth Doctor and Peri sought to vacation aboard the *Lankester* (sic), a cargo ship en route from the Cape of Good Hope to New Orleans. The *Lankester*'s chief mate, Jacques De Requin, was smuggling two captured mermaids – Anthrotrite and her daughter, Galatea – to sell them for profit. Other mer-people, led by Anthrotrite's father Nereus, breached the ship's under-carriage. Anthrotrite died, the *Lankester* sank and the mer-people captured de Requin to torment him. The Doctor and Peri returned Galatea to her grandfather, and convinced him to discretely rescue any *Lankester* survivors. As part of these events, the Doctor was drafted to serve as a medical professional attached to the Merchant Navy.

On 12th December, 1901, John Lafayette, a linguist, accidentally travelled along a space-time path to ancient Babylon.[1847]

The War Doctor introduced his associate, the Squire, to Proust.[1848] **Jack Harkness dated Proust for a while, and claimed the man was rather immature.**[1849] **Jack was married at least once.**[1850] Jack Harkness met a precognitive named Sam who had just returned home from the Boer War.[1851] In the same year, Jack, Emily Holroyd and Alice Guppy defeated a shadowy terror that brutalised the imagination.[1852]

In 1902, Archibald Lethbridge-Stewart had a night of indiscretion with his sister-in-law, Lillian, while his brother Alistair was away. Gordon Conall Lethbridge-Stewart, the future father of Brigadier Alistair Lethbridge-Stewart, was born nine months later, still in 1092, and regarded as Alistair and Lillian's son.[1853]

On 10th March, 1902, Archie logged Object 3019, a weapon, into the Torchwood Archive.[1854] Baden-Powell taught the Doctor the rudiments of tracking.[1855] By 1902, there were Polynesian/alien hybrids on Easter Island again. They used the teleport device to resettle their forefathers' homeworld. The explorer Stockwood was still alive, and planned to return to the alien homeworld also.[1856]

Sarah Bernhardt starred in *Hamlet* at the New Regency Theatre.[1857] The Doctor told P.G. Wodehouse – who was

---

1841 "About seven years" after the 1894 component of *Iris: Enter Wildthyme*.

1842 *TW: From Out of the Rain*, off a newspaper reported dated "August 11th 1901".

1843 *The Mind Robber*

1844 *Byzantium!* (p179). No date given, but McKinley was shot 6th September, 1901, and died eight days later.

1845 *Demon Quest: The Demon of Paris*. Toulouse-Lautrec died 9th September, 1901.

1846 Dating *Cryptobiosis* (BF subscription promo #3) - The date is given.

1847 *Benny: Walking to Babylon*

1848 *The Eleventh Doctor Year Two*: "The Then and the Now". Marcel Proust lived 10th July, 1871 to 18th November, 1922.

1849 *TW: Dead Man Walking*

1850 As strongly implied by a photo of Jack and an unidentified woman in *TW: Something Blue*. *The Torchwood Archives* (BBC) state that the marriage occurred "in the early 1900s". The eleventh Doctor mentions "all of Jack's stag parties" in *The Wedding of River Song*.

1851 *TW: Trace Memory*. Sam is 96 in 1967, and says that he met Jack when he was 31 (p184-185). The second Boer War ended in 1902.

1852 *TW*: "Hell House"

1853 The Haisman Timeline (expanding upon *Twice Upon a Time*), and *Leth-St: The Forgotten Son* (ch8).

1854 *TW: The Torchwood Archive* (BF)

1855 *The Silent Stars Go By*. Lt General Robert Baden-Powell, a.k.a. Lord Baden-Powell, served in India and Africa from 1876 to 1910, and authored many books on the art of reconnaissance and scout training.

1856 *Eye of Heaven*

1857 *J&L S3: Swan Song*. No year given, but Bernhardt debuted as Hamlet in the silent film *Le Duel d'Hamlet* (1900), and would have been more likely to have continued in the role prior to a leg injury she incurred in 1905. Gangrene forced an amputation in 1915, although her acting career did continue.

1858 *Circular Time*: "Autumn". Wodehouse lived 1881-1975, but the date is otherwise arbitrary.

1859 *The Suffering*. Raffles is a fictional "gentleman thief" created by Arthur Conan Doyle's brother-in-law, E.W. Hornung, as something of a mirror reflection of Sherlock Holmes. The first collection of Raffles stories was published in 1899; the last by Hornung – a novel, *Mr. Justice Raffles* – saw print in 1909.

1860 *Wishing Well*

1861 "One hundred and seven Earth years" before "Ghosts of the Northern Line".

1862 *Leth-St: Night of the Intelligence* (ch13). Actor David Spenser was 33 when he played Thomni in *The Abominable Snowmen* [1935], so we might imagine the character was born in 1902.

saddened because he didn't know what he was writing about – that it sounded as if he had a story that was trying to get out.[1858] The first Doctor learned some housebreaking skills from A.J. Raffles.[1859] In 1902, Rupert Gaskin started building the Gaskin Tunnel, hoping to find the lost highwayman's gold rumoured to be beneath a well in Creighton Mere. The construction was abandoned when Gaskin died from influenza.[1860]

The Corialiths of Masma engineered memory devices to house the mental engrams of their dead. A Corialith came to Earth with one such Mnemosyne unit, but was feared by members of the public and killed. The young Mnemosyne sequestered itself in the alcoves of the Northern Line.[1861]

Only six months old, Thonmi was taken to the Det-Sen Monastery. The Abbot Songsten recognised him as a reincarnation of the master Thonmi Sambhota: the inventor of the Tibetan script, and minister to the Emperor Songstan Gambo.[1862]

The Second Incursion of Fang Rock

1902 - HORROR OF FANG ROCK / BEAST OF FANG ROCK[1863] -> Earth was now strategically important for the Rutans in their war with the Sontarans. According to the Doctor, the Rutans "used to control the whole of Mutters Spiral once".

The second of the Rutans thrown back from the future landed at the Fang Rock lighthouse, unaware that it had been relocated in time. **The fourth Doctor and Leela arrived at Fang Rock as the Rutan scout murdered the three lighthouse keepers, and also a quartet including**

Lord Henry Palmerdale. Prior to his demise, one of the lighthouse keepers – Benjamin Albert Travers, the uncle of Professor Edward Travers – followed instructions passed down by his family and concealed a rod of a Rutan osmic projector in the lighthouse's generator room, for Anne Travers to find decades on. An astral-projecting Owain Vine witnessed some of the Fang Rock murders.

The Doctor and Leela destroyed both the scout and its mothership, which had been sent back in time by Anne. Investigators concluded that one of the lighthouse keepers, Reuben Whormby, was responsible for the deaths, and then killed himself.

1902 - FORTY-FIVE: "False Gods"[1864] -> The Time Lord formerly worshipped as Thoth was now "Jane Templeton", an associate of Howard Carter. She directed him to excavate what she believed to be Userhat's tomb, hoping that her TARDIS was located inside. The Ship was dying, and caused temporal disruption that drew the seventh Doctor, Ace and Hex to the tomb. The Doctor convinced Jane that her TARDIS had to be euthanised in the heart of a sun, and she duly went back in time to do so.

1902 - REVENGE OF THE JUDOON[1865] -> A lizard-like alien altered his form and became "Professor Challoner", the head of a British secret society that investigated extreme science: the Cosmic Peacemakers. Challoner wanted to take over the world by installing Edward VII as a global emperor, and to this end involved Sir Arthur Conan Doyle – whose memory of Challoner's plot was erased.

The tenth Doctor and Martha landed at Balmoral Castle

1863 Dating *Horror of Fang Rock* (15.1) and *Leth-St: Beast of Fang Rock* (*Leth-St* novel #3) - The Terrance Dicks novelisation of *Horror of Fang Rock* and the story's contemporary publicity material set it "at the turn of the century". Electric power was introduced to lighthouses around the turn of the century. Fang Rock is in the English Channel ("five or six miles" from Southampton) and is particularly treacherous, and was probably upgraded early on.

There's a reference to King Edward. As fan Alex Wilcock has noted, although the Doctor's style of dress if often referred to as "Edwardian", this is the only *Doctor Who* TV story set in the Edwardian period (and there's not a frock coat to be seen). *The Programme Guide* offered the date "1909", *The Terrestrial Index* claimed "1904". *The TARDIS Logs* suggested "c. 1890", *The Doctor Who File* "early 1900s". *The TARDIS Special* gave the date "1890s". *Timelink* makes a convincing case for 1902, based on mumbled references to Salisbury and Bonar Law. *About Time* sifted the evidence and decided, "The early twentieth century... King Edward is mentioned, so it must be between 1902 and 1910". *Whoniverse* (BBC,

p94) places *Horror of Fang Rock* "a decade or so" before 1913.

Leth-St: Beast of Fang Rock seems to settle the matter by repeatedly stating that *Horror of Fang Rock* happened in "1902". In the same book, an initial Rutan incursion happened in "1822" and "1823", in accordance with Reuben mentioning, in the TV story, that the Beast was last seen "eighty years ago", and young Vince later claiming this was "back in the twenties".

Beast of Fang Rock establishes that the slain lighthouse worker Ben was Professor Travers' uncle – not unreasonably, as Ben is the right age, and his surname isn't given on screen. The same novel entails the Rutan scout who details the withdrawal from Mutter's Spiral being some decades out of time and failing to realise it, but the Doctor doesn't quibble with the scout's assessment as being wrong for this era.

1864 Dating *Forty-Five: "False Gods"* (BF #115a) - It's "1902".

1865 Dating *Revenge of the Judoon* (*Quick Reads* #3) - The back cover gives the year; in the story the Doctor says it's "the very beginning of the twentieth century".

while Edward VII was there... only to find that the castle had vanished. They recognised this as the work of the Judoon, who had been tricked into aiding Challoner under a false warrant. Martha interviewed Doyle about the Peacemakers while the Doctor used the TARDIS to locate Balmoral – which was in the Arabian Desert. He also met Baden-Powell, who was investigating the disappearance. Challoner had established Temporal Reversion devices that could eliminate all of Britain's rivals, but the Doctor got Balmoral back to its normal location and convinced the Judoon of Challoner's duplicity. The Judoon left, and Challoner fell victim to his own device. The Doctor and Martha departed for a working holiday as they cleared out Challoner's Temporal Reversion devices from all the world's capitals.

1902 - DINOSAURS ON A SPACESHIP[1866] **->** The eleventh Doctor left his friend, the African big game hunter John Riddell, with two "disappointed" dancers after claiming that he was just popping out for some liquorice. The Doctor returned seven months later to recruit Riddell to help with a crisis in the year 2367. Afterward, Queen Nefertiti left the Doctor's company and settled with Riddell on the African plains.

The Doctor was technical advisor on *A Trip to the Moon* (1902).[1867] In 1902, Monroe Stahr saw a film about the unearthing of an Egyptian tomb that would later inspire him to finance the movie *The Curse of the Scarab*.[1868]

1903 (Spring) - THE WANDERER[1869] **->** The alien Dahensa sent out a probe, a Wanderer, to collect intelligence data about other races, but the device experienced temporal flux and started harvesting information from the future at a rate of a thousand years per day. The first Doctor, Ian, Barbara and Susan happened upon the device in Siberia around the turn of the century. Ian befriended a peasant named Grigori – who was actually Grigori Rasputin. He prompted the Wanderer to discharge its data into his mind, giving him knowledge of the centuries to come. The Dahensa captured Ian and Susan while trying to claim the Wanderer, but the Doctor altered the Wanderer in such a way that turned the Dahensa into petroleum.

The Doctor used the TARDIS' telepathic circuits to strip the Wanderer data and short-term memory from Rasputin's mind before depositing him at the Summer Garden in St Petersburg. It was possible that Rasputin would experience recollections of these events in dreams. The travellers dumped the Dahensa spaceship in the Tura River.

@ The eighth Doctor drank absinthe in Prague, 1903.[1870]

1866 Dating *Dinosaurs on a Spaceship* (X7.2) - The year is given.
1867 *The City of the Dead*, "Prisoners of Time".
1868 "The Curse of the Scarab". It's "forty years" before the story, but that's clearly rounding up as the Melies' silent movie *Trip to the Moon* is referenced, and that was released in 1902.
1869 Dating *The Wanderer* (BF CC #6.10) - The blurb says that it's "Siberia at the end of the 19th Century", but Barbara estimates that "it's around the turn of the century, maybe a bit later", prompting Ian to later say that it's "only sixty years from our own time". Rasputin is in his "early 30s" and was born 21st January, 1869, supporting a slightly later dating. Historically, Rasputin arrived in St Petersburg in 1903. It's specified as being Springtime.
1870 "The Fallen"
1871 *Year of the Pig*. Toby's fan Alice Bultitude later shows him film footage of this event – even though 1903 is rather early for footage of this kind.
1872 *Jubilee*
1873 Dating *The Sleep of Reason* (EDA #70) - We're told it's "Thursday 24th December 1903" at the start of this section (p22).
1874 "One hundred years" before *SJS: Buried Secrets*.
1875 Dating *Iris S3: Iris Rides Out* (BF Iris #3.2) - The year is given. Carnacki, the star of short stories by William

Hope Hodgson, also appeared in *Foreign Devils*. The Sigsand Manuscript appears in Hodgson's stories.
1876 Dating *Starborn* (BF CC #8.9) - It's "early twentieth century Earth", far enough prior to the modern day that Barbara feels a little insulted when Vicki suggests that this time is just as "primitive" as her native era. The story takes place prior to the final scene of *The Romans*, where Vicki finally gets to tell her story about Nero.
1877 Dating *Freakshow* (BF promo #9, DWM #419) - The year is given.
1878 *Moonflesh*
1879 FP: *The Brakespeare Voyage* (ch3).
1880 FP: *Spinning Jenny*. Howkins' husband Bill is "twenty-seven and a half" (ch2) in 1931, and is "a little older" (ch7) than her.
1881 *Only Human*
1882 One hundred years before *Catch-1782*.
1883 *The Romans*
1884 "Centuries" before *The Murder Game, The Final Sanction*.
1885 *The Tomorrow Windows*. *Peter Pan* was published in 1905.
1886 *Casualties of War*. Pankhurst was a founder of the British suffragette movement. She was chained to Number Ten in 1905.
1887 *Smith and Jones*
1888 "The Lost Dimension"

In the summer of 1903, Toby the Sapient Pig attended a gathering of creative minds in Vienna. By 1913, owing to his addled memories, Toby would believe that all present were pigs.[1871]

> (=) The TARDIS' simultaneous arrival in 1903 and 2003 massively disrupted the timelines. In 1903, the Doctor helped the English defeat the Daleks, who had attacked Central London. Only two Daleks survived and were taken captive. The first World War still happened, but the British used the captured Dalek technology to take control of the whole world. The British government locked the Doctor and Evelyn in the Tower of London for propaganda purposes, and Evelyn starved to death.[1872]

1903 (December) - THE SLEEP OF REASON[1873] **->** The Sholem-Luz were creatures that could tunnel through the Time Vortex, and were attracted to mental turmoil as part of their life-cycle. In December 1903, a Sholem-Luz was drawn to Mausolus House, an asylum. The Sholem-Luz essence infected an Irish wolfhound, which became monstrous and triggered a series of murders. Joseph Sands, the nephew of a Mausolus House patient, slew the creature and burned its corpse in a fire that had started in a chapel on the grounds. The eighth Doctor arrived through a time corridor from around 2004, and the second Sholem-Luz accompanying him also perished in the fire. Not wishing to relive the twentieth century over again, the Doctor went into suspended animation for about a hundred years.

Dr Thomas Christie, the governor of Mausolus House, found a dog's tooth – all that remained of the Sholem-Luz – and made a pendant from it. It reappeared a century later.

Parts of *The Book of Tomorrows* had been lost over the centuries, but now the Orphans of the Future stole it entirely. By the early twenty-first century, their number included scientists, philosophers, inventors and other key individuals in Europe and North America.[1874]

1904 - IRIS S3: IRIS RIDES OUT[1875] **->** By now, Thomas Carnacki had fought the Faceless Sisters of Ealing Common. He also possessed the Sigsand Manuscript: the runic incantation of the Lucifer Codex, an algorithm that purported to decode the nature of evil.

Sir Donald Marshall fell on hard times financially, and sought to bargain with a demon to maintain his estate, Mocata Grange. Marshall's summoning ritual forged a wormhole to the domain of the Hog Lord, but unleashed a number of side effects, such as several of the Hog-Lord's man-pigs appearing dead in Marshall's flowerbeds. The supernatural expert Carnaki looked into these events, and

met Iris Wildthyme and Panda when the wormhole drew Iris' bus off course. They journeyed to the Hog Lord's realm, and convinced him to aid them in sealing the wormhole. Upon their return to Mocata Grange, Iris and Panda fled the Monstron Time Destroyer pursuing them.

Iris later paid Carnacki a visit, as she was impressed by his chest tattoos, and wished to intimately share her own tattoo of a bumblebee riding a bike.

c 1905 - STARBORN[1876] **->** Vicki's attempt to tell Ian and Barbara about her adventures in Rome was interrupted when the TARDIS landed in early twentieth-century London. The star-ascended Stella, trying to retroactively avert her destiny, brought Vicki into contact with a medium: Madame Violet. Stella presented herself as Vicki's ghost, and gave her the Doctor's ring to destroy – an act, she claimed, that would stop Vicki dying when the TARDIS next landed. Vicki saw through Stella's deception, and pocketed the Doctor's ring as Stella's essence faded, and Vicki and Violet lost their memories of this encounter.

1905 - FREAKSHOW[1877] **->** The fifth Doctor, Tegan and Turlough visited Buzzard Creek, Arizona, and saw a travelling carnival: Thaddeus P Winklemeyer's Menagerie of Medical Marvels. The freaks on display were alien beings, and Winklemeyer was actually a Vmal, an alien who propagated via micro-organisms that he sold to the crowd as an "elixir of life". The travellers thwarted Winklemeyer's plans, alerted galactic authorities as to his actions and took his captives home.

The famed explorer Nathaniel Whitlock met the Sioux warrior Silver Crow in 1905, and acquired his services as a hunting companion. Whitlock also took possession of Silver Crow's Moonflesh.[1878] Ella Staunton, a beloved of Robert Scarratt of the Great Houses, was born in 1905.[1879] Elizabeth Howkins, an accomplished ritualist, was born.[1880] The Doctor once went for a stroll in Edwardian Bromley.[1881] The National Foundation for Scientific Research, UK, originated as a group of private researchers that adopted the name and gained charity status after World War II. The organisation eventually leased a house from Melanie Bush's great-uncle.[1882] **The Doctor trained the Mountain Mauler of Montana.**[1883]

The Kalarians turned Ockora into a holiday resort, and, not realising the Ockorans were intelligent, hunted them for sport.[1884] An alien gave J.M. Barrie the idea for *Peter Pan*, based on a popular extra-terrestrial story.[1885]

@ The Doctor claimed to have chained Emmeline Pankhurst to the railings outside 10 Downing Street.[1886] **Pankhurst stole the Doctor's laser spanner.**[1887] Emmeline Pankhurst gifted Romana with a parasol.[1888]

The chess master Swapnil Khan and his daughter Queenie Glasscock were present during a chess tournament in Nuremberg, 1906, where Rudolf Spielmann played David Prezepiorka. The Doctor's train was delayed by anarchists on the line at Baden-Baden.[1889]

In 1906, Jack Harkness set up a bank account that gathered interest for at least a century.[1890]

Emily Winter Leaves the TARDIS

1906 - "Final Sacrifice"[1891] **->** Eliza Cooper had met Jack Harkness by this point.

Robert Lewis and Eliza Cooper of Torchwood visited Alexander Hugh, Professor of Advanced Sciences at Oxford, and his assistant Annabella. Hugh had built a time portal using repulsors from an alien tripod that crashed in Surrey, and the batteries from a giant metal man recovered from the Thames. But when the four of them stepped through the portal, intending to arrive just five minutes into the future, they found themselves twenty thousand years and five star systems away from their starting point.

The tenth Doctor and Emily Winter eventually gave Hugh a lift back home. The Doctor concluded that the slain Annabella was a fixed point in space and time – she should have lived, while Emily should have died. To correct the situation, Emily left the Doctor's company twenty years before she had met him, and adopted Annabella's identity. Funded by horse-betting information that the Doctor provided, Emily/"Annabella" came to own a theatre in Peckham, to discover the comic actor Archie Maplin, and to create United Actors Studio with him.

Jack Harkness first happened upon the uninhabited Tretarri housing district after enjoying a good night with a sailor and a showgirl together. An invisible force kept him from entering the location. Over the next century, he would make fourteen attempts to do so.[1892]

(=) 1906 (March) - TW: THE HOUSE THAT JACK BUILT[1893] **->** Jack Harkness was the first owner of Jackson Leaves, a Cardiff house built in 1906. Interdimensional beings who fed off paradoxes were drawn to Jack and retroactively inserted themselves into the house's history, causing all who lived there to die violently. Jack was secretly the lover of both the realtor who sold him the house, Alison, and her fiancé Miles. The exchange of vows at their wedding was extremely awkward, each of them worried that the other had discovered their involvement with Jack.

The day after Miles and Alison were married, he drowned her. An older version of Jack altered history so he didn't purchase the house – the interdimensional beings were consequently woven into a massive paradox, and consumed themselves.

In the amended history, Alison lived and had a son, Gordon Cottrell.

The San Francisco Earthquake

1906 (17th-18th April) - DC 2: THE GIFT[1894] **->** By using a psychic weapon, the Gift, to amplify the 1906 San Francisco earthquake, the Time Lord Caleera hoped to scuttle the eighth Doctor's history by prematurely destroying the city where he would be "born" in future. The Doctor, Liv and Helen consigned the Gift to the TARDIS' power house, and the earthquake unfolded as history said. Afterward, the Doctor and his friends found a note with the words "Hello, Sweetie", and went to the specified coordinates to confront Caleera and the Eleven...

Azathoth and her army of Rakshassi were destroyed in the San Francisco earthquake of 1906, following the

---

1889 *The Magic Mousetrap*
1890 *TW: Miracle Day*
1891 Dating "Final Sacrifice" (IDW *DW* Vol. 1, #13-16) - A caption tells us it's "1906". Lewis says "the British Empire will rise again", but actually, it was still in good shape in 1906. The tripod is presumably a reference to *The War of the Worlds*; the remains of the "giant metal man" recovered from the Thames presumably refers to the CyberKing (*The Next Doctor*), in defiance of it looking on screen as if it was completely disintegrated.
1892 *TW: The Twilight Streets*
1893 Dating *TW: The House That Jack Built* (*TW* novel #12) - In the corrected timeline, a report written by Alice Guppy concerning temporal flux that occurred "last night" – the same night that Jack first seduces Alison, it seems – at Jackson Leaves is dated to "17th March, 1906".
1894 Dating *DC 2: The Gift* (BF *DC* #2.3) - The San

Francisco Chronicle names the day as "April 17th, 1906". Historically, the earthquake struck at 5:12am on the morning of 18th April. The eighth Doctor notes that he died/was reborn in San Francisco in "93 years' time" (in 2000, *Doctor Who – The Movie*). Mention is made of the performer Enrico Caruso, who was on stage in *Carmen* a few hours before the earthquake hit.
1895 *All-Consuming Fire*
1896 *Vampire Science*
1897 *Mastermind*
1898 Dating *ST: "Forgotten"/Mastermind* (BF *Short Trips* #17p and BF *CC* #8.1) - "Forgotten" names the exact days, and *Mastermind* confirms the year. *Mastermind* entails the body-hopping Master living on Earth throughout the twentieth century, and expands upon his arrival there in "Forgotten" (the sixteenth and final story in Big Finish's *The Centenarian* collection, which is otherwise outside the remit of *Ahistory*). "Lady Louisa

Doctor's intervention.[1895] The vampire Weird Harold was buried alive in the San Francisco earthquake.[1896]

The Master Spends 106 Years on Earth

The decaying Master was trapped on Earth from 1906 to 2012, without benefit of his TARDIS, and forced to take new host bodies in an effort to stay alive...[1897]

1906 (24th-25th June) - ST: "Forgotten" / MASTERMIND[1898] **->** Still possessing the abilities of a morphant deathworm, the Master had survived within the TARDIS' Eye of Harmony following his confrontation with the Doctor in San Francisco, 1999. He escaped, as a cloud of gas, by mentally influencing a friend of the Doctor – the 100-year-old Edward Grainger – to briefly open the Eye, then reprogrammed the TARDIS to go to the day of Grainger's birth: 25th June, 1906. The vaporous Master possessed Sir George Steer to kill Grainger in his crib, but was thwarted by the Graingers' maid, Violet, and returned to being a gas. The TARDIS failed to register any trace of the Master, and so the eighth Doctor returned the elder Grainger to 2006. Afterward, the Master possessed Violet's fiancé Richard and murdered her...

A few months later, the Master discovered that everybody he inhabited went into decline, returning him to a decaying state. He transferred his essence into a young sailor outside a bar, and slowed that body's rate of decay with chemicals for five years. Meanwhile, the Master's TARDIS, disguised as a grandfather clock, was found in the Valley of Kings and lost to its owner for a century. It was eventually housed within UNIT's Vault.

In 1906, Charles Gaskell and a Torchwood team discovered advanced alien cryo-tech that could be used to freeze the dead.[1899] A 5.2 earthquake wracked Swansea on 27th June, 1906. It was suspected that Torchwood Cardiff suffered aftershocks, and that a number of its personnel died.[1900]

(=) 1906 (24th December) - THE CHIMES OF MIDNIGHT[1901] **->** The eighth Doctor and Charley discovered the inhabitants of an Edwardian manor house were trapped in a time-loop. The servants were brutally murdered, but at midnight time would roll back two hours and the process would repeat itself. The Doctor found that the house was imprinted with the murders and that Edith Thompson – one of the servants – would later work for the Pollard family. Edith had killed herself in 1930 upon learning of Charley's death in the R-101 accident, but Charley's paradoxical arrival in 1906 left history confused as to whether Edith had cause to kill herself or not. The Doctor decisively talked Edith out of killing herself, ending the time-loop.

Emily Winter, a companion of the tenth Doctor, was born in 1907.[1902] In the same year, Gerald Carter assumed command of Torchwood Cardiff.[1903] The Doctor visited in Brighton in 1907.[1904]

(=) c 1907 - TIMEH: THE SIDEWAYS DOOR[1905] **->** An alternate version of Honoré Lechasseur killed Professor Roche, a member of the Academy of Fine Arts Vienna who recommended against Adolf Hitler's admission as an art student. This cleared the way for Hitler's successful application, preventing him in future from joining the Nazi Party.

1907 (15th November) - THE DARKNESS OF GLASS[1906] **->** The Caversham Society gathered on Michael's island to commemorate the hundredth anniversary of Manning Caversham's death. The fourth Doctor and Leela stopped one of the Society members, Joseph Holman, from an ill-advised attempt to liberate and control the demon Caversham had restrained in a window in 1807. The demon-infested window shattered and largely washed out to sea, and the Doctor and Leela kept enough bits to prevent the creature from again manifesting.

and Mr Pollard", Charley Pollard's parents, are among the guests at the Graingers' party ("Forgotten").

1899 TW: The Twilight Streets (p133). The equipment doesn't seem able to revive frozen people, so it presumably compliments the cryo-tech that Torchwood has been using since Victorian times, as evidenced with Jack in 1901.

1900 This event is only mentioned in The Torchwood Archives (BBC), which is a useful secondary source but hardly sacrosanct. However, until another explanation is offered, this might well explain the fate of Emily Holroyd's Torchwood crew.

1901 Dating The Chimes of Midnight (BF #29) - The date is given.

1902 Emily says she is "19" in "Silver Scream".

1903 There's conflicting dates about this – Gerald's biography on Torchwood.org.uk says he took charge in 1907; The Torchwood Archives (BBC) says it was 1910.

1904 Pier Pressure

1905 Dating TimeH: The Sideways Door (TimeH #10) - The Academy rejected Hitler twice, in 1907 and 1908.

1906 Dating The Darkness of Glass (BF 4th Doc #4.2) - It's "one hundred years ago, to the night" since Caversham died on 15th November, 1807.

1907 Dating FP: Warlords of Utopia (FP novel #3) - Marcus was born on 8th January 2661, by the Roman calendar, which measures from the founding of Rome (753BC). So Scriptor was born on 8th January, 1908. This

= 1908 - FP: WARLORDS OF UTOPIA[1907] **->** Marcus Americanius Scriptor was born on Roma I, a parallel Earth where the best of all possible outcomes had occurred to the Roman Empire. It was a utopian civilisation that encompassed the world, from the cities under the ice caps to cities built on and under the oceans – such as Atlantis. The world had existed in five centuries of unbroken peace. It was the perfect world, although half the population were slaves. Scriptor's family ruled North America, and he lived on a family estate that took up the whole of Manhattan. America was a backwater, although an Atlantean astrologer gave Scriptor's family hope that their new son would bring them glory.

On the day Scriptor was born, a mysterious old man arrived in the Forum in Rome, using a time ring. He was one of thirteen members of the Great Houses apparently fleeing the War in Heaven.

The Tunguska Incident

The third Doctor, Jo Grant and Liz Shaw watched the Tunguska explosion in 1908.[1908] The Warlock alien arrived on Earth in the meteorite that landed in Tunguska.[1909] **Alien bacteria arrived with the meteorite.**[1910] **The Tunguska Scroll, which told the story of Horath and his final resting place, was recovered from the site.**[1911] The UNIT Vault contained what was thought to be a part of Sontaran scoutship that crashed at Tunguska... or it could just have been a rusted lump of metal.[1912]

The vessels assigned to the Dalek Project encountered a storm in the Time Vortex. Two of the ships survived and emerged into real space – one exploded in Siberia, 1908, with no survivors, while the other crash-landed in Kent and remained hidden before enacting its new objective at Hellcombe Hall.[1913] An alien hallucinogenic was recovered

from Tunguska that would facilitate development of the Sen-Gen AI.[1914]

The Tunguska blast of 1908 should have knocked Earth off its axis, but didn't thanks to the protective insulation of a few tens of thousands of trees.[1915]

1908 (30th June) - BIRTHRIGHT[1916] **->** Half of the seventh Doctor's TARDIS fell through time to June 1908 and exploded in the wastes of Tunguska in Siberia. It disintegrated on impact; historians attributed this event to a meteorite strike.

1908 - THE EMERALD TIGER[1917] **->** Lord Edgar Forster led an expedition to India to collect samples for the Zoological Society in London, but his group encroached upon the hidden valley held by the were-tiger Shardul Khan and his siblings Ayyappa and Dawon. Khan slaughtered Forster – the dead lord's wife, Adele, survived, but was separated from their young son John. She sealed off the cave entrance to the hidden valley with dynamite.

Ayyappa became gravely wounded after a confrontation with his brother, and was found, amnesiac, near the Carrabba Caves. In time, he became known as Professor Narayan, the head of Mythology and Folklore at the University of Calcutta. Dawon accepted the young John Forster as her cub.

Vislor Turlough's great-grandfather ran a smuggling operation, and used the dimensional vault established by his own great-grandfather to house contraband. Turlough's ancestor betrayed his fellow smugglers and was killed. The vault's security system slaughtered his murderers, but also pulverised the royal treasure of Trion.[1918]

Constance Clark, a companion of the sixth Doctor, was born.[1919] **In Lahore, 1909, some men under the command of Captain Jack got drunk and ran over a "chosen**

---

is the same day, in our version of history, that William Hartnell was born.
1908 *The Wages of Sin*
1909 *Warlock* (p353).
1910 *Dalek*
1911 *SJA: Enemy of the Bane*
1912 *Tales from the Vault*
1913 *The Dalek Project*
1914 *CM S1: Artificial Intelligence*
1915 *In the Forest of the Night*
1916 Dating *Birthright* (NA #17) - Page 202 cites the meteorite strike's historic date of 30th June, 1908. On the events attributed to the Tunguska incident, see the Unfixed Points in Time sidebar. Alternatively, perhaps the location is a space-time nexus (akin to the Cardiff Rift) that drew several items to the same point, where many of them exploded together.

1917 Dating *The Emerald Tiger* (BF #159) - Lord Edgar names the year, and Professor Narayan is found "eighteen years" before the 1926 portion of the story.
1918 Estimated as three generations prior to *Kiss of Death*.
1919 Constance turns 35 in *The Middle*, with a biological scan noting her age-change to the very minute. Flip, a little astonishingly, opens that story wishing Constance a happy 35th birthday, having (one presumes) correctly calculated to the day how much time she's spent aboard the TARDIS. Constance joined the TARDIS in 1944 (*Criss-Cross*), and went home the same year in *Quicksilver*, so we might imagine she was born in 1909 – depending on how much time one wants to deduct because she's been TARDIS travelling. Miranda Raison was 37 when she first played Constance.

one" – a little girl with a connection to the spirit world, and who was protected by fairy creatures. The next week, the fairies killed fifteen of Jack's men on a train. Jack was the only survivor.[1920] M LeDuc of Torchwood visited the Paris Air Show in 1909.[1921]

The Doctor bought Inuit garb from the explorer Robert Peary as Peary journeyed north, and also owned snow-shoes belonging to Peary's associate Matthew Henson.[1922] The Doctor personally knew the performer/Chinese giant Chang Woo Gow, and regarded him as a marvellous fellow and a good dancer. Gow finally retired and opened a tea-room in Bournemouth. Elsewhere, Toby the Sapient Pig and Nurse Albertine saw Mrs Lillian Washbourne on stage at a theatre in Cincinnati.[1923]

The Sea Devils engineered the Ravenscaur Disaster, a massive undersea earthquake in Scotland, to separate the Raven Peninsula from the mainland.[1924]

1909 (February to 24th April) - BIRTHRIGHT[1925] ->

The secret society the New Dawn, led by Jared Khan, attempted to stabilise the Great Divide with the future and bring the Chaarl back to this time. Some Chaarl broke through and murdered a number of people in the East End. Khan hypnotised Margaret Waterfield, Victoria's aunt, to further his schemes, and then had her killed. The seventh Doctor left Benny and Ace in this time while he dealt with matters elsewhere. The Doctor was a member of the same club as Prime Minister Herbert Henry Asquith, and had Asquith get Benny out of a spot of trouble.

The Doctor's TARDIS time-rammed itself to stop Khan's plans, and half of the Ship – with Khan's mind inside – fell through time to June 1908 and exploded in the wastes of Tunguska in Siberia. The Chaarl were trapped in one of the surviving TARDIS' inner dimensions.

1909 (mid September) - STING OF THE ZYGONS[1926]

-> The tenth Doctor and Martha discovered a Zygon colony in the Lake District and wiped them out.

At Christmas 1909, the Doctor gave composer Maurice Ravel a pocketwatch bearing the Prydonian seal – and arranged for Ravel to receive the watch many years previously, before they had met.[1927] Picasso painted the twelfth Doctor's portrait, and used his eyebrows as an expression of Cubism.[1928]

A new incarnation of Drax lost his Cockney accent while perpetrating a long-con against George V.[1929]

1910 (13th-17th October) - PARADOX LOST[1930] ->

Amy, Rory and the artificial person Arven travelled to London, 1910, in an experimental time vessel to rendez-vous with the eleventh Doctor, but materialised on 13th October, three days before his arrival. Their timeship created the very rip in space-time that they had been investigating, enabling the extra-dimensional Squall to get a foothold in the universe.

The Doctor arrived in the TARDIS on 17th October, and reunited with his friends. Professor Archibald Angelchrist, a retired secret serviceman who had investigated paranormal threats such as tentacled creatures in the Thames, extra-terrestrial viruses and ancient entities awakening from tombs underneath Edinburgh, helped the Doctor banish the Squall back to their home dimension. Arven was heavily damaged and fell into the Thames. It would meet the Doctor, Amy and Rory's past selves in 2789.

While studying at Cambridge, Dorian Gray became friends with Evan Morgan. During a visit to the Vandermeer family bookshop, Morgan persuaded the owner to sell him Kronos Vad's *History of Earth* (Vol. 36,379).[1931] An Acridian, Overseer Zim, came to Earth and set up a profitable mind-swapping operation in Bramfield.[1932]

The eleventh Doctor met Mata Hari – "an interesting woman", he claimed – in a Paris hotel room. He was busy toasting Jammy Dodgers as she disrobed.[1933] The eleventh Doctor, Amy and Rory laid the groundwork for an escape from Alcatraz by altering the blueprints of the

---

1920 *TW: Small Worlds*. A caption gives the date. The *Torchwood* website said this was when Jack was a time-travelling con man, but as he's commanding troops and survives the fairy attack, it's more likely that this is the Jack who lived through the twentieth century.

1921 *TW: The Dying Room*

1922 *Brotherhood of the Daleks*. The most famous of Peary's expeditions was in 1909.

1923 Some "years" before *Year of the Pig*.

1924 *The Twelfth Doctor Year Two*: "Clara Oswald and the School of Death". Clara says in issue #1 that this happened in 1907; captions in issue #3 say it was early March 1909.

1925 Dating *Birthright* (NA #17) - It is "Thursday 15 April 1909" on p23, and Benny has been stranded "two months" (p24) by then. She departs on "24 April" (p203).

1926 Dating *Sting of the Zygons* (NSA #13) - The TARDIS lands "16 September 1909" and the adventure takes at least three days.

1927 *J&L* S11: *Maurice*, possibly to commemorate Ravel finishing *Gaspard de la nuit* in 1908.

1928 "The Pestilent Heart". Picasso's Cubism period lasted 1909-1912.

1929 *The Trouble with Drax*. George V was born in 1865 and reigned 1910-1936.

1930 Dating *Paradox Lost* (NSA #48) - The days are provided at the start of each relevant chapter.

1931 "More than seventeen years" before *Worlds BF: The Feast of Magog* [June 1927].

1932 "Sixty years" before *3rdA: The Hidden Realm*.

1933 *Pond Life*. Mata Hari moved to Paris in 1903, and was arrested and executed there in 1917.

Federal Penitentiary building, and hiding equipment behind a deceptively weak piece of a wall marked with "Amy 4 Rory".[1934] Francis and Muriel Wilberforce of Pease Pottage were married in 1910.[1935]

The Doctor saw Earth tremors in Peru in 1910.[1936] In same year, Torchwood Cardiff reorganised their archive.[1937] Torchwood had an Internet at its disposal.[1938]

Gareth Robert Owen, a freelance agent for Torchwood and the son of the founder of G.R. Owen's department store, found a being akin to a tiny butterfly in a crashed spaceship in 1910. To prevent Torchwood weaponising the alien, Owen merged with the creature and relocated G.R. Owen's Department of Curiosities to a pocket dimension. The two of them lived there in a timeless state.[1939]

Humans associated with the criminal aliens in Wolfenden realised that the aliens' technology could be fuelled by brain chemicals related to memory. In the decades to follow, visitors to Wolfenden were robbed of some of their memory chemicals and then released, largely none the wiser.[1940] Andrew Carnegie's wealth aided the eleventh Doctor in buying out SERVEYOUinc.[1941]

c 1910 - THE CATALYST[1942] -> Lord Joshua Douglas, an Edwardian gentleman, became a companion of the third Doctor. He was gone from home for a year, but returned looking ten years older and claiming that he'd been off in Peru. The Z'nai emperor H'mbrackle II, having been imprisoned in a quarantine tesseract accessible from Joshua's home, escaped and exacted vengeance by killing Joshua, his wife and their daughter Jessica. A group of Z'nai arrived through time in a Z'nai Angel of War to retrieve their emperor, but fell prey to a Z'nai-killing virus. The fourth Doctor and Leela trapped H'mbrackle II where "nobody would find him", and purified Joshua's home by burning it down.

1911

The dancer Ernestina Stott was born around 1911.[1943] **The Doctor said 1911 was "an excellent year, one of my favourites".[1944] The Nine Travellers were surveyed in 1911.[1945] In 1911, the Doctor was due to take a lesson in either flying a biplane or knitting.[1946] On 13th March, 1911, the *Hunstanton Chronicle* reported Mr Alfred Mason's insistence that his dead wife, a victim of the Night Travellers, could be resurrected if the flask containing her stolen life-essence was found.[1947]**

1911 - WORLDS BF: KRONOS VAD'S HISTORY OF EARTH (VOL. 36,379)[1948] -> Iris Wildthyme's efforts to reach London, June 1911, caused her bus to land at Cuidad Juarez during the Mexican Revolution. She and her friends spotted Pancho Villa before continuing on...

1911 (11th-12th June) - WORLDS BF: THE ADVENTURE OF THE BLOOMSBURY BOMBER / KRONOS VAD'S HISTORY OF EARTH (VOL. 36,379)[1949] -> The Gomagog, marauders from another dimension, had killed every version of themselves in parallel histories. Their aggression spread to our reality, where they warred against countless civilisations.

Dr Alexander Korvo, an acolyte of the Gomagog,

1934 "Escape Into Alcatraz". The main building of the Alcatraz Federal Penitentiary was constructed as a military prison in 1910-12, and was first used as a federal prison after renovations in August 1934.

1935 *The Wrong Doctors*

1936 *The English Way of Death* (p46).

1937 *TW: Slow Decay*

1938 "A century" prior to *TW: Ghost Train*, although it isn't especially clear what this means.

1939 *TW: Department X*

1940 "One hundred years" before *SJA: The White Wolf*.

1941 *The Eleventh Doctor Year One*: "The Rise and Fall". Carnegie lived 1835-1919.

1942 Dating *The Catalyst* (BF CC #2.4) - The year isn't given, but the Douglas family lives in an Edwardian house, and comes across as an Edwardian family. The suffragette movement (which peaked in 1912) is topical enough for Lady Douglas to view it with contempt. Douglas' first name, "Joshua", isn't mentioned until *The Time Vampire*.

It's here said that Joshua travelled with a Doctor who was an "old man"; *The Time Vampire* specifies that it's

the third Doctor (a "white-haired man who wore a bright red jacket"). Joshua travelled with the Doctor for about a decade – such a massive duration of time in the third Doctor's lifetime is most likely to have occurred in the interim between *The Green Death* and *The Time Warrior*, when he's no longer exiled, companionless and possibly – in wake of Jo Grant's departure – looking for a reason to spend some time away from Earth.

1943 She is 21 according to the sleeve notes of *Hornets' Nest: The Dead Shoes*.

1944 *Pyramids of Mars*

1945 *The Stones of Blood*

1946 *The Impossible Astronaut*

1947 *TW: From Out of the Rain*

1948 Dating *Worlds BF: Kronos Vad's History of Earth (Vol. 36,379)* (*Worlds BF #1.4*) - The First Battle of Ciudad Juarez lasted 7th April to 10th May, 1911.

1949 Dating *Worlds BF: The Adventure of the Bloomsbury Bomber/Kronos Vad's History of Earth (Vol. 36,379)* (*Worlds BF #1.2, 1.4*) - Holmes datelines the letter he writes to Watson pertaining to events in *The Bloomsbury Bomber* as "June 20th, 1911". The latter story specifies

learned that a crucial book of prophecy (Kronos Vad's *A History of Earth* Volume 36,379) resided in one of five bookshops in Bloomsbury and Holborn, but failed to determine which one. Korvo's surrogate blew up four of the bookstores, prompting concern from officials that the bombings were related to the impending coronation of George V. Mycroft Holmes suspected otherwise, and asked his brother Sherlock to look into the matter. John Watson was recuperating from a fever in Switzerland.

> (=) One of Korvo's bombs destroyed the Vandermeer family's bookshop and killed Sherlock. Iris Wildthyme, accompanied by Captain Turner, Jenni Marcel and Zack Hoffman, reversed this fortune by defusing the bomb, then returned to the bookshop a century on.

Sherlock exposed Korvo's complicity in the bombings, but the man escaped.

The Doctor's First Encounter With Sutekh

1911 - PYRAMIDS OF MARS[1950] -> The fourth Doctor and Sarah Jane landed at the Old Priory, on the future site of UNIT HQ. They discovered that the servants of Sutekh were planning to release him from his imprisonment. The Doctor trapped Sutekh in a time corridor, eventually destroying him.

Sutekh side-stepped the time corridor at the last instant, but became trapped in a pocket realm: an Eternals' void. The tenth Doctor later defeated him. Sutekh's body was destroyed, but his mind survived, and would attempt to manufacture a new physical form in the twenty-seventh century. The seventh Doctor trapped Sutekh's mind within a self-perpetuating time loop.[1951]

The pipe organ was recovered from the Old Priory and later secured in the UNIT Vault.[1952]

1911 (late October) - MOONFLESH[1953] -> The fifth Doctor and Nyssa happened upon Whitlock Manor in Suffolk as Nathaniel Whitlock hosted a weekend hunting excursion. Hannah Bartholemew, a member of the Order of the Crescent Moon – a group that believed that humanity existed in the thrall of extraterrestrials – scraped pieces off Whitlock's Moonflesh rock for analysis, and thereby awakened the Takala energy creature within. A cadre of hunter-seekers from the Takala Empire arrived to capture the rogue, which the Doctor and Silver Crow returned to dormancy by performing the Ghost Dance.

Hannah Bartholemew took advantage of a glitch in the TARDIS' door to stow herself aboard the Ship. With the Doctor and Nyssa, she journeyed to both an Arrit tomb ship in an unknown era, and the Scientific Outpost for Research and Development of Inter-Dimensional Energies (SORDIDE) in the pioneering days of the Earth Empire, where she remained.[1954]

The King's Regulations were published in 1912.[1955] **The Royal Flying Corps was formed in 1912.**[1956] Francis Wilberforce Jr, the son of Francis and Muriel Wilberforce, was born that year.[1957]

Xznaal, an Ice Lord, was struck by the state of the withered plant life on his home planet of Mars.[1958] The downfall of Imperial China was sealed when the Celestial Toymaker lost a game.[1959]

The city of Cornucopia, situated on an unnamed planet in the Tau Ceti System, served as one of the biggest spaceports until a ship made from psychic metal – looking outwardly like a golden ziggurat – appeared in the skies overhead. The resultant radiation storm isolated

that Korvo's bomb "killed" Holmes on June 11th, and the action continues to the next day.
1950 Dating *Pyramids of Mars* (13.3) - Laurence Scarman says it's "nineteen hundred and eleven".
1951 Two stories released within a year of one another – *The Tenth Doctor Year Two*: "Old Girl" and *NAofBenny V2: The Pyramid of Sutekh* – describe differing means by which Sutekh gained a reprieve from death in *Pyramids of Mars*. Reconciling the two isn't so difficult – he physically survives the fourth Doctor's trap by escaping into a holding dimension, but meets his end while battling the tenth Doctor... but his mind endures nonetheless, for the seventh Doctor to deal with. Any failure on Sutekh's part to acknowledge the former story probably owes to his obliteration and rebirth in-between – harrowing, even for a demigod. Afterward, his disembodied mind meets the fourth Doctor and Leela in *Kill*

the Doctor!/The Age of Sutekh.
1952 *Worlds DW: The Screaming Skull*, playing off *Pyramids of Mars*.
1953 Dating *Moonflesh* (BF #185) - The blurb gives the year. The coming winter represents the tenth anniversary of Audrey Whitlock's death in December 1901, and it's been "six years" since Nathaniel Whitlock met Silver Crow in 1905. The Doctor judges the time of year as "late October, I'd say".
1954 *Moonflesh, Tomb Ship, Masquerade*.
1955 *The War Games*
1956 *Ghost Light*
1957 *The Wrong Doctors*
1958 "Eighty-five" years before *The Dying Days* (p175).
1959 *The Nightmare Fair*. Imperial China came to an end in 1912. The Toymaker's interest in China is doubtless meant to explain his attire.

Cornucopia, making all but visual landings impossible. Cornucopia developed a crime-based economy in the recession to come, and was run by five Conspiracy Classes: the Assassins Alliance, the Blackmailers Collusion, the Hijackers Guild, the Kidnappers Federation and ThiefCorp. Police were outlawed on Cornucopia, and the top Crime Lords adhered to a strict Conspiracy Code. The ziggurat's pilot had died, and so the ship ejected its ignition key – which came to be known as the Star of Solitude – to attract a clever individual who could serve as a replacement. The ship was named one of the Eight Wonders of the Universe.[1960]

> (=) A historical deviation caused colleagues of the self-sacrificing Captain Oates to drag him back to camp, where they died together.[1961]

The Sinking of the *Titanic*

Charley Pollard, a companion of the eighth Doctor and (later) the sixth Doctor, was born the day the *Titanic* sank.[1962] **The *Titanic* sank, although the Doctor claimed that he had nothing to do with that... The ninth Doctor warned the Daniels family not to board the *Titanic* and was photographed with them. However, he boarded the ship, and ended up clinging to an iceberg.[1963]**

The eleventh Doctor owned a napkin from the *Titanic*.[1964] Ibrahim Hadmani, a time-traveling colleague of Erimem, stood on the Irish coast as the *Titanic* sailed into the Atlantic, and took a picture of it on his iPhone.[1965]

1912 (14th April) - THE LEFT-HANDED HUMMINGBIRD[1966] **->** On the sinking *Titanic*, the seventh Doctor prevented Huitzilin – also called the Blue – from acquiring the Xiuhcoatl, an Exxilon weapon capable of manipulating molecules. It could transmute or destroy matter. Huitzilin manifested but was killed.

1912 (April) - MASTERMIND[1967] **->** Having escaped the Doctor's TARDIS in 1906, the decaying Master hoped to avoid the oncoming First World War, but – his knowledge of Earth history being less than absolute – unwisely booked passage aboard the *Titanic*. He rushed to claim a seat on a lifeboat, and arrived in America in a weakened state. The Master possessed Mr Ferrel, a member of the Hudson Dusters street gang, and within months became the group's leader. As "Don Maestro", he oversaw much of New York's criminal activity for twenty years.

1912 - THE SUFFERING[1968] **->** In Piltdown, the skull of the female leader from the fourth galaxy was excavated and thought to be the "missing link" between ape and man. The leader's consciousness influenced women to start an uprising against men at a suffrage rally in Hyde Park. The first Doctor, Steven and Vicki combined efforts to defeat the leader, then fulfilled history by replacing her skull with a human cranium and the jawbone of an ape.

1912 (30th-31st October) - GRACELESS: THE FOG[1969] **->** An asteroid destroyed the Cheshire town of Compton, dispersing extra-terrestrial energy in such a way as to obliterate the town without leaving a crater. The impact rippled through time and space, attracting the living Key-tracers Abby and Zara. They interacted for a time with the last echoes of the townsfolk killed in the event.

The British government bought out the land where Compton once stood, and the army erected new buildings, further making the memory of the town lost to history.[1970]

Around 1913, Harding Wellman died while mountaineering in Switzerland.[1971] A Wyndham Lewis painting was amongst the artifacts later taken to the Earth colony of Jegg-Sau, and found ruined there.[1972] **Lydia Childs joined Torchwood** in 1913, and would serve as the secretary of Torchwood Cardiff until the early 1920s.[1973] In 1913,

---

1960 "About a century" before "The Cornucopia Caper". The ziggurat is one of the "Eight Wonders of the Universe", but it's unclear if this is the same (greatly reduced, in this era) designation used in *Death to the Daleks*, or something altogether different. "Hunters of the Burning Stone" establishes Cornucopia as being situated in Tau Ceti.

1961 *The Algebra of Ice* (p13). Oates died 17th March, 1912.

1962 *Neverland*. She was eighteen years, five months and twenty-one days old when she met the Doctor (in *Storm Warning*), according to *The Chimes of Midnight*. However, that would seem to mean that Charley was born 14th April (the night the iceberg struck *Titanic*) as opposed to 15th April (when *Titanic* went under).

1963 The Doctor mentions the *Titanic* in *Robot*, but

tells Borusa in *The Invasion of Time* that "it had nothing to do with me". The ninth Doctor's involvement with the *Titanic* was cited in *Rose* and *The End of the World*.

1964 *Plague of the Cybermen*

1965 *Erimem: Buccaneer*

1966 Dating *The Left-Handed Hummingbird* (NA #21) - The story takes place on the *Titanic*, and the date is confirmed on p221.

1967 Dating *Mastermind* (BF CC #8.1) - The Hudson Dusters existed from the late 1890s to the mid-1910s.

1968 Dating *The Suffering* (BF CC #4.7) - It's "the year of our Lord, nineteen hundred and twelve". This particular Hyde Park rally seems to be fictional; other suffrage rallies took place there in real life, as when 250,000 people marched there in June 1908.

1969 Dating *Graceless: The Fog* (*Graceless* #1.2) - Amy

anthropologist Manuel Gamio discovered a part of the Great Temple of the Aztecs.[1974]

1913 - YEAR OF THE PIG[1975] -> The sixth Doctor and Peri sought to relax at the Hotel Palace Thermae in the Belgian municipality of Ostend. Also in residence were Toby the Sapient Pig, Nurse Albertine, Toby's admirer Alice Bultitude and the mentally confused Inspector Alphonse Chardalot. The Doctor deduced that Toby and Chardalot were actually brothers, the result of genetic experiments carried out some decades previous. The two siblings were reunited, and the Doctor believed they were perhaps better off not knowing details about their origins.

The Doctor happened upon Proust at this time, and made a point of grabbing the reclusive man by the shoulders, calling him Marcel, breathing port fumes up his nose and telling him exactly what he thought of the central character in *Swann's Way*. The actress Lillian Washbourne died in a fire. Chardalot gave Peri a stuffed monkey that was believed to hail from the gift shop of Madame Ensor, the mother of the Belgian painter James Ensor.

Owing to a mishap with a temporal fission grenade that Chardalot possessed, the sky was briefly filled with exploding cows.

The Doctor saved St Peter Port from some terrible threat on Halloween 1913. He could not save the life of young Celia Doras.[1976] The Doctor and Ace independently visited the premiere of the ballet *The Rites of Spring* in 1913.[1977]

Sir Toby Kinsella went to school with Jeffrey Broderick, who took bets on a fight that Kinsella engineered between a rugby captain and a boy who stole his mother's oatcakes. One of the combatants received a broken nose and two

fractured ribs.[1978] Kinsella was raised Catholic.[1979]

1913 (September to 11th November) - HUMAN NATURE (TV) / THE FAMILY OF BLOOD[1980] -> To escape the Family of Blood – expert hunters who wanted the DNA of a Time Lord – the tenth Doctor used a Chameleon Arch to become human and hide in 1913. With Martha's help, the amnesiac Doctor became a teacher at Farringham School and fell for nurse Joan Redfern. The Family arrived on Earth in their invisible spacecraft and confronted Smith, who had no idea he had been the Doctor. Martha helped the Doctor resume his true nature, and the Time Lord swiftly and ruthlessly granted the Family their wish for immortality by imprisoning them all for eternity.

The First World War

World War I began 28th July, 1914, and ended 11th Nov, 1918.

The Nemesis statue passed over the Earth in 1913, heralding the First World War.[1981] The eleventh Doctor thought it possible that Gavrilo Princip was acting under Dalek control when he assassinated Archduke Franz Ferdinand and his wife, triggering World War I to the benefit of the Dalek Project.[1982]

Captain Jack discovered that the Bad Penny had triggered events that endowed sailors at Tiger Bay, Cardiff, with alien material. This turned them into bestial, wrinkled creatures – the Weevils – that ate people. He chucked the Bad Penny into the Rift, then cleared out the main Weevil nest with a flamethrower. As it was 1914, Jack worried that the Bad Penny was somehow responsible for the

procures a copy of *The Manchester Guardian* dated to "Wednesday, 6th of November, 1912", which is "a week" after the story takes place. She and Zara arrive in Compton the night before the catastrophe.
1970 "A year" after *Graceless: The Fog*.
1971 "Some fifty years" before *Winter for the Adept*.
1972 *Benny S5: The Relics of Jegg-Sau*. Lewis, a co-founder of the Vorticist art movement, lived 1882-1957. His work was exhibited as early as 1912.
1973 From Torchwood.org.uk and *The Torchwood Archives* (BBC). Childs is seen in the photograph of the 1918 Torchwood in *TW: To the Last Man*, alongside Gerald Carter, Harriet Derbyshire, Douglas Caldwell and Dr Charles Quinn.
1974 *The Left-Handed Hummingbird* (p58).
1975 Dating *Year of the Pig* (BF #89) - The year is given, and specified on the back cover. Proust lived 1871-1922, and *Swann's Way* – his seven-volume, semi-autobiographical novel – was published between 1913 and 1927. The Ostend gift shop run by James Ensor's mother is historical, and some items in the store

inspired Ensor's painting.
1976 *Just War*
1977 *Lungbarrow, Vampire Science*.
1978 *CM S1: Artificial Intelligence*. Hugh Ross was 65 when he played Kinsella in *Counter-Measures* Series 1 [1964], so we might imagine that the character was born in 1899. That would beg the question, however, of why Kinsella wasn't called up to serve in World War I – if he was, we're never told of it.
1979 *CM S2: The Fifth Citadel*
1980 Dating *Human Nature* (TV)/*The Family of Blood* (X3.8-3.9) - Martha shows the Doctor a newspaper dated "Monday November 10th 1913", and a poster for the Annual Dance – which occurs the following day – yields the date of "November 11th". The Doctor has been on Earth "two months", so since early September.
1981 *Silver Nemesis*
1982 *The Dalek Project*. Ferdinand was killed on 28th June, 1914. The Doctor's suspicions that the Daleks were behind the event are neither confirmed nor denied.

onset of World War I.[1983]

The immortal Captain Jack served in the First World War.[1984] The sarcophagus carrying the second Hornet Swarm materialised at the Cromer Palace of Curios at 2 am on 14th April, 1914. This triggered a fire, and the Swarm perished as the Palace burned down.[1985]

John Watson passed by Buckingham Palace on 4th August, 1914, and was swept up in a crowd celebrating His Majesty's Government declaring war on Germany. Two days beforehand, Sherlock Holmes and Watson had defeated Von Bork, an agent of the Kaiser who tried to steal documents related to Britain's defence plans. Watson accepted a Colonelcy from his old regiment, and was headed to France when Mycroft Holmes and Bernice Summerfield asked for his help. They solved a mystery involving a malfunctioning piece of Time Lord circuitry.[1986]

Francis Wilberforce of Pease Pottage died in 1914, in World War I.[1987] Patrick O'Sullivan, the brother of Molly O'Sullivan, volunteered to serve in World War I, but was killed on his first day of service in France. Another brother, Liam O'Sullivan, stayed in Ireland but was killed by an English sentry.[1988] Alistair Lethbridge-Stewart's grandfather served in Military Intelligence in World War I.[1989]

John Smith and Wolsey the TARDIS Cat

1914 (April) - HUMAN NATURE (NA)[1990] -> Wanting to learn more about human emotions, the seventh Doctor acquired nanites that transformed his Time Lord body into that of a human, and stored his biodata and memories in a small pod. He mentally became "John Smith" – a persona crafted by the TARDIS – and worked as the house master at Hulton Academy for Boys in the village of Farringham in Norfolk. Benny posed as Smith's niece. Smith and a teacher, Joan Redfern, soon fell in love.

The shapechanging Aubertides pursued the TARDIS to Farringham – consuming the Doctor's biodata would greatly extend their lifespans and enable them to produce enough offspring to overwhelm Gallifrey, then countless worlds. Most of the Aubertides were killed in a pitched battle; Smith saved Joan by exchanging his mind with that of the Doctor, and then died while inhabiting the body of

---

1983 *TW: The Torchwood Archive* (BF), explaining the origin of the Weevils from the TV series.
1984 *Utopia*
1985 *Demon Quest: Sepulchre*
1986 *Benny: Secret Histories:* "A Gallery of Pigeons"
1987 *The Wrong Doctors*
1988 *DEyes: X and the Daleks*
1989 *Leth-St: The Daughters of Earth* (ch2).
1990 Dating *Human Nature* (NA #37) - It is "April" (p17) "1914" (p16).

ARE THERE TWO HUMAN NATURES, NOW?: Well, yes. The 2007 television story *Human Nature/The Family of Blood* is an adaptation of the New Adventures novel *Human Nature*, both written by Paul Cornell.

In varying degrees, the new series has done this four other times so far: *Dalek* was based on elements of *Jubilee* (a Big Finish audio also by Rob Shearman), *Rise of the Cybermen/The Age of Steel* resulted from an attempt to adapt the audio *Spare Parts* by Marc Platt (the finished product was a different story altogether, but Platt still received a credit), *The Lodger* (TV) came about when Gareth Roberts revamped his tenth Doctor *DWM* comic of the same name, and Steven Moffat used the central idea and the name of the main character of his *Annual 2006* story ("What I Did On My Christmas Holidays by Sally Sparrow") as the basis of *Blink*. All four of these examples are clearly different stories – the Cyberman ones explicitly take place in different universes, in fact – and it's easy enough to believe they could all happen to the Doctor, given a little coincidence.

The idea of coincidence is stretched to and probably beyond breaking point by the two *Human Natures*, however. There's nothing in the TV story to explain how both could happen. Yet this chronology counts both stories, as it counts both *Shadas*, so some explanation is probably needed.

There are a number of possibilities:

1) Both happened, and it's all a coincidence. There are differences, some of them pretty serious ones: they take place in different years; the school is called Hulton in the novel and Farringham in the TV story; the Doctor is in a different incarnation with a different companion and becomes human for a different reason; he fights different aliens. The Joan Redferns he falls for are different ages and have different histories. So the Doctor has a similar adventure twice – luckily, it's one that involves him losing his memory, so the second version of "John Smith", at least, wouldn't notice the redundancy.

2) Both happened, and it's not a coincidence. We're told in the TV story that the TARDIS chose the landing point. Perhaps it's deliberately picked a situation that "worked" in similar circumstances. It seems a little odd – if not actively cruel – for the TARDIS to pick on another Joan Redfern, though.

3) The original was erased from history... possibly as a result of the Time War, the events of the novel *Human Nature* no longer "happened" (this does not automatically suppose that the whole of New Adventures did not "occur", however). The Big Finish version of *Shada* establishes that in this situation, there would be a timeline gap that needs filling, but that a different incarnation of the Doctor can play the part.

1991 *No Man's Land.* Dudgeon says the Mons conflict started 22nd August, 1914, although some resources say it technically was initiated on the 23rd. Real-life

the Aubertide leader, August. The sole surviving Aubertide, Greeneye, escaped by turning himself into a cow – but met his fate in a slaughterhouse.

The Doctor and Joan parted ways, but not before she gifted him with her cat, Wolsey, as a memento.

The Battle of Mons

During World War I, the first conflict between England and Germany occurred at the Battle of Mons. The English Captain Dudgeon luckily survived when his platoon was wiped out, and he later claimed to have seen one of the Angels of Mons: guardians from on high who sought to protect the British troops.[1991] Jack Harkness was vaguely acquainted with author/mystic Arthur Machen.[1992]

1914 (21st August) - THE TENTH DOCTOR YEAR ONE[1993] **->** As soldiers in Belgium braced to defend the town of Mons from the Germans, Jamie Colquhoun's mate Henry revealed that he wanted to marry Jamie's sister Margaret. However, a Weeping Angel fed off Henry's life, and sent him back to the Tay Bridge disaster.

> (=) The carnage of the Battle of Mons awoke the Dark Matrix. The British Expeditionary Force saw the form of Jack the Ripper over the battlefield.[1994]

The Creation of the Forge

The elder god Weyland influenced the creation of the Forge as a tool he could use against Fenric. A future member of the Forge, Captain Lysandra Aristedes, would unknowingly become one of Weyland's game pieces.[1995]

1914 (14th October) - PROJECT: TWILIGHT[1996] **->** The Forge, a secret project to improve the stock of soldiers, experimented on prisoners to create a race of "twilight vampires". One of the subjects, Amelia, a.k.a. Twilight Seven, became vampiric on 12th September, 1914. On 14th October, the vampires overpowered their creator, Dr Abberton, and fled. Abberton took the vampire formula to survive his wounds, and became known as Nimrod.

The Doctor was in Folkstone during the German bombardment of Antwerp in October 1914, and met a young woman named Jessica Borthwick. Under fire, she shuttled Belgian refugees across the channel in her yacht.[1997]

1914 (Christmas Day) - "The Forgotten"[1998] **->** The ninth Doctor and Rose found themselves in the trenches of the 11th Battalion Bedfordshire Regiment, and the Doctor celebrated the holiday by organising a football match between the two sides. The man in charge of this section of the trench, Captain Harkness, had been shot in the head and taken to hospital – he survived without a scratch.

The Twelfth Doctor Regenerates

1914 (25th December) - TWICE UPON A TIME[1999] **->** The Testimony Foundation lifted Captain Archibald Hamish Lethbridge-Stewart – who had been fated to die in Ypres – from history, but a timeline error diverted him to 1986. The twelfth Doctor, alongside the first Doctor, arranged for Archibald to return a few hours forward... just in time for the Christmas Armistice of 1914, which saved Archibald's life. The Doctors agreed to look in on Archibald's family in future.

The first Doctor returned to 1986 to undergo his regeneration. The twelfth Doctor visited with Testimony-made avatars of Bill Potts, Nardole and Clara Oswald, and regained his memories of the latter. Departing from his friends, he allowed his own regeneration to progress...

soldiers did report seeing the angels that Dudgeon describes, but they're commonly regarded as the result of battle trauma, urban legends and perhaps deliberately targeted propaganda.

1992 *TW: Consequences:* "The Wrong Hands". Machen, a Welsh author responsible for the legend of the Angels of Mons, lived 1863-1947.

1993 Dating *The Tenth Doctor Year One* (Titan 10th Doc #6-9, "The Weeping Angels of Mons") - A caption names the year.

1994 *Matrix*

1995 *Gods and Monsters*

1996 Dating *Project: Twilight* (BF #23) - The exact days are given.

1997 *Brotherhood of the Daleks*

1998 Dating "The Forgotten" (IDW *DW* mini-series #2) - The date is given. Private Benton may be an ancestor (the grandfather?) of UNIT's Sergeant Benton.

1999 Dating *Twice Upon a Time* (X10.13) - The exact day is given.

CAPTAIN ARCHIBALD LETHBRIDGE-STEWART: *Twice Upon a Time* ends with the World War I captain who accompanies the first and twelfth Doctors finally identifying himself as "Captain Archibald Lethbridge-Stewart" – a name-drop so profound, it gives the twelfth Doctor pause, given his long history with Archibald's family.

In interviews, Mark Gatiss (who played Archibald) out-and-out stated that the character was intended as the Brigadier's grandfather. This isn't actually said within the fiction, however, and potentially clashes with the extensive family tree of the Brigadier as laid out in the *Lethbridge-Stewart* novels. To smooth out this difficulty, the short story *Leth-St:* "What's Past is Prologue" and

Archibald retained no memory of meeting the Doctors.[2000]

1915

Professor Travers began his search for the Yeti...[2001] A copy of Waddell's *Among the Himalayas* convinced Edward Travers, age 16, that yeti were real, and he spent the next twenty years trying to prove it.[2002] Charles Arthur Cromwell of Torchwood was born on 6th March, 1915.[2003] The sixth Doctor had mint-condition gas masks from the Second Battle of Ypres, 1915.[2004]

(=) The Already Dead kidnapped Corporal Francis Morgan of the Welsh Fusiliers to serve as the living core component of a temporal fusion device.

A Vortex Dweller retroactively prevented Morgan's abduction, and he died instead.[2005]

Molly O'Sullivan Joins the TARDIS, Leaves

(=) c 1915 - DEyes: THE GREAT WAR / X AND THE DALEKS[2006] **->** Distraught from Lucie Miller's death, the eighth Doctor set course for the end of time to gain some perspective about the universe. Straxus, an agent of the Gallifreyan CIA, intercepted the TARDIS and said the Time Lords had foreseen that an unknown alien power would attempt to destroy the universe, as part of a scheme centred round an unnamed woman in France, World War I. The Doctor identified the woman as Molly O'Sullivan – formerly a chambermaid to the Donaldson family, and currently in France to protect her mistress, Kitty Donaldson, as part of the Voluntary Aid Detachment. A Time Vortex disturbance centred on Molly killed many in the vicinity, including Kitty. The Daleks attempted to capture Molly as part of their alliance with the renegade Time Lord Kotris, but the Doctor and Molly went on the run in the TARDIS...

After Kotris' actions were erased from history, Molly left the Doctor's company to continue caring for Kitty.

1915 (7th May) - THE SIRENS OF TIME[2007] **->** The fifth Doctor was on a merchant ship that was torpedoed by

Leth-St: The Man from Yesterday tacitly established that Archibald was officially the Brigadier's great-uncle, but biologically his grandfather owing to a night of infidelity with his sister-in-law Lillian (the Brig's grandmother). The Haisman Timeline provides further details about the Brigadier's grandfather increasingly realising the truth of this.

2000 The Haisman Timeline, clarifying *Twice Upon a Time*.
2001 "Twenty years" before *The Abominable Snowman*.
2002 *Leth-St: Night of the Intelligence* (ch11).
2003 *TW: Trace Memory*.
2004 *Recorded Time and Other Stories*: "Paradoxicide". The battle was 22nd April to 25th May, 1915.
2005 *TW: The Undertaker's Gift*. The book is a little contradictory concerning Morgan's abduction/death – it's said on page 90 that Torchwood investigated his disappearance after the war in 1919, and yet when his kidnapping is retroactively prevented, page 239 claims that "he was dead by 1915".
2006 Dating *DEyes: The Great War* and *DEyes: X and the Daleks* (BF *DEyes* #1.1, 1.4) - World War I began in 1914, but it's before America joined the war in 1917. Molly writes that it's an "uncommonly sunny day".
2007 Dating *The Sirens of Time* (BF #1) - The date is given.
2008 *The Eaters of Light*. The *Lusitania* sank 7th May, 1915.
2009 *The Curse of Davros*

2010 Dating *White Darkness* (NA #15) - "On the wall, a calendar of 1915 had just been turned to the August page" (p22).
2011 *The Dalek Project*
2012 *The Cabinet of Light* (p85).
2013 *Just War*
2014 Dating "The First" (*DWM* #386-389) - The exact days are given. The expedition is historical, and renowned as the last great (albeit failed) crossing of Antarctica.
2015 "The Age of Ice", "The Crimson Hand".
2016 *The Night Witches*
2017 Dating *Players* (PDA #21) - The date is given (p69).
2018 *The Wages of Sin*
2019 *The Magic Mousetrap*. The brothers started performing "before the war", but the Empire Theatre didn't open until April 1915, as a music hall starring Marie Lloyd.
2020 *2ndD* V1: *The Mouthless Dead*. The Battle of Jutland happened 31st May to 1st June, 1916.
2021 *The Elixir of Doom*, "twenty years" before 1936.
2022 *Human Nature* (NA)
2023 *The Family of Blood*
2024 *Storm Warning*
2025 *Eater of Wasps*
2026 "Time Bomb!"

a U-boat. He was captured and posed as a German secret agent. He escaped shortly before the U-boat torpedoed the RMS *Lusitania*. The Doctor failed to save the *Lusitania*, but in doing so prevented the future murder of Alexander Fleming, the discoverer of penicillin. Without it, the world would have suffered from plagues and fallen prey to the Second Velyshaan Empire.

Nardole heard a strange story about the sinking of the *Lusitania*.[2008] Davros foresaw that if Napoleon won the Battle of Waterloo, the French Empire would swiftly become dominant in Europe, and achieve absolute autocracy and great scientific progress with a century.[2009]

1915 (August) - WHITE DARKNESS[2010] -> The seventh Doctor, Benny and Ace arrived in Haiti as a civil rebellion against President Sam started. Lemaitre, an ancient man working on behalf of the Great Old Ones, was raising an army of zombies. They planned to open a gateway from their realm to Earth, and to conquer Europe. The Doctor destroyed Lemaitre and his base with a bomb.

In 1915, Daleks working toward the Dalek Project shot down Ralph Hellcombe's plane, turned him into a Dalek agent and reunited him with Lord Hellcombe, his father. A grateful Lord Hellcombe put his factories at the Daleks' disposal, working on what he thought was a weapon that would end the War. Similarly, the Daleks killed the son of Erik Graul, a German industrialist, and framed the Allies for the death. A vengeful Graul agreed to produce proto-Daleks at a factory in Belgium.[2011]

In 1915, Mr Sun was imprisoned for killing a professor of economics, who was later revealled as an Austrian spy.[2012] Arthur Kendrick distinguished himself by second-guessing the U-boat commanders on the Atlantic convoys. He would serve as an Admiral in World War II.[2013]

1915 (12th-13th September) - "The First"[2014] -> Tall crystalline beings, the Skith, were explorers of the Four Galaxies. They coveted knowledge to such an extent, they would acquire samples from planets, then eradicate their inhabitants or infect them with Skith crystals and turn them into Skithself. The Skith drove the Viskili, Mammox and pig-like Byndalk to extinction.

The tenth Doctor and Martha found that the Skith were interfering with Ernest Shackleton's trans-Antarctic expedition aboard the *Endurance*. A whale was transformed into a Skith octopoid, and zoologist Robert Clark progressively turned into Skithself. Together with Shackleton and the legendary adventurer-photographer James Francis Hurley, the travellers opened a rift and sent the Skith and their spaceship – Oppressor One – into the sun. Clark returned to normal, and Shackleton's expedition failed as history recorded.

The Skith leader survived, wounded, on Earth. It retained some knowledge of time travel that had been copied from the Doctor's mind when he was briefly turned into Skithself.[2015] The second Doctor owned one of Ernest Shackleton's compasses.[2016]

1915 (18th November) - PLAYERS[2017] -> The second Doctor arrived in No Man's Land using a time ring. He saved Winston Churchill from an ambush engineered by two Players, the Count and the Countess. The next day, he saved Churchill again, this time with the help of Jeremy Carstairs and Jennifer Buckingham. Carstairs joined Churchill's staff. The Doctor escaped a German firing squad by using the time ring.

The scientist Nikita Kuznetzov saw the devastation at Tunguska.[2018] Harry Randall and his twin brother Herbert – both of whom became trapped in the Toymaker's domain – performed as comic funambulists. The two of them, or possibly just Harry, topped the bill at the Empire Theatre in Penge.[2019]

Ben Jackson's uncle fought in the battle of Jutland, where he witnessed a thousand men perish on the *Invincible* when its ordnance detonated. A direct hit on the *Lion* caused a fireball that killed sixty men.[2020]

Iris Wildthyme sometimes enjoyed inserting anachronisms into black and white films, and appeared as an extra in *Boudica*, a film starring Vita Monet. Iris took a bottle of transmogrifying elixir to a cast party, having mistaken the liquid for Bombay Sapphire. Monet nabbed the elixir, and over the next two decades transformed her five husbands into monsters (the bloody count, the lizard man, the leopard boy, the living skeleton and the human jelly) that starred in her films. Iris semaphored in *Boudica* to her future self that Vita had taken "something dangerous", but before she could convey more, the scene cut away to Monet carving into Roman soldiers.[2021]

The Somme

The Battle of the Somme took place on 14th July, 1916. Richard Hadleman survived, treated by Timothy Dean, a former student of Dr John Smith of Aberdeen.[2022] **Tim Latimer saved himself and his schoolmate Hutchinson on a First World War battlefield, thanks to a premonition he'd had some years earlier.**[2023] Lance Corporal Weeks, later the chief steward aboard the *R-101*, fought at the Somme.[2024] Roger Gleave, a future police inspector, witnessed the devastation.[2025]

A time-hopping Death's Head appeared prior to the first battle of the Somme, blasted a tank and left.[2026] The UK Ministry of Defence created longevity pills with material from a Martian meteorite, and designated Corporal Paul Reynish as the first of a corps of never-aging soldiers.

Reynish fought at the Somme, but remained the only soldier on the books with an extended lifespan.[2027] Private Michael Thomas survived while his fellows died trying to capture Mametz Wood at the Somme.[2028]

The immortal Helena posed as Lt Helena English, an ambulance driver in France, 1916.[2029]

1916 (July-August) - THE TENTH DOCTOR YEAR ONE[2030] -> The Weeping Angels operated with impunity on the battlefields of World War I, as the conflict provided an excuse for why soldiers went missing. The tenth Doctor and Gabby found themselves in No Man's Land in Germany, and aided a Scottish soldier, Jamie Colquhoun, in trapping a group of Angels in an underground tunnel. Despite Jamie and Gabby's attraction for one another, he insisted on staying behind to aid the war effort.

The Many Deaths of Rasputin

On one of their missions, the crew of the *Teselecta* converted their ship to look like Rasputin – but made the mistake of rendering him as green.[2031]

wih - Two days before Rasputin's death, Faction Paradox took him away to the Eleven-Day Empire, where he became Father Dyavol, an advisor to Cousin Anastasia. In his place, the Faction supplied a duplicate Rasputin generated in a remembrance tank. The Great Houses sensed something amiss with Rasputin's history and attempted to rewrite the duplicate's biodata, even as the Celestis put their mark of indenture on him. The faux Rasputin effectively became three zombies in one, and the prolonged manner of his death embarrassed all concerned.[2032]

1916 (December) - THE WAGES OF SIN[2033] -> The third Doctor, Jo Grant and Liz Shaw arrived in St Petersburg as members of the city's elite, concerned about Father Grigori Rasputin's growing influence over Empress Czarina Alexandra, conspired to murder him. Jo befriended Rasputin and saved him from death by poisoning, but the conspirators repeatedly shot and beat Rasputin, still failing to kill him. The conspirators finally had Rasputin thrown into a frozen river. The Doctor refrained from action as Rasputin drowned, fulfilling history. Six weeks later, the Russian Revolution overthrew Tsar Nicholas II.

1917 - THE ROOF OF THE WORLD[2034] -> Lord Davey discovered an alien pyramid in the Himalayas when his expedition was wiped out in a storm. He was killed and replaced with a doppelganger. The fifth Doctor, Peri and Erimem arrived in Darjeeling, where Erimem met Davey and was possessed by the same force. A black cloud descended, killing dozens of people... including Erimem. The Doctor deduced this was an attempt on the part of the Great Old Ones to take control of the world, and that Erimem was still alive. Peri froze the cloud with liquid nitrogen. The pyramid was buried beneath an avalanche.

2027 *P.R.O.B.E.: When to Die.* The Battle of the Somme happened 1st July to 18th November, 1916.
2028 *2ndD V1: The Mouthless Dead.* The attempt to capture Mametz Wood happened 7th-12th July, 1916.
2029 *Erimem: Three Faces of Helena*
2030 Dating *The Tenth Doctor Year One* (Titan 10th Doc #6-9, "The Weeping Angels of Mons") - The action takes place at the Somme during World War I. A caption says it's "July 1916" in issue #6, but it's labelled as "August 1916" by issue #8, seemingly without that much time passing in-between.
2031 *Let's Kill Hitler.* Presumably Rasputin wasn't the target of their attack, as they were impersonating him.
2032 *FP: The Book of the War*
2033 Dating *The Wages of Sin* (PDA #19) - The date is given (p21). *Zagreus* confirms that the Doctor has met Rasputin.
2034 Dating *The Roof of the World* (BF #59) - It's 1917 according to the back cover.
2035 *Storm Warning*
2036 *The Devil Goblins from Neptune*
2037 *Singularity*
2038 *Leth-St: The Daughters of Earth* (ch2).
2039 "A hundred years" before *Vortex Ice.*
2040 *The Next Life*

2041 "About sixty years" before the 1977 portion of *The Valley of Death.*
2042 Dating *No Man's Land* (BF #89) - The year is given.
2043 Dating *The Dalek Project* (BBC original graphic novel #2) - The year is given.
2044 *Planet of Giants, The Alchemists.*
2045 *The War Games*
2046 *The Sea Devils*
2047 *Delta and the Bannermen*
2048 *Divided Loyalties*
2049 *Eternity Weeps*
2050 *Byzantium!, The King of Terror.*
2051 *The Empire of Death.* Luckner lived 1881-1966.
2052 *Mad Dogs and Englishmen*
2053 *Torchwood.org.uk.* Harriet appears in *TW: To the Last Man.* Caldwell is pictured with her.
2054 *TW: Small Worlds*
2055 "A hundred years" before *Face the Raven.*
2056 *Criss-Cross*
2057 Dating *The Haunting of Malkin Place* (BF 4th Doc #6.5) - The Doctor intervenes the night before the Third Battle of Ypres, which commenced on 31st July, 1917.
2058 Dating *The Way Through the Woods* (NSA #45) - It's "autumn 1917, shortly after closing time" (p19).

On 16th April, 1917, the Doctor and Lenin played tid-dlywinks on the train journey that returned Lenin from Switzerland to Russia. After that, the Doctor met Empress Alexandra.[2035] The Doctor was present in Russia during the October Revolution, met Lenin and became a Hero of the Revolution.[2036] The Doctor regarded Lenin as a "disagree-able man with terrible breath".[2037] Alistair Lethbridge-Stewart's grandfather was in Russia during the 1917 revo-lution.[2038]

Miners spooked the cyborg-squid sleeping in Chihuahua, Mexico, and it reduced a hundred of them to skeletons.[2039] As a child, Charley Pollard saw the Crystal Palace. She also learned French from her Uncle Jacques.[2040] The Luron named Godrin enabled local tribesmen in the Amazon to "recover" the diary of Professor Perkins, hoping that the document would lure technologically proficient humans to the Valley of Death.[2041]

1917 - NO MAN'S LAND[2042] **->** An agent of the Forge, posing as "Lieutenant-Colonel Brook" of the British army, undertook experiments to refine his soldiers' killing instinct. The Forge also wanted to know if psychological trauma could endow people with time sensitivity or pre-cognition. Soldiers at Charnage Hospital near Arras in France were subjected to psychological refinement in the "hate room", and made to "kill" dummies of German troopers. Brook sent a squad to No Man's Land when a wounded trooper, Private Taylor, informed him of an old church on an excellent vantage point there. Due to Brook's conditioning, the British soldiers slaughtered one another.

The seventh Doctor, Ace and Hex destroyed Brook's research, and Brook was killed by his own callous men. The Doctor postulated that perhaps the unhinged Private Taylor had indeed demonstrated precognition.

1917 - THE DALEK PROJECT[2043] **->** The Dalek Project moved into its final phase, with Lord Hellcombe and Erik Graul's factories working to produce Dalek ground forces respectively for the Allies and the Germans. The Daleks hoped to trigger a war to end all wars, in which they could assess how humans dealt with certain defeat. The eleventh Doctor intervened as the two Dalek forces converged on human soldiers in France, and reprogrammed the German Daleks to attack the UK-made ones. All Daleks on the battlefield were destroyed, and the surviving Dalek Project spaceship crashed into a trench system. It would remain buried for a hundred years.

The Doctor returned, accompanied by Professor Angela Todd, from dealing with the revived Dalek ship in 2017, and had tea with his friend Corporal Ted Anderson.

The first Doctor and Susan were caught in a Zeppelin raid at some point during the war.[2044] **A First World War battlefield near Ypres was kidnapped by** the War Lords.[2045] **The Doctor claimed to have been wounded at the Battle of Gallipoli.**[2046] **Burton, later a camp leader at Shangri-La in 1959, fought in the War using his sabre in hand-to-hand combat.**[2047] The Toymaker kidnapped two British soldiers from Ypres.[2048]

Turkish soldiers during the First World War claimed to have seen The Ark of Ages on Mount Ararat.[2049] The Doctor saw the Battle of Passchendale.[2050] The Doctor met the noted sailor Felix von Luckner.[2051]

In 1917, Reginald Tyler started writing the fantasy epic *The True History of Planets* while on leave from soldiering in France.[2052]

Harriet Derbyshire was recruited from Oxford **to join Torchwood Cardiff. Douglas Caldwell,** formerly a draughtsman in the Royal Engineers, **joined Torchwood Cardiff** during World War I.[2053] **In 1917, the Cottingley Fairies photographs caused a sensation – even Sir Arthur Conan Doyle thought they were genuine. Decades later, the girls who took the pictures admitted they were fakes, but Torchwood would have reason to suspect they were real.**[2054]

A violent act occurred on Mayor Me's trap street in London – the last such disturbance the locale would experience for a century.[2055] Constance Clarke returned to London from Nyasaland as a young girl, after her father died of tuberculosis. She finished her schooling in England, and studied Modern Languages at Somerville College.[2056]

(=) 1917 (30th July) - THE HAUNTING OF MALKIN PLACE[2057] **->** A Warrior Historian from the future died in the Third Battle of Ypres. An 18-year-old British soldier, Maurice, used the Historian's dam-aged time watch to go home to Malkin Place, but four years on. The fourth Doctor retroactively averted the resultant time vacuum by jumping back with the same watch, and persuading Maurice to not go home. Maurice instead died saving a fellow soldier, Jack, who was important to the web of time as a future editor of war stories and poetry.

To reunite with the second Romana and the TARDIS, the fourth Doctor spent the next five years living in Paris and his Baker Street abode, hiding out in the attic to avoid himself as needed. He also grew a moustache.

1917 (autumn) - THE WAY THROUGH THE WOODS[2058] **->** As part of their investigations into the people who had gone missing in Swallow Woods, the eleventh Doctor and Amy dropped off Rory to observe barmaid Emily Bostock. Rory and Emily were transported into a pocket dimension that Reyn the were-fox used to save the odd person from his sentient spaceship.

1917 (Christmas) - LETH-ST: "What's Past is Prologue"[2059] **->** By now, Alistair Lethbridge-Stewart Sr. had spent some years serving in Russia. The Lethbridge-Stewart family celebrated Christmas together. Alistair Sr. caught his nearly 15-year-old son, Gordon, trying to enlist by lying about his age. As Gordon and his uncle Archibald were the spitting image of one another, Alistair suspected that Gordon was Archibald's son, not his.

1918

wih - Russia made the switch from the Julian calendar to the Gregorian one in 1918, when the 31st January was immediately followed by 14th February. Cousin Anastasia claimed these lost thirteen days and founded the Thirteen-Day Republic, a rival to Faction Paradox's Eleven-Day Empire.[2060]

The Doctor was present on 23rd March, 1918, when the Chinese conjuror Chung Ling Soo died on stage in London. Soo was performing in the Wood Green Empire, and perished when his bullet-catching act went wrong.[2061]

wih - Grand Duchess Anastasia Nikolaevna, Tsar Nicholas II's youngest daughter, was recruited to join Faction Paradox and became known as Cousin Anastasia. History recorded that Anastasia was executed along with her family on 17th July, 1918.[2062]

Around 1918, the Doctor and Cornelius literally crossed swords in an adventure that involved a Newcastle coal

mine and Leopard Men.[2063] The British military captured a Sontaran named Brak when he crashed to Earth. He was brought to England in 1918, and would be kept under paralysis until World War II.[2064]

By the Doctor's estimate, the radiation in the field behind the local church in Klimtenburg should have passed.[2065]

> = The Doctor met Mao Zedong when the man was a librarian.[2066]

The Spanish Flu Pandemic

@ 1918 (March to August) - CASUALTIES OF WAR[2067] **->** The eighth Doctor investigated reports of the walking dead in Hawkswick in Yorkshire. Befriending the village midwife, Mary Minnett, he discovered that the traumatic memories of wounded soldiers convalescing at Hawkswick Hall were empowering the Dark Forces: psychic energy that pre-dated the age of scientific reason, and was laden in humankind like a race memory. The Doctor entered a netherworld created by the Dark Forces and caused a psychic backlash, destroying them. It was possible that the dispersion of the Dark Forces caused the Spanish Flu epidemic.

@ The Doctor kept the last letter Mary wrote to him (on 22nd August, 1918).[2068] An influenza epidemic in 1918

2059 Dating *Leth-St:* "What's Past is Prologue" (*Leth-St* short story) - The day is given.
2060 *FP: The Book of the War, FP: Warring States.*
2061 *Assassin in the Limelight*
2062 *FP: The Book of the War, FP: Warring States* (p52).
2063 *The Coming of the Terraphiles*
2064 *Sontarans: Old Soldiers*
2065 "The next century or so", the Doctor estimates, after *Plague of the Cybermen* (p90).
2066 *Unbound: Sympathy for the Devil.* Mao had this occupation 1917-1919.
2067 Dating *Casualties of War* (EDA #38) - The story begins on " 19 March, 1918" (Prologue). Mary writes a final letter to the Doctor on "22nd August" (Epilogue).
2068 *Eater of Wasps*
2069 *Birthright*
2070 *Pier Pressure.* The armistice with Germany was signed in France on 11th November, 1918.
2071 Dating *TW: To the Last Man* (*TW* 2.3) - The year is given. Tommy is 24 and was born 7th February, 1894, so events in 1918 must occur after that day. *The Torchwood Archives* (BBC) claims that he was killed on 28th October, 1918, so events in *To the Last Man* – set three weeks beforehand – presumably occur in the same month.
2072 Dating *TW:* "Rift War" (*TWM* #4-13) - The year is given.

2073 Dating *DEyes 2: The White Room* (BF *DEyes* #2.2) - The story ends on Armistice Day: November 11th, 1918.
2074 *DEyes 2: Time's Horizon/Eyes of the Master.*
2075 *DEyes 3: Rule of the Eminence.* It's a bit vague as to where, exactly, Molly goes after ending her travels with the Doctor. *Dark Eyes 4* entails the Doctor and Liv looking for Molly in 1921.
2076 "Twelve years" before *The English Way of Death* (p83).
2077 *Time in Office.* Hitchcock lived 1899-1980, started his film career in 1919.
2078 *Storm Warning.* The Treaty of Versailles, which brought World War I to a close, was signed 28th June, 1919.
2079 *The Time Museum.* Date unknown, but this being the TARDIS, it's hard to believe that Ian was there absent an important historical event. One candidate would be the signing of the Treaty of Versailles.
2080 *The Magic Mousetrap*
2081 *Worlds BF: The Feast of Magog*
2082 *Matrix*
2083 Dating *The Memory Cheats* (BF CC #6.3) - The month and year is given.
2084 Dating *Toy Soldiers* (NA #42) - The main action of the book starts "25 September 1919" (p39).

and 1919 killed more people than the Great War itself.[2069]

The West Pier in Brighton absorbed the cheerful feelings of its visitors – the malevolent aliens from Indo subsisted off these emotions, and grew stronger. However, the armistice that ended World War I created such a widespread feeling of relief, the aliens were temporarily subdued.[2070]

1918 (October) - TW: TO THE LAST MAN[2071] **-> The Rift caused St Teilo's Hospital in Cardiff to overlap with itself in the twenty-first century, an act that endangered both time zones. Gerald Carter and Harriet Derbyshire of Torchwood were instructed by a future projection of Thomas Reginald Brockless – a soldier at St Teilo's recovering from shellshock – to find and cryo-freeze his past self. They did so, enabling Torchwood in future to close the Rift by sending Tommy back through it. Tommy resumed being shellshocked on his return to 1918; three weeks later, he was returned to France and executed for cowardice.**

1918 - TW: "Rift War"[2072] **->** Gerald Carter and Harriet Derbyshire disrupted a group of stone circle worshippers by "borrowing" a tank from the military. Rift activity briefly juxtaposed them with Ianto and Tosh in 2008, where they saw their friend and colleague Jack Harkness.

Molly O'Sullivan Rejoins the TARDIS, Leaves

1918 (November) - DEyes 2: THE WHITE ROOM[2073] **->** As World War I drew to a close, Molly O'Sullivan squatted in the Doctor's house at 107 Baker Street. The abode contained a priest hole, as the Doctor knew that he would one day need to hide a pontiff there.

Exposure to the time-active virus KX-variant 243 had thrown a Viyran back to 1918, and it conducted viral experiments on humans at the Blackwell Convalescent Home. The TARDIS' arrival generated temporal particles that activated the dormant KX virus, resulting in another Viyran being pulled back to 1918. The eighth Doctor convinced the Viryans that their No. 1 priority was to eradicate Patient Zero, causing them to label each other as such and destroy one another. He also realised that the virus was a closed loop – it would endure in the Viyrans' corpses, and draw them back to its year of origin.

The retrogenitor particles within Molly reactivated when the Doctor casually touched her, and they left in the TARDIS to investigate this mystery and also share new adventures together. Molly gave the keys to the Doctor's house to an associate of hers, David Walker.

The TARDIS deliberately took the Doctor and Molly two millennia into the future, to the very edge of the universe. The Celestial Intervention Agency looked for Molly in 1918, but failed to find her.[2074] Following the end of the Eminence War, Narvin brought Molly back to her native time.[2075]

An agent of the Bureau arrived from the future (circa 2386) and adopted the name Percival Closed.[2076] Tegan challenged the Doctor's claim that he gave Hitchcock the idea to simultaneously zoom in and move the camera.[2077]

Brigadier General Tamworth was part of the Versailles delegation, and foresaw that reparations against Germany would further a bigger conflict.[2078] At some point in his travels with the Doctor, Ian Chesterton visited Versailles.[2079]

Following an incident on a rowing boat on Lake Balaton, the summer of 1919, Mrs Elsa Kerniddle would never speak again. She was later transported into the Celestial Toymaker's realm.[2080] The disgraced Alexander Korvo aided the UK secret service during the War. Charges against him were dropped, and he returned home.[2081]

> (=) In the world of the Dark Matrix, the Jack the Ripper killings started again after the Great War. Ghostly Rippers begin terrorising London. There was mass panic, despite summary executions for suspects. The government withdrew to Edinburgh.[2082]

1919 (August) - THE MEMORY CHEATS[2083] **->** The second Doctor, Jamie and Zoe were in Tashkent, Uzbekistan, as the Bolsheviks took command of the North, and were expected to spread their control to the South. The letters of Richard Lansing detailed how school children were going missing, and said a deformed man was responsible. Lansing and his wife Elizabeth were killed before discovering the truth. It was possible that a kind alien observer was collecting some children to take back to its homeworld, and spare them the horror of warfare on Earth. It was also possible that the Lansings had died because Zoe accidentally agitated the creature into killing them. In Zoe's native time, she and her defence council were unable to agree on exactly what had taken place, and how this matter resolved.

1919 (late September) - TOY SOLDIERS[2084] **->** Investigating the mysterious disappearance of children across post-War Europe, the seventh Doctor, Benny, Roz and Chris discovered that they had been kidnapped by the Recruiter, a device transporting beings from many worlds to act as soldiers in the fourteen-hundred-year war that had ravaged the planet Q'ell. The Recruiter had been built to destroy the Ceracai race, but the Doctor reprogrammed it to rebuild the devastated planet.

Harriet Derbyshire was killed, age 26. Gerald Carter retired from active Torchwood service, but remained a consultant.[2085] **The Doctor drank with Lloyd George when he was Prime Minister.**[2086]

The Nineteen Twenties

The Doctor acquired a copy of the 1920 book *Every Boy's Book of the English Civil War*. He would later lose it in 1648.[2087] The Doctor met movie producer Harold Reitman in England in the 1920s.[2088] He helped Joyce with *Ulysses*.[2089] The Doctor knew author F. Scott Fitzgerald.[2090]

The fourth Doctor regarded "the roaring twenties" as "one of the three great periods in Earth history".[2091] The ancestors of the Sidewinder Syndicate became stranded on Earth, the 1920s, and adopted gangster-fashion as their own.[2092]

In the 1920s, Blue Tit birds in Southampton learned to tear the tops off milk bottles and drink the cream inside. Soon, Blue Tit birds more than a hundred miles away were exhibiting the talent – even though the birds rarely flew more than fifteen miles – and by 1947, the habit was universal among the species. This owed to morphic resonance, a collective memory held within a planet's morphogenetic field, and passed on to each new generation of life. The same effect was witnessed in monkey creatures four million years in the future, on the planet Endarra.[2093]

The Doctor met the Czech composer Leos Janacek.[2094] River Song enjoyed herself at "outrageous" parties in the 1920s, many of them hosted by the ladies' badminton team. According to River, Princess Victoria had a "lethal backhand".[2095]

The twin brothers Edward and Vincent Travers became estranged, and didn't see each other for the half-century

prior to their deaths.[2096] @ The Doctor studied Ba Chai in Peking, the 1920s.[2097]

A predatory force that lived in art, the Red Lady, killed young Francis McCallum's parents – but he trapped the fiend in a crayon drawing, and blinded himself to prevent her escape. Over the decades, McCallum used his inheritance to purchase other artworks that the Red Lady inhabited, further restraining her.[2098] The Doctor witnessed a cargo cult in the Melanesian Islands.[2099]

At university, Tobias Kinsella was thick as thieves with fellow students Hassan Al-Nadyr and Mikael, and well as a young lecturer, John Routledge. Upon learning that Mikael was a Russian spy, Kinsella had the Secret Service apprehend his friend. He was turned over to Russia, and would spend the next decade in a Russian gulag. Ex-Nazi geneticists working for Russia experimented on Mikael, making him resistant to aging.[2100]

1920

The time traveller Honoré Lechasseur was born.[2101] Jean-Henri, Honoré's father, abandoned his son and Honoré's mother, Evangeline Lechasseur.[2102] As part of their analysis to repair an ailing sun, the Key tracers Abby and Zara read *A Determination of the Deflection of the Light by the Sun's Gravitational Field, from Observations Made of the Total Eclipse of May 29, 1919* (1920).[2103] The Aquilion visited Earth in 1920 and acquired some Assam tea.[2104]

2085 *TW: To the Last Man*. Harriet is said to be killed "the year after" an undated photo of Gerald Carter's Torchwood team is taken; *The Torchwood Archives* (BBC) dates her death to 1919, confirming that the photo was taken in 1918. There's conflicting reports of when Gerald stops leading Torchwood Cardiff – Torchwood. org.uk says he held himself responsible for Harriet's death and "retired from active service soon afterwards", but *The Torchwood Archives* (BBC) says he remained in charge until 1926.
2086 *Aliens of London*. No date is given, but Lloyd George was Prime Minister 1916-1922.
2087 *The Roundheads*
2088 *Dying in the Sun*
2089 "The Final Chapter"
2090 *The Crooked Man*. Fitzgerald lived 1896 to 1940; his best-known work, *The Great Gatsby*, was published in 1925.
2091 *The Auntie Matter*
2092 *House of Cards*
2093 *Scaredy Cat*
2094 *Downtime* (p262). Janacek lived 1854-1928. His later works are among his most prized, but the Doctor's claim that Janacek "didn't even get into his stride as a composer until he was in his eighties" is strange, given

that Janacek died age 74.
2095 *DC 2: The Sonomancer*. Princess Victoria, the second daughter of King Edward VII, lived 1868-1935.
2096 "Fifty years" before *Leth-St: The Dreamer's Lament* (ch3).
2097 *To the Slaughter*
2098 The background to *DC 1: The Red Lady*.
2099 *The Warehouse*, "in the early twentieth century", so presumably following World War I. Cargo cults resulted from a primitive people observing the transport capabilities of more advanced civilisations, and praying for material wealth.
2100 *CM: Who Killed Toby Kinsella?*
2101 He's 29 in *TimeH: The Tunnel at the End of the Light* (p16), which appears to take place in early 1950 – although he might have already had a birthday, in which case he was born in 1921.
2102 *TimeH: The Sideways Door*
2103 *Graceless III: Consequences*. The work was published in 1920.
2104 *Signs and Wonders*
2105 Dating *2ndD V1: The Mouthless Dead* (BF CC #10.1) - The TARDIS instruments initially claim that it's "5681" by the Hebrew calendar, whereupon the Doctor flips through the options and says, "Here we are –

1920 (10th November) - 2NDD V1: THE MOUTHLESS DEAD[2105] -> A train clipped the TARDIS outside Canterbury, prompting the second Doctor, Ben, Polly and Jamie to exit the Ship while it healed. The Unknown Warrior was being transported from Dover for burial in Westminster Abbey, and the collective sorrow of millions funneled through the TARDIS' damaged telepathic circuits, giving substance to memories of fallen soldiers. The walking dead killed a signalman, destroying him with the grief they embodied. Private Michael Thomas was reunited with his fiance, Frances, and the love they shared coalesced in the King's sword attached to the Unknown Warrior's casket, dissipating the dead.

1920 (5th December) - BLINK[2106] -> The Weeping Angels transported Kathy Nightingale from 2007 to Hull in 1920. She would marry Benjamin Wainright and live out her life in her own past.

(=) 1921 (Spring) - DEyes 4: A LIFE IN THE DAY / DEyes 4: THE MONSTER OF MONTMARTRE[2107] -> The physically ailing Dalek Time Controller – now the only Dalek survivor of an eradicated timeline, and ostracized from its own kind – sought to re-shape Earth's history via the temporal scar created by Molly O'Sullivan's personal timeline. An infusion of retrogenitor particles linked the Controller to Molly's life, and it collaborated with the bald Master to turn Earth into a Dalek factory. They repurposed the Pagoda Tower into what was effectively a giant Dalek.

The eighth Doctor and Liv arrived in London, 1921, to check up on Molly. The two of them resided at the Ritz for two weeks, as one of the Doctor's former selves was occupying 107 Baker Street. Androids working for the Dalek Time Controller tracked down the travellers, stole the TARDIS and attempted to cover their escape with a temporal grenade. Martin Donaldson – Kitty Donaldson's brother – was caught in the blast, and the resultant time-loop accorded Martin a single day to repeatedly spend time with Liv and secretly fall in love with her. Martin's efforts enabled the Doctor and Liv to escape the loop and follow the TARDIS' chronon trail. They believed Martin dead, but the loop continued, and Martin awoke in his own bed.

The Time Controller completed the Pagoda by incorporating the TARDIS into its workings. The Doctor retrieved his Ship, but was drawn in it to forty years in the future. The Master tricked Liv into tracking the Doctor there...

Molly O'Sullivan lived out the next four decades on an Earth that increasingly fell to the Dalek Time Controller.[2108]

1921 - TIMEH: THE SEVERED MAN[2109] -> The Cabal of the Horned Beast was now powerful enough to enthrall the village of Middleton Basset using a time-creature. The time travelling Honoré Lechasseur and Emily Blandish broke the Cabal's hold over the time-creature, freeing the townsfolk.

c 1921 - THE DALEKS' MASTER PLAN[2110] -> While hiding from the Daleks, the TARDIS landed briefly on a film set in Hollywood.

Gregorian. It's November 1920. "The Unknown Warrior's funeral is slated for "tomorrow" at Westminster Abbey; he was buried there on 11th November.

2106 Dating *Blink* (X3.10) - Benjamin's newspaper names the day and year.

2107 Dating *DEyes 4: A Life in the Day/The Monster of Montartre* (BF *DEyes* #4.1-4.2) - The year and season are given. It's a bit odd that *Dark Eyes 3* ended at a point when the Doctor and Molly knew they couldn't reunite for fear of attracting attention from various cosmic powers and imperiling her life, but writer Matt Fitton says: "The Doctor knows it would be dangerous to actually meet Molly, but the fact that her eyes are still dark [meaning she still possesses retrogenitor particles] is of grave concern to him". For this reason, it seems, the Doctor and Liv look in on Molly a few years after her return to this era.

The Dalek Time Controller here seeks to create a New Dalek Paradigm that includes Dalek Strategists, but the effort ultimately seems unrelated to the New Dalek Paradigm that shows up in *Victory of the Daleks*.

The Controller cites red Daleks as its intended Time Strategists, when Daleks of that colour in *Victory of the Daleks* are mere drones.

2108 *DEyes 4: Master of the Daleks*

2109 Dating *TimeH: The Severed Man* (*TimeH* #5) - A time-sensitive tells Honoré and Emily that they're in 1921 (p108). Strangely, though, *TimeH: Echoes* p10 seems to state that these events happened in 1924.

2110 Dating *The Daleks' Master Plan* (4.4) - The script for episode seven, "The Feast of Steven," specified a date of "1919," but publicity material released on 1st October, 1965, stated that the TARDIS lands in "California 1921". The film being made is a talkie, which means this must be after the release of *The Jazz Singer* in 1927. Numerous Hollywood personalities are seen or hinted at in the episode. Actor Rudolph Valentino made his debut in 1914, but was only really famous after *The Sheik* in 1921. Actor Douglas Fairbanks Sr. debuted in 1915, but he wasn't "big" (as he is described in the episode) until *The Three Musketeers* in 1921. Chaplin's debut was 1914, but the film we see in production strongly resembles *Gold*

c 1921 - DotD: SMOKE AND MIRRORS[2111] -> The Tremas Master, trapped in the imploding dimension that was formerly realised as Castrovalva, psionically projected his consciousness to Earth via a surviving Ovid sphere kept at a fairground. He convinced Harry Houdini – who had a history of tearing down his idols, including the conjuror Jean Eugene Robert-Houdin – to turn against his old friend, the Doctor.

Houdini summoned the fifth Doctor, Adric, Tegan and Nyssa via a psionic beam, on the pretence of investigating a medium using impossible methods of deduction. He tried and failed to drown the Doctor, then decried his change of heart. The Doctor and his allies stopped the Master from fully manifesting on Earth, and – on instructions from the eleventh Doctor – returned the sphere to the Ovids.

The Ovids were so impressed with Tegan and the return of their sphere, they eventually shared the secrets of their psychic-kinetic technology with humanity.[2112]

Eileen Le Croissette (later Younghusband), an associate of Brigadier Lethbridge-Stewart and Professor Travers, was born in 1921.[2113] The Russian mineralogist Leonid A Kulik visited the area of the Tunguska explosion in 1921, but failed to locate the impact site.[2114]

1922

The ninth Doctor, having lived on Earth since 1894, started going to a particular dance hall in Birmingham every night following New Year's, to meet Rose Tyler when she materialised there.[2115]

In 1922, a foreigner staying at Tullock Inn vanished on Tullock Moor, kidnapped by the Zygons.[2116] **Dr Judson was crippled before this time.**[2117] The Threshold set up offices on Earth's moon in 1922.[2118] Muriel Wilberforce became chairwoman of the Pease Pottage Women's Institute in 1922, and served longer than anyone

---

Rush (1924). Bing Crosby didn't go to Hollywood until 1930. *DWM* writer Richard Landen claimed a date of "1929", *The TARDIS Special* offered "c.1920".

2111 Dating *DotD: Smoke and Mirrors* (*Destiny of the Doctor* #5) - The blurb says that it's "England in the 1920s", and the Doctor comments that it's "around the turn of the 1920s". Houdini died in 1926, and here displays an interest in spiritually communing with his mother, who passed in 1913. It's after Houdini has vilified Robert-Houdin, which notably happened with his book *The Unmasking of Robert-Houdin* (1908).

2112 *DotD: The Time Machine*

2113 *Leth-St: The Flaming Soldier*, mirroring Younghusband's real-life birth on 4th July, 1921.

2114 *The Wages of Sin*

2115 *9thC: The Other Side*. While this a romantic notion, see this story's Dating notes for a simpler solution.

2116 Angus relates the story in *Terror of the Zygons*.

2117 According to Commander Millington, the accident happened "over twenty years" before *The Curse of Fenric*, and Judson appears to blame Millington for it. The novelisation, also written by Ian Briggs, confirms that Millington was culpable.

2118 "Wormwood"

2119 *The Wrong Doctors*

2120 *TW: Trace Memory*

2121 *TW: The Twilight Streets*

2122 *The Movellan Grave*. Carter appears in *Forty-Five*: "False Gods", but didn't discover Tut's tomb until 1922.

2123 Dating *The Haunting of Malkin Place* (BF 4th Doc #6.5) - The year is given. It's "Autumn weather". *The Turn of the Screw* (1898) leaves the reader uncertain as to whether ghosts are involved or not.

2124 Dating *9thC: The Other Side* (BF *The Ninth Doctor Chronicles* #1.3) - The year and month are given. The whole "Doctor living on Earth for twenty-eight years to

catch up with Rose scenario" could've been avoided, had he simply asked her for Adam's phone number while chatting with her from 1894.

2125 *TimeH: Kitsune*

2126 *Assassin in the Limelight*. This is said to have taken place in "the summer of 23 or 24", but Fender was more at his height in the former year, as England dropped him after 1924.

2127 "The Age of Ice". The likely suspect here is *The Life of Ernest Shackleton* (1923), published a year after Shackleton's death, but it's unclear who did the censoring as UNIT didn't yet exist.

2128 *Illegal Alien*

2129 *Iris S2: The Panda Invasion*. Historically speaking, the claim is a strange one. Eric Blair, a.k.a. George Orwell, wasn't incarcerated but did serve as an imperial policeman in Burma from 1922 to 1927. Perhaps Iris was imprisoned and Orwell was her jailor.

2130 *The Wreck of the World*. The *Flying Scotsman*, built in 1923, is currently owned by the National Railway Museum in York.

2131 *Graceless III: The Edge*

2132 Dating "Four Doctors" (Titan mini-series #1-2, 5) - A caption gives the year.

2133 Dating *River S1: The Boundless Sea* (BF *The Diary of River Song* #1.1) - An academic says that King Tut's tomb was discovered "last summer" – a less-than-accurate remark, as it was found on 4th November, 1922, and opened 16th February, 1923.

2134 Dating *Paradox Lost* (NSA #48) - The exact day is given (p233).

2135 Dating *Timewyrm: Exodus* (NA #2) - Part Two of the novel is set during the Munich Putsch, which took place between the 8th and 9th of November 1923. A textbook quoted in the novel erroneously gives the month as "September" (p95).

else in the role, until her death in 1964.[2119] Sao Paulo, 1922, was the site of a Vondrax visitation.[2120]

In the same year, Jack Harkness once again failed to enter the Tretarri housing district, but engaged in some "sexual deviancy" with a young lady in the back of the Torchwood Daimler he'd requisitioned.[2121]

The fourth Doctor owned a Gladstone Bag; with it, he'd helped Howard Carter to find King Tut's tomb.[2122]

1922 (Autumn) - THE HAUNTING OF MALKIN PLACE[2123] **->** While lodging at his Baker Street house, the fourth Doctor and the second Romana decided to take a steamtrain to Rye, to question Henry James if ghosts were involved in *The Turn of the Screw*. They diverted to deal with ghostly happenings at Malkin Place, and found that a young soldier, Maurice, had escaped from World War I using time tech: a time watch. The resultant time vacuum was pulling Maurice back to 1917, and drawing the essences of future-born children to Malkin Place. The Doctor slipped back with the time watch and restored history. Maurice died in Ypres, and the Doctor reunited with Romana after having lived out the intervening five years.

Malkin Place was inhabited by a bona fide ghost: that of Mrs Mountford, killed in 1742.

1922 (November) - 9thC: THE OTHER SIDE[2124] **->** The Bigon Horde's temporal tsunami left Rose Tyler at a dance hall in Birmingham. She phoned the ninth Doctor in 1894, and he lived through the interceding twenty-eight years to rejoin her. They called Adam Mitchell in 2012, who opened a portal so they could return to that year. The Bigon Horde followed.

1923

Zoo animals killed during an earthquake in Tokyo, 1923, became vengeful spirits, and were contained within a haunted house later built on the same locale.[2125] The Doctor watched a cricket game featuring Percy George Herbert Fender – whom he regarded as the finest cricketer ever to captain England.[2126]

Material pertaining to the Skith was embargoed from Ernest Shackleton's biography.[2127] Miss Simone performed at the Palace Theatre, Northampton, in 1923. After her death, her spirit became the manager of a hotel for the deceased at the end of time.[2128]

In 1923, George Limb, a member of military intelligence, failed to convince his superiors that the British should side with Hitler.[2129] Iris Wildthyme spent a night in a cell with George Orwell.[2130]

The *Flying Scotsman*, the first steam locomotive to reach 100 mph, was built. In future, it would be preserved aboard *The World*.[2131]

(=) 1923 - "Four Doctors" (Titan)[2132] **->** The tenth Doctor and Gabby stopped the Cybermen from thieving the French gold reserves in Paris, 1923, whereupon Gabby stopped for crepes while the Doctor disposed of the Cyber-tech. Meanwhile, the eleventh Doctor and Alice dealt with radiation monsters emerging from the Seine, and Alice stopped in the same café as Gabby while the eleventh Doctor went to purchase some 1920s *bandes dessinee* (Franco-Belgian comics). Clara secretly approached Gabby and Alice, and asked them to help her prevent a multi-Doctor meeting on Marinus that was foretold to end with the universe's destruction.

To Clara's dismay, the tenth, eleventh and twelfth Doctors tracked down their companions and started arguing. The quarrelling tenth and twelfth Doctors poked one another, causing a paradox in the café – which was a fixed point in time – that attracted a pack of Reapers. In fleeing, the Doctors and their companions docked their respective TARDISes together, but wound up on the planet Marinus...

An older version of Gabby burst into the café, having been strategically thrown back in time by a Weeping Angel, and told everyone their plans had gone hideously wrong. Deciding upon a different course of action made the older Gabby vanish, her timeline erased. The Doctors and their friends decided they would still go to Marinus, but on their own terms...

Afterwards, the Doctors and their companions returned to the café to have a leisurely chat, but respectfully went their separate ways after glimpsing the ninth Doctor and Rose inside.

c 1923 - RIVER S1: THE BOUNDLESS SEA[2133] **->** River Song hoped to get away from it all for a bit, and established herself as a visiting archaeology professor in the UK. Bertie Potts – officially a British consul, but actually a clone working for the Rulers of the Universe – observed River as she investigated a recently discovered tomb in Mesopotamia, and destroyed lethal microbots freed from within. The microbots killed Potts, but not before he gave River an invitation to a party in a Magellanic Cloud, where she confronted the Rulers...

1923 (23rd October) - PARADOX LOST[2134] **->** The eleventh Doctor brought the AI unit Arven to live with the retired Professor Archibald Angelchrist, figuring they could both use the company.

1923 (9th November) - TIMEWYRM: EXODUS[2135] **->** The seventh Doctor and Ace witnessed the Munich Putsch, an attempted coup organised by a young Adolf Hitler, so the Doctor could gain Hitler's confidence and sway events in future. A man with energy weapons fired upon the time travellers – it was the War Chief, who was operating in this era to aid the Nazis, but the Doctor didn't recognise him.

1924

The Doctor borrowed a rucksack from George Mallory and Andrew Irvine before their final assault on Everest in 1924. He warned them not to lose their gloves, lest they lose their lives, but he never saw from them again – possibly because he'd failed to return Mallory's gloves.[2136] In 1924, the Panoptican Theatre was converted into an 850-seater and renamed the Beacon Film Theatre.[2137] Iris Wildthyme's bus had a constant supply of fresh water thanks to an inter-dimensional, time-travelling pipeline to a Canadian lake in 1924.[2138]

The last remnants of Marshall Sezhyr's Ice Army fell into in-fighting, and his most devout followers were slaughtered – chained out onto the surface of Mars to face the Red Dawn. One group gathered relics from his shrine and escaped to Earth.[2139]

On 28th February, 1924, Jack Harkness showed up at Torchwood India in Delhi armed with dance records, and seduced the group's leader: Eleanor, the Duchess of Melrose. Britain's hold over India was coming to an end, and Jack had orders to relocate Torchwood India's holdings

back to the home country. On 29th February, the Duchess and her associates used a piece of alien tech left behind – a "time store" – to halt the passage of time inside an old colonial mansion. They carried on for decades, unaging, as the world changed around them.[2140]

1924 - TW: THE TORCHWOOD ARCHIVE (BF)[2141] ->
Captain Jack's reclamation of the alien artefacts at Torchwood India threw the Duchess into such a rage, she sent Jack an item that he'd missed: Object One, along with the bad luck surrounding it.

Rachel Jensen, a member of Counter-Measures and an associate of the seventh Doctor, was born. As a child, she spent a lot of time at one of the oldest synagogues in London.[2142] The Monk offered his companion Tamsin "Caesar's very own Caesar salad".[2143] A Toymaker captive, Lola Luna, was a denizen of the Weimar cabaret circuit.[2144]

Mars' orbit drew the Red Planet closer to Earth than it had been in centuries. To better detect radio signals from Mars, National Radio Silence Day commenced in the United States on 21st August, 1924. Select parties discovered that the signals contained a chant of the name "Sutekh" over and over.[2145]

2136 *Circular Time*: "Spring". George Mallory and Andrew Irvine perished while attempting to climb Everest in June 1924, which perhaps makes the Doctor and Nyssa's light-hearted banter about the topic a little inappropriate.
2137 Torchwood.org.uk, elaborating on *TW: From Out of the Rain*.
2138 First mentioned in *The Scarlet Empress*, with year specified in *Iris: Enter Wildthyme*.
2139 "Forty-three years" before *Thin Ice* (BF).
2140 *TW: Golden Age*. The specific days are given – which is fortunate, as the time between 1924 and 2009 is variably rounded as "eighty years", "about eighty years", "over eighty years", and "nearly ninety years". The Duchess offhandedly suggests that Torchwood India collected, amongst other things, Yeti spheres and a one-eyed yellow idol from the north of Kathmandu. It's difficult to imagine *The Abominable Snowmen* taking place before 1924 (this book dates it to 1935), so perhaps she's just being whimsical about having such items.
2141 Dating *TW: The Torchwood Archive* (BF *TW* special release #1) - The year is given.
2142 *CM: Who Killed Toby Kinsella?* Pamela Salem, who plays Jensen, was 39 when she filmed *Remembrance of the Daleks* [1963], so we might imagine that her character was born in 1924.

2143 *The Resurrection of Mars*. It's a common misconception that "Caesar salad" originated with Julius Caesar – it actually started with Caesar Cardini, who is said to have created it during a 4th of July rush on his restaurant in 1924. Cardini died in 1956.
2144 *The Magic Mousetrap*. The Weimar lasted from 1919-1933, and the height of its cabaret was 1930-ish, but Lola presumably performed before *The Magic Mousetrap* takes place in 1926.
2145 *NAofBenny* V2: *The Vaults of Osiris*
2146 Dating *The Clockwise Man* (NSA #1) - The date is given.
2147 Dating *FP: Warlords of Utopia* (FP novel #3) - Scriptor is "18" when this sequence of events starts.
2148 *FP: The Book of the War*
2149 *Leth-St: The Forgotten Son* (ch5).
2150 *Island of Death*
2151 *TW: Miracle Day*
2152 "Twenty years" before *Daleks Among Us*.
2153 Dating "The Futurists" (*DWM* #372-374) - It is "two decades into the new century", and the Doctor says it is 1925 later in the story.
2154 Dating "Theatre of the Mind" (*DWM* #496) - The year is given.
2155 Dating *Black Orchid* (19.5) - The Doctor says it is "three o'clock, June the eleventh, nineteen hundred and twenty-five".
2156 *And You Will Obey Me*, a reference to *Black Orchid*.

1924 (October) - THE CLOCKWISE MAN[2146] -> The ninth Doctor and Rose arrived to visit the British Empire Exhibition, and quickly discovered that a creature that ticked had committed a series of attacks. Shade Vassily, a war criminal from the planet Katuria, had been tracked down to Earth by the socialite Melissa Heart – actually a disfigured alien hunter. The Katurians used clockwork technology, but the Doctor prevented Vassily and Heart's conflict from destroying London.

= c 1924 - FP: WARLORDS OF UTOPIA[2147] -> On Roma I, Scriptor came to the attention of the Emperor and was commissioned to write the history of the Hercules Bridge that linked Europe to Africa. Following this, he decided to write a history of the Forum in Rome, and learned of the mysterious old man who'd materialised the day he'd been born. He also made many contacts, and married Angela, the daughter of a Scottish merchant.

A few months later, Scriptor tracked down the old man in a Swiss hospital and located his time ring. Scriptor accidentally followed the old man to another universe (Roma II) where Rome never fell, but had not prospered quite as much as his own. Scriptor and his family negotiated trading deals between the two universes, keeping their monopoly on travel between them – and the existence of other Romes – a closely-guarded secret. He soon mapped hundreds of other Romes – Roma III, where Yung Lo had won the coin toss and moved the Chinese court to Rome; Roma IV, where the Christians were a political force; Roma V, where the Mediterranean had been drained to irrigate the Sahara; Rome VI, a matriarchy; and so on. Lacking any understanding of parallel universes, the Roman philosophers believed that each of these Romes orbited a different sun in their own universe.

On Rome CLII, the asteroid that killed the dinosaurs in most universes arrived sixty-five million years late, and wiped out a Roman civilisation that pitted dinosaurs against each other in their arenas. On this ruined world, Scriptor killed a mysterious monster that had been tracking the thirteen Great House members who'd fled their universe, and had murdered seven of them. Scriptor took the seven time rings the monster had collected – now armed with eight such devices, Scriptor's family expanded the scope of their operations considerably. The existence of other Romes became public knowledge on Roma I.

1925

wih - The earliest iteration of Faction Hollywood, an off-shoot of Faction Paradox, could be traced back to 1925, although Faction Paradox proper would have little to do with the group after the 1940s.[2148]

Gordon Conall Lethbridge-Stewart and Mary Gore, the future parents of Alistair Lethbridge-Stewart, were married in 1925.[2149] In 1925, the Doctor stopped the time traveller Studs Maloney importing hooch from the twenty-fifth century.[2150] **The American CIA acquired a photo of Jack Harkness that was taken in 1925.**[2151]

Daleks loyal to Davros conquered the planet Azimuth, and although the seventh Doctor and Ace defeated them with cleverness and a judiciously applied baseball bat, a few survivors remained in a secret research facility. They worked on Project 9001: an undertaking to grow a clone that Davros' mind could inhabit when his original body inevitably died. The resultant clone, named Falkus after Skaro's second moon, was born a purebred Kaled and rose through the Daleks' ranks, eventually assuming the position of Supreme Dalek. Monument Plaza, which had been a burial pit under the Dalek occupation, became home to a statue of Ace – naked, wielding a baseball bat and inscribed with the word "Liberty" – to commemorate Azimuth's liberation.[2152]

1925 - "The Futurists"[2153] -> The tenth Doctor and Rose landed in Milan, because Rose wanted an ice cream. The Futurists were holding a meeting, and a strange green glow heralded the materialisation of a futuristic city – which quickly started to crumble. The TARDIS transported the Doctor and Rose to Cardiff in the late third century.

1925 - "Theatre of the Mind"[2154] -> In New York, Harry Houdini exposed the "psychic" Madame Tarot as a fraud – only to discover she was under the thrall of an intelligent alien crystal forged to resemble a crystal ball, and which fed upon weakness and despair. Houdini summoned the twelfth Doctor and Clara with his signal-watch. By imagining the thing that made them feel most free, the trio overloaded the crystal, but Tarot still died.

1925 (11th June) - BLACK ORCHID[2155] -> The explorer George Cranleigh was believed killed by Indians while on an expedition in the Amazon in 1923. Cassell and Company published his book *Black Orchid*. George's fiancée, Anne Talbot, eventually became engaged to his brother Charles. Yet George hadn't died. The Kajabi Indians had horribly disfigured George because he stole their sacred black orchid, but the chief of a rival tribe rescued him. George was kept hidden away at Cranleigh Hall. The fifth Doctor, Tegan, Nyssa and Adric were guests at the hall when George broke out, and fell to his death while trying to abduct his former fiancée.

The fifth Doctor believed that he owned the Cranleigh Cup.[2156]

1926

Ian Gilmore, a future commander of Counter-Measures and associate of the seventh Doctor, was born.[2157] Gordon James Lethbridge-Stewart, brother of Alistair, was born in March 1926.[2158]

A famous author of boys' stories for *The Ensign* magazine vanished at his home in 1926.[2159] On 4th June, 1926, the SS *Bernice* inexplicably vanished in the Indian Ocean. The ship had left England in early May, and the last anyone ever saw of it was on 2nd June, when it left Bombay.[2160]

The Doctor's account at the Singapore Hilton went unpaid from 1926 to decades afterwards. He settled the bill, with a gold brick, in 2008.[2161] The Doctor watched Babe Ruth hit three home runs for the Yankees in 1926.[2162] The Doctor lost a baseball signed by Babe Ruth on the planet Semtis, while battling the Shroud.[2163]

1926 - "The Gods Walk Among Us"[2164] -> In Egypt, archaeologists unearthed Sontar's tomb. The Sontaran within was still alive after fifty-five hundred years, and killed the archaeologists – but their Egyptian bearers dropped a stone slab on the alien, apparently killing it.

Emily Winter Joins the TARDIS

1926 (late June) - "Silver Scream" / "Fugitive" / "Final Sacrifice"[2165] -> The tenth Doctor investigated a static point in space and time connected to Emily Winter, a hopeful starlet. He attended a Hollywood party thrown by Archibald Maplin, and met actor Maximilian Love (the biggest thing to hit Hollywood since Rudolph Valentino) as well as studio-runner Matthew Finnegan. The Doctor learned that an alien Terronite from the future, Leo Miller, was posing as human and using an ancient device to chemically alter the part of the brain that controls optimism. The device let Miller transfer the hopes and dreams

2157 Gilmore first appeared in *Remembrance of the Daleks* [1963] and features in Big Finish's *Counter-Measures* audios. The placement here derives from actor Simon Williams' birth year of 1946, which suggests that the character of Gilmore was born circa 1922
2158 In *Leth-St: The Forgotten Son* (ch11), in which Gordon's twelfth birthday is slated for late March, 1938.
2159 *The Mind Robber*
2160 *Carnival of Monsters*. The Doctor has heard of the disappearance of the SS *Bernice*, but we see it vanish from the MiniScope and apparently return to its native time at the end of episode four. Perhaps the ship didn't arrive home safely after all. Alternatively, perhaps the Doctor's actions alter history, although this would make for something of a paradox.
2161 *The Girl Who Never Was*
2162 *Illegal Alien* (p83).
2163 *Shroud of Sorrow* (p164). Babe Ruth lived 1895-1948.
2164 Dating "The Gods Walk Among Us" (*DWM* #59) - The year is given in the opening caption.
2165 Dating "Silver Scream" (IDW *DW* Vol. 1 #1-2) - A caption in issue #1 states that it's "1926", although when the Doctor returns to the scene in "Fugitive", the caption says "1927". It's 1926 again when we see Maplin's party once more at the end of "Final Sacrifice". Matthew specifies in "Don't Step on the Grass" that he met the Doctor in "late June 1926", which would concur with a mention of Rudolph Valentino that implies he's still alive – he died suddenly in August that year. Bizarrely, in "Don't Step on the Grass", the Doctor wonders why Matthew – a native of 1926 – has never read *The Lord of the Rings*, which was published in 1954.
2166 Dating *The Magic Mousetrap* (BF #120) - The year is given. This adventure appears to finish with two "pieces" of the Toymaker still lodged in Ace's mind. The

Toymaker claims he deliberately gave up his powers just to know what it was like to lose, but that could just be hyperbole.
2167 *The Magic Mousetrap, Gods and Monsters*. The awareness the chessboard gives the Doctor leads to confrontations with elder gods in *Lurkers at Sunlight's Edge, House of Blue Fire, Project: Nirvana* and the Black TARDIS Trilogy: *Protect and Survive, Black and White, Gods and Monsters*.
2168 Dating *The Unicorn and the Wasp* (X4.07) - The Doctor sniffs the air and states it's the "1920s", then later finds a newspaper giving the date as "8 December 1926". Christie's disappearance on that day is a matter of historical record; she was found on 19th December.
2169 *Iris S5: Looking for a Friend*
2170 *The Androids of Tara*. José Raúl Capablanca y Graupera lived 1888-1942. He spent six years as a world chess champion, ending in 1927.
2171 Dating *The Emerald Tiger* (BF #159) - The Doctor names the adventure's starting date as "December the 31st, 1926", and hails its conclusion the next day as "1st January, 1927", "a new year". In support of this, a hot air balloon operator has a 1924 rifle, the Gujarat protests of 1925 happened "last year", and 1908 is cited as being "eighteen years ago". A little clumsily, Adele claims that "the monsoon season was over six months ago" – in India, it lasts June to September. Calcutta was renamed Kolkata in 2001.
2172 "Fellow Travellers". This may or may not be a reference to *The Abominable Snowman*. If so, it's unclear which character Ella's grandfather was.
2173 *TW: Trace Memory*
2174 *Serpent Crest: Tsar Wars*
2175 Dating *Real Time* (BF BBCi #1) - Dr Goddard identifies the date of Cyber-infection.

of individuals into Love, making him more charismatic and successful. The Doctor thwarted the Terronites and saved Emily's life – but this changed history, as she was fated to die. A squad of Judoon arrested the Doctor, and took him to the Shadow Proclamation to stand trial.

Upon his return, Emily and Matthew joined the Doctor on his travels. Emily's older self, passing as Annabella Primavera, had also attended Maplin's party. The Doctor helped Maplin to secure funding for his films; in future, Maplin starred in *The Fun Fair, The Great Oppressor* and *Future Times*.

1926 - THE MAGIC MOUSETRAP[2166] ->

Ludovic Comfort served as director of the Hulbrook sanatorium in Switzerland. He was captured by the Celestial Toymaker, and spent ten years playing games including electric shock tiddlywinks and poison-tipped pin the tail on the donkey.

> (=) The seventh Doctor, Ace and Hex and other people in the Toymaker's domain defeated the mandarin, turning him into a wooden doll. The Doctor believed that the Toymaker's powers and identity would fade if separated for long enough, and had everyone present – save for Ace and Hex – eat one piece of the Toymaker. Everyone believed they'd been transported back to the Hulbrook sanatorium, 1926, but the Toymaker's realm was mimicing the locale.
>
> Four weeks passed. The still-wooden Toymaker revived and made his foes play games, winning back many splinters of himself. The chess master Swapnil Khan and his daughter Queenie manipulated gameplay until Swapnil and the Toymaker were trapped on an electrocuted board. So long as Swapnil didn't make his final move, neither of them could leave without burning to death. Theoretically, the board could remain viable for two thousand billion years.

Swapnil mustered enough mental force to return everyone save himself and the Toymaker to the real Hulbrook sanatorium in 1926. The game-losers remained in the shape of toys.

The presence of a giant chessboard in the sanatorium alerted the Doctor that some of the elder gods were becoming more active, and he began making plans to curtail them.[2167]

1926 (8th and 19th December) - THE UNICORN AND THE WASP[2168] ->

The tenth Doctor and Donna arrived at Eddison Manor, where Agatha Christie was just one of the guests of Lady Clemency Eddison. Another guest, Professor Peach, was murdered and suspicion fell on a mysterious jewel thief: the Unicorn, who was after Lady Eddison's necklace, the Firestone. Soon after, Donna was attacked by a giant wasp – a Vespiform from the Silfrax Galaxy.

The Doctor solved the mystery... Reverend Golightly killed Professor Peach when he learned that Golightly was Lady Eddison's illegitimate son. The Firestone was a Vespiform telepathic recorder which contained Golightly's true identity – he was also a Vespiform. Golightly abducted Christie, but after a car chase, he drowned. He was mentally tethered to Christie's mind through the Firestone, and as he died, she lost her memory of these events. The Doctor dropped Christie in Harrogate, knowing that history dictated that she would be found after having gone missing for ten days. It was possible that Christie's subconscious remembered details of this adventure that would be incorporated into her novels, including the creation of Miss Marple. The Unicorn escaped.

Iris dedicated a Polaroid taken on Christmas Eve, 1926, to her best friend in the world: Panda.[2169]

1926 (31st December) to 1927 (1st January) - THE EMERALD TIGER[2170] ->

The TARDIS landed at the Foucault train station in Calcutta, as the fifth Doctor – accompanied by Tegan, Turlough and the older Nyssa – wished to see the legendary cricket match between All India and the Marylebone Cricket Club, with Arthur Gilligan leading the latter.

The influence of the trans-mogrifying Emerald Tiger crystal had spread throughout the fauna in Shardul Khan's valley, and infected Nyssa. Professor Narayan regained his memories of being the were-tiger Ayyappa, and with his sister Dawon confronted their tyrannical brother Khan – who killed both of them. Lady Adele Forester obliterated Khan and the Emerald Tiger crystal with dynamite. The resultant energy release from the crystal re-invigorated Nyssa, outwardly making her look as youthful as she did when she left the Doctor on Terminus.

In 1927, the Doctor watched the Cuban grandmaster Capablanca play chess.[2171] In the same year, the second Doctor met Ella's grandfather in Tibet. From this time, his family became caretakers of the Doctor's house in Kent.[2172] The Vondrax killed people in Siberia, 1927.[2173] The Doctor was in the movie *Metropolis* (1927).[2174]

> (=) 1927 - REAL TIME[2175] -> The Cybermen succeeded in infecting Earth with a techno-virus that transformed living beings into cybernetic ones. Most of the human race died from shock, and all animals perished. The cybernetic survivors fell under Cybermen domination. Evelyn Smythe was reportedly the virus' original carrier, having travelled back to this year after being infected in 3286.

1927 (May) - THE EMPTY HOUSE[2176] -> The Groog were a race of tall, blue-grey aliens with a knot of tentacles and toadstool-like organs for faces. Some Groog were nice, but others "devoured" whole planets in the name of the Groog Empire.

A Groog ship collided with the TARDIS, throwing the Doctor's Ship temporally out of phase with its surroundings. The TARDIS landed near Winchester, Hampshire, and brought Rory back into synch with local time, but the eleventh Doctor and Amy were left as ghost-like figures who unknowingly caused a series of spooky incidents. The pair believed the Groog had taken Rory and two locals captive, but in fact the aliens were protecting their charges from the "apparitions". The Doctor and Amy returned to the TARDIS and re-calibrated their personal time fields, ending the misunderstanding.

1927 (July) - TW: MIRACLE DAY[2177] -> Jack Harkness met Angelo Colasanto, an Italian immigrant, on Ellis Island after Angelo stole Jack's visa. The two of them became lovers, and infiltrated bootlegging operations in Little Italy, New York. They fulfilled Jack's mission by destroying one of the Trickster's Brigade – a parasite considered as vermin on at least one hundred and fifty worlds, and served as dinner on another. The Trickster had hoped that the parasite would lay eggs in Franklin Roosevelt's brain, driving him mad and changing world history so the Trickster could feed off the resulting chaos. Jack was temporarily shot dead while killing the parasite – he went to Los Angeles, even as Angelo was arrested and sentenced to a year in prison.

1927 (August) - WORLDS BF: THE FEAST OF MAGOG[2178] -> Having returned from a short spell in Barcelona, Dorian Gray attended a party at the south Wales country estate of his friend Evan Morgan. At Morgan's request, Alexander Korvo held a séance to coincide with The Feast of Magog, when the barriers between realities were thin. Korvo summoned a demonic force that called itself Legion, and possessed Pamela St John-Edwards: a beloved of both Dorian and Morgan. The Legion found the copy of Kronos Vad's *A History of Earth* (Volume 36,379) in Morgan's possession, and set fire to Pamela's body while trying to destroy it. Dorian saved the book, but deemed Pamela lost and repelled the Legion by killing her. Korvo lost his nerve while trying to run Dorian over, and died in a car crash.

The next day, Dorian and Morgan returned Vad's chronicle to the Vandermeer bookshop. Dorian again met Sherlock Holmes at Korvo's funeral, and assured him the book was in safe hands.

The Doctor met Dame Nellie Melba, a noted Australian opera soprano, and learned her party piece: how to shatter glass with your voice.[2179] The Doctor met Sigmund Freud and knew Marie Curie intimately.

2176 Dating *The Empty House* (BBC *DW* audiobook #19) - The Doctor sniffs the rain and concludes that it's "May 1927, maybe 28". Amy later finds a letter, the postmark of which confirms the former.

2177 Dating *TW: Miracle Day* (TW 4.7) - The year is twice given in captions. Angelo and Jack watch fireworks set off for the 4th of July celebrations, and Jack mentions that Franklin Roosevelt will be elected governor of New York "this November" (actually incorrect – that happened in November 1928, not 1927). The visa permit that Jack forges for Angelo bears the starting date of 2nd June, 1927, the expiration date of 9th December. The Trickster's Brigade is a recurring villain in *The Sarah Jane Adventures*.

2178 Dating *Worlds BF: The Feast of Magog* (*Worlds BF* #1.3) - Dorian names the month and year.

2179 *The Power of Kroll*, and also mentioned in *Serpent Crest: Aladdin Time*. Dame Nellie Melba lived 1861-1931.

2180 *Doctor Who – The Movie*. It's possible these encounters were all on the same visit: Freud lived 1865-1939, Marie Curie 1867-1934, and Puccini 1858-1924. The only date given is that the Doctor was with Puccini shortly before he died.

2181 *The Devil Goblins from Neptune*

2182 *Relative Dementias*. This is possibly a misremembering of *Doctor Who – The Movie*. The Doctor name-dropped Puccini in that story, but it was Leonardo da Vinci who had the cold.

2183 *The City of the Dead*

2184 *Grimm Reality*

2185 *Borrowed Time* (p126).

2186 *The Curse of the Black Spot*

2187 *Phantasmagoria*

2188 "Silent Scream"

2189 *The Helm of Awe*

2190 Dating *TW: Miracle Day* (TW 4.7) - Angelo has been locked away for "a year" when Jack re-enters his life, and Jack's torture in the basement is later referenced as occurring in "1928".

2191 Dating *The Glamour Chase* (NSA #42) - The exact day is given (p23).

2192 *Timewyrm: Revelation* (p50), *The Ghosts of N-Space* (p147) and *Unnatural History* (p164). The Blinovitch Limitation Effect was first mentioned in *Day of the Daleks* (and subsequently in *Invasion of the Dinosaurs* and *Mawdryn Undead*). Episodes of New *Who* (particularly *The Big Bang* and *A Christmas Carol*) indicate the Limitation Effect has lost its potency, somehow.

2193 "Eighty years" before *TW: From Out of the Rain*, according to Captain Jack. *The Torchwood Archives* (BBC) dates the Travellers' encounter with Christina – seen as an old woman in the TV story – to 1928.

He met Pucchini[2180] in Milan.[2181] Puccini had a cold.[2182]

@ The eighth Doctor had sessions with Freud, hoping to jog his memory.[2183] He told Freud that he had a phobia of silverfish.[2184] Sigmund Freud told his friend the Doctor: "Vell Doctor, ven confronted vis ze unbelievable, ze human brain goes into shock!"[2185] **The Doctor had fond memories of Freud's comfy sofa.**[2186]

The Doctor owned a copy of *Wisden's Almanac* from 1928.[2187] The tenth Doctor's runaround with Leo Miller in Hollywood, 1926, inspired director Buster Keaton regarding the filmography of the silent film *Steamboat Bill Jr.* (1928).[2188] The Doctor enabled the Bronte sisters to visit Hollywood.[2189]

The Three Families Gain Capt. Jack's Blood

1928 - TW: MIRACLE DAY[2190] **->** Jack Harkness reunited with Angelo Colasanto upon Angelo's release from Sing Sing prison in New York. Angelo believed that Jack's resurrection powers stemmed from the devil, and turned him over to the superstitious residents of Little Italy. Jack was repeatedly killed in the basement of the Giordano Butcher Shop, coming back to life every time.

A trio of men with the surnames Ablemarch, Costerdane and Frines sensed that Jack represented an opportunity, and embarked on a partnership – they paid $10,000 for the contents of the butcher's basement. Angelo regretted his actions and freed Jack, but Ablemarch, Costerdane and Frines retained Jack's spilt blood and formed The Three Families. Jack judged that Angelo would be better off without him, and exited his life. Angelo remained inspired by Jack, and devoted the rest of his life to finding a means of living forever. He monitored Jack for decades to come.

The Three Families went into the world and became shadow players – one family specialised in finance, one in politics and one in the media. They systematically erased all records of their bloodlines, purging the names Ablemarch, Costerdane and Frines from history. Angelo had some early affiliation with the Families, but was ostracised because he had loved a man.

1928 (14th August) - THE GLAMOUR CHASE[2191] **->** The Tahnn wiped out the English town of Little Cadthorpe while searching for the missing Weave spaceship *Exalted*. They refrained from destroying Earth, fearing the wrath of the Shadow Proclamation.

Aaron Blinovitch formulated his Limitation Effect in the reading room of the British Museum in 1928. He authored *Temporal Mechanics*, and was a member of Faction Paradox.[2192] The Night Travellers recognised that the advent of cinema had numbered the days of their circus shows. They opted to endow themselves onto film containing their images; one such reel wound up in the basement archives of the Electro Cinema in Cardiff.[2193] Jack Harkness once cruised the Kurfurstendamm in Berlin with Christopher Isherwood.[2194]

The Young Life of Alistair Gordon Lethbridge-Stewart

Although much was known of the life of Brigadier Lethbridge-Stewart, some contradictions remained.[2195]

Alistair Gordon Lethbridge-Stewart, a longtime associate and friend of many incarnations of the Doctor, was born on 22nd February, 1929, in Bledoe.[2196] His paternal grandmother was Lillian McDougal, a.k.a. "Granny McDougal".[2197] He would attend grammar school in the nearby Liskeard. As a boy, he was not enamoured by stories his father told him of life in the RAF.[2198]

2194 *TW: A Day in the Death.* Isherwood, a novelist, resided in Berlin from 1929 to 1933. His meeting with Jack could have easily have happened in another year, but it's perhaps relevant – given that Jack was involved – that Isherwood at this time capitalised upon Berlin's relative sexual freedom to indulge his taste for "pretty youths" (*The Telegraph*, 18th May, 2004).

2195 The *Lethbridge-Stewart* novel range, along with its supplementary materials, repeatedly nail down the Brigadier's history in copious amounts of detail. In doing so, however, it overlooks broad details about the Brigadier's life given by Barry Letts – the producer of the third Doctor era, which heavily featured the character – in *Island of Death*, and yet acknowledges the Brig's Granny McDougal, as created by Letts in *The Ghosts of N-Space*.

The *Lethbridge-Stewart* novels claim to take place in a separate timeline, owing to the Great Intelligence having altered the Brigadier's history in September 1939 (see The Haisman Timeline sidebar). That wouldn't explain, however, the aforementioned discrepancies in the Brigadier's upbringing prior to that.

2196 *Leth-St: The Forgotten Son, Leth-St: Top Secret Files*, The Haisman Timeline. In *The Forgotten Son* (ch 11), Lethbridge-Stewart turns nine on that day (the same day that actor Nicholas Courtney died) in 1938. Additionally, he's "16" in 1945, some "months" after his father is reported killed earlier in that year. All of this squares with there being "three years" between Alistair and his brother Gordon, who was born in 1926 (ch11). Nicholas Courtney, who played Lethbridge-Stewart, was born 16th December, 1929.

2197 *Leth-St: Night of the Intelligence* (ch2).

2198 *Leth-St: The Forgotten Son* (chs. 7-8, 11).

Lethbridge-Stewart never lived in Scotland. His father's family had stayed there while his father moved to England and met his mother.[2199]

Lethbridge-Stewart was an only child whose mother died when he was young. He was raised by his father and Granny McDougal. He was raised in Simla, India, and his happiest memories were of summers there. His father rose to the rank of Colonel.[2200]

> (=) When Lethbridge-Stewart was six or seven, he was heartbroken to lose a red balloon, and had a recurring nightmare about it for the rest of his life.

The eighth Doctor caught the balloon and returned it.[2201] Lethbridge-Stewart left India for prep school in England when he was eight.[2202] As a schoolboy, Alistair Lethbridge-Stewart hated his history teacher – a bore named Linbury – so became rather bad at History.[2203]

1929

Olive Hawthorne, a white witch living in Devil's End, and an acquaintance of the third Doctor, was born along with her younger twin sister Poppy.[2204]

In 1929, Lord Barset led an expedition to Antarctica aboard his ship, the *Rochester*. A base that contained "lizard men" was discovered, and disaster ensued. The *Rochester* sank and all hands were lost, save for one member found with Lord Barset's diary of the mission. The man died shortly afterwards, screaming about monsters, but the journal was later passed down to Barset's grandson.[2205]

The base was a Silurian shelter, and UNIT would investigate it in the 1970s.[2206] The *Daily Telegraph* of 12th April, 1929, noted rumours that an Antarctic expedition had been lost after finding a city of intelligent reptiles.[2207]

The Fang Rock lighthouse became automated in 1929.[2208] As Dr Helena Bennett, the immortal Helena opened a clinic for the poor in Edinburgh, 1929.[2209]

1929 - THE AUNTIE MATTER[2210] -> The Valjax enjoyed meditative seclusion until a spacebourne virus wiped out their population. One of the survivors, Zenobia Brabazon, crashed to Earth, and endured by transferring her consciousness into new host forms. She lived at Bassett Hall in the village of Bassett-on-Hamble, Hampshire, and hypnotised "her nephew" – a hapless fellow named Reginald – into procuring fresh host bodies as part of his search to find a wife.

The fourth Doctor sent the TARDIS flitting off to a thousand worlds, to make the Black Guardian tire of pursuing the Ship, and lodged with the first Romana near Bassett-on-Hamble for a week until the TARDIS returned for them. Romana went out to read the scientific literature of the age, forcing the Doctor to recruit their maid, Mabel Dobbs, as a companion proxy to ask challenging questions of him. The two Time Lords separately learned of Zenobia's murder spree, and ended it by blowing up Bassett Hall, with Zenobia inside. As the Doctor and Romana argued over which of them deserved credit for stopping the alien threat, Reginald proposed to Mabel.

1929 - THE HOUNDS OF ARTEMIS[2211] -> An expedition found the temple of Artemis in Smyrna, Eastern Turkey, and released the psychic parasite inside. The eleventh Doctor and Amy helped to bind the creature in iron once more, and a group of local psionics re-buried its

2199 *Leth-St: Moon Blink*.
2200 *Island of Death* by Barry Letts, contradicting the history of Lethbridge-Stewart given in *Leth-St: The Forgotten Son*. Granny McDougal was first mentioned in Letts' *The Ghosts of N-Space*, and is mentioned in the *Lethbridge-Stewart* novels, including *Leth-St: Night of the Intelligence*.
2201 *The Shadows of Avalon* (p3, 271).
2202 *Island of Death*.
2203 *Leth-St: The Flaming Soldier* (ch2).
2204 Olive Hawthorne appeared in *The Daemons*. The spin-off work *Daemons: White Witch of Devil's End* refrains from giving hard dates pertaining to her life, but progresses from her teenage years up to the character's passing in its year of release (2017). Actress Damaris Hayman, who played Olive, was born 16th June, 1929.
2205 *Frozen Time*, reflecting events from the Audio-Visuals story *Endurance*. Nick Briggs, who wrote *Frozen Time*, starred as the Doctor in that adventure.
2206 *The Scales of Injustice*, also referring to *Endurance*.

2207 "City of Devils", and yet another reference to *Endurance* by *The Scales of Injustice* author Gary Russell. By 2012, the loss of the expedition is publicly acknowledged, not just rumoured.
2208 *Leth-St: Beast of Fang Rock* (ch2).
2209 *Erimem: Three Faces of Helena*
2210 Dating *The Auntie Matter* (BF 4th Doc #2.1) - The blurb says that it's "England in the 1920s". The Doctor broadly says it's the time of "Gershwin, Fitzgerald, Hemingway, flappers, men in spats, diamonds as big as the Ritz". Romana seeks to read the newest theories published by Niels Bohr (1885-1962) and Werner Heisenberg (1901-1976) – the former had founded the Niels Bohr Institute in 1920 and won a Nobel Prize in Physics in 1922, and the latter had work published by 1925. In *The Sands of Life*, the Doctor says – presumably in reference to *The Auntie Matter* – that the last newspaper he read was dated "1929".
2211 Dating *The Hounds of Artemis* (BBC *DW* audiobook #11) - The year is given.

temple. The Doctor provided the expedition's only survivor, Bradley Stapleton, with the location of a genuine temple of Artemis, guaranteeing the man's career.

1929 (summer) - THE STEALERS FROM SAIPH[2212]->

The Saiph had possessed an archaeologist and spent some decades establishing energy reception points in Antibes, Thessalonica, Tobruk, Tunis and Tangiers. Using an elemental converter aboard an orbiting satellite, the Saiph hoped to create an energy ring that would change the chemical composition of the Mediterranean Sea, turning it into a breeding ground for them. The fourth Doctor and the first Romana, having vacationed for some weeks at the Hotel du Cap in Antibes, France, torched the Saiph.

Cindy Wu's Boyfriend Dies

1929 - THE TENTH DOCTOR YEAR TWO[2213] -> The

tenth Doctor, Gabby and Cindy relaxed in New Orleans, and Cindy started up a romance with Roscoe Ruskin: the lead trumpeter of the Storyville Players. Roscoe's improvisational talents let a creature made of music – the King Nocturne – to enter our dimension. It made plans to colonise Earth by replicating through their music. Roscoe died resisting the creature, which the Doctor trapped within an entire century's worth of Earth tunes. It would escape centuries on, and its offspring would menace the human colony on Wupatki.

1929 - BLOOD HARVEST[2214] -> As gangland violence

escalated in Chicago, the enigmatic Doc McCoy opened a speakeasy right in the middle of disputed territory. The Doc and his moll Ace saved Al Capone's life. The seventh Doctor was tracking down the eternal being Agonal, who had amplified the gang warfare to feed his lust for violence.

The vampire Yarven travelled to Earth from E-Space aboard the Doctor's TARDIS.

Yarven became a progenitor of many of Earth's vampires. Villagers in Croatia overpowered and buried him alive, and he would remain trapped until 1993.[2215] The Doctor couldn't remember if Al Capone or Genghis Khan told him that villains often wanted records detailing exactly how bad they'd been.[2216]

The Brigadier's car, a Humber 1650 Open Tourer Imperial Model, was built in 1929.[2217] The Shroud tentatively extended itself into people susceptible to psychic influence. On 20th August, 1929, it connected with a young boy named Ben, after his dog died.[2218] The Canavatchi engineered the Wall Street Crash of October 1929 to hinder humankind's development.[2219]

Lord Tamworth witnessed the arrival of the Engineer Prime of the telepathic Triskele on Earth. He was promoted to "Minister of Air", and oversaw preparations to use the R-101 airship to return the Engineer Prime to its people.[2220]

The Nineteen Thirties

The Urbankans began to receive radio signals from Earth.[2221] **The Doctor met the cricket player Donald Bradman, and once took five wickets for New South Wales.**[2222] Rita Hayworth taught the Doctor how to chacha. On another occasion, she instructed the Doctor and River Song in the art of the rumba.[2223]

2212 Dating *The Stealers from Saiph* (BF CC #3.12) - Romana's narration tells us, "It was the summer of 1929." Somewhat uniquely for a Doctor/first Romana story, this audio takes place between *The Armageddon Factor* and *Destiny of the Daleks*.

2213 Dating *The Tenth Doctor Year Two* (Titan 10th Doc #2.11-2.12, "The Jazz Monster"/"The Music Man") - A caption here says it's the Jazz Age, which lasted through the 1920s and ended with the onset of the Great Depression. *The Tenth Doctor Year Two*: "The Infinite Corridor" entailed the Doctor stating his intent to visit the *beginning* of jazz, and the recap in issues #12 and #13 say it's "the height" of the Jazz Age. Nonetheless, in *The Tenth Doctor Year Two*: "Old Girl", Cindy reads an online entry that the Storyville Players disbanded, for unknown reasons, "in 1929".

There's a bit of fluff in the continuity circuits in that the Doctor mentions Rose having a holiday romance (of sorts) with a man named Bruno – presumably a mistaken reference to Bruno Langley, who played Adam Mitchell (*Dalek*, *The Long Game*). Less likely, it means singer Bruno Mars (born Peter Gene Hernandez,

in 1985), although it's unclear how that would fit into the emotional arcs of Series 1 and 2. Or, the Doctor has become *so* terrible with names that when he says "Bruno", he actually means "Mickey".

2214 Dating *Blood Harvest* (NA #28) - The blurb states it is 1929. The book is set during Prohibition (1919-1933), but while Al Capone is at liberty. In May 1929, Capone was sentenced to prison time for carrying a concealed weapon, so *Blood Harvest* occurs before that. He saw release in 1930; his more infamous conviction on tax evasion charges happened in 1931.

2215 *Goth Opera*

2216 *Borrowed Time*

2217 His student Ibbotson, nicknamed "Hippo", identifies the car in *Mawdryn Undead*.

2218 *Shroud of Sorrow* (p57).

2219 *The King of Terror* (p179).

2220 "One night last winter" before *Storm Warning*.

2221 *Four to Doomsday*

2222 *Four to Doomsday*. No date given. Donald Bradman was born in 1908, playing for Australia from 1928-1948.

During the 1930s, the League of Nations set up a secret international organisation, LONGBOW, to deal with matters of world security. It found itself, on occasion, dealing with unexplained and extra-terrestrial phenomena.[2224] The Doctor discussed the theoretical Philosopher's Stone (not the Khamerian-created one) with psychiatrist Carl Jung.[2225]

The Silurian Triad was revived. These were Ichtar, Scibus and science advisor Tarpok.[2226]

In the 1930s, a matador named Manolito trained the Doctor in the basics of his art, and the Doctor and his friend Ernest Hemingway ran with the bulls in Pamplona.[2227] The tenth Doctor got drunk with Hemingway on the banks of the Seine. In future, the Doctor would lose this memory to the Memeovax.[2228] Hemingway never forgave the Doctor for beating him at Tiddlywinks.[2229] The Doctor stressed to Hemingway the importance of grace over fire, as they consumed daiquiris in Harry's Bar.[2230]

The Doctor was friends with the philosopher Wittgenstein.[2231] He worked with the Three Stooges in Hollywood, and was the fourth Stooge.[2232] Firestone Finance was founded in Cardiff, the 1930s, as a front to acquire and sell alien technology for profit – until the business did so well selling war bonds, it became a legitimate bank.[2233]

Between 1932 and 1940, Odd Bob the Clown – an aspect of the Pied Piper – abducted at least one hundred and four children across America.[2234] The people of Parakon discovered rapine, a crop that when processed could be used as a foodstuff or a building material. For the next forty years, the Corporation that marketed rapine ruled the planet unopposed, supplanting nations, governments, armies and all competition.[2235] An escape pod carrying the criminal Zimmerman landed in England, where he met a woman named Rachel. He became known as

---

2223 *DC 3: The Doomsday Chronometer.* Hayworth lived 1918-1987. Her most active period as a dancer was in the 1930s, when she was credited as "Rita Cansino".

2224 *Just War*

2225 *Option Lock.* No date given. Jung lived 26th July, 1875, to 6th June, 1961.

2226 "Around forty years" before *The Scales of Injustice*.

2227 *Deadly Reunion.* No date given. Hemingway lived 1898-1961.

2228 "Thinktwice". Hemingway lived 1899-1961. He appears in good health during his meeting with the Doctor, and was much less so after being nearly killed in a plane crash in 1952.

2229 *Death Match*

2230 *The Twelfth Doctor Year One*: "The Hyperion Empire"

2231 *The Hollows of Time.* Ludwig Wittgenstein lived 1889-1951.

2232 *Paradise 5.* The Stooges were effectively active from 1925 until Larry Fine had a stroke in January 1970.

2233 *TW: Department X*

2234 *SJA: The Day of the Clown*

2235 "Forty years" before *The Paradise of Death* (p131).

2236 "Thirty years" before *No More Lies*.

2237 *TW: From Out of the Rain*, with *The Torchwood Archives* (BBC) specifying that Jack did this undercover work in the "early 1930s".

2238 *TW: Almost Perfect*

2239 *Luna Romana.* Schrodinger lived 1887-1961, and won the Nobel Prize in 1934.

2240 *The Silurian Candidate*, presuming the seventh Doctor isn't buffaloing Ace with for the fun of it. Pavlov (1849-1936) started conducting work on dogs as early as the mid-1880s, but won the Nobel for his research into gastric functions of dogs and people in 1904. Erwin Schrodinger, however, didn't develop his superposition theory until 1935.

2241 *Pier Pressure.* Billy is obviously a young William Hartnell, who appeared in both films.

2242 *Hexagora.* Flynn lived 1909-1959. His first starring role was *Captain Blood* (1935).

2243 "At least" fifteen years before *Pier Pressure*.

2244 "Fifty years" before *The Labyrinth of Buda Castle*. The BBC started daily radio broadcasts earlier than that, in 1922, but it presumably took a critical mass of signals to begin restoring Frid.

2245 Dating *The Wormery* (BF #51) - It is some point in "the thirties".

2246 Dating *The Twelfth Doctor Year Three*: "The Boy with the Displaced Smile" (Titan 12th Doc #3.2) - Year known, but the setting suggests Americana of yesteryear, and uses imagery from *American Gothic* by Grant Wood (1930). A caption says it's the twelfth Doctor's "last solo" trip in the TARDIS (meaning before he takes up residence at St Luke's University, presumably).

2247 Dating *TW: Exodus Code* (TW novel #19) - The year is repeatedly given. The Helix Intelligence's sigil is discovered "in January, right before Lent" (ch3).

2248 Dating "A Wing and a Prayer" (*DWM* #462-464) - The Doctor and Amy both agree that it's "1930". Johnson says that her sister Irene committed suicide "last year", which happened in 1929. Prior to this, as Johnson also mentioned, she experienced a bad breakup (from Swiss businessman Hans Arregger). The England to Australia flight that Johnson is here undertaking happened 5th to 24th May, 1930.

2249 Dating *The English Way of Death* (MA #20) - The date is given (p23).

2250 Dating *The Silent Scream* (BF 4th Doc #4.3) - Audio films have recently put silent ones out of business, a trend that started with *The Jazz Singer* (released 6th October, 1927). The blurb says it's the "late 1920s", Romana says it's "1930". There's no mention of the Great Depression, usually acknowledged as starting on Black Tuesday (29th October, 1929), but that was followed by

"Nick Zimmerman", turned over a new leaf and spent the next thirty years with her in wedded bliss.[2236]

Jack Harkness went undercover with a travelling show, billing himself as a man who couldn't die, while looking into rumours of the Night Travellers. He found no trace of them.[2237] During the 1930s, Jack went to the Weimar Republic to investigate reports that some prominent National Socialists were peddling in alien technology. He entirely failed in his mission owing to a number of parties and other distractions.[2238]

The Doctor and Romana were acquainted with both Erwin Schrodinger and his cat.[2239] Ivan Pavlov turned inconsolable after his dog disappeared off after Schrodinger's Cat. Even the naming of the Pavlovia after him failed to lift his spirits.[2240]

A young actor named Billy appeared in *I'm an Explosive* (1933) and *While Parents Sleep* (1935). He would come to befriend the music hall comedian Max Miller.[2241] The Doctor sparred with Errol Flynn.[2242]

The stage musician Professor Talbot performed on Brighton's West Pier, which led to his encountering the Indo aliens. Talbot was killed, but the aliens' energy animated his body, and his mind became focused on gaining widespread recognition and authority. He was presumed dead, but would resurface in 1936.[2243]

The cold data caused by the advent of radio slowly restored the entombed Zoltan Frid, and facilitated his freedom some decades on.[2244]

? 1930 - THE WORMERY[2245] **->** On a planet affected by a dimensional nexus point, worms evolved with a precognitive ability. Appalled to see themselves turning into hairy, complex beings, the worms divided into factions to derail their future. The "anti faction" group sought to turn the universe into total chaos, preventing development of any type. The "pro faction" group allied with the club singer Bianca, hoping to freeze the universe in a single perfect moment. Additionally, a group of shadow beings – the potential future selves of the worms, held in a state of flux – searched for a means of becoming corporeal.

The nightclub "Bianca's" now existed in a dimensional nexus, accessible via special taxis that shuttled patrons through dimensional portals. The club was Iris Wildthyme's TARDIS, with its exterior looking like 1930s Berlin. The sixth Doctor and Iris arrived separately at Bianca's club, and exposed Bianca as the embodiment of Iris' darker natures. The worm factions and their shadow selves each tried to exploit the club's extra-dimensional nature to their advantage. The Doctor used his TARDIS to Time-Ram the nightclub, which severed its dimensional links and returned its patrons to their native times. This defeated the worms and their shadows, and transferred the wreckage of the club to Berlin. Bianca escaped.

? 1930 - THE TWELFTH DOCTOR YEAR THREE[2246] **->** The twelfth Doctor stopped an emo-parasite from the Oblivion Shallows from feeding upon the people of Sweet Haven.

1930

1930 - TW: EXODUS CODE[2247] **->** The Helix Intelligence buried within the Earth was slowly dying, and required Captain Jack Harkness' advanced fifty-first century DNA to heal itself. The Intelligence formed a sigil – three circles, representing the balance needed in the world above, below and the here and now – in igneous rock in the Sacred Valley of the Andes, Peru. Jack investigated the sigil in a Hawker's Hornet, but his pilot, Renso, prevented the Helix Intelligence from claiming him. The Helix Intelligence struggled on until the twenty-first century.

1930 (May) - "A Wing and a Prayer"[2248] **->** The Howling Swarm, a group of cosmic insects, made war against other hives of the great web on behalf of their Great Mother. One Swarm drone, Koragatta, developed more autonomy and fled to the deserts near Baghdad, 1930. Three Swarm hunters scanned for Koragatta, causing a sandstorm that delayed aviator Amy Johnson as she attempted to break Bert Hinkler's record of flying around the world. The eleventh Doctor and Clara happened upon Johnson as the Doctor visited his friend Omar, "the finest fez merchant in Mutter's Spiral", to buy a new fez.

Koragatta absorbed the energy of localized oil and gas deposits, growing to monstrous size. He then fled through space-time with the Doctor and Omar, mentally tapping the Doctor's knowledge of hyper-dimensional travel to create a wormhole, but the Doctor facilitated Koragatta's death. The Great Mother vowed to destroy Earth to avenge her spawn, but the Doctor convinced her to spare the planet on behalf of its most dominant and magnificent life form: ants.

1930 (June) - THE ENGLISH WAY OF DEATH[2249] **->** The TARDIS arrived in London during an inexplicable heat wave, as the fourth Doctor needed to return some library books. He, the second Romana and K9 stumbled upon a group from the thirty-second century (the Bureau) that were using time corridor technology to send retired people to the English village of Nutchurch. While the Doctor put a stop to that, Romana confronted the sentient smell Zodaal, an exiled would-be conqueror from the planet Vesur. Zodaal was trapped in a flask.

1930 - THE SILENT SCREAM[2250] **->** A time traveller, Dr Julius, collected memorabilia from silent movie stars. Julius funded a new movie project, Hammerstein Studios' *Fires of Fate*, to attract the celebrities, then transferred many of their body parts – teeth, hair, even their voices – to two-dimensional lifeforms, his Celluoids. The fourth Doctor, with the second Romana and K9, shifted Julius' voice into his own system. The victimized Celluoids turned upon Julius' equipment and body, destroying the Studio.

The BBC was considering a TV adaptation of the book *Black Orchid*. Josephine Laws passed along the ArkHive amulet to her 16-year-old daughter Josie Laws McRae on 14th July, 1930 – the same day that *The Man with the Flower in His Mouth* was broadcast.[2251] **The Here protected Earth from a meteoric incident in the Curuca River, Brazil.**[2252]

In 1930, Douglas Caldwell transferred to Torchwood London to work in research and development.[2253] **Around 1930, the fourth Doctor visited Tigella and saw the Dodecahedron.**[2254] The Doctor bought Jacques Cousteau

his first set of flippers.[2255] Jacques Cousteau taught the Doctor about sharks.[2256] **In the US census of 1930, the population of Manhattan was 1,867,000.**[2257] Grenwell Damian Fleming built a home on what became known as Fleming's Island, and murdered his wife there in 1930.[2258]

Charley Pollard Joins the TARDIS

1930 (5th October) - STORM WARNING[2259] **->** The TARDIS landed on the doomed airship *R-101* during its maiden voyage, and the eighth Doctor discovered Charley Pollard, a stowaway. Lord Tamworth, a government minister, ordered the ship to a higher altitude and it docked with an alien vessel. The British had arranged to return a crashed alien to its own people, the Triskele. A faction of the Triskele became aggressive when the Lawgiver that kept them in check died. The Doctor eased the situation, and Tamworth stayed with the Triskele as an advisor. The

a period of cautious optimism – massive bank failures didn't start happening until the last third of 1930.

2251 *The Wheel of Ice* (p91). *The Man with the Flower in His Mouth* was the first piece of British-produced TV drama. *Black Orchid* featured in the *Doctor Who* story of the same name.

2252 *In the Forest of the Night*. A meteoric airburst struck the Curuca River on 13th August, 1930, but was of far less magnitude than the Tunguska incident.

2253 From Torchwood.org.uk.

2254 "Fifty years" before *Meglos*.

2255 "Children of the Revolution". In *The Devil Goblins of Neptune*, the third Doctor (as his internal monologue conveys to the reader) lies to Captain Yates that he "taught Jacques Cousteau everything he knows".

2256 *The Murder Game*. No date is given.

2257 *TW: Miracle Day*

2258 *5thB: Iterations of I*

2259 Dating *Storm Warning* (BF #16) - It is stated that it is "early in October 1930"; the *R-101* historically began its maiden flight on 4th October, 1930, and crashed the next day. The date is confirmed in *Minuet in Hell* and *Neverland*. According to *The Chimes of Midnight*, Charley was born the day the *Titanic* sank (or, rather, the night the ship hit the iceberg), and was eighteen years, five months and twenty-one days old when she met the Doctor.

2260 *Charley S1: The Fall of the House of Pollard*, reversing course on *The Chimes of Midnight*, in which the Doctor seemed to resolve a time paradox by convincing Edith to *not* commit suicide.

2261 Dating *Daleks in Manhattan/Evolution of the Daleks* (X3.4-3.5) - Martha finds a newspaper just after the TARDIS lands, and it sets the date as "Saturday 1 November 1930". Construction of the Empire State Building commenced on 17th March, 1930, and it officially opened on 1st May, 1931.

2262 *The Stolen Earth, Journey's End.*

2263 At least twenty years before *TimeH: The Tunnel at the End of the Light*.

2264 *TimeH: Peculiar Lives*. The blurb specifies this as happening "between the wars", i.e. World War I and II, and a member of *homo peculiar*, Percival, was a 15 year old "five years" prior to 1950 (p21), meaning he was born in 1930.

2265 Dating *Seasons of Fear* (BF #30) - The play starts with the Doctor saying it's the "cusp of the years 1930 and 1931".

2266 *Charley S1: The Fall of the House of Pollard*, referencing *Seasons of Fear*.

2267 *The Rapture*

2268 "The Final Chapter"

2269 The island resurfaces "four years, three months and six days" prior to *Lurkers at Sunlight's Edge*.

2270 Dating *TimeH: The Sideways Door* (TimeH #10) - Honoré's mother is killed "four months" before he turns 12 (p19), and he was born in either 1920 or 1921 (likely the former). A little confusingly, page 16 says that Honoré's grandmother raised him "from early childhood" – not a term that's typically attributed to an 11 year old.

2271 Dating *The Eleventh Doctor Year One* (Titan 11th Doc #1.3, "What He Wants") - A caption gives the year. Johnson died in 1938, age 27. His music didn't take off until later, with the release of *King of the Delta Blues* (1961). Johnson's undocumented life led to the urban legend that he'd achieved fame via a Faustian pact.

2272 The Haisman Timeline. Chorley first appeared in *The Web of Fear*.

2273 The Haisman Timeline. Douglas is an original creation of the *Lethbridge-Stewart* novels.

2274 Torchwood.org.uk, elaborating on *TW: From Out of the Rain*.

R-101 was damaged upon its return, and the Doctor and Charley escaped as it crashed in France. The Doctor realised that Charley was meant to have died in the crash.

Charley Pollard's diary was recovered from the wreckage of the *R-101* and given to her parents. At some point, Louisa Pollard discovered the body of a household maid, Edith Thompson, who died by her own hand.[2260]

1930 (1st November) - DALEKS IN MANHATTAN / EVOLUTION OF THE DALEKS[2261] **->** The tenth Doctor and Martha discovered that homeless people in New York had been going missing from a Hooverville, a community of victims of the Great Depression living in Central Park. The people had been abducted by the Cult of Skaro – the last four surviving Daleks, who had fled the Battle of Canary Wharf in 2007 via temporal shift. The Daleks required human subjects for their genetic experiments, and were turning them into pig slaves. The final experiment was undertaken by their leader, Dalek Sec, who converted himself into a "human Dalek".

The Daleks planned to draw energy from a solar flare down through the Empire State Building, and use it to create a new race of human Daleks. The Doctor sabotaged the attempt, and the resultant human Daleks rebelled. In the ensuing conflict, every Dalek and Dalek hybrid was destroyed save for Dalek Caan – who escaped via a temporal shift.

Dalek Caan penetrated the time lock established around the Last Great Time War, and succeeded in rescuing Davros from it.[2262] Half-human creatures dubbed "Subterraneans" took to living in an underground cavern near the Constitution Hill tube station in London.[2263]

(=) Their leader escaped to find a better life. He became the famed poet Randolf Crest, writing such works as *The Darkness That Hides as Kind*.

Honoré Lechasseur and Emily Blandish changed history so that Crest never left his people.

Advanced humans from the future sought to spur their own creation, and mentally influenced the founding of the British Hampdenshire Programme, an undertaking to create supermen. It produced genetically modified children of the species *homo peculiar*.[2264]

1930 (31st December) - SEASONS OF FEAR[2265] **->** The immortal Sebastian Grayle found the eighth Doctor and Charley in Singapore, and boasted that he'd already killed the Doctor in the past. The Doctor set about investigating the matter, heading for Britain in 305 AD.

Charley Pollard's parents received word that their daughter had been seen in Singapore.[2266] The Doctor fought in the Spanish Civil War with the father of future bar owner Gustavo Riviera. Later, he brought Gustavo to refuge in Ibiza.[2267] The Doctor was Dali's house guest.[2268]

The island with the citadel of the Carnash Coi re-surfaced near Alaska. While three Carnash Coi continued sleeping, a fourth adopted human form and set out to reconnoitre Earth. The scout passed as Clarence Penrose Doveday, but his human aspect became so dominant, he forgot his supernatural origins. Doveday's memories surfaced as dreams, and the stories he wrote based upon them appeared in such pulps as *Shuddersome Tales* and *Weird Tales of Cosmic Horror*.[2269]

c 1931 - TIMEH: THE SIDEWAYS DOOR[2270] **->** When Honoré Lechasseur was 11, two serial killers – the blood ritualists John and Wayne Carter, whom the papers dubbed the "Royal Street Vampires" – killed his mother. The adult Honoré witnessed the event with Emily Blandish, but let history run its course. Afterwards, the younger Honoré was raised by his Grandmother Delecrolix.

1931 - THE ELEVENTH DOCTOR YEAR ONE[2271] **->** The eleventh Doctor and Alice, along with the stowaway John Jones, visited the Dockery Plantation in Mississippi to watch future jazz legend Robert Leroy Johnson (a.k.a. the King of the Delta Blues) perform. The Doctor was already friends with Johnson, having given him a copy of *The Best of Robert Johnson* for his birthday.

The SERVEYOUinc Talent Scout cut a nefarious deal with Johnson's audience, bringing them under his thrall. The Doctor also fell under the Scout's control, but Alice, Jones and Johnson rescued the Doctor in Bessie – which the TARDIS had augmented into a pick-up – and freed everyone present by amplifying the sonic screwdriver's signals through the Ship. Johnson gave Jones some music lessons, improving his skills.

Harold Barrington **Chorley, a sensationalising journalist, was born** in April 1931. He grew up in Monaghan, Northern Ireland.[2272] Walter Douglas, a classmate and close friend of Alastair Lethbridge-Stewart, was born in May 1931.[2273] In 1931, the Beacon Film Theatre was renamed the Electro.[2274] Maria de Naglowska's occult mirror later became the property of Jennifer Alford.[2275]

1931 (June) - FP: SPINNING JENNY[2276] **->** The employees at a calico works factory in Strines offered prayers to the machines there – that they not consume their hair, or arms, and so on – and unexpectedly incarnated a newborn Loa. One of the workers, a young Elizabeth Howkins, christened it "Spinning Jenny". The newborn Loa's long-running combat with another of its kind, Baron Samedi, was responsible for years when industry would flourish, then collapse.

Baron Samedi's wife, the Loa Maman Brigitte, caused a factory fire – during the fracas, Spinning Jenny consumed Howkins' husband Bill. Per its life cycle, Spinning Jenny was thrown back to the start of the Industrial Revolution, pulling Howkins in its wake.

A much-older Howkins returned to this era. Using Baron Samedi's knife, Howkins cut Bill free from Jenny's flesh, but he remained a shade of his former self. The Baron tricked Jenny into feeding Bill a particular kind of flower, which through Bill's link to Jenny poisoned her.

1932

Aviatrix Diane Holmes incorrectly thought Amelia Earhart disappeared in 1932.[2277] Professor Richard Lazarus was born around 1932.[2278] Mrs Wibbsey was a fan of the movie star Mimsy Loyne.[2279] The Doctor helped to guarantee actor Clark Gable's fame by sticking a fake moustache on him.[2280] The eleventh Doctor knew a military code that had been on record since 1932, and instructed those receiving it to stand aside for its bearer, "however harebrained [their] actions might seem".[2281]

1932 (April 12th) - "A Matter of Life and Death"[2282]
-> The eighth Doctor and Josie visited Briarwood House as the Nixi spaceship buried there completed a 200-year hibernation cycle, and set about awakening the Nixi king. The ship transformed those within the house into wood-like servants for the king, but the Doctor and Josie found

the ship's hibernation key, and put the king to sleep for another two centuries.

1932 (summer) - HORNETS' NEST: THE DEAD SHOES[2283] -> The fourth Doctor arrived in Cromer and was drawn to the Cromer Palace of Curios, run by Mrs Fenella Wibbsey. There he met the dancer Ernestina Stott, whose one-woman performance of *The Nutcracker* was running on the Pier. They found a display cabinet with a pair of old ballet shoes that still contained withered feet, but Ernestina stole the shoes.

The Doctor saw Ernestina dance, which she did with supernatural brilliance – aided by the shoes. He also watched Ernestina flying, but got her to safety. Mrs Wibbsey was revealed to be possessed by the Hornets, and shrunk the Doctor and Ernestina, setting them down in a large Victorian dolls house. The Doctor again made contact with the Hornets, who said they met him in 1832 (something which had not yet happened from the Doctor's perspective). The Doctor returned himself and Ernestina to their normal scale, but the Hornets released Mrs Wibbsey and took control of Ernestina, forcing her to dance. The Doctor removed the shoes, freeing her. Mrs Wibbsey had residual traces of the Hornet influence, so the Doctor brought her to the twenty-first century.

1933

Otto Kreiner moved from Germany to England, soon meeting and marrying Muriel Tarr. They would become the parents of the eighth Doctor's companion Fitz.[2284]

2275 *Benny B3: Legion: Shades of Gray.* Naglowska lived 1883-1936. She published a collection of works by the occultist Paschal Beverly Randolph, on the topic of sex magic and mirrors, in 1931.

2276 Dating *FP: Spinning Jenny* (FP novel #11) – The month and year are given.

2277 *TW: Out of Time.* Earhart really disappeared in 1937.

2278 Lazarus declares he is "seventy-six years old" in *The Lazarus Experiment,* which is set in 2008.

2279 *Demon Quest: Starfall.* She meets the actress, after a fashion, in the 1970s.

2280 *Shroud of Sorrow.* Gable hated facial hair. He was forced to grow a real moustache for the stage play *Love, Honor and Betray* (1930) - a faux one kept falling off during the lovemaking scenes – but it's fake in *Strange Interlude* (1932), the first motion picture in which he appears with it.

2281 *The Forgotten Army.* The code was presumably originated for the Doctor's personal benefit, but it's not said how this came about.

2282 Dating "A Matter of Life and Death" (Titan 8th Doc #1-5) - The travel-list the Doctor obtained in issue

#1 names the exact day.

2283 Dating *Hornets' Nest: The Dead Shoes* (BBC fourth Doctor audio #1.2) - It's stated a number of times in this story and the previous one that it's 1932. *Hornets' Nest: The Stuff of Nightmares* says it's "July"; the sleeve notes for *The Dead Shoes* include a newspaper clipping dated "13th June 1932", and which dates events to "last week". Mrs Wibbsey's first name is never spoken, but appears in the sleeve notes of *The Dead Shoes*.

2284 *Frontier Worlds*

2285 "About seventy-eight years" before *TW: Miracle Day.*

2286 *Charley S1: The Fall of the House of Pollard*

2287 An (admittedly sexist) colleague of Helen estimates that she's thirty in *DC: The Red Lady* (set in 1963). That seems plausible, as Helen says she's been at the National Museum "four years longer" than a coworker who gains a promotion.

2288 The Haisman Timeline

2289 *Leth-St: Travers & Wells: Other Wars, Other Worlds*

2290 *Eater of Wasps*

2291 *Mad Dogs and Englishmen*

2292 *The Year of Intelligent Tigers*

Jack Harkness saw the Pacific Ocean, and wouldn't do so again until the twenty-first century.[2285]

Charley Pollard's parents, Richard and Louisa Pollard, diminished their fortune searching for their lost daughter. After three years of doing so, Richard retreated into his office in their London townhouse and – while pretending to write a history of the Saxe-Coburgs – read fantastical stories by Jules Verne, J.M. Barrie, Arthur Conan Doyle and other such works that Charley had enjoyed.[2286]

Helen Sinclair, a companion of the eighth Doctor, was born.[2287] Edward Travers and Margaret Goff married in August 1933.[2288] Upon their marriage, Edward's father gifted him with a family heirloom: a ring bearing a kontron crystal.[2289]

@ The eighth Doctor spent much of 1933 in the South Seas, and claimed to have gotten a tattoo there. He now had a criminal record in England.[2290] While in the South Seas, he saw magic performed.[2291] He served about the ship *Sarah Gail*, where he learned to play the violin[2292] and read a report of wasps attacking a train outside Arandale.[2293] At some point, he visited Australia and Hangchow.[2294]

1933 (January) - THE ALCHEMISTS[2295] **->** With the TARDIS having landed in Berlin and disguised itself as an advertising pillar, the first Doctor and Susan found a merchant to exchange their Roman aurei for local currency. The merchant believed the "new" coins derived from attempts by Fritz Haber – the chemist who synthesized ammonia, revolutionizing Germany's agriculture and war efforts – to separate gold from seawater. A British secret service agent, Pollitt, worried that Germany would become rich off Haber's efforts, and kidnapped the Doctor as he visited the Kaiser Wilhelm Institute Building to meet with such geniuses as Einstein, Heisenberg, Planck, Schrodinger and Wigner. Susan helped her grandfather to escape, and they left in the TARDIS.

1933 (August) - EATER OF WASPS[2296] **->** An alien device from the future caused wasps to mutate into killers. The eighth Doctor, Fitz and Anji encountered a trio of Time Agents who were seeking the device. The Time Agents decided to sterilise the area with a nuclear explosion, but the Doctor disarmed their nuclear weapon, and also smashed the mutagenic device.

c 1933 - "The Doctor and the Nurse"[2297] **->** The eleventh Doctor and Rory witnessed a giant gorilla in New York... then rectified the situation upon realising that it was a normal-size gorilla, and that New York had been shrunk.

c 1933 - MASTERMIND[2298] **->** The decaying Master's health again went in decline, and he took over the body of Don Maestro's son Michael.

By 1933, Germany had become aware that werewolves existed. Such non-humans were ordered to register with the government, and werewolves loyal to the party were reportedly used to sense dissenters. Several werewolves were rounded up and incarcerated for a year in a camp equipped with silver wire. A man from the Schutzstaffel (the SS, the Nazi Party's "praetorian guard") pressed the desperate werewolves into the service of the state.[2299] In 1933, Cuevas discovered a part of the Great Temple of the Aztecs.[2300]

1934

John **Benton, a member of UNIT and associate of the third and fourth Doctors, was born.**[2301]

1934 - THE EYE OF THE GIANT[2302] **->** The *Constitution III* was beached upon an uncharted island of Salutua in the

---

The Year of Intelligent Tigers, referring to events in *Eater of Wasps.*
2294 *History 101.* This was possibly during his second bout of world travelling in the sixties and seventies.
2295 Dating *The Alchemists* (BF CC #8.2) - The Doctor initially estimates that it's "around November 1932", but Susan more definitively says that it's "January 1933", that Hitler will (as he did in real life) seize power at end of month and that Faber will die the following year (on 29th January, 1934). Mention is made of a "mysterious packing crate" the Doctor keeps in the TARDIS, undoubtedly a reference to the Hand of Omega (*Remembrance of the Daleks*); see also *The Beginning*.
2296 Dating *Eater of Wasps* (EDA #45) - The Doctor estimates "it is probably the 1930s. If pushed, I'd have to say 1933. Twenty-seventh of August in fact" (p10).
2297 Dating "The Doctor and the Nurse" (IDW Vol. 4

#3-4) - Rory says it's "1930s New York". *King Kong* debuted in 1933.
2298 Dating *Mastermind* (BF CC #8.1) - It's "just over twenty years" since the Earthbound Master took over his last body in 1912.
2299 *Wolfsbane* (p90).
2300 *The Left-Handed Hummingbird* (p58).
2301 A tricky one to place. John Levene, who portrays Benton, was born 24th December, 1941, which – allowing that Benton's birth is subject to UNIT Dating – seems fair enough. However, the independent film *Wartime* depicts Benton and his brother as being (to look at the boys on screen) at least age ten in 1944. Benton's first name isn't given on screen, but was first cited as "John" (surely after Levene himself) in *Wartime*.
2302 Dating *The Eye of the Giant* (MA #21) - "The time is the eighth of June, nineteen thirty-four" (p42).

South Pacific. The third Doctor and Liz Shaw arrived at the island using a time bridge portal, and discovered a spacecraft in a volcanic crater. Animal and plant life on the island was subject to gigantism: giant crabs roamed the beach, bats the size of men flew at night, and the forest was hypertrophied. The Doctor discovered that drugs created by the Semquess, the most skilled bioengineers in the galaxy, were responsible for the mutations. The drugs had been brought to Earth fifty years before by Brokk of the Grold. The Semquess had tracked him, and now they apparently destroyed him. Brokk, though, used the properties of the Semquess drug to merge with Grover's young wife Nancy and leave Earth.

1934 - LURKERS AT SUNLIGHT'S EDGE[2303] **->** Emmerson Whytecrag III, a millionaire white supremacist, sought to ritualistically summon the power of the Carnash Coi. The beasts consumed Whytecrag, but the seventh Doctor, Ace and Hex succeeded in once again submerging the Carnash Coi's island-citadel and putting the monstrosities within to sleep. C.P. Doveday failed to escape the citadel before this happened, and also entered hibernation.

The eleventh Doctor claimed to own a carpet bag given to him by Mary Poppins.[2304] The Doctor pursued the Master across Berlin, and met Himmler and the future "Butcher of Prague", Reinhold Heydrich.[2305] On 30th June, 1934, the German-imprisoned werewolves were unleashed at a hotel housing men loyal to Ernst Roehm's Sturmabetilung ("Storm Division", a.k.a. stormtroopers). One of the werewolves, Emmeline Neuberger, bit a silver chain around a man's neck and was rendered unconscious. She was subsequently overlooked, and escaped into the German woods.[2306]

(=) 1934 (22nd December) - BIG BANG GENERATION[2307] **->** To boost tourism, a resident in New South Wales, Australia, fabricated aboriginal legends pertaining to the Three Sisters rock formation. Bavarian archaeologist Thomas G. Schneidter explored the area to find *die Glanz*, a.k.a. the Pyramid Eternia lodestone, a.k.a. the Glamour, and present it to the Chancellor of Germany. The twelfth Doctor and Benny arrived as the lodestone released a pulse that erased Schneidter's wife from history. The Doctor quieted the lodestone, then stressed to Schneidter that he must remain in New South Wales and entrust his offspring with guarding the lodestone until it was needed. Schneidter agreed, and the Doctor and Benny returned to 2015.

2303 Dating *Lurkers at Sunlight's Edge* (BF #141) - The year is given.
2304 *The King of Terror* (p103).
2305 *Magic of the Angels* (ch7). The film *Mary Poppins* (1964) was based on a series of children's books published 1934-1988.
2306 *Wolfsbane*. Page 93 says the werewolves were taken from the camp on 29th June, 1934; the hotel slaughter occurred the following evening. Historically, Hitler moved against Roehm and his Sturmabetilung because they could have staged a *coup d'etat*. He ordered the Sturmabetilung leaders to congregate at the Hanselbauer Hotel in Bad Wiesse near Munich, which is where the massacre in *Wolfsbane* evidently takes place. The purge is sometimes referred to as "The Night of the Long Knives".
2307 Dating *Big Bang Generation* (NSA #59) - The exact day is given (ch8). In real life, a non-aboriginal Katoomba local, Mel Ward, made up an "aboriginal" legend concerning the Three Sisters in the late 1920s or early 1930s.
2308 *The Highest Science* (p257).
2309 *The Time of Angels*. Woolf lived 1882-1941.
2310 *TW: Miracle Day*
2311 *Leth-St: Night of the Intelligence* (ch2).
2312 *Mastermind*. Prohibition was repealed on 5th December, 1933. Siegel lived 1906 to 20th June, 1947, when he was shot to death. Lansky fared better, living

1902 to 1983.
2313 *The Nightmare of Black Island*
2314 *The Unicorn and the Wasp*
2315 *The Sword of the Chevalier*. Rathbone lived 1892-1967. He and Flynn duelled in such films as *Captain Blood* (1935) and *The Adventures of Robin Hood* (1938).
2316 Dating *The Abominable Snowmen* (4.2) - According to the Doctor, this story occurs "three hundred years" after events that the monk Thonmi says took place in "1630". In *The Web of Fear*, Victoria agrees with Anne Travers' claim that the Travers Expedition took place in "1935".

In *Downtime*, Victoria says *The Abominable Snowmen* happened "fifty years" before 1984 (pgs. 41, 43). Charles Bryce says that Travers discovered *Yeti Traversii* in "1936" (p65) – not necessarily the same year that *The Abominable Snowmen* takes place, even though Travers goes in pursuit of a Yeti at story's end.

Whoniverse (BBC, p97) throws up its arms to say the Great Intelligence's gambit with the Yeti happened "probably in the late 1920s or 1930s (accounts vary as to the exact date)". *A History of the Universe in 100 Objects* tags its Yeti Control Sphere entry as "circa 1930" and "in the early 1930s" (p78).

The Haisman Timeline places this story in "October", the month that most of its episodes were broadcast. *Timelink* didn't quibble with the year being 1935. *About Time* thought the incidental evidence – particularly

1935

The seventh Doctor and Bernice failed to meet Virginia Woolf and went to the theatre instead. In the audience was twenty-fifth century explorer Gustaf Heinrich Urnst, who had been transported there by a Fortean Flicker.[2308] **The Doctor was on Virginia Woolf's bowling team.**[2309] **In 1935, Victor Podesta, an eyewitness to Jack Harkness' torture and resurrection in Little Italy, 1928, wrote and published the short story "The Devil Within" based upon what he'd seen.**[2310]

James Lethbridge-Stewart and Raymond Phillips coined James' paternal grandmother as "Granny McDougal" upon learning her maiden name in 1935.[2311]

The repeal of Prohibition and crackdowns by New York law enforcement curtailed the decaying Master's criminal enterprises, so he moved to Las Vegas in 1935 and became the owner of the La Casa Del Maestro casino. The Boulder Dam (later the Hoover Dam) supplied electrical power for the Master's experiments, but he refrained from interfering directly with history, fearful of detection by the Celestial Intervention Agency or the Doctor. The Master soon controlled all of Las Vegas' casinos, but made it appear that the likes of Bugsy Siegel and Meyer Lansky were in charge.[2312]

A Cynrog spacecraft crashed in Wales. The pilot died after implanting segments of his memories in eight local children.[2313] **The Agatha Christie novel *Death in the Clouds* was first published in 1935.**[1499] The Doctor learned the art of fencing from swashbuckler Basil Rathbone, as did Rathbone's on-screen opponent, Errol Flynn.[377-042]

The Great Intelligence Attacks Det-Sen

1935 - THE ABOMINABLE SNOWMEN[2316] -> The second Doctor, Jamie and Victoria arrived in the Himalayas. They found that the Yeti were menacing the Det-Sen Monastery and an expedition led by Professor Travers. The Yeti were robots built on behalf of the Intelligence – a powerful being of pure thought that attempted to manifest physically. The Doctor banished

it from Earth. The High Lama Padmasambhava was at last freed from the Intelligence's control and expired.

1935 (October) - LETH-ST: "The Creatures in the Cave" -> Having just left the Doctor's party, Edward Travers followed what he hoped was a natural-born yeti into a cave. He observed a row of the Intelligence's yeti, and then experienced a burst of white light...

The defeated Great Intelligence sent its surviving Yeti, and its servant Jemba-wa, through a time portal to the 1960s in preparation to invade the London Underground decades on. Edward Travers was caught in its wake, and found himself in 1965.[2317] The Timelash beam disrupted Edward Travers' return to his own era, and spirited him and – H.G. Wells, from the past – away to a parallel version of England in 1899...[2318]

After Padmasambhava was lost, Thomni became the abbot of Det-Sen.[2319] Eventually, Professor Travers discovered a breed of flesh-and-blood Yeti that became classified as *Yeti Traversii*.[2320]

= The Inferno Earth version of Edward Travers died in an avalanche in Tibet, 1935.[2321]

1935 - DotD: ENEMY ALIENS[2322] -> A fatigued eighth Doctor and Charley returned to the TARDIS, having prevented an army of granite behemoths animated by the insane sculptor Hamish Dorian Ernst from running amok in Bloomsbury, London. In the last two days, they had survived a Faberge egg bomb, met a living painting and shared tea with author Vita Sackville-West. The papers would mention the strange case of "smashed statues" in Bloomsbury, and report that Ernst had committed suicide.

The TARDIS passed along a garbled message from the eleventh Doctor that mentioned William Tell. The eighth Doctor and Charley found a stage performance in which "Mr William Tell, Europe's most memorable memory man" delighted audiences by reciting an array of statistics... that secretly contained coded messages for a German spy cell. One of the spies, Hilary Hammond, killed Tell to silence

---

Travers privately financing his expedition (more likely before the Wall Street crash) and the automatic benefit of doubt that he's truthful because he's an Englishman – better matched 1925-1928.

The *Lethbridge-Stewart* novels, starting with *Leth-St: The Forgotten Son* (chs. 1, 3, 12), are very consistent in claiming that *The Abominable Snowmen* happened in "1935". In *Leth-St: Times Squared*, Edward Travers is brought forward from that year following the Great Intelligence's defeat at Det-Sen.

2317 *Leth-St: Times Squared*

2318 *Leth-St: Times Squared, Leth-St: "Time and Again"*

– both leading into *Leth-St: Travers & Wells: Other Wars, Other Worlds*.

2319 *Downtime, Leth-St: Night of the Intelligence* (ch13).

2320 *Downtime* (p62), per the end of *The Abominable Snowmen*.

2321 *Leth-St: The Schizoid Earth*, alluding to *The Abominable Snowmen*.

2322 Dating *DotD: Enemy Aliens* (*Destiny of the Doctor* #8) - The blurb gives the year. The Doctor says it's "toward the less distinguished end of 1935..." Vita Sackville-West, an author and poet who was involved with Violet Trefusis and Virginia Woolf, lived 1892-1962.

him, then presented himself to Charley as a secret service agent. Charley declined Hammond's marriage proposal, offered as a means of giving her new credentials when she was suspected of Tell's murder.

The Doctor and Charley exposed Hammond's duplicity, and inadvertently assisted genuine secret service operatives in busting up the spy ring's base of operations in Scotland. They also scared off a group of alien conquerors by hijacking a broadcast of *Music Box*, and directly messaging the would-be invaders a warning from the eleventh Doctor that Earth was protected.

The conquerors' defeat eliminated psychic interference that would have hampered the Doctor's broadcasts to the insectoid Creevix.[2323]

1936

Ian Chesterton, a companion of the first Doctor, was born.[2324] Fitz Kreiner, a companion of the eighth Doctor, was born in Hampstead on 7th March, 1936.[2325] Regimental Sgt Samson Ware, an associate of Alistair Lethbridge-Stewart, was born April 1936.[2326]

u – **Mike Yates, a future UNIT captain and associate of the third** and fourth **Doctor**s, was born. He spent much of his childhood near Inverness, and had links to Aberdeen on his mother's side.[2327]

Private Gwynfor Evans was born in June 1936, Llanfairfach, as the youngest child of Dyfan and Norma Evans. He was named after his mother's sister, Gwynnie. Owing to his father's infidelity, Gwynfor's mother abandoned the family. Dyfan Evans worked as a driver, so often left Grynfor in the care of his grandmother and ailing grandfather.[2328] Alun Travers, the son of Edward and

Margaret Travers, was born July 1936. He would become a history teacher at the Oxford College of Further Education.[2329] When Alistair Lethbridge-Stewart was seven, his brother James gave away his books to their Uncle Mario, Granny McDougal's second cousin.[2330]

Sir Henry Rugglesthorpe and his family become playthings of the Toymaker.[2331] **In October 1936, the Doctor joined Mao Tse-Tung on the Long March.**[2332] The first Doctor visited the court of Edward VIII.[2333] After most filmmakers had relocated to the West Coast of America, Starlight Studios remained on the East Coast. Rock Railton and Giddy Semestre were its biggest icons.[2334]

The seventh Doctor and Mel met German racing driver Emil Hartung in Cairo. The Doctor accidentally inspired Hartung to develop aircraft that could avoid radar detection. Hartung won the Cairo 500 thanks to the modifications the Doctor made to his car.[2335]

@ The eighth Doctor made a visit to Highgate.[2336]

1936 (Sunday) - THE GLAMOUR CHASE[2337] -> The eleventh Doctor, Amy and Rory stopped some Tahnn from destroying the Weave stranded in the English town of Shalford Heights. Some of the Weave (including 6011, the Doctor's former acquaintance) had perished, and three locals – including the archaeologist Enola Porter – agreed to crew the ship and take it away from Earth. Owain, having guarded the Weave for six thousand years, finally died.

1936 (Autumn) - THE ELIXIR OF DOOM[2338] -> Iris Wildthyme and Jo Grant stopped at Vita Monet's monster-movie production company, Cosmic Studios, to reclaim the transmogrifying elixir Monet had taken from Iris some twenty years ago. Monet had imprisoned her headlining monster-husbands, and the human jelly defiantly burst

2323 *DotD: The Time Machine*
2324 According to an early format document for the series, dating from July 1963, Ian is "27". Then again, William Russell, born in 1924, certainly looks older than that on screen.
2325 *The Ancestor Cell* (p126), based on the writers' guidelines. He was "27" in *The Taint*. His year of birth is "1935" in *Escape Velocity*. He celebrates his birthday on 7th March in *Interference*.
2326 The Haisman Timeline, the supplemental material to *Leth-St: Moon Blink*.
2327 Going by actor Richard Franklin's birth year of 1936, and subject to UNIT dating. *DotD: Vengeance of the Stones* contains the details about his childhood.
2328 *Leth-St: The Life of Evans* (ch1), *Leth-St: "The Feast of Evans".* The Haisman Timeline specifies the month of his birth; Llanfairfach features in *The Green Death*.
2329 *Leth-St: Night of the Intelligence* (ch2).
2330 The Haisman Timeline
2331 *Divided Loyalties*

2332 *The Mind of Evil.* The Long March was a massive retreat on the part of the Chinese Communist Army to elude the Kuomintang Army. It granted the Communists a needed respite in the north of China.
2333 *The Cold Equations.* Edward ruled 20th January, 1936, to 11th December of the same year.
2334 "At least two years" before *The Angel's Kiss.*
2335 *Just War*
2336 *Grimm Reality*
2337 Dating *The Glamour Chase* (NSA #42) - The year is repeatedly given. According to p59, it's a Sunday. The Doctor rattles off a list of the "true greats" of archaeology (p139), but as he does so while expressly lying to Enola Porter that she's going to number among them (and as the list includes at least one real-life fraud, Shinichi Fujimura) the whole thing looks so improvised, it's probably best to not take it seriously.
2338 Dating *The Elixir of Doom* (BF CC #8.11) - The year is given. Iris says that *Movieland Dreams* #75, dated to "Autumn 1936," is "this month's issue".

itself to scuttle production of *Leopard Boy Meets the Human Jelly*. The eighth Doctor, randomly present at one of Monet's parties, sang a Venusian lullaby to stop the monsters from rampaging. Vita's operations were curtailed, and her first husband, the Bloody Count, escaped.

1936 (November) - CHARLEY S1: THE SHADOW AT THE EDGE OF THE WORLD / THE FALL OF THE HOUSE OF POLLARD[2339] ->

In Scotland, 1936, an airplane spotted the temple constructed by the Viyrans' creators. Expeditions there fell prey to an Amythist virus conducted through the Ever-and-Ever Prolixity, which devolved human males into savage ape-like creatures. The Viyrans studied the female survivors' natural immunity until Charley Pollard arrived via a Prolixity portal. She returned through it after convincing the Viyrans to release their captives and cure the males...

Finding herself in an incorporeal state, Charley made mental contact with a psychic, Michael Dee. Richard and Louisa Pollard's financial situation had further eroded, and they were selling their Hampstead estate. They had supplied no dowry for their eldest daughter, Margaret, who had married an American and was touring the States.

Dee convinced the Pollards to hold a séance that drew Charley back to reality. She was reunited with her parents until a Viyran retrieval squad took her back to the future. Unknown to Charley, the Viyrans revised her parents' memories so that they forgot she existed. Richard vaguely remembered Charley's suggestion about investing with the industrialist William Morris, and decided to do so.

@ 1936 (November) - WOLFSBANE[2340] ->

The eighth Doctor had returned to England, and been rejected several times after submitting short stories to *Astounding Stories* magazine. Harry Sullivan disembarked to explore when the fourth Doctor's TARDIS stopped on Earth, but the Ship inexplicably dematerialised. Stranded, Harry met the eighth Doctor. Lady Hester Stanton, believing herself the reincarnation of Morgan le Fay, performed magic rituals to wake the land and bind it to her. She hoped to rule England from behind-the-scenes, with her son George taking Edward VIII's place. Stanton magically compelled the werewolf Emmeline Neuberger to assist her.

Stanton's spells began to awaken the land, and a wood dryad expelled the slumbering swordsman Godric. He possessed the Holy Grail, which Harry used to make the Earth swallow Stanton – and the Grail also. Emmeline, instinctively desiring a mate, bit Harry.

The fourth Doctor and Sarah returned for Harry, and took Godric back to his native time. Some reports suggest Harry turned into a werewolf and killed Sarah, then was killed by the Doctor; some suggest Harry returned home and secretly became a werewolf during the full moon; and some say the Doctor cured Harry's condition.

The eighth Doctor believed Harry, Stanton and Godric had all died, and made gravesites to stop anyone getting curious about them or the Grail. He introduced Emmeline to his friends in the British Ministry, but they experimented on her in the hope of creating lupine soldiers.

1936 (30th November) - "The Eagle of the Reich"[2341] ->

The phoenix egg buried near the Crystal Palace pulled the TARDIS off course from its target destination of the Great Exhibition, 1851. The eleventh Doctor, Amy and Rory found that Dr Sophie Renard of the Societe Archeologique, who was excavating the site of the Palace's disused pneumatic railway, was actually Professor Kriemhilde Steiner of the Nazi Black Science Division. Steiner sought the phoenix egg as a thousand-year power source for the Reich, but was incinerated while laying hands on it. The egg hatched, and the newborn phoenix left for its home dimension – causing a fire that burnt the

---

Iris seems even more addled than normal, as she claims that she doesn't have any extra lives – that she's "more like [Jo] than a [Time Lord]", and yet she mentions meeting the eighth Doctor and "Sam" (almost certainly Sam Jones) on Hypero – which she did in *The Scarlet Empress*, a story in which she regenerated. Jo, a little confusingly, says she hasn't met the eighth Doctor before (which she did, in *Genocide*).

2339 Dating *Charley S1: The Shadow at the Edge of the World* and *Charley S1: The Fall of the House of Pollard* (CP #1.2-1.3) - The year is given in both stories, and the latter specifies the month as "November". Sir William Morris (1877-1963) founded Morris Motors Limited, which made Spitfires and other war materials. Charley's parents mention that they haven't heard from her sister Sissy (*Gallifrey I: A Blind Eye* [1939]) and a strange business involving "the Grangers, all that time ago"

(*Short Trips:* "Forgotten" [1906]).

2340 Dating *Wolfsbane* (PDA #62) - Harry is abandoned on 27th November, 1936, according to p24. Harry's fate is left ambiguous due to the presence of multiple timelines, which were finally compressed to one history in *Timeless. Sometime Never* says the Council of Eight had a hand in engineering Harry's "death".

2341 Dating "The Eagle of the Reich" (IDW *DW Special 2012*) - Historically, the Crystal Palace burned down on Monday, 30th November, 1936 – meaning a slight bit of discontinuity happens when a custodian here tells the Doctor's trio that they can't go in because the Palace is "closed Sundays". Churchill was, in real life, among those viewing the building as it burned down. The eleventh Doctor's group next arrives at the Crystal Palace's opening, in 1851, in "Hypothetical Gentleman".

Crystal Palace to the ground. Winston Churchill was among those who watched the blaze, and told the Doctor that it was the end of an era. The Doctor's trio resumed their journey to 1851.

1936 (December) - WOLFSBANE[2342] -> The TARDIS rematerialised after leaving Harry behind two weeks in the past, and the fourth Doctor and Sarah found his "tombstone". They pieced together what had occurred during the previous fortnight. The Doctor rescued Emmeline from the Ministry, and drew enough blood from her to ritualistically send the land back to sleep. She departed back to Germany; the Doctor and Sarah went back to find Harry.

1936 (December) - PLAYERS[2343] -> King Edward VIII sought to dissolve the British government, hoping to vest more power with Nazi sympathizers. The sixth Doctor aided Winston Churchill in coercing the King to abdicate the throne, threatening to charge him with treason. This thwarted the schemes of the Players, who were engaged in a game of historical alterations.

The Doctor and Peri stopped at Cholmondeley's bank, where the Doctor's account had amassed one hundred twenty years of compound interest.

1936 (December) - PIER PRESSURE[2344] -> In Brighton, a string of murders gave rise to stories of "the Phantom Bloodsucker of Preston Park", a killer who preyed upon the blood of fresh young maidens. The sixth Doctor and Evelyn encountered the famous music hall comedian Max Miller, and found the reportedly dead Professor Talbot as an agent of the Indo aliens. The Doctor feared the aliens would gain much power by feeding off the emotional trauma of the impending World War II, and short-circuited their energy with a piece of Gallifreyan zinc. This allowed Talbot to finally die, dissipated the aliens' mass and embedded their essence within Brighton's West Pier.

The Doctor estimated that the essence of the Indo aliens from 1936 would corrode the West Pier, and probably consume its metal entirely in sixty or seventy years.[2345]

1937

If rumours at St Luke's University Bristol, 2017, could be believed, the twelfth Doctor had been lecturing there for fifty years, perhaps even seventy.[2346]

@ The amnesiac eighth Doctor was in London at this time.[2347] **The Doctor and Clara went to dinner in Berlin, 1937, but didn't nip out after the pudding to kill**

2342 Dating *Wolfsbane* (PDA #62) - It's 11th December, 1936 (p49).
2343 Dating *Players* (PDA #21) - The date is given (p150).
2344 Dating *Pier Pressure* (BF #78) - The year is given. Mention that *Charlie Chan at the Opera* is currently showing in Brighton is potentially a glitch, as some documentation indicates it wasn't distributed in the UK until 8th January, 1937. Miller states that he's 40; he's approximating, because he would have been 42 at the time.
2345 *Pier Pressure.* This refers to the West Pier's real-life decay. It partially collapsed on 29th December, 2002, then further caved in on 20th January, 2003.
2346 A claim that Bill makes in *The Pilot*, but possibly nothing more than office tittle-tattle. If it was true, it would entail the twelfth Doctor showing uncharacteristic restraint – not just with steering clear of Earth's crises all that time, but actually retiring from adventuring and contenting himself with just teaching class, which doesn't sound like him at all. There's no sign in Series 10 that the Doctor has judiciously obeyed Nardole's instructions and left the TARDIS to collect dust in the corner for decades, only to throw such incredible discipline out the window once he meets Bill. If Series 10 teaches us nothing else, it's that the Doctor is woeful at both staying put and sneaking away without Nardole noticing. (See The Doctor's Age sidebar for more.)
2347 *History 101*
2348 *Kill the Moon*

2349 It's said that the plane was made "about forty years" before *The Valley of Death*. Only 199 Ford Trimotors were made, from 1925 to 1933.
2350 "Tooth and Claw" (*DWM*). Threshold's involvement and the date are confirmed in "Wormwood".
2351 Dating *Benny* S10: *Secret Origins* (Benny audio #10.4) - The year is given.
2352 *TimeH: The Sideways Door.* The *Hindenburg* went down on 6th of May, 1937.
2353 Dating *History 101* (EDA #58) - It's "Barcelona, 1937" (p1).
2354 *The Shadow of Weng-Chiang* (p208).
2355 *Superior Beings* (p58).
2356 Dating *Leth-Set:* "The Bledoe Cadets and the Bald Man of Pengriffen" (*Leth-St: HAVOC Files* #3.1) - The year and month are given.
2357 Dating *The Shadow of Weng-Chiang* (MA #25) - The date is given (p1).
2358 *Leth-St: The Forgotten Son* (chs. 4,11), following on from *The Name of the Doctor*.
2359 *Leth-St: The Forgotten Son* (chs. 4,11).
2360 *Leth-St: The Schizoid Earth*
2361 The Haisman Timeline
2362 *Leth-St:* "The Lost Skin"
2363 *Ghost Ship*
2364 *TW: Miracle Day*
2365 *J&L* S3: *Swan Song.* This dating is somewhat arbitrary, as the date of Jago's death isn't known, but it must occur before the New Regency's destruction in 1940.
2366 *Leth-St: The Showstoppers*

Hitler.[2348] Godrin's slow-time field created a Second Bermuda Triangle above the Valley of Death, which caused a Ford Trimotor – a.k.a. a "goose" airplane – to be lost to it.[2349]

In 1937, the eighth Doctor and Fey Truscott-Sade fought psychic weasels in Russell Square. Soon after, the Threshold implanted a perceptual relay unit in Truscott-Sade's brain, enabling them to monitor what she saw.[2350]

1937 - BENNY S10: SECRET ORIGINS[2351] **->** As part of his crusade against the Deindum, Irving Braxiatel endowed Frost, a Nazi officer, with an extended lifespan and tasked him with destroying Buenos Aires. Frost wouldn't accomplish this mission until the late twenty-sixth century.

> (=) Alternate versions of Honoré Lechasseur and Emily Blandish prevented the *Hindenburg* disaster, enabling continued use of dirigibles.[2352]

1937 - HISTORY 101[2353] **->** Sabbath sent an agent to Barcelona to track down the Absolute, a being from the future that had acquired information about his activities. This disrupted history, which in turn corrupted the Absolute's perceptions. The eighth Doctor, Anji and Fitz arrived and discovered that the Picasso painting *Guernica* had been altered. The Doctor sent Fitz to Guernica itself to check events. The Doctor restored reality and the Absolute returned home. These events inspired Eric Blair, also known as the writer George Orwell.

Aviatrix Amelia Earhart disappeared, possibly because she flew into one of the Dragon Paths, lines of magnetic force.[2354] The Doctor had Amelia Earhart's flying jacket.[2355]

1937 (a weekend in July) - "The Bledoe Cadets and the Bald Man of Pengriffen"[2356] **->** James Lethbridge-Stewart, Henry Barnes, Raymond Phillips and Jemima Fleming fancied themselves as the Bledoe Cadets: a club available for adventuring and detective work. They refused to let James' brother Alistair join, as he was too young. Alistair and James summoned the police to rescue Henry when Mad Jim Cliskey, an escaped convict from Dartmoor, held him prisoner in the Pengriffen fougou. James still refused to name Alistair as a Cadet, but Alistair was thrilled, as the Cliskey business had been so exciting!

1937 (August) - THE SHADOW OF WENG-CHIANG[2357] **->** The fourth Doctor, the first Romana and K9 were drawn to Shanghai while searching for the Key to Time. They stumbled across the Tong of the Black Scorpion's plan to recover their "god" Weng-Chiang (Magnus Greel) from the zygma beam experiment. The Doctor followed the Tong's leader, H'sien-Ko – the daughter of the stage magician Li H'sien Chang – to the holy mountain of T'ai Shan. There, the Doctor found the Tong had constructed the world's first nuclear reactor to achieve the power needed to retrieve Greel. The Doctor narrowly prevented a temporal paradox by time-ramming Greel's Time Cabinet, hurling it back to 1872.

The Great Intelligence Changes Alistair Lethbridge-Stewart's History

A splinter of the Great Intelligence survived Clara Oswald's assault on its temporal duplicates by inveigling itself into the history of one of its foes, Alistair Lethbridge-Stewart. In September 1937, the Intelligence-shard found Alistair's brother Gordon receptive to its influence, and infiltrated his mind as Maha, his "imaginary friend".[2358]

1938

In late March 1938, the piece of the Great Intelligence within Gordon Lethbridge-Stewart Jr goaded the young boy into leaping to his death at Golitha Falls. The Intelligence-shard took refuge in the nearby Remington Manor, and would later animate Gordon's dead form.[2359]

> '= In the Inferno-Earth reality, young Alistair Lethbridge-Stewart died at Golitha Falls, but his brother James lived.[2360]

In April 1938, Gordon Lethbridge-Stewart wrote a letter admitting that he knew his true parentage, but that he considered Alistair Sr. his true father. A family solicitor kept the letter, to be delivered to Alistair Sr. upon Gordon's death.[2361] When Harold Chorley was seven, his brother Lawrence beat their abusive father to death with a rolling pin. The authorities believed their father died falling down the stairs, but Harold would later leverage the truth against his brother, the journalist Larry Greene.[2362]

Ghosts were sighted on the *Queen Mary* in 1938.[2363] **In 1938, the entire Podesta family – which had ties to the Three Families – changed their names and disappeared from the public record.**[2364]

Swan Lake was first performed at the New Regency some time after the death of the theatre's legendary impresario, Henry Gordon Jago. It was a huge success.[2365] A German diving experiment captured a siphonophore, a creature of the deep seas, in 1938, and turned it over to Vilhelm Schadengeist.[2366]

The Shepherd and the Shepherdess had overseen a billion worlds in their native universe, but fled through a gateway as their realm rotted into nothingness. Seeking to recreate their home in our reality, they sought out Kurt Schalk – an unremarkable clerk working in Berlin – and endowed his dreams with the blueprints for a Persuasion machine: a device that could overcome the will of any being, anywhere. Schalk and his assistant, Lukas Hinterberger, would spend years trying to craft such a machine on the Reich's behalf.[2367]

1938 (8th April) - TIMEH: THE ALBINO'S DANCER[2368]
-> Honoré and Emily fulfilled history pertaining to events in the Albino's bunker by damaging and hiding a time-belt.

1938 - "The Curse of the Scarab"[2369] **->** The fifth Doctor and Peri landed in what they thought was an Egyptian tomb, but which was actually a Hollywood film set. The movie *The Curse of the Scarab* was beset with problems, including Raschid Karnak, the uncommunicative lead, who played the Mummy. Director Seth Rakoff was under a great deal of pressure from the studio boss, Monroe Stahr. Peri led Karnak to his dressing room, where he choked and scarab beetles started emerging from his mouth. A robot Mummy killed Stahr. The Doctor discovered more deactivated Mummies in a control centre inside a prop pyramid. Karnak was there, and told them he was cursed by the beetle god Kephri. He used the Grimoire of

Anubis to resurrect Kephri. A plague of locusts was released as Kephri manifested. The Doctor held it in place with an ankh, and had a robot Mummy destroy it. The film set was destroyed in a fire.

At one point during this encounter, Peri was abducted by Threshold.

Mels Regenerates into River Song

1938 - LET'S KILL HITLER[2370] **->** The *Teselecta* – a robot vehicle crewed by four hundred and twenty-one miniaturized justice agents, whose mission was to pull the greatest villains in history from the end of their lives and punish/torture them – travelled through time to capture Adolf Hitler, but arrived too early in his timestream. The *Teselecta* shifted to pose as a Nazi officer and approached Hitler just as the TARDIS, with the eleventh Doctor, Amy, Rory and Mels aboard, crashed through the window of Hitler's office. Rory locked Hitler in a cupboard, but Mels was hit by a stray bullet... which triggered her regeneration into the body

2367 *Persuasion*. Schalk and Hinterberger spend "years" rather than decades working on the Persuasion machine, and Schalk implies that his dreams started "before the war" (generally regarded as starting with the invasion of Poland on 1st September, 1939). There's no evidence that the Shepherd and Shepherdess' home universe is the one before our own, or that they have any affiliation with the Great Old Ones.

2368 Dating *TimeH: The Albino's Dancer* (*TimeH #9*) - The exact day is given, p1.

2369 Dating "The Curse of the Scarab" (*DWM* #228-230) - The date is given.

2370 Dating *Let's Kill Hitler* (X6.8) - The date is given in a caption. In all of the *Doctor Who* stories that involve Hitler, this is the only one where he actually sees the TARDIS.

2371 Dating *The Angel's Kiss: A Melody Malone Mystery* (BBC Series 7 ebook #1) - Melody/River narrates (ch1): "I checked the calendar – 1938. I hadn't planned on cleaning [my office] until at least 1946." The story is a prequel to *The Angels Take Manhattan* – Julius Grayle makes a cameo appearance, Kliener's Weeping Angel is presumably the one seen on screen in Grayle's study, and River is already established as Melody Malone in the TV story.

As the paradox that wipes out the Angels at Winter Quay annuls much of *The Angels Take Manhattan* from history, it's unclear how much events leading up to it are scrubbed from the timeline also. One possibility is that Kleiner's Angel – which seems to be operating independently from the Winter Quay Angels – does survive the paradox, struggles on to 2012, and is the one responsible for Amy and Rory being forever sepa-

rated from the Doctor.

2372 Dating *The Angels Take Manhattan* (X7.5) - The exact day is given.

2373 Rory writes to his father in *P.S.* than he and Amy are stuck in New York "fifty years before I was born". Presuming he was born around the same time as Amy, in 1989, it seems that the two of them are indeed sent back to 1938, and began their new life from there. The supplemental material to *Summer Falls and Other Stories* suggests that as part of their new identities, Amy and Rory tell people that they lived in New York prior to World War II.

2374 *The Bells of Saint John*, and the supplemental material to *Summer Falls and Other Stories*

2375 Dating *Invaders from Mars* (BF #28) - The date is given, although the Welles play was actually broadcast on 30th October, not the 31st. Big Finish claims to have deliberately changed the date as part of the historical alterations affecting the second season of McGann audios. There are a couple of further anachronisms, such as a mention of the CIA and Welles not knowing about Shakespeare, which are explained in *The Time of the Daleks*.

2376 Dating *Fiesta of the Damned* (BF #215) - The blurb states that it's "1938". The Doctor says, "The Battle of Ebro River has just been fought" – historically, that occurred July to November 1938, and represented a crushing defeat for the Republicans. Franco's Nationalists are slated to capture Catalonia, Tarragona and Barcelona "in a few months", which happened in January and February 1939.

2377 *Timeless*. The bookshop is said to be on Charing Cross Road, but it was on Euston Road in *Time Zero*.

of the person the Doctor's group knew as River Song.

Programmed by the Silence to kill the Doctor, Melody kissed him using lipstick laced with poison from the Judas Tree before heading out into Berlin. The justice agents identified Melody as the criminal River Song and began torturing her – but Amy sabotaged the *Teselecta*, forcing its crew to transmat to safety. The TARDIS taught Melody to fly her, enabling Melody to rescue Amy and Rory from the *Teselecta*'s interior.

The dying Doctor asked Melody to find River Song and whispered something to her that profoundly affected her. Amy used the *Teselecta* records to prove that Melody *was* River Song, whereupon River sacrificed her remaining regenerations to save the Doctor's life. The Doctor, Amy and Rory took the exhausted River Song to the fifty-first century to recover.

1938 - THE ANGEL'S KISS[2371] -> River Song set up shop in New York and worked on unconventional cases as the detective Melody Malone, the sole employee of the Angel Detective Agency. A weakened Weeping Angel forged an agreement with Max Kliener, the head of Starlight Studios and the producer of *Lady Don't Shoot*. The Angel harvested time energy from Kleiner's celebrities, healed itself with some of the proceeds and devoted the rest to creating short-lived duplicates of its victims. In this way, Kliener had a constant supply of Rock Railtons and Giddy Semestres at his disposal. River shut down Kliener's operation after one of the Railtons asked for her help, and Kliener crumbled to dust after accidentally kissing the Angel. Despite River's efforts, the still-diminished Angel was loaded onto a truck and taken away...

Amy and Rory Williams Leave the TARDIS

(=) 1938 (3rd April) - THE ANGELS TAKE MANHATTAN[2372] -> The Weeping Angels converged upon New York City and took over most of its statues. The Winter Quay apartment block, located near Battery Park, was turned into a battery farm: a prison in which the Angels could send victims back in time in a recurring loop and feed upon the resultant time energy.

River Song, operating as "Melody Malone", happened upon Rory when an Angel sent him back from 2012. The eleventh Doctor and Amy broke through the time distortion surrounding New York, and found that Rory was fated to be sent back again to die in Winter Quay as an old man. Rory and Amy killed themselves, creating a paradox that poisoned the Angels' food supply and averted Winter Quay from being established. The resultant historical revision sent the Doctor and his friends back to 2012...

One Angel survived to 2012, and again sent Rory back to this era. As the fractured timelines in New York meant that the TARDIS couldn't return there without destroying the city, Amy had the same Angel send her back so she could join her husband. Amy and Rory had each other, but would never see their friends or family again.[2373] In future, Amy would become a writer and editor of children's books. *The Angel's Kiss*, a Melody Malone mystery, was the first book she read when she arrived in New York.[2374]

1938 (31st October) - INVADERS FROM MARS[2375] -> An alien spaceship crashed in New Jersey and was looted by the gangster Don Chaney, who discovered a bat-like being aboard. Chaney hired the Russian physicist Yuri Stepashin to develop an atom bomb from the advanced technology, hoping to give America an advantage over Germany. The eighth Doctor and Charley found conflict brewing between Chaney and his rival, Cosmo Devine, who wanted to sell the technology for the Nazis.

The alien split into thirty beings and threatened to go on a rampage, but the aliens Streath and Noriam subdued the pilot as part of a protection racket. Devine convinced Streath and Noriam that their weapons could seize control of Earth without the need for deception. The Doctor went to CBS Studios and had Orson Welles stage a second, private performance of *War of the Worlds* for the aliens' benefit, hoping to make them think that the formidable Martians had already invaded Earth. The plan failed. Stepashin detonated his atom bomb aboard the aliens' spacecraft while it was in orbit, destroying them.

1938 (Winter) - FIESTA OF THE DAMNED[2376] -> Following the Battle of Ebro River in the Spanish Civil War, Republican soldiers led by Juan Romero took shelter in the town of Farissa. Air bombing activated a buried Godseed – an alien weapon of war programmed to rewrite a local population's DNA – that turned the Farissa residents into hybrid creatures resembling Cuelebres, creatures from Spanish mythology. The seventh Doctor, travelling with Mel and Ace, created a human-compatible Godseed that returned everyone to normal, and then tricked Nationalist bombers into destroying the rogue Godseed. Romero turned down Mel's offer to come with the TARDIS crew, and continued the fight against General Franco's forces.

The eighth Doctor left a copy of Fitz's journal, entitled *An Account of An Expedition to Siberia*, in a second hand bookshop for his past self to find.[2377] @ In 1938, the amnesiac Doctor bought Fitz's journal from a bookshop on Euston Road.[2378]

Adolf Hitler gained the Validium Arrow, a piece of the Nemesis statue. The Nemesis itself passed over Earth, heralding Germany's annexation of Austria.[2379]

1938 (Christmas) - THE DOCTOR, THE WIDOW AND THE WARDROBE[2380] **->** The eleventh Doctor destroyed a threatening alien spaceship, and donned an impact suit as he fell to Earth. A young mother, Madge Arwell, helped him get back to the TARDIS. As his helmet was on backwards, she never saw his face.

1939

Anne Margaret **Travers, an associate of the second Doctor and Alistair Gordon Lethbridge-Stewart, was born to Edward** and Margaret **Travers** on October 28th, 1938.[2381] Edward Travers inherited a house in London from his father, Lyndon Travers.[2382]

Lance Corporal Sally Wright was born in March 1939.[2383] When her father Dyfan died, Wright discovered that she was from his second family. Gwynfor Evans was her half-brother.[2384]

In Antarctica, the Nazis started construction of a huge underground base that was shaped like a swastika.[2385] **A photo of Jack Harkness from 1939 wound up in the American CIA archives.**[2386] Circa 1939, a pair of

Cybermen from the thirtieth century arrived accidentally in Jersey. They secretly took control of Peddler Electronic Engineering in London.[2387] **In 1939, a failed attempt to open Devil's Hump, "the Cambridge University Fiasco", took place.**[2388] **A fez-wearing eleventh Doctor found his way onto a Laurel and Hardy movie.**[2389]

In 1939, the Doctor dined with a capricious host who served their guests dolphin brains.[2390] The Doctor fixed the central-heating boiler at the radar shadow factory at Cowbridge House, Malmesbury, in the winter of 1939.[2391] Petty Officer Wren Charlotte Bibby disappeared without a trace in 1939, another victim of the Keynsham Triangle.[2392]

1939 - "Tooth and Claw" (DWM)[2393] **->** The eighth Doctor and Izzy were summoned to Varney's island in the Atlantic, where eccentric guests – including Fey Truscott-Sade, an old friend of the Doctor – were served the meat of endangered animals by Varney's monkey servants. Truscott-Sade worked for British Intelligence, and suspected that Varney was creating biological weapons for the Nazis. In truth, Varney had drugged everyone's champagne with a microbe derived from his ancestors, and this turned the guests – the Doctor and Fey included – into vampires.

Varney served the last of the Curcurbites – an alien construct fuelled by blood. The Doctor destroyed the Curcurbite by poisoning his own blood and allowing the

2378 *Time Zero*

2379 *Silver Nemesis*

2380 Dating *The Doctor, the Widow and the Wardrobe* (X7.0) - It is three years before the story's main action.

2381 The Haisman Timeline, the supplemental material to *Leth-St: Moon Blink*. Anne is "thirty years old" in *Leth-St: Beast of Fang Rock* and *Leth-St: "Legacies",* which matches with actress Tina Packer being twenty-nine when she appeared in *The Web of Fear* (subject to UNIT Dating). Anne's ancestor, Archibald Goff, died "almost a hundred years before she was born" (*Beast*, ch10) in "September 1839" (ch1) - if *Moon Blink* is right, it's actually a bit more than a century.

2382 "Some thirty years" before *Leth-St: Beast of Fang Rock,* so doubtless after *The Abominable Snowmen.*

2383 *Leth-St: Night of the Intelligence* (ch4).

2384 *The Shadow in the Glass*

2385 The Haisman Timeline

2386 *TW: Miracle Day*

2387 "A year or two back" before *Illegal Alien.*

2388 *The Daemons*

2389 *The Impossible Astronaut.* The movie appears to be *The Flying Deuces* (1939).

2390 *The Next Life*

2391 *The Crawling Terror* (ch13).

2392 *Leth-St: The Dreamer's Lament*

2393 Dating "Tooth and Claw" (*DWM* #257-260) - It's "1939", according to the opening caption.

2394 Dating *Gallifrey I: A Blind Eye* (*Gallifrey* #1.4) - The

exact day is given.

2395 *Resistance.* The start of the war is generally dated to 1st September, 1939, when Germany invaded Poland.

2396 *Quicksilver*

2397 *The Web of Fear*

2398 *Energy of the Daleks*

2399 *Project: Twilight*

2400 *Doctor Who and the Pirates*

2401 *The Sins of Winter*

2402 *Ghost Ship*

2403 *Endgame* (EDA)

2404 *Wishing Well*

2405 *Hide.* Presuming talk of "the war" means World War II, Palmer must have (remarkably) done much or all of this as a teenager. That, or he's older than actor Dougray Scott was, age 46, when he filmed *Hide.*

2406 *CM S2: Manhunt*

2407 *Heart of TARDIS.* This was "several years" before Crowley's reported death in 1947 (p6).

2408 *Heart of TARDIS*

2409 *Mastermind*

2410 *FP: The Brakespeare Voyage* (ch7).

2411 *Leth-St: Night of the Intelligence* (ch7).

2412 Dating *Timewyrm: Exodus* (NA #2) - Part Three of the novel is set in "1939" (p111).

2413 Dating *Breaking Bubbles and Other Stories*: "An Eye for Murder" (BF #188c) - The year is given. The Doctor and Peri hear Prime Minister Neville Chamberlain's radio announcement declaring war with

construct to feed off him... this returned the Doctor to normal, but left him gravely ill. Izzy and Fey got him back to the TARDIS, knowing they would have to take the Doctor to Gallifrey if he was going to survive.

Sissy Pollard Kills Herself

1939 (3rd September) - GALLIFREY I: A BLIND EYE[2394] **->** The arms and secrets broker Mephistopheles Arkadian summoned President Romana to the Vienna-Calais express on Earth, 1939, and offered to identify the party behind the theft of a timonic fusion device if she turned a blind eye to his activities concerning Charley Pollard's sister, Cecila "Sissy" Pollard. Sissy had been appointed the Munich representative of the League of English Fascists by Sir Oswald Mosely, and had met Hitler himself. One of Arkadian's clients hoped to kill, stuff and sell her as a Nazi collectible.

Romana, Leela, CIA Coordinator Narvin and CIA agent Torvald found that Sissy's boyfriend, Erich Kepler, was actually an earlier incarnation of Torvald. An embittered isolationist disgusted with Romana's policies, Kepler had averted Sissy's historic suicide by a river in Munich. Kepler threatened that unless Romana allowed the Time Lords to erase her from history, he would use Sissy – much like her sister – to unleash anti-Time throughout the universe. Moreover, Torvald had arranged the theft of the timonic fusion device, in a further bid to discredit Romana.

The incumbent Torvald confessed that he was actually Andred – who had regenerated during the gunfight in which Torvald had died. Narvin removed Kepler's memories of these events; Torvald would die as history dictated. Leela and Andred remained estranged. Knowing she'd never be regarded as anything other than an amusement to the Nazis, and a traitor to the British, Sissy killed herself.

The Second World War

Polly Wright's parents were married a month before World War II broke out. Her father Edward was a doctor, and her mother was a proper society lady, being one of the Bessingham-Smiths. They lived in a big old house in the country. Edward had an elder brother Charles, and a younger brother Randolph.[2395] Flip Jackson's great-grandfather flew planes during World War II.[2396]

During the war, bunkers were built in the London Underground, including one at Covent Garden.[2397] During World War II, a secret tunnel was built under Charing Cross station for, if events warranted it, the emergency evacuation of the National Gallery and its treasures. Only the Prime Minister and the Doctor knew that this route existed.[2398] The Doctor knew his way around the secret tunnels under the Thames used during the Second World War.[2399]

The Doctor advised Winston Churchill on policy.[2400] Churchill gave the Doctor his own postcode.[2401]

During World War II, the *Queen Mary* was used as a troop ship and torpedoed. Soldiers died, leading people to suspect the ship was haunted.[2402] Beings of light from Altair III observed the Second World War.[2403] Gaskin Manor in Creighton Mere was used as a convalescent home during World War II.[2404]

Alec Palmer, an operative of Her Majesty's government, worked during the war to disrupt U-Boat operations in the North Sea and destroy European railway lines. He also participated in Operation Gibbon, which involved carrier pigeons. American airmen stationed at Caliburn House heard the Caliburn Ghast.[2405] Charles Waverly served as Ian Gilmore's commanding officer during his cadetship.[2406]

Occultist Aleister Crowley summoned the demon Jarakabeth.[2407] During World War II, the United States feared that collective Nazi belief could alter the fabric of reality. The US government hired writer J.R.R. Tolkien and his contemporaries to infuse world culture with a greater sense of what was fantasy, and what was reality.[2408] The decaying Master furthered his experiments by co-opting the nuclear research at Los Alamos.[2409]

> (=) wih - The War in Heaven created time-fisulas in which the Nazis spread their influence into space, until House Lineacrux moved to erase the effort.[2410]

> = World War II never happened on Inferno-Earth, and so the Republic and Stalin divided up Europe.[2411]

1939 (early September) - TIMEWYRM: EXODUS[2412] **->** The seventh Doctor, having inveigled his way into Hitler's confidence as "Herr Doktor Johann Scmidt" with Ace as his "niece, Fräulein Dorothy Scmidt", told Hitler that if he invaded Poland, the British would declare war on Germany. Hitler refused to believe him, but the Doctor was proved right – which made Hitler trust him all the more.

Hitler had risen to power, doubly aided by the War Lords and the Timewyrm nestled within his mind. The War Lords hoped to build a "War Lord universe" by giving the Nazis space travel, whereas the Timewyrm wanted to divert the course of history. The Doctor exposed the War Lords' plans to betray the Nazis, and the forces of Reichsmarshal Goering slaughtered them. The War Lords' influence ended with the destruction of their base, Drachensberg Castle.

1939 (3rd September) - BREAKING BUBBLES AND OTHER STORIES:"An Eye for Murder"[2413] **->** Dr Ruth Horowitz of St Ursula's College performed invisibility experiments on a light-refracting, petrified alien eye

handed down by her grandmother. The sixth Doctor and Peri prevented a Nazi, Dr Maria Backhouse, from stealing the eye on behalf of the Reich. The eye's invisibility effect proved unstable, and disintegrated Backhouse.

As the Second World War started, a few people in England felt that their country should fight alongside the Nazis. Ratcliffe was one such person, and he was imprisoned for his belief.[2414]

The British government wanted the Sontaran Brak to create weapons for use in World War II. Brak synthesised Kobalt Blue, a malleable substance that could power projectile and energy weapons – and hoped that it would either spur humanity into becoming foes worthy of the Sontarans, or push Earth's governments into destroying one another. However, the government's development of Kobalt Blue never got past the testing stage.[2415]

1939 (December) - CHURCHILL: THE ONCOMING STORM[2416] **->** A Gallifreyan Auger Stone – a product of the Last Great Time War, made to upgrade the intelligence of ground troops – fell to Earth on 22nd November, 1939. Army engineers recovered the Stone from the Thames on 23rd November; in December, it was brought to the attention of Winston Churchill, who was currently serving as First Lord of the Admiralty. Churchill had met different incarnations of the Doctor before, and here met the ninth Doctor as he attempted to stop an octet of mechanical beings, Reactive Automated Trail Seekers (RATS), from obtaining the Auger Stone to improve their AI. As the Doctor feared, the Stone accelerated the RATS' intelligence so much, it destroyed them.

UNIT in the Forties

Lethbridge-Stewart would later attend Holborough with Teddy "Pooh" Fitzoliver. Lethbridge-Stewart's Granny McDougal died when he was 13[2417], and he later won the

---

Germany, which happened on 3rd September, 1939.

2414 *Remembrance of the Daleks*

2415 *Sontarans: Old Soldiers*

2416 Dating *Churchill: The Oncoming Storm* (*The Churchill Years* #1.1) - The blurb says it's "late 1939"; Churchill's narration establishes the time as "December 1939". Churchill served as First Lord of the Admiralty twice, from 1911-1915, and again from 3rd September 1939 to 11th May, 1940. For the ninth Doctor, this entails a trip to World War II separate from *The Empty Child/The Doctor Dances*.

2417 *The Paradise of Death* (p25).

2418 *Island of Death*

2419 *Business Unusual*

2420 *Old Soldiers*

2421 *Leth-St: The Forgotten Son* (ch8).

2422 *Unbound: Masters of War*

2423 In *The Rescue*, Vicki claims that Barbara ought to be "550" years old. As *The Rescue* is set in 2493, this means Barbara was born in 1943 – making her twenty in 1963, and therefore too young to be a history teacher. Jacqueline Hill was born in 1931, and was 34 when *The Rescue* was made – meaning that Vicki is clearly rounding down. The finalised Writers' Guide for the first series said Barbara was "23", although she certainly seems older.

2424 *Leth-St: Beast of Fang Rock*

2425 *The Spectre of Lanyon Moor*

2426 *Matrix*

2427 *Leth-St: The Schizoid Earth*

2428 *Illegal Alien* (p211). The Nazis occupied Jersey on 1st May, 1940.

2429 *TW: Sleeper*

2430 *Leth-St: "The Last Duty".* Younghusband lived, in real life, 1921-2016. The *Lethbridge-Stewart* range folds

itself into her memoirs (*One Woman's War*, 2011, and *Eileen's War*, 2016), also published by Candy Jar Books.

2431 *Leth-St: "The Lock-In"*

2432 Dating *The Nemonite Invasion* (BBC *DW* audiobook #3) - The date is given, and the story takes place at the start of the Dunkirk evacuation, which took place from 26th May to 4th June, 1940.

2433 Dating *Timewyrm: Exodus* (NA #2) - The story coincides with the historical evacuation of Dunkirk, and the Doctor exorcises the Timewyrm from Hitler's mind shortly prior to that.

2434 Dating *DEyes: Fugitives* (BF *DEyes* #1.2) - The Doctor says that it's "the 29th of May, 1940", during the evacuation of Dunkirk. He and Molly land near the East pier housing the HMS *Grenade*, which was sunk by German divebombers on the same day.

2435 *Just War*

2436 *The Ultimate Adventure*. Churchill delivered the speech on 4th June, 1940.

2437 *The Nemonite Invasion*

2438 *Resistance*, in which it's said that his "third birthday" occurs in the summer of 1943.

2439 *Grimm Reality*

2440 *The Turing Test* (p59).

2441 Details given of the HMS *Capulet* are at odds with the historical record. In real life, a German U-boat sank the British motor tanker HMS *Capulet* in the Atlantic Ocean on 2nd May, 1941. In *Phantoms of the Deep*, the *Capulet* goes down in the Pacific Ocean (where the Mariana Trench is located) following pursuit (according to a captain's log entry dated to 7th July, 1940) of a Japanese destroyer.

2442 Dating *Illegal Alien* (PDA #5) - Tomorrow's date, "14 November 1940" is given (p20).

Public Schools Middleweight Cup during his last year at Fettes.[2418] Lethbridge-Stewart and John Sudbury went to the same school.[2419]

When a young Alistair Gordon Lethbridge-Stewart told his father that he was going to join the army, the senior Lethbridge-Stewart said, "In life, as on the field of battle, there are old soldiers and there are bold soldiers, but there are very few old, bold soldiers."[2420] Alistair Lethbridge-Stewart and his childhood friend Raymond Phillips visited Redgate Smithy at Trethevy Quoit in the early 40s.[2421]

> = Alistair Gordon Lethbridge-Stewart had to abandon his hope of joining the Air Force, as he suffered from too much vertigo.[2422]

1940

Barbara Wright, a companion of the first Doctor, was born in 1940 and lived in Bedfordshire for a time.[2423] Many records pertaining to Fang Rock were lost in 1940, when an air attack leveled Trinity House in London.[2424] Radar equipment on Lanyon Moor was subject to mysterious interference, and the men stationed there suffered from mental illnesses.[2425]

> (=) On the Earth of the Dark Matrix, Britain had to use its army to fight civil disorder, not Hitler. The Americans intervened, and took control of the United Kingdom before defeating Hitler.[2426]

> = In Spring 1940, on In-Between Earth, unidentified spaceships attacked humanity by dropping large objects from the stratosphere. Alastair (sic) Lethbridge-Stewart's parents died, and his brother James didn't return from a battle at Helsinki.[2427]

The Nazis occupied Jersey. Colonel Schott found a dormant Cyberman army in the Le Mur engineering factory.[2428] **The British military sealed off a mineshaft just outside Cardiff in the 1940s, and in future used it to store nuclear weapons.**[2429]

Eileen Younghusband, a filter officer in the Women's Auxiliary Air Force, signed the Official Secrets Act in 1940.[2430] Pearl Hammond witnessed fighting in the Pyrenees, including a strange mist that appeared on a harvest moon, and caused weapons to misfire.[2431]

The Miracle of Dunkirk

1940 (26th May) - THE NEMONITE INVASION[2432] ->

Aliens terraformed the homeworld of the leech-like Nemonites and culled them. One Nemonite fled into space in a crystalline sphere, and sought to initiate a breeding cycle that would create millions of offspring – enough to possess the population of an entire planet.

The tenth Doctor and Donna were in hot pursuit of the rogue and arrived at Dover Castle, the tunnels of which contained a British navy centre under the command of Vice Admiral Bertram Ramsay. The Nemonite spawned thousands of offspring that were contained aboard a British submarine. A Naval rating named Fossbrook – whom Donna had become enamoured with – sacrificed himself to blow up the vessel.

British forces were trapped at Dunkirk, but Ramsay was reluctant to initiate Operation Dynamo (a strategy for saving the troops using civilian vessels) for fear of the blow to morale if the civilians involved were killed. At the Doctor's recommendation, Ramsay initiated the operation.

1940 (May) - TIMEWYRM: EXODUS[2433] -> Hitler, still emboldened by the Timewyrm within him, became jubilant as his armies scored many successes. German forces had reached Abbeville in France. At Hitler's command post of Felsennest, the seventh Doctor and Ace exorcised the Timewyrm from Hitler's mind. This left Hitler weakened, and the Doctor persuaded him to halt the German advance on Dunkirk. This enabled the Miracle of Dunkirk – the rescue of hundreds of thousands of British and French soldiers in a makeshift fleet of civilian boats – to occur and mark a turning point of the war.

> (=) 1940 (29th May) - DEyes: FUGITIVES[2434] -> Stymied in their efforts to reach Gallifrey, the eighth Doctor and Molly O'Sullivan briefly visited Dunkirk during the evacuation. They quickly departed, with the Daleks hot on their tail...

The seventh Doctor remembered being at Dunkirk during the evacuation.[2435] The Doctor met Winston Churchill after Dunkirk, and inspired him to make his famous "We will fight them on the beaches..." speech.[2436]

In early June, Donna visited Fossbook's mother, and delivered a letter that he'd written to her.[2437] Polly Wright's oldest brother was born in the summer of 1940.[2438]

@ The eighth Doctor visited Lancashire in the forties and met aliens from Antares 5.[2439] He failed to join the RAF, unable to prove he was a British subject. He left England, spending two years in South America and Africa.[2440]

The HMS *Capulet* sank during World War II, and fell into the Mariana Trench. The alien spaceship trapped there assessed the psychic potential of Midshipman Jack Hodges, and put him into stasis while it awaited the arrival of more humans.[2441]

1940 - ILLEGAL ALIEN[2442] - > A time-travelling Cyberman, injured by a Luftwaffe bomb in London, instinctively sought blood plasma to heal its damaged

components. It began a murder campaign and gained a reputation as "the Limehouse Lurker". The seventh Doctor and Ace destroyed it.

The time travellers discovered that George Limb, a former Foreign Office secretary, had given Cyber-technology to both the Allies and the Nazis as a means of sparking a technology race. Limb escaped using a Cybermen time machine, but the Doctor's intervention eradicated much of the errant Cyber-technology, plus destroyed the Nazi Cyber-conversion base in Jersey. However, a pump house containing hundreds of Cybermen cocoons survived, and was discovered by private detective Cody McBride.

= c 1940 - FP: WARLORDS OF UTOPIA[2443] **->**
While exploring parallel Romes, Scriptor crossed a great Divide between universes. He arrived in a new order of realities, ones where Hitler was winning World War II. On one of these worlds, Germania V, he met and slept with a parallel version of his wife Angela, and helped the British army fight SS officers parachuting in to kidnap the British royal family.

Returning across the Divide, Scriptor developed a plan to liberate all these Nazi Earths. Few differences existed between these realities (the point of divergence came in 1918, at the end of World War I), and

the Romans quickly alighted on winning strategies. The plan failed for the first time on Germania LXI; Scriptor soon met Abschrift – one of the Cwejen – and realised that the Nazi worlds were co-ordinating with one another.

There was also a "Hitler wins" Earth – the one perfect iteration of the idea. The Hitler of that world had set up a Council of Hitlers from other parallels. These Nazis were using atomic weapons to devastate Britain. The tide was turning across the Nazi worlds, and Scriptor was captured.

(=) 1940 - 1963: FANFARE FOR THE COMMON MEN[2444] **->** The TARDIS briefly arrived in 1940 because its target year, 1957, was walled off behind a time lock. The fifth Doctor conceded defeat and returned to 1963.

The Blitz

The German bombing attacks on Britain began 7th September, 1940, and ended 11th May, 1941.

The "original" Jack Harkness – an American pilot whose name would be adopted by a Time Agent in

---

2443 Dating *FP: Warlords of Utopia* (FP novel #3) - Scriptor arrived on the first Nazi Earth in time to hear the original broadcast of Churchill's "Fight them on the beaches" speech, which was delivered 8th June, 1940.
2444 Dating *1963: Fanfare for the Common Men* (BF #178) - The Doctor names the year, and it's during the Blitz (which lasted September 1940 to May 1941).
2445 *TW: Captain Jack Harkness.* The Battle of Britain lasted 10th July to 31st October, 1940.
2446 *J&L S3: Chronoclasm*
2447 *Just War.* The date is given as 1941 (p4), but that is a mistake and should read 1940.
2448 *The Lazarus Experiment.* Lazarus names the year as 1940. The Doctor refers to having seen the horrors of the Blitz, which he did in *The Empty Child/The Doctor Dances,* as well as in a number of the novels.
2449 *The Twelfth Doctor Year One:* "The Hyperion Empire"
2450 *Worlds DW: The Reesinger Process*
2451 *CM S3: The Concrete Cage*
2452 *The Alchemists*
2453 *CM S1: The Pelage Project*
2454 *DotD: Hunters of Earth*
2455 Dating "The Doctor and the Nurse" (IDW Vol. 4 #3-4) - As a caption indicates, the TARDIS has arrived on the right place and day, but entirely the wrong year.
2456 "Thirty years" before *The Web of Fear. Leth-St: Night of the Intelligence* (ch11) says this happened when Anne Travers is "barely two", so it's probably late 1940.

2457 *CM S2: The Fifth Citadel*
2458 Dating *FP: Spinning Jenny* (FP novel #11) – The month and year are given (ch17).
2459 "A few months" before *Victory of the Daleks,* and presumably after Dunkirk, or Churchill would have deployed the Ironsides then. The Daleks seen here seem to be survivors from the events of *Journey's End.* (The Doctor: "When we last met, you were at the end of your rope, finished." Dalek: "One ship survived." The Doctor: "And you fell back through time, crippled, dying.") In the Monster File on the DVD extras, writer Mark Gatiss states that "The last three Daleks who survived Davros and the Reality Bomb have arrived back in 1940".
2460 "A month" before *Victory of the Daleks.*
2461 *SJA: The Mark of the Berserker*
2462 Dating *Victory of the Daleks* (X5.3) - No year given. The story takes place during the Blitz (September 1940 to May 1941) and there's reference to St Paul's being hit – it was never hit in real life, but there was a famous near-miss that destroyed much of the surrounding area on 29th December. This might be when the story is set, but there's no evidence of it being around Christmas. When we see Bracewell and Churchill again, in *The Pandorica Opens,* the caption tells us it is 1941.
2463 *Victory of the Daleks, A Good Man Goes to War.*
2464 *Quicksilver*
2465 *Criss-Cross*
2466 *The Shield of the Jotuun*

1941 – killed twenty-six opponents during the Battle of Britain.[2445] At 8:47 pm on 12th October, 1940, a bomb destroyed a hotel next to the New Regency Theatre, which as a consequence was torn down. Elliot Payne linked his location in the Victorian Era to the very minute that the bomb fell, destroying a group of Time Eaters (and evidently himself) when it detonated.[2446]

The seventh Doctor and Bernice arrived in Guernsey in December 1940. Bernice went undercover as Celia Doras, the daughter of a local landlady.[2447] **As a child, Richard Lazarus was caught up in the Blitz and became obsessed with immortality.**[2448]

Clara Oswald's grandmother hid in the London Underground tunnels during the Blitz.[2449] The Reesinger Estate took heavy damage during the Blitz.[2450] A layer of subterranean metallic ore had long been a source of madness in St Anton's, as it created an imbalance of brain fluids by focusing the moon's gravitational energy. The Blitz cracked the ore layer, intensifying the effect. Mrs Jeffries caught Roderick Purton purloining items, and he bludgeoned her to death with an antique clock.[2451]

The first Doctor and Susan found themselves in the London Blitz.[2452] Ken Temple, a future industrialist, lost his entire family during the Blitz while he was off at sea.[2453] Mayfield Terrace, a street in London, took heavy damage during the Blitz. An extraterrestrial weapon designed to agitate the local population – a prelude to an invasion – became entombed there, and remained inert until 1963.[2444]

1940 (17th October) - "The Doctor and the Nurse"[2445] -> The TARDIS landed during the Blitz, having misfired in an attempt to skip ahead a few hours in 1814. The eleventh Doctor and Rory saved the spy and future author Ian Fleming from fallen rubble and an undetonated German bomb, and Rory wound up inspiring the creation of James Bond.

Needing funds, **Professor Travers sold one of the Great Intelligence's yeti to a collector,** Emil **Julius Silverstein.**[2446] When an invasion looked inevitable, four citadels were constructed under London so that operations could continue in secret if Germany prevailed.[2447]

1940 (December) - FP: SPINNING JENNY[2448] -> Spinning Jenny was thought to be either a Loa of Vengeance or of Democracy – two concepts fighting for supremacy in World War II, as exemplified by German bombs falling upon Manchester. Elizabeth Howkins, now in her eighties, had become more adept at ritualistic time travel and visited this year from 1854. Cousin Isabella's secret backer – a woman endowed with power, whom Howkins' shadows were inclined to obey – tried to recruit Howkins to help restore Faction Paradox. Howkins declined, and left to reunite with her husband. The unidentified woman used James Braddock's enhanced biodata to open a portal and take her leave.

A single Dalek ship had fallen back in time following the Reality Bomb gambit in 2009. The few Daleks aboard needed to draw the Doctor out of hiding, and fashioned an independent-thinking android: Professor Edwin Bracewell. He presented the Daleks to Churchill as his own inventions: the "Ironsides", war machines powerful enough to change the course of the war.[2459] Churchill had concerns about the Ironsides and telephoned the Doctor, requesting his presence.[2460] Park Vale barracks was hit by a German bomb in December 1940, burying the Berserker pendant there.[2461]

1940 (end of December) - VICTORY OF THE DALEKS[2462] -> The eleventh Doctor and Amy responded to a summons from the Doctor's old friend Winston Churchill. It was a month since Churchill phoned the Doctor, and in that time he'd come to see the advantages of Bracewell's machine soldiers: the Ironsides. The Doctor was horrified to learn that the Ironsides were actually Daleks – they had obtained the final remaining Dalek Progenitor, but were not genetically pure enough to activate it. The Doctor's identification of his foes as Daleks triggered the Progenitor, and it spawned "a new Dalek paradigm": five new, genetically pure Daleks with the designated functions of Scientist, Strategist, Drone, Eternal and Supreme. These Daleks exterminated the impure Daleks, and threatened to destroy the Earth with an Oblivion Continuum planted in Bracewell. The Doctor deactivated the Continuum, but the Daleks escaped.

Bracewell's knowledge temporarily enabled a few British airplanes to become space-worthy and fight the Daleks. The Doctor later took the aircraft through time to help rescue Amy from Demons Run.[2463]

Constance Clarke

Constance met her future husband, Henry Clarke, when he was a dashing sub-lieutenant, straight from university.[2464] Constance Clarke joined Bletchley Park in 1940, and was on duty the night Alan Turing and his colleagues made a breakthrough in their cryptography efforts in Spring 1941.[2465] Constance's great-uncle Jasper lived alone in the country, spending his days talking to his dog and shooting rabbits out of his breakfast room window.[2466]

1941

The birth of Allison Williams, a future member of Counter-Measures, was difficult and left her mother unable to have more children.[2467] In 1941, the Doctor was present when a group of Alpha Centauri were stranded in Shanghai and panicked.[2468] Lydia Childs of Torchwood died in 1941.[2469] Dr Charles Quinn of Torchwood was killed during an air raid in World War II.[2470] Eileen Le Croissette joined the air force in 1941. She went to a private showing of *Metropolis* in Berlin, on the same day she was almost arrested for impersonating a Nazi guard.[2471]

The Lone Centurion dragged the Pandorica free from a warehouse hit by incendiary devices during the Blitz. This was his last recorded appearance.[2472] The Doctor occasionally visited his married friends, the painters Diego Rivera and Frida Kahlo, after a strange incident involving them in 1941.[2473]

Thomas Erasmus Flanagan, age eight, was evacuated to Cardiff in 1941. He never saw his mother or sister again, and momentarily got lost at the railway station. He was adopted, and lived out his life in Cardiff.[2474]

1941 (2nd January) - TW: TRACE MEMORY[2475] -> The time-jumping Michael Bellini visited the day a German bomb destroyed his childhood home, killing his mother.

Aviatrix Amy Johnson vanished after her plane crashed. The Celestial Toymaker had kidnapped her.[2476]

1941 (5th January) - "A Wing and a Prayer"[2477] -> History dictated that aviator Amy Johnson would drown in the Thames during a ferry flight, but as her body was never recovered, the eleventh Doctor and Amy secretly rescued her. They arranged for Johnson to continue her sky travels on an alien planet.

1941 - THE PANDORICA OPENS[2478] -> The painting *The Pandorica Opens* was found in an attic in France. Professor Bracewell showed Churchill the painting, and Churchill telephoned the Doctor about it. The TARDIS redirected the call so that Churchill spoke to River Song, who was at Stormcage prison in the future.

1941 (Saturday, 20th January) -> TW: CAPTAIN JACK HARKNESS[2479] -> Captain Jack and Toshiko Sato arrived from the twenty-first century, having entered a temporal shift in the Ritz, a Cardiff dance hall. They met an American pilot named Captain Jack Harkness – the man whose identity "our" Jack stole while operating as a con man – and who was due to die the following day. Jack befriended his namesake before the Rift re-opened, and he and Tosh returned home.

The original Jack Harkness died on 21st January. His squadron was out on a training mission, and two formations of Messerschmitts surprised them. The

2467 *CM S3: The Forgotten Village*
2468 *The Shadow of Weng-Chiang* (p23).
2469 From *The Torchwood Archives* (BBC)
2470 Torchwood.org.uk
2471 *Leth-St: The Flaming Soldier* (chs. 1, 5).
2472 *The Big Bang*; the year is named as 1941.
2473 *The Tenth Doctor Year One*: "Revolutions of Terror"
2474 *TW: Ghost Machine*
2475 Dating *TW: Trace Memory* (TW novel #5) - The exact day is given, p30.
2476 *Divided Loyalties* (p46). It's possible that the eleventh Doctor's revision to history in "A Wing and a Prayer" deprives the Toymaker of the opportunity to capture Johnson.
2477 Dating "A Wing and a Prayer" (DWM #462-464) - Johnson died on 5th January, 1941.
2478 Dating *The Pandorica Opens* (X5.12) - The date is given in a caption. No explanation is given for why Bracewell, who seemingly went into hiding in fear of being deactivated (*Victory of the Daleks*) is working for Churchill again. Bracewell's black glove, indicating the hand he lost in *Victory of the Daleks*, proves that *The Pandorica Opens* comes after that story.
2479 Dating *TW: Captain Jack Harkness* (TW 1.12) - The story takes place on 20th January, 1941 (as is stipulated

on the dance hall poster), and the original Jack Harkness is fated to die the following day.
2480 *The Empty Child*
2481 *TW: Captain Jack Harkness*
2482 Dating *The Empty Child/The Doctor Dances* (X1.9-1.10) - The date is repeatedly given as 1941. Jack says it's the "height of the Blitz", which ended 16th May.

In *TW: Everything Changes*, military records claim that Captain Jack Harkness failed to report for duty on 21st January and was presumed dead. Some fans and commentators have adopted this date for *The Empty Child* two-parter, under the assumption that Jack was "presumed dead" because he left on that date with the Doctor and Rose. However, it's stipulated in *TW: Captain Jack Harkness* that the original Captain Jack Harkness died on 21st January, and "our" Jack admits that he falsified the military's records to cover up the man's death. The reference to Harkness "failing to report for duty", then, must refer to the genuine article, not "our" Jack.

It is unlikely that "our" Jack would start passing as "Jack Harkness" before the original has died; nor does it ring true that he takes the name, experiences the events of *The Empty Child/The Doctor Dances* and departs in the TARDIS all in a twenty-four hour period. Moreover, *The Empty Child* states that the Doctor and

Captain destroyed three of the enemy, but was hit and couldn't bail out because his plane was on fire.

… and, earlier in "our" Jack's timeline, he arrived in 1941 to perpetrate a con job.[2480] He had never met the original Jack Harkness, but adopted his name after falsifying the records.[2481]

Jack Harkness Joins the TARDIS

1941 - THE EMPTY CHILD / THE DOCTOR DANCES[2482] -> Captain Jack Harkness, a con-artist and former Time Agent from the fiftieth century, attempted to scam the ninth Doctor and Rose by crashing a Chula ambulance capsule into London. The capsule dispatched sub-atomic nanogenes that attempted to heal a gas-masked boy who'd been killed by a German bomb. The nanogenes were unfamiliar with human physiology and concluded that the masked, torn-up child was indicative of the human race. The child revived as a hollow, gas mask-wearing individual who was looking for his mummy.

The Doctor and Rose arrived "a few weeks, maybe a month" afterwards. The nanogenes had become airborne and started restructuring people into gas mask-wearing figures *en masse*. Jack admitted his con job to the Doctor and Rose, and the three of them deduced that a young woman named Nancy was the child's mother. The nanogenes recognised Nancy as such and examined her, creating a more suitable template of the human form. The affected humans were restored, and the Doctor programmed the nanogenes to deactivate. Jack took up travel with the Doctor and Rose.

1941 (1st-6th March) - JUST WAR[2483] -> The seventh Doctor, Bernice, Roz and Chris investigated reports of a new Nazi weapon. Roz and Chris joined the Scientific Intelligence Division to find out what the British knew, and Bernice went undercover in Guernsey. The German scientist Hartung had built two radar-invisible planes, *Hugin* and *Munin,* which he had started developing before the British had even invented radar. *Hugin* exploded on a test flight, killing Hartung. Bernice was captured and tortured, but Roz blew up *Munin,* denying it to the Nazis.

River Song and Helen Sinclair smashed an antique stained glass window to acquire a key to the Revelation Sect's holdings. As it was May 1941, during the Blitz, a bomb obliterated all trace of their vandalism.[2484]

1941 (7th June) - SJA: LOST IN TIME[2485] -> Clyde Langer was transported back in time to obtain a piece of chronosteel discovered beneath the Rhineland. Hitler believed the item was Thor's Hammer, an object of great power. A team of Germans tried to use the chronosteel to block a radar system in the English village of Little Maulding – the first step of a German invasion that would catch the English by surprise. A local boy, George Woods, aided Clyde in alerting the authorities, and the German force was captured. Clyde returned to 2010 with the chronosteel.

c 1941 (Friday to Saturday) - TW: THE DYING ROOM[2486] -> Oberfuhrer Hans Grau of the SS reined in Germany's Institute of Alien Technology, renaming it Project Hermod. Meanwhile, M LeDuc, a Torchwood operative, went undercover in Nazi-occupied Paris with Gabriel, a human-looking alien. Gabriel's innate ability to manipulate genetics caused increasing numbers of Aryan troopers to fatally mutate in accordance with their sins. Grau also perished, after LeDuc tricked him into giving away Project Hermod's name and location. Gabriel's contagion would eventually kill five thousand German soldiers. LeDuc recruited a double agent, Madame Berber, into Torchwood's ranks.

1941 (7th August) - TW: "Overture"[2487] -> An alien race had seeded sleeper agents onto Earth – a means of

---

Rose don't turn up until "a few weeks" or perhaps "a month" after the alien probe has landed. "Our" Jack presumably passes as "Captain Jack Harkness" during that time, as he has no way of knowing when the targets of his con-job – the Doctor and Rose – will arrive.

The most likely scenario, then, is that the original Jack Harkness dies on 21st January, the time-travelling con man (whose real name – for all we know – might well be "Jack") adopts his identity shortly thereafter, the con man gets cosy with the soldiers seen in *The Empty Child* and the Doctor and Rose land "a few weeks" or "a month" later – meaning February 1941 is the most probable time for this story to occur.

The *Torchwood* website says that Captain Jack disappeared on 5th January, which doesn't fit what we're told on screen.

2483 Dating *Just War* (NA #46) - The main action of the book starts on "the morning of 1 March 1941" (p5).

2484 *DC 3: The Doomsday Chronometer*

2485 Dating *SJA: Lost in Time* (SJA 4.5) - The precise date is given.

2486 Dating *TW: The Dying Room* (BF *TW* #18) - The blurb says it's "Paris, 1940s". The German occupation of France happened 22nd June, 1940 to 25th August, 1944; *The Dying Room* seems to happen during its early days (Berber: "So many are fleeing the city, when the Germans allow them to leave"). "Yesterday morning" happened on a Friday.

2487 Dating *TW: "Overture"* (*TWM* #25) - The day is given.

monitoring the human race prior to it developing a space empire. The sleeper agents were activated upon hearing a specific song; Captain Jack's future self in 2607 sent back a sonic failsafe that he thought would safely deactivate the agents, but it killed them instead.

1941 (18th August) - THE TWILIGHT STREETS[2488]

-> Torchwood Cardiff was now composed of Dr Matilda B Brennan, Llinos King, Gregory Phillip Bishop, Jack Harkness and a Welshman named Rhydian. To test Jack, Bilis Manger disrupted the group's operations – Jack killed an enthralled Tilda Brennan, and failed to save Bishop, his lover, from being incinerated. The Hub was currently accessed by a warehouse; in future, this would become a pizza parlour.

1941 (Autumn) - CHURCHILL: HOUNDED[2489] ->

Major Wheatley of MI-5 worried that Winston Chuchill's fits of depression, his "black moods", might derail Churchill's leadership ability during the war. Wheatley embarked upon a scheme to control Churchill via a primal spirit from the Indian sub-continent that manifested as a huge black dog, but Churchill's secretary, Hetty Warner, summoned the eleventh Doctor with a letter addressed to "The Doctor, the TARDIS, somewhere". The dog killed Wheatley, but the Doctor cobbled together a device that would manifest Churchill's despair as a rival canine. Warner died trying to implement the plan. When Churchill's resolve kept him from generating a black dog, the Doctor created one from his own dark side, and his beast tore the Indian black dog to pieces.

Constance Clark Dies, for a Time

c 1941 - STATIC[2490] -> At the village of Abbey Marston, the RAF discovered a stone circle capable of snatching people from the moment of their deaths. Unknown parties

had engineered the circle to generate duplicate bodies for the minds of the deceased, then return their original forms to avert a paradox. The RAF used the circle to glean intelligence from fallen soldiers, but shut down the operation when the sixth Doctor and Constance stopped bodiless entities – the Static – from hijacking the resurrection process and overrunning Earth.

While stopping the Static, Constance perished in a fire. The Doctor facilitated her return to life by tasking a survivor, Percy Till, with standing guard over the circle for four decades.

1941 (Winter) - "Instruments of War"[2491] -> In the Sahara, members of the Eighth Sontaran Battle Fleet allied with Tuareg tribesmen affiliated with the Nazis, to find the long-lost Sontaran Warsong: a world engine capable of weaponising entire planets. A Rutan spy disguised as Reich-hero Heinz Bruckner found and activated the Warsong. The twelfth Doctor and Clara, as aided by Field Marshal Erwin Rommel, phoned Winston Churchhill to send in an air strike – a time-buying tactic while the Doctor disrupted the Warsong's harmonics and destroyed it. The Doctor and Clara left, knowing that Rommel would be compelled to commit suicide after the failure of Operation Valkyrie.

Tobias Kinsella recruited Edward Travers to work for the Fourth Operational Corps in November 1941. Travers' children, Anne and Alun, consequently spent a great deal of time with their uncle and aunt, Sebastian and Kathleen Goff.[2492]

1941 (2nd November) - "The Way of All Flesh"[2493]

-> The eighth Doctor and Izzy arrived in Mexico during the Day of the Dead festival. While the Doctor tracked a strange energy reading, Izzy was run over and rescued by the artist Frida Kahlo. The ghost of Frida's father appeared.

2488 Dating *TW: The Twilight Streets* (*TW* novel #7) - The exact day is given, p17.
2489 Dating *Churchill: Hounded* (*The Churchill Years* #1.2) - Churchill's narration names the year and season. In real life, Churchill described his manic depression as a "black dog".
2490 Dating *Static* (BF #233) - It's during World War II, but the Doctor cautions that it's "a few years too early" for Constance to return to her old life, which she verifies is in "1944".
2491 Dating "Instruments of War" (*DWM* #481-483) - A caption gives the month and year; the Nazis have "encamped for the winter". It's after the *Ark Royal* was sunk, on 14th November, 1941. Operation Valkyrie, a failed effort to kill Hitler, happened in July 1944.
2492 The Haisman Timeline, *Leth-St*: "The Dogs of War",

Leth-St: Night of the Intelligence (ch14).
2493 Dating "The Way of All Flesh" (*DWM* #306, 308-310) - The date is given.
2494 Dating "Me and My Shadow" (*DWM* #318) - The date is given.
2495 Dating "As Time Goes By" (IDW Vol. 3 #13-16) - The Doctor to Amy and Rory: "This is Casablanca in 1941. It's the only way out of Europe to avoid the Nazis, and they should be marching in here any minute." Historically, the British-American North African Campaign to secure Casablanca did occur later, in November 1942.

The Silurians here regard the Doctor as a fairy tale akin to the "Breargan wolfsnake or the venomous sea devil" – not a notion that's supported in any other *Doctor Who* story, especially as his main encounters

The Doctor met the aliens responsible, the Torajenn. Their mistress, Susini of the Wasting Wall, was a necrotist – she created art from the death of the innocent. The Torajenn wanted to have their natural bodies restored using her technology. The Torajenn were vulnerable to loud sounds, and Frida and Izzy set off fireworks to prevent them from killing the revellers. The Doctor destroyed them, but aliens arrived and kidnapped Izzy.

1941 (November) - "Me and My Shadow"[2494] -> Fey Truscott-Sade was fighting Nazis in Austria, using her "Feyde" powers as a last resort, when she was summoned by the eighth Doctor to help find Izzy.

1941 - "As Time Goes By"[2495] -> The eleventh Doctor, Amy and Rory visited Casablanca to buy the Doctor a new fez, and uncovered a Silurian plot to overly hydrate the air, then collapse the city with an earthquake and generate a tidal wave to wipe out all life on Earth's surface. The Doctor ended the plan, and warned the Silurians in question not to venture back onto Earth's surface unless they desired peace.

1941 - NAofBENNY V2: THE VAULTS OF OSIRIS[2496] -> The seventh Doctor and Ace attempted to retrieve the secondary Eye of Horus from Egypt before German soldiers claimed it for the Fuhrer. Contact with the Eye flung the Doctor back to ancient Egypt, even as the TARDIS – operating to pre-programmed coordinates – took Ace to the twenty-seventh century Mars to collect Bernice Summerfield. The soldiers made off with the Eye.

Toshiko Sato's grandfather stayed in London after the attack on Pearl Harbor, but was persecuted for his ethnicity.[2497] Basement sections D-3 and D-4 of the Torchwood Hub were built in 1941 and 1942, under cover of the work being part of Britain's war effort.[2498]

1941 (Christmas) - THE DOCTOR, THE WIDOW AND THE WARDROBE[2499] -> Madge Arwell's husband, Reg, was killed in action over the Channel. She decided to postpone telling their children, Lily and Cyril, about it until after Christmas so as not to ruin the holiday. They evacuated to a house owned by their Uncle Digby in Dorset – the eleventh Doctor had got there before them, and prepared the place to give the children the perfect Christmas. Part of this involved wrapping up a dimensional portal to a planet that was a winter wonderland. Cyril opened his present early, and fell through to the year 5345. The Doctor and Lily went after him, and Madge soon followed.

Using her memories of home, Madge navigated the Time Vortex and returned the Doctor and her family back to England. This acted as a beacon for her husband's bomber, which arrived outside Uncle Digby's house in time for the family to celebrate Christmas.

1941 (December) to 1942 (March to 27th April) - LETH-ST: THE FLAMING SOLDIER[2500] -> Gulliver Base was built in Bratton, Wiltshire to study the *Shrike* (a.k.a. "the Miracle") – a recovered spaceship belonging to the alien pirates, the Flight. Section Officer Eileen Le Croissette, as Guillver's filter officer, met Professor Edward Travers when he crafted Orville, a robotic pilot for the Miracle. The Flight reclaimed the *Shrike*, but a German air raid compelled them to time-jump forward some decades. To Le Croissette's astonishment, a man emerged from a time portal – her future friend, Major James Randall – and cried out "Eileen" before dying. She retained the three golden control coins in his possession.

In future, the Duke Guest House hotel was built on the site of Gulliver Base. The RAF tasked Le Croissette, as the hotel's manager, with keeping watch over the area.

---

with them are yet to come in the 1970s (*Doctor Who and the Silurians, The Sea Devils*), 2020 (*The Hungry Earth/Cold Blood*), and circa 2084 (*Warriors of the Deep*).
2496 Dating *NAofBenny* V2: *The Vaults of Osiris* (*NAofBenny* #2.2) - The year is given. The secondary Eye of Horus appeared in *Pyramids of Mars*.
2497 *TW: Captain Jack Harkness*. Pearl Harbor was attacked on 7th December, 1941.
2498 *TW: Trace Memory*
2499 Dating *The Doctor, the Widow and the Wardrobe* (X7.0) - A caption says Reg is shot down "three years later" than the day Madge first met the Doctor. The telegram she receives states that he was shot down on

the "20th". In *The Doctor: His Lives and Times* (p233), the same telegram specifies that Captain Arwell went missing during an air operation the night of 18/19th Dec 1941". A second caption states that the Arwells arrive at Uncle Digby's house on "Christmas Eve". Madge later tells Droxil she is from "1941".
2500 Dating *Leth-St: The Flaming Soldier* (*Leth-St* novella #2) - The relevant months are repeatedly named. The action ends on "twenty-seventh of April, 1942" (ch9) with the Bath Blitz, which killed more than four hundred people.

1942

Ben Jackson and Polly Wright, companions of the first and second Doctors, were both born in 1942. The Jackson family lived near a brewery.[2501] Polly had four brothers, and was the second-born in her family.[2502] She was from Chelsea.[2503]

Gerald Carter of Torchwood died in 1942.[2504] The husband of Henrietta Goodhart, a future friend of Wilf Mott, was killed during the bombing of Singapore. They had been married for only three days.[2505] **The immortal Captain Jack served in the Second World War.**[2506] **The German battleship *Bismarck* was sunk.**[2507] **The Doctor once claimed to have been wounded at El-Alamein in Egypt.**[2508] He drove an ambulance at El Alamein and was registered as Dr John Smith, 55583.[2509] The Doctor visited Buda Castle in 1942, when it served as a military hospital.[2510]

Captain Anthony Rogers was part of an early space experiment, possibly as far back as 1942. He was hard-wired into satellite technology that was later sold to the Deselby Matango company, and remained in such a state for centuries.[2511]

@ The eighth Doctor rented a flat in Bloomsbury, and lived there for almost a decade from 1942.[2512] The Star of Solitude was stolen from a merchant on Cornucopia, and came to reside in a ThiefCorp vault.[2513]

Ralf Klein, a spy for the British, became attached to Kurt Schalk's Persuasion machine project and spent three years relaying information back to England. Mutter, his lover and a radio room worker, aided his endeavours.[2514] The Davros clone Falkus came of age, and began to secretly govern the planet Azimuth. The authorities brought about peace by erasing the past – it became illegal to recount anything that took place during the occupation, or to even speak the word "Dalek".[2515]

2501 According to a plot synopsis issued on 20th May, 1966, Ben and Polly are both "24" at the time of *The Smugglers*. Michael Craze (Ben) was then 24, Anneke Wills (Polly) was 23. The document also gave Polly's surname as "Wright", which is never used on screen, but is mentioned in the Missing Adventure *Invasion of the Cat-People*. In the same book, Polly says she was brought up in Devon. A science article in *The Doctor: His Lives and Times* (p22) nudges Polly to being slightly older, claiming she was age "25" when she worked for Professor Brett (*The War Machines*).

In *The War Machines*, Kitty, the manageress of the Inferno nightclub, remarks that they rarely get anyone "over twenty" into the club, which might suggest that Ben and Polly are a little younger. Mind, neither of them look younger than twenty, and *The Murder Game* reaffirms their birth year as 1942. *Resistance* concurs that Polly was born before 1944, and *The Forsaken* dates Ben's birth to December 1942.

2502 *Resistance*
2503 *The Night Witches*
2504 Torchwood.org.uk. *The Torchwood Archives* (BBC) claims that Gerald died during the Blitz in January 1941, possibly juxtaposing his fate with the one the website attributes to Charles Quinn.
2505 *Beautiful Chaos* (p105). The first air raid on Singapore occurred on 8th December, 1941, followed by a respite until the prolonged Battle of Singapore (29th December, 1941, to 15th February, 1942).
2506 *Utopia*
2507 The Doctor knows of the *Bismarck* in *Terror of the Zygons*.
2508 *The Sea Devils*. Two World War II battles were fought at El-Alamein, an Egyptian town, in 1942. The first lasted 1st to 27th July. The second, 23rd October to 4th November, saw the Allies forcing the Axis to retreat back to Tunisia.

2509 *Autumn Mist*, *The King of Terror* (p241).
2510 *The Labyrinth of Buda Castle*
2511 *Benny S8: The Tub Full of Cats*, presuming Rogers' claims can be given any credit.
2512 *Endgame* (EDA)
2513 "Seventy years" before "The Cornucopia Caper".
2514 *Daleks Among Us*
2515 "Three years" before *Daleks Among Us*.
2516 The background to *CM S4: New Horizons*.
2517 Dating *The Girl Who Never Was* (BF #103) - The date is given.
2518 Dating *The Forsaken* (BF EA #2.2) - The month and year are given, and the action occurs a "week" after the invasion of Singapore, which capitulated to Japanese forces on 15th February, 1942.
2519 Dating *The Scapegoat* (BF BBC7 #3.5) - The Germans are currently occupying Paris (1940-1944). The Doctor says his regenerative powers won't save him if he's decapitated – this contradicts what occurs to another Time Lord in *The Shadows of Avalon*, but as the Doctor is here in danger of being beheaded for sport, he could just be bluffing to save his current life.
2520 Dating *Mad Dogs and Englishmen* (EDA #52) - The date is given.
2521 Dating *Dethras* (BF 4th Doc #6.4) - The blurb and the participants identify the submarine as originating in World War II. The Doctor and Romana determine that it's the same time zone, as the Zarcarri were active in "the first half of the twenty-first century".
2522 Dating *The Shadow in the Glass* (PDA #41) - The date appears on p217. This contradicts *Timewyrm: Exodus*, which the Doctor says is his first meeting with Hitler.
2523 Dating *Erimem: The Beast of Stalingrad* (Erimem novel #2) - The year is given. It's some "months" (Part One) into the siege of Stalingrad, which lasted 23rd August, 1942 to 2nd February, 1943.

The Nazis discovered Vril – a legendary substance said to power amazing machines, grant eternal life and more – in the Arctic in 1942. The German scientist Hendrich Muller translated inscriptions detailing how to distill Vril, but feared the consequence of the Nazis obtaining such a wonder-liquid. Muller destroyed much of his work and, after the war, fled Germany to Britain.[2516]

1942 (15th January) - THE GIRL WHO NEVER WAS[2517] -> The Japanese laid siege to Singapore, which was defenceless after the Imperial Navy sank the HMS *Repulse* and HMS *Prince of Wales*. The SS *Batavia* was one of the last ships out of the harbour, having been chartered by the smuggler Byron – the ship's contraband included part of Adolf Hitler's private gold supply.

The TARDIS left Charley Pollard on board the *Batavia*, then returned to 2008 when the Cybermen compelled Byron to modify equipment that "translocated" the vessel to the year 500,002. The eighth Doctor, arriving separately from 2008, sent a recall signal that pulled the *Batavia* back to 1942. Byron's grandson, also originating from 2008, forced the reunited Doctor and Charley to transport him to 500,002, so he could plunder the Cyber-ship there.

Japanese torpedoes struck the *Batavia*; its passengers took to lifeboats, but were killed by Japanese mines. The *Batavia*, with a cache of Cybermen in its hold, took to "bouncing" through time and would be seen in 2008. Madeleine Fairweather, a seaman, was the sole survivor of the event. Exposure to Cyber-signals rendered her amnesiac, and she spent the next sixty-five years thinking her name was "Charlotte Pollard". The Byron family took her in, and she later birthed a son.

1942 (mid-February) - THE FORSAKEN[2518] -> Following the Japanese invasion of Singapore, Private James Jackson – the future father of Ben Jackson – was among soldiers who withdrew to the nearby island of Kenga to await evacuation. The Forsaken – an alien that fed on fear – stalked and killed most of Jackson's unit. The second Doctor, accompanied by Ben, Polly and Jamie, quelled his own fear, and made the Forsaken itself afraid of death, causing the fiend to consume itself. James left for Britain to start a family, and thought "Polly" was quite a nice name, should he have a daughter. Ben would be born in December 1942.

c 1942 - THE SCAPEGOAT[2519] -> A group of goat-like Barok aliens had amalgamated themselves into French society. The "scapegoat" of their tribe had crafted a career as "Max Paul, the most assassinated person in the world". Paul would be brutally killed on stage – past performances had seen him cut into pieces, crushed, shot by firing squad, stabbed, strangled, burnt, as well as his being blown up in *Testing, Testing*, and lynched in *Last Post*. After each "death", the Baroks used a quantic reanimator to turn back time and heal Paul's injuries.

The quantic reanimator was losing its potency, and required power from a time machine. The Baroks projected a quantic beam that snagged the TARDIS while the eighth Doctor and Lucie were en route to the Moulin Rouge, 1899. Paul was appearing at the Theatre des Baroques in Paris, and Lucie found herself performing alongside him in *The Executioner's Son* – in which Paul was guillotined. The Doctor finally relocated the Baroks back to their homeworld, which had recovered from the cosmic disaster that occurred there two millennia ago. Paul snuck away with a slinky female Barok.

1942 - MAD DOGS AND ENGLISHMEN[2520] -> In the nineteen-forties, various Oxford academics and writers such as Tyler and Cleavis started meeting as the Smudgelings. All was well until the necromancer William Freer was invited to join – before long, the other members started to mock Tyler's work. The eighth Doctor discovered that Freer had put Tyler in psychic contact with Dogworld, and compelled Tyler to rewrite *The True History of Planets*. The Doctor left for London and met Noel Coward, who was in on Freer's scheme. Later, Coward refused to help some talking kittens from Pussyworld.

c 1942 - DETHRAS[2521] -> After invaders largely wiped out his people, the Zarcarri, the scientist Dethras cracked the secret of hyper-evolution. A strategist, Flague, teleported a British submarine away from Earth during World War II – Dethras turned the crewmen into soldiers that could hyper-evolve to thrive in any environment, then realised the depths of Flague's hunger for vengeance and fled with his charges. The fourth Doctor and the second Romana relocated Dethras and the soldiers to a stable ecology; they would remain undiscovered for a thousand years. Historically, Flague was due to die after crossing the wrong people.

1942 (August) - THE SHADOW IN THE GLASS[2522] -> The sixth Doctor and the Brigadier arrived at a Berlin ballroom party, where the Doctor presented himself to Hitler as "Major Johann Schmidt" of the Reich. The time travellers acquired a sample of Hitler's blood for analysis.

1942 (Winter) - ERIMEM: THE BEAST OF STALINGRAD[2523] -> Erimem and her friend Andrea Hansen jumped through time to the German siege of Stalingrad. The Drofen Horde, fearsome aliens from Monocertos who per galactic treaty fed on the dead, had unlawfully started eating the living as well. Erimem persuaded German and Russian soldiers to shell the Horde's spaceship, destroying it. A survivor of the Horde, Isabella Zemanova, age 22, immigrated to Britain.

1942 - THE NIGHT WITCHES[2524] -> The second Doctor tried to teach Polly, Ben and Jamie to fly the TARDIS, but instead of the Winter Palace in 1782, they found themselves north of Stalingrad during World War II. The 588th Soviet Regiment – an all-female pilots division – prepared to hold the line against the German Panzer advance. Polly looked identical to the Night Witches' best pilot, Tatiana Kregki, and the travelers thwarted Tatiana's efforts to pose as Polly and exit the war. The Doctor's party left, not knowing the imminent battle's outcome.

In November 1942, there were reports of vampires in Romania.[2525] Steinmann oversaw the first test of Germany's V-1 rocket at Peenemünde in December.[2526]

Captain Jack became close to a 17-year-old woman named Estelle Cole, whom he met at the Astoria ballroom a few weeks before Christmas. They pledged to spend the rest of their lives together, but he was posted abroad, and she volunteered to work the land. He would renew their friendship decades later in the twenty-first century, while posing as his own son.[2527] On Christmas Eve of that year, the Nazi Oskar Steinmann oversaw the first test of the "flying bomb" at Peenemunde.[2528]

1943

Liz Shaw, a companion of the third Doctor, was born in Stoke-on-Trent, 1943, to Ruben Shaw.[2529] Margaret Travers died in April 1943.[2530]

In 1943, the toy store owner Mr Sun walked out of his shop in Covent Garden and was never seen again. A week later, the shop was bombed and vanished as if it had never existed. It soon reappeared.[2531] Honoré Lechasseur was posted to England in 1943.[2532] **When Angela Price was a little girl, her grandmother, Emily Morris, gave her the chronosteel key and a newspaper clipping that Sarah Jane had left behind in 1889. Morris tasked her granddaughter with returning the key to Sarah on the date of the clipping: 23rd November, 2010.**[2533]

The Doctor thought novelist Roald Dahl had a "dark sense of humour".[2534]

> (=) The English Empire retook the American colonies, but there was a revolt in 1943. The future American Prime Minister's grandfather led the army that put it down.[2535]

The Seventh Doctor Bests Fenric

1943 (May) - THE CURSE OF FENRIC[2536] -> The seventh Doctor and Ace arrived at a military base on the Yorkshire coast which housed the ULTIMA machine, an early computer. The Russians sent a squad to capture the machine, but the British had anticipated this by booby-trapping it to detonate a lethal toxin, waiting for a time when the Russians became their enemies. Fenric, an ancient being trapped by the Doctor, had engineered the situation to free himself and roused an army of Haemovores to help his bid. The Doctor convinced the Ancient Haemovore to destroy Fenric.

The Doctor visited the German High Command around this time.

2524 Dating *The Night Witches* (BF EA #4.1) – The blurb gets its wires crossed, claiming that it's "1942", but also that the Night Witches (active 1942 to 1945) are defending against the Germans' Operation Barbarossa... which ended 5th December, 1941. The fiction itself is more vague, but suggests it's earlier in the war than later – the oncoming Panzers are the "vanguard" of the German army, and Tatiana shows exhaustion from having flown thirty-two missions (the Witches flew more than eight hundred of those before the war's end). There's mention of snowfall, so it's a cold time of year.
2525 "Six months" before *The Curse of Fenric*.
2526 *Just War* (p252).
2527 *TW: Small Worlds*. Jack's relationship with Estelle lasted weeks, at most, but it was serious enough for them to have a photograph (with Jack in uniform) taken together.
  It isn't specified whether Estelle met Jack while he was working as a con man prior to *The Empty Child*, or while he was immortal and living through the entire twenty-first century. The latter seems more likely for a couple of reasons. Such a heartfelt relationship appears more characteristic of the slightly bitter, emotionally withdrawn and immortal Jack than the carefree con man who knows he's working to the clock and is possibly involved with Algy (*The Empty Child*). Additionally, it's specified that Jack met Estelle "a few weeks before" Christmas, yet it's unlikely that he started using the name "Jack Harkness" until the original died in January 1941 (*TW: Captain Jack Harkness*). Unless Estelle thinks the "son" has a different surname to his father (unlikely, although in truth she never calls him anything other than "Jack"), her meeting him in December 1940 seems suspect.
  An earlier dating is probably preferable, as the odds of Jack and Estelle keeping in touch increase as World War II comes to a conclusion. However, the Torchwood website dates some final correspondence between Jack and Estelle to 1944.
2528 *Just War*
2529 *The Devil Goblins of Neptune* (p10). Actress Caroline John, who played Liz, was born in 1940. Liz's father was named in *P.R.O.B.E.: The Devil of Winterborne*.
2530 The Haisman Timeline
2531 *The Cabinet of Light* (p86).
2532 *The Cabinet of Light* (p17).

Fenric survived his defeat at the seventh Doctor's hands, but was cast, formless, into the outer darkness. He spent years there recovering, and would again confront the Doctor at the dawn of time.[2537]

In the later stages of the war, the painter Amelia Ducat manned an ack-ack gun in Folkestone.[2538] **The UNIT Master kidnapped a V1 from the skies over Cambridgeshire using TOM-TIT.**[2539] Melanie Bush's grandfather died during the war.[2540] A time warp meant a World War II soldier bowled a cricket ball instead of a hand grenade.[2541] A German fighter crashed in the River Tees following a collision with a Q'Dhite spaceship.[2542]

@ 1943 - THE TURING TEST[2543] **->** The eighth Doctor met the British spy/novelist Graham Greene in Sierra Leone, where they encountered pale-skinned humanoids.

Rachel Jensen worked with cryptographer Alan Turing on codebreaking.[2544] The Reverend Foxwell, a friend of the Doctor, was a leading mind at the Naval Cryptographic Section at Bletchley, and worked with Alan Turing.[2545] The Philadelphia Experiment created a rift that interacted with the upper dimensions containing fairy creatures: the Sidhe.[2546]

1943 (26th October) - THE MACROS[2547] **->** American military researchers applied Einstein's unified field theory in an attempt to bend light around the USS Eldridge, hoping to develop invisibility for use in the war. The sixth Doctor and Peri went to Washington, D.C., where they tried, and failed, to retroactively prevent the effort – dubbed the "Philadelphia Experiment" – from proceeding. The Eldridge was caught in a time-looping rift, and would remain stuck there until 2010.

Later, the American government covered up the loss of the USS Eldridge by claiming it had been renamed the Leon and given to Greece.

In November 1943, Lt Commander Henry Clarke left his wife Constance to serve in the war.[2548]

1944

Eileen Le Croissete married Peter Younghusband in 1944.[2549] Olive Hawthorne's grandmother died. The military discharged Olive's father owing to injuries he'd sustained, and he became a dairy foreman.[2550]

In 1944, Belgium, Honoré Lechasseur was caught in a German booby trap in Belgium and severely injured. He spent the next few years in a Dorset hospital, proving his doctors wrong by walking again. He rarely slept, and began having strange visions.[2551]

John Benton's brother Christopher accidentally fell to his death while the two boys were out playing. The boys' father, an army sergeant, was blown to pieces by a grenade in a town in Normandy.[2552] The Doctor visited a set of rooms beneath Cadogan Castle, and there saw Winston Churchill work on Operation Daylight, a covert operation that worked toward the liberation of France.[2553]

2533 SJA: Lost in Time. Date unknown, but actress Rowena Cooper was born in 1935, and so fits the timeframe of being Morris' granddaughter.

2534 The Twelfth Doctor Year One: "The Hyperion Empire". Time unknown, but Dahl lived 1916-1990. His first novel, The Gremins, was published in 1943.

2535 Jubilee

2536 Dating The Curse of Fenric (26.3) - Ace says that the year is "1943". The script stated that the time is "1943 – probably May".

2537 Gods and Monsters

2538 The Seeds of Doom

2539 The Time Monster

2540 Just War

2541 "Forty years" before "The Tides of Time".

2542 "Fifty years" before "Evening's Empire".

2543 Dating The Turing Test (EDA #39) - It's "in January 1943" (p116).

2544 Who Killed Kennedy, taking its cue from the Remembrance of the Daleks novelisation.

2545 The Hollows of Time

2546 Autumn Mist

2547 Dating The Macros (BF LS #1.8) - The day is given. The mythos around the Philadelphia Experiment claim it commenced around 28th October, 1943. Autumn Mist offers an alternative explanation for what happens to the Eldridge - it's possible to reconcile the two if the ship wasn't entirely destroyed in The Macros, enabling the eighth Doctor to find it in a still-dephased state and make use of it in 1944. (Alternatively, see Unfixed Points in Time.) The "cover up" story of the Eldridge mirrors the real-life explanation for what became of the vessel.

2548 "Almost a year" before Quicksilver, and providing the background details to Criss-Cross. The latter story says that Henry Clarke left home in "November".

2549 Leth-St: The Flaming Soldier (ch7).

2550 The film version of Daemons: White Witch of Devil's End says Olive's grandmother passed when Olive was small. The novelisation alternatively pins the same grandmother's passing to "a few years" before Daemons: White Witch of Devil's End: "The Inheritance", when Olive is in her late teens.

2551 The Cabinet of Light

2552 The independent film Wartime, based upon some graffiti that reads "CB + JB 1944".

2553 "About forty years" before Rat Trap. Both Operation Daylight and Cadogan Castle are fictional; D-Day actually commenced, under the codename

wih - Eleonora Albertova Kruger, one of the iterations of Cousin Anastasia, died in Bulgaria in 1944.[2554]

Ian Gilmore's unit perished, save for him and Tom Carver, on a bridge at Arnhem as part of Operation Market Garden.[2555] The Doctor knew Field Marshal Bernard Montgomery, who swore by duffel coats.[2556]

Data collectors in the United Kingdom started conducting Mass Observation during World War II, to find patterns by studying people's eating habits, place of residence and more. The committee formed to slave the information to calculating machines examined life expectancy first, as it was easiest. The group endured for decades, and came to call themselves the Death Watch.[2557]

The UK government initiated a eugenics program to produce an army of super-soldiers. Tobias Kinsella, Charles Waverly, Reginald Kent and Professors Deacon and Barrisford helped initiate the project, and oversaw the distribution of experimental drugs to women having difficulty conceiving. One of the women involved – Waverly's wife, Lady Catherine Waverly – bore a sickly daughter named Emma. Charles Waverly arranged Emma's schooling aboard, and monitored the mutations the program had endowed her with.[2558] One mother enrolled in the program, Mary Culver, told Kinsella that she had miscarried – but had her son, Ray, raised in secret with a distant uncle.

Other children born to the programme demonstrated increasing levels of psychosis in adulthood, and were kept sedated in secretive clinics.[2559]

1944 (February) - RESISTANCE[2560] **->** The second Doctor, Polly, Ben and Jamie became separated in German-occupied France following a scuffle with the Milice (the French Gestapo). Polly found herself face to face with a downed British pilot: her father's brother, Randolph Wright, who was historically slated to die in a German POW camp. She abandoned her friends in a bid to save her uncle from his fate, only to realise that her "uncle" was a spy. The real Randolph Wright had already been captured, and the spy had been using his biographical details as a cover story. A French resistance member shot the spy dead, and Polly was reunited with her friends.

1944 (21st March) - THE CRAWLING TERROR[2561] **->** The Wyrresters, large scorpion-like creatures from the planet Typholchaktas in the Furey-King Maelstrom, reverse-engineered transmat technology left by aliens in the form of stone circles, and transmitted the schematics for a compatible circle to Earth. Codebreakers Alan Turing, Gordon Welchman, Dilly Knox and Dr Judson worked to translate the message. The Nazis did so first, and con-

---

Operation Neptune, on 6th June, 1944.

2554 *FP: The Book of the War*. The joke here is that Anastasia, following her downfall concerning the Thirteen-Day Republic debacle, was triplicated and made to live as three women who, in real life throughout the twentieth century, claimed to be the "lost" Grand Duchess Anastasia. Anastasia's remains were conclusively identified in 2008.

2555 *CM S1: Threshold*. Operation Market Garden was a massive Allied offensive which entailed, among other things, the capture of several bridges between Eindhoven and Nijmegen in the Netherlands. Its failure scotched Allied hopes of ending the war by Christmas 1944. The Germans captured the Arnhem bridge on 20th September of that year. In *The Assassination Games*, Gilmore and Sir Toby Kinsella wrongly refer to Operation Market Garden as being code for the Shoreditch Incident (*Remembrance of the Daleks*).

2556 *Beyond the Ultimate Adventure*. Montgomery used the coat to distinguish himself to his troops. He served in both World Wars, but was promoted to field marshal in September 1944.

2557 *The Last Post*. Mass Observation was a UK social research group from 1937 to the mid-1960s.

2558 *CM S2: Manhunt*

2559 *CM S2: Sins of the Fathers*

2560 Dating *Resistance* (BF CC #3.9) - The back cover says it's "February 1944"; the same month and year appear on Polly's train ticket.

2561 Dating *The Crawling Terror* (NSA #57) - The day is given (chs. 10, 12).

2562 Dating *Criss-Cross* (BF #204) - The Doctor claims that World War II will end "this time next year" (Germany surrendered on 8th May, 1945). It's before Operation Overlord (the Allied code-name for the Normandy invasion, which commenced on 6th June, 1944) and "Stauffenberg" (the attempt to assassinate Hitler on 20th July, 1944). Dr Schwartzman remarks that it's "lovely weather for the time of year". The story's author, Matt Fitton, said: "Spring 1944 is about right, though I'm careful not to be too specific! The opening scenes take place some weeks prior to the arrival of Agents Spark and Tulip - so maybe around Feb/Mar, with the rest of the story late April/May and just before Overlord."

Constance has been at Bletchley Park for "four years", and she "wasn't there long" in "Spring 1941". At Bletchley, the Doctor occupies the former office of John Tiltman – he was promoted to Brigadier and made Deputy Director of the Government Code and Cypher School in 1944. Alan Turing is currently at Hanslope Park developing the Delilah system; work on that started in May 1943 and carried over into 1944, but it wasn't finished in time for use in the war.

The Doctor claims that the TARDIS has been in his Bletchley Park office "these last few months", and Constance treats him as something of a new boy - but he takes some credit for referring engineer Tommy Flowers to codebreakers Max Newman (Turing introduced the two of them in February 1943) and W.T.

structed what they thought was a Wonderweapon – *Die Glocke*, The Bell – as part of Project Chronos while the British did the same in Ringstone as part of Project Big Ben. The German endeavour failed, but Aleister Crowley, working for British counter-intelligence, deduced that the circle required ley line energy.

The activated Ringstone circle brought a Wyrrester through to Earth, but the twelfth Doctor arranged a Luftwaffe bombing run that destroyed the creature and the circle. Researcher Jason Clearfield fell under the thrall of Wyrrester venom, which also gave him near-immortality. He laboured for seventy years to aid the Wyrrester cause.

Constance Clarke Joins the TARDIS

1944 (Spring) - CRISS-CROSS[2562] **->** By now, the Doctor had signed the Official Secrets Act several times. Constance Clarke was the leading WREN at Wavendon House, Bletchley Park. She'd not heard from her husband – Lt Commander Henry Clarke, who worked for Naval intelligence – since the start of the year.

Different races of sentient energy waves engaged in a radiation war that divided the spectrum. One of the war-participants, the Waveform, fled to a lower frequency and became trapped in Earth's radio waves. The Waveform's distress signal immobilized the TARDIS as the Doctor tried to go fishing at a lovely little spot on the Isis. To crack the signal, the Doctor faked credentials and installed himself at Bletchley Park in one of John Tiltman's old offices.

Agents of the Reich inadvertently freed the Waveform, which intended to conquer all radio frequencies and make use of Earth in the radiation war. Aided by Constance, the Doctor used the Park's Colossus machine to create a binding cipher keyed to the Waveform's name, and contained the creature within an alien reconnaissance pod. Constance opted to travel with the Doctor in the restored TARDIS.

The First Elizabeth Klein Goes to Colditz, Gets Tricked into Erasing Her Own History

1944 / (=) 1944 - COLDITZ[2563] **->** The seventh Doctor and Ace were quickly captured when the TARDIS landed at Colditz Castle.

(=) The Doctor realised that one of his interrogators, Klein, had travelled back from a future where the Nazis had developed laser technology from the components of Ace's walkman, won the war by dropping nuclear bombs on New York and Moscow, and secured the TARDIS. Ace had been killed, but the Doctor had given himself a second chance by regenerating and posing as "Schmidt" – a scientist who helped Klein determine how to operate the TARDIS.

In one version of events, the Doctor's manipulations caused Klein to keep Ace alive, averting the errant history. The Doctor and Ace escaped Colditz while Klein, now the only survivor of her timeline, fled to South America. She sheltered with a colony of National Socialists, and requalified for medicine.

Owing to events in 2044, the version of Klein who visited Colditz was erased from history. The Colditz paradox was somehow resolved without her involvement.[2564]

The eleventh Doctor took part in a failed breakout from a World War II POW camp.[2565] **@** The eighth Doctor met Joseph Heller, an American pilot, in a military hospital.[2566]

1944 - DEADLY REUNION[2567] **->** Second Lieutenant Alistair Gordon Lethbridge-Stewart served in Intelligence during World War II. He was assigned to update the British army's maps of the Greek islands.

On the island of Zante, Lethbridge-Stewart encountered the Greek gods Demeter, Persephone and Hermes, who were attempting to lead quiet, domestic lives. The Greek god Hades hoped to provoke a world conflict even more

---

Tuttle. Fitton commented: "The Tommy Flowers bit is a result of compressing some of the back story – I'd imagined the Doctor had flitted in and out and visited Churchill, Turing and company, lending a hand with building Colossus in his previous travels. I don't think the Doctor has been at Bletchley more than a few months, but because I cut all that down to save lots of exposition, we're left with that apparent Flowers anachronism – oops!"

The Doctor fondly muses about the work of code-breaker Alfred "Dilly" Knox, who died 27th February, 1943, but it wasn't Fitton's intention that the two had actually met. Some of Robbie Flint's background is based on the real-life double agent Eddie Chapman,

a.k.a. Agent Zig-Zag. Also, Flint mentions having cut a deal with MI5 to protect his family members, including his "toerag" cousin Billy (Fitton's *An Ordinary Life*).

2563 Dating *Colditz* (BF #25) - The date "1944" is given. The detail about New York and Moscow being bombed comes from "Klein's Story". *A Thousand Tiny Wings* relates what happens to Klein between 1944 and when she next meets the Doctor.

2564 *The Architects of History*

2565 *The Impossible Astronaut*

2566 "Five months" before *The Turing Test*.

2567 Dating *Deadly Reunion* (PDA #71) - The date is given (although as already noted, it makes Lethbridge-Stewart older than most other stories would have him).

devastating than World War II, which would cripple humanity and allow him to rule Earth. The god Poseidon, at Persephone's request, ended Hades' scheme and cast him back into the underworld. Persephone and Lethbridge-Stewart became lovers, but she used water from the River Lethe to make him forget these events.

During the Normandy landings, Jason Kane's grandfather was killed when a sniper hit his lucky crucifix and it became lethal shrapnel.[2568] Captain Davydd Watson saw visions during the Normandy landings, an effect of an experiment by the organic computer Azoth.[2569] The long-lived Corporal Paul Reynish was part of the Normandy landings.[2570]

During the nineteen-forties, two Gaderene scouts – members of an insectoid race whose homeworld was dying – arrived on Earth via an unstable transmat process. One of them matured into the calculating Bliss, but her brother mutated into a dragon-sized Gaderene that covered itself in mud and went dormant. Bliss lost the ninth key – a small jade shard – to the Gaderene transmat, but British Wing Commander Alec Whistler discovered it in the aftermath of an explosion at Culverton Aerodrome. Without the key, Bliss could only bring Gaderene embryos,

not adults, through to Earth.[2571]

In 1944, the Toymaker kidnapped US Marine Mark Conrad.[2572]

1944 - THE SHADOW IN THE GLASS[2573] **->** On 17th May, 1944, a British fighter plane shot down a Vvormak spacecruiser as it passed over Turelhampton, England. The Vvormak were in stasis, but the ship's gravitational field rendered it immobile. Unable to relocate the ship, the British military sealed off the area for fifty years as part of a cover story.

Private Gerrard Lassiter stole the Vvormak ship's main navigation device as a talisman. It could project images of the future, and became known as the Scrying Glass. Gunther Brun, a German trooper, killed Lassiter in France and took the device, only to lose it to Colonel Otto Klein in a game of cards. Two weeks later, Reichsfuher Heinrich Himmler learned of the device and ordered Klein to hand it over to him. Himmler then gave it to a group of Tibetan mystics for study.

In July 1944, the sixth Doctor persuaded Churchill to help smuggle him into France, and infiltrated the Reich Records Department as "Colonel Johann Schmidt". In August 1944, Hitler became curious about other items left

---

2568 *Death and Diplomacy*
2569 *The Taint*
2570 *P.R.O.B.E.: When to Die*. The Normandy landings commenced on 6th June, 1944.
2571 "Thirty years" before *The Last of the Gaderene*.
2572 *Divided Loyalties*
2573 Dating *The Shadow in the Glass* (PDA #41) - The date is given (p29).
2574 Dating *Mastermind* (BF CC #8.1) - Exact year unknown, but this seems to happen during World War II.
2575 Dating *Quicksilver* (BF #220) - The Doctor and Constance struggle to nail down how long it's been since *Criss-Cross* [Spring 1944]. Constance judges, from the state of her mail, that it's "still 1944, at least", but that she's been gone "months" rather than weeks. She later notes that the trees have "autumn leaves", and apologizes to her director that "Three months' leave from Bletchley was just the ticket. Though I'm afraid I may have ended up taking slightly longer." She also notes that it's been "almost a year" since her husband left home in (according to *Criss-Cross*) November 1943. Kinvar notes that he detected the TARDIS "a few months ago". Finally, in *Static*, Constance up and names her year of origin as "1944".
2576 Dating *Autumn Mist* (EDA #24) - The story takes place during the Battle of the Bulge. The Doctor confronts the Beast in *The Taint*.
2577 *SJA: Lost in Time*
2578 Dating *The Turing Test* (EDA #39) - The story takes

place over several months, and ends with the Allies bombing Dresden, which occurred in February 1945.
2579 *The Marian Conspiracy*, which takes place circa 2000, says she is "55. A Big Finish press release, however, claims she was 65 in 1999, suggesting a much earlier birth date of 1934. Big Finish Producer Gary Russell says *The Marian Conspiracy* should be favoured whatever the press release says.
2580 Harry celebrates his 41st birthday in *Harry Sullivan's War*, set circa 1986 but subject to UNIT dating. Ian Marter, who played Harry and also wrote *Harry Sullivan's War*, was born in 1944.
2581 She's "24" in *Leth-St: Times Squared* (ch2), which dates itself to 1969.
2582 *No Future*
2583 *New CM* S1: *Troubled Waters*. The UK and the US bombed Dresden on 13th-15th February, 1945.
2584 *TW: Trace Memory*
2585 "Next March" after *The Shadow in the Glass*.
2586 *The Shadow in the Glass*
2587 *TimeH: Peculiar Lives*
2588 *DotD: Hunters of Earth*
2589 *The Haisman Timeline*
2590 *Leth-St: The Forgotten Son* (ch7).
2591 *The Haisman Timeline*
2592 *Leth-St: Night of the Intelligence* (ch4).
2593 *Leth-St: Night of the Intelligence* (ch7).
2594 Dating *Leth-St: The Schizoid Earth* (*Leth-St* novel #2) - The year is given (ch13). In real life, Tesla died in January 1943.

at the Turelhampton site, and authorised the Doctor, as "Schmidt", to participate in a raiding party. The raid occurred on 18th August.

c 1944 - MASTERMIND[2574] **->** Mob bosses in Las Vegas sent an assassin, Ms Morelli, to kill the decaying Master, but he hypnotised her into turning her gun on herself. The Master better incorporated the mafia into his operations and increasingly went into seclusion.

1944 (Autumn) - QUICKSILVER[2575] **->** Constance Clarke asked the sixth Doctor to bring her home, feeling she'd neglected her affairs for too long. She received word that her husband, Henry, had been killed in the line of duty... although he'd actually run away with one of his intelligence contacts, a woman named Ana. Henry had come into possession of a piece of Vilal technology that threatened to upend history. The troll-like Vilal followed as the Doctor and Constance skipped ahead to the next instance of its use, in 1948.

1944 (December) - AUTUMN MIST[2576] **->** The eighth Doctor, Sam and Fitz were split up when they arrived during the Battle of the Bulge. Sam was injured, the Doctor served as a medic, and Fitz found himself serving as a corporal in the German army. Sam's injuries were fatal, but she was rescued by the Sidhe. A rift had formed between our realm and theirs, but the Doctor trapped the anarchic King of the Sidhe, Oberon, aboard the dephased USS *Eldridge*. Oberon perished as the Doctor deployed the *Eldridge* into the rift, sealing it. It was expected that another aspect of Oberon would take his place. The rift's closure enabled the Beast to arrive on Earth and begin feeding upon humanity.

George Woods enlisted in the Army when he was 16, and fought in the Battle of the Ardennes, a.k.a. the Battle of the Bulge. He survived, and would work in the field of radar development in the 50s and 60s.[2577]

@ 1944/5 - THE TURING TEST[2578] **->** The cryptographer Alan Turing intercepted a unique code transmitted from Dresden, concluding that it was alien in origin. The eighth Doctor had befriended Turing, and suggested they contact the signal's originator. They allied themselves with the spy Graham Greene. The Doctor also approached American pilot Joseph Heller, promising to get him out of the army if he flew the Doctor and Turing to Dresden. An English officer, Elgar, was revealled as an assassin out to kill the mysterious pale-skinned aliens. The Doctor killed Elgar and the aliens beamed away from Earth, leaving the Doctor behind as the Allied bombing of Dresden began.

1945

Evelyn Smythe, a companion of the sixth Doctor, was born around 1945.[2579] **Harry Sullivan, a companion of the fourth Doctor and member of UNIT, was born around the same time.**[2580] Adrienne Kramer, a future brigadier-general of UNIT and an associate of the eighth Doctor, was born.[2581]

On 13th February, 1945, the seventh Doctor and Bernice witnessed the destruction of Dresden.[2582] Ian Gilmore also saw the assault on Dresden.[2583]

Charles Arthur Cromwell joined Torchwood in 1945.[2584] In March, the Doctor flew a Mark VIII Halifax bomber.[2585] The Tibetans charged with keeping the Scrying Glass were murdered on 25th April, 1945. In the years to follow, it would fall into the hands of Adolf Hitler's son.[2586]

In 1945, members of *homo peculiar*, fearing that evolution would go the route of exterminating them or *homo sapiens*, took to living in seclusion at a number of retreats. *Peculiar Lives*, a "scientific romance" by Erik Clevedon based upon his meeting with Percival, one of *homo peculiar*, was published.[2587] Colonel Rook – later a teacher at Coal Hill School – served in World War II, and was in Germany in 1945.[2588]

Edward Travers first met Eileen Le Croissette (later Younghusband) in March 1945.[2589]

Gordon Lethbridge-Stewart Snr, now a wing commander in the Royal Air Force, was declared missing in action, and believed dead, in early 1945. Some months later, his widow Mary gave their house in Bledoe to the Philips family, whose home had been severely damaged in the war. She moved with her son Alistair to Lancashire, to live her sister and brother-in-law, Isobel and Thomas Davies. The splinter of the Great Intelligence in Remington Manor erased Alistair's memories of his dead brother Gordon. It did the same to Mary, and secreted another piece of itself in the space this created in her mind.[2590]

Alistair Lethbridge-Stewart Sr received Gordon's letter conceding his true parentage in 1945, and resolved to discuss with his brother Archibald.[2591] Age 16, Alistair Lethbridge-Stewart witnessed the war-damage in Cornwall and decided to pursue a career as an officer. His grandfather in Scotland was pleased. His mother wasn't, but conceded it's what his father would have wanted.[2592]

= On the Inferno Earth, Mary Lethbridge-Stewart died, but her husband Gordon lived.[2593]

= 1945 - LETH-ST: THE SCHIZOID EARTH[2594] **-> On In-Between Earth, Nikola Tesla led a last-ditch survival effort aboard the airship *Phoenix*. The discovery of an alien power-converter facilitated a system designed to launch twenty person-bearing capsules into the past, to warn humanity of its**

downfall. However, the capsules' journeys deviated, and they landed at various points on our Earth and the Inferno Earth.

Colonel Lethbridge-Stewart of our Earth and Major James Lethbridge-Stewart of Inferno-Earth were aboard the *Phoenix* as it came under assault and launched its capsules. Tesla returned them to their respective worlds as the *Phoenix* erupted in flames. Before the end, the Alistair Lethbridge-Stewart of this reality – Alastair (sic), age 15 – was sent through to the Inferno Earth, 1959.

1945 (Monday, 30th April) - THE SHADOW IN THE GLASS[2595] **->** The sixth Doctor, the Brigadier and journalist Claire Aldwych arrived from 2001 with Hitler's adult son, and the men entered Hitler's bunker. The Doctor easily portrayed Hitler's son as a madman, and Hitler, failing to recognise his offspring, shot him dead. The Nazis disposed of the body in a nearby water tower. The Allies would later mistake the corpse for a double of Hitler, killed for an unknown reason.

Martin Bormann, one of Hitler's aides, killed Claire and substituted her body for that of Eva Braun. Hitler committed suicide. A pregnant Eva was flown to a submarine in Hamburg. She later gave birth to a son named Adolf. He was raised at the secret Nazi base in Antarctica.

The Second Iteration of Elizabeth Klein

1945 (late April) - DALEKS AMONG US[2596] **->** Kurt Schalk had made great advances in developing a Persuasion machine, but discovered his prototype's sphere of influence only extended 50 km. More troublingly, the operator's mind had to be free of all doubts and emotional liabilities, lest these manifest in the machine's targets. Such an unbending ideologue was required that nobody human, not even the Fuhrer, would suffice.

Schalk decided that a "designer baby" grown to precise specifications could operate the machine. Such a child – a female – was gestated, in Schalk's laboratory, using genetic material from Schalk and Elizabeth Volkenrath (regarded as a terror among the Nazi elites). The child was a blank slate, intended as the first of a legion of clones who would saturate the globe with Germany's influence via mass-produced Persuasion machines.

The seventh Doctor's historical deletion of the Elizabeth Klein he met at Colditz shifted the timelines until her lifetime found a new form to inhabit: the blank-minded girl born in Schalk's laboratory. As the Americans advanced into Germany, the adult Elizabeth Klein arrived, from the planet Azimuth, in the TARDIS in search of her origins.

Ralf Klein stole Schalk's child, vowing to escape to London with his beloved, Mutter, and raise the girl as their own. He briefly met Elizabeth, and mistook her for Volkenrath. Acknowledging the compassion he sensed in "Volkenrath", Ralf vowed to name his adopted daughter Elizabeth after her. Klein grew up thinking Ralf and Mutter were her parents, with no knowledge of her true heredity.

2595 Dating *The Shadow in the Glass* (PDA #41) - The date is given (p23, 147).
2596 Dating *Daleks Among Us* (BF #177) - The month and year are given, and coincide with the final Allied advance into Germany. The Reichstag was captured on 30th April, the same day that Hitler committed suicide.
2597 Dating *Daleks Among Us* (BF #177) - The month and year are given. Klein doesn't seem worse for wear (all things considered) from her imprisonment, and expects the Russians to execute her in short order, so she's probably not locked up for long following her capture. It's also possible that the Doctor found it expedient to retrieve Klein before their arrival in the same month in Dusseldorf, to keep her already convoluted timeline as clean as possible.
2598 "The Broken Man"
2599 *Magic of the Angels*. Trafalgar Square's VE Day celebration happened on 8th May, 1945.
2600 Dating *Forty-Five*: "Casualties of War" (BF #115c) - The Doctor provides the specific day.
2601 Dating *Persuasion* (BF #175) - The Doctor says that it's "the outskirts of Dusseldorf, Germany, May 1945", and also that Hitler has died (he killed himself on

30th April). *Daleks Among Us* sees Klein return to Schalk's laboratory, at the end of April, "three weeks" before these events. The Doctor's comment that it's "just one month after [Germany] was liberated by American forces" depends upon how you define terms, but Berlin unconditionally surrendered on 7th May, 1945. The TARDIS moves in space, not time, when it relocates from Dusseldorf to Minos.
2602 *Daleks Among Us, Starlight Robbery*.
2603 Dating *Daleks Among Us* (BF #177) - The Doctor says that they've returned to Minos "as close to our moment of departure [in *Persuasion*] as I dare".
2604 Dating *Leth-St*: "In His Kiss" (*Leth-St HAVOC Files* #2.1) - The Haisman Timeline says it's "Summer 1945", but the story opens right before the school holidays, "in the Spring sunshine", and spans some weeks. Jemima is "sixteen". The father of her child remains unknown – Jemima knows it's not Henry (hence her regret that if they *had* fooled around, she could've convinced him the child was his), and editor Andy Frankham-Allen says it's not James' ghost, as such things don't exist in the *Lethbridge-Stewart* books.

Hunted by the Allies, Volkenrath met Klein while searching for Schalk. At gunpoint, Klein revealed what she knew about the Doctor, the Daleks, the TARDIS and events on Azimuth. Volkenrath used the Ship's Fast Return Switch to go to Azimuth, leaving Klein behind. The Russians thought that Klein was Volkenrath, and imprisoned her.

1945 (May) - DALEKS AMONG US[2597] **->** The seventh Doctor and Will Arrowsmith, disguised as Stormtroopers, liberated Elizabeth Klein from imprisonment by the Russians. As this left the three of them on the run on the Eastern Front – totally bereft of allies and with the TARDIS buried about 76 km away, and the Sixth Russian Tank Corps and a pack of angry wolfhounds chasing them – the Doctor suggested that Klein look upon this not so much as a rescue effort as an *adventure!*

The Doctor once tried to stop General Montgomery from punching General Patton into a plate of steamed dumplings, when Winston Churchill entered the room and shouted: "Doctor! If you won't win the blasted war for me, at least rescue the hors d'oeuvre." On May 8th, 1945, Churchill issued a permanent order in file DI89/A45/K76, stamped "Operation Blue Box", that the Doctor should receive full security clearance on all post-war operations.[2598]

Kylie Duncan and Amber Reynolds, two young victims of the Weeping Angels, arrived in Trafalgar Square during the VE Day celebration there. They would live out their lives, and meet the eleventh Doctor (who wasn't present at the Trafalgar festivities), Amy and Rory in 2012.[2599]

1945 (9th May) - FORTY-FIVE: "Casualties of War"[2600] **->** Joey Carlisle, a thief, stole a cache of alien tech belonging to the Forge, and came into possession of a bracelet called a Truthsayer. The Deons, lawkeepers from the Anurine Protectorate, used such devices to make suspects tell the truth. The seventh Doctor, Ace and Hex tracked the bracelet's psychic emissions during the VE Day celebrations. Carlisle and his mother lived next door to Ace's mother and grandmother on Old Terrace in Streatham, and so Ace briefly visited her mother, who was currently age three.

1945 (third week of May) - PERSUASION[2601] **->** The seventh Doctor and Elizabeth Klein – with Will Arrowsmith aboard the TARDIS as a stowaway – arrived in Dousseldorf, Germany, May 1945, in search of the German scientist Kurt Schalk.

Both human and extraterrestrial parties sought Schalk's work on the Persuasion machine, and he had used his prototype device to *persuade* his assistant – Lukas Hinterberger – that he *was* Schalk, and to *persuade* himself that he was Hinterberger. The Doctor's party found "Hinterberger" – actually Schalk with a case of mistaken identity – in Schalk's deserted laboratory. "Hinterberger" mistook Klein for Volkenrath, and agreed to lead her group to "Schalk" – who had fled to the Greek isle of Minos.

The Shepherd and Shepherdess who furthered Schalk's work had grown withered away from their universe, and needed the life force of others to survive. Those attached to the Persuasion project regarded the duo as *Struwwelpeter*, after the 1845 children's book *Shockheaded Peter* by Heinrich Hoffman. The Doctor feared the disruption and death the *Struwwelpeter* could cause, and offered to transport them to the lush and healing world of Newpeerlessness. They agreed – learning too late that Newpeerlessness was a Time Lord prison planet. For extra security, the Doctor materialised the TARDIS around Newpeerlessness and miniaturised it within the Ship's Star Chamber – which already contained a minor galaxy from the Tear of Ragged Restoration.

The Spivalins – renowned as "lords of the galactic index, ravagers of the interstellar exchange" – captured "Schalk", but the Kletcht, a race of space-faring asset strippers, bought out the entire Spivalin Empire to acquire "Schalk" and his prototype Persuasion machine. The Doctor, Klein and Will went after "Schalk", failing to realize that they'd let the genuine article – still thinking he was Hinterberger – run away into the woods...

The Daleks captured the real Schalk and took him to their base on the planet Azimuth. The Doctor, Klein and Will wrongly tracked Hinterberger to the future, at an auction held by Garundel Galactic, but eventually realised their error and returned to 1945...[2602]

1945 (May) - DALEKS AMONG US[2603] **->** The seventh Doctor, Elizabeth Klein and Will Arrowsmith went back to Minos, hoping track down Kurt Schalk. Klein feigned drunkenness and splashed alcohol on a Dalek left behind to exterminate anyone pursuing Schalk, causing the Dalek to incinerate when it fired its weapon.

With Schalk's trail entirely cold, the Doctor's party went to consult with the Wraiths of Lemuria to find him...

1945 (Spring to Summer) - LETH-ST: "In His Kiss"[2604] **->** Jemima Fleming and Henry Barnes were now, as her mother put it, "courting". Nonetheless, Jemima rewarded Alistair Lethbridge-Stewart with his first-ever kiss when he saved Lottie Greenwood from drowning in a pond. Jemima had visions of James Lethbridge-Stewart's shade calling out to her from Draynes Wood. She became pregnant soon afterward, but miscarried after four months. Jemima accepted Henry's marriage proposal, and they saw Alistair off as the Lethbridge-Stewart family – following his father being lost in the war – moved away.

When people asked, Alistair Lethbridge-Stewart said his first kiss was Imelda Clark, in Coleshill – but it was actually Jemima Fleming.[2605]

Lucia Moretti of Torchwood was born on 18th June, 1945.[2606] A reservoir of pain and suffering, possibly representing humanity's darker nature, became concentrated in an area of England during perihelion: a point in mid-August when our reality and its reality became closest. The dark force was believed to have manifested in dozens of murderous individuals throughout the centuries – and on 13th August, 1945, it compelled young Daniel O'Kane to kill his parents and two sisters.[2607]

= 1945 - ATOM BOMB BLUES[2608] -> The seventh Doctor and Ace arrived in Los Alamos, where the Manhattan Project was about to culminate in the detonation of the first atom bomb. The Doctor identified one of the scientists, Ray Morita, as someone from the twenty-first century of a parallel universe. The Doctor made contact with a jellyfish-like alien, Zorg, and went to Los Angeles to confront the Chapel of the Red Apocalypse: a cult that had been a front for a spy ring.

Ace learned that *she* was in a parallel universe, and that Ray was from her reality, lured to the alternate history by a love of Duke Ellington music. In the proper timeline, a musicians' union strike meant much of his work was never recorded, but the strike didn't take place in the other universe.

The Doctor and Ace uncovered a plot to alter the equations of the Manhattan Project to unleash enough power to destroy this universe, tipping history in Japan's favour across the multiverse. The Doctor defeated the plan, the atom bomb test concluded as history recorded and the Doctor took Ray home – with his precious records.

William Bishop, an adjutant of Brigadier Lethbridge-Stewart, was born August 1945.[2609]

1945 (5th August, 2nd September) - "Sky Jacks"[2610] -> Toward the end of World War II, the United States military initiated three game-changing strikes against Japan. The nuclear bombs Fat Man and Little Boy were respectively slated for deployment against Nagasaki and

2605 *Leth-St:* "The Enfolded Time"
2606 *TW: Children of Earth*
2607 *P.R.O.B.E.: The Zero Imperative*
2608 Dating *Atom Bomb Blues* (PDA #76) - The story is set on the eve of the first A-Bomb tests.
2609 *Leth-St: The Forgotten Son,* the Haisman Timeline.
2610 Dating "Sky Jacks" (IDW Vol. 4 #9-12) - The caption gives the date: "5th August, 1945". The nuclear strikes against Hiroshima and Nagasaki happened on 6th and 9th August. In the epilogue, the Doctor says that it's "September 2nd, 1945... Victory in the Pacific Day!" The term applies to both the announcement of Japan's surrender (15th August in Japan, 14th August in the US due to time zone differences), the follow-up celebrations and – in this case – the formal signing of the surrender document on 2nd September.
2611 Dating *Daleks Among Us* (BF #177) - The Daleks capture Schalk in May 1945 (following *Persuasion*) and take him to Azimuth via a time capsule, but it's not said how much, if any, actual time displacement this entails. For Schalk, "six months" pass on Azimuth as the Daleks restore his memories and syphon the Persuasion machine blueprints out of his mind. If the trip to Azimuth doesn't involve time travel, then, the Doctor, Klein and Will must show up there around December 1945. If time travel is involved, the story could occur in any of a myriad of periods.
Tipping the scales in favour of an earlier dating, Falkus – from his position as Supreme Dalek – says that he's purged what details Davros could remember of the Doctor's interrogation (in *Genesis of the Daleks*) and programmed into the first Daleks' memory banks

before they betrayed him. (This is something of an odd claim, as it's debatable if there's a moment in *Genesis of the Daleks* episodes five and six when Davros could have conceivably done this.) Presuming that Falkus has access to the entire datanet of the Daleks he's allied with, his amendments must have occurred before the Daleks invade Earth (circa 2167, even though the Doctor told Davros that it happened in "the year 2000"; see the dating notes on *The Dalek Invasion of Earth*), as the Daleks have no foreknowledge of the event.
For Davros, this story takes place after Skaro's destruction (*Remembrance of the Daleks*), and although he leaves Azimuth in a time capsule to reunite with his Daleks, it's once again unstated how much time travel is needed for him to do just that. (Davros says he's leaving for "some far distant place", nothing more.) The mental torment he receives at the Wraiths' hands, and his eventual escape from them, and could lead to the manner in which he's found at the start of *War of the Daleks*.
2612 *TW: The Undertaker's Gift*
2613 *Just War*
2614 "Memorial"
2615 *Heart of TARDIS*
2616 "The Broken Man"
2617 "Operation Proteus"
2618 "Thirty years" before *The Paradise of Death* (p79).
2619 *CM S1: Threshold*
2620 *CM S4: Rise and Shine*
2621 *The Wrong Doctors*
2622 *Leth-St: The Showstoppers*

Hiroshima, and a third, Big Momma, was targeted on Kyoto. Japanese Zero planes attacked the *Sky Jack*, the airplane carrying Big Momma, north of Iwo Jima and killed half the crew. The two survivors, Sgts Gunner and Lasseter, radioed the failure of their mission as the *Sky Jack* entered an unidentified vortex in the sky. They arrived at Tipperary Station – a floating base within the environs of the Doctor's TARDIS – and remained there for three years of their personal time. The attempt to annihilate Kyoto was lost to history.

The eleventh Doctor returned those trapped at Tipperary Station to their native times, and left Sgts Gunner and Lasseter to experience Victory in the Pacific Day, the end of the war between the US and Japan.

? 1945 (December) - DALEKS AMONG US[2611] -> The Daleks who captured Kurt Schalk on Minos, 1945, took him to their hidden base on the planet Azimuth. They restored Schalk's true persona, but the Persuasion machine blueprints in his mind could not be extracted without causing data corruption. The Supreme Dalek, secretly the Davros clone Falkus, agreed that Schalk could become the Fuhrer of the Daleks – a delaying tactic while the blueprints were copied from Schalk as he slept.

Davros had become separated from his Daleks following Skaro's destruction, and went to Azimuth in pursuit of them. He failed to realise Falkus' origins and elevated stature, and spent months thinking himself at liberty while the Daleks monitored his every move.

At the seventh Doctor's request, the ghostly Wraiths of Lemuria consulted their database of criminals and located Schalk. The Doctor, Elizabeth Klein and Will Arrowsmith attempted to capture the man, but Klein increasingly realised that her origins were bound up in Schalk's work. The Doctor pre-programmed the TARDIS to take Klein back to Schalk's laboratory in Dusseldorf, April 1945, and instructed her to come back using the Fast Return Switch.

Klein's biological mother, Elizabeth Volkenrath, returned in the TARDIS instead, posed as her daughter and volunteered to operate the Daleks' Persuasion machine – the purpose for which Klein had been born and bred. Falkus agreed, envisioning that Klein-clones could use the Persuasion machine to mentally dominate alien races, and even to persuade their very hearts and the electrical impulses of their brains to *stop*. He envisioned that whole populations – whole solar systems and galaxies, even – would just *stop*.

The machine's power ran away from Volkenrath – and she commanded all Daleks on Azimuth to *stop*, slaying them, and ordered all clone matter present to dissolve, turning Falkus to goo. Will released the Shepherd – who was alone, as the weakened Shepherdess had expired – from the TARDIS' Star Chamber to counter-act the out-of-control machine. Volkenrath made the Shepherd *stop*, but

the effort of slaying a near-omnipotent being overloaded the Persuasion machine, killing her.

Davros escaped in a Dalek time capsule... which the Doctor redirected to Lemuria, where the Wraiths set about haunting the Daleks' creator. The Doctor and Will then left for Germany, the past, to rescue Klein.

Aftermath of World War II

Captain Jack and a platoon of commandoes rounded up fugitive Nazis in Berlin at the end of World War II.[2612]

The Russians captured Emil Hartung's research into stealth aircraft, and took it to a vault in the Kremlin. Generalleutnant Oskar Steinmann was found guilty (along with twenty-two others) of Nazi war crimes and sentenced to life imprisonment at Nuremberg.[2613]

Brian Galway was killed in North Africa during World War II. His 12-year-old brother, Simon, attended a memorial service on 20th December, 1945. The Doctor placed the surviving consciousness of the Telphin, a peaceful race wiped out by the Chaktra, inside the boy.[2614]

After World War II, the American military experimented to see if widespread belief could alter the laws of physics. The residents of the Midwest town Lychburg were brainwashed with transceivers, creating thousands of people who simultaneously believed whatever the military wanted. An experiment to make the people believe "the gates of Hell were opening", however, created an unstable dimensional rift. The military tried to level the project with a low-yield nuclear device, but only succeeded in knocking Lychburg out of Earth's dimension entirely.[2615]

The ousting of the Nazis from Prague, 1945, benefited Yuri Azarov, who had ties to Russia and set up a KGB network in the city. Azarov's mind formed a connection with the centuries'-old Golem of Prague, and he used the Golem as an enforcer.[2616] After the war, the British government set up Operation Proteus to create illegal chemical weapons.[2617] The Parakon named Freeth began to visit Earth, accounting for some UFO sightings over the next thirty years.[2618]

Professor Heinrich Schumann, a German war criminal, was recruited to work at British Rocket Group.[2619] Sir Keith Kordel, unknowingly one of the Light Sleepers, helped to sponsor British Rocket Group.[2620] Muriel Wilberforce worked at the Pease Pottage Post Office after World War II, and would continue doing so well past retirement age.[2621]

At the end of World War II, the Nazi scientist Vilhelm Schadengeist physically and mentally merged with the siphonophore in his possession. The Americans relocated the resultant hybrid, codename: Factotum, as part of Operation Paperclip.[2622]

The twelfth Doctor misunderstood that one of Clara's students, Evie Hubbard, was supposed to conduct an *imaginary* interview with Winston Churchill,

and arranged a conversation with the genuine article.[2623] Following World War II, the secondary Eye of Horus was hidden from Sutekh's followers in plain sight, as part of a museum display in Egypt.[2624]

> (=) A time bubble caused the village of Stockbridge to vanish. Authorities said a bomber had destroyed the town, and the mystery of its disappearance gave rise to the Psychic Investigation Group (PIG).[2625]

The Doctor met Einstein.[2626] The Rani briefly kidnapped Albert Einstein.[2627] Albert Einstein's efforts to build a time machine caused a fez he owned to interact with its future self, as owned by his friend the Doctor, which created a temporal window that transported him to the Doctor's TARDIS. A green liquid that Einstein was experimenting on splashed in his face, temporarily transforming him into an Ood. Einstein's hair remained exceptionally frizzy upon his return to normal – the Doctor complimented the look, saying it made Einstein appear more "sciencey". The Doctor returned Einstein to 18th September, 1945, after admitting that the toothbrush he'd borrowed from him some time ago had been destroyed by the Daleks.[2628] Einstein was among a talented few who could harness the power of quantum mathematics, Iris Wildthyme thought.[2629]

The Doctor appeared in a couple of noir films, and regarded Humphrey Bogart as the only man who could beat him at chess.[2630] Seven-year-old James Wilton and his sister Stephanie found Rees' music box, enabling Rees to possess Stephanie's mind.[2631]

u – Jo Grant, a companion of the third Doctor and member of UNIT, was born.[2632]

1946 (20th May) - FP: THE BRAKESPEARE VOYAGE[2633] -> Robert Scarratt, a member of the Great Houses, became infatuated with Ella Staunton: a prostitute working in a Tempest Hey brothel in Liverpool. A man named Thomas Hendron murdered Staunton on 20th May, 1946, and lied that "another man" was in the vicinity to throw authorities off the scent. By positioning himself nearby during Staunton's death, Scarratt wove himself into the historical narrative as the "other man", and hoped this would avoid the temporal destabilization inflicted upon members of the Great Houses' Second Wave. Staunton was found guilty of Staunton's murder and hanged in the Walton Gaol on 17th July.

1947

John Jones, a future rock star and companion of the eleventh Doctor, was born.[2634] In 1947, the first Doctor and Dodo helped a weapons convoy reach Scapa Flow in Scotland.[2635] As governor of India, the father of broadcaster Timothy Vee acquired a mind-altering statue of an Indian god. He brought it back to England after India obtained independence.[2636]

2623 *The Woman Who Lived*

2624 *NAofBenny V2: The Vaults of Osiris*

2625 Variously said to occur at the end of World War II and about "sixty years" before *The Eternal Summer*, set in 2009.

2626 *The Stones of Blood*. No date given. Einstein lived 1879-1955, publishing his Special and General Theories of Relativity in 1905 and 1915 respectively. He also appeared in *Time and the Rani*, but it isn't made clear if he and the Doctor already knew one another. Einstein and the eleventh Doctor are already chummy, however, in *Death is the Only Answer*.

2627 *Time and the Rani*. A scene showing the Rani kidnap Einstein was deleted from the camera script.

2628 *Death is the Only Answer*

2629 *Iris* S4: *Iris at the Oche*

2630 *DotD: Night of the Whisper*. Bogart lived 1899-1957, and starred in such noir films as *The Big Sleep* (1946) and *Key Largo* (1948).

2631 *Worlds DW: The Reesinger Process*, "five years" after the Blitz.

2632 Based upon actress Katy Manning being born in 1946, but subject to UNIT dating.

2633 Dating *FP: The Brakespeare Voyage* (FP novel #8) - The exact day is given (ch3).

2634 Alice, who met Jones in 1962, names him as "a twenty year old" in *The Eleventh Doctor Year One*: "The Sound of Our Voices". However, Jones is (thematically) a carbon copy of David Bowie (real name: David Robert Jones), who wasn't born until 1947. Perhaps it's best to assume that Alice was rounding, since Bowie did indeed start performing in 1962, at age 15.

2635 *Masters of Earth*

2636 *J&L* S5: *The Age of Revolution*. India gained independence in 1947.

2637 *Leth-St: The Forgotten Son* (ch7), "a couple of years" after 1945.

2638 *Leth-St*: "The Slow Invasion"

2639 Dating *Daemons: White Witch of Devil's End* (story #1, "The Inheritance") - Olive notes in the novelisation that her twin sister Poppy has turned 18, and Olive's appointment as guardian of Devil's End – although it's not said – seems to rely upon her having attained that age (her alleged successor, Bryony, is also 18 in *Daemons*: "Hawthorne Blood"). The internal narrative of "The Inheritance" comes a bit unstuck, however, in saying that "a few years"/"two years" after her appointment, Olive is "only 17". The film version of that scene includes two "World War II servicemen" walking by – not that World War II is necessarily still happening.

Mary Lethbridge-Stewart and her son Alistair moved to Coleshill.[2637] When Anne Travers was nine, she nearly drowned during a trip to the seaside.[2638]

Olive Hawthorne
Appointed Guardian of Devil's End

1947 - DAEMONS: WHITE WITCH OF DEVIL'S END[2639] -> A gateway in Devil's End served to attract evil influences, and so a guardian – always of Hawthorne blood – stood against such forces. Lobelia, the elder sister of Olive Hawthorne's grandmother, appeared to Olive late one night and named her as the next guardian. Lobelia bestowed upon Olive her grimoire, then departed for the next plane of existence... but only after warning that sacrifices might be required. The next day, Olive's twin sister Poppy went missing, and would not return until the end of Olive's life.

1947 - DYING IN THE SUN[2640] -> The second Doctor, Ben and Polly called in on the Doctor's old friend, movie producer Harold Reitman, but found he had been murdered. Star Light Pictures were about to release *Dying in the Sun*, and the Doctor was surprised that such a poor movie had received such rave reviews. The telepathic Selyoids were affecting the audience's perceptions of the film. The movie's producer, De Sande, was intent on using their powers to dominate the world. The Doctor caused a plane crash that killed De Sande, but this released the Selyoids present in De Sande's body. Their dispersal meant that Hollywood would remain a place of extreme emotions.

1947 - GHOSTS OF INDIA[2641] -> The tenth Doctor tried to satiate Donna's craving for curry, but arrived in Calcutta ten years later than he had planned, while India was in the throes of its independence struggle. They met Mohandas "Mahatma" Gandhi, and soon discovered that a weed-like alien, the Jal Kalath named Darac-7, was creating outlawed Gelem Warriors for use by the Hive Council of its homeworld. The Gelem were created by absorbing violent impulses, and when Darac-7 forced Gandhi into the Gelem-making machine, it exploded, killing Darac-7. The Doctor and Donna wished Gandhi farewell, and the Doctor solemnly informed Donna that Gandhi was fated to die in January, the following year.

Clara Oswald had an argument with Gandhi.[2642]

c 1947 - "The Professor, the Queen and the Bookshop"[2643] -> C.S. Lewis wrote *The Professor, the Queen and the Bookshop*, in which little Amelia and Rory wandered into Phoenix Books – a time-travelling bookshop – and met the Professor who managed it. They arrived in the realm of the White Queen, where it was always winter – not Christmas – and trapped her in a book. J.R.R. Tolkien thought that Lewis' story was rubbish, but one of the Inklings sharing their company at the Eagle and the Child pub – the eleventh Doctor, accompanied by Amy – suggested that the story might work better with a wardrobe.

The twelfth Doctor said he was personal friends with C.S. Lewis, and had told him about Narnia: a place that the despotic witch Jadis briefly turned into a frozen hell.[2644] The seventh Doctor took his friend, J.R.R. Tolkien, through time to attend the wedding of Bernice Summerfield and Jason Kane.[2645]

The Roswell Incident

The CIA captured a Nedenah ship at Roswell. One alien was autopsied, the others were taken to Area 51.[2646] **The collector Henry Van Statten had artifacts from Roswell in his private museum.**[2647] The Roswell incident was an alien "fender-bender", according to the Doctor.[2648] The Doctor managed to explain away why he was masked and holding forceps above a slabbed alien body at Roswell, 1947, while a camera sat in the corner of the room.[2649]

On 13th June, 1947, ambassador Seruba Velak – a "Grey Alien" – was en route to negotiate an alliance against the Viperox when pirates shot down her saucer. Her ship crashed outside Roswell, and the US Air Force took her to Area 51. Her husband, Rivesh Mantilax, was fighting the Viperox and unable to mount a rescue attempt for six years.[2650]

The Doctor knocked over a paint pot and inspired

2640 Dating *Dying in the Sun* (PDA #47) - Early on, a newspaper is dated "12 October 1947" (p17).
2641 Dating *Ghosts of India* (NA #25) - The year is given.
2642 *Under the Lake*
2643 Dating "The Professor, the Queen and the Bookshop" (DWM #429) - It's prior to Lewis writing *The Lion, the Witch and the Wardrobe*, the manuscript of which was finished in March 1949.
2644 *Deep Time* (ch11). It's possible the eleventh Doctor did this, following "The Professor, the Queen

and the Bookshop".
2645 *Happy Endings*. Tolkien's wedding gift is a first edition of *The Hobbit*, which was published in 1937.
2646 *The Devil Goblins from Neptune*, and also referred to in *The Face of the Enemy*.
2647 *Dalek*
2648 *Peacemaker*
2649 *The Wheel of Ice* (p159).
2650 *Dreamland* (DW). The date is given in a caption. See the Unfixed Points in Time sidebar.

Jackson Pollock, an American artist, around this time. Pollock gave the Doctor a painting, *Azure in the Rain by a Man Who'd Never Been*.[2651]

The rituals of black arts practitioner Edward Alexander Crowley had summoned a Jarakabeth demon to Earth. The demon impersonated Crowley after his death at Hastings, 1947. The US security service Section Eight approached "Crowley" in the hope that his Hermetic Arts could be adopted for military use. The Crowley demon would become the head of the DIvisional department of Special Tactical Operations (Provisional) with Regard to Insurgent and Subversive Activity (DISTO(P)IA), a government branch designed to counter subversion.[2652]

1948

On 30th January, 1948, Mohandas "Mahatma" Gandhi was assassinated.[2653] A year after the first crash, a Nedenah rescue mission was shot down over Roswell.[2654] The Doctor bought a stuffed owl for Sarah in 1948. It was one of the items she packed when she left his company.[2655]

Ian Gilmore participated in the Berlin Airlift.[2656] **The Doctor liked the 1948 Olympics opening ceremony so much, he went back to see it again.**[2657] Torchwood acquired some alien artifacts at auction in 1948.[2658] **Wilf Mott was too young to fight in the Second World War, but joined the British Army and served as a private in Palestine, 1948.**[2659]

Barbara Wilson and Eddie Smith, the future parents of Sarah Jane Smith, met while serving coffee in a Navy, Army and Air Force Institutes (NAAFI) canteen. They were married after he proposed by passing her a note asking her to become "Mrs Smith".[2660]

Lloyd and Devina Collins, the future parents of Jess Collins – a friend of the twelfth Doctor – met aboard the *Empire Windrush*.[2661]

Constance Clark Leaves Her Husband

1948 (March) - QUICKSILVER[2662] **->** Henry Clarke had married Ana, and was living with her in Vienna as "Harry Cook", a linen trader. She was pregnant with his child. The Vilal component in Clarke's possession had been parlayed into a new communications system, part of Operation Quicksilver. The sixth Doctor and Constance Clarke arrived to investigate as the Vilal pursuing them happened upon the Doctor's wedding invite from Flip Jackson, and used its biodata to transport her through time – as potential leverage against the Doctor – with a vortex scoop. Constance realised the depth of her husband's betrayal to their marriage. The Doctor used Quicksilver's psychic influence to force a cease-fire upon the Vilal and their rivals, the insectoid Zerith.

Henry and Ana left to begin a new life in Bucharest, even as Constance and Flip decided to keep travelling with the Doctor.

2651 *Divided Loyalties.* Pollock was influential to the abstract expressionism movement.
2652 *Heart of TARDIS*
2653 *Ghosts of India*
2654 *The Devil Goblins from Neptune* (p240).
2655 *Interference.* We see it in *The Hand of Fear*.
2656 *CM S1: Artificial Intelligence.* The Airlift occurred 24th June, 1948 to 12th May, 1949, in response to the Soviet Union blockading parts of Berlin under Western control.
2657 *Fear Her*
2658 *TW: Slow Decay*
2659 *The End of Time*
2660 *SJA: The Temptation of Sarah Jane Smith.* No date given, but this is before Sarah Jane is born in 1951.
2661 *"The Pestilent Heart".* The *Empire Windrush* became renowned for transporting a group of West Indian immigrants from Jamaica to the UK in 1948.
2662 Dating *Quicksilver* (BF #220) - The year is given. Henry flips through a newspaper and sees mention of the Treaty of Brussels; that happened on 17th March, 1948.
2663 *FP: The Labyrinth of Histories,* extrapolating from the godfather's grandfather being conceived circa February 1899.
2664 *Leth-St: The Forgotten Son* (ch15).

2665 *Leth-St: Night of the Intelligence* (ch7). *Nineteen Eighty-Four* was published in 1949.
2666 Dating *The Cabinet of Light* (TEL #9) - The year is 1949, according to p14 and the back cover blurb. *TimeH: Peculiar Lives* specifies that the pyjama-clad Emily was found wandering the streets of London in "late 1949" (p13). The Doctor admits that his own memories are "hazy", and so he might be conflating the story of his last regeneration with the one in *Doctor Who – The Movie*. (Alternatively, it might have happened exactly as he claims.)

Emily's amnesia is attributed to Mestizer's agents attacking her. Given the murky recollections of everyone involved, though, it could stem from the blow to the head she receives at the end of *TimeH: Child of Time*.
2667 *TimeH: Child of Time*
2668 Dating *TimeH: The Winning Side* (TimeH #1) - The *Time Hunter* novella series picks up in wake of events in *The Cabinet of Light;* the year is variously reiterated as 1949. Pages 7 and 78 say that Emily is "killed" on a "cool, crisp December night".
2669 "Twenty years" before *The Underwater Menace*.
2670 *The Scales of Injustice.* No date is given.
2671 *Return of the Living Dad.* This happened in "the fifties" (p66).
2672 *Instruments of Darkness*

1949

Godfather Sabbath of Faction Paradox was born.[2663]

> (=) Alistair Lethbridge-Stewart's brother Gordon was fated to die in 1949, and his soul reincarnated in 1951, but the Great Intelligence's machinations caused him to perish more than a decade sooner.[2664]

> = *Nineteen Eighty-Four* didn't exist on Inferno Earth, nor did Kentucky Bourbon.[2665]

Honoré Lechasseur and Emily Blandish

1949 - THE CABINET OF LIGHT[2666] **->** An unknown incarnation of the Doctor – one who believed he had regenerated after visiting "the city by the bay" and being shot after meeting "a beautiful lady with no pity" – arrived in London with his companion, Emily Blandish. Agents working for Mestizer, a nemesis of the Doctor, attacked them – Emily helped the Doctor to escape, but Mestizer's agents captured the Doctor's time cabinet. The trauma of the event rendered Emily amnesiac. She was found wandering the streets of London, and became known in the press as "the Girl in Pink Pyjamas" (and occasionally "the Girl in the Pink Bikini"). She was used to promote clothes rationing.

To retrieve his property, the Doctor sought help from an expatriate and time sensitive named Honoré Lechasseur, who chiefly worked as a "fixer" – a trafficker of goods in a largely, but not entirely, legal fashion. Honoré observed the Doctor confronting Mestizer, and light from the Doctor's time cabinet started her house on fire. The Doctor, Mestizer, the house and the cabinet all disappeared. Afterwards, Honoré and Emily struck up a partnership.

By now, the Doctor was regarded as a "hobgoblin" or "myth" in the underground community. Legends claimed he variously gave fire to humankind, burned London in 1666, kidnapped the crew of the *Mary Celeste* and built Stonehenge with his bare hands.

Honoré and Emily's future selves watched as she was found, wandering the London streets, in her pyjamas.[2667]

1949 (December) - TIMEH: THE WINNING SIDE[2668]

-> Emily found that she was a "time channeller" who could travel through time and space in conjunction with a time-sensitive such as Honoré. They investigated the appearance of Emily's body beneath Hammersmith Bridge – part of a divergent timeline triggered when a civil servant, Simon Brown, released nuclear secrets to the entire world. Emily and Honoré erased this errant history after travelling to it in the year 1984, and Emily prevented her death by letting go of her "killer", a time-sensitive named Radford, during a time jump.

The Nineteen Fifties

In the early nineteen-fifties, Professor Zaroff – "the greatest scientist since Leonardo" – vanished.[2669] The testing of nuclear weapons, plus an increase in dumping of toxic waste, destroyed many Silurian shelters.[2670]

Albinex the Navarino arrived down a faulty time corridor from the far future.[2671] In Jamaica, the 1950s, the Doctor met the ornithologist James Bond and took him to the 1800s to see a live dodo. The Doctor later introduced writer Ian Fleming to Bond, who served as inspiration for Fleming's super-spy novels.[2672] The Doctor met the Cuban guerrilla leader Che Guevara.[2673] **UFOs were fashionable in the fifties.**[2674]

Amy and Rory agreed with the eleventh Doctor that American hot dogs from the 1950s were the best hot dogs of all.[2675] Jack Harkness thought the food of the 1950s was horrid.[2676] Torchwood collected about a dozen items of alien technology that came through the Rift in the 1950s.[2677]

The Doctor met John F. Kennedy in the 1950s.[2678] The patents of Ken Temple, an industrialist, revolutionised British manufacturing in the 1950s.[2679] In the 1950s, the Soviets sanctioned hothouse experiments into psychic phenomena, which entailed children being locked up for years.[2680] Iris Wildthyme was friends with actor-songwriter George Formby.[2681] The slow-time field generated by the Luron Godrin created a Second Bermuda Triangle above the Valley of Death, causing a DC4 plane to be lost to it.[2682]

2673 *Psi-ence Fiction.* No date is given.
2674 According to the Doctor in *Dreamland* (*DW*).
2675 *The Eye of the Jungle*
2676 *TW: Department X*
2677 *TW: Slow Decay*
2678 *Shroud of Sorrow* (p110). This happens "just before [the Doctor] accidentally got engaged to Marilyn Monroe at Frank Sinatra's house" (*A Christmas Carol*). It's not specified that the Doctor met Kennedy *at* that party, which is fortunate, because Kennedy was

merely a Congressman from Massachusetts in 1952, so would have been far less likely to be palling around with Sinatra et al. The impetus for Kennedy's alleged affair with Marilyn Monroe – her singing "Happy Birthday" to him – came much later, in 1962.
2679 *CM* S1: *The Pelage Project*
2680 *CM* S2: *Peshka*
2681 *Iris* S4: *Iris at the Oche.* Formby lived 1904-1961.
2682 *The Valley of Death.* DC4s were produced 1942-1947, and are here said to be "from" the 1950s.

The Doctor took fencing lessons from Errol Flynn, and thought the man had "the most enormous" ego.[2683] The Cambridge Five, a notorious spy ring, actually had nine members. The UK government kept the existence of four of them secret.[2684]

The TARDIS fully arrived on Hoy, Scotland, having left Ian and Barbara behind during a botched materialisation in 1956. The first Doctor allowed the local spay wife/witch Janet McKay and select others to believe he was a protective spirit, the Wissfornjarl, as he needed help hiding the TARDIS under a barrow. He spent some years enjoying good company and good books, waiting to reunite with his friends.[2685]

u – Overseer Zim conspired to turn Bramfield into a New Town, to attract victims for his Mind Thresher.[2686]

Lethbridge-Stewart in Korea

Alistair Lethbridge-Stewart was posted to Korea, and served there with Walter Douglas.[2687] Lethbridge-Stewart was in Korea as a private, during his National Service. Second Lt Spencer Pemberton became an invaluable mentor to him.[2688]

Lethbridge-Stewart's service in Korea marked the first time he killed someone with his bare hands: a bayonet down his opponent's collar bone. Captured for a time, he received poor treatment from the Korean People's Army.

When his National Service ended, Lethbridge-Stewart left Japan and was on the reserve list for eighteen months.[2689]

When Lethbridge-Stewart was 21, he spent a time in New York on the way back from Korea.[2690] Lieutenant Lethbridge-Stewart spent some time in Sierra Leone. One day, while lost in the forest, he met Mariatu, eldest daughter of Chief Yembe of the Rokoye village. Mariatu went to the city with Lethbridge-Stewart, returning alone a few years later with her son, Mariama.[2691]

1950

Mentally influenced by the Player Myrek, President Truman approved Operation Kali, a psychic warfare programme.[2692] Kenneth James Valentine, a former policeman who was at D-Day, joined Torchwood Cardiff in 1950.[2693]

Ian Gilmore met Dr Nadia Jovenka, a medic assisting the civilian population in Berlin, 1950. She was recalled to Russia as Stalin isolated the East from the West.[2694] At some point, Gilmore was posted in Calcutta and experienced gastronomic turmoil after eating a seafood madras.[2695]

Gwynfor Evans' grandfather died of black lung in 1950; his grandmother passed soon after. Grynfor's father taught him, at age 14, to drive so he could avoid working in the pit.[2696] Dr Ronald Fletcher carried out the first kidney transplant in the UK in 1950. Not long after, he joined a band of time-travelling surgeons.[2697]

2683 *Robot of Sherwood.* Flynn lived 1909-1959, and rose to fame with his first starring role in *Captain Blood* (1935).

2684 *CM S1: Artificial Intelligence.* The Cambridge Five were recruited in the 1930s, and operated at least until the early 1950s. Members included Kim Philby and Donald Maclean, both seen in *Endgame* (EDA).

2685 Some "years" before *The Revenants.*

2686 "Almost twenty-five years" before *3rdA: The Hidden Realm.*

2687 *Leth-St: The Forgotten Son* (chs. 10, 13), *Leth-St: The Schizoid Earth, Leth-St: Moon Blink* (ch6, supplemental material). The Korean War happened 1950-1953. Lethbridge-Stewart must have served there starting in 1950, as *Leth-St: The Forgotten Son* (ch3, epilogue) accords him "nineteen years" of service, in a book that dates itself to 1969.

The Devil Goblins of Neptune says that a 21-year-old Lethbridge-Stewart (born February 1929, according to the *Lethbridge-Stewart* books) routed through New York on his way back from Korea. If so, either he was simply on leave for a bit, or his incarceration in a Chinese prison camp happened that year and he was sent home afterward.

2688 *Leth-St:* "The Ambush"

2689 *Leth-St: Night of the Intelligence* (ch4).

2690 *The Devil Goblins from Neptune* (p37).

2691 *Transit,* when Lethbridge-Stewart is a lieutenant. The placement here is coincides with his military service as laid out in the *Lethbridge-Stewart* novels.

2692 "About a year" before *Endgame* (EDA).

2693 *TW: Trace Memory,* extrapolating from the fact that Valentine's paper trail vanishes in that year, and his records were later purged by Torchwood.

2694 *CM S1: Artificial Intelligence*

2695 *CM S2: The Fifth Citadel*

2696 *Leth-St: The Life of Evans* (ch2).

2697 *TW: Visiting Hours,* taking liberties with history. In real life, Charles Rob and William Dempster performed the first deceased kidney transplant in the UK in 1955; Michael Woodruff did the first live one in 1960.

2698 *Leth-St: Night of the Intelligence* (ch7); Dylan is "nine" when he arrives on our Earth in 1959.

2699 Dating *TimeH: The Tunnel at the End of the Light* (*TimeH* #2) - The cover bears the year, and when all is said and done, Honoré and Emily return to their starting point of "early 1950" (p150).

2700 *TimeH: The Clockwork Woman; TimeH: Kitsune; TimeH: The Severed Man; TimeH: Echoes.* Honoré and Emily tend to return home after each adventure, and the intros to each novella (as well as some internal references, including *The Severed Man,* pgs. 60-61, 106; *Echoes,* p9) reiterate that they originate from 1950.

2701 Dating *TimeH: Peculiar Lives* (*TimeH* #7) - The

= Dylan Jensen Lethbridge-Stewart, the son of the Inferno Earth's James Lethbridge-Stewart, was born in 1950.[2698]

(=) 1950 - TIMEH: THE TUNNEL AT THE END OF THE LIGHT[2699] **->** Mestizer resurfaced and took command of the Subterraneans. They committed an escalating number of murders while helping her find a time-sensitive that she could use to escape.

Honoré and Emily went back in time and stopped the Subterraneans' leader from leaving them, which retroactively prevented Mestizer from knowing they existed.

Honoré and Emily made further time-jumps, and had adventures pertaining to a clockwork woman in 1805; an impending apocalypse in Japan, 2020; the murderous Cabal of the Horned Beast in 1921; and a trapped time entity in London, 1995.[2700]

1950 (June) - TIMEH: PECULIAR LIVES[2701] **->** The future humans that had created *homo peculiar* now sought to eliminate them, as their timeline depended upon *homo peculiar* dissipating its essence through humanity. Members of *homo peculiar* defeated this goal by mastering time-channelling, and took to living in future eras where animal and plant life were in abundance on Earth, but humankind was absent.

On "a hot summer's night", Honoré and Emily left for Antioch, 1098.[2702]

c 1950 - IRIS S5: AN EXTRATERRESTRIAL WEREWOLF IN BELGIUM[2703] **->** Captain Turner emerged from the Time Vortex in the English countryside, and was found in a ditch by Chloe, a young woman he'd already met in future. The two of them became smitten. Iris came to collect her time-lost friend, but spied the young lovers from afar and left Turner and Chloe to a happy future together.

1951

Owain Vine, the reincarnation of Alistair Lethbridge-Stewart's brother James, part of the Great Intelligence's cycle of existence and treated as Alistair's "nephew" was born in April 1951 – as was his twin, Lewis.[2704] **The radio telescope was invented.**[2705] **The last witchcraft act on the English statute books was repealed in 1951.**[2706] Rupert Locke, a resident of Jackson Leaves, was convicted of six violent rapes in 1951.[2707] **Mrs Randall, a future nursing home resident who would meet Sarah Jane Smith, was named Miss Ealing of 1951.**[2708] A vicious alien species inspired *The Day of the Triffids*.[2709]

A computer built to regulate space trains, cars and buses was left at loose ends once its humanoid creators were lost in an undisclosed incident. In 1951, the Rift transported a Cardiff train leaving from Platform 4 for Grangetown to the computer's world. The train driver died, but the computer kept itself occupied by copying him and building trains to shuttle the replicants about.[2710]

(=) 1951 (13th February) - TIMEH: THE SIDEWAYS DOOR[2711] **->** Jonah Rankin, a time sensitive, accidentally transported Honoré and Emily to a parallel reality where their alternate selves had brazenly used their abilities to avert World War II and make other changes. The temporal amendments were such that history began to unravel. Honoré and Emily escaped as their counterparts were transported to parts unknown by a fatally wounded Rankin.

---

month and year are given as June (pgs. 13, 41, 82), and an epilogue references some incidental events on "early July" (p127) and "5th September" (p129).

2702 *TimeH: Deus Le Volt.* Honoré mentions some relaxation of rationing in the United Kingdom, as historically occurred in May 1950.

2703 Dating *Iris S5: An Extraterrestrial Werewolf in Belgium* (BF Iris #5.7) - Chloe says that World War II "ended almost five years ago".

2704 "Forty years" after *Pyramids of Mars*.

2705 *Leth-St: The Forgotten Son*, the Haisman Timeline; Owain is "18" in *Leth-St: Times Squared* [1969].

2706 *The Daemons*

2707 *TW: The House That Jack Built.* This event still occurs even once the house's history is revised.

2708 *SJA: Eye of the Gorgon*

2709 *TW: Exodus Code* (ch36). *The Day of the Triffids* was published in 1951.

2710 *TW: Ghost Train*

2711 Dating *TimeH: The Sideways Door* (TimeH #10) - After Honoré and Emily cross over into the parallel reality, page 32 reads: "The masthead on *The Times* confirmed the date was the same as it had been that morning: 13 February 1951." While this would seem to mean that it's 13th February in Honoré and Emily's native reality as well, *TimeH: Child of Time* – set in either late November or December 1951 – claims (p12) that events in *The Sideways Door* happened only "weeks" ago. The only way to reconcile this is to assume that some time displacement does occur when they cross from one Earth to another, but that's certainly not the impression one gets here.

1951 (23rd February) - TIMEH: THE ALBINO'S DANCER[2712] **->** Emily and the Albino – a half-human, half humanoid crimelord – travelled back some months to a bunker the Albino owned, as did Honoré and Catherine Howkins, one of the Albino's dancers. They were present as Leiter and Catherine's younger self – fugitives from the Sodality – arrived at the bunker using time belts. Honoré saved Catherine's younger self when the bunker exploded; she believed that Emily had perished, when in fact her older self had died instead. The Albino was also killed in the explosion – which so gravely wounded a man named Burgess, he would become the Albino in future.

Sarah Jane Smith – a companion of the third and fourth Doctors, an associate of the tenth Doctor and a thwarter of alien evil-doers – was born between 1st and 21st May, 1951, in the village of Foxgrove, to Eddie and Barbara Smith.[2713] On 30th June, 1951, Catherine Howkins was hired as an exotic dancer for the Albino.[2714]

1951 (18th August) - SJA: THE TEMPTATION OF SARAH JANE SMITH[2715] **->** When Sarah Jane Smith was three months old, her parents mysteriously left her in her pram along the side of the road in the village of Foxgrove, then were killed when their car struck a tractor that had broken down in the lane. She would be raised by Lavinia Smith, her father's sister.

> (=) The Trickster enabled Sarah Jane to travel back from 2009 and prevent her parents' death, creating a parallel timeline in which the Trickster devastated Earth. Sarah's parents accepted that their survival had crippled the world, and sacrificed themselves to restore history.

In Autumn 1951, the surviving members of a race that had evolved on Jupiter's moon Europa left their dying habitat, but were caught in Earth's gravity well. The ship crashed near Delphin Isle in the North Sea: the home to a top-secret UK base established for high-ranking Cold War defectors. The Delphin Isle staff began dissecting the ship's crew, but the Europans deployed a natural secretion they used to mentally commandeer their food source. They maintained secret control of the base for decades.[2716]

1951 (4th November) - TIMEH: THE ALBINO'S DANCER[2717] **->** Catherine Howkins happened upon Honoré and thanked him for saving her life last February – in an explosion where Howkins believed that Emily had

---

2712 Dating *TimeH: The Albino's Dancer* (*TimeH* #9) - The exact day is repeatedly given.
2713 According to *SJA: Whatever Happened to Sarah Jane?*, Sarah was "13" by mid-July, 1964. *SJA: The Temptation of Sarah Jane Smith* establishes that she was "three months old" in August 1951, suggesting she was born in May. We can further narrow the date as *SJA: Secrets of the Stars* says that Sarah is a Taurus, which lasts 20th April to 21st May.
In *SJA: Goodbye, Sarah Jane Smith*, Sarah says she was "23" when she met the Doctor (in *The Time Warrior*) - the same as her age given on screen in *Invasion of the Dinosaurs* (although in the novelisation of that story, she's "22"). Elisabeth Sladen, who played Sarah, was born in 1948. In the format document for the proposed *K9 and Company* series, it's stated that Sarah was born in "1949". She was "about 30" in the spin-off novel *Harry Sullivan's War* (suggesting a birth date of 1955), and *Evolution* (p242) says she was born "over sixty years" after 1880.
2714 *TimeH: The Albino's Dancer*
2715 Dating *SJA: The Temptation of Sarah Jane Smith* (*SJA* 2.5) - The precise date is given.
2716 *The Defectors*
2717 Dating *TimeH: The Albino's Dancer* (*TimeH* #9) - The exact day is repeatedly given, and while it's stated within the text and on the cover that Honoré and Emily now originate from 1951, the introduction – as with the previous six *Time Hunter* novellas – continues to stub-

bornly insist that it's 1950.
2718 *TimeH: The Sideways Door*
2719 Dating *TimeH: Child of Time* (*TimeH* #11) - This is the final *Time Hunter* novella. It's reiterated that it's still 1951. The day is given (p15), and it's been "a couple of weeks" (pgs. 12, 15) since the previous novella.
2720 Dating *Timewyrm: Exodus* (NA #2) - In Part One of the novel, the Doctor proclaims it to be the "Festival of Britain, 1951" (p5). At the end of the novel, the Doctor and Ace arrive at the real Festival of Britain.
2721 Dating *Endgame* (EDA #40) - The year is given (p242).
2722 *Father Time* (p58).
2723 *Zagreus*, again judging by a historical simulation.
2724 Dating *Real Time* (BF BBCi #1) - The date is given, episode one, track 1.
2725 *The Plotters*. If we take the writers' guidelines at face value, she would have been 12 at the time.
2726 *TW: Out of Time*
2727 *The Legends of River Song*: "Picnic at Asgard"
2728 *Cuddlesome*. It's not stated when this occurs, but Timothy West, who plays Turvey, was born in 1934 – making 1952 as good a dating as anything else.
2729 *Leth-St: The Forgotten Son* (ch4).
2730 *Leth-St: The Life of Evans* (ch1).
2731 Dating *The Nowhere Place* (BF #84) - The date is given.

died. Honoré, Howkins, Emily and the Albino used various means to go back to February, all of them intent on uncovering the truth about the incident.

Honoré and Emily briefly travelled to a parallel reality in which their alternate selves were abusing their powers.[2718]

1951 (1st December) - TIMEH: CHILD OF TIME[2719]

-> Honoré and Emily examined the corpse of a woman from the future, which caused them to travel to 2586. After learning of Emily's origins, they returned to 1951 and looked forward to new adventures together.

> **(=) 1951 - TIMEWYRM: EXODUS**[2720] **->** Following the total defeat of the British army at Dunkirk in 1940, the German army swept across the Channel and landed at Folkestone. Britain fell in six days. Churchill and thousands of suspected troublemakers were executed. Oswald Mosley was installed as Prime Minister, and Edward VIII was crowned. Unsure what to do with Britain, the Nazi High Command let the country fall into ruin.
>
> All able-bodied men were conscripted as slave workers and shipped to the continent. In 1951, the Festival of Britain took place in London to celebrate ten years of Nazi victory. The Germans planned to have a man on the moon in this year. The seventh Doctor and Ace realised that history had been altered. They travelled back and averted this timeline with the destruction of Drachensberg Castle in 1939.

After they defeated the War Lords and Timewyrm, the Doctor and Ace visited the real Festival of Britain and discovered that history was back on course.

@ 1951 - ENDGAME[2721] **->** The seventh Doctor (and Ace) saw the eighth Doctor at the Festival of Britain, but neither recognised the other.

The Players decided on a new game, seeing which among them could provoke a nuclear holocaust on Earth. Kim Philby, a member of British intelligence and a double agent for the Soviet Union, recruited the eighth Doctor to defeat the Players.

President Truman became abnormally hostile to China, and the Doctor discovered the president was under the influence of the Player Myrek. As Philby suspected, another Player – the Countess – was manipulating Stalin. The Doctor ended the Players' control of the Russian leader and Truman. Returning to America, the Doctor tricked the Players into killing each other. The Doctor declined a job at the White House and returned to London.

@ The eighth Doctor was present in the Soviet Union during a high profile chess match played in 1951.[2722] In 1951, the Dionysus Project in Cardington opened a doorway to the Divergents' domain. This killed the researchers Dr Stone and the Reverend Matthew Townsend.[2723]

> **(=) 1951 - REAL TIME**[2724] **->** With the Cybermen firmly in control of Earth, a group of human rebels crafted an organic techno-virus capable of destroying the Cybermen's artificial implants. They used a Chronosphere to dispatch Dr Reece Goddard to 3286, the year in which the Cybermen altered history, in the hope of averting this timeline altogether.

1952

Barbara Wright worked at Hampstead High School for girls in 1952.[2725] **Pilot Diane Holmes flew from England to Australia in just four days.**[2726] The Doctor owned a gold medal from the 1952 Olympics in Helsinki.[2727]

Ronald Turvey went to university to read biochemistry when he was 18, but bullies tore his beloved teddy bear, Mr Cuddles, to shreds. In the years to come, Turvey was infected with the Tinghus: a member of a race of psychic parasites. He felt as if the ghost of Mr Cuddles was talking to him, and would found a toy company.[2728]

Raymond Harold Phillips, a childhood friend of Alistair Lethbridge-Stewart, was dismissed as a kook after publishing *The Hollow Man of Carrington Lodge* (1952), an account of the "supernatural presence" (actually an avatar of the Great Intelligence) that haunted Draynes Wood.[2729]

Sixteen-year-old Gwynfor Evans was drafted in 1952, and posted to the Corps of Engineers as a driver. Such was his cowardice and haplessness, he would spend the next eighteen years as a Private.[2730]

1952 (7th September) - THE NOWHERE PLACE[2731]

-> Scientists working on behalf of the British War Office were stationed RAF Hill Lankton Base, and the Oxford-educated Trevor Ridgely was assigned to work on rocket propulsion there. Trevor doodled the rudimentary design for a star drive-equipped ship, and although he never worked toward the completion of such a device, his sketch planted the seed of his idea. Someone would return to Trevor's sketch in future, spot something he'd overlooked and help to facilitate humankind's journey into the stars.

The sixth Doctor and Evelyn arrived from 2197, and encountered Trevor on the *Ivy Lee*, the last Turret-class train in service, as it was passing through Stapely Moor. Representatives of the original race that evolved on Earth hoped to trick the time travellers into facilitating the loss of Trevor's sketch – and thereby subvert humanity's star-travel – but the Doctor and Evelyn thwarted the plot and returned to the future.

(=) In Klein's history, the Third Reich controlled Africa. When the Mau Mau rebelled in 1952, waves of German aircraft obliterated their tribal areas.[2732]

The First Elizabeth Klein Joins the TARDIS

1952 (October) - A THOUSAND TINY WINGS[2733] ->
The Chaliss had evolved as a species of intelligent little birds – a rarity in the universe, owing to their inability to work tools with wings. They would nestle on a humanoid – a "mule", of sorts – in their hundreds, thousands even, and thereby achieve a group consciousness.

One such Chaliss gestalt arrived in Kenya as the Mau Mau rebelled against the British. It intended on using humanity as test subjects in the creation of a "universal plague" that could be tailored and sold to various parties. As different races wiped themselves out, the Chaliss would amass enough economic might to control the galaxy.

(=) The Elizabeth Klein who escaped from Colditz was now in Kenya, owing to her fascination with the dark continent. She had a full laboratory in Nairobi, but abandoned it when the uprising started. The seventh Doctor happened upon Klein as she sheltered in a farmhouse, and together they killed the Chaliss birds, whose "mule" died soon afterwards. A British subject, Mrs Sylvia O'Donnell, was tasked with seeing that a dome the Chaliss had built was buried, forever trapping the contagion within. The Doctor hoped to broaden Klein's philosophies by letting her see other worlds, and made her his new companion.

Owing to Klein's removal from history in 2044, the Doctor defeated the Chaliss without her involvement.

(=) In Klein's history, Hans De Flores was "the Führer's favourite". The Nazis sent builders to construct new cities in the devastated Kenya, but the carpet bombing in 1952 had released the Chaliss contagion. Within three years, most of the builders were dead. The Führer assigned Klein to take a team of doctors and investigate, but they were evacuated before making any progress. It was years before the Nazis dared return to Africa.[2734]

1952 (December) - AMORALITY TALE[2735] -> The third Doctor and Sarah Jane sought to investigate a warp shadow, and arrived prior to a killer smog descending on London. The Doctor set up shop as a watchmaker. Sarah

---

2732 *A Thousand Tiny Wings*

2733 Dating *A Thousand Tiny Wings* (BF #130) - The back cover vaguely declares that it's "Kenya, the 1950s", but to judge by everyone's anxieties, the Mau Mau uprising (1952-1960) has just begun. A BBC Overseas Service radio broadcast relates how the Kenyan governor, Sir Evelyn Baring, has declared a state of emergency just two weeks after taking office, and how the authorities have already arrested one hundred leaders of the insurgency, including rebel spokesperson Jomo Kenyatta (later Kenya's first prime minister) – all of which occurred on 20th October, 1952.

Annoyingly, and despite all the historical detail that indicates an October 1952 dating, *The Architects of History* dates this story to "1953" – although the version of Klein who works for UNIT might be rounding when she says that.

2734 *A Thousand Tiny Wings*. De Flores appeared in *Silver Nemesis*.

2735 Dating *Amorality Tale* (PDA #52) - It's "Wednesday, December 3, 1952" (p12).

2736 *J&L S5: The Age of Revolution*

2737 *Maker of Demons*

2738 Dating *A Christmas Carol* (X6.0) - The year is given. Monroe *was* between marriages, as it happens, in 1952.

2739 Dating *Night and the Doctor*: "Good Night" (Series 6 DVD minisode) - No year given, but it's commonly assumed (not unreasonably) in fandom that "Marilyn" refers to Marilyn Monroe, who married the Doctor in *A Christmas Carol*. Mention of the biplane suggests that she's forced to make her way home without benefit of time travel.

2740 *Nightshade* (p111).

2741 *Escape Velocity* (p196).

2742 *The Dying Days* (p52). Sherpa Tenzing Norgay and Edmund P. Hillary were the first to conquer Everest, on 29th May, 1953.

2743 *TW: Exodus Code* (ch14). Hillary lived 1919-2008.

2744 *The Suffering*. In real life, *The Times* published evidence of the hoax in November 1953.

2745 *The Catalyst*. The type of race isn't specified.

2746 "Five years" before *Dreamland* (DW).

2747 *Dreamland* (DW). *SJA: The Vault of Secrets* specifies that the Men in Black were first active in 1953.

2748 Trueman is 56 in *SJA: Secrets of the Stars*, set in early November, 2009, so he was born in either 1952 or 1953. Trueman-actor Russ Abbott is somewhat older than the part he played, having been born 16th September, 1947.

2749 "Ghosts of the Northern Line"

2750 *The Mists of Time*

2751 *3rdA: Storm of the Horofax*

2752 *Mastermind*, "two decades" prior to 1973.

2753 "Twelve years" before *CM S2: Manhunt*.

2754 *TW: Ghost Mission, TW: Outbreak*

2755 Dating *The Torchwood Archive* (BF *TW* special release #1) - The year is given.

2756 Dating *The Idiot's Lantern* (X2.7) - The story's climax coincides with the coronation of Queen Elizabeth II, with the Doctor and Rose arriving the day before.

found out that a war was brewing between the Ramsey and Callum gangs. Callum was actually a member of the Xhinn, a ruthless alien species, and the killer smog was actually a Xhinn weapon. The Doctor destroyed the Xhinn scoutship, which deterred their main fleet from attacking.

Ellie Higson saw the Great Smog of 1952. At some point, she enrolled in the Royal Ballet school, and would make use of the resultant fighting skills in 1968.[2736] The seventh Doctor successfully crossed "sing a duet with Frank Sinatra" off his bucket list, but felt lucky to escape with his life, as Sinatra wasn't a very good sport.[2737]

1952 - A CHRISTMAS CAROL[2738] -> The eleventh Doctor, the teenage Karzan Sardick and Abigail Pettigrew visited Hollywood. The Doctor was supposed to do a duet with Frank Sinatra, but accidentally got engaged to Marilyn Monroe. They were married at a locale the Doctor later insisted wasn't a real chapel. In the same year, the Doctor met Albert Einstein and Father Christmas – whom the Doctor better knew as "Fred" – at Sinatra's hunting lodge.

? 1952 - NIGHT AND THE DOCTOR: "Good Night"[2739] -> A euphonium-bearing eleventh Doctor bid goodbye to River Song after they'd dealt with a possessed orchestra on a moonbase. He asked her to tell a woman named Marilyn that she would have to take a biplane home...

1953

The science fiction serial *Nightshade* was first shown by the BBC in 1953. It would run for five years.[2740] @ The eighth Doctor quickly became a fan of the show.[2741]

The Doctor was the first man to climb Everest, giving mountaineers Tenzing Norgay and Edmund Hillary a hand up.[2742] Captain Jack once raced Hillary to a summit, but wasn't present at Hillary's climb of Mount Everest.[2743]

The notorious Piltdown Man skull was exposed for what it was: a human cranium with the jawbone of an ape attached.[2744] Joshua Douglas, a companion of the third Doctor, won first prize in a race in 1953 and was awarded a metal cup.[2745] **Rivesh Mantilax was shot down attempting to rescue his wife from Area 51. He was found and kept safe by a group of Native Americans led by Night Eagle.**[2746]

In 1953, the Alliance of Shades – an extra-terrestrial organisation dedicated to keeping advanced technology from primitive worlds such as Earth – deployed robots presenting themselves as Men in Black to perform recovery operations. The tenth Doctor would encounter a quartet of Men in Black – Mr Dread, Mr Fear, Mr Terror and Mr Apprehension – during his visit

to Area 51 in 1958.[2747]

Martin Trueman was born at exactly the right moment, exactly the right time, for him to later serve as a channel for the power of the Ancient Lights.[2748]

The Doctor made a hobby of seeing *The Mousetrap*, and watched every production from 1953 to at least 2009.[2749]

u – Jo Grant's grandfather died when she was seven.[2750] When Jo Grant was at school, she wanted to work at a monkey sanctuary in Africa.[2751]

The decaying Master, living on Earth throughout the twentieth century, extended the lifespan of his bodies to forty years, but sequestered himself in a sterile penthouse to eliminate the risk of infection.[2752]

Tara Cassington died in Switzerland, aged 15, from a broken neck at a finishing school that received funds from Commodore Charles Waverly. The commodore's daughter, Emma Waverly, adopted Cassington's identity.[2753]

Norton Folgate

Norton Folgate, a Torchwood One agent from 1953, projected himself into the future to assess Sgt Andy Davidson's performance in the field. Folgate claimed that in his era, Torchwood worked to curtail a black market for alien artefacts – including a deadly Bandril staser – which flourished owing to spaceships shot down during World War II.[2754]

1953 - TW: THE TORCHWOOD ARCHIVE (BF)[2755] -> Norton Folgate betrayed Torchwood and covertly furthered the Committee's interests. He stole Object One from Torchwood, and positioned them to dismantle the Mandrake gangster operation. The government mistakenly believed that Torchwood had ties to London's drug trade.

The Coronation of Elizabeth II

1953 (1st-2nd June) - THE IDIOT'S LANTERN[2756] -> An alien became an energy being after her people executed her, and fled to Earth in 1953. The Wire, as she was now called, conscripted Mr Magpie of Magpie's Electricals to supply cheap televisions in the run-up to the coronation of Queen Elizabeth II. This enabled the Wire to feed off the electrical energy of viewers' brains, which turned them blank-faced. The Wire wanted to connect with the twenty million people expected to watch the Coronation, and regain her corporeal body.

The tenth Doctor and Rose arrived on Florizel Street in London and learned of the Wire's intentions. The Doctor sabotaged the transmitter at Alexandra Palace, which trapped the Wire onto a Betamax tape (that the Doctor intended to tape over) and restored her victims to health.

The Wire killed Mr Magpie before she was captured, but his company would prosper without him.[2757]

Ian Chesterton was raised Church of England. When TV was still a novelty, he'd spend Saturday afternoons with his father, showing support for the home team. Ian saw Spanish Armada films starring Errol Flynn, Bette Davis and Flora Robson, and his hero was Sir Francis Drake.[2758] One summer after the war, Ian Chesterton frequently wound up in his father's dark room, developing pictures after days out to Brighton or Southend.[2759]

1953 (20th November) - TW: TRACE MEMORY[2760]
-> An Arctic expedition discovered a Vondraxian Orb, and sent it via a Scandinavian cargo ship to Torchwood Cardiff. The Orb reacted badly to the presence of the Rift and exploded – a dock worker, Michael Bellini, absorbed the Orb's energy and was flung back to 1941.

c 1953 (Winter) - AN ORDINARY LIFE[2761] -> A psychic parasite that had harmlessly existed in Earth's oceans "for centuries, millennia even" dominated Michael Newman, an immigrant to England from Jamiaca, as he went on a fishing trip in the East Indies. Through him, the parasite replaced London dockworkers with force-grown doppelgangers, while the originals were kept in stasis.

Seeking energy with which to multiply, the parasite latched onto the passing TARDIS' telepathic circuits and drew the Ship off course. The parasite's minions captured the first Doctor and the TARDIS, both of which went dormant to fend off the parasite's mental assault. Steven and Sara spent some weeks erroneously thinking the Doctor had left them stranded, but eventually rescued their friend and ruined the parasite's operations. Sara threw the para-

site's node heart into the sea and blasted it with her pistol, believing that its remains would harmlessly emulate plankton and other marine life.

> (=) In 1953, the second President of the English Empire celebrated the fiftieth Jubilee of victory by executing one of his two captive Daleks.[2762]

The Toymaker beat Le Chiffre at baccarat.[2763] An archaeological dig at Mynach Hengoed in 1953 uncovered an alien spaceship, which Torchwood acquired.[2764]

On 18th December, 1953, a plane with three people on board fell through the Rift in Cardiff. They would emerge from it in late 2007.[2765]

Lethbridge-Stewart at Sandhurst[2766]

With Spencer Pemberton's sponsorship, Second Lt Alistair Lethbridge-Stewart enrolled at Royal Military Academy Sandhurst in early 1954. On his first day there, he became reacquainted with a fellow cadet and one of his most enduring friends: Walter Douglas. A few weeks later, Douglas introduced him to Officer Cadet Leslie Johnston. The trio became so thick as thieves, they were known as the Holy Trinity.

Despite this, Johnston became ever-resentful of his friends' accomplishments. Lethbridge-Stewart was posted to the Scots Guards, Johnston to the Royal Signals. In 1958, Johnston made unsolicited advances on Corporal Joseph Rainey's fiance, resulting in a fistfight. Johnston received prison time and a dishonourable discharge, and the rage he displayed at his trial made Lethbridge-Stewart realise that Johnson had secretly hated him all the while at

---

2757 Use of the Magpie Electricals logo has become a running joke for the new series design team, and is seen on various electronics in *The Runaway Bride*, *The Sound of Drums*, *Voyage of the Damned*, *Day of the Moon*, *TW: The Undertaker's Gift*, *The Lost Magic* and *The Lie of the Land*. It's on a banner in *The Beast Below*, and on equipment in the TARDIS in *The Eleventh Hour*, *Vincent and the Doctor* and *Before the Flood*. A shop of electronics equipment in *Wave of Destruction* [1964] includes a "Magpie Deluxe".

2758 *The Flames of Cadiz*

2759 *The Dark Planet*

2760 Dating *TW: Trace Memory* (*TW* novel #5) - The exact day is given, p27.

2761 Dating *An Ordinary Life* (BF EA #1.4) - The blurb, Sara and Steven all ballpark the era as "1950s Earth/London". Elizabeth II is Queen, so it's after her ascension to the throne on 6th February, 1952. Steven narrates that "the first snow of winter was falling over London". Two weeks later, he mentions a "winter afternoon gloom".

2762 *Jubilee*

2763 "End Game" (*DWM*). Le Chiffre is the villain in the first James Bond novel, *Casino Royale* (1953).

2764 *TW: Slow Decay*

2765 *TW: Out of Time*

2766 *Leth-St: Night of the Intelligence* (ch4) definitively has the Brigadier start at Sandhurst in early 1954; *Leth-St: Top Secret Files* says he graduated in 1956.

2767 *Leth-St: Night of the Intelligence* (ch4).

2768 In *Mawdryn Undead*, the 1983 Brigadier talks of "thirty years of soldiering". He doesn't have a moustache in the regimental photograph seen in *Inferno*. He is a member of the Scots' Guards in *The Web of Fear*. Other information here comes from *The Invasion* and *The Green Death*.

2769 *Leth-St: The Showstoppers*

2770 *TW: Trace Memory*

2771 *The Bells of Saint John*. An ebook of *Summer Falls* (credited to Amelia Williams, but actually written by James Goss) states 1954 as its original year of publication. There's no real way of telling how much of the

Sandhurst. They would not see each other for eleven years.[2767]

Alistair Gordon Lethbridge-Stewart attended Sandhurst with Billy Rutlidge. Once his training was complete, Lethbridge-Stewart grew his moustache, joined the Scots' Guards and was stationed for a time at Aldgate.[2768]

Soon after his academy days, Alistair Lethbridge-Stewart became acquainted with Sgt Samson Ware.[2769]

1954

In March 1954, Torchwood Cardiff carried out an inventory of its alien tech that took all five of its staff the best part of a month to complete.[2770] *Summer Falls*, **a children's book by Amelia Williams, was released** in 1954.[2771] **Brenda Williams, the mother of Rhys Williams, was born.**[2772] Iris and Captain Turner met Noel Coward on Capri.[2773] The first Doctor and Susan met Noel Coward.[2774]

Graham Greene received a tape from Alan Turing that explained his contact with the Doctor.[2775] Circa 1954, the student Astrabel Zar vacationed on Gadrahadradon, a haunted planet that facilitated glimpses into the future. Zar received instructions from his future self on how to build Tomorrow Windows, devices that would similarly display images of future times. He would later pass on the secret of building Tomorrow Windows to one of his own students, Charlton Mackerel.[2776]

Warlord Hagoth's group of Zygons infiltrated the music business, then branched out into humankind's industrial operations. Their goal was to spur industry in a way that would promote global warming and damage the ozone layer – making Earth more habitable for Zygon-kind.[2777]

George Limb survived being catapulted through time and landed in 1954. He loosely learned to navigate his time machine between 1940 and 1962, but his journeys created many alternate timelines. Limb's final trip resulted in his being left in 1954 while his time machine jumped on ahead to 1959. He waited five years to retrieve it.[2778]

1954 - "The Good Soldier"[2779] **->** The seventh Doctor and Ace drove up to a diner in the Nevada desert and found it full of American soldiers. The area lifted into space and docked with a flying saucer, which in turn docked with its mothership... and Cybermen emerged from the sand. The Doctor told Ace that the Mondasian Cybermen would have attacked Earth before 1986 if they'd had the right weapon... and that they were standing in it.

Meanwhile, the Cybermen had learned how to control human minds, and required aggression – which they lacked themselves – to power their warship. They installed Colonel Rhodes, the leader of the soldiers, into the device. Ace interfaced with the system, detaching the flying saucer. The Cybermen pursued, but the Doctor and Ace overloaded their reactor, destroying the warship.

1954 (Summer) - DAEMONS: WHITE WITCH OF DEVIL'S END[2780] **->** Olive Hawthorne became so enamoured of a vampire named Victor, she offered to let him turn her. Instead, Victor came to resent his undead existence, and – to protect Olive from his corruption – met with her one more time in daytime, and let the sunlight destroy him.

story within – involving a young girl named Kate, an enigma posed by the painting *The Lord of Winter*, and a Doctor-like character named the Curator – actually happened within the *Doctor Who* universe, and how much is Amelia's invention.

2772 She's "63" in *TW: Visiting Hours* [2017]. Nerys Williams, who plays Brenda here and in *TW: Something Borrowed*, was born more than a decade earlier, in 1941.

2773 *Iris S5: Dark Side*. Coward vacationed on Capri in 1954, and while there wrote "A bar on the Piccola Marina". According to *Mad Dogs and Englishmen*, Iris and Coward meet again in 957.

2774 *The Sleeping City*. Coward lived 1899-1973.

2775 *The Turing Test*. "Six months" after Turing's suicide (7th June, 1954; p104), "forty-six years" before the year 2000 (p105).

2776 "Fifty years" before *The Tomorrow Windows* (p274).

2777 "Decades" prior to *The Zygon Who Fell to Earth*.

2778 *Loving the Alien* (p188-189).

2779 Dating "The Good Soldier" (*DWM* #175-178) - "It's 1954" according to the Doctor. The Cybermen resemble those from *The Tenth Planet*, and that's specified in dialogue. The Cybermen report to Mondas Control.

2780 Dating *Daemons: White Witch of Devil's End* (story #2, "Half Light") - No date given. The townsfolk look upon Olive as a spinster – Olive remarks in the film version of *White Witch* that "An unmarried woman in her thirties was considered an old maid", but the label was actually saddled upon unmarried women earlier than that. We've arbitrarily decided that Olive is about 25, spacing out the passage of time between *Daemons*: "The Inheritance" (when she's 18) and *Daemons*: "The Poppet" (when she's in her forties). In keeping with that, Olive's final meeting with Victor (which happens "on a hot summer's day") occurs a month before a total eclipse settled upon the United Kingdom, which historically happened on 30th June, 1954.

(=) 1954 (mid-Summer) - IRIS S5: MURDER AT THE ABBEY[2781] **->** Iris Wildthyme's companion, Captain Edwin Turner, struck up a romance with Chloe, the niece of Lady Fothergill, but she was allergic to nuts... and murdered via a sandwich surreptitiously laced with mashed almonds. Iris and Turner deduced that Chloe's death was related to a Russian spy ring run by Lord and Lady Fothergill and their servants, the Albertsons. The duo exposed the operation, and turned the perpetrators over to MI-5.

Peter Allen Tyler, the future father of Rose Tyler, was born 15th September, 1954.[2782]

1954 (9th November) - THE WITCH HUNTERS[2783] **->** The first Doctor, Ian, Barbara and Susan arrived after visiting Salem during the witch trials. Susan was distressed to think that some of the residents would be burnt as witches, and used the TARDIS' Fast Return Switch in a bid to go back and save them. Returning to 1954, the time travellers attended the premiere of *The Crucible* in Bristol.

Later, the Doctor brought the condemned Rebecca Nurse to this era to view *The Crucible* and see memorials to the victims of the Salem witch trials.

1955

In 1955, Chris Parsons was born. The Doctor visited Chris' future College, St Cedd's Cambridge.[2784] Captain Jack signed items into the Torchwood Cardiff archive.[2785] Clara Oswald's grandmother met her grandfather when she saw him on a pier on a rainy day.[2786] Alistair Lethbridge-Stewart's grandmother died in 1955.[2787]

Winston Churchill was no longer prime minister, and in his retirement authored history books. The eleventh Doctor, accompanied by a young Kazran Sardick, granted Churchill's wish to learn more about history from Julius Caesar himself. They departed for 55 BC...[2788]

When Allison Williams was 14, she had a fling with Jack Maddocks over the Easter holidays.[2789] In 1955, a fire gutted the tower of the lighthouse at Fang Rock, but left its generator room intact.[2790] Vincent Travers' daughter Deborah married, and took the surname Walker.[2791]

In 1955, the Good Thinking Project created mind-reading nano-viruses from alien technology, and accidentally spurred an outbreak of violence among its human test subjects. Jack Harkness realised Norton Folgate's duplicity to Torchwood. Good Thinking was curtailed, but only after Jack was burned alive, alongside all of the test subjects. Decades later, Ianto Jones would discover that Torchwood had no record of Folgate's death.[2792]

(=) In an errant timeline, George Limb saved the life of actor James Dean. The alternate Dean served as Limb's assistant in the proper reality.[2793]

(=) To undo events at Colditz Castle, the seventh Doctor arrived at a border-crossing checkpoint in the Reich-controlled West. He arranged for himself to be gunned down, and regenerated in secret while the Nazis took the TARDIS away. He spent the next six years helping people evade the Reich's ethnic cleansing programs.[2794]

c 1955 - "Prisoners of Time"[2795] **->** In Los Angeles, the tenth Doctor adapted the Griffith Observatory's telescope so Martha could see an image of Gallifrey as it looked before the Time War. Soon after, they stopped two Dominators and their Quarks from enslaving humanity with subliminal messages slipped into a motion picture.

Adam Mitchell kidnapped Martha, but the Doctor over-

2781 Dating *Iris S5: Murder at the Abbey* (BF *Iris* #5.4) - It's the same year that bacon rationing ended in the UK following World War II, in 1954. Turner says it's "the middle of summer". The "happy ending" that Iris allows Turner and Chloe circa 1950, in *Iris S5: An Extraterrestrial Werewolf in Belgium*, would presumably entail overwriting these events so Chloe's murder never occurred.

2782 *Father's Day*

2783 Dating *The Witch Hunters* (PDA #9) - The date is given, p68. The Fast Return Switch first appeared in *The Edge of Destruction* (see the Fast Return Switch sidebar).

2784 *Shada*

2785 *TW: Slow Decay* (p84).

2786 *The Time of the Doctor*, as roughly extrapolated from actress Sheila Reid being born in 1937.

2787 *The Devil Goblins from Neptune* (p56), *The King of Terror* (p126).

2788 *Churchill: Living Memory*. Churchill's second tenure as prime minister ended 6th April, 1955. His *A History of the English-Speaking Peoples*, a four-volume history of Britain that began with Julius Caesar's invasions of Britain, was released 1956-58.

2789 *CM S3: The Forgotten Village*

2790 *Leth-St: Beast of Fang Rock* (ch2).

2791 "Fifteen years" before *Leth-St: The Dreamer's Lament*.

2792 *TW: Outbreak*

2793 *Loving the Alien*. Dean died 30th September, 1955.

2794 "Klein's Story", confirming the 1955 dating given in *Colditz*.

2795 Dating "Prisoners of Time" (IDW *DW* mini-series) - The Doctor estimates from a truck that it's "the mid-1950s", an era that the fashions, design and state of movie-making all suggest.

CYBERMEN ... FASHION VICTIMS?: *When we first published this sidebar in 2012, we postulated that although it had become commonplace to regard all strains of Cybermen (save for the Cybus Industries models) as having some inheritance from Mondas, perhaps they were in fact multiple, and separately developed, races. Since then,* The Doctor Falls *came out and said exactly that, with the twelfth Doctor explaining: "[Cybermen] happen everywhere there's people. Mondas, Telos, Earth, Planet 14, Marinus... People get the Cybermen wrong. There's no evil plan, no evil genius. Just parallel evolution... People plus technology minus humanity."*

Nonetheless, as the questions and answers posed by this sidebar still seem relevant – and it's always possible that a future story declares the Doctor to be wrong, or inadvertently contradicts what is said in The Doctor Falls *– we've folded the post-2012 Cybermen stories into it, applied some light revision, and otherwise let it stand.*

Does the variation in design between the Cybermen actually symbolise anything, and how helpful is it to the dating process? It's a similar question to that of the Klingons in *Star Trek* – there's a real-life reason (generally related to budgets and audience expectations) as to why they look different in the sixties and the eighties, but is there a reason *within* the fiction?

On television, it's not even clear that the characters "see" any difference between different models of Cybermen. Ben instantly recognises the Cybermen in *The Moonbase*, even though they bear little resemblance to the ones he saw in *The Tenth Planet*. Notably, he doesn't so much as comment that they've been redesigned – something that might be relevant to say, if one is evaluating the capabilities of the alien invaders that are besieging one's moonbase. Ben is hardly alone in this, as many other characters fail to make the same observation (just to name a few, the Doctor, Polly, Jamie, Zoe, Brigadier and Sarah Jane all encounter different versions of the Cybermen). On screen at least, it's rare to see an old model once a new one has been introduced (except for the flashback in *Earthshock*, the head in a museum in *Dalek* and *World Enough and Time/The Doctor Falls*).

We almost never see two versions of the Cybermen together (again, *World Enough and Time/The Doctor Falls* is an exception that proves the rule). Yet the development doesn't appear to be linear in terms of fictional history – it's strictly linear in terms of the order the Doctor meets them. Without wanting to get unduly philosophical, the television episodes we see are a *representation* of reality, not a window on it – unless there's an unrevealed canonical reason as to why (for instance) the Silurians have zips down their backs in *Warriors of the Deep*. We're seeing things as convincingly as the BBC can render them, so it's entirely possible that – to the characters – the Cybermen from *The Tenth Planet* look identical to the ones in *The Moonbase* and *Earthshock*.

In the books, audios and comic strips, the distinction is made rather more often – for example, the Doctor notes that the Cybermen in "The Good Soldier" are the same design as the ones from *The Tenth Planet*.

If we take it as read that the characters *do* see different models of Cybermen, the significance could be functional. Perhaps the Cybermen from *The Tenth Planet* are adapted for Arctic conditions, the ones in *The Moonbase* and *The Wheel in Space* for low gravity operation and so forth. This seems unlikely, though – the Cybermen we see are almost always intent on roughly the same thing: marching into a human military installation and taking it by force.

It may well be that what we think of as one race is, in fact, many. Elsewhere in the *Doctor Who* universe, it seems to be a common stage of evolution for an organic race to remove "weaknesses" using cybernetic implants. Not every race does so – the Gallifreyans don't, for example, and humans apparently only ever do so in a limited fashion (as seen in, say, *Warriors of the Deep* or *The Long Game*). But a fair number of the Doctor's adversaries are cyborgs – the Daleks, the Sontarans and the Ice Warriors all are to at least some extent. Perhaps "Cyberman" is just the name of the end result when one of the human-like races that seem to exist on countless planets independently (or semi-independently) discards their organic form for a cybernetic one. Following the dictates of pure logic, technology and elegance, they all come up with roughly the same design for their cybernetic bodies. (And therefore there must be some overwhelming logical imperative for those handles on their helmets.) In the parallel universe of *Rise of the Cybermen/The Age of Steel*, Lumic seems to create Cybermen practically identical to the ones from our universe (name, handles and all) – and the Doctor, Rose and the Daleks all identify them.

There's no reason why these various Cyber Races couldn't cooperate, or even see themselves as part of the same "ethnic" or "political" group – it seems logical enough, and the Cybermen of a parallel universe offer an alliance with the Daleks in *Doomsday*. It might explain the discrepancies in the accounts of their origins, sphere of influence and levels of technology – as well as their appearance – across the series.

So perhaps the design indicates a lineage – the Cybermen of *The Invasion* and *Revenge of the Cybermen* are of one lineage, the ones of *Earthshock* and *Silver Nemesis* another. Surprisingly, while not entirely unproblematic, this does work.

Here is a list of different models, as well as the years and planets they are from. In the case of books and audios, cover art was considered as evidence if the text didn't specify. Note that, as elsewhere in the book, it's been assumed that the Cybermen we see aren't time travellers unless explicitly stated. The Cybermen of the far future clearly acquire time travel – it's usually stated

continued on page 1315...

came the memory-fog preventing him from remembering the abduction of his former companions. The Doctor contacted Frobisher by focusing the Griffith telescope on the Great Chronal Rift of Xandaragorus Minor, and asked his friend to infiltrate Adam's base of operations.

1956

Maxwell Edison, a Stockbridge resident and friend of the fifth, eighth, tenth and twelfth Doctors, was born in 1956.[2796] **Lavinia Smith published her paper on the teleological response of the virus when her niece, Sarah Jane, was five years old.**[2797] **Amy and Rory, living out their days in New York, adopted Anthony Brian Williams in 1956.**[2798]

u – Alistair Lethbridge-Stewart met Fiona, his future wife.[2799]

In 1956, the Doctor met a Jesuit palaeontologist in Africa.[2800] The vampires of Los Angeles culled their own kind to hide their numbers.[2801] Joseph Heller told Kurt Vonnegut, future author of *Slaughterhouse-Five* (1969), about his meeting with the Doctor.[2802]

Ben Jackson, age 14, stowed away on a cargo ship bound for Singapore. The captain discovered him and offered him a job.[2803] The Doctor prevented Santa Mira from being taken over by aliens in 1956.[2804] The French colony of Kebiria was granted independence in 1956. Civil war started almost immediately.[2805]

By 1956, the Grimoire of Anubis had fallen into the hands of comedian Joey Bishop.[2806] Before he was shipped off to Cyprus in 1956, Samson Ware saw Lethbridge-Stewart. They wouldn't meet again for about a decade.[2807]

Pearl Hammond, formerly of the Special Operations Executive and Bletchley, was now a barmaid on Kentish coast. In 1956, she convinced Lethbridge-Stewart to vio-

late orders and shelter his men in her pub, protecting them from an alien mist.[2808]

1956 - THE REVENANTS[2809] **->** The TARDIS partly arrived on the Isle of Hoy, Orkney, Scotland, then continued some years into the past after Ian and Barbara had exited the Ship. The two of them met the local witch Janet McKay, and were reunited with the first Doctor, who had spent the intervening time waiting for them. The TARDIS' double presence further animated the Marsh Wains – the muddy remnants of alien minds long dead – to seek out a mind powerful enough to pull their psyches together. McKay's mind let the psyches to reintegrate, and they were reborn in human form as the Marsh family. They would peacefully live on Hoy for decades.

1957

A replica version of the 1957 edition of Agatha Christie's *Death in the Clouds* was produced in the year five billion.[2810] Douglas Caldwell of Torchwood died in 1957.[2811] **Miss Kizlet became the Great Intelligence's thrall when she very young, and grew up devoted to its aims.**[2812] Allison Williams' father regretted that his wife never bore him a son, and "drove her away". After leaving Lower Burford for university, Allison was estranged from him for nearly a decade.[2813]

A little boy, later called the Landlord, found some alien woodlice, the Dryads, in the garden. The Dryads turned his dying mother Eliza into living wood, saving her life. As a grown man, the Landlord let the woodlice feed upon six of his tenants every twenty years, in return for them sustaining the life of his mother. The first such feeding occurred in 1957.[2814]

2796 Max celebrates his 60th birthday in "The Stockbridge Showdown" [2016].

2797 *The Time Warrior*

2798 *P.S.*

2799 *The Scales of Injustice*. Fiona forecasts the Brig phoning her based on "fifteen years" of late-night calls of him saying she won't see him for a week. The Haisman Timeline specifies that she and the Brig "re-meet" one another in 1971.

2800 *The Pit* (p98).

2801 *Vampire Science*

2802 *The Turing Test* (p207).

2803 *Invasion of the Cat-People* (p31).

2804 "Last year" according to *First Frontier* (p68), and a reference to the original *Invasion of the Bodysnatchers*.

2805 *Dancing the Code*

2806 "The Curse of the Scarab"

2807 *Leth-St: The Showstoppers*

2808 *Leth-St:* "The Lock-In"

2809 Dating *The Revenants* (BF promo #10, DWM #448) - The year is given. The idea that the first Doctor spends a few years in his personal lifetime waiting for Ian and Barbara to turn up on Hoy creates a bit of discontinuity with *The Rescue*, in which they quietly console him after Susan's "recent" departure (although from Ian and Barbara's point of view, it would seem recent).

2810 *The Unicorn and the Wasp*

2811 From Torchwood.org.uk.

2812 *The Bells of Saint John*, extrapolating from actress Celia Imrie being born in 1952.

2813 "Nine years, four months, seventeen days" before *CM S3: The Forgotten Village*.

2814 The Doctor and Bill estimate this all began "seventy years" before *Knock, Knock*, which would make the Landlord slightly older than actor David Suchet (age 70

...continued from page 1313

that they've stolen the technology, but it seems equally clear that the Cybermen of *The Moonbase* or *The Invasion*, say, aren't time travellers.

Type I: *World Enough and Time/The Doctor Falls* (Mondas colony ship), *Spare Parts* (when created, Mondas), *The Silver Turk* (1873, Mondas), "Junkyard Demon" ("pioneers", Mondas), "The Good Solider" (1954, Mondas), *The Tenth Planet* (1986, Mondas).

Note: It seems pretty clear that these are the early Cybermen, exclusively from Mondas.

Type II: *The Harvest* (2021), *The Moonbase* (21st century, ?), *The Wheel in Space* (21st century, ?), *Iceberg* (21st century), *The Tomb of the Cybermen/Return to Telos* (c.2486, Telos), *Benny: The Crystal of Cantus* (2606, the planet Cantus), *Illegal Alien* (time travellers from the 30th century).

Notes: Again, it's easy to group these together as the model of Cybermen who survive Mondas' destruction and attempt to attack twenty-first century Earth, then retire to their Tombs on Telos. The Cybermen in *The Wheel in Space* are from roughly the same time period, and a slight variation on this model.

Until the Cybermen relocate to Telos, it's unclear where they are based after Mondas' obliteration. David Banks speculates in his *Cybermen* book that they are based on a planet on the edge of the solar system, and links this to the Planet 14 mentioned in *The Invasion*.

The Cybermen from *Illegal Alien* come from the thirtieth century. The book only refers to the mask as having "teardrops" – a feature of the type of Cyberman seen in *The Invasion* and *Revenge of the Cybermen*, which would fit with the dating. The cover of *Illegal Alien*, however, reuses a photograph from *The Wheel in Space*, another design with "teardrops".

While *The Harvest* is an audio and we don't see Cybermen involved (they're not shown on the cover), the reference to *The Wheel in Space* suggests the Cybermen are the same type in both stories.

Type III: *The Invasion* (UNIT Era), *The isos Network* (UNIT Era), *Human Resources* (2006), *Killing Ground* (22nd century, nomads), *Legend of the Cybermen* (early 22nd century), "Assimilation 2" (2267), *Sword of Orion* (2503, Telos), *Kingdom of Silver* (circa 2505), *Cyberman 1* and *2* (2515-2516), *Last of the Cybermen* (c.2530), *Benny: Silver Lining* (2604), *Revenge of the Cybermen* (29th century, nomadic survivors of Cyber Wars), *The Girl Who Never Was* (time travellers grounded on Earth, 500,002).

Notes: On the whole, this also seems to form a distinct group that generally has a nomadic existence (i.e. they are based in spaceships, rather than having a home planet). At least one group of these Cybermen existed before *The Tenth Planet* (the ones we see in *The Invasion*). These Cybermen fight wars against early

human colony planets, and also the Cyber War referred to in *Revenge of the Cybermen*.

David Banks (in his book *Cybermen* and novel *Iceberg*) states that there was an early schism among the Cybermen – one group stayed on Mondas and only reluctantly adopted full cybertisation (the group here named as the Type I Cybermen), while another embraced the technology (and became the Type III seen in *The Invasion*).

The covers of *Human Resources* and *Legend of the Cybermen* depict Cybermen of the same type as *The Invasion*, and are set before the discovery of Telos. The Cybermen in *Iceberg* itself are a hybrid version – Cybermen who survived *The Invasion*, in part because they've adapted technology from the Cybermen seen in *The Tenth Planet*.

As noted above, despite the cover image, it's possible that the Cybermen in *Illegal Alien* are of this type.

It may or may not be significant that the Cybermen in *The Invasion* wear their chest units the other way up to the ones in *Revenge of the Cybermen*. The chest units are the same prop, and there's a circular detail on it – on the top in *The Invasion*, the bottom in *Revenge of the Cybermen*.

One of these Cybermen ended up in Vorg's MiniScope in *Carnival of Monsters*, and it's also the type of Cyberman the Doctor remembers in *The War Games*.

Type IV: "Throwback" (future, Telos), "Black Legacy" (unknown timezone, Empire), "Deathworld" (unknown timezone, Empire).

Notes: The comic strip stories are all apparently set when the Cybermen have an interstellar Empire (see "Do The Cybermen Ever Have an Empire?"). They resemble the Type III, but with a slightly more streamlined designed, and far more visible rank insignia.

Type V: *Attack of the Cybermen* (future, Telos), *Earthshock* (2526), *Silver Nemesis* (1988, hope to create a "new Mondas"), "Exodus/Revelation/Genesis" (unknown), "Kane's Story" (4650, "Empire").

Notes: *Attack of the Cybermen* and *Earthshock* could be near-contemporary stories (they are in this chronology). Both the Type IV (as seen in *Revenge of the Cybermen*) and Type V (*Attack of the Cybermen*) Cybermen fought and lost the Cyber War; Type V might be the upgraded model, developed during the fighting, although *Cyberman 2* seems to be the genesis of the *Earthshock* models, refining the *Attack of the Cybermen* versions.

However, *Silver Nemesis* (where the Cybermen are slightly redesigned) and "Kane's Story" are outliers. We don't have a date for "Exodus/Revelation/Genesis". The simplest explanation for a group of Cybermen who want a New Mondas in 1988 (*Silver Nemesis*) is that they're survivors from Mondas' destruction in 1986

continued on page 1317...

(=) The time-traveling Lenny Kruger altered the Beatles' personal histories by going to 1957 and delaying the elimination of national service. Kruger time-locked this year, but the fifth Doctor obtained the time-key needed to undo this errant history.[2815]

= c 1957 - FP: WARLORDS OF UTOPIA[2816] **->** Scriptor had been a captive of the Nazis for sixteen years. The Council of Hitlers had made many gains, and Scriptor and Abschrift spent a lot of time together. Abschrift was from True Earth, and believed the Roman and Nazi Earths had been created by mysterious forces, very possibly to create armies to fight in the War in Heaven. The Nazi Worlds had, by now, launched attacks across the Divide and conquered one of the Roman Earths. The Hitler of Germania I had produced a son, August Hitler.

Scriptor escaped his captors, but failed to kill August. The Nazis destroyed a huge Roman invasion force with nuclear weapons. The Romans launched a massive counterattack, taking world after world.

1957 (18th September) - "Agent Provocateur"[2817] **->** The tenth Doctor and Martha materialised from the year five billion at Ainsworth Point, Cumbria. Martha was shot, and so the Doctor rushed her to Ainsworth House. They encountered Silas Wain – an agent provocateur working to test the Doctor on behalf of the Elite Pantheon of higher beings. Martha deduced that one of her nurses was a Catkind, and the Doctor discovered that Wain had been building a pan-dimensional sonic weapon – that their rival, Professor Tharlot, promptly stole. The Elite Pantheon returned the Doctor and Martha to the year five billion.

u – The Doctor became a member of the Progressive Club, a gentleman's club in Mayfair.[2818] Edwin Pratt became the vampire Slake in 1957.[2819] Ace had a British Rail Card from 1957, the only form of ID she carried.[2820]

The Master Regenerates

1957 (4th October) - FIRST FRONTIER[2821] **->** On May Day 1957, the first *Sputnik* was destroyed before it completed an orbit of the Earth. News of this failure was never made public.

The Doctor visited the first official *Sputnik* launch at least twice. The same day, there was intense UFO activity over Corman Air Force Base in New Mexico, and the USAF engaged alien spaceships. These were the Tzun, now a race divided into three subspecies. They planned to cause a war between Washington and Moscow, then step in and pose as humanity's saviours. The Tremas Master was helping them, but Ace shot the Master – who had used Tzun technology to upgrade his Trakenite body to be more akin to a Time Lord one – and caused him to regenerate. The seventh Doctor prevented chaos from ensuing as the Master betrayed the Tzun and destroyed their mothership.

On the 15th of the same month, a Time Lord using the name Louis approached Johannes Rausch, who possessed a degree in metallurgy from the University of Vienna. Louis

---

when this was filmed). Either way, the Landlord must have been quite the young entrepreneur, bagging his first victims at about age 17.

2815 *1963: Fanfare for the Common Men.* National service in the UK went into decline in 1957, ended in 1960.
2816 Dating *FP: Warlords of Utopia* (FP novel #3) - Scriptor gives the date.
2817 Dating "Agent Provocateur" (IDW *DW* mini-series #1) - It has been "twelve years" since the war, and Martha sees a newspaper with the date on it.
2818 "Thirteen years" before *The Devil Goblins from Neptune.*
2819 *Vampire Science*
2820 "Ground Zero"
2821 Dating *First Frontier* (NA #30) - It's "October 4th, 1957" (p6). The Tzun Master next appears in *Happy Endings.*
2822 *Unregenerate!* The dating is awry, as radio broadcasts suggest this is the day of *Sputnik's* launch (4th October), yet Louis claims the date is "the 15th".
2823 The Doctor mentions C19 in *Time-Flight*, in connection with contacting UNIT.
2824 *The Scales of Injustice* (p205), *Leth-St: Night of the*

Intelligence. C19 is referred to in a number of novels, particularly Gary Russell's *The Scales of Injustice, Business Unusual* and *Instruments of Darkness*, where it's a shadowy branch of British intelligence that keeps the existence of aliens under wraps by cleaning up alien artifacts left over from their various incursions (a little like Torchwood, then). *Leth-St: Night of the Intelligence* sees C19 given authority over the wayward Vault, which features in Russell's books.
2825 *Alien Bodies. Sputnik II* was launched 3rd November, 1957.
2826 *1963: The Space Race*
2827 *Mad Dogs and Englishmen*
2828 *Escape Velocity*
2829 *Rags* (p185); this happened 30th August to 5th September, 1958.
2830 *Shada*
2831 *SJA: The Last Sontaran*, no date given.
2832 *SJA: The Day of the Clown*, no date given.
2833 *TW: Children of Earth*
2834 *TW: Almost Perfect*
2835 *Beautiful Chaos* (p163).
2836 "Agent Provocateur"

offered to make Rausch's life highly successful if Rausch agreed to take part in a painless procedure the day before he died. Rausch agreed, and the two of them would meet again almost fifty years later.[2822]

Department C19 was set up in Britain[2823] in the late fifties as an offshoot of the Civil Defence programme.[2824]

Sputnik II launched and carried Laika the dog into orbit. The third Doctor later recovered her body and buried it on the planet Quiescia.[2825] General Mikhail Leonov was the last face that the dog Laika saw before she was placed into Sputnik 2 and launched into outer space. An alien probe embedded within a contained black hole detected signals emanating from Earth, and sought to offer aid to its inhabitants. The probe found Laika, alone and abandoned, and found humanity wanting. It helped Laika return to Earth in 1963.[2826]

In 1957, Noel Coward met Iris Wildthyme at the Royal Variety Performance. Their friendship led to Iris giving Noel a pair of pinking shears capable of cutting the Very Fabric of Time and Space, enabling him to time travel. Multiple Cowards began operating in various time zones.[2827]

1958

@ The eighth Doctor was present when the Atomium – a monument representing an iron crystal magnified 165 billion times – was unveiled in Brussels.[2828] The Ragman stoked racial violence between Teddy Boys and Afro-Caribbean immigrants in Notting Hill and Notting Dale.[2829]

In 1958, the Doctor again visited St Cedd's College.[2830] **As a child, Sarah Jane would look out her window and fall asleep counting the stars, dreaming about what was out there in space – and having no idea that she would one day explore it.**[2831] **The Pied Piper visited Sarah Jane Smith when she was a child, instilling in her a fear of clowns.**[2832]

John Frobisher, a future civil servant, was born in Glasgow in 1958.[2833] "When You Discover You're Not Who You Thought You Were", a Torchwood document pertaining to body dislocation and misplacement, was last revised in 1958.[2834] In the same year, the Doctor played washboard in a skiffle band, The Geeks, which featured Brian "Ahab" Melville. Joe Meek was going to produce the group's album, but it didn't come to pass.[2835]

The tenth Doctor and Martha had a milkshake in Wisconsin, 1958.[2836] In 1958, Operation Piper attempted to genetically engineer rats smart enough to spy on Russia, and pool information in a gestalt

...continued from page 1315

(*The Tenth Planet*). Although it's not mentioned, they could be survivors from *Attack of the Cybermen*. Perhaps they're from the base on the moon that's mentioned and not accounted for – those Cybermen wanted to change history to prevent the destruction of Mondas, so perhaps their back-up plan would be to create "New Mondas".

What's interesting is that the Cybermen in *Attack the Cybermen* definitely have a stolen time travel vessel, there's some evidence that the ones in *Earthshock* are time travellers, and the ones in *Silver Nemesis* are after Gallifreyan technology. So we might be able to assume that the Type V Cybermen are all be Cybermen from the twenty-sixth century, with limited knowledge of time travel they've acquired from stolen technology.

This design seems to have a comeback around the Davros Era, according to "Kane's Story".

Type VI: *Real Time, Radio Times* eighth Doctor strips, *The Reaping*, "The Flood".
Notes: The Cybermen continue to evolve, and by the far future they're on the verge of extinction and apparently have one strategy: acquire a time machine and go back into history to change it.

Type VII: *The Eleventh Doctor Year One* (312, unknown), *The Next Doctor* (1851, fell back through time, Pete's World; includes "Cyber-King" model), *Rise of the Cybermen/The Age of Steel* (2007, Pete's World), *Army of Ghosts/Doomsday* (2007, Pete's World), *The Pandorica Opens/The Big Bang* (102, went through Cracks in Time, unknown), *Closing Time* (c.2012, unknown), "Assimilation 2" (2386, unknown), *A Good Man Goes to War* (River Song Era, mobile Twelfth Cyber Legion).
Notes: First seen as the creations of Cybus Industries in a parallel universe. *A Good Man Goes to War* is the first time this model is seen without the Cybus Industries logo, perhaps suggesting that "our" Cybermen incorporated the technology into their own, or that the design was developed independently in the main *Doctor Who* universe.

Type VIII: *World Enough and Time/The Doctor Falls* (Mondas colony ship), *Dark Water/Death in Heaven* (2016, Earth), *The Time of the Doctor* (? 5100 to 6000, unknown), *Nightmare in Silver* (c.199,900, Hedgewick's World), *Hell Bent* (Gallifrey: Twelfth Doctor Era, unknown).
Notes: These Cybermen operate under the directions of a group consciousness, the Cyberiad. We first see them in *Nightmare in Silver*, but they recur in other timezones. It's possible there are stages of their evolution we don't see, but *The Doctor Falls* indicates they represent an immediate "upgrade" from the Mondasian Cybermen.

mind: the Rat King.[2837]

Professor Edgar Nelson-Stanley dug up the talisman of the Gorgons in Syria, and gave it to his wife Bea. A Gorgon turned Bea to stone, but the talisman returned her to normal. One of the two remaining Gorgons was killed.[2838] Sgt Samson Ware received an honourable discharge in 1958.[2839]

On 23rd April, 1958, the Motor Torpedo Boat *Heroic* sank in a storm in the Thames. Elliott Payne translocated one of the doomed sailors, Johnny Skipton, to Victorian times as an experiment. The shades of Skipton's drowned crewmen went back via a time break and retrieved him, giving them all eternal rest.[2840]

Experiments on the alien hallucinogenic recovered from Tunguska were conducted in Prague, 1958.[2841] McCusky's Peptic Purgative Pills, a form of concentrated rhubarb and vinegar, was marketed as an excellent means of voiding the stomach.[2842] The United States developed Project A119 as a means of detonating a nuclear bomb on the moon as a show of strength.[2843]

John Smith and the Common Men

The natives of the planet Bional had a biology that absorbed energy as they achieved higher levels of fame. The Bional authorities banned photographs, recordings and anything else that could facilitate an ongoing adoration of any of their number. The Bional named Klyneln, later known as Lenny Kruger, craved such power but was unwilling to assume the risk involved. He captured three of his fellow Bionals (Mayanas from the Court of Caldy, Jecomyn from the Convent of Heath and Kapraban from the Wheel of Contact), erased their memories and brought them to Earth. The trio respectively became known as Mark Carville, James O'Meara and Korky Goldsmith, with flesh suits disguising their true natures even from themselves. They began performing as the rock band the Common Men.[2844]

1958 - DREAMLAND (*DW*)[2845] **-> The tenth Doctor arrived in Dry Springs, a town not far from Area 51, looking to eat chili at a diner. He met waitress Cassie Rice and ranch worker Jimmy Stalkingwolf, and saw an ionic fusion bar sitting on the counter – a souvenir from a flying saucer crash five years before.**

Azlok, Lord Knight of the Imperial Viperox War Horde, brought his Viperox to Earth in search of the survivor from that crash: Rivesh Mantilax. A Viperox queen set about birthing a Viperox swarm, even as Azlok allied himself with Colonel Stark of the United States Air Force (USAF). Mantilax had built a genetic-targeting weapon with the potential to wipe out every Viperox in the universe, and Stark hoped to modify the device for deployment against Russia.

2837 *Rat Trap*

2838 "Fifty years" before *SJA: Eye of the Gorgon.*

2839 *Leth-St: The Showstoppers*

2840 *J&L S3: Dead Men's Tales*

2841 *CM S1: Artificial Intelligence*

2842 "Ten years" before *J&L S5: The Case of the Gluttonous Guru.*

2843 "A few years" before *1963: The Space Race* (in real life, this apparently happened in 1958). While the US government has never officially recognised the project, a former NASA official released documents proving its existence in 2000.

2844 The background to *1963: Fanfare for the Common Men*. Carville claims in 1970 that he, O'Meara and Goldsmith met a total of twelve years beforehand.

2845 Dating *Dreamland* (*DW* Red Button animated story) - A caption conveys that it is "eleven years" since 1947, and the Doctor confirms that it's "1958". The Department in the *K9* series also calls the operation to recover alien ships "Fallen Angel". The Doctor twice says he "always wanted" to go to Area 51. See the Unfixed Points of Time sidebar.

2846 *Dreamland* (*DW*). The Doctor is almost certainly referring to Retcon, as seen in *Torchwood*, and may be unaware that they actually created it in the late 90s – according to *The Torchwood Archives* (BBC) – i.e. only forty, not fifty, years on.

2847 *SJA: Prisoner of the Judoon*

2848 Dating *Spiral Scratch* (PDA #72) - Rummas gives the year.

2849 *Spiral Scratch*

2850 Dating "Tuesday" (*DW Annual 2011*) - The year is given.

2851 Dating *Bad Therapy* (NA #57) - The date is given (p1).

2852 Dating *1stD V2: The Bonfires of the Vanities* (BF CC 11.3) - The blurb says it's "the late 1950s", and Ben names the day. Lewes hosts the UK's biggest Bonfire Night (commemorating not just Guy Fawkes Night, but the burning of seventeen Protestants at the stake), which always begins on 5th November – unless that's a Sunday, in which case it's the 4th.

2853 Date unknown, but Angela Bruce was born in 1951, so was about 38 when she played Bambera in *Battlefield* [c.1997].

2854 *Leth-St: Night of the Intelligence* (ch7).

2855 Dating *Delta and the Bannermen* (24.3) - The Tollmaster says that the bus will be going back to "1959", and the date is confirmed by a banner up in the dance hall at the Shangri-La resort. Hawk's line that "this is history in the making" implies this is the first American satellite, but that was actually *Explorer I*, launched on 31st January, 1958.

The Doctor reunited Mantilax with his wife, Seruba Velak, who was being kept prisoner as part of the USAF's Operation Fallen Angel – a programme that examined and detained extra-terrestrials. The Viperox swarmed, but the Doctor adapted Mantilax's genetic device to repel them with ultrasonics – they returned home to Viperon, and had to stay at least a light year's distance from Earth. Although the Viperox had laid waste whole galaxies, the Doctor knew they would evolve into a benevolent race. The Grey Aliens returned home in their repaired flying saucer.

President Eisenhower did not know aliens existed, or were being kept in Area 51.

The American government currently used a gas to crudely wiped memories. The Doctor said that a truly effective amnesia drug would not be discovered for another fifty years.[2846] The technical details of the alien spacecraft taken to Area 51 were later retrieved by Androvax.[2847]

1958 - SPIRAL SCRATCH[2848] -> Professor Joseph Tungard was exiled to Britain for dissent against the new Soviet government in Bucharest. On the journey to London, he and his wife Natjya met Dr Pike and his granddaughter Monica. The Tungards settled in England, where Joseph began an affair with Monica… who was secretly an alien Lamprey, a creature that fed on temporal energy

The sixth Doctor and Mel arrived at Wikes Manor in Suffolk, forewarned that a girl called Helen Lamprey was about to vanish from her birthday party. Timelines were beginning to overlap, and alternate versions of the Doctor and Mel appeared. Helen Lamprey vanished, as history had been altered so that she, not her mother, died a number of years ago in a house fire. Mel now had a sister.

The Doctor and Mel followed Helen's father, Sir Bertrand, to London where he met Monica and the Tungards. Monica revealed her identity as a Lamprey, and that she sought to destroy those who might threaten her plans to feed on damage to the timelines. This triggered Sir Bertrand's memory, and he revealed he was also a Lamprey. The two Lampreys fought, unleashing storms of temporal energy that aged bystanders to death.

The Doctor realised that Helen Lamprey was half-human, half-Lamprey and therefore vital to Monica's plans. He and Mel left in the TARDIS for the planet Carsus. Many sixth Doctors from alternate realities crossed over to combat the Lamprey, and quite a few died overwhelming it with their chronon energy. Mel's Doctor held the Lamprey in place while his fellows overwhelmed it – the Lamprey died, but the Doctor absorbed a fatal dose of chronon energy. The surviving Doctors returned home while Mel and her Doctor left in the TARDIS, and were snared in the Rani's tractor beam...

> = In an alternate universe, the sixth Doctor and half-Silurian Melanie Baal visited Helen Lamprey's birthday party… on a space station in Earth orbit.[2849]

1958 - "Tuesday"[2850] -> Sir Reginald Offord Troupe, an exiled royal, allied with alien Vroon warriors in an attempt to capture the throne of England, then the world. While the eleventh Doctor was stuck in a prison cell on Gibraltar, Rory was crowned King of England following a mishap with the psychic paper. Amy stirred the Vroon workers into revolution, and Troupe was arrested.

(A) Peri Meets the Seventh Doctor

1958 (October) - BAD THERAPY[2851] -> The first of the Krontep warlords, Moriah, had taken up residence on Earth. Operating from the Petruska Psychiatric Research Institute, Moriah sought to construct Toys – genetic duplicates of people that could become whomever their owner desired. He wanted a Toy that would replicate his late wife Petruska, but some of the Toys became increasingly independent. Moriah had a metamorphic device, disguised as a black cab, that would round up any Toys who escaped.

The seventh Doctor and Chris arrived, and a young man named Eddy Stone, actually a Toy, died in front of the TARDIS. Meanwhile, the Doctor's former companion Peri, having spent twenty-five years as King Yrcanos' wife, travelled down a gateway from Krontep to Earth. She aided the Doctor against Moriah. The Doctor created a Toy of Petruska for Moriah, who believed himself unworthy of her love and was killed by his creations. The Doctor also took Peri home to the 1980s.

lgtw - c 1958 (5th November) - 1STD V2: THE BONFIRES OF THE VANITIES[2852] -> The burnt alien in Lewes caused unrest on Bonfire Night by deploying androids disguised as Guy Fawkes effigies. The first Doctor, Polly and Ben saved the town, and made the alien leave Earth. Two Time Lords in the Last Great Time War blocked a Dalek assault on the Doctor's timeline here.

1959

Brigadier Winifred Bambera, a member of UNIT and associate of the seventh Doctor, was born.[2853] By 1959, Alistair Lethbridge-Stewart had attained the rank of captain.[2854]

1959 - DELTA AND THE BANNERMEN[2855] -> The first US satellite was launched, and almost immediately it was lost. CIA agents across the world were put on alert, and agents Weismuller and Hawk tracked it to a holiday camp in Wales, England. A Nostalgia Trips group arrived through time at the holiday camp, and their members included the Chimeron Queen. The seventh Doctor and Mel helped to defeat a group of Bannermen trying to kill the Queen. Billy, a mechanic at the camp, underwent conversion into a Chimeron to help the Queen re-propagate her race.

One Bannerman survived, albeit deafened and amnesiac. He ended up with Isaac Summerfield's group.[2856] Dr Nadia Jovenka, a Russian scientist, defected to the West.[2857] James Aster was shot between the eyes during a card game gone wrong on the Burmese border. Emma Waverly later made use of his identity.[2858]

= **1959 - LETH-ST: THE SCHIZOID EARTH**[2859] -> Owing to the space-time-displacing properties of the *Phoenix* capsules, Colonel Lethbridge-Stewart found himself on the Inferno Earth in 1959. He encountered his "brother", the Major James Lethbridge-Stewart of this reality, and both were transported to In-Between Earth in 1945. After meeting the Nikola Tesla of that Earth, James returned home.

James' father, Gordon Lethbridge-Stewart, served as the Republic's Director of External Security. A *Phoenix* capsule arrived containing an alternate version of Alastair (sic) Lethbridge-Stewart, age 15. As his son had died years ago, Gordon groomed the boy for a military career.

= In the "Inferno" universe, the British Republic fought the Bannermen and destroyed them. Components from the alien starship allowed them to engineer space shuttles within ten years.[2860]

(=) The uncle of Ruby Porter was lost in Swallow Woods in 1959, when he was 15. Ruby's grandmother became so sad, it motivated Ruby to become a police officer.

The eleventh Doctor prevented the capture of Ruby's uncle, and so she became a history lecturer.[2861] Rachel Jensen bumped into one of her classmates, the journalist Hilary de Winter, at a reunion.[2862]

2856 *Return of the Living Dad*
2857 "Six years" before *CM* S1: *Artificial Intelligence.*
2858 "Six years" before *CM* S2: *Manhunt.*
2859 Dating *Leth-St: The Schizoid Earth* (*Leth-St* novel #2) - The year is repeatedly given. In-Between Earth is so named because it lies "between" our world and Inferno-Earth. Captain Marianne Kyle, seen here, is very probably the same Inferno-reality character who appears in the David McIntee novels *The Face of the Enemy* and *Bullet Time*. The 15-year-old Alastair Lethbridge-Stewart seen here grows up – with benefit of brainwashing drugs that age him faster than normal – to become the Brigade Leader seen in *Inferno*.
2860 *The Face of the Enemy* (p248).
2861 *The Way Through the Woods*
2862 "Five or six years" before *CM* S4: *Clean Sweep.*
2863 *TW: Submission*. In real life, the *Trieste* reached its maximum depth on 23rd January, 1960.
2864 *Imperial Moon*
2865 *UNIT: Snake Head*
2866 *SJA: The White Wolf*. It's suggested that Sarah loses a "whole year" of her life owing to this event, although this is hard to take literally, as she never notices the discrepancy.
2867 Dating *Loving the Alien* (PDA #60) - Ace gains a tattoo that dates the year as 1959 (p24). The Doctor similarly remarks on the year as 1959 (p33). The newspaper on the cover specifies it's "November" 1959.
2868 *Synthespians* ™
2869 *Ghost Ship*. No date is given.
2870 *Millennial Rites* (p159). The Mods and Rockers gangs were two British youth movements during this time.

2871 *Vincent and the Doctor*. Picasso started his art career in 1900; he died in 1973.
2872 *Leth-St: Moon Blink* (supplemental material).
2873 *Leth-St:* "Eve of the Fomorians", and – surely – another Quatermass reference.
2874 *DC 4: Ship in a Bottle*
2875 *The Zygon Who Fell to Earth*
2876 *A Death in the Family*. Lowry, famed for his renderings of Salford and its surrounding areas, lived 1887-1976.

2877 Torchwood.org.uk, elaborating on *TW: From Out of the Rain.*
2878 *TW: The House That Jack Built*. No date is given; Clarke immigrated to Sri Lanka in 1956, and lived there until his death in 2008.
2879 The psychspace – and the musician's native time – is variously given as "the late 1950s" and "the 1960s" in the undatable "Forever Dreaming".
2880 *Heart of Stone*. Ali was born in 1942, was a professional boxer from 1960 to 1981.
2881 *Leth-St: The Showstoppers* (chs. 10, 14).
2882 "Space Squid". Godzilla first appeared in 1954, so it's some time after that.
2883 *Zamper*. Milton Keynes was build as part of the third wave of the New Towns programme, so this happened during the sixties.
2884 *Iris S3: The Midwinter Murders*
2885 *TW: Exodus Code*
2886 *DC 3: The Doomsday Chronometer*
2887 The decade before *Leth-St: The Dreamer's Lament.*
2888 *1963: The Space Race*. Eisenhower was president 1952-1960.

The bathyscaphe *Guernica*, built in Spain and a twin to the *Trieste*, became the first vessel to reach the depths of the Mariana Trench. The alien trapped there possessed one of the two crewmen: Captain Samuel Doyle, age 50. The other, Henry Goddard, died after recording his last words on 9th August, 1959. The alien began to feed off Doyle's memories, and awaited rescue. The US government covered up the failure of the *Guernica's* mission, and the *Trieste* would be celebrated after successfully descending into the Trench the following year.[2863]

In October 1959, the Russian probe *Lunik 3* scanned the moon crater where the Phiadoran safari park once stood. The Russians named it Tsiolkovskii, after a teacher who wrote a paper on rocket travel.[2864] Prior to the twenty-first century, the last reported sighting of a vrykolaka – a type of vampire – was in 1959.[2865] When Sarah Jane was eight, she and her aunt Lavinia visited the rectory in Wolfenden during a "harvesting period" – when the aliens in the town extracted human memory chemicals. The two of them forgot that they'd ever visited the village.[2866]

Death and Replacement of Ace

(=) 1959 - LOVING THE ALIEN[2867] -> George Limb's time-jumps created an alternate timeline where he was Prime Minister. The populace was cybernetically augmented, which eliminated disease and somewhat created a utopia, but overcrowding became a problem. The British Space Agency was tasked with facilitating travel to other timelines as a means of expansion.

In the proper history, the Americans and British jointly launched a Waverider space vehicle, piloted by Colonel Thomas Kneale. However, the ship that returned hailed from the cyber-human reality, and was piloted by an alternate version of Captain Davey O'Brien. International tensions increased over the incident. The cyber-human Britain attempted to send its warships through to the proper reality, but a nuclear strike devastated the alternate Britain and ended the threat.

Limb's assistant, an alternative version of James Dean, died while destroying Limb's time machine. Limb committed suicide in fear of undergoing cyber-conversion.

Before his death, Limb shot and killed Ace. The seventh Doctor took up travel with a virtually identical Ace that hailed from one of the timelines Limb had created.

The Nineteen Sixties

The Doctor met the artists Francis Bacon and Lucian Freud in Soho in the sixties, and thwarted one of the Master's schemes.[2868] The Doctor met *Lord of the Flies* author William Golding.[2869] The Mods and Rockers guarded the Library of St John the Beheaded during the sixties.[2870] **The Doctor thought Pablo Picasso was a "ghastly old goat", and tried and failed to get him to paint more conventionally.**[2871]

Anne Travers studied for several years at both the Victoria University of Manchester and Cambridge University.[2872] Anne Travers was one of Bernard's students.[2873] Helen Sinclair's grandmother discovered she was ill, and died a few years later.[2874]

A man named Trevor enjoyed success as a sixties folk singer, but he died late in the decade in a motorcycle accident. The record company that handled Trevor's songs, Satsuma, hushed up his death and put his body into cryogenic suspension in accordance with his last wishes.[2875] Ace met L.S. Lowry up North at a cotton mill full of polymorphic soot monsters, and ended up owning a napkin with his drawings of stick men.[2876]

In the sixties, the Electro Theatre in Cardiff hosted the likes of Cila Black, *The Who* and the Walker Brothers.[2877] Captain Jack shared some "wonderful summers" with Arthur C. Clarke in Colombo, Sri Lanka.[2878]

The minds of a musician, a painter, a poet and a mathematician wandered into a peaceful psychspace that resembled Britain, but was the home dimension of a psychic squid. They later sacrificed themselves to destroy the squid and save the eleventh Doctor and Amy.[2879]

The Doctor used to spar with Muhammad Ali.[2880] In Lisbon, 1963, CIA agent Tyrone Hanssen encountered Vilhelm Schadengeist, and was hypnotised into killing one of his avatars, Wing Commander Maurice Shepstone, with strychnine.[2881]

On a visit to Japan, the eleventh Doctor's companion Kevin the Tyrannosaur was mistaken for Godzilla.[2882] When the TARDIS landed on mid-twentieth century Earth, Benny Summerfield visited Milton Keynes to settle an archaeological debate. She returned to the Ship happy to be proved right, and with boxes of shoes.[2883]

Bernard Duncan became famous as a writer of detective stories featuring a one-armed, washed-up inspector and his lesbian sidekick. Duncan also penned cherished novelisations of rare 1960s TV shows.[2884] A cabal of physicists in the 1960s hypothesized that part of an astral force, splintered by the Big Bang, resided in the core of the Earth.[2885]

In the 1960s, and with some help from a sonic crowbar, River Song and Helen Sinclair nicked the eighth piece of the Doomsday Chronometer hidden by the Revelation Sect in the Vatican.[2886] Professor Travers researched the mystery of the Keynsham Triangle off and on for a decade, but failed to solve it.[2887]

The United States secretly constructed Moonbase Eisenhower on the far side of the moon. In the event of nuclear war, it would house a small, viable population until the Earth was habitable again.[2888]

UNIT in the Sixties

u – A secret bunker was built in Whitehall.[2889]

Human space probes were being sent "deeper and deeper" into space.[2890] Earth Reptile Shelter 429, near the Channel Islands, revived.[2891]

Liz Shaw attended Newnham College at Cambridge during the 1960s, and met fellow student Jean Baisemore there during Freshers' week. They became close friends, with Jean teaching Liz – who was something of a prude – about the wonders of life beyond the lecture hall. Jean argued with Liz about the existence of life on other planets, and Liz shot her down in flames.[2892]

Lethbridge-Stewart met Heinrich Konrad, a German officer, during a NATO exercise in the sixties.[2893]

1960

The Doctor was awarded an honorary degree from St Cedd's in 1960.[2894] He visited Anne Doras and her husband in Guernsey, 1960. They had a daughter called Bernice. The same year, convicted Nazi Oskar Steinmann was released from prison on medical grounds.[2895]

With the cancellation of the Blue Streak missile programme, Sir Gideon Vale began developing the Starfire ballistic system as a low-cost alternative.[2896] The sentient black hole aiding Laika also saved Pchyolka and Mushka, two other dogs sent into space.[2897]

Hendrich Muller founded the altruistic company New Horizons, but died before the completion of its work.[2898]

> = In the 1960 of a world where the Second World War never ended, Gus – a companion of the fifth Doctor – joined the US Air Force to join the fight. After two years, he saw combat.[2899]

c 1960 - CHURCHILL: THE CHARTWELL METAMORPHOSIS[2900] **->** The eleventh Doctor arranged for Lily Arwell to become a nurse to Winston Churchill, and asked her to keep an eye on his dear friend in his retirement. Churchill felt the weight of his years, and assisted an insectoid alien – a Proscoran, the last of his kind – in experiments that Churchill hoped would yield a youth-restoring potion. Secretly, the Proscoran intended to use humanity as raw material in which to birth his race anew. Arwell summoned the Doctor as the Proscoran transformed another of Churchill's staff, Mrs Whitaker, into a Proscoran queen. Churchill saved the Doctor by running the Proscoran through with a garden fork, and the Doctor both captured the queen and transported the remaining Proscoran eggs to a world where they could thrive. The Doctor also agreed to take Churchill and Arwell in the TARDIS, by a route of his choosing, to stay with Churchill's friends in the French Riviera.

> **(=) 1960 - 1963: FANFARE FOR THE COMMON MEN**[2901] **->** Lenny Kruger's historical alterations in 1957 prevented the Beatles from achieving fame, and he increasingly positioned the Common Men to take

---

2889 "Twenty years" before *Invasion of the Dinosaurs*.
2890 "For the last decade" before *Spearhead from Space*.
2891 "About ten years" before *The Scales of Injustice*.
2892 *The Blue Tooth*
2893 *Old Soldiers*
2894 *Shada*
2895 *Just War*
2896 *1963: The Assassination Games*. The military cancelled Blue Streak as a missile programme in 1960, but it continued as a potential satellite launcher.
2897 *1963: The Space Race*. In real life, Puchyolka and Mushka died aboard Sputnik 6, which launched on 1st December, 1960.
2898 "Just over five years" before *CM S4: New Horizons*.
2899 "4-Dimensional Vistas". Gus has been "three years in the air force", and has been fighting since "last year".
2900 Dating *Churchill: The Chartwell Metamorphosis* (*The Churchill Years* #1.4) - Churchill is currently in "my dotage, my detestable dotage", although the Doctor tells the man he has "years left in you". Churchill's fitness was variable in his later years – he was physically unable to travel to America in 1963, when Congress named him as the first-ever honorary citizen of the

United States, but remained MP for Woodford until 1964. He died, age 90, on 24th January, 1965.
Arwell met the eleventh Doctor in *The Doctor, The Widow and the Wardrobe* [1941].
2901 Dating *1963: Fanfare for the Common Men* (BF #178) - The year is given. National Service ended "three years ago" (in 1957).
2902 Dating *Mad Dogs and Englishmen* (EDA #52) - "It's 1960!" (p118).
2903 Dating *No More Lies* (BF BBC7 #1.6) - No year is given, but the upper and lower boundaries of this story's dating can be deduced. Rachel's brother references "You Are My Sunshine" (1939) and the Time Lords' temporal barrier is currently preventing the Doctor and Lucie from getting any closer to her era than 1974 (per *Horror of Glam Rock*). There's no mention of a war being on or rationing, so the action is less likely to take place in the 1940s. The season is suggested in that the garden party is held outdoors, and some of the action occurs in Nick and Rachel's "summer house".
2904 According to her tombstone in *The Rings of Akhaten*. The date marks the debut of *Pathfinders in Space*, an ITV show developed by Sydney Newman. Elena's full name is given in *Death in Heaven*.

their place. Nyssa fell back in time to 1960 with Kruger from late October 1963, and met the Common Men in Hamburg during their early days. The fifth Doctor recovered Nyssa while following an older version of Kruger, who warned his earlier self how their scheme had gone awry in 1970. The Krugers conditioned Korky Goldsmith to serve as a buffer between the other Commen Men, to help the group endure longer. The future Kruger returned to 1970. Shock troops from a future where Kruger succeeded and became the Emperor Paternis came back to kill the Doctor and Nyssa on his behalf. The pair escaped to 1966 in Kruger's time vessel, which was disguised as the Pfannkuchen Club. Kruger erased the Common Men's memories of the Doctor and Nyssa.

1960 - MAD DOGS AND ENGLISHMEN[2902] **->** Fitz met Iris Wildthyme in Las Vegas, where she had found fame as the diva Brenda Soobie. Her companion of sixty years, the poodle Martha, had been manipulating Iris to alter history. Iris helped the eighth Doctor defeat the poodles, then left for further adventures with her new companions Fritter the poodle and Flossie the cook.

c 1960 (summer) - NO MORE LIES[2903] **->** Nick Zimmerman modified his time technology and created a mini-time loop, hoping that he and his dying wife Rachel could eternally enjoy a garden party. This drew the attention of time-eaters – the Tar-Modowk, who rode Vortisaurs. Accompanied by Lucie, the eighth Doctor erased the Tar-Modowk from existence. Zimmerman was forced to deactivate the time-loop, and Rachel died soon afterwards.

Elena "Ellie" Alison Ravenwood, the mother of Clara Oswald, was born 11th September, 1960.[2904]

Tegan Jovanka

Tegan Jovanka, a companion of the fifth Doctor, was born 22nd September, 1960.[2905] Tegan's middle name was Melissa. Her father was named William.[2906]

Tegan Jovanka lived on a cattle station, far off in the countryside, when she was small. She got lost, at age seven or eight, when her mother took her to see Aboriginal cave drawings. Soon afterward, young Tegan witnessed a traditional Aboriginal dance staged for tourists. The combination of the two strange events gave her nightmares for years.[2907] Tegan's uncle had a farm.[2908] Tegan grew up with horses.[2909] Her cousins did blast mining in Australia.[2910]

She spent her childhood in Caloundra, near Brisbane.[2911] Tegan's Serbian grandfather told her vampire stories.[2912] One of Tegan's fondest memories was flying in a single-engine Cessna Skyhawk with her father.[2913]

1961

Reconstruction of the Fang Rock lighthouse began in 1961.[2914] Archie, the Torchwood archivist, received a telegram from Her Majesty to congratulate him on turning one hundred years old.[2915] Ken Temple saw Rachel Jensen present a paper on quantum cryptography.[2916] Lethbridge-Stewart spent some time in Berlin, 1961.[2917]

Counter-Measures is Founded

The Intrusion Counter Measures Group (ICMG) was founded in 1961 as a science-led team, with military backup, assigned to protect the United Kingdom from hostile powers.[2918] Group Captain Gilmore was appointed leader.[2919] Counter-Measures' charter accorded it the option of removing suspected aliens from access to hazardous materials.[2920] Sir Toby Kinsella oversaw construction of the

---

2905 According to her character outline, Tegan is "21" when she meets the Doctor (in *Logopolis*, set in 1981). Originally she was to be 19, until the production team were told that legally air hostesses had to be 21 or older. Clarifying the issue, *The Gathering* has Tegan celebrating her 46th birthday on 22nd September 2006. Janet Fielding was born in 1957, which might suggest that she's three years older than the character she played. However, fandom often presumes that Tegan spent three years travelling with the Doctor (the duration of Fielding's time on screen), which would suggest that – like Fielding – Tegan is 49 when *The Gathering* takes place.
2906 *Divided Loyalties*
2907 *5thB: Psychodrome*
2908 *Equilibrium*
2909 *The Peterloo Massacre*

2910 *The Contingency Club*
2911 *The King of Terror*
2912 *Goth Opera*
2913 *The Cradle of the Snake*
2914 *TW: The Torchwood Archive* (BF), extrapolating from Archie being 38 in *TW: The Victorian Age* [1899]. The script to *The Torchwood Archive* is a bit out of synch with this, dating Archie's 100th birthday to "1970".
2915 *Leth-St: Beast of Fang Rock* (ch2).
2916 "A few years" before *CM S1: The Pelage Project*.
2917 *The King of Terror* (p255).
2918 *Who Killed Kennedy* (p69), *Leth-St:* "The Dogs of War". The ICMG first appears in *Remembrance of the Daleks*, and features in Big Finish's *Counter-Measures* audios.
2919 *Who Killed Kennedy* (p69).
2920 *CM S2: The Fifth Citadel*

Keep as a prison to house threats identified by Counter-Measures and other agencies.[2921]

The Beatles at the Cavern Club

The third Doctor, Jo and Mike Yates hoped to see the Beatles perform at the Cavern Club, 1961... if the TARDIS could get them there.[2922] Captain Jack went to the Beatles' debut at the Cavern Club in Liverpool, on the off-chance that the Doctor would turn up at such a nostalgic event. When the Doctor failed to show, Jack enjoyed himself with a party of student nurses in Biba shirts.[2923] The eleventh Doctor claimed that 96% of the audience at the Beatles' first show at the Cavern Club, 1961, were time travellers... as was John Lennon.[2924]

1961 - "The Time of My Life"[2925] **->** The tenth Doctor and Donna saw the Beatles perform at the Cavern Club. Donna had John Lennon autograph a CD of an album that the Beatles hadn't written yet for her mother.

> (=) In an alt-timeline where the Common Men achieved the fame meant for the Beatles, the group performed in the Cavern Club in Liverpool, 1961.[2926]

Molly O'Sullivan is Laid to Rest

> **(=) 1961 - DEyes 4: MASTER OF THE DALEKS**[2927] **->** Four decades on, the Dalek Time Controller had created a Dalek army that had conquered Earth and renamed it New Skaro. Daleks numbering in the millions were created using raw material from humanity, Sontarans and Draconians. Mary Carter, formerly known as Molly O'Sullivan, had been doing missionary work in Africa when the Dalek war machine surged across Europe, and been spared – although her husband was killed.
>
> The eighth Doctor's TARDIS was drawn to the epicentre of this errant history: Dalek operations in

Moscow. The bald Master, having manipulated Liv Chenka, arrived to incorporate the Doctor's Ship into the still-damaged Dalek Pagoda. The Time Controller instead incorporated the Master's TARDIS, thus cementing this alternate history into being, and then moved to dispense with the Master's services. The Master activated a sub-routine he'd slipped into the newborn Daleks, making them turn on one another. In the chaos to follow, the Dalek Time Controller captured Molly and Liv, and escaped in the Doctor's TARDIS to find the creator of the Eminence, Marcus Schriver, in the future. The Doctor followed in the Master's TARDIS, which broke the Pagoda's hold on history and stranded his old enemy.

Molly's eventual salvation of Earth's timeline restored her own history, in which she performed missionary work and had a family. Following the elder Molly's demise at the Eye of Orion in future, the Doctor and Liv pledged to bring her body home, and bury her in her own soil.[2928]

lgtw - 1961 - WD S3: THE SHADOW VORTEX[2929] **->** As the whole of Earth, 1961, was vulnerable to temporal manipulation, the Time Lords fighting the Last Great Time War established a quantum barrier around it to prevent Dalek incursion.

> (=) A human defector, "Lara", converted the West Berlin Science Academy's isotron into a Shadow Vortex: a gateway through which millions of Daleks would invade and destroy Earth post-1961, depriving the Doctor of so many useful allies that he would be erased from time. The War Doctor surrounded Lara and the Vortex with his TARDIS, and brought them into contact with their past selves, which consigned them to a universe where they paradoxically couldn't exist.

2921 *CM S4: The Keep*.

2922 *3rdA: The Havoc of Empires*. The Beatles made 292 appearances at the club, from 1961-1963.

2923 *TW: Almost Perfect*. Historically, this happened on 9th February, 1961.

2924 Dating "The Time of My Life" (*DWM* #399) - This can't be the Beatles' *first* performance at the club, or Captain Jack would have spotted the Doctor there (*TW: Almost Perfect*). The Beatles played at the club more than once in 1961, and were first spotted there by Brian Epstein on 9th November.

2925 *The Eleventh Doctor Year One*: "What He Wants".

2926 *1963: Fanfare for the Common Men*. The Beatles regularly played the Cavern Club in their early days.

2927 Dating *DEyes 4: Master of the Daleks* (BF *DEyes*

#4.3) - It's "forty years" after the 1921 component of the story.

2928 *DEyes 4: Eye of Darkness*

2929 Dating *WD S3: The Shadow Vortex* (BF *WD* #3.1) - The year is given. It's apparently Autumn or Winter, as the Berlin Wall was constructed "in August" (historically, that happened on the 13th of that month).

2930 Confirmed in *The Seeds of Death*.

2931 "Fifty years" before "Down to Earth".

2932 "Three years" before *CM S1: Artificial Intelligence*.

2933 *Leth-St: The Showstoppers, Leth-St*: "Schadengeist's First Love".

2934 "Klein's Story"

2935 *Salvation* (p5).

2936 *The Flames of Cadiz*

In 1961, Yuri Gagarin became the first human to travel in space.[2930] The Doctor materialised in the middle of a battle between the Trylonians and Zorians, causing both sides to scatter. The Trylonian commander Lum-Tee fled to Earth and hid in a small English village.[2931]

Allison Williams started dating Julian St Stephen, a psychologist, in 1961.[2932] On 13th October, 1961, Vilhelm Schadengeist physically and mentally merged with his siphonophore. The resultant hybrid received the codename Factotum.[2933]

> (=) In Klein's reality, Adolf Hitler died in 1961. Prior to this, technology harvested from alien incursions had been locked away in a Berlin depository, its existence denied because Hitler was loathe to admit the superiority of alien intelligences. With his passing, limitations on researching such tech were eased, and the Reich's ruling body became torn with internal divisions.[2934]

1962

Dorothea Chaplet, a companion of the first Doctor, was sent to live with her great-aunt Margaret when her parents died. At her new school, she was given the nickname "Dodo".[2935] Barbara Wright went on holiday to Spain in 1962, returning with a toy donkey and a sword-shaped letter opener from Toledo.[2936]

Rachel Jensen began working on artificial-intelligence experiments at Cambridge.[2937] She failed to realise that page 4, paragraph 24, of her contract designated all of her current and future research as the intellectual property of Her Majesty's Government. Jensen and Professor Jeffrey Broderick worked together at Cambridge for years.[2938] Jensen became involved with one of her colleagues at

Cambridge, Henry Cording. They drifted apart after she never answered his marriage proposal one way or another.[2939]

Section Eight used the dark arts to end the Cuban Missile Crisis.[2940] A small party of Muslims passed into Avalon.[2941] The starship of the alien scientist Raldonn crashed in Britain, killing the co-pilot. He was set to work on Operation Proteus, and began using it as a cover for other experiments on humans.[2942]

@ It was the eighth Doctor's idea that the Beatles should wear suits.[2943] The Doctor was friends with the Beatles.[2944] The Doctor travelled the world in the sixties and seventies.[2945] He visited India.[2946]

The Doctor spent some time at a Buddhist temple in Thailand, searching for a dragon. His search took twenty-five years and he travelled across China, Vietnam and Siam. He found the dragon, but it's not known what subsequently happened.[2947] During the 1960s, the Doctor spent some time learning ventriloquism from Edgar Bergen of *The Edgar Bergen and Charlie McCarthy Show*.[2948]

lgtw - One Dalek fell through time at the end of the Last Great Time War, crashing to Earth in the Ascension Islands. Damaged and unresponsive, it spent the next fifty years being passed from one private collection to another, ending up being bought by Van Statten.[2949] Another Dalek fell from the sky off the coast of Brazil, and would spend a half-century languishing in South America.[2950]

Percival Noggins, a mind-controlled factory manager, was born around 1962.[2951] The Doctor observed Wernher von Braun as he struggled with a prototype rocket for America's space programme.[2952] Sgt Ruben Hicks sneakily acquired a guitar, and taught Lethbridge-Stewart a few chords in 1962. A few months later, Hicks died in Korea.[2953]

2937 "Two years" before *CM S1: Threshold*.
2938 *CM S1: Artificial Intelligence*
2939 New *CM S2: The Splintered Man*
2940 *Heart of TARDIS* (p197).
2941 "Fifty years" before *The Shadows of Avalon*.
2942 "Many months" before "Operation Proteus", and more than four months because Raldonn was there to detect the Doctor's arrival on Earth.
2943 *Trading Futures*
2944 *Magic of the Angels* (ch9).
2945 *Father Time*. This is one reason that the Doctor doesn't bump into himself during the UNIT era.
2946 "Twenty-seven years" before the third part of *Father Time*.
2947 *The Year of Intelligent Tigers*
2948 *Dark Progeny*. The success of this depends upon when the Doctor trained with Bergen – who was very popular, but let his ventriloquism skills lapse while

working in radio. Later in Bergen's career, the McCarthy doll would mock Bergen for moving his lips.
2949 It arrived "at least fifty years" before *Dalek*.
2950 "Fifty years" before *UNIT S5: Encounters: The Dalek Transaction*, indicating the Earthfall in *Dalek*.
2951 This happened forty-seven years before *Hornets' Nest: Hive of Horror*, according to the sleeve notes.
2952 *Persuasion*. Wernher von Braun (1912-1977), considered the father of rocket science, was among hundreds of Nazi engineers who migrated to the United States following World War II. The prototype the Doctor observed could have been part of the Saturn rocket programme – the pinnacle of von Braun's career, initiated in 1962, and used later in the decade to help America first step foot on the moon.
2953 "Fifteen years" after 1947, according to *The Devil Goblins from Neptune*.

American scientists worked out how to operate the navigation system of their captured Nedenah spaceship.[2954]

(=) The Common Men performed in Morecambe and London in 1962.[2955]

(=) 1962 - "Klein's Story"[2956] **->** Elizabeth Klein was researching physics at Cambridge when Major Eunice Faber recruited her to examine alien technology in Berlin. They became romantically involved, and he told her of the capture of the Doctor's time machine in 1955. Soon after, the eighth Doctor, posing as "Johann Schmidt", made contact with Klein and offered to help her determine the Ship's secrets. They worked together for the next three years.

1962 - "Escape Into Alcatraz"[2957] **->** The Blowfish named Mako owed money to the wrong Silurian, and thought it best to hide in Alcatraz prison for a decade, disguised by a shimmer suit as the convict Luchessi. Mako had saved the Doctor's life from the ice pirates on Cygnus Delta, and so the eleventh Doctor travelled back to aid his friend after reading in the newspaper that Mako would die during a prison riot. Alien bounty hunters tried to claim the price on Mako's head, but the Doctor triggered the riot with help from Malone, the so-called King of Alcatraz, who was fearful of being probed by aliens. Mako was mistakenly thought dead beneath a rockfall, but escaped. The Doctor strongarmed the bounty hunters into presenting the news coverage of Mako's demise to their employers, so he could live in peace.

John Jones, Superstar, Joins the TARDIS

1962 - THE ELEVENTH DOCTOR YEAR ONE[2958] **->** The eleventh Doctor brought Alice to the first public performance of John Jones, a musician destined for superstardom with such albums as *Abanazar's Madness*, and under such monikers as "the Chameleon of Pop", "the Tall Pale Earl" and "Xavi Moonburst"... but found that Jones was a talentless, meek fellow in a boring suit. The Doctor tried to salvage the evening by taking Alice back to 1931 to see Robert Leroy Johnson perform, but Jones stowed away in the TARDIS...

Jones' many adventures with the Doctor and Alice helped him develop as a person and a musician. The Doctor and Alice returned Jones to 1962, where he gave his debut performance to a star-struck crowd. From a distance, Alice saw her late mother in the audience.

In time, Jones would become the greatest pop star in the universe, and travel about in his own spaceship.[2959]

Minnie Hooper, a friend of Wilfred Mott, got trapped in a police box on August bank holiday in 1962.[2960] Melanie Bush's sister Annabelle was born 4th October, 1962.[2961]

1962 (22nd October) - SHROUD OF SORROW[2962] **->** The eleventh Doctor and Clara took Mae Callon, a newspaper reporter they met while defeating the Shroud, back in time to see her dying grandmother one last time.

1962 (23rd November) - THE LIGHT AT THE END[2963] **->** The fifth Doctor arrived at 59A Barnsfield Crescent in Totton, Hampshire – the home of Bob Dovie and his family – but the TARDIS smashed Dovie's chimney on arrival. By acclimating Dovie to the TARDIS' interior, the Doctor prevented a conceptual bomb the cadaverous Master had planted in 1963 from detonating.

While looking into the Starfire missile programme, the seventh Doctor campaigned for Parliament as "John Rutherford". He avoided his usual pseudonym of "John Smith", knowing that Lanarkshire would elect an MP of the same name in 1970.[2964]

2954 *Leth-St:* "The Band of Evil"
2955 *1963: Fanfare for the Common Men*
2956 Dating "Klein's Story" (BF #131a) - The year is given. Reference is made to the Reich possessing a Drahvinian power core, which suggests that the Drahvins from *Galaxy 4* are spacefaring in this era, but it's of little help in dating that story.
2957 Dating "Escape Into Alcatraz" (IDW *DW Special 2012*) - The year is given. The riot/escape involving Mako is fictional, but the same year saw one of the prison's most infamous escape efforts, when Frank Morris and brothers Clarence and John Anglin fled the island on a life-raft made from raincoats. It's never been properly determined if they drowned while doing so or got clean away, but their story was dramatised as *Escape from Alcatraz* (1979) starring Clint Eastwood,

Patrick McGoohan and Danny Glover.
2958 Dating *The Eleventh Doctor Year One* (Titan 11th Doc #1.3, #1.15, "What He Wants"/"The Comfort of the Good") - A caption gives the year in both stories. David Bowie, the obvious inspiration for Jones, started performing in 1962.
2959 *The Eleventh Doctor Year Three:* "Remembrance"
2960 *The End of Time*
2961 *Spiral Scratch*
2962 Dating *Shroud of Sorrow* (NSA #53) - The day is given (p247).
2963 Dating *The Light at the End* (BF DW 50th Anniversary story) - It's exactly one year prior to the shenanigans at Dovie's house on 23rd November, 1963.
2964 *1963: The Assassination Games*. The Doctor campaigns "several months" before his win circa May 1963.

Pre-History

The Gallu, demon-creatures from the Underworld, were "older than the world, older than time".[1]

A demonic force, the Mother of Shadows, was imprisoned billions of years ago.[2] Another demonic force, summoned by Alexander Korvo in 1927, claimed to have watched over the Earth since humanity's distant ancestors first climbed down from the trees.[3]

History

The Gallu consumed souls in ancient Babylon and other cultures prior to encountering Dorian Gray in 1900.[4] The Vikings felled the Icelandic forests to build their ships, but left alone one inhabited by lycanthropes.[5]

Ollantay's flute was among the items later found in Jennifer Alford's collection of supernatural items.[6]

In the tenth century, three dragons – a red one (the tester), a jade one (representing wealth) and a white one (redemption) – were ritualistically trapped by the playing of a game of mahjong, which entailed the building of walls. The twittering of sparrows within the game pacified the dragons, who remained bound until the 1950s.[7]

The vampire Ivor entered into a pact with a siryn in the early seventeenth century, and in time they travelled with a carnival. The siryn's song lured in customers, but she needed to eat one human heart per day to survive.[8]

A mother lost her first five children to natural causes, but birthed a sixth – a son – on Christmas Eve. As her son's health failed, the mother bargained with an old woman in the forest for his life. The mother forfeited her own life, but her heart replaced her son's ailing one. As an old man, the son discovered that he would never die – if he kept har-

vesting replacement organs from the living.[9]

Tobias Matthews, a future lover of Dorian Gray, went to a circus in 1724 over his mother's objection, and became infatuated with one of its handlers, Ivor. The siryn that Ivor served maimed Toby – to save the young man's life, Ivor sired him as a vampire. The circus moved on, and Toby would next see Ivor in 2014.[10] Toby's father had left him at a young age.[11]

Lord Elliot Marwick commissioned a tapestry to celebrate the wedding of his first-born son in 1759. Successive generations of Marwicks were thought to add images of themselves to the work, but, in truth, the tapestry claimed the Marwicks' souls – and trapped them screaming – upon their deaths.[12]

In 1783, Johann van Kirk purchased land in what would become Los Angeles. Generations of his family would regularly sacrifice young people on behalf of the Mother of Shadows.[13] Deacon Brodie became a fine cabinet maker in Edinburgh, but also operated as a master thief by keeping keys to everything he built. In a university vault, Brodie found a key that enabled its user to transfer bodies. The authorities captured Brodie and hung him on a gallows that he'd constructed, but he survived by swapping forms.[14]

Maleficums from Napoleonic times would wind up in the collection of Jennifer Alford.[15]

A string of preventable factory deaths in Suffolk, the 1830s, resulted in creation of a supernatural black smoke, which vengefully killed a dozen industrialists. The smoke became trapped in its victims' corpses, which were buried at the Church of St. Giles.[16] The vampire Toby Matthews was personally acquainted with William Wordsworth.[17]

---

1 *DG* S1: *This World, Our Hell.*

2 "Billions of years" before *DG* S5: *Valley of Nightmares.*

3 *Worlds BF: The Feast of Magog*

4 *DG* S1: *This World, Our Hell.* The Gallu hail from Babylonian and Assyrian mythology.

5 *DG* S4: *Inner Darkness.* It's believed that Norse settlers came to Iceland in the second half of the ninth century.

6 *Benny* B3: *Legion: Shades of Gray,* referencing the Quechua dramatic play *Ollantay.* Differing theories exist as to the play's origin; it possibly survived in oral tradition, and the earliest known manuscript belonged to the priest Antonia Valdes (1744-1816). *Shades of Gray* has a bit of a misnomer in calling the item "Quena Ollantay's flute", as Quena is the type of flute in question, not the main character's name or title.

7 "A thousand years" before *DG* S1: *The Twittering of Sparrows.*

8 "Five hundred years" before *DG* S3: *Heart and Soul.*

9 "Hundreds of years" before *DG: Desperately Seeking Santa.*

10 *DG* S3: *Heart and Soul*

11 *DG* S3: *The Darkest Hour*

12 *Benny* B3: *Legion: Shades of Gray,*

13 *DG* S5: *Valley of Nightmares*

14 "One hundred thirty years" before *DG: The Prime of Deacon Brodie.*

15 *Benny* B3: *Legion: Shades of Gray,.* The word "maleficium" more typically refers to an act of black magic rather than a magical item.

16 *DG* S4: *His Dying Breath*

17 *DG* S1: *The Heart that Lives Alone.* Wordsworth lived 7th April, 1770 to 23rd April, 1850.

Dorian Gray

Dorian Gray

There were differing accounts about Dorian Gray's history; this is one of them.[18]

Dorian Gray, an immortal and hedonist, was born on 8th November, 1862. His mother would sometimes play Schumann's *Prophet Bird* to aid him to sleep.[19] The name Dorian was Gaelic for "stormy weather." Dorian studied a book of Norse mythology in his family library.[20] After the deaths of Dorian's parents, he was raised by several governesses, then a boarding school.[21]

Dorian Gray's father died "a few years" before Dorian turned ten, and shortly after the birth of Dorian's younger sister, Isadora Victoria Gray. The two children were soon adopted by their aunt and uncle, as their father's passing left their mother so grief-stricken, she was institutionalized. Isadora had friends, but Dorian – having witnessed the damage friendship perpetrated on his mother – preferred books to people.[22]

1879 (August) - DG S2: RUNNING AWAY WITH YOU[23] -> When Dorian Gray was sixteen, his aunt and uncle hired a new housekeeper, Constance Harker. Dorian's aunt went to Scotland to visit her ailing father for a week, and took his sister Isadora with her. Dorian's uncle was called away on business suddenly, and left him in Constance's care. Dorian lost his virginity to Constance, and in so doing was instilled with a sense that youth was to be prized, and age feared.

Although Constance and Dorian never had sex after that day, a supernatural creature that had latched onto Dorian as his "imaginary friend" deemed Constance a threat to their relationship, and pushed her down the stairs to her death. Dorian was never formally accused of causing Constance's demise, but her passing left a cloud of suspicion over him. A part of Dorian never truly grew up, and so his "imaginary friend" remained with him, and would again manifest in 2012.

The Picture of Dorian Gray

The 18-year-old gentleman Dorian Gray sat for a portrait as painted by his friend, Basil Hallward. The beauty of the picture was such that Dorian claimed that he would give his soul if only the picture could age while he remained forever young, rather than the reverse. Basil Hallward's friend from Cambridge, Lord Henry Wooton, met Dorian and mentored him into a life of depravity. Dorian fell in love with a young stage performer, Sibyl Vane, but later deemed her unworthy of him and terminated their engagement – which prompted Sibyl to take her own life.[24]

Other people – including Loretta Delphine – also sold their souls to gain immortality, but Dorian Gray lasted longer than most.[25]

Oscar Wilde visited St. Joseph, Missouri, a few days after Jesse James was shot dead.[26] Richard Dadd died 7th January, 1886 – he was an asylum patient who had murdered his father, thought himself under the influence of Osiris and painted many works with supernatural themes. Wilde had interviewed Dadd, and suspected that Dadd's evil taint had infected his paintings and sketches, and through them contaminated London's moral fibre.[27]

Oscar Wilde Meets Dorian Gray

A few months after the birth of his second son, Vyvyan, Oscar Wilde entered a Paris bookshop to find a copy of *Le Pere Goriot* by Balzac. There he happened to meet Dorian Gray. The two of them quickly became friends and, in time, had an affair until Wilde returned to London.[28]

Emma Elizabeth Smith, one of the non-canonical Ripper victims and possibly a victim of Richard Dadd's spirit, was murdered on 3rd April, 1888.[29]

---

18 See *The Picture of Dorian Gray* sidebar for the alternative.
19 *DG* S2: *Running Away With You*, *DG: We Are Everywhere* and *DG: The Prime of Deacon Brodie*.
20 *DG* S4: *Freya*
21 *DG* S4: *The Abysmal Sea*
22 *DG* S2: *Running Away With You*, extrapolating from Dora's given age and year of death in *DG: The Twittering of Sparrows*.
23 Dating *DG* S2: *Running Away With You* (*DG* #2.5) - The month and year are given. The lethal "imaginary friend" seems akin to the entity in *Benny* B3: *Legion: Shades of Gray*.
24 The broad developments in *The Picture of Dorian Gray*, as confirmed in *DG: Ghosts of Christmas Past*. The latter story claims that Sibyl died, and Dorian became immortal, "thirty years" prior to c.1912.
25 *DG* S3: *The Darkest Hour*, *DG* S2: *The Picture of Loretta Delphine*.
26 *DG* S1: *This World, Our Hell*. James died 3rd April, 1882.
27 *DG* S5: *One Must Not Look at Mirrors*
28 *DG* S5: *One Must Not Look at Mirrors*. Vyvyan was born 3rd November, 1886, so Dorian and Oscar presumably meet in early 1887.
29 *DG* S5: *One Must Not Look at Mirrors*

THE PICTURE OF DORIAN GRAY: Big Finish's *The Confessions of Dorian Gray* series works on the premise that Dorian Gray was a real person who befriended Oscar Wilde, who passed off Dorian's life story as fiction in his novel *The Picture of Dorian Gray* (1890). Between Series Two and Three of *Confessions*, Big Finish also released an audio adaptation of Wilde's book.

Confessions broadly acknowledges the events of *The Picture of Dorian Gray* – that Dorian bargained away his soul to gain immortality and the transference of his sins into a portrait of him; that he betrayed the young stage performer Sibyl Vane, who killed herself; that he impulsively murdered the painter Basil Hallward, and so on. *DG: Ghosts of Christmas Past* is a direct sequel to *Picture*, both confirming that the key points of *Picture* took place, and also crossing over with Big Finish's *Sherlock Holmes* series.

It's difficult to count the audio version of *The Picture of Dorian Gray* itself, however, as part of the *Confessions* canon. Not only does it so adhere to Wilde's novel that Dorian dies at the end (not necessarily an impediment for a supernatural immortal, but *Confessions* never references the incident), *DG: Running Away With You* fronts a backstory for Dorian that is so at odds with *Picture*, it can only be assumed that Wilde changed some of Dorian's personal details while keeping intact the tale of his infernal bargain and the hedonism to follow.

The Picture of Dorian Gray audio establishes that Dorian was born in 1852, and that his hateful grandfather raised him after both his parents died. Very hard dates are also provided on Dorian's activities from 1872 (when Hallward completes Dorian's portrait) to 1890 (when Dorian murders the man). By contrast, *DG: Running Away With You* establishes that Dorian was either born in 1862 or 1863 (he's "17" in 1879), *DG: The Mayfair Monster* cites him as "137 years" old on 31st December, 1999 (so, he was born in 1862); and *DG: We are Everywhere* and *DG: The Prime of Deacon Brodie* definitively specify that he was born on 8th November, 1862 (thereby ruling out most of the timeline given in *Picture*, unless we're to believe that Dorian sat for his portrait, went to a bawdy house in Whitechapel with Lord Henry Wooton and had a devastating engagement and romance with Sibyl – all at age nine). *Running Away With You* also relates that Dorian's sister Isodora was born not long after him; that their father *did* die, but their mother was institutionalized; and that they were both adopted by a reasonably kind (if aloof) aunt and uncle. There's no sense that Dorian was raised by his grandfather, although he does later recall (*DG: The Needle*) that the man did business with JC Parker, an investment bank.

Ghosts of Christmas Past casts its lot with *Running Away With You*'s timeline, doubly claiming that Dorian became immortal (meaning, when he sat for his portrait) and Sibyl Vane committed suicide "thirty years" prior to circa 1912 (*Picture* says both of those incidents happened a decade earlier, in 1872). *Ghosts* also claims

that Dorian blackmailed the chemist Alan Campbell owing to the potential scandal of an illegitimate daughter; in *Picture*, it's because Campbell is a closeted homosexual who shared a steamy fortnight with Dorian in Cairo. *The Prime of Deacon Brodie* also specifies that Dorian sat for his portrait at age 18 – meaning the repeated claims in *Confessions* that Dorian outwardly looks "barely twenty" (*DG: The Immortal Game*, *Ghosts of Christmas Past*, etc.) are the result of people rounding up a little, based upon his body posture and intellect.

While *The Picture of Dorian Gray* has been left out of this appendix for the aforementioned reasons, anyone preferring to accommodate it should note the following dates it provides:

• **1852:** Dorian Gray is born (he's "37, almost 38" on 4th June, 1890).

• **1872 (June):** Dorian, having been back in London for "barely two months", stops by the homestead of his friend, the painter Basil Hallward, on 3rd June and meets an associate of Hallward's from Oxford: Lord Henry Wooton. Dorian expresses sadness that he will age while his picture remains young, and vows that he would give his very soul to make the reverse come true. The portrait is delivered to Dorian's house on 10th June, the same day that Wooton takes Dorian to an upscale bawdy house in Whitechapel. Hallward's portrait of Dorian adopts a more sneering look, as if it were absorbing Dorian's sins and debauchery.

• **1872 (August to September, 30th November):** Dorian watches a performance of *Romeo and Juliet* in the East End on 1st August, and falls in love with the female lead, 17-year-old Sibyl Vane. On 8th August, they visit Kensington Gardens. On 2nd September, Hallward and Wooton return from abroad and learn of Dorian's relationship with Sibyl. He invites his friends to witness her performance as Juliet, but it's so leaden and uninspiring, Dorian feels humiliated and spitefully terminates their engagement. The next day, Dorian regrets his words and decides to reconcile with Sibyl, but learns that she killed herself with a vial of prussic acid. On 30th November, Dorian tells his friends that he's leaving the country in two days to travel.

• **1870s and 1880s:** Dorian travels widely, going to Paris (December 1872); the Riviera to meet Wooton (1st March, 1873); Venice (17th February, 1874); the Highlands, to go hunting with Wooton ("fifteen years" before 1890); Cairo (1877); the Orient for more than a year; Shanghai (30th April, 1881); back to London, briefly (3rd August, 1883); Cairo again, where he has a short-lived love affair with King's College graduate Alan Campbell (2nd to 20th October, 1885).

• **1890 (June):** Dorian returns to his home in Mayfair after many years away. On 4th June, he learns from Wooton that stories of his incorrigibleness while overseas have reached London society. Hallward finds the

continued on Page 1331

1888 (summer to 30th September) - DG S5: ONE MUST NOT LOOK AT MIRRORS[30] **->** Dorian Gray happened upon Oscar Wilde in London, and they once more became secret lovers. Wilde found himself unsettled by Dorian's callousness, especially in the company of Dorian's associate Walter van Kirk. Such was their depravity that Wilde worried that Dorian, van Kirk or both were committing the Whitechapel murders – and so followed them one night as they enjoyed drinks on the town. To Wilde's eyes, Richard Dadd's spirit seemed to be present as the third Ripper victim, Elizabeth Stride, was killed. Dorian aided a distraught Wilde after the incident, took him home, and they later renewed their friendship.

Dorian Gray found that he wasn't aging, while his picture was indeed absorbing his sins and becoming more corrupt. When Basil Hallward expressed concern about Dorian's morality, Dorian showed Hallward his portrait – then, on impulse, stabbed him to death. Dorian blackmailed the chemist Alan Campbell into destroying Hallward's body. Hallward had been due to leave for Paris, so his disappearance went unnoticed for a time.[31]

The Picture of Dorian Gray

Oscar Wilde wrote *The Picture of Dorian Gray* based upon Gray's actual life, but passed it off as a work of fiction. The story's success made Gray's name more infamous, but not the man himself. Wilde and Gray's friendship waned, and Gray would not see Wilde, nor Wilde's friend Robert Ross, until shortly prior to Wilde's death.[32] Dorian owned a copy of *The Picture of Dorian Gray* signed for him by Wilde.[33]

In 1891, Inspector Lestrade asked Sherlock Holmes to investigate Basil Hallward's disappearance. Holmes determined that Hallward had been murdered, and correctly assessed the involvement of chemist Alan Campbell – but erroneously concluded that Campbell had murdered Hallward. The media learned of Holmes' suspicions, and the resultant publicity ruined Campbell's reputation. Campbell was thought to have killed himself, but used his knowledge of chemistry to fake his demise.[34]

---

30 Dating *DG* S5: *One Must Not Look at Mirrors* (*DG* #5.1) - The blurb names the year, when the Ripper murders occurred (the first canonical one happened on 31st August, 1888). Dorian and Oscar get reacquainted over a "hot, bloody summer", and the story ends with Elizabeth Stride's death on 30th September, leaving open-ended the degree to which Dadd was actually involved in the Ripper killings, or what ended the murder spree.
31 A turning point in *The Picture of Dorian Gray*, confirmed in *DG: Ghosts of Christmas Past*.
32 *DG* S1: *This World, Our Hell* claims that Dorian and Wilde last saw each other "nine [years]... maybe ten" prior to 1900. Similarly, Dorian last saw Ross – who was born 25th May, 1869 – when the man was "twenty". The *speed* with which *The Picture of Dorian Gray* was apparently published following Dorian's murder of Hallward is a little dizzying – *DG: Ghosts of Christmas Past* claims that Hallward's disappearance raised some alarm with the authorities in 1891, suggesting Hallward died the previous year, and yet *The Picture of Dorian Gray* was first published in the July 1890 issue of *Lippincott's Monthly Magazine*.
33 *DG* S3: *Blank Canvas*
34 The background to *DG: Ghosts of Christmas Past*. Holmes doesn't seem to have noticed that Oscar Wilde published a novel in 1890 that fingered Dorian Gray, whom Holmes interviewed, as Hallward's killer.
35 *DG: Ghosts of Christmas Past*
36 *DG* S1: *The Twittering of Sparrows*. Date unknown; it's not even clear if this occurs before or during Dorian's exile from London. Isodora here has sex for the first time, having been born in 1870. The Eiffel tower was constructed in 1889; Gustave Eiffel lived 1832 to 1923;

Edison 1847 to 1931.
37 *DG* S5: *Angel of War*
38 *DG: All Through the House*
39 *DG* S4: *Human Remains*
40 Or so Victoria claims in *DG* S3: *Displacement Activity*.
41 Dating *DG* S1: *This World, Our Hell* (*DG* #1.1) - The story opens in "Paris, November 1900", and ends with Dorian reading a *Times* obituary (published 1st December, 1900) on Wilde, who died 30th November. The story is predicated on an infamous Wilde quote, delivered in his final days: "My wallpaper and I are fighting a duel to the death. One of us has got to go."
42 Dating *DG* S4: *Banshee* (*DG* #4.5) - The blurb claims that it's "Country Meath, 1900," but Dorian's narration says it's "Autumn 1902".
43 "More than seventeen years" before *Worlds BF: The Feast of Magog* [June 1927].
44 *DG* S2: *Murder on 81st Street*
45 *DG* S1: *The Houses in Between*
46 Dating *DG: Ghosts of Christmas Past* (*DG* #1.X) - The days are given, but no year is named. *Worlds BF: The Adventure of the Bloomsbury Bomber* establishes that Dorian and Sherlock last met "almost fifteen years" prior to August 1927, which would favour a dating for *Ghosts of Christmas Past* of circa 1912, if not that exact year.

The numerous incidental statements made about this adventure broadly agree that it happens in the early 1910s... Dorian says that Sherlock interviewed him pertaining to Basil Hallward's murder "almost twenty years ago" in 1891, and that he hasn't been back in London in that same amount of time. The case entailed Sherlock making what is now a "20-year-old deduction"; similarly, Alan Campbell allegedly killed himself "almost twenty years ago". Holmes has been gone from

Dorian's Self-Exile from London

Dorian Gray left London, and didn't return for two decades.[35]

Dorian, his sister Isodora, Thomas Edison and the engineer Gustave Eiffel spent the evening together on the left bank in Paris, including the top of the Eiffel Tower. Isodora wrote something in a guest book that made Edison blush. Dorian stormed off while outside Notre Dame, infuriated because a waiter or waitress turned down his advances. Isodora lost her virginity that night to Filippe, one of Dorian's lovers, but would not see her brother again until the 1950s, in Singapore.[36] During his "grand tour" away from London, Dorian Gray visited the Church of St. Jean and saw its prized Angelus bell.[37]

The Brigadoon Hotel was built in Kensington in 1893.[38] Dorian Gray's medical history became a lot less well documented after 1895.[39] The Lowell Foundation was established when its founder, the great-grandmother of Victoria Lowell, moved to England at the turn of the century.[40]

The Death of Oscar Wilde

1900 (November) - DG S1: THIS WORLD, OUR HELL[41] **->** Dorian Gray received word that his old friend Oscar Wilde was dying, and went to the man's final residence: the Hotel D'Alsace in Paris. The Gallu, creatures of the underworld, looked upon Paris as a modern-day Babylon in terms of corruption, and had taken to consuming the bodies and souls of the hotel-patrons. The hotel manager, Genevieve Moreau, profited from the deaths by claiming the patrons' belongings. Being soulless, Dorian was immune to the Gallu's power, and he maneuvered the fiends into feasting upon Moreau instead. Dorian facilitated a priest giving Wilde last rites – a means of protecting him from the Gallu – and then left Paris. Soon afterward, he read Wilde's obituary in the *Times*.

1902 (Autumn) - DG S4: BANSHEE[42] **->** Dorian Gray had caused another minor scandal in the papers, so decided to accompany his associate Robert Mardling to a house in Ireland: a rundown abode in a bog that Mardling had won in a game of baccarat. A tormented banshee tethered to the housekeeper, Mary O'Tubridy – who was the last of her line, and terminally ill – besieged the house. The banshee wanted to scream one last time, but could only do so prior to a violent death. Dorian promised to kill O'Tubridy, enabling the banshee to scream, then ended O'Tubridy's life with an axe.

continued from Page 1329

rampant tales of Dorian's debauchery unsettling, and, mere hours before he's due to leave for Paris, visits Dorian's home on 4th June to talk about the hideous rumours. Dorian shows Hallward his baleful portrait... and, feeling encouraged by the picture to do so, stabs Hallward to death. The next day, Dorian summons Dr Alan Campbell – now a respected husband and father of two – and threatens to expose him as a homosexual if he didn't use his knowledge of chemistry to destroy Hallward's body. Campbell complies, and Hallward's absence goes unnoticed for some time, as he'd announced his departure for Paris.

Ghosts of Christmas Past picks up these storylines, claiming that Sherlock Holmes investigated Hallward's disappearance – and interviewed Dorian – in 1891, but wrongly concluded that Campbell murdered Hallward. Campbell fakes his death, beginning a bid to revenge himself on Dorian and Sherlock twenty years later.

• **1890 (10th – 12th August):** Sibyl Vane's brother Jim confronts Dorian in London on 10th August, 1890. On 12th August, Dorian and Wooton go hunting on Sir Geoffrey Clouston's estate, where Jim Vane – while stalking Dorian – is accidentally shot dead by Clouston. Dorian becomes lethargic in the weeks following Jim's death.

• **1890 (1st September):** Dorian learns from Wooton about a doctor at St. Thomas' – Alan Campbell, he believes – who was being blackmailed and shot himself. An increasingly desperate Dorian vows to do good deeds, but his picture remains unchanged. Enraged, Dorian stabs at his portrait with the knife he used to murder Hallward. Dorian's manservant Victor hears the commotion, and finds his master dead on the floor, supernaturally withered and aged.

While studying at Cambridge, Dorian Gray became friends with Evan Morgan. During a visit to the Vandermeer family bookshop, Morgan persuaded the owner to sell him Kronos Vad's *History of Earth* (Vol. 36,379).[43] Dorian studied some Hebrew at Cambridge.[44]

In 1911, Dorian Gray seduced a stage performer, Mary Sawyer – and terminated their relationship as she tried to tell him she was pregnant with his son. Such was Sawyer's shame, she burned down the music hall where she worked, killing herself and her unborn child.[45]

The Death of Henry Wooton, Dorian's First Meeting With Sherlock Holmes

c 1912 (23rd to 24th December) - DG: GHOSTS OF CHRISTMAS PAST[46] **->** Sherlock Holmes had been absent from London for the past "nine or so years", and was living in Sussex while John Watson checked on 221B Baker Street from time to time. Dorian Gray was in

Madrid, having been "ejected" from Paris. Watson spent Christmas with his wife's family.

As part of his revenge scheme against Dorian and Sherlock, Alan Campbell learned that Mycroft Holmes visited his brother each year for Christmas dinner, and so poisoned Mycroft's associate: Lord Henry Wooton. Dorian, Mycroft and by extension Sherlock returned to London to attend Wooton's funeral, whereupon Campbell stole Dorian's portrait and threatened to destroy it unless Dorian met Sherlock in Piccadilly Circus, decried him as a liar and shot him dead by midnight on Christmas Eve. Dorian and Sherlock also found themselves haunted by the "ghosts" of Sybil Vane (actually Campbell's illegitimate daughter, Jemma Mortindale) and a young James Moriarty.

Reclaiming his portrait, Dorian aided Sherlock in confronting Campbell and Mortindale in the East End theatre where Sibyl Vane once performed. Campbell and Mortindale were tricked into confessing their culpability in Wooton's death, and promptly arrested.

Sherlock returned to Sussex, as his bees needed attending... leaving Dorian to ponder that the "James Moriarty" they'd spied had nothing to do with Campbell's machinations, and was perhaps a supernatural force after all.

1913 (Spring) - DG S2: THE IMMORTAL GAME[47] ->

Dr Henry Jekyll was now living in Worthing as a professor of chemistry and lecturer of medicine at Aldersgate, "Sir Edward Montague", and kept his home address secret from his other self. The UK government funded Montague's efforts to create a new type of inhibition-free soldier, and he field-tested his research in India and Paupa New Guinea. His "half-brother" vehemently disagreed with the conclusions of his work.

Dorian Gray visited a royal banquet with King George V in attendance, then went to a park and, over the course of three weeks, observed Montague and his "half-brother" separately advancing a chess game against one another. Montague befriended Dorian, prompting his "half-brother" to trick Dorian into revealing Montague's location. Realising his mistake, Dorian raced to Montague's house to find it – and much of Montague's research – on fire, and the man's wife dead from the blaze. Montague left, acknowledging he was safer from his "brother" if he lived in isolation. Dorian spied Montague's four-year-old son, thought lost in the fire, amidst the rooftop shadows – with a supernatural glint in his eye.

London for "nine or so years"/"close to a decade". Moriarty died "twenty years ago" (presumably in 1893, when "The Final Problem" was published). Sibyl died, and Dorian became immortal, "thirty years" ago.

The story relies upon both Dorian and Sherlock having been gone from London for a long time, and needing something as dramatic as Wooton's death to lure them back. *The Adventure of the Bloomsbury Bomber* places Dorian as studying in Cambridge circa 1910, and although those events necessitate that he quickly visit a London bookshop, it's safe to assume that he otherwise avoids the city until *Ghosts of Christmas Past* rolls around. The same can, give or take, be said for Sherlock, although he does investigate the Bloomsbury explosions at his brother's request in June 1911.

47 Dating *DG S2: The Immortal Game* (DG #2.4) - Dorian names the year and season. Jekyll is outwardly in his "late 50s, early 60s", presumably reflecting the publication of *Strange Case of Dr. Jekyll and Mr Hyde* on 5th January, 1886. The story erroneously claims that the Immortal Game – a legendary chess match between Adolf Anderssen and Lionel Kierseritzky – happened "49 years ago", and vaguely implies that Dorian witnessed the contest. In actuality, the game was held 21st June, 1851 – about 62 years before this story, and quite a while before Dorian was born.

48 *DG S5: Angel of War*

49 Dating *DG S5: Angel of War* (DG #5.2) - The blurb cites the year, which follows the Battle at Mons in 1914.

50 *DG: All Through the House*. It's said that the hotel

disappeared from public view in "1916", but the only survivor of the original occultists dates these events to "Christmas 1915".

51 Dating *DG: The Prime of Deacon Brodie* (DG #2.X) - Historically, German Zeppelins conducted the first-ever air raid on Scotland on 2nd April, 1916. In France, Dorian says he's "almost sixty", which is rounding up some from his birth in 1862 (see *The Picture of Dorian Gray* sidebar).

52 *Worlds BF: The Feast of Magog*

53 *DG S4: The Enigma of Dorian Gray*

54 Dating *DG: The Prime of Deacon Brodie* (DG 2.X) - The blurb says it's "Edinburgh, 1920", and Dorian says it's "two years" out from the Great War (which ended 11th November, 1918). It's late enough in October that Brodie's night costume seems feasible "on Halloween". The story concludes on Saturday, which in 1920 would mean either 26th October or 2nd November, with Dorian awakening from his confrontation with Brodie "three days" later.

55 *DG S2: The Picture of Loretta Delphine*

56 *DG S2: Murder on 81st Street*

57 Dorian and Parker keep bumping into each other socially, but don't see each other in the "thirteen years" prior to *DG S2: Murder on 81st Street* [1939].

58 Dating *Worlds BF: The Feast of Magog* (Worlds BF #1.3) - Dorian names the month and year.

59 Dating *DG S4: His Dying Breath* (DG #4.4) - Eva and the blurb name the year. Dorian says their relationship continued "as the autumn slid into a dank and chill winter".

Private Stuart Knight claimed to have witnessed the Angels protecting the Allies at Mons.[48]

1915 - DG S5: ANGEL OF WAR[49] **->** Dorian Gray volunteered for service in World War I – to impress a girl, Lettie Holdsworth, with his bravery so she would have sex with him. He became a Lieutenant, and met Captain James Anderson on the battlefield in France. Private Stuart Knight insisted he had seen the Angels at Mons, and went deeper into No Man's Land to try to find the Angelus bell: an object said to summon an angel if struck three times. Dorian and Anderson followed, but Knight became violently unhinged and was shot dead by Anderson. Afterward, Dorian and Anderson became lovers.

A group of occultists checked into the Brigadoon Hotel on Christmas 1915, and performed a demonic ritual they hoped would save them from the horrors of World War I. The occultists summoned a manifestation of Lucifer... and, failing to control him, opted to seal off the hotel and trap Lucifer within. The Brigadoon disappeared, along with the hundred residents inside, and would reappear on Christmas Day each year to attract new victims.[50]

1916 (Spring) - DG: THE PRIME OF DEACON BRODIE[51] **->** Dorian Gray served in World War I under the command of his lover, Captain James Anderson. They enjoyed leave from the War in the Spring, but unexpectedly witnessed German Zeppelins dropping bombs on Scotland. They returned to the trenches in France, where James became trapped during a German assault. Dorian surrendered his gas mask to James and seemingly "died" in his place, but revived to find his comrades gone. Listed as dead, Dorian returned to London, where he indulged in "art, music, literature and beauty" for the rest of the war.

The disgraced Alexander Korvo aided the UK secret service bureau during the War. The charges against him were dropped, and he returned home.[52] Adam Notting, a lover of Dorian Gray, was born in Crystal Palace, 1920.[53]

1920 (late October to early November) - DG: THE PRIME OF DEACON BRODIE[54] **->** Deacon Brodie had established Brodie's department store in Edinburgh as a front for his illicit body-swapping operation. Dorian Gray received a copy of James Anderson's poetry of the war, recognised himself in some of it and sought out his ex-lover in Edinburgh. Anderson initially rejected Dorian, having grieved for his loss during the Great War. Brodie approached Dorian with an offer to let him swap bodies for 24 hours, which enabled Dorian to befriend Anderson in another form. Anderson deduced Dorian's identity, and aided him as Brodie attempted to keep Dorian's body for himself, leaving Dorian in a body with terminal lung disease. Dorian captured Anderson and hung his immortal body so many times, Anderson returned Dorian to his proper body.

Dorian recovered from the experience to find James gone, horrified by Dorian's actions. En route back to London, Dorian spied Brodie escaping on another train.

Loretta Delphine, the murderous owner of the Hotel Delphine in Florida, tortured and killed about twenty of the local gang bosses in her hotel's secret dungeon. The authorities arrested Delphine, but she escaped. Delphine's pact with demonic forces enabled her essence to live on in a picture of herself that hung above the hotel's fireplace.[55]

Dorian Gray Meets Dorothy Parker

The poet and satirist Dorothy Parker first met Dorian Gray in a boarding house. She was playing backgammon in a hallway, and he came running down the stairs wearing a kimono and lipstick.[56] Parker happened upon her friend Dorian Gray while he sitting in a bathtub playing a game of Consequences. On another occasion, she unexpectedly ran out of a bullfight to throw up in the street, and randomly found him standing there.[57]

1927 (August) - WORLDS BF: THE FEAST OF MAGOG[58] **->** Having returned from a short spell in Barcelona, Dorian Gray attended a party at the south Wales country estate of his friend Evan Morgan. At Morgan's request, Alexander Korvo held a séance to coincide with The Feast of Magog, when the barriers between realities were thin. Korvo summoned a demonic force that called itself Legion, and possessed Pamela St. John-Edwards: a beloved of both Dorian and Morgan. The Legion found the copy of Kronos Vad's *A History of Earth* (Volume 36,379) in Morgan's possession, and set fire to Pamela's body while trying to destroy it. Dorian saved the book, but deemed Pamela lost and repelled the Legion by killing her. Korvo lost his nerve while trying to run Dorian over, and died in a car crash.

The next day, Dorian and Morgan returned Vad's chronicle to the Vandermeer bookshop. Dorian again met Sherlock Holmes at Korvo's funeral, and assured him the book was in safe hands.

1929 (Autumn to Winter) - DG S4: HIS DYING BREATH[59] **->** In London, Dorian Gray enjoyed an era of jazz, gin and dancing, and took up with a young woman named Eva Granger. An earth tremor released the black smoke buried at the Church of St. Giles in the 1830s, and it resumed murdering those who had done harm to others. Billy Fielding, Granger's childhood sweetheart, became jealous of her relationship with Dorian and murdered her. Dorian allowed the smoke to kill Fielding, then trapped the smoke in a bottle and threw it out to sea.

Dorian Gray learned how to make Molotov cocktails in Madrid, the 1930s.[60] In the same decade, Dorian took a degree in ornithology.[61] The immortal in need of replacement organs killed a man dressed as Santa Claus in the 1930s... and, for good measure, kept his outfit.[62]

Maria de Naglowska's occult mirror later became the property of Jennifer Alford.[63] A casket belonging to Rabbi Loew, a central figure in the legend of the golem, was found in Czechoslovakia, 1935, and placed on display in a New York museum.[64] James Anderson went to speak with his publisher in 1935, and chanced upon Dorian Gray in the street. The two of them graciously pretended not to know one another.[65]

Dorian Gray watched the Crystal Palace burn.[66] Dorothy Parker remembered little of 1936 and 37, when she secretly co-wrote some of the Broadway Brats films.[67] A bored Dorian Gray had his appendix removed without anesthetic – just to see what it felt like – at the Melrose Hospital, 1937. The immortal appendix that Dorian left behind grew in the hospital's basement, subsisting off medical waste.[68]

1939 (April) - DG S2: MURDER ON 81ST STREET[69] -> Julius Metzger, the owner of a Chicago freight company, lent much support to a pro-Nazi organisation: the German American Bund. Appalled by Metzger's beliefs, Professor Bloom revived the golem on display in an antiquities exhibition, and had the creature eliminate Metzger. Dorian Gray and his friend Dorothy Parker happened upon one another in Greenwich Village, and pursued the golem as it turned on Bloom and killed him. By changing the inscription on the golem's forehead to the Hebrew word for "dead", Dorian made the golem go dormant once more. The police, having no love for the German American Bund, claimed that Metzger and Bloom died of aneurysms, and that any witness saying otherwise must have been high on reefers. Dorian and Parker took their leave of the authorities, and went out for a nice breakfast.

James Anderson finally wrote down the strange events pertaining to Dorian Gray in No Man's Land, 1915.[70]

1940 (29th December) to 1941 (1st January) - DG S1: THE HOUSES IN BETWEEN[71] -> A Luftwaffe strike on London killed nearly two hundred people, in what was dubbed the Second Great Fire of London. Dorian Gray had moved his portrait to a United Savings Bank vault, and watched the carnage from atop the *Daily Mail* building before returning to his home in Mayfair. The next day, an ethereal force attacked Dorian via memories of his betrayal of Mary Sawyer in 1911. Dorian destroyed the force by

---

60 *DG* S4: *Freya*

61 *DG* S4: *The Abysmal Sea*

62 *DG*: *Desperately Seeking Santa*

63 *Benny* B3: *Legion: Shades of Gray*. Naglowska lived 1883-1936. She published a collection of works by the occultist Paschal Beverly Randolph, on the topic of sex magic and mirrors, in 1931.

64 *DG* S2: *Murder on 81st Street*

65 *DG* S5: *Angel of War*

66 *DG*: *All Through the House*

67 *DG* S5: *Valley of Nightmares*

68 *DG* S4: *Human Remains*

69 Dating *DG*: *Murder on 81st Street* (*DG* #2.3) - The blurb gives the year. It's "two months" after some twenty thousand people attended a German American Bund rally in Madison Square Garden, which in real life happened on 20th February, 1939.

70 "Twenty five years" after *DG* S5: *Angel of War*.

71 Dating *DG* S1: *The Houses in Between* (*DG* #1.2) - The story begins on "December 29th, 1940", and continues on the next day; the Second Great Fire of London indeed happened on those two nights. Dorian is recovered two days after that, on 1st January.

72 *DG* S3: *Echoes*

73 Dating *DG*: *Frostbite* (*DG* #4.X) - It's "two years on" from World War II. The blurb says that it's "1947... on Christmas Eve". The *Dorian Gray* audios don't revolve or explain Harker's schemes/intentions toward Dorian.

74 Dating *DG* S5: *Valley of Nightmares* (*DG* #5.3) - It's the "Summer of 1948", and "165 years" after 1783. Dorian catches Parker fibbing about her age, and makes her admit to being "54" – but even *that* must be a white lie, as she was born 22nd August, 1893, so she's 55 if not 56. *The Fan* (1949) was Parker's last film; the next year, she was blacklisted as a Communist.

75 Dating *DG* S4: *The Living Image* (*DG* #4.8) - The blurb and Dorian state that it's "England, 1949". It's after clothes rationing ended (on 15th March, 1949). Dorian and Scarlet go to see Vivien Lee (she played Scarlet O'Hara in *Gone With the Wind*) in *A Streetcar Named Desire* at the Aldwych - it's not necessarily the first performance, but the show historically opened on 11th October, 1949.

76 Dating *DG* S4: *The Enigma of Dorian Gray* (*DG* #4.1) - The year is given. Dorian ends matters with Notting on "15th November".

77 *DG* S1: *The Twittering of Sparrows*. In real life, the *MV Joyita* went overdue on 6rd October, 1955, before being found with nobody aboard on 10th November. Dorian leaves London "a few years" before meeting up with his sister in Singapore.

78 Dating *DG* S1: *The Twittering of Sparrows* (*DG* #1.3) - The story occurs after the crew of the *MV Joyita* was lost [October 1955], and not long before the People's Action Party won governance of Singapore in 1959. In *DG*: *All Through the House*, Dorian specifies that his sister died in "1956".

running into a burning building to set himself afire, and was pulled from the rubble two days later.

In 1941, Dorian Gray was in the Galapagos Islands, and didn't return to England for "some time".[72]

1947 (24th December) - DG: FROSTBITE[73] **->** Tiring of the scarcity and queues in post-war Britain, Dorian Gray went to Manhattan to spend Christmas Eve in Rockefeller Plaza. He wound up ice-skating with a woman who kissed him in Central Park on the stroke of midnight... then discovered that she'd poisoned him with the toxin of a golden dart frog. His assailant, Mina Harker, left after vowing that this was her first strike against him...

No documentation exists pertaining to Harker's intentions toward Dorian, or how the business between them resolved.

1948 (Summer) - DG S5: VALLEY OF NIGHTMARES[74] **->** Dorothy Parker struggled as a Hollywood screenwriter, but was commissioned to adapt an Oscar Wilde comedy, *Lady Windermere's Fan*, for film. She had not seen Dorian Gray since New York, 1939, but now asked him to give personal insight on her script. The two of them attended a party in Hollywood with such luminaries as John Wayne, John Ford, Joan Crawford and *Ben Hur* star Ramon Novarro, but soon discovered that Maximus Films head Walter van Kirk had achieved the 1001 "witnesses" (the skulls of his family's victims) needed to loose the Mother of Shadows into our dimension. Dorian shattered some of the skulls, ruining the ritual and causing the Mother to consume van Kirk.

1949 - DG S4: THE LIVING IMAGE[75] **->** On the Brighton to London Express, Dorian Gray and businessman Jonathan Moore discovered they were the spitting image of one another. Moore asked Dorian to double for him on an outing with his wife Scarlet to a Tennessee Williams play, while Moore slipped away to a gentleman's club. Dorian agreed, interested in the challenge of posing as a normal person.

Moore asked Dorian to take his place for longer periods, and enjoyed increasing amounts of debauchery. Dorian went out with Scarlet for "their anniversary"... and seduced her, breaking the one rule Moore had imposed upon him. Moore sought to end his swapping with Dorian, prompting a tense confrontation at the Moore home. Scarlet discovered her husband's duplicity and fled with their son... but in her haste drove her car into a trolley bus. Dorian saved the child as the car's fuel tank exploded, killing Scarlet and Moore, and let the authorities reunite the boy with his remaining family.

1952 (November) - DG S4: THE ENIGMA OF DORIAN GRAY[76] **->** At the University of Salford, Dorian Gray pursued a degree on English literature and became lovers with Adam Notting – laterally the university's head of computing research – for two weeks in November. Notting built BEAST, a computing system smart enough to write poetry, but learned of Dorian's immortality and from it conceived a new means of developing artificial intelligence: the BEAUTY system. Dorian sensed that Notting was becoming too attached to him and left the university.

Isodora Gray's husband, Charles Rigby, had died during a Japanese attack in World War II. She set sail aboard the merchant vessel *Joyita* for Singapore, but the mockery proffered during a game of mahjong by a fellow passenger, Mr. Lee, caused the three dragons bound in the vicinity to break free and attack the ship. The *Joyita* was later found abandoned – Isodora alone had survived on a lifeboat and reached Singapore. The weakened dragons had taken refuge in her body.

Dorian Gray left London and travelled the world, taking an interest in the routes of famous people that had gone missing, but failed to solve any of the mysteries surrounding them. He also followed the route Sir Thomas Raffles took to Singapore before establishing it as a colony, and hoped to discover what befell of the *Joyita*.[77]

The Death of Isodora Gray

1956 - DG S1: THE TWITTERING OF SPARROWS[78] **->** Isodora Gray had collected reports of her brother Dorian's exploits, and kept a scrapbook with stories that enigmatically described him as Immortal Beloved, the Englishman Who Ages Not and the Grayzion. Group Captain Alistair Bellamy befriended Isodora in Singapore, and played mahjong with her every morning – a ritual that kept the three dragons nestled within her subdued. Nonetheless, the dragons killed Bellamy, and compelled Isodora to write to her brother, as they hoped to transfer their essences into his immortal body.

Isodora implored Dorian to kill her before the dragons broke free – and he did so, breaking her neck. She was the last family member that Dorian knew. He encased Isadora's body in a lead chest to bind the dragons, and paid a premium to bury her in a nameless, deep grave on the Sienne, near the Eiffel Tower. As Isadora's executor, Dorian gave her estate to the Bellamy family.

Dorian Gray

The Present Day

Dorian Gray first met Alyssa Symes in 1964, at the Marquis Club, where he was performing with his band.[79]

1964 (March) - DG S2: THE LORD OF MISRULE[80] ->

Lenny Starr, a music producer and member of a séance group, developed the Hexatron: a device that transmitted sound in six dimensions, enabling spirits to hear his music. The Hexatron let a spirit incarnate on Earth as a man named Otto, who set about spreading Starr's music far and wide via a rocker band called the Gravediggers. Meanwhile, Dorian had become the star of a rival mod band named Dorian Gray and the Hedonists. Dorian favoured the mods simply because he didn't like brylcreem.

Dorian realised that Otto amplified his audience's baser instincts, and intended to compound the effect until a wave of brutality overtook all of humanity. By slipping amphetamines into Otto's tea, Dorian caused Otto's next performance in London to go into overdrive – the audi-ence rushed onto the stage, tore him apart and ate him. Afterward, Dorian retired from being a pop star.

1968 - DG S4: THE ENIGMA OF DORIAN GRAY[81] ->

A terminally ill Adam Notting had copied his mind into the BEAUTY system's RAM so it could prompt his failing memory. After Notting's death, the BEAUTY AI sent Dorian Gray an invitation to its decommissioning at the University of Salford. Dorian realised that BEAUTY was a crude copy of Notting that could do little more than talk to itself, and let the system be shut down.

Jennifer Alford's collection of supernatural items came to include the Crimson Pearl.[82]

The Nineteen-Seventies

Alyssa Symes and Dorian Gray met again in Beirut, where Dorian inadvertently stoked political tensions owing to a woman possessed in a café. Dorian and Symes escaped and struck up a relationship, travelling the world together

---

79 DG S4: The Abysmal Sea

80 Dating DG S2: The Lord of Misrule (DG #2.2) - Dorian states that it's "March 1964", and upon returning to London reports that "Spring was in the air". The blurb cites that it's "England, 1964."

81 Dating DG S4: The Enigma of Dorian Gray (DG #4.1) - The year is given. Dorian attempted a degree at Salford "more than ten years" ago, in 1952.

82 Benny B3: Legion: Shades of Gray, presumably referencing the Crimson Pearl from the Big Finish Dark Shadows audio of the same name. That story ended with Quentin Collins throwing the pearl into the ocean.

83 "Four years" before DG S4: The Abysmal Sea. Fighting erupted between Christian Phalangists and Palestinian guerrillas in Beirut on 28th March, 1970.

84 Date unknown, but it's prior to DG S4: Human Remains.

85 Dating DG S4: The Abysmal Sea (DG #4.6) - Dorian cites the month and year. Nixon has resigned (he did so on 8th August, 1974), "Kung Fu Fighting" is at the "top of the charts" (it entered the UK Singles Chart on 17th August, 1972, but didn't actually hit No. 1 until 21st September), and Turkey and Greece are on the brink of war (tensions ran high that year, especially after Turkey invaded Cyprus on 20th July, and kicked out the Greek population in its North).

86 Dating DG S4: Freya (DG #4.2) - Dorian names the year and season.

87 DG S3: We Are Everywhere

88 Dating DG S1: The Heart That Lives Alone (DG #1.4) - Dorian's narration broadbrushes the time as "the 80s", but the blurb specifies the year, and the season is given. A partygoer dresses as Marty McFly from Back to the Future; it debuted in the UK on 4th December, 1985.

89 Dating DG S1: The Heart That Lives Alone (DG #1.4) - "Several months" elapse after Dorian and Toby's first meeting in Summer 1986, and the story concludes in "August" of the next year.

90 Dating DG: Trick or Treat (DG #4b) - The date is given as "October 31st", this being a Halloween story. There's flourishes of modernity such as a telephone and takeaway menus, but while it's tempting to date the story to its release in 2015, this marks the first time that Dorian has skipped Halloween... something one might expect him to have done during his despondency following Tobias Matthews's death in Summer 1987 (DG S1: The Heart That Lives Alone).

91 DG: The Mayfair Monster

92 "Twenty years" before DG S2: The Picture of Loretta Delphine.

93 Dating DG S4: Human Remains (DG #4.3) - The blurb says "London, 1998."

94 Dating Benny B3: Legion: Shades of Gray (Benny box set #3.2) - No year given. Dorian says, "I am so very old now, my friend. I have seen and done so much. I have written history", meaning it's well past his native time of the 1800s. He and Spencer are discrete about their relationship at high society parties, but it's unclear if it's because homosexuals are more closeted in this era, or simply because Spencer doesn't like people butting into his private life. Scott Hancock, the writer of this story, commented over email: "No specific date in mind [for the Gray and Price sequences], though I recall it most likely being the turn of the 20th century".

95 Dating DG: The Mayfair Monster (DG #3.X) - The year and seasons are given.

for the next four years.[83] Dorian spent a week in a basement dive in Shanghai, and didn't lose his wallet once.[84]

1974 (August) - DG S4: THE ABYSMAL SEA[85] -> Having island-hopped for about a month, Dorian Gray and Alyssa Symes set sail for Crassus. A kraken sank the RHS *Pericles*, but died when Dorian and Alyssa lured it over a volcanic vent. Alyssa ended things with Dorian, as he was ill-suited to settle down with her.

1974 (Winter) - DG S4: FREYA[86] -> Dorian Gray had not stopped traveling since his relationship with Alyssa ended. To the North of Stockholm, he happened upon the goddess Freya, who was living in a house in the forest. A monstrous troll sought revenge because Freya had killed its family, and although Dorian tricked the creature into falling into a frozen lake, it pulled Freya under also.

The Nineteen-Eighties

Luke Edward Glass, a future tormentor of Dorian Gray, was born 15th July, 1983.[87]

Dorian Gray and Toby Matthews

1986 (Summer) - DG S1: THE HEART THAT LIVES ALONE[88] -> Dorian Gray became smitten with Tobias Matthews upon meeting him at a masked soiree on the Royal Cresent in Whitby, and was doubly intrigued when Toby dismissed him as "nothing special".

1987 (Summer) - DG S1: THE HEART THAT LIVES ALONE[89] -> By this point, Oscar Wilde was the most famous person Dorian Gray had been friends with. After several months of trying to get on a better standing with Tobias Matthews, Dorian discovered that Toby was a vampire... when Toby slaughtered a woman he'd been keeping in his home to "tide him over". Dorian and Toby became lovers, with Toby easing his hunger by feeding off his immortal partner.

Toby agreed to let Dorian paint his portrait, but was so haunted by seeing his bearing for the first time in centuries, he increasingly lost the will to live. In August, Dorian held Toby as a sunrise turned his beloved to ashes.

? 1987 (31st October) - DG: TRICK OR TREAT[90] -> For the first time in his life, Dorian Gray recused himself from the parties, revelry and candy giving ceremony of Halloween. While drinking whiskey at home, Dorian saw such apparitions as a young girl covered in blood, her throat slit, and his own reflection telling him: "You let us in." Dorian found that his drawing room furniture had been rearranged into a state of perfect balance, and heard the girl say *trick* before the clock chimed midnight and

Halloween ended. He concluded that however crass and commercial Halloween had become, its traditions were keeping evil spirits at bay.

The Nineteen-Nineties

Still grieving for Toby, Dorian Gray fared poorly throughout the 1990s. He endured phases of "killing" himself with drugs, a noose, a toaster dropped in the bathtub, lighting a cigarette after drinking petrol, and more.[91]

Loretta Delphine's spirit escaped from her picture, and reanimated her dismembered victims to create a zombie army in the Florida Everglades. Dorian and his associate, Isha Grant, ended the threat and heard Delphine declare, "I can and will and have justified all and every perversion of the art of murder", as they again trapped her in her picture. Grant continued working at the Hotel Delphine to guard the picture and raise her daughter, Kayla. Dorian left, having grown so familiar and tired with the United States, he vowed to never again step foot there.[92]

1998 - DG S4: HUMAN REMAINS[93] -> Dorian Gray's ennui became such that he went to the Melrose Hospital to have his appendix removed once more. The appendix that Dorian had left there in 1937 had been nurtured into a monstrous form as part of Project Ascelpius, and was inhabited by the collective soul of the patients who had died at Melrose. To stop the creature feeding off the living, Dorian destroyed it in a fire.

c 1999 - BENNY B3: LEGION: SHADES OF GRAY[94] -> The Collector, a conceptual being with whom the immortal Dorian Gray had once broken a deal, stalked the dreams of Dorian's associates. It possessed the body of Dorian's lover, Spencer Price – whom Dorian killed, mournfully, to prevent the Collector fully manifesting.

1999 (Summer to Autumn) - DG: THE MAYFAIR MONSTER[95] -> The artist Natallie Isaacs had became famous after painting the portrait of the Secretary General of the United Nations, then seducing the man and providing fodder for his divorce proceedings. Meanwhile, Dorian Gray attempted to move past his suicidal despondency, secured his portrait in a personal vault at the Bank of London, and resorted to prolonged drinking. Aware of Dorian's supernatural nature, Natallie "randomly" approached Dorian and gained his confidence. The two of them regularly checked into hotels across the country for all manner of activities...

1999 (31st December) - DG: THE MAYFAIR MONSTER[96] **->** Natallie Isaacs dialed back on her time with Dorian, causing him to become desperate for her company. On New Year's Eve, Natallie rejoined Dorian and falsely claimed that, owing to a brain tumour, she had only four weeks to live. In a display of intimacy, Dorian insisted on taking Natallie to the Bank of London and showing her his portrait. At the stroke of midnight, Natallie repeatedly stabbed Dorian and made off with the item...

The Twenty-First Century

2000 (January to February) - DG: THE MAYFAIR MONSTER[97] **->** Natallie Isaacs set about copying Dorian's portrait by hand, hoping to crack the secret of its immortality granting powers, then sell such abilities to elite clients for a massive profit. Her efforts caused much of Dorian's age and sin to return, making him so infirm that he relied upon the charity of a Bank of London security guard named Tom. Dorian's occasional forays outside his house resulted in the media reporting that "the Mayfair Monster" was wandering about town. Tom aided Dorian in locating Natallie in Shoreditch – showing Natallie's portrait-copies to Dorian greatly restored him, and his original portrait fully returned his youth and vigour. Dorian vowed to keep his portrait closer at hand, but let Natallie go because she was so diverting.

After their flight was cancelled, a school group became trapped in the Brigadoon Hotel.[98]

2007 (January) - DG S1: THE FALLEN KING OF BRITAIN[99] **->** Having travelled so much of the world, Dorian Gray sought to boost his personal revenues by embarking on a career as the banker "Charles White". Dorian peddled cocaine on the side, and became lovers with a coworker, Simon Darlow, until demons in the cocaine-powder killed two of Dorian's associates. Visions of past acquaintances and victims haunted Dorian until he vowed to end use of the cocaine. Simon realised that his feelings for Dorian weren't reciprocated, and left him.

Construction of the Needle office complex on Leadenhall Street, London, uncovered many bodies felled by the Black Death. The investment company behind the Needle left the bodies there, as it was cheaper than relocating them.[100]

2009 (December) to 2010 (January) - DG S4: INNER DARKNESS[101] **->** Eluding yet another scandal, Dorian Gray went to Iceland to see the Northern Lights, and ran afoul of lycanthropes living in an isolated wood. One of their number, Askell Brimson, warned Dorian that the full moon would drive the lycanthropes to pure savagery, and advised him to escape along a secret path. Brimson provided Dorian with a gun, but was unable to

96 Dating *DG: The Mayfair Monster* (*DG* #3.X) - The day is given. There's no sense of the reality warping events of *Doctor Who – The Movie* occurring at the stroke of midnight, but, as with *TW: Fractures*, there wouldn't be, owing to the different time zones involved.
97 Dating *DG: The Mayfair Monster* (*DG* #3.X) - Dorian is incapacitated with age and sin for "a couple months" following the New Year. *DG S3: The Darkest Hour* establishes that Victoria Lowell's organisation aided Natallie's efforts against Dorian.
98 "Fourteen years" before *DG: All Through the House.*
99 Dating *DG S1: The Fallen King of Britain* (*DG* #1.5) - The month and year are given. Dorian says he has now enjoyed "over a hundred years of life". The White Rabbit pub on London's Embankment, a recurring locale in Big Finish's *Doctor Who* and Bernice Summerfield audios, is featured.
100 "Five years" before *DG S3: The Needle.*
101 Dating *DG S4: Inner Darkness* (*DG* #4.7) - The blurb supplies the year. Dorian names the month as "December", with the story finishing "a month" later.
102 Dating *DG S2: The Picture of Loretta Delphine* (*DG* #2.1) - Dorian narrates that it's "Florida, Summer 2012", in agreement with the blurb. The story saw release in July 2013.
103 Dating *DG S2: Running Away With You* (*DG* #2.5) - Dorian's narration calls his time of death as "23.59 on Friday the 26th of October, 2012". He first noticed odd

things happening in the flats "a couple of months ago", on "21st of the 8th, 2012". The blurb also gives the year as "2012", although the story wasn't released until August 2013. Thematically, Dorian's demise mirrors the end of *The Picture of Dorian Gray.*
104 "Six months" before *DG S3: The Needle.* The locale is a fictional analogue of the Spire (see *The Bells of Saint John*).
105 Dating *The Confessions of Dorian Gray* Series 3 – The series saw release in November 2014, and opens "two years" after Dorian died [26th October, 2012] in *DG S2: Running Away With You.* It's been "seven years, almost eight" since Dorian last saw Simon Darlow in *DG S1: The Fallen King of Britain* [January 2007], and "thirty years" since Toby died in *DG S1: The Heart That Lives Alone* [Summer 1987].
　Dorian remarks in *DG S3: Displacement Activity* that it's been "barely six weeks" since he was resurrected in *DG S3: Blank Canvas*, meaning the whole of Series 3 occurs in that timespan. The bulk of it occurs in the third episode, *DG S3: We Are Everywhere*, in which Luke Glass repeatedly murders Dorian from 30th September to 25th October, and probably a few days on either side. The remainder of the series happens in rapid succession – certainly, *DG S3: The Needle* quickly follows *Blank Canvas*, and *DG S3: Echoes* picks up minutes after *We Are Everywhere.*

control his own inner wolf and pursued the man. Dorian shot Brimson dead and escaped to London – and, a month later, found that Brimson's attack had given him the lycanthrope taint. Dorian's portrait absorbed the condition into itself, adopting a glint of yellow in its eyes.

2012 (Summer) - DG S2: THE PICTURE OF LORETTA DELPHINE[102] ->

A splinter of Loretta Delphine's consciousness infected police sergeant Kayla Grant, causing her to murder her mother Isha and about twenty other people. "Kayla" summoned Dorian Gray to Florida, and intended to possess his immortal body. Kayla resisted Delphine's influence long enough to soak her mother's house with kerosene, enabling Dorian to light the property ablaze. Delphine fled Kayla's burning body into her picture, but Dorian torched that also, destroying her.

2012 (26th October) - DG S2: RUNNING AWAY WITH YOU[103] ->

Dorian Gray had inherited his childhood estate from his uncle, and long ago had it converted into flats. The supernatural "imaginary friend" that Dorian had acquired in his youth found Constance Harker's spirit within the flats and trapped her. Failing to get Dorian's attention, the Friend began murdering Dorian's tenants.

Realising the Friend's true nature, Dorian returned to his home in Mayfair, went to the attic and looked at his portrait – which he hadn't seen in years. To protect others from his past and future mistakes, Dorian slashed at his picture with one of Basil Hallward's pallet knives. The picture's canvas rewove, and Dorian's image became young once more as Dorian re-absorbed his sins and died as an old man. The Friend was dispersed, and Constance's soul was freed. Dorian's consciousness remained in his picture, made to relieve his memories.

Construction was finished on the Needle office complex.[104]

2014 (September to October) - THE CONFESSIONS OF DORIAN GRAY SERIES 3[105] ->

Two years after his death, Dorian Gray was officially listed as missing. Three thrillseekers – Joe, Richard and Sophia – broke into Dorian's disused house in Mayfair and found the frame that normally held his portrait was empty. Dorian's soul, which had inhabited the portrait for decades, manifested as an older version of Dorian, and enacted a ritual sacrifice that would enable a soul to escape Hell. The portrait-Dorian stole Joe's voice, Richard's body and Sophia's youth, which resurrected the actual Dorian Gray while his sin-riddled soul returned to the confines of its portrait...

A restored Dorian went to draw on the £1.5 million he kept with White Stallion Investments – an account managed by his former lover, Simon Darlow – and met with Simon at the newly constructed Needle office complex as

it emptied out for the weekend. The spirits of plague victims, whose bodies had been callously left beneath the Needle, caused such a disturbance that the building suffered subsidence. The ghosts released Dorian and Simon to disclose the truth about their fate.

Victoria Lowell, a member of the enigmatic Lowell Foundation, brought Dorian to the attention of serial killer Luke Glass. He introduced himself to Dorian by poisoning the man's coffee, and found Dorian an ideal victim – Glass could murder Dorian over and over again, never leaving a body as evidence. On 30th September, Dorian awoke to find he'd been murdered in his sleep, and his sheets were bathed in blood. He subsequently experienced death by exposed electrical wire in shower (3rd October), a Ricin-laced book (the 7th), a severed brake line (the 13th), gas (the 18th), suffocation (the 19th), a blow to the head while taking out the bins (the 21st), drowning (23rd) and stabbing (the 25th). Dorian's resignation of his fate prompted Glass to innovate: he imprisoned Dorian in a room that flooded twice a day, drowning Dorian unless he preferred to kill himself with a variety of instruments provided. Dorian turned the tables on Glass and drowned the man.

Lowell approached Dorian under false pretences, and directed him to investigate Gwynne Smith, AKA Madame Pandora, a fortune-teller at a New Age shop. Pandora owned a supernatural Heart's Desire Tarot deck that granted wishes to her clients, but soon after caused their deaths. Dorian destroyed the bloodthirsty Tarot deck in a fire, but only after he'd drawn the card that symbolizing his greatest desire: The Lovers. As a result, Dorian's love Tobias Matthews was restored to life...

Toby's sire, the vampire Ivor, sensed Toby's resurrection and through him targeted Dorian. The siryn that Ivor served needed to feast upon a heart a day, and – as an immortal – Dorian seemed a ready-made source of hearts. Dorian's ever-regrowing heart failed to nourish the siryn, as he had no soul. Toby dispatched Ivor and saved Dorian; together, they imprisoned the siryn inside a weighted oil drum and dropped her into a lake.

Lowell – actually representing an organization that sought to destroy all things supernatural – manipulated Dorian and Toby into attending a gallery unveiling, ostensibly to aid them in stealing an artifact from its collection: the Eternity Canvas. Instead, Lowell made off with the Salisbury Bloodstone, went to Dorian's house in Mayfair and harnessed the bloodstone's power of resurrection to manifest the soul within Dorian's portrait. Lowell believed Dorian's soul was uniquely suited to dispatch the man, but the portrait-Dorian rewarded Lowell's trust by stabbing her eyes out and killing her. The portrait-Dorian came for Dorian, who realised that the bloodstone had been fuelled by Toby's love for him. By rebuking Toby's affections, Dorian banished his soul back into its picture.

The infernal being that Dorian had bargained his soul

with was present at the gallery, wearing the form of Lord Henry Wooton. A conflicted Toby spurned Dorian, but later returned to ask Dorian if he was interested in a fresh start...

Unknown to Toby, Dorian's soul came to reside within him – as part of a scheme to release the manifestation of Lucifer trapped within the Brigadoon Hotel.[106]

2015 (1st-26th December) - DG: DESPERATELY SEEKING SANTA / ALL THROUGH THE HOUSE[107] ->

Simon Darlow visited Dorian Gray's house to inform him that Victoria Lowell's organisation, the Skin-Walkers, had sought to keep Dorian away from the Brigadoon Hotel in Kensington. Before Simon could speak to Dorian, Toby hypnotised the man into forgetting all about Dorian, Lowell and the hotel.

The immortal killer adorned as Santa Claus had slept through most of 2015, but awoke on 1st December and began harvesting organs to keep his body-shell going. The Santa-killer realised that Dorian's organs only granted limited relief, but Toby's vampire organs could convey extended hardiness. Dorian and Toby savaged the Santa-killer, but he plundered a passerby of his organs and lived on...

On Christmas Night, Toby talked Dorian into a stay-

over at the Brigadoon Hotel, which had, as was its custom, appeared in Kensington for just the one day per year. The manifestation of Lucifer trapped within the hotel threatened that the lovers would never leave... unless Dorian agreed to reclaim his soul (while keeping his immortality), so that Lucifer could hitch a ride out of the hotel and then depart. Dorian agreed, failing to realise that his soul was already within Toby. As Dorian regained his soul, Lucifer moved into the void it left and took over Toby's form. Unable to bring hell to the whole of Earth, Lucifer left after vowing to make Dorian's life a living hell in 2016...

=? 2016 - DG S5: EVER AFTER[108] ->

After Lucifer possessed Toby, Dorian Gray awoke on New Year's Day to find himself institutionalised. His portrait was "gone". Everyone believed he was one of his cover identities, "Charles White". Acquaintances from Dorian's past appeared as different people – including Victoria Lowell, who presented herself to Dorian as his mother. Dorian doubted his own identity, until the embodiment of his portrait briefly appeared at the foot of his bed.

"Dorian's mother" authorised him to receive a lobotomy, to destroy his Dorian Gray identity. Lucifer performed the procedure, and – as Dorian flatlined

---

106 *DG: All Through the House*

107 Dating *DG: Desperately Seeking Santa/All Through the House* (*DG #4X*) - The narrator says that Santa Claus' killing spree starts on "December the 1st, in the year of our Lord 2015" and continues throughout the month. The confrontation between Dorian, Toby and Lucifer happens on the evening of Christmas Day, with the aftermath seen into the next morning. It's said to be Dorian and Toby's "first proper Christmas together", suggesting their relationship hadn't quite settled in the aftermath of *The Confessions of Dorian Gray* Series 3 [2014].

The Lucifer-manifestation seen here is played by Gabriel Woolf, who portrayed Sutekh in *Pyramids of Mars* and the Beast in *The Impossible Planet*, perhaps suggesting that all three are aspects of the same being.

108 *Dating DG S5: Ever After* (*DG #5.4*) - This is the last of Big Finish's *The Confessions of Dorian Gray* audios, and – quite obviously – it ends on an ambiguous note. We're not told if Lucifer created the institution scenario, or if it's happening only in Dorian's head, or something else altogether. Lucifer vowed in *DG: All Through the House* [Christmas Eve, 2015] that he would torment Dorian, and that "2016 is going to be very interesting". If time holds any meaning in the institution, then, it's likely that year.

In *The Confessions of Alexander Vlahos* interview audio, Vlahos and series producer Scott Hancock discuss how *Dorian Gray* listeners do accept *Benny* B3:

Legion: Shades of Gray [2618], the very first story in which Vlahos played the character, as canon. We might imagine, then, that Dorian survives Lucifer's torture, that he never reunites with Toby (as the narrator claimed in *All Through the House*), but that he does, at the latest, have possession of his portrait again in the twenty-second or twenty-third century, but loses it again until the twenty seventh.

109 Dating *Benny* B3: *Legion: Shades of Gray* (Benny box set #3.2) - Benny's associate Jack, in viewing these events via a séance with Benny and Ruth, estimates that it's the "twenty-second, twenty-third century, at a guess".

111 Dating *Benny* B3: *Legion: Shades of Gray* (Benny box set #3.2) - Caitlin was first spotted "about a year or so ago" on "November 27th, 2616", and it's "fifteen months" after she caused Isobella Klempe's death. Benny concludes, after witnessing these events in a séance, "that asylum was definitely present day".

112 Dating *Benny* B3: *Legion: Shades of Gray* (Benny box set #3.2) – The séance that Benny, Jack and Ruth convene in *Shades of Gray* occurs "about a year or so" after Caitlin was first spotted on "November 27th, 2616" and "fifteen months" after Isobella Klempe's death, which triangulates to suggest that story – and presumably the rest of the *Benny: Legion* box set – happens in 2618. Supporting that, Benny's son Peter says he's "eighteen" in *Everybody Loves Irving*, which matches with his being born in 2600 (*Benny: The Glass Prison*).

– declared that his face was the last Dorian would see before he died. Dorian realised that the soul was a terrible reality: it could be bought and sold and bartered away, or poisoned and made perfect, but everyone had one.

The Future

c 2200 - BENNY B3: LEGION: SHADES OF GRAY[109]

-> Jennifer Alford, a con artist, attracted Dorian Gray's attention by displaying the soul-stealing Marwick Tapestry at the Montesquieu Gallery, a venue that specialized in Trotman digital watercolours. Gray accepted an invitation to view Alford's private collection of supernatural artifacts, which enabled Alford to capture Gray long enough to steal his portrait on behalf of her employer, the Collector. The next day, Gray escaped and found that the Marwick Tapestry had claimed Alford's soul. Gray and his portrait would remain separated until the twenty-seventh century.

2618 - BENNY B3: LEGION: SHADES OF GRAY[110] ->

Drs Warrilow and Hawke of the Firebrand medical facility asked Dorian Gray, an expert on the supernatural, to consult on two deaths related to a patient named Caitlin. Gray discovered that Caitlin was an "imaginary friend" made real, who caused the deaths of people she associated with. He advised Warrilor and Hawke to just leave Caitlin alone, then departed. The Collector entered the facility afterward, pledged to come for Gray, and watched as Caitlin killed the doctors.

2618 - BENNY B3: LEGION: SHADES OF GRAY[112] ->

The immortal Dorian Gray received word that his portrait – lost to him for centuries – was held at Triptic House on Legion City's outskirts. Gray anonymously hired Bernice Summerfield, who was accompanied by her colleagues Jack and Ruth, to retrieve his property. Benny, Ruth and Jack found the portrait and held a séance through which they experienced scenes from Gray's involvement with the Collector. Gray entered Triptic to reclaim his portrait, and Benny's trio left him alone to ponder it.

What became of Dorian Gray after Legion City is unknown.

Fixed Points in Time

The new *Doctor Who* has introduced the concept of "fixed points in time" as a shorthand, of sorts, to address a problem with time travel that classic *Doctor Who* always had, but was hesitant to discuss. Namely, why does the Doctor treat the past of modern-day Earth as if it's sacrosanct, but happily intervene in events set in Earth's future? To a time traveller, most if not all of history should be the past from *some* vantage point, meaning that the nexus points of both Earth's "past" and "future" history should be treated with equal weight.

Even David Whitaker (*Doctor Who*'s first script editor, and the show's biggest proponent of the "You cannot change history, not one line" approach to time travel) is somewhat hypocritical about this. On Whitaker's watch, it's literally impossible for Barbara to alter Aztec history (*The Aztecs*), and efforts to change Napoleon's timeline are doomed to failure (the final scene of *The Reign of Terror*). However, given the chance to overthrow the Daleks who have conquered Earth (conventionally, without benefit of time travel) circa 2167, the Doctor and his friends without hesitation do so (*The Dalek Invasion of Earth*). Whitaker's successors favoured the view that altering history *was* possible, but the dichotomy of leaving Earth's past alone while mucking about with its future remained. The slaughter of the Huguenots in Paris, 1572, must be allowed to play itself out (*The Massacre*), but stopping Mavic Chen and the Daleks from building a Time Destructor in the year 4000 is fair game (*The Daleks' Master Plan*).

In the early Silurian stories (*Doctor Who and the Silurians*, *The Sea Devils*), the third Doctor further complicates matters by advocating an accord between humanity and the Silurians that he must know – as a matter of established history – didn't happen. It's fairly evident that Malcolm Hulke, Terrance Dicks, et al, were more concerned with the stories' morality play than the temporal implications of the Doctor's viewpoint, but the lack of any explanation has been conspicuous by its absence.

In the new series, moments/events that must, at all cost, happen to preserve the integrity of history are called "fixed points in time". The phrase has become fairly common currency, despite the tenth Doctor stressing to Adelaide Brooke in *The Waters of Mars* that it's all conjecture, not established fact. ("I mean, it's only a theory... but I think certain moments in time are fixed. Tiny, precious moments. Everything else is in flux, anything can happen, but those certain moments, they have to stand. This base, on Mars, with you, Adelaide Brooke, this is one vital moment. What happens here must always happen.") Whatever his uncertainty about the topic, though, the Doctor so strongly believes that the devastation of Pompeii (*The Fires of Pompeii*) is a "fixed point in history" that he and Donna kill twenty thousand people to make it happen. On a lesser scale, (but still deadly), the Silence in "The Doctor and the Nurse" regard the London Beer Flood of 1814 as a fixed point – so much so, one of their operatives uses explosives to make it happen.

In *Cold Blood*, and in an echo of past Silurian stories, the eleventh Doctor says that human and Silurian representatives in 2020 can craft an accord between their races because "There are fixed points through time, where things must always stay the way they are. This is not one of them. This is an opportunity, a temporal tipping point. Whatever happens today will change future events, create its own timeline, its own reality." That isn't a very satisfactory explanation, though... wouldn't the successful brokering of such a deal in 2020 overwrite all of the fixed points in time *after* that? Would the timetable of Adelaide Brooke's mission to Mars still hold true if humanity had gained access to Silurian technology about three decades beforehand? It's fair to say that *Cold Blood* doesn't actually answer the problems inherent in the Pertwee Silurian stories, it just more directly acknowledges that they exist.

The consequence of averting a fixed point in time isn't consistently rendered... when River Song subverts a fixed point in time by not shooting the eleventh Doctor (*The Wedding of River Song*), it instantly causes all of time and space to occur at the same moment. But when the tenth Doctor prevents Adelaide Brooke from dying in *The Waters of Mars*, nothing appears to happen in the interim before she fulfills upon the fixed point by committing suicide. The Reapers appear when Rose saves her father in *Father's Day*, but that might owe to her intervening in her personal history, not a fixed point. The comic story "Ripper's Curse" seems confused about this – the eleventh Doctor (seemingly forgetting everything he learned in *The Waters of Mars*) says that every victim of Jack the Ripper is "a static point in space and time, they can't be altered", then he, Amy and Rory *do* intervene anyway, and incur no penalty when one victim is swapped for another. Perhaps a "static point" is different from a "fixed point", but it isn't explained how. Further complicating this, *The Wedding of River Song* claims that Lake Silencio, 2011, is a "still point in time" that can be used to create a "fixed point", but doesn't actually define what a "still point" is or how one comes about.

Later on, the eleventh Doctor tells Amy in *The Angels Take Manhattan* that if she joins Rory in the past (and he sees their tombstones), it will create "fixed time" and lock down her fate, meaning that the Doctor will never see her again. Does this create a "fixed point", however? The language is syrupy enough that perhaps it doesn't. Perhaps he's just using the term "fixed" to describe the temporal rule that once somebody sees their own fate, no temporal trickery to undo it is allowed – but the end result if they tried might be different than *The Wedding of River Song* (albeit still very, very undesirable).

River S3: My Dinner with Andrew operates on the assumption that since it's set at a restaurant outside of the universe's causality, the Doctor's death at Lake Silencio being a fixed point (*The Impossible Astronaut*) doesn't apply and he can easily shuffle off this mortal coil beforehand. As it happens, the fifth Doctor dies for a short while until that's temporally reversed, and his doing so makes the stars in the sky go dark (as with *The Name of the Doctor*).

War Master: Only the Good: The Good Master entails a special case, featuring as it does a sentient fixed point in time *and* space on the planet Arcking – literally a talking pinprick of energy that grants temporal healing to those on Arcking's surface until a historically appointed hour when it's grounded out by touch (like discharging a static build-up from one's shoes) and Arcking falls. Had the War Master succeeded in harnessing this fixed point, we might have learned more about its characteristics – but, mercifully for those involved in the Last Great Time War, he doesn't.

The final way that the new series addresses "fixed points in time" is that Captain Jack is named as one following Rose's resurrecting him in *The Parting of the Ways*. (The Doctor in *Utopia* on Jack's immortality: "You're a fixed point in time and space. You're a fact. That's never meant to happen.") This deviates from the established use of "fixed point in time", but it at least has a certain internal logic: if Jack is, effectively, a mobile set of space-time coordinates that are impervious to being nullified, it might follow that his body could restore itself after being pulped (*TW: Children of Earth*). What effect becoming a "fixed point" had on Jack's blood is more open to interpretation – in *TW: Miracle Day*, the Blessing recalibrates itself after scanning Jack's blood, and Rex Matheson becomes similarly immortal owing to an infusion of Jack's blood and highly unusual circumstances. It remains to be seen if Rex himself is now a "fixed point", or just someone who can heal mortal injury.

The Shakespeare Notebooks

As if reconciling Shakespeare's history throughout *Doctor Who* wasn't challenging enough (see the Shakespeare sidebar), *The Shakespeare Notebooks* – a short story anthology released in 2014 – goes fairly berserk in claiming that multiple incarnations of the Doctor and his companions interacted with (basically) any Shakespeare play one cares to name. The clear and obvious intent of the project was to have fun with it all and not give much of a toss about continuity, but this does leave the book in something of a limbo state where canon is concerned. *Are* we to construe

that these events / play drafts presented in *The Shakespeare Notebooks* were inspired by some actual event within the *Doctor Who* universe... or is it all a huge exercise in taking the piss? Even the Prelude to *The Shakespeare Notebooks* leaves matters a bit opaque, claiming that the documents within have been "discovered recently" and, while very exciting to behold, are of somewhat questionable origin.

Some of the impetus behind the text entails Shakespeare realising, in the wake of *The Shakespeare Code*, that he's met the Doctor many times before, and trying to collect his notes, journals and play drafts to make sense of it all. While that playfully acknowledges *The Shakespeare Code* presenting itself as the Doctor and Shakespeare's first meeting, in defiance of their having met other times in the tie-in properties, it doesn't serve to reconcile pre-existing stories of the Doctor and Shakespeare such as *The Time of the Daleks*, etc. – rather, it just piles on new ones.

The best compromise, then, is probably to list out the main developments of *The Shakespeare Notebooks* for benefit of anyone wishing to give its stories due consideration, while – given the strong possibility that it's all apocryphal – leaving them out of the main *Ahistory* timeline.

In *The Shakespeare Notebooks*, we find:

• Shakespeare's first thoughts on *Hamlet* entail the eleventh Doctor appearing from his blue box to speak to the main character.

• An early draft of *As You Like It* includes numerous *Doctor Who* references, including "The cosmos is a stage, and all, from thou to Fenric, merely players..."

• The second Doctor, Jamie and Zoe act as the witches in *Macbeth*.

• The eleventh Doctor crops up in *Cymbeline*.

• The fifth Doctor sat down with Shakespeare and actor Richard Burbage in late 1601 to chat about *Twelfth Night*.

• On 24th June, 1594, Shakespeare recorded in his dream diary a vision he experienced featuring the first Doctor, elements of the planet Vortis (*The Web Planet*) and a troupe of Sontarans performing *The Most Glorious Defeat and Most Deserv'd Death of the Trifling Rutan Foe at Fang Rock*. It

• A variant opening of *Henry V* reveals that the Battle of Agincourt in 1415 intersected with the Last Great Time War.

• A draft of *Romeo and Juliet* includes the eleventh Doctor, Amy, Rory, a Sontaran cloning vat, a Teselecta-class ship (*Let's Kill Hitler*), an Auton and a Zygon.

• The tenth Doctor and Donna appear in the working notes of *The Tempest*, with the Doctor's catchphrase "Allons-y" inspiring the name of Alonso, King of Naples.

• The line "Exit, pursued by a bear" in *The Winter's Tale* replaces the original scene, of someone exiting into a blue box.

• The eleventh Doctor blunders into the action of Act V,

Appendix

Scene iii of *The Winter's Tale*, thinking a statue of Hermione is a Weeping Angel.

• An early version of *Antony and Cleopatra* includes the Mara (*Kinda* et al).

• An alternative version of *Troilus and Cressida* relates some events of the TV story *The Myth Makers* (which was itself inspired by the play).

• Romana factors into a draft of *Pericles* during the search for the Key to Time (Season 16).

• *Coriolanus* was originally set in a land called Tara (*The Androids of Tara*).

• An extract of *Master Faustus* (written by Christopher Marlowe) entailed a demonic pact facilitated by the Master. The text ends with the Daleks exterminating Marlowe.

• The sixth Doctor and Peri appear in *As You Like It*.

• Reviews comment upon a performance of *Double Falsehood*, thought an adaptation of Shakespeare's *Cardenio*, that features the ninth Doctor.

• The gravedigger scene from *Hamlet* includes the fourth Doctor looking for another Fendahl skull (*Image of the Fendahl*).

• The script of *Timon of Athens* includes the Axons.

• The fourth Doctor rewrote some of *Hamlet* (in accordance with *City of Death*), and the sixth Doctor provided notes for *Julius Caesar*.

• The lost Shakespeare play *Ye Unearthly Childe* retells the story of *An Unearthly Child*.

• In his will, Shakespeare left his wife their second-best bed, as it was the one they regularly slept in. The tenth Doctor acquires Shakespeare's *best* bed – the one kept in the spare room, for guests and on nights when Shakespeare was plagued by his imagination – as it contains a fleet of killer alien trees kept docile by the Doctor applying some psychically absorbent "memory hay" from the Bulrushes of Lethe. To Donna's dismay, the Doctor flips the mattress and lets her sleep on it, to test that the trees remain dormant.

From Wildthyme With Love

From Wildthyme With Love (2013), the third Iris Wildthyme release from Snowbooks, presents a special problem in terms of canonicity, in that it's a series of letters written between Iris and Panda as the former larks about through time and space in her bus, and the latter jaunts about on his own with a Time Scrunchy. The pair correspond with one another about their adventures, which are very obvious parodies of *Doctor Who* stories.

Given the unreliability of the two narrators, it's hard to know exactly how much to regard their claims as canon – Iris and Panda are, after all, renowned tellers of tall tales and heavy consumers of spirits, one of whom has a track record of appropriating other people's stories as her own (much to the Doctor's outrage in *The Scarlet Empress*, also written by Paul Magrs). With the various Iris Wildthyme

books and audios, shamelessly recycling *Doctor Who* and other SF and fantasy series as adventures featuring Iris is part of the point – a central premise of the Iris series, after all, is the question, "What if the Doctor were a boozing middle-aged woman in outrageous attire, who has a time machine disguised as the No. 22 double-decker bus to Putney Common, and is best friends with a talking stuffed panda?"

That said, while *Ahistory* has repeatedly treated the Iris stories as canon (particularly as the reader/listener can almost always see or hear the events in question), it's asking a bit much – from a metafictional point of view – to vest much stock in the claims of two characters who are inherently so unreliable. For all we know from Iris and Panda's letters, *From Wildthyme With Love* could be a game of fabricated one-upmanship between the two of them.

What follows, then, is a breakdown of the escapades chronicled by Iris and Panda, truthfully or not, as well as mention of the *Doctor Who* stories they're based on...

Iris Wildthyme wrote to Panda that she...

• ... visited a dead planet with lots of blond blokes living in the woods together, wearing a heavy amount of blue eyeshadow (letter #1, *The Daleks*).

• ... found a secret conference of space delegates, including the Prime Minister of the Solar System and something that looked like an evil Christmas tree (#3, *The Daleks' Master Plan*).

• ... joined a dance troupe grooving to "Sacred Flame, Sacred Flame..." (#5, *The Brain of Morbius*).

• ... met the descendants of the blue-eyeshadow boys on a jungle planet, and found a disco beneath an ice volcano (#7, *Planet of the Daleks*).

• ... ran around as if in a silent movie on Christmas Day (#9, *The Daleks' Master Plan*).

• ... found space cabbages buried in the permafrost, and resolved the situation by making a Stir Fry of Doom (#11, *The Seeds of Doom*).

• ... spent months in a caravan as part of Marco Polo's harem (#13, *Marco Polo*).

• ... came down with the dreadful lurgy, met a professor in Holby Space City, fought a giant prawn, and acquired a robotic companion, PAND-R (#15, *The Invisible Enemy*).

• ... solved games in a living city on Sexxilon (#17, *Death to the Daleks*).

• ... found a luxury spa on a mining planet, only to have the server robots try to massage and pummel everyone to death (letters #19, 21; *The Robots of Death*).

• ... was stuck on an island surrounded by a foaming-acid sea, and fended off men in rubber suits while looking for five special keys (#23, *The Keys of Marinus*).

• ... found Synthetic Men in sarcophagi of ice, deep underground (#25, *The Tomb of the Cybermen*).

• ... aided MIAOW and her ex-companion Jenny against a gestalt entity that assumed the form of a gigantic bin bag of vomit, and commanded a robot bear (#27, *The Web of Fear*).

• ... materialized inside a TV set, then emerged into a TV show room in London, circa 1974, as a stegosaurus smashed through the window (#29, a blend of *Carnival of Monsters* and *Invasion of the Dinosaurs*).

• ... joined a cult whose prized possessions included a glowing skull, an Egyptian sarcophagus, a giant spider and a roomful of mirrors that could transport people to the Victorian era (#31, *Image of the Fendahl*, *Pyramids of Mars*, *Planet of the Spiders*, *The Evil of the Daleks*).

• ... encountered the Cosmic Puppet Master at an amusement arcade in Blackpool (#33, *The Nightmare Fair*).

• ... realised that a Space-Age Butlins camp was overrun by crabs (#35, *The Macra Terror*).

• ... enjoyed a lentil bake and stuffed mushrooms at a Welsh hippy commune, but failed at making mushroom vodka in the bath (#37, *The Green Death*).

• ... was aghast as a cadre of fiendish scientists created a growing virus, and PAND-R used it to become enormous (#39, *Robot*).

• ... found herself in a drafty castle, and discovered that King John was actually a cyborg from the future (#41, *The King's Demons*).

• ... met the spirit of her bus sin a small enclave universe, at a junkyard in time (#43, *The Doctor's Wife*).

• ... prevented the genocide of reptile people at the Earth's core (#46; *Doctor Who and the Silurians*).

• ... invited all of her friends to a great big knees-up at the village of Hobbes End, May Day 1972 (letters #48, 50; *The Daemons*).

Panda, having taken Iris' Time Scrunchy, wrote to her that he...

• ... met a high-class lady married to a count who kept a time machine in his basement (letter #2, *City of Death*).

• ... saw a flying saucer landing on Putney Common (#4, *The Daleks' Master Plan*).

• ... spotted a stegosaurus after buying sweets at a Woolworths in 1974 (#6, *Invasion of the Dinosaurs*).

• ... enjoyed Christmas on a cruise liner, where a waitress sacrificed herself on a fork lift to stop a saboteur (#8, *Voyage of the Damned*).

• ... discovered a time traveler cloning dinosaurs, transforming people into trees, and running a gay bathhouse in nineteenth-century Darlington (#10, *The Mark of the Rani*).

• ... undertook a mission for MIAOW, and wound up meeting two other Pandas (who could only communicate with him via Skype) in an anti-matter universe (#12, *The Three Doctors*).

• ... met some charming lesbians in a stone circle in southern England, circa 1978, and retired to their bungalow for hot sausage sandwiches (#14, *The Stones of Blood*).

• ... was put on trial, by someone with absurd headgear, for continued interfere in galactic history (#16, *The Trial of a Time Lord*).

• ... found himself involved in the Tim War (sic), a conflict at the level of meta-reality (#18, referencing the Last Great Time War).

• ... suckled the teats of a cyber-plesiosaurus posing as the Loch Ness Monster in Scotland (#20, *Terror of the Zygons*).

• ... escaped from numerous monsters and met five incarnations of Iris, with five buses (#22; *The Five Doctors*).

• ... joined a future version of Iris on her travels, and with her found a land of primitive tribes, invisible monsters and a ten-story high bust of himself carved into a mountain range (#24, *The Face of Evil*).

• ... pitted wits against the Cosmic Puppet Master and the King of the Land of Fictional Spin-offs (#26, *The Celestial Toymaker* and *The Mind Robber*).

• ... found an alternate-reality Earth, and witnessed an alternative origin for the Synthetic Men (#28, *The Rise of the Cybermen*).

• ... had a race against time on a spaceship falling into the sun (#30, 42).

• ... landed in Verailles, where the future Iris indulged in horse-jumping through mirrors, fighting clockwork fops, having a dalliance with a young lady in a big frock (#32, *The Girl in the Fireplace*).

• ... witnessed Iris' future self blowing up the parties involved in the Tim War (#34, the Last Great Time War).

• ... got stuck in the year five billion, at an Earth colony that resembled the M25, and met a giant head in a bucket – formerly an omnisexual travel agent named Mr Derek – who said with his dying breath: "Watch out for crabs" (#36, *Gridlock*).

• ... told Ngaio Marsh, at a country house party in the 1930s, that he loved her murder mysteries and had never heard of Agatha Christie (#38, *The Unicorn and the Wasp*).

• ... met some cavemen (#40, *An Unearthly Child*).

• ... was stuck down a well, and encountered a large, hairy green ball bag that looked suspiciously like a scrotum (#42, *The Creature from the Pit*).

• ... saw the words "Time Gentlemen, Please" repeated over and over, and met T.S. Eliot while pursuing disembodied aliens intent on possessing the minds and forms of the Faber Twentieth Century Poets (#44; the Series 1 "Bad Wolf" storyarc, with some generalised Russell T. Davies-style foreshadowing).

• ... talked with a head in a box, who said that Iris would soon confront "The Penultimate Question" (#45, *The Wedding of River Song*).

• ... went back to assassinate Hitler, and shoved him into a cupboard (#47, *Let's Kill Hitler*).

• ... accepted Iris' invitation to join her at Hobbes End, May Day 1972 (#49; *The Daemons*).

There are a number of stories without the references needed to place them in any meaningful relation to the rest of universal history.

Some (such as *The Celestial Toymaker*) take place in a reality completely detached from the universe's timeline. Other stories simply fail to provide (or aren't interested in providing) more evidence beyond the fact that they occur "on an alien planet in the future". Given the entire duration of human development into space, this isn't particularly helpful, presuming the humanoids featured in the story are human in the first place. Without more clues as to how such stories relate to human history or another documented event, a proper dating is impossible. A story such as *Anachrophobia* looks for all the world like placement on the timeline should be attainable, but the evidence (or lack thereof) says otherwise.

The following stories are among those that defy a proper dating. The TV stories are listed in broadcast order; the books, audios and comics are listed alphabetically.

TV Stories

The Chase (2.8, the sequence on Aridius – although it has to take place after the Daleks launch their time machine, as the Doctor and companions see that on the Time-Space Visualiser, which can only see into the past)

Galaxy 4 (3.1)

The Daleks' Master Plan (3.4, the sequences on Tigus and the ice planet)

The Celestial Toymaker (3.7, occurs in the Toymaker's domain)

The Mind Robber (6.2, in the Land of Fiction, a timeless dimension)

Carnival of Monsters (10.2)

The Ribos Operation (16.1, the White Guardian sequence)

The Horns of Nimon (17.5)

Castrovalva (19.1, the non-Earth sequences)

Enlightenment (20.5)

The Five Doctors (20.7, the first Doctor's kidnap and the Eye of Orion sequences)

"Born Again" (*Children in Need* sketch #1, post-regeneration scene in the TARDIS with tenth Doctor and Rose)

"Time Crash" (*Children in Need* sketch #2, scene in the TARDIS with the fifth and tenth Doctors)

Amy's Choice (X5.7, occurs in the TARDIS)

Meanwhile in the TARDIS (Series 5 DVD minisode; occurs in the TARDIS)

Death is the Only Answer (*Doctor Who Confidential* minisode)

"Time" (*Comic Relief* sketch #1, occurs in the TARDIS)

"Space" (*Comic Relief* sketch #2, occurs in the TARDIS)

The Girl Who Waited (X6.10, although mention of Disneyland Clom, and the presence of a Mona Lisa and a Venus de Milo, broadly suggests that it's the future)

Clara and the TARDIS (Series 7 DVD minisode; occurs in the TARDIS)

Inforarium, The (Series 7 DVD minisode)

Rain Gods (Series 7 DVD minisode)

Rings of Akhaten, The (X7.8, events on Akhaten)

The Name of the Doctor (X7.14, sequence with Clara in the sixth Doctor's TARDIS and the finale, with the Doctor and Clara somewhere in the Doctor's personal timeline)

Caretaker, The (X8.6; the planet of the sand piranhas)

Novels and Novellas

Anachrophobia (EDA #54)

Beltempest (EDA #17)

Citadel of Dreams (TEL #2)

Coldheart (EDA #33)

Crooked World, The (EDA #57)

Doctor Trap, The (NSA #26)

Dreams of Empire (PDA #14)

Eight Doctors, The (EDA #1, the Eye of Orion sequence)

Frontier Worlds (EDA #29)

King's Dragon, The (NSA #41; the Doctor's remark on page 224 that Prime Directives are "So twenty-third century. So very retro", isn't very helpful, even presuming he can be taken literally)

Match of the Day (PDA #70)

Nightdreamers (TEL #3)

Parallel 59 (EDA #30)

Shell Shock (TEL #8)

Shining Darkness (NSA #27)

Sky Pirates! (NA #40)

Ultimate Evil, The (BF Missing Episodes novelisation #2)

Audios

Absolution (BF #101)

Afterlife (BF #181, flashback to the planet Palinor)

Age of Endurance, The (BF EA #3.1; Ian mentions how humans fought naval battles in sailing ships "centuries back", but seems to be speaking from his modern-day viewpoint, not whatever time-zone he's standing in)

Anachronauts, The (BF CC #6.7, extended TARDIS sequences, and a mental construct in Steven Taylor's mind)

Aquitaine (BF #209)

Art of Death (BBC DW audiobook #15)

Blood of Erys, The (BF #183)

Blood of the Daleks (BF BBC7 #1.1-1.2; events on Red Rocket Rising)

Breaking Bubbles and Other Stories: "Breaking Bubbles" (BF #188a) and "Of Chaos Time The" (BF #188b)

Cannibalists, The (BF BBC7 #3.6)

Child, The (BF CC #7.6)

Circular Time: "Spring" (BF #91, events on the planet of the bird-people)

City of Spires (BF #133, occurs in the Land of Fiction)

Company of Friends, The: "Fitz's Story" (BF #123b)

Cortex Fire (BF #225b)

Creatures of Beauty (BF #44)

Daleks Among Us (BF #177, Wraiths of Lemuria sequences – although the Wraiths' database of criminals and their descendants is so extensive, it's likely the far future)

Dark Eyes (BF 8th Doc box set #1; events on the planet Halaka and the Mesceroni care facility)

Dark Husband, The (BF #106)

Darkening Eye, The (BF CC #3.6, flashback story)

Dead London (BF BBC7 #2.1, occurs in an alien's mind)

Doomsday Quatrain, The (BF #151, occurs on alien planet made to simulate sixteenth-century Earth)

Drowned World, The (BF CC #4.1, flashback story)

Eleven, The (*Doom Coalition* #1.1; the planet of the interdimensional spider-god)

Elite, The (BF LS #3.1)

Embrace the Darkness (BF #31)

Empathy Games (BF CC #3.4, flashback story)

Fear of the Daleks (BF CC #1.2)

Fifth Traveller, The (BF EA #3.2)

Forever Trap, The (BBC DW original audiobook #2)

Four Doctors, The (BF subscription promo #9, a.k.a. #142b; the Jariden sequences)

"*Fragile Yellow Arc of Fragrance, The*" (BF LS #2.1b)

Genesis Chamber, The (BF PHP #2.1)

Her Final Flight (BF subscription promo #2)

Holy Terror, The (BF #14)

Immortal Beloved (BF BBC7 #1.4; the participants are human, but this isn't very helpful for dating purposes)

Invasion of E-Space, The (BF CC #4.4)

... Ish (BF #35)

Last of the Titans (BF promo #1, DWM #300)

Legacy of Death (BF 4th Doc #5.4)

Legend of the Cybermen (BF #135, Land of Fiction sequences)

Light at the End, The (BF DW 50th anniversary release; events in the Vess weapons factory, situated in a pocket dimension)

Masters of Luxor, The (BF LS #3.7)

Memory Bank, The, and Other Stories: "The Memory Bank" (BF #217a) and "The Becoming" (BF #217d)

Nekromanteia (BF #41)

Night's Black Agents (BF CC #4.11, occurs in the Land of Fiction)

No Place Like Home (BF promo #3, DWM #326)

1001 Nights: "My Brother's Keeper" (BF #168b)

1001 Nights: "Smuggling Tales" (BF #168d)

Paradox Planet, The (BF 4th Doc #5.3; K9 identifies the people of the planet Aoris as "humanoids", but doesn't say they're from Earth)

Planet of the Rani (BF #205; the Teccaurora Penitentiary sequences happen "97 years" after *The Rani Elite*)

Prisoner of the Sun (BF BBC7 #4.8)

Psychodrome (BF 5th Doc boxset #1.1)

Queen of Time, The (BF LS #4.2; takes place in the realm of Hecuba, the Celestial Toymaker's sister)

Quinnis (BF CC #3.6, occurs in the Fourth Universe)

Rani Elite, The (BF #194)

Recorded Time and Other Stories: "Paradoxicide" (BF #150b)

Recorded Time and Other Stories: "Question Marks" (BF #150d)

Red (BF #85)

Revenge of the Swarm (BF #189; opening scene on Polisipodron, the planet of jewels)

Ringpullworld (BF CC #4.5)

Scenes from Her Life (BF DC #3.2; occurs in the Vortex)

Scherzo (BF #52; occurs in-between realities)

Second Doctor, The V1: *The Edge* (BF CC #10.4)

Shadow Planet (BF #226a)

Sirens of Time, The (BF #1, sixth Doctor segment)

Solitaire (BF CC #4.12, occurs in the Toymaker's domain)

Something Inside (BF #83)

Story of Extinction, The (BF CC #10.2; events on the planet Amyryndaa)

Subterranea (BF 4th Doc #6.6)

Three Companions, The: "Polly's Story" (serialized back-up story; BF #120-129)

Time Museum, The (BF CC #7.1, events at the Time Museum itself)

Time Reef (BF #113a)

Time Works (BF #80)

Tomb Ship (BF #186)

Warehouse, The (BF #202; the Doctor takes as given that it's Mel's future, but doesn't quantify)

War Master, The: Only the Good (events on Gardezza, Arcking and Elidh's agrarian community)

War to End All Wars, The (BF CC #8.10; flashback story on the planet Comfort)

Wishing Beast, The (BF #97)

World Apart (BF #226b)

Wreck of the Titan, The (BF #134, occurs in the Land of Fiction)

You are the Doctor and Other Stories: "Come Die With Me" (BF #207b)

Audios (spin-off series)

Benny: Many Happy Returns (Benny 20th anniversary special; hypothetical projection of aged Bernice after she escapes from her nursing home to an archaeological dig)

Benny: Missing Persons: In Living Memory (Benny box set #5.5, events at the Epoch's base of operations outside of time and space)

Diary of River Song, The S3: *My Dinner with Andrew* (BF #3.3; happens at a restaurant outside of space-time)

Gallifrey: Spirit (Davidia sequences)

Graceless: The End (*Graceless* #1.3; warpship sequences)

Graceless IV: The Room (*Graceless* #4.2)

Iris S4: Whatever Happened to Iris Wildthyme? (Iris audio #4.1)

Kaldor City: "The Prisoner" (supplemental story on "The Actor Speaks" CD featuring Paul Darrow, stated as taking place three days after *Kaldor City: Checkmate*, but likely occuring from Landerchild's perspective within the Fendahl gestalt)

Kaldor City: Storm Mine (*Kaldor City* #1.6, stated as taking place eighteen months after *Kaldor City: Checkmate*, but likely occurs from Blayse's perspective within the Fendahl gestalt)

K9: The Choice (BBV audio #13)

K9: The Search (BBV audio #16)

Minister of Chance, The, episodes one to five (the final scene entails the Minister revealing that the story takes place on a world once called "Terra", but there's no evidence that it is Earth, or in which era it occurs even if that's true)

Comics

"Are You Listening / Younger and Wiser" (*DWM 1994 Summer Special*)

"Autonomy Bug" (*DWM* #297-299)

"Beautiful Freak" (*DWM* #304)

"Betrothal of Sontar, The" (*DWM* #365-367)

"Black Legacy" (*DWW* #35-38)

"Body Electric, The" (Titan Free Comic Book Day #1a)

"Cat Litter" (*DWM* #192)

"Chameleon Factor" (*DWM* #174)

"Changes" (*DWM* #118-119)

"Character Assassin" (*DWM* #311)

"City of the Damned" (*DWW* #9-16)

"Crossroads of Time" (*DWM* #135)

"Culture Shock" (*DWM* #139)

"Doctor and the Nurse, The" (IDW Vol. 4 #3-4; four random jumps, one of which looks like feudal Japan)

Eleventh Doctor Year One, The (Titan 11th Doc #1.11, "Four Dimensions")

Eleventh Doctor Year Two, The (Titan 11th Doc #2.3, "Pull to Open", occurs in the TARDIS)

Eleventh Doctor Year Three, The (Titan 11th Doc #3.6-3.7, "The Memory Feast", as well as events on the planet Zoline in #3.9, 3.11, "Strange Loops". The music of Kenny G vexes the Doctor in a lift in the latter story, but that might owe to his having the temporal bends.)

"End of the Line" (*DWW* #54-55)

"Enlightenment of Ly-Chee the Wise, The" (*The Incredible Hulk Presents* #10)

"Exodus / Revelation / Genesis" (*DWM* #108-110)

"Fabulous Idiot" (*DWM Summer Special 1982*)

"Fangs of Time" (*DWM* #243)

"Final Quest, The" (*DWW* #8)

"Follow That TARDIS" (*DWM* #147)

"Food for Thought" (*DWM* #218-220)

"Forever Dreaming" (*DWM* #433-#434, occurs in the dimension of a psychic squid)

"Forgotten, The" (IDW *DW* mini-series #2, tenth Doctor sequences)

"Four Doctors" (Titan mini-series; the planet with the Museum of Terrible Fates)

"Funhouse" (*DWM* #102-103)

"Ground Control" (IDW *DW* Annual 2010, "Doctor and Donna being chased by killer bow-wielding pandas" sequence)

"Happy Deathday" (*DWM* #272)

"John Smith and the Common Men" (*DWM* #467, occurs in the Guardian of Sorrow's hellscape)

"Keepsake" (*DWM* #140)

"K9's Finest Hour" (*DWW* #12)

"Land of Happy Endings" (*DWM* #337; dream sequence in the TARDIS)

"Land of the Blind" (*DWM* #224-226)

"Laundro-Room of Doom" (Titan Free Comic Book Day #1c; set in the TARDIS)

"Last Word, The" (*DWM* #305)

"Life of Matter and Death, A" (*DWM* #250)

"Matter of Life and Death, A" (Titan 8th Doc #2)

"Nature of the Beast" (*DWM* #111-113)

"Oblivion" (*DWM* #323-328; story's main events)

"Once in a Lifetime" (*The Incredible Hulk Presents* #1)

"Outsider, The" (*DWW* #25-26)

"Party Animals" (*DWM* #173)

"Planet of the Dead" (*DWM* #141-142)

"Prisoners of Time" (second Doctor adventure at the Frenko Bazaar – although the baddies deem Jamie valuable because he's "from the past"; fourth Doctor adventure on the planet Agratis; eighth Doctor and Grace adventure in the city of Brendais; ninth Doctor and Rose adventure on the Grand and Glroisu monument to Drake Ayelbourne of Altair VII; Clara Oswald kidnap; Adam's base of operations, said to exist in a limbo "somewhen, in a place between places" and "in between time periods")

"Religious Experience, A" (*DWM Yearbook 1994*)

"Rest and Re-Creation" (*DWM Yearbook 1994*)

"Return of the Daleks" (*DWW* #1-4, eight hundred years after previous Dalek invasion)

"Room with a Déjà vu" (IDW *DW* one-shot #5)

"Run, Doctor, Run" (IDW *DW* Annual 2011)

"Salad Daze" (*DWM* #117)

"Ship Called Sudden Death, A" (*DWM Summer Special 1982*)

"Silent Knight" (IDW *DW* Vol. 2, #12; arguably non-canonical, a bit of holiday silliness)

"Sins of the Fathers" (*DWM* #343-345)

"Sky Jacks" (IDW Vol. 4 #9-12; occurs within the TARDIS)

"Slimmer!" (*The Incredible Hulk Presents* #11)

"Space in Dimension Relative and Time" (Titan 11th Doc #6)

"Spam Filtered" (IDW *DW* Vol. 2 #1, unnamed in single issue, entitled in trade paperback)

"Spirits of the Jungle" (*DWM* #489-491)

"Stairway to Heaven" (*DWM* #156)

"Stitch in Time!, A" (*The Incredible Hulk Presents* #6)

Tenth Doctor Year Two (Titan 10th Doc #2.10, "Infinite Corridor, The", occurs in the TARDIS)

Tenth Doctor Year Three, The (Titan 10th Doc #3.6-3.8, 3.10-3.11, the Doctor's visits to Mechma Onzlo III Station in the "third most populous and formidable Draconian Era", and the Vortex Butterfly's rogue solar system)

"Tesseract" (IDW Vol. 1, #7-8)

"Time and Tide" (*DWM* #145-146)

"Time Fraud" (IDW *Doctor Who Special 2012*; events on the planet Helion)

"Time of My Life, The" (*DWM* #399, Zyglot courtship, swamp, clock creature, vampire goth cannibals, psychic parasite and Donna goodbye message sequences)

"Timeslip" (*DWW* #17-18)

"To Sleep, Perhance to Scream" (IDW *DW Annual 2010*)

"Touchdown on Deneb 7" (*DWM* #48)

Twelfth Doctor Year One, The (Titan 12th Doc #1.16, "Relative Dimensions", occurs in the Celestial Toyroom)

Twelfth Doctor Year Two, The (Titan 12th Doc #2.14-2.15, : "Invasion of the Mindmorphs"; trips to see the mating dance of the Abraxas Manta Whales, the colliding galaxies of Myrax and Aurora, the Oasis of M'Noa, the Kangastangs of Xebedee and the alleged utopia of Zarma)

"TV Action" (*DWM* #283)

"Uninvited Guest" (*DWM* #211)

"Universal Monsters" (*DWM* #391-393)

"Whispering Gallery, The" (IDW *DW* one-shot #1)

"Who's That Girl!" (*The Incredible Hulk Presents* #8-9)

"Woman Who Sold the World, The" (*DWM* #381-384)

"Your Destiny Awaits" (IDW *DW Annual 2011*, desert planet and "Kevin chases aliens" sequences)

INDEX

SPECIAL NOTE: For easier reference, the volumes of *Ahistory* Fourth Edition are numbered 1000 and up for Volume 1, 2000 and up for Volume 2, and 3000 and up for Volume 3.

Bold numbers indicate main story entries for each adventure (the same information is found in the Table of Contents) . Plain-text numbers indicate a story reference in the footnotes. This index also lists characters, alien races, planets and organisations that appear in three or more stories. Characters are alphabetical based upon their most commonly used name, followed by a quick description of that character and the media (TV, audios, etc) in which they *first* appeared.

Big Finish box sets, for the most part, are listed under the box set title, then the individual stories therein. (The format is a bit inconsistent – whenever possible, we've gone with whatever's on the cover.)

To save space, Titan's comics are listed under *The Tenth Doctor Year One, The Eleventh Doctor Year One,* etc. We've anticipated a collection of *The Ninth Doctor Year One.*

Jago, Henry Gordon (theatre impressario, investigator of the supernatural, close friend of Professor Litefoot; associate of fourth Doctor, sixth Doctor, other Doctors and Leela; TV) (born) 1174, (young adult life, interaction with future self) 1186-1187, (involvement with stage performer Ruby Valentine) 1193, (meets Litefoot, fourth Doctor and Leela during the Weng-Chiang affair) 1205, (investigates infernal affairs with Litefoot) 1208-1213, (meets sixth Doctor, travels in TARDIS, winds up stuck in 1968 before returning to own time, 1893) 1214-1215, (more investigations with Litefoot) 1215-1225, (meets son, Henry Jr.) 1223

Janus Conjunction, The (EDA #16) 2220, 3073, 3078, 3080, 3082-**3083**, 3121

Jamie McCrimmon (second Doctor companion, mid-18th-century Highlander; TV) (joins TARDIS, leaves TARDIS) 1147, (now married to Kirsty McLaren, with many bairns) 1157, (recruited by sixth Doctor for one last mission) 1157, (death) 1040

Jason Kane (rogue; husband, then ex-husband, then partner of Bernice Summerfield; acclaimed writer of extra-terrestrial erotica; novels) (born) 2125, (leaves abusive family) 2152, (marries Benny) 2264, (separates from Benny) 2179, (reunites with Benny) 3154, (hits it big writing xenoporn) 3156, (death) 3172

Jaws of Orthrus (K9 1.8) **3031**, 3298

Jenny (genetic daughter of the tenth Doctor; TV) (generated, gains bowship) 3325-3326, (meets twelfth Doctor) 2335

Jenny Flint (wife, cohort and maid of Madame Vastra; TV) (meets Vastra and the Doctor) 1183, (as partner of Vastra) 1204

Jess Collins (friend of the twelfth Doctor, college student; comics) (boyfriend dies) 2095, (Doctor lodges with Collins family for a half year) 2096, (as adult working at National Gallery) 2296

"Jetsam" (*TWM* #3) **2234**, 3116, 3408

Jigsaw War, The (BF CC #6.11) **3208**

Jo Grant (third Doctor companion, UNIT operative; TV) (born) 1300, (hired as Doctor's assistant) 2067, (leaves UNIT to marry Clifford Jones) 2079, (shown as divorced from Jones, with one child) 2157, (meets Sarah Jane and tenth Doctor, shown as married to Jones, with seven children) 2269

John Hart, Captain (former Time Agent; frenemy and lover of Captain Jack Harkness; TV) (partnered with Harkness) 3307, (runs con job on Harkness) 2228, (coerced into terror campaign against Torchwood) 2240

"John Smith and the Common Men" (*DWM* #467) 1348

Jorjie Turner (friend of K9; TV) (born) 3021, (meets K9) 3030

Journey to the Centre of the TARDIS (X7.11) 2364, 2380, 2444, 3198-**3199**

Journey's End (X4.13) 1189, 1266, 1282, 2205, 2211, 2234, 2240-**2242**, 2244, 2253, **2287**, 2305, 2347, 2360, 2372, 2429, 2439-2440, 3139-3140, 3219, 3288-3289

Joy Device, The (Benny NA #22) 3096, **3158**

Joyride (Class novel #1) 2166, 2327, **2338**

Jubilee (BF #40) 1234, 1244, 1291, 1310, **2182**, 3288

Judas Gift, The (Benny audio #8.2) 1070, 1100, 3121, 3148, 3156, 3158, 3170-**3171**, 3172, 3320

Judgement Day (SJA audiobook #10) 1032, 1062, 1064, 1144, 1172, 2081-2082, 2092, 2277-**2278**, 3153, 3178-3179, 3406

Judgement of Isskar, The (BF #117) 1051, **1057**-1058, 3344-**3345**, **3408**

Judgement of the Judoon (NSA #31) 2277, 3112-3113, **3117**

Judgment of Sutekh, The (FP audio #2.6) **1055**, 1150-**1151**, **2414**

Judoon (rhino-like peacekeepers, shock troops of the Shadow Proclamation; TV) (first appearance) 2224

Juggernauts, The (BF #65) 3281-3282, 3284-**3285**, 3327

"Junkyard Demon" (*DWM* #58-59) 1315, **3116**, 3257

"Junkyard Demon II" (*DWM* Yearbook 1996) **3116**

Jupiter Conjunction, The (BF #160) 3096, **3098**

Just War (NA #46) 1158, 1182, 1243, 1246, 1264, 1272, 1280, 1282, **1285**, 1290-1291, 1298, 1322, 2020, 2072, 2138, 2212, 2344, 3010, 3134, 3142, 3156,

3210, 3213

Justice of Jalxar, The (BF 4th Doc #2.4) **1228**, 1231

K9 (robot dog; various K9s are companions to the fourth Doctor, Leela, Romana and Sarah Jane Smith; TV) (Mark 1 given to the fourth Doctor) 3299, (Mark 1 leaves TARDIS with Leela; the Doctor unpacks Mark 2) 2397, (Mark 2 leaves TARDIS with Romana) 3235-3236, (Doctor gives Mark 3 as gift to Sarah Jane Smith) 2117, (destruction of K9 Mark 1) 2419, (indeterminate Mark takes up residence in year 2050) 3029

K9 and Company (18.7-A) 1206, 1306, 2030, 2050, 2088, 2116-**2117**, 2122, 2170, 2208, 2232, 3030

K9 and the Beasts of Vega (*The Adventures of K9* #2) 2396, **3300**

K9 and the Missing Planet (*The Adventures of K9* #4) **3378**

K9 and the Time Trap (*The Adventures of K9* #1) 2357, 2396-**2397**

K9 and the Zeta Rescue (*The Adventures of K9* #3) 2396-**2397**

K9 Series 1 **3029**

"K9's Finest Hour" (*DWW* #12) 1348

Kadiatu Lethbridge-Stewart (descendant of Brigadier Lethbridge-Stewart, adventurer in time and space, seventh Doctor associate; novels) (meets seventh Doctor) 3054

Kaldor City (futuristic locale, society reliant on advanced robots) (founding) 3192, (sub-section on) 3204, (robot revolt, Fendahl attack) 3207, (as interstellar trader) 3228

Kaldor City (Magic Bullet audios; spinoff of *The Robots of Death*; a season-long story, with a coda; *Occam's Razor*, *Kaldor City* #1; *Death's Head*, *Kaldor City* #2; *Hidden Persuaders*, *Kaldor City* #3; *Taren Capel*, *Kaldor City* #4; *Checkmate*, *Kaldor City* #5; *Storm Mine*, *Kaldor City* #6) 3192, 3204, **3206**, **3207**, 3208, 3228

Kaldor City: Metafiction (*Kaldor City* #1a) 3204, 3206-**3207**

Kaldor City: "The Prisoner" (supplemental story on "The Actor Speaks" CD featuring Paul Darrow) 1348, 3207

Kaleds (forefathers of the Daleks; TV) (war against the Thals begins) 1073, (war ends, Kaleds either die or become Daleks) 1089

Kalendorf (insurrectionist fighting the Daleks; audios) (meets Susan Mendes) 3325, (death reported) 3329

Kamelion (robotic fifth Doctor companion; TV) (joins TARDIS) 1104-1105, (destruction) 2127

"Kane's Story" (*DWM* #104) 1315, 1317, **2130**, 3263, **3285**

Kaston Iago (hired gun operating out of Kaldor City, quite probably was Avon on *Blake's 7*; audios) (background) 3205, (begins working for Uvanov) 3206, (absorption into the Fendahl) 3207

Katarina (first Doctor companion, handmaiden to Cassandra in ancient Troy; TV) (joins TARDIS) 1067, (death) 3267

Kate Stewart (UNIT commander, daughter of Alistair Lethbridge-Stewart, associate of eleventh and twelfth Doctors; independent films) (born) 2056, (estrangement from father) 2138, (son Gordon born) 2142, (reunites with father) 2149, (in command of UNIT) 2305

Keeper of Traken, The (18.6) 1096, 1110, 2114-**2115**, 2360, 2371, 2377, 2379, 2392, 2396, 2401, 3236

Keepsake (BF #112b) **3123**-3124, **3278**

"Keep, The" (*DWM* #248-249) 3238, 3302, **3304**, 3318

Key to Time, the (extremely powerful artifact broken into six segments; TV) (forging of the Key in the Chaos Pool) 3408, (fourth Doctor and first Romana tasked with finding the Key) 2398, (assembly of the Key, dissipation) 3402, (second hunt for the Key to Time initiated; the Key's destruction) 3408

Keys of Marinus, The (1.5) 1036, **1038**-1039, 1070, 1344

Kill the Moon (X8.7) 1035, 1274, 2161, 2170, 2316, 2322-**2323**, 2401, 3012, 3020, 3022-3025, **3028**, 3037, 3050

Killing Ground (MA #23) 1315, 2138, 3050, 3065, 3070, 3073, 3076, **3077**, 3078, 3128, 3179, 3263, 3354

Kinda (19.3) 1344, 3210, **3223**, 3242

King of Sontar, The (BF 4th Doc #3.1) 2396, 3126-**3127**

King of Terror, The (PDA #37) 1051, 1075, 1101, 1110, 1114, 1122, 1154, 1248, 1263, 1270, 1288, 1312, 1323, 2047, 2096, 2098, 2116, 2140, 2156, 2162-**2163**, 2176, 2374, 3018, 3020, **3034**

King's Demons, The (20.6) **1104**, 1345, 2118

King's Dragon, The (NSA #42) 1346

Kingdom of Silver (BF #112) 1118, 1315, **3122**, 3278

Kingdom of the Blind, The (Benny audio #6.2) 3048, 3166-**3167**

Kingmaker, The (BF #81) 1112, **1114**, **1115**, 1128-**1129**, 2084, 2360, 3074, 3338, 3414

Kiss Kiss, Bang Bang (TW 2.1) **2228**, 3056, 3306, 3308

Kiss of Death (BF #147) 1053, 1096, 1140, 1238, 2109, 2122-**2123**, 3246

Kitsune (TimeH #4) 1108, **1109**, 1254, 1304, **3012**

"Klein's Story" (BF #131a) 1293, 1312, 1324, **1326**, 2024-**2025**, 2091

Knock, Knock (X10.4; 2017) 1314, 2102, 2154, 2166, 2193, 2329, **2335**

Korven, The (K9 1.3) 3026, **3209**, 3030, 3098, 3180

Krillitane Storm, The (NSA #36) **1102**

Krillitanes (winged tenth Doctor foes; TV) (first appearance) 2208

Kroton (eighth Doctor companion, free-thinking Cyberman; comics) (develops emotions, left drifting in space) 3121-3122, (revives, joins the TARDIS) 3244-3245, (leaves the TARDIS) 2167

Krotons (crystalline aliens; TV) (generation) 3028, (first appearance) 3331